FAMILY LAW, GENDER AND THE STATE

The third edition of this work on family law, comprising text, cases and materials, provides not only an explication of legal principle but also explores, primarily from a feminist perspective, some of the assumptions about, and constructions of, gender, sexual orientation, class and culture that underlie the law. It examines the ideology of the family and, in particular, the role of the law in contributing to and reproducing that ideology. Structured around the themes of welfare, equality and family privacy, the book aims to offer the benefits of a textbook while also giving students a wide-ranging set of materials for classroom discussion. As well as providing a firm grounding in family law, the text sets the law in its social and historical context and encourages a critical approach by students to the subject. It provides an ideal introduction to family law for undergraduates, but will be equally helpful for postgraduate students of family law for whom it provides a challenging selection of materials set within a theoretical framework rich in ideas and arguments.

Family Law, Gender and the State

Third Edition

Alison Diduck
and
Felicity Kaganas

·H A R T·
PUBLISHING

OXFORD AND PORTLAND, OREGON
2012

Published in the United Kingdom by Hart Publishing Ltd
16C Worcester Place, Oxford, OX1 2JW
Telephone: +44 (0)1865 517530
Fax: +44 (0)1865 510710
E-mail: mail@hartpub.co.uk
Website: http://www.hartpub.co.uk

Published in North America (US and Canada) by
Hart Publishing
c/o International Specialized Book Services
920 NE 58th Avenue, Suite 300
Portland, OR 97213-3786
USA
Tel: +1 503 287 3093 or toll-free: (1) 800 944 6190
Fax: +1 503 280 8832
E-mail: orders@isbs.com
Website: www.isbs.com

© Alison Diduck and Felicity Kaganas 2012

British Library Cataloguing in Publication Data
Data Available

ISBN: 978-1-84946-149-8

Typeset by Forewords, Oxford
Printed and bound in Great Britain by
TJ International Ltd, Padstow, Cornwall

Preface to the Third Edition

In the six years since we wrote the preface to the second edition, the changes within family law have been dramatic. And we fear that by the time this book is published, the law will have changed yet again. If the planned withdrawal of legal aid from private law disputes goes ahead, contact and residence disputes (or if the proposal in the *Final Report* of the Family Justice Review is implemented, child arrangements orders) will be confined to the wealthy or to those people prepared to represent themselves. And even they will, if the Family Justice Review proposals are incorporated into legislation, be expected to consider mediation first.

As was the case in relation to the first and second editions, we aim to explain and explore the law in its social context. We focus not only on the law but also on family policy to examine, primarily from a feminist perspective, how the family is constructed and regulated in contemporary British society. We have continued to rely on a range of materials that are not all strictly legal in order to do so.

The structure of the book has changed; we have moved towards a more traditional structure. In the previous editions we used a case method to illustrate how the law would play out in our imagined scenarios. Our aim was to demonstrate, among other things, how family cases can present the lawyer with a number of intertwined issues and problems. However, we reluctantly came to the conclusion that, for the purposes of teaching, this structure made the book too fragmented and difficult to navigate. We have therefore removed all the case scenarios.

This edition is in two parts. The first outlines the nature of families and family relationships. The second part is divided into three sections, each focusing its analysis of the law and policy on one of the principles we believe to be key in shaping both law and policy: equality, welfare and family privacy.

Yet again, for reasons of space, we have left gaps unfilled. These include the financial consequences of death and bankruptcy, child abduction and the legal position of older family members.

We hope that we have stated the law correctly as at July 2011.

While this book was in press two important developments occurred. The first was publication of the *Final Report* of the Family Justice Review and the second was the long-awaited decision of the Supreme Court in *Jones v Kernott*. We have added short postscripts to Chapters 6, 10 and 14 referring to these, but were not able to discuss them in any detail. The Family Justice Review *Final Report* reiterates many of the recommendations made in the Interim Report, but also makes some new ones. We discuss the recommendations regarding section 8 proceedings at the end of Chapter 10 and the recommendations regarding child protection proceedings at the end of Chapter 14. *Jones v Kernott* clarified the principles developed in *Stack v Dowden* regarding the determination of the beneficial interests in a house acquired in joint names by an unmarried couple who intended it to be their family home. We refer in the postscript to Chapter 6 to the joint judgment of Lady Hale and Lord Walker, but while the Court was unanimous in the result, Lords Collins, Kerr and Wilson disagreed on the conceptual and practical differences between 'inferring' and 'imputing' intention to the parties.

As always we remain indebted to those who gave us encouragement in writing this book and we thank in particular Richard Hart and his editorial team at Hart Publishing. We are also grateful for research assistance provided by Yuvraj Joshi and Naureen Shameem. Finally, we thank our families for their forbearance and humour.

Alison Diduck
Felicity Kaganas
November 2011

Contents

Table of Cases

xv

Table of Legislation

INTERNATIONAL/REGIONAL

Council of Europe

European Union

NATIONAL

United Kingdom

OTHER

Australia

Canada

Ireland

New Zealand

South Africa

Sweden

PART I

FAMILIES AND RELATIONSHIPS

PART I

FAMILIES AND RELATIONSHIPS

1

Law and 'The Family'

I. FAMILIES AND SOCIETIES

In the light of recent family law reforms, it may be provocative, if not downright peculiar, to suggest that the idea of the family in English law is dependent for its meaning on the monogamous sexual relationship (either actually or symbolically) between a man and a woman, or to say that much of the law concerning the formation and adjustment of family relationships highlights the importance of this heterosexual union and retains it, at least symbolically, at its core. Yet, despite recent changes to the laws that constitute and give legal meaning to 'family', 'parent' or 'spouse', changes that seem to create alternative bases for family formation, we wish to counsel caution in conceding too quickly the decline of the heterosexual gendered norm in family law. We shall make this case in more detail below, and for now wish simply to make the point, by way of introduction, that despite the variety of connections between people that could make their relationship a familial one, there is a particular type of conjugal unit that remains at the foundation of what law understands to be family.

This legal meaning of family sometimes corresponds with and sometimes contradicts popular or personal meanings of family. If you were asked, for example, to define your family, you might include all those people who live in your household irrespective of whether you are biologically related to them, or you might include some or all biological relatives who live outside your household. Your answer may depend upon the reason for the question. Which members of your family do you think you ought legally to be required to support financially? Which members of your family should be required to support you? Which members of your family provide you with emotional and physical security? For whom would you sacrifice most? It is interesting that when children were asked to identify members of their families they did not refer simply to those who held a formal status in relation to them, but tended to refer to ties of affection as being the essence of family life and they identified love and the quality of the relationship as being crucial to making someone a 'proper' parent (Smart, Neale and Wade 2001).

So, can we say then that families are created by affective and emotional ties between people? And if we can say this for some purposes, can we say it for all? What if the idea of the family in English law were dependent for its meaning exclusively upon the existence of a parent–child relationship, or were based solely on the giving of mutual affection and emotional support? On the other hand, what if affection and emotion were irrelevant to creating and sustaining a legal family? What if it were an economic interdependence between two or more people that distinguished families from other groups of people?

3

US scholar Martha Fineman suggests, from a feminist perspective, that the notion of a family should rest upon a 'mother–child' relationship. She is careful to say, however, that men as well as women could perform the 'mother' role:

> In my newly redefined legal category of family, I would place inevitable dependents [*sic*] along with their caregivers. The caregiving family would be a protected space, entitled to special, preferred treatment by the state.
>   The new family line, drawn around dependency, would mark the boundaries of the concept of family privacy. The unit would also have legitimate claims on the resources of society. Specifically, I envision a redistribution or reallocation of social and economic subsidies now given to the natural family that allow it to function 'independently' within society. Family and welfare law would be reconceived so as to support caretaking as the family intimacy norm.
>
> (Fineman 1995: 231–32)

> I propose Mother/Child as the substitute core of the basic family paradigm. Our laws and policies would be compelled to focus on the needs of this unit. Mother/Child would provide the structural and ideological basis for the transfer of current societal subsidies (both material and ideological) away from the sexual family to nurturing units. (ibid: 233)

> Two additional theoretical caveats are necessary. First, I believe that men can and should be Mothers. In fact, if men are interested in acquiring legal rights of access to children (or other dependents) [*sic*], I argue they must be Mothers in the stereotypical nurturing sense of that term—that is, engaged in caretaking. Second, the Child in my dyad stands for all forms of inevitable dependency—the dependency of the ill, the elderly, the disabled, as well as actual children. (ibid: 234–35)

> Mothering should be thought of as an ethical practice, as embodying an ideal of social 'goodness'. As an idealized notion, motherhood should not be confined to women but be a societal aspiration for *all* members of the community. (ibid: 235)[1]

In a later work,[2] Fineman argues that a reconceptualisation of family based on the idea of dependency would transform notions about our relationship to the state.

> [I]n our political ideology, dependency is considered to be a private matter. It is the family, not the state or the market, that assumes responsibility for both the inevitable dependent [*sic*]—the child or other biologically or developmentally dependent person—and the derivative dependent [*sic*]—the caretaker. The institution of the family operates structurally and ideologically to free markets from considering or accommodating dependency. The state is cast as a default institution, providing minimal, grudging and stigmatized assistance should families fail.
>
> (Fineman 2004: 228)

> [But] [i]f the existence of a certain type of family is a prerequisite for the coherent development of our concepts of the 'public' market and the state, what happens when we are forced to concede that there have been widespread and not easily reversible changes in the way we think about and practice family … ?
>   What social expectations apply to the relationships among the state, market and man (outside his former category as 'husband') or woman (outside her former category as 'wife')? How do

---

[1] See also Herring (2010a, 2011) who advocates that family and therefore family law should be concerned with what he calls the 'sexless family' and focus on care in relationships. Diduck (2008a) suggests that 'family' is about care of dependants.

[2] See Reece (2008) for a review of Fineman's thesis.

we begin to decide what is the appropriate set of social relations and expectations to address the child's claim upon society and its institutions for provision of the goods necessary to meet her or his material, social, and emotional needs? If the family that would have provided the historic answer to this latter question no longer exists, our old reliable background begins to crumble. Further complicating this confrontation is the fact that the family is not isolated in its changes. Transformations in the family were provoked by (and further provoke) changes in other institutions. Therefore, our existing ideology about such matters as the appropriateness of state intervention and regulatory action must also be reconsidered, perhaps shifted, in the context of change. (ibid: 235–36, references omitted)

In the UK, Patricia Morgan (1995) writing from a 'New Right' perspective, suggested that a parent–child dyad as the basis of 'family' exists already by default, but that the consequences for society are dire. She argues that giving legal recognition as 'family' to a single parent and her child contributes to social ills such as juvenile delinquency, unemployment and poverty. The Centre for Social Justice, a Conservative policy centre, agrees:

Politicians and policy makers in Britain have typically shied away from distinguishing between family structures. They have become scared that they may upset someone if they talk of two parent families. Too many hide behind the mantra that it is just about personal choice and that Government has no opinion. Yet it is the government which has to pick up the cost of family breakdown, and not just the direct costs, (£20–24bn) but also the many indirect costs such as increased drug and alcohol abuse, debt, educational underachievement, unemployment and crime.

We reject the notion that policy can or should be wholly neutral. Evidence shows different family structures to have different outcomes, and therefore policy should support that which is in the best interests of society. Committed, in particular married, couple relationships produce the best outcomes for adults and children. Children do best when living with both biological parents. If you have experienced family breakdown as a child you are more likely to experience family breakdown as an adult. (Centre for Social Justice 2010: 8)

Irrespective of one's political point of view, then, it seems that the idea that the form or organisation of families is integrally related to the shape and organisation of societies is not contentious. Further, this is not a new insight. Frederick Engels wrote many years ago that the rise in dominance of that which we now know as the conjugal or nuclear family was related to the rise of private property and capitalism and the dominance of men over women. Compare his view of this phenomenon, written in 1884, with that of sociologist Talcott Parsons, who makes many of the same points in 1949, although from a very different political perspective.

As regards the legal equality of man and woman in marriage, the position is no better. Their legal inequality, bequeathed to us from earlier social conditions, is not the cause but the effect of the economic oppression of the woman. In the ancient communistic household, which comprised many couples and their children, the task entrusted to the women of managing the household was as much a public, a socially necessary industry as the procuring of food by the men. With the patriarchal family and still more with the single monogamous family, a change came. Household management lost its public character. It no longer concerned society. It became a *private service*; the wife became the head female servant, excluded from participation in social production. Not until the coming of modern large-scale industry was the road to social production opened to her again—and then only to the proletarian wife. But it was opened in such a manner that, if she carries out her duties in the private service of her family, she remains excluded from public production and unable to earn; and if she wants to take part in public industry and earn independently, she cannot carry out family duties. And the women's position in the factory is the position of women in all lines of business, right up to medicine and the law. The modern individual family is founded on the open or concealed domestic slavery of women, and modern society is a mass composed of these individual families as its molecules. In the great majority of cases today, at least among the possessing classes, it is the husband who is obliged to earn a living and support his family, and that in itself gives him a position of supremacy without any need for special legal privileges. Within the family he is the bourgeois and the wife represents the proletariat. In the industrial world, however, the specific character of the economic oppression burdening the proletariat is visible in all its sharpness only when all the special legal privileges of the capitalist class have been abolished and the complete legal equality of both classes established ... . And in the same way, the peculiar character of the supremacy of the husband over the wife in the modern family, the necessity of creating real social equality between them and the way to do it, will only be seen in the full light of day when both possess complete equality of rights. Then it will be plain that the first condition for the liberation of women is to bring the whole female sex back into public industry, and that this in turn demands the abolition of the monogamous family's attribute of being the economic unit of society. (Engels 1978: 84–86)

Monogamy arose from the concentration of larger wealth in the hands of a single individual—a man—and from the need to bequeath this wealth to the children of that man and of no other. For this purpose, the monogamy of the woman was required, not that of the man, so this monogamy of the woman did not in any way interfere with open or concealed polygamy on the part of the man ... .

... With the transfer of the means of production into common ownership, the monogamous family ceases to be the economic unit of society. Private housekeeping is transformed into a social industry. The care and education of the children becomes a public affair; society looks after all children alike, whether they are born of wedlock or not. (ibid: 87–88)

Talcott Parsons writes:

What a crucially important structural role is played by the marriage relationship—far more so than in most kinship systems—has already been pointed out. As a structurally unsupported relationship resting largely on emotional attraction, it must be protected against the kind of stresses that go with severe competition for prestige between the members. It is well known that segregation of role is in general one of the main mechanisms for inhibiting potentially disruptive competition. The functional importance of the solidarity of the marriage relationship to our kinship system may therefore be presumed to be a major factor underlying the segregation of the sex roles in American society, since sex is the primary basis of role differentiation for marriage partners ... .

Structurally the most fundamental aspect of the segregation of the sex roles seems to be with reference to the occupational system. Especially in the structurally crucial middle-class area of our society, the dominant mature feminine role is that of housewife or of wife and mother. Apart from the extremely important utilitarian problems of how adequate care of household and children are to be accomplished, the most important aspect of this fact is that it shields spouses from competition with each other in the occupational sphere, which, along with attractiveness to women, is above all the most important single focus of feelings of self-respect on the part of American men. In this sector of society the largest part of the gainful employment of women is that of unmarried girls and of women living outside normal family relationships. There has been a notable check in the tendency for women to enter the higher occupational careers; for example, the proportion of women in the professions of medicine and law has remained approximately constant for more than a generation. Only a minority of such career women carry full normal family responsibilities, including the care of young children. Finally, when in the middle classes married women are gainfully employed, in a large proportion of cases it is in a job rather than in a career. Such employment is ordinarily not in competition with that of men of the same class status and ordinarily does not produce a comparable proportion of the family income.

(Parsons 1949: 192–94, footnotes omitted)

In the first place, structural analysis clearly shows that, if the United States is to remain and develop further as a democratic, urbanized, industrial society, with a large measure of equality of opportunity, the range of possible family structures which are compatible with its type of society is very narrow. As it is, our family system is responsible for serious limitations on the ideal of equality of opportunity. But any considerable shift in the direction, for instance, of the family types found in peasant societies would undoubtedly entail serious consequences for the rest of the social structure. Such a family type may well be more stable than our own, but if this stability must be purchased at the expense of drastic reduction in the productivity of our economy and drastic limitations of the realizability of our democratic values, is it worth the price? (ibid: 200–01, footnotes omitted)

So we see that, to both of these writers, the organisation of people into traditional, patri- archal nuclear families is a necessary element of industrial and post-industrial capitalist society. Anderson, a more contemporary sociologist, presents yet a different view. He suggests that modern capitalist societies are in many ways antithetical to the values and morality that we consider a part of the 'traditional' family and that the conjugal or nuclear family is neither the result nor the cause of modern industrial or post-industrial capitalism:

We now know, of course, that the fundamental proposition here—family form and process as a functional consequence of the demands of industrial society—is hopelessly over-simple. The historical premise is incorrect, since over most of Britain and much of the rest of Western Europe and North America the typical domestic group has been small and simple in structure, at least since medieval times; where this group was larger and more complex (which was usually only among the more affluent), it was servants and not kin who were responsible. In the Euro- pean peasant family, as in our own, day-to-day family life was centred around the conjugal pair. While a sense of solidarity with wider kin was clearly present in some sections of the popula- tion, and was at times used as an important reference point in social action, at no time in the past one thousand years (with the possible exception of a few remote areas such as Scotland north and west of the Highland Line) has kinship been the dominant basis for social organiza- tion, certainly in Britain and probably anywhere in Western Europe; for most of the population, ties even with siblings have probably been of no greater significance than they are today. Indeed, it is a special irony that at least some forms of early industrialization in Britain actually increased people's dependence on kin (and even their ability to live with them and near them) to a level unknown for hundreds of years (at least) before.

Moreover, in as far as the family system did change with industrialization, detailed histori- cally-based analysis of the processes involved suggests that any simple model of industrialization *causing* family change is grossly oversimplified. Firstly, the early methods both of capital accu- mulation and of labour recruitment were largely extensions of pre-existing social processes. In order to recruit and retain labour, industrial employers often had to adapt to the expectations of their potential labour force by, for example, employing families rather than individuals in the early textile mills and by conniving with parents to ensure the employment of under-age chil- dren, by taking on paternal functions for young girls such as guarding their morals and even finding them spouses, and by respecting kinship and community ties in recruitment, promotions and work allocation. Secondly, the association of family change with industrialization obscures the fact that the new features of modern family forms first emerge, not in the early factory towns, but much earlier in the homes of the bourgeoisie and, in the rest of society, in areas like those regions of England where large scale capitalist farming based on hired day labour emerged following enclosure, and in the proto-industrial areas of Europe in the 18th century where domestic production for local use became transformed into domestic production for an anonymous market through the intervention of a capitalist merchant class. In an important sense, therefore, far from industrialization causing changes in the family, changes in production and in domestic life in the direction of modern forms of production and of domestic social organization went together; one without the other was impossible and both were reflections of much more profound structural and value changes. Thus, both can only be understood as a function of this historically specific transformation. It must, therefore, follow that in other societies, with different family traditions and different ideologies of modernization, different outcomes are to be expected in both industrial and family functioning and form.

(Anderson 1980: 35–36, footnotes omitted)

Anderson, therefore, like Engels and Parsons, but without Engels' cause-and-effect analysis, or Parsons' functionalism, suggests that the 'look' of families and the organisation of society are linked, and that changes in both are linked in turn to changes in society. He lists society's 'structural and value changes' as the family's relationship to production, changes in the roles of children within families, demographic changes, technological developments, the undermining of close community supervision of families and changes in the 'basic values underlying interpersonal relations in the whole society ... during the transition from a patriarchal and even feudalistic peasant society to a capitalist industrialised one, based theoretically on principles of citizenship' (Anderson 1980: 56). In response to those who wish to return to this historical notion of the 'traditional family', he concludes that

the history of the Western family shows quite clearly that we cannot go back to a strict conformity to the family morality that we have inherited from the past without also—which is clearly impossible—reverting to the economic and social relations of the past. We are not peasants anymore and thus cannot sustain a peasant morality. We have to develop new institutions and new behaviours to cope with new situations. (ibid: 58)

More recent sociological and historical interest in families has also focused upon the apparent connection between social conditions and family relationships, and the view is that family change 'can be understood in relation to evolving employment patterns, shifting gender relations, increasing options in sexual orientation and cross-cultural influences in a multi-cultural society' (Smart et al 2001: 17). Families are 'transforming themselves in relation to post-industrialism and the major structural changes of late modernity' (ibid). Indeed, Smart and Neale (1999) posit that after years of uninterest, sociology recently has become interested in families again. Much of this new sociology of the family identifies individualisation as the key phenomenon that, near the end of the twentieth century, affected our relationships with the state and the international polity as much as it did our relationships with intimates. Beck and Beck Gernsheim (1995), for example, identify individualisation, globalisation and women's liberation as primary factors in what they see as our need constantly to make and remake our biographies, our identities and relationships. To them our biographies and the commitments and relationships we choose in relation to them are flexible, unwritten, personal works in progress and have produced 'post-familial families'. These families have moved from being communities of need to elective affinities.

Whereas, in pre-industrial society, the family was mainly a community of need held together by an obligation of solidarity, the logic of individually designed lives has come to the fore in the contemporary world. The family is becoming more of an elective relationship, an association of individual persons, who each bring to it their own interests, experiences and plans and who are each subjected to different controls, risks and constraints.

As the various examples from contemporary family life have shown, it is necessary to devote much more effort than in the past to the holding together of these different biographies. Whereas people could once fall back upon rules and rituals, the prospect now is of a staging of everyday life, an acrobatics of balancing and coordinating ... . Since individualization also fosters a longing for the opposite world of intimacy, security and closeness, most people will continue— at least in the foreseeable future—to live within a partnership or family. But such ties are not the same as before, in their scope or in their degree of obligation or performance ... . As people make choices, negotiating and deciding the everyday details of do-it-yourself relationships, a 'normal chaos' of love, suffering and diversity is growing and developing.

This does not mean that the traditional family is simply disappearing. But it is losing the monopoly it had for so long. Its quantitative significance is declining as new forms of living appear and spread—forms which (at least generally) aim not at living alone but at relationships of a different kind: for example, without a formal marriage or without children; single parenting, conjugal succession, or same-sex partnerships; part-time relationships and companionships lasting for some period in life; living between more than one home or between different towns. These in all their intermediary and secondary and floating forms represent the future of families or what I call the contours of the 'post-familial family'.

(Beck and Beck-Gernsheim 2002: 97–98, references omitted)

Another influential perspective has been provided by Anthony Giddens (1992). Giddens also sees relationships changing as individualisation becomes more reflexive. He described revolutions in sex, love and gender relations as producing a 'transformation of intimacy' in which relationships last only as long as the partners continue to get something from them. As a result of this 'transformation', obligation and commitment in relationships has become negotiable rather than remaining static and subject to externally prescribed norms. To him, these are 'pure relationships' and are based upon contingent, 'confluent love'. While they may be more fragile than traditional relationships based upon romantic love, he says they are more democratic and fulfilling. Jeffrey Weeks (2002) uses these ideas to identify 'families of choice' within the gay and lesbian communities, and speculates that these new affinities could come to define all forms of intimacy.

These theories highlight social change, risk and disembeddedness as the conditions of modern times and they postulate changes in our ways of living to cope with these conditions. These changes mean a new importance in relationships of intimacy for negotiability, individuality, and the search for an authentic and fulfilled self. For the most part, however, most of these new sociologists of family are not doomsayers. Giddens, for example, declares that the pure relationship is a more democratic family form than the traditional family and Beck-Gernsheim's post-familial family does not signal the end of family, simply its taking on a new form. The role of law and the state in this view becomes to recognise and support these new ways of 'doing family' (Morgan 1996).

Others agree that historical changes are occurring, but see them as dangerous (Deech 2009a; Centre for Social Justice 2010). They would say that the way in which individuality and disaffiliation have become contrasted with obligation/duty in the new millenium represents a crisis. Their solution is to reassert the good of marriage, tradition and obligation. Rather than acknowledge and support the post-familial family, they say there are both moral and social reasons why law and policy must discourage it and encourage individuals toward marriage and the traditional family (see also Morgan 2000; Finnis 1994).

Yet others query whether individualisation with its presumed retreat from commitment has been as dominant a trend either socially or personally as is commonly believed (Smart 2007). Feminist critiques of Beck and Giddens, for example, suggest that both present an androcentric point of view, representing the ideology of a privileged few—usually men— who, because of their greater wealth and lesser child-rearing and other caring responsibilities, are able to move on from commitment easily (Mulnari and Sandell 2009). They are worried about the ways in which these theories of late modernity have 'captured the European sociological imagination' and that '[e]specially within the field of family studies the use of Beck's and Giddens' theories are extensive, often both as broad, sweeping framing statements about what world "we" live in' (Mulinari and Sandell 2009: 494). Whatever view one takes on new sociologies of family and intimacy, we agree with Smart that theoretical reflection generates a refinement of ideas and excites innovative empirical work; recent reflections, including individualisation theory, have injected debate and excitement into the study of families and relationships (Smart 2007: 24–25).

One further view of changing sociological approaches to family is to refuse to see family as an entity at all. Giddens and Beck and Beck-Gernsheim see family as a 'thing', as a group of people bound together by choice, biology or law such as marriage or civil partnership. From other sociological perspectives, however, family is to be seen as 'less of noun and more of an adjective or, possibly, a verb. "Family" represents a constructed quality of human interaction or an active process rather than a thing-like object of detached social investigation' (Morgan 1996: 16; Morgan 1999). On this view, the object of study becomes what people do rather than the form of relationships they adopt. The term 'family practices' has been coined to capture the 'family' quality of interactions of everyday living, so that

> activities which on their face seem immediately to be 'about' family are included in this term, but, importantly, so are activities which may not seem so obviously to be family matters. Accessing public transport, eating breakfast, working overtime and voting, for example, can all be studied as family practices. (Diduck 2003: 28)

Q What are the advantages and disadvantages of understanding family to be a noun or object? What are the advantages and disadvantages of understanding family to be something one does rather than as a unit in which one resides?

Methodological and theoretical problems have been identified in many of the above analyses of family history and family sociology, but despite these problems, as Anderson suggests, we may still conclude that the way in which people choose to structure their affective and economic relationships both affects and is affected by social mores and economic conditions in any society. Our changing family practices may be a result of changing social norms or may precede them. Normative influences go both ways. Social norms interact with legal ones so that the effects of discourses of individualisation, rights, morality, equality or care can be uncovered in both (Diduck 2008a).

Demographic research confirms that we are indeed living in different types of relation-ships. The Office for National Statistics (ONS) reported that in 2010 there were 17.9 million families in the UK. Families were defined as a married, civilly partnered or cohabiting couple with or without children, or a lone parent with at least one child (ONS

2011a). The ONS also reported that there were 7.5 million one-person households and 0.8 million households consisting of two or more related adults (ibid). From these figures we see that marriage, civil partnership and cohabitation now appear to be socially 'acceptable' lifestyle choices in Britain. But perhaps the choices do not end there. For many, being a part of a relationship and sharing one's life with another does not require either state sanction or cohabitation. 'Living apart together' (LAT) has become a recognised sociological and demographic term and researchers in Britain are beginning to explore its legal and social policy implications (Haskey and Lewis 2006). According to Haskey (2005), around one in three people aged 16–59 who are neither co-residentially cohabiting nor married and living with their spouse are in a LAT relationship. Many choose to enter into these relationships and many are forced into them by employment or other circumstances, but maintaining independence while at the same time being in a 'relationship' is a common feature. Unlike cohabitation and civil partnership, both of which remain marriage-like, LAT challenges one of the markers of marriage/conjugal coupledom by disassociating it from common residence. In this way, LAT, unlike contemporary cohabitation, may be a real example of a new way to affiliate. Perhaps like cohabitants did years ago, those living in a committed, sexually exclusive, intimate yet non-co-residential relationship must learn to manage their version of autonomous intimacy with external norms of what it means to be a 'couple'.

Shifting meanings of 'family' and relationship may be coming from other quarters as well. Weeks also found that the term 'family' has become an 'important rallying point' for many self-identified non-heterosexuals:

> Increasingly, the term is being deployed by many people to denote something broader than the traditional relationships based on lineage, alliance and biology, referring instead to kin-like networks of relationships based on friendship, choice and commitment ... . [U]se of the term suggests a strong perceived need to appropriate the sort of values and comforts that the family is supposed to embody. (Weeks 2002: 218)

This could mean that 'the stories many non-heterosexual men and women tell about families of choice are creating a new public space where old and new forms jostle for meaning, and where new patterns of relationships are being invented' (ibid: 219).

Diduck (2008a)[3] sums up the changes as follows:

> Most people interested in family sociology and family law seem to agree that families are changing. Whether we look simply at the demographic data or at the more nuanced research that demonstrates changes in the nature, manifestations and experiences of personal commitment and responsibility, we all have to admit that something is happening. Some of us may be pleased by the changes and some of us disconcerted or even frightened by them, but research shows that 'family life' for many of us is lived outside the heteronuclear married norm and includes forms of group marriage, serial monogamy, unmarried different or same sex cohabitation, non co-resident intimate partnerships or living apart together, step-parenthood and or lone parenthood, not to mention other household communities including the non-conjugal home-sharers with whom the Law Commission had so much trouble in 2002 and disregarded in 2006. Sociologists tell us that these relationships are important to people; they provide stability, intimacy, care, and companionship. They are central to people's core values. Family sociologists further tell us that friendship practices are changing so that there may be a blurring of lines

[3] See also Diduck (2008b).

between friends and family. In all of these new family practices, connectedness operates in more various ways than simply through sexual intimacy or blood. (Diduck 2008a: 251)

She then wonders how law has responded to these changes.

What is law's relationship with these ambiguous or at least flexible family practices? What is family law to make of these other forms of 'connectedness', or, more to the point, of their personal and social consequences? One view is that family law has simply and appropriately responded to them. Whether we see these relationships as new or as only newly acknowledged, law has in the last decade extended its jurisdiction remarkably rapidly to encompass many of them simply by acknowledging them as family connections. On this view, family law itself really hasn't changed; it has simply extended its remit to permit a wider range of people and relationships within it.

Another view, however, is that family law has not so much responded to social change as it has participated in it. Expanding family law may have helped to facilitate changing family practices and new 'personal familiarities' and in this way has worked together with actual behaviour to legitimize the increasing diversity of ways in which we arrange our personal living. On this view, law is connected to the actions of people such that both constituencies are engaged in a continual process of 'meaning making'. Family law and family practices 'mutually shape each other as people challenge the partiality of legal conceptions through social action *and* challenge social patterns through legal discourse'. Meaning making does not begin from scratch, however, connection and mutuality 'invest legal forms with new meanings by reference in part to the meanings that are already established'. (ibid: 251–52)

II. FAMILIES AND THE LAW: QUESTIONING SOME ASSUMPTIONS

Family Ideology

It has been said that law has moved from a definition of family based on its form, to one based upon its functions.[4] This may be true, but still begs the question of what its appropriate functions are. We suggest that many of those functions and much of their legal regulation—that is, much family law—takes its shape and is given meaning through a particular idea of, or ideology[5] of, the family. O'Donovan discusses family ideology in this way:

What is the ideology of the family which contributes to the maintenance of present structures? For evidence of views of law-makers we can turn to the statements of politicians and of the judiciary—the traditional establishment. The family is presented in the Britain of the 1990s as the bedrock of traditional values and common sense ... .

In political rhetoric the family serves many purposes. It is totem, emblem of stability, reassurance and common sense. It can be used to reject challenges to established authority and to castigate critics as 'trendy'. It also serves to be made guilty, to be blamed for crime rates,

---

[4] See discussion below, pp 26–27.
[5] For a discussion of ideology, see eg Eagleton (1991); Purvis and Hunt (1993); Hunt (1985); Easton (1976); Havas (1995); Laclau and Mouffe (1985).

delinquency, illiteracy. Yet it can stand against the state as bulwark against intrusion and interference. Thus, Ferdinand Mount, one-time Cabinet office advisor:

> The family's most dangerous enemies may not turn out to be those who have openly declared
> war. It is so easy to fight against the blatant cruelty of collectivist dictators … . It is less
> easy to fight against the armies of those who are 'only here to help'—those who claim to
> come with the best intention but come armed, all the same, with statutory powers and
> administrative instruments: education officers, children's officers … welfare workers and all
> the other councils … which claim to know best how to manage our private concerns.

The family does not have to establish its credentials, its origins, its sources—it just is whatever
it is. It contains, as Goodrich says of law, the tradition of inescapable institutions—repeti-
tion … . As one former government minister puts it, the family:

> poses strength and resilience, not least in adversity. Loyalty to the family ranks highest of
> all, higher even than loyalty to the state. It is not accident … that dictatorships, whether of
> the Left or the Right, seek first to devalue and then to destroy the family.
>
> (O'Donovan 1993: 39–40, references omitted)

The idea or ideology of the family, then, comprises a timeless, traditional nuclear, private,
ideal family form, which may or may not have existed historically in a majority of households, if at all (see Gillis 1997; Diduck 2003: ch 2), and as we have seen, certainly exists
only in a shrinking number today. Despite this, however, the ideology of the family
informs much of family law- and policy-making. Gittins explains:

> [I]t soon becomes evident that a wide gap exists, and has existed, between discourses about 'the
> family' and how individuals actually live their lives … . Many studies have failed to differen-
> tiate between what preachers, politicians and philosophers say a family should be and how
> people in fact live and interact in social groups that are defined as families. Much of Lawrence
> Stone's work (1977), for instance, is really an analysis of changing family ideology rather than
> a study of actual patterns of family life. Demographers, on the other hand, have tended to
> concentrate on household structures and demographic events alone without reference to values,
> discourses or ideology. Yet both aspects need to be understood.
>
> Linked to this question is the question of what relationship exists between people's material
> circumstances, the ways in which they live their lives, and discourses and ideologies of how
> they should live their lives. The extent to which one determines or influences the other is a
> highly controversial problem which cannot be resolved here (if, indeed, anywhere). What I want
> to consider, however, is the ways in which a number of sometimes contradictory discourses
> about 'the family' are exercised in and through the media, religious institutions, the educational
> system and social policy generally to create an overall 'ideology of the family'.
>
> Discourses within this ideology include prescriptions and proscriptions on gendered behav-
> iour, ethnic relations (eg, social disapproval of mixed marriages), age, masculinities and
> femininities. Overall, an amalgam of discourses combine to create a dominant representation of
> what a family should be like. This representation changes over time, but nonetheless is presented
> as something universal. For the past few decades this ideal has been of a young, married,
> heterosexual, white, middle-class couple with two children—a boy (older) and a girl, all of
> whom live together in their own house. The husband is the main breadwinner and the wife is
> a full-time housewife/mother who may, however, work part-time. The assumption of this ideal
> family's normality has influenced, and continues to influence, social policy and the ways in
> which laws are formulated and implemented for the population overall. (Gittins 1993: 2–3)[6]

---

[6] On family ideology generally, see Dewar (1992); Collier (1995b); Havas (1995); Barrett and MacIntosh
(1991).

One of the themes of this book, then, is that there are close and necessary connections between the way people choose to order their affective and parenting relationships, law and the organisation of the social and economic world, and that these connections are mediated through family ideology. In law, just as in business, in the popular media, and in other aspects of modern life, a particular form of 'family' is held out as ideal, even while other forms may in some circumstances be deemed 'good enough'. More and more people and relationships are being let into the family 'club', providing they look like or function like the ideal.[7] This is not to say that laws regulating families do not change over time or that changes in family practices do not precede legal change. Founded as it is in a liberal democratic polity, however, and filtered through family ideology, law's engagement with family relations has tended to rely upon a number of foundational assumptions, and we now turn to unearthing those assumptions and their implications for families.

In the liberal vision of the family, its social function is to provide a financially autonomous, physically and emotionally fulfilling enclave for its members. This idea of family rests on a few assumptions. First, it assumes a division between that which we know of as the private—the realm of the 'home'—and the public—the realm of politics and market or 'work'. The second assumption is that the need for the type of physical and emotional fulfilment obtained from the liberal family is inherent in human nature, or that we are destined 'naturally' to form private and monogamous heterosexual couples and procreate. The third assumption upon which the functionalist liberal vision of the family rests is that the family is the 'safe' place in which care and nurture dominate over competition and danger.

We will question each of these assumptions in turn.

1. Public and Private

This view of a private versus a public sphere of life is reflected in a number of political and social visions as well as legal rules. It emerges in the historical work discussed earlier, from Engels to Parsons to Anderson. One view of the divide is ascribed to German sociologist Ferdinand Tonnies (O'Donovan 1985: 4–5). Tonnies contrasted a pre-modern society characterised by social harmony in which relationships were mediated by love, duty, common understanding and purpose—*Gemeinschaft*—with modern commercial society characterised by individualism, competition and formality— *Gesellschaft*. His two ideal types of society have come to be used as metaphors for the private realm of family life and the public realm of market relations. Other writers suggest that the origins of a public/private dichotomy can be traced to Aristotle. Freeman, for example, says:

> It can be traced to Aristotle. Men by nature were intended to live in a polis in which the highest good could be attained. Women, slaves and children did not and could not participate in the unfolding of goodness and reason which was the 'common heritage of co-equal participants in perfect association'. They were confined to the oikos, the household, a non-public sphere. The good at which the household aimed was a lesser good. Women, accordingly, achieved only the limited goodness of the 'naturally ruled' a goodness that was, of course, different in kind from that of the naturally ruling. (Freeman 1985: 166–67, endnotes omitted)

Freeman and others (eg Rose 1987) observe how Aristotle's public/private notion became

---

[7] Diduck (2005a) has called this the familialisation of society.

a part of the more recent liberal philosophy on which contemporary English law is based. O'Donovan describes the separation as follows:

> The idea that private and public can be distinguished is imbued in legal philosophy and informs legal policy. 'One of the central goals of nineteenth-century legal thought was to create a clear separation between constitutional, criminal, and regulatory law—public law—and the law of private transactions—torts, contracts, property and commercial law'. This division is not confined to distinguishing relations between individual and state from relations between individuals. It also draws a line dividing the law's business from what is called private. Although this boundary between the private and public shifts over time, the existence of the distinction and the notion of boundary are rarely questioned.
>
> The dichotomy between private and public as unregulated and regulated has its origins in liberal philosophy. The seventeenth-century liberal tradition as represented by Locke posits a distinction between reason and passion, knowledge and desire, mind and body. This leads to a split between the public sphere in which individuals prudently calculate their own self-interest and act upon it, and a private sphere of subjectivity and desire. As Roberto Unger describes it: 'In our public mode of being we speak the common language of reason, and live under laws of the state, the constraints of the market, and the customs of the different social bodies to which we belong. In our private incarnation, however, we are at the mercy of our own sense impressions and desires.' The liberal conception is of man as a rational creature making rational choices and entering the political sphere for his own ends.
>
> Nineteenth-century liberal thought, as expressed by John Stuart Mill, continued the tradition of the private/public split. In his feminist work *On the Subjection of Women* the solution for Mill was the grant to women of full equality and formal rights with men in the public sphere. From public equality, he believed, would follow a transformed family, a 'school of sympathy in equality' where the spouses live 'together in love, without power on one side or obedience on the other'. Yet he did not propose the merging of the two spheres but rather sanctioned the division of labour in which women remain in the realm of subjectivity and the private. Thus he argued: 'When the support of the family depends, not on property but on earnings, the common arrangement, by which the wife superintends the domestic expenditure, seems to me in general the most suitable division of labour between the two persons.' Women's role was to remain that of loving and softening men in the domestic realm. Mill's views on household management overlooked the connection between economic power and dominance in the home. Economic inequality leads to an imbalance of power. The division of labour whereby one spouse works for earnings and the other for love encapsulates the public/private split.
>
> (O'Donovan 1985: 8–9, references omitted)

As each of these writers implies,[8] the separation of life into a public and a private sphere has enormous repercussions for what we believe to be the state's responsibility for assisting families. As more and more types of relationships become subsumed within the private sphere of the family, the state's responsibility for supporting individuals correspondingly lessens (Diduck 2005a). The public/private separation also has political implications for claims to justice made by family members. As Philipps says:

> [The public/private divide] functions ideologically to draw boundaries around what properly constitutes the subject of politics and what is considered the legitimate scope of political claims ... . These boundaries, which are shifting, serve to limit arbitrarily the reach of liberal ideals such democracy, equality, justice and liberty. Political claims based on these ideals are effectively confined to a limited public sphere created and defined by marking it off from the

---

[8] See also Fineman (2004).

family or domestic sphere, and from the market. An expansion of private responsibility for human welfare will therefore tend to depoliticize women's social reproductive labour and to delegitimate any claims to equality based on this work. (Philipps 2002: 45, references omitted)

Finally, the public/private split also affects relations between members of families. It enshrines values in legal and social policy, for example, that explain the reluctance, until relatively recently, of police officers to 'intervene' in domestic violence situations,[9] it normalises the economic dependence of women upon men,[10] and it has operated to legitimate the 'objectification' of children.[11] Herring also reminds us that the idea of family relations as private may also have class implications: '[F]or those reliant on social housing and benefits the home can be seen as replete with social intrusion' (Herring 2011: 21). He goes further: 'In fact, the state may police families in less obvious ways than direct legal intervention: health visitors, teachers, neighbourhood watch schemes and social workers could all be thought a form of policing of families outside of formal legal regulation'(ibid).[12]

Some theorists, however, have been concerned to question the public/private dichotomy and to test its taken-for-granted status. These writers have suggested that a split between public and private is not a naturally occurring social phenomenon but, rather, is socially constructed. It, like the idea of the family, is ideological. Nikolas Rose explains:

> Analyses of the legal regulation of marriage, divorce, sexual behaviour and domestic violence are deployed to show that the ideology of individual choice and personal freedom in the private domain of home and family legitimates a refusal by public authorities to intervene into certain places, activities, relationships and feelings. Designating them as personal, private and subjective makes them appear to be outside the scope of law as a fact of nature, whereas in fact non-intervention is a socially constructed, historically variable, and inevitably political decision. The state defines as 'private' those aspects of life into which it will not intervene, then, paradoxically, uses this privacy as the justification for its non-intervention. Like *laissez faire* in the market, the idea that the family can be private in the sense of outside public regulation is a myth. The state cannot avoid intervening in the shaping of familial relations through decisions as to which type of relations to sanction and codify and which types of dispute to regulate or not regulate. (Rose 1987: 64–65)

Indeed, by not 'intervening' in so-called private matters, the state is taking a decision to support the status quo which can be considered a form of intervention or, at least, regulation

Much has been written on the reification of a public/private divide in the area of family law,[13] including that which questions its usefulness as an analytical device (Collier 1995b: 66–67). In fact, if we adopt Morgan's (1996) view of family as an adjective or a verb, then all manner of public engagements have 'family' aspects to them, so that laws about, for example, employment, public transportation and political citizenship are all family matters. We do not have the space here to review the literature in its entirety, but for our purposes we wish to note the assumptions in law about the existence and the propriety of such a separation, and to question how these assumptions inform and affect laws governing families. We take the view, as Diduck and O'Donovan (2006) do, that the 'legal

---

[9] See Chapter 12 below.
[10] See Chapters 5 and 6 below.
[11] See Chapters 4 and 11 below.
[12] See also Donzelot (1980) and Chapters 5 and 14 below.
[13] See, eg, Eekelaar (2000).

regulation of private, *family* relations are also about the regulation of *social and political* relations; they are about the nature and value of dependence and independence, about the balance of social and economic power and about the part that law plays in this regulation' (Diduck and O'Donovan 2006: 1)

Thus, while many take the view that families are private units and are not the business of law unless something 'goes wrong', we, like Rose, and Diduck and O'Donovan, take the view that the very definitions of what a family is, or what is right or wrong for it, is a legal matter. This belies the privacy rhetoric which banishes law from the 'healthy', functioning family. This liberal view of the private family is belied further, not only by law's place relative to the family, but also by the place of other public institutions such as religion and 'the market'. In conjunction with law, each influences the constitution of families in any historical time and place.

2. The Private Nuclear Family as Natural

The development of the private family and its separation from the social world are often presented as inevitable; writers such as Parsons see a split between a particular form of family and the rest of society as having evolved naturally with increasingly progressive social conditions. However, although we believe that there is a connection between social conditions and family forms, we wish to question the degree to which this version of the family can be assumed to be natural or the product of evolutionary forces.

For early anthropologists and theorists of the family the evolution of capitalist society, and hence of the families which formed or were formed by that society, was understood in Darwinian terms as a social manifestation of the 'survival of the fittest':

> During the second half of the 19th century, a number of social and intellectual developments—among them the evolutionary researches of Charles Darwin; the rise of 'urban problems' in fast-growing cities; and the accumulation of data on non-Western peoples by missionaries and agents of the colonial states—contributed to what most of us would now recognize as the beginnings of modern social science. Alternately excited and perplexed by changes in a rapidly industrializing world, thinkers as diverse as socialist Frederick Engels and bourgeois apologist Herbert Spencer—to say nothing of a host of mythographers, historians of religion, and even feminists—attempted to identify the distinctive problems and potentials of their contemporary society by constructing evolutionary accounts of 'how it all began'. At base a sense of 'progress' gave direction to their thoughts whether like Spencer they believed 'man' had advanced from the love of violence to a more civilized love of peace or, like Engels, that humanity had moved from primitive promiscuity and incest toward monogamy and 'individual sex-love'.
>
> (Collier et al 1982: 36–37)

While later theorists denied a belief in linear social progress toward one universal image of family, many (eg Linton 1949) continued to have recourse to a belief in what was 'natural' to explain family forms and functions.

As Barrett and McIntosh (1991: 26) point out, any appeal to the 'natural' of the idea of the family serves an ideological function by giving legitimacy to the moral and socio-political claims the family is able to make:

> It is in the realm of gender, sexuality, marriage and the family that we are collectively most seduced by appeals to the natural. In this realm the shifting mores of practice are solidified, some to be sanctified and others condemned. The prevailing form of family is seen as inevitable, as naturally given and biologically determined. (ibid: 27)

To make the claim that a certain form of the family is 'natural' gives the claimant a rhetorical advantage. He or she does not have to admit the moral or political aspects of the claim while at the same time can dismiss all opposition as 'unnatural'.

It is our position that the nuclear family's place in the social history of industrialisation, capitalism and liberal political morality is not a result of natural forces. Indeed, its link with that time period is questionable.[14] While humans have most probably always had some need to organise themselves into units which meet needs of affection, sex, safety and nurture, the shape that that unit takes is based upon more than simply 'instinct' or nature. Historians and sociologists alike suggest that there is a direct and dialectical relationship between, for example, 'family' and production, subsistence or labour, and in more modern times, 'family' and taxation policy, and 'family' and immigration, for example, but whether the relationship relies upon the 'naturalness' of this family is debatable. Historians have disagreed, for example, on the timing and causes of the emergence of the intimate, companionate family founded upon romantic love, on the transition from (or indeed existence of) an extended multigenerational family, and on the role of gender and the place of children within the family.[15]

Thus, with the exception perhaps of its place in religious discourse, the 'natural family unit' so eulogised in contemporary political rhetoric can be seen as anything but natural. Mount (1982) even questions the 'naturalness' of the 'traditional' family within the established church, by suggesting that it has only relatively recently appropriated the 'traditional' family into its discourse.

3. The Family as Protection

The third unstated assumption of the liberal view of the family is that emotional, economic, physical and psychological succour are provided in this unit. We saw earlier how Tonnies' *Gemeinschaft* and *Gesellschaft* can be used as theoretical models for this view. 'The family' is assumed to be a unit that provides care and allows individual freedom to flourish, and represents the last bastion against the harshness of either individual competition, according to Tonnies, or collectivism, according to more modern theorists such as Mount. Prime Minister Margaret Thatcher captured the more modern view when she proclaimed that, '[t]here is no such thing as society. There are individual men and women and there are families' (*Woman's Own* 1987: 10). But as cases of child abuse are revealed,[16] and as the numbers of battered women continue to outnumber places available for them in refuges,[17] more writers have come to question the idea that individuals are necessarily protected within the 'the family' and, accordingly, they argue that it should not be immune from intervention. Freeman, for example, writes:

> [I]f women and children are dependents, all that non-intervention achieves is protection of the dominance of men against women, adults against children. When Goldstein, Freud and Solnit tell us that a policy of minimum coercive intervention by the state accords with their 'firm belief as citizens in individual freedom and human dignity' we have to ask 'whose freedom?' and 'what dignity'? In a world of basic structural inequalities of which the family is a microcosm, individual freedom can be so exercised as to undermine not only the liberty of others but also their human dignity. Bill Jordan put the point well when he wrote that 'the case against inter-

---

[14] See Davidoff et al (1999) and sources cited therein.
[15] See, eg, Gillis (1997); Davidoff et al (1999); Diduck (2003); and sources cited therein.
[16] See Chapter 13 below.
[17] See Chapter 12 below.

vention in family life often rests on the freedom of more powerful members (usually husbands in relation to wives and parents in relation to children) to exercise their power without restriction'. (Freeman 1985: 168–69, references omitted)

Certainly in many families mutual respect, affection and nurture prevail. The law no longer permits physical chastisement of a wife by her husband, rape in marriage has been recognised as a crime, and, broadly speaking, the beating of children has come to be called child abuse. We shall explore later in more detail, however, the extent to which the traditional nuclear family lives up to the functional ideal assumed by law, but for our purposes now, we wish to identify the assumption as a problematic one.

III. WHAT IS FAMILY LAW?

Thus far we have suggested that that unit which we know of as the family is not capable of any easy definition. Who is included in the definition of 'family' may differ depending upon whether what is being constructed is a sociological model, an anthropological model or an economic or legal model. Perhaps it depends upon what we want the family to represent or to do. Moreover, people in Britain currently arrange their social, economic and sexual lives in many different ways. Yet, despite this multiplicity of family forms, there is an ideology of the family which relies upon, and in turn reinforces, assumptions which imply that it is possible to construct a single definition of family. Those assumptions centre on the notion of separate spheres and family privacy, on the image of the family unit as a source of affection and protection, and on the belief in the inherent 'naturalness' of the traditional family form. It is, therefore, as much the ideology of the family as families themselves which sets the stage for the study of family law. As US family law scholar, Fran Olsen, states:

> [T]he family and roles within the family are constituted by law and state intervention in the family is not an analytical concept but rather an ideological one. Family law is an arena for the ideological struggle over what it means to be a mother, daughter, wife and so forth ... one of the most important questions about any legal decision is how it affects political and ideological struggles. (Olsen 1992: 209)

Family law, then, has to address crucial questions: how and in what situations do institutions of the state become involved in (and in the consequences of) our choice of sexual partners, our decisions whether and with whom to have children, and the manner in which we choose to live, share our money or rear our children? In law, just as in sociology, history or anthropology, the answers to these questions often reflect a judgement about the value of the family unit in question relative to the dominant ideology of the family at any given historical moment. It is an awareness of this judgement that we wish readers to maintain throughout this book. We also wish to underline the relationship between the conditions of families and social conditions as well as that between law and social conditions. Neither families nor law can be conceptually or materially separated from the social and economic context that plays a part in shaping them.

What do these relationships and contingencies mean for the study of family law, especially if, as Katherine O'Donovan suggests, the very 'black box' we construct as 'family

law' is part of the ideology of the family (O'Donovan 1993: 25)? Diduck (2008a) describes
some of the history of family law:

> Many scholars date the birth of 'family law' as the modern concept we know today in Britain
> at some time after the Second World War. Before that, the law regulating the family was frag-
> mented into disparate parts and in addition to the law of property and testamentary law, included
> topics such as the law of husband and wife and the law relating to infants. Blackstone's direct
> legacy is perceptible here as is the legacy of the common law tradition in which the 'develop-
> ment of the concepts, categories and divisions of the common law is bound with the concrete
> problems that arise in individual cases'. The law, in other words, was made by the judges, and
> the 'family law' cases that came before them traditionally were indeed cases about marriage and
> divorce, about settlement of property and about the liability for contracts and criminal actions
> of children. And so, despite the broad range of laws that might be seen to 'directly affect' the
> family, those fragments that were deemed to be family law and that eventually were gathered
> together under that heading reflected the concerns of those who were able to bring their causes
> before the courts: the propertied and middle class (usually men) for whom validity of marriage
> and divorce was profoundly important for establishing the legitimacy of their line and the
> legitimate passage of property along it. Laws that 'directly affected' the poor were simply not
> seen as family law at all. These laws were administered by the Magistrates or were contained
> within and administered as part of the Poor Law and reflected a class based division which
> arguably has left its mark on family law today. Few family law textbooks even today contain
> chapters on income support, jobseekers' allowance, tax, employment or public housing.
>
> Probert suggests that a fragmented and segregated body of family law makes sense however,
> in the context of segregated (middle class) family living historically, in which children and
> servants were allocated to separate quarters within the household. The Victorian family just did
> not look like or live like families do now, so Victorian family law should not be expected to
> look like it looks now. She makes the reasonable point to which I shall return below, that 'the
> fact that earlier concepts of family law do not always resemble our own should not obscure the
> fact that they may have been better suited to the law and the families of their own time'. She
> reminds us that there was in fact a text book published in 1885 entitled *The Law of Domestic
> Relations* which included a chapter on Master and Servant.
>
> Eventually, around the 1950s, however, a coherent body of law became conceptualized
> specifically as 'family law'. It was first taught at the London School of Economics by Professor
> Otto Kahn-Freund whose continental background may have influenced his pursuit of family law
> as a separate doctrinal discipline. The first textbook with family law in its title was published
> in 1957 and brought together the black letter law concerning the parties' status as husband and
> wife and the property entitlements that came with it. There was neither discussion of children's
> welfare nor of the public law relating to children, nor indeed of many of the public consequences
> of marriage and divorce. This state of affairs changed over the years, however, until Cretney
> could say that by the year 2000 'there was in place a system [of family law] constructed on
> rational principles'.
>
> Among the many reasons for the gathering together in the immediate post-war period of a
> body of case law under the heading family law may be that the subject of the law—a particular
> form of family—became politically important at that time, at least ideologically, in a formal,
> conceptually clear way. (Diduck 2008a: 258–59, references omitted)

[But] if just as changes in the social world—the entrenching of a particular family form at a
particular historic time as the subject of family law—was a part of the creation of a coherent
notion of 'family law', perhaps contemporary social changes may signal a time now for a challenge to that coherent notion. (ibid: 266)

Others have taken up the challenge. Eekelaar notes the changes in family practices in the twentieth century and asks 'Do we need to try to bring these [new forms of relationships] under some concept of "family"?' (Eekelaar 2006: 31). He proposes we abandon the label 'family law' in favour of 'personal law'. Probert (2004b) wonders if a return to the old term 'domestic relations law' might be appropriate.

Whatever we call it, family law must cope with subjects who do not act as the rational reasonable men paradigmatic of other areas of law. It 'engages with areas of social life and feeling—namely love, passion, intimacy, commitment and betrayal—that are … riven with contradiction or paradox' (Dewar 1998: 468). Dewar (1998, 2000) suggests that for this and other reasons, family law can be described as 'chaotic'. He says that family law exhibits normative incoherence or uncertainty and that this stems from uncertainty about its proper role or purpose. Is family law to enforce rights between family members, or to promote their welfare, for example, or is it to maximise utility and pursue an optimal outcome? (Dewar 1998: 490) Is it to enforce rules or exercise discretion?[18] As we shall see, what we call family law does all of these things, but as we said above, its choices at any given moment or in any given case reflects a judgement about the value of the relationship in question relative to its particular social and political context.

Our approach in this book is to open up the study of family law to one which encompasses more than simply the statutes and cases that regulate relations between conjugal partners or parent and child. We seek to identify also those who are not so regulated, and try to understand reasons for both the exclusions and inclusions. Secondly, our approach to family law also acknowledges that regulation occurs at normative and informal levels as well as at the level of formal law. Thirdly, family law in this book is also the law of public support, employment, personal taxation, education, immigration, international human rights, housing and crime. Finally, we suggest that an understanding of the law in each of these areas is incomplete without further understanding of the economic and social policy affecting each. Through this broad meaning of 'family law' we hope to undermine to some degree the ideology of the family which keeps O'Donovan's black box closed.

Let us now examine how our relationships are regulated directly by legal definition of them. Law assumes a certain place in society for something called a family, but like sociology and anthropology, it has difficulty in defining exactly what that entity looks like.

IV. THE LEGAL FAMILY

There is no statutory definition of family, and there is really no common law definition either. How can law, which demands certainty, cope with this lacuna? There are, in reality, only a few situations in which this question is raised in law. In one example, courts were called upon to determine whether a surviving tenant was a member of the deceased's 'family', for if so, that surviving tenant retained statutory rights to the home. In this series of cases, the closest thing to a legal definition the courts created was the statement that a family is what the ordinary man on the street thinks it is. This reliance upon 'common sense' or popular perception (or ideology?) is illustrated in the case of *Sefton Holdings v*

---

[18] But see Diduck (2008a) who sees more normative consistency in family law than Dewar identifies.

Cairns.[19] Here, the Court of Appeal was called upon to determine whether the relationship between two women who lived as sisters for 45 years was a family relationship for the purposes of the Rent Act 1977. Lloyd LJ said:

> The question is whether the defendant, Miss Florence Cairns, is entitled to protection under the Rent Acts, that is to say, whether she is a statutory tenant under s 2 of the Rent Act 1977. The answer depends on the meaning to be given to the word 'family' in para 7 of Part I of Sch 1 to that Act.
>
> The facts are that the plaintiffs, Sefton Holdings Ltd, are the landlords of the premises in question. They let it to Mr Richard Gamble some time between 1939 and 1941 when the house was built. Mr Gamble died in 1965. His daughter, Ada, then succeeded to the tenancy. Miss Ada Gamble died in 1986. The defendant came to live with Mr and Mrs Gamble and their daughter Ada in 1941. She was then 23 and single. Both her parents had died. Her boyfriend had just been killed in the war. Miss Ada Gamble asked her parents if they would take the defendant in, which they did. They treated her as their own daughter. She called them 'Mom and Pop'. She has lived in the same house ever since. She is now some 70 years of age.
>
> On 6 June 1986, shortly after Miss Ada Gamble died, the plaintiffs served on the defendant a notice to quit. The defendant claims that she is entitled to remain on in the house as a statutory tenant under para 7 of Part I of the first schedule, which provides as follows:
>
> > [The court went on to quote the section which states that a statutory tenancy passes automatically on the death of the first tenant to a member of that tenant's family who was residing with him or her at the time of death.]
>
> … So what we have to decide in this case is whether the defendant is a member of her family who was residing with her at the time of, and for the period of 6 months immediately before, her death. The defendant was clearly residing with Miss Ada Gamble at the time of Miss Ada Gamble's death. But was she a member of Miss Ada Gamble's family? That is the question. The county court judge has decided that she was, and there is now an appeal to this court.
>
> … It has been held over and over again that, in deciding whether a person is a member of another person's family, we must give the word 'family' its ordinary, everyday meaning. We cannot extend that meaning in order to cover what might appear to be a hard case; we must not let affection press upon judgment … . (109–10)

Various attempts have been made by the courts from time to time to define the word 'family', by identifying various categories within which a person would be a member of another person's family. But Lord Diplock did not embark on that task in *Joram Developments Ltd v Sharratt*, and I do not propose to embark on that task myself. All I would say is that, in approaching this case, I have found it useful to bear two matters in mind. First, there is the distinction drawn by Viscount Dilhorne *in Joram Developments Ltd v Sharratt* … between being a member of a family and being a member of the household. Secondly, there is the distinction between being a member of the family and living as a member of the family. There is no doubt that the defendant lived as a member of the family, and that may be why the judge decided this case in her favour. But the question we have to ask ourselves is not whether she lived as a member of the family, but whether she was a member of the family. I am clear that she was not, and that the man in the street would take the same view. (112)

Sir Roualeyn Cumming-Bruce agreed.

With some feeling of regret, I agree.

I have been aided by the guidance given by Lord Dilhorne in the speech to which Lloyd LJ

---

[19] [1988] 2 FLR 109.

has referred. It seems to me clear beyond a peradventure that the plaintiff in this case became a member of the household of Mr and Mrs Gamble and, in spite of her age of 23, was offered and accepted a high degree of kindness and support which led the judge to make the finding that she reminded herself that in 1941 young women of 23 did not by and large live in the independent way that so many young women do today. Mr and Mrs Gamble were giving her a home and they took her in as a daughter, and in every way treated her as such ... .

Like Lloyd LJ, it is with diffidence that I am moved to differ from the view of a county court judge familiar with the local circumstances of the Liverpool environment; but the question is a question of law, although, like all questions of law, it involves a nice appreciation of the relevant factors. Through the now mounting line of cases which deal with the meaning of the word 'family' in the context of the relevant schedule it is to be observed that in no case has the court found it possible to identify the necessary ingredient or quality that distinguishes a familial nexus from a nexus less than familial. The approach of the courts has been to look at all the circumstances and to then seek to answer the question: 'What would an ordinary person characterize the relationship as?' For the reasons explained by Lord Dilhorne, I do not myself think that, putting the test in that way (accepting that it has been so frequently), it really adds very much to the question: 'What is the ordinary meaning of someone being a member of somebody else's family?' To be a member of a family is *different* from being treated as a member of the family. (112)

The court here recognises that circumstances in 1941 may have been different from those in 1987 and also recognises that 'the local circumstances of the Liverpool environment' may have been relevant to the County Court judge who first heard the case. An awareness of these specificities is important in formulating definitions of a concept such as 'family' which is so dependent upon social understandings, and yet the court then goes on to say that those specificities must be put aside to determine 'questions of law'. It is possible to criticise this decision on the basis of the court's formal and positivistic separation of law from social conditions, especially as the court then purports to answer the 'legal' question by reference to 'all the circumstances' and 'what an ordinary person would characterise the relationship as'.

Q In your view, could the court have legitimately found that Mrs Cairns was a member of Miss Gamble's family? What about Mr Michalak, who came from Poland and lived with Mr Lul from 1985 to Mr Lul's death in 1998. The judge found that Mr Michalak subsisted on Mr Lul's good graces towards him. They were distantly related, and Mr Michalak addressed Mr Lul by a Polish word which translated to 'Uncle'. M cooked some meals for L, did some of his shopping, and gave him a helping hand with his washing, particularly towards the end of his life when he was sometimes incontinent. The court found that while M was helping to care for L, he was not a full-time carer. It found there was no emotional bond, that theirs was in no sense a loving or caring relationship. Rather, M merely had a relationship of respect for the older man and therefore could not be said to be a part of Mr Lul's family so as to entitle him to remain in the flat on Mr Lul's death. (See *Michalak v LB Wandsworth* [2002] 4 All ER 1136 CA.) Do you agree? How would you characterise their relationship?

O'Donovan has reviewed the *Sefton Holdings* decision and others in which courts have attempted to identify family for different purposes, and finds that 'law privileges certain forms [of family] and denies recognition and benefits to others, while simultaneously denying that a coherent definition of family exists' (O'Donovan 1993: 39). Let us critically analyse this statement by examining some of the later cases. First, let us contrast two cases in which same-sex conjugal relationships were at issue.

In *Harrogate Borough Council v Simpson*[20] the court had to decide whether the defendant, who had lived in a lesbian relationship, was entitled to remain in a council house after her partner, the tenant, had died. The court considered the Housing Act 1980 which provided that a secure tenancy vested in a member of the tenant's family on the death of the tenant, and included as family those who lived together as husband and wife. The question was whether the two women, for this purpose, qualified as 'family'. The court below answered no. Counsel for the respondent argued that cohabitation had become acceptable in society and that, save for the bearing of children, the relationship between the women was characterised by the same factors as heterosexual cohabitation: family values, monogamy and permanence. Watkins LJ said:

> That the views of the public have changed with regard to the association of man and woman is to be derived from the judgments in *Dyson Holdings Ltd v Fox* [1976] QB 503. In that case the defendant had lived with the tenant of the house as if she were his wife for 21 years until his death in 1961. They had never married. They had no children. After his death the defendant continued to live in the house, for which she paid rent as if she were his widow. Proceedings were brought to evict her. It was held that the owners of the house were entitled to recover possession of it. On appeal it was held that the question whether the defendant was a member of the tenant's family was to be answered according to the understanding of the ordinary man, using the word 'family' in its popular sense, as at the time of the tenant's death in 1961.

In his judgment Bridge LJ said at 512G:

> It is clear, however, that *Gammans v Ekins*, following *Brock v Wollams* [1949] 2 KB 388, proceeded on the basis that the question who is a 'member of the tenant's family' is to be answered according to the understanding of the ordinary man, and this test has been consistently applied in all the other cases decided on this provision. Now, it is, I think, not putting it too high to say between 1950 and 1975 there has been a complete revolution in society's attitude to unmarried partnerships ... . The ordinary man in 1975 would, in my opinion, certainly say that the parties to such a union, provided it had the appropriate degree of apparent permanence and stability, were members of a single family whether they had children or not ... .
> ... Counsel for the plaintiffs contends that, if Parliament had wished homosexual relationships to be brought into the realm of the lawfully recognized state of a living together of man and wife for the purpose of the relevant legislation, it would plainly have so stated in that legislation, and it has not done so. I am bound to say that I entirely agree with that. I am also firmly of the view that it would be surprising to the extreme to learn that public opinion is such today that it would recognize a homosexual union as being akin to a state of living as husband and wife. The ordinary man and woman, neither of 1975 nor in 1984, would in my opinion not think even remotely of there being a true resemblance between those two very different states of affairs. That is enough, I think, to dispose of this appeal, which, for the reasons I have provided, I would unhesitatingly dismiss. (94–95)

In this case the court refers to two previous cases of heterosexual cohabitation. Between the time of *Gammans v Ekins*, decided in 1950, and *Dyson Holdings v Fox*, decided in 1976, the view of the 'ordinary man' was said to have changed so as to come to accept unmarried heterosexual cohabitants as a family.

---

[20] [1986] 2 FLR 91 (CA).

Q Do you think that the court could have accepted the position argued by counsel for the respondent and adopted the same position with respect to same-sex cohabitants?

Q Who is the 'ordinary person' to whom the court looked?

The second case is *Fitzpatrick v Sterling Housing Association Ltd.*[21] In this case, F lived for 18 years with T in a 'longstanding, close, loving and faithful, monogamous, homosexual relationship' (47). When T, the tenant, died, F sought to remain in the flat, either as T's surviving spouse or as a surviving member of his family. The court was unanimous that for the purposes of the Rent Act 1977 he did not qualify as a surviving spouse, but the majority found that he was member of T's family. Like the courts before them, the court dealt with the issue as a matter of the interpretation of words.

> This expression [family] is not a term of art; that is, it is not a technical term with a specific meaning. It is a word in ordinary usage, with a flexible meaning. The statutory succession provisions have been amended several times, but to this day family has remained unamended, undefined and unparticularised. Parliament has left it to the courts to determine, in any given case, whether a particular individual falls within the description. (41)

> I must also mention the 'ordinary person' test enunciated by Cohen LJ in *Brock v Wollams* [1949] 2 KB 388, 395. He suggested that the trial judge should ask himself this question: would an ordinary person, addressing his mind to the question whether the defendant was a member of the family, have answered 'Yes' or 'No'? This oft-quoted test has tended to bedevil this area of the law. It may be useful as a reminder that family is not a term of art. But the test gives uncertain guidance when, as here, the members of the Court of Appeal and also your Lordships are divided on how the question should be answered. Contrary to what seems implicit in this form of question, the expression family does not have a single, readily recognisable meaning. As I have emphasised, the meaning of family depends upon the context in which it is being used. The suggested question does not assist in identifying the essential ingredients of the concept of family in the present context.
> The concept of the family has undergone significant development during recent years, both in the United Kingdom and overseas. Whether that is a matter for concern or congratulation is of no relevance to the present case, but it is properly part of the judicial function to endeavour to reflect an understanding of such changes in the reality of social life. Social groupings have come to take a number of different forms. The form of the single parent family has been long recognised. A more open acceptance of differences in sexuality allows a greater recognition of the possibility of domestic groupings of partners of the same sex. The formal bond of marriage is now far from being a significant criterion for the existence of a family unit. While it remains as a particular formalisation of the relationship between heterosexual couples, family units may now be recognised to exist both where the principal members are in a heterosexual relationship and where they are in a homosexual or lesbian relationship. (51–52)

Q Do you agree with the way the court explained the ordinary person test?

The next issue was what the essential elements of family were.

---

[21] [2001] 1 AC 27.

The problem in the present case is to determine what, short of blood or marriage, may evidence the common bond in a partnership of two adult persons which may entitle the one to be in the common judgment of society a member of the other's family. It seems to me that essentially the bond must be one of love and affection, not of a casual or transitory nature, but in a relationship which is permanent or at least intended to be so. As a result of that personal attachment to each other, other characteristics will follow, such as a readiness to support each other emotionally and financially, to care for and look after the other in times of need, and to provide a companionship in which mutual interests and activities can be shared and enjoyed together. It would be difficult to establish such a bond unless the couple were living together in the same house. It would also be difficult to establish it without an active sexual relationship between them or at least the potentiality of such a relationship. If they have or are caring for children whom they regard as their own they would make the family designation more immediately obvious, but the existence of children is not a necessary element. Each case will require to depend eventually upon its own facts. (51)

And

The hallmarks of the relationship were essentially that there should be a degree of mutual interdependence, of the sharing of lives, of caring and love, of commitment and support.

And finally,

Where sexual partners are involved, whether heterosexual or homosexual, there is scope for the intimate mutual love and affection and long-term commitment that typically characterise the relationship of husband and wife. This love and affection and commitment can exist in same sex relationships as in heterosexual relationships. In sexual terms a homosexual relationship is different from a heterosexual relationship, but I am unable to see that the difference is material for present purposes. As already emphasised, the concept underlying membership of a family for present purposes is the sharing of lives together in a single family unit living in one house. (44)

Q Can you list the factors required to found a legal family? Why do you suppose conjugality has such central importance? What, in your view are the essential characteristics of the legal family? On this see Cossman and Ryder (2001).

It seems, then, that law's attempts to define the family now follow a functional approach; the common sense of family life is now about what it does, rather than what it is. The functional approach to defining families has been described as progressive—it demands that legal rights and obligations flow from the way a relationship functions rather than from the form that it takes. Millbank[22] describes it in these terms:

Functional family approaches accord with a core objective of feminist legal scholarship and law reform projects—to centre 'lived lives' rather than legal doctrine or formal legal categories. Not coincidentally, therefore, many of the proponents of functional family approaches in relationship law are feminist and progressive scholars, who embrace the idea of dynamic change in law to reflect changing social practices. By positing law's role as reflecting and assisting actual families' experiences and needs, rather than as encouraging or mandating a particular family form, functional family approaches run directly counter to normative approaches to law such as the

[22] See also Glennon (2008).

so-called 'channelling' purpose of family law. The 'channelling function' has been expressed as one which 'supports social institutions which are thought to serve desirable ends', such as marriage, by 'channelling' people towards them. In this competing view, law's role is to tell people, both individually and collectively, how they should form families (and, to a greater or lesser extent, to provide inducements for those who listen to these messages, and impose punitive consequences on those who do not). Not coincidentally, proponents of the normative or channelling approach to family law are often conservative scholars and religious organisations, who wish to maintain established legal traditions and use them to (attempt to) stem or reverse changing social practices. (Millbank 2008: 156)

The functional approach adopted in the *Fitzpatrick* case allowed Mr Fitzpatrick to remain in his home of many years. But we must also remain aware of the 'functions' of family identified by the House of Lords. They remain within an ideal in which conjugality and the privatisation of care and dependency are central. In this way, law's model is still the private, heterosexual, traditional family. While the range of people who may be allowed into it may have increased, the norms by which they must live remain the same (Diduck 2001a, 2005a). Indeed it is ironic that at the same time as policy seems increasingly to be moving away from the view that marriage should be the only state-sanctioned intimate relationship, the test for others is the degree to which they are 'marriage-like' (Cossman and Ryder 2001). Law's normative vision of 'the family', with marriage as the benchmark, is reproduced each time a court is called upon to decide whether a particular living arrangement is 'familial' or not, but this vision is said to be that of the 'ordinary public' rather than that of the court. It is also reproduced when courts decide matters which appear to be peripheral to defining 'family'. For example, what vision of family is reproduced in these words from decisions which appeared to be about the living arrangements of children?

> I shall take a great deal of convincing that it is right that an adult male should be permanently unemployed in order to look after one small boy.[23]

And

> [I]n my opinion both Bracewell J and, in the Court of Appeal, Thorpe LJ failed to give the gestational, biological and psychological relationship between CG and the girls the weight that that relationship deserved. Mothers are special.[24]

Q In the light of all of these cases, consider O'Donovan's assertion regarding law's outward denial that a definition of family is possible. Construct arguments for and against her position.

The concept of family is also important in EU law and the law of the European Convention on Human Rights (ECHR), which, by virtue of the Human Rights Act 1998, has direct effect on domestic law. In EU law, the definition of 'family' is important because a Member State of the EU must permit the family members of an EU national to enter,

---

[23] *B v B (Custody of Children)* [1985] FLR 166, 174. The Court of Appeal here was quoting the trial court, and in fact overturned the trial court's decision by awarding care and control of the child to the father.

[24] *Re G (Children) (residence: same-sex partner)* [2006] UKHL 43; [2006] 2 FLR 629, per Lord Scott. The dispute here was between the gestational mother of children and her former same-sex partner.

live and work in that state. The original definition of 'family' was a narrow one, being limited to legal spouses and children and parents who were dependent (Salford 2002). It has since broadened, but only slightly. 'Family' for the purposes of free movement within the EU means the EU citizen's spouse, civil partner, child under 21 and other children who are dependent and their spouses and civil partners, and dependent direct relatives in the ascending line—that is, the citizen's dependent parents or parents-in-law or grandparents or grandparents-in-law. Further, the host Member State shall, in accordance with its national legislation, facilitate entry and residence of any other family members who are dependants or who require the care of the EU citizen and a partner with whom the EU citizen has a durable relationship.[25] According to Salford, the definition 'is premised on the traditional and increasingly exclusive notion of the legally married, nuclear and economically functional model' (Salford 2002: 411) and while it has been extended to those registered same-sex partnerships and to all cohabitants in 'durable relationships', it arguably still follows the old model.

The European Court of Human Rights (ECtHR) takes a slightly different approach.

> The Strasbourg institutions, for their part, although still limited in their interpretation of 'family' for the purposes of Article 8 ECHR[26] (in that they too favour the legally married, heterosexual union), have gone some way towards acknowledging modern patterns of family life. For instance, they apply what is commonly referred to as the 'reality test' whereby de facto family relationships are taken into account when considering whether or not 'family life' exists. In other words, the Court and Commission draw a distinction between family *relationships* and family *life*, acknowledging that one is not necessarily synonymous with the other to trigger the protection of Article 8. Instead, they assess the reality of the ties between the family members as well as evidence of close personal links such as a relationship of emotional (as opposed to merely economic) dependency between the parties. This contrasts with the ECJ's more formulaic approach whereby the existence of genuine family *life* is irrelevant for the purposes of activating family rights under the free movement provisions. (Salford 2002: 413, emphasis in original)

This means that European human rights law protects the right to family life of divorced parties with children,[27] of unmarried cohabitants with children[28] and even of unmarried parties with children who have never cohabited.[29] In 2010 it finally recognised that a family life might also exist between same-sex partners without children. In *Schalk and Kopf v Austria*,[30] Schalk and Kopf complained that Austria's prohibition on same-sex marriage violated not only their Article 12 right to marry and found a family[31] but also

---

[25] EU Directive 2004/38/EC. See also the case of C-34/0 *Ruiz Zambrano v Office national de l'emploi* (ONEm) (ECJ 2011) in which the Grand Chamber of the European Court of Justice held that the non-EU parents of a child who is resident in and a citizen of an EU Member State have the right to live and work in that state. To find otherwise would violate the rights of the child who is an EU citizen.

[26] Art 8 ECHR, now incorporated into the Human Rights Act 1998, states:

   1. Everyone has the right to respect for his private and family life, his home and his correspondence.
   2. There shall be no interference by a public authority with the exercise of this right except such as is in accordance with the law and as is necessary in a democratic society in the interests of national security, public safety or the economic well-being of the country, for the prevention of disorder or crime, for the protection of health or morals, or for the protection of the rights and freedoms of others.

[27] *Berrehab and Koster v The Netherlands* (1989) 11 EHRR 322.
[28] *Keegan v Ireland* (1994) 18 EHRR 342.
[29] *Boughanemi v France* (1996) 22 EHRR 228.
[30] *Schalk and Kopf v Austria* [2010] 30141/04 ECHR.
[31] See discussion in Chapter 2 below.

constituted discrimination under Article 14 in conjunction with Article 8. The ECtHR found that while states still possessed a wide margin of appreciation regarding same-sex marriage, the applicant's Article 8 rights were engaged:

90. It is undisputed in the present case that the relationship of a same-sex couple like the applicants' falls within the notion of 'private life' within the meaning of art 8. However, in the light of the parties' comments the Court finds it appropriate to address the issue whether their relationship also constitutes 'family life'.

91. The Court reiterates its established case-law in respect of different-sex couples, namely that the notion of family under this provision is not confined to marriage-based relationships and may encompass other de facto 'family' ties where the parties are living together out of wedlock. A child born out of such a relationship is ipso jure part of that 'family' unit from the moment and by the very fact of his birth (see Elsholz v Germany [2000] ECHR 25735/94, para 43; Keegan v Ireland [1994] ECHR 16969/90, para 44; and also Johnston v Ireland [1986] ECHR 9697/82, para 56).

92. In contrast, the Court's case-law has only accepted that the emotional and sexual relationship of a same-sex couple constitutes 'private life' but has not found that it constitutes 'family life', even where a long-term relationship of cohabiting partners was at stake. In coming to that conclusion, the Court observed that despite the growing tendency in a number of European States towards the legal and judicial recognition of stable de facto partnerships between homosexuals, given the existence of little common ground between the Contracting States, this was an area in which they still enjoyed a wide margin of appreciation (see Mata Estevez v Spain [2001] ECHR 56501/00, with further references). In the case of Karner (cited above, para 33), concerning the succession of a same-sex couples' surviving partner to the deceased's tenancy rights, which fell under the notion of 'home', the Court explicitly left open the question whether the case also concerned the applicant's 'private and family life'.

93. The Court notes that since 2001, when the decision in Mata Estevez was given, a rapid evolution of social attitudes towards same-sex couples has taken place in many member States. Since then a considerable number of member States have afforded legal recognition to same-sex couples (see above, paras 27–30). Certain provisions of EU law also reflect a growing tendency to include same-sex couples in the notion of 'family' (see para 26 above).

94. In view of this evolution the Court considers it artificial to maintain the view that, in contrast to a different-sex couple, a same-sex couple cannot enjoy 'family life' for the purposes of art 8. Consequently the relationship of the applicants, a cohabiting same-sex couple living in a stable de facto partnership, falls within the notion of 'family life', just as the relationship of a different-sex couple in the same situation would.

95. The Court therefore concludes that the facts of the present case fall within the notion of 'private life' as well as 'family life' within the meaning of art 8. Consequently, art 14 taken in conjunction with art 8 applies.

Interpretation of Article 8 in the UK in some ways lags behind the European courts and in some ways has anticipated it. In *Ghaidan v Mendoza*,[32] another defining family case for the purposes of an inherited tenancy, the House of Lords utilised Section 3 HRA to read provisions of the Rent Act compatibly with the Human Rights Act 1998. Lord Nicholls sets out the issue:

---

[32] [2004] 3 All ER 411; [2004] UKHL 30.

4. ... Paragraphs 2 and 3 of Schedule 1 to the Rent Act 1977 provide:

2(1) The surviving spouse (if any) of the original tenant, if residing in the dwelling-house immediately before the death of the original tenant, shall after the death be the statutory tenant if and so long as he or she occupies the dwelling-house as his or her residence.

(2) For the purposes of this paragraph, a person who was living with the original tenant as his or her wife or husband shall be treated as the spouse of the original tenant.

3(1) Where paragraph 2 above does not apply, but a person who was a member of the original tenant's family was residing with him in the dwelling-house at the time of and for the period of 2 years immediately before his death then, after his death, that person or if there is more than one such person such one of them as may be decided by agreement, or in default of agreement by the county court, shall be entitled to an assured tenancy of the dwelling-house by succession.

5. On an ordinary reading of this language paragraph 2(2) draws a distinction between the position of a heterosexual couple living together in a house as husband and wife and a homosexual couple living together in a house. The survivor of a heterosexual couple may become a statutory tenant by succession, the survivor of a homosexual couple cannot. That was decided in *Fitzpatrick's* case. The survivor of a homosexual couple may, in competition with other members of the original tenant's 'family', become entitled to an assured tenancy under paragraph 3. But even if he does, as in the present case, this is less advantageous. Notably, so far as the present case is concerned, the rent payable under an assured tenancy is the contractual or market rent, which may be more than the fair rent payable under a statutory tenancy, and an assured tenant may be evicted for non-payment of rent without the court needing to be satisfied, as is essential in the case of a statutory tenancy, that it is reasonable to make a possession order. In these and some other respects the succession rights granted by the statute to the survivor of a homosexual couple in respect of the house where he or she is living are less favourable than the succession rights granted to the survivor of a heterosexual couple.

Baroness Hale's words capture the spirit of the majority:

142. Homosexual couples can have exactly the same sort of inter-dependent couple relationship as heterosexuals can. Sexual 'orientation' defines the sort of person with whom one wishes to have sexual relations. It requires another person to express itself. Some people, whether heterosexual or homosexual, may be satisfied with casual or transient relationships. But most human beings eventually want more than that. They want love. And with love they often want not only the warmth but also the sense of belonging to one another which is the essence of being a couple. And many couples also come to want the stability and permanence which go with sharing a home and a life together, with or without the children who for many people go to make a family. In this, people of homosexual orientation are no different from people of heterosexual orientation.

143. It follows that a homosexual couple whose relationship is marriage-like in the same ways that an unmarried heterosexual couple's relationship is marriage-like are indeed in an analogous situation. Any difference in treatment is based upon their sexual orientation. It requires an objective justification if it is to comply with article 14. Whatever the scope for a 'discretionary area of judgment' in these cases may be, there has to be a legitimate aim before a difference in treatment can be justified. But what could be the legitimate aim of singling out hetero-sexual couples for more favourable treatment than homosexual couples? It cannot be the *protection* of the traditional family. The traditional family is not protected by granting it a benefit which is denied to people who cannot or will not become a traditional family. What is really meant by the 'protection' of the traditional family is the *encouragement* of people to form traditional families and the *discouragement* of people from forming others. There are many reasons why it might be legitimate to encourage people to marry and to discourage them from living together

without marrying. These reasons might have justified the Act in stopping short at marriage. Once it went beyond marriage to unmarried relationships, the aim would have to be encouraging one sort of unmarried relationship and discouraging another. The Act does distinguish between unmarried but marriage-like relationships and more transient liaisons. It is easy to see how that might pursue a legitimate aim and easier still to see how it might justify singling out the survivor for preferential succession rights. But, as Buxton LJ [2003] Ch 380, 391, para 21, pointed out, it is difficult to see how hetero-sexuals will be encouraged to form and maintain such marriage-like relationships by the knowledge that the equivalent benefit is being denied to homosexuals. The distinction between heterosexual and homosexual couples might be aimed at discouraging homosexual relationships generally. But that cannot now be regarded as a legitimate aim. It is inconsistent with the right to respect for private life accorded to 'everyone', including homosexuals, by article 8 since *Dudgeon v United Kingdom* (1981) 4 EHRR 149. If it is not legitimate to discourage homosexual relationships, it cannot be legitimate to discourage stable, committed, marriage-like homosexual relationships of the sort which qualify the survivor to succeed to the home. Society wants its intimate relationships, particularly but not only if there are children involved, to be stable, responsible and secure. It is the transient, irresponsible and insecure relationships which cause us so much concern.

The result of this decision was that the Rent Act provision was read as if it said *'as if they were his or wife or husband'.*[33] In addition, it shows that the *culture* of human rights may have influenced family law in more subtle ways and become a part of the 'rules', outside what appears as traditional family law, which inform and constitute our familial lives.[34]

V. 'CHOICE' AND OUR FREEDOM TO CHOOSE HOW TO ORDER OUR FAMILIAL LIVES

We have stated that the state, often through law, encourages or discourages certain relationships by reference to family ideology, which is in turn interpreted through other social and political imperatives the state identifies as important from time to time. This means that tensions between imperatives may have to be mediated through family ideology. Family law, for example, must cope with policies to protect individuals from exploitation at the same time as protecting their autonomy,[35] to protect both the welfare and the rights of family members,[36] the integrity of the unit and the autonomy of the individuals within it[37] and the potential conflict between a parent's or partner's social and personal respon-

---

[33] See also *Nutting v Southern Housing Group Ltd* EWHC 2982 (Ch); [2005] 1 FLR 1066 in which Evans-Lombe J held that in order to find that cohabitants in this case of the same sex qualified as 'spouses' for the purposes of the Housing Act 1988's provisions for succession to tenancies, the important factors were whether the relationship was an 'emotional one of lifetime commitment' (para 9) that was 'openly and unequivocally displayed as such to the outside world' (para 17). See also *Secretary of State for Work and Pensions v M* [2006] UKHL 11; [2006] 2 FLR 56, in which the House of Lords held (Baroness Hale strongly dissenting) that a woman's relationship with her same-sex partner did not engage her Art 8 rights for the purposes of a claim that she was discriminated against relative to opposite-sex partners for the purposes of calculation of her child support payments. The ECtHR held on 28 September 2010 that it did not need to decide the Art 8 issue, as the applicant's rights under Protocol 1 and Art 14 were breached (*JM v UK* Case No 37060/06) (ECtHR).

[34] See further discussion in Chapter 7 below in the context of financial orders—ancillary relief law.

[35] See, eg, Chapter 7 below regarding financial orders—ancillary relief.

[36] See, eg, Chapter 11 below regarding children.

[37] See, eg, Chapter 3 below regarding the dissolution of formal unions.

sibility.[38] And children have a central role in the ideology of the family both in terms of the legal regulation of decisions to reproduce and in terms of legal arrangements for their care.[39]

Sometimes the context in which people make reproductive decisions is an aggressive and obvious state policy, such as China's one-child policy, and sometimes it is only indirectly related to reproduction. The Civil Partnership Act 2004, for example,[40] allows registered civil partners to acquire responsibilities for their partner's children, which can be seen as promoting the welfare of children, but also as promoting the economic interests of society.

> When the social responsibilities of the welfare state are being peeled away, lesbian and gay men are voluntarily offering to take on the responsibilities of other men, women and children. The state interest in conscripting lesbians and gay men, along with the more usual targets of divorced fathers into the taking on the costs of family support has long been clear. (Adam 2004)

At still other times, the social/legal context is less obviously related to a population or family policy. Gillian Douglas (1991) notes that a state can be described as anti-natalist, such as contemporary China, where overpopulation is perceived as a problem, or it can be pro-natalist, as many Western European states have been in the past. Sometimes a pro-natalist policy is eugenic in nature, when it seeks to increase only certain segments of its population. Examples are Britain in the late nineteenth and early twentieth centuries and, more blatantly, Nazi Germany in the 1930s and 1940s. As we observed earlier, the reasons that a state might be interested in regulating its population and the units in which that population lives are manifold, and include the fact that rises and falls in population rates and the burden of public and private economic responsibilities have enormous social and economic implications. They also affect the age and size of the population, which in turn affects public spending on health, social security and pensions. They also affect education policy and the composition of the labour force. The United Kingdom after World War II, for example, adopted a strong pro-natalist stance with cultural messages and financial rewards encouraging procreation within the traditional nuclear family.

Other economic, cultural and social mechanisms that a state may adopt to influence the forms its families take include some of the following (see Douglas 1991: 2–13):[41]

1. Regulation of who, if anyone, has access to medical/technological procedures which control reproduction. For example, a state could render criminal the provision of birth-control devices or abortion as part of a pro-natalist stance. Romania in the 1980s under the Ceaucescu regime is an example of this position. Alternatively, a state could selectively enforce such criminal provisions, with the effect of demonstrating a pro-natalist stance for some segments of the population only. Nazi Germany is an example of a state with this policy, and it has been argued that a more contemporary example can be found in the United States, where the feminist demand for women's 'reproductive freedom' means for some, usually white, middle-class women, freedom to choose abortion, and for others, usually poor, often African American women, freedom from forced sterilisation or coerced abortion. Related to this policy is also the question of

---

[38] See, eg, Chapter 5 below on family state relations.
[39] See, eg, Chapter 4 below.
[40] See Chapter 4 below.
[41] See Chapter 5 below.

what the state does about infertility. A state's policy on population and family may be determined by examining to whom reproductive treatments are offered and how they are regulated (Langdridge and Blyth 2001). In England and Wales, the Human Fertilisation and Embryology Acts 1990 and 2008 do not provide strict rules regulating decisions regarding eligibility for fertility treatment, preferring to leave such decisions to clinics and medical professional guidelines. The Act does, however, provide that all decisions about treatment must take the welfare of any potential child into account.[42]

2. In a society where marriage is revered morally, encouraged socially and privileged legally, the minimum age of legal marriage demonstrates the degree to which the state wishes to encourage people to enter into this privileged form of relationship. It also has a profound effect on the rate of population growth. Although increasing numbers of unmarried women are having babies, state policy concerning procreation is reflected in the age at which it approves the formation of a heterosexual relationship through marriage. The age of legal marriage in China, for example, is 20 for women and 22 for men, reflecting China's anti-natalist policy. In England and Wales the minimum age at which men and women can marry is 16, but between the ages of 16 and 18 parental or court permission is required.[43]

3. The state can provide either financial incentives or penalties for a person to marry or have children. The most obvious incentive is some form of family allowance or child benefit provision. Indirect financial reward in the form of tax breaks for married couples, children or child-care is also an indication of a state's population and family policy, as is the provision of child-care and universal free education. England and Wales makes only moderate provision in this category. While the Conservative manifesto before the 2010 general election promised to introduce a tax incentive for marriage and civil partnership, the coalition government has not, to date, implemented this this promise. A small but still universal child benefit is paid to carers, although it will from 2013 become means tested; a child tax credit is paid to some parents; and education or training is mandatory until age 18, but only begins at age 5. Child-care before the age of 5 is not universally provided by the state, and the state neither requires nor encourages employers to provide either child-care or paid time off from work for nursing sick children, visits to schools, or any of the responsibilities that flow from rearing children. It does provide, however, some unpaid parental leave, carer's leave, lengthy maternity leave and short paternity leave. Finally, the law allows for parents of young or disabled children to request flexible working and employers are under a duty to consider the request seriously.[44] While some of these provisions appear to compare favourably with other jurisdictions, the differences in maternity leave and paternity leave do say something about what is considered to be the appropriate division of labour in the family.

4. Cultural factors can influence us in our decision to have children. Frequent vilification in the press of single mothers means that parenthood as a status for women who live without male partners is discouraged. On the other hand, the cultural status of (married or partnered) parenthood appears to be high in the UK now. It is interesting to note as well that cultural messages to have children or not to have children tend to be directed at women only, as though men are not involved at all in the process![45]

---

[42] See further Chapter 4 below.
[43] See Chapter 2 below; Marriage Act 1949, s 3, as amended by Sch 12, para 5 of the Children Act 1989.
[44] See Chapter 5 below.
[45] See Chapters 4 and 5 below.

5. The degree to which a society can be characterised as patriarchal influences population rates as well. In general, there is a correlation between large families and male dominance over women and between small families and societies where women are more economically independent and are more equal decision-makers in society (United Nations 1996).

Q Can you think of any other influences within law or social or popular culture which may have an effect on our decisions how to order our familial lives?

VI. CONCLUSIONS

We identified above some presumptions on which the 'liberal' understanding of 'the family' rests and suggested that they also form a part of law's understandings of family. Our approach in this book is to reveal them so as to offer a critical view of family law and policy in England and Wales. We will also offer a perspective that treats gender, class, sexual orientation and generation as important both implicitly and explicitly in the legal regulation of relationships. Our approach will highlight three themes that we feel have emerged in family law in the new millenium. They are equality, welfare and family privacy.

Equality between the sexes has been a continuing part of family law and policy over the past three decades (Hale 1998). It usually takes the form of a formal equality or sameness approach in which the men and women of family living become the de-gendered 'spouses' and 'parents' of family law, and much law and policy reform is committed to pursuing this aim. In the light of the foundational assumptions about family living and family law, we will explore both this goal and its implications for the family lives of men women and children.

The second theme we see in contemporary family law is the increasing importance of welfare in determining 'good' family practices. We note, however, that welfare is a contestable concept and its primacy, particularly in the context of an also increasing rights conciousness, may mean different things for, and have different effects upon, different legal subjects depending on where they are situated in the gender–class–generational matrix.

Finally, we explore the importance in family law of liberalism's divide between the 'public' and the 'private'. The 'ideal' family of law resides in the private sphere, and while we see challenges to that placement in contemporary law and policy, we also explore the resiliency of the ideological divide in much law, practice and policy.

FURTHER READING

J Bridgeman, H Keating and C Lind (eds), *Responsibility, Law and the Family* (Dartmouth, Ashgate, 2008).

J Eekelaar, *Family Law and Personal Life* (Oxford, OUP, 2006).

L Glennon, 'Obligations Between Adult Partners: Moving from Form to Function?' (2008) 22 *In't J of Law, Policy and the Family* 22.

DHJ Morgan, *Family Connections* (Cambridge, Polity, 1996).

2

Personal Relationships and Legal Status

Can we say that law and social pressures favour marriage above other family forms? What evidence do we have either for or against such a statement? As we saw in Chapter 1, the, at least, symbolic marital relationship remains central in social and legal ideas of the ideal family. Or perhaps it is not for marriage per se that the most privilege in law is reserved, but rather it is a particular family form, albeit one that is most closely accommodated by marriage, which is favoured by law and encouraged by the state (Smart 1984)? As the 'defining family' cases already discussed demonstrate, certain roles within relationships attract the legally beneficial 'family' label, while others do not. Parker (1990) also suggests that it is the *form* of the family unit which is important to the state and not whether that form has undergone any formal or religious ritual to legitimate it. He studied patterns of informal marriage and cohabitation in England and Wales from 1750 to 1989 and found that the state at that time appeared increasingly to be recognising unmarried cohabiting relationships as acceptable forms of family.[1] He posits possible reasons for this:

One can now find some reference to cohabitation in virtually every nook and cranny of law which has an impact on domestic relationships (and I am by no means confining this to 'family law') ... .

A common explanation ... is to say that it is a response to the increase in informal marriage. Whilst the growth in cohabitation may be a necessary condition, it is not a sufficient one, however. A fuller explanation is obviously because people think that it is right that these references appear. This still leaves the difficult question of why there has been such a shift in the sense of justice to permit juridification of informal marriage in such a relatively short period of time. Why has the space opened up?

In my view the answer is to be found in the changing strategy of family regulation. As marriage is displaced by family, wifedom by motherhood and the support/dependency structures of the patriarchal family assume greater importance than the legal form, it is actually counter-productive to the real purpose of social policy to exclude from regulation a family type that is so obviously here to stay. If income support is paid to a married couple at a lower rate than to two single people then the State loses money if an unmarried couple is treated as two single people. If the allocation of resources, such as public sector housing, ignores informal marriage then the State is manifestly not bolstering the private family (within which children are brought up and women are supported by men). If law-makers are forced to deny what claimants regard as their rights by relying on medieval-sounding arguments about morality then the ideology of justice which gives popular legitimacy to the legal system is severely threatened. Even those judges who have rejected a property claim through preference for individualistic principles of

---

[1] Even if not as legally equivalent to marriage (Probert 2009).

trust law cover themselves by saying that the answer lies with Parliament (see, for example, Fox LJ in *Burns v Burns* [1984] 1 All ER 244 at 255g). (Parker 1990: 148–49)

If Parker's observations were correct in 1990, it follows that we should be seeing continued legal accommodation of marriage-like relationships. After all, people are living in these types of relationships in increasing numbers. Statistics show, for example, that the number of opposite-sex cohabiting couple families in the UK increased from 2.1 million in 2001 to 2.8 million in 2010, and the number of same-sex cohabiting couple families increased from 45,000 in 2001 to 51,000 in 2010 (ONS Statistical Bulletin 2011a). How has the law responded to these changes in our partnering behaviour? And what of other changes that some see as occurring in patterns of intimate living? Indeed, it seems that people are organising their personal relationships in increasingly diverse ways that do not include monogamous conjugality or even co-residence. According to some sociologists, our 'new' family forms include now (in reality, probably always have included) forms of group marriage, serial monogamy, non-co-resident intimate partnerships or living apart together (LAT), non-conjugal homesharing and other household communities (Carling 2002; Budgeon and Roseneil 2004), and that all these relationships are important to people in providing intimacy, care and companionship. They are central to people's core values but fit increasingly uneasily in the category 'family' (Budgeon and Roseneil 2004). Sociologists also tell us that our friendship practices are changing so that there may be a blurring of lines between friends and family (Roseneil and Budgeon 2004; Roseneil 2004). Rather than the romantic love relationship being the basis for care, those more fluid ones, involving the sharing of lives and intimacy, now provide this basis. In this chapter we will examine Parker's thesis about changing strategies of family regulation in the light of all these changes in our intimate living.

I. MARRIAGE AS A SOCIAL INSTITUTION

Before we examine in more detail Parker's analysis of the changing relationship between families and the state and support for, and the law relating to, marriage and marriage-like cohabitation, let us first explore the legal and social relationship between marriage and family, for, to many, the two are inextricably linked. Marriage, despite apocalyptic analyses of the 'soaring' divorce rate and the 'death' of the family, is still a (surprisingly, some might say) popular institution. While rates for first marriages have been dropping since 1961 when it was 74.9 per 1,000 for men and 83 per 1,000 for women (Population Trends 2004: 118), the (provisional) rate in 2009 was still a healthy 21.3 for men and 19.2 for women over the age of 16 (ONS 2011b). 65% of all marriages in 2009 were first marriages for both partners and 35% were remarriages for one or both of them (ONS 2011b). Indeed, marriage retains such an inportant place in contemporary consciousness that many of those who are legally excluded from it argue that their exclusion violates their basic human rights.[2]

How can we explain the British love affair with marriage, particularly from the point of view of women? Research from the 1970s for example, showed that marriage had dif-

---

[2] *Wilkinson v Kitzinger* [2007] 1 FCR 183; *B v UK* [2005] 3 FCR 353; *Bellinger v Bellinger* [2003] UKHL 21; *Schalk and Kopf v Austria* [2010] 30141/04 ECHR

ferent effects for men and women. It was said that marriage tended to 'endow men with a better lifestyle, greater freedom and more power, while it has the opposite effect on women, limiting, impoverishing and rendering them vulnerable to abuses of power by their husbands' (Auchmuty 2004: 105, citing Bernard 1973). Recent research across 15 countries from the WHO world mental health survey, however, found that marriage (versus never being married) was associated with reduced risk of mental health disorders for both men and women (Scott et al 2010). It also found, however, that some gender differences remained. Marriage's protection against depression was stronger for men and its protection against substance abuse was stronger for women. The researchers observe that this effect could be consistent with a gender role interpretation 'such that women's marital roles are less satisfying or involve more chronic strain than men's' (Scott et al 2010: 1502). Marriage's slightly stronger protection for women against substance abuse may also be associated with gender roles, in this case, being the primary caretaker of children (ibid: 1503). Indeed 'a longitudinal study of the 1958 British cohort found that heavy drinking occurred to a similar degree among married men regardless of parental status, but reduction in heavy drinking among women who married was associated primarily with becoming a parent' (ibid). Further, while employment with no other role constraints is associated with mental health benefits, the combination of employment with responsibility for children is associated with increased distress in women (ibid: 1502). It thus seems that while marriage may indeed be good for us, it, or at least the gender roles traditionally associated with it, confer benefit differently to men and women. 'Gender differences in role strains and role constraints contribute to the gender differences that we find in the association between getting married and depression and subtance use onset in individuals' (ibid: 1502).

There are also statistics which show that for women, at least, poverty is almost as likely an outcome of divorce as financial security (Weitzman 1985; Bailey and Bala 1998; Douglas and Perry 2001; Fisher and Low 2009).

> The stark conclusion is that men's household income increases by about 23 per cent on divorce once we control for household size, whereas women's household income falls by about 31 per cent. *There is partial recovery for women, but this recovery is driven by repartnering*: the average effect of repartnering is to restore income to pre-divorce levels after nine years. Those who do not repartner tend to be older and have children. For these individuals ... the long term economic consquences of divorce are serious. (Fisher and Low 2009: 254, emphasis added)

Nevertheless, it seems that, as a social institution, marriage represents an idealised rite of passage into adulthood. It marks a heterosexual couple's readiness to assume the 'normal' responsibilities of adulthood, including home-owning, child-rearing, legitimate and exclusive sexual activity, and financial independence from parents. Further, its iconic and ideological status as a desirable precondition for 'family' gives marriage a social legitimacy that other types of relationships do not have. Through a combination of these social factors, the private monogamous couple relationship becomes the model to which we aspire to demonstrate our successful transition into adulthood.

Sociologists of the family Berger and Kellner (1980) provide a comparable explanation for the appeal of marriage in contemporary society. Relying upon the work of French sociologist Emile Durkheim, they suggest that marriage offers a state in which the individual is protected from *anomie*, a state of alienation from and anxiety about what is perceived as a normless and ailing society. They accept psychological research which presents those who are married as happier, more emotionally stable and mature than their unmarried counterparts, but they then argue that the analysis must not stop there; we must look to why married people feel so happy and psychologically healthy. In answer to this question, Berger and Kellner suggest that measuring psychological states such as mental health is misleading without recognition that both one's reality and relationship to it are socially constructed. To them, the compulsion to legitimate the marital world in today's psychological terms of 'emotional stability' is part of the same process as that which was used historically to legitimate it in traditionally religious terms.

> [C]ontemporary psychology functions to sustain this precarious [marital] world by assigning to it the status of 'normalcy', a legitimating operation that increasingly links up with the older religious assignment of the status of 'sacredness' ... . Whether one legitimates one's maritally constructed reality in terms of mental health or of the sacrament of marriage is today largely left to free consumer preference. (Berger and Kellner 1980: 320–21)

Berger and Kellner are thus suggesting that we look behind our assumptions about the naturalness or normality of our marriage behaviour and the consequent psychological satisfaction we get from being married and therefore 'normal', to examine the process of how that behaviour *comes to be understood* as normal and therefore satisfying. In earlier times the validation process was achieved through religious discourse, while in modern times it is through the more legitimate (for us) discourses of psychology and sociology.

Others (eg Gillis 1985) suggest that since Victorian times, at least for women, economic factors are the most important drivers of our desire to marry:

> [T]he single greatest factor was the evolution of industrial capitalism which undermined the independence of the family economy and consigned to men the role of principal breadwinner and to women the destiny of dependent wife and mother. From the 1840s onward women lost their place in the economy that offered them the highest wages and the greatest independence. (Gillis 1985: 241–42)[3]

Ferdinand Mount, on the other hand, offers yet another perspective from which to view marriage. He equates families with marriage and romantic love.[4] His 1982 book is entitled *The Subversive Family* and is subtitled *An Alternative History of Love and Marriage*. He postulates that the married conjugal union is a subversive institution, one which is based on romantic love and which provides protection and freedom from an interfering church and state. According to Mount's thesis, men and women have always freely chosen their relationships with one another based upon love, and have always formalised those relationships according to a marriage ritual. The church and the state only latterly became interested in those relationships in order to exert control over the population, and so, to Mount, the married conjugal family is not the bedrock of church and state, but rather it subverts them. He concludes his book with the following words explaining the appeal of marriage:

> It can only be said, in the most hesitant fashion possible, that it may be because marriage still seems to be the most interesting enterprise which most of us come across. With all its tediums and horrors, it has both more variety and more continuity than any other commitment we can

---

[3] Gittins also suggests that the most powerful force inducing people to marry is economic (see Gittins 1993: ch 5), notwithstanding popular acceptance of what she calls 'the ideology' of romantic love (ibid: 73).

[4] See also Diduck (2003: ch 2) and sources cited therein.

make ... . Marriage and the family make other experiences, both pleasant and unpleasant, seem a little tame and bloodless. And it is difficult to resist the conclusion that a way of living which is both so intense and so enduring must somehow come naturally to us, that it is a part of being human. (Mount 1982: 256)

Part of what Mount calls the 'appeal of marriage' may be explained by marriage's link with romantic love and indeed recent research into why people choose to marry confirms this link. Hibbs et al (2001) found that 30% of their respondents cited love as their primary reason for marrying. Research also shows, however, that people marry for other reasons, including a desire to conform to parent's wishes, religious prescription and cultural norms (Eekelaar and Maclean 2004), a belief that marriage was the natural next step in the progression of their relationship (Hibbs et al 2001; Lewis 1999), and most importantly because marriage was seen to be an expression of their commitment, not only to each other (Lewis 1999; Reynolds and Mansfield 1999; Hibbs et al 2001; Eekelaar and Maclean 2004), but to a way of living (Reynolds and Mansfield 1999). Eekelaar (2007) found that people married for a variety of reasons, which he divided into the following categories: compliance with convention; external manifestation of an internal state; symbolic confirmation of the completion of an internal process; provision of a famework within which completion of an internal process is intended to develop; and achievement of pragmatic objectives (Eekelaar 2007: 418). He observes that marriage had value for people, but the nature of that value was not the same for all (ibid: 418).

Alternative explanations for the continuity of marriage in Western society, then, rely upon assumptions about the psychological characteristics of individuals and groups, the idea that marriage is what people do when they are 'in love', and religious doctrine, law or economic necessity. Marriage is also thought to provide stability to families and to society and it is thought to be the best context in which to rear children (Centre for Social Justice 2010, 2011), even though these beliefs about the stability and social 'good' of marriage are questionable. Miles, Pleasance and Balmer (2009) report, for example, the importance of age and socioeconomic circumstances rather than relationship status per se as factors that contribute to relationship breakdown. Further, the Institute for Fiscal Studies reports that after controlling for differences between married and cohabiting couples such as parents' education, occupation, income, housing tenure and relationship quality, any previously noted differences in children's cognitive and social and emotional development at ages 3 and 5 are not statistically significant (Goodman and Greaves 2010). And again, it is difficult to say whether relationship quality reflects selection into marriage or any positive benefits of marriage itself (ibid).[5]

Marriage as a social institution is more than the behaviour of actors reacting to either rational or irrational stimuli, however. According to O'Donovan (1993: 57) the artefacts and ceremonies around marriage give it the status of icon or totem. According to Gillis as well, the married state required and continues to require 'powerful symbolic reinforcement to give it the stability the conjugal bond by itself [does] not provide' (Gillis 1985: 259).

According to O'Donovan:

[M]arriage endures as symbol. The marriage order, like the legal order, is a matter of what is lived, accepted and made familiar, or family. It may be presented as private but it is reinforced everywhere in public and in political discourse. Marriage has its own rituals, children,

---

[5] For a review of the US literature, see Brown (2010).

coupledom, Saturday nights out, reunions, a familiar tradition learned and transmitted at home. It does not have to be rational, its origins are sacred, it can call on mythology, an unconscious reservoir of memories, emblems, a fictive narrative. (O'Donovan 1993: 57)

Despite the number and variability of explanations for why people marry, including those which rely upon the psychological, the mythical-social, the legal, the economic and historical appeals to nature, people still tend to regard marriage as the ultimate commitment one can make to a sexual or emotional partner. Marriage, for many, is still the ultimate goal for those wishing to *really* settle down. Is, however, the social and emotional importance attached to marriage an adequate explanation for the level of legal significance which is attached to that form of commitment? Heterosexual couples who choose not to marry tend to express similar levels of commitment and obligation to each other and to share many of the same values as those who marry (Lewis 1999; Eekelaar and Maclean 2004), yet their relationships do not attract the same legal privileges.[6] The policy of the current coalition government is unclear. Conservative policy is to encourage marriage, through, for example, tax breaks which were promised during the 2010 election, but Liberal Democrat policy is to empower parents and not 'preach' to families.

Marriage thus holds a paradoxical place in English law and policy. It is said to be both important and not important to social stability and children's welfare. The various explanations for the 'good' of marriage, however, do not explain the type of commitment law requires of people, nor do they explain legal exclusions from the categories of potential spouses. It is to these matters that we now turn. If marriage is truly emotionally fulfilling, psychologically and socially stabilising, and economically advantageous for individuals and for society, why are its terms of entry so circumscribed?

II. MARRIAGE AS A LEGAL INSTITUTION

Legal scholar Eric Clive questioned in a provocative 1980 article whether marriage was a necessary legal concept at all. He did not comment upon marriage as a social institution, but proposed that the legal concept of marriage is a technical matter which has no real relationship to the social institution of marriage (Clive 1980: 71). He reviewed the relevance of marriage to criminal law, to the law of contract, tort and taxation, as well as the many laws dealing with financial provision for dependants, and concluded that the legal status of marriage added nothing to how justice was done in these areas, and in many cases it only unduly complicated matters (ibid: 77). He agreed that personal commitments between people, or various forms of families, will undoubtedly continue to exist, but that ascribing legal status to those relationships was in most cases unnecessary, and in others unjust.

Martha Fineman has made this argument as well:

[W]e should abolish marriage as a legal category and with it any privilege based on sexual affiliation. I want to emphasize I am addressing only the *legal* significance of marriage. There would be no special legal rules governing the relationships between husband and wife or defining the consequences of the status of marriage as now exist in family law. In fact, these categories would no longer have any legal meaning at all. Instead, the interactions of female

[6] See below pp 68–72.

and male sexual affiliates would be governed by the same rules that regulate other interactions in our society—specifically those of contract and property, as well as tort and criminal law. The illusive equality between adults in sexual and all other areas would thus be asserted and assumed, a result that to many will be symbolically appealing. Women and men would operate outside of the confines of marriage, transacting and interacting without the fetters of legalities they did not voluntarily choose. Of course, people would be free to engage in 'ceremonious' marriage; such an event would, however, have no *legal* (enforceable in court) consequences ... . Any legal consequences would have to be the result of a separate negotiation.

(Fineman 1995: 228–29)

For many, however, Clive's and Fineman's view is unrealistic or, worse, morally wrong. There must, they would argue, be a connection between law and marriage. One of the themes of this chapter is to test Clive's and Fineman's as yet socially unacceptable position by questioning the assumed necessity for society of *legal* marriage.

We shall first examine what marriage is in law and the social and sexual assumptions on which it is based by examining the rules about entry into it.

III. GETTING MARRIED

Given that marriage remains a popular institution for heterosexual adults who wish to live with one another, how does one go about actually legally doing it, and what does it mean for us legally once we do?

There is no statutory definition of marriage, although the Matrimonial Causes Act 1973 (MCA 1973) defines those marriages which are void or voidable at law. A void marriage is one that is considered to be non-existent ab initio. There is no need for a court to render the marriage non-existent; a decree or declaration of nullity by a court is merely declaratory of the parties' status. A void marriage can be attacked by a party to it or a third party even after the death of one of the parties. A void marriage is one where the parties have undergone some form of ceremony of marriage, but there was a fundamental flaw in that ceremony. On granting a decree of nullity the court retains the jurisdiction to make financial provision orders,[7] property adjustment orders[8] and pension-sharing orders,[9] and a void marriage must thus be distinguished from a non-marriage, in which the parties' ceremony was nothing like a marriage,[10] in which case the court has no powers to make orders for ancillary relief. In *Hudson v Leigh*[11] the court was asked to set out the condi-

---

[7] S 23 MCA 1973.

[8] S 24 MCA 1973.

[9] S 24A MCA 1973.

[10] Contrast *Geries v Yagoub* [1997] 1 FLR 854, in which a marriage was held to be void where the parties had undergone a religious ceremony in a church and then held themselves out as and believed themselves to be married, with *Ghandi v Patel* [2002] 1 FLR 603, in which a Hindu ceremony in a restaurant was held to be a non-, rather than a void, marriage. See also Probert (2002); *Burns v Burns* [2007] EWHC 2492; [2008] 1 FLR 813 in which a marriage conducted in a hot-air balloon over California was held to be a void marriage; and *B v I* [2010] 1 FLR 1721 in which because the claim for nullity was statute barred, the Court found a forced marriage to be a non-marriage. Where there is doubt as to the validity of the ceremony or there is insufficient evidence as to its validity, a presumption of marriage may be applied, and the longer the parties have cohabited assuming they were married, the stronger the presumption and clear and cogent evidence is required to displace it. See *Chief Adjudication Officer v Bath* [2000] 1 FLR 8.

[11] [2009] EWHC 1306, [2009] FLR 1129; permission to appeal denied in *Leigh v Hudson* [2009] EWCA Civ 1442.

tions that distinguished a void marriage from a non-marriage. It declined to do so, but did offer the following factors:

[79] In the result, it is not in my view either necessary or prudent to attempt in the abstract a definition or test of the circumstances in which a given event having marital characteristics should be held not to be a marriage. Questionable ceremonies should I think be addressed on a case by case basis, taking account of the various factors and features mentioned above including particularly, but not exhaustively:

(a) whether the ceremony or event set out or purported to be a lawful marriage;
(b) whether it bore all or enough of the hallmarks of marriage;
(c) whether the three key participants (most especially the officiating official) believed, intended and understood the ceremony as giving rise to the status of lawful marriage; and
(d) the reasonable perceptions, understandings and beliefs of those in attendance.

In most if not all reasonably foreseeable situations, a review of these and similar considerations should enable a decision to be satisfactorily reached.

Finally, a voidable marriage is one that is valid until declared otherwise by a court of competent jurisdiction, at which time the court's decree takes retrospective effect. A voidable marriage may not be challenged after the death of one of the parties and may not be challenged by a third party.[12]

There is legislation requiring certain formalities of marriage, breach of some of which render a marriage void or voidable.[13]

According to the MCA 1973:

11. A marriage celebrated after 31 July 1971 shall be void on the following grounds only, that is to say—

(a) that it is not a valid marriage under the provisions of the Marriage Acts 1949–86 (that is to say where—
    (i) the parties are within the prohibited degrees of relationship[14];
    (ii) either party is under the age of sixteen[15]; or
    (iii) the parties have intermarried in disregard of certain requirements as to the formation of marriage);[16]
(b) that at the time of the marriage either party was already lawfully married;
(c) that the parties are not respectively male and female;
(d) in the case of a polygamous marriage entered into outside England and Wales, that either party was at the time of the marriage domiciled in England and Wales.

For the purpose of paragraph (d) of this subsection a marriage is not polygamous if at its inception neither party has any spouse additional to the other.

---

[12] On the history of eligibility to marry see Cretney (2003a: ch 2).
[13] See the Marriage Act 1949, as amended from time to time.
[14] See s 1 Marriage Act 1949 and first schedule to that Act.
[15] The age of capacity to marry at common law was 14 for a boy and 12 for a girl. The minimum age now is 16 (s 2 Marriage Act 1949) but children between the ages of 16 and 18 may marry only with the consent of persons with parental responsibility for them, or a court (s 3 Marriage Act 1949). The capacity to marry of a mentally disabled adult was considered in the case of *Sheffield City Council v E and Another* [2004] EWHC Fam 2808 in which the court held (para 141) that the relevant questions were (i) did the person understand the nature of the marriage contract (which was in essence, a simple one)? And (ii) did the person understand the duties and responsibilities that normally attached to marriage?
[16] See s 49 Marriage Act 1949.

Section 12 of the MCA 1973 provides that a marriage shall be voidable on the following grounds only:[17]

(a) that the marriage has not been consummated owing to the incapacity of either party to consummate it;

(b) that the marriage has not been consummated owing to the wilful refusal of the respondent to consummate it;

(c) that either party to the marriage did not validly consent to it, whether in consequence of duress, mistake, unsoundness of mind or otherwise;

(d) that at the time of the marriage either party, though capable of giving a valid consent, was suffering (whether continuously or intermittently) from mental disorder within the meaning of the Mental Health Act 1983 of such a kind or to such an extent as to be unfitted for marriage;

(e) that at the time of the marriage the respondent was suffering from venereal disease in a communicable form;

(f) that at the time of the marriage the respondent was pregnant by some person other than the petitioner;

(g) that an interim gender recognition certificate under the Gender Recognition Act 2004 has, after the time of the marriage, been issued to either party to the marriage;

(h) that the respondent is a person whose gender at the time of the marriage had become the acquired gender under the Gender Recognition Act 2004.[18]

The judicial definition of marriage most commonly referred to is from a nineteenth-century case, *Hyde v Hyde and Woodmansee*.[19] The court said that marriage is 'the voluntary union for life of one man and one woman to the exclusion of all others' (ibid: 133). This is a deceptively simple definition. Yet, despite its Victorian heritage, it has not been overruled directly and its main principles can be seen to have been incorporated in the MCA 1973.

The *Hyde v Hyde* definition reveals its Western roots in church or canon law,[20] and that it continues in force, and, in effect, is paralleled by sections 11 and 12 of the MCA 1973, reveals the continued influence of the established Church in English marriage law.[21] *Hyde v Hyde* and its implicit incorporation into the 1973 MCA raise a number of questions. For example, *Hyde v Hyde*'s 'voluntariness' requirement has been recast into the 'valid consent' requirement of subsections 12(c) and (d). What, however, did the court mean by 'voluntary' in 1866, and how has this been translated into the legal meaning of 'valid consent' more than a century later? For example, do social or familial pressures render the choice to marry involuntary or the consent to marriage invalid?

---

[17] But see s 13 and discussion below regarding bars to relief where these grounds are alleged.

[18] Words inserted by the Gender Recognition Act 2004.

[19] *Hyde v Hyde and Woodmansee* [1866] *L Rev* 1 P & D 130, where a potentially polygamous marriage contracted in the Mormon faith was not regarded as valid in English law.

[20] Indeed, the court spoke of marriage 'as understood in Christendom' (ibid: 133).

[21] See on this Bradley (1996).

IV. THE LANGUAGE OF CONSENT

The question of consent has often been raised in the context of arranged marriages in an effort to distinguish them from forced marriages. Munby J captures the dominant judicial and policy view in a 2006 decision, *NS v MI*:[22]

> [2] Arranged marriages are perfectly lawful. As I emphasised in *Re SA (Vulnerable Adult with Capacity: Marriage)* [2005] EWHC 2942 (Fam), [2006] 1 FLR 867, at para [26], such marriages are not, of course, in any way to be condemned. On the contrary, as Singer J said in *Re SK (an Adult) (Forced Marriage: Appropriate Relief)* [2004] EWHC 3202 (Fam), [2006] 1 WLR 81, sub nom *Re SK (Proposed Plaintiff) (an Adult by way of her Litigation Friend)* [2005] 2 FLR 230, at para [7], arranged marriages are to be supported as a conventional concept in many societies. And for that very reason they are, I emphasise, not merely to be supported but to be respected.
>
> [3] Forced marriages, in contrast, are utterly unacceptable. I repeat what I said in *Re K, A Local Authority v N* [2005] EWHC 2956, (Fam) [2007] 1 FLR 399, at para [85]:
>
>> 'Forced marriage is a gross abuse of human rights. It is a form of domestic violence that dehumanises people by denying them their right to choose how to live their lives. It is an appalling practice. As I said in *Singh v Entry Clearance Officer, New Delhi* [2004] EWCA Civ 1075, [2005] 1 FLR 308, at para [68]:
>>
>>> "forced marriages, whatever the social or cultural imperatives that may be said to justify what remains a distressingly widespread practice, are rightly considered to be as much beyond the pale as such barbarous practices as female genital mutilation and so-called 'honour killings'."
>>
>> No social or cultural imperative can extenuate and no pretended recourse to religious belief can possibly justify forced marriage.'

The traditional view was that for consent to be vitiated the party must have been acting out of fear of an immediate threat to life, limb or liberty.[23] In *Hirani v Hirani*,[24] however, the Court of Appeal adopted contract law principles to fashion a different test to determine valid consent. Ormrod LJ said:

> The crucial question … in these cases is whether the threats, pressure or whatever it is such as to destroy the reality of consent and overbears the will of the individual. It seems to me that … this is a classic case of a young girl, wholly dependent on her parents being forced into a marriage with a man she has never seen in order to prevent her (reasonably from her parents' point of view) continuing in an association with a Muslim which they would regard with abhorrence. But it is as clear a case as one would want of the overbearing of the will of the petitioner and thus invalidating or vitiating her consent. (p 234)

This alternative test appears to ask whether the party's will was overborne, rather than asking about fear for life or limb. It has been confirmed in *NS v MI*:[25]

> [30] There are many different ways of expressing the concept that what a person says may not

---

[22] [2007] 1 FLR 444.
[23] See eg *Singh v Singh* [1971] 2 All ER 828; *Singh v Kaur* (1981) 11 Fam Law 152.
[24] [1982] 4 FLR 232.
[25] [2007] 1 FLR 444; see also *P v R (Forced Marriage: Annulment)* [2003] 1 FLR 661.

be binding upon him or of describing how pressure, or whatever it is, may destroy the reality of consent and overbear the will. One well-known metaphor is illustrated by a passage from an American writer (Bishop, *Commentaries on the Law of Marriage and Divorce* (6th edn, 1881), vol 1, p 177, para 210) cited with approval by Sir Jocelyn Simon P in *Szechter (orse Karsov) v Szechter* [1971] P 286, at 297:

> 'Where a formal consent is brought about by force, menace, or duress—a yielding of the lips, not of the mind—it is of no legal effect. This rule, applicable to all contracts, finds no exception in marriage.'

...

[31] To this I would add a number of subsidiary points.

[32] The first is that, as Sir Jocelyn Simon P pointed out in *Szechter (orse Karsov) v Szechter* [1971] P 286, at 297, although in the nature of things the source of the fear and the agent of duress will generally be the the other party to the marriage, this is not necessarily so.

[33] The second is that there are, of course, many ways in which such duress or coercion may be brought to bear, a point illustrated by the well-known passage in the summing up of Sir JP Wilde to the jury in *Hall v Hall* (1868) LR 1 P&D 481, at 482. That was a probate case, but the point is equally applicable in the present context:

> 'pressure of whatever character, whether acting on the fears or the hopes, if so exerted as to overpower the volition without convincing the judgment, is a species of restraint under which no valid will can be made. Importunity or threats, such as the testator has not the courage to resist, moral command asserted and yielded to for the sake of peace and quiet, or of escaping from distress of mind or social discomfort, these, if carried to a degree in which the free play of the testator's judgment, discretion or wishes, is overborne, will constitute undue influence, though no force is either used or threatened. In a word, a testator may be led but not driven; and his will must be the offspring of his own volition, and not the record of some one else's.'

[34] To this I would only add that, as Lindley LJ observed in a famous passage in *Allcard v Skinner* (1887) 36 ChD 145, at 183, 'the influence of one mind over another is very subtle'. Moreover, one has to have regard to the relationship between the parties. As I remarked in *Re SA (Vulnerable Adult with Capacity: Marriage)* [2005] EWHC 2942 (Fam), [2006] 1 FLR 867, at para [78], where the influence is that of a parent or other close and dominating relative, and where the arguments and persuasion are based upon personal affection or duty, religious beliefs, powerful social or cultural conventions, or asserted social, familial or domestic obligations, the influence may, as Butler-Sloss LJ put it in *Re T (Adult: Refusal of Treatment)* [1993] Fam 95, [1992] 2 FLR 458, at 120, and 477 respectively be subtle, insidious, pervasive and powerful. In such cases, moreover, very little pressure may suffice to bring about the desired result.

[35] The third point is this. The test is a subjective, not an objective, one.

...

[36] The fourth point is that although the standard of proof is the ordinary civil standard of the balance of probability, due regard must of course be had to the principle expounded by Lord Nicholls of Birkenhead in the well-known passage in his speech in *Re H and Others (Minors) (Sexual Abuse: Standard of Proof)* [1996] AC 563, [1996] 1 FLR 80, at 586 and 95–96 respectively that the more serious the allegation the more cogent is the evidence required to overcome the unlikelihood of what is alleged and thus to prove it.[26] And the court must be

---

[26] Note that this point has now been overruled by *Re B* [2008] UKHL 35; [2008] FLR 141, in the context of child protection.

careful to ensure, particularly perhaps where a nullity suit is undefended, that a proper case is being put forward and not one contrived to enable a spouse to escape from a perfectly lawful and proper marriage which has turned out to be irksome ... .

[37] The fifth point is this. The court must be alert to the possibility of forced marriage – something more prevalent than some would care to admit – and robust in its response to it. But we must always equally be careful not merely to distinguish been arranged marriage and forced marriage but also to guard against the risk of stereotyping. As I said in *Re K*, at para [93]:

> 'We must guard against the risk of stereotyping. We must be careful to ensure that our understandable concern to protect vulnerable children (or, indeed, vulnerable young adults) does not lead us to interfere inappropriately—and if inappropriately then unjustly—with families merely because they cleave, as this family does, to mores, to cultural beliefs, more or less different from what is familiar to those who view life from a purely Euro-centric perspective.'

This test raises difficult issues, however. How far, for example, should a law premised and reliant upon the existence of a rational individual will, a notion which is itself based upon relatively modern philosophical concepts of liberal individualism, regulate traditional/ religious lives based in other philosophical foundations entirely?[27] Munby J's notion of consent would not invalidate a marriage contracted in a context within which marriage is seen as a family or collective event in which the interest/will of the individual becomes subsumed within the interest/will of the group. Neither do these notions acknowledge the gendered notions of the individual and *his* consent which inform contract law[28] as well as the law of duress in marriage.

Q Does the Court's reasoning here, in *Hirani* and *P v R*, mean that the traditional practices of many cultural and religious groups violate English law? On the other hand, does the test merely reproduce in law stereotypical understandings of passive and obedient Asian women who are overcome by coercive traditions?[29]

It is clear that many arranged marriages do not overbear the will of the participants and the law is concerned to distinguish them from forced marriages, which do. Forced marriages are considered a form of domestic violence and will be discussed in Chapter 12 in that context. Sometimes, however, as we noted above, the issue of consent is not so clear. Where, for example, is the line to be drawn between concepts such as encouragement and coercion, loyalty and exploitation, or indeed, social embarrassment and social degradation? Sometimes drawing a clear dichotomy between consent and coercion is not appropriate.

The forced versus arranged marriage debate, for example, may draw upon notions of 'free will' and 'coercion' which can both obscure the nature of the paradigm legal subject and invoke a colonialist view of culture. Anitha and Gill observe that 'forced marriage is constructed as a culturally sanctioned aberration from the norm of freely contracted marriages, and little attention is given to the many ways in which all women located within a matrix of structural inequalities can face social expectations, pressure and constraint in matters of marriage' (Anitha and Gill 2009: 166). They go on: 'Women within ... [minority] communities are re-presented as particularly oppressed and lacking in agency,

---

[27] On this and on the gender implications of the test, see Lim (1996). See also Bradney (1994).
[28] See Williams (1991) and Lim's (1996) use of Williams' analysis.
[29] See on this Lim (1996); Anitha and Gill (2009).

unlike the putatively liberated women in the West who are seen as "educated, as modern, as having control over their own bodies and sexualities, and the freedom to make their own decisions"' (ibid: 166, reference omitted). They seek to draw attention to 'the myriad ways in which women, whatever their culture, ethnicity, religion or class, experience pressure to marry, thereby also culturalising the concept of coercion in marriage within mainstream communities' (ibid: 168) and to present consent and coercion in relation to marriage as two ends of a continuum, 'between which lie degrees of socio-cultural expectation, control, persuasion, pressure, threat and force' (ibid: 165).

John Gillis (1985) offers a historical perspective, but he suggests that by 1914 many marriages were contracted either by young women afraid of the social repercussions arising from being 'left on the shelf', or by those marrying for economic reasons. It is extremely unlikely, however, that, had the *Hirani* reasoning been applied to them, the consent of these parties would have been found to be invalid. Their will was not overborne by threats of economic suffering or economic pressure.

Q When, in your view, does social pressure or financial or emotional coercion amount to an 'overbearing of the will'? Consider this question in the light of the statistics above regarding the financial effects of divorce and re-partnering upon women, or of minority ethnic women feeling social pressure to marry.

It is in the light of our earlier discussion of the psychosocial and economic importance to many of marriage that we must evaluate the law which maintains that marriages are entered into by the parties freely and voluntarily. Such a formulation of marriage rests on the liberal assumptions of the exercise of a free and private choice to marry and is reinforced each time courts use the language of 'overbearing of the will' to vitiate consent. Judicial reasoning of this type which preserves the institutional status quo and the ideology of marriage and family may, as Smart says, reflect law's concern to preserve marriage as a purely private arrangement construed as being the result of individual choice and freedom to exercise that choice, despite the fact that the terms of the contract are unspecified. It can thus be held up as an example of the 'private sphere *par excellence*' (Smart 1984: 118).

We can unpick the liberal foundations of marriage law further by examining so-called 'immigration marriages'. Immigration law allows husbands or wives of non-British (or EU) spouses to sponsor their spouses' entry into the UK and provides that as long as this sponsorship remains in effect the non-British spouse is protected from deportation.[30] Those entering the UK as spouses or fiancé(e)s must obtain an entry clearance as such and immigration officials issuing these entry clearances are expected to focus upon whether the marriage is genuine, whether the couple intends to live together permanently as husband and wife, whether the marriage is subsisting and whether the parties have met. The circumstances of marriages will continue to be scrutinised closely in order to determine whether or not the marriage is a 'genuine' one. 'Genuineness', in these cases, is not related to consent, however, but is related to another of the assumptions underlying marriage which allow it to maintain its status as icon of the private sphere: that, at least in modern times, it is based upon affection or romantic love (Stone 1990; Diduck 2003).

---

[30] This rule also applies to fiancé(e)s. For a recent consideration of the Rules in the context of Art 12 of the European Convention on Human Rights see *R (on the Application of Baiai and others) v Secretary of State for the Home Department* [2008] UKHL 53.

While the genuineness of romantic intentions may be a factor for immigration law, it is not for validity of marriage. In *Vervaeke v Smith*[31] the petitioner, a Belgian national and a prostitute who was about to be deported as a result of her convictions for soliciting, went through a ceremony of marriage with a UK national, a 'down and out' who married her allegedly for £50.00 and a ticket to South Africa (147). Without going through any form of divorce, she later married an Italian national. Her Italian 'husband' died, and at issue was her entitlement, as his widow, to any of his estate. In order to be so entitled she had to prove that her first 'marriage' was invalid. In dismissing her appeal from her petition, Hailsham LC in the House of Lords first approved the words of the trial judge and then extended them:

> Where a man and a woman consent to marry one another in a formal ceremony conducted in accordance with the formalities required by law, knowing that it is a marriage ceremony it is immaterial that they do not intend to live together as man and wife … . It is immaterial that they intend the marriage to take effect in some limited way … . To hold otherwise would impair the effect of the whole system of law regulating marriages in this country, and gravely diminish the value of the system of registration of marriages on which so much depends in a modern community.
>
> I have no doubt that [this doctrine] would extend to a marriage as here celebrated between a British to a foreign national in circumstances where the ceremony was intended to achieve the status of British nationality in the foreign national by means of marriage and the private arrangement between the parties was simply to limit their personal relationships to the achievement of the status of married person with a view to acquiring British nationality for the previously alien partner. (148–49)

The House of Lords relied in this passage on the public policy behind the law. It may be argued that in reaching this decision, they identified a conflict between two of the foundations of 'proper' marriage, which meant that the parties to a valid marriage were nonetheless parties to a non-genuine marriage. Apart from the basic question why immigration law should look behind marriage law at all, this clash between two of the ideological bases of marriage, and the laws in respect of them, raises the difficult question phrased by Hayes and Williams as follows:

> [W]here an asylum seeker marries in an attempt to avoid deportation to a country where he reasonably fears that he will be imprisoned, probably tortured, and even killed, is this a sham, [immigration but nonetheless valid] marriage, or a[n invalid] marriage entered into as a result of duress? (Hayes and Williams 1995: 397)[32]

---

[31] [1982] 2 All ER 144.

[32] There is much consternation expressed in the media about 'sham' or immigration marriages. The most recent effort to control them is a direction from the Church of England that the traditional practice of reading the banns before weddings should be stopped if either of the people is a foreign national from outside Europe. They are instead to be referred to a registrar to obtain a licence, and if they insist upon marrying in the Church, their details are to be passed to the UK Border Agency (Travis, *The Guardian* 2011). See also Marriage Act 1949 Pt 3.

V. THE PERMANENT HETEROSEXUAL UNION

The second difficulty raised by *Hyde v Hyde*'s legal definition of marriage lies in how we are to construe the word 'union'. What kind of union must there be? Is it a physical union? A financial one? An emotional one? Some legal light can be shed upon these questions by reference to the consummation requirement in MCA 1973 subsections 12(a) and (b) which has its basis in canon law.[33]

Notwithstanding that embedded within the ideology of marriage is romantic love, there is no requirement for that in the statute, nor is there one mandating commitment, respect, economic interdependence or emotional fulfilment. It is the physical, heterosexual union which is fundamental to marriage. Cases that have attempted to define the nature of that union-consummation for the purposes of marriage law have clearly established its heterosexual, and, arguably, phallocentric nature. Even though sexual practices are many and varied, only one particular sex act qualifies as legal consummation. Richard Collier describes the leading case on consummation as follows:

> The case of *D-e v A-g (falsely calling herself D-e)* [1845] 1 Rob Ecc 280 (p 1039) is the cornerstone of the cases on the place of sexual intercourse in marriage. Indeed it was later to be described (Per Willmer LJ in *SY v SY (Orse W)* [1963] p 55) as 'a statement of commanding authority'. In the leading judgement, Dr Lushington declared that the court were 'all agreed that, in order to constitute the marriage bond between young persons, there must be the power, present or to come, of sexual intercourse' (p 1045). He then proceeded, in a passage which is worth quoting at length, to define the legal meaning of sexual intercourse:
>
>> Sexual intercourse, in the proper meaning of the term, is ordinary and complete intercourse; it does not mean partial and imperfect intercourse; yet, I cannot go to the length of saying that every degree of imperfection would deprive it of its essential character. There must be degrees difficult to deal with; but if so imperfect as scarcely to be natural, I should not hesitate to say that, legally speaking, it is no intercourse at all. I can never think that the true interest of society would be advanced by retaining within the marriage bonds parties driven to such disgusting practices. Certainly it would not tend to the prevention of adulterous intercourse, one of the greatest evils to be avoided' (p 1045).
>
> This is the crux of Lushington's reasoning in *D-e v A-g*. First, intercourse (giving pleasure) is not in itself sufficient. It is admitted that intercourse has taken place in this case but it was not 'real' (ordinary/proper/natural) intercourse. 'Ordinary' and 'natural' must therefore have some meaning. Second, the 'disgusting practices' which might follow from 'unreal' intercourse are one of the 'greatest evils' against the 'true interest of society'. These are the consequences of a legal recognition of 'imperfect' sexual intercourse in marriage. What sexual intercourse involves is a specific interaction of the male and female body (genital connection, penis/vagina) and what non-marital intercourse (adultery) might lead to is social disorder:
>
>> 'Without the power [to consummate] neither of the two principal ends of matrimony can be attained, namely, a lawful indulgence of the passions to prevent licentiousness, and the procreation of children, according to the evident design of Divine Providence' [p 1045].
>
> There is in law a 'true' sexual intercourse which is capable of consummating a marriage. Other 'unnatural' connections and non-penetration, be it due to structural impediment or psychological inability, are not sufficient to consummate a marriage. What such a construction does, of course, is to marginalise sexual practices outside the frames of the heterosexual matrix. It is, simply,

---

[33] Note, however, s 13(1)(a) and (b), which states that a marriage in which the parties understood there was not to be a sexual relationship cannot later be avoided on the ground of inability or refusal to consummate.

penetration which defines sexual intercourse in law (see also O'Donovan 1993 p 46). What constitutes the 'natural' quality of the genitals, however, is far from clear and would appear to vary from case to case. (Collier 1995b: pp 152–53)

> **Q** What does Dr Lushington's reasoning tell us about the role of marriage in English law and society? Is it to provide a legitimate outlet for one form of sexual expression or is it to procreate? See on this *Cowen v Cowen* [1946] P 36, [1945] 2 All ER 197 (CA) and *Baxter v Baxter* [1948] AC 274, [1947] 2 All ER 886 (HL). How does this judgment fit with the *Vervaeke* case above? Why do you think conjugality or this form of sexual expression of monogamy is so important to law?

The court in *Hyde* spoke of the sexual union in marriage being for life. But does the phrase 'for life' literally mean that? Does this mean that 'unions', even active heterosexual ones, if they are intended to last only for a limited period, are not legal marriages?[34] In some cases it might not, as *Vervaeke* illustrates. It is true that marriages now are legally dissoluble, but the dominant view is that divorce is a matter of last resort—it is to be resorted to only when the marriage has irretrievably broken down. Most parties believe, and the traditional marriage ceremony reinforces that belief, that marriage is for life, notwithstanding that a 'way out' is offered if things become intolerable. Official Reports over the years on marriage and divorce law have recognised without question the lifetime commitment implied in marriage even when advocating possible forms of divorce. The Royal Commission on Marriage and Divorce reported in 1956, for example, that the basis of its approach to considering possibilities for a new divorce law included reinforcing marriage as a lifetime commitment:

> The Western World has recognised that it is in the best interests of all concerned—the community, the parties to a marriage and their children—that marriage should be monogamous and that it should last for life. It has also always recognised that owing to human frailty, some marriages will not endure for life, and that in certain circumstances it is right that a spouse should be released from the obligations of marriage.
>
> (Royal Commission on Marriage and Divorce 1956: 7, para 35)

The language of lifetime commitment and individual responsibility for the success or failure of that commitment also pervaded the Law Commission's 1990 Consultation Paper *The Ground for Divorce* which led eventually to the ill-fated Family Law Act 1996.[35]

> The aim of supporting those marriages which can be saved can be distinguished from the aim of upholding the institution of marriage itself. For some of our respondents, as for our predecessors, it was important that divorce law should send the right messages, to the married and the marrying, about the seriousness and the permanence of the commitment involved. We agree.
>
> (Law Commission 1990: 10, para 3.4)

According to these official representations, it is law's business to reinforce 'messages' regarding the desirability of and the responsibility for the permanent heterosexual rela-

---

[34] Lack of intention to remain married for life is one of the grounds for annulment in the Catholic Church.
[35] See Chapter 3 below.

tionship entered into by the parties. On this view, if marriages fail, rather than looking to outside factors or to the nature of the institution itself as a possible source of the problem, it is the individuals and their failure to negotiate successfully their social and emotional responsibilities—the 'human frailties' identified in the 1956 report—which are believed to be to blame. It is this view which underlines government and popular support for the provision of marriage preparation classes (Advisory Group on Marriage and Relationship Support 2002; DWP and DfE 2011); for information booklets to be distributed by clergy and registrars on the rights and responsibilities of marriage (Home Office 1999); and counselling and therapy in times of relationship stress (Advisory Group on Marriage and Relationship Support 2002; DWP and DfE 2011). It may also explain continued demands to retain the notion of fault in divorce law.[36] Arguably this view also exacerbates the feelings of personal failure which are experienced by many when their marriages do not 'work out'. 'If counselling or therapy does not help us to see how to mend our relationships, the failure remains ours—it is a failure of our love or our commitment' (Diduck 2003: 40).[37]

VI. ONE MAN AND ONE WOMAN

According to *Hyde v Hyde* and subsection 11(c) of the MCA 1973, the union must be between one man and one woman. This requirement is conceptually problematic for a couple of reasons. The first is the exclusivity required. Group marriage, polygamy[38] or, for that matter, certain premarital sexual liaisons[39] may invalidate a marriage on a strict construction of this requirement. Polygamy is also prohibited by the criminal law of bigamy.[40] We can examine some explanations for the monogamy requirement by reference to those jurisdictions in which polygyny[41] is or has been practised on a wider scale than in England.[42]

Examining the prohibition on polygyny that was in force in South Africa in 1991, Kaganas and Murray suggested that the privileging of the Christian companionate model of marriage rested originally on ethnocentric, racist views of 'the heathen society' (Kaganas and Murray 1991: 119) and on interpretations of Christianity, morality, the evolutionary 'naturalness' of the nuclear family and the 'rightful place of women' (ibid: 121). If we dismiss the first four justifications as remnants of the pernicious effects of colonisation and dominance, we are left with the argument that polygyny is antithetical to the values of equality inherent in a democratic society. Kaganas and Murray addressed these equality-based objections to polygyny:

The first concern, that there is something inherently unequal in a family structure which

---

[36] See Chapter 3 below.
[37] See also Chapter 3 below.
[38] See amended s 11(d).
[39] See s 12(e), (f) MCA 1973.
[40] Offences Against the Persons Act 1861 s 57.
[41] The term 'polygamy' is used to denote a marriage in which there is more than one spouse of either sex. The term 'polygyny' refers specifically to marriage in which the law permits the man more than one wife.
[42] On the regulation of polygyny from a rights perspective, see Banda (2003). See also Fox (1992) in which he discusses the approaches of US courts to the polygyny of the Mormons of Utah state. Many of his arguments and conclusions are similar to those below.

comprises one man and many women, is dubious. It is not self-evident that the apparently symmetrical relationship of one woman to one man provides the *only* formula for equality within marriage. A variation of the argument might be that the relationship is unequal and degrading for women because, while each woman in a polygynous marriage is committed to a single man, she has to compete with a number of other women for his attention and a share of the family's material resources. This also fails to withstand scrutiny. It is possible, outside the very specific and historically quite recent notions of romantic love and companionable marriage, that each wife's attentions are also divided among her husband, other members of her family and the community in which she is living. This point is well made in a study on polygyny in Nigeria by Ware when she notes that '[w]hether one considers that women who have to share a husband are underprivileged depends upon the value placed upon husbands'. Furthermore, while it is true that wives are dependent on their husbands for access to resources, they are not necessarily prejudiced by the introduction of new wives; in many polygynous societies, additional wives increase the wealth of the group rather than deplete it.

The power that polygyny may give husbands to introduce new wives and thus to determine the composition of the family, raises different issues. On the face of it, the equality objection here is easily dealt with by making the introduction of new wives a matter to be decided jointly by the husband and any existing wives. Indeed, this is already the case in Indonesia. However, a formal requirement of consent may be worth very little and we are likely to mistrust a wife's consent when it is exacted in a society in which men dominate. But this means that the problem lies in the society in which polygyny is practised rather than in the institution itself.

(Kaganas and Murray 1991: 127–28, footnotes omitted)

They argued that there is nothing inherent in polygyny which requires the oppression of women, and others have agreed that it does not cause the breakdown of the fabric of society (Fox 1992). Rather, it is the patriarchy in any society which can render any family form degrading or oppressive.[43] They concluded that we 'should re-examine the basis of our objections to polygyny' (Kaganas and Murray 1991: 134).[44]

> **Q** How, if at all, would you regulate polygyny or 'group marriages', especially in the light of the sociological work referred to above which suggests that commitment, interdependence, care and support may be shared by more than two people at a time?

The second difficulty with the one man/one woman requirement includes both the subtle issue of determining a precise definition of 'man' and 'woman'—and the far more obvious question of why it is only persons of the opposite sex who are permitted to marry. Let us look first at the man/woman requirement, put in statutory form by section 11(c) of the MCA 1973. We assign sex and gender to people on the basis of a number of different biological, social and psychological factors. In a series of cases between 1970 and 2003 the courts were called upon to determine the *legal* meaning of 'man' and 'woman', and in effect, therefore, of marriage.

---

[43] The law in South Africa has since changed to accord recognition to polygynous marriages entered into in terms of indigenous customary law. The Recognition of Customary Marriages Act 1998 was also intended to remedy the inferior position of women under customary law and gives customary husbands and wives equal status (s 6). In addition, it provides for the fair distribution of assets for the first family when the husband marries a second wife. However, it is reported that, in practice, the position of women in customary marriages has not changed in jurisdictions which have attempted to introduce legal equality and doubts have been expressed as to whether the same result will obtain in South Africa (Mamashela 2003).

[44] See also Shah (2003); Rehman (2007).

In the first and most famous, *Corbett v Corbett (orse Ashley)*,[45] the respondent, Ashley, was a post-operative transgendered person. She had undergone male to female gender reassignment surgery before her marriage to Corbett. The marriage failed and the petitioner, Corbett, sought a decree that their marriage was void because both parties at the time of the marriage were persons of the male sex, or, in the alternative, because the marriage was never consummated. Medical and psychological evidence was called and the court found that there were a number of criteria by which we assign the sexual identity of a person. A person could be identified as being of one sex or another by chromosomal factors, by examination of gonads or genitals, by his or her psychological or social identification, or by looking at hormonal or secondary sex characteristics. The issue before the court, then, was which of these factors ought to determine a person's *legal* sex for the purpose of marriage? In choosing only biological indicators to determine sex, the decision says much about beliefs in biological determinism and the immutability of sex and their reinforcement through the legitimising authority of law, as well as about the nature of the legal marriage relationship:

> [S]ex is clearly an essential determinant of the relationship called marriage, *because it is and always has been* recognised as the union of one man and one woman. It is the *institution on which the family is built*, and in which the capacity for *natural heterosexual intercourse* is an essential element. (48, emphasis added)

Let us examine closely the italicised words. First, the court comes to a conclusion about the essential determinants of marriage and goes on to establish the basis on which the conclusion is drawn. How convincing is it, however, in terms of legal argument and proof, to say that something ought to be the case simply (1) because it is and (2) because it always has been, especially where no evidence is relied upon to establish either state of affairs? This form of legal reasoning demonstrates a conservative approach to the judicial role and the power of judicial rhetoric to accept a contention as axiomatic and thus to dismiss any need for evidence to prove it or legal authority to validate it. We can make similar observations about the second assumption connecting, with no stated authority, marriage and the (only legally legitimate, it seems) family. In relation to the kind of sexual behaviour which is essential, the 'natural' is called in aid. That which is 'natural' is one type of heterosex, but more than that, it is heterosex in marriage. The Supreme Court of Canada provides a contrasting, less conservative approach to legal reasoning when considering an argument about the historical and natural meaning of marriage:

> First, it is argued, the institution of marriage escapes legislative redefinition. Existing in its present basic form since time immemorial, it is not a legal construct, but rather a supra-legal construct subject to legal incidents. In the *Persons* case, Lord Sankey, writing for the Privy Council, dealt with this very type of argument, though in a different context. In addressing whether the fact that women never had occupied public office was relevant to whether they could be considered 'persons' for the purposes of being eligible for appointment to the Senate, he said at p 134:
>
>> The fact that no woman had served or has claimed to serve such an office is not of great weight when it is remembered that custom would have prevented the claim being made or the point being contested.
>>
>> Customs are apt to develop into traditions which are stronger than law and remain unchallenged long after the reason for them has disappeared.

[45] [1970] 2 All ER 33.

The appeal to history therefore in this particular matter is not conclusive.

Lord Sankey acknowledged, at p 134, that 'several centuries ago' it would have been understood that 'persons' should refer only to men. Several centuries ago it would have been understood that marriage should be available only to opposite-sex couples. The recognition of same-sex marriage in several Canadian jurisdictions as well as two European countries belies the assertion that the same is true today.

Second, some interveners emphasize that while Lord Sankey envisioned our Constitution as a 'living tree' in the *Persons* case, he specified that it was 'capable of growth and expansion within its natural limits' (p 136). These natural limits, they submit, preclude same-sex marriage ... .

The natural limits argument can succeed only if its proponents can identify an objective core of meaning which defines what is 'natural' in relation to marriage. Absent this, the argument is merely tautological. The only objective core which the interveners before us agree is 'natural' to marriage is that it is the voluntary union of two people to the exclusion of all others. Beyond this, views diverge. We are faced with competing opinions on what the natural limits of marriage may be. (*Reference Re: Same Sex Marriage* 2004 SCC 79, paras 25–27)

While some may argue that accepting monogamous union as natural is problematic, the point here is that the court acknowledged that there may be differing views about a state of affairs or even an entity that is purported to be 'natural'. The California Supreme Court has also adopted more expansive reasoning in response to arguments about history or tradition justifying law:

The state's protracted denial of equal protection cannot be justified simply because such constitutional violation has become traditional. ... Advocates of [a ban on interracial marriages] asserted that because historically and culturally blacks had not been permitted to marry whites, the statute was justified. Thus argument was rejected by the Court ... [in *Perez v Sharp* (1948) 32 Cal 2d 711]. ... Simply put, same-sex marriage cannot be prohibited simply because California has always done so before. (Coordination Proceeding, Marriage Cases, San Francisco County Superior Court; Tentative Decision, Kramer J, 14 March 2005, 7–8)[46]

Let us continue with the *Corbett* judgment. Once the court had declared the legal essence of marriage, it went on to state:

The question then becomes, what is meant by the word 'woman' in the context of marriage, for I am not concerned to determine the 'legal sex' of the Respondent at large. Having regard to the essentially heterosexual character of the relationship which is called marriage, the criteria must, in my judgment, be *biological* for even the most extreme degree of transsexualism in a male or the most severe hormonal imbalance which can exist in a person with male chromosomes, male gonads and male genitalia cannot reproduce a person who is naturally capable of performing the *essential role of a woman in marriage*. In other words, the law should adopt in the first place, the first three of the doctors' criteria, ie the *chromosomal, gonadal and genital* tests, and if all three are congruent, determine the sex for the purpose of marriage accordingly, and ignore any operative intervention. (48, emphasis added)

The italicised parts of this passage make it clear that Ormrod LJ believes that the essential role of a woman in marriage is biological and related in some way to chromosomes, although the precise value of the X chromosome is not made clear, given its post-treatment physical invisibility. One possible conclusion is that chromosomes in some way convey to

---

[46] See also *Home Affairs v Fourie* [2005] ZACC 19, a decision of the Constitutional Court of South Africa.

Ormrod LJ the essence of a person, an essence which, having been engendered by the magical caprice of nature, ought to be respected by humans. The essential role of a woman in marriage is also related, according to Ormrod LJ, to having female gonads, although the non-functioning of these sexual reproductive organs does not preclude a valid marriage being contracted by a person who is sterile. The potential capacity to reproduce, then, in some way, but not finally, determines the role of a woman in marriage. Finally, Ormrod LJ declares that the essential woman in marriage must have the genitals of a woman, implying that having her vagina penetrated is one of the essential roles of woman in marriage.

Corbett remained the authority in English law until 2004, despite its reasoning and conclusions having been rejected by courts in other jurisdictions and also despite having been subjected to criticism by the European Court of Human Rights (ECtHR).[47] Until 2002, however, the Court's criticisms did not extend so far as to find that the UK's position on the immutability of gender violated a person's right to marry and found a family under Article 12 of the European Convention on Human Rights (ECHR). Rather, the Court said that while the UK was bound to keep the matter under review in the light of 'scientific and social developments', designating who was able to marry came within a state's margin of appreciation.[48] But the Court finally lost patience with the UK in 2002.

In that year the ECtHR decided two cases[49] that set the government in motion toward legislation that became the Gender Recognition Act 2004. The following extracts from the ECtHR's judgment in *Goodwin* discuss the interpretation of Articles 8 and 12 ECHR in the context of the marriage of trans-gender persons.

[97] The Court recalls that in the cases of Rees, Cossey and Sheffield and Horsham the inability of the transsexuals in those cases to marry a person of the sex opposite to their re-assigned gender was not found in breach of Article 12 of the Convention. These findings were based variously on the reasoning that the right to marry referred to traditional marriage between persons of opposite biological sex, the view that continued adoption of biological criteria in domestic law for determining a person's sex for the purpose of marriage was encompassed within the power of Contracting States to regulate by national law the exercise of the right to marry and the conclusion that national laws in that respect could not be regarded as restricting or reducing the right of a transsexual to marry in such a way or to such an extent that the very essence of the right was impaired. Reference was also made to the wording of Article 12 as protecting marriage as the basis of the family.

[98] Reviewing the situation in 2002, the Court observes that Article 12 secures the fundamental right of a man and woman to marry and to found a family. The second aspect is not however a condition of the first and the inability of any couple to conceive or parent a child cannot be regarded as *per se* removing their right to enjoy the first limb of this provision.

[99] The exercise of the right to marry gives rise to social, personal and legal consequences. It is subject to the national laws of the Contracting States but the limitations thereby introduced must not restrict or reduce the right in such a way or to such an extent that the very essence of the right is impaired.

[100] It is true that the first sentence refers in express terms to the right of a man and woman to marry. The Court is not persuaded that at the date of this case it can still be assumed that

[47] A detailed discussion of the case law and policy can be found in the first edition of this book at pp 51–56.
[48] *Rees v United Kingdom* (1987) 9 EHRR 56; *Cossey v UK* [1991] 2 FLR 492; *Sheffield and Horsham v UK* [1998] 2 FLR 928.
[49] *Goodwin v UK* [2002] 2 FLR 487; and *I v UK* [2002] 2 FLR 518.

these terms must refer to a determination of gender by purely biological criteria. There have been major social changes in the institution of marriage since the adoption of the Convention as well as dramatic changes brought about by developments in medicine and science in the field of transsexuality. The Court has found above, under Article 8 of the Convention, that a test of congruent biological factors can no longer be decisive in denying legal recognition to the change of gender of a post-operative transsexual. There are other important factors [including] the acceptance of the condition of gender identity disorder by the medical professions and health authorities within Contracting States, the provision of treatment including surgery to assimilate the individual as closely as possible to the gender in which they perceive that they properly belong and the assumption by the transsexual of the social role of the assigned gender. The Court would also note that Article 9 of the recently adopted Charter of Fundamental Rights of the European Union departs, no doubt deliberately, from the wording of Article 12 of the Convention in removing the reference to men and women. ...

[104] The Court concludes that there has been a breach of Article 12 of the Convention in the present case. (511–12, all references omitted)

In 2003 the House of Lords concurred [50] that section 11(c) of the MCA 1973 violated the ECHR, but rather than read that section compatibly with Articles 8 and 12 (as it did the word 'spouse' in the *Mendoza* decision discussed in Chapter 1) it issued a declaration of incompatibility. Neither did the court make the other order sought by the parties, namely a declaration pursuant to section 55 of the MCA 1973 that the marriage they celebrated in 1981 (Mrs Bellinger was a post-operative transgendered woman) was valid. Lord Nicholls thought the matter was one better dealt with by Parliament because of its vast and diverse repercussions:

Recognition of Mrs Bellinger as female for the purposes of section 11(c) of the Matrimonial Causes Act 1973 would necessitate giving the expressions 'male' and 'female' in that Act a novel, extended meaning: that a person may be born with one sex but later become, or become regarded as, a person of the opposite sex.

This would represent a major change in the law, having far reaching ramifications. It raises issues whose solution calls for extensive enquiry and the widest public consultation and discussion. Questions of social policy and administrative feasibility arise at several points, and their interaction has to be evaluated and balanced. The issues are altogether ill-suited for determination by courts and court procedures. They are pre-eminently a matter for Parliament, the more especially when the government, in unequivocal terms, has already announced its intention to introduce comprehensive primary legislation on this difficult and sensitive subject.

(1052, paras 36–37)

He also thought that the issue of when one's gender was changed was too complicated to be dealt with by the courts:

By what criteria are cases such as these to be decided?

But the problem is more fundamental than this. It is questionable whether the successful completion of some sort of surgical intervention should be an essential prerequisite to the recognition of gender reassignment. If it were, individuals may find themselves coerced into major surgical operations they otherwise would not have. But the aim of the surgery is to make the individual feel more comfortable with his or her body, not to 'turn a man into a woman' or vice versa. As one medical report has expressed it, a male to female transsexual person is no less a woman for not having had surgery, or any more a woman for having had it.

[50] *Bellinger v Bellinger* [2003] UKHL 1; [2003] 1 FLR 1043.

These are deep waters. Plainly, there must be some objective, publicly available criteria by which gender reassignment is to be assessed. (1053, paras 440–42)

Finally, the question of recognising an acquired gender went to the fundamental meaning of marriage:

Marriage is an institution, or relationship, deeply embedded in the religious and social culture of this country. It is deeply embedded as a relationship between two persons of the opposite sex. There was a time when the reproductive functions of male and female were regarded as the primary raison d'être of marriage. The Church of England Book of Common Prayer of 1662 declared that the first cause for which matrimony was ordained was the 'procreation of children'. For centuries this was proclaimed at innumerable marriage services. For a long time now the emphasis has been different. Variously expressed, there is much more emphasis now on the 'mutual society, help and comfort that the one ought to have of the other'.

Against this background there are those who urge that the special relationship of marriage should not now be confined to persons of the opposite sex. It should be possible for persons of the same sex to marry. This, it is said, is the appropriate way to resolve problems such as those confronting Mrs Bellinger.

It hardly needs saying that this approach would involve a fundamental change in the traditional concept of marriage. Here again, this raises a question which ought to be considered as part of an overall review of the most appropriate way to deal with the difficulties confronting transsexual people. (1054, paras 46–48)

The law is now governed by the Gender Recognition Act 2004. This Act provides that a person of at least 18 years of age can make application to a Gender Recognition Panel for a gender recognition certificate on the basis of living in the acquired gender or having changed gender according to the law of another country.[51] If issued, the certificate means that the person's gender becomes, for all purposes, the acquired gender.[52] A full gender recognition certificate cannot be issued if a person is married.[53] In that case an interim certificate may be issued which will take effect once the marriage comes to an end. The application for a gender recognition certificate must include reports made by two professionals, one of whom must practice in the field of gender dysphoria, and the panel must be satisfied that the applicant has or has had gender dysphoria, has lived in the acquired gender for the immediately preceding two years'and intends to live in the acquired gender until death.[54] There is no requirement for gender reassignment surgery.

In the context of these decisions about the validity of marriage, UK law has thus re-examined the meaning of gender. It is no longer assumed to be biological and therefore immutable. But rather than also re-examining the meaning of (sex in) marriage, the combined effect of the Gender Recognition Act 2004 and the *Bellinger* decision seems merely to reinforce old meanings. According to Diduck (2003),[55] while these decisions, along with the Gender Recognition Act 2004, allow that gender is changeable,

[r]ather than accept a fluid definition of marriage to account for that changeability, [they] require a choice to be made to fix identity so that intimate partners [can] make an orthodox, heterosexual marriage. Further, the basis for choice of gender identity remain[s] rooted in a medical

---

[51] S 1.
[52] S 9; except that it does not affect a person's status as the father or mother of a child (s 12).
[53] S 4.
[54] S 3.
[55] See also Sandland (2003).

or psychiatric dysfunction. It [is] seen as an abnormality that [can] be remedied by law for the purpose of encouraging 'normal' traditional marriage. (Diduck 2003: 204)

Collier (1995b) attempted to deconstruct the law's preoccupation with heterosex in marriage before these changes. He said:

> The transsexual cases, basing marriage on a biological dichotomy, ignore the 'social' aspects of marriage relationship and focus instead on the sexual. If marriage 'depends on sex and not on gender' then legal discourse is valorising one particular medical interpretation of the relationship of sex and gender. Compassion, consideration, empathy and the ability to love and understand are all subordinated within an economy of masculinity which privileges intercourse above all else in the constitution of the marriage relationship. Other forms of human contact and pleasure are denied legal validity within a position which takes it for granted that there is a fundamental difference between men and women, and that heterosexuality is normal.
>
> (Collier 1995b: 130, references omitted)

Q Do you think his comments are still relevant?

O'Donovan's strategy is to analyse marriage law by reference to who is excluded from marriage (O'Donovan 1993: 49–59). She argues that, by excluding all but one man and one woman from the privileged legal institution of marriage, the law ensures the orderly access of men to women's bodies, and to any children of the union. The political implications of this arrangement for her are clear:

> Legal theorists have deconstructed marriage to point up the gendered nature of its terms. Yet others find a solution in a freely negotiated contract to be agreed by the partners. Contract as the model of political relations and the justification of the state is presented as a solution to marriage difficulties, as a principle of social association, and as a means of creating social relationships, such as couple agreements. This is reinforced by pointing to entry into marriage as free and voluntary. Recent work on family and social contract raises doubts about this line of reasoning. In her powerful book *The Sexual Contract* Carole Pateman criticises the limitations of social contract theory in justifying current political arrangements. The sexual contract, which predated the social contract, gave men conjugal mastery over women, realised through marriage. Readings of major social contract theorists from Hobbes to Rousseau confirm that the family is taken as natural, as pre-given. Marriage, the foundation of family, ensures the subordination of women, which is presented as inevitable. The free individuals who contract in the social contract are male. The issue of whether or not women contract freely into the sexual contract is unresolved, and the way out for political theorists is to tell patriarchal stories in which marriage and family are 'natural' ... .
>
> Although women are taking control of their sexuality and bodies, there remain contradictions surrounding women and contract in relation to political theory and to marriage. The positing of the family as 'natural', pre-dating the state, in political philosophy leaves unspecified social understanding of that unit. There can be no doubt that the fathers of social contract theory wrote in the context of subordination, at a time when married women could not contract, as their legal existence was subsumed under that of their husband. For Pateman the notion of the free, contracting citizen of the modern state remains tainted by its origins in male individualism and female subordination. (O'Donovan 1993: 58–59, references omitted)

O'Donovan uses Pateman's work to tie together the two underlying premises of English marriage law, that it is a free and voluntary union, but that it is one which only a man and a woman may enter into together. For her, the ideological power of the first masks the political implications of the second.

The other difficulty, of course, with the 'one man and one woman' requirement as it is reproduced in section 11(c) MCA is that it precludes two people of the same sex from marrying. For many, this exclusion from what can be considered at best a problematic institution is not cause for concern. Auchmuty (2004), for example, highlights that for many feminists, such as O'Donovan, Fineman and Pateman, the institution of marriage is too burdened with historical and ideological baggage and is therefore 'irredeemable'. Many lesbians and gay men who are excluded from marriage thus have no wish to enter into it, claiming that to support same-sex marriage denies legal and social recognition of what is *different* about same-sex relationships; to them the claim for the right to marry is merely a claim for the right to assimilate into a patriarchal institution.[56] Others, however, see same-sex marriage as an opportunity not 'to participate in traditional family life, but to redefine what counts as family' (Auchmuty 2004: 111, citing Calhoun 2000); it would provide the opportunity to reshape marriage 'into a *genuine* relationship between equals' (Auchmuty 2004: 109, emphasis in original).

Others still see the issue in terms of rights and discrimination (Hale 2004; Murphy 2004).[57] But thus far Article 12 of the ECHR has not been interpreted by any court to permit the marriage of same-sex couples.[58] However, courts in South Africa, Canada and the US, which have written constitutions, have done so and may provide guidance on the possible directions European courts may take in the future. The Ontario Court of Appeal put it this way in 2003:

[5] Marriage is, without dispute, one of the most significant forms of personal relationships. For centuries, marriage has been a basic element of social organization in societies around the world. Through the institution of marriage, individuals can publicly express their love and commitment to each other. Through this institution, society publicly recognizes expressions of love and commitment between individuals, granting them respect and legitimacy as a couple. This public recognition and sanction of marital relationships reflect society's approbation of the personal hopes, desires and aspirations that underlie loving, committed conjugal relationships. This can only enhance an individual's sense of self-worth and dignity.

[6] The ability to marry, and to thereby participate in this fundamental societal institution, is something that most Canadians take for granted. Same-sex couples do not; they are denied access to this institution simply on the basis of their sexual orientation. ...

[107] [S]ame-sex couples are excluded from a fundamental societal institution—marriage. The societal significance of marriage, and the corresponding benefits that are available only to married persons, cannot be overlooked. Indeed, all parties are in agreement that marriage is an important and fundamental institution in Canadian society. It is for that reason that the claim-ants wish to have access to the institution. Exclusion perpetuates the view that same-sex relationships are less worthy of recognition than opposite-sex relationships. In doing so, it offends the dignity of persons in same-sex relationships. (*Halpern v AG* (2003) 65 OR 3d 161)[59]

---

[56] See Auchmuty (2004) and sources cited therein.

[57] There is a voluminous literature on same-sex marriage as a rights issue. For a review of some of this, see Auchmuty (2008a).

[58] In the UK see *Wilkinson v Kitzinger (no 2)* [2006] EWHC 2022; [2007] FCR 183, and in the ECHR see *Shalk and Kopf v Austria* [2010] 30141/04 ECHR.

[59] www.ontariocourts.on.ca/decisions/2003.

In England and Wales, however, these human rights arguments were not successful. In *Wilkinson v Kitzinger*[60] two women who were legally married in Canada applied to the High Court to have their relationship recognised in the UK as a marriage rather than as a civil partnership. Potter P found no violation of Article 12's right to marry and found a family, nor of Article 8 in conjunction with Article 14. He said:

[118] It is apparent that the majority of people, or at least of governments, not only in England but Europe-wide, regard marriage as an age-old institution, valued and valuable, respectable and respected, as a means not only of encouraging monogamy but also the procreation of children and their development and nurture in a family unit (or 'nuclear family') in which both maternal and paternal influences are available in respect of their nurture and upbringing.

[119] The belief that this form of relationship is the one which best encourages stability in a well regulated society is not a disreputable or outmoded notion based upon ideas of exclusivity, marginalisation, disapproval or discrimination against homosexuals or any other persons who by reason of their sexual orientation or for other reasons prefer to form a same-sex union.

[120] If marriage is, by longstanding definition and acceptance, a formal relationship between a man and a woman, primarily (though not exclusively) with the aim of producing and rearing children as I have described it, and if that is the institution contemplated and safeguarded by art 12, then to accord a same-sex relationship the title and status of marriage would be to fly in the face of the Convention as well as to fail to recognise physical reality.

[121] Abiding single sex relationships are in no way inferior, nor does English law suggest that they are by according them recognition under the name of civil partnership. By passage of the CPA, United Kingdom law has moved to recognise the rights of individuals who wish to make a same sex commitment to one another. Parliament has not called partnerships between persons of the same-sex marriage, not because they are considered inferior to the institution of marriage but because, as a matter of objective fact and common understanding, as well as under the present definition of marriage in English law, and by recognition in European jurisprudence, they are indeed different.

Q At the time of writing, eight couples in England have a case before the ECtHR seeking the right of opposite-sex couples to register a civil partnership (see below) and the right of same-sex couples to marry. Do you agree that the prohibition of same-sex couples from marriage violates their rights? That the prohibition of opposite-sex couples from civil partnership violates theirs? Auchmuty (2008a) thinks there might be rights violations, but is not worried about it:

The irony is that marriage is in long-term decline across the western world. It is entirely possible that it is only by opening it to same-sex couples like Wilkinson and Kitzinger that it will survive another generation or two. In a society where the differences in legal status between spouses and cohabitants are disappearing, imperfectly understood, and not much cared about, Kitzinger and Wilkinson's insistence on the need for formal equality seems pedantic, even irrelevant. Worse still, it may impede a natural *extra-legal* movement towards substantively equal treatment for all family forms. 'In actively pursuing same-sex marriage or partnership regulation we sell ourselves short and give up on the possibilities and alternatives that exist for legitimizing the diverse ways in which we live and love', Catherine Donovan points out.

---

[60] [2006] EWHC 2022; [2007] FCR 183. For an alternative 'judgment' in this case, see Harding (2010) and commentary on it by Monaghan (2010).

The potential for same-sex couples to remake the institution of marriage in finer form is much more limited than the potential for other and perhaps better ways of living to evolve gradually and naturally as they are doing. 'My concern is that lesbians and gay men will relax into the complacency of being married', warns Victoria Clarke, '... and be too busy registering at Harvey Nichols to transform the institution from within.'

One lesson from this case is that formal equality claims are not always progressive. Goals may be worthless or even unworthy, some institutions better dismantled or abandoned. Marriage is one of these. Wilkinson and Kitzinger have written: 'We believe that no civil institution should be reserved for heterosexuals only, any more than it should be reserved for whites or "Aryans" only.' But whether you see marriage as an oppressive bastion of male power, as the second-wave feminists did, or simply as outmoded and irrelevant, as many contemporaries do, the goal should surely be to get rid of it, or at least to let it die out of its own accord — not to try to share in its privileges, leaving the ineligible out in the cold.

Wilkinson and Kitzinger further claim that: 'Demanding the right to marry is not equivalent to endorsing ... the traditional symbolic meaning of marriage'. But by representing marriage as so important and desirable *in itself*, their case may simply reinforce conservative ideas about the primacy of marriage and the inferiority of other family forms, speeding a return to the days when those of us outside the privileged institution—the unattached, the divorced, those 'living in sin', and single parents, whether heterosexual or homosexual—were criticised, patronised, and pathologised. We are beginning to see the first signs of a turning back of the clock in the Labour government's doubling of the value of the inheritance tax exemption for transfers between spouses and civil partners, thus doubly disadvantaging the unmarried, and the Conservative opposition's pledge to match it. At the moment when it is easier to be unmarried than ever before in history, all this legal energy and expense seems at best wasteful, at worst counter-productive. (Auchmuty 2008a: 497–98, references omitted)

We shall see that, like some other jurisdictions, the UK has chosen to rectify perceived and actual discrimination against same-sex couples by introducing a system of registration of their partnerships, by which couples will obtain many, if not all, of the rights and responsibilities of marriage. The UK's scheme was, for the Department of Trade and Industry which sponsored the Civil Partnership Bill in Parliament in 2003, an 'important equality measure for same-sex couples' (DTI 2003a: 13, para 1.2). It was said that the proposal, which has now become the Civil Partnership Act 2004, would

provide for the legal recognition of same-sex partners and give legitimacy to those in, or wishing to enter into, interdependent, same-sex couple relationships that are intended to be permanent. Registration would provide a framework whereby same-sex couples could acknowledge their mutual responsibilities, manage their financial arrangements and achieve recognition as each other's partner. Committed same-sex relationships would be recognised and registered partners would gain rights and responsibilities which would reflect the significance of the roles they play in each other's lives. This would encourage more stable family life. (ibid)

Q Do you agree with the view that a form of registration of partnerships remedies discrimination against same-sex partners?

The California Superior Court took the view that it did not:

The idea that marriage-like rights without marriage is adequate smacks of a concept long rejected by the courts: separate but equal. In *Brown v Board of Education of Topeka, et al*, (1952) 347 US 483, 494, the Court recognized that the provision of separate but equal educational opportunities to racial minorities 'generates a feeling of inferiority as to their status in the community that may affect their hearts and minds in a way unlikely ever to be undone.' Such logic is equally applicable to the State's structure granting substantial marriage rights but no marriage. (Coordination Proceeding: Marriage Cases 2005: 9)

VII. THE CIVIL PARTNERSHIP ACT 2004

The first attempt in Britain to formulate a scheme of registered civil partnerships was intended to apply both to same-sex and opposite-sex partners[61] but partly on the grounds that to do so would undermine marriage, it was withdrawn.[62]

Instead, the UK took the position that registration should be available only for those for whom marriage was unavailable, and, as we saw above, on the basis of equality, promoted and passed the Civil Partnership Act 2004. A civil partnership is 'a relationship between two people of the same sex' (section 1(1)) which is formed when they register their partnership in accordance with the Act. The government was keen to distance civil registration from marriage:

> It is a matter of public record that the Government has no plans to introduce same-sex marriage. This consultation document is about a civil partnership registration scheme.
>
> (DTI 2003a: 13, para 1.3)

> We have considered the position of opposite-sex couples, many of whom now choose to cohabit instead of marrying, and other people who live together in a close supportive household environ-ment. The Government believes that these situations are significantly different from that of same-sex couples who wish to formalise their relationships but currently are unable to do so.
>
> (ibid: para 1.4)

It is not made clear exactly what the 'significant difference' is between the situations of same-sex and opposite-sex cohabitants; certainly protecting against economic vulnerability and providing rights and formal recognition are important in both situations. Perhaps the difference is simply the legal inability of same-sex partners to formalise their relationships, and if so, then the government's position seems to reinforce the view that opposite-sex partners should simply get married if they want the legal benefits and protection that comes with that status.

Further, as much as civil partnership is said to be distinct from marriage, a close reading of its terms and the rights and responsibilities it confers reveals that it creates a legal status which displays virtually all the characteristics of a civil marriage. The civil partnership document must be signed by the parties, two witnesses and the registrar before it is registered.[63] Like marriage, a civil partnership is for life, terminating only on death, dissolution or annulment.[64] There are other similarities to marriage as well, including the requirement of monogamy (neither of the partners must already be in a marriage or other civil partnership), legal age (the partners must be over the age of 18 or if between 16 and 18 have parental consent) and exclusion from the prohibited degrees of

---

[61] Lord Lester's Civil Partnerships Bill (2002).

[62] At the time of writing a case is pending before the ECt HR claiming that the prohibition of opposite-sex couples from registering a civil partnership constitues a violation of Arts 8 and 14.

[63] S 2.

[64] S 1(3).

relationship.[65] There are also requirements as to the formalities of the registration procedure, including the place of registration,[66] the provision of notice of the proposed partnership and a waiting period.[67] And, like marriage, a civil partnership may be void or voidable if defective in certain ways, although note that the non-consummation and venereal disease grounds are not available as they are in marriage.

49 Grounds on which civil partnership is void

Where two people register as civil partners of each other in England and Wales, the civil partnership is void if

(a) at the time when they do so, they are not eligible to register as civil partners of each other under Chapter 1 (see section 3),

(b) at the time when they do so they both know—

    (i) that due notice of proposed civil partnership has not been given,

    (ii) that the civil partnership document has not been duly issued,

    (iii) that the civil partnership document is void under section 17(3) or 27(2) (registration after end of time allowed for registering),

    (iv) that the place of registration is a place other than that specified in the notices (or notice) of proposed civil partnership and the civil partnership document, or

    (v) that a civil partnership registrar is not present, or

(c) the civil partnership document is void under paragraph 6(5) of Schedule 2 (civil partnership between a child and another person forbidden).

50 Grounds on which civil partnership is voidable

(1) Where two people register as civil partners of each other in England and Wales, the civil partnership is voidable if—

(a) either of them did not validly consent to its formation (whether as a result of duress, mistake, unsoundness of mind or otherwise);

(b) at the time of its formation either of them, though capable of giving a valid consent, was suffering (whether continuously or intermittently) from mental disorder of such a kind or to such an extent as to be unfitted for civil partnership;

(c) at the time of its formation, the respondent was pregnant by some person other than the applicant;

(d) an interim gender recognition certificate under the Gender Recognition Act 2004 (c.7) has, after the time of its formation, been issued to either partner;

(e) the respondent is a person whose gender at the time of its formation had become the acquired gender under the 2004 Act.

(2) In this section and section 51 'mental disorder' has the same meaning as in the Mental Health Act 1983 (c. 20).

51 Bars to relief where civil partnership is voidable

(1) The court must not make a nullity order on the ground that a civil partnership is voidable if the respondent satisfies the court—

(a) that the applicant, with knowledge that it was open to him to obtain a nullity order, conducted himself in relation to the respondent in such a way as to lead the respondent reasonably to believe that he would not seek to do so, and

---

[65] Ss 3 and 4.
[66] S 6.
[67] Ss 8–17.

(b) that it would be unjust to the respondent to make the order.

(2) Without prejudice to subsection (1), the court must not make a nullity order by virtue of section 50(1)(a), (b), (c) or (e) unless—

(a) it is satisfied that proceedings were instituted within 3 years from the date of the formation of the civil partnership, or
(b) leave for the institution of proceedings after the end of that 3 year period has been granted under subsection (3)

...

(5) Without prejudice to subsection (1), the court must not make a nullity order by virtue of section 50(1)(d) unless it is satisfied that proceedings were instituted within the period of 6 months from the date of issue of the interim gender recognition certificate.

(6) Without prejudice to subsections (1) and (2), the court must not make a nullity order by virtue of section 50(1)(a) or (e) unless it is satisfied that the applicant was at the time of the formation of the civil partnership ignorant of the facts alleged.

In later chapters we will examine the legal effects of civil partnership, but it seems clear that it is meant to resemble marriage. Indeed, it has been described as 'ingenious' (Stychin 2005)—it is virtually marriage in all but name.[68] By the end of 2009 the total number of civil partnerships formed in the UK from December 2005 when the Act came into force was 40,237 (ONS 2010a). Early research shows the meaning and significance of the Civil Partnership Act for same-sex couples. Shipman and Smart's (2007) early research demonstrated that while for many couples equality and legal rights were important, love, commitment and respect from the wider family were equally as important in people's decisions to register their partnerships.[69]

VIII. THE HISTORY OF MARRIAGE

We have thus far examined the law regulating entry into marriage and civil partnership, which arguably helps us to understand the meaning and importance of marriage and the marriage-like relationship, and we now wish to utilise another approach to examine that meaning. Dire predictions about the breakdown of the fabric of society caused by fewer people marrying, it seems, have always been with us (Thane 2010). Usually, as we will see, they are accompanied by predictions of the dire consequences of the removal of women from their homemaking and child-rearing roles. If we look at the debate around the legal regulation of marriage in the eighteenth and nineteenth centuries, it may help us to place contemporary debate around the social and legal meaning of marriage into historical and political perspective.

Historically, the status of husband and wife and the regulation of that status were matters only for the individuals concerned, their families and their immediate community. The church was concerned with peoples' spiritual well-being, and so the canons of the Roman Catholic Church declared that marriage was a holy estate. Other than that declaration, though, the church did not have much to say about how one would enter into that

---

[68] See also Auchmuty (2004). Note also that non-consummation is not a ground for voidability.
[69] See also Mitchell et al (2009).

holy estate, other than to say it was by agreement and physical consummation. Rules governing who could enter into it were limited to specifying minimum ages of 12 for girls and 14 for boys and to rules prohibiting marriage within certain degrees of relationship by blood (consanguinity) and by marriage (affinity). Throughout medieval times the consent of the parties, provided it was spoken in the present tense, was sufficient to make a valid marriage. Here we see the canonical beginnings of the voluntariness and the consummation requirements in the MCA 1973.

The privacy of these arrangements did not cause problems for the majority of people, but when questions of property arose, the private and informal nature of the marriage created difficulties for those concerned about the orderly transmission of their property. Partly to meet the needs of greater certainty required by the propertied classes, the church then created a set of formal rituals to go along with the exchange of consents. These rituals included the exchange of vows in a church, publicising the intention to marry in the form of banns and placing a ring on the wife's finger. As time went on, the rituals became more strict and included restricting the times of the day during which the vows could be exchanged.

The ecclesiastical rituals became more socially accepted in time, and those who required formal recognition because they wanted to avoid later problems of proof then began to use them more and more. Property disputes were a matter for the common law courts which came to require the evidence of the formal religious ceremony in order to decide questions of property transmission.

The majority of the population for whom property questions were irrelevant had no need to conform to the rituals of the church, yet despite the cost of such rituals—which put them out of reach of many people—in the first half of the eighteenth century large numbers of people who wished to be regarded as married, nonetheless observed the rites and rules it demanded (Probert 2009). For others, social, if not legal, legitimacy for their unions was achieved in other ways. Gillis (1985) writes, for example, of forms of community rituals which varied from place to place, but which were deeply rooted in custom and authority to provide moral, social and financial legitimacy to unions.

In addition to the 'common' folk, those who were not interested in the church wedding included young people who wished to marry without the parental consent required by the church for those under 21, those who could not afford the church rituals, couples disparate in age or religion, or those who desired privacy for other personal reasons (Gillis 1985). These people were 'marrying' according to local custom or by using the services of rogue ministers at the Fleet prison in London (Gillis 1985; Parker 1990, 1987; Stone 1990). These 'informal' marriages may not have conformed to church requirements, but were usually regarded functionally and socially as marriages.

The private ordering of familial lives was unregulated formally by law until the mid-eighteenth century. It is not clear whether Parliament acted at that point because private ordering of relationships had become increasingly unacceptable to upholders of the propertied and increasingly patriarchal order (O'Donovan 1985), or because 'popular customs of all kinds increasingly came under attack by a ruling class fearful of their public order consequences' (Parker 1987: 144) or simply because it dealt with the specific concern of particular forms of clandestine marriage (Probert 2009).[70] The consequences for the propertied classes of clandestine marriage were more than simply public-order consequences,

---

[70] See Probert (2009: 210–20) for discussion of the various theories explaining passage of Lord Hardwicke's Act.

however. The legal doctrine of coverture and the rule of primogeniture ensured that propertied men could maintain, or indeed increase, their wealth through a union with a woman, who lost virtually all legal identity upon marriage. By the eighteenth century, the aristocracy realised that clandestine marriages meant that they lost control over the orderly transmission of their wealth. In this political context, if young people continued to marry whomever they wanted to in these clandestine ceremonies, it was almost seen as a threat to property and patriarchy (O'Donovan 1985: 48).

The House of Lords had a number of times attempted to promote bills invalidating clandestine marriages, but the House of Commons refused to pass them. Finally, a bill was presented in the Lords by the Lord Chancellor, Lord Hardwicke, in 1753. The debate that accompanied its passage is illustrative.[71]

> How often have we known of the heir of a good family seduced, and engaged in a clandestine marriage, perhaps with a common strumpet? How often have we known a rich heiress carried off by a man of low birth, or perhaps by an infamous sharper? What distresses some of our best families have been brought into, what ruin some of their sons and daughters have been involved in, by such means, every gentleman from his own knowledge may recollect.
>
> (O'Donovan 1985: 45)

Lord Hardwicke's bill proposed that all marriages were required to be performed in the Church of England in order to be valid. Further, all such church marriages had to be entered in the church register and no marriage of anyone under the age of 21 years was valid without the consent of parents or guardians. The Act was to apply to all, except members of the Royal Family, Jews and Quakers.

Q What aspects of Lord Hardwicke's bill can you see remaining in the MCA 1973?
In the Marriage Act 1949?

One of the arguments against the bill was that it would enable the aristocracy to create a closed and increasingly wealthy caste for itself. Another was that it would have a ruinous effect upon the poor; it would be expensive, inconvenient and would therefore result in a rise of concubinage, bastardy and infanticide. Despite these arguments, the bill was passed and became law in 1753.[72] According to O'Donovan, Gillis describes it as 'an undisguised triumph of property, patriarchy and male dominance generally' (O'Donovan 1985: 49), and Cretney notes that it gave the Church of England a virtual monopoly over marriage (Cretney 2003a: 6).

Enforcement of the law was placed within the jurisdiction of the secular courts, so that any member of the clergy who was convicted of disobeying it was subject to a penalty of 14 years' transportation.

Nevertheless, a number of forms of relationship formation remained popular, and although Probert (2009) argues that the numbers are not as great as some historians have suggested, it is likely that to the people who practised them and to their communities they were respectable and proper. But they left no public record. Perhaps the best known of

---

[71] Although Probert (2009) cautions that because one is able to find support for any number of explanations for the Act in parliamentary speeches and further that we can only guess at the motivations of those who voted in favour but did not speak, 'any explanation that posits a single cause shoud be regarded as flawed' (Probert 2009: 212).

[72] An Act for the Better Prevention of Clandestine Marriages 1753.

the evasive tactics was marrying across the border in Scotland in Gretna Green. In the period after the Act to the end of the eighteenth and beginning of the nineteenth century, informal marriages were more than just the remnants of 'folk life'; they were actually a powerful challenge to the law of the patriarch, church and state (Gillis 1985; Parker 1990).

Women in particular often preferred these informal marriages because the doctrine of coverture only applied upon formal marriage. If a woman wished to maintain her separate legal identity, an informal marriage would give her legitimacy in the eyes of her community without legally disabling her through a state-sanctioned marriage.

Lord Hardwicke's Act remained the primary law relating to marriage until 1836 when an entirely civil ceremony became legal.[73] This new provision providing for marriage at a Registry Office assisted those who could not meet the 1753 requirements. Initially, the working classes were hesitant to use the civil service because it was associated by them with the Poor Law Administration. But later, by the 1870s, the Registrar became the resort of pregnant women and other persons who did not want the full publicity of a church wedding. But then:

> [b]y the mid-19th century an age of conformity had begun which only began to fragment with the increase in cohabitation after the Second World War. For many working class people in about 1850 alternatives to formal marriage were becoming decreasingly attractive. The amendment to the Poor Law in 1834 made legal marriage increasingly important for women's economic survival. Towns and cities became more anonymous so that there was less effective community pressure on a man to marry or support a woman if she had a child by him. The bourgeois family model slowly filtered down to the working class so that alternative forms became less thinkable.
> (Parker 1990: 74–75)

The 1836 Act completed the move to the secularisation of marriage. The state now had control over marriage. It needed to know clearly who was married to whom for the purposes of the distribution of benefits and burdens. 'A centralised bureaucratic state could not tolerate the ambiguities of the pre-Hardwicke era' (O'Donovan 1985: 48).[74]

After 1836, statutes regulating marriage have dealt mainly with the formalities of the wedding itself,[75] with Cretney characterising those of the 1990s as demonstrating a Thatcherite approach to administrative efficiency and consumerism: 'There was an underlying belief in exposing public services to the pressures of consumer demand, competition and market forces, and this led the government to propose giving the public a greater choice of marriage ceremony' (Cretney 2003a: 30). He observes that the 1994 Marriage Act allowing marriages to be solemnised in 'approved' premises effectively 'privatised' civil marriage (ibid: 31).

And then, of course, 2004 brought the Civil Partnership Act, which as we saw, offers marriage 'in all but name' to an even broader class of people. Yet, even after their most recent reforms, the marriage and civil partnership legislation retain their restrictions on age and proximity of family relationship. Both the Marriage Act 1949 and the Civil Partnership Act contain prohibitions based on consanguinity and affinity. The minimum age

---

[73] Marriage Act 1836.

[74] Cretney observes that the 1836 Act met the interests of both the state and the church: the state had an interest in being able to determine whether or not a person was married, with all the legal consequences that flowed from that status, but its interest in the actual ceremony was limited to ensuring its recognition as binding by both parties (Cretney 2003a: 9).

[75] See discussion in Cretney (2003a: ch 1).

for legal marriage or civil partnership now is 18. However, the minimum age is 16 if there is parental consent or the court consents.[76]

> **Q** Why was it important that the law allow parents some control over their children's decisions to marry? How real was this control? What were restrictions on age at marriage meant to achieve? What reasons are there today for such control? See also Hamilton (1996) regarding the case of a 13-year-old who contracted a 'marriage' under Islamic law. What were restrictions on marriage between blood relations designed to achieve? What reasons can you think of for such restrictions today?

IX. FORMAL AND INFORMAL RELATIONSHIPS

We have dealt so far with the way in which personal relations are regulated by legal assignment of eligibility to participate in marriage and by the creation of an alternative legal status that, while 'like' marriage, is not marriage. We have also discussed the historical context in which that regulation developed. Implicit in these discussions was the idea that non-formalised relationships between adults entailed little, if any, legal regulation. However, the distinct legal consequences of married/civilly registered and non-married/civilly registered cohabitation may serve as a form of post-hoc regulation of relationships. We turn now to the legal effect that legal status has upon individuals (Clive 1980).

The legal effect of marriage is no longer that described by Blackstone in the eighteenth century whereby husband and wife became one in law and the wife's legal existence was subsumed under that of the husband (Blackstone 1778: 442). But we can see remnants of this situation in contemporary law (for example, in the question of whether a husband and wife can be co-conspirators)[77] and custom (for example, the tradition of a wife giving up her name and taking her husband's).

In addition, the remnants of laws which treated unmarried cohabitants in all cases as legal strangers can also be discerned. There is currently no obligation upon unmarried/ unregistered people to support each other financially during or at the end a relationship, and if an cohabiting partner dies intestate, the bereaved partner has no automatic right to inherit from the estate.[78] Other examples of legal situations in which married/registered and unmarried/unregistered partners are treated differently include the scope of parental responsibility assigned to unmarried as opposed to married fathers[79] and the lack of legislated proprietary rights in the family home for cohabiting partners.[80] On the other hand, there are some situations in which the legal gap between married/registered partners and cohabitants is narrowing. Married women may now contract in their own name as if they were unmarried, and we saw in Chapter 1 some similarity of treatment, for example, in the succession to tenancy cases. In addition, 'spousal' (now often called 'partners'') ben-

---

[76] Marriage Act 1949 s 3, as amended by Children Act 1989 Sch 12. The Church of England ceremony itself, although no longer required for validity, still contains elements of the pre-Hardwicke ritual. See generally, Cretney (2003a).

[77] *Midland Bank Trust Co Ltd v Green (No 3)* [1982] Ch 529 (CA); Criminal Law Act 1977 s 2(2)(a).

[78] See Inheritance (Provision for Family and Dependants) Act 1975.

[79] See Chapters 4 and 8 below.

[80] See Chapter 6 below.

efits are sometimes provided to cohabiting partners pursuant to employment contracts or other private contracts.

Regulation of legal burdens and benefits to cohabiting partners relative to their married/registered counterparts has proceeded in England and Wales on an ad hoc or piecemeal basis in response to increasing numbers of people who are choosing to live in 'informal' marriage-like arrangements. In 2001 there were reported to be 2,129,000 opposite-sex cohabiting couple families and 45,000 same-sex cohabiting couple families in the UK (ONS 2011a). In 2010 those numbers increased to 2,737,000 and 51,000 respectively (ibid). The current ad hoc approach whereby in some situations cohabitants are treated in law as though they are married (eg for income support purposes), sometimes as similar but still inferior to married couples (eg for protection from domestic violence under the Family Law Act 1996) and sometimes as legal strangers (eg for the purposes of financial or property division on relationship breakdown) has been described as a 'legislative and judicial lottery' (Barlow and James 2004: 156).[81] It is thus not surprising that there is no clear definition for all purposes of 'cohabitant' in English law. Like the definition of 'family' discussed in Chapter 1, it often depends upon why the question is being raised. Contrast, for example, the definition in the Fatal Accidents Act 1976 of those entitled to bring an action for a wrongful action causing death, with the definition developed by the courts to determine who is living together for the purposes of obtaining social security benefits. In addition to spouses and civil partners of the deceased, the Fatal Accidents Act includes

1 (3)(b) any person who—

(i) was living with the deceased in the same household immediately before the date of the death; and

(ii) had been living with the deceased in the same household for at least two years before that date; and was living during the whole of that period as the husband or wife [or civil partner] of the deceased.

The court, on the other hand, has developed six 'signposts' for identifying cohabitation for benefits purposes, namely co-residence; stability; financial support; a sexual relationship; children; and public acknowledgement.[82]

This piecemeal approach contrasts with the approach taken in other jurisdictions which have adopted comprehensive legislation providing for public and private support and property rights for unmarried cohabitants.[83]

---

[81] See Herring (2011) for a comprehensive review of the legal rights and responsibilities of unmarried cohabitants.

[82] *Crake v Supplementary Benefits Commission* [1982] 1 All ER 498.

[83] Some of these provisions are over 20 years old. In 1984 New South Wales in Australia passed its de facto Relationships Act which provides for the right of unmarried cohabitants to claim either property readjustment or support on the breakdown of the relationship. In Sweden the Law on Cohabitees (Joint Homes) legislation provides for, among other things, a right on separation to division and distribution of property acquired for joint use, and modest succession rights (Bradley 1996: 98–100). In both of these jurisdictions it is important to note the class of cohabitants who fall under the jurisdiction of the laws. In New South Wales de facto partners for the purposes of a maintenance application are those who have lived in a domestic relationship as husband and wife for not less than two years. The Swedish law applies to 'relationships involving cohabitation in which an unmarried woman and an unmarried man live together in circumstances resembling marriage' (Bradley 1996: 214).. In contrast to this, the Norwegian Law on Joint Households applies to two or more unmarried persons over 18 who have lived together for at least two years, and so includes relatives, students and friends as well as cohabitees (Bradley 1996: 214). In Scotland, see the more recent Family Law (Scotland) Act 2006.

There have been attempts in recent years to remedy the disadvantage suffered by dependent or otherwise vulnerable cohabitants on the death of their partner or breakdown of their relationship.[84] In relation to their home, the Law Commission's discussion paper on the rights of cohabitants and other 'homesharers' in the family home (Law Commission 2002) considered the possibility of devising a scheme which would distribute fairly shares in a shared home. The Commission found it impossible to do so, however, at least through changes in property law. It said:

> [W]e have identified, in the course of this project, a wider need for the law to recognise and to respond to the increasing diversity of living arrangements in this country. We believe that further consideration should be given to the adoption—necessarily by legislation—of broader-based approaches to personal relationships, such as the registration of certain civil partnerships and/or the imposition of legal rights and obligations on individuals who are or have been involved in a relationship outside marriage.
>
> (Law Commission 2002: Executive Summary, para 15)

It seemed to be advocating a relationship-based approach which would confer rights and responsibilities upon cohabitants as a result of their cohabitation. This was the approach taken by the Law Society (Law Society 2002) and by a number of academics.[85] It was taken forward to the Law Commission in 2007 (Law Commission 2007). The Law Commission acknowledged that providing remedies for cohabitants either during cohabitation or on its breakdown was controversial. In the end, it limited its study to the rights and obligations of cohabitants on relationship breakdown, confirming that no such obligations ought to inhere in the non-formalised relationship itself. We shall therefore discuss the Law Commission's project in Chapter 7 where we focus upon the financial consequences of relationship breakdown.

In the end, we seem to be left with the same controversy. There are those who oppose new measures to recognise legally cohabitation on the ground that to do so would undermine the institution of marriage (Centre for Social Justice 2010). And there are others who oppose change on the ground that it would undermine the autonomy and choice of those who had consciously chosen not to marry or register their relationship to subject them to a marriage-like regime (Deech 2010). On the other hand, especially in the light of the prevalence of the 'common law marriage myth' (Barlow and James 2004), many feel that there ought to be statutory redress available for the economic vulnerability experienced by many cohabitants, particularly on separation, and that this would accord with people's expectations and recognise the reality of their family lives (Barlow et al 2005, 2008).

Opposition to these measures comes not only from family traditionalists. Some feminist and other critical scholars suggest that if law and policy are truly to reflect our new and diverse partnering and living patterns, perhaps conferring rights and benefits only upon those couples who look most like married couples, whether same-sex or different-sex, does not go far enough. A legislative scheme for cohabitants on this view simply reinforces the heterosexual conjugal couple as the paradigm legal and social relationship and the privilege that is, and indeed ought to be, attached to it. The Law Commission in 2002 recognised the difficulty of accommodating in law our changing family practices that do not conform to that paradigm relationship:

---

[84] See Chapter 7.
[85] See, eg, Barlow and James (2004).

There is also an increasing problem concerning persons who are not in any sense 'a couple', but who live together for mutual support or caring. They may or may not be related, but their financial affairs become somewhat inextricably intertwined. This is not by any means a homogenous group. (Law Commission 2002: para 1.31(4))

As we saw, it was not able in 2002 to devise a scheme to accommodate these non-conjugal homesharers and they were outside the terms of reference set for the more recent project. Yet arguably that accommodation is precisely what is needed. The Law Commission of Canada observed in 2002 the same growing diversity in Canadian family life and it concluded that recognising and supporting the great variety of caring personal adult relationships is an important state objective, along with valuing equality and autonomy, personal security, privacy, freedom of conscience and religion, while at the same time maintaining coherence and efficiency in the law. In the light of these principles, it concluded that the distinction between conjugal and non-conjugal relationships is inconsistent with the value of equality, since conjugality is not an accurate marker of the qualitative attributes of personal adult relationships that are relevant to practical legislative and policy objectives. Further, it assumed that the state's role should be neutral regarding the roles that people assume in their personal relationships, and therefore instead of simply arguing that some relationships currently excluded should be included in legal recognition, it proposed that we start from square one and look at the way governments have relied upon relational status in allocating rights and responsibilities. It criticised this traditional reliance on status, and instead proposed a legislative regime that accomplishes its goals by relying less on whether people are living in certain kinds of relationships and more on whether a particular characteristic of the relationship was relevant to the particular state goal. Since different laws have different objectives, the characteristics of the relationship deemed to be relevant should differ as we move from one law to another. And while sometimes some characteristics of the relationship would be important and other times they would not be, conjugality would never be important (Law Commission of Canada 2002). As Roseneil observes, the effect of such an approach on law and policy might mean, for example, framing work-life policies 'in terms of the range of important personal relationships and commitments within which people live their lives' (Roseneil 2004: 415) rather than narrowly with reference to relationship status.

This idea has been tested in the courts in the UK and in Strasbourg. In *Burden v UK*[86] the Grand Chamber of the ECtHR found that there was something distinctive about the conjugal marriage relationship which entitled the state to provide tax benefits for it. Two 'spinster sisters' who lived together claimed that they ought to be entitled to the inheritance tax relief offered to married and civilly registered partners. The Court disagreed. Rosemary Auchmuty (2009) considers the implications of both their action and the result:

Joyce and Sybil Burden are elderly sisters who have lived together all their lives. They own a house in Marlborough, inherited from their parents 30 years ago, whose value (together with adjoining land) had risen to £875,000 by January 2006 when their case was heard. Each possessed in addition investments worth about £150,000 and they shared the ownership of two other properties worth £350,000 in total. Each sister had willed her property to the other. They had long been aware that, when one of them died, the other would face a substantial inheritance tax bill because the threshold for the 'nil rate' band was less than the value of property owned by each sister.

[86] [2008] 2 FLR 787.

The sisters applied to the European Court of Human Rights, claiming discrimination by the UK under Article 14 of the European Convention on Human Rights (ECHR) in the application of Article 1 of Protocol 1 because, while spouses and civil partners may leave their property to each other free of inheritance tax, this exemption is not available to other individuals who live together in similar mutually caring relationships like theirs. (Auchmuty 2009: 205–06)

On the substantive issue as to whether the UK was in violation of Article 14 in conjunction with Article 1 of Protocol 1, a majority of 15 of 17 judges found against the Burdens, but for different reasons from the majority in the lower court. Where the latter had left open the question as to whether the sisters were in an analogous position to a married couple or a civil partnership, the Grand Chamber found that they were decidedly *not*: 'the relationship between siblings is qualitatively of a different nature to that between married couples and homosexual civil partners'. The 'essential difference', according to the court, was the consanguinity of siblings, which ruled out the possibility of marriage or a civil partnership in English law. It was the making of a choice to enter a legally sanctioned relationship—a choice which, of course, the Burdens could not make—that set marriage and civil partnerships apart from other domestic couplings. 'Rather than the length or the supportive nature of the relationship, what is determinative is the existence of a public undertaking, carrying with it a body of rights and obligations of a contractual nature.' Since, in the Grand Chamber's view, the two relationships were not comparable, it followed that there was no breach of the Convention and no need to consider whether the discrimination was proportionate or served a legitimate aim. (ibid: 209, references omitted).

In truth, however, this was not really a case about civil partnerships. It was a case about tax; about spousal privilege (and the extension of that privilege to gays and lesbians who register their partnerships); and about old age and vulnerability. (ibid: 211)

Thirty years ago, feminists called for an end to the privileging of marriage and the nuclear family, and for recognition and acceptance of the variety of ways people actually live, the relationships and family forms we choose (or find ourselves in), and the households we create. The Burdens' legal challenge has forced a consideration of why the UK government, in allocating privileges such as tax exemptions, chooses to recognise one kind of caring relationship—that of two committed but unrelated individuals in a marriage or marriage-like relationship—and not another—that of two committed but *related* individuals. In this sense, the Burdens' claim for equal treatment as an alternative family form *was* a feminist claim, and may yet yield positive results. (ibid: 217–18, references omitted)

Q How would you legislate for the rights and obligations of unmarried partners or homesharers? Whom would you include within the scope of your legislation? See generally, on the development of the law relating to unmarried cohabitation, Cretney (2003a: ch 13).

X. SUMMARY AND CONCLUSION

The legal approach to regulating relations between intimates is, as we saw, connected with the political and social economy of a state. It is also, however, intimately connected with custom, tradition and religious beliefs held by dominant communities within the state. Perhaps this is what Parker means when he suggests that our study should be focused more upon what we mean by marriage itself, than on any differences between formal and informal marriage. Marriage is still the referent; other partnerships are alternatives to it. Marriage in England and Wales is accorded a privileged social status which provides a place for the legitimate expression of heterosexual desires, imbuing other types of sexual activity and other relationships with a lesser status. The married unit is the economic unit upon which state financial policy is based and has its modern beginnings in concern for the orderly transmission of property within families. It is the institution which most easily, even though not exclusively, accommodates the model of family preferred by other state institutions and is presumed to be the model which best promotes the welfare of children. It is, however, also a model which can be adapted in an increasingly egalitarian society, as is demonstrated by recent changes in the law that appear to give legitimacy to other family models, but on closer inspection do so only if they are sufficiently 'marriage-like' (Cossman and Ryder 2001). Entry into it or refusal of it is still considered the private and individual 'choice' of the parties. It is the model on which the modern regulation of adult relationships is based, and that regulation displays, we suggest, elements of all three of our themes: equality, welfare, and a divide between public and private.

Q Do we now have a three-tiered system, with marriage at the top, followed by civil partnership and then by unmarried cohabitation?

We can now return to Clive's and Fineman's thesis and the subversive questions become: what is the *legal* value of the religious or social ritual of marriage? Does it make sense simply to assimilate civil partnership into that model? Would you feel comfortable living in a society in which decisions to form households were validated socially without the necessity of their legal validation? Why should a religious ritual or social rite of passage confer any more legal status upon a person than a first holy communion, a confirmation, a debutante's 'coming out' or a bar mitzvah?

FURTHER READING

F BANDA, 'Global Standards: Local Values' (2003) 17 *International Journal of Law, Policy and the Family*.

A BARLOW, S DUNCAN, G JAMES and A PARK, *Cohabitation, Marriage and the Law* (Oxford, Hart Publishing, 2005).

S CRETNEY, *Family Law in the Twentieth Century: A History* (Oxford, Oxford University Press, 2003).

J EEKELAAR and M MACLEAN, 'Marriage and the Moral Bases of Personal Relationships' (2004) 31 *Journal of Law and Society* 510.

S PARKER, *Informal Marriage, Cohabitation and the Law 1750–1989* (Basingstoke, Macmillan, 1990).

S ROSENEIL and S BUDGEON, 'Cultures of Intimacy and Care Beyond "the Family": Personal Life and Social Change in the Early 21st Century' (2004) *Current Sociology* 135.

C SMART, *The Ties That Bind* (London, Routledge and Kegan Paul, 1984).

C STYCHIN, 'Family Friendly? Rights, Responsibilities and Relationship Recognition' in A Diduck and K O'Donovan (eds), *Feminist Perspectives on Family Law* (London, Cavendish, 2006).

3

Dissolution of Legal Relationships: The Process and its Consequences

I. DIVORCE—INTRODUCTION

2009 was the sixth consecutive year that the number of divorces in England and Wales fell. It was in fact the year with the lowest number of divorces since 1974 (ONS 2011c). In 2009 the divorce rate in England and Wales decreased by 6.3% to 10.5 divorcing people per thousand married population, representing the lowest divorce rate since 1977, when there were 10.3 divorcing people per thousand married people (ibid). Of all decrees awarded to one partner (rather than jointly to both), 67% were awarded to the wife (ibid).

Divorce, like marriage and cohabitation, is firmly entrenched as part of our familial and social lives. Also like cohabitation it is viewed in different ways. Some see divorce as a means of escape from an unhappy, dangerous or unfulfilling marriage, while others see it as too frivolously chosen and another symptom of a retreat from social and personal responsibility (Deech 2009a). Some see it as an expression of autonomy, while others see it as an expression of selfishness. Finally, divorce, like cohabitation, has also been linked to poorer outcomes for children (Centre for Social Justice 2010), although this too is disputed.[1]

In whatever way one views it, however, it is difficult to think about divorce without reference back to the law and policy on marriage. As we saw in Chapter 2, entry into marriage is considered to be a voluntary matter, and marriage has always been regarded as a sort of hybrid, resembling both a contract and a binding vow.[2] The state's regulation of marriage takes many forms, and it relies upon social and ideological forces as much as it does on law.[3] Perhaps surprisingly, however, regulation of marriage occurs also through divorce law. In any event, while entering into marriage is relatively easy as long as both partners satisfy the formal requirements,[4] ending a marriage has never been quite so simple. In the first part of this chapter we will explore not only the law of divorce, but will also present different views of the moral, religious, economic and social policies behind that law. We will then discuss the law regulating dissolution of civil partnerships which largely mirrors dissolution of marriage by divorce.

---

[1] See Chapter 8 below.
[2] See *Hyde v Hyde and Woodmansee* [1866] L Rev 1 P and D 130.
[3] See Chapter 2 above.
[4] See Chapter 2 above.

II. THE HISTORY OF DIVORCE

The early history of formal divorce[5] in England and Wales begins with canon law (Finer and McGregor 1974: 85–87). The ecclesiastical courts treated marriage as indissoluble and, in the case of validly contracted marriages, granted only a limited form of relief in certain circumstances. A divorce *a mensa et thoro* could be granted on proof of a matrimonial offence, but had the effect only of a modern judicial separation. However, the law of nullity was developed in order to 'provide a legitimate avoidance of the rigours of the doctrine of indissolubility' (Finer and McGregor 1974: 86).

So, until the seventeenth century those who could afford to had to petition the ecclesiastical court for divorce. Although, theologically, this court could not break the bond that God had created, it could declare that that bond had never existed in the first place and grant a divorce *a vinculo*. The impediments to a validly contracted marriage usually dealt with lack of capacity to marry or lack of proper consent to marriage.[6] Successfully challenging the validity of the marriage in one of these ways meant, of course, that any children were rendered illegitimate and their entitlement to property defeated. But it did have the effect of allowing the parties to marry again.

The first 'modern' way to escape from a valid marriage was the development in the seventeenth century of what became known as parliamentary divorces (Stone 1990: 309–11). Finer and McGregor (1974: 92) explain that this new remedy was developed primarily to secure succession to peerages and property but later filtered down from the aristocracy to the merchant class.[7]

Adultery was the sole ground for parliamentary divorce. For a wife's petition to succeed, her husband's adultery had to be 'aggravated' by bigamy, incest or an unnatural vice. It was thought that '[s]hort of this, she suffered no "very material injury" and she ought not to resent her husband's unfaithfulness' (Cornish and Clark 1989: 379).[8] Husband petitions, on the other hand, became so common and the rules so routinised that, in 1840, a select committee of the House of Commons was set aside to hear divorce petitions. However, ecclesiastical proceedings and parliamentary divorces were still meeting the needs only of the propertied classes.[9] For those who were not wealthy, there was no legal exit from marriage.

Yet just as the poor often symbolically challenged the laws of church and state in their means of marrying, they often did the same in their means of divorcing. One of the most popular means of 'divorce' was desertion. For others, ritual was important to symbolise to the couple and to the community that the relationship was over by mutual agreement of the parties. In some parts of England the custom of wife-selling was practised in which a man put a halter around his wife's neck and led her to the open cattle market to 'auction' her to the highest bidder. Usually, these auctions were prearranged, and by agreement

---

[5] See, for the history of divorce law generally, Stone (1990); McGregor (1957); Cornish and Clark (1989); Cretney (2003a); summaries in Finer and McGregor (1974); Royal Commission Report (1956).

[6] See Chapter 2 above.

[7] See also Anderson (1984).

[8] Cornish and Clark (1989: 379) go on: '[i]n the period to 1857, only four women would ever succeed in securing a divorce Act'. See also Finer and McGregor (1974: 94).

[9] For those who did not wish to litigate at all but for whom property was of some concern, settlements drafted by conveyancers were available to deal with separation and property matters, if not full divorces. See Stone (1990: part VII).

between the husband, wife and new partner. They represented an important symbolic end to one relationship and beginning of another (O'Donovan 1984). Folk custom served the same purpose for the poor as parliamentary divorce did for the rich; it served as public notice of the end of a marriage.

For many, however, desertion was the route out of marriage. It was relatively easy for a migrant worker or man who wished to enlist to get 'lost' in pre-industrial England, and deserted wives accounted for about 6% of all women in south-east England who applied for Poor Relief in the eighteenth century (Stone 1990: 142). However, by the nineteenth century, the large number of deserted wives posed problems for the parishes which became responsible for them. In addition, the influence of liberals such as Mill and Bentham, the lobbying of women and reforms directed at the separation of church and state led to the press taking up the cause of divorce reform (Cornish and Clark 1989: 383).[10] A Royal Commission was set up in 1852 to investigate the matter.[11] The history of divorce from that time to the present becomes the history of proposals for reform countered by resistance to reform based upon fears for the health of society caused by an increasing divorce rate and the undermining of the institution of marriage.

While the government argued publicly in the 1850s that divorce reform would promote equality by bringing divorce from the door of only the rich man to the 'humblest classes' (Stone 1990: 371), Stone argues that this was a fallacious claim; the government had no intention of creating equality in accessibility of divorce. It seems that the motives and the morals of the 'humbler' classes were always suspect.

> To virtually all legislators, the poor were seen as a threatening, immoral, dissolute mass of people to whom it would be extremely dangerous to extend the facility of easy divorce. ... [It] might, it was argued, undermine what elements of stability existed in working-class families. In any case, there was no evidence at all that the poor were demanding divorce. (Stone 1990: 374)

Rather, the object of reform was to abolish the separate and 'chaotic' distribution of jurisdiction over separation and divorce among Parliament, church courts and common law courts. The real significance of the first Act relating to divorce, passed in 1857, was, then, that it met this object; it made divorce a secular matter. The law, in reality, however, did not change that much. The Divorce and Matrimonial Causes Act 1857 removed the procedure from the ecclesiastical court and Parliament to the common law courts—a process that was cheaper but not cheap, thereby allowing divorce a little lower down the social scale—while keeping in place the old grounds for obtaining a divorce.[12] Divorce *a mensa et thoro* was similarly transformed into judicial separation. Collusion and connivance were absolute bars to divorce. The Act did not, in the end, achieve the equality of accessibility it apparently promised to the poor, and it never was intended to achieve

---

[10] Cretney (2003a: 162) observes that the impetus for change also came from the review of the probate jurisdiction of the Ecclesiastical Courts, resulting in the creation of the Court of Probate in 1857 and questions about what to do with the courts' remaining jurisdiction over matrimonial causes.

[11] It was chaired by Lord Campbell, and reported in 1853: see Royal Commission on Divorce and Matrimonial Causes (1853).

[12] A husband could petition on the ground of adultery and a wife could petition on the grounds of incestuous adultery; bigamy with adultery; rape; sodomy; bestiality; adultery with such cruelty as would have entitled her to a divorce *a mensa et thoro*; or adultery with desertion for two years. See the Divorce and Matrimonial Causes Act 1857, s XXVII.

complete equality between men and women, but it did probably address some of the concerns of the middle classes.[13]

Divorce reform did not reappear as a political issue until 1909 when another Royal Commission was convened.[14] According to Stone, there were three stimuli to demands for further reform: the increasing erosion of beliefs in general religious 'truths' and the general secularisation of society; the scandals and absurdity of the collusion required by so many in order to obtain a divorce; and the growing movement, particularly among middle-class women, for women's equality in the public sphere, and also a move towards greater equality between the classes (Stone 1990: 391–92). The Commissioners, reporting in 1912, were split.

> A Majority Report advocated reform of the legal machinery for divorce and offered reasons to justify it. A Minority Report, signed by three members, opposed all the important proposals on the grounds that they would make divorce easier; that this would merely create more divorces; and that any extension of the causes for divorce beyond female adultery were against the express words of Christ.
>
> The Majority Report was a remarkable document for its day. It set out three principles. The first was that there should be equality of access between both rich and poor and men and women. Over this there was ostensibly not much dispute. The second was that divorce should be regarded as merely a legal mopping-up operation after the spiritual death of a marriage. The third was that in any society there is no necessary correlation between the number of divorces and the level of sexual immorality. (Stone 1990: 393)

While pressure for reform continued (Cretney 2003a: 214–16), political debate was interrupted by the First World War and only continued after 1918. In 1923 the next piece of legislation was passed.[15] The only amendment it made to the law was to equalise the ground of adultery as between men and women. 'So, in an age which was doing a good deal formally to give women equality with men, there passed away the notion of the husband's "accidental adultery" and with it the most egregious application of the double standard' (Cornish and Clark 1989: 397).

In 1937 yet another divorce reform Act was passed,[16] this time extending the grounds for divorce beyond adultery to include desertion for three years, cruelty, habitual drunkenness and incurable insanity. The preamble to the Bill reveals the changes in perception of the 'problem' of divorce which allowed such provisions to pass into law:

> The preamble to the act, written by AP Herbert, stated that its object was to offer true support for marriage; protection for children; the removal of hardship for the unhappily married; the reduction of illicit unions; the elimination of unseemly litigation; the relief of consciences of the clergy; and the restoration of due respect for the law. (Stone 1990: 401)

Herbert thus presented his Bill not as a force for change but as a source of stability (Cretney 2003a: 51). Although the law now appeared to grant formal equality between spouses with regard to grounds for divorce, Smart argues that that goal was undermined

---

[13] See generally Cretney (2003a: ch 5).

[14] The Gorrell Commission's terms of reference were to inquire into 'the present state of the law and the administration thereof in Divorce and Matrimonial Causes, and Application for Separation Orders, especially with regard to the position of the poorer classes in relation thereto' (Cretney 2003a: 209). See on this period generally, Cornish and Clark (1989: 393–98); Cretney (2003a: ch 6).

[15] Matrimonial Causes Act 1923.

[16] Matrimonial Causes Act 1937. On this Act generally, see Cretney (2003a: ch 7).

by differential interpretations in the courts: women were often held to higher moral and sexual standards than men, and grounds for divorce often were interpreted differently for men than for women (Smart 1984: 27–53). Rather than divorce legislation, it was probably the introduction of Legal Aid in 1948 which did most towards achieving greater practical equality in divorce, given the differences in men's and women's incomes and wealth.[17] Certainly, statistics show a great increase in the rate of divorce after the extension of legal aid in 1949 (Smart 1984: 33), though the end of the Second World War was another influence.

In the 1950s another Royal Commission on Marriage and Divorce was struck to consider and explain the reasons for the higher, though stable, rate of divorce[18] while having 'in mind ... the "need to promote healthy and happy married life and to safeguard the interests and well-being of children"' (Royal Commission 1956: 7).

Q Review the mandates and objectives of the various commissions and reports on divorce. What themes do you see emerging in divorce reform debate?

While the Commission had a very wide remit, the main issue before it was the ground for divorce, and on this question it was divided. Only one Commissioner recommended that divorce be available in the absence of any 'matrimonial fault'. The remaining 18 signatories to the 1956 Report were split nine members to nine on whether divorce should be granted on the ground only of the 'irretrievable breakdown of the marriage' (provable by separation for seven years or more, with some adding the proviso that divorce would not be available if one of the spouses objected and others adding the proviso that the separation be attributable to the unreasonable conduct of the respondent spouse), rather than on the ground of one spouse having committed a matrimonial offence. Cretney et al characterise the outcome as designating the role of law as being to 'give relief where a wrong had been done', rather than to provide a 'dignified and honourable means of release from a broken marriage' (Cretney et al 2002: 273). Those in favour of the new ground argued their case as follows:

> 70. (vii) We think that the time has come to recognise that matrimonial offences are in many cases merely symptomatic of the breakdown of marriage, and that there should also be provision for divorce in cases where, quite apart from the commission of such offences, the marriage has broken down completely ... .
>
> (ix) ... We do not believe that the introduction of this new principle of divorce into the law will lessen respect for marriage and undermine it as an institution. On the contrary, by basing dissolution of marriage on a complete breakdown of that union, we are, we think, heightening the respect for true marriage, for the emphasis is then placed on marriage as a real union for life. It is impossible to ignore the fact that at the present time the matrimonial offence is in very many cases only a means of obtaining a dissolution of marriage desired by both parties. Our proposal avoids the distasteful expedient of committing a matrimonial offence to give cause for

---

[17] See also Cretney (2003a: 306–18).

[18] The Morton Commission discussed factors such as the 'complexity of modern life'; the conditions of modern life including scarce housing, earlier age at marriage and the 'greater demands made of marriage, consequent on the spread of education, higher standards of living and the social and economic emancipation of women'; newer attitudes towards sex and modern psychology which encouraged 'self-expression'; and a general 'dangerous' tendency to take the responsibilities of marriage less seriously (Royal Commission, 1956: 8–10, paras 43–49). See also Smart (1984: 36–38); Cretney (2003a: 327–43).

divorce, lessens undesirable publicity and dispenses with the often unwarrantable assumption that one spouse is more to blame than the other. (Royal Commission 1956: 23–24).

The contrary view was expressed as follows:

69. (ii) We believe that the consequences of providing the 'easy way out' afforded by divorce by consent would be disastrous to stability in marriage. The inevitable result would be the granting of divorces in cases where no real necessity for the remedy had arisen ... . People would then come to look upon marriage less and less as a life-long union and more and more as one to be ended if things began to go wrong, and there would be a real risk that widespread divorce would come to be an accepted feature of our society. As those attitudes spread they would undermine, and ultimately destroy, the concept of life-long marriage.

(iii) ... We are deeply concerned about the effect on children of the present divorce rate; their suffering would be multiplied if divorce were to become more widespread. The best home for children is of course a happy home, but in our opinion (and most of our 'expert' witnesses confirmed this) children can put up with a good deal of friction between their parents so long as the home remains intact ... .

...

(vii) ... But whether there are children or not, the State must be concerned in the maintenance of a marriage and in its dissolution, because the state has an overriding responsibility to ensure, in the interests of the community, that the institution of marriage is upheld.

(viii) ... [To] give people a right to divorce themselves would be to foster a change in attitude to marriage which would be disastrous for the nation. (Royal Commission 1956: 14–15)

> **Q** Note that each 'side' argues that its position buttresses, rather than undermines, marriage as an institution. Which argument do you favour? Smart characterises the question as whether the law ought to see marriage as a contract between the spouses and the state, or as one simply between the spouses (Smart 1999b).
>
> Note also that the religious aspects of divorce were no longer argued by either side, but that recourse is had to morals, to the interests of children and to the interests of society. Children are considered seriously for the first time in the divorce reform debate and, yet again, the dependence of the stability of society upon the institution of marriage is assumed rather than argued for.

Nothing was to come of this Royal Commission Report for several years, but Stone suggests that it presented the germ of the idea of no-fault divorce to an increasingly secular society (Stone 1990: 409). Interestingly, the idea was taken up by a group set up by the Archbishop of Canterbury—concerned at the rate of illegitimacy—which produced its own report in 1966 favouring no-fault divorce and suggesting that irretrievable breakdown of marriage be the only ground for divorce (Archbishop of Canterbury's Group 1966). The newly created Law Commission supported this proposal in its report also published in 1966. Some of the Law Commission's conclusions are summarised as follows:

120. (1) The objectives of a good divorce law should include (a) the support of marriages which have a chance of survival, and (b) the decent burial with the minimum of embarrassment, humiliation and bitterness of those that are indubitably dead ...

(3) Four of the major problems requiring solution are:

(a) The need to encourage reconciliation. Something more might be achieved here; though little is to be expected from conciliation procedures after divorce proceedings have been instituted

(b) The prevalence of stable illicit unions. As the law stands, many of these cannot be regularised nor the children legitimated

(c) Injustice to the economically weaker partner—normally the wife

(d) The need adequately to protect the children of failed marriages.

(Law Commission 1966: 53–54)[19]

Q Do you agree with these objectives? Note their similarities and differences from previous commissions and reports.

The time appeared to be right for change, and the result of the two reports was a compromise position: while irretrievable breakdown should be the sole ground for divorce, breakdown would be proved by evidence of one or more of five facts, three of which were, in effect, the matrimonial offences of adultery, cruelty and desertion.[20] Marriage-saving remained important, though, and it was thought that the parties should be encouraged to attempt reconciliation wherever possible. Thus, the Divorce Reform Bill did not remove fault from divorce law entirely, and its purpose included facilitating reconciliation (Cretney 2003a: 378).

Arguments in favour of the no-fault provisions of the Bill included claims that it did no more than reflect changes already occurring in society, and that rather than undermining family life and marriage, it strengthened both by allowing the many stable but illegitimate unions to become legitimate (Stone 1990: 407). Indeed, Smart asserts:

> Arguably, this legislation marked a shift away from the traditional method of controlling family life through restriction and limitation on movement and change, towards regulating it by providing directions for this movement and change. The direction in which individuals were invited to go was away from an unsatisfactory marriage towards a second more satisfactory one. Quite simply, the solution to the divorce problem was seen as (re)marriage. ... In the debates in the House of Commons, MPs spoke of divorce as the process by which individuals could leave miserable relationships in order to start new, legitimate, fulfilling ones. Moreover, although there was concern over the effects of divorce on children at this time, this concern was also submerged by the faith in the stabilising power of the re-constituted family. (Smart 1999b: 7–8)

One can view the Divorce Reform Act 1969, with its at least symbolic acknowledgement of marriage breakdown as the only ground for divorce, as a remarkable piece of legislation. It can also be seen as remarkable in the way in which it reconciles the competing ideas of marriage as both a contract between individuals and between the individuals and the state, and in the way in which it continues to promote marriage saving as an appropriate part of divorce law.

The Act was subsequently consolidated with other legislation, including the Matrimonial Proceedings and Property Act 1970, into the Matrimonial Causes Act 1973 (MCA), and remains the law today. The history of divorce reform does not end here though. These substantive changes were followed by procedural changes that have had an equally—if not more—dramatic effect on the availability and nature of divorce. Both the Law Commission and the Archbishop's group envisaged that a court would examine the evidence and

---

[19] See also Cretney (1996b).
[20] See generally Cretney (2003a: 355–75).

only then determine whether the marriage had indeed irretrievably broken down. This vision has been gradually abandoned and a 'special procedure' was first established in 1973 for the simplest of the undefended divorce cases, and then extended in 1977 to all undefended divorce cases. The special procedure means that the parties do not have to appear in court, but their documents are scrutinised by a district judge who then satisfies herself/himself that the petitioner is entitled to a decree of divorce. The documents are checked for procedural as well as substantive regularity.[21] Very little opportunity is provided to the parties or the court to query any of the allegations in the documents and in effect this means that undefended divorce has become an administrative rather than judicial procedure.[22] In practice, about 99% of divorces are undefended and granted under the special procedure rules (LCD 1993: para 2.7). The Family Procedure Rules (FPR) 2010 state:

7.20—(1) This rule applies where an application is made under rule 7.19 [an application for a decree nisi or conditional order of dissolution under the Civil Partnership Act 2004].

(2) If at the relevant time the case is an undefended case, the court must—

(a) if satisfied that the applicant is entitled to—
  (i) in matrimonial proceedings, a decree nisi or a decree of judicial separation (as the case may be); or
  (ii) in civil partnership proceedings, a conditional order or a separation order (as the case may be),

so certify and direct that the application be listed before a district judge for the making of the decree or order at the next available date;

(b) if not so satisfied, direct—
  (i) that any party to the proceedings provide such further information, or take such other steps, as the court may specify; or
  (ii) that the case be listed for a case management hearing.

III. THE MATRIMONIAL CAUSES ACT 1973

The MCA 1973 opens as follows:

1. (1) Subject to section 3 below, a petition for divorce may be presented to the court by either party to a marriage on the ground that the marriage has broken down irretrievably.

(2) The court hearing a petition for divorce shall not hold the marriage to have broken down irretrievably unless the petitioner satisfies the court of one or more or the five following facts; that is to say—

(a) that the respondent has committed adultery and the petitioner finds it intolerable to live with the respondent;
(b) that the respondent has behaved in such a way that the petitioner cannot reasonably be expected to live with the respondent;

---

[21] *Santos v Santos* [1972] Fam 247; *Pounds v Pounds* [1994] 1 FLR 775.

[22] Cretney (2003a: 383) suggests that rather than minimising the bitterness and distress of divorce, the special procedure may have increased them, because parties no longer have the opportunity of answering allegations made in the petition or venting their grievances in court.

(c) that the respondent has deserted the petitioner for a continuous period of at least two years immediately preceding the presentation of the petition;

(d) that the parties to the marriage have lived apart for a continuous period of at least two years immediately preceding the presentation of the petition ... and the respondent consents to a decree being granted;

(e) that the parties to the marriage have lived apart for a continuous period of at least five years immediately preceding the presentation of the petition ... .

(3) On a petition for divorce it shall be the duty of the court to inquire, so far as it reasonably can, into the facts alleged by the petitioner and into any facts alleged by the respondent.[23]

(4) If the court is satisfied on the evidence of any such fact as is mentioned in subsection (2) above, then, unless it is satisfied on all the evidence that the marriage has not broken down irretrievably, it shall, subject to [section 5] below, grant a decree of divorce.

(5) Every decree of divorce shall in the first instance be a decree nisi and shall not be made absolute before the expiration of six months from its grant unless the High Court by general order from time to time fixes a shorter period ... .[24]

2. (1) One party to a marriage shall not be entitled to rely for the purposes of section 1(2)(a) above on adultery committed by the other if, after it became known to him that the other had committed that adultery, the parties have lived with each other for a period exceeding, or periods together exceeding, six months.

(2) Where the parties to a marriage have lived with each other after it became known to one party that the other had committed adultery, but subsection (1) above does not apply, in any proceedings for divorce in which the petitioner relies on that adultery the fact that the parties have lived with each other after that time shall be disregarded in determining for the purposes of section 1(2)(a) above whether the petitioner finds it intolerable to live with the respondent.

(3) Where in any proceedings for divorce the petitioner alleges that the respondent has behaved in such a way that the petitioner cannot reasonably be expected to live with him, but the parties to the marriage have lived with each other for a period or periods after the date of the occurrence of the final incident relied on by the petitioner and held by the court to support his allegation, the fact shall be disregarded in determining for the purposes of section 1(2)(b) above whether the petitioner cannot reasonably be expected to live with the respondent if the length of that period or of those periods together was six months or less.

(4) For the purposes of section 1(2)(c) above the court may treat a period of desertion as having continued at a time when the deserting party was incapable of continuing the necessary intention if the evidence before the court is such that, had that party not been so incapable, the court would have inferred that his desertion continued at that time.

(5) In considering for the purposes of section 1(2) above whether the period for which the respondent has deserted the petitioner or the period for which the parties to a marriage have lived apart has been continuous, no account shall be taken of any one period (not exceeding six months) or of any two or more periods (not exceeding six months in all) during which the parties resumed living with each other, but no period during which the parties lived with each other shall count as part of the period of desertion or of the period for which the parties to the marriage lived apart, as the case may be.

(6) For the purposes of section 1(2)(d) and (e) above and this section a husband and wife shall

---

[23] Undefended divorces now proceed according to the special procedure: see above. It is difficult to say that the Court can offer more than a review of procedural regularity. See also FPR 2010 R 7.20.

[24] The period of time between the decree nisi and decree absolute is now six weeks. Under the FPR 2010 R 7.1, these orders are known collectively as 'matrimonial orders'.

be treated as living apart unless they are living with each other in the same household, and references in this section to the parties to a marriage living with each other shall be construed as references to their living with each other in the same household. ...

3. (1) No petition for divorce shall be presented to the court before the expiration of the period of one year from the date of the marriage.

(2) Nothing in this section shall prohibit the presentation of a petition based on matters which occurred before the expiration of that period.

...

5. (1) The respondent to a petition for divorce in which the petitioner alleges five years' separation may oppose the grant of a decree on the ground that the dissolution of the marriage will result in grave financial or other hardship to him and that it would in all the circumstances be wrong to dissolve the marriage.

(2) Where the grant of a decree is opposed by virtue of this section, then—

(a) if the court finds that the petitioner is entitled to rely in support of his petition on the fact of five years' separation and makes no such finding as to any other fact mentioned in section 1(2) above, and

(b) if apart from this section the court would grant a decree on the petition, the court shall consider all the circumstances, including the conduct of the parties to the marriage and the interests of those parties and of any children or other persons concerned, and if of opinion that the dissolution of the marriage will result in grave financial or other hardship to the respondent and that it would in all the circumstances be wrong to dissolve the marriage it shall dismiss the petition.

(3) For the purposes of this section hardship shall include the loss of the chance of acquiring any benefit which the respondent might acquire if the marriage were not dissolved.

6. (1) Provision shall be made by rules of court for requiring the solicitor acting for a petitioner for divorce to certify whether he has discussed with the petitioner the possibility of a reconciliation and given him the names and addresses of persons qualified to help effect a reconciliation between parties to a marriage who have become estranged.

(2) If at any stage of proceedings for divorce it appears to the court that there is a reasonable possibility of a reconciliation between the parties to the marriage, the court may adjourn the proceedings for such period as it thinks fit to enable attempts to be made to effect such a reconciliation.

Note that there is no provision for joint petitions: one party must petition the court and designate the other as respondent. Whoever petitions must establish that his or her marriage has broken down irretrievably and prove that one of the five facts applies to him or her. Let us now break down these provisions to illustrate how courts have interpreted them.

The Ground for Divorce

Section 1(1) Irretrievable Breakdown

This is the sole ground for divorce and on its face does not seem to require any fault by one of the parties. But this subsection is to be read with the others: evidence of breakdown is insufficient if one of the five facts is not also proved, and evidence of one of the facts is insufficient if irretrievable breakdown is not proved, although it is not necessary to show that the fact relied upon caused the irretrievable breakdown.[25] So, in *Buffery v Buffery*,[26] for example, after 21 years of marriage the parties had grown apart, could not communicate and had nothing in common. The court found their marriage had broken down irretrievably, but simply establishing this ground without also establishing one or more of the five facts was not sufficient to dissolve their marriage. Mr and Mrs Buffery were unable to establish one or more of them and so were unable to divorce notwithstanding the breakdown of their marriage.

Adultery

The first of the five facts is section 1(2)(a): adultery by the respondent. Note that the petitioner cannot rely upon his or her own adultery and that both adultery and intolerability have to be proved. The intolerability need not be because of the adultery.[27] Adultery is voluntary sexual intercourse by one of the parties with a third party of the opposite sex and requires some element of penile–vaginal penetration.[28] It may be proved by the respondent's admission on the prescribed form in the special procedure and the co-respondent need not be named. This fact must be considered in the light also of section 2(1) and (2). Here the legislation encourages reconciliation. First, it makes provision for the adultery, in effect, to be 'forgiven' if the parties live together for more than six months after it is discovered. Second, any efforts they make to try to live together after the adultery is discovered that do not last for six months cannot be held against the petitioner in establishing the intolerability element of the fact.

Behaviour

Section 1(2)(b) is the behaviour fact. It is often referred to as 'unreasonable behaviour', but a close reading shows that the petitioner is not alleging the respondent's behaviour is unreasonable; he or she is alleging that in the light of the behaviour any expectation that he or she continue to live with the respondent is unreasonable. Once again, the petitioner cannot rely upon his or her own behaviour. The test of reasonableness has both a subjective and an objective element to it. The Court of Appeal in *Buffery* confirmed the test as follows:

> Would any right-thinking person come to the conclusion that this husband has behaved in such a way that his wife cannot reasonably be expected to live with him, taking into account the whole of the circumstances and the characters and personalities of the parties (per May LJ, 468, quoting Roskill LJ in *Livingstone-Stallard*).[29]

The court must determine if a reasonable person would think it was reasonable for that petitioner to continue to live with that respondent. Behaviour need not be intentional and it may be unreasonable to expect the petitioner to tolerate it even where it is the result of

---

[25] *Pheasant v Pheasant* [1972] 1 All ER 587 and *Stringfellow v Stringfellow* [1976] 2 All ER 539.

[26] [1988] 2 FLR 365.

[27] *Cleary v Cleary* [1974] 1 All ER 498 (CA).

[28] *Sapsford v Sapsford and Furtado* [1954] P 394; [1954] 2 All ER 373; *Dennis v Dennis* [1955] P 153; [1955] 2 All ER 51 (CA).

[29] *Livingstone Stallard v Livingstone Stallard* [1974] Fam 47. See also *Pheasant v Pheasant* [1972] 1 All ER 587.

illness and there is no blameworthiness on the part of the respondent. In *Thurlow v Thurlow*[30] the wife suffered from illness. After attempting to look after her at home, the husband eventually had her admitted to hospital, saying he could no longer cope. He petitioned for divorce based on the behaviour fact. The court takes up the facts here:

> She has remained an in-patient ever since. In his agreed report dated July 20, 1972, the consultant psychiatrist in charge of her case, who had known the wife as a patient for many years, made the following, among other, observations: 'She is the subject of almost life-long epilepsy of a mild type and this is still quite actively disabling requiring very full medical treatment.' He then described the other, and more severe, neurological disorder which he suspected was also starting to manifest itself, and added:
>
>> 'Mentally she has slowly deteriorated severely both on the intellectual and emotional sides. Her husband recently made noble efforts to care for her at home but she had to return to full nursing and hospital care despite his unusually courageous efforts. Her long-term outlook is very poor and she will probably require indefinite institutional care and with diminishing appreciation of the circumstances.'
>
> From my observation of the husband I also concluded that he had done all that lay within his powers to cope with his wife during the final three weeks. He was not only unable to do so but the stress imposed upon him in trying to look after her was having a significant effect upon his own health. He made a genuine, sustained and considerable effort but was forced to give up.
>
> Since July 1, 1972, the husband has only visited his wife on one occasion. In view of his previous laudable efforts to care for her up to this time this is somewhat surprising. His explanation was that there wasn't any marriage left and that he was doing everything and getting no help and no response in return. His final visit to the wife was in July 1972 when he asked her whether she would agree to a divorce. The wife at first said she would agree and then changed her mind. In a medical report dated January 30, 1975, the consultant in charge of the wife's case states that she wishes to maintain her marital status and he confirms that there is not any cause for hope of the reversal of her condition. At some time in 1973 the husband met another lady whom he wishes to marry. He started the present proceedings for divorce in May 1973.
>
> The husband's case therefore consists of allegations of both negative and of positive behaviour on the part of the wife. The negative behaviour alleged and proved is that between the middle of 1969 and July 1, 1972, she gradually became a bedridden invalid unable to perform the role of a wife in any respect whatsoever until she reached a state in which she became unfitted even to reside in an ordinary household at all and required to be removed to a hospital and there reside for the rest of her life. The positive behaviour alleged and proved is that during the same period she displayed bad temper and threw objects at her mother-in-law and caused damage by burning various household items such as towels, cushions and blankets. From time to time she escaped from the home and wandered about the streets causing alarm and stress to those trying to care for her.
>
> I am satisfied that by July 1972 the marriage had irretrievably broken down and since the wife, tragically, is to spend the rest of her life as a patient in a hospital the husband cannot be expected to live with her. But the question remains as to whether the wife's behaviour has been such as to justify a finding by the court that it is unreasonable to expect him to do so. I accept the submission made on behalf of the wife that it is not sufficient to identify a state of affairs wherein there is a dead marriage coupled with an impossibility of cohabitation. It must be shown that it is the behaviour of the respondent which justifies a conclusion by the court that the petitioner cannot reasonably be expected to endure cohabitation. (per Rees J, 39–40)

In granting the decree nisi of divorce the court reiterated that to do so need not imply

---

[30] [1975] 2 All ER 979.

any blameworthiness on the part of the respondent. In effect, as the same judge said in another case, the court in these situations makes a 'value judgement' about the behaviour in question. In *Richards v Richards*[31] Rees J held it was not unreasonable to expect Mrs Richards to continue to live with Mr Richards' moodiness, occasional violence, spells of silence and staring, wandering around at night and accusations of Mrs Richards' infidelity, brought on by what both parties characterised as his 'nervous breakdown'. Notwithstanding the irretrievable breakdown of their marriage, the court found that his behaviour was not such that she could not reasonably be expected to live with him.[32]

In general, the older cases indicate that the behaviour needs to be fairly serious, but the more recent evidence is that the court will not judge too strictly that which one partner claims is unreasonable for him or her. The Law Society has suggested that 'virtually any spouse can assemble a list of events, which, taken out of context, can be presented as unreasonable behaviour sufficient on which to found a divorce petition' (The Law Society, Family Law Sub-Committee 1979, in Law Commission 1988a: para 3.8). In over half of the cases in 2009 where the divorce was granted to the wife, the husband's behaviour was the fact proven (ONS 2011c).

Finally, note that the provisions relating to the behaviour fact also have encouragement to reconcile built in. Section 2(3) allows the court, for the purposes of determining the reasonableness of the expectation that the petitioner ought to continue living with the respondent, to take into account the continued cohabitation of the spouses after the last incident relied upon in the petition only if the cohabitation lasts for more than six months. This section appears to encourage parties to attempt reconciliation without fear that such an attempt would make it more difficult to establish the behaviour fact if the attempt fails.

Desertion

Section 1(2)(c), the desertion fact, is rarely used. Desertion requires an unjustified withdrawal from the married state without the consent of the other spouse and with the intention to remain permanently separated. It requires both a separation and an intention to end the marriage. The separation requirement can be met if the parties remain under the same roof if they do not share a household. Conversely it may not be met if they are physically living apart without the intention to end the marriage, such as if one is posted overseas by the military or is in prison. More will be said on the separation elements below in relation to the separation facts. For the purposes of desertion, however, the key is that the 'innocent' spouse does not consent to the deserter's intended absence. Section 2(4) states that that intention may be inferred by the court in certain circumstances if the respondent was incapable of continuing it. Finally, note also section 2(5) which states that the continuous period of two years desertion (like the two years (section 1(2)(d)) or five years (section 1(2)(e)) living apart) will not be interrupted by the parties resuming cohabitation for up to six months, but that those periods of cohabitation shall not count as part of the time of desertion or living apart. This again appears to encourage attempts at reconciliation.

---

[31] [1972] 3 All ER 695.
[32] See also *Birch v Birch* [1992] 1 FLR 564, where the husband's dogmatic and chauvinistic behaviour towards a sensitive wife was held to be behaviour with which she could not reasonably be expected to live.

Separation

Finally, section 1(2)(d) and (e) constitute the separation facts. If the parties have lived apart for two years the decree will be granted if they consent to the divorce. If they have lived apart for five years, the decree can be granted without consent. 'Living apart' means not living in the same household (section 2(6)) and can occur if the parties are living under the same roof. This happpens, for example, where one of the parties simply cannot afford to move out. The court will look to whether they share meals, a bedroom and social time together. Sometimes parties remain under the same roof for other reasons. In *Mouncer v Mouncer*[33] they wished to maintain some semblance of normalcy for the sake of the children. This meant, however, they failed to establish they were living apart.

> [S]ometime in November 1969, the wife left the matrimonial bedroom. Thereafter she slept with the girl in one bedroom and the husband slept with the boy in the other. From then until 12 May 1971, when the husband left 49 Belmont Road, and went to live with his mother once more, the position remained unchanged. The wife and husband, although in separate rooms, usually took their meals together, cooked by the wife, often but not always in the company of one or both of the children. Two or three days a week the husband attended a meeting at his place of work. The cleaning of the house continued to be done by the wife, except on Fridays and Saturdays when she went out to work all day, and on those occasions it was done by the husband. 49 Belmont Road has a dining room, a living room, two bedrooms, a kitchen and a bathroom. The evidence does not suggest that any of these rooms was particularly allocated to either husband or wife except to the extent that the husband and the boy slept in one room and the wife and the girl in the other; and husband and wife, when they respectively cleaned the house, made no distinction between one part of the house and the other. In his evidence the husband referred to one of the rooms (not his bedroom) as 'the room we lived in'. The wife, however, did no washing for the husband. He made his own arrangements for that to be done elsewhere. The only reason why the husband continued to live in this way at 49 Belmont Road was his wish to continue to live with and help to look after the children.
>
> (per Wrangham J, 290–91)

Given the current emphasis placed upon sharing childcare in the 'post-separation family', it is arguable that to refuse a divorce in these circumstances today would be less likely, but it is equally arguable that it was harsh on the Mouncers, who were simply acting in the interests of their children.

Both the desertion and the separation facts require a mental and physical element. The mental element for living apart was considered by the Court of Appeal in *Santos v Santos*:[34]

> If these words [living apart] import an element additional to physical separation, can that element depend on a unilateral decision or attitude of mind; if so, must its existence be communicated to the other spouse; and, in any event, how can it be identified so that it is in practice capable of judicial determination?
>
> Obviously this element is not one which necessarily involves mutual consent, for otherwise the new Act would not afford relief under head (e) in that area where it was most plainly intended to be available—where the 'innocent' party adheres to the marriage, refusing to recognise that in truth it has ended, often despite the fact that the 'guilty' one has been living with someone else for very many years. So it must be an element capable of being unilateral: and it

---

[33] [1972] 1 All ER 289.
[34] [1972] Fam 247.

must, in our judgment, involve at least a recognition that the marriage is in truth at an end—and has become a shell, to adopt a much-used metaphor.

If the element can be unilateral in the sense of depending on the attitude of mind of one spouse, must it be communicated to the other spouse before it becomes in law operative? That is a question that gave particular concern in the course of the argument. There is something unattractive in the idea that in effect time under head (e) can begin to run against a spouse without his or her knowledge. Examples discussed included men in prison, in hospital, or away on service, whose wives, so far as they knew, were standing by them: they might, perhaps, thus be led to fail to take some step which they would later feel could just have saved the marriage. On the other hand, communication might well be impossible in cases where the physical separation was due to a breakdown in mental health on the part of the other spouse, or a prolonged coma such as can occasionally occur. Moreover, need for communication would tend to equate heads (d) and (e) with desertion—which comes under head (c)—something unlikely to be intended by the legislature. Moreover, bowing to the inevitable is not the same thing as intending it to happen.

In the end we have firmly concluded that communication by word or conduct is not a necessary ingredient of the additional element.

On the basis that an uncommunicated unilateral ending of recognition that a marriage is subsisting can mark the moment when 'living apart' commences, 'the principal problem becomes one of proof of the time when the breakdown occurred'—as was stated in the Virginia Law Review article, vol 52 (1966), p 70. How, for instance, does a judge in practice discharge the unenviable task of determining at what time the wife of a man immured long term in hospital or one serving a 15 year sentence changes from a wife who is standing by her husband (in the sense of genuinely keeping the marriage alive till he recovers or comes out) to one who realises the end has come but visits him merely from a sense of duty arising from the past? Sometimes there will be evidence such as a letter, reduction or cessation of visits, or starting to live with another man. But cases may well arise where there is only the oral evidence of the wife on this point. One can only say that cases under heads (d) and (e) may often need careful examination by the first instance judge and that special caution may need to be taken. In some cases, where it appears that the petitioning wife's conduct is consistent with a continuing recognition of the subsistence of the marriage, automatic acceptance of her uncorroborated evidence inconsistent with such conduct would not be desirable. On the other hand, there can be cases where a moment arrives as from which resumption of any form of married life becomes so plainly impossible, eg on some grave disability becoming known to be incurable, that only slight evidence is needed—for the nature of the breakdown is so patent.

The difficulties arising from some of these problems at one stage led to hesitation as to whether after all 'living apart' in this particular Act might not refer merely to physical separation. But there are at any rate two cogent reasons against holding that the standard meaning does not apply. First, in any statute in which those words are used the same problems are normally inherent to a considerable degree - and it cannot be said that they have such a special impact in the Act of 1969 as to lead to the inference that the standard meaning is negatived. Secondly—perhaps more importantly—there are the injustices and absurdities that could result from holding that 'living apart' refers merely to physical separation; these, in our judgment, outweigh any hard cases or difficulties that can arise from the standard interpretations. (260–61)

Therefore, 'living apart' referred to in grounds (d) and (e) is a state of affairs to establish which it is in the vast generality of cases arising under those heads necessary to prove something more than that the husband and wife are physically separated. For the purposes of that vast generality, it is sufficient to say that the relevant state of affairs does not exist whilst both parties recognise the marriage as subsisting. That involves considering attitudes of mind; and naturally the difficulty of judicially determining that attitude in a particular case may on occasions be great. But the existence of such a difficulty cannot be in point, for heads (d) and (e) are not the only ones in which the identification of an attitude of mind is required: indeed the whole concept of a breakdown being 'irretrievable' may involve coming to conclusions on attitudes of mind, when an issue is raised under section 2(3).

We have deliberately refrained from speaking unequivocally of 'all cases' (as opposed to 'the vast generality of cases') arising under heads (d) and (e) for the same reason that we have not sought to attempt any definition either of 'consortium' or of 'absence of consortium': similarly we have gone no further than to specify the attitude of mind that precludes its being said that the parties are living apart. (263)

Recall that the separation facts also allow parties to attempt reconciliation (section 2(5)).

Divorce based on the fact that the parties have lived apart for two years and consent to the divorce (section 1(2)(d)) is the closest the law in England and Wales offers to divorce by consent.[35] Perhaps one of the reasons English law does not permit divorce by consent is its history of using divorce law as a means of marriage saving. As we have seen, built into the law is encouragement for the parties to attempt reconciliation. And there are other provisions also which impose a duty to consider the possibility of recon-ciliation. Section 3(1) bars the parties from commencing divorce proceedings during their first year of marriage, and subsections 6(1) and (2) place responsibilities on both the courts and the parties' legal representatives to consider the possibility of the parties' reconciliation.[36]

The law's distaste for divorce by consent is also implied in the bars and protections built into the Act to ensure that the court can offer protection to vulnerable spouses. The five-year separation fact in section 1(2)(e) was originally described as a 'Casanova's charter', allowing as it did an ostensibly innocent spouse to be divorced against her will. Protection for innocent deserted spouses was put into place in section 5 in terms of which the court must dismiss the petition if in all the circumstances the court finds that the dissolution of the marriage will result in grave financial or other hardship to the respondent and that it would be wrong to dissolve it. Financial hardship includes loss of pension rights.[37] Other hardship can include social and religious hardship.[38] '[A]ll the circum-stances' includes the wishes of the parties and the children. Note that this is the second part of a two-part test. Both must be proved.

In addition, some cases of religious hardship may now be ameliorated by section 10A, which allows the court to withhold the decree absolute until both parties have declared that they have taken all steps required to dissolve the marriage in accordance with their religious practices. This section applies now only to Jewish divorces whereby the parties are not deemed divorced in Jewish law until the husband delivers to the wife a divorce document called a 'get'. Section 10A prevents the husband from refusing to obtain the religious divorce by delivering the get to his wife if he wishes to obtain a civil divorce. Finally, section 41 requires the court to consider arrangements for any children of the family. The court can delay the divorce if it feels an order under the Children Act 1989 is appropriate. The parties complete a form on which they answer questions about arrange-ments for children. In practice, however, this section is rarely used to delay the decree (Douglas et al 2000).

---

[35] This can be contrasted with divorce law in Scotland which provides for divorce after one year living apart with consent and two without consent: see Family Law (Scotland) Act 2006.
[36] See also FPR 2010 R 7.6.
[37] *K v K (Financial Relief: Widow's Pension)* [1997] 1 FLR 35.
[38] *Banik v Banik* [1973] 3 All ER 45.

IV. DIVORCE REFORM 1969–2010

While the MCA 1973 remains the law, the issue of divorce reform has continued to vex governments. Perhaps the compromise nature of the 1969 reforms made continuing debate inevitable. Smart suggests also that by the 1980s the 'optimistic scenario in which families happily re-constituted themselves did not materialise' (Smart 1999b: 9). In the light of cultural shifts in the meanings of parenthood and shifts in patterns of employment, it became evident that, 'for many women with children, remarriage was unlikely, unattractive or even financially irresponsible' (ibid). However, in the 1980s and 1990s context of increased public spending on divorced spouses and their children, increased expenditure on legal aid, perceptions of the effects of conflict and divorce on children and the former Conservative government's 'back to basics' and 'family values' political rhetoric, a moral panic of sorts appears to have been created by the increase in the rate of divorce.[39] In 1988 the Law Commission presented a discussion paper proposing further reform of divorce law (Law Commission 1988a), and followed this paper with a Report (Law Commission 1990) in which it presented the view that divorce ought to be treated in law as a process over time rather than as a single event. The particular proposals could also be seen as a means of reducing the upwardly spiralling legal aid budget in family matters. The government therefore adopted the Report in a Consultation Paper issued by the Lord Chancellor's Department (LCD 1993) and followed this with a White Paper (LCD 1995a). A Bill[40] was published in 1995 and the Family Law Act (FLA) was passed in 1996. Part II of the Act, dealing with divorce, will not become law and Part III, dealing with legal aid, has been repealed, but in many ways their legacy lives on in policy and procedural reform.

Before we examine this legacy, let us first look at the criticisms of the existing law. Are they still valid? The Law Commission, like other commissions before it, agreed that its brief was twofold: to buttress rather than to undermine the stability of marriage and to allow the 'empty shell' of an already broken down marriage to be destroyed with maximum fairness and a minimum of distress and bitterness (Law Commission 1990). While the objectives had not changed much from previous commissions, this time it was also suggested that there was an overwhelming belief that the current law was confusing and unjust. The Law Commission's (1990) six main criticisms of the 1973 Act were:

(a) It Is Confusing and Misleading

2.8 There is a considerable gap between theory and practice, which can lead to confusion and lack of respect for the law. Indeed, some would call it downright dishonest. There are several aspects to this. First, the law tells couples that the only ground for divorce is irretrievable breakdown, which apparently does not involve fault. But next it provides that this can only be shown by one of five 'facts', three of which apparently do involve fault ... .

2.9 Secondly, the fact which is alleged in order to prove the breakdown need not have any connection with the real reason why the marriage broke down ... .

2.10 The behaviour fact is particularly confusing. It is often referred to as 'unreasonable behaviour', which suggests blameworthiness or outright cruelty on the part of the respondent; but this

---

[39] In 1971 there were 73,666 decrees absolute granted in England and Wales; in 1981 144,763; in 1991 158,301; and in 1996 156,692 (Population Trends 117, 2004: 74).

[40] The Family Law Bill 1995.

has been called a 'linguistic trap'[41] because the behaviour itself need be neither unreasonable nor blameworthy: rather its effect on the petitioner must be such that it is unreasonable to expect him or her to go on living with the respondent, a significantly different and more flexible concept which is obviously capable of varying from case to case and court to court ... .

2.11 Finally, and above all, the present law pretends that the court is conducting an inquiry into the facts of the matter, when in the vast majority of cases it can do no such thing.

(Law Commission 1990: 5–9)

Q Do you agree that the current law is confusing and misleading? What arguments would you make against this accusation?

(b) It Is Discriminatory and Unjust

...

2.13 The fault-based facts can ... be intrinsically unjust. 'Justice' in this context has traditionally been taken to mean the accurate allocation of blameworthiness for the breakdown of the marriage.[42] Desertion is the only fact which still attempts to do this ... . A finding of adultery or behaviour certainly need not mean that the respondent is any more to blame than the petitioner for the breakdown of the marriage. ...

2.14 This inherent potential for injustice is compounded by the practical problems of defending or bringing a cross-petition of one's own ... .

Q Do you agree that 'justice' includes the allocation or recognition of blame in divorce cases? The Law Commission's earlier paper (1988a) reported that usually both parties were equally to blame for the end of the marriage. Do you agree?

(c) It Distorts the Parties' Bargaining Position

2.15 ... Questions of the future care of children, distribution of family assets, and financial provision are all governed by their own legal criteria ... . Yet negotiations may also be distorted by whichever of the parties is in a stronger position in relation to the divorce itself.[43] The strength of that position will depend upon a combination of how anxious or reluctant that party is to be divorced and how easy or difficult he or she will find it to prove or disprove one of the five facts.

Q Given the centrality of mediation in divorce proceedings (see Chapter 15), does this cause you any concern?

(d) It Provokes Unnecessary Hostility and Bitterness

2.16 A law which is arbitrary or unjust can exacerbate the feelings of bitterness, distress and

---

[41] *Bannister v Bannister* (1980) 10 Fam Law 240, per Ormrod LJ.

[42] See on this Whelan (1995) and particularly in that volume N Barry. For a contrary view, see Ellman (1997). One must also ask whose sense of justice is being denied. If the majority of divorces are instigated by wives, it is usually husbands who feel that, because the decision to leave was not theirs, they should not be punished by sharing any of 'their' assets with their wives (Davis et al 1994: 51–53). Indeed, Ellman (1997: 227) indicates that wives usually feel satisfied with their divorces and the results of their divorces.

[43] See Ellman (1997).

humiliation so often experienced at the time of separation and divorce. Even if the couple have agreed that their marriage cannot be saved it must make matters between them worse if the system encourages one to make allegations against the other … .

Q **Is there anything the law can or should do to ease the pain of relationship breakdown?**

(e) It Does Nothing to Save the Marriage

2.17 None of this is any help with the law's other objective, of supporting those marriages which have a chance of survival. The law cannot prevent people from separating or forming new relationships, although it may make it difficult for people to get a divorce. The law can also make it difficult for estranged couples to become reconciled. The present law does make it difficult for some couples—in practice a very small proportion—to be divorced, but it does so in an arbitrary way depending upon which facts may be proved. It also makes it extremely difficult for couples to become reconciled … .

2.18 … An undefended decree can be obtained in a matter of weeks. If both parties are contemplating divorce, the system gives them every incentive to obtain a 'quickie' decree based on behaviour or separation, and to think out the practical consequences later.[44]

(f) It Can Make Things Worse for the Children

2.19 … The children themselves would usually prefer their parents to stay together. But the law cannot force parents to live amicably or prevent them from separating. It is not known whether children suffer more from their parents' separation or from living in a household in conflict where they may be blamed for the couple's inability to part … . Children who suffer most are those whose parents remain in conflict.

2.20 … [T]he present law can, for all the reasons given earlier, make the conflict worse. It encourages couples to find fault with one another and disputes about children seem to be more common in divorces based on intolerable behaviour than in others.

Q **Do you accept these criticisms of the current law? If so, what options for reform are there? Some jurisdictions chose to adopt a divorce system based on separation of the parties for a minimum period. This option is said to have the advantage of requiring the parties to experience living apart from each other, with all of the financial and emotional consequences that entails, before they divorce.[45] Other options are to allow divorce by consent of the parties or divorce on the unilateral demand of one party, as in Sweden (Bradley 1996). These options were rejected by the Law Commission because, among other things, it was said that to adopt either would allow the state to abdicate its interest in sustaining marriage and determining when marriages should be ended. In your view, are these compelling interests that the state should accommodate in its divorce law? See Ellman (1997) and Whelan (1995) for contrary views on this question.**

Deech (2009a) makes another complaint about the current law:

[O]ver the last 40 years or so we have abandoned, in terms of approbation/disapprobation, law

---

[44] Ibid.
[45] See, eg, Canada, The Divorce Act 1985; and Davies (1993).

and categorisation, any pressure to conform to basic, long unchallenged tenets of private morality. At the time I applauded the liberalising laws of the 1960s and still think that on balance they did more good than harm—the legalisation of abortion and homosexuality, the ending of the criminalisation of suicide, the stigmatising of illegitimacy and the liberalising of contraception and divorce. Yet the effect, when taken all together a few decades on, is to live in a society where there are no constraints on private morality, no judgmentalism, no finger wagging or name calling, only acceptance of anything that anyone does, short of the criminal law, in the name of the pursuit, if not of individual happiness, then at least individual choice. It is not possible, it seems to me, to raise a generation in that permissive framework and then expect those self same people to go into politics and behave with the utmost scrupulousness and regard for the public purse and approval, to behave in a way that bears public scrutiny and accountability and takes into account the cost to others and the future of cherished constitutional institutions. So individual happiness is pitted against, and prevails over the good of, one's family and others. (Deech 2009a: 1049)

In order to deal with what she sees as a flight from morality she proposes more than one reform. The first is a return to acknowledging fault (the judgementalism and finger-wagging she sees as important in society) and the second is to introduce a waiting period before the divorce is made final. Here she describes the first.

The failure to recognise any fault on behalf of one party or the other does rankle: in some marriages, but by no means all, there is clearly fault, as popularly understood, on one side or the other and it is odd that this cannot be referred to. There is no other area of law where such attempts are made to ignore causation and blame and this failure may make for more resentment in the separate but parallel proceedings for maintenance and property and maybe in making arrangements for the children. The reintroduction of fault, at least in maintenance proceedings, might send a message that behaviour in marriage is a serious issue. Its removal as a concept has taken away some leverage from spouses seeking to block the divorce proceedings and induced an inability to understand why one is paying for someone who, in general parlance, was 'guilty'.

On balance I would not advocate any wholesale reform of the divorce grounds themselves. All those whose marriages have broken down can easily obtain divorces under the existing law, so there is no need to 'liberalise' it—on the contrary. Indeed, any reform is dangerous. Each successive attempt in the twentieth century to bring the statute law into line with 'reality' has resulted in an increase in the divorce rate. Every increase results in greater familiarity with divorce as a solution to marital problems, more willingness to use it and to make legislative provision for its aftermath. The pressure on the divorce system leads to a relaxation of practice and procedure in divorce, then to a call for a change in the law to bring it into line with reality, and then to yet another increase in divorce. This is the spiralling process which Parliament should not encourage, for the sake of the children if nothing else. (ibid: 1053)

Deech is not alone in proposing a return to a fault-based system. Some suggest that a court's acknowledgement of fault for the breakdown of the marriage serves the interests of justice by acknowledging wrongdoing and proclaiming the moral and social importance of marriage (Herring 2011: 129, quoting Baroness Young). Others, while they would not necessarily wish a return to fault-based divorce, contend that the parties themselves often feel an emotional or psychological need to apportion blame, or at least to have their wrong acknowledged (see Day Sclater 1999 and discussion below). Among the counter-arguments, of course, is that it is usually difficult, if not impossible to identify one party who was completely at fault for the breakdown of a marriage, and to attempt to do so would merely exacerbate bitterness between them, rather than alleviate it.[46]

Deech goes on to propose a further change in divorce procedure:

> My own remedy would be an introduction of a waiting period to stop divorce being so quickly granted, even where the ground is one of the speedy ones. I would add to the present grounds of divorce a provision that no decree shall be granted until at least 12 months have elapsed from the service of the petition (the start of the formalities). This would ensure that no petitioner would be free to remarry for at least 1 year after the beginning of the process, regardless of the reasons for the divorce. Others have called strongly for a 3 month cooling off period before proceedings can start in which finances and the impact of the divorce can be explored. During this period no financial proceedings could be launched, for they inflame the situation and the purpose of waiting would be to discover what was practicable and what could not be afforded. The waiting period could also be used to explore alternative dispute resolution procedures as an alternative to court. Most importantly it could be used to provide information to the parties about their future and the way the legal proceedings work. Having said that, some pilot trials of providing information to divorce petitioners have not worked well, because it has been done to groups, and has led to more insistence on seeing a lawyer, rather than less.
>
> (ibid, references omitted)[47]

Q Do you agree that 'quickie divorces' are a problem and that a waiting period should be introduced?

Others take issue with the correlation between divorce reform and the rate of marriage breakdown. Richards argues:

> There is a widespread view that the number of those who divorce is determined by the ease or difficulty of the legal process. In the widest sense this is, of course, true—if divorce is not possible, it cannot happen. However, as the example of Ireland shows, the absence of a divorce process does not ensure that all couples remain living together or, indeed, married. The process of marital breakdown should be distinguished from the various legal processes that those whose marriages have ended use (or do not use) to regularise their situation … .
>
> The views in Phillips (*Putting Asunder: A History of Divorce in Western Society* (CUP, 1988)) represent a consensus among researchers and informed commentators:
>
>> divorce law reforms had little or nothing to do with setting off the most recent [ie 1960–70s] divorce rate increases. In almost all countries divorce rates had begun to rise before legal reforms were enacted or came into force, and the widespread introduction of no-fault divorce legislation during the 1970s was partly a response to increased divorce, not a cause of it. (p 620)
>
> … There are those who have, and will, argue that the proposed legislation [the FLA 1996] will make divorce 'easier' and so increase the numbers. Such arguments miss the point; for most couples the difficulty or ease of divorce lies not in negotiating the legal procedures but in the inevitably painful process of reaching a decision to end a relationship and the enormous emotional, social and economic upheavals that are involved in uncoupling.
>
> (Richards 1996: 151–53)

---

[46] For a good discussion of the arguments for and against a fault-based divorce system, see Herring (2011: 128–131).

[47] This is not the first time Deech has made this argument. See Deech (1994: 121).

Q Do you find Richards' arguments convincing? Does Deech confuse rates of marital breakdown with rates of divorce? Is there anything that law can do about marital breakdown? Can it be argued that the symbolic value of the law is as important as its practicalities, so that the message law gives to the public about the 'ease' or 'difficulty' of divorce must not be ignored?[48]

The option chosen by the Law Commission and implemented in the FLA 1996 was said to make divorce both 'easier' and 'more difficult'. A 'process over time' option was said best to meet the government's objectives of a new divorce law:

> to support the institution of marriage; to include practicable steps to prevent the irretrievable breakdown of marriage; to ensure that the parties understand the practical consequences of divorce before taking any irreversible decision; where divorce is unavoidable, to minimise the bitterness and hostility between the parties and reduce the trauma for the children; and to keep to the minimum the cost to the parties and the taxpayer. (LCD 1995: 18, para 3.5)

Q Note the similarities and differences between these objectives, written in 1995, and those in 1912, 1937, 1956 and 1966.

V. THE LEGACY OF THE FAMILY LAW ACT 1996

Section 1 FLA 1996 sets out a number of general principles designed to provide guidance to courts and professional personnel involved in the divorce process. It is in force, and despite its specific reference to Parts II and III which never came into force, sets out clearly the current policy with respect to divorce.

1. The court and any person, in exercising functions under or in consequence of Parts II and III, shall have regard to the following general principles—

(a) that the institution of marriage is to be supported;
(b) that the parties to a marriage which may have broken down are to be encouraged to take all practicable steps, whether by marriage counselling or otherwise, to save the marriage;
(c) that a marriage which has irretrievably broken down and is being brought to an end should be brought to an end
   (i)   with minimum distress to the parties and to the children affected;
   (ii) with questions dealt with in a manner designed to promote as good a continuing relationship between the parties and any children affected as is possible in the circumstances; and
   (iii) without costs being unreasonably incurred in connection with the procedures to be followed in bringing the marriage to an end; and
(d) that any risk to one of the parties to a marriage, and to any children, of violence from the other party should, so far as reasonably practicable, be removed or diminished.

We immediately see that this part of the FLA has a dual focus: both to end and to save

---

[48] Sometimes, the public gives messages to law. In a referendum in May 2011 53% of the Maltese electorate voted in favour of introducing divorce in Malta, previously the only EU country not to permit divorce. In July the Bill was signed into law. The Philippines and the Vatican are now the only states that prohibit divorce (BBC News 2011).

marriages, and it is arguable that these dual, indeed conflicting, goals contributed to the unworkability of the divorce parts of the Act and to their eventual abandonment (Walker 2004). We shall provide an overview of the statutory provisions rather than their details[49] and suggest that their vision of the good divorce and the good divorcing subject continues to drive divorce policy and procedure (Diduck 2003).[50]

The sole ground for divorce under the FLA 1996 was irretrievable breakdown of marriage, which was to be evidenced by one or both parties lodging with the court a 'statement of marital breakdown', waiting a prescribed period of time for 'reflection and consideration' (at least nine months) beginning two weeks after making the statement, and then, having reflected upon the breakdown and having considered arrangements for their future, lodging with the court a further statement that the marriage had irretrievably broken down. The court would then grant the divorce if it was satisfied that the parties had made satisfactory arrangements for the future, including arrangements settling financial matters between them and for any children of the marriage. No party, however, was entitled to make the initial statement of marital breakdown, unless he or she had first attended an 'information meeting', that had two principal objectives:

> The first was to direct attention to the issues which it was felt people contemplating taking steps to end their marriage needed to consider. The second was to ensure that these people were given information on the various options for the resolution of difficulties, including the availability of marriage support services, mediation and legal services. (Walker 2004 Executive Summary)

There are novel aspects of both the procedure and the 'message' (Eekelaar 1999) of the FLA 1996. Procedurally, 'fault' was finally removed from the law; irretrievable breakdown was to be evidenced solely by living apart. The second novel aspect of the legislation was that divorce was to be a decision taken solely by the parties; the Act provided, in effect, for divorce by consent. These two changes supported a revised vision of marriage: that it is about the relationship between the individuals concerned rather than about the relationship between them and the state. The third novel procedural aspect of the Act was the way in which it directly promoted, indeed required, the previously only implicitly encouraged relationship between law and applied social work (Cretney 2003a: 390) at various stages of the process. This last element of the Act was important in order to give effect to a number of new 'messages' the Act was designed to 'radiate' (Eekelaar 1999),[51] including the idea that divorce was not a one-off event, but rather was to be seen as part of a family's life course; it was a transition rather than an ending. Further, the message was that parties ought to be able to manage that transition in a responsible way if sufficient information and counselling were provided to them (at the information meetings and meetings with a marriage counsellor) and that they would then reflect upon it (during the period of reflection and consideration) and see that the responsible divorce was one which was conflict-free and harmonious (and so choose to mediate rather than litigate outstanding issues between them). In general the 'FLA 1996 was intended to do more than simply provide a new framework for divorce. It was intended to effect a cultural shift in how people view marriage and divorce, and also to effect behavioural change' (Diduck 2003: 58).

One of the ways in which that change was to be encouraged was through the provision

---

[49] For a detailed discussion of the provisions, see the first edition of this volume, pp 427–35.
[50] See also Walker (2004).
[51] See also Dewar (1998).

of information at the mandatory information meetings. However, the results of pilot projects undertaken with those meetings indicated that while people do want information about divorce law, they want information that is relevant to them and their circumstances (Walker 2004), and that while they thought information about the importance of reducing conflict and its effects on children was 'useful' (Walker 2001: 829), having that information did not necessarily translate into the 'crude behavioural changes anticipated by government' (Diduck 2003: 59). People still wanted advice from solicitors. And yet, while the mandatory information meetings have been consigned to history (for now), government seems to retain its belief that people's behaviour can be influenced by providing them with the 'right' information.

Building upon the results of the pilot projects, the then government believed that family law solicitors were best placed to provide that information. It set up more pilot projects, known as Family Advice and Information Networks (FAINS) which later became the Family Advice and Information Service (FAInS). The goal of these services is described by the researchers who evaluated them over their five years of operation:

> The Family Advice and Information Networks were ... designed to build on best practice in family law and existing support services and they sought to provide a holistic and comprehensive response to the concerns, difficulties and problems people experience when relationships break down. The idea was to develop a seamless service through which family law clients would receive tailored information, help and advice and be encouraged to use other services whenever it was appropriate to do so. The holistic approach would entail an enhanced first meeting between a solicitor and a client, during which a wide range of matters would be discussed and a personalised action plan (PAP) drawn up. Thereafter, the solicitor would manage the progress of the case, ensuring that appropriate referrals were made to other services.
>
> (Walker et al 2007)

The results of the evaluation were that the FAInS had little effect either on solicitors' practice or on client satisfaction (Walker et al 2007). Policymakers, however, were undeterred. A new form of 'holistic' information service was proposed in the Interim Report of the The Family Justice Review (2011). The Review acknowledged first that there is little that law or policy can do to prevent marriage breakdown itself, even though they may have a role to play in how that breakdown is managed:

> 105. The state cannot fix fractured relationships or create a balanced, inclusive family life after separation where this was not the case before separation. Court is generally not the best place to resolve these disputes. Where possible, disputes should be resolved independently or using dispute resolution services such as mediation, when it is safe to do so. Parents who choose to use the court system must understand it will not be a panacea. Courts will only make an order where this is in the best interests of a child. Further, where the court does make an order, this may well not be in line with one or both parents' expectations or wishes. People need to expect that court should be a last resort, not a first port of call.

It proposed a new point of reference for separating partners:

> 114. *An online information hub and helpline should be established* to offer support and advice in a single, easy-to-access point of reference at the beginning of the process of separation or divorce. This will help people to make informed decisions regarding how best to resolve the issues they face as part of their separation. The hub will also contain information to ensure that those who feel they are at risk can swiftly alert support services. It would collate:

clear guidance about parents' responsibilities towards their children whether separated or not, including their roles and responsibilities as set out in legislation;

information and advice about services available to support families, whether separated or not;

information and advice to resolve family conflicts, including fact-sheets, case studies, peer experiences, DVD clips, modelling and interactive templates to help with Parenting Agreements;

advice about options for supported dispute resolution, which would highlight the benefits of alternative forms of dispute resolution, including mediation, and Separated Parents Information Programmes (PIPs);

information about court resolution, should alternative dispute resolution not be suitable, and costs of applications;

support for couples to agree child maintenance arrangements;

guidance on the division of assets; and

what to do when there are serious child welfare concerns.

115. Where individuals feel, after they have accessed the hub, that they do need further help or the service of the court to resolve any outstanding issues, *it should be compulsory that they meet a mediator*, trained and accredited to a high professional standard, *who should*:

assess the most appropriate intervention, including mediation and collaborative law, or whether the risks of domestic violence, imbalance between the parties or child protection issues require immediate referral to the family court; and

provide information on local dispute resolution services and how they could support parties to resolve disputes. (emphasis in original)

Under the ill-fated FLA 1996 people were to take personal responsibility for acting on the information they received. They were to reflect upon it, consider it and, ideally, in its light, either to choose a therapeutic intervention for their marriage, or choose to divorce responsibly by submerging conflict. In this way, the Act has been described as radiating another 'message': in this case a new social and individual moral agenda around divorce (Eekelaar 1999; Diduck 2003; Reece 2003) that provides a new way of regulating it (Smart 1999b; Reece 2003). Rather than imposing upon divorcing couples a morality of externally defined obligation or duty (such as a law based upon punishment and matrimonial fault), the Act redefined as moral those choices people take reflectively and responsibly (Reece 2003) so as to produce the 'good', harmonious divorce. Engaging in counselling and particularly in mediation were two of the ways in which their moral choices were to be exercised under the FLA 1996, and we can see that these messages remain in current marriage and divorce policy and procedure.

Finally, the message that divorce is a transition in family life rather than a one-off event is also one which has remained beyond the 1996 Act. Imperatives directed toward saving marriages are now recast into saving families, and the conflict-free divorce is designed to do this by producing the harmonious 'post-divorce family' (Day Sclater 1999; Smart 1999b).

Although Part II of the FLA 1996 may not be with us, through procedural changes in its image designed to provide information, to encourage mediation[52] and counselling and to 'save' families, the ideal divorce described therein, may be:

> The ideal divorce manages families, it brings new forms of families into the ideal family net—in this case a post-divorce family which must take up where the pre-divorce one failed and be forever stable, co-operative and harmonious. It is a non-threatening family (Day Sclater 1999 p 15) and it can be achieved by the 'good' divorce which is harmonious and characterised by rational appraisal and behaviour which plans properly for the future … [i]t keeps families together' (Day Sclater 1999 p 177). It is a bad divorce that tears families apart—it is 'conflict ridden, accusatory, costly … and associated with the legal process' (Day Sclater 1999 p 176).
>
> (Diduck 2003: 66)

Current divorce law is thus in many ways contradictory. It expresses the preoccupations and compromises of both the 1960s and the new millennium. It displays a tension between theory and practice about whose interests are to be protected by divorce law: the state's or the individual's (Cretney 2003a: 391). Further, its substantive provisions about fault, for example, contrast with its procedural ones about harmony. The effect of this tension can be serious for divorcing individuals.

> The dominant saving marriages [and reducing conflict] agenda points to—indeed it requires—a focus on the 'we' at a time when, psychologically, many spouses are concerned primarily, for a host of complex reasons, with a project of (re)development, (re)assessment and defence of the 'me', of the divorcing self. (Collier 1999: 261)

The way in which divorce law and practice deal with the 'we' and the 'me' can have profound consequences for divorcing individuals. Day Sclater's (1999) study of the psychodynamics of divorce demonstrates that 'emotions, conflicts and anger are normal psychological parts of coping with loss, separation and reconstruction of identity, yet divorce law and process reject the relevance of feelings, or at least assume they are "manageable"' (Diduck 2003: 65). Further, while an opportunity to revisit and understand the past is an important part of an individual's building of his or her post-divorce identity, the process allows only a focus on the future of the 'new' family.[53]

VI. THE CIVIL PARTNERSHIP ACT 2004

As we saw in Chapter 2, the Civil Partnership Act 2004 (CPA) provides for the creation of a new legal status for same-sex partners, and regulates acquisition of that status in ways that are very similar to that of marriage. The Act provides also for the dissolution of civil partnerships. There were 41 dissolutions of civil partnerships in 2007—the first year dissolutions were available—180 in 2008 and 351 in 2009 (ONS 2011b). 'By the end of 2009 .9% of all male civil partnerships in the UK had ended in dissolution, while 2.3% of all UK female civil partnerships had ended in disssolution' (ibid). Because civil part-

---

[52] And see also the Green Paper on Legal Aid Reform (Ministry of Justice 2010a), which proposes the removal of public funding for legal representation from all family matters where domestic violence is not an issue. Mediation, however, will continue to be funded.

[53] On the different experiences of men and women of divorce, see Day-Sclater (1999); Smart and Neale (1999).

nerships were modelled on marriage and divorce law, the one ground for dissolution of the civil partnership is that it has broken down irretrievably and this must be established by one or more facts. But just as consummation is not required for the civil partnership to be valid, adultery is not one of the permitted facts to establish its breakdown.

Section 37(1)(a) of the CPA empowers the court to make a dissolution order, which dissolves a civil partnership. Section 37(2)(a) states that such an order is a conditional order and section 38(1)(a) that it may be made final after six weeks. Section 41(1) states that no application for a dissolution order may be made within the first year of the civil partnership. We see so far the same provisions as those which apply in divorce proceedings, and indeed section 42 imposes on both solicitors and the court the same requirements to take measures to encourage reconciliation of the civil partners as are imposed in divorce proceedings. The similarities with divorce continue:

[44]

(1) Subject to Section 41, an application for a dissolution order may be made to the court by either civil partner on the ground that the civil partnership has broken down irretrievably.

(2) On an application for a dissolution order the court must inquire, so far as it reasonably can, into—

(a) the facts alleged by the applicant, and
(b) any facts alleged by the respondent.

(3) The court hearing an application for a dissolution order must not hold that the civil partnership has broken down irretrievably unless the applicant satisfies the court of one or more of the facts described in subsection (5)(a), (b), (c) or (d).

(4) But if the court is satisfied of any of those facts, it must make a dissolution order unless it is satisfied on all the evidence that the civil partnership has not broken down irretrievably.

(5) The facts referred to in subsections (3) and (4) are—

(a) that the respondent has behaved in such a way that the applicant cannot reasonably be expected to live with the respondent;
(b) that—
    (i) the applicant and the respondent have lived apart for a continuous period of at least 2 years immediately preceding the making of the application ('2 years' separation'), and
    (ii) the respondent consents to a dissolution order being made;
(c) that the applicant and the respondent have lived apart for a continuous period of at least 5 years immediately preceding the making of the application ('5 years' separation');
(d) that the respondent has deserted the applicant for a continuous period of at least 2 years immediately preceding the making of the application.

[45]

(1) Subsection (2) applies if—

(a) in any proceedings for a dissolution order the applicant alleges, in reliance on Section 44(5)(a), that the respondent has behaved in such a way that the applicant cannot reasonably be expected to live with the respondent, but
(b) after the date of the occurrence of the final incident relied on by the applicant and held by the court to support his allegation, the applicant and the respondent have lived together for a period (or periods) which does not, or which taken together do not, exceed 6 months.

(2) The fact that the applicant and respondent have lived together as mentioned in subsection

(1)(b) must be disregarded in determining, for the purposes of Section 44(5)(a), whether the applicant cannot reasonably be expected to live with the respondent.

(3) Subsection (4) applies in relation to cases where the applicant alleges, in reliance on Section 44(5)(b), that the respondent consents to a dissolution order being made.

(4) Rules of court must make provision for the purpose of ensuring that the respondent has been given such information as will enable him to understand—

(a) the consequences to him of consenting to the making of the order, and

(b) the steps which he must take to indicate his consent.

(5) For the purposes of Section 44(5)(d) the court may treat a period of desertion as having continued at a time when the deserting civil partner was incapable of continuing the necessary intention, if the evidence before the court is such that, had he not been so incapable, the court would have inferred that the desertion continued at that time.

(6) In considering for the purposes of Section 44(5) whether the period for which the civil partners have lived apart or the period for which the respondent has deserted the applicant has been continuous, no account is to be taken of—

(a) any one period not exceeding 6 months, or

(b) any two or more periods not exceeding 6 months in all,

during which the civil partners resumed living with each other.

(7) But no period during which the civil partners have lived with each other counts as part of the period during which the civil partners have lived apart or as part of the period of desertion.

(8) For the purposes of Section 44(5)(b) and (c) and this section civil partners are to be treated as living apart unless they are living with each other in the same household, and references in this section to civil partners living with each other are to be read as references to their living with each other in the same household.

...

[47]

(1) The respondent to an application for a dissolution order in which the applicant alleges 5 years' separation may oppose the making of an order on the ground that—

(a) the dissolution of the civil partnership will result in grave financial or other hardship to him, and

(b) it would in all the circumstances be wrong to dissolve the civil partnership.

(2) Subsection (3) applies if—

(a) the making of a dissolution order is opposed under this section,

(b) the court finds that the applicant is entitled to rely in support of his application on the fact of 5 years' separation and makes no such finding as to any other fact mentioned in Section 44(5), and

(c) apart from this section, the court would make a dissolution order.

(3) The court must—

(a) consider all the circumstances, including the conduct of the civil partners and the interests of the civil partners and of any children or other persons concerned, and

(b) if it is of the opinion that the ground mentioned in subsection (1) is made out, dismiss the application for the dissolution order.

(4) 'Hardship' includes the loss of the chance of acquiring any benefit which the respondent might acquire if the civil partnership were not dissolved.

[48]

(1) The court may, on an application made by the respondent, rescind a conditional dissolution order if—

(a) it made the order on the basis of a finding that the applicant was entitled to rely on the fact of 2 years' separation coupled with the respondent's consent to a dissolution order being made,

(b) it made no such finding as to any other fact mentioned in Section 44(5), and

(c) it is satisfied that the applicant misled the respondent (whether intentionally or unintentionally) about any matter which the respondent took into account in deciding to give his consent.

(2) Subsections (3) to (5) apply if—

(a) the respondent to an application for a dissolution order in which the applicant alleged—
    (i) 2 years' separation coupled with the respondent's consent to a dissolution order being made, or
    (ii) 5 years' separation,

has applied to the court for consideration under subsection (3) of his financial position after the dissolution of the civil partnership, and

(b) the court—
    (i) has made a conditional dissolution order on the basis of a finding that the applicant was entitled to rely in support of his application on the fact of 2 years' or 5 years' separation, and
    (ii) has made no such finding as to any other fact mentioned in Section 44(5).

(3) The court hearing an application by the respondent under subsection (2) must consider all the circumstances, including—

(a) the age, health, conduct, earning capacity, financial resources and financial obligations of each of the parties, and

(b) the financial position of the respondent as, having regard to the dissolution, it is likely to be after the death of the applicant should the applicant die first.

(4) Subject to subsection (5), the court must not make the order final unless it is satisfied that—

(a) the applicant should not be required to make any financial provision for the respondent, or

(b) the financial provision made by the applicant for the respondent is—
    (i) reasonable and fair, or
    (ii) the best that can be made in the circumstances.

(5) The court may if it thinks fit make the order final if—

(a) it appears that there are circumstances making it desirable that the order should be made final without delay, and

(b) it has obtained a satisfactory undertaking from the applicant that he will make such financial provision for the respondent as it may approve.

We see that the law regarding the dissolution of civil partnerships is virtually the same as the law of divorce. The only difference is that heterosexual spouses may establish irretrievable breakdown of their marriage by reason of adultery, while same-sex partners may not. The DTI (2003b) stated that while adultery was not included among the dissolution facts, sexual infidelity could found an application for dissolution proceedings within the behaviour fact:

Adultery has a specific meaning within the context of heterosexual relationships and it would not be possible nor desirable to read this across to same-sex civil partnerships. The conduct of a civil partner who is sexually unfaithful is as much a form of behaviour as any other. Whether it amounted to unreasonable behaviour on which dissolution proceedings could be grounded would be a matter for individual dissolution proceedings. (DTI 2003b: 36)

Q Do you agree that adultery has a very specific meaning in heterosexual marriage that does not apply in civil partnerships? What is that meaning? Do you agree that it would not be desirable to extend it to same-sex civil partnerships?

VII. NULLITY AND JUDICIAL SEPARATION

We saw in Chapter 2 the requirements for valid marriages[54] and civil partnerships.[55] A party may seek a decree of nullity on establishing one of those grounds, provided one of the bars does not apply. For some couples, a decree of nullity is preferable to a divorce or dissolution order for religious reasons.

On granting a decree of nullity, a court can make an order for ancillary relief, now called a financial order, just as it can on making a decree of divorce or dissolution order. We shall discuss the financial implications of relationship breakdown in Chapter 7.

Q Herring (2011: 67) tells us that in 2008 200 annulments were granted by the courts and raises the question of whether annulment should be retained in the law at all. In your view, why does the law retain the concept of a void marriage or civil partnership? Why does it retain the concept of a voidable one? Should these be treated differently?

Where parties have objections to divorce or dissolution, they also have the option of obtaining a separation order. Because one's legal status does not change upon separation, one is not required to obtain the sanction of the court in order to separate from a spouse or civil partner, and of course, many couples live apart without applying for a court order. However, for those who do need to make their separation formal, the law makes provision for an order currently termed a 'judicial separation' decree.

The MCA 1973 provides in section 17 that a petition for a decree may be made on the grounds of the existence of any of the five facts mentioned in section 1(2) applicable to divorce, namely adultery, behaviour, desertion, two-year separation with consent and five-year separation without consent. The CPA 2004 also provides for judicial separation,[56] allowing either civil partner to make an application for a separation order on the ground that one of the four facts exists.[57] Further, the court shall grant a decree of judicial separation (under the MCA; a separation order under the CPA) if it is satisfied on the evidence of any of those facts and there are no children to whom consideration of a section 8 (Children Act 1989) order ought to be given.[58] The court is not concerned to establish that

---

[54] See MCA 1973 ss 11, 12 and 13 and Chapter 2 above.
[55] See CPA 2004 ss 49, 50 and 51 and Chapter 2 above.
[56] S 37(d) CPA.
[57] S 56(1). The facts are unreasonable behaviour, two-year separation with consent, desertion and five-year separation without consent.
[58] S 17(2) MCA; s 56(3) CPA.

the marriage or the civil partnership has broken down irretrievably.[59] The same provisions for the special procedure apply in separation cases as in divorce and dissolution cases. In separation cases under either the MCA or the CPA, just as in divorce or dissolution cases, there are provisions also relating to the solicitor's and the court's exploration of reconciliation[60] and the court's acceptance of negotiated settlements.[61] Unlike in the case of divorce or dissolution, the petition or application is not barred during the first year of marriage or civil partnership, and the decree or order takes effect immediately on being granted. The main difference between a judicial separation and a divorce or dissolution is, of course, that the marriage or civil partnership continues. This obviously has implications for matters such as pensions and other financial obligations.[62]

If one is not concerned to maintain one's legal status as a husband, wife or civil partner, for religious reasons for instance, why would one seek a judicial separation? Some relief, such as the protection from violence or occupation of the family home, may be granted without a judicial separation. However there are certain financial remedies which only become available once a decree or order is granted. Financial provision orders, property adjustment orders or orders for the sale of property under the MCA 1973 can only be made after a decree of separation,[63] and under the CPA 2004 only on making a separation order.[64] Another reason one might wish to petition for judicial separation is that proof of the fact in the separation proceedings may be relied upon in subsequent divorce or dissolution proceedings.[65] This means that a party may obtain financial relief along with a judicial separation in the hope that a reconciliation is possible, but leave the way open to petition for divorce on the same ground (subject to the reconciliation provisions) if all hope fails (Conway 1997; Lowe and Douglas 2007: 303).

VIII. CONCLUSION

What does the history of divorce tell us about the way in which law and society regulate our relationships? Indeed, what effect *can* the law regulating dissolution of relationships have upon the breakdown of some relationships and the creation of new ones? Many, including sociologists, historians and psychologists, have attempted to explain rising rates of marriage breakdown, but no conclusive answers have been agreed (Stone 1990: 410–16). Stone suggests that a combination of factors, including 'changes in social, religious, and moral values, which seem to have been permanently affected by two world wars, together with the by-products of medical and contraceptive technologies, the rise of service econ-

---

[59] S 17(2) MCA; s 56(2) CPA

[60] S 17(3) MCA referring to s 6 MCA; s 42 CPA.

[61] S 17(3) MCA referring to s 7 MCA; s 43 CPA.

[62] Although the provisions relating to devolution of estates on intestacy do not apply if one spouse dies while living separately under an order (s 18(1) MCA) or one civil partner dies while separated from the other (s 57 CPA).

[63] Although interim orders are available once the petition is filed, and s 27 provides that maintenance may be ordered in situations where one spouse has failed to provide reasonably for the other: see Chapter 6 below. Further, one may wish to rely upon the more limited jurisdiction of the magistrates in the DPMCA 1978 to make financial provision orders.

[64] Schedule 5 of the CPA 2004 makes provision for financial relief, including property adjustment orders and sale of property orders, that corresponds to provision made in connection with marriages under the MCA 1973; schedule 6 makes provision that corresponds with relief available under the Domestic Proceedings and Magistrates' Courts Act 1978 in connection with marriages. See s 72 CPA.

[65] S 4 MCA; s 46(3) CPA.

omies, and the opening of the labour market to married women' (ibid: 416), have contributed to increased rates of marital breakdown. Deech (2009a) suggests there are moral questions involved. Richards (1995a) suggests that the nature of marriage itself has changed, making relationships more vulnerable. Recall our discussion in Chapter 1 of the 'transformation of intimacy': people now expect their partners to meet their emotional, sexual and companionate needs, and are more prepared to move on if they don't.

The way in which law regulates our exit from unsatisfactory relationships says much about the nature of those relationships. By insisting upon their judicial dissolution, and by refusing to allow divorce or dissolution by consent, the law states clearly that it is not merely the parties' interests which are at stake; there is also a public interest in maintaining, or at least regulating, relationships. Law's negotiation of the public/private divide in matters of divorce and dissolution of civil partnerships is thus a delicate one. On the one hand, the law must allow individuals some autonomy in making intimate decisions about partnering and separating, and individuals are expected to take personal responsibility for those decisions, yet on the other hand, the public interest in those decisions is clearly asserted.

Q Do you agree with the balance that has been struck between the public and the private in the law of divorce and dissolution?

Q Recall that in 2009 67% of divorce decrees were granted to the wife in England and Wales. The most frequent fact on which divorce was granted to a woman was the unreasonable behaviour (*sic*) of her husband. Does this statistic surprise you, given the different economic consequences for men and women of divorce? What explanation can you give for this statistic?

Q Stone suggests that comparisons of current divorce rates with past times may be misleading because of the failure to realise the role played in the past by premature death in dissolving marriages (Stone 1990: 421). Stone's figures show that the proportion of marital dissolutions by death or divorce in England and Wales at the early stages of marriage was much the same for the cohort marrying in 1826 as for that marrying in 1980 (ibid: p 410). What conclusions can you draw from this suggestion?

Q Are marriage and divorce two sides of the same coin? Is divorce law the best place for implementing state policy on marriage? Why is this policy implemented at this stage? Would we tolerate any more regulation of how we enter into our relationships? Finally, why does state policy on civil partnerships appear to mirror almost exactly that on marriage?

4

Parent–Child Relationships

We suggested in Chapter 1 above that the couple relationship, based upon the traditional heterosexual relationship, is central to the ideology of the family. Our view, like Fineman's (2004), is that this 'sexual family' as she called it, retains a powerful hold on family law and policy and influences ideas about what are assumed to be 'good' family relationships. One of the bases for the centrality of the 'sexual family' is the benefit that relationship is assumed to confer upon society and upon the individuals in it, not least upon children. We have also seen, however, that a great many adults do not arrange their familial lives around this relationship, nor do children live only in heterosexual nuclear family units. Yet, despite some accommodation in law and policy for these 'new family forms', we suggest that the sexual family has not been displaced by them.

We now turn to the relationship between children and adults. Laws concerning those relationships affect not only adult responsibilities for the care of children, but also the regulation of reproduction itself. In the first part of this chapter we will examine the social and legal ordering of reproduction and the issues raised in the legal determination of who is a parent. In doing so, we focus as much upon those to whom the labels 'parent', 'mother' or 'father' may not attach as upon those to whom they may.

We will examine the way in which legal rules sometimes recognise and sometimes create a connection between adult and child to forge a legal relationship. Although our focus will be on parenthood as a *legal* construct, parenthood (like childhood) is also a biological phenomenon and a socially constructed category—motherhood and fatherhood themselves are only 'natural' to the extent that it takes genetic material from a male and a female to begin a new life. And, as we shall see, the law takes cognisance of understandings of parenthood that span the biological and the social.

In this chapter we shall also examine the meaning of parenthood in law. Throughout the chapter, we will seek to situate the assignment of parenthood and the rights and responsibilities that come with that assignment within the context of equality, the ideologies of welfare and familialism and their place in the public/private divide.

I. BECOMING A PARENT: RIGHTS AND THE REGULATION OF REPRODUCTION

Disproportionate research into assisting women's reproductive capacities and the plethora of techniques that have been developed for use on women's bodies are examples of how reproduction is seen almost exclusively as a matter of and about women. As Sheldon states, '[r]eproduction has been seen as women's business and it is the bodies of women which have been understood as posing the greatest threat to the foetus. Men's relationship to reproduction has been constructed as distant, and largely vicarious' (Sheldon 1999: 138; Sheldon 2006). Even if there is, as Collier and Sheldon (2008) observe, a movement away from these traditional and dominant understandings of reproduction as primarily a female concern, it is a challenge to see how law can recognise men's reproductive needs without undermining or denying women's needs, given the significant biological and social differences at play (Collier and Sheldon 2008: 64–65). Collier and Sheldon note, for example, that many putative fathers feel marginalised by their exclusion from reproductive decision-making and concerns (ibid: 37–67) and that healthcare professionals 'are increasingly encouraged ... to recognise men's own needs as reproductive agents' (ibid: 65). However, to speak of formal sex equality in the context of reproduction is problematic (Kingdom 1991), and we must not therefore lose sight of the fact that any rights relating to reproduction, as well as legislation, medical procedures or social or moral discourse concerning reproduction, have always and necessarily affected women and men in very different ways.

Historically, the valorisation of maternity was as important to the first wave of the feminist movement as it was to upholders of patriarchy. To both, however, the characteristics of the idealised mother were race-specific (Lewis 1980), class-specific (Lewis 1980, 1992) and status-specific, encouraging motherhood only within marriage (Smart 1992; Spensky 1992). In this context, and in the context of an increasingly influential evangelical movement and other organised movements promoting 'moral purity', advocates for legal and freely available methods of birth control, for example, were often seen to be advancing an 'unnatural' course of action for middle-class married women. For women who did not meet the standard of the proper Victorian mother—poor, unmarried and often not white— birth control and sterilisation were encouraged. In the twenty-first century, the image of 'traditional' motherhood as woman's 'natural' role remains relatively strong, as does its perceived power to shape the good society (Diduck 1995; Phoenix 1996).

Fatherhood, historically, meant something different. Fatherhood was primarily concerned with the transmission of the family name and property to legitimate heirs. Fathers in the twenty-first century may not now be so preoccupied with their heirs, and the image of fatherhood is changing somewhat to incorporate the notion of the 'involved' father. Nevertheless Collier has argued that a particular form of hegemonic masculinity survives in which masculinity is defined according to a divide between the heterosexual/potent/ virile man and the homosexual/impotent/non-virile one; the impotent/non-virile man is constructed as a threat to the institution of marriage, and not really a man at all (Collier 1995b: 150–51; see also Collier 2010). Further, he has argued that the masculinity of the potent/virile man must be manifested in a 'respectable' way—within marriage—so as to create mature, safe fatherhood.

> **Q** The above perspectives suggest that motherhood is seen as a natural fulfilment of a woman's instinct, while fatherhood is seen as a necessary expression of appropriate or safe masculinity. Do you agree that these understandings play a part in the gendering of parenthood? How might they differently affect the legal regulation of reproduction?

The notion of gender-neutral reproductive rights is, then, a questionable one. Nonetheless, a number of international documents[1] appear to recognise reproductive rights in some sense, but their substance is not always entirely clear. How, for example, are we to interpret Article 12 of the European Convention on Human Rights (ECHR) and Fundamental Freedoms, or Article 16 of the Universal Declaration of Human Rights (UDHR)? Article 12 ECHR states: 'Men and women of marriageable age have the right to marry and to found a family, according to national laws governing the exercise of this right.' Article 16 UDHR states: 'Men and women of full age, without any limitation due to race, nationality or religion, have the right to marry and found a family.' And, of course Article 8 ECHR, the right to respect for one's private and family life, seems also to be important in the context of reproduction. It is arguable that some right to procreate appears to be protected by these Articles, but it also appears that that right is circumscribed to some degree. It may be helpful to recall that these documents were drafted in the aftermath of the atrocities perpetrated by the National Socialist regime in Germany and as a response to Nazi laws permitting forced sterilisation of segments of the population deemed undesirable (Bock 1991). In the context of a society practising forced sterilisation, the purpose of a right to reproduce seems clear, but in a society where this kind of treatment is not socially, morally or legally sanctioned, the substance of the right has yet to be determined especially in the light of the margin of appreciation the European Court of Human Right (ECtHR) offers to signatory states.[2] However Articles 12 and 8 have been considered recently in the context of reproduction in the ECtHR.

In *Dickson v UK*,[3] the wife was 45 years old. Her husband was serving a life sentence for murder. He had a number of years left to serve before his tariff was up, which meant that the wife would be at least 51 years old before she and her husband might be able to conceive a child. When the prison service refused on policy grounds to grant them facilities for artificial insemination, the Dicksons claimed a breach of their rights under Article 8 ECHR. In finding that their rights were not violated Lord Auld said in the Court of Appeal decision:

> It seems to me that concern, not only for the public attitude to the exercise by prisoners of certain rights in prison which they would take for granted outside, and concern for the rights of a putative child in the upbringing it would receive depending on the circumstances and the length of imprisonment involved, are highly relevant circumstances, for the purposes of Article 8.2. (para 20)

Concern for the potential child's 'rights' or 'welfare' might, in other words, justify restricting an adult's reproductive decisions. In the European Court, the United Kingdom put forward this policy as well as two others in defending the *Dickson* appeal. It argued that (i) losing the opportunity to beget children was an inevitable and necessary consequence of imprisonment; (ii) to allow prisoners guilty of certain serious offences to conceive children would undermine public confidence in the prison system by circumventing punitive and deterrent elements of the sentence; and (iii) the long-term absence

---

[1] See Douglas (1991: 22–25) and generally, Jackson (2001). Further, the Platform for Action agreed at the Fourth World Conference on Women held in Beijing China in September 1995 recognised reproductive rights that 'rest on the recognition of the basic right of all couples and individuals to decide freely and responsibly the number, spacing and timing of their children and to have the information and means to do so, and the right to attain the highest standard of sexual and reproductive health' (1996: para 95).

[2] See also Hale J (1996: 8).

[3] ECHR Grand Chamber 44362/04 (2007) on appeal from *Dickson v Premier Prison Service Ltd, Secretary of State for the Home Department* [2004] EWCA Civ 1477.

of a parent would have a negative impact on any child conceived, and therefore on society as a whole.

The Dicksons' complaint was upheld, however. The Grand Chamber found, first, that Article 8 was applicable because the refusal of artificial insemination facilities concerned private and family life, which incorporated the right to respect for their decision to become genetic parents. A person retained his Convention rights on imprisonment, so any restriction on those rights had to be justified. The Chamber further confirmed that there could be positive obligations inherent in a state's duty to secure respect for private and family life, which could involve the adoption of measures even in the sphere of relations between individuals. In response to the Secretary of State's policy arguments, the court found that although the inability to beget a child was a consequence of imprisonment, it was not an inevitable one given the availability of artificial insemination facilities. It found that prisoners' rights should not be automatically forfeited based purely on what might offend public opinion. Finally, the state's positive obligations to ensure the effective protection of children did not extend to preventing potential parents from attempting to conceive a child in circumstances such as those in the instant case, especially as the wife was at liberty and able to care for any child conceived until her husband's release. The policy in this case did not allow for any real weighing of the competing public and individual interests and prevented the required assessment of whether a restriction was proportionate. This meant that the policy fell outside any acceptable margin of appreciation, and there had, therefore, been a breach of Article 8 ECHR.

The second recent case to consider reproductive rights under the ECHR and the Human Rights Act 1998 (HRA) was one in which discrimination was alleged and so the court was required to identify and balance competing rights. In *Evans v Amicus Healthcare and Others*[4] the issues were the meaning of certain provisions of the Human Fertilisation and Embryology Act 1990 (HFEA) and whether those provisions breached any of the claimant's rights under the ECHR. After being diagnosed with ovarian cancer, Ms Evans, together with her then partner Mr Johnston, sought in-vitro fertilisation (IVF) treatment. They executed the required consents and embryos were fertilised and frozen for later implantation in Ms Evans' womb. After treatment for cancer, including the removal of her ovaries, but before implantation, however, the couple split up and Mr Johnston wrote to the clinic advising them that the embryos should be destroyed; he was, in effect withdrawing his consent for them to be used. Because withdrawal of his consent and destruction of the embryos would have ended any possibility of Ms Evans ever having a child genetically related to her, she sought, among other things, declarations that Mr Johnston could not withdraw his consent, that she could lawfully be treated with the embryos and that the relevant provisions of the HRA 1998 allowing a person to withdraw consent at any time for the 'use' of the embryos breached her rights under Articles 8, 12 and 14 of the ECHR. She did not allege discrimination between men and women, however. Instead she alleged discrimination between fertile and infertile women.

The Court of Appeal agreed that Ms Evans' Article 8 rights (to respect for her private life—her bodily integrity) were engaged by the state regulating the conditions in which she could have an embryo transferred into her. Even though it was not argued before it, the court also took the opportunity to comment upon the issue of gender, rights and

---

[4] [2004] EWCA Civ 727; [2005] Fam 1. All refs are to [2005] Fam 1. The decision was upheld by the Grand Chamber of the ECHR in *Evans v UK* 6339/05 [2007] 1 FLR 1990 on the grounds, inter alia, that because there was no consensus among European states on these 'moral and legal issues', states must be given a broad margin of appreciation. For an alternative, feminist, judgment in the *Evans* case, see Harris-Short (2010).

reproduction. It found that just as Ms Evans' rights were engaged by the provisions of the HFEA 1990, Mr Johnson's rights were also affected. Because both parties' rights had to be respected, the policy of requiring ongoing consent satisfied Article 8(2). According to Arden, LJ:

110 ... The personal circumstances of the parties are different from what they were at the outset of treatment, and it would be difficult for a court to judge whether the effect of Mr Johnston's withdrawal of his consent on Ms Evans is greater than the effect that the invalidation of that withdrawal of consent would have on Mr Johnston. The court has no point of reference by which to make that sort of evaluation. The fact is that each person has a right to be protected against interference with their private life. That is an aspect of the principle of self-determination or personal autonomy. It cannot be said that the interference with Mr Johnston's right is justified on the ground that interference is necessary to protect Ms Evans's right, because her right is likewise qualified in the same way by his right. They must have equivalent rights, even though the exact extent of their rights under article 8 has not been identified.

111 The interference with Ms Evans's private life is also justified under article 8(2) because, if Ms Evans's argument succeeded, it would amount to interference with the genetic father's right to decide not to become a parent. Motherhood could surely not be forced on Ms Evans and likewise fatherhood cannot be forced on Mr Johnston, especially as in the present case it will probably involve financial responsibility in law for the child as well.

Q Do you agree that the balance of rights between these parties must be 'equivalent'? Are men and women so differently situated with regard to reproduction that attempting to accord them equal or equivalent rights will be of little use? See on this Sheldon (2004, 2010).

The final recent case we wish to consider raises, like *Evans*, issues of discrimination but, like *Dickson*, also involves consideration of human rights alongside the regulation of family forms. In *SH and Others v Austria*[5] the complainants were two heterosexual couples. One couple challenged Austrian legislation regulating assisted reproduction that prohibited the use of donated sperm in IVF, although use of donated sperm was permissible if it were introduced directly into the woman's body; and the second couple challenged the provision that prohibited in all cases the use of donor ova.

With two strong dissents, the ECtHR confirmed, following *Dickson v UK*, that 'the right of a couple to conceive a child and to make use of medically assisted procreation for that end comes within the ambit of Article 8, as such a choice is clearly an expression of private and family life'. It concluded that 'Article 8 of the Convention therefore applies to the present case' (para 60).

The complainants alleged that they were discriminated against as compared with other couples who did not require donated gametes and thus that Article 14 also applied. The ECtHR found that both couples made their case successfully. In response to the Austrian government's arguments related specifically to couple number 2, in which the government raised its social policy prerogative regarding regulating family forms, the court said:

79. The Government also submitted that *in vitro* fertilisation raised the question of unusual relationships in which the social circumstances deviated from the biological ones, namely the

---

[5] Case No 57813/00 [2010]. The case was referred to Grand Chamber and a decision is pending at the time of writing.

division of motherhood into a biological aspect and the aspect of 'carrying the child' and perhaps also a social aspect.

80. The Court observes that, according to the Constitutional Court's decision of 14 October 1999, the Austrian legislator was guided by the idea that medically assisted procreation should take place similarly to natural procreation, in particular that the basic principle of civil law—*mater semper certa est, pater est quem nuptiae demonstrant*—should be maintained by avoiding the possibility that two persons could claim to be the biological mother of one and the same child and to avoid disputes between a biological and a genetic mother in the wider sense.

81. The aim of maintaining legal certainty in the field of family law by keeping a long-standing principle of this field of law as one of its basic features certainly has its merits. Nevertheless, unusual family relations in a broad sense are well known to the legal orders of the Contracting States. Family relations which do not follow the typical parent–child relationship based on a direct biological link, are nothing new and have already existed in the past, since the institution of adoption, which creates a family relationship between persons which is not based on descent but on contract, for the purpose of supplementing or replacing biological family relations. From this matter of common knowledge the Court would conclude that there are no insurmountable obstacles to bringing family relations which would result from a successful use of the artificial procreation techniques at issue into the general framework of family law and other related fields of law.

Q This case has been heard by the Grand Chamber and we are awaiting its decision. Do you take from these three human rights cases a right to procreate, as well as a right to not procreate (certainly under Article 8 and possibly under Article 12 ECHR)? What scope is given to states to limit this right? What weight is given to sex equality in these rights? What weight is given to the 'sexual family'?

II. DILUTING THE RIGHT TO REPRODUCE: WELFARE AND THE 'SEXUAL FAMILY'

As we saw above, there is room even in the interpretation of human rights for policy to privilege certain family forms over others. For the majority of the population the decision to conceive children, although taken in the context of specific material and ideological conditions, remains private, and rights are usually not invoked at all. For others, conceiving a child requires medical or legal intervention and so the decision to embark upon parenthood becomes more of a public concern, and therefore more amenable to 'rights-talk'. We argue, however, that as we saw above, 'rights-talk' does not always reflect the dominant framework in which these reproductive matters are decided.

According to the Human Fertilisation and Embryology Authority about one in seven couples in the UK are affected by infertility (HFEA 2010: 3). Infertility is defined as 'failing to get pregnant after two years of regular unprotected sex' (ibid). The Human Fertilisation and Embryology Authority licenses and regulates clinics in the UK that provide treatment for infertility. The legal aspects of this treatment—assisted reproduction—are governed by the Human Fertilisation and Embryology Acts 1990 and 2008 and the regulations promulgated under them. These Acts adopt a disease model of infertility, however, which is often inappropriate for prospective clients. First, framing the services as treatments for 'infertility' ignores those who are medically capable of procreating, but for whom heterosexual intercourse is not an option. Second, infertility is more than a physical matter; it has a strong social component. Morgan writes, for example, of society's 'parenthood mystique' (Morgan 1989: 72), a part of which is society's view of a childless heterosexual couple as a deviant, selfish or incomplete family. The Warnock Report on Human Fertilisation and Embryology, published in 1984 and dealing with the social, ethical and legal implications of assisted reproduction, put it in these terms:

> Childlessness can be a source of stress even to those who have deliberately chosen it. Family and friends often expect a couple to start a family, and express their expectations either openly or by implication ... . For those who long for children, the realisation that they are unable to found a family can be shattering. It can disrupt the picture of the whole of their future lives. They may feel that they will be unable to fulfil their own and other people's expectations. They may feel themselves excluded from a whole range of human activity and particularly the activities of their child rearing contemporaries. In addition to the social pressure to have children, there is for many a powerful urge to perpetuate their genes through a new generation. This desire cannot be assuaged by adoption. (Warnock Report 1984: 8, para 2.2)

In addition to social pressure upon (married) couples to 'found a family', people face individual pressures as well. For men, fertility is associated with power (Dewar 1989; Morgan 1989) and a hegemonic masculinity (Collier 1995b, 2010), and the maternal role for women is valorised as their 'true' or natural role even by the medical profession (Stanworth 1987: 15). There is a strong argument that, instead of seeking to meet 'demand' by devoting high-tech medical resources to enabling more people to have children, we should instead acknowledge that the demand is at least partly a result of hegemonic ideas about women's 'true' role, and 'promote attitudes which accept childlessness and enable women (especially) to fulfil themselves in other ways than parenthood' (Douglas 1991: 107).

It may be that the pressures to reproduce are not felt or are resisted by a significant proportion of people, however. Recent statistics on fertility in England and Wales show a trend towards later childbearing and smaller families. The total fertility rate in 2009 was 1.94 children born per woman, a slight drop from 1.96 in 2008, but the highest since 1973 (ONS Fertility 2010b). The average age of the mother for all live births in the UK was 29.4 (ibid). In 2009, UK fertility rates for women aged 35–39 and 40+ continued to increase, in line with this long-term trend. However, fertility fell slightly among women aged 30–34, in contrast to recent years. Despite this fall, women in their early thirties continued to have the highest fertility of any age group. There was a small decrease in the fertility rate of women in their twenties in 2009 (ibid). Furthermore, it is estimated that around 17% of all women remain childless (Portanti and Whitworth 2009: 12). It is thought that, while lack of a partner is associated with childlessness, a woman's own engagement with the labour market and her (higher) social class are also significant (ibid: 19).

Q Can you draw a distinction between 'childlessness' and 'infertility'? Should treatment be available in both circumstances? Douglas says

> On the other hand, a person may seek treatment to relieve her state of childlessness. She may be capable of conceiving through sexual intercourse, but prefers to avoid this, perhaps because she has failed to find a partner with whom she wishes

to share her life or bring up a child ... . For example, a woman who undergoes a 'premature menopause' at the age of 30 will be regarded as 'infertile'. She is likely to be sympathetically treated if she and her partner seek assisted reproduction; she will be accepted as having a clinical need for treatment. A woman who undergoes menopause at the age of 45, on the other hand, and then asks for treatment may be told that she has left it too late. Her childlessness is something she should have done something about sooner; in other words, it is due to her choice. Her desire for a child is nothing more than that—a desire. (Douglas 1993: 55)

The HFEA 1990 as amended by the 2008 Act sets out the requirements for the licensing of clinics, but, with the exception of section 13(5) (as amended by section 14(2)(b) of the 2008 Act) it does not lay down rules concerning entitlement to treatment. Section 13(5) requires licensed treatment centres to take account 'of the welfare of any child who may be born as a result of the treatment, (including the need of the child for supportive parenting), and of any other child who may affected by the birth'.[6]

This section replaces the previous statutory guidance that the welfare of the child included his/her need 'for a father'. It is arguable that this reform was necessary, not only for human rights equality reasons (Wallbank 2004) but also because the basis upon which it was there in the first place reflected common-sense notions of welfare and fears about fatherless families. The change, however, argue McCandless and Sheldon (2010a) may not be that great in practice. Clinical practitioners, they suggest, were already employing a permissive interpretation of the old section (ibid: 219) and the Guidance issued by the HFEA regarding interpretation of the new need for 'supportive parenting' is equally liberal.

Supportive parenting is a commitment to the health, well being and development of the child. It is presumed that all prospective parents will be supportive parents, in the absence of any reasonable cause for concern that any child who may be born, or any other child, may be at risk of significant harm or neglect. Where centres have concern as to whether this commitment exists, they may wish to take account of wider family and social networks within which the child will be raised. (HFEA Code of Practice Guidance Notes 2009)

The Code of Practice in which this paragraph is found gives substance to the discretion given to professionals in the broad framework of the statute. The Code is subject to ministerial approval and is available to the public, but there is no legal sanction if a clinic is found to have violated it. On one hand, this type of regulatory regime provides flexibility which could prove advantageous to individual clients. On the other hand, it leaves individual medical practitioners with almost unfettered discretion over the reproductive lives of many people. The courts, furthermore, are reluctant to police this discretion. Decisions about treatment are not justiciable, so if a person feels aggrieved by a refusal of treatment, her only recourse is judicial review of the decision. In *R v Ethical Committee of St Mary's Hospital*[7] the court refused to look behind the criteria established by the clinic with respect to treatment decisions provided that the rules of administrative law, such as procedural fairness, were adhered to.

The guidelines in the Code of Practice direct centres to bear in mind the requirements

---

[6] For recent discussion of the legislative history of this section, see Smith (2010); McCandless and Sheldon (2010a, b); People and Science Policy Ltd (2006). For a discussion of the section it replaced, see Douglas (1993); Jackson (2001, 2002); Wallbank (2004).

[7] [1988] 1 FLR 512.

of section 13(5)[8] and direct them to consider a number of factors in this regard, including treating parties fairly and without discrimination (HFEA 2009 section 8.7), considering the prospective parents' commitment to raise children, their ability to provide a stable environment, their immediate and family medical histories, their ages and their ability to provide for the child's needs and the risk of harm to children (HFEA 2009 sections 8.9, 8.10). Centres are expected to take medical and social histories of each patient and to make enquiries of their GPs; refusal of patients to provide this information is a factor to be taken into account in the decision to provide treatment (HFEA 2009 section 8.13).

We see, then, that regulation of assisted reproduction is not exclusively legal, medical, moral, financial or bureaucratic, but rather takes a multidisciplinary approach. We see also that medical professionals must take their decisions after considering two different perspectives: the welfare of the child required by section 13(5) and the fitness of the patient as assessed by the guidelines (Douglas 1993).

> **Q** In your view, does this multifaceted approach resolve satisfactorily the balance between patients' rights and child welfare? Would you provide in vitro fertilisation treatment for the following (give reasons):
>
> (a) a single, 26-year-old unemployed woman who has had a hysterectomy;
> (b) a single, 37-year-old, fertile, professional woman;
> (c) two 30-year-old women in a stable, long-standing lesbian relationship;
> (d) a married professional couple where the wife has a history of prostitution and the husband, with a low sperm count, has a conviction for living off the earnings of prostitution;
> (e) a married heterosexual couple, the husband aged 29 and the wife 50;
> (f) a married heterosexual couple in their late 20s, who have two children, where the husband has immotile sperm and has been unemployed for two years.
>
> Do you think the courts and the legislature have struck the right balance between a pure rights-based approach and a pure welfare approach to freedom from interference in reproductive decisions?

III. REGULATION OF REPRODUCTION: THE RIGHT NOT TO REPRODUCE

Contraception

Like the right to reproduce, the assertion of a right not to reproduce is not a straightforward matter. Different means of contraception have been utilised by men and women for centuries. Throughout the years, however, one can identify a waxing and waning in their social and legal acceptability. Douglas provides a concise history:

> In England, up to 1860, a variety of pamphlets advocating and explaining contraception sold well and enjoyed a wide circulation. In particular, a manual called the Fruits of Philosophy, by

---

[8] S 8A HFEA 2009.

Charles Knowlton sold for many years, until a bookseller who published an illustrated edition was convicted of distributing obscene literature. To challenge this effective ban on the book, Charles Bradlaugh, who had founded the Malthusian League in 1860 to spread information about the need for birth control, together with Annie Beasant republished Knowlton's book and sold it openly. They were tried for publishing an obscene libel. The jury found that the book was 'calculated to deprave public morals, but entirely exonerated the defendants from corrupt motives in publishing it'. The practice by married couples of birth control increased after the trial, which received enormous publicity, and the birth-rate in Britain actually began to fall from 1877.

At the turn of the century, a new impetus for birth control emerged in the spread of eugenic theory, loosely based on Darwin's theory of evolution. It was argued that the human stock could be improved if 'better' people had children, and less superior specimens did not. This view was adopted particularly in the United States where it was used to sanction the often involuntary sterilisation of those deemed mentally defective, on the ground that this deficiency would be passed on to offspring. Such attitudes never received judicial or legislative formulation in England, although the Brock committee did examine the issue of sterilising the mentally handicapped in 1934.

The 20th century saw the founding of birth control societies which provided both contraceptive information and services, and of the coming to prominence of the contraception campaigners Marie Stopes in Britain and Margaret Sanger (who invented the term 'birth control') in the United States. In 1930, the Minister of Health issued a memorandum allowing local authorities to give contraceptive advice in cases where further pregnancy would be 'detrimental to health'. In fact, this memorandum was ignored, and contraception remained a private matter for individuals themselves, perhaps after consulting their doctor or private birth control clinic, until the late 1960's.

Its practice was, nonetheless, widespread. Surveys carried out from the turn of the century reveal that, beginning with the wealthy and then spreading to the working class, contraception was an increasingly accepted part of married life. (Douglas 1991: 42–44, footnotes omitted)[9]

For a time contraception was thought to violate the very purpose of marriage, and this view is still held today by many religions. It was reflected also in early cases. In *Cowen v Cowen*[10] the Court of Appeal found that a marriage could not be consummated if the husband wore a condom during intercourse or withdrew before ejaculation. This decision was eventually overruled,[11] but evidences the importance of maternity, or potential maternity, to married women, and paternity to married men. In contrast, use of contraceptives was encouraged among the 'lower orders' and, as Douglas states above, many of the 'feminist' pioneers of the birth-control movement advocated it for eugenic reasons. Contraception and contraceptive advice are now freely available on the NHS for most sexually active women,[12] but again many feminists have suggested that birth control continues to be viewed differently depending upon whether the patient is poor and black or middle class and white (Cox 1990; Roberts 1993).[13] Smart theorises abortion in a similar way. She suggests that legal concern about abortion increased when married women began having abortions (Smart 1992: 19). Finally, although there is some interest in developing a contraceptive pill for men, comparatively little research has been undertaken in this area.

---

[9] See also Jackson (2001: 11).

[10] [1946] P 36; [1945] 2 All ER 197.

[11] See *Baxter v Baxter* [1948] AC 274.

[12] See *Gillick v West Norfolk and Wisbech Area Health Authority* [1986] AC 112; [1985] 3 All ER 402; [1985] 3 WLR 830; [1986] 1 FLR 224. Despite this decision, which permits doctors to provide contraceptives to children under the age of 16, the UK has the highest rate of teenage pregnancy in Europe (Jackson 2001: 16).

[13] See Jackson's (2001) discussion of issues of contraception in developing countries.

Abortion

Abortion is regulated in England and Wales by the criminal law, by the Offences Against the Person Act 1861, the Infant Life Preservation Act 1929 and the Abortion Act 1967 as amended, and by healthcare policy and practice. The Offences Against the Person Act provides the starting point for the criminal law of abortion. According to sections 58 and 59, all abortions are unlawful.

58 Every woman being with child who, with intent to procure her own miscarriage, shall unlawfully administer to herself any poison or other noxious thing, or shall unlawfully use any instrument or other means whatsoever with the like intent, and whosoever, with intent to procure the miscarriage of any woman, whether she be or be not with child, shall unlawfully administer to her or cause to be taken by her any poison or other noxious thing, or shall unlawfully use any instrument or other means whatsoever with the like intent, shall be guilty of felony.

59 Whosoever shall unlawfully supply or procure any poison or other noxious thing, or any instrument or thing whatsoever, knowing that the same is intended to be unlawfully used or employed with intent to procure the miscarriage of any woman, whether she be or be not with child, shall be guilty of a misdemeanour.

Similarly, the destruction of a 'viable' foetus is a crime pursuant to the Infant Life Preservation Act 1929.

1(1) Subject as hereinafter in this subsection provided, any person who, with intent to destroy the life of a child capable of being born alive, by any wilful act causes a child to die before it has an existence independent of its mother, shall be guilty of felony, to wit, of child destruction, and shall be liable on conviction thereof on indictment to penal servitude for life:

Provided that no person shall be found guilty of an offence under this section unless it is proved that the act which caused the death of the child was not done in good faith for the purpose only of preserving the life of the mother.

(2) For the purpose of this Act, evidence that a woman had at any material time been pregnant for a period of twenty-eight weeks or more shall be prima facie proof that she was at that time pregnant of a child capable of being born alive.

Defences to both of these crimes are provided by the Abortion Act 1967:

1(1) Subject to the provisions of this section, a person shall not be guilty of an offence under the law relating to abortion when a pregnancy is terminated by a registered medical practitioner if two registered medical practitioners are of the opinion, formed in good faith—

(a) that the pregnancy has not exceeded its twenty fourth week and that the continuance of the pregnancy would involve risk, greater than if the pregnancy were terminated, of injury to the physical or mental health of the pregnant woman or any existing children of her family; or

(b) that the termination is necessary to prevent grave permanent injury to the physical or mental health of the pregnant woman; or

(c) that the continuance of the pregnancy would involve risk to the life of the pregnant woman, greater than if the pregnancy were terminated; or

(d) that there is a substantial risk that if the child were born it would suffer from such physical or mental abnormalities as to be seriously handicapped.

(2) In determining whether the continuance of a pregnancy would involve risk of injury to

health as is mentioned in paragraph (a) or (b) of subsection (1) of this section, account may be taken of the pregnant woman's actual or reasonably foreseeable environment ... .

5(1) No offence under the Infant Life Preservation Act shall be committed by a registered medical practitioner who terminates a pregnancy in accordance with the provisions of this Act.[14]

Apart from the criminal law, abortion is regulated in the way that Health Authorities and Health Trusts negotiate the priority given to abortions as an NHS-funded medical procedure, and in the way in which individual physicians exercise the discretion given to them by the Abortion Act to make decisions about who is entitled to an abortion. So long as their discretion is exercised in good faith, courts usually will not question the decision (Sheldon 1996). Sheldon reviewed the leading cases on abortion in the English courts and concluded:

> The court decisions which I have outlined share an acceptance of abortion as a matter for medicine and a consequent judicial reluctance to intervene or to second-guess the decisions made by doctors. What the courts did in these cases is actively to protect and entrench the monopoly of doctors, while policing those marginal cases which did not fall within the bounds of good medical practice. This accords both with the assumption that abortion is a technical matter to be decided by doctors and a long tradition of leaving the regulation and control of medical practice largely to the medical profession itself. (Sheldon 1996: 106)

As Sheldon has emphasised elsewhere (Sheldon 1993), MPs debating the bill which was to become the Abortion Act 1967 did not question placing the responsibility for decisions regarding termination of pregnancy upon medical practitioners rather than upon the women concerned. Indeed, one MP asked: 'Who is the mother to make the judgment?'

It appears that the great majority (96%) of abortions are funded by the NHS,[15] and the British Pregnancy Advisory Service (BPAS)[16] anticipates that, despite changes to commissioning arrangements being considered by the coalition government, the level of public funding is unlikely to be reduced (BPAS 2011). In addition, it reports that the availability of abortion has been improved by the fact that publicly funded abortions are carried out in the independent sector. So although a significant minority of medical students surveyed a recent study said they would conscientiously object to performing an abortion (Strickland 2011: 3), it seems that most women seeking an abortion, particularly early abortion, can find treatment.

The regulation of abortion, whether formal or informal, raises a number of issues. The first is the basis upon which abortion is legally and philosophically defensible at all. Defenders of abortion often speak of a woman's right to choose abortion, invoking a right to bodily autonomy. However, many argue that the legality or morality of abortion cannot be resolved by reference simply to a right to bodily autonomy. As we stated earlier, one person's right usually gives rise to another's competing right, and in the abortion context that competition usually is phrased in terms of women's right to bodily integrity versus a foetus's right to life, and sometimes also places a woman's right to bodily integrity in competition with a man's right to reproduce. Despite the difficulty for many of resolving

---

[14] Before this amendment was added by the HFEA 1990, the relationship between the ILPA and the Abortion Act was at times unclear. See, eg, *Rance v Mid-Down Health Authority* [1991] 1 QB 587; and *C v S* [1988] QB 134.

[15] While waiting times may vary according to area, most do not exceed three weeks for a first referral (Abortion Rights undated).

[16] This is a body claiming to be 'Britain's largest single abortion provider' (Bpas undated).

these contests (eg Dworkin 1995), both have been resolved legally in England in favour of the woman. In *C v S*[17] a man attempted to obtain an injunction in order to prevent his pregnant girlfriend from having an abortion. The court found that the legislation did not require the consent of anyone but the patient and the doctors and that this procedure did not violate any rights of the 'father'. In *Paton v UK*[18] the married 'father' made the same argument before the European Commission of Human Rights which held with respect to his rights:

> [The Commission] observes that any interpretation of the husband's and potential father's right, under Article 8 of the Convention, to respect for his private and family life, as regards an abortion which his wife intends to have performed on her, must first of all take into account the right of the pregnant woman, being the person primarily concerned in the pregnancy and its continuation or termination, to respect for her private life … . In the present case, the Commission, having regard to the right of the pregnant woman, does not find that the husband and potential father's right to respect for his private and family life can be interpreted so widely as to embrace such potential rights as claimed by the applicant, ie a right to be consulted, or a right to make applications, about an abortion which his wife intends to have performed on her. (416–17)[19]

Q Why do you think the court weighed the balance in favour of the woman? Could it have had something to do with the greater physical risk she takes in the reproductive process?

On the question of the foetus's right to life, the English courts have been consistent in their view that a foetus is not a person until born and so can have no legal rights until then.[20] In *C v S* the plaintiff argued that he was also bringing the action on behalf of the foetus as its next friend, but the court found that such an action was impossible. The European Commission of Human Rights in *Paton* also considered this matter:

> The Commission has considered whether Article 2 [which begins 'Everyone's right to life shall be protected by the law'] is to be construed as recognising an absolute 'right to life' of the foetus and has excluded such an interpretation on the following grounds.
> The life of the foetus is intimately connected with, and cannot be regarded in isolation from, the life of the pregnant woman. If Article 2 were held to cover the life of the foetus and its protection under this Article were, in the absence of any express limitation, seen as absolute, an abortion would have to be considered as prohibited, even where the continuation of the pregnancy would involve a serious risk to the life of the pregnant woman. This would mean the 'unborn life' of the foetus would be regarded as being of a higher value than the life of the pregnant woman … .
> The Commission finds that such an interpretation would be contrary to the object and purpose of the Convention. It notes that, already at the time of the signature of the Convention (4 November 1950), all High Contracting Parties, with one possible exception, permitted abor-

---

[17] [1988] QB 135; [1987] 1 All ER 1230.

[18] (1981) 3 EHRR 408.

[19] In Canada and the USA notification of or consent by the 'father' is not required either. See *Tremblay v Daigle* (1990) 62 DLR (4th) 634; and *Planned Parenthood v Danforth* 428 US 52 (1976).

[20] See *Re MB (Medical Treatment)* [1997] 2 FLR 426; *St George's Healthcare National Health Service Trust v S, R v Collins, ex parte S*, [1998] 3 WLR 936; [1998] 2 FLR 728. Contrast this view with the Constitution of the Republic of Ireland, for example: Art 40(3) which acknowledges 'the right to life of the unborn'.

tion where necessary to save the life of the mother, and that, in the meanwhile, the national law on termination of the pregnancy has shown a tendency towards further liberalisation. (415)[21]

The most recent statement on abortion to come from the ECtHR confirms that abortion does fall within the scope of one's Article 8 right to respect for private life.[22] Two applicants were prohibited in Irish law from obtaining an abortion in Ireland on the grounds of their health and well-being. The court found that in its broad concept of private life, including the right to personal autonomy and to physical and psychological integrity, Ireland's 'prohibition of the termination of the first and second applicants' pregnancies sought for reasons of health and/or well-being amounted to an interference with their right to respect for their private lives' (para 216). However, on the question of whether that breach was justified, based on Ireland's moral concern to protect the right to life of the unborn, the court found that

> it is not possible to find in the legal and social orders of the Contracting States a uniform European conception of morals including on the question of when life begins. By reason of their 'direct and continuous contact with the vital forces of their countries', State authorities are in principle in a better position than the international judge to give an opinion on the 'exact content of the requirements of morals' in their country, as well as on the necessity of a restriction intended to meet them. (para 223)

It found therefore that the prohibition pursued a legitimate aim and did so proportionately and thus remained within the broad margin appreciation afforded to states on these questions, notwithstanding the 'consensus amongst a substantial majority of the Contracting States of the Council of Europe towards allowing abortion on broader grounds than accorded under Irish law' (para 235). The third applicant's pregnancy constituted a risk to her life. She had a rare form of cancer, and although the Irish constitution made provision for assessing abortion in these contexts, the government had not implemented those provisions. The court found that in this context Article 8 imposed positive obligations on the state which it failed to meet and this failure constituted a breach of C's Article 8 rights (para 267).

Douglas sums up the multifaceted arguments around abortion 'rights':

> The demand for reproductive freedom seems to derive ultimately from the idea of having control over one's own body. This has two aspects. First, there is the right not to have one's body interfered with against one's will. This has received general, though not complete, legal recognition, through tort and criminal law protecting against assault.
>
> The second aspect is less well-established. Here, what is claimed is the right to do with one's body as one wishes. This right has not been generally conceded by the law, which imposes a variety of restrictions upon it … . However, it may be relied upon where use of contraceptives is in issue, since relatively few nowadays would argue that such use is immoral.
>
> The claim to autonomy in the sense of doing as one wishes with one's body is harder to sustain where abortion or control over childbirth are concerned, for the issue may then become one of competing rights, any right to life of the foetus versus the right to autonomy of the woman. Pro-abortionists may argue that the foetus is akin to an invader, whom the woman has the right to repel. English law has given some recognition to this argument. For example, it

---

[21] See also *Kelly v Kelly* [1997] 2 FLR 828 (Ct of Sess) where the Scottish court denied a man an order preventing his estranged wife from having a lawful abortion. It also found that a foetus had no legal persona.
[22] *A, B and C v Ireland* case no 25579/05 (para 213) decision 16 December 2010.

permits abortion on the basis that, inter alia, the presence of the foetus is a threat to the woman's health or general welfare. Sterilisation of a woman with a severe learning difficulty has been justified by a Law Lord on the basis that pregnancy 'would be an unmitigated disaster' for her.

Anti-abortionists stress the innocence and helplessness of the foetus, imprisoned in the womb, in their calls for its protection from the mother. Such an approach diverts attention away from the interests of the woman who carries the foetus. But viewing the foetus as some hostile invader of the woman's womb is equally unsatisfactory. Neither approach really encompasses the complexity and uniqueness of reproduction. We may ultimately have to conclude that it is not like other life situations, and therefore cannot be dealt with by means of analogies, however ingenious. It may be necessary to find a different way of looking at the question, perhaps by viewing the mother and foetus as a unit.

This is not to argue that the foetus is a part of the mother, like any other bodily organ, to be dealt with by her as she wishes. This view cannot be sustained in the light of our scientific understanding of the development of the foetus. Equally importantly, it is to be doubted whether women view the child they carry merely as a part of themselves, whether they wish to have the child or not. Rather, it is to seek to recognise the intimate connection between the woman and the foetus she carries, based on the immutable reality that, while it remains in her uterus, its growth depends entirely upon her health and strength, and she ultimately is responsible for its nurture. Equally, she, and no one else, is directly affected by the presence of the foetus in her womb. Kant's principle that no one should be used merely as a means, but always as an end in themselves, would seem to be appropriate here. No woman should be required to take on the responsibility and the risks of pregnancy, for the benefit of the foetus, unless she is willing to do so. And no one else is better placed to decide what should happen to that foetus.

(Douglas 1991: 16–18, footnotes omitted)

Q To what degree has English law adopted this approach? This approach means that a pregnant woman and a foetus may be regarded neither as two autonomous rights-bearing individuals, nor as one, embodied by the woman. What implications does such a view have for our understanding of the liberal legal subject?

Douglas goes on:

This [her argument above] is not an argument which the law has adopted. Rather, it has entrusted decision-making during pregnancy to the medical profession rather than to the woman herself. Legal abortion is dependent upon the certified opinion of two registered medical practitioners. Although English courts have not yet been prepared to sanction control over the movements of a pregnant woman in order to safeguard her foetus, the law offers little freedom to a woman to determine how she will give birth, upholding a medical monopoly on the right to attend a woman in childbirth and hence restricting her choice of attendants and mode of childbirth.

The law therefore gives the woman a right to control her capacity to reproduce through contraception, through its recognition of a right to bodily autonomy in the sense of non-interference. But once the child has been conceived, her freedom to have an abortion depends upon a balance which gradually shifts in the foetus's favour, though never so far as to favour the life of the foetus over that of the woman. (ibid: 18, footnotes omitted)

Q In your view, has English law struck an appropriate balance between the woman, the man, the state and the foetus? On the legal history of abortion, see Smart (1992) and Douglas (1991). On patient autonomy and abortion generally, see Jackson (2001: ch 3) in which she argues that 'abortion law should no longer consist in a set of defences to the crime of abortion, but rather should, like the rest of British medical law, be informed by the guiding principle of patient self-determination' (ibid: 72). Finally, see Sheldon (1997) on abortion law generally.

Conclusion

Our freedom to make decisions to reproduce must be examined in the context of the extent to which people, particularly women, are able to control their fecundity. We have attempted to show that notwithstanding that these decisions are often framed within a rights discourse, legal management of reproduction decisions is not easily, or even usually, made in those terms. Instead, the state regulates many decisions about reproduction through discourses rooted in problematic notions about welfare, paternalism and the ideologically powerful 'sexual family'. When rights language is invoked, the meaning or content of the right is not always clearly articulated. Indeed, in the abortion context, Clarke (1989) suggests that if anyone at all has any *rights*, it is doctors.

IV. MOTHERS AND FATHERS: THE 'FRAGMENTATION'[23] OF PARENTHOOD?

We said above that parenthood in law spans the biological and the social. In addition to recognising the biological parent,[24] the law also recognises, for example, the 'psychological parent' (Goldstein et al 1980a, 1980b),[25] who is that person to whom the child has bonded emotionally and psychologically, and the 'social parent',[26] who is the person who undertakes the day-to-day care for the child. As Baroness Hale observed in *Re G (children)*:[27]

> There is a difference between natural and legal parents. Thus, the father of a child born to unmarried parents was not legally a 'parent' until the Family Law Reform Act 1987 but he was always a natural parent. The anonymous donor who donates his sperm or her egg under the terms of the Human Fertilisation and Embryology Act 1990 is the natural progenitor of the child but not his legal parent. (para 32)

Further, designation of parenthood implicates complex issues of rights and welfare. Some may consider that to promote both, the law ought to prioritise a child's 'natural parent', usually understood in biological terms. But in the interests of the welfare of the child, Baroness Hale observed that even 'natural parenthood' can be broken down:

---

[23] We have drawn here on Collier and Sheldon's idea of the 'Fragmentation of Fatherhood' (Collier and Sheldon 2008).

[24] See, eg, s 20(1) Family Law Reform Act 1969.

[25] See *Re M (Child's Upbringing)* [1996] 2 FLR 441 (CA) for an example of a case in which the concept of 'psychological parent' was accepted by the courts: per Ward LJ, 54–55.

[26] See, eg, the definition of 'child of the family' s 52(1)(a) of the MCA 1973 and Sched 5 para 80(2) of the CPA which includes a child of one of the parties to a marriage or civil partnership. See also Baroness Hale's judgment in *Re G (children)* [2006] UKHL 43.

[27] [2006] UKHL 43.

33. There are at least three ways in which a person may be or become a natural parent of a child, each of which may be a very significant factor in the child's welfare, depending upon the circumstances of the particular case. The first is genetic parenthood: the provision of the gametes which produce the child. This can be of deep significance on many levels. For the parent, perhaps particularly for a father, the knowledge that this is 'his' child can bring a very special sense of love for and commitment to that child which will be of great benefit to the child (see, for example, the psychiatric evidence in Re C (MA) (An Infant) [1966] 1 WLR 646). For the child, he reaps the benefit not only of that love and commitment, but also of knowing his own origins and lineage, which is an important component in finding an individual sense of self as one grows up. The knowledge of that genetic link may also be an important (although certainly not an essential) component in the love and commitment felt by the wider family, perhaps especially grandparents, from which the child has so much to gain.

34. The second is gestational parenthood: the conceiving and bearing of the child. The mother who bears the child is legally the child's mother, whereas the mother who provided the egg is not: 1990 Act, s 27. While this may be partly for reasons of certainty and convenience, it also recognises a deeper truth: that the process of carrying a child and giving him birth (which may well be followed by breast-feeding for some months) brings with it, in the vast majority of cases, a very special relationship between mother and child, a relationship which is different from any other.

35. The third is social and psychological parenthood: the relationship which develops through the child demanding and the parent providing for the child's needs, initially at the most basic level of feeding, nurturing, comforting and loving, and later at the more sophisticated level of guiding, socialising, educating and protecting. The phrase 'psychological parent' gained most currency from the influential work of Goldstein, Freud and Solnit, Beyond the Best Interests of the Child (1973), who defined it thus:

'A psychological parent is one who, on a continuous, day-to-day basis, through interaction, companionship, interplay, and mutuality, fulfils the child's psychological needs for a parent, as well as the child's physical needs. The psychological parent may be a biological, adoptive, foster or common law parent.'

When thinking about parents and children, then, we may need to distinguish between parentage (the biological link between parent and child), parenthood (legal recognition of that link), and the legal duties and rights that sometimes come with those statuses: parental responsibility (Bainham 1999).

Parental responsibility is a concept created by the Children Act 1989. It encompasses all the rights and duties that parents have with respect to their children.[28] We will discuss parental responsibility in more detail below and in Chapter 8 but for now wish to underline that it provides a clear example of one way in which parenthood has been fragmented in law: parental responsibility can be held by any number of people who, usually, are able to exercise it independently of other holders of it.

Parenthood can be fragmented in these ways, but also more obviously, by gender. Motherhood, in other words, may mean something different from fatherhood.[29] And more fundamentally, gender is also important when we look at the ease with which motherhood and fatherhood themselves may be fragmented. Collier illustrates the different relationships with a child that a man can have and the role that law plays in those relationships:

---

[28] S 3 Children Act 1989.
[29] For further discussion, see pp 184–85 below.

[W]e can, at the outset, distinguish between paternity and fatherhood. 'Fatherhood' is the social construct through which the law has historically sought to attach men to children. It is not a unitary concept and there is (as we shall see) no one fatherhood in law. A distinction may be made therefore, between 'paternity', signifying a biological but not necessarily social connection with a child, 'biological fatherhood', which embraces the biological and social fathering relationship, and 'social fatherhood' in which the 'role' of fathering and all the obligations it involves, occurs but without the presence of a biological relationship between man and child. All of these are instances of men's relationships with children which have been established in law. It is once paternity is proved that there may be a legal relationship between a man and a child ... but the bundle of rights, obligations and duties which make up parenthood do not automatically follow from a finding of paternity. Thus although the terms are often used synonymously, *paternity* is different from *fatherhood*. The former refers to the legal status of men who have biologically fathered a certain child or children. In a sense it is the law which 'gives' a man the status of fatherhood through recourse to the concept of paternity.

(Collier 1995b: 184–85, references omitted)

He also reminds us that law can, in other circumstances, override biology in assigning fatherhood: the 'presumption of legitimacy' operates to attach the status of legal fatherhood to the husband of the child's mother, even if there is evidence that he is not the biological father (ibid: 184).[30] Finally, legal fatherhood does not necessarily imply that a man has legal responsibility to care for, visit or even acknowledge a child.[31]

Despite the fact that a child can only have one *legal* father at any one time,[32] Collier and Sheldon (2008) suggest that law is beginning to find a place for different men to fulfil the different aspects of 'fatherhood'.[33] They offer examples of law countenancing more than one father in a child's life and suggest that fragmentation of fatherhood in this way challenges the symbolic value of the need for an 'authentic' father to complete the nuclear family.

Motherhood, on the other hand, is not so easily 'fragmented' into its social, psychological and biological parts. It is difficult to find examples of law countenancing more than one mother in a child's life, notwithstanding that motherhood and maternity have become categories that are increasingly detachable from each other. Advanced techniques of assisted reproduction together with the law of adoption mean that a child may have up to four 'real' mothers (a genetic mother, a gestational mother, a commissioning social mother and an adoptive mother), not to mention social or psychological relationships created through fostering or step-parent situations.

As it does with fatherhood, law accepts some maternal relationships and overrides others in determining legal motherhood and in allocating rights and responsibilities to mothers. But it is impossible, outside of adoption cases as we shall see below, for law to find a place for more than one woman to fulfil different aspects of motherhood. As Diduck observes, first quoting Mykitiuk (2001):

Whereas paternity is a construction allowing fatherhood to be established in a variety of ways— including choice—maternity is a unitary construction where women can be deprived of the

---

[30] But see now Thorpe LJ in Re H and A (children) [2002] EWCA Civ 383; [2002] 2 FCR 469 discussed below pp 159–62, and see *O v L (Blood Tests)* [1995] 2 FLR 930; *K v M (paternity: contact)* [1996] 1 FLR 312 for applications of this principle.

[31] See Chapter 8 below.

[32] See, eg, adoption below.

[33] See also Sheldon (2005).

status if both the biological and social roles are not fulfilled. The naturalization of maternity by law has precluded legal thinking about the distribution of maternity in a manner similar to determinations of paternity (Mykitiuk 2001).

O'Donovan and Marshall reflect upon even feminists' apparent inability to separate mother-hood from maternity (2006); it seems that men have a choice about parenthood that women do not have (Boyd 2007). (Diduck 2007: 479)

Diduck reminds us further of Boyd's suggestion that law may accommodate different types of fatherhood as a type of 'affirmative action' for them required by 'men's histori-cally more fragile social ties to children and the now diminished capacity of the marriage tie to provide them (Boyd 2007)' (ibid: 479).

In the next part we will outline the ways in which law assigns the status of parenthood, and explore potential explanations for those assignments. For, as Jackson (2006) states, while it is usually presented as a question of fact, the determination of which of the features that are normally associated with parenthood should be singled out as identifying the 'real' mother or father of a child, is actually a question of judgement. We will then examine the legal, social and material meaning of that status. In other words, first we will address who, in law, is a parent, and then we will examine what, in law, parenthood means, both to the parent and to the child. It is here that the fragmentation of parenthood may also be relevant; as Baroness Hale said in *Re G*:

> To be the legal parent of a child gives a person legal standing to bring and defend proceedings about the child and makes the child a member of that person's family, but it does not necessarily tell us much about the importance of that person to the child's welfare. (para 32)

V. WHO IS A PARENT? BECOMING A MOTHER

Biological Mothers

Western European culture[34] recognises a link between a child and the woman who has borne that child. In most cases the same woman provides the gametes and bears the child, and the combination of these biological facts usually gives rise to a legal relationship with all of its attendant responsibilities.[35] With the advent of methods of assisted reproduction, however, an egg may be donated by one woman and implanted in the womb of another, genetically unrelated woman who will then carry and give birth to the child. Both can be called the biological mothers of the child. In such cases, the question becomes whether the law should assign rights and responsibilities to the genetically related mother or to the carrying mother.

At present, the law prioritises the carrying woman. Legal motherhood in cases where a woman has received an embryo implant through a licensed clinic is determined by section 33(1) of the HFEA 2008:[36]

---

[34] See Kandel (1994) for other possibilities.

[35] There are exceptions, however. See, for example in France *accouchement sous x*, discussed below pp 127–28.

[36] This re-enacts s 27(1) HFEA 1990.

> The woman who is carrying or has carried a child as a result of the placing in her of an embryo or of sperm and eggs, and no other woman, is to be treated as the mother of the child.

Consider, however, section 20(1) of the Family Law Reform Act 1969:

> In any civil proceedings in which the parentage of any person falls to be determined, the court may, either on its own motion or on an application by any party to the proceedings, give a direction—
>
> (a) for the use of scientific tests to ascertain whether such tests show that a party is or is not the father or mother of that person ...

This section allows for the taking of non-invasive bodily samples in order to perform DNA profiling, which can establish accurately the genetic parentage of a child.

We may thus see two competing biological priorities at work in determining legal motherhood. When one becomes a mother through sexual intercourse, or without the assistance of a licensed clinic, the law assigns maternity through the genetic connection, although of course in these cases the genetic mother will always be the carrying mother. When one obtains donated gametes with assistance at a licensed clinic, however, the genetic link is disregarded and the gestational link takes precedence. A number of explanations are offered for this prioritisation of bearing and delivering a child.

The Warnock Committee appointed to report on various aspects of assisted reproduction considered the ethical, moral, legal and technological issues around the donation of gametes and felt that donations should be encouraged as a means of assisting infertile couples.[37] To this end, it recommended relieving the donors of any legal obligations or responsibilities for children resulting from their donations (Warnock Committee 1984). The desire to encourage donations may be one reason that the law confers legal status on gestational mothers rather than genetic mothers when licensed assistance is provided. Another might be that the law recognises the commitment and health risks undertaken by the carrying woman (Douglas 1991: 129). Perhaps a further justification for the rule might be that there should be some recognition of a psychological and physical 'bonding' between woman and foetus, which many suggest takes place in the womb. However, the Warnock Committee, in its discussion of surrogacy,[38] did not consider this factor to be significant and appeared to accept arguments that, because little is known about a bonding process in utero, 'no great claims should be made in this respect' (Warnock Committee 1984: 46).

The Warnock Committee's view of maternal–foetal bonding is in sharp contrast to that of some anthropologists and psychologists who suggest that a great deal is indeed known about pre-birth bonding, and that what is known supports the view that bonding—'the intense emotional attachment between two organisms resulting from the totality of the psychophysical interactions' (Fox 1992: 74)—begins before birth and continues at parturition. Anthropologist Robin Fox states:

---

[37] One of the arguments against legalising egg (or sperm) donation was that the process introduces a third party into marriage, an institution traditionally denoting an exclusive relationship (see Chapter 2 above). Donation was thus seen as a moral wrong akin to adultery and as constituting a threat to the 'family unit'. See, eg, Tallin (1956); *MacLennan v MacLennan* 1958 SLT 12; Bartholomew (1958). The Committee did not accept these objections as sufficiently weighty to justify banning the process. See, however, *SH and others v Austria* Case No 57813/00 [2010] pp 111–12 above.

[38] See below pp 130–34.

The emotional bonding of the mother and child starts before birth. This bonding will eventually become essential to the healthy emotional development of the child as the mother's milk (in preformula days) is essential to its physical development. The evolutionary function of the preparturition bonding is presumably to prevent the mother from rejecting the infant at birth ... . One of the most important cues in mother-infant bonding is that of voice ... . It is not surprising therefore that students of neonate behaviour have noted a marked preference for the mother's voice in the newborn. (Fox 1992: 78)[39]

On the other hand, many suggest that such connections are only the result of society's 'socio-economic requisites' (Jenks 1996: 42) or cultural imperatives that have succeeded in constructing women but not men as 'natural caregivers'. Yngvesson suggests that, for law, this means that the mother–child dyad is 'naturalised' as an 'intimate, emotionally charged connection' which patriarchy manifests as 'outside' the boundary of the law, whereas fatherhood, grounded as it is property rights over the child, is fundamentally 'within' the law (Yngvesson 1997: 38–39).[40] It is ironic, then, that it is the 'naturalised' maternal bond that is automatically accorded legal status, while as we shall see below, the 'rational' paternal bond is not.

As O'Donovan observes, this means a woman in England and Wales cannot give birth and refuse motherhood, even if only for six weeks (O'Donovan 2000: 73).[41] 'Giving birth makes a woman a mother in English law. Even if the child is to be placed for adoption, or is born to a woman acting as a surrogate for another, or is not genetically related to the birth giver, parturition makes motherhood' (ibid).

In contrast, in France[42] it is perceived as a woman's right to give birth anonymously and remain permanently free from any legal bond with the child (O'Donovan 2000; Lefaucheur 2004), and the ECtHR has upheld her right to do so under Article 8 ECHR. While the child also has a right under Article 8 to know his or her identity and circumstance of birth, in *Odievre v France* the Grand Chamber held that the two had to be balanced along with the general social interest and France's law was within its margin of appreciation.[43]

The ideal situation is and will remain that even a woman who is pregnant under difficult circumstances—which characterise the situation at issue in the present and similar cases where women today have opted for anonymity when giving birth—should be able to give birth under circumstances that ensure her and her baby's safety and make it possible for the child to know the mother's identity, even if it is immediately adopted by a new family. When however, a woman for whatever reason finds that this is not an option in her case—which it may be difficult for anyone else fully to appreciate—human rights should none the less mediate in favour of her being able to give birth under circumstances that ensure her and her baby's safety, even if she insists on remaining anonymous vis-a-vis the child. It would be plainly inhumane to invoke human rights to force a woman in this situation to choose between abortion or a clandestine birth; the latter always holds a potential of jeopardising the mother's and/or the child's health and, if worst comes to worst, could be life threatening and/or result in the child being stillborn. ((2004) EHRR, para OIII15)

---

[39] For a feminist view of this connection, see Rothman (1989).
[40] See also Diduck (1998, 1999a).
[41] A woman may not consent to adoption or to a parental order under the HFEA 2008 in the first six weeks after giving birth. See below pp 130–34, 139–41.
[42] And Italy and Luxembourg: see *Odievre v France* ECtHR (2004) EHRR 43; [2003] 1 FCR 621, para 19.
[43] There was a strong dissenting minority judgment in this case.

Q In the case of *Re B (Adoption by One Natural Parent to Exclusion of Other)* [2001] I FLR 589 CA, Hale LJ stated that carrying and giving birth to a child is sufficient to create a 'family life' (for the purposes of Article 8) between a woman and child even if they are separated at birth (para 38) and this finding was approved by the House of Lords even though the decision was overturned on other grounds ([2001] UKHL 70; [2002] I FLR 196 at para 30 per Lord Nicholls). How, if at all, does this decision reflect either of the views on maternal–foetal bonding? How does the French law do so? Which do you prefer?

Q Do you agree with the law's resolution of the priority between genetic and gestational mothers? What arguments can you make for or against section 33(1) HFEA?

All of the arguments above assume that the law should designate only one woman as the child's mother. An alternative view is that the quest for one exclusive legal mother simply reproduces the 'sexual family' and the heteronormativity of law in which parenthood cannot be understood outside of the heterosexual paradigm. What if we were to 'recognise the maternity of both the genetic mother and the gestational mother and involve them both in the child's social rearing' (Kandel 1994: 168).[44] Indeed, inter-partner egg sharing is becoming increasingly popular among lesbian partners who are doing just this and research with them demonstrates that while it may be difficult sometimes for them and their children to embrace the idea of two *mothers*, they have far less difficulty in embracing the idea that there are two carers, each involved in the activity of 'mothering' (Diduck 2007).

The Adoption and Children Act 2002 and the Civil Partnership Act 2004 seem to acknowledge this legally, as does the new status provision for female parents in the HFEA 2008. The HFEA requires the civil partner of a woman who receives treatment to be designated as the female parent of the child unless she did not consent to that treatment. It also permits a woman to be designated as a 'female parent' of a child born to a woman who receives treatment, if they agree 'female parenthood conditions'.

42 Woman in civil partnership at time of treatment

(1) If at the time of the placing in her of the embryo or the sperm and eggs or of her artificial insemination, W was a party to a civil partnership, then subject to section 45(2) to (4), the other party to the civil partnership is to be treated as a parent of the child unless it is shown that she did not consent to the placing in W of the embryo or the sperm and eggs or to her artificial insemination (as the case may be).

43 Treatment provided to woman who agrees that second woman to be parent

If no man is treated by virtue of section 35 as the father of the child and no woman is treated by virtue of section 42 as a parent of the child but—

(a) the embryo or the sperm and eggs were placed in W, or she was artificially inseminated, in the course of treatment services provided in the United Kingdom by a person to whom a licence applies,

(b) at the time when the embryo or the sperm and eggs were placed in W, or W was artificially

---

[44] See Kandel (1994) further for anthropological research on 'shared mothering'. See also Langdridge and Blythe (2001) and Jackson (2006).

inseminated, the agreed female parenthood conditions (as set out in section 44) were met in relation to another woman, in relation to treatment provided to W under that licence, and

(c) the other woman remained alive at that time,

then, subject to section 45(2) to (4), the other woman is to be treated as a parent of the child.

44 The agreed female parenthood conditions

(1) The agreed female parenthood conditions referred to in section 43(b) are met in relation to another woman ("P") in relation to treatment provided to W under a licence if, but only if,—

(a) P has given the person responsible a notice stating that P consents to P being treated as a parent of any child resulting from treatment provided to W under the licence,

(b) W has given the person responsible a notice stating that W agrees to P being so treated,

(c) neither W nor P has, since giving notice under paragraph (a) or (b), given the person responsible notice of the withdrawal of P's or W's consent to P being so treated,

(d) W has not, since the giving of the notice under paragraph (b), given the person responsible—

    (i)   a further notice under that paragraph stating that W consents to a woman other than P being treated as a parent of any resulting child, or

    (ii) a notice under section 37(1)(b) stating that W consents to a man being treated as the father of any resulting child, and

(e) W and P are not within prohibited degrees of relationship in relation to each other.

On the one hand, these provisions seem to challenge the 'sexual family' and law's heteronormativity. Yet, as McCandless and Sheldon (2010)[45] point out:

> [T]he sexual family model continues to resonate in a steadfast resistance to the possibility that a child can have two 'mothers' (or indeed [as we shall see] two 'fathers'). The two parent model thus also appears to encompass an assumption of what might be loosely termed 'parental dimorphism', by which we mean that the two parents are seen as occupying complementary yet different legal roles. ... The 2008 Act [HFEA 2008] further provides that references elsewhere in law to 'father' should be taken to include 'female parent'.
>
> This points to another significant dimension of the sexual family: that it is rooted in the idea of complementarity, assuming a fundamental difference in how parental status is acquired. ... motherhood is firmly grounded in gestation (and this holds significance per se, rather than merely standing as a proxy for a genetic link). Law's interest in genetic links has thus tended to be focussed on fathers. Indeed, ... the possibility of acquiring either motherhood or 'female parenthood' through a genetic link is explicitly addressed and excluded in the 2008 Act [s 47].[46] The grounds for such exclusion are not readily evident. No rationale was given for it in the explanatory notes accompanying the 2008 Act and there is no discussion of it in the Parliamentary debates, suggesting that it either passed unnoticed or was felt to be entirely uncontroversial. Two explanations were offered for the provision during the course of our interviews. First, and almost certainly most significantly, was the perceived need to avoid any future possibility that two women might each claim to be recognised as the mother of a child citing, respectively, gestational and genetic connections. Such claims would be most likely to arise in the context of a lesbian couple who wish both to enjoy a biological connection with a future child and therefore choose to create an embryo from one partner's ova, which will be implanted in the other partner. ... [R]ecognising two women as parents in this way would [also] leave open the possibility that a third party might also attempt to assert legal parenthood. Second, it was suggested to us that the provision might reflect concerns about mitochondrial DNA donation, seeking to

---

[45] See also Diduck (2007).

[46] S 47 provides that a woman is not to be treated as the parent of a child merely by virtue of egg donation.

head off the possibility that a donor might assert some parental claims on this basis. While such a provision appears unnecessary given the clear definitions of legal motherhood and female parenthood provided in the statute, this section might be taken as providing what one inter-viewee suggested to be 'clarity' and, another, a 'belt and braces' approach.

Whether legally necessary or not, this explicit rebuttal of any possibility that female parent-hood might be grounded in genetic links serves to emphasise the distinction between how we think about motherhood and fatherhood: while genetic connections are very relevant to estab-lishing fatherhood, legal motherhood is a status emphatically grounded in gestation.

(McCandless and Sheldon 2010: 193–94, references omitted)

Q How would you determine the legal motherhood of a child? How does this provision reconcile the arguments of the Austrian government raised in the *SH and others* case discussed above? How, if at all, can the law accommodate more than one legal mother? There is a large body of work on this: see, for example, Jackson (2006), Harrison (1995), Wallbank (2004, 2010), Lind and Hewitt (2009), Jones (2010, 2011), Smith (2010), Probert (2004), and Langdridge and Blyth (2001). This issue arises again in the context of adoption, where the law has difficulty reconciling the privacy of adoptive families with continued contact with birth mothers in 'open adoptions' (see below and Yngvesson 1997), and surrogacy (see below).

In summary, then, in terms of the HFEA 1990 together with the HFEA 2008 (eg section 33(1), genetic relationships do not necessarily create legal relationships between women and children, but gestational relationships always do. These Acts also create a brand new legal status for some women, seemingly based upon intention alone: female parenthood. Finally, the Acts limit to two the number of parents a child may legally have. As McCan-dless and Sheldon observe in their review of the reform of the HFEA 1990, other jurisdictions permit more than two parents to be named on a child's birth certificate, '[y]et in the UK, despite the lack of political or cultural consensus on what actually makes someone a parent, the idea that a child may benefit from having more than two parents appears to have been too radical to have merited any discussion' (McCandless and Sheldon 2010: 193).

Sometimes the woman who carries the foetus to term does not intend to rear the child after its birth, and may be carrying the child as part of a business arrangement or as an act of generosity toward another person. In this case, we see legal motherhood determined by intention and social parenthood.

Surrogacy

The persistence of the exclusivity of parenting within the ideal of the nuclear family has also led to a search for a 'real' mother in the context of surrogacy arrangements. We have seen how the law resolves the genetic/gestational mother choice in favour of gestational mothers in assisted-reproduction contexts, but in surrogacy arrangements, the choice is between the gestational mother and the intended social, or commissioning, mother (who might, of course, also be the genetic mother!). Complicating the legal issue further is the social understanding of motherhood and surrogacy, as revealed in the language of the discourse itself. Morgan (1989), for example, highlights the social understandings of motherhood revealed by naming the carrying mother instead of the commissioning mother as the surrogate. This seems odd, given the priority ascribed to gestational mothers in other contexts. But Morgan defends this use of language, recognising that it is another example of 'the use and elision of language to appear to make one set of circumstances more natural, thereby less objectionable, therefore commanding support among right-thinking people' (Morgan 1989: 60). The contrary view would be 'that it is the person ... who takes and rears the child rather than she who gives birth who is properly the sur-rogate. The woman giving birth is *the* mother, not the surrogate' (ibid: 56). Surrogacy in this way may 'fragment motherhood' (Cook et al 2003a: 4) conceptually, but as we shall see, the law does not tolerate this fragmentation.

Q Does one's identification of the 'real' mother depend upon one's definition of motherhood or mothering?

Surrogacy can occur where the surrogate receives sperm from the commissioning father, or it can occur where she receives an embryo from both commissioning parents.[47] It is only when surrogacy has been arranged through a licensed clinic and the surrogate has either been artificially inseminated or implanted with an embryo or sperm and egg that the HFEA is engaged, however. As we have seen, regardless of the surrogate's intention, she is, pursuant to section 33(1) of the HFEA 2008, the legal mother of the child. In order to give legal effect to the surrogacy arrangement, then, the intended social mother must either adopt the child[48] or she can apply together with her partner under section 54 of the HFEA 2008 for a parental order.[49] The relevant parts of section 54 read as follows:

54 (1) On an application made by two people ("the applicants"), the court may make an order providing for a child to be treated in law as the child of the applicants if—

(a) the child has been carried by a woman who is not one of the applicants, as a result of the placing in her of an embryo or sperm and eggs or her artificial insemination,

(b) the gametes of at least one of the applicants were used to bring about the creation of the embryo, and

(c) the conditions in subsections (2) to (8) are satisfied.

(2) The applicants must be—

(a) husband and wife,

(b) civil partners of each other, or

(c) two persons who are living as partners in an enduring family relationship and are not within prohibited degrees of relationship in relation to each other.

(3) Except in a case falling within subsection (11), the applicants must apply for the order during the period of 6 months beginning with the day on which the child is born.

(4) At the time of the application and the making of the order—

(a) the child's home must be with the applicants, and

(b) either or both of the applicants must be domiciled in the United Kingdom or in the Channel Islands or the Isle of Man.

---

[47] Statistics on the frequency and success of surrogacy arrangements are difficult to compile due to the informal nature of many surrogacy arrangements.

[48] As in *Re MW (Adoption: Surrogacy)* [1995] 2 FLR 759.

[49] As in *Re Q (Parental Order)* [1996] 1 FLR 369.

(5) At the time of the making of the order both the applicants must have attained the age of 18.

(6) The court must be satisfied that both—

(a) the woman who carried the child, and

(b) any other person who is a parent of the child but is not one of the applicants (including any man who is the father by virtue of section 35 or 36 or any woman who is a parent by virtue of section 42 or 43),

have freely, and with full understanding of what is involved, agreed unconditionally to the making of the order.

(7) Subsection (6) does not require the agreement of a person who cannot be found or is incapable of giving agreement; and the agreement of the woman who carried the child is ineffective for the purpose of that subsection if given by her less than six weeks after the child's birth.

(8) The court must be satisfied that no money or other benefit (other than for expenses reasonably incurred) has been given or received by either of the applicants for or in consideration of—

(a) the making of the order,

(b) any agreement required by subsection (6),

(c) the handing over of the child to the applicants, or

(d) the making of arrangements with a view to the making of the order,

unless authorised by the court.[50]

The effect of a parental order is the same as an adoption order: the parental status of the birth parents is extinguished in favour of the commissioning parents. And note that there must be two parents. A parental order may not be made in favour of one person. An order in favour of two same-sex parents would adopt the language of parents, rather than 'mother' and 'father'.

The HFEA 2008 must be read in conjunction with the Surrogacy Arrangements Act 1985 which prohibits third parties from becoming involved in commercial surrogacy arrangements[51] and provides that no surrogacy arrangement or contract is enforceable by or against any of the parties.[52] Thus any arrangement concerning the care of the child after birth is enforceable only if it is construed as a consent within the meaning of section 54 HFEA 2008, rather than as a contractual term agreed when the arrangement was originally made.[53]

English law thus displays an almost reluctant acceptance of surrogacy, but England and Wales are not alone in their apparent ambivalence. There is little international consensus on the legal treatment of surrogacy. As Cook et al, point out, some jurisdictions 'ban surrogacy altogether. Some have opted for partial bans while introducing rules to designate and regulate what is permissible. Some have voluntary guidelines and some have eschewed any form of regulation at all' (Cook et al 2003a: 2). They say that these differences might be evidence of the 'sense of profound anxiety and ambivalence' (ibid: 4) that surrogacy evokes.

---

[50] See *Re S (Parental Order)* [2010] 1FLR 1156 and *Re X (Foreign Surrogacy)* [2009] 2 FCR 312 where the courts retrospectively approved payments in excess of expenses because neither the children nor the women appeared, in these cases to have been exploited.

[51] S 2 Surrogacy Arrangements Act 1985.

[52] S 1A.

[53] For a good review of the law of surrogacy, see Hale LJ's judgment in the case of *Briody v St Helens and Knowsley Health Authority* [2001] EWCA Civ 1010; [2002] QB 856; [2001] 2 FLR 1094.

Surrogacy is problematic for traditional notions of 'mother', 'father' and 'family' when it introduces a third (or even fourth) party into reproduction, when it introduces contractual or 'public' arrangements into 'private' affairs and when it fragments motherhood. Surrogacy makes motherhood negotiable and confounds both social and biological bases of claims to parenthood. (ibid: 4)

Many of these concerns were highlighted by the Warnock Report (1984) which only grudgingly accepted that surrogacy might be acceptable in some cases. In many ways, however, these are real concerns. Surrogacy might indeed disrupt traditional ideas of 'family' and of motherhood. Probert, for example, cites research that shows that most surrogates do not form attachments with the child they bear (Probert 2004a: 276) but that many expect to play some role in the child's life as a special aunt or godmother (ibid: 277).

Q Would these disruptions to 'motherhood' or 'family' be consistent with the welfare of children? With the welfare of other members of the 'family'? With changing family practices?

There are other objections one could have to surrogacy.[54] One could, for example, object to it on the grounds that it is exploitative and simply reduces women to the status of incubators—Margaret Atwood's chilling novel, *The Handmaid's Tale* (1985), presents a dystopic vision of established and enforced surrogacy. Conversely, one could view surrogacy as one of the most altruistic acts that one woman can perform for another, and say that to argue that it is 'unnatural' relies upon patriarchal views of motherhood, 'maternal instincts' and 'natural' connections.[55] Or one could put forward arguments focusing on autonomy and say that a woman should be entitled to do as she wishes with her own body.[56] Finally, one may be concerned that surrogacy renders the resulting child a commodity to be 'sold' or given away.[57] Surrogacy is an issue that arouses strong feelings in many, although it may be the case that it is not so shocking to the public consciousness as it was when the first cases were reported in the press[58] in the 1980s resulting in the quick passage of the Surrogacy Arrangements Act 1985.[59]

Q How, if at all, would you regulate surrogacy arrangements? To whom would you assign the status of legal motherhood? What if the surrogacy arrangement breaks down? In such cases the court will apply the welfare principle in considering whether to make a residence order in favour of one of the parties.[60]

---

[54] See generally, Jackson (2001: ch 6); and Brazier et al (1998).

[55] But see Ragone (2003).

[56] See Jackson (2001).

[57] On the arguments generally, see Jackson (2001: ch 6) and sources cited therein; Rothman (1989); Fox (1992); Freeman (1989a); Zipper and Sevenhuijsen (1987); Marshall (1994); Smart (1989); Cook et al (2003b).

[58] In England, see *Re C* [1985] FLR 846; in the USA, see *In the Matter of Baby M* (1988) 537 A 2d 1227 (NJ Sup Ct). Brazier et al reported that the public has come to accept surrogacy (Brazier et al 1998: para 4.5).

[59] The Warnock Report (1984) also recommended criminalisation of commercial surrogacy. Warnock's view of the arguments against surrogacy can be found in paras 8.10–8.12 of the Report. The Brazier Report (Brazier et al 1998) made a number of recommendations for increased regulation of surrogacy and for new legislation, but none has been implemented.

[60] See eg *A v C* [1985] FLR 445; *Re P (Surrogacy: Residence)* [2008] Fam Law 18; *Re N (a child)* [2007] EWCA Civ 1053.

Q To what degree does the state regulate the different types of biological motherhood? Do you see evidence of motherhood being fragmented in this regulation?

Non-biological Mothers

As we have seen, section 54 of the HFEA 2008 enables legal motherhood to be assigned to a woman who may have no biological connection at all with a child, provided that her husband or male partner has such a connection. In this case, it may be said that the intention to become a mother, or social motherhood, is prioritised over biology. Another situation in which the intention to become a mother is given legal effect is adoption, a legal relationship created by the Adoption and Children Act 2002. In addition, there are other ways in which the law recognises one's intention to become a mother, but creates something short of full parental status. These include residence orders which confer parental responsibility,[61] guardianship, special guardianship and, to a lesser extent, fostering. We will deal first with adoption. While we proceed with our discussion of adoption in the context of motherhood, much of it relates to legal fatherhood as well. Adoption creates the legal status of 'parent', but where there are differences between mothers and fathers in the context of adoption, we will highlight them.

Adoption[62]

Adoption in English law is entirely a creature of statute, and a relatively recent one at that. There is no common law equivalent, and adoption may not be effected in any way other than by a court order. English law does not, therefore, recognise private adoption agreements, or any form of 'customary adoption'.[63] Adoption results in the legal transfer of all rights and responsibilities from one family to another.[64] Section 67 of the Adoption and Children Act 2002 reads as follows:

(1) An adopted person is to be treated in law as if born as the child of the adopters or adopter.

(2) An adopted person is the legitimate child of the adopters or adopter and, if adopted by—
(a) a couple, or
(b) one of a couple under section 51(2),
is to be treated as the child of the relationship of the couple in question.

(3) An adopted person—
(a) if adopted by one of a couple under section 51(2), is to be treated in law as not being the child of any person other than the adopter and the other one in the couple, and

---

[61] S 12 Children Act 1989. See Chapter 8 below.

[62] The Adoption and Children Act 2002, together with the Adoptions with a Foreign Element Regulations 2005; The Adoptions Agencies Regulations 2005 SI 2005/392; The Restrictions on the Preparation of Adoption Reports Regulations 2005 SI 2005/1711; The Suitability of Adopters Regulations 2005 SI 2005/1712; Adoption: National Minimum Standards (DoE 2011) and the Hague Convention on the Protection of Children and Co-operation in respect of Intercountry Adoption regulate intercountry adoptions. We will not discuss these in this chapter, but for a good review see Bainham (2005: 767–74) and sources cited therein.

[63] For a discussion of aboriginal child-rearing and adoption philosophies in Australia see Butler (1989).

[64] Adoptive parent–child relationships are also included in the list of prohibited relationships between people lawfully allowed to marry (see Marriage Act 1949, Sch 1 and Chapter 2 above).

(b) in any other case, is to be treated in law, subject to subsection (4),[65] as not being the child of any person other than the adopters or adopter;

but this section does not affect any reference in this Act to a person's natural parent or to any other natural relationship.

The first adoption legislation in England and Wales was the Adoption Act 1926.[66] It was said to evidence a desire to give legal effect to those de facto relationships that had developed as a result of family upheaval caused by war and industrialisation (Barton and Douglas 1995), to provide children for childless couples and to relieve the stigma upon unmarried women who had children; in short, it was seen as a solution to the problem of what to do with illegitimate children (Lewis 2004: 237). Over the next five decades, however, construction of the problem shifted and with it the interests to be prioritised by the legislation shifted as well. In the period after the Second World War, for example, adoption was partly aimed to serve children's interests by enabling them to be raised in 'proper families' and partly to serve adult interests by enabling them to form 'proper families' (Spensky 1992). And by the 1970s social priorities had shifted yet again. The Adoption Act 1976 appeared to prioritise the interests of children over those of adults, but partly because of the changing nature of the pool of adoptable children, a new interest came to the fore, that of the state (Lewis 2004: 238). Thus, what were once two policy objectives vying for supremacy at different historical moments became three, and by 2002 the third seemed to have won: adoption came to be seen as a solution to the problems of the childcare system (ibid).

> **Q** What changing social conditions may have brought about these policy shifts? Do changing notions of acceptable motherhood or acceptable families have any role to play in this thinking? Spensky (1992), for example, argues that in the 1950s homes for unmarried mothers and the practice of placing their children for adoption in 'proper' nuclear families functioned to 'legitimate' all three parties: the child, the childless married couple and the unmarried mother.[67]

Further, the priority given to the interests of either birth parents or adoptive parents has also shifted over time. Lewis notes that the Houghton Report, which preceded the Adoption Act 1976, is said to have favoured adoption and the interests of adoptive parents over those of birth parents (Lewis 2004: 240). By the mid-1980s, she says, favour had swung back toward birth families (ibid: 242). And in the 1990s, a White Paper (Department of Health et al, 1993) and the Adoption Bill 1996 that followed it reflected a mixed view, combining the then Conservative government's commitment to 'family values', family privacy, swift and punitive intervention for families deemed to have failed, and profound suspicion of professions and professional ideology (Lewis 2004: 244).[68] The focus of the Adoption and Children Act 2002, in turn, appears to prioritise the interests of yet another party, the state, over those of adopters or birth families.

Leading up to the Adoption and Children Act 2002 was the Prime Minister's Review

---

[65] Adoption by natural parent.

[66] For an excellent review of the history of adoption in England and Wales, see Cretney (2003a: ch 17).

[67] See also Reeves (1993) who outlines the role played by moral, economic and spiritual discourses to encourage unmarried women to give their children for adoption.

[68] For a discussion of this Bill and the consultations that led to it, see the first edition of this book.

of Adoption (PIU 2000).[69] This focused clearly upon the potential adoption of children who were 'looked after' by local authorities, rather than upon the adoption of babies or of children by step-parents or other relatives. Based upon the assumption that permanence and stability promoted the welfare of looked-after children, it promoted adoption, rather than long-term foster care, as the preferred method of achieving it (Lewis 2004). It aimed to increase the number of looked-after children who were adopted, and recommended changes to social work policy and practice and to the law.

The White Paper that followed[70] stated unequivocally that the government's aim was to promote the wider use of adoption (para 1.13).[71] Included among its recommendations were: to create national standards for adoption services, including a national register of adopters and timescales within which decisions for most children should be reached (paras 4.5 and 4.6); to ensure that the welfare of children was paramount in all decisions about their future (para 4.14); to provide a range of permanency options in addition to adoption and long-term fostering (para 5.2); to increase the pool of potential adopters (paras 6.16–6.19); and to provide after-adoption support for both adopted people (paras 6.41–6.46) and adopters (paras 6.26–6.40). These recommendations have, for the most part, been incorporated into the Adoption and Children Act 2002,[72] sometimes in controversial ways. What follows is not a detailed review of the Act and the procedures for adoption, but rather an overview which focuses on these recommendations, the assumptions upon which they are based and the legal form required to implement them.[73]

The Goal—Increasing Adoption[74]

It is clear that the government believed that adoption is beneficial for children, or at least that it is better than being looked after by a local authority. This confidence in the benefits of adoption was expressed in the White Paper:

> 1.12 … research shows that children who are adopted when they are over six months old generally make very good progress through their childhood and into adulthood and do considerably better than children who have remained in the care system throughout most of their childhood. These children are also better adjusted than children who grow up in institutions. Adoption of older children has positive, though to varying degrees, effects on all aspects of their development. (White Paper 2000)

Commentators, however, note that the research about the benefits of adoption is ambiguous at best.[75] Beihal et al (2009) studied the outcomes and feelings of children in long-term foster care and those who had been adopted. They concluded that 'despite the lack of legal security in long-term foster placements, 'stable long term foster care may be very successful in providing emotional security and positive outcomes for children' on measures of emotional and behavioural difficulties and participation and progress in school (Beihal

---

[69] For a discussion of the Review, see Barton (2000).

[70] Secretary of State for Health (2000). Hereafter called 'White Paper'.

[71] Point 2 of the Executive Summary sets a target of increasing by 40% by 2004–05 the number of looked after children adopted, and to exceed this, if possible, by a 50% increase (Secretary of State for Health 2000: 5).

[72] And associated legislation, regulations and guidelines. See discussion below.

[73] For a detailed review of adoption law, see Bainham (2005: ch 7); Harris-Short and Miles (2011: 13).

[74] There were 4,655 adoption orders made in 2009. This represents a period of relative stability in numbers after a 9.7% fall between 2005 and 2006 and a steady fall during the 1980s and 1990s (ONS 2010c: Adoption).

[75] See, eg, Thoburn (2003); Eekelaar (2003b); Lewis (2004); cf Triseliotis (2002).

et al 2009: 5). In effect, the research does seem to show that permanence and stability are important to a child's welfare but it is open to question whether adoption ought to be presumed to be the preferable means of providing this permanence.

Finally, given that Article 8 ECHR has been said to protect one's right to know one's identity,[76] the legal form of adoption, the complete replacement of one family with another, may be out of step with human rights ideals. It may also be out step with changing family practices. As Lewis comments:

> In the increasingly messy world of family formation and change, children may have a number of mother figures and father figures. Furthermore, the messiness is no longer hidden and gives rise to less and less stigma. In this context, the notion of giving a child a new legal status in a new family looks increasingly anachronistic. (Lewis 2004: 251)

It may be these shifting family practices which have influenced recent social work practice and statutory guidance on adoptions, however. Permanency and stability are still the goals for children's placements, yet privileging the adoption placement over other arrangements promotes a version of the traditional, private nuclear family with all of its attendant responsibilities for the care and (financial) support of children, and effects a 'wholesale transfer in legal terms'[77] of family status. Yet, as we shall see, many adoptions are nonetheless able to take into account the increasingly complicated ways in which family lives are lived.

National Standards

Other than certain relatives of a child or people acting pursuant to an order of the High Court, it is only an approved adoption agency that may make arrangements for adoption.[78] Not only are adoption agencies, ie all local authorities and voluntary adoption societies registered under the Care Standards Act 2000,[79] exclusively *permitted* to arrange adoptions, they are *required* to maintain adoption services.[80] In order to achieve the goal of increasing the number of looked-after children who are adopted, the White Paper announced the perceived need for further and tighter regulation of the way adoption agencies do this.

> 4.5 The National [Adoption] Standards set out what children, prospective adopters, adoptive parents and birth families can expect from the adoption process, and the responsibilities of adoption agencies and councils, so that all parties receive a fair and consistent service where they live. They are underpinned by a set of values, which stress the importance to each child of having a permanent family, where they are safe. They put the child's needs at the centre of the adoption process.

> 4.6 The Standards include timescales within which decisions for most children should be reached and action taken to ensure that children are not kept waiting for a family. (White Paper 2000)

Section 3 of the Adoption and Children Act 2002 sets out the basic requirements for the facilities and services that adoption agencies must provide. The way in which adoption

---

[76] See eg *Odievre v France* above.
[77] *Re B (a child)* (adoption order) [2001] EWCA Civ [2001] 2 FLR 26, per Hale LJ, para 24.
[78] Adoption and Children Act 2002 s 92.
[79] Ibid, s 2.
[80] Ibid, s 3.

services are discharged is regulated by guidelines[81] and a number of statutory instruments.[82] The most recent National Adoption Standards (DfE 2011b) take up issues such as determining the child's wishes and feelings (Standard 1), promoting a child's positive behaviour and relationships, health and educational attainment (Standards 3, 5 and 7), recruiting adopters and matching children with them (Standards 10 and 13), and the involvement of birth families in the adoption plan (Standards 8 and 12). Statutory Guidance on Adoptions (DfE 2011a) directs permanence planning by requiring local authorities to plan for a permanent home for the child at the four-month case review,[83] to set clear timescales for achieving the plan and, where adoption has been identified as the plan, to ensure that the adoption panel will make its recommendation within two months of the decision being taken (DfE 2011a: ch 2, paras 1 and 2). All children who are looked after by local authorities for four months must, therefore, be considered for adoption. Guidelines are also set for clear timescales and criteria to be applied at all stages of the adoption process, including preparing, assessing and approving prospective adopters (ibid: ch 3), matching and proposing a placement (ibid: ch 4), reviewing placements (ibid: ch 5), safeguarding and permitting access to adoption records (ibid: ch 6), issues of post-adoption contact (ibid: ch 7) and supporting adopters (ibid: ch 9).

Adoption and Welfare

The Adoption and Children Act 2002 brings adoption law into line with the principles in the Children Act 1989. Section 1 implements the paramountcy principle, the principle of no delay and the no-order principle:

1 Considerations applying to the exercise of powers

(1) This section applies whenever a court or adoption agency is coming to a decision relating to the adoption of a child.

(2) The paramount consideration of the court or adoption agency must be the child's welfare, throughout his life.

(3) The court or adoption agency must at all times bear in mind that, in general, any delay in coming to the decision is likely to prejudice the child's welfare.

(4) The court or adoption agency must have regard to the following matters (among others)—

(a) the child's ascertainable wishes and feelings regarding the decision (considered in the light of the child's age and understanding),
(b) the child's particular needs,
(c) the likely effect on the child (throughout his life) of having ceased to be a member of the original family and become an adopted person,
(d) the child's age, sex, background and any of the child's characteristics which the court or agency considers relevant,
(e) any harm (within the meaning of the Children Act 1989 (c 41)) which the child has suffered or is at risk of suffering,
(f) the relationship which the child has with relatives, and with any other person in relation to whom the court or agency considers the relationship to be relevant, including—

---

[81] DfE (2011a).
[82] There are a number of statutory instruments related to adoption. See in particular The Adoption Agencies Regulations SI 2005/389
[83] Four weeks plus three months. See Chapter 14 below.

(i)   the likelihood of any such relationship continuing and the value to the child of its doing so,

(ii) the ability and willingness of any of the child's relatives, or of any such person, to provide the child with a secure environment in which the child can develop, and otherwise to meet the child's needs,

(iii) the wishes and feelings of any of the child's relatives, or of any such person, regarding the child.

(5) In placing the child for adoption, the adoption agency must give due consideration to the child's religious persuasion, racial origin and cultural and linguistic background.

(6) The court or adoption agency must always consider the whole range of powers available to it in the child's case (whether under this Act or the Children Act 1989); and the court must not make any order under this Act unless it considers that making the order would be better for the child than not doing so.

The welfare test applies at all stages of the adoption process, from choosing prospective adopters to placing a child for adoption to making the order itself and any conditions for contact to attach to it. We shall consider the effect of the welfare test at each of these stages, beginning with the paramountcy of welfare at the placement and order stages.

This section represents a significant change from the previous legislation. Under the Adoption Act 1976 welfare was only the court's 'first' consideration when making an adoption order and it was not an explicit factor in deciding whether to 'free' a child for adoption.[84] Neither an adoption order (without first freeing) nor a freeing order could be granted unless the birth parents consented or the court dispensed with their consent on the basis that they were withholding it 'unreasonably'. According to the leading case, *Re W*,[85] the test was an objective one. The court was required to determine whether a reasonable parent in the same situation would withhold agreement to the adoption of her child.

But who is the reasonable mother? Perhaps the reasonable mother ought *never* to agree to give up her child, or perhaps she ought *always* to be supremely altruistic and agree to give up her child whenever a better chance for that child's future can be found. Perhaps reasonable behaviour lies somewhere between these two extremes. In any case, the legal determination of reasonableness was potentially problematic. Our comments in Chapter 1 about the gendered nature of the liberal, reasonable individual may be complicated further by research suggesting that 'reasonableness' may also be race- and class-specific. Poor or indigenous mothers may be constructed as unreasonable if they 'cling' to their children, and as reasonable if they readily give up their children (Kline 1995)[86] to be 'properly' cared for. In contrast, middle-class, white women may be more easily stigmatised as 'bad' mothers if they contradict their 'maternal instincts' by giving up their children too easily, and classed as reasonable if they put up a fight. The 'unreasonableness' test was objectionable, therefore, on a number of grounds.

The Adoption and Children Act 2002 has dealt with this issue by incorporating the paramountcy test not only when the court is deciding to make the adoption order, but also

---

[84] It was, however, considered as part of the reasonableness test: see below and discussion in Bainham (2005: 291–96) and Choudhry (2003). 'Freeing' for adoption had been the process under the 1976 Act by which Local Authorities obtained the court's approval to place a child for adoption.

[85] [1971] AC 682.

[86] In the context of the reasonable father, see *Re D* [1977] AC 602.

when deciding whether or not to dispense with consent to make a placement order. Placement orders replace freeing orders.

21 Placement orders

(1) A placement order is an order made by the court authorising a local authority to place a child for adoption with any prospective adopters who may be chosen by the authority.

(2) The court may not make a placement order in respect of a child unless—

(a) the child is subject to a care order,
(b) the court is satisfied that the conditions in Section 31(2) of the 1989 Act (conditions for making a care order) are met, or
(c) the child has no parent or guardian.

(3) The court may only make a placement order if, in the case of each parent or guardian of the child, the court is satisfied—

(a) that the parent or guardian has consented to the child being placed for adoption with any prospective adopters who may be chosen by the local authority and has not withdrawn the consent, or
(b) that the parent's or guardian's consent should be dispensed with.

This subsection is subject to section 52 (parental etc consent).

(4) A placement order continues in force until—

(a) it is revoked under section 24,
(b) an adoption order is made in respect of the child, or
(c) the child marries or attains the age of 18 years.

52 Parental etc consent

(1) The court cannot dispense with the consent of any parent or guardian [including special guardian] of a child to the child being placed for adoption or to the making of an adoption order in respect of the child unless the court is satisfied that—

(a) the parent or guardian cannot be found or is incapable of giving consent, or
(b) the welfare of the child requires the consent to be dispensed with.

(2) The following provisions apply to references in this chapter to any parent or guardian of a child giving or withdrawing—

(a) consent to the placement of a child for adoption, or
(b) consent to the making of an adoption order (including a future adoption order).

(3) Any consent given by the mother to the making of an adoption order is ineffective if it is given less than six weeks after the child's birth.

(4) The withdrawal of any consent to the placement of a child for adoption, or of any consent given under section 20, is ineffective if it is given after an application for an adoption order is made.

(5) 'Consent' means consent given unconditionally and with full understanding of what is involved; but a person may consent to adoption without knowing the identity of the persons in whose favour the order will be made.

(6) 'Parent' (except in subsections (9) and (10) below) means a parent having parental responsibility.

Does this mean that once adoption is found to best serve the welfare of the child, parental consent will always be dispensed with? According to recent authorities, the answer is unclear, but might be yes, even though the decisions are not phrased in that way. Rather, the matter seems to be resolved by the welfare of the child being subsumed within her or her parents' Article 8 rights.[87] In *Re P (a child)*[88] the Court of Appeal found that a parent's Article 8 rights to respect for family life were engaged by an application to place a child for adoption and that 'any adoption or placement order made without parental consent in accordance with section 52(1)(b) of the 2002 Act, must be proportionate to the legitimate aim of protecting the welfare of the child' (per Wall J, para 119). The way in which the court then conducted its assessment of welfare, however, stressing as it did the child's welfare *over his whole life*, seems to suggest, as Harris-Short and Miles observe (2011: 906), that meeting this welfare test, in effect, is all that is necessary to dispense with consent. Harris-Short and Miles worry that this approach may not comply with Strasbourg jurisprudence, despite the court's reference to the ECHR (ibid: 907).[89] This is so, even though in *EH v X London Borough Council*[90] the Court of Appeal confirmed that in applications for placement orders courts must consider explicitly the Children Act 1989, the section 1(4) welfare factors under the Adoption and Children Act 2002, the rights of the parents and children under the ECHR, and proportionality (per Wall LJ, para 98). It said that the trial court's findings that

> The interests of these children is to approve the local authority's care plan for adoption and make care orders and I do so. The welfare of these children positively demands and requires that the consent of each parent to adoption be dispensed with. I accordingly dispense with their consent on the basis that it is in the interests of these children to be placed for adoption and I accordingly make placement orders in respect of both children (para 97)

were 'wholly inadequate' (para 97). Finally, in *Re S (Adoption Order or Special Guardianship Order)*[91] the Court of Appeal also considered that the parties' Article 8 rights must be taken into account. The court, it said 'must be satisfied that its order is a 'proportionate response to the problem' (per Wall LJ, para 49), and that if all else was equal after conducting the welfare test, the appropriate order was the one that interfered with family life least.

> **Q** Some argue that the welfare test is too broad a test to use for dispensing with consent to placement for adoption or for adoption itself; one can always find a 'better' family situation particularly if the birth parents are poor. Do you agree? See on this Choudhry (2003) who reviews the case law and academic literature on interpretations of the paramountcy principle in the light of the Human Rights Act. She concludes that the current practice in the context of adoption, which acts to sever the legal relationship of birth relatives, may not be consistent with Article 8 ECHR but proposes that a reinterpretation is possible which would be consistent with it. This approach, she says, requires an equal balancing of the

---

[87] For a discussion of rights and welfare, see Chapter 9 below.
[88] [2008] EWCA Civ 535; [2008] 2 FLR 625.
[89] See *Johansen v Norway* case no 17383/90 (1997). See also on this Choudhry and Herring (2010).
[90] [2010] EWCA Civ 344; [2010] 2 FLR 661.
[91] [2007] EWCA Civ 54.

interests and claims of all prior to the elevation of any one interest. See also Choudhry and Herring (2010).

Q In *M v FH (A Local Authority)* [2011] EWCA Civ 273; [2011] 2 FLR 123 (*sub nom Re A (Father: Knowledge of Child's Birth)*), the Court of Appeal held that the courts would not sanction the withholding of information about the existence of a child from his or her parent, or dispense with service of notice on that parent or, in effect, dispense with that parent's consent to adoption, in anything other than exceptional circumstances where there were strong countervailing factors. In this case, the mother wished to have the child adopted without notifying her husband of the birth. She claimed that her husband had mental health problems which rendered his behaviour unpredictable and violent. Is this a different test from the one above?

We can also see from these provisions whose consent is required and also whose consent is not required to a placement order or adoption order. First, the consent of arguably the most important person in the process is not required. The child, irrespectve of her or his age, is not required to consent to the proceedings.[92] The Act does, however, require the child's wishes and feelings to be taken into account as a part of the welfare test,[93] and it is likely that the older the child, the more weight will be given to his or her views. Further, the Regulations require the adoption agency to ascertain the wishes and feelings of the child when it is first considering adoption as an option,[94] and on its review of a placement for adoption once the child is living in the placement,[95] but there is no duty to consult the child on the question of placement itself. In that case, the adoption agency only has an obligation to explain to the child its decision to place her for adoption.[96] Otherwise, there are references throughout the guidance and standards to adoption agencies' duties, as a matter of practice, to ascertain the wishes and feelings of the child,[97] but none that demand those wishes and feelings to be given effect.[98]

The other obvious gap in the list of persons from whom consent to adoption is required relates to fathers without parental responsibility. While their consent is not required, however, Article 8 ECHR will protect their right to be notified and possibly joined as a party to the proceedings.[99] The Regulations may also protect this right for fathers before the matter proceeds to court. Regulation 14 of the Adoption Agencies Regulations 2005 requires agencies, when they are considering adoption for a child, to provide counselling and information for, and to ascertain the wishes and feelings of, the parent or guardian of the child and others, and this requirement extends to a father without parental responsibility if the agency knows his identity,[100] and if the agency is satisfied that it is appropriate so to include him.[101] In this case the agency must also ascertain whether he wishes to

---

[92] This is in contrast to a number of other jurisdictions, including Scotland in which the consent of children over the age of 12 is required.

[93] S 1(4)(a).

[94] The Adoption Agency Regulations 2005 Reg 13.

[95] Ibid, Reg 36(5)(a).

[96] Ibid, Reg 33(4).

[97] See DfE (2011a: ch 2, para 20) and DfE (2011b: Standard 1).

[98] On incorporating a child's views into the welfare test, see discussion in Chapter 11 below.

[99] See *Re B (Adoption by One Natural Parent to Exclusion of Other)* [2001] 1 FLR 589 CA and full discussion of the case law in Chapter 8 below.

[100] The Adoption Agency Regulations 2005 Reg 14(3).

[101] Ibid, Reg 14(4)(a).

acquire parental responsibility for the child or intends to apply for a residence or contact order under the Children Act 1989 section 8.[102] The agency also must, if it considers it appropriate, notify in writing a father to whom Regulation 14(3) applies, of its decision regarding placing a child for adoption.[103]

> [Q] Why would it be, or not be, in a child's best interest to have such a father noti-
> fied? Why would it be, or not be, a child's right, to have such a father notified?
> Or is it a matter of the father's right? See *M v FH (A Local Authority)* above. Do
> these provisions for including the child and the father without parental respon-
> sibility go far enough? How, if at all, would you change them?

The paramountcy of welfare also raises issues about who is considered to be suitable to adopt. The Adoption and Children Act 2002 states that an adoption order may be made in favour of a couple if both are over 21 years old, or if one of them is the child's mother or father and is at least 18 years old.[104] Section 144(4) states that a 'couple' means a married or civilly registered couple or 'two people (whether of different sexes or the same sex) living as partners in an enduring family relationship'. The symbolic significance of this legal acknowledgement of same-sex parenthood must not be underestimated, and this position has now been accepted in the ECtHR. The court has not found a 'right' to adopt, but, where adoption is permitted, states must not discriminate unlawfully against potential applicants.[105]

While it remains unclear as to what an 'enduring family relationship' might mean, it is clear that these decisions will depend upon the facts of the case. Recall our discussion in Chapter 1 regarding the controversy around unmarried cohabitants and the law. How does one assess whether a non-formalised relationship is 'enduring'? In *Re T (a child)*[106] Hedley J shed some light on this question by stating that sometimes co-residence is not even required: 'What is required is: first, an unambiguous intention to create and maintain family life, and secondly, a factual matrix consistent with that intention. That is clearly a question of fact and degree in each case.'

The Adoption and Children Act 2002 also allows for one person to adopt a child if that person is over the age of 21 and is not married[107] or a registered civil partner.[108] A person is also eligible to adopt if he or she is the (same-sex or opposite-sex) partner of a parent of a child.[109] If the lone prospective adopter is married to someone other than the parent[110] or is a registered civil partner of someone other than a parent,[111] he or she is eligible if the spouse or partner cannot be found. Similarly a married person or civil partner can

---

[102] Ibid, Reg 14(4)(b).

[103] Ibid, Reg 33(3)(b). See also DfE (2011a: ch 2, paras 35–43).

[104] S 50 Adoption and Children Act 2002.

[105] *EB v France* case no 43546/02 (2008) where the court found that French law which permitted adoption by a single heterosexual applicant discriminated against single gay or lesbian adopters. And see *In re P and others* [2008] UKHL 38; [2008] 2 FLR 1084 (*sub nom Re P (Adoption: Unmarried Couple)*), where the House of Lords found that Northern Irish legislation prohibiting unmarried couples from adopting violated Articles 14 and 8.

[106] [2010] EWHC 964 para 16; [2011] 1 FLR 1487 (*sub nom Re T and M (Adoption)*).

[107] S 51((1).

[108] Amendment made by the Civil Partnership Act 2004 s 79(4).

[109] S 51(2). S144(7) states that 'a person is a partner of a parent if the person and the parent are a couple but the person is not the child's parent'.

[110] S 51(3).

[111] S 51(3A) inserted by the Civil Partnership Act s 79(5).

adopt alone if he or she is separated and the separation is likely to be permanent or if the spouse or partner is incapable of making a joint application by reason of ill health. Finally, in limited circumstances,[112] a parent may adopt his or her own child to the exclusion of the other parent. In these cases the purpose of the adoption order would be to 'take away, rather than give, since the focus is on the *termination* of the parental status of the other parent' (Bainham 2005: 277).

The court faced this issue in a case in which a mother gave birth to a daughter without informing the father of the pregnancy. Immediately after the birth she turned the baby over to hospital staff and requested that the baby be adopted. The father found out about the birth only by chance and with the mother's co-operation obtained parental responsibility for the baby and began to care for her. He then wished to secure the child's future in his own care and applied, with the mother's consent, for an adoption order. The mother only wanted an annual photograph and progress report to be provided through the local authority. The Official Solicitor representing the child at trial opposed the adoption order, as although he regarded the mother's lack of interest in the child as 'lamentable', he submitted that it would not be in the child's best interests to deprive her of a mother. The adoption order was granted at first instance but overturned by the Court of Appeal on a number of grounds.[113] Hale LJ gave the leading judgment, finding that an adoption order infringed the mother's Article 8 rights because an adoption did not meet a pressing social need in this case and was a disproportionate response to the child's current needs. She said:

> [40] ... it is difficult to argue that there is a pressing social need to deprive A of all legal relationship with one half of her family of birth ... she already has a full and secure legal and factual relationship with her father. If there is any need to give her more, it can be provided for in a package of orders along the lines discussed [such as specific issues orders, prohibited steps orders and s 91 orders under the Children Act 1989]. In my view, it would be a disproportionate response to her current needs to turn her from the child of two legal parents, with two legal families, into the child of only one parent, with only one legal family.

The House of Lords[114] disagreed and restored the adoption order. It said there was no reason to set aside the trial judge's exercise of discretion in finding that A's best interests would be served by adoption. Lord Nicholls stated: 'Given the mother's attitude to A from the moment of A's birth, and her consent, adoption by the father was in A's best interests' (para 27) and on all the evidence, the trial judge was entitled to form this view (para 28).

It is tempting to say that their different conclusions in this case may have been at least in part influenced by the courts' respective assessments of the mother. In the Court of Appeal, Hale LJ regarded the mother's actions as responsible rather than 'lamentable' (para 21). She said

> [h]ard though it may be for many to understand, she has recognised that she is not the maternal type and does not want to have children. She made responsible arrangements for her first child and was planning to do the same for A. She wants what is best for her, understands the father's position, and says that she will not interfere'. (para 20)

---

[112] S 51(4): where the other parent is dead or cannot be found; where there is no other parent by virtue of s 28 HFEA 1990; or there is some other reason justifying the adoption.

[113] *Re B (Adoption by One Natural Parent to Exclusion of Other)* [2001] 1 FLR 589 (CA).

[114] *Re B (a child) (sole adoption by unmarried father)* [2001] UKHL 70; [2002] 1 FLR 196.

In contrast, Lord Nicholls in the House of Lords made no direct reference to the mother's actions. His indirect references, however, suggest that he took a different view of them. While acknowledging that 'permanent exclusion of the child's mother' is a 'drastic and detrimental consequence', he stated that 'how serious this loss is likely to be depends on the circumstance of the case' (para 22). He then had to find that there existed the statutory 'other reasons' for making the adoption order, and said that 'abandonment, or persistent neglect or ill-treatment of the child, could be instances' (para 23) of such 'other reasons'.

Q Can you make an argument that unstated beliefs and assumptions about the meaning of motherhood and fatherhood inform the decision in this case?

The Adoption and Children Act 2002 and the human rights cases refer only to general capacity to adopt, and leave to regulations the role of adoption agencies to determine the suitability of individual adopters. However, the statute at the same time stresses that where the potential adopters are a couple, 'proper regard is had to the need for stability and permanence in their relationship'.[115] Adoption agencies are mandated to screen and interview all potential adopters and must take medical and social histories, family histories, education, employment and income histories, and make personality assessments including asking why that person wants to adopt and their views on child-rearing. They must carry out police and neighbourhood checks and obtain references.[116] Exercise of the discretion given by the Act to adoption agencies raises many issues about who, in law as well as in social work theory and practice, is suitable to become a parent. And the focus of investigations may be upon mothers, as in their search for 'normality' social workers may assume that mothers, rather than fathers, will be the primary carers of children. Prospective adoptive parents undergo extensive checks and interviews which are more intrusive even than those undergone by applicants for fertility treatment.

While there was evidence that in the past the welfare of the child was perceived to be met best by the traditional nuclear family (Campion 1995), the new policy of promoting adoption for looked-after children, the changes in the law regarding same-sex parenting as well as changes in social work practice have led to greater acceptance of 'non-traditional' applicants, especially for older children and those who would otherwise be difficult to place. This has meant that the old 'benchmarks' are no longer applicable; as Katz comments, 'it is no longer self-evident what is required of a "good enough" parent' (Katz 2000: 218). He says that social workers therefore include a good deal of gut feeling and experience rather than research in their assessments of prospective adopters, which means they tend to favour either the cultural norm or whatever happens to be in current favour at the time (ibid: 219). Adoption practice is, he says suffused with myths, assumptions and cultural values. So, for instance he argues, the stance that openness is vital for children would hold, 'no matter what research demonstrated' (ibid: 227). In general, despite the regulations, guidelines and standards, professionals are faced with a difficult task in trying to 'hold in mind the needs and phantasies of all points in the adoption triangle [child, adopter, birth family] (ibid: 229). The issues of openness and racial/cultural/religious matching have, in the recent past, been particularly prominent in social work practice.

---

[115] S 45.
[116] See DfE (2011a: ch 3, paras 26–48); DfE (2011b: Standard 4); Adoption Agencies Regulations 2005 SI 389/2005, particularly para 35 and Sch 4 Pt 1.

Q Consider the wording of the following passage from the White Paper (Department of Health et al 1993) in the light of our discussion of ideology and common sense in Chapter 1:

4.28 The judgments that adoption agencies and their staffs need to make are inherently difficult, and do not become any less so as society becomes more complex and varied. Nevertheless, they should be careful always to take approaches which are based on commonsense and objective professional assessment and avoid reliance on ideology. (8)[117]

And now compare with the current Statutory Guidance (DfE 2011a: ch 4, para 4):

But by being informed by research, being realistic and consider a prospective adopter who can meet most of the child's identified needs, and seeking families in-house, from other adoption agencies—local authorities and voluntary adoption agencies (VAAs)—consortia, and the Adoption Register will put the child in an excellent position of being placed quickly with a new, safe and loving family. *If the prospective adopter can meet most of the child's needs, the social worker must not delay placing a child with the prospective adopter because they are single, older than other adopters or does [sic] not share the child's racial or cultural background.* (emphasis in original)

Do you see a difference in approach?

Placing a child with adopters who do not share the child's ethnic, religious or cultural background is a sensitive and controversial issue.[118] We have seen that section 1(5) of the Adoption and Children Act 2002 requires agencies to consider these factors in placing a child for adoption, and there is also reference to these factors in the Guidance (DfE 2011a: ch 4):

7. A prospective adopter can be matched with a child with whom they do not share the same ethnicity, provided they can meet the child's other identified needs. The core issue is what qualities, experiences and attributes the prospective adopter can draw on and their level of understanding of the discrimination and racism the child may be confronted with when growing up. This applies equally whether a child is placed with a black or minority ethnic family, a white family, or a family which includes members of different ethnic origins.

8. All families should help children placed with them to understand and appreciate their background and culture. Where the child and prospective adopter do not share the same background, the prospective adopter will need flexible and creative support to be given by their agency. This should be in the form of education and training, not just simplistic advice, provided in a vacuum, on learning their children's cultural traditions or about the food/cooking from their birth heritage. The support plan should consider how the child's understanding of their background and origin might be enhanced. This can include providing opportunities for children to meet others from similar backgrounds, and to practise their religion—both in a formal place of worship and in the home. Maintaining continuity of the heritage of their birth family is important to most children; it is a means of retaining knowledge of their identity and feeling that although they have left their birth family they have not abandoned important cultural, religious

---

[117] See Jolly and Sandland (1994) on this.
[118] Barn (2000: 112) makes the point that in practice 'transracial' has meant the placement of minority ethnic children in white homes.

or linguistic values of their community. This will be of particular significance as they reach adulthood.

We see an attempt here to resolve the controversy. Many believe that transracial adoption is not in the best interests of children because it inhibits them from developing a positive racial identity, it subjects them to identity confusion or social ostracism, or because it can be seen as an example of colonialisation of ethnic minorities by the white majority.[119] The evidence of the benefits or otherwise of transracial adoption is inconclusive. Many children fare well in transracial or transcultural placements while others do not. It seems that current policy is to consider a 'same-ethnicity' placement to be in a child's welfare, but that as a factor, ethnicity should not outweigh other factors.

Q Do you think the policy strikes the right balance? Hayes (2003) argues that the research on outcomes for children in transracial placements is positive, or at least neutral, and therefore that the requirement to consider ethnicity as a factor in adoption placements is based upon nothing but ideology. Do you agree? Even if it were, does it mean the requirement should be abandoned?

The importance of a child knowing[120] and being secure in his of her identity is also raised in what have come to be known as open adoptions. As we saw above, in many ways the concept of 'open adoption' is contrary to the notion of adoption itself, but several studies have demonstrated that adopted children fare better when they are aware of their adopted status, when they have information about their birth parents and, in many cases, when they have the opportunity to make or maintain contact with their birth families. This research (eg Walby and Symons 1990; Triseliotis 2000; Smith and Logan 2002) suggests that all people have a need to understand or have some knowledge of their identity, history or roots, and that to accommodate this desire is not only compatible with adoption, but is in the best interests of children. This thinking contrasts with that of the 1960s when it was believed that a clean and absolute break from the birth family was in a child's best interests (Rowe 1966), adoption was shrouded in secrecy and it was inconceivable to allow continued contact with birth families. That thinking has changed is clear. The Guidance (2011a: ch 5) encourages adopters to share information about the child's circumstances by way of a 'life story book' and a later life letter:

48. The child's life story book helps them explore and understand their early history and life before their adoption. It is important therefore for it to be written in a simple and age-appropriate style and that the language and terms used are agreed with the prospective adopter before the book is handed over. For example, some prospective adopters use the term 'tummy mummy' as a way of explaining to the child who their biological mother is, whereas other prospective adopters use different terms. The explanation of why the child was adopted should not include explicit or distressing details. This information needs to be given to the child at a time when they are emotionally able to cope and understand the information. Consideration should be given on whether the surname of the birth parents, family and others should be included in the life story book.

49. The child's birth parents, family, foster carers and other people who know the child should be encouraged to be involved in putting together the contents. They may also be able to provide

---

[119] See on this, Barn (2000) above; Murphy (2000); Hayes (2003) and sources cited therein.
[120] On the child's right to know his identity, see Fortin (2009a: 468–81).

memorabilia significant to the child such as the child's hospital birth wristband; soft toys, letters, and celebration cards; first drawings and paintings, and photographs of birth parents, siblings, family members and other people who are important to the child. Where appropriate, this memorabilia should be stored safely in a suitable box—a 'memory box'.

50. The life story book and 'memory box' should be co-ordinated by one person, preferably the child's social worker, and given to the child and prospective adopter in stages. The first stage is at the second statutory review of the child's placement with the prospective adopter. The completed life story book should be presented within ten working days of the adoption cere-mony, ie the ceremony to celebrate the making of the adoption order.

Later life letter: AAR 35

51. A social worker who knows the child, preferably the child's social worker, should prepare the later life letter for the child. The letter should explain the child's history from birth and be sufficiently detailed so that in the future the adolescent child, or young adult, will have factual details about their birth family and their life before adoption, and so be able to understand why they could not live with their birth family, and why they were adopted. The letter should be given to the prospective adopter within ten working days of the adoption ceremony, ie the ceremony to celebrate the making of the adoption order.

The Adoption and Children Act 2002 itself requires adoption agencies to keep information on adoptions, including identifying information about persons involved, and provides for when that information can be disclosed.[121] Further, the Act requires the maintenance of an Adoption Contact Register[122] and an Adopted Children Register.[123] The first is a reg-ister that enables adopted persons and their birth relatives to contact each other where they both want to do so, and the second is a register that enables an adopted adult to gain access to her or his birth records. Sometimes just having the information about one's birth family is sufficient, but often adoptees need more. There are, they feel, key aspects of their identity that are missing (Triseliotis 2000). In these situations, and to answer ques-tions about the circumstances of their adoption, they may search for their birth families and the information provided by these registers will assist them. Furthermore, research (Triseliotis et al 2005) shows that contact and reunion might be good for all parties in the so-called 'adoption triangle'.

Providing information or encouraging contact are different, however, from making an adoption order with a condition of contact attached to it. Open adoptions of these sorts fly more directly in the face of what an adoption is supposed to be, and the general judicial attitude has been to attach contact conditions only where they have been previ-ously agreed by the adoptive family.[124] As to whether post-adoption contact is in the best interests of the child, Neil (2003)[125] can only conclude after a comprehensive review of the issues and the research that it depends upon the individual child and his or her cir-cumstances. While contact might be beneficial for older children, or help to resolve some

---

[121] Ss 56–65. See also The Disclosure of Adoption Information (Post-Commencement Adoptions) Regula-tions 2005 SI 2005/888, which applies to adoptions made after the 2002 Act, and The Adoption Information and Intermediary Services (Pre-Commencement Adoptions) Regulations 2005 SI 2005/890, which applies to adults adopted before the 2002 Act came into force.

[122] Ss 80 and 81; DfE (2011b: Standard 16).

[123] Ss 77–79. See also the Adopted Children and Adoption Contact Registers Regulations 2005 SI 2005/924.

[124] Smith and Logan (2002) note, however, that many adoptive families find it a burden to maintain and facilitate contact with birth families.

[125] See also Eekelaar (2003b); Smith and Logan (2002).

children's identity questions or their feelings of rejection, it is by no means of universal benefit.

The White Paper (2000) contained the rather ambiguous statement that 'a child's needs to maintain links to their birth family ... should always be considered, and ... where appropriate, the local social services should make arrangements to meet the lifelong needs of the child' (para 6.43). The Adoption and Children Act 2002 itself is silent on post-adoption contact, except to require the court, before making an adoption order, to consider whether there should be arrangements made for contact.[126] Before adoption, however, an application for contact may be made with or after a placement order,[127] and regulations also require adoption agencies and adoption panels to consider contact issues throughout each stage of their planning process, from the initial consideration of adoption as a plan,[128] through recommendations made about adoption placements,[129] and on placement.[130] Finally, the National Minimum Standards (DfE 2011b) ensure that contact is always considered in work with the child (Standard 8), and Chapter 7 of the Statutory Guidance (DfE 2011a) explains the duties of an adoption agency in relation to contact.

Recent research has found that factors associated with poor contact outcomes are when:

> Birth relatives have poor adjustment to the adoption and poor acceptance of the child's dual connection; Birth relatives or adopter(s) have poor commitment or negative attitudes towards the contact; A lack of connection is evident between the child and the birth relative during contact or there is a fear of loss of connection resulting from the structure or quality of the contact (eg infrequent, highly formal); There is a lack of trust and insecurity in the relationship between the child and the adopters; The child is struggling to cope with emotional and behavioural problems; The contact includes a birth relative who has severely neglected or abused the Child; There are poor relationships between the adopters and the birth relative. (ARI 2010: 4)

Factors associated with successful contact are when:

> There is a commitment to contact, a positive attitude and an awareness of the benefits on all sides; There is a clear connection between the child and the birth relative alongside a developing sense of trust and security in the adoptive family; The birth relative can accept the child's adoption and their own change of role in the child's life; There are 'good enough' relationships between the adoptive family and the birth relative; There is a consensus between the birth relative and the adoptive parent(s) about what is in the child's best interests; Birth relatives and adopters can make efforts to demonstrate that they value each other's roles in the child's life. (ibid)[131]

Post-adoption contact is thus always an issue for adoption agencies and courts and the

---

[126] S 46(6).

[127] Ss 26–27. The difficulty with contact during placement before an adoption order is made, however, is that it may frustrate bonding between the child and the prospective adopters. In *Gorgulu v Germany* [2004] 1 FLR 894 the ECtHR held that a German court which had suspended contact between an unmarried father and his child who had been living with foster parents for two years with a view to eventual adoption had violated the father's Art 8 rights. The suspension of contact precluded any form of family reunion between the child and the father.

[128] The Adoption Agencies Regulations 2005 Reg 13 requires the agency to ascertain the child's wishes and feelings about contact and Reg 14 the parent or guardian's wishes and feelings about it.

[129] Reg 18(3)(a) requires the adoption panel to consider contact when it makes its recommendation.

[130] Reg 46 requires the adoption agency to consider arrangements for contact on placing a child with an adoptive family.

[131] See also Neil et al (2011).

empirical research about its benefits remains uncertain.[132] For those older, looked-after children whom adoption policy now targets, however, it may be important. The difficulty is that adoption still purports to replace one family entirely with another and it is only slowly beginning to be recognised that people often can feel a part of more than one family at a time. Post-adoption contact requires 'an acknowledgement that children are not exclusively "owned" *either* by their birth parents *or*, subsequently, by their adoptive parents' (Smith and Logan 2002: 290) and promotes the view that adoptive relationships should be based upon 'reciprocal obligations' (ibid). Smith and Logan observe, however, that this change would represent a fundamental challenge to both adoption legislation and judicial attitudes (ibid).

And judicial attitudes may be changing. In *Re P (a child)*,[133] after noting that historically post-adoption contact between a child and his birth family was perceived as highly exceptional, the court indicated that the jurisprudence was in need of review in the light of the Adoption and Children Act 2002. Wall LJ said:

> 146. Since 1995, the value of contact post adoption has been identified in a number of the cases, notably by Ward LJ in Re G (Adoption: Contact) [2002] EWCA 761, [2003] 1 FLR 270 and in the dissenting speech of Baroness Hale of Richmond in the Northern Ireland case of Down Lisburn Health and Social Services Trust v H [2006] UKHL 36; [2007] 1 FLR 12, both of which, of course, were decided without specific reference to the 2002 Act. However, as we understand it, the position has remained not only that contact orders post adoption are unusual, but, as was said in Re R (Adoption: Contact) [2005] EWCA Civ 1128 at paragraph 49; [2006] 1 FLR 373 at 385, that whilst contact post adoption was 'more common' the jurisprudence was clear, and that 'the imposition on prospective adopters of orders for contact with which they are not in agreement is extremely, and remains extremely unusual'.

> 147. All this, in our judgment, now falls to be revisited under section 26 and 27 of the 2002 Act, given in particular the terms of sections 1(4)(f), 1(6) and (7) and 46(6). In our judgment, the judge in the instant case was plainly right to make a contact order under section 26 of the 2002 Act, and in our judgment the question of contact between D and S, and between the children and their parents, should henceforth be a matter for the court, not for the local authority, or the local authority in agreement with prospective adopters.

> 154. We do not know if our views on contact on the facts of this particular case presage a more general sea change in post adoption contact overall. It seems to us, however, that the stakes in the present case are sufficiently high to make it appropriate for the court to retain control over the question of the children's welfare throughout their respective lives under sections 1, 26, 27 and 46(6) of the 2002 Act; and, if necessary, to make orders for contact post adoption in accordance with section 26 of the 2002 Act, under section 8 of the 1989 Act. This is what Parliament has enacted. In section 46(6) of the 2002 Act Parliament has specifically directed the court to consider post adoption contact, and in section 26(5) Parliament has specifically envisaged an application for contact being heard at the same time as an adoption order is applied for. All this leads us to the view that the 2002 Act envisages the court exercising its powers to make contact orders post adoption, where such orders are in the interests of the child concerned.

Q Do you agree with the court's view? Do you think that this change is in the interests of children?

---

[132] Recent research (Neil 2009) confirms that one cannot make blanket predictions about the impact of contact on children.

[133] [2008] EWCA Civ 535. See also *Re J (Adopted Child: Contact)* [2010] EWCA Civ 581.

Q How has the nature of adoption changed over the years? What, if any, role in a child's life would you reserve for a 'former' mother after adoption? A 'former' father, grandparent or sibling? What, if any, say would you allow the child in this matter? What, if any, say would you allow the adoptive parents? Have these changes complicated the private, nuclear family ideal?

Q Before we leave our discussion of legal motherhood, recall that we said above that a child may not be designated legally motherless at birth. In what situations, however, has law created the status of legally motherless children?

Increasing the Range of Permanency Options—Special Guardianship

The White Paper (2000) said:

> 5.8 Adoption is not always appropriate for children who cannot return to their birth parents. Some older children do not wish to be legally separated from their birth families. Adoption may not be best for some children being cared for on a permanent basis by members of their wider birth family. Some minority ethnic communities have religious and cultural difficulties with adoption as it is set out in law.[134] Unaccompanied asylum seeking children may also need secure, permanent homes, but have strong attachments to their families abroad. All these children deserve the same chance as any other to enjoy the benefits of a legally secure, stable permanent placement that promotes a supportive, lifelong relationship with their carers, where the court decides that is in their best interests.

The Adoption and Children Act 2002 thus created the status of special guardianship.[135] Sections 14A–G of the Children Act 1989 govern the making, variation, discharge, effect and support of special guardianship orders.[136] They are a form of foster-plus: a special guardianship order does not terminate the status of birth parents; they share parental responsibility with the special guardians(s). But, like birth parents who share parental responsibility with each other, special guardians can exercise their parental responsibility to the exclusion of any other person with parental responsibility.[137] Those who are entitled to apply for special guardianship are the same as those who are entitled to apply for section 8 orders or residence and contact orders pursuant to section 10(5) of the Children Act 1989[138] and specifically includes local authority foster parents and relatives with whom the child has lived for at last one year. It is clear that special guardianship is intended to be utilised as part of the focus upon 'looked-after' children,[139] and now that policy is focusing upon utilising and supporting family and friends as carers of children,[140] special guardianship may take on increased importance for them.

Special guardianship is presented as an alternative form of permanency planning for children, but as the extract above makes clear, as 'second best' to adoption. This view has been said to be out of line with other views of permanency planning.

---

[134] Islamic law does not, for example, recognise adoption.

[135] For a historical view of similar provisions in English law, see the second edition of this book; Cretney (2003a) and *Re S (a child) (adoption or special guardianship order)* [2007] EWCA Civ 54; [2007] 1 FLR 819.

[136] See also the Special Guardianship Regulations 2005 SI 2005/1109.

[137] Children Act 1989 S 14C.

[138] See Chapter 10 below.

[139] See Chapters 13 and 14 below.

[140] DfE (2010b).

Not all countries are as zealously wedded as the UK to the gold standard of adoption. Indeed, the UK and USA are positively isolated on the world stage in their pro-adoption approach to permanency planning, with only Canada and Norway expressing a similar interest. New Zealand and Australia both have a small number of adoptions, with formalised kinship placements much preferred for looked after children. In New Zealand, the 'total removal of parental rights is seen as such a draconian measure ... that it is viewed as a civil liberty issue', with the deeming of a child as born to the adopters considered 'repugnant' and an 'unnecessary distortion of reality'.

(Hall 2008: 364, references omitted)

If special guardianship does provide for children's and carers' senses of security, then we might think that adoption should be ordered only when special guardianship is not adequate. However, the Court of Appeal has offered slightly different guidance on this, referring to the welfare of the child. In *Re S (a child) (adoption order or special guardianship order)*[141] Wall LJ said:

44 It is important to note also that the statutory provisions draw strong and clear distinctions between the status of children who are adopted, and those who are subject to lesser orders, including special guardianship. As we have already pointed out, the considerations in relation to adoption in the expanded check-list contained in section 1 of the 2002 Act require the court to address the question of the child's welfare throughout his life. We do not think this point needs any further explanation or emphasis. Its consequences are, however, significant.

45 Thus, although section 14C(1) of the 1989 Act gives special guardians exclusive parental authority, this entitlement is subject of a number of limitations. ...

46 ... in addition to the fundamental difference in status between adopted children and those subject to special guardianship orders, there are equally fundamental differences between the status and powers of adopters and special guardians. These, we think, need to be borne in mind when the court is applying the welfare checklist under both section 1(3) of the 1989 Act and section 1 of the 2002 Act.

47 Certain other points arise from the statutory scheme:—

  (i)   The carefully constructed statutory regime (notice to the local authority, leave requirements in certain cases, the role of the court, and the report from the local authority—even where the order is made by the court of its own motion) demonstrates the care which is required before making a special guardianship order, and that it is only appropriate if, in the particular circumstances of the particular case, it is best fitted to meet the needs of the child or children concerned.

  (ii) There is nothing in the statutory provisions themselves which limits the making of a special guardianship order or an adoption order to any given set of circumstances. The statute itself is silent on the circumstances in which a special guardianship order is likely to be appropriate, and there is no presumption contained within the statute that a special guardianship order is preferable to an adoption order in any particular category of case. Each case must be decided on its particular facts; and each case will involve the careful application of a judicial discretion to those facts.

  (iii) The key question which the court will be obliged to ask itself in every case in which the question of adoption as opposed to special guardianship arises will be: which order will better serve the welfare of this particular child?

48 The special nature of the jurisdiction also has implications for the approach of the courts:—

---

[141] [2007] EWCA Civ 54.

(i) In view of the importance of such cases to the parties and the children concerned, it is incumbent on judges to give full reasons and to explain their decisions with care. Short cuts are to be avoided. It is not of course necessary to go through the welfare check-list line by line, but the parties must be able to follow the judge's reasoning and to satisfy themselves that he or she has duly considered it and has taken every aspect of it relevant to the particular case properly into account.

(ii) Provided the judge has carefully examined the facts, made appropriate findings in relation to them and applied the welfare check-lists contained in section 1(3) of the 1989 Act and section 1 of the 2002 Act, it is unlikely that this court will be able properly to interfere with the exercise of judicial discretion, particularly in a finely balanced case. ...

(iii) In most cases (as in these three appeals) the issue will be, not the actual placement of the child, but the form of order which should govern the future welfare of the child: in other words, the status of the child within the particular household. It is unlikely that the court need be concerned with the alternative of making "no order" under section 1(5) of the 1989 Act and 1(6) of the 2002 Act.

(iv) For the same reason, the risk of prejudice caused by delay (to which section 1(2) of the 1989 Act rightly draws attention) may be of less pivotal importance. Indeed, in many cases, it may be appropriate to pause and give time for reflection, particularly in those cases where the order in being made of the court's own motion. ...

49 We would add, however, that, although the 'no order' principle as such is unlikely to be relevant, it is a material feature of the special guardianship regime that it is 'less intrusive' than adoption. In other words, it involves a less fundamental interference with existing legal relationships. The court will need to bear Article 8 of ECHR in mind, and to be satisfied that its order is a proportionate response to the problem, having regard to the interference with family life which is involved. In choosing between adoption and special guardianship, in most cases Article 8 is unlikely to add anything to the considerations contained in the respective welfare checklists. Under both statutes the welfare of the child is the court's paramount consideration, and the balancing exercise required by the statutes will be no different to that required by Article 8 . However, in some cases, the fact that the welfare objective can be achieved with less disruption of existing family relationships can properly be regarded as helping to tip the balance.

Special guardianship orders within pre-existing family relationships

50 It is clear from the White Paper that special guardianship was introduced at least in part to deal with the potential problems arising from the use of adoption in the case of placements within the wider family ... .

51 A particular concern is that an adoption order has, as a matter of law, the effect of making the adopted child the child of the adopters for all purposes. Accordingly, where a child is adopted by a member of his wider family, the familial relationships are inevitably changed. This is frequently referred to as the 'skewing' or 'distorting' effect of adoption, and is a factor which the court must take into account when considering whether or not to make an adoption order in such a case. This is not least because the checklist under section 1 of the 2002 Act requires it to do so:—see section 1(4)(f) ('the relationship which the child has with relatives.'). However, the weight to be given to this factor will inevitably depend on the facts of the particular case, and it will be only one factor in the overall welfare equation.

Q Research into the first two years of its availability shows that special guardianship was broadly meeting carers' expectations. 'They felt it was providing them with sufficient parental responsibility and legal security while enabling children to retain a link with their birth parents' (Wade et al 2009: 3). Wade et al further found that 'most children were reported to be faring well, especially in relation to their health, attachments and emotional well-being' (ibid). Would it surprise you to learn that 86% of special guardians in the first two years were relatives of the children, with the majority being grandparents (ibid; see also Hall 2008)? 1,260 special guardianship orders were made in 2010 in England (DfE 2011c).

Consider the following view offered by Hall (2008: 376) in the light of the court's guidance above:

> Special guardianship offers an opportunity not only to reduce the number of children in care, but also more fundamentally to review the prevailing approach to permanence planning and to bring the UK into line with Convention-compliant least interventionist principles and international practice. This study suggests that so far, both opportunities have apparently been missed.

Do you agree that there should be readier recourse to special guardianship?

Other Ways to Become a Parent—Guardianship

A status akin to that of motherhood (or fatherhood) is conferred on a person appointed as guardian of a child. The historical concept of guardianship[142] of children was done away with in the Children Act 1989 and, as Bainham notes, '[h]enceforth, parents would just be parents and guardianship would be confined to non-parents who stepped into the shoes of deceased parents' (Bainham 2005: 226).[143] Guardianship is provided for in sections 5 and 6 of the Children Act 1989, which state, inter alia, that guardians may be appointed either by a parent with parental responsibility for a child, a guardian or by a court. The guardian, who need not be biologically related to a child, is in a position analogous to, but not identical with, a parent, in that he or she has full parental responsibility for the child.[144] Bainham describes guardianship as follows:

> Guardianship differs significantly from all other forms of social parenthood. It is by far the least regulated, the appointment of guardians being largely a private matter not subject to public scrutiny, judicial or otherwise. It is also the most far-reaching in its legal effects since it carries some of the incidents which are normally associated with natural parenthood but which fall outside the concept of parental responsibility. Yet the status of guardianship, although closely resembling parenthood, is not identical. For example, guardians are not liable for child support as parents are. More importantly, they may voluntarily disclaim their appointment, whereas the obligations of parenthood are imposed by operation of law and may not be voluntarily relinquished or transferred. The status of guardianship may also be revoked by court order, whereas parenthood survives all court orders except adoption. (Bainham 2005: 226)

Q Does it strike you as incongruous that although guardianship is the most 'far-reaching in its legal effects of all forms of social parenthood', it is also the least regulated? Bainham (2005) further reminds us that the Law Commission reviewed in 1985 the question of whether there ought to be restrictions or

---

[142] The married father was the guardian of his children.
[143] See Bainham (2005: 225–30) generally on guardianship. See also Law Commission (1985a).
[144] S 5(6).

checks on people appointed as guardians, but rejected the idea. What do you suppose was the policy behind this decision?

Guardianship only comes into operation where parents with parental responsibility are deceased.

Parental Responsibility: Residence Orders

We have seen in the law of guardianship an example of law conferring the responsibilities of parenthood upon people who are not parents at law in order to enable them to carry out the responsibilities of parents. Another category of persons upon whom law confers the responsibility of parents is that of persons who obtain a residence order under the Children Act 1989. The award of a residence order carries with it parental responsibility[145] which lasts while the order remains in force.[146] However, such an order does not affect the status of a parent: a person with parental responsibility does not lose it simply because another person subsequently also acquires parental responsibility.[147]

Social Motherhood—No Legal Status

In addition to forms of social motherhood which are regulated by law, there are those relationships between adults and children which do not carry the same degree of legal status, but nevertheless do impose some responsibility upon the adult involved. We include in this category foster mothers and stepmothers, but, again, the rules for acquiring foster parent or step-parent status are generally the same for women as for men. Because the frequency with which they are acquired differs between men and women, however, we will address them in the contexts in which they are most likely to occur. We will discuss foster parenthood in this section under motherhood, and will address step-parenthood in the following section on fatherhood.

Foster Parents

Foster parents are people who provide substitute care, usually assumed to be temporary, for a child whose parents are unable to provide it. In some situations, long-term fostering is seen as an acceptable permanence plan for a child, usually as a preferable alternative to institutional care,[148] or, as stated in the White Paper (2000: para 5.12): '[Long-term fostering] has proved particularly useful for older children with strong links to their birth families, who do not want or need the formality of adoption or "special guardianship".' Generally, fostering reflects the belief that a private family is the better setting in which to care for children. By acting as substitute parents, foster parents take on the role of a child's social parents and are responsible for the day-to-day care of the child, although they do not have parental responsibility for the child. They have only weak legal status, therefore, but are in a position to decide day-to-day matters such as whether to authorise emergency medical treatment for a child. Section 3(5) of the Children Act 1989 states that:

---

[145] See Chapter 8 below.

[146] S 12(2) of the Children Act 1989. S 12(3) places some limitations on parental responsibility in these circumstances: it does not confer the right to consent to adoption or to appoint a guardian for the child. See Chapter 10 below for a discussion of recent case law in making residence orders.

[147] Children Act 1989 s 2(6).

[148] Although institutional care is now being said to be appropriate for older children. See Chapter 14 below.

A person who

(a) does not have parental responsibility for a particular child; but
(b) has care of the child

may (subject to the provisions of this Act) do what is reasonable for the purpose of safeguarding or promoting the child's welfare.

Informal fostering arrangements have been utilised by parents throughout history, and parents continue to be able to choose informal foster carers privately. The law does not intervene in any way to regulate these fostering arrangements if the parents choose foster carers who are relatives within the meaning of the Children Act. However, if the carers are not relatives, are not applicants for adoption and do not have parental responsibility for the child, they are 'private' foster carers within the meaning of the Act and are regulated by Part IX of the Act.

Regulations under the Children Act require private foster carers to notify local authorities either that they intend to act or are acting as private foster carers, and local authorities are then required to ensure that the home meets minimum standards and to monitor the placement to ensure that the welfare of the child is not in danger.[149] While monitoring private foster placements was not high on local authorities' list of priorities (Barton and Douglas 1995: 107), and so private arrangements were subject to minimal supervision, the 2005 regulations now require the local authority to monitor private arrangements closely.[150]

If private foster parents wish to obtain a clearer legal status, they may apply for a residence order which will give them parental responsibility. In order to apply, they need permission from the court[151] unless they have the consent of those with parental responsibility[152] or unless the child has been living with them for at least three years.[153]

Public or local authority foster care is also the subject of direct legal regulation. Regulation of public care originated as a result of the baby-farming scandals of the last century (Barton and Douglas 1995: 104), and is seen as part of local authorities' duty to care for children in need. Section 22 of the Children Act gives local authorities the power to place children in foster care. A person can become a local authority foster parent only after undergoing stringent checks of suitability similar to those carried out for prospective adoptive parents.[154] And a person remains a foster parent only so long as the local authority agrees. The foster carer must be able to work with the local authority, usually with the long-term goal of returning the child to her parents or to the placement of the child for adoption, and her ability to apply to court for parental responsibility or adoption was therefore circumscribed under the Children Act 1989.

But, as we have seen, the policy announced in the White Paper (2000) identified permanence for looked-after children as a priority, and while adoption was seen as the preferred means of achieving that permanence for children, there was also support given

---

[149] S 67 and Sch 8 of the Children Act 1989; The Children (Private Arrangements for Fostering) Regulations 2005 SI 2005/1533.

[150] See Replacement Children Act 1989 Guidance on Private Fostering (DCSF 2005). This is a response to the death of Victoria Climbie at the hands of her aunt and the aunt's partner. Victoria was placed in the care of the aunt pursuant to a private fostering arrangement.

[151] Children Act 1989 S 10(2)(b).

[152] Ibid, s 10(5)(c) (iii).

[153] Ibid, s 10(5)(b).

[154] Sch 2, Part II, s 12; Fostering Services (England) Regulations 2011 SI 2011/581; DfE (2011d, e).

to long-term fostering for certain children. Hall (2008) describes current use of long-term fostering:

> Long-term foster care placements in the UK are generally used for children 'for whom adoption is not appropriate', namely older children, children with ongoing and significant relationships with birth parents and children with close carer attachments for whom a placement move would not be appropriate. Long-term fostering is also much more likely to be the plan for children with emotional and/or behavioural problems, or with a history of severe abuse, given the child's difficulties in forming attachments (clearly connected to the risk of placement disruption and failure), the increased ability of foster carers to know how to gain access to resources and professional help and support, and the need for post-placement support (including respite care and residential placements).
>
> Foster care has its limitations, not least in that parental responsibility for the child is retained by the 'corporate parent' (the local authority), significantly restricting the powers and responsibilities of foster carers to act independently. Foster care placements are always prone to change, even if intended as long-term, and by their nature are therefore considered inherently 'fragile', lacking in sufficient permanence, security and certainty. Despite the considerable benefits they can offer many children, these placements have come to be popularly dismissed as 'not quite good enough' (Hall 2008: 361)[155]

While 'focused support' and 'better permanence planning' (White Paper 2000: para 5.13) were seen as necessary for fostered children, the Adoption and Children Act 2002 has also made it easier for local authority foster carers to formalise their 'parental' relationships with their foster children more quickly than was previously the case. Local authority foster carers may give notice of their intention to adopt the child,[156] or make application for special guardianship of the child,[157] after fostering for one year. Finally, should a local authority foster carer wish to obtain parental responsibility for the child in her care, she may only apply for permission from the court to obtain a residence order (which carries parental responsibility), with the consent of the local authority or after the child has lived with her for one year,[158] unless she is a relative of the child.[159] Research indicates, however, that not many foster carers take up these opportunities. There were, it was found, 'three principal disincentives: first, the child's high level of needs and the ongoing need for social work support; second, the carer's unwillingness to lose out financially; and third, in relation to residence orders, fear of the difficulties of sharing parental responsibility with the birth parents' (Hall 2008).

In the event of a contested application, the court would be faced with deciding whether the best interests of the child lay with her 'social parents'—the foster carers—or with her (usually) biological parents—those with parental responsibility. Although law may be increasing its recognition of biological status in some areas of child law, it is not the case that biology automatically prevails. The welfare test may demand a different outcome.

The courts are, however, wary of overriding the parents' wishes in order to choose the 'better' home for the child. Respect for the privacy of the family ensures that while courts will be circumspect in their decisions to interfere with the biological relationship the

---

[155] See also Beihal et al (2009); Triseliotis (2002).
[156] Adoption and Children Act 2002 s 42(4).
[157] Children Act 1989 s 14A(5)(d).
[158] S 10(5A) of the Children Act 1989. Introduced by the Adoption and Children Act 2002 to reduce period from three years.
[159] S 9(3).

welfare of the child prevails and that any 'presumption' in favour of a 'natural parent', if
it ever existed at all, certainly in private law cases, has no part in the welfare test.

The law regarding the weight that 'natural parenthood' should have in private disputes,
either in the form of 'parental rights' or in assessing the child's welfare, has been clarified
by the Supreme Court. In *Re B (a child)*[160] a grandmother was granted a residence order
regarding her grandson who had lived with her his whole life. His father, who had staying
contact, appealed the order, relying upon Lord Nicholls' words in *Re G*[161] that 'in the
ordinary way the rearing of a child by his or her biological parents can be expected to be
in the child's best interests, both in the short term and, more importantly, in the longer
term. ... A child should not be removed from the primary care of his or her biological
parents without compelling reason' (para 2). The Supreme Court made it clear that Lords
Nicholls' comment was set firmly in the context of the child's welfare (para 34, per Lord
Kerr for the court). His Lordship went on as follows, quoting from Baroness Hale's
opinion in *Re G*:

> 33. ... She said this at paragraph 30.
>
> 34.
>
>> [30] My Lords, the [Children Act 1989] brought together the Government's proposals in
>> relation to child care law and the Law Commission's recommendations in relation to the
>> private law. In its Working Paper No 96, *Family Law: Review of Child Law: Custody* (1986),
>> at para 6.22, having discussed whether there should be some form of presumption in favour
>> of natural parents, the Law Commission said:
>>
>>> 'We conclude, therefore, that the welfare of each child in the family should continue to
>>> be the paramount consideration whenever their custody or upbringing is in question
>>> between private individuals. The welfare test itself is well able to encompass any special
>>> contribution which natural parents can make to the emotional needs of their child, in
>>> particular to his sense of identity and self-esteem, as well as the added commitment
>>> which knowledge of their parenthood may bring. We have already said that the indications
>>> are that the priority given to the welfare of the child needs to be strengthened rather than
>>> undermined. We could not contemplate making any recommendation which might have
>>> the effect of weakening the protection given to children under the present law.'
>>
>> Nor should we. The statutory position is plain: the welfare of the child is the paramount
>> consideration. As Lord MacDermott explained in *J v C* [1070] AC 668, 711, this means that
>> it 'rules upon or determines the course to be followed'. There is no question of a parental
>> right. As the Law Commission explained: 'the welfare test itself is well able to encompass
>> any special contribution which natural parents can make to the emotional needs of their
>> child' or, as Lord MacDermott put it, the claims and wishes of parents 'can be capable of
>> ministering to the total welfare of the child in a special way'.
>
> 37. This passage captures the central point of the *In re G* case and of this case. It is a message
> which should not require reaffirmation but, if and in so far as it does, we would wish to provide
> it in this judgment. All consideration of the importance of parenthood in private law disputes
> about residence must be firmly rooted in an examination of what is in the child's best interests.
> This is the paramount consideration. It is only as a contributor to the child's welfare that parent-
> hood assumes any significance. In common with all other factors bearing on what is in the best
> interests of the child, it must be examined for its potential to fulfil that aim. There are various

---

[160] [2009] UKSC 5; [2010] 1 FLR 551.
[161] [2006] UKHL 43.

ways in which it may do so, some of which were explored by Baroness Hale in *In re G*, but the essential task for the court is always the same.

Q Refer back to our discussion about the paramountcy of welfare in adoption placement orders, and adoption orders. Would this reasoning be followed in that context?

Q For a good discussion of the case law and interpretation of the paramountcy principle in cases involving foster carers, see Fortin (2009a: 519–34). She says the courts say it is appropriate to privilege the biological parents only when all other factors are equal[162] and argues that this 'other things being equal' formula requires a comparison of the two homes (ibid: 525). Is this a similar test to the one used in private law disputes between parents?

Fortin notes (2009: 525–26), however, that the courts apply this formula to achieve the same result as ensued from the application in earlier case law of an approach which placed the evidential burden on the foster carers; in effect the foster parents still have to persuade the court that the child's welfare 'positively demands the displacement of the parental right'.[163] She then goes on to consider whether the ECHR could affect this line of cases and concludes that, while parents can invoke Article 8, so can foster carers who have been caring for the child. She says it would be 'regrettable' if the ECHR was used to 'justify and outmoded myth about ... a "psychological blood bond"' (ibid: 530, reference omitted).

Q In what ways does foster caring either conform to or challenge notions of the private nuclear family? What role, if any, is left for the state in caring for children?

VI. WHO IS A PARENT? BECOMING A FATHER

Both a biological connection between a man and a child and a social connection can give rise to legal consequences. Historically the law relied upon a combination of both connections to do so. It was thought that the uncertainty of biological paternity (often reinforced by misogynist assumptions about women's predilection for deception in reproductive matters) required presumptions in law to render certain rules about paternal responsibility and the passing of family property in a patrilineal legal order. Carol Smart put it in these terms:

[U]nlike motherhood, fatherhood has posed complicated problems for a legal system that has based the ownership and inheritance of property on descent through the male line—on that is, patrilineal and primogenital ordering. Paternity has been a continuing 'problem' for the patriarchal family in Western Europe ... and this is manifest in the tortuous complexity of the legal system designed to protect the descent of property and privilege. (Smart 1987: 99)

---

[162] *Re H (a minor) (custody: interim care and control)* [1991] 2 FLR 109, 112–13, interpreting *Re K (a minor)* [1991] 1 FLR 57.

[163] *Re K (a minor) (ward: care and control)* [1990] 3 All ER 795, 798.

Before DNA testing could establish paternity conclusively, the legal response to this 'problem' was the presumption of legitimacy, or the presumption of paternity (Smart 1984). This presumption, which designates a woman's husband as the father of any children born to her, still remains, but in the light of scientific and social advancements, doubt has been cast upon its usefulness. In *Re H and A (Children)*[164] Thorpe LJ said:

> [30] ... I question the relevance of the presumption [of legitimacy] or the justification for its application. In the 19th century, when science had nothing to offer and illegitimacy was a social stigma as well as a depriver of rights, the presumption was a necessary tool, the use of which required no justification. That common law presumption, only rebuttable by proof beyond reasonable doubt, was modified by s 26 of the Family Law Reform Act 1969 by enabling the presumption to be rebutted on the balance of probabilities. But as science has hastened on and as more and more children are born out of marriage it seems to me that the paternity of any child is to be established by science and not by legal presumption or inference.

In this case the court considered that ascertainment of the 'truth' of the children's biological paternity outweighed even the husband's statement that he would leave the family if he were found not to be their biological father. The law seems to have accepted the value of biological familial relationships (perhaps as a result of the decline in the proportion of children born to married parents or to the increased numbers and power of fathers living separately from their children), but it has also had to reconcile this with the traditional social importance attached to marriage and family.

Whereas in the past courts tended to prioritise, in the interests of the child's welfare, the stability of the family and would refuse to order tests where that stability would be disrupted, the trend now appears to be toward ascertaining biological 'truth' over maintaining social arrangements. It appears to have supplanted the older case law that suggests that such tests do not promote the welfare of the child if they are ordered in the face of opposition from the mother, because they would disrupt a settled family relationship.[165] Some of the ways in which courts have achieved this reconciliation is to suggest that it is in the public interest that the 'truth' be known',[166] that it is in child's best interests to know,[167] and indeed that he or she may have a right under Article 7 of the UN Convention on the Rights of the Child[168] and Article 8 ECHR[169] to know the truth about her or his origins. Bainham (1999, 2008a, 2008b) and Eekelaar (2006) have written in support of law following that genetic 'truth'. Bainham asserts it is a matter of protecting autonomy:

---

[164] [2002] EWCA Civ 383; [2002] 2 FCR 469.

[165] See *K v M (Paternity: Contact)* [1996] 1 FLR 312; *Re F (A Minor: Paternity Test)* [1993] 1 FLR 598; *O v L (Blood Tests)* [1995] 2 FLR 930; and Conway (1996). See also *J v C* [2006] EWHC 2837 (Fam); [2007] 1 FLR 1064 (*sub nom Re J (Paternity: Welfare of Child)*), in which the court did not order tests immediately in the face of evidence that to do so would harm the child.

[166] *Re H (a minor) (Blood Tests: Parental Rights)* [1997] Fam 89 (CA).

[167] Even though welfare is not 'paramount' in these questions. See, eg, *Re T (Paternity: Ordering Blood Tests)* [2001] 2 FLR 1190; *Re D (Paternity)* [2006] EWHC 3545 (Fam); [2007] 2 FLR 26, in which the court ordered tests over the strong objection of the child.

[168] *Re H (Paternity: Blood Test)* [1996] 2 FLR 65; *Re G (Parentage: Blood Sample)* [1997] 1 FLR 360; *Re R (A Minor) (Blood Test: Constraint)* [1998] 1 FCR 41. Art 7(1) states: 'The child shall be registered immediately after birth and shall have the right from birth to a name, the right to acquire a nationality and, as far as possible, the right to know and to be cared for by his or her parents'. See also *S v McC* [1972] AC 24; *Re G (A Minor) (Blood Test)* [1994] 1 FLR 495; Fortin (2009).

[169] *See Re T (paternity; Ordering Blood Tests)* above; *Mikulic v Croatia* [2002] 3 FCR in which the child had a right to know her paternity as a part of her right to respect for private life; and *Odievre v France* (above) in which that right is limited.

The key point is that individuals wish to exercise personal autonomy and to take their own decision about whether or not biological links are important to them. They are not required to give any reason for this. It is not for the state, or their parents or anyone else to dictate whether biological parentage is, or is not, important to them. It is fundamentally an individual choice which ought to be respected. The issue is how the child's choice can be meaningfully protected *during childhood.* (Bainham 2008b: 347)

Eekelaar suggests keeping the 'truth' from children amounts to adults acting in their own interests and denying that right to their children.

Adults can create legal truths which are at odds with physical truth. They may deliberately disguise physical truths. When they do that, you can be sure that it is in order to project the social order constructed by the adults into the future. ... [T]his knowledge [of physical truth] allows the individual to confront the world as it is *on his own terms,* and influence solutions according to his perception of his interests given the physical truth. But with physical truth forever obscured, society's new members are doomed to manipulation.

(Eekelaar 2006: 74, emphasis in original)

Not all commentators agree. Diduck sees it as a biological determinism that cannot be separated from the reinforcement of the position of fathers in families.

Now that we *can* know the biological—or at least genetic—'truth', it seems that in the interests of our well-being, we *must* know. And not only must we know, it has now become our right to know. ... This rediscovered deference to biological determinism in the form of respect for genetic 'truth' has been accomplished in law by linking it to both welfare and rights. Once again, gender issues loom large in both these links. First of all, disputed parentage was traditionally and still is virtually always about disputed paternity and so the 'universal principles' about a child's need to know his or her *identity* developed from responses to questions about a child's *paternity.* Adopting the gender neutral language of identity or origins simply masks the importance thus attributed to knowledge of paternal lineage. ... It should thus not be surprising to note the next step that was taken: connecting 'the child's right to identify both natural parents and the value to the child of creating a social relationship between them'. While 'the assumption that the birth tie automatically guarantees a beneficial in built affinity between parent and child is surely naïve', cases concerning disputes between biological parents and `social parents' began to reinforce that assumption. ... the association of biology with welfare may have been motivated in part by a fear of 'social engineering', but this explanation does not go far enough to rebut the preponderance of evidence which disputes any inherent moral, developmental, psychological or other value to a child created by a blood connection with carers. Given that the link between genetic relationship and welfare was established in a context that included a concern to reassert paternal authority/rights in the family, that evidence must surely be necessary.

(Diduck 2007: 468–71, references omitted)

Fortin also worries that the focus on the child's right to know his paternity may really reflect adult concerns.

Surely a child has a right not to know the identity of his father, if he himself believes, with some grounds, that his entire life would be disrupted by such knowledge? Indeed, the view that *all* children have a right to know their parents' identity may sometimes achieve more harm than good, given the danger of the two issues being confused—the child's need to know about his origins and his possible need for a social relationship with his biological parent.

(Fortin 2009b: 340)

When dealing with applications from putative fathers, it is arguable that the domestic courts are extending a child's right to know beyond its appropriate boundaries ... the disputes being litigated have little to do with children's right to know their origins. The ... applications brought by putative fathers are not brought to provide the child with information alone, they are the initial stages of attempts to establish a social relationship between father and child based on assumptions about biological connectedness. The putative fathers' assumption that once the biological ties between father and child have been clearly identified, they should be fulfilled by a social relationship produces an elision of the right to know the parent's identity with the right to have a relationship with that parent. ... such an elision concentrates the court's attention on the putative father's position and his own interests—countered by those of the mother—These are adult centred arguments which spring from adult centered disputes over children who are treated as the property of those who can establish biological connectedness. (ibid: 354)

Finally, Smart suggests that privileging scientific 'truth' over other 'truths' may not always serve the interests of all family members.

It is easy therefore to interpret the gradual adoption of genetically determined reproductive truth as a story of progress away from harmful or murky practices towards a more enlightened and scientifically informed approach to relationships. However, there is another way to interpret the relationships between culturally elevated truths, secrets and forms of knowing. The need for a certain kind of secrecy at different times and in different circumstances can be interpreted as a response to social vulnerability. In this way secrets might serve as a form of protection against economic hardship, social rejection or personal denunciation. An emergent insistence on genetic truth and transparency may simply create other forms of vulnerability, especially if cultural mores and familial norms have not changed greatly. The availability of scientific certainty over such things as paternity cuts across delicate social and personal relationships, and while the secrets that a mother might wish to keep could be harmful, the truth proclaimed by a man who renounces fatherhood may be equally damaging. So alongside this potential re-alignment of relationships it is important to remember the extent to which these are also relationships of power. The drive towards genetic truth in familial relationships presumes that openness is good because it creates a level playing field of knowledge. However, family members themselves may not be on an equal footing and so this kind of openness may simply bring with it different forms of vulnerability. ... the legal insistence on only one kind of truth, namely genetic, in family relationships may simply promote the claim to truth of science above other claims concerned with caring, relationality and the preservation of kinship bonds. There may be better ways of managing the complex issues that arise from messy relationships and human reproduction than through the use of legal regulation. (Smart 2009: 564–65)

Q Do you think the presumption of paternity/legitimacy should be retained? Do you think that the prioritisation of genetic links has gone too far?

The man named on the child's birth certificate is also presumed to be the child's father.[170] Where the mother is not married, she alone has responsibility to register the child's birth, and if she does so with the (unmarried) father, he will also obtain parental responsibility.[171] This position was seen as unsatisfactory for a number of reasons. Some thought it gave mothers too much power (Bainham 2008a), and it was thought to undermine policies directed toward child support, responsible parenting, gender equality and engaging fathers in families. As a result, a new section has been inserted into the Births and Deaths

---

[170] Births and Deaths Registration Act 1953 s 34(2).
[171] Children Act 1989 s 4.

Registration Act by the Welfare Reform Act 2009 requiring mothers to give details of the child's father to the registrar unless, inter alia, she does not know his identity or whereabouts, he is dead, he lacks mental capacity or she has reason to fear for her safety if he is contacted.[172] Once identified, the father will be contacted and required to make a statement either acknowledging or disputing paternity.

Both the presumption created by the birth certificate and the presumption of legitimacy can be rebutted by evidence on a balance of probabilities, but remain in law in order to achieve certainty. They have the effect also of conferring parental responsibility on the presumed father. As we have seen, however, not all biological fathers have parental responsibility or other social or legal responsibilities for their children.

Fatherhood—The Significance of Biology

Section 56 of the Family Law Act 1986 enables a child to seek a declaration that he or she is the legitimate child of his or her parents. Section 55A of the same Act enables a person to seek a declaration that a person is or was the parent of another person. If the applicant is anyone other than the child, the other parent, the possible parent himself or herself,[173] or the Secretary of State in a dispute about child support,[174] the court must determine first that the applicant has sufficient personal interest in the finding.[175] The court may refuse to hear the application if it considers that to determine the application would not be in the best interests of the child.[176] Finally, the declaration, once made, is binding on all persons.[177]

The best evidence the court can have before it to determine parentage (technically both motherhood and fatherhood) is scientific evidence, as Thorpe LJ said in the *Re H and A* case above, and under section 20 of the Family Law Reform Act 1969 the court has the power to direct the use of scientific tests in order to determine parentage and for the taking of bodily samples to complete those tests. Consents to take the bodily samples are required from all persons over the age of 16[178] and from a person with care and control of a child under 16 in respect of whom bodily samples must be taken. If the person does not give the required consent the bodily sample may be taken from the child anyway if the court considers it would be in the child's best interests.[179] Finally, section 23(1) of the Family Law Reform Act 1969 provides that if any person fails to comply with a direction to provide samples for testing, the court may draw whatever inferences it deems appro-

---

[172] The Births and Deaths Registration Act 1953 s 2A, 2B. These sections are not yet in force, with the government saying that the law is still under consideration. See further Chapter 8 below. For a debate about this reform, see Bainham (2008a) and Wallbank (2010). Bainham argues that the reforms may not have gone far enough and that the concerns of vulnerable women and children should have no impact on the purpose of birth registration, which is simply to provide a record of biological truth. Wallbank, on the other hand, opposes such a formal notion of equality between parents that marginalises women's concerns about fathers' actual responsibility toward children and valorises an aspirational view of fatherhood. See also Sheldon, who sees in the reform a 'policy optimism both about the desire of fathers to be more involved with their offspring and the likely success of initiatives in parenting as a means of addressing broader social problems' (Sheldon 2009: 375).

[173] Sub-s 55A(4).

[174] Child Support Act 1991 s 27.

[175] Family Law Act 1986 s 55A(3).

[176] Ibid, s 55A(5).

[177] Ibid, s 58(2).

[178] Ss 21(1) and (2).

[179] S 21(3). See discussion above.

priate from the refusal. This includes drawing an inference 'as to the very fact which was in issue, namely the child's actual paternity'.[180]

It does not automatically follow, however, that a declaration of paternity will carry with it any legal, social or emotional responsibilities or privileges. If the man is married to the legal mother of the child, then this biological confirmation of the presumption of legitimacy merely confirms his status as legal father. If the mother of the child is married to another man, however, the declaration of parentage, even if based upon an adverse inference drawn from a refusal to take the test, may rebut the presumption of legitimacy[181] to place the biological father in the position of an unmarried father under the Children Act with respect to parental responsibility.[182]

These provisions for determining a child's paternity offer a contrast to the former 'bastardy' or affiliation proceedings which were *quasi*-criminal in nature, and which required that a woman's testimony regarding her child's paternity be corroborated. In effect, they appeared to have been designed almost to give the putative father a 'sporting chance to get away with it' (Barton and Douglas 1995: 200), and their complicated and criminal nature deterred and stigmatised women who were forced to rely upon them (Finer and McGregor 1974). In the past, paternity suits were usually used to determine a support obligation on the part of the father, and it is interesting to note that, while in many cases this is still the case, such declarations are now often sought by men who wish to establish a legal connection to children.

Where an unmarried man[183] is identified as the biological father of a child, he is included within the category 'parent' under a number of statutes. However, that label carries only limited legal rights and responsibilities. He is liable for support of the child pursuant to the Child Support Act 1991, and may as of right make certain applications under the Children Act 1989,[184] for example, but has no parental responsibility under the Children Act unless he meets the conditions under the Children Act 1989.[185] As we saw above, he may have the right to be notified about certain proceedings concerning his child, such as adoption proceedings, but, unlike a mother's biological connection to her child, his mere biological connection does not create for him and his child a family life to be recognised under Article 8 ECHR. To do this he must establish a 'close personal tie' with the child.[186] Sometimes biological paternity, then, carries only a legal status, with few rights or responsibilities attached.

In other cases, a biological connection will create no legal status at all. In these situations, the law simply disregards a known biological connection entirely. An example of this is the, admittedly now rare, case where the mother or the court does not wish to disturb the presumption of legitimacy by directing scientific tests. Another example of legal rules overriding biological relationships is when a man donates sperm under the auspices of a licensed authority: as sperm donor he has no legal relationship with any resulting children.

The first legal regulation of fatherhood in the context of assisted reproduction, the

---

[180] *Re A (A Minor) (Paternity: Refusal of Blood Test)* [1994] 2 FLR 463; *Secretary of State for Work and Pensions v Jones* [2003] EWHC 2163; [2004] 1 FLR 282.

[181] See, eg, *F v Child Support Agency* [1999] 2 FLR 244; *Secretary of State for Work and Pensions v Jones*, above.

[182] See below, and Chapter 8.

[183] We use this term here to mean unmarried to the child's mother.

[184] See further Chapter 8 below.

[185] Children Act 1989 s 4. See Chapter 8 below.

[186] *G v Netherlands* [1993] EHRR CD 38. See also discussion in Chapter 8 below and cases cited therein.

Family Law Reform Act 1987, provided that where a child was born to a married woman as a result of artificial insemination by donor (AID), no man other than her husband was to be treated as the child's father unless it was shown that the husband did not consent to the insemination.[187] Following the Warnock Committee's recommendation that AID was not necessarily ethically objectionable and that donors should have no legal responsibilities toward resulting children (Warnock Committee 1984: para 4.22), section 28(6)(a) of the HFEA provides that where the donation is made and used with the consent of the donor, in a manner consented to by the donor, by a licensed clinic under the authority of the HFEA, he is not to be treated as the father of the child.

One of the reasons for excluding donors from any legal responsibility for their offspring was to encourage people to donate gametes. Until 2005 it was thought that, for the same reason, donations must always remain anonymous, although non-identifying information as to physical and social characteristics could be entered upon a register and disclosed on application[188] to an applicant. From 1 April 2005, children who were conceived after that date are entitled to receive identifying information such as the name and date of birth of the donor,[189] and the HFEA 2008 made further changes to the information stored and able to be provided to both the child and the donor.[190] The donor, for example, may now access non-identifying information about any children conceived through the use of their gametes.

> **Q** Recall the discussions above of identity in the context of open adoption and paternity disputes. Outline the arguments for and against donor anonymity.

> **Q** As a result of its 2011 Consultation on Donation, the Human Fertilisation and Embryology Authority announced that donors should be permitted to place conditions on the use of their sperm and eggs, but to issue guidance qualifying this permission according to different contexts. This is a potentially controversial decision. 'For example, should a sperm donor be permitted to specify that their sperm cannot be used (or alternatively, can only be used) to treat a lesbian, or a single woman, or a woman of a particular ethnicity, religion or age?' (Starr 2011).

Sperm is relatively easy to collect and to donate and artificial insemination is not a high-tech procedure. AID may occur on an informal basis between friends, and in these cases the above sections of the HFEA do not apply. In such cases, biological evidence or, if applicable, the presumption of legitimacy will determine legal fatherhood but the social role these fathers play varies from arrangement to arrangement. Dunne's research shows, for example, that lesbian mothers overwhelmingly organised donor inseminations informally (Dunne 2000: 15) and that it was not unusual for the donors to have regular contact with their offspring (ibid: 160). Fathers sometimes took on the role of 'kindly uncle' (ibid: 18, 22) and sometimes were actively engaged in parenting (ibid: 28). And finally, this form

---

[187] S 27.

[188] S 31 HFEA 1990.

[189] The Human Fertilisation and Embryology Authority (Disclosure of Donor Information) Regulations SI 2004/1511, para 2(3). Fears that the removal of anonymity would deter donors proved unfounded; although there was a slight drop in numbers in 2004 and 2005, the numbers returned to their pre-reform rates in 2007 and 2008 (HFEA 2011: Donor Statistics).

[190] See ss 31–35.

of AID also had the effect of increasing the child's kin network: sometimes the father's parents enthusiastically accepted the role of grandparents (ibid: 24), while other times they did so less enthusiastically (ibid: 30).

Fatherhood—The Significance of Intention

The HFEA 2008 states:

35 Woman married at time of treatment

(1) If—

(a) at the time of the placing in her of the embryo or of the sperm and eggs or of her artificial insemination, W was a party to a marriage, and

(b) the creation of the embryo carried by her was not brought about with the sperm of the other party to the marriage, then, subject to section 38(2) to (4), the other party to the marriage is to be treated as the father of the child unless it is shown that he did not consent to the placing in her of the embryo or the sperm and eggs or to her artificial insemination (as the case may be).

(2) This section applies whether W was in the United Kingdom or elsewhere at the time mentioned in subsection (1)(a).

36 Treatment provided to woman where agreed fatherhood conditions apply

If no man is treated by virtue of section 35 as the father of the child and no woman is treated by virtue of section 42 as a parent of the child but—

(a) the embryo or the sperm and eggs were placed in W, or W was artificially inseminated, in the course of treatment services provided in the United Kingdom by a person to whom a licence applies,

(b) at the time when the embryo or the sperm and eggs were placed in W, or W was artificially inseminated, the agreed fatherhood conditions (as set out in section 37) were satisfied in relation to a man, in relation to treatment provided to W under the licence,

(c) the man remained alive at that time, and

(d) the creation of the embryo carried by W was not brought about with the man's sperm, then, subject to section 38(2) to (4), the man is to be treated as the father of the child.

37 The agreed fatherhood conditions

(1) The agreed fatherhood conditions referred to in section 36(b) are met in relation to a man ('M') in relation to treatment provided to W under a licence if, but only if,—

(a) M has given the person responsible a notice stating that he consents to being treated as the father of any child resulting from treatment provided to W under the licence,

(b) W has given the person responsible a notice stating that she consents to M being so treated,

(c) neither M nor W has, since giving notice under paragraph (a) or (b), given the person responsible notice of the withdrawal of M's or W's consent to M being so treated,

(d) W has not, since the giving of the notice under paragraph (b), given the person responsible—

  (i) a further notice under that paragraph stating that she consents to another man being treated as the father of any resulting child, or

  (ii) a notice under section 44(1)(b) stating that she consents to a woman being treated as a parent of any resulting child, and

(e) W and M are not within prohibited degrees of relationship in relation to each other.

(2) A notice under subsection (1)(a), (b) or (c) must be in writing and must be signed by the person giving it.

(3) A notice under subsection (1)(a), (b) or (c) by a person ("S") who is unable to sign because of illness, injury or physical disability is to be taken to comply with the requirement of subsection (2) as to signature if it is signed at the direction of S, in the presence of S and in the presence of at least one witness who attests the signature.

38 Further provision relating to sections 35 and 36

(1) Where a person is to be treated as the father of the child by virtue of section 35 or 36, no other person is to be treated as the father of the child.

39 Use of sperm, or transfer of embryo, after death of man providing sperm

(1) If—

(a) the child has been carried by W as a result of the placing in her of an embryo or of sperm and eggs or her artificial insemination,

(b) the creation of the embryo carried by W was brought about by using the sperm of a man after his death, or the creation of the embryo was brought about using the sperm of a man before his death but the embryo was placed in W after his death,

(c) the man consented in writing (and did not withdraw the consent)—

    (i) to the use of his sperm after his death which brought about the creation of the embryo carried by W or (as the case may be) to the placing in W after his death of the embryo which was brought about using his sperm before his death, and

    (ii) to being treated for the purpose mentioned in subsection (3) as the father of any resulting child,

(d) W has elected in writing not later than the end of the period of 42 days from the day on which the child was born for the man to be treated for the purpose mentioned in subsection (3) as the father of the child, and

(e) no-one else is to be treated—

    (i) as the father of the child by virtue of section 35 or 36 or by virtue of section 38(2) or (3), or

    (ii) as a parent of the child by virtue of section 42 or 43 or by virtue of adoption, then the man is to be treated for the purpose mentioned in subsection (3) as the father of the child

40 Embryo transferred after death of husband etc. who did not provide sperm

(1) If—

(a) the child has been carried by W as a result of the placing in her of an embryo,

(b) the embryo was created at a time when W was a party to a marriage,

(c) the creation of the embryo was not brought about with the sperm of the other party to the marriage,

(d) the other party to the marriage died before the placing of the embryo in W,

(e) the other party to the marriage consented in writing (and did not withdraw the consent)—

    (i) to the placing of the embryo in W after his death, and

    (ii) to being treated for the purpose mentioned in subsection (4) as the father of any resulting child,

(f) W has elected in writing not later than the end of the period of 42 days from the day on which the child was born for the man to be treated for the purpose mentioned in subsection (4) as the father of the child, and

(g) no-one else is to be treated—

(i) as the father of the child by virtue of section 35 or 36 or by virtue of section 38(2) or (3), or

(ii) as a parent of the child by virtue of section 42 or 43 or by virtue of adoption, then the man is to be treated for the purpose mentioned in subsection (4) as the father of the child.

(2) If—

(a) the child has been carried by W as a result of the placing in her of an embryo,

(b) the embryo was not created at a time when W was a party to a marriage or a civil partnership but was created in the course of treatment services provided to W in the United Kingdom by a person to whom a licence applies,

(c) a man consented in writing (and did not withdraw the consent)—

   (i) to the placing of the embryo in W after his death, and

   (ii) to being treated for the purpose mentioned in subsection (4) as the father of any resulting child,

(d) the creation of the embryo was not brought about with the sperm of that man, (e) the man died before the placing of the embryo in W,

(f) immediately before the man's death, the agreed fatherhood conditions set out in section 37 were met in relation to the man in relation to treatment proposed to be provided to W in the United Kingdom by a person to whom a licence applies,

(g) W has elected in writing not later than the end of the period of 42 days from the day on which the child was born for the man to be treated for the purpose mentioned in subsection (4) as the father of the child, and

(h) no-one else is to be treated—

   (i) as the father of the child by virtue of section 35 or 36 or by virtue of section 38(2) or (3), or

   (ii) as a parent of the child by virtue of section 42 or 43 or by virtue of adoption, then the man is to be treated for the purpose mentioned in subsection (4) as the father of the child.

We see from section 35 that if a woman is married at the time she receives treatment her husband is to be treated as the father of any child unless it can be shown he did not consent to the treatment. Here we see a version of the old presumption of paternity applied in assisted-reproduction situations. Importantly, he must have consented to the actual treatment that was provided. In *Leeds Teaching Hospitals NHS Trust v A*[191] Mr and Mrs A sought IVF treatment together in which his sperm was to be injected into her egg. After a successful pregnancy Mrs A gave birth to twins, but it emerged that her egg had been mistakenly fertilised with Mr B's sperm rather than with her husband's sperm. The question before the court was whether the old section 28(2) HFEA 1990 (which adopted the same wording as the new section 35 HFEA 2008) applied to the situation so as to designate Mr A the father of the twins. In observing that the section 28(2) question revolved around the question of consent to treatment (para 27), Butler Sloss P said:

28. Mr A certainly gave his consent to the placing in his wife of 'an embryo'. The embryo actually placed in Mrs A was a fundamentally different embryo from one that might have been created by the use of Mr A's sperm. Mr A has indicated that he does not wish to seek to withdraw his consent and wishes to take advantage of the irrebuttable presumption set out in section 28(2) and become the legal father. It is not, however, a matter of endorsement by the husband of his consent. The question whether the husband consented is a matter of fact which

---

[191] [2003] EWHC 259; [2003] 1 FLR 1091.

may be ascertained independently of the views of those involved in the process. On the clear evidence provided in the consent forms Mr A plainly did not consent to the sperm of a named or anonymous donor being mixed with his wife's eggs. This was clearly an embryo created without the consent of Mr and Mrs A.

In the result, because Mr A did not consent to the treatment that Mrs A actually received, the twins' paternity fell to be determined by the common law rules and Mr B was their legal father. Mr A would be required to apply for a residence order conferring upon him parental responsibility or, in the alternative to adopt the twins he intended to raise with his wife.

According to section 36, if a woman (W) who receives treatment has no husband (who would be treated as father) or civil partner (who would be treated as female parent), a man (M) whose sperm was not used in the treatment will be treated as father if the agreed fatherhood conditions in section 37 apply. Those conditions primarily relate to consent to being so treated, and note that they do not require M and W to be cohabiting or even in an 'enduring' relationship. They do, however, assume the possibility of a sexual relationship, as M and W must not be within the prohibited degrees of relationship.[192] Sections 39 and 40 provide for similar fatherhood attribution, even if the treatment was provided after the death of the gamete donor or intended father.

Fatherhood by intention in these situations mixes awkwardly sometimes with fatherhood by biology. In surrogacy through a licensed clinic, for example, it means that if sperm is donated to a surrogate by an intended social father (a commissioning father), he is not the legal father despite either his intention or his genetic contribution; rather the husband of the surrogate is the legal father of the child unless he did not consent to the insemination. If he did not consent, scientific tests would establish a genetic connection with the commissioning father, who would then be in the position of an unmarried father with the surrogate as legal mother. The commissioning (biological) father and his partner (if he has one) may then be granted a section 54 parental order with the consent of the surrogate and her husband. Otherwise, he could apply to adopt the child or to obtain parental responsibility under the Children Act.[193]

Where the sperm is donated to a woman by a third party (as opposed to the commissioning father) through a licensed authority, the donor has no legal role as parent, the surrogate is the legal mother, and the surrogate's husband is the legal father unless he did not consent. If he did not consent, or if she has no husband or man who fulfils the agreed fatherhood conditions, the child is legally fatherless until an adoption order or a section 54 parental order (if the surrogate was implanted with gametes from the commissioning wife/female partner) is made in favour of the commissioning couple, at which point the male partner then becomes a father. There would be no father required to consent to the order. Generally then, where donated sperm is provided through a licensed authority, a donor will not be treated as a father, but a consenting husband will be so treated. The overriding factor for assigning fatherhood in all of these situations seems to be a man's consent and intention to be, or not to be, a father and no assumptions are made about mystical or biological 'bonds' of fatherhood. But the consent must be clear and unambiguous.

Let us review the implications of the law's apparently mixed pro- and anti-biologism.

---

[192] The same conditions appear in s 44 HFEA 2008 as the 'agreed female parenthood conditions' discussed above. See McCandless and Sheldon (2010b).

[193] As the biological father, he can rely on s 4 of the Children Act 1989.

On the one hand, fatherhood by consent is contrary to law's privileging of biology and things 'natural' but, on the other, it contradicts this position when there is a marriage or marriage-like partnership to privilege above nature. It is still the case, as it was even before the advent of new reproductive technologies, that it is *'marriage* and not the blood tie that confers automatic paternity upon men and creates a legal relationship between children and their fathers' (Smart 1987: 101). Reliance upon this relationship, now in extended form, continues to privilege the 'sexual family'. Smart argued in 1987 that increased assertion by women of 'autonomous' motherhood is disruptive of the idealised nuclear family, and so law has responded by '[extending] the legal concept of paternity and [enhancing] paternal rights' (ibid: 99; see also Diduck 1995; Boyd 2007).

> **Q** Review the ways we have discussed so far in which fathers are given legal status.
> Is Smart's position still persuasive now, over 20 years later?

While fatherhood was always based more upon intention than motherhood, it seems that law now offers fathers a 'double element of choice. A man who is not married to the mother of his child can choose to recognize that child as his own, while married men can choose to deny paternity on the basis of genetic evidence' (Mykitiuk 2001: 772). Women's choices about motherhood are, as we saw earlier, far more constrained. Boyd comments that the increasing fragmentation—or extension—of fatherhood in this way could be seen also as a valuing of paternal ties while women's socially constructed care-giving ties to children remain taken for granted and undervalued (Boyd 2007: 65).[194]

Collier and Sheldon take up this theme. They see the law's recent engagements with fatherhood as more complicated, however. They argue that law's recent focus on father-hood is 'open-ended, fluid and fragmented' (Collier and Sheldon 2008: 234). They see contradictions and tensions in the way that law sees and treats fathers, particularly in their role in the still powerful 'sexual family' ideal and the 'simultaneous pull' to recognise 'those familial, caring relationships which are significant to children, whether they occur in a (hetero)sexual family or not' (ibid: 235). While the genetic link between fathers and children has enjoyed new vigour in law, they suggest that this has not been won at the expense of other visions of fatherhood (ibid) and situate their observations firmly in the context of recent government policy of engaging fathers, of fathers' new family practices, of policies of gender equality, and shifting understandings of masculinity and the 'man of law' (see also Collier 2010).

Adoption

Men may become adoptive fathers if they apply and qualify jointly with their wives or partners and, in theory, single men can apply to adopt, just as single women can.

> **Q** Before we leave our discussion of legal fatherhood, consider in what situations
> a child may be legally fatherless.

---

[194] See also Diduck (2007).

Social Fatherhood—No Legal Status

This category of fathers encompasses stepfathers and foster fathers. Because much of the discussion above related to foster mothers applies to foster fathers, we will not repeat it here. Conversely, much of the discussion on stepfathers which follows here applies to stepmothers, but we discuss step-parenthood in this section because men are far more likely to become full time step-parents than women. 84% of stepfamilies in Great Britain in 2006 consisted of a stepfather and a natural mother compared with 10% of families with a stepmother and a natural father (ONS 2007).

Step-parents

A man becomes a stepfather by the simple act of either marrying a woman who is the mother of a child and with whom that child lives or entering into a civil partnership with a man who is that child's father. Entry into step-parenthood, therefore, is entirely unregulated by law, other than by the law of marriage or civil partnership.[195] The step-parent is a social parent, but, like a foster parent, he has no automatic parental responsibility for the child. This situation places step-parents in an ambiguous legal position and often an awkward emotional one. Bainham describes it in these terms:

> The step parent is in a potentially awkward position from the start. He (or she) is part of a family unit and has a regularised relationship with the natural [*sic*] parent through marriage, but lacks a regularised relationship with the children in the family. Thus while the step parent undoubtedly is in most cases in loco parentis and has de facto care of the children, he lacks the parental responsibility which would put him on an equal footing with his spouse and legitimate his standing to be fully involved in upbringing … . While the relationship between the adult partners may be viewed as a partnership of equals, the relationship between them and the child is clearly not equal in law. In the event of disagreement, the natural [*sic*] parent (by virtue of parental responsibility) has the sole authority on any issues affecting the children. This is a situation which has all the potential for conflict between the spouses and between the step parent and the children. (Bainham 2005: 232–33)

This awkward position may be exacerbated when the couple are not married or registered civil partners, as they may then be perceived to have even less formal status. It also cannot be separated from research which suggests that children from stepfamilies are overrepresented in many negative statistics such as those relating to looked-after children, young runaways or child abuse (Smith 2003: 197). They may experience anger, depression, anxiety and resentment when one of their parents repartners and, particularly in adolescence, they may feel conflicted and disengage from their families.[196] Step-parents also may feel anxious and experience emotional conflict.[197] There is also research, however, which suggests that, like any family living, stepfamily living is complicated, but that children and adults learn to adapt to its complexities (Smith 2003; Parentline Plus 2005). Their adaptation in practice to become functional families is something that has only relatively recently come to be reflected in the law. Current legal discourse tries to recon-

---

[195] See Chapter 2 above.
[196] Parentline Plus 2005.
[197] Feijten et al (2011).

cile the competing needs for children for families or social parenthood (in this case recognising the authority and responsibility of the stepfather) and their biological ties (in this case recognising the need for contact and on-going parental responsibility of the non-resident father).[198] Its resolution for stepfathers is to provide ways for them to acquire legal status in relation to their stepchildren, without the non-resident biological father losing his status.

A step-parent can acquire legal status in relation to the child—parental responsibility— by agreeing with his partner who has parental responsibility (and any other parent who has parental responsibility) or by applying to the court for an order of parental responsibility.[199] Until he does so, or if he is not married to or not civilly registered with the child's parent, he remains only a de facto carer unless the relationship is formalised legally through an application for a residence order, which can be made only with the permission of the court, with the consent of those with parental responsibility[200] or after living with the child for three years.[201] Until the Adoption and Children Act 2002, the only other alternative for step-parents was joint adoption with their new spouse, but this alternative meant that not only was the non-resident parent's parental responsibility extinguished, the resident parent had to adopt her own child. Now, a cohabiting, married or civilly registered 'partner' may apply to adopt the child singly. While this is an improvement over the old situation, an adoption order would still operate to extinguish the status of the child's other parent. This is a situation which is not always desirable.

> **Q** Particularly in the light of the acceptability of 'serial monogamy', some scholars, such as Masson, suggested that the law needed to provide some increased status or rights for step-parents, including automatic parental responsibility on marriage (Masson 1989). Do these reforms, in your view, strike a fair balance between stable family life for children and continued importance of biological relationships?

Conclusion

Let us return to the themes we identified at the beginning of this chapter: equality, welfare/paternalism; and the public/private divide. We wished also to examine the strength of the ideology of the 'sexual family' within these themes. We looked first at the issue of legal and state regulation of parenthood status. Barton and Douglas (1995), drawing on the earlier work of Douglas and Lowe (1992), identify a continuum along which the degree of regulation runs 'from minimal, if any, control in the case of the carrying woman who happens to be unmarried, to a lengthy state investigation into the applicant's suitability to be a parent in the case of adoption' (Barton and Douglas 1995: 50). Regulation can be

---

[198] Edwards et al suggest that the law that emphasises biological over social ties is 'seeking to shift people's opinions in a particular direction', one which 'not only ignores the view that children need families, but requires biological parents to construct a social tie that most people feel is unworkable' (Edwards et al 1999: 101). They also suggest that the law exhibits a class bias, as their findings showed a significant class difference in the value people ascribe to each discourse, with working-class stepfamilies unanimously adopting a social family preference, none linking emotional relationships to biological status (ibid: 92), and middle-class families generally linking emotional connection, parental rights and responsibilities to biological status (ibid: 90).

[199] Children Act 1989 s 4A.

[200] S 10(5)(c) (iii).

[201] S 10(5)(b).

in the form of legislation and direct legal coercion, or it can be in the form of control or governance through non-legal agents, such as the social workers who determine the suitability of applicants for adoption and who visit the homes of foster carers or the physicians who decide appropriate candidates for infertility treatment. We saw in this regulation some apparent challenge to the 'sexual family' norm but also its 'tenacious' hold on the legal imagination (McCandless and Sheldon 2010b).

We saw also the way in which the welfare of the child is understood as remaining within in the sexual family when law must decide who are his or her 'parents'. Law also incorporates a form of gender equality which invokes and embraces ideas of new family practices and in particular a new, fragmented fatherhood. In addition, adoption reforms, the creation of the new legal status of 'female parent' and of statuses acquired by parental orders and special guardianship orders, and clearer recognition of the role of step-parents all appear to give credence to this proposition, even while new biological interventions become available for facilitating much desired biological parenthood and human rights are prayed in aid of acknowledging that identity. As we have maintained, however, these two trends may not be paradoxical, gender makes a difference in both the experience and the legal regulation of parenthood.

It is here, with the possibility of gender differences in mind, that we shall begin our discussion of what being a parent means in law.

VII. WHAT DOES IT MEAN TO BE A PARENT?
DAY-TO-DAY RESPONSIBILITIES

The first thing one can say about a parent's responsibility to his or her children is that they have some responsibility to look after their children and to nurture them. We will examine in Chapter 5 below the ways in which law may or may not enforce a parent's moral and social responsibility to rear well adjusted and healthy children. In this section we will examine the minimum standards the law lays down for defining a child's best interests and for parents' responsibilities to maintain them. That the standards have varied over the years reflects ever-changing notions of parental rights and responsibilities,[202] children's welfare,[203] and private and state responsibility for protecting it.[204]

In his *Commentaries on the Laws of England*, Blackstone divided what we would call parental 'rights and responsibilities' into parental 'duties and powers'. He summarised the duties of parents toward legitimate children as including maintenance, protection and education. The power of parents over their children he summarised as follows:

> The power of parents over their children is derived from the former consideration, their duty; this authority being given them, partly to enable the parent more effectually to perform his duty, and partly as a recompense for his care and trouble in the faithful discharge of it. And upon this score the municipal laws of some nations have given a much larger authority to the parents, than others. The Ancient Roman laws gave the father a power of life and death over his children; upon this principle, that he who gave had also the power of taking away.
>
> (Blackstone 1778: 452)

---

[202] See Chapter 8 below.
[203] See Chapter 9 below.
[204] See Chapter 5 below.

The power of a parent by our English laws is much more moderate, but still sufficient to keep the child in order and obedience. He may lawfully correct his child, being under age, in a reasonable manner, for this is for the benefit of his education. The consent or concurrence of the parent to the marriage of his child under age, was also *directed* by our ancient law to be obtained: but now it is absolutely *necessary*; for without it the contract is void ... . A father has no other authority over his son's *estate*, than as his trustee or guardian; for, though he may receive the profits during the child's minority, yet he must account for them when he comes of age. He may indeed have the benefit of his children's labour while they live with him, and are maintained by him; but this is no more than he is entitled to from his apprentices or servants. The legal power of a father (for a mother, as such, is entitled to no power, but only to reverence and respect) ... over the persons of his children ceases at the age of twenty one; for they are then enfranchised by arriving at years of discretion, or that point which the law has established (as some must necessarily be established) when the empire of the father, or other guardian, gives place to the empire of reason. Yet till that age arrives, this empire of the father continues even after his death; for he may by his will appoint a guardian to his children. (ibid: 452–53)

Q What is the nature of the family relationship and the state–family relationship evoked by Blackstone's description?

Parental Responsibility

Prior to the Children Act 1989, the law spoke of 'guardianship', 'parental rights and duties' or the 'rights and authority' of parents (Law Commission 1988b: para 2.4). The Law Commission was concerned that the language of rights that predominated at the time reflected an outmoded authoritarian model of parenthood and failed to recognise that contemporary parenthood is characterised by responsibilities rather than rights (ibid: para 2.1). The concept of parental responsibility is one of the key innovations of the Children Act 1989 and is designed to shift the emphasis away from rights and to form the basis of a coherent legal framework for the allocation of responsibility and decision-making powers concerning children. As Bainham (1999) has said, and as we saw above, parental responsibility must be distinguished from parentage and parenthood. All mothers and married parents automatically have parental responsibility, unmarried fathers can acquire it, as can local authorities, step-parents, guardians and special guardians, adopters and those who have a residence order in respect of a child. We have seen above how a number of these 'parents' acquire parental responsibility, and will look at unmarried fathers in Chapter 8 below, but for now wish to note that one of its distinguishing features is that it can be held by any number of people,[205] who do not have to be either biological or social parents of a child. Where parental responsibility vests in more than one person, each of them may act independently in meeting that responsibility, except where, as in the case of the marriage of the child, statute requires the consent of each,[206] or where there is a duty to consult.[207] When it is held by married parents it can never be lost, except by adoption. In any case, parental responsibility cannot be abandoned or transferred although it is possible

---

[205] Children Act 1989 s 2(5).
[206] Ibid, s 2(7).
[207] See Chapter 8 below.

to arrange for some or all of it to be met by someone, or agencies such as schools, acting on behalf of the person with parental responsibility.[208]

Parental Responsibility under the Children Act

Parental responsibility is defined in section 3(1) of the Children Act 1989: 'In this Act 'parental responsibility' means all the rights, duties, powers, responsibilities and authority which by law a parent of a child has in relation to the child and his property.' Thus, the incidents of parental responsibility were left to the common law, unlike in Scotland, for example, where the incidents of parental responsibility are listed in the Children (Scotland) Act 1995.[209]

The Children Act definition has, in fact, been described as a 'non-definition'.[210] Despite a number of calls for detailed codification of these rights and duties over the years (Barton and Douglas 1995: 115–16), the legislature has declined to specify in any detail what might be encompassed by this very general definition.

Q How would you define parental responsibility? Why do you think Parliament was reluctant to be more specific?

When debating the possibility of providing a complete list of parental rights and duties, the Law Commission observed that this 'would clearly be a large task involving consideration of many difficult and controversial areas ... . We doubt whether the list could ever be comprehensive' (Law Commission 1985b: para 1.9). The list would need to change from time to time to meet differing needs and circumstances and to take account of the child's age and maturity (Law Commission 1988b: para 2.6). The legislature's decision in favour of a very general definition may therefore be attributable to a perceived need to preserve flexibility and to enable the law to take account of changing circumstances and of differences between children.[211]

The Law Commission acknowledged that the change in terminology from rights to responsibilities would make little difference in substance (ibid: para 2.4) and the wording of section 3(1) of the Children Act makes it necessary, in order to interpret it, to look to those rights, duties and powers traditionally recognised by the law. Barton and Douglas, reviewing the literature, conclude that:

> If the legal agenda can be inferred from the conventional lists of issues involving some or all of those with parental authority, it might be itemised, roughly by the age of the child, like this:
>
> (1) physical possession, home, protection and contact;
> (2) name;
> (3) education and religion;
> (4) discipline and punishment;
> (5) medical treatment;

---

[208] S 2(9). In addition, as we saw with foster parents, a person who does not have parental responsibility but who has actual care of a child may do what is reasonable to safeguard or promote the child's welfare (s 3(5)). This would cover, eg, decisions relating to medical treatment in the event of an accident.

[209] S 1(1).

[210] Lord Meston, Hansard (HL), vol 502, col 1172.

[211] Lowe (1997) argues that more clarity along the Scottish lines is needed in England, particularly since the concept of parental responsibility is gaining international acceptance and usage.

(6) travel and emigration;
(7) property and contracting;
(8) legal proceedings;
(9) services;
(10) marriage;
(11) disposing of the child's corpse.   (Barton and Douglas 1995: 114)

The emphasis in the Children Act on responsibilities rather than rights is consonant with
the general aim of the law reformers to introduce a legal framework that is fundamentally
child-centred. This aim reflected the direction in which the law was already developing;
even prior to the enactment of this statute, parental rights were being cast by the courts
in terms of the duties owed by parents to children.[212]

> **Q** To what extent does Blackstone's account of parents' duties and powers
> resemble parental responsibility under the Children Act? Blackstone's account
> of paternal authority over children is one illustration of the privacy accorded
> that relationship by a non-interventionist eighteenth- and nineteenth-century
> state, in which even the most brutal forms of child abuse became a matter
> of public concern only later in the nineteenth century (Dingwall and Eekelaar
> 1988).[213] What type of care does the law require in the twenty-first-century ver-
> sion of the liberal state which privileges both parental autonomy (Blackstone's
> *powers*) and children's welfare (his *duties*)?

Criminal Responsibility

As a general rule, the law only imposes criminal liability as a result of a positive act
(Williams 1983: 146; Ashworth 1995: 104–5; cf Norrie 1993). It is contrary to notions of
the autonomy of the individual to hold a person liable for his or her failures to act, and
so, with a few exceptions, omissions cannot form the basis of criminal liability (Ashworth
1995: 108–09). One of those exceptions is where there is a pre-existing duty to act, and
the parent–child relationship is said to create such a duty. Bainham states that a parent's
duty to protect a child arises from his or her parental responsibility (Bainham 2005: 617).
In addition, others, 'who have "responsibility" for children, in the less technical sense of
assuming their physical care' are subject to a duty to protect children, so that their failure
to do so can give rise to criminal liability (ibid).[214]

Criminal acts committed by parents against children can include any offences against
the person, including sexual offences. Parents can be prosecuted under the Sexual Offences
Act 2003 for sexual offences against their children in the same way that strangers can,
but parents, along with other named relatives and carers, are also subject to special
criminal laws respecting sexual offences. The old criminal offence of incest (with respect
to children) has been replaced with the offences of sexual activity with a child family
member[215] and inciting a child family member to engage in sexual activity.[216] 'Child'

---

[212] See *Gillick v West Norfolk and Wisbech Area Health Authority* [1986] 1 AC 112.
[213] See Chapter 13 below.
[214] And see Children and Young Persons Act 1933 s 1(1) and (2)(b).
[215] S 25 Sexual Offences Act 2003.
[216] S 26.

means anyone under the age of 18 in these sections, and 'family' is broadly defined to include parent, grandparent, brother, sister, half-brother, half-sister, aunt or uncle, foster parent or former foster parent, and, if they have lived in the same household, step-parent (even if unmarried to the child's parent) cousin, stepbrother or sister or someone who has been involved in caring for or training the child.[217] In addition, there are a series of sexual offences that may be committed by people who are in positions of trust respecting a child.[218] These include people who care for children in care homes, institutions, residential homes and the like.[219]

The Offences Against the Person Act 1861 outlaws assault by anyone, including parents against their children, but in some cases the law does permit parents to chastise their children physically. In some cases, parents,[220] unlike strangers, are able to rely upon the right, described by Blackstone, and protected in Section 1(7) of the Children and Young Persons Act 1933, to administer punishment to a child. Until 2005 this defence was available to any charge, but section 58 of the Children Act 2004 has removed the defence from charges of wounding or causing grievous bodily harm and assault causing actual bodily harm under the Offences against the Person Act 1861 and child cruelty under the Children and Young Persons Act 1933. Even where the defence is available, the corporal punishment must be 'moderate and reasonable'.[221] Once this defence is raised to a charge, the burden of proof is on the prosecution to prove that the assault went beyond those limits.

Views vary greatly on the morality, the legality and indeed the effectiveness, of corporal punishment of children. Supporters say that a 'loving smack' (or more) is effective as a means of discipline and that prohibiting corporal punishment would mean that minor or trivial incidents could be prosecuted as criminal offences. Opponents argue that it teaches children that violence is an appropriate reaction to conflict, that it actually harms children's psychological development and that it can too easily escalate into serious abuse. The clearest argument against hitting children, no matter with what force, is that it infringes their rights under the ECHR and the UN Convention on the Rights of the Child. In *A v UK (Human Rights: Punishment of Child)*[222] the ECtHR heard a case that set in motion changes to the long-standing view in the UK that all corporal punishment was a private matter of child discipline. In this case a stepfather beat his 9-year-old stepson with a garden cane on several occasions, causing severe bruising. He raised the defence of lawful chastisement to a charge of assault occasioning actual bodily harm and was acquitted. A took the matter to the ECtHR alleging, among other things, a violation of his right under Article 3 of the ECHR not to be subjected to torture or to inhuman or degrading treatment or punishment. The European court held that the law did not provide adequate protection against treatment or punishment contrary to Article 3. The government's response was to issue a Consultation Document (Department of Health 2000a) but it limited its terms of reference immediately:

[217] S 27.

[218] Ss 16–24.

[219] Ss 21–22. For commentary and discussion see Bainham (2005: 620–28).

[220] It also protects those to whom parents have delegated the power to chastise: see *Sutton London Borough Council v Davis* [1994] 1 FLR 737. For a good summary see Law Commission (1995) Consultation Paper 139 Part XI and Fortin (2009a: 326ff).

[221] For changing interpretations of moderate and reasonable, see *R v Hopley* (1860) 2 F and F 202; *R v Derriviere* (1969) 53 Cr App R 637; and *R v Smith*, 2 November 1994 (CA); *A v UK* [1998] 2 FLR 959; *R v H* [2001] EWCA Crim 1024; [2001] 2 FLR 431. See also Fortin (2009a: 325–34; Smith, (2004).

[222] [1998] 2 FLR 959.

1.5 The Government fully accepts the need for change. The harmful and degrading treatment of children can never be justified. We have made it quite clear, however, that we do not consider that the right way forward is to make unlawful all smacking and other forms of physical rebuke and this paper explicitly rules out this possibility. There is a common sense distinction to be made between the sort of mild physical rebuke which occurs in families and which most loving parents consider acceptable, and the beating of children.

The government seemed to be relying upon the results of an ONS survey in 1998 in which 85% of respondents agreed it was sometimes necessary to smack a naughty child over 5 years old; 53% if the child was over 2 years old, and 13% if the child was under 2 years old (DoH 2000a: 21). And the English public seems still to be quite unequivocal in its support of corporal punishment. While parents' attitudes towards smacking have shifted over time, it is less likely to be used/have been used by current parents and there is often a correlation between parents' opinions on smacking and their age (with younger parents tending to hold more negative opinions about smacking than older parents), around half of all parents think it is sometimes necessary to smack a naughty child (DCSF 2007: 1). The majority of parents think the law should allow parents to smack their children (ibid).

Perhaps it is not surprising that in the light of this popular sentiment, the government has gone no further than the Children Act 2004 amendments to reform the law directly. It found that more far reaching reform was not required under the ECHR, since the coming into force of the Humant Rights Act meant that any court considering a reasonable chastisement defence would be bound to take into account the *A v UK* judgment, which said that the factors relevant in determining whether there was a breach of Article 3 were the nature and context of the defendant's behaviour, its duration, its physical and mental effect upon the child, and the age and personal characteristics of the child. Since then, there has been some suggestion that a further factor has been added to the list: the reasons given by the defendant for administering the punishment.[223]

> **Q** Do you think the government has responded adequately to the *A v UK* case? In addition to the ECHR, Article 37 of the UN Convention on the Rights of the Child states: 'No child shall be subjected to cruel, inhuman or degrading treatment or punishment.' Since 1991 corporal punishment has been banned in children's homes[224] and foster placements;[225] it has been outlawed in state schools since 1987;[226] and since 1998[227] in all schools.[228] Finally, since 2003 child-minders have not been allowed to administer corporal punishment to children in their care.[229]

> **Q** Freeman says the current law on smacking is a statement about how children are regarded in society: '[N]othing is a clearer statement of the position that

[223] *R v H* above. See generally, Smith (2004).
[224] Children's Homes Regs 1991, SI 1991/1506, Reg 8(2)(a).
[225] Foster Placement (Children) Regs 1991, SI 1991/910.
[226] Education (No 2) Act 1986 s 47; Education (Abolition of Corporal Punishment) (Independent Schools) Regs 1987, SI 1987/1183; Education (Abolition of Corporate Punishment) (Independent Schools) (Prescribed Categories of Persons) Regs 1989, SI 1989/1825, which together abolish corporal punishment in schools wholly or partly funded by the state, or where pupils' education is subsidised by the local authority or the government.
[227] Education Act 1996 s 548(1), as amended by School Standards and Framework Act 1998.
[228] The prohibition was upheld by the House of Lords in *R (on the application of Williamson) v Secretary of State for Education and Employment* [2005] UKHL 15; [2005] 1 FCR 498. See further discussion below.
[229] Day Care and Child Minding (National Standards) (England) Regulations 2003 SI 2003/1996, para 5.

children occupy in society, a clearer badge of childhood, than the fact that children alone of all people in society can be hit with impunity' (Freeman 1997a). Do you agree? For an excellent discussion of the issues, see Herring (2011: 471–74).

In addition to these minimal standards set by the criminal law regarding sexual offences and offences against the person,[230] there are other offences relating to the mistreatment or death of children while in someone's care. The Children and Young Persons Act 1933 creates offences relating to the mistreatment and neglect of children by their carers.[231] The relevant wording of the legislation is as follows:

1(1) If any person who has attained the age of sixteen years and has responsibility for any child or young person under that age, wilfully[232] assaults, ill-treats, neglects, abandons, or exposes him, or causes or procures him to be assaulted, ill-treated, neglected abandoned or exposed, in a manner likely to cause him unnecessary suffering or injury to health (including injury to or loss of sight, or hearing, or limb, or organ of the body, and any mental derangement), that person shall be guilty of a misdemeanour, and shall be liable—

(a) on conviction on indictment, to a fine or alternatively, or in addition thereto, to imprisonment for any term not exceeding ten years;

(b) on summary conviction, to a fine not exceeding [the prescribed sum] or in addition thereto, to imprisonment not exceeding six months.

(2) For the purposes of this section—

(a) a parent or other person legally liable to maintain a child or young person, or the legal guardian of the young person, shall be deemed to have neglected him in a manner likely to cause injury to his health if he has failed to provide adequate food, clothing, medical aid or lodging for him, or if, having been unable otherwise to provide such food, clothing, medical aid or lodging, he has failed to take steps to procure it to be provided under the enactments applicable in that behalf. ...

(3) A person may be convicted of an offence under this section—

(a) notwithstanding that actual suffering or injury to health, or the likelihood of actual suffering or injury to health, was obviated by the action of another person ... .

(7) Nothing in this section shall be construed as affecting the right of any parent, or (subject to section 548 of the Education Act 1996) any other person, having the lawful control or charge of a child or young person to administer punishment to him.[233]

And the Domestic Violence, Crime and Victims Act 2004 creates the offence of causing or allowing the death of a child or vulnerable adult:

---

[230] See also Children and Young Persons Act 1933 s 1(2)(b) regarding death of a child by suffocation while in bed with another who was under the influence of drink.

[231] The Act also deals with employment restrictions for children, begging, sale of tobacco to children and other matters.

[232] In *R v Sheppard* [1981] AC 394 the House of Lords interpreted the word 'wilfully' as including an element of *mens rea* or intention to commit the offence. See the discussion of this in Barton and Douglas (1995: 138–39).

[233] Recent examples of prosecutions under this section include *R v AG* [2003] EWCA Crim 3046 (causing unnecessary suffering); *R v L (Yasmin)* [2003] EWCA Crim 1146 (neglect by leaving a young child alone at home); and see also *Re A (Children) (Conjoined Twins: Surgical Separation)* [2001] 2 WLR 480; [2001] 1 FLR 1 for a discussion of the requirement to provide medical treatment.

5 The offence

(1) A person ('D') is guilty of an offence if—

(a) a child or vulnerable adult ('v') dies as a result of the unlawful act of a person who—
   (i)   was a member of the same household as V, and
   (ii) had frequent contact with him,
(b) D was such a person at the time of that act,
(c) at that time there was a significant risk of serious physical harm being caused to V by the unlawful act of such a person, and
(d) either D was the person whose act caused V's death or—
   (i)   D was, or ought to have been, aware of the risk mentioned in paragraph (c),
   (ii) D failed to take such steps as he could reasonably have been expected to take to protect v from the risk, and
   (iii) the act occurred in circumstances of the kind that D foresaw or ought to have foreseen.

(2) The prosecution does not have to prove whether it is the first alternative in subsection (1)(d) or the second (sub-paragraphs (i) to (iii)) that applies.

(3) If D was not the mother or father of V—

(a) D may not be charged with an offence under this section if he was under the age of 16 at the time of the act that caused V's death;
(b) for the purposes of subsection (1)(d) (ii) D could not have been expected to take any such step as is referred to there before attaining that age.

(4) For the purposes of this section—

(a) a person is to be regarded as a 'member' of a particular household, even if he does not live in that household, if he visits it so often and for such periods of time that it is reasonable to regard him as a member of it;
(b) where v lived in different households at different times, 'the same household as V' refers to the household in which V was living at the time of the act that caused V's death.

(5) For the purposes of this section an 'unlawful' act is one that—

(a) constitutes an offence, or
(b) would constitute an offence but for being the act of—
   (i)   a person under the age of ten, or
   (ii) a person entitled to rely on a defence of insanity.
Paragraph (b) does not apply to an act of D.

(6) In this section—

'act' includes a course of conduct and also includes omission;
'child' means a person under the age of 16;
'serious' harm means harm that amounts to grievous bodily harm for the purposes of the Offences against the Person Act 1861 (c 100);
'vulnerable adult' means a person aged 16 or over whose ability to protect himself from violence, abuse or neglect is significantly impaired through physical or mental disability or illness, through old age or otherwise.

(7) A person guilty of an offence under this section is liable on conviction on indictment to imprisonment for a term not exceeding 14 years or to a fine, or to both.

This offence is designed to deal with cases in which a child (or vulnerable person) dies as a result of conduct by a member of his or her household which puts him or her at serious risk of physical harm and it is not clear which of two people actually caused the death. An offence is committed if the adult household member actually caused the death, or if they were aware or ought to have been aware of the risk, they foresaw or ought to have foreseen the act causing the death, and they failed to take reasonable steps to protect the child from the risk. The prosecution does not have to prove which of these situations applies to the person(s) charged.

Education

Most people agree that education is a good in and of itself. Children in England, however, were not required to attend school until 1880. Prior to that, education was provided on a private fee-paying or charitable basis, with schools often being run by the church (Cunningham 1995). Many schools for the poor were run by charities with the specific aim of teaching children (Protestant) Christian values (Cunningham 1995: 119–20)

And the aims of the state were not always child-centred in providing for compulsory elementary education.

> The state's purpose in making schooling compulsory went beyond a desire to ensure that every child was taught the three Rs; it wanted to instil morality, and patriotism, and to train children in regular habits. (Cunningham 1995: 157)

Barton and Douglas also make this point: 'As industrial processes developed in complexity, employers saw the advantages in having a disciplined and at least partly-skilled labour force and therefore supported the expansion of elementary education' (Barton and Douglas 1995: 256).

They go on:

> There were tensions, first, between the needs of the economy for a skilled (or drilled) workforce and those of parents to support their families with the help of older offspring, and secondly, between the right of the state to assert what should be taught and the right of parents to control what their children learnt. Such tensions were reflected in the low leaving age, which permitted parents to turn their children into economically productive units, but only as soon as industry could make use of them, and the control over the curriculum of Her Majesty's Inspectorate whose annual inspections led to a strong ethos of 'teaching to the test'. (ibid: 266)[234]

The state, then, accepted responsibility in the nineteenth century for educating its youth, but it also placed on parents a responsibility to ensure that their children received this education.

Determining a child's education is an incident of parental responsibility. This means that parents can decide on the type of education their children receive,[235] and the ethos of the education system since the 1980s has been to encourage parents to exercise a 'choice' in their children's education and to give them more say in the running of schools. Education has in this way become seen as a consumer commodity amenable to the 'rules' of the market. The consumer is, however, the parent rather than the child. The general principle underlying the Education Act 1996 is, in fact, that children shall be educated in

---

[234] See also Dingwall and Eekelaar (1988).

[235] Where those with parental responsibility disagree about the child's education, they may seek a specific issue order or a prohibited steps order under s 8 Children Act 1989. See Chapter 10 below for a full discussion.

accordance with the wishes of their parents,[236] and this position has the backing of the ECHR. Article 2 of the First Protocol of the ECHR states:

> No person shall be denied the right to education. In the exercise of the functions which it assumes in relation to education, and to teaching, the state shall respect the right of parents to ensure such education and teaching in conformity with their own religious and philosophical convictions.

The scope of this Article was tested in a case in which parents (and teachers) of children at Christian independent schools argued that the prohibition on corporal punishment infringed their rights under it to ensure that their children were educated according to their religious and philosophical convictions.[237] They argued that corporal punishment was required by their religious convictions. The House of Lords agreed that while these rights were engaged, the ban on corporal punishment pursued a legitimate aim, was not disproportionate and therefore was a measure Parliament was entitled to take.

Parents nonetheless have great discretion in determining their children's education. They also have responsibilities, though. After a series of statutory measures, the obligation of parents today to ensure that their children are provided with an education is found primarily in the Education Act 1996. It places parents under a duty to ensure that children of compulsory school age—between the ages of 5 and 16—receive education suitable to their needs, ability, aptitude and age.[238] Some parents attempt to provide this education for their children at home.[239] Where parents fail to secure the regular attendance of a registered pupil at school, they have committed an offence[240] punishable by a fine, three months imprisonment or by the issuing against them of an education penalty notice[241] by the headteacher, his or her delegate or the local education authority. The penalty notice requires the parent to pay a fine in lieu of criminal proceedings being brought. If a parent fails to demonstrate that the child is otherwise receiving a suitable education, the local education authority may issue a school attendance order[242] and if the parent fails to comply with it he or she has also committed an offence.[243] Otherwise the local education authority can apply for a parenting order[244] or request that the parent enter into a parenting contract under the Anti Social Behaviour Act 2003.

Q Should parents be guilty of a criminal offence if children are not sent to school? What about the parents of a 14 year old who regularly truants?

Civil proceedings may also be brought in the event of children's failure to attend school. The local education authority can apply for an Education Supervision Order under the

---

[236] Education Act 1996 s 9.

[237] *R (on the application of Williamson) v Secretary of State for Education and Employment* [2005] UKHL 15; [2005] 1 FCR 498. They also claimed the prohibition violated their right to freedom of religious expression under Art 9 of the ECHR.

[238] Ss 7 and 8. See also Education and Skills Act 2008 which is not yet in force, requires young people to remain in education or training until age 18.

[239] See Monk (2009).

[240] Education Act 1996 s 444.

[241] Ibid, s 444A; Education Penalty Notice Regulations 2004 SI 2004/181.

[242] Education Act 1996 s 437.

[243] Ibid, s 443.

[244] Crime and Disorder Act 1998.

Children Act 1989[245] which requires the supervisor to 'advise, assist, befriend and give directions to' the child and his or her parents so as to secure that the child is properly educated.[246] In extreme circumstance a care order may be made.[247]

You will notice that the first part of Article 2 of Protocol 1 of the ECHR states that 'no person shall be denied the right to education'. This seems to suggest that education is a right belonging to the child, rather than to her parents. And Article 28 of the UN Convention on the Rights of the Child requires states to:

> recognise the right of the child to education, and with a view to achieving this right progressively and on the basis of equal opportunity ...
>
> (a) make primary education compulsory and available free to all ...
> (b) encourage the development of different forms of secondary education ... make them available and accessible to every child, and take appropriate measures such as the introduction of free education and offering financial assistance in case of need;
> (c) make higher education accessible to all on the basis of capacity.

> **Q** What does it mean to have a right to education? Can that right be enforced by children against parents? By children or parents against the state? See on this *R (on the application of Holub) v Secretary of State for the Home Department* [2001] I WLR 1359. Against a school? Does Article 2 protect the right of children or the rights of parents? See generally on children's rights and education, Fortin (2009a: ch 6) and Meredith (2001). See generally on education law, Harris (2007). See also the Education and Skills Act 2008 which will place a duty on all people in England to participate in education or training until age 18.

> **Q** How, in your view, ought the responsibility for educating children to be divided between family members and schools? Does it depend upon what is being taught? Does it depend upon the age of the child? Consider these questions in the light of the discussion of nursery provision for under fives in Chapter 5 below, where one of the justifications for universal provision was its educational value for younger children.

Housing and Healthcare

The Children and Young Persons Act 1933 makes it an offence for a parent to fail to provide adequate lodgings for a child, or to fail to procure adequate lodgings according to the appropriate statutory provisions.

The Children and Young Persons Act 1933 also makes specific mention of a parent's duty to provide medical aid for a child, and stipulates that a parent who fails in that duty is deemed to have neglected the child. The state also assumes a responsibility for the medical care of children through the National Health Service, and the court is sometimes called upon to make decisions in respect of medical treatments. As is the case with education, however, the question is how the balance between state responsibilities and parental responsibilities is to be struck. We discuss this in Chapters 5 and 11 below and

---

[245] S 36 and Part III Sch 3.
[246] Sch 3 Para 12(1)(a).
[247] *Re O (A Minor) (Care Order: Education: Procedure)* [1992] 2 FLR 7.

we also discuss in Chapter 11 the third dimension added to this issue: that of the *child's* role in the decision-making process.

VIII. BEING A MOTHER, BEING A FATHER AND BEING A CHILD

Mothers and Fathers

Parents' legal responsibilities towards their children are outlined by law in gender-neutral terms. Indeed, reading the statutes, one would not think there is any longer a difference between the responsibilities of mothers and (married) fathers in law. The creation of the new de-gendered 'legal parent' (who could be either a man or a woman) in law may only confirm this view. Recent feminist work has suggested, however, that *social* prescriptions about good mothers and good fathers are often reflected in and reinforced by legal prescriptions. Scholars have written, for example, of the ideologies of motherhood and fatherhood and noted that the two bear different meanings when reflected in legal duties and responsibilities of parents.[248]

Q What activities or characteristics come to your mind when you think of mothering? What about fathering?

Collier (1995a, b) has written how the absent, authoritarian breadwinner was traditionally the 'father' of law, and Smart (1991), Fineman (1995), and Smart and Sevenhuijsen (1989) show how mothering has traditionally meant nurturing and physical care. As all of these writers suggest, however, there is nothing biologically predetermined about these developments. Others agree:

> Ruddick (1997) also suggests that in modern Western societies the ideal father is defined by the functions of provision, protection and authority/legitimation (p 207). Crucially, however, while she recognises that mothers also fulfil these functions, they do so in a more immediate way, so that fathers provide 'distantly'—away from home—mothers more closely and intimately; fathers protect against physical intrusion or 'an uncertain and dangerous world', mothers adopt an additional focus on daily dangers or emotional suffering; and fathers represent the reality of the 'world' and its authority to judge and punish while mothers represent the comforts of home and 'soft love' (pp 207–11). Her observations have been confirmed in empirical research which shows that these gendered roles for parents are deeply entrenched in peoples' ideals of family life (Warin, *et al*, 1999, Hatten, *et al*, 2002). She states, of course, that there is nothing inherent about these characteristics, and indeed images of the 'new' caring, sharing father who changes nappies and experiences emotional intimacy with his child have abounded in the last decade or so. That men *can* 'mother' in this way is not disputed (see also Fineman 1995) and presumably this means also that women can 'father', but social and economic conditions and ideologies of motherhood, fatherhood and childhood conspire to make this type of degendered parental work difficult. (Diduck 2003: 85)

---

[248] See, eg, Diduck (1993, 1995); Boyd (1996); Smart (1991); Collier (1995a, b); Smart and Sevenhuijsen (1989); Smart and Neale (1999).

Recently, Collier (2010) and Collier and Sheldon (2008) have suggested that the traditional idea of 'father' has become more complicated. They trace a 'coming together of economic, cultural and political developments [which] has served to reframe the question of what constitutes a "good father" and responsible "family man" in law' (Collier and Sheldon 2008: 133). At the same time, however, they recognise a 'coexistence of change and continuity' (ibid: 134): 'The "father as breadwinner" model and the masculinities with which it has been associated, have not been supplanted in law. Rather, they exist alongside and in tension with the new ideology of the "father as carer"' (ibid: 136). As we shall see in Chapters 5 and 6 below, the challenges this complication poses for policy and for fathers themselves is clear in negotiations, for example, of policies directed at 'helping parents' (Kaganas 2010b) and work–family balance.[249]

Despite popular accounts of the 'new' father who cares intimately for his children, therefore, what we may see now is a new fatherhood infused with a degree of uncertainty and ambiguity which is fed by hegemonic masculinities, new forms of intimacy and current government policy to promote active parenting by both parents (Collier and Sheldon 2008). There is less uncertainty about motherhood, however. Even where parents profess to desire the co-parenting ideal, most settle into the typical pattern where mothers become primary caretakers and fathers provide 'distantly' (Hatten et al, 2002; Ellison et al 2009). In Smart, Neale and Wade's study, 'basically fathers were one step removed from their children and their relationship with them was sustained via their relationship with the mother' (Smart et al 2001: 47). And children themselves often see mothers as the parent who is 'the main source of physical and emotional care', and fathers as 'someone to do things with' (James 1999: 192).

The roles that heterosexual parents play in their children's lives may thus be constrained by a gender ideology that arguably is supported by legal and cultural institutions. Research with same-sex parents also demonstrates that while they often are able to redefine the boundaries, meaning and content of parenthood, and while they do not have to conform to gender scripts and can 'make it up' as they go along (Dunne 2000: 13), many also fall into gendered patterns of work and care (Gabb 2005; Burns et al 2008).

Children

Henricson and Bainham argue that it has always been the family that the state has been concerned to support rather than the individual rights of family members (Henricson and Bainham 2005: 11), and on this view the way that motherhood or fatherhood is supported by law and policy does reflect government's ideas of the good family from time to time.[250]

However Henricson and Bainham also note that there is now a 'perceptible trend towards policies that place *children* and their rights much higher up the political agenda' (ibid: 9, emphasis added). This is evident, they say, from the provisions of the UN Convention on the Rights of the Child (ibid: 21), the EU Charter (ibid: 28) and the European Constitution (ibid: 30).[251] This new focus on children's rights[252] implies, and/or stems from, a perception of children as separate and independent persons and legal personalities.

---

[249] See also Collier (2010), particularly chs 4, 5 and 7.

[250] See also Collier (2001).

[251] See, on the constitution, Schuurman (2003).

[252] Henricson and Bainham do not regard the primacy accorded to children's rights or welfare as legitimate; they argue that this could lead to the undervaluing of the rights of other family members in contravention of

'The story of the acceptance of the notion of children's rights,' they note, 'is very largely one of gradual recognition of [children's] independent status as juristic persons and not mere adjuncts of their parents or constituent members of a family' (ibid: 31).

Traditional ideas of children as objects of concern who can and should be moulded and socialised within the school and the private family have also been challenged by researchers who have engaged directly with children. Perceptions of children now encompass the image of the child as an active participant in home and public life. Yet the image of the child as an object of care or concern also persists. Kaganas and Diduck explain:

> The newly complex paradigm child incorporates two previously competing images of the child. The first is the child as incompetent and dependent. This child is vulnerable because he or she is in the process of development toward self or personhood. This child is one whose welfare is to be prioritised over rights because he or she is not yet fully capable of exercising rights competently. This child needs to be protected. The image is rooted in philosophical ideas of the child as 'becoming' a fully rational subject, and incorporates images of the child as evil, inno-cent or as a blank slate. It also incorporates socialisation theory as well as ideas in developmental psychology suggesting that there is a teleological progression through various and fixed devel-opmental stages of maturation. It can be described as a romantic developmentalist view of the child and has a veneer of common sense about it. It appears to be the dominant paradigm in which educationalists, psychologists and child welfare professionals, including CAFCASS prac-titioners, work.
>
> However, in contrast to this, sociologists studying childhood have begun to take seriously the idea of the child as 'being'. Rather than seeing childhood as a 'biologically determined' and universal stage, which is characterised by incompetence or irrationality, and through which all children pass on their way to completion as autonomous adults, they see it as a socially constructed space or as a variable concept. On this view, children need not necessarily be conceived of as inactive mounds of clay to be formed by socialising agents, by nature or by structural forces over which they have no control. Instead, it becomes possible to put forward alternative images of children and these, according to James and Prout, have gained currency: 'Looking at children not only as outcomes of social processes but as actors within them has gained widespread acceptance'. Indeed, they highlight this as an 'emergent paradigm' for the study of childhood and identify as one of the key features of this approach the need to see children 'as active in the construction and determination of their own social lives, the lives of those around them and of the societies in which they live'. With this kind of paradigm, it becomes possible to ascribe to children the characteristics of reflexivity and agency and to see them as participants in the project of late modern individualisation. In this paradigm, children have the capacity to exercise a form of agency, a type of post-liberal autonomy, and to affect and influence their environment, conditions, attachments, detachments and self-identity. More than this, they are assigned an increasing degree of responsibility for doing so.
>
> Both the romantic developmentalist child and the autonomous reflexive child are idealised constructs. While they are in many ways dichotomous ideals, we suggest that both contribute to the new ideal child of law. Their simultaneous presence reflects an ambivalence within the legal ideal, an ambivalence most clearly apparent in criminal law. And, while there can be little doubt that it is the dependent, romantic child that is still dominant in private family law, we are of the view that it is possible to detect in this field of discourse too increasing references to children's autonomy and responsibility.
>
> This blending of paradigms is more than a way for law to reconcile the long-standing tension between the child as subject and as object. While that attempted reconciliation is important, we suggest that what is also important is the process and the discourse through which it is pursued.

the ECHR They also point out that the CRC recognises the importance to children of their parents and other family members (Henricson and Bainham 2005: 21).

It may, in other words, reflect a more general drive to recruit children into a broader social project of promoting 'active citizenship'. (Kaganas and Diduck 2004: 961–62, references omitted)

Q Do you agree that law reflects a 'blended paradigm' child? How has law constructed childhood in education law? In adoption law? In determining a child's parentage?

Q What do the authors mean by 'active citizenship'? How, if at all does law promote it?

The new way of 'seeing' children is described by Neale as being 'not simply as welfare dependants but as young citizens with an active contribution to make to society' (Neale 2004: 1). She goes on to define children's citizenship as 'an entitlement to recognition, respect and participation' and asserts that these are 'basic needs' which are 'crucial to children's well-being' (ibid). Children's citizenship, she says, is 'both a need and a right' (ibid: 9). What needs to be done, she says, is to find ways of integrating citizenship and welfare more effectively into public policy and of extending the principles of citizenship to younger children (ibid: 2).

The concept of citizenship deployed here embraces consultation in the sense of 'listening and responding to children' and entails 'inviting children to communicate and take part in decision making about matters that affect them' (ibid: 3). Those children who wish to participate should be able to do so while the wishes of those who do not should be respected (ibid: 4). This move to participation, she observes, necessitates a change in the way that children are perceived and a change in the relationships between children and adults both in the public and the private arenas. The dominant 'welfare paradigm', she says, constructs children as 'relatively incapable and vulnerable to harm, and therefore in need of strong guidance, control and support from responsible adults', particularly if they are young (ibid: 8). Children's welfare is defined by adults. In contrast, an approach that rests on the idea of citizenship enables children to be seen as people with strengths and competencies, competencies born of experience rather than age and so potentially present in young children (ibid: 8).[253]

Adults, contends Neale, have to recognise that children are people 'in their own right' and that 'they have their own ways of understanding the world and are capable of defining their own needs, rights, interests and responsibilities' (ibid: 9). Adults should not necessarily control children but, instead, support them 'as they begin to take responsibility for their own lives' (ibid). At the same time, children do have to be protected.

This tension between welfare and rights/autonomy is apparent in the telling distinction that is made between participation and choice. Children, Neale points out, prefer to make decisions 'collaboratively with supportive adults rather than autonomously' (ibid: 4, 10). They 'will accept adult responsibilities to make final decisions as long as these are based on open communication and the reasons for particular decisions are made transparent' (ibid). 'Granting citizenship to children, then, is not the same thing as granting them autonomous political rights, nor does it detract from their welfare needs' (ibid: 10).

We have seen that there has, indeed, been a move towards eliciting children's views on

---

[253] See Marchant and Kirby (2004) who contend that even infants' wishes should be taken into account when decisions and plans are made. Of course, young children's wishes might be overridden, they say, but adults should develop ways of communicating with them to enable them to express preferences. Presumably, however, those expressions of preferences are always subject to adult interpretation.

a number of issues in the public sphere such as adoption, health and education,[254] and children's views are more frequently taken into account in court proceedings impacting on their family lives.[255] Encouraging consultation with young people[256] and facilitating their participation in some form was an important part of New Labour policy. Whether children's views have a significant influence on decisions is open to doubt, however. Willow, for example, found that, in relation to consultation with children under 12, there was little evidence of noticeable impact and what there was, tended to be 'one-off and small scale' (Willow 2004: 23).[257] Nevertheless the rhetoric of participation is clearly apparent[258] and children are described, like their adult counterparts, as 'customers' of services (DfES 2001: 6).

What is striking, however, is that much of the talk focused not only on the benefits to children and young people of being heard, but on the importance of teaching them to become responsible citizens. This is undoubtedly linked to the government's continuing concerns about promoting social inclusion and its 'war on anti-social behaviour' (Henricson and Bainham 2005: 35).[259] Yet Henricson and Bainham suggest that the government was concerned to promote children's welfare rather than rights in its social exclusion strategy (ibid: 44). And even the remit of the Children's Commissioner, they say, is concerned with outcomes for children rather than children's rights (ibid: 61).

The coalition government's 'Big Society' agenda sits alongside its continuation of a form of the previous government's social exclusion strategy. The 'Big Society' is intended to 'encourage greater participation in local decision making and to shift ownership of assets and of initiative into the hands of local individual, groups and communities' (Fisher and Gruescu 2011). In a study entitled *Children and the Big Society*, however, the authors conclude that the agenda remains disconnected from children and families (ibid: 49) and that more could be done to encourage children's and young people's participation in planning and building the communities they wish to live in. In this and in most policy about children, the image of the child as an autonomous actor is closely constrained within the framework of welfare. The idea of the child as responsible citizen is imbued with ideas of socialisation. And the idea of consulting children does not necessarily include giving effect to their wishes.

Q Does government policy on children's citizenship reflect Neale's view of children's citizenship?

As we saw, children themselves tend to differ on whether they want to exercise decision-making rights. Those who do want to have some meaningful influence over their social and material lives do not necessarily wish to be independent decision-makers. Nevertheless, they do not want to be shut out from the decision-making process either. They simply wish to have a voice (Smart, Neale and Wade 2001: 122), both in legal processes concerning them and in their everyday family practices.

---

[254] See Willow (2004).

[255] See Chapter 11 below. For example, children's attendance at court may be becoming more acceptable.

[256] As Marchant and Kirby (2004) say, it is young people, rather than very young children, who are normally consulted. See DfES (2001: 5) and see also DfES (2005).

[257] On decisions where parents split up, see May and Smart (2004); James et al (2003).

[258] See, eg, CYPU (2001: 1, 6); DCA (2003a: 5, 21); DCA, DfES and DTI (2005: para 52).

[259] Regarding the then Labour government's strategy to reduce poverty and promote social inclusion, see Henricson and Bainham (2005: 39ff).

These studies have found that children also see themselves with a degree of autonomy in their construction of family and relationships. They negotiate care and support in a democratic way within their families ... . 'They viewed themselves not simply as children needing care but as young people who wanted to talk to others and be listened to, trust others and be trusted, and engage in open and meaningful communications. ... In other words, children value a democratic style of family life' (Smart, Neale and Wade 2001, p 58) in which they are active participants.

(Diduck 2003: 82)

> **Q** How, if at all, can parents accommodate this 'new' child? How can law either support them or inhibit them from doing so? Consider for example, the law on corporal punishment.

IX. CONCLUSION

We have seen how the law maintains a balance between public and private responsibility for children, but that the balance weighs in favour of private parental responsibility. We have raised questions about how the law assigns parenthood, and raised issues concerning parental autonomy and the public interest in parenting, and have complicated the matter further by introducing issues of gender and of children's autonomy. We have also considered that parents may be the same sex and that this factor may influence parenting in practice.[260] Throughout, we have inferred that much of the law and policy about parents and children is concerned primarily to promote and preserve a particular version of the family. While there are concessions made in law to new and 'messy' family practices, that version still looks remarkably like the heterosexual, nuclear, or traditional, family that we examined in Chapter 1 above. We have also inferred that that family may be perceived as being 'in crisis' and therefore to require discipline, or a form of remoralisation (Day Sclater and Piper 2000), and that law's choices in assigning parenthood and the responsibilities that go with that assignment are a part of that remoralisation project. We shall develop these observations further in the following chapters, in which specific questions arise as to how parents and children negotiate the legal ordering of their day to day lives.

FURTHER READING

A BAINHAM, 'Parentage, Parenthood and Parental Responsibility: Subtle, Elusive, Yet Important Distinctions' in A Bainham, S Day Sclater and M Richards, *What is a Parent?* (Oxford, Hart Publishing, 1999).

S CHOUDHRY, 'The Adoption and Children Act 2002, The Welfare Principle and the Human Rights Act 1998—A Missed Opportunity?' (2003) 15 *CFLQ* 119.

R COLLIER, *Men, Law and Gender, Essays on the 'Man' of Law* (Abingdon, Routledge, 2010).

R COLLIER and S SHELDON, *Fragmenting Fatherhood, A Socio-Legal Study* (Oxford, Hart Publishing 2008).

R COOK, S DAY SCLATER and F KAGANAS (eds), *Surrogate Motherhood: International Perspectives* (Oxford, Hart Publishing, 2003).

---

[260] For a discussion of transgender parents, see McCandless and Sheldon (2010b).

G Dunne, 'Opting into Motherhood: Lesbians Blurring the Boundaries and Transforming the Meaning of Parenthood and Kinship' (2000) 14 *Gender and Society* 11.

J Fortin, *Children's Rights and the Developing Law*, 3rd edn (London, Butterworths, 2009).

C Henricson and A Bainham, *The Child and Family Policy Divide* (York, Joseph Rowntree Foundation, 2005).

E Jackson, 'What Is a Parent?' in A Diduck and K O'Donovan (eds), *Feminist Perspectives on Family Law* (London, Cavendish, 2007).

F Kaganas and A Diduck, 'Incomplete Citizens: Changing Images of Post-Separation Children' (2004) 67 *MLR* 959.

J Lewis, 'Adoption: The Nature of Policy Shifts in England and Wales 1972–2002' (2004) 18 *Int'l J of Law, Policy and the Family* 235.

M Maclean and J Eekelar, *The Parental Obligation* (Oxford, Hart Publishing, 1997).

J McCandless and S Sheldon 'The Human Fertilisation and Embryology Act 2008 and the Tenacity of the Sexual Family Form' (2010) 73 *MLR* 175.

A Prout and A James, 'A New Paradigm for the Sociology of Childhood? Provenance, Promise and Problems' in A James and A Prout (eds), *Constructing and Reconstructing Childhood* (London, Routledge, 2003).

EB Silva (ed), *Good Enough Mothering? Feminist Perspectives on Lone Motherhood* (London, Routledge, 1996).

C Smart, B Neale and A Wade, *The Changing Experience of Childhood Families and Divorce* (Cambridge, Polity Press, 2001).

J Triseliotis, J Feast and F Kyle, *The Adoption Triangle Revisited A Study of Adoption, Search and Reunion Experiences (Summary)* (London, BAAF, 2005).

5

The Family–State Relationship:
Social Policy

I. FAMILY LIVING AND SOCIAL POLICY

It has always been a feature of welfare states to provide support and assistance for their citizens. That assistance comes in the form of services or financial provision. In the past, welfare policy and legal initiatives targeted employment, housing, economic or health outcomes, all of which clearly affected family relationships and family life, but were not directed at families per se. It is only relatively recently that we can say the UK has had a specific 'family policy' that targets the well-being of families as a part of an integrated government policy across diverse social welfare issues. That policy arguably creates and regulates the direct relationship between families and family members with the state and in doing so has a profound influence upon partnering decisions, caring decisions and decisions to become parents, and upon our ability to implement these decisions. State policies in areas such as childcare, employment, taxation, welfare and housing[1] provide the context in which we 'do' family and either facilitate or complicate family life.

> Welfare states have long been important actors in social and family life. While they vary in the degree to which they focus explicitly on the family, states have typically sought to secure family functioning, reproduction, and care provision against destructive tendencies of the market. The growth and development of the welfare state itself could be seen as countering 'pure' individualisation processes—a function of state intervention epitomised historically, by such diverse measures as the ban on child labour, regulation of working time, the development of social security for workers, and the granting of entitlements to those who provide care. Family law is a complementary part of such state intervention, intended to institutionalise mutual obligations and rights within couples and between family members and to cover some risks of those who face disadvantages in earning an income (typically women).
>
> (Daly and Scheiwe 2010: 178, references omitted).

We shall take the introduction of a specific family policy in England and Wales to have occurred in the late 1990s after the election of the New Labour government. This was a time when demographic changes associated with increased women's employment, changes in family forms and changes in the contributions that men and women make to the family (Lewis 2009: 4) were recognised formally and it coincided also with changes in labour

---

[1] Also relevant are education policies and law, disability, asylum, neighbourhood renewal and criminal justice.

markets and welfare state restructuring (ibid: 6). '[T]he decline of the male breadwinnner model, the changing nature of risk, an increasing degree of economic independence for women, and the desire to modernise social protection systems to match the goal of a less standardised and more flexible working life' (ibid 2009: 8) meant that families took on a new importance in social security policy. *Supporting Families*, the 1998 consultation document published by the newly elected government, recognised this importance and in proposing widespread changes to both policy and family law,[2] impliedly recognised that family law is a part of any state's social security provision. Following that document, the government set up the National Family and Parenting Institute (now the Family and Parenting Institute) a National Childcare Strategy and launched the Sure Start programme in 1998.[3] In 1999 the Prime Minister Tony Blair also announced the government's aim to cut child poverty by one-half by 2010 and eradicate it by 2020.

Since 1999 family and social security policy has been further 'modernised' by a focus on social exclusion, child development and 'work–life balance' for both mothers and fathers. The coalition government has maintained this focus which has become a part of its 'Big Society' agenda (Fisher and Gruescu 2011). The family's relationship with the state has changed greatly during this time, but these changes arguably continue to draw upon long-standing gendered principles and values (Daly and Scheiwe 2010: 195) which, while formally gender neutral, affect women and the children in their care disproportionately to men. We shall discuss these policies in the following areas: child poverty, work and benefits; support and compulsion for parents; work–life balance; and housing.

II. CHILD POVERTY, WORK AND BENEFIT:
SERVING TWO MASTERS?

In Britain, the 'contested—and shifting—boundary between state and private responsibility' (Fox Harding 1996: 108) for support has been negotiated differently at different times. The history begins with the first official legislation providing for public responsibility to support those who were not able to support themselves. The Tudor Poor Law of 1601 was concerned with controlling labour and the movement of people, but also sought to provide for their support by placing obligations upon kin to contribute and to reimburse the parish for support already extended. That law has been called a separate system of family law for the poor (ten Broek 1963–64), or a third system of family law (Finer and McGregor 1974: 268).[4] According to ten Broek:

> The poor law was thus not only a law *about* the poor but a law *of* the poor. It dealt with a condition, and it governed a class. The special legal provisions were designed not to solve the causes and problems of destitution but to minimise the cost to the public of maintaining the destitute. They were accordingly concomitants of the central concept and great achievement of the poor law—the assumption of public responsibility for the support of the poor—and the necessity it entailed of keeping public expenditure down. (ten Broek 1963–64: 268)

---

[2] See discussion in Chapter 7 below.
[3] Sure Start programmes provide a range of education, health and parenting support in disadvantaged areas.
[4] According to Finer and McGregor (1974), the first two were the common law, which regulated the family lives of the bulk of the population, and the law of trusts and the canon law, which regulated the family lives of the rich and powerful.

The modern history of state support for the poor begins with the Poor Law of 1834. Finer and McGregor say that this Act:

> under the influence of Malthus, imported Elizabethan severities into the society of early industrialism. On this view, poverty was an inescapable part of the natural order of society. Hence it was a leading principle in 1834 to reinforce the distinction between the ordinary poor and paupers, between poverty and destitution, by treating the indigent in accordance with the master formula of 'less eligibility' ... .
>
> ... [L]ess eligibility was to be enforced by abolishing all forms of assistance for able-bodied paupers and their families in their own homes, and by requiring them to be relieved in a workhouse. The workhouse would impose severely deterrent conditions upon its inmates as well as subjecting them to a loss of civil rights, separation from their spouses, and a deliberately imposed stigma of pauperism. It would, therefore, serve both to test the genuineness of destitution—the so-called workhouse test—and to provide an incentive for the pauper to become an independent labourer. In the commission's report, the inmates of the workhouse were to be classified into groups ranging from the impotent aged to the able-bodied and treated with a discriminating severity related to the degree of their moral delinquency.
>
> (Finer and McGregor 1974: 114–15)[5]

Q How would you describe the state's responsibility for supporting families in these laws? Is it closer to the public or the private end of the continuum?

This legislation remained in effect until after the Second World War, when legislation based upon Sir William Beveridge's 1942 report was enacted, first in relation to family allowances in 1945[6] and then as part of the primary foundation of the modern welfare state, the 1946 National Insurance Act and the 1948 National Assistance Act. The idea behind the Beveridge Report was that a compulsory scheme of social insurance paid in return for contributions from earnings was the best way the state could contribute to those families in need. Beveridge did recognise that there would continue to be a residual need for those persons who were not able to work and were therefore not entitled to such contributory benefits, and so he proposed the creation of a 'safety net' of means-tested non-contributory benefits.

Beveridge did not envisage 'workers' to be a gender-neutral category.

> The welfare and appropriate role of women occupied a central place in the Beveridge schema. The man and his wife as a team, the subsidiary nature of female employment, the sanctity of the family as an economic and moral entity, along with the principles of insurance and subsistence, were the main philosophical tenets underlying Beveridge's proposals. While concerned to give official recognition to the (unpaid) work that women had always done, Beveridge also ensured that women would be retained in their traditional role. 'In the next thirty years housewives as mothers have vital work to do in ensuring the adequate continuance of the British race and of British ideals in the world'. Given this function, it is hardly surprising to find that for Beveridge men's support of their wives was a lifelong obligation, that married women normally did no or negligible paid work and that couples who lived together with regular sexual relations and shared expenses were always heterosexual. Beveridge's fundamental assumption about married women was that public income maintenance was secondary for them because of the

---

[5] And see Finer and McGregor (1974) as well on reactions to the Poor Law and on its break up. For the gendered basis of this law, see Daly (1994).

[6] The Family Allowances Act 1945 was passed as a result of decades of campaign, not least by early feminists such as Eleanor Rathbone. See also Pascall (1997).

security offered by men in marriage. Single women—a minority of women—were, however, to be treated like men. (Daly 1994: 786)

The principle that family members are responsible for relatives was first consolidated in 1601. Since then, there have been changes to that responsibility,[7] but even the 1948 Act did not derogate from it entirely. Finer and McGregor describe the changes as follows:

> The National Assistance Act 1948 decreed, 'The existing Poor Law shall cease to have effect', and set up the National Assistance Board. It restricted the liable relative obligation to husbands and wives and to parents and children, but it relieved children of the existing statutory duty to support their parents. The Act imposed maintenance obligations equally on both spouses, and did not, in its own terms, make these obligations conditional on the continuance of cohabitation or the absence of matrimonial offence on the part of the spouse to whom the obligation was due. But a decision in the High Court restricted the absolute terms of the statute and relieved a spouse of the support obligation in respect of another who was adulterous or in desertion. The powers of the National Assistance Board in respect of liable relatives were transferred unaltered to the Supplementary Benefits Commission by the Ministry of Social Security Act 1966.
>
> (Finer and McGregor 1974: 148)

Supplementary benefits were changed to Income Support in 1988 and since then a number of other changes have been made to the system which, arguably, have rendered it unrecognisable from its origins. Daly argues that British income maintenance provisions, then and continuing into the 1990s, displayed a

> complex interplay of programmes oriented to the support of families and family obligations. Thus, the family is most commonly the unit of reference, especially in social assistance, and male and female access to welfare is constructed in such a way as to encourage family obligations. Provisions are gendered to the extent that women and men are assigned different roles and responsibilities. Men are, as far as possible, constructed as providers, and maintainers of family well-being. The possibility of them being full-time fathers is more or less eliminated: they are encouraged, if not compelled, to be economically active. Thus, men receive payments mainly if they experience labour market-related contingencies: accident, illness, redundancy, unemployment. British women, in contrast, are encouraged to be carers, although, increasingly on a part-time basis. Provisions at various stages have re-inforced a caring role for women. They have also generally constructed this work as unpaid, although the introduction of contingency, non-contributory benefits for carers in recent years moves some way towards state subsidisation of this form of work. Women have also been typically constructed as dependents of men. The case of widows provides a good example. For long treated more generously than other solo mothers, in effect their privilege derives from the rights of their husbands and traces its roots to the male obligation to maintain. The case of other solo mothers is more complex and appears to be underpinned by an emphasis on their motherhood role. Thus labour market participation for them is not encouraged to the same degree as it is for other people dependent on state support. (Daly 1994: 793)

Q Daly's comments are pertinent to the Beveridge Report itself and to the legislation enacted pursuant to it. Keep Daly's words in mind as we continue our review of British welfare provision. Are Daly's ideas supported by those rules?

---

[7] See, eg, the Poor Law Act 1927.

Policy shifted in 1999. The trends that emerged in those shifts were

> from social support to social inclusion via employment; from measures of decommodification (that enable people to leave the labour market for due cause) to ways of securing commodification; and from unconditional benefits to benefits that are heavily conditional on work or training.
>
> (Lewis 2009: 7–8)

'[C]rucially', this recast work–welfare relationship was extended to women as well as men (ibid: 8). It was a part of government strategy to tackle child poverty and what was perceived to be a culture of welfare dependency. In 'incentivising' work (understood only as paid work), New Labour policy was that 'work is the best form of welfare' (James 2009). Further, this shift chimed with economic shifts and increasing 'individualisation', in which

> the aspect of a person's status that counts above all now is their relationship to the labour market whereas in the past family-related status, especially marital status, was much more dominant among the criteria governing entitlement to welfare state services and benefits. The demand for individualised social security claims as individual rights, rather than as derived rights depending on marriage to an insured person, was a prominent subject of legal and social policy debate during the 1990s and a policy goal pursued by the EU.
>
> (Daly and Scheiwe 2010: 180, references omitted)

Current government policy confirms this thinking. It also confirms that late twentieth and early twenty-first century welfare policy is located within a child welfare discourse that is merged with ideas about public order and personal responsibility. But the dominant theme that encompasses these social concerns is child poverty and the family's responsibilty to alleviate it. Consider this extract from the coalition government's first document on child poverty (DWP and DfE 2011) in which very little seems to be said about unemployment levels or minimum wage as causes of child poverty, but a great deal is said about the 'family'.

> [This document] is set against the backdrop of the Child Poverty Act 2010, which established income targets for 2020 and a duty to minimise socio-economic disadvantage. This strategy meets the requirement to set out the proposed measures to make progress between 2011 and 2014. It is also set against the backdrop of a Spending Review that placed a very high priority on improving the life chances of children and the protection of vulnerable families, while also making crucial progress in reducing the nation's fiscal deficit.

> This Government is committed to eradicating child poverty but recognises that income measures and targets do not tell the full story about the causes and consequences of childhood disadvantage. The previous Government's focus on narrow income targets meant they poured resources into short-term fixes to the symptoms of poverty instead of focusing on the causes. We plan to tackle head-on the causes of poverty which underpin low achievement, aspiration and opportunity across generations. Our radical programme of reform to deliver social justice will focus on combating worklessness and educational failure and preventing family and relationship breakdown with the aim of supporting the most disadvantaged groups struggling at the bottom of society.

> Addressing the root causes of poverty and not just the symptoms means recognising the importance of the context in which a child is raised, alongside factors including education and income. That is why we are committed to supporting strong families. We also know that effective

parenting is critical to enabling children to flourish. As part of this Government's drive to make our society more family-friendly, this strategy also sets out how we will enhance relationship and parenting support.

This, alongside a drive to achieve higher social mobility for all, and help families out of poverty and onto and up the ladder, is our strategy for eradicating child poverty once and for all.

Focusing on the causes of poverty

1.31 It is clear that many of the major barriers that disadvantaged families struggle to overcome are complex and that families require support from a wide range of different, traditionally separate, services. *Our structural reform programme aims to create a system that is joined-up both across government and through local areas and organisations.*

1.32 Evidence on the key drivers suggests that our approach to tackling the causes of intergenerational cycles of poverty must include:

- *tackling worklessness*: reforming the welfare system so that people are able to work their way out of poverty;
- *tackling debt*: building financial capability among families to support informed decision making and the avoidance of debt;
- *strengthening families*: enhancing relationship and parenting support to strengthen family relationships and the home environment;
- *tackling educational failure*: improving educational attainment, through a new focus on the early years, and the introduction of the Pupil Premium, so that schools are empowered and incentivised to help the most disadvantaged pupils achieve; and
- *tackling poor health*: introducing a public health approach based on the life course for addressing the wider social determinants of health and building self-esteem, confidence and resilience from infancy with stronger support for the early years.

Current Law: Tax and Social Benefits

Jobseeker's Allowance (JSA) is the primary benefit for those with no or low income. It is available for those working less than 16 hours per week. Receipt is, however, conditional: it requires the claimant to be available for and actively seeking work and to sign a 'jobseeker's agreement'. There are two types of JSA. Contribution-based JSA may be claimed if one has paid enough National Insurance contributions (NICs). It is payable for a maximum of 182 days. Income-based JSA is based on income and savings and may be claimed if no or insufficient NICs have been paid. Both types of JSA require a 'jobseeker's agreement', which sets out the steps the claimant will take to find work. A person will be required to come into a Jobcentre when asked to, at least once every two weeks, to sign a statement saying that they have been looking for work and nothing has changed that could affect their JSA. If one is not free to accept work, does not look for training or work, does not have a current 'jobseeker's agreement', one could be disqualified from receiving JSA. Further, if one turns down work or leaves a job or training without valid reason, the JSA can be lost.

Until the 1980s it (then called NI unemployment benefit) included extra amounts for child dependants. The Jobseeker's Act 1995 repealed additional allowances for adult dependants of the unemployed.

In conjunction with claims for JSA the New Labour government introduced a series of 'New Deals', including the New Deal for Lone Parents, the New Deal for Young People and the New Deal for Partners, the latter being intended to reduce the number of workless households. Joining a New Deal is mandatory if one is aged between 18 and 24 and has been in receipt of JSA for 6 months, and if one is over the age of 25 and has claimed JSA for 18 months. New Deals offer enhanced assistance in finding work and require enhanced commitment from the claimant, or there is a risk of losing the benefit. Joining the other New Deals is not mandatory, but if claimants or partners join, they receive enhanced assistance with finding employment.

The third income replacement benefit is Income Support (IS). IS is the basic means-tested scheme of benefits for those who are not able or expected to work. Categories of people who are not expected to seek work and who are therefore eligible for IS include lone parents, parents on maternity or paternity leave, and those with significant caring duties. Only one member of a family may claim income support and cohabitants, same-sex or different-sex, may be included as a family for this purpose. IS is no longer paid for children. To get money for children, one must claim Child Tax Credit instead (see below).

Because eligibility for IS does not depend upon availability for work, it is the primary benefit available for lone parents. However, even though she is not expected actively to seek work, a lone-parent claimant for IS must attend a job-focused interview as a condition of receiving the benefit. IS is only available while her youngest child is under the age of 7 (from October 2011, age 5) at which point she will transfer to JSA. It is thought that she is, from that point, 'available for work'.

IS is also a 'passport' to other benefits such as free school meals, free prescriptions, and free dental care and eye tests. In addition, once a claimant satisfies the IS requirements, the claimant automatically qualifies for Housing Benefit and Council Tax Benefit. Housing Benefit and Council Tax Benefit are means-tested benefits payable to people on low incomes to assist them in paying rent or council tax. In the Social Security Act 1986 it was provided that up to 100% of eligible rent was provided for, but in 1996 the regulation changed so that local authorities now have a discretion to pay a lesser sum, in the light of 'local considerations'. Both benefits include premiums for children and carers.

There are two further benenfits available for those who are not expected to seek work. If one is unable to work due to disability or ill health, one can claim Incapacity Benefit (before 2008) or Employment and Support Allowance (for new claims after 2008). These claims begin with a medical assessment to determine one's capacity or fitness for work. Tougher assessments are being made for Employment and Support Allowance, and after initial assessments in 2010, 66% of claimants were found 'fit for work'. However,

> Citizen's Advice has reported 'grave concern' at the numbers found fit for work. It concludes that the assessment does not effectively measure fitness for work and is producing inappropriate outcomes. ... In the new system, many men and women with lesser health problems will be therefore pushed onto JSA instead, or out of the benefits system altogether if they are denied income-based JSA because of other household income. (Kenway et al 2010)

Other benefits are available specifically for families, and examples are Pension Credit[8] and grants from the Social Fund (SF), which provide help for one-off expenses. The SF is a publicly funded source of meeting the cost of single sudden and heavy expenses for those who need them. There is a one-off maternity grant to pregnant women or new mothers,

---

[8] See further Chapter 6 below.

which is available to meet all of the costs of a new baby. Further, loans are available for crisis events or high-cost items such as winter coats for children, but these are determined solely at the discretion of the SF officers. There is no right of appeal of an SF officer's decision, only provision for judicial review of the decision.

The Tax Credits Act 2002 introduced the Child Tax Credit and the Working Tax Credit. Both create tax advantages for those caring for children, but because they come in the form of tax credits depend upon one having an income against which to credit them. The Child Tax Credit consists of a family element, a child element and a small baby element, payable in the first year of a child's life; the family element is payable to any family responsible for a child, while the child element is payable for each qualifying child for which the carer is responsible. Unlike the Child Tax Credit, which is payable even if the carer is on IS or income-based JSA, the Working Tax Credit requires that the claimant is in paid employment for a minimum of 16 hours per week. It is payable to those who qualify financially, whether they have caring responsibilities or not. The amount received depends on the level of income and caring responsibilities, and is designed to provide greater benefits to those with lower incomes. It includes elements that take account of caring responsibilities: there is a lone-parent element and, importantly, a childcare element to help working carers who spend money on 'approved' or 'registered' childcare.

Currently, the state also provides a universal benefit to carers of children. Child Benefit was seen as an important part of the government's strategy to combat child poverty. It is provided as a universal cash payment paid to the parent with care, assumed to be the mother unless the mother applies for another person to receive it. The coalition government announced in 2010, however, that from 2013, Child Benefit will be withdrawn from all families where one parent's income falls within the higher tax rate (currently about £44,000 per year).

> **Q** Universality is an issue upon which it is difficult always to find agreement. Many argue, for example, that finite resources should be targeted at the most needy, and that paying child benefit to wealthy parents either does not make financial sense or is inequitable. Others argue that it is the principle of state support for families that is important, and universality evidences the idea that all children are important to the state and that the state has some responsibility for them. It enhances social integration. Write a short paragraph identifying the pros and cons of universal child benefit.

> **Q** In 2004 the Child Trust Funds Act was passed. The government issued a voucher worth £250.00 to start an account for all children born on or after 1 September 2002. The voucher was issued automatically to all carers receiving Child Benefit so that they can start a long-term non-taxable savings fund from which only the child, on turning 18, could withdraw funds. Children in families receiving Child Tax Credit received an extra amount. The fund was designed to teach children about finances and the benefits of saving. The coalition government announced the end of CTFs for all children born after January 2011. While this fund was not designed to assist families with the immediate needs of raising children, how might it have benefited children and carers in their day-to-day lives?

> **Q** Article 26 of the United Nations Convention on the Rights of the Child, to which Britain is a signatory, provides that states parties must:

recognise for every child the right to benefit from social security ... taking into account the resources and the circumstances of the child and persons having responsibility for the maintenance of the child, as well as any other consideration relevant.

Article 27 requires states to:

recognise the right of every child to a standard of living adequate to the child's physical, mental, spiritual, moral and social development.

Construct an argument that Britain has met its international obligations under these provisions. Construct an argument that it has not.

Q Some (eg Morgan 1995) suggest that the two-parent family is discriminated against by Britain's fiscal policies. In what way might this argument be accepted or rebutted?

We have seen that the primary imperative behind New Labour's social security policy was to move people from welfare into work, and that this policy was implemented by setting a number of 'work-focused' conditions for entitlement and by increasing the incentives to 'make work pay'. They were increased further in the Welfare Reform Act 2009. Section 1 of that Act amended the Jobseeker's Act 1995 to include a 'work for your benefits' scheme. The scheme has not been fully implemented, but is currently being piloted across four jobcentre areas in England[9]. This reform, in the context of other reforms in the last ten years, appears to target lone parents (mothers) in particular:

'conditionality' is the term used by the Department of Work and Pensions (DWP) to describe what it describes as the quid pro quo at the heart of the reforms. It is stated to be 'a clear bargain that almost everyone on benefits would be expected to take active steps towards work, but where those expectations are based on an individual's needs and circumstances'. In the new proposals [now statute], workfare, or the imposition of work-related responsibilities on parents claiming benefits, is also directly connected with the government's goal to reduce child poverty by half by 2010/11, as a step towards a longer-term commitment to eradicate it by 2020, a commitment currently being placed on a statutory footing with the Child Poverty Bill [now Act]. Although one reason why the UK suffered higher child poverty rates than nearly any other industrialized nation in the late 1990s was the increase in families where no-one was in work, household worklessness has affected dual-parent and lone-parent families alike and in-work poverty is a persistent problem in the UK. Nevertheless, the targeting of lone parents' economic activity in the UK welfare reforms continues a longstanding policy focus on engaging 'lone parents' in paid employment as the answer to child poverty. As around nine out of 10 lone parents are women it is necessary to cast a critical feminist eye over the proposals. Targeting 'lone parents' means targeting 'lone mothers' and, overwhelmingly, low-income women.

(Grabham and Smith 2010: 82, references omitted)

These policies, based on 'a shift towards a "work for your benefit" approach to welfare, combine a more punitive and surveillance-led attitude to benefit claimants with a privatization of welfare services. Discourses of empowerment and personal responsibility' run throughout them (ibid: 84, reference omitted). On the one hand they can be criticised as assuming that claimants do not want to work (ibid); and on the other as relying mistakenly upon the assumption that the benefit claimant will act as a rational economic actor and

---

[9] The Jobseeker's Allowance (Work for Your Benefit Pilot Scheme) Regulations SI 2010/1222.

consider only the economic implications of his or her actions (Barlow and Duncan 2000a, 2000b; Barlow et al 2002; Rafferty and Wiggan 2011). These 'rationality' and 'morality' mistakes not only risk alienating some claimants, particularly mothers, but also have the potential to result in unfairness to them.

The welfare reform policies of successive New Labour governments, and now the coalition government, mark a significant shift 'away from the traditional social insurance model of social security' (Wikeley 2002: 8).[10] But their effect on mothers is inconsistent. 'Work' is not incentivised for partnered mothers in the same way as it is for lone mothers, signifying an assumption that the 'family' or 'family law' will continue to act as security for them.

The language in which these policies have been promoted mirrors that by which other policy shifts (such as in Child Support and private pension provision) have been presented: the language of personal and individual responsibility. In the context of social security:

> These initiatives reflect ... the ... government's emphasis on reciprocity or 'welfare contractualism' as the basis for a reformed welfare state. In particular, this ideology holds that, as a condition of eligibility for benefit, the state may legitimately enforce the citizen's responsibilities, most notably the responsibility to work or at least to engage in active job search and training. (Wikeley 2002: 8)

Plant goes further and suggests that the reforms may actually transform political and philosophical notions of citizenship.

> The first view of citizenship is that it is a *status* which is not fundamentally altered by virtue, or lack of it, of the individual citizen, and irrespective of whether the individual citizen is making a recognised contribution to society. As a basic status that comes through membership of a particular political community, citizenship implies a set of rights; these rights are of two sorts: rights to be left alone ... that is to say negative rights; and positive rights to the economic and social conditions of citizenship—health, education and welfare. On this view, status and membership are the crucial issues in relation to rights, not whether a particular citizen makes a positive contribution to society as a whole. ... The rights are linked to the possession of common needs for security, health and education. As common needs their moral force should be recognised by society and the means of their satisfaction financed out of general taxation. ...
>
> The second, and alternative, view of citizenship places much less emphasis on rights and focuses instead upon *obligation, virtue and contribution*. On this view, citizenship is not a kind of pre-existing status, but rather something that is developed by contributing to the life of society—it is an *achievement* rather than a *status*. The ideas of reciprocity and contribution are at the heart of this concept of citizenship: that individuals do not and cannot have a right to the resources of society unless they contribute to the development of that society through work or other socially valued activities, if they are in a position to do so. Citizenship has to be earned, it is not a given. (Plant 2003: 154–55, emphasis in original)

If changes to social security are indeed a part of broader changes in ideas of citizenship, it is worthwhile asking who is most easily accommodated and who is usually excluded from the new model of British citizenship. First, by linking citizenship to employment this policy is dangerously dependent upon the market order in general and the labour market in particular (Plant 2003: 164). Those whose jobs are most vulnerable in such

---

[10] See generally Wikeley (2007).

markets will be most easily excluded from citizenship, and those who cannot be active in the labour market for other reasons are equally at risk of social and political exclusion. Disabled people, children[11] or people who care for others outside of the market, ie on the private side of the public/private divide, are the most obvious candidates for such stigmatisation and exclusion. And as long as women remain the primary source of unpaid care in society, the gender implications of it are clear.

Further, designating as valuable or worthy of earning citizenship rights only *paid* labour is also problematic for women, children and others who face legal, moral, social or physical barriers to entering the workforce. Carers particularly are in a push–pull situation. At the same time as it valorises paid work for all, government policy also valorises 'the family', an institution, as we have seen, to which roles are clearly assigned. Its primary role is the care of dependants. While carers are also dependent because they depend upon resources in order to undertake that care, those resources are assumed to be provided by the self-sufficient family (Fineman 2004: ch 2) and welfare reforms that prioritise 'workless households' rather than 'workless individuals' collude in this assumption (Bennett 2002).[12] It seems that the reforms aim to reduce 'dependency' but only dependency on the state, not dependency on other individuals (ibid).

Finally, basing entitlement to, and the amount of, IS upon the 'family' rather than upon the individual makes the assumption that the money received is distributed equitably among 'family' members. However, Lister et al studied couples with children in receipt of means-tested social security benefits and found that spending patterns *and* expectations regarding those patterns were highly gendered.

> Men prioritized personal spending money more highly than women, who typically took responsibility for vigilant restraint over both their own and their partners' spending, going without themselves to prioritize their children's needs. In practice, the distinction between 'individual' and 'collective' expenditure was sometimes muddied; men tended to legitimate elements of their 'individual' spending as having a collective benefit and to define women's 'collective' spending on their children as 'individual'. The latter reflected a belief, shared by men and women, that responsibility for meeting children's everyday needs was the woman's domain.
>
> (Lister et al 1999: 205–06)

The coalition government announced further reform proposals in 2010 (DWP 2010a). While the overall policy has not changed, the form of benefit will, should the Welfare Reform Bill 2011, before Parliament at the time of writing, become law.

> We would propose to use a set of principles to guide reform. They could be to:
> - ensure that people can see that the clear rewards from taking all types of work outweigh the risks;
> - further incentivise and encourage households and families to move into work and to increase the amount of work they do, by improving the rewards from work at low earnings, and helping them keep more of their earnings as they work harder;
> - increase fairness between different groups of benefit recipients and between recipients and the taxpayer;
> - continue to support those most in need and reduce the numbers of workless households and

---

[11] For a discussion of children and young people in social security law, see Wikeley (2001). He describes the ideological underpinning of the poor law as 'mask[ing] both paradoxes and conflicts in the law's treatment of children and young people as nascent full members of the community' (223).

[12] See also Bennett (2005).

children in poverty and ensure that interactions with other systems of support for basic needs are considered;

- promote responsibility and positive behaviour, doing more to reward saving, strengthening the family and, in tandem with improving incentives, reinforcing conditionality;

- automate processes and maximise self service, to reduce the scope for fraud, error and overpayments. This could include a responsive and immediate service that saves the taxpayer significant amounts of money and ensures compliance costs for employers, at worst, no worse than under the current system; and

- ensure that the benefits and Tax Credits system is affordable in the short and longer term.

(DWP 2010a para 18)

The different benefits will be replaced by one universal benefit.

Universal Credit is an integrated working-age credit that will provide a basic allowance with additional elements for children, disability, housing and caring. It will support people both in and out of work, replacing Working Tax Credit, Child Tax Credit, Housing Benefit, Income Support, income-based Jobseeker's Allowance and income-related Employment and Support Allowance. (DWP 2010b: para 7, Executive Summary)

13. The clear financial incentive provided by Universal Credit will be backed up by a strong system of conditionality; unemployed people who can work will be required to take all reasonable steps to find and move into employment. Conditionality will be responsive to an individual's circumstances—reflecting, for example, that whilst the majority should move into full-time work, for some people there may be temporary periods when part-time work is appropriate (for example, for some lone parents).

14. Strengthened conditionality will in turn be supported by a new system of financial sanctions. The new sanctions will provide greater incentives for people to meet their responsibilities.

> **Q** In what ways is welfare and social security policy consistent with the model of the private family? In what way is it consistent with the individual earner model? Do you think it strikes an appropriate balance between public and private responsibility for citizens' well-being? Is social security law still 'family' law' for the poor?

Social Security Law and Gender[13]

The Fawcett Society draws on analysis from the Institute for Fiscal Studies (IFS) on the impact of the recent and proposed tax and benefit changes on men and women. It found that single women are hit harder than single men, couples and multifamily households by the current government's tax and benefits changes and that lone parents, over 90% of whom are women, are, on average, among the biggest losers as a result of the reforms (Fawcett Society 2011: 2). According to the Fawcett Society:

The move to push more lone parents into paid work comes at a time when … barriers look set to increase further as opportunities in the labour market diminish. In particular, the rapidly declining number of jobs in the public sector—which has been quicker than the private sector to adapt to women's maternity and care needs through providing more quality flexible and part

---

[13] See also Featherstone (2009).

time jobs—will further exacerbate the barriers lone parents face to securing suitable work. A significantly smaller pay gap exists in the public sector (11.6%) than in the private sector (20.8%). (Fawcett Society 2011: 8)

Government support for lone parents to enter into work is also being reduced, for example a grant to help support lone parents with the costs associated with training has recently been axed.

As Gingerbread has reported, accessing appropriate and affordable childcare remains a significant hurdle for many single parents seeking work.

Recent research from the Daycare Trust shows that only 45% of local authorities report sufficient childcare provision for children aged 5–11. Furthermore, the cost of childcare in the UK, which is ranked as amongst the highest in the world, is rising year-on-year. For example, the cost of an out-of-school club has risen by 12.5 per cent since 2009, far above the rate of inflation.

Meeting such costs is set to get even harder for single parents due to changes to the Working Tax Credit which amount to a 10% cut in the amount of childcare costs that low-income families can expect to be covered by the state. As the Treasury states in its *'Overview of the impact of Spending Review 2010 on equalities'*, published alongside the 2010 Comprehensive Spending Review, *'The reduction in support through the childcare element of tax credits ... will particularly affect women in lone parent households'*—60% of the recipients of the childcare element are working single parents.

A recent survey conducted by Working Mums provides evidence that changes to the Working Tax Credit are already having a marked impact on the ability of mothers—many of whom will be lone mothers—to combine work and childcare. The survey found that 24% of mothers have had to give up work as a result of the changes.

Conflicting messages

At the same time as the coalition government introduces wide-scale welfare reform with the intention of 'making work pay', they are reducing the level of support for childcare and training costs that help lone parents into work. Meanwhile, universal credit proposals create disincentives for mothers in couples seeking paid employment where their partner is already working/seeking work. (ibid: 9–10, references omitted)

III. SUPPORT AND COMPULSION FOR PARENTS

The justification for almost all state policy on families is to promote the welfare of children. Just as concerns about child poverty drive welfare and income support, concerns about children's life 'outcomes' drive much of the support services available for families. However, as James (2009) reminds us, these policies usually adopt a view of children as 'human becomings' rather than as 'human beings'.[14] Piper (2008) describes it as a policy of 'investment' in children. 'One element that does not emerge strongly from government policies is a concept of children as people with rights and voices of their own; the UN Convention on the Rights of the Child is rarely referred to' (James 2009: 7).

Every Child Matters (2003) not only investigated the child protection system and the

---

[14] See further Chapter 13 below and Piper (2008).

circumstances around the death of Victoria Climbie, but set out desired outcomes for children which focused not only on their well-being as children,[15] but also upon ways to prevent their future offending or social exclusion. It advocated a policy of early intervention. As a result, Children's Trusts were set up 'to ensure that services for children were well coordinated at local level' (James 2009: 4), Children and Young People's Plans were introduced by which local authorites could improve local strategic planning. But parents were the main policy focus. 'Parents and the home environment they create are the single most important factor in shaping their children's well-being, achievements and prospects' (James 2009, quoting the foreword of *Every Parent Matters* (DfES 2007: 3)).

We usually think of parenthood as entailing rights and responsibilities toward a child as well as the autonomy to exercise those rights and responsibilities.[16] There are other incidents of parenthood, however; incidents that are less readily amenable to legal management, yet are governed directly and indirectly by legal precepts. A parent not only has the responsibility to feed, clothe and educate a child; he or she also has a moral responsibility to care for a child emotionally, socially and psychologically, and to prepare the child successfully for assuming the responsibilities of adult life.[17] It is as much this aspect of parenthood that we think of when we speak of child-rearing as it is the provision of material nurturance and protection from harm. It is this aspect of parenthood that may be most closely managed by social policy. What does it mean, though, to rear a child 'successfully' and how can the state help parents to do so? Further, this question blurs the image of the successful child and the successful parent.

Theories from both psychology and sociology emphasise processes of maturation, self-reliance, individuation and socialisation in a child's development, and it is seen primarily as the parents' role to facilitate successfully the child's progression through the various developmental stages. Freud, for example, theorises a series of psychosexual stages through which a child progresses, developing from his or her id, to heeding an ego and superego, so that he or she becomes a socially well-adjusted individual. Too much or too little gratification at any of the stages may result in fixation at that stage or regression to it, both of which are pathological (Freud 1905).

Other developmental psychologists who have influenced Western thinking (and law)[18] include Kohlberg (1984), who identified stages in the development of moral judgement which, in a healthy individual culminated in individual principles of conscience; Piaget (1952), who characterised child development in terms of cognitive development—the progressive emergence of more logical forms of thought which led ultimately to the development of idealism and the ability to understand the hypothetical; and Erikson (1980), who theorised a child's psychosocial development as the resolution of a series of crises or conflicts through which the individual progresses to a healthy adult personality.[19]

Sociology, too, has had something to say about a parent's proper role in rearing children. One theory, analysed and criticised from a variety of perspectives, is that of *socialisation*. Socialisation has been defined as 'the process by which an individual incorporates the attitudes and behaviours considered appropriate by any group or society … .

---

[15] See Chapters 13 and 14 below.

[16] See Chapter 4 above and Chapter 8 below.

[17] See O'Neill (1979) and Archard (1993); see also Chapter 4 above.

[18] See the discussion of *Gillick* below and Smart et al (2001).

[19] See also Gilligan (1982) in which the author challenges traditional studies of a child's stages of moral and personality development by suggesting that developmental theories have been built on observations of boys and men, excluding and marginalising the motives and morality of girls and women. See discussion generally in Diduck (2003), and Smart, Neale and Wade (2001).

It is learning the culture or the ways of a group; the process encompasses both the teachers and the learners, the socializing agents and the socialized' (Adams 1975: 137).

Talcott Parsons, the functionalist sociologist (1949),[20] 'saw society as an organism concerned to ensure its continued perpetuation through time, and socialisation as the process through which this was accomplished' (Diduck 2003: 78). He placed great responsibility upon families and parents as socialising agents, declaring, for example, that it was in 'the family' that girl children learn how to be women and boy children learn how to be men in contemporary society.[21] Perhaps now, more than ever before, parents are held to be primarily responsible for instilling in their children an 'appropriate' morality and level of industriousness and responsibility. Their employment status is seen as offering a role model for children and New Deal and family-friendly work practices encourage parents and carers to see themselves as partners with the state and with the market, vested with the responsibility of becoming better citizens by moving from dependency into independence and importantly, also by 'ensuring that their children behave responsibly and are sufficiently informed and educated to become citizen workers themselves' (Williams 2004: 29). To assist parents in carrying out their roles as socialisers, government has, among other things, created a Parenting Fund to strengthen services in the voluntary sector, established a national body to train Parenting Practioners, offered parenting classes in Children's Centres, provided funding for Parent Support Advisors in schools and expanded parent telephone helplines.

Socialisation, however, also occurs in the broader societal context as well as in families. Television, school, popular culture and religious involvement, mediated through families, can influence a child's socialisation. And so can direct government involvement. Citizenship classes are now a part of the national curriculum,[22] evidencing government's concern with socialising children according to particular precepts. Finally, in *Youth Matters* (DfES 2005), the government built upon the policy begun in *Every Child Matters* to create and co-ordinate services to teenagers, with the aim, inter alia, of encouraging young people to see themselves as 'citizens', by encouraging among them a culture of voluntary work (DfES 2005: ch 4).

Much of this activity aimed at producing responsible citizens can be seen as a response to a perceived 'crisis' in the family and as part of broader social project in which the family is disciplined, or 'remoralised' (Day Sclater and Piper 2000) to cope with this crisis, partly by attributing increased decision-making responsibility to it and by inculcating personal responsibility for those decisions in its members. This view shares something with that of French sociologist Jacques Donzelot (1980). Donzelot relies upon notions of surveillance and tutelage through the realm of the social in which the popular stratum (the working class) is familialised. To him, in the nineteenth century there was a change from government *of the family* to government *through the family* through increased supervision of and intervention in families. This was not accomplished directly by the state as agent, however, but by various interventions in various different settings, which meant that in the nineteenth century 'the independent authority of families gave way to social management through families' (Barrett and MacIntosh 1991: 98). Donzelot's presentation of socialisation, then, is as a means of governing or policing families.[23]

---

[20] See Chapter 1 above.

[21] See also Chodorow (1978) on mothers and daughters, and Dennis and Erdos (1993) on fathers. Dennis and Erdos present the view that the lack of a father figure in the family harms society.

[22] Education Act 2002 s 84 and 85.

[23] See also Vaughan (2000) and further Chapter 13 below.

It is arguable that recent policies show signs of that 'governance'. 'New Labour governments have evidenced a preoccupation with "the governance of parenting"' and what Lubcock has termed a new phase of "performance managed parenting"' (Piper 2008: 83–84, references omitted). The current coalition government has also focused upon parents in its child poverty strategy.

3.8 A key influence on the early development of children is what has become known as the 'home learning environment', in other words the activities that parents undertake with pre-school children. Evidence also shows that children's development is linked to aspects of the home such as the aspirations of parents and children, the level of education that their parents achieved and the level of conflict in the adult couple relationship.

3.9 Promoting good parenting is not primarily a job for the Government. *What is needed is a much wider culture change towards recognising the importance of parenting, and how society can support mothers and fathers to give their children the best start in life.*

3.10 Parents want to be able to turn to trusted organisations for support and advice at times of stress or difficulty. The Department for Education is providing around £60 million in grant allocations for voluntary and community organisations each year in 2011–12 and 2012–13. This will help support the delivery of national priorities for children and young people including parenting support and mediation.

3.11 We know that many families (not just those with young children) would welcome more information and support with raising their children. We want to see a culture where the key aspects of good parenting are widely understood, and where all parents recognise that they can benefit from advice and support on parenting skills. Just as many new parents choose to access ante-natal education, we want access to parenting advice and support once a child is born to be considered the norm. (DWP and DfE 2011: 38, references omitted and emphasis in original)

In addition to disciplinary techniques, the government has also adopted other, more coercive parenting strategies to create good children, the good mothers and fathers who will rear them, and therefore the good families and good society presumed to result. Policy has shifted from 'parental responsibility' to 'parenting responsibly'; it marks 'a transition from authority to accountability' (Piper 2008: 100).

Criminal Responsibility

Before coming to power in 1997, Tony Blair used the memorable slogan 'tough on crime, tough on the causes of crime' to define New Labour's approach. The 'causes of crime' originally referred to social problems such as poverty and unemployment. However, policy increasingly focused on the quality of parenting as a cause of crime, both in the short term for teenagers and in the long term for young children. Initiatives designed to intervene in parenting have been introduced alongside a focus on behaviour that is 'anti-social' rather than criminal, with young people in particular targeted by fast track penalties such as Anti-Social Behaviour Orders (ASBOs). (James 2009: 9)

This was not a view specific to New Labour, however. In the White Paper (Home Office 1990a) which preceded the Criminal Justice Act 1991, the Conservative government proposed a new offence be created for parents who failed to prevent their children from offending.

Crime prevention begins in the home. Parents have the most influence on their children's development. From their children's earliest years parents can, and should, help them develop as responsible, law-abiding citizens. They should ensure that their children are aware of the existence of rules and laws and the need for them; and that they respect other people and their property ... .

When young people offend, the law has a part to play in reminding parents of their responsibilities. (Home Office 1990a: 40, paras 8.1 and 8.2)

Few people would disagree with the first part of this statement. Many, however, disagreed with the latter part, which went on to propose a new criminal offence for a parent's failure to prevent her or his child from offending. It was argued in particular that making someone liable for the criminal behaviour of another constituted a violation of human rights, that the difficulties of proving a 'failure' to prevent behaviour were insurmountable, and that those who were likely to be punished most frequently and most severely were households already in financial or emotional difficulty.[24]

The proposed new offence was not included in the Criminal Justice Act 1991, but the combined effect of its provisions and those in the Criminal Justice and Public Order Act 1994 were to require parents to pay any fines for which their children were liable;[25] to enter into a recognisance of not more than £1,000 if the court deemed it appropriate; to take proper care of and control of their child and to be liable to a fine if they unreasonably refused to enter into such a recognisance;[26] and to be liable to be bound over where children refuse to complete community sentences.[27] Taking further these provisions for parents' responsibility for their children's behaviour, the Crime and Disorder Act 1998 gave the court the power to make a 'parenting order' if it would be desirable to prevent their children's anti-social, truanting or criminal behaviour.[28] A parenting order requires parents to attend counselling or parenting classes. And the Anti-social Behaviour Act 2003 states that a court making an ASBO against someone under the age of 16 must make a parenting order against his or her parents if the court is satisfied that it would be desirable. The Act also makes provision for voluntary parenting contracts to be entered into by parents with local education authorities or youth offending teams.

> **Q** Can a parent's responsibility to rear well-adjusted and law-abiding children be transformed into an enforceable legal duty to do so? What arguments are there for creating such a legal duty? What are the arguments against? Can responsibility for children's criminal behaviour be located with anyone apart from the child himself or herself? Bainham (2005: 657) sees these provisions as reflecting a paradoxical view of children and parents. Apart from seemingly violating basic ideas of criminal responsibility, these views of children and parents *both* being responsible for a child's criminal or anti-social behaviour are contrary to the view held elsewhere in child law that a parent has only dwindling control of

---

[24] On the issue of parental liability for children's actions, see Boyd (1990), Barton and Douglas (1995: 280–82) and sources cited therein.

[25] The CYPA 1933 s 55 governs the duty of the court to order a parent or guardian to pay a fine in respect of a child, unless to do so is unreasonable or the parent or guardian cannot be found. See further the Criminal Justice Act 1988; the Criminal Justice Act 1991, amending the CYPA 1933 s 55 by adding subsection 1B. In *A v DPP*, *The Times*, 18 April 1996, where the child was being accommodated by a local authority, it was unreasonable to expect the parents to pay the fine. See also Criminal Justice Act 1991 s 57.

[26] Criminal Justice Act 1991 s 58.

[27] Criminal Justice and Public Order Act 1994 (Sch 6, para 50).

[28] Crime and Disorder Act 1998 s 8.

a child as she gets older. Parents here are assumed to be in control of their children and responsible for their behaviour.

Q Research shows that most parenting orders are made against mothers (Piper 2008). Kaganas (2010b) observes that Sure Start programmes are used by mothers more frequently than by fathers. 'Parenting responsibly', like most active parenting, seems also to be a gendered responsibility. Why do you think this is?

Gillies notes the two imperatives around which parenting policy is constructed: public order (criminal justice) and children's future opportunities. This means, she says, that poor families are targeted for services.

The twin concerns of criminal and social justice are used to construct a powerful moral case for intervening and shaping the parenting practices of working-class families. Unregulated, poor parents spawn damaged, antisocial children destined to live a life of poverty and crime, while those made aware of their responsibilities are supposedly empowered to rewrite their family's destiny. On the basis of this reasoning, only the most selfish, uncaring or stupid would reject advice and guidance designed to improve their children's life chances. This moral justification has underpinned an increasingly coercive and authoritarian approach to family policy, which has seen ever greater use of compulsion, fines, and imprisonment. (Gillies 2008: 100)

But she identifies a lack of consensus around what parenting responsibly might mean in this context. She criticises policy that is 'grounded in middle class privilege' (ibid: 112), and argues that parenting practices and values are always grounded in social and economic realities.

In contrast to a more middle-class preoccupation with passing on privilege, the socially excluded parents in my research struggled to preserve their limited resources. However, in the process they actively inculcated their children with crucial survival skills. Working-class mothers and fathers were emotionally and practically engaged in helping their children negotiate disadvantages and challenges that were considerably less likely to trouble middle-class children or their parents. My research suggests that the different values that working-class parents hold in relation to their children's development need to be recognized in terms of a distinct moral logic guiding parenting practice. Such parents viewed their role in terms of caring for, protecting, and loving their children rather than teaching or cultivating them. (ibid: 103)

Q Do you agree that the 'governance' or 'discipline of families through 'parenting support services' is an issue of class? Of gender?

IV. WORK–LIFE BALANCE

Historically, the family's task of combining paid and unpaid work has been considered a private matter. 'However, since the late 1990s, at the European Union (EU) level and in member states, this policy field has increasingly been recognised as having a significant bearing on some of the new challenges facing modern welfare states' (Lewis 2009: 2), and reconciling work and care has come onto national and EU agendas. In the UK, work and family balance came to be an explicit policy goal in 1997 with the advent of New Labour. It was thought to be able to address a number of social concerns, including achieving higher employment rates and thus increasing competitiveness and growth, addressing the needs of an ageing society by enabling women to work and thereby improving the dependency ratio, offering a solution for child poverty and promoting children's education (Lewis 2009: 2–3). Yet, despite the fact that the family–work balance is, as Lewis also reminds us, a profoundly gendered issue, gender equality in most EU Member States has only been a secondary goal, if it is articulated at all (ibid: 3).

Policy in the UK has tended to be gender neutral and to focus primarily on the 'work' (understood only as paid work) side of the balance. It addresses 'care work only insofar as it impinges on employment goals' (Lewis 2009: 3). While, as we saw in Chapter 4, and will see again in Chapter 6, both mothers and fathers have adapted both their family lives and their employment lives in recent years, and tend to express a desire for the equal sharing of paid and unpaid work, men's increased time in unpaid work in the home has not kept up with women's increased time in paid work outside it. Thus, gender divisions and inequalities remain in both paid and unpaid work. The gender pay gap stands at around 15.5%. According to the Equality and Human Rights Commission (EHRC):

> The gender pay gap is lowest for the under 30s, rising more than five-fold by the time workers reach 40. It is influenced by a number of factors: lower pay in sectors where women are more likely to choose careers, the effect of career breaks and limited opportunities in part-time work. The level of earnings penalty is strongly mediated by levels of education but is not eliminated, even for the best-qualified women. (EHRC 2010: 27)

As far as unpaid work goes:

> Many parents display practical attitudes and hold modern values, but the arrangements they put in place for work and childcare are often constrained along traditional lines. Over three quarters of mothers state that in day-to-day life they have the primary responsibility for childcare in the home. There are significant differences between the perceptions of men and women about whether they share responsibility for childcare equally. Whilst a third of men believe that they share equally, only 14 per cent of women agree. (Ellison et al 2009: 11)

Finally gender also makes a difference when it comes to other aspects of family living. Women, for example, are much more likely to combine childcare with leisure activities than are men (Lewis 2009: 52) and to assume more of the responsibility for coordinating and allocating tasks (ibid).

A recent EHRC study found that working parents were having a tough time of it generally.

> Over half (53 percent) of parents say their current arrangements are 'by necessity rather than choice'

> Working mothers and fathers typically have very different working weeks. Among mothers, 36 percent work part-time. Fathers are most likely to work 40–49 hours a week

> Less than half (46 percent) of parents agree it is possible to meet the needs of their children as well as their own work, or career, needs

> Only 31 percent agree that parents have a choice about whether to spend time with their children or at work, while 48 percent disagree

60 percent of parents think fathers should spend more time with their children. Asked if they spend enough time with their own children, 44 percent of men and 23 percent of women say they do not

Half of fathers and nearly a third (31 percent) of mothers think they spend too much time at work, while nearly half (46 percent) of mothers think their partner spends too much time at work

Current arrangements cause tension and stress for 25 percent of parents. (EHRC 2009: 17–18)

Both government and the EHRC are interested in creating a different work culture in the UK and policy is focused on improving choice for parents, 'through increasing both the time available to care for young children (through leave and flexible working policies) and the time available to work (increasing childcare availability and its affordability through tax credits)' (James 2009: 18). We shall discuss this focus on 'choice' in both of these crucial elements of obtaining a 'work–family balance'. By way of introduction, however, the EHRC (2009) final report, *Working Better*, reminds us that a gender-neutral focus on 'choice' must take into account, yet often fails to do so, the realties of how parents live their day-to-day family lives:

> It is clear that the current leave arrangements offer widely different choices, and create widely different constraints, for men and women. Many women's career prospects are damaged after they have children. The gender pay gap more than trebles when women reach their 30s as a result of the financial penalties associated with motherhood. Women often take part-time work in lower paid jobs and—let us be clear here—that may be out of choice. But there is strong evidence that it is not all based on choice.
>
> More than half of part-time workers are working below their potential because it is the only way they can combine paid employment with caring for children or older relatives. The Women and Work Commission has estimated that Britain is losing £15bn–£23bn per year due to the under-use of women's skills.
>
> The division of labour in the home remains very unequal, however. In couples where both partners are employed, women do an average of 15 hours of housework a week while men do five hours, research shows. Cohabiting women do more domestic chores than single women, while cohabiting men do less than men living on their own.
>
> It appears that the unequal sharing of household tasks can shift significantly as women gain earning power and status at work. A Canadian study found that housework becomes more evenly shared in a couple as the wife's income rises. In couples where the woman earns $100,000 or more, paid work and housework are more likely to be split equally between partners.
>
> A rebalancing of housework should result as more women reach earnings parity with their partners, or out-earn them. However, in Britain the gender pay gap has actually increased, and women's progress to the top of organisations is stagnating or even regressing in most sectors, as reported in the Commission's Sex and Power 2008 study.
>
> Given these persistent inequalities, it is perhaps understandable that far more policy energy has been devoted to enhancing maternal employment than to promoting paternal caring. Yet the promotion of active fatherhood may well be crucial in removing the obstacles that prevent women achieving their full potential at work. (EHRC 2009: 24)

Employment Law and Policy

Employment law and policy have focused on giving more rights to employees so as to improve parents' choices about their work–family balance. As we observed, policy in this regard became explicit with the election of New Labour in 1997. The government announced its *Work–Life Balance Campaign* in 2000 (James 2009) which aimed to increase awareness of employers of the benefits of work–life balance policies. Radical changes were then made in the Employment Act 2002, and further reform followed swiftly. Let us begin with the relationship in law between reproduction/reproductive behaviour and employment.

Employment and Reproduction

In the nineteenth century medical warnings about damage to reproductive capacity justified 'protecting' women from various types of employment. It was thought, for example, that prolonged standing was not only cruel and painful for women, but caused irreparable harm to their ability to reproduce and therefore that work as shop assistants could lead to sterility:

> Woman is badly constructed for the purposes of standing eight or ten hours upon her feet. I do not intend to bring into evidence the peculiar position and nature of the organs contained in the pelvis, but to call attention to the peculiar construction of the knee and the shallowness of the pelvis, and the delicate nature of the foot as part of a standing column. *The knee joint of a woman is a sexual characteristic* ... . The Ontario Bureau of Industries also noted in its annual report in 1885 that women were subject to 'fainting spells and spasms' apparently as a direct result of prolonged standing. (Backhouse 1991: 263, reference omitted)

Concern about women's reproductive capacity also excited calls to restrict women's work in factories:

> Specifying the potential for damage to 'internal organs', Dr Bergin shocked the legislators by insisting that because 'her conformation is entirely different from that of a man' a woman factory worker would almost certainly face 'sexual weakness'. He quoted from a leading American physician and public health advocate:
>
>> Amongst the women of factory operatives, much more than among the general population ... deranged states are present, eg, leucorrhea, and too frequent and profuse menstruation; cases also of displacement, flexions and versions of the uterus, arising from the constant standing and the constant heat of and confinement in the mills. (ibid: 270, reference omitted)

Protecting women's reproductive capacity also served as justification for keeping women out of universities:

> The 'horror' of disabled children was presumed to be the obvious consequence of female studies ... . [An American doctor] abhorred the prospect of young women studying during menstruation:
>
>> Instead of resting both body and mind for a few days, [the pupil] is expending the nerve-force which should give tone to the uterus, and exhausting menorrhagia occurs, which of

course, in turn places the system in a still worse position for the next period ... . This terrible routine may go on til the health is completely broken down ... . Other disturbances of the uterine functions ..., and incomplete or non-development of the reproductive organs take place as a consequence of mental overstrain during early menstruation. The tendency to sterility ... is attributed ... to a diversion of the vital forces from the reproductive system to the brain. (ibid: 298, reference omitted)

These medical opinions are, in the light of modern medical and technological knowledge, of historical interest only. However, the issues they raise about women's supposed biological imperative to reproduce and the tension this creates with employment are still alive today. Immediately we are faced with the question whether legislation which was, and is, aimed to 'protect' women from industrial health hazards is indeed protective, or is instead exclusionary and discriminatory. Just as contemporary medical knowledge has discredited the notion that studying damages women's reproductive systems, it has also alerted us to new and legitimate hazards to the reproductive health of both women and men, notwithstanding that disproportionate focus remains upon women's reproductive bodies (Thomson 1996; Sheldon 1999). Hence, questions of how to understand the equity of protective legislation remain, as does its influence upon the decision and the ability to reconcile childcare responsibilities and earning. As Bacci reminds us:

The question of the impact of industrial health hazards upon the fetus and the pregnant woman has become even more controversial that earlier in the century. Some companies in America, Britain and elsewhere are excluding women of childbearing age from work processes where there is a known danger to the fetus, unless they can prove themselves sterile. (Bacci 1990: 135)

One interesting point made by Bacci in this context is the assumed exclusivity of the relationship between women and reproduction:

The suggestion that 'women's' protections be extended to men raises another important theoretical point. On first appearances the fact that some women were forced to undergo sterilisation to save their jobs, to 'sacrifice their "femaleness"' in Joan Bertin's words, seems a prime example of women being compelled to fit into a workplace designed for men. But Bertin also makes the point that 'hazards are often ignored or minimised, except when they involve female aspects of reproduction' and that men are wrongly presumed invulnerable 'to the effects of chemical exposures until conclusive and undeniable evidence of hazard has been amassed' ... . Women have been constructed as *vulnerable* for a multitude of political and economic reasons— to keep them in certain jobs and out of others, and to keep them reproducing—but men have been constructed as *invulnerable* for economic and political reasons as well, mainly to obviate the necessity of creating genuinely healthy working conditions. This may be a 'male norm', but it is probably a norm many men would now prefer to reject. Putting reproduction onto the political agenda has revealed that neither men nor women are the neutered automatons of liberal theory, although the sexual division of labour has made it easier for men to approximate this model. (ibid: 146–47, references omitted)

Bacci concludes that the solution would be 'to make so-called "women's standards" effective standards for all' (ibid: 142). In other words, '[i]f a workplace is not safe for pregnant workers, therefore, it is not safe' (ibid: 153).

In the nineteenth century the arguments about women working outside the home rested not only upon biological fears, but also upon the effect of outside work upon the health of the family:

Coupled with the reproductive argument was the concern that working wives and mothers were not able to attend to their domestic responsibilities, and thus could not provide a proper home-life for their offspring. The point was not that women were doing work other than child care. Women had always done so, especially before industrialisation had moved so much production away from the home. It was rather that in the home women had combined their productive work with child care. In the factories this was virtually impossible. (Backhouse 1991: 186)

In the 1844 House of Commons debate over the Hours of Labour in Factories Bill Lord Ashley spoke eloquently about the unnaturalness of working women, resulting not only to their usurpation of male privileges, but also to the moral downfall of the family, leading one to speculate about the link between the two. Working women, he said, formed themselves into clubs, where they would come together to drink, sing and smoke, neglecting their children. The effect, he said, was to create within families 'disorder, insubordination and conflict' (Cairns 1965: 68).

In the 1990s the argument changed slightly; women's employment was said either to be one of the causes or predictors of divorce, or to contribute to the undermining of men as marriage partners, both of which, in turn, are said to be damaging to children and to traditional families.[29] And now, as we have seen, the argument has changed yet again. The policy is work for all, even if for partnered mothers on a part-time basis. Whether this policy reflects the reality of women's lives, however, is questionable. Let us begin with pregnancy.

Maternity Rights

Pregnancy in employment is dealt with in a number of different legislative provisions,[30] many of which were implemented as a result of European law.[31] Included in them is the right to paid time off for antenatal treatment and a rule that dismissal from employment as a result of pregnancy is deemed to be unfair dismissal in Britain.[32] Research conducted by the Equal Opportunities Commission in 2004 found, however, that 7% of women had either been dismissed, made redundant or treated so badly they felt they had to leave their jobs as a result of their pregnancy, maternity leave or return to work following absence for maternity (Adams et al 2005: vii). Further, 'forty five per cent had experienced tangible discrimination, such as denial of training opportunities and changes to job descriptions' (ibid). Overall, three-quarters of mothers of young children had encountered some form of 'discrimination, workplace unpleasantness or poor employer practice either while they were pregnant, while on maternity leave or on their return to work' (ibid: 71). The researchers also found that this treatment has an impact upon the attachment that women feel to the labour market (ibid: 73). Rights of Women sums up the research:

[29] See a series of publications from the Institute of Economic Affairs, including Morgan (1995).

[30] See primarily the Equality Act 2010; Employment Rights Act 1996; Employment Act 2002; Work and Families Act 2006; and various statutory instruments. It is also unlawful to treat a woman less favourably because she is undergoing IVF treatment or is intending to become pregnant.

[31] See Council Directive 92/85 on the introduction of measures to encourage improvements in the safety and health at work of pregnant workers and workers who have recently given birth or are breast-feeding; Pregnant Workers Directive 92/85/EC; and the Part Time Workers Directive 97/81/EC ensuring that part time workers are treated no less favourably than full time workers.

[32] The Equality Act 2010 prohibits employers from dismissing an employee or treating her less favourably because of her pregnancy.

In 2005 the Equal Opportunities Commission (EOC) estimated that 30,000 women lose their jobs each year as a result of being pregnant while research conducted by the EOC in 2003 found that 25% of employers asked could not refer to a single statutory entitlement for pregnant women. The same study found that nearly 25% of women who made an employment tribunal claim had been dismissed within hours of telling their employer they were pregnant while one in five women returning from maternity leave were given lower grade jobs.

(Rights of Women 2011: 20)

We see in these statistics the questionable role that law has in influencing behaviour or attitudes.

At present, all women are entitled to 52 weeks maternity leave regardless of their previous length of service with their employer. Adopters are entitled to the same leave and pay provisions that we shall discuss in the context of maternity. If a couple adopts jointly, one of them is entitled to adoption leave and one to paternity leave (discussed below).

Two weeks of maternity leave are mandatory. Other than that, it is up to the woman to decide how to arrange her leave. The first 26 weeks are Ordinary Maternity Leave (or Ordinary Adoption Leave) and the second are Additional Maternity Leave (or Additional Adoption Leave). During both periods of leave, women retain all the benefits of the terms and conditions of their employment, except for those relating to remuneration. At the end of Ordinary Maternity Leave, a woman has the right to return to the same job under the same terms and conditions as before she began her leave. The right to return to work after Additional Maternity Leave is a right to return to the job in which she was employed before her absence or, if it is not reasonably practicable for the employer to permit her to return to that job, to another job which is both suitable for her and appropriate for her to do in the circumstances. Women who have 26 weeks of consecutive service at the 15th week before the birth of their expected baby qualify for Statutory Maternity Pay (SMP). SMP lasts for 39 weeks. It is payable at two rates: an earnings-related rate (90% of average earnings) payable for the first six weeks of the maternity pay period and a standard rate for the remaining 33 weeks,[33] subject always to a maximum of 90% of previous earnings. A pregnant woman/new mother who is not eligible for SMP is likely to be eligible for Maternity Allowance or IS instead. Maternity Allowance is payable at a lower rate than SMP.

Paternity Rights

The Employment Act 2002, which came into force in 2003, granted fathers[34] Statutory Paternity Leave (including for adoptions) for the first time. To be eligible for Statutory Paternity Leave the applicant must intend to be fully involved in the child's upbringing and intend to use his leave to care for the child and support the mother. He must be either the biological father of the child or the mother's partner or the adopter or partner of the adopter. Fathers who have completed six months of service with their employer at the 15th week before the baby is due may take one or two consecutive weeks' paternity leave at any time in the eight weeks following the baby's birth. These fathers are entitled to Statutory Paternity Pay (SPP) during their paternity leave, payable at the same rate as

---

[33] Individual employment contracts or collective agreements may offer enhanced remuneration.

[34] And now, same-sex female partners.

SMP. The Work and Families Act 2006 also introduced provisions for 'additional paternity leave' of up to six months provided the mother has returned to work. The practical effect is to give parents the option of dividing a period of paid leave entitlement between them. The two types of leave are legally separate, however—the mother does not 'share' her leave with her partner. To the extent that additional paternity leave is taken during the mother's 39-week maternity pay period it will be paid at the same rate and in the same way as SMP. These provisions came into effect in 2011.

The introduction of Statutory Paternity Leave is certainly welcome and goes some way toward enhancing new fathers' bonding with children, but the gross disparity between maternity and paternity leave provisions makes clear that the expectation remains that the mother is primarily responsible for the early development of the child. Indeed, the UK now has the longest maternity leave entitlement of any EU Member State (Lewis 2009: 167). It means also that men's choices about combining parenting with work are constrained. Although they are paid at the same rate as SMP, given that men in full-time employment earn on average over 15% more than women in full-time employment, Statutory Paternity Leave may not be a real option for families when income is sorely needed. The EHRC (2009) reports findings from a MORI poll for the Chartered Institute for Personnel and Development which found that four out of five fathers would take their leave entitlement if flat-rate payments were increased to 90% of full pay (EHRC 2009: 24). Finally, fathers must take their leave within eight weeks of the baby's birth, in consecutive blocks of one or two weeks. If they choose to take only a week when their baby is born, they forfeit the second week.

Despite these limitations, more than half of fathers in the EHRC survey conducted in 2009 took the two-week Statutory Paternity Leave (Ellison et al 2009). Just over a third of them did not take paternity leave at all. The remaining 10% said they were not eligible. The survey reports that the main reason for men not taking paternity leave is that they cannot afford to lose pay around the birth of their child. They mentioned also that workload and employer resistance were other constraints: one in five fathers said they were too busy or their employer would not be happy if they took it. In all, however, nearly 90% reported that they would have liked to take it (EHRC 2009: 24). The EHRC also reports that only 4–8% of eligible fathers are expected to take up the right to additional paternity leave (ibid: 25). This is disappointing on its own terms, but in conjunction with the package of other leave provisions offered to carers, it could be argued that even they further entrench the gendered nature of childcare (Weldon-Johns 2011).

Parental Leave and Flexible Working

As a result of the EC Parental Leave Directive in 1996[35] parents may also be entitled to unpaid parental leave to care for their child or make arrangements for the child's welfare. Both parents may qualify, if they have completed one year's service with their employer by the time they want to take the leave. They are entitled to 13 weeks per child (18 if the child is disabled), which can be taken up to the child's fifth birthday (or 18th if the child is disabled) or during the first five years after an adoption placement.

All employees have the right to take a reasonable period of time off work to deal with

---

[35] Directive 96/34/EC; now in the Employment Act 2002.

emergencies involving dependants. Dependants are spouses, partners, children, parents or anyone who lives with the employee as part of his or her family.

Finally, all employees have the right to request flexible working patterns if they have completed 26 weeks of work for their employer and have not made such a request in the last 12 months. The request would be for a change in hours, times or place of work so as to accommodate care for a child until age 17 or a dependent adult. Employers have a statutory duty to consider seriously the request but can reject it for business reasons.

Finally, James (2009) reminds us that one 'family-friendly' measure the government has not implemented fully is the 1993 EU Working Time Directive, which stipulates a maximum 48-hour work week. The UK position is to continue to permit employees to opt out of the rule.

Although these allowances reflect a changing attitude toward helping families balance their work and family lives, many parents continue to find it difficult to take their full leave entitlement due to financial reasons.

> The current [pre 2011] leave system for parents of young children gives the right to 80 weeks of leave in total, before the child is five years old: up to 52 weeks for the mother (the last 13 weeks unpaid), up to two weeks for the father, and up to 13 weeks for each the mother and father. The current policy is characterised by a long period of maternity leave at low pay (after the initial six weeks) or unpaid; a short period of paternity leave at low pay; and a system of parental leave which has low incentives for take-up—being inflexible (it must be taken in blocks of full weeks) and unpaid. (EHRC 2009: 33)

The long hours culture of work also contributes to a family-unfriendly work–life balance, as does the (perceived) resistance of many employers. Given that 70% of flexible working parents in the EHRC survey confirmed that it enables them to spend more time with their children, and a similar proportion reported that it improved the quality of family life (Ellison et al 2009: 13), it is important to understand why more parents do not request it. Ellison et al found that the key reasons for not requesting flexible work were fear of being marked out as not committed to the job, and fear that flexible working would negatively affect chances of promotion. For women, fear of their request being refused and worry about the reaction of colleagues were also concerns (ibid: 66).

The evidence about parents' attitudes to work–family balance is mixed. On the one hand, fathers do wish to be more involved in childcare (70%), although interestingly, 65% also said that women are naturally better at caring for children (Thompson et al 2005: vii) and only one in five had made some sort of adjustment to their working pattern in order to spend time with the new baby (ibid: viii). It is also interesting that employers showed support for fathers' involvement with children, but fathers reported feeling that only about half of their employers would be supportive of more than two weeks leave (ibid: ix).[36]

Weldon-Johns (2011) comments that the package of leave provisions, far from bringing about a 'change of landscape in UK work-family rights' (Weldon-Johns 2011: 25), actually entrenches the gender division of caring responsibilities. She identifies three main reasons. First, the package is inflexible (ibid: 27). Second,

> [T]he lack of earnings-related pay during leave has raised concerns regarding fathers' utilization of work–family rights. The flat-rate statutory paternity pay level notably contrasts with the initial earnings-related statutory maternity pay and draws an unnecessary and arbitrary distinc-

---

[36] See also Collier (2010), particularly ch 6 on the views of male lawyers on work and fatherhood.

tion between maternity and paternity leave, thereby according a lower value to paternal care and suggesting that it is a secondary or supplementary right. (ibid: 28)

Further, the unpaid nature of parental leave makes it particularly difficult for low-earning or single-parent families to use it (ibid).

In research conducted in 2006, it was found that only 1% of the total number of employees, or 6% of working parents with dependant children, studied, used the right to parental leave. ... [R]esearch indicates [taking leave] is connected with payment during leave. This reflects the distinctions in earnings between men and women and that fathers continue to be defined in terms of their earning role. This was evident in research conducted in 2008–2009 which revealed that 38% of parents still agree that earning is the fathers' responsibility. However, Dermott argues that caution should be exercised here when attempting to define fatherhood in terms of the traditional breadwinning role, because other factors, such as age and partner's employment status, are better predictors of men's labour-market commitment. While it is certainly the case that there is a variety of factors influencing labour-market commitment, breadwinning remains a key component of the male identity and so has an influence on fathers' work–family decisions.
(Weldon-Johns 2011: 28, references omitted).

Thirdly, she comments that the whole package is based upon a particular approach to the work-family balance which is based upon women's model of work, or a 'female model of balance' (Dermott 2006: 631). The package of rights focuses on periods of withdrawal from the labour market as opposed to facilitating care while remaining in employment, which may be more attractive to men. In this way it reinforces the idea, despite rhetoric or 'sound bites' (Weldon-John 2011), about fathers as carers, that the 'work–family' balance is all about women. Lewis (2009) describes this model as a 'gender participation model', designed 'to enable women to enter the labour market, and to leave it "for cause" (namely, to care)—rather than enabling women and men to be able to make a real choice to engage in paid and/or unpaid work' (Lewis 2009: 16–17). They remain, largely, policies to ease the burden on women who perform both (ibid: 17), and together with tax and benefit policies, ones to enable employment (ibid: 77).

Finally, the current maternity, paternity and parental leave arrangements impact differently on the choices and constraints for different groups of parents.

Around 25 percent (La Valle et al 2008) of lone mothers do not qualify for SMP. Those lone mothers who do qualify are far more likely than "couple" mothers to rely on it alone, without additional employer maternity pay. This is because they are more likely to be in jobs offering less favourable maternity provisions. (EHRC 2009: 26)

Q Comment upon the current approach in the UK to family-friendly working. Lewis (2009) notes that the phrase 'work–family balance' was changed in government rhetoric to 'work–life balance'. Does this change in language reflect a change in approach?

Childcare

We stated in Chapter 1 that a state's policy respecting the type of families it encourages, in terms both of family form and family privacy, can be demonstrated by, among other things, the support it provides for the care of children. Until recently, policy in England and Wales was based upon and reinforced the assumption that childcare was predominantly the private concern of the conjugal family, in practice the mother. As a result, very little was done in the public arena about childcare,[37] in the form of either financial support or service provision. According to the Family Studies Centre in 1995, this meant that for the 52% of mothers with children under the age of 5 and the 75% of mothers with youngest children aged between 5 and 11 who were employed outside the home, childcare was usually arranged privately through the family or a friend or neighbour (Hartrais 1994; Rodger 1995; Millar and Worman 1996; Windebank 1996). Statistics compiled in April 1996 by the National Children's Bureau showed that fewer than 1% of children aged between 0 and 4 were cared for in local authority day nurseries or family centres and 9% were cared for by registered childminders. Fox Harding commented on the situation as follows:

> State child-care provision of nurseries, playgroups and nursery schools for younger children, and playschemes out of school hours for older children is restricted in Britain. Not only is provision not universal, but it is mostly limited to children and families deemed to have problems. A contrast is often drawn with the war years when nursery provision was widespread, in order to free women for paid work. Mothers now turn to a range of systems for child care while they are working: husbands, relatives and other informal carers; registered (or unregistered) childminders and nannies; private and employer-provided nurseries, and so on.
>
> (Fox Harding 1996: 33–34)[38]

Since the 1990s, however, policy has shifted. Two objectives lay behind the shift: to support disadvantaged families during the children's early years and in this way improve their life chances; and to enable mothers to move into the labour market, 'so reducing child poverty and increasing economic competitiveness and growth' (James 2009: 19). One of the first policy documents published by the new government in 1998 was its National Childcare Strategy. It also launched the Sure Start programme in 1998 and in 2004 the government announced its ten-year strategy for childcare (HM Treasury et al 2004). The aims of that strategy, or the 'vision' at its heart, were:

> a childcare system where: parents are better supported in the choices they make about work and family responsibilities; childcare is available to all families and is flexible to meet their circumstances; childcare services are among the best quality in the world; and all families are able to afford high quality childcare services that are appropriate for their needs.
>
> (HM Treasury et al: 2004: para 1.10)

The strategy document is important and interesting for a number of reasons. First, it is one of the few 'official' statements linking good quality childcare to child development and not merely to parental (or rather, maternal) employment. Second, it concedes that the 'market' may not be appropriate as the exclusive regulator of childcare provision. Finally, it acknowledges that the availability of good quality childcare is an issue with specific relevance for women's well-being. Chapter 2 of the document sets out the government's policy rationale. It was based upon three ideas: that childcare is good for children and for

---

[37] For a discussion of why feminist mobilisation around the issue of childcare in Britain was so modest, see Randall (1996).

[38] See also Canaan's (1992) work on family centres, showing how they were used for 'problem' families only.

society; that it is good for parents' employability; and that it should be based upon parental choice.

The document reviews the literature on the effect of childcare on child development.[39] It points to research confirming the value of 'consistent one to one care' in a child's first year but acknowledges that any negative effects of full-time maternal employment in this year can be offset by high-quality care from others, including fathers (para 2.15). It also points to the mixed findings with respect to childcare from ages 1–3, but again acknowledges that any negative effects on child development arising from high levels of group care of poor quality can be avoided by good quality care. In fact, good-quality care can boost children's cognitive skills, social skills and development (para 2.16). The evidence also shows that involvement in 'high quality early years education [at ages 3 and 4] can lead to better educational and social outcomes for children (para 2.17) and that childcare for school age children can improve a child's 'educational attainment and behaviour' (para 2.19). The government concludes that the policy implications of these findings are related to the quality of childcare as much as to its supply.

The document also links childcare with child poverty. It refers to the Child Poverty Review (HM Treasury et al 2004) issued with the 2004 Spending Review, which states government's goals as halving child poverty by 2010 and eradicating it by 2020 (ibid: 5). Childcare became a part of this goal when the government stated that 'child poverty is about more than just income' and promised that government would ensure 'work for those who can and support for those cannot' (ibid). The provision of good-quality, accessible childcare was part of the strategy to combat child poverty that focused on parental employment:

> Children's economic well-being is largely determined by the employment status of their parent or parents.
>   The likelihood of parents engaging in work depends on a wide range of interlinked factors. Macroeconomic stability and a flexible labour market are key and are complemented by policies to encourage and support people to move off welfare and into work. This can be achieved through a combination of bringing parents into contact with the labour market, improving the financial returns to work and addressing key barriers to work such as problems acquiring childcare. (HM Treasury et al 2004: paras 3.1, 3.2)

And then the childcare strategy went one step further. It linked not only children's economic wellbeing, but also their social and psychological wellbeing to parental employment:

> Children growing up in households connected to the labour market are likely to have a better understanding of the link between educational attainment and its consequences for later life. Parental employment is also linked to improved performance in education when a child is older. For the adults involved, employment can bring benefits of increased self-esteem, extended social networks, a greater sense of control, and reduced mental health problems. These can all have positive consequences for children. By contrast, children from workless households are less likely to have home environments conducive to learning, and are more likely to fail to attain at school and to be workless in later life.
>
> (ibid: para 2.28)

While the childcare strategy was about helping 'parents' and 'households' to connect to

---

[39] Annex A to the document summarises the evidence.

the labour market, it recognised that having children has a far greater impact on the working lives of mothers than on fathers. The document states that maternal employment was at 64% in 2002 (para 2.33), but that around 40% of these women worked part time. Further, while the percentage of women in professional and managerial roles had increased from 25% to 33% during the previous ten years, in 2001 over 70% of those in receipt of the National Minimum Wage were women (para 2.36). As we have seen, despite asserted changes in attitude and behaviour, motherhood clearly matters to a woman's (work) life in a way that fatherhood does not to a man's (work) life.

> ... One study showed that women returning to the labour market after a one year gap experi-enced a 16.1% drop in earnings compared to their previous job, while men experienced a drop of about 6.5%. Another study estimated that each year in full-time employment increased hourly earnings by three per cent. By contrast, each year of part-time working was found to decrease hourly earnings by one per cent, in addition to losing out on the three percent increase. Simi-larly, each year of interruption to employment for child care and family care reduced hourly earnings by one per cent, again in addition to losing out on the three per cent increase from full-time employment. (HM Treasury et al 2004: para 2.44)

The final point we wish to make about the childcare strategy document is the way in which it acknowledges that the childcare market cannot be an efficient or effective regu-lator of childcare services. Contrary to other messages about one's personal and individual responsibility for children, for work and for family choices, and contrary also to incen-tives designed to appeal to that personal responsibility, this part of the document acknowledges some social responsibility for aspects of those choices. It states that there are benefits to childcare that may not be captured by the market.

> [P]arents do not receive all the benefits generated by their work, but they must meet all the costs of working: parents, as with all workers, capture some of the benefits generated by their work in wages, but the rest is shared with their employers and the rest of society in the form of higher economic growth. Employers may have some incentive to help parents share childcare costs, as if a parent is forced to give up work the employer loses their share of the benefits that were generated by the parent's work. ...
> ... parents must meet the costs of childcare immediately, whereas the benefits from remaining attached to the labour market when their children are young may extend over many years. (ibid)

The government's ten-year strategy for childcare, therefore, included creating childcare places for all families with children up to age 14 who need it. Its success can be measured by more recent statistics about the availability and use of childcare. There were around 2.5 million OFSTED-registered childcare places in England in 2008, a 33% increase from 2003. Of these, 1,684,800 were provided by full daycare settings, sessional providers, after-school and holiday clubs, and childminders and 817,400 places were registered in early-years provision in maintained schools (Campbell-Barr and Garnham 2010: ix). There is free early years' education of 12.5 hours per week (rising to 15 in 2013) (DWP and DoE 2011) for 3 and 4 year-olds available in nurseries and playgroups during school terms. Employers in England and Wales are not obliged to provide daycare facilities for their workers' children, although they are given tax relief if they do.[40]

  Further,

---

[40] ICT(EP)A 2003 S 318. And employers can provide in lieu of income of up to £55.00 per week, childcare vouchers. They will be free of tax and NI payments to the parent and to the employer.

In 2008 in England, 5.5 million children aged 0–14 were receiving childcare overall; 3.8 million were receiving formal provision and 2.9 million were receiving care from informal providers. Three and 4 year-olds were the most likely to receive childcare, with 90 per cent in some type of childcare and 10 per cent in none. Eighty-six per cent of 3 and 4 year-olds received formal and 39 per cent informal childcare. The figures reflect the universal offer of free part-time early years education for this age group, as well as a greater general need for childcare for pre-school children compared with older children. This contrasts with 0–2 year-olds, of whom 59 per cent received some type of childcare, with 38 per cent receiving formal and 37 per cent receiving informal childcare. Twelve to 14 year-olds were least likely to be receiving childcare, with 50 per cent in some type of childcare; 26 per cent receiving formal and 27 per cent receiving informal childcare. (Campbell-Barr and Garnham 2010: x, reference omitted).

Childcare is an integral part of family–life balance, at least for mothers:

The evidence suggests that the availability of informal care, childcare arrangements that fit with mothers' working hours, good quality and affordable childcare, and the availability of appropriate jobs with flexible arrangements, are all key factors that enable mothers to work outside the home. A substantial minority of lone mothers were able to work because they received childcare subsidies through working tax credits.

Analysis of mothers who were not in employment shows that a substantial proportion reported childcare as a barrier to work. It was mainly mothers in couples who could afford to stay at home (ie did not need the money), while a substantial minority of lone mothers could not 'afford' to work (ie not earn enough to make it worthwhile). The proportion of mothers who were not working because they did not want to lose their benefits has declined considerably since 1999, probably due to the introduction of tax credits which have made work financially more attractive to families with low earning potential. Lack of flexible employment continues to be an obstacle to employment, particularly for lone mothers not in employment.

(Campbell-Barr and Garnham 2010: xv).

The previous government set itself different targets to meet in the years up to 2020, and the current coalition government has not upset these. Like the previous government, it connects 'early years provision' for children with combating child poverty (DWP and DoE 2011: ch 3). While policy for some time in the 2000s could be said to have been moving closer to the models in countries such as Denmark, Norway and Sweden where extensive public daycare has been available for many years and state commitment to its provision is seen not only as a policy which advances equality between the sexes by easing women's access to employment, but as one in which the best interests of children are promoted (Bradley 1996: 115, 171, 201),[41] it is arguable that that movement, or at least that focus for movement has stalled. Even so, childcare provision has come a long way from 1996, when Millar and Warman (1996) examined the availability of daycare services in the 15 Member States of the EU plus Norway. This part of their research was aimed at 'how the role of the state is defined *vis à vis* the role of the family' (Millar and Warman 1996: 29). Their research shows that at the time, Britain could be grouped with Ireland, Portugal and Spain in assuming that childcare is intended for '"problem" children, those deemed at risk in some way or with particular needs' (ibid: 31) rather than for 'meeting the needs of mothers (or parents) to combine child-rearing with paid work' or 'as having a primarily educational role for children and so be the entitlement of all children' (ibid: 31).

Fox Harding described the daycare debate in the 1990s in these terms:

---

[41] But, for the contrary view, see Morgan (1996).

Finally, the issue of day care throws into relief the underlying ideological debate about family responsibility, and especially maternal responsibility. The day care debates highlight a struggle over the state–family boundary and over what is properly a public/private area of responsibility. Broadly, the state's expectation in Britain is that parents/mothers will care for young children during the day, and this is conveniently reinforced by post-war theories of child development which suggested that day care outside the family was damaging. However, recent research indicates that much depends on the *quality* of day care; it is not adverse *per se* (National Children's Bureau, 1993). Nevertheless, publicly provided state care is construed as a 'welfare' provision for a minority of families with special problems, for whom it is seen as helpful; otherwise mothers will care (or make their own arrangements). The effects of this are that working parents/ mothers must turn to a range of other (possibly unsatisfactory) non-state alternatives, or indeed leave children alone: a situation beginning to attract media attention and public concern in the early 1990s. The assumption that day care is a 'private' matter may be highly damaging to children. (Fox Harding 1996: 171)

Q How does the current provision for childcare construct the public/private boundary in terms of responsibility for childcare? How does it influence the construction of motherhood and fatherhood?

Work and Family and the State: Some Observations

We have seen that both paid and unpaid work are gendered activities. Both men and women try to achieve a balance in their work and family lives, for their own satisfaction, as well as for their children's welfare. Many women try to achieve this compromise in their employment and family lives by working outside the home on a part-time basis. But with its advantages, part-time work also has its disadvantages. Apart from the financial disadvantage it creates in terms of the ability to acquire property and pension provision in later life,[42] part-time work can create a host of other disadvantages for women. Warren, (2003), for example, suggests that policy that focuses only upon a balance between work and family ignores other important aspects of one's life; we balance other domains in our lives, including leisure and financial security, and that taking these other domains into account shows that female part-timers in lower-level jobs showed the least satisfaction with their financial security and with the social aspects of their lives. She concludes that the work–life system is multidimensional and not two-dimensional and that policymakers should take this into account in assessing the benefits and disadvantages associated with working part-time. Morris and Nott also note the complicated moral and financial negotiations undertaken by part-time working mothers:

> Particularly significant are the findings in the Survey on Part-timers on why women choose to work at all. The disadvantages were numerous and obvious: those with children, for example faced horrendous problems of child care, especially in school holidays or when a child was ill. Most of the respondents said they felt guilty about combining work with other responsibilities, continually feeling that one suffered at the expense of the other. Apart from having to juggle their two roles there are also problems concerning the work itself: part time work tends to be in lower skilled jobs and because the pay is also low there are problems with tax and particularly with national insurance … .
>
> And yet, despite the multifarious problems, these women still go out to work. Money is

---

[42] See Chapter 6 below.

clearly an important motivating factor, though the extent to which this was true varied amongst the respondents and it is notable that many referred to the feeling of independence it gave. Other factors mentioned were the social contacts work engenders plus the mental stimulation and self-esteem. (Morris and Nott 1995: 59)

These complicated negotiations are compounded still further when one factors in the responsibilities of being a 'good mother' or a 'good father'. According to Neale and Smart (2002):

> The identities of the mothers in our sample appeared to be bound up primarily with their relationship with their children. They were more likely to start with an imperative to care ... . They also recognised the economic imperatives of raising children and may have extended their role to accommodate this ... . In contrast, the identities of most of the fathers in our study remained bound up primarily with their employment. They were likely to start with an imperative to secure paid work ... . They were also likely to recognise the imperative to care for their children, and some extended their role to accommodate this. (Neale and Smart 2002: 196)

Barlow et al looked at the 'cost–benefit analysis' employed by lone mothers about their decisions to enter into paid work and found that most saw 'their moral and practical responsibility for their children as their primary duty and for many (although not all) this responsibility to be a good mother is seen as largely incompatible with significant paid work' (Barlow et al 2002: 113).[43] And so, contrary to the 'message' of social security and employment policy, which seems now to have shifted from a male breadwinner model to a dual earner or one and one half earner model (Lewis 2002), 'those lone mothers who chose not to take up paid work, far from falling into a deviant sub-culture that abhors self-reliance and social responsibility [and now, the welfare of their children!], did so on the basis of what they believed to be the morally proper thing to do as a mother' (Barlow, et al 2002: 113).

As it stands now, many employers accommodate men even less than women. Full-time British male workers work the most hours of any of their EU counterparts—a mean of 46 hours per week (O'Brien and Shemilt 2003: 13). Ellison et al report that 39% of all parents work between 40 and 49 hours per week on average, with 46% of fathers doing so (Ellison et al 2009: 34). British work patterns still tend to be family-unfriendly for all parents, and can be contrasted with Swedish state policy, for example, in which children's interests were material in restructuring employment patterns:

> This [protecting children's interests] is reflected in extensive statutory holiday entitlements and the long term commitment to a six hour day. Employment rights—parental leave, paternity leave, leave for parents of sick children, leave to attend school 'contact' days—are based on the assumption that both parents are employed and that both should have time and energy for their children. (Bradley 1996: 111)[44]

Flexible or family-friendly work was seen to provide some help, but while much of British industry is committed to flexible working hours, that commitment has usually been driven by competitive pressures, or labour market fluctuations. Further, Brannen et al note the difference between flexible and family-friendly working practices:

---

[43] See also Duncan et al (2003); Barlow and Duncan (2000a, 2000b); Rafferty and Wiggan (2011).

[44] The origins of the Swedish policy stem from a number of influences, from pronatalism to acceptance of more state control over reproductive and family matters to feminism (Bradley 1996).

The distinction between 'flexible' and 'family friendly' working practices can easily become blurred. 'Family friendly' practices may be 'flexible'—but not all 'flexible' practices are family friendly'. It has been suggested that

> family friendly practices can be defined as a formal or informal set of employment terms and conditions which are designed to enable an employee to combine family responsibilities with employment ... . Whilst family friendly practices are designed to suit both employee and employer, flexible working practices may not be so accommodating towards the former and may be designed more for the employer than the employee.

> ... 'Flexibility' in patterns of work takes many forms: flexible daily, weekly and annual hours; compressed working weeks; shiftworking; alternatives to full-time permanent working, including temporary contracts, sub-contracting, part-time working and job-sharing; and working part or all of the time at or from home. (Brannen et al 1994: 8, reference omitted)

To summarise thus far: reflected in a lack of adequate childcare facilities outside the family and a historical lack of interest on the part of business or government to assist workers with family responsibilities, care of children was deemed to be a private matter for the family rather than a matter for universal support by the state. Recently, however, family-friendly work and childcare have appeared on the government agenda. The rationale for this shift is said to include the welfare of children and the welfare of the economy. Tied in with welfare policy, the government hopes to reduce the number of 'workless' households by providing economic and service incentives for all to work, at least part-time. One's responsibility to society and to one's family, one's very citizenship (Plant 2003),[45] appears to hinge upon one's economic productivity. And yet, while the ideologies of proper motherhood and fatherhood remain entrenched and women tend to resolve the conflict between the imperative to care and the imperative to earn by taking up part-time work, their 'citizenship' or relationship with the state is affected differently from men's. For mothers, arrangements for paid work and care often affect not only their levels of stress and feelings of guilt, but also the kind of work they are able to obtain and the hours they are able to work in order to accommodate the dual responsibility which is expected of them. Additionally, expectations of men, although changing, mean that many are deprived of the fulfilment they might have through a stronger relationship, based upon more than 'breadwinning' alone, with their children (Hatten et al 2002; O'Brien and Shimelt 2003; Collier 2010). It is partly these effects upon heterosexual parents and their children which the Scandinavian policy, for example, was designed to counter.[46]

Daly and Scheiwe (2010) see the change from marriage to parenthood as the state's preferred vehicle of support and control as involving a challenge to the gender order. But with policy emphasis on gender neutral 'parenting' and 'choice', 'women disappear within the family, and the compatibility of employment and care is designed as a female project rather than as a programme treating equally individuals with care obligations' (Daly and Scheiwe 2010: 190),[47] and the gender order remains intact.

---

[45] See further below, and above pp 200–01.

[46] Dunne's (2000) research seems to demonstrate that lesbian parents are able to negotiate childcare in a more egalitarian way because they perceived themselves as free of sex role stereotypes and assumptions. See further Chapter 4 above and Chapter 6 below.

[47] See also Lewis (2009); EHRC (2009).

V. HOUSING

Britain's housing policy[48] has undergone radical changes since the middle of the twentieth century. In the 1950s and 1960s, for example, rented accommodation was the primary form of housing, and local authorities provided close to one-third of it (Morris and Nott 1995). Throughout the 1980s however, the government's policy was actively to encourage owner occupation of housing through its 'right to buy' legislation. As a result, local authorities now provide only a relatively small proportion of the housing stock.[49] They do have some obligation to house, however, and local authority controlled housing is currently allocated according to rules set out in the Housing Act 1996 as amended. Local authorities are also required to comply with the provisions of the Homelessness Act 2002 and with regulations. In addition, they must take into account the relevant Codes of Guidance.[50]

The Housing Act 1996 was originally drafted under the Conservative government in the context of debates and media coverage about supposed abuses of the system. In particular it was claimed, with little evidence, that the priority accorded to people with dependent children under the homelessness legislation was providing teenagers with an incentive to become pregnant and claim council tenancies (Pascall et al 2001: 294). Women, particularly young women, were blamed for 'creating pressures on housing supply, for free-riding and for displacing worthier two-parent families from their place on the housing lists' (ibid: 293). The Housing Act 1996 changed the statutory duty upon local housing authorities to provide only temporary rather than permanent accommodation for the homeless, so that permanent accommodation would normally be allocated only through the housing register.

With the advent of the Labour government, policy again changed. The Labour agenda focused less on the promotion of the nuclear family and more on notions of community, need and social exclusion. A Green Paper (DETR and DSS 2000) was published setting out the 'key principles' for housing policy. These concerned choice; an adequate supply of decent housing to meet needs; giving responsibility to individuals who are able to do so to house themselves; improving the quality of housing; reducing barriers to work; supporting vulnerable people; tackling all forms of social exclusion; and promoting sustainable development (para 1.5). The government's proposals specifically in relation to homelessness were intended to 'ensure that unintentionally homeless people in priority need are provided with temporary accommodation until they obtain suitable settled accommodation (in either the public or private sector)' (para 9.42). In addition the aim was to 'ensure our most vulnerable citizens are protected by the homelessness safety net' (para 9.42). The reforms were also designed to open up the possibility of assisting non-priority applicants for housing such as childless couples and homeless single people who are not vulnerable (para 9.58).

The Homelessness Act 2002, including its amendments to the Housing Act 1996, as

---

[48] See generally, Pascall (1997: ch 13).

[49] Registered social landlords are increasingly significant providers of social housing (DETR and DSS 2000: para 1.20).

[50] Housing Act 1996 s 182. The relevant codes are the Code of Guidance on the Allocation of Accommodation (ODPM 2002); The Code of Guidance on the Allocation of Accommodation: Choice Based Lettings 2008; Homelessness Code of Guidance for Local Authorities 2006; and the Supplemental Guidance on Intentional Homelessness 2009.

well as its Code of Guidance (ODPM 2002), were designed to implement the government's key principles. First, the legislation broadened potential access to housing. Anyone can now apply for accommodation except for specified categories of people from abroad who are designated ineligible,[51] or people whose conduct makes them unsuitable tenants.[52] Second, the legislation has been amended to remove the time limit on the local authority's duty to house those in need of emergency accommodation. Section 193 of the Housing Act 1996 no longer restricts the duration of the duty to two years[53] and simply provides that the authority has a duty to ensure that accommodation is available to an applicant who is eligible, homeless, has a priority need and has not become homeless intentionally.[54] Third, authorities now have a discretion to offer accommodation to those who are not in priority need.[55] Where the applicant has a priority need but is intentionally homeless, there is a duty to provide accommodation for such time as the authority considers will provide him or her with a reasonable opportunity to find his or her own accommodation.[56] Housing authorities also have a duty to take reasonable steps to enable those in priority need and threatened with homelessness, but not intentionally so, to remain in their accommodation.[57] However, in addition to these duties, housing authorities now have new powers. They are permitted to allocate accommodation to those who are unintentionally homeless but who are not in priority need.[58] They also have a discretion to help those not in priority need but who are not intentionally threatened with homelessness, as well as those who are in priority need but who are intentionally threatened with homelessness, to remain in their homes.[59]

Those who have a priority need for accommodation[60] in terms of the statute are people who are homeless or threatened with homelessness as a result of an emergency such as a flood, households with dependent children, and households that include a pregnant woman or a vulnerable person. A person fleeing domestic violence in their home is deemed unintentionally homeless and in priority need.[61]

The duties of local authorities to provide temporary or emergency accommodation, then, depend on whether the homeless person is in priority need and on whether their plight is the result of an intentional act or omission. The statute also distinguishes between different categories of people in relation to the allocation of settled accommodation. All applicants for housing, including those already in temporary accommodation, are allocated permanent housing in accordance with a housing scheme. In addition, the scheme

[51] S 160A Housing Act 1996 as amended. Those subject to immigration control are not eligible unless they fall within prescribed classes, such as people granted refugee status, exceptional leave to remain or indefinite leave to remain. See The Allocation of Housing (England) Regulations 2002, SI 2002 No 3264. See also ODPM (2002: ch 4) on eligibility.
[52] S 160A(7) Housing Act 1996 as amended. Such persons can be treated as ineligible. This extends also to cases where a member of the applicant's household's behaviour is in issue.
[53] The main homelessness duty in s 193 persists until it is brought to an end by circumstances specified in that section. These include an offer of an assured tenancy or a refusal of a final offer of accommodation.
[54] Prior to the 2002 amendments, this duty was limited if the authority was satisfied that other accommodation was available in the area; it was obliged only to provide advice and assistance to enable the applicant to find accommodation him- or herself. This limitation has now been repealed.
[55] The statute also places a duty on authorities to provide advice and assistance to those who are homeless or threatened with homelessness if they are intentionally so or if they do not have priority needs.
[56] S 190(2) Housing Act 1996.
[57] S 195(2) Housing Act 1996 as amended. A person is threatened with homelessness if it is likely that he or she will be homeless within 28 days (s 175(4) Housing Act 1996).
[58] S 192(3) Housing Act 1996 as amended.
[59] See s 195(8)–(9) Housing Act 1996 as amended.
[60] See s 189 Housing Act 1996.
[61] For further discussion, see Chapter 12 below.

must give 'reasonable preference'[62] to certain categories of people including those who are homeless, those who are homeless and owed a duty under section 193, those who are threatened with homelessness and owed a duty under section 195(2), those who are in unsatisfactory housing conditions, those who need to move on medical and welfare grounds, and those who need to move where failure to move will cause them or others hardship.[63] The scheme may also be framed so as to give additional preference to people within the reasonable preference categories who have urgent housing needs.[64]

The effect of the legislation is to retain the priority status based on pregnancy and dependent children. However, there is a discretion to help unintentionally homeless people who do not qualify for priority status. Moreover, all homeless persons, including those who are single and those who are childless must be given reasonable preference in the allocation of accommodation.

When it comes to securing the housing need of children, it is often social services rather than the housing authority that appears to bear responsibility. Where an application under the housing legislation is made on behalf of the child in an attempt to circumvent the intentional homelessness provisions, the House of Lords has decided that the local authority should find other means of meeting its obligation. (Barton and Douglas 1995: 251–52).[65] Parents who are ineligible or intentionally homeless may turn instead to social services. Section 213A of the Housing Act 1996 is designed to enable social services to be apprised of the situation where a young person is or is likely to be homeless. Where someone applies for housing but is ineligible or intentionally homeless, that person must be asked to consent to social services being notified if a person under 18 lives with him or her. Provided there is consent, social services must be told of the situation so that they can take action.

Local authorities have duties under Part 3 of the Children Act 1989 and it may be necessary for social services and the housing authority to work together to fulfil these. Section 17 provides that:

(1) It shall be the general duty of every local authority …

(a) to safeguard and promote the welfare of children within their area who are in need; and

(b) so far as is consistent with that duty, to promote the upbringing of such children by their families, by providing a range and level of services appropriate to those children's needs.

Section 20(1) places a duty upon local authorities to

provide accommodation for any child in need within their area who appears to them to require accommodation as a result of—

…

---

[62] S 167(2) Housing Act 1996 as amended.

[63] S 167 Housing Act 1996 as amended. It is not apparent that the hardship ground would necessarily be appropriate to prioritise victims of domestic violence. See the discussion of these grounds in ODPM (2002: paras 5.16–5.17). However the Code of Guidance provides, as an example under the category of medical or welfare grounds, '[t]he need to recover from the effects of violence (including racial attacks) or threats of violence, or physical, emotional or sexual abuse' (ODPM 2002: Annex 3).

[64] S 167(2) Housing Act 1996 as amended. The revision of the Code of Guidance gives as an example, people who are victims or at risk of domestic violence (ODPM 2002: para 5.18). See Chapter 12 below.

[65] See also *R v Oldham Met BC, ex parte Garlick and Related Appeals* [1993] AC 509; Gilbert (1993); Loveland (1996).

(c) the person who has been caring for him being prevented (whether or not permanently, and for whatever reason) from providing him with suitable accommodation or care.[66]

Social services may ask the housing authority to provide advice and assistance in the exercise of its functions under Part 3 and the housing authority is obliged to provide such 'advice and assistance as is reasonable in the circumstances'.[67] Similarly, section 27 of the Children Act 1989 provides that housing authorities are obliged to respond to a request for help from social services in fulfilling its duties under that Act. So, for example, housing authorities and social services may have to consult in cases where a household includes a child in need who requires accommodation for welfare or medical reasons[68]

However, the obligation to co-operate is circumscribed; it applies only where co-operation is compatible with the duties of the authority asked for help and if rendering help would not unduly prejudice the discharge of its functions.[69] And the duty under section 213A(5) of the Housing Act 1996 is limited to what is 'reasonable'. Neither of these provisions, it seems, can be used to force a housing authority to provide accommodation to the carers or family of a child who is in need as a result of the fact that the adults with whom he or she lives are homeless. Social services has the power, but has no obligation under Part 3, to provide housing for the families or carers of children.

A child whose family is homeless and ineligible for help under housing legislation may be assessed as being in need. However section 17, the House of Lords has held,[70] is a general provision and does not confer absolute, enforceable rights on individuals (paras 91, 135); the only remedy is judicial review. Moreover, section 17 is not primarily designed to deal with the rehousing of children in need to enable them to live with their families: 'housing is the function of the local housing authority' (para 92). To use section 17 in this way would have the effect of turning the social services department of a local authority into another kind of housing authority with priorities that differ from those set down in housing legislation (para 93).

Section 20 does oblige the local authority to provide children with accommodation if their carers are unable to provide them with suitable accommodation and it is not open to them to refer the child to the homeless person's unit.[71] However, there is no duty in the Children Act[72] to ensure that the carers are given accommodation; the duty is exclusive to the child. And while to place children in accommodation apart from their parents constitutes an interference with family life,[73] whether a decision taken under Part 3 is compatible with Article 8 of the ECHR depends on the facts of each case.[74]

---

[66] See also ss 17(1) and 27(2).

[67] S 213A(5) Housing Act 1996 as amended.

[68] Included as one of the categories meriting reasonable preference in s 167(2) Housing Act 1996.

[69] S 27(2) Children Act 1989. See *R v Northaven DC, ex parte Smith* [1994] 2 AC 402, [1994] 3 All ER 313.

[70] *R (on the application of G) v Barnet London Borough Council; R (on the application of W) v Lambeth London Borough Council; R (on the application of A) v Lambeth London Borough Council* [2003] UKHL (2004) 57 1 FLR 454.

[71] *R (On the application of G) v Southwark London Borough Council* [2009] UKHL 26; [2009] 2 FLR 380. See also *R (M) v Hammersmith and Fulham London Borough Council* [2008] UKHL 14; [2008] 1 WLR 535 in which the House found that when a child approached a housing association seeking housing, she should have been referred to the children's authority for assessment under the Children Act 1989.

[72] *R (on the application of G) v Barnet London Borough Council; R (on the application of W) v Lambeth London Borough Council; R (on the application of A) v Lambeth London Borough Council* [2003] UKHL (2004) 57 1 FLR 454. The court rejected the argument that s 23 created such a duty (paras 102–04).

[73] See *Kutzner v Germany* [2003] 1 FCR 249.

[74] *R (on the application of G) v Barnet London Borough Council; R (on the application of W) v Lambeth London Borough Council; R (on the application of A) v Lambeth London Borough Council* [2003] UKHL (2004) 57 1 FLR 454, para 69.

Assistance with housing is also provided by way of financial assistance. Housing Benefit is a means-tested benefit payable to tenants in both private and social housing. Tenants in social housing can claim 'eligible rent', which includes the rent and charges for some services such as laundy services, but does not include water, heat, lighting or cooking charges. Local Housing Allowance, the assistance for people renting in the private sector, is set at a maximum based on the rents in the local area. Changes made to this benefit in the 2011 budget of the coalition government mean that it will be restricted if tenants are occupying what is thought to be accommodation too large for their needs, usually counted by number of bedrooms. Single people under 25, for example, will be restricted to the rate for a single room in a shared house, rather than a one-bedroom flat. The maximum rate for any tenant will be for a four-bedroom house, regardless of the number of people living in it. Extra money will be provided, however, for a room for carers.

In 2010 the coalition government published a consultation document regarding reform of housing law (2010 DfCLG). The proposals are focused upon giving local authorities and registered landlords, such as housing associations, greater discretion to determine the type of tenancies they offer to claimants, to whom they offer them and the conditions under which they are offered. It is proposed, for example, to introduce a new level of rent payable for social housing tenants—called 'affordable rent'—which will be higher than social rent, but lower than market rent. If the tenant on receiving this still cannot afford to pay his/her rent, he/she will be eligible for housing benefit (paras 2.5, 2.6). It is also proposed to create a new form of 'flexible' tenancy for a range of fixed periods (paras 2.11, 2.12). It is proposed to give local authorities discretion to determine who qualifies for social housing, ie which categories of applicants to put on waiting lists (Chapter 4), but duties to the most vulnerable, including homeless people, would be maintained, while giving local authorities more 'flexibility' on how to achieve them (Chapter 6). These proposals are contained in the Localism Bill 2011, making its way through Parliament at the time of writing.

> **Q** Article 27(3) of the UN Convention on the Rights of the Child requires states, in the case of need, to provide material assistance and support programmes, particularly with regard to nutrition, clothing and housing. In your view, has the UK met its obligation under this Article?

VI. CONCLUSION

We have looked at the relationship of families with the state. This relationship is about the balance struck between public and private responsibility for care work—the work that families do. Family policy affects how easily we can 'do' this family living, which includes our paid and unpaid work. In this policy our obligations to our family members and the state's obligations to us have shifted over the years. '[T]here is a double repositioning going on: individuals are being repositioned vis-a-vis family, state and market and family-related functions and agency are being repositioned vis a vis those of the state and market' (Daly and Scheiwe 2010: 194).[75] Responsibility is now more privatised, and, with the 'Big Society' localised, than ever. It seems the residual role the state has retained has been to encourage that responsibility and accountability. This might not create such a precarious

---

[75] See also Diduck (2005a, 2008a).

position for vulnerable carers, if other social supports were also not concurrently being eroded.

FURTHER READING

L ADAMS, F MCANDREW and M WINTERBROTHAM, *Pregnancy Discrimination at Work: A Survey of Women* (London, Equal Opportunities Commission, 2005).

A BARLOW and S DUNCAN, 'New Labour's Communitarianism, Supporting Families and the "Rationality Mistake": Part I' (2000) 22(2) *Journal of Social Welfare and Family Law* 23.

——, 'New Labour's Communitarianism, Supporting Families and the "Rationality Mistake": Part II' (2000) 22(2) *Journal of Social Welfare and Family Law* 129.

A BARLOW, S DUNCAN and G JAMES, 'New Labour, the Rationality Mistake and Family Policy in Britain' in A Carling, S Duncan and R Edwards (eds), *Analysing Families: Morality and Rationality in Policy and Practice* (London, Routledge, 2002).

S DUNCAN et al, 'Motherhood, Paid Work and Partnering: Values and Theories' (2003) 17 *Work, Employment and Society* 309.

J LEWIS, *The Politics of Motherhood: Child and Maternal Welfare in England 1900–1939* (London, Croom Helm, 1980).

——, *Work Family–Balance, Gender and Policy* (Cheltenham, Edward Elgar, 2009).

S SEVENHUIJSEN, *Citizenship and the Ethics of Care* (London, Routledge, 1998).

M THOMSON, 'Employing the Body: The Reproductive Body and Employment Exclusion' (1996) 5 *Social and Legal Studies* 243.

M THOMPSON, L VINTER and V YOUNG, *Dads and their Babies: Leave Arrangements in the First Year: Working Paper Series No 37* (London, Equal Opportunities Commission, 2005).

PART II

THE PRINCIPLES AND THE LAW

Section 1: Equality

INTRODUCTION

In the next three sections we will discuss the law in the context of three principles which we see as underpinning contemporary family law. The principles are equality, welfare and family privacy. In dividing our discussion this way we do not mean to suggest that the principles do not overlap. Indeed, as we stated in Chapter 1, they work together to inform the way that families, family practices and family relationships are governed by law. This section, Chapters 6–8 will introduce the first of these principles, that of equality between the adult partners to a relationship, and will illustrate it in two contexts.

In Chapter 6 we explore the law's impact upon economic ordering in households, including income generation and distribution, spending and the acquisition of wealth in the form of property and property rights. On the face of it, there is little *direct* legal regulation of the ways in which members of families order their economic and financial affairs, yet law and social policy play a large part in influencing indirectly both a family's financial arrangements and how its members determine the use of their resources. We wish to explore the impact on these determinations of the principles of formal and substantive equality, individualism, co-operation and family ideology.

When partners are or have been married or in a registered civil partnership the court has jurisdiction, and wide discretion, to make orders regarding all of their property and finances, no matter how or when acquired. The court exercises its discretion with the aim of achieving 'fairness' between the parties. There are no statutory guidelines as to what 'fairness' means, or as to how best to achieve it, although the statutes that govern financial relief on separation, divorce, nullity or dissolution of civil partnerships contain lists of factors for the court to consider when it is deciding if and how to exercise its powers to achieve fairness. In Chapter 7 we look at how, if at all, that principle is or should be informed by some idea of equality.

Secondly, questions may arise as between parents, and between parents and third parties, concerning the authority to make decisions about children's upbringing. In addition, when parents separate, arrangements have to be made for their children's residence and care. In relation to parental responsibility in particular, and to some extent residence and contact, the law has been shaped, at least in part, by the principle of equality. Parental responsibility is discussed in Chapter 8 from this perspective.

In these three chapters we seek to explore the development of equality as it has been adopted in family law, and present alternative conceptions of what it might mean. We will raise questions about the appropriateness of various notions of individual equality in families and the impact of gender on those notions. In both the 'public' sphere of work and wealth creation and the 'private' sphere of family care, the relationship between the sexes has been characterised by increasing formal or liberal equality which, we argue, has had serious implications for women's and children's well-being. In this way, these chapters also reflect law's concern with welfare and the public/private divide.

Our discussion begins with finances and property. While we include in this discussion the distribution of income and property on the dissolution of both marriages and civil partnerships, both the legislative scheme regulating that distribution and the principles used to interpret it were developed in the context of heterosexual marriage and divorce and the structural and ideological considerations and assumptions about sex and gender roles that inform(ed) those institutions. Further, the law regarding the fair or 'rightful' ownership of, and ways of sharing, family finances and property was, and we suggest still is, impossible to separate from ideas about the ownership and acquisition of property generally, the 'rightful' places of men and women in society and their consequent implications for men's and women's relative abilities to accumulate wealth.

The same gendered analysis can made of parenting. While children may have parents who are of the same sex, and the principles about the responsibility parents bear to their children are the same in all cases, those principles were developed in the context of mothering and fathering, family practices that are profoundly gendered. And so, while we incoroprate here the law's treatment of same-sex families, these chapters are located in a section about gender equality because we believe the legacy of family law's gendered and gendering practices remains intact today.

6

Household Economics

In this chapter we explore the law's impact upon the economic ordering of households, including income generation and distribution, spending and the acquisition of wealth in the form of property and property rights. On the face of it, there is little *direct* legal regulation of the ways in which members of families order their economic and financial affairs. Once again, however, law and social policy play a large part in influencing indirectly both a family's financial arrangements and how its members determine the use of their resources.

We divide this chapter into three main parts. The first will deal with household income. We will examine questions such as how household income is generated and by whom it is generated, while the second deals with how it is distributed among members of the household and who controls that distribution and on what basis. The third part will focus upon the acquisition of property and the determination of interests in property.

The theme running through this chapter, as in all chapters in this part, is the way in which principles of formal and substantive equality interact with the ideology of the family.

I. FAMILY INCOME

A household's income may come from private or public sources. By private sources, we mean the wages or salaries of those members who engage in paid labour, or income generated by any family business in which a family member has an interest. By public sources we mean income which comes directly from the state in the form of contributory or non-contributory benefits and indirectly in the form of state-provided services.

Waged Income

The degree to which law and policy influence the accumulation of a family's income from this outside private source is largely dependent upon the form the family takes. So, because law regulates the labour of adult, able-bodied men less rigorously than it does the labour of women and those under the age of 16 (Daly and Scheiwe 2010),[1] families consisting only of adult able-bodied men will have less legal 'intervention' to contend with

---

[1] See below, pp 243–46 on children's work.

in relation to how they accumulate income and then distribute it between their members. The 'free market' in which these men exchange labour, goods or services for money also constructs few social difficulties or 'barriers' for them, although immigration status, race and racism still play a part in structuring the opportunities of many.[2] On the other hand, families which include women and children, or families which comprise women and children only, will be more affected both by legal regulation of the members' opportunities for employment and by unofficial and social regulation which either inhibits or enhances those opportunities. Similarly, and as we have seen in previous chapters, whether or not the adults in the family are legally attached to each other or to the children also affects the degree of legal intervention in their family finances; some legal relationships create obligations of support.

> **Q** Legal regulation of the 'traditional' (able-bodied male) labour market, the predominant source of household income, is different from regulation of the 'non-traditional' labour market (women, children and disabled men). The National Minimum Wage Act 1998, for example, excludes a number of categories of employees and employers, including those living and working in their employer's home and restrictions on the maximum number of hours worked are limited to those in the Working Time Regulations 1998 , which also excludes domestic servants. Statutory limits on the type and hours of work children may undertake are stricter than those applicable to adults,[3] and there are legal restrictions on the entry of children into certain occupations. What forms of indirect legal or social regulation of the labour market can you think of? How might this indirect regulation affect a household's income? Consider also the effect of 'race' or nationality on employment and the Equality Act 2010.

Direct and indirect regulation of the labour market is important because English law makes it clear that, at least regarding adults, whoever earns income has all legal rights to it.

The Historical View

At common law the doctrine of coverture meant that, on marriage, a wife's personal property became her husband's, and this included her earnings from paid work. Indeed, it was for this reason that, both before and after Lord Hardwicke's Act,[4] many working women may have chosen not to marry formally, but rather to enter into informal marriages, or to 'live tally' with their partners (Parker 1987, 1990; but see Probert 2009). It was not until the Married Women's Property Acts 1870 and 1882, passed after decades of

---

[2] According to the Department for Work and Pensions, in 2008–09 around two-fifths of households with heads from ethnic minority backgrounds were in a low-income bracket, around twice the rate for those who were of white British descent (DWP 2010). According to the Equality and Human Rights Commission, in 2009 the employment rate for Asian people was 59.3%, for black British people 57.8%, and for British white people was 74.8% (EHRC 2009).

[3] See below, pp 243–46.

[4] An Act for the better prevention of clandestine marriages 1753. See also Gillis (1985); Lemmings (1996); Parker (1990, 1987); and Chapter 2 above.

campaigning by women, that married women became entitled to keep their property, including their wages.[5]

These Acts did not pass without opposition. A newspaper editorial in the 1860s argued that such a change in the law would completely alter the relationship between husband and wife, and questioned whether it was sound policy to do this 'for the sake of a particular class of wives' (Pahl 1989: 20).

The 1882 Married Women's Property Act established the system of separate property for spouses, which remains, in effect, the law today[6]—according to Pahl, the legislation 'can be seen as the greatest transfer of resources from married men to married women which has ever taken place' (Pahl 1989: 22).

Which members of families are easily able to earn has long been a matter of interest not only from the perspective of traditional family law but also in the context of labour law[7] and welfare law (Beveridge 1942).[8] In the nineteenth century and the first part of the twentieth century, it was thought that in families consisting of men, women and children, it was men who contributed income to the family by working outside the home for pay; women maintained the home by working unpaid inside the family. Not only was this arrangement accepted socially, but global economic figures and gross national products of countries were calculated based upon the assumption that the work that (usually) men did outside the home for remuneration was real work, while the work that (usually) women did in the form of reproduction and homemaking was not.[9] Indeed, as we have seen in Chapter 5, such an understanding of historical arrangements leads to statistics which indicate growing numbers of women working outside the home being construed today, just as they were in the 1880s,[10] as revealing a peculiarly modern trend. Recent historical work has suggested, however, that the traditional breadwinner/homemaker arrangement, which has been called the bourgeois family model because of its origins in the middle classes, was dominant only within certain segments of society at particular historical times and was not nearly so pervasive or universal as is popularly thought.

Women and Work

In medieval and early modern societies, for example, women contributed not only to household and farm work, but also to family incomes (Oakley 1985; Hudson and Lee 1990). Further, although industrialisation is often cited as the point at which the sexual division of labour in families became entrenched, even during this period, the bourgeois family model was not universal. Hudson and Lee have reviewed the history of female labour in Europe, and conclude that women's work was persistently under-recorded in historical records (Hudson and Lee 1990: 20). Nevertheless, they do identify patterns of a 'traditional' division of labour between married men and women, and provide some explanation for the withdrawal of married women from the workplace. With respect to

---

[5] See generally Holcombe (1983) and Auchmuty (2008).
[6] See below, pp 252–54.
[7] As in agitation by trade unions for the 'family wage'.
[8] See below and Chapter 5 above.
[9] James (1994: 173) estimates that women's unpaid work—in agriculture, food production, reproduction, and household activities—accounts for as much as 50% of a country's GNP.
[10] See Pahl (1989: 20).

late eighteenth–early nineteenth-century industrialisation, they indicate that the *ideology* of the family was important.

> [F]emale employment during the century or so before 1945 saw greater emphasis on the role of single women and a diminished degree of participation in the formal economy by married women. In Britain in 1911, for example, 69% of all single women worked, but only 9.6% of married women [did] … .
>
> In attempting to explain the long-term determinants of the nature and extent of women's employment, life-cycle and age-related earning patterns were clearly important. Low levels of male wages especially in the less-skilled sectors during the nineteenth century along with large family size made it essential that women earned an income both before marriage and at least during the early years of marriage until children were old enough to replace the wife's income through their own wage-earning activities … .
>
> Changes in the extent of married women's employment in the nineteenth and early twentieth centuries also reflected the growing dominance of the bourgeois family model, in which the breadwinner was the husband and the wife and children the dependants … . The Victorian ideal of the 'angel in the house', reflecting the influence of evangelicism and the over-riding view of women as domestic beings was clearly evident by the 1830s and 1840s, and this idealisation of femininity … limited adult women to a narrowly defined role as wives and mothers. Diffusion of the bourgeois family model within nineteenth century European society was underpinned and reinforced by a concept of the sexes which embodied great mental and emotional distinctions. The emergent medical profession, with its image of women as conspicuous consumptives also helped to maintain the view of women as invalid, weak, delicate and invariably prone to illness.
>
> … Formal teaching of girls in schools was equivalent to 'professional mothering' and any higher education was pursued primarily in order to train women for their domestic role … . Increasing official concern with the potential deleterious effects on family welfare, particularly in relation to infant and child mortality, of full-time work by married women also tended to encourage the primacy placed upon domestic responsibilities. Similarly in the late 1940s and 1950s the emphasis by psychologists on maternal adequacy as the key to 'normal' child develop-ment played a role in militating against the active participation of married women in the labour force. (Hudson and Lee 1990: 21–22, footnotes omitted)

As regards the working class, the authors point out that

> [n]otions of respectability were well entrenched within sections of the working class (for example, carding buttons at home was regarded as more respectable than making matchboxes). Status consciousness and increasing social stratification within the working class may well have reinforced the cult of domesticity and contributed to the low profile of women's work and its contribution to the family income. (ibid: 23, footnotes omitted)

Davidoff et al also note how in the nineteenth century the cult of domesticity permeated both the working classes, perhaps partly as a way to 'lock men, particularly young men, into steady work' (Davidoff et al 1999: 18), and the middle classes in which 'wifely femininity became associated with being the mistress of a household, and masculinity with elevating the *need* to work to a moral and respectable *duty* to do so' (Diduck 2003: 140). The drive for the 'family wage' and protective labour legislation were also important influences in the dominance of the nineteenth-century cult of domesticity. An important point to note, however, is that while women's participation in the *formal* economy was limited, their place in the *non-formal* economy, doing home or outwork which was not officially recognised, was more prominent (Hudson and Lee 1990: 29). Women supple-mented men's low or seasonal wages by undertaking work such as childminding, cleaning and washing, work that could mean the difference between survival and starvation (ibid: 30–31).

Married working-class women, then, have always assumed an important role in their families' economic livelihoods, although the middle-class cult of domesticity which measured a man's status by the idleness of his dependants gradually began to pervade working-class homes. As a result, women's earnings came to be seen as supplementary or as their own 'pin money', and these understandings contributed to justifications for keeping women's wages lower than men's. Even today, women tend to be defined as 'secondary earners'. The importance of these understandings for relationships within heterosexual families should not be underestimated. In 1989, social policy researcher Jan Pahl reported on interviews with 102 married couples about their sources of income and patterns of money management. She found that the power of the 'secondary earner' assumption continued even when women contributed a greater proportion of their income to the family coffers than did men. Husbands were perceived by both spouses as breadwinners and, therefore, as entitled to the privileges that attended this status:

> Inequality in the wider society meshes with inequality within the household. A woman may contribute a higher proportion of her earnings to housekeeping than her husband, but her income is still likely to be regarded as marginal; a man may contribute a lower proportion of his earnings, but he still feels justified in spending more than his wife on leisure because *both define him as the breadwinner*. (Pahl 1989: 170, emphasis added)

The sources we have cited refer only indirectly to law. Law does not require men to take on the role of family breadwinner, nor is there a statutory requirement that women assume the role of homemaker. Contemporary law professes to be disinterested in relation to the sex of both workers and parents and claims to operate on an assumption of equality between the sexes. It says, in effect, that how men and women choose to order their working lives is a private decision to be made by them alone. We have seen, however, that a combination of low-wage work for women and the assumptions in the labour market about both men and women encourages the traditional division of labour in heterosexual households, which, while the relationship is intact, may not be a problem. If, however, the partners go their separate ways, the economic consequences for each are very different.

Living outside of these gendered assumptions may allow many same-sex partners to negotiate their respective roles in a more open way (Dunne 1999; Weeks 2002). One of the respondents in Dunne's research with cohabiting lesbian couples expressed it in this way:

> I suppose because our relationship doesn't fit into a social norm, there are no pre-set conditions about how our relationship should work. We have to work it out for ourselves. We've no role models in terms of how we divide our duties, so we've got to work it out afresh as to what suits us … . We try very hard to be just to each other and … not exploit the other person.
>
> (Dunne 1999: 73)

As in the past, though, we must look today to the non-formal economy to gain a deeper understanding of family income patterns. First, significantly more women than men fall into the category of homeworkers—those engaged in baking, knitting, sewing, computing, clerical work, selling, hairdressing, teaching and childminding (Morris and Nott 1995: 56). These occupations, which may be unrecorded or under-recorded in formal employment statistics, are less likely to receive employment protection and benefits including

National Insurance, pensions or sick pay. Further, both formal and informal domestic labour is performed predominantly by women, often by migrant women, and, when unrecorded, or performed by a 'close member of the family', is not subject to statutory protections.[11] Secondly, women may work without pay within a family business, just as they do within the family home, and it seems that this phenomenon is most common among some ethnic minority communities which are characterised by close ties within the extended family (Anthias and Yuval-Davis 1993: 85–86, 119; Breugel 1994; Morris and Nott 1995).

Let us review the picture we have painted so far with regard to the generation of household incomes. Generally, the 'traditional' assumption that in heterosexual households, particularly in married households, men earn and women do not, or that women generally do not earn if they have children, can be challenged with reference to both modern and historical sources. Women do work outside the home, and are therefore able to contribute income as well as services to the household economy. We have also seen, however, that statistics concerning employment may not include many homeworkers, family workers or informal domestic workers. These statistics also do not include unpaid work in the home or family business, which, while not ascribed monetary value, are forms of work that are of crucial importance to the family and national economy. And it is overwhelmingly women who perform this labour, even if they also work for pay. However, researchers have identified what they call an 'economy of gratitude', whereby if men demonstrate that they are *aware* of the inequality in the division of unpaid work and compensate with emotional support, their partners might be 'mollified', and both might accept that a 'fair' arrangement had been reached (Lewis et al 1999: 53–57).

We have seen that the 'traditional' arrangement is changing; both men and women now contribute to the family financially, but they are not always able to do so on an equal basis, and the old assumptions about male breadwinners and female homemakers still have some purchase socially. Scott and Dex report that the employment rates for women with children under 5 increased by 10% between 1992 and 2004. while the employment rates for men in those households remained constant (Scott and Dex 2009: 47). They also report that as the number of paid hours for these women increased by three hours per week, the number of hours of unpaid housework decreased from 24.7 to 18.7 (ibid: 48). They go on: '[B]y contrast, men's paid and unpaid work hours changed very little over this period' (ibid: 48). Full-time working mothers in fact do twice the number of hours of housework per week as their full-time working partners (14 vs 7) although they work on average fewer full-time hours (39 vs 46) (ibid). We can conclude from this research, from the research about childcare and employment policy initiatives we reviewed in Chapter 5, and from our discussion of the gendered nature of parenting in Chapter 4, that while there are indeed shifts in how we perceive our place and our obligations in intimate relationships, these have not yet transcended family ideology with its gendered assumptions about 'traditional' family roles, the liberal public/private dichotomy which designates only paid work as work, or the way we actually 'do' family.

> If women do less paid work outside the home than men, then it seems only equitable that they should do more unpaid work in the home than men. In principle, the female partner could do more paid work than the man, but the relative wage rates are against this choice and in favour of women's specialisation in home work. Men will able to earn more per hour, on average, than

---

[11] For the 'close relative' exclusion, see Employment Rights Act 1996 s 161. On domestic labour generally, see eg Gregson and Lowe (1994).

women. So it is more efficient for the man to work, and thus, he accumulates more human capital which brings in higher wages in future. But this reinforces the unequal wage rates for men and women and locks women into unpaid home work. Does this matter? If the couple have committed themselves to living together as a unit, then they both stand to gain financially by this gender specialisation. In the past, couples were happy to do this, but times are changing. It is now seen as riskier for the woman to compromise her earning potential. She needs to maintain human capital (in terms of work experience and training) to cope with future uncertainties, such as unemployment or divorce. Moreover the traditional female career pattern has exerted a heavy penalty on older women who are reliant on state pensions. (Scott and Dex 2009: 55)

Vogler sums up the difficulties:

Both men and women now participate in the labour market as 'individuals' with their 'own' incomes, and intimate relationships are almost invariably regarded as partnerships between equals, in which all resources are ideally shared equally, regardless of who contributes what to the household. At the same time, however, men still earn more than women, while women are still seen as responsible for unpaid caring and household tasks. In these circumstances the problem couples face is that individual autonomy and equality are inevitably in tension with each other, because equality requires higher earners to give up a degree of individual autonomy and control over their 'own income' in order to redistribute equally within the couple.

(Vogler 2009: 62)

As the division of household labour is gendered, it may not be surprising that partners of the same sex tend to report more egalitarian negotiations in dividing it (Dunne 1999; Weeks et al 1999; Weeks 2002).

Q Consider these observations in the light of how financial equality is negotiated in the context of the ideology of the family.

A Contextual Perspective

Statistics reflecting earnings in families by necessity measure a family's situation at a particular point in time. Patterns of income are not static, however. A family member's earnings during his or her lifetime depend upon many factors, including the stage he or she is at in the family's or individual's lifecycle. Grassby (1991) identifies three sub-cycles in a household's economic cycle, although we may argue that her model is based upon the patriarchal 'traditional' model of the family which assumes that a worker has no family responsibilities. The first of Grassby's sub-cycles is the employment sub-cycle in which the early years of employment provide a basis for experience or seniority-building, the middle years provide increased revenue and the final years provide the best earning years and the basis upon which pension levels are usually determined.[12] The other two subcycles are the saving and spending sub-cycles, which are often in direct conflict with each other. Saving is difficult in the early years when income is at its lowest and spending is at its highest, especially if there are children, and so spending predominates at that point, leaving saving for the future and for when income increases.

---

[12] We may also argue here that this 'traditional' cycle may have changed with recent changes in patterns of employment, whereby workers in their later years are more vulnerable to redundancy and where workers are told they must no longer expect 'jobs for life'. See on this Equal Opportunities Commission (1995: 33).

Q Household income, who earns it and how the earnings may be saved and must be spent, therefore, all change depending upon the point in the household's economic cycle at which one is looking. What other variables would you suggest influence this model if we were examining a family consisting of a 22-year-old woman, her 50-year-old mother, and her 1-year-old child?

Added to this view of a household's economic cycle over its life is the particular life stage of the individuals. According to the Equality and Human Rights Commission:

> More than 80% of men of working age are in employment from their late 20s to their early 50s. The proportion who are in employment declines sharply after the age of 60. Women are much less likely than men to be employed full-time or self-employed in their early 30s (due to caring responsibilities), and if they return to work are more likely to take and remain in part-time employment. (EHRC 2010: 390)

Let us examine household income in the later lifecycle, the time during which income comes through pensions accrued during working life. While the state provides a basic flat-rate pension,[13] it is based upon NI contributions made during one's employment. To qualify for the full state pension one must have 30 years of contributions. If one is not eligible on this basis, one might be eligible on the basis of contributions made by one's husband, wife or registered civil partner, but that rate is only a proportion of the rate payable from personal contributions. Until 5 April 2010 the state pension age was 60 for women and 65 for men, but after this date women's state pension age began to rise; it will be 65 in 2020. After that, both women's and men's state pension age is to rise to 66 by 2026 and then to 67 by 2036, and to 68 by 2046.

The basic pension is low and if it is one's only source of income one may be entitled to the means-tested Pension Credit to top it up. There is also a second tier of state pension, so-called Additional State Pension, that increases the amount payable, again based on earnings and again claimable (at a reduced rate) by the widow(er) of the pensioner. These second-tier pensions do allow certain carers to build up 'credits' during years out of the workforce; carers who are in receipt of carers' allowance and who remain out of the workforce to care for a child under the age of 6 will build up credits at the low earnings threshold. The Additional State Pension is primarily aimed at low earners, however, leaving those on middle or high incomes to join occupational or personal pension schemes.[14]

Occupational and private pension schemes typically provide a retirement income based upon contributions made by the employee and employer during the employee's working life. They assume a model of full-time 40-year employment in order to calculate the amount necessary for an adequate retirement income, and typically make no concession for carers (Ginn 2003: 494). 'Contribution rates, resting periods, retirement benefits and

---

[13] See Pensions Act 2007. See also, however, the consultation paper *A State Pension for the 21st Century* (2011) in which the coalition government is seeking views for simplifying the state pension system.

[14] The Pensions Act 2008 introduced a series of reforms to enable and encourage individuals to save more for retirement. The 2008 Act was followed by Draft Workplace Pension Reform Regulations on which the government was consulting at the time of writing. These reforms focus on the use of auto-enrolment into workplace pension schemes, from which an individual would need to actively opt out, to build private saving. The 2008 Act will not come into force until 2012. The coalition government plans to supplement it with further legislation, currently in the form of the Pensions Bill 2011 which also proposes to require members of public sector pension schemes to increase, or to start making, contributions towards the costs of providing pensions under public sector employment schemes.

other terms at the heart of retirement income schemes are all selected on the premise that forty years are available to accumulate enough' for retirement (Smith 2001: 520). And herein lies the problem for women. While women have the same ability formally to accrue these pensions as men, we have seen that their patterns of work differ markedly from the 40-year full-time model on which pension accrual and entitlement are based. If a woman was or is married, she may have the benefit derived from her husband's contributions, but if she is single or divorced when she reaches pensionable age, particularly if she has had caring responsibilities, she faces the very real possibility of poverty.

> [T]he different way in which women dispose of their time, divided between the labour force and household production, is crucial [to retirement income]. Because of this most women spend less than half the years spent by men in paid employment. A woman's years in the workforce are broken by child care and shortened by elder care. They are also mostly part-time because of the enduring practice of women doing the greater share of household production even when employed. In truth women oscillate between household production and the labour force. In the former they earn little or nothing towards retirement. What they gain from the latter is diminished further by lower pay rates and lower promotion. (Smith 2001: 520)

It is clear, therefore, that full-time employment is crucial for building private pension entitlements (Ginn and Arber 1996; Ginn 2003) and women's exclusion from these entitlements has recently come onto the public and political agenda (Price 2007, 2009).[15]

Income generation during different parts of a family's lifecycle thus affects other parts of the cycle. Attribution of value, in money terms or otherwise, to some types of labour (in the public sphere) and ignoring the value of other types of labour (in the private) means that in the later cycle as well as in the earlier women tend to be poorer relative to men, and the wealth they do 'earn' is often derived from their status as a 'wife'. The lack of social and economic recognition of 'home' work obviously has implications for individual women, but it may also say something about the relative value ascribed generally in British society to 'women's work'.

Children and Work[16]

Adult women and men are often not the only members of households to bring in income. We stated earlier that children's employment is relatively strictly regulated by law, but children continue to participate in both the formal and informal economies in Britain. According to the European Trades Union Institute, up to 40% of 13–15 year olds and nearly 25% of 11 and 12 year olds were working in undeclared part-time jobs in the UK (Paone 2006: 35). Children also engage in unpaid labour in the home, by babysitting and helping with household chores. This work, like women's work in the home, has traditionally been ignored when the family economy is studied. In addition, children often

---

[15] See Price (2009) for a comprehensive and detailed study of the effect over the life course of partnership forms, parenting, earning and gender. These factors will continue to have a profound effect upon later life income and poverty levels as long as pension systems remain dependent upon involvement in paid work and earnings levels. She concludes: 'To the extent that work biographies remain highly gendered, private pension systems will continue to disadvantage women. ...[And] it is not only work biographies but also gendered cultural norms [of women as "second earners" and as dependent upon men] which influence women's participation in third tier pension schemes' (Price 2009: 278–79).

[16] For an overview, see Bainham (2005: 679–88).

contribute to the family's finances by generating their own pocket money or money which becomes a part of the household budget. It has been found that nine-tenths of children performed in the non-formal economy by doing household jobs, half performed babysitting duties for families and neighbours, three-quarters ran errands, 26% worked in the family business, and many were responsible for light work on family farms (Bond 1996: 300).

Regulation of children's hours of work and types of work is by both UK domestic law and international instruments.[17] The primary domestic legislation is the Children and Young Persons Act 1933, as amended primarily by the Children (Protection at Work) Regulations 1998[18] which implement the EC Directive on the Protection of Young People at Work.[19] Taken together, they regulate the work of 'children', who are defined as those under the legal school-leaving age of 15, and who should be distinguished from 'young people', defined as those between ages 15 and 18.[20] The 1933 Act provides that no child under the age of 14 shall be employed in any work other than as an employee of a parent in light agricultural or horticultural work on an occasional basis.[21] Children are also prohibited from doing any work other than 'light work': work which does not jeopardise a child's safety, health, development, attendance at school or participation in work experience.[22] The Act also provides limits on the hours children may work per day and per week, and also for ensuring that they have at least two consecutive weeks off work during school holidays.[23]

Section 18(2), however, empowers the Secretary of State to make regulations providing for exceptions for children aged 13 for certain types of work and in relation to conditions of employment.[24]

Taken together, the UK and EU provisions represent a movement away from historical views of the role of children and of child labour in the family.[25] That view, held by even the most compassionate of reformers in the nineteenth century, is described by Cunningham as follows:

> The utilitarians did not object to child labour in principle, only to its excess. Time in childhood, they argued, must be set aside for schooling and physical growth. But beyond that, and beyond a certain minimum age, there was no reason why children should not go to work and contribute to the family economy. (Cunningham 1995: 142)

Cunningham explains the movement away from this view as a type of Romanticism cap-

---

[17] See eg Hamilton and Watt (2004).

[18] SI 1998/276.

[19] Council Dir 94/33/EC.

[20] There are fewer restrictions on the work of young people, who, for the most part, are treated as adults, with the exception of some specific requirements imposed upon their employers regarding health and safety at work. (Health and Safety (Young Persons) Regulations 1997 SI 1997/135). See Bainham (2005: 688).

[21] S 18(1).The minimum age at which children can be employed in such work is 13. (Children (Protection at Work) Regulations 2000 (Nos 1 and 2) SI 2000/1333 and SI 2000/2548. See Bainham (2005: 683).

[22] S 18(1) and (2A).

[23] S 18(1).

[24] See also s 20 in relation to street trading and also ss 24, 25, 37 and 39 of the Children and Young Persons Act 1963 regarding children's work in performances, the Education Act 1996, which requires children's attendance in school between the ages of 5 and 16 (s 8, as amended by the Education Act 1997) and the Education and Skills Act 2008 which requires their attendacne in trainning or education untial age 18. Regulations concerning the working time for adolescents—those aged between 15 and 18—are included in the Working Time Regulations 1998 and the Working Time (Amendment) Regulations 2002 SI 2002/ 3128.

[25] See generally, Piper (2008).

tured by and propounded both by Romantic literati such as Wordsworth and Elizabeth Barrett Browning and by campaigners for the emancipation of the slaves who were able to deploy similar arguments about children (ibid: 140). While the state had long regulated the employment of children, they introduced the notion that children had a right not to work at all (ibid: 138).

Bond explains the movement in slightly different terms:

> Whereas the family environment had earlier provided a means of production for peasant families, the process of industrialization demanded that workers move away from the family and compete in the labour market as individuals. Although at first, children continued to be involved in providing the family with a livelihood, the physical separation was reinforced by the gradual imposition upon working-class families of bourgeois ideology, which recognized a man's status by the domesticity of his wife and children and demanded legislation designed to restrict the participation of women and children in the labour market. Several other factors also influenced the legislation: the recognition that the cheap labour of children was undercutting the wages paid to adults; a humanistic concern with the exploitation of children; and an understanding that since children were the key to the country's future economic and military well-being, the preservation of their health was important. (Bond 1996: 297–98)

She attributes some of this process to an ideology of family privacy whereby the family was separated from the public world of the market, but points out that that same ideology was also responsible for much of the resistance to child labour legislation in the nineteenth century. For example, it was thought that restricting children's labour in mines and factories was an unwarranted intrusion into parental control over children (ibid: 298), and she suggests that the ideology of family privacy is what continues to maintain contemporary private exemptions from child labour restrictions, such as those which create exceptions where children are employed by parents in light agricultural work or street trading.

There is a sense in middle-class society that children work 'so as to learn the value of an honest day's labour' or 'to learn the value of money', rather than to contribute to the family's finances. Indeed, current understandings of childhood are such that the child himself or herself is the antithesis of the worker. Modern childhood is supposed to be the stage at which one does not have the responsibilities of adulthood and when one is supposed to be innocent and free to play and to learn and to mature.[26] In many respects, this is the legacy of the nineteenth-century Romantic notions of childhood as a period of innocence. Cunningham quotes one American campaigner as saying 'the term child labor is a paradox for when labour begins ... the child ceases to be' (Cunningham 1995: 144).

Q Does British law reconcile the identities 'worker' and 'child' in a satisfactory way? In your view, can they be reconciled? Is your view influenced by your view of what childhood represents, or an ideology of childhood?

---

[26] See, eg, on views of childhood Bar-On (1997); Diduck (1999a); Archard (1993); Jenks (1996); Prout (2005); see Chapter 4 above.

Other Income

Income for families may come from another private source in the form of support payments made by non-resident spouses or civil partners, ex-spouses or ex-civil partners and parents. Once again, these obligations stem from the common law duty of a husband to maintain his wife and legitimate children, but now are enshrined in legislation which may extend the obligation beyond both the marriage bond and the old category of legitimacy. Support on separation, divorce or dissolution of civil partnership is at the discretion of a court or may be negotiated between the separating parties. The law is contained in the Matrimonial Causes Act 1973 (MCA) as amended,[27] the Civil Partnership Act 2004 (CPA),[28] and the Domestic Proceedings and Magistrates' Courts Act 1978,[29] and it provides for interim and final orders, for negotiated agreements and for lump sums as well as periodic payments. Support for children is provided for in the Children Act 1989,[30] the MCA 1973 and CPA 2004 (as above), the Domestic Proceedings and Magistrates' Courts Act (as above) and the Child Support Act 1991, amended. Each of these obligations will be discussed in Chapter 7. Finally, as we saw in Chapter 5, income for families also comes directly from the state. We raise these benefits and maintenance payments here simply to highlight that for many families, primarily single-parent families, they form a significant proportion of family income.

II. SHARING INCOME AND PROPERTY IN FAMILIES

With the exception of that earned by middle-class children, we tend to assume that money received by individuals from waged work or from the state is usually pooled in the family coffers and shared fairly, if not equally, for the benefit of all. The way in which money is distributed from those coffers among family members is only regulated directly to the extent that the law imposes a mutual obligation of support upon civil partners or spouses and upon parents to support their children. The spousal obligation stems from the common law duty of a husband to support his wife (Finer and McGregor 1974; Cretney 2003a), and is now enshrined in statute as a reciprocal obligation between spouses and civil partners. The legislation is limited in scope and effect, however. It does not apply to cohabitants at all,[31] and it refers only to 'reasonable maintenance'. The duty imposed on parents to support their legitimate children stems from the common law, although it has been called an 'imperfect duty' and historically was one for which the common law provided no enforcement mechanism (Smart 1987; see also Cretney 2003a). So-called illegitimate children were the responsibility of the parish and the mother until bastardy proceedings for child maintenance were introduced in 1871,[32] which in 1957 became

---

[27] Part II ss 21–40.
[28] Sch 5 Pt 9.
[29] Ss 1–8 and 19–32.
[30] S 15.
[31] And does not automatically apply to void marriages: *J v S-T (Formerly J) (Transsexual: Ancillary Relief)* [1997] 1 FLR 402 (CA).
[32] The Bastardy Act 1733, amended in the Bastardy Laws Amendment Act 1871.

affiliation proceedings.[33] Support for children is now enshrined in the Children Act 1989, the MCA 1973 and, more controversially, the Child Support Act 1991, as amended.[34]

Maintenance During the Relationship

As we have said, cohabitants have no legal duty to support or to contribute to the support of the other. Parents, however, whether they are married to each other or not, are legally obliged to contribute to the support of their children. We shall examine the child support obligation on separation in Chapter 7. Here we wish to draw attention to those circumstances where the law does intervene about the level of support married or civilly registered partners can expect from the other during the currency of their relationship. Partners in a marriage or civil partnership who have instituted divorce, nullity or dissolution proceedings may apply for maintenance from the other pending suit,[35] but even those who have not instituted proceedings may apply for an order if the respondent has not provided reasonably for them or a child of the family. Section 1 of the Domestic Proceedings and Magistrates' Court Act 1978 reads as follows:[36]

> Either party to a marriage may apply to a magistrates' court for an order under section 2 of this Act on the ground that the other party to the marriage—
>
>> has failed to provide reasonable maintenance for the applicant; or
>> has failed to provide, or to make a proper contribution towards, reasonable maintenance for any child of the family; or
>> has behaved in such a way that the applicant cannot reasonably be expected to live with the respondent; or
>> has deserted the applicant.

MCA 1973 section 27 and CPA 2004 Schedule 5, Part 9 also permit an application for an order for periodic payments or a lump sum if the respondent has failed to maintain reasonably the applicant or a child of the family. As is the case in the magistrates' courts, 'reasonableness' is a question of fact, but in determining an application under the MCA, the court must have regard to the factors in section 25(2) MCA.[37]

Distribution of income among family members apart from these duties of support is unregulated by law. Social science research tends to equate the living standards of dependants with those of the breadwinner, assuming that the altruistic and co-operative nature of the family means that income is allocated equally among all. Pahl put it in these terms:

> When a single person lives alone he or she is likely to be both the main earner and the main spender for that household. If an economist were to analyse the consumer behaviour of such an individual there would be a substantial body of economic theory on which to draw. When two or more adults live in the same household economists have traditionally treated that household as though it were an individual and have assumed that the same economic principles of micro-economics apply ... . But can we assume that individuals and households behave in similar

---

[33] Affiliation Proceedings Act 1957.
[34] See, generally, Finer and McGregor (1974), Barton and Douglas (1995), and MacLean and Eekelaar (1997). See also Chapter 2 above.
[35] MCA 1973, s22 and 22A, and CPA 2004, Schedule 5, Part 8.
[36] See also CPA 2004, Schedule 6, Part 1.
[37] See Chapter 7 below.

ways? Where one individual is the main earner and another the main spender what social and economic processes shape the allocation of money within that household?

    ...

    In reality, of course, income is earned by individuals, not households, and goods and services are purchased not by households but by individuals. However, 'by a heroic simplification the separate identities of men and women are merged into the concept of the household. The inner conflicts and compromises of the household are not explored'.

    By treating it as though it were an individual, the household has become a sort of black box, within which the transfer of resources between earners and spenders has been rendered invisible.

(Pahl 1989: 3–4, references omitted)

Her research, published in 1989, opened up that black box and provided an important source of information for policymakers and theorists on how income is distributed between husbands and wives, how the distribution is explained by them, and how it affects power and spending patterns within households. We have alluded to this and other research above. Let us examine first Pahl's groundbreaking research.

Pahl interviewed 102 couples, both separately and together, to seek to determine how gender, generation, life course, marriage ideology and trends toward more egalitarian marriages influence the allocation of money and the responsibility for controlling it.

She identified four general systems of money management in families. The first was *wife management* or the *whole wage* system. In families adopting this system one partner, usually the wife, 'is responsible for managing all the finances of the household and is also responsible for all expenditure, except for personal spending of the other partner' (Pahl 1989: 67).

The second system was the *allowance* system, where, typically:

> the husband gives his wife a set amount every week or month, to which she adds her own earnings, if any. She is then responsible for paying for specific items of household expenditure, while the rest of the money remains in the control of the husband and he pays for other items. Thus he has access to the main source of income, while she only has access to that part of it which he chooses to give her. (ibid: 69)

The third pattern was the *pooling* system or *shared management*. 'Pooling couples have a joint account or common kitty into which both incomes are paid and from which both draw. Thus both have access to the income entering the household and expenditure responsibilities are more or less shared' (ibid: 71).

Finally, she identified the *independent management* system:

> The essential characteristic of this system is that both partners have an income and that neither has access to all the household funds. Each partner is responsible for specific items of expenditure, and though these responsibilities may change over time, the principle of separate control over income and separate responsibility for expenditure is maintained. (ibid: 74)

She then distinguished between management (the day-to-day tasks of money management) and control (such as decision-making) of finances, and found that although a large number of wives managed money, fewer controlled it (ibid: 90). She drew the following conclusions:

Where a wife controls the finances she will usually also be responsible for money management; where a husband controls finances he will usually delegate parts of money management to his wife. Thus where a wife controls finances she will usually be responsible for paying the main bills and for making sure that ends meet, as well as for buying food and day-to-day necessities. Where a husband controls finances he will typically delegate to his wife the responsibility for housekeeping expenses, sometimes giving her a housekeeping allowance for this purpose. Marriages where the wife controls the money and the husband manages it are rare. Finally, there is a small number of marriages where the husband both controls and manages the money; Wilson described male control of expenditure as a deviant pattern which has serious consequences for women and children. The evidence suggests that when a husband both controls and manages the money there is likely to be extreme inequality between husband and wife and deprivation on the part of the wife and children. (ibid: 91)

Pahl suggested that the way in which couples choose to allocate income and responsibility depends upon a number of factors, including assumptions about gender roles and the 'natural' marriage and family; psychological characteristics attributed to the partners such as interest and skills in money management; expenditure patterns including which partner is responsible for spending on particular items; practicalities such as who has easiest access to banks and supermarkets and the working hours of the partners; socio-economic variables such as household income level and the wife's proportionate contribution to the total income; and cultural variables such as generation and geographical region of residence (ibid: 122). Further, while the couples themselves tended to give explanations for their particular arrangements in terms of psychological characteristics or practicalities, Pahl's analysis of the results showed that 'the socio-economic circumstances of peoples' lives, and the beliefs which shaped their views of the world, often had greater explanatory power' (ibid: 120):

> Household income is an important variable [in explaining patterns of management and control] when income is low: when money is short, so that managing it is a demanding chore rather than a source of power or pleasure, then typically women manage and control finances. At higher incomes the source of that income becomes important. If only the husband is in employment he tends to control the money, and to delegate management of a part of it to his wife ... [Ideology] can be used as a justification: wives are seen as better at management when money is short, while husbands are defined as financially knowledgeable when there is more money and when the wife's work is unpaid ... .
>
> ... For some the psychological characteristics appear to dominate: money is controlled by the person with the greatest financial skills. However, being defined as having financial skills can itself be the product of ideological assumptions about the nature of femininity or masculinity. For other couples practicalities appear to dominate, with bills being paid by whoever can get to the bank, or by the partner whose earnings go monthly into the bank rather than by the one who is paid weekly in cash. However, working hours and forms of payment themselves reflect economic forces and social status. (ibid: 121)

Pahl also looked at patterns of spending and her conclusions follow:

> Where wives control finances a higher proportion of household income is likely to be spent on food and day-to-day living expenses than is the case where husbands control finances; additional income brought into the household by the wife is more likely to be spent on food than additional money earned by the husband. Additional support for these hypotheses comes from the finding that husbands are more likely to spend more on leisure than wives. (ibid: 151–52)

More recent research has confirmed Pahl's findings. Mothers tend to exhibit stronger preferences than fathers for putting the children's financial needs before their own individual needs for leisure (Walker et al 1994; Lister et al 1999), and women tend generally, compared with men (perhaps because men tend to have more time on their hands?), to minimise their own needs for leisure or personal spending; luxuries such as these tend to be viewed by men as 'needs' and by women as 'wants' (Walker et al 1994; Burgoyne 2004). Finally, women tend to prioritise spending to benefit children (Ringen and Halpin 1997; Lister et al 1999)

In some ways, of course, this ideology has shifted over the years. Much of the recent sociological literature demonstrates, for example, that most heterosexual couples would describe their relationship as a partnership of equals. Pahl's more recent research (Pahl 2005) found that patterns of money management in the UK and elsewhere reflect this equality and also individualisation in relationships; there has been a shift over the years from 'pooling' to a more independent forms of financial management. In the light of this individualisation, Pahl was interested to examine how much money these individuals retained under their own control and what they were expected to pay for out of that money. She reported that despite their independent management of money, women were overwhelmingly responsible for paying for women's clothes (90% of all household spending on this item), children's clothes (85%), food (80%) and childcare/school expenses (78%), while men paid 73% of all household spending on alcohol, 69% on motor vehicles, 66% each on repairs to the house and meals out, and 65% on gambling (Pahl 2005: 388). She concludes:

> When household finances are managed independently, both partners may enjoy a sense of autonomy and personal freedom, so long as their incomes are broadly equivalent. However, if the woman's income drops, for example when children are born, while at the same time her outgoings increase, because she is expected to pay the costs of children, the situation may change, … despite all the aspirations towards equality in relationships, gender inequalities in earnings and gender differences in spending priorities may mean that in certain circumstances individualisation in couple finances is a route to inequality. (ibid: 389)

It seems that the individuals in contemporary relationships, like those in the relationships of their parents' generation, must find ways to resolve what Vogler calls 'the tensions at the heart of all intimate relationships between, on the one hand, individual autonomy versus commitment to the welfare of the couple as a collective unit, and on the other, equality versus inequalities in power and living standards between individuals within the same relationship' (Vogler 2009: 60).

Q Burgoyne (2004) observed that in marriages where the woman is the main breadwinner, women were more likely to 'relinquish the power that usually comes to men with this role', possibly in an attempt to 'minimise the potential discomfort that the men might feel in occupying a non-normative, dependent position' (168). What role can or should law play in challenging assumptions about men and women's social identities as workers and breadwinners? Review the maternity and paternity leave provisions described in Chapter 5.

Q Pahl (1989) suggested that her results should be seen as having important implications 'for all who are concerned about the living standards of children, about the employment of women and about tax and employment policies which affect families' (152). If you were a policymaker, what would you think are these implications, and how would they influence your recommendations for policy on child poverty and employment law? See also Cantillon and Nolan (1998).

Pahl (1989) studied only married partners, and she questioned whether her results would be consistent for cohabiting partners including same-sex partners, and whether there might be any ethnic variations in her results. Since her groundbreaking work, some of her questions are being answered. Vogler et al (2008) and Vogler (2009) report that the formality of marriage is not determinative in money management systems. The differences between married and cohabiting heterosexual couples becomes significant only for young, childless and older, post-marital cohabiting couples. Cohabiting parents, in other words, tend to organise their finances similarly to married parents. Douglas et al (2009a, 2009b) also found that patterns of money management among heterosexual cohabitants were not correlated with other features of their relationships; they tended to keep their finances separate, but the day-to-day organisation of finances was determined by a number of different variables. Further, Burns et al (2008) found that the values of fairness, equality and independence were utilised by lesbian and gay respondents in their money management systems but that where income levels differed, a higher status was nonetheless often afforded to the higher earner:

> In the presence of a strong *norm* of equality based upon 50/50 contributions (and despite a *practice* of proportionate payments), disparate incomes (re)produce inequalities with regard to control, entitlement, decision-making and autonomy in both the individual management and partial pooling systems. (Burns et al 2008: 499)

The power and influence of the higher earner was not, however, the same as that in traditional heterosexual relationships. Partners who earned less money did not, for example, tend to do more housework as lower-earning women in heterosexual relationships often do (ibid).

III. ACQUIRING PROPERTY

A family's wealth can be measured not only by its income, but also by the value of any real or personal property its members own or control. For most of the history of family law in Britain, however, the regulation of family property was of concern to only a small proportion of the population; the majority did not own any land or other significant assets. Indeed, the histories of both 'traditional' family law and the common law are in many ways the history of the law of property as it was developed by and for the landed and industrialist classes. The ownership of property, particularly of home ownership, has to some degree been democratised in recent years, but it still remains largely a middle-class concern.

Within households, decisions about property, like those about money, tend to remain a matter for private arrangement (Morris and Nott 1995); the law has very little to say about how family members use and allocate their property except in the event of bankruptcy or if the family unit breaks up as a result of separation or death. At that point, the property that family members have accumulated can be redistributed and, in cases of divorce or dissolution of civil partnership, the court has a very broad discretion with respect to redistribution of property among family members. In the absence of such events, there is little scope for the law to intervene. Nevertheless, property ownership may still be significant in the way it affects families, primarily, as we have seen above, in that it may influence dynamics such as power and authority in the family. We will discuss financial and property adjustment on separation, divorce and civil partnership dissolution in Chapter 7, and will focus now on how wealth in the form of property is accumulated and distributed within households.

Current rules about family property stem from the nineteenth-century Married Women's Property Acts which applied the notion of individual and separate ownership of property to husband and wife in the same way as it applied between legal strangers. As we noted earlier, this was a radical development at the time, introducing the idea of formal equality which remains the basis of the law of family property today. Separate ownership and formal equality mean that whoever purchases and has legal title to an item of property has all the rights of ownership in it, including the right to keep, mortgage or dispose of it, and the right to realise its value on disposition. These property rights apply, in theory, to any item of property, even to those assets which appear to be 'family property' such as the family car or the family home, although there are some special rules which govern the family home. The strict common law rules of ownership were first tempered only by the gradual development of rules of equity which provide that a beneficial interest in property, as distinct from a legal interest, may be acquired by someone who does not have legal title to it.

We will address the general law of property as it applies to family members, but will not focus upon the intricacies of the common law tenures in land, the legislation such as the Land Registration Act 2002, or the general rules of equity.[38] Our focus instead will be upon the theme of separate ownership of family property and the principle of formal equality that underlies it.

Separate Property

At common law, the owner of property has discretion over how to deal with it, whether the owner lives together with another person in a family relationship or not. This has always been the case for cohabitants, but only in the nineteenth century did it become so for married individuals. The early history of the law of property as between husbands and wives begins with the common law doctrine of coverture in terms of which the wife's legal personality was subsumed under that of her husband. In exchange, the husband was under an obligation to support his wife for life. Finer and McGregor (1974) describe the law in the nineteenth and early twentieth centuries in these terms:

> [T]he common law virtually stripped a woman, on marriage, both of her existing property and of her capacity to acquire property for herself in the future. All of the wife's personal chattels, including money, which she owned at the date of marriage, or which she acquired thereafter, whether by her own efforts or not, became the husband's absolute property. Any debt owed to

---

[38] For clear and often insightful expositions of the law in respect of the family home, see Lowe and Douglas (2007); see also The Law Commission discussion paper (Law Commission 2002), which provides an excellent overview of the law.

the wife became the husband's if he chose to collect it. The husband took the income of the wife's leaseholds; he could sell them in her lifetime and take the proceeds for himself; and they became his property absolutely if his wife predeceased him. The husband was entitled to the sole management of his wife's freeholds, and took a life estate in the whole of them as soon as there was any issue of the marriage born alive. ...

The origins of this regime owed less to biblical metaphor than they did to the practical demands of the feudal overlord. But it was part of the stock-in-trade of the seventeenth century common lawyers to justify it by reference to the Book of Genesis ... .

Theologically sound or not, a doctrine which to so large an extent delivered up a woman's property to her husband was not acceptable to the propertied classes ... .Hence, from the latter part of the sixteenth century onwards, the lawyers busied themselves on behalf of their clients in inventing and refining devices to protect a woman's property from the ravages to which her marriage exposed it. The devices grew up within equity—the system of law developed by the Chancellor to ease the rigidities of the common law—and were recognised and enforced by the court of Chancery ... .

Dicey described these developments by saying 'There came, therefore, to be not in theory but in fact, one law for the rich and another for the poor. The daughters of the rich enjoyed, for the most part, the considerate protection of equity, the daughters of the poor suffered under the severity and injustice of the common law'. This was certainly true; but it is to be remarked that equity served a socio-economic purpose more fundamental than guaranteeing the comforts of rich men's daughters. The essence of the arrangements which equity upheld was the preservation of wealth within the kinship group which had provided it.

(Finer and McGregor 1974: 96–97, references omitted)

Thus there was in the nineteenth century quite a sophisticated system of equity for the property of the rich, the common law of coverture for the wages and small businesses of middle classes, and the Poor Law for the labouring or unemployed poor. A clear discrimination between rich and poor was maintained in the law, which was just as clear as the legal discrimination between men and women. Political writers and intellectuals of the time captured the intellectual movement toward equality and liberalism and, at the same time, women lobbied Parliament to change the law (Holcombe 1983). Eventually a series of reforming statutes was enacted. As Finer and McGregor note, however, these did not 'assimilate the property rights of married and single women', but extended 'to all married women the limited advantages of the "separate property" regime which legal ingenuity and private enterprise had until then conferred on the few' (Finer and McGregor 1974: 110). The Law Reform (Married Women and Tortfeasors) Act 1935 finally enabled a married woman to acquire, hold and dispose of any property 'in every respect as though she were single'.

These reforms were consistent with the politics of liberalism, individualism and formal equality in the nineteenth and early twentieth centuries which brought about other political 'revolutions' such as the abolition of the slave trade and the enfranchisement of women and the non-property-holding majority.[39] They meant that men and women, in marriage as in other spheres of life, were to be treated equally in terms of property acquisition and allocation. Whoever acquired the property owned it. This separation of property and formal equality between men and women continues as the foundation of property law within families today.[40]

---

[39] See, eg, 2nd and 3rd Reform Acts 1867 and 1884 and the Representation of the People Act 1918 extending the franchise to women over 30 and all men.

[40] For a detailed and typically excellent review of the legal history in this field, see Cretney (2003a: ch 3).

Q What does formal equality mean for the allocation of wealth between men and women in society generally as well as in families? Do men and women have equal access to the wealth needed to acquire property? A quotation from Sir Jocelyn Simon in 1964 is insightful:

But men can only earn their incomes and accumulate capital by virtue of the division of labour between themselves and their wives. The wife spends her youth and early middle age in bearing and rearing children and in tending the home; the husband is thus freed for his economic activities. Unless the wife plays her part the husband cannot play his. The cock bird can feather his nest precisely because he is not required to spend most of his time sitting on it. (Simon 1964)

In your view, are his remarks still relevant today? Construct an argument that there is symbolic value in the law espousing formal equality between men and women in families. Construct an argument that a legal strategy of formal equality serves simply to mask real inequalities and so to perpetuate them.

Today, proprietary rights in property can be gained pursuant to acquisition of legal ownership, whether sole or joint, or to acquisition of a beneficial interest in property. The law governing the acquisition of legal title to property is formally gender neutral and impervious to marital status. Ownership in land is evidenced by registration pursuant to the Land Registration Act 2002—whose name is on the title?—or for the decreasing instances of unregistered land, by the Law of Property Act 1925. Yet, while it operates on the basis of the principles of formal equality, in the context of the system of separate property, the law may, in effect, prejudice the non-earning partner, usually the woman. As we have seen, women are usually the primary caretakers of children, and they often give up work to take on this role. When they do earn, their earnings are on average less than those of men. Loss of income and the purchasing power that comes with that income means that women tend to have less money and so less opportunity to acquire property in their own names. In order to ameliorate the plight of women in this position, courts have, in the past, invoked the equitable principles governing the acquisition of beneficial ownership. In this way, courts sought to recognise the contributions women made to families.

Beneficial Ownership: Express Trust

A beneficial interest in property arises where the legal owner is said to hold the property on trust for someone else. It can be created by an express declaration of trust, which must be in writing.[41] Putting the family home (or any other property) in joint names may not be enough even though it will lead to a presumption that the owners intend to share the equitable interest in the property.[42] If the property is unregistered land, the purchasers are advised to state clearly their intention regarding equitable ownership.

---

[41] Law of Property Act 1925 s 53(1)(b)
[42] *Stack v Dowden* [2007] UKHL 17; [2007] 1 FLR 1858.

Implied Trusts

Where there is no written declaration of trust the law can sometimes imply one. Where a person who is not the legal owner of property has made contributions to its acquisition that the law regards as sufficient, the law will imply that he or she has acquired an interest in the property. The effect is that the legal owner holds the property in trust for both himself or herself and the non-owning party. This means that the legal owner would have to consult the beneficial owner before selling or mortgaging the property and, if it is sold, that the latter obtains an interest in the proceeds of sale. While these rules of equity apply to all owners of property, the courts have recognised that 'familial' relationships may be amenable to special treatment. Equity in this way ameliorates some of the hardship of the formal equality of the common law, but its discretionary nature means that decisions about the type of contribution sufficient to create the beneficial interest may vary with 'the length of the Chancellor's foot'.

Resulting Trust[43]

The first type of implied trust is the resulting trust. A person who is not the legal owner of property can establish a resulting trust where she makes a direct financial contribution to the purchase price of the property. Her beneficial ownership then is said to result from the contribution. In *Tinsley v Milligan*[44] the parties together purchased a bed-and-breakfast establishment. Although Milligan contributed money to the purchase of the house, title to it was registered in Tinsley's sole name. When their relationship broke down, Milligan was able to establish to the satisfaction of the majority of the House of Lords that she had a proprietary interest in the property by virtue of the trust resulting from her financial contribution to its purchase.

Until recently, there was some uncertainty about the proportion of the interest the contribution created. On the one hand there was a series of cases such as *Springette v Defoe*[45] in which the actual amount, or proportion of the contribution to the price of the property, determined the proportion of the beneficial share. On the other hand, there were cases such as *Stokes v Anderson*[46] and *McHardy*[47] in which the court found that the contribution was not intended to quantify the interest, but rather was evidence of a common intention to share the property, the interests then being determined according to the parties' intentions as could be inferred from all the circumstances and principles of fairness. In 1995 Lord Justice Waite in the Court of Appeal decision of *Midland Bank v Cooke*[48] said:

> I confess that I find the differences of approach in these two cases[49] mystifying. In the one a strict resulting trust geared to mathematical calculation of the proportion of the purchase price provided by cash contribution is treated as virtually immutable in the absence of express agree-

---

[43] See also Law Commission (2002) for a comprehensive review of the law.
[44] [1994] AC 340.
[45] [1992] 2 FLR 388.
[46] [1991] 1 FLR 391.
[47] *McHardy and Sons v Warren* [1994] 2 FLR 338.
[48] [1995] 2 FLR 915.
[49] Referring to *Springette* and *McHardy*.

ment; in the other a displacement of the cash-related trust by inferred agreement is not only permitted but treated as obligatory. (942)

Where there was no evidence of the parties' intentions as to the amount of the beneficial share, or even where the parties themselves said they had no agreement, the court held that equity still had a role in inferring one. Waite LJ said:

> When people, especially young people, agree to share their lives in joint homes, they do so on a basis of mutual trust and in the expectation that their relationship will endure. … For a couple embarking on a serious relationship, discussion of the terms to apply at parting is almost a contradiction of the shared hopes that have brought them together. There will inevitably be numerous couples, married or unmarried, who have no discussion about ownership, and who perhaps advisedly make no agreement about it. It would be anomalous, against that background, to create a range of home-buyers who were beyond the pale of equity's assistance in formulating a fair presumed basis for the sharing of beneficial title, simply because they had been honest enough to admit they never gave ownership a thought or reached any agreement about it. (927)

On this basis, the court found that the whole course of dealing between the parties, including what took place during the time they cohabited in it, was evidence of what they intended at the time of acquisition of the property.

Midland Bank v Cooke, and indeed the bulk of the case law on beneficial ownership, has since been considered by the House of Lords.[50] As we shall see, their more recent formulation of the issues, while confirming the 'whole course of dealing' approach, seems to suggest that the resulting trust has fallen out of favour, with preference to be given to the common intention constructive trust.

Common Intention Constructive Trust

A party seeking to establish a constructive trust of this nature must show that the parties had a common intention that she would have a share in the property, that she reasonably relied upon (acted upon) that common intention and that her reliance caused her some detriment. In the context of the family home, where she has moved into her partner's property, or where the family property is registered in one name alone, each of these requirements can present difficulties for the applicant. First, establishing the common intention itself may be difficult because the realities of life are such that very few couples discuss the nature of the ownership of their home, meaning that the claimant must convince the court to infer the common intention from other evidence. As we shall see below, the courts have stated that direct contribution to the purchase price or mortgage, and little else, will do to establish that intention. If this is true, then it may be difficult for a woman in a 'traditional' relationship to make the kind of contributions that the law regards as relevant to evidencing a common intention to share the ownership, as opposed merely to the occupation or use of property. Courts have, to a large degree, relied upon gender stereotypes in making their decisions and failed to take account of the disadvantages created for those who conform to traditional gender roles. In effect, courts often refuse to recognise as a relevant contribution anything that a 'normal' husband or wife would do

---

[50] *Stack v Dowden* [2007] UKHL 17; [2007] 1 FLR 1858.

in relation to property. This means that 'normal' wives who contribute to the running of the household by means of labour and childcare may find these contributions discounted.

And even if she is successful in establishing the first part of the test, the claimant must then satisfy the court of her detrimental reliance on that understanding of intent. Again, evidence said by courts to establish detrimental reliance must be conduct that that would not reasonably have been undertaken in the absence of an expectation of an interest in the house. At this stage as well, the homemaker may be at a disadvantage.

Two steps are necessary, therefore to establish a constructive trust in property. Let us examine each of them in turn.

Common Intention

First, a common intention to share must be proved. According to the leading case of *Lloyds Bank plc v Rosset*:[51]

> The first and fundamental question which must always be resolved is whether, independently of any inference to be drawn from the conduct of the parties in the course of sharing the house as their home and managing their joint affairs, there has at any time prior to acquisition, or exceptionally at some later date, been any agreement, arrangement or understanding reached between them that the property is to be shared beneficially. The finding of an agreement or an arrangement to share in this sense can only, I think, be based on evidence of express discussions between the parties, however imperfectly remembered and however imprecise the terms may have been. Once a finding to this effect is made it will only be necessary for the partner asserting the beneficial interest against the partner entitled to the legal estate to show that he or she has acted to his or her detriment or significantly altered his or her position in reliance on the agreement in order to give rise to a constructive trust or proprietary estoppel. ...
>
> In sharp contrast with this situation is the very different one where there is no evidence to support a finding of an agreement or an arrangement to share, however reasonable it might have been for the parties to reach such an agreement if they had applied their minds to the question, and where the court must rely entirely on the conduct of the parties both as the basis from which to infer a common intention to share the property beneficially and as the conduct relied on to give rise to a constructive trust. In this situation, direct contributions to the purchase price by the partner who is not the legal owner, whether initially or by payment of mortgage instalments, will readily justify the inference necessary to the creation of a constructive trust. But as I read the authorities, it is at least extremely doubtful whether anything less will do. (132–33)

It is clear, then, that common intention can be established most easily if there is an express agreement between the parties, whether oral or in writing. On occasion, the courts have interpreted a statement by the party as evidencing such an agreement in spite of the fact that, on the face of it, it appears to mean the exact opposite. In *Grant v Edwards*,[52] for example, the owner told his cohabitant that he would have put the house in their joint names, except that to do so would have jeopardised the divorce settlement with her previous spouse. Similarly, in *Eves v Eves*[53] the legal owner told his cohabitant that he would have put the house in their joint names, but that he could not because she was under 21 years old. In both of these cases the court found the necessary common intention in these statements. In *James v Thomas*,[54] however, Mr Thomas' comments to Ms James in the

---

[51] [1991] 1 AC 107; [1990] 1 All ER 1111. All page references are to the Appeal Cases.
[52] [1986] Ch 638; [1987] 1 FLR 87.
[53] [1975] 1 WLR 1338 (CA).
[54] [2007] EWCA Civ 1212.

course of their 15-year cohabitation that improvements they were making to the house would benefit them both were held by the court to imply benefit to their use and enjoyment of the house rather than their beneficial ownership of it (para 33). In general, the court will look to see whether, 'at any time prior to the acquisition of the disputed property, or exceptionally at some later date, [there have] been discussions between the parties, leading to any agreement, arrangement or understanding between them that the property is to be shared beneficially'.[55]

The situation is more difficult if there is no agreement. In this case, the court may be asked to infer a common intention from the conduct of the parties. Inferring a state of mind from conduct is always a tricky matter, and these cases are no exception. Direct financial contributions to acquisition or regular payments towards the mortgage will usually be straightforward evidence of a common intention, as Lord Bridge stated in *Rosset* above.[56]

What if, however, one party pays all the household expenses, thus freeing up the other to pay the mortgage instalments? According to Lord Bridge in *Rosset*, this indirect financial contribution to the purchase price of the home would not qualify as evidence of a common intention. Nevertheless, a decision of the High Court has provided some indication that the courts may be more willing to adopt this analysis than in the past. In *Le Foe v Le Foe and Woolwich plc*[57] it held that indirect financial contributions to the mortgage will be sufficient to evidence the requisite common intention. In this case, the wife's contribution to the home was to pay for day-to-day domestic expenditure, thus freeing up the husband's income to pay the mortgage, service charge and outgoings. It was, as the court found, an 'arbitrary allocation of responsibility' (para 10). The court accordingly took the view that, although the wife had made no cash contribution to the mortgage, she had made indirect contributions to the mortgage, sufficient for it to infer the common intention that the wife would have a beneficial interest in the home.

It is in privileging financial contributions that the courts have tended to disadvantage women: recall the research discussed above on who pays for what in heterosexual relationships and the research on who does what work in them. In *Gissing v Gissing*,[58] although the wife, during the course of a 26-year marriage, paid for furnishings, for laying a lawn and for her own and the children's clothes, these expenditures were not found to evidence a common intention that she should acquire a beneficial interest in the matrimonial home. In *Burns v Burns*[59] the parties cohabited for 19 years. The woman cared for their children full time in the couple's early years together, and her financial contributions began some time after the property was acquired. She contributed to housekeeping, purchased clothes, furniture, a dishwasher and redecorated the interior of the home, while carrying out domestic work in the home. Once again, these contributions were found insufficient to prove a common intention that she should acquire a proprietary interest in the home.

In *Burns*, as in *Gissing* before it, the female partners also performed traditional 'wifely' labour which did not satisfy the court of the parties' intention to share ownership of their homes.[60] Indeed, in *Burns* the court said:

---

[55] *H v M (Property: Beneficial interest)* [1992] 1 FLR 229, 231.
[56] See also *Lightfoot v Lightfoot-Brown* [2005] EWCA Civ 201.
[57] [2001] 2 FLR 970.
[58] [1971] AC 886; [1970] 3 WLR 255; [1970] 2 All ER 780.
[59] [1984] Ch 317; [1984] FLR 216.
[60] For a while it seemed that labour of an unusual kind might suffice to establish to the satisfaction of the courts the elusive common intention. In *Cooke v Head* [1972] 1 ELR 518; [1972] 2 All ER 38 the woman demolished a shed and did some building work on the property. This, according to the court, was 'much more

If the woman makes no 'real' or 'substantial' financial contributions towards either the purchase price, deposit or mortgage instalments by the means of which the family home was acquired, then she is not entitled to any share in the beneficial interest in that home even though over a very substantial number of years she may have worked just as hard as the man in maintaining the family in the sense of keeping the house, giving birth to and looking after and helping to bring up the children of the union. (FLR 242)

Q Comment here on the court's use of the words 'real' and 'substantial.'

And in Rosset itself:

Up to 17 December 1982 [Mrs Rosset's] contribution to the venture was: (1) to urge on the builders and to attempt to coordinate their work ... . (2) to go to the builders' merchants and obtain material required by the builders ... and to deliver the materials to the site ... . (3) to assist her husband in planning the renovation and decoration of the house. In this, she had some skill over and above that acquired by most housewives. She was a skilled painter and decorator who enjoyed wallpapering and decorating, and, as her husband acknowledged, she had good ideas about this work. In connection with this, she advised on the position of electric plugs and radiators and planned the design of the large breakfast room and the small kitchen of the house; (4) to carry out the wall papering of Natasha's bedroom and her own bedroom, after preparing the surfaces of the walls and clearing up the rooms concerned before the papering began; (5) to begin the preparation of the surfaces of the walls of her son's bedroom, the den, the upstairs lavatory and the downstairs washroom for papering ... . (6) to assist in arranging the insurance of the house ... . (7) to assist in arranging a crime prevention survey ... . (8) to assist in arranging the installation of burglar alarms. (per Lord Bridge, 129–30; quoting from Judge Scarlett at trial)

In this case, the wife was attempting to establish a proprietary interest in the property (held in her husband's name alone, and paid for by him alone from trust funds and a bank overdraft) in order to protect her share from the bank which had brought an application for an order of possession. Mr Rosset, had, without his wife's knowledge, executed a charge in favour of the bank in order to obtain an overdraft, on which he subsequently defaulted before the couple separated. Mrs Rosset and her two children, aged 1 and 6, were staying in the house when the bank's application came before the court.

Lord Bridge of Harwich, writing for a unanimous court, gave the judgment. First, he stated the issue before the court.

The question the judge had to determine was whether he could find that before the contract to acquire the property was concluded they had entered into an agreement, made an arrangement, reached an understanding or formed a common intention that the beneficial interest in the property would be jointly owned. I do not think it is of importance which of these alternative expressions one uses. Spouses living in amity will not normally think it necessary to formulate or define their respective interests in property in any precise way. The expectation of parties to every happy marriage is that they will share the practical benefits of occupying the matrimonial home whoever owns it. But this is something quite distinct from sharing the beneficial interest in the property asset which the matrimonial home represents. (127–28)

---

than most women would do' and it helped to gain her a one-third interest in the family home. In *Eves v Eves* (above), Lord Denning, but no other members of the Court of Appeal, thought that the fact that she helped with painting and heavy construction-type work, including breaking up concrete and demolishing a shed, evidenced the requisite common intention (1340).

Q Would parties to a 'happy marriage' ever form a common intention to share beneficial ownership of property as distinct from sharing 'practical benefits' of occupancy? Do you agree that expectations of sharing the practical benefits of occupancy are distinct from expectations of sharing beneficial interest in the property?

He then went on, first quoting the findings of Judge Scarlett:

I am satisfied that in 1982 the common intention expressed by [Mr and Mrs Rosset] in conversation between themselves was that Vincent farmhouse should be purchased in the name of [Mr Rosset] alone, because funds would not be available from [his] family trust in Switzerland unless the purchase was made only in his name. In addition, however, it was their common intention that the renovation of the house should be a joint venture, after which the house was to become a family home to be shared by [the parties] and their children.

I pause to observe that neither a common intention by the spouses that a house is to be renovated as a 'joint venture' nor a common intention that the house is to be shared by parents and children as the family home throws any light on their intentions with respect to the beneficial ownership of the property. (130)

His Lordship went on to determine ownership in the home:

It is clear from these passages in the judgment that the judge based his inference of a common intention that Mrs Rosset should have a beneficial interest in the property under a constructive trust essentially on what Mrs Rosset did in and about assisting in the renovation of the property between the beginning of November 1982 and the date of completion on 17 December 1982. Yet by itself this activity, it seems to me, could not possibly justify any such inference. It was common ground that Mrs Rosset was extremely anxious that the new matrimonial home should be ready for occupation before Christmas if possible. In these circumstances, it would seem the most natural thing in the world for any wife, in the absence of her husband abroad, to spend all the time she could spare and to employ any skills she might have, such as the ability to decorate a room, in doing all she could to accelerate progress of the work quite irrespective of any expectation she might have of enjoying a beneficial interest in the property. The judge's view that some of this work was work 'on which she could not reasonably have been expected to embark unless she was to have an interest in the house' seems to me, with respect, quite untenable. (131)

Q What conduct by Mrs Rosset might have sufficed as evidence of a common intention that she should have an interest in the house? Would it be the most 'natural thing in the world' for Mrs Rosset to have hammered nails or knocked down or put up walls?

Q On this analysis, in the absence of an agreement or understanding, can a partner with no income and no savings ever claim a beneficial interest in the property? What are the implications for men and for women of this analysis? If a partner has an income, would you advise her to pay for food and household bills, or to pay the mortgage? But could it not be said to be the 'most natural thing in the world' for a partner to contribute to the mortgage payments if she is in employment?

> **Q** What do these cases tell you about the courts' assumptions about the marriage relationship? In your view, do husbands and wives who conform to traditional gender roles 'intend' common ownership of their home?

Dicta from a recent decision of the House of Lords has suggested that the *Rosset* test for inferring common intention may be changing. *Stack v Dowden*[61] was a case under the Law of Property Act 1925 in which legal title was held in joint names, but there was no declaration as to the interests held by each. As we have seen, however, putting the home in joint names creates a presumption that beneficial ownership is to be held jointly in equal shares. Ms Dowden provided the deposit on the home and the mortgage was joint. Over the course of their 20-year cohabitation she was the higher earner and her contribution to the property was greater. When the parties separated she sought to rebut the presumption of equal shares and claimed a larger share of the interest in the property. The House of Lords found that the onus was on her—the party seeking to rebut the presumption—and that it was a difficult task to do so, but Baroness Hale found that, in the context and circumstances of this case, Ms Dowden was successful. Because Ms Dowden had contributed more to the purchase price, the parties had kept their money in separate accounts and had divided the household accounts rigidly, Baroness Hale for the majority found that their relationship was not a 'partnership' in which joint ownership was intended.[62]

> **Q** In the light of the recent research discussed above indicating that independent forms of money management are increasingly common among couples (and see Douglas et al 2009), was Stack and Dowden's arrangement that 'unusual'?

While this case was said to be 'very unusual' (per Baroness Hale, para 92) and was concerned with joint names, the court was still looking for the 'common intention' that it looks for in sole-names cases such as *Rosset*. On this point, Baroness Hale suggested that Lord Bridge may have set the hurdle 'rather too high' (para 63) for establishing common intention, and Lord Walker wondered whether, even if Lord Bridge was right in 1990, the 'law had moved on':

> Lord Bridge's extreme doubt 'whether anything less will do' was certainly consistent with many first-instance and Court of Appeal decisions, but I respectfully doubt whether it took full account of the views (conflicting though they were) expressed in *Gissing v Gissing* (see especially Lord Reid [1971] AC 886 at pp 896G–897B and Lord Diplock at p 909D–H). It has attracted some trenchant criticism from scholars as potentially productive of injustice (see Gray & Gray, Elements of Land Law, 4th ed [(2005)], paras 10.132 to 10.137, the last paragraph being headed 'A More Optimistic Future'). Whether or not Lord Bridge's observation was justified in 1990, in my opinion the law has moved on, and your Lordships should move it a little more in the same direction. (para 26)

Baroness Hale in the Privy Council confirmed this view again in *Abbott v Abbott*:[63]

> The Court of Appeal appears to have attached undue significance to the dictum of Lord Bridge

---

[61] [2007] UKHL 17; [2007] 1 FLR 1858.
[62] See, however, *Fowler v Barron* [2008] EWCA Civ 377; [2008] 2 FLR 831. For a detailed discussion of these cases and their implications, see Harris-Short and Miles (2011).
[63] [2007] UKPC 53; [2008] 1 FLR 1451.

in *Lloyd's Bank plc v Rosset*, in particular as to what conduct is to be taken into account in quantifying an acknowledged beneficial interest. The law has indeed moved on since then. The parties' whole course of conduct in relation to the property must be taken into account in determining their shared intentions as to its ownership. (para 19)

The difficulty is how these words can be interpreted. What does the phrase 'whole course of conduct' mean? There is evidence that despite its potential erosion of the strict *Rosset* test, early Court of Appeal cases since *Stack v Dowden* have taken a restrictive approach to it.[64] It is to be hoped that this question will be resolved soon. In 2011 the Supreme Court heard the case of *Jones v Kernott*,[65] another case like *Stack* in which a separating cohabitant sought to claim more than 50% of the interest in the family home. The decision is pending at the time of writing. The Supreme Court will consider whether a court can properly infer an agreement by an unmarried couple, who hold a property in equal shares at the date of their separation, to the effect that thereafter their respective beneficial interests should alter. Because this is a joint-names case, however, any comments the Supreme Court makes regarding common intention will be only obiter dicta in regard to sole-names cases such as *Rosset*. The height of the 'hurdle' it set may yet remain the same.

Reliance and Detriment

In addition to a common intention, evidenced either by an express agreement or by conduct, the court must also find that the person seeking to establish the existence of a trust relied upon that intention to her detriment. If the common intention is evidenced by the payment of money, that conduct, ie the payment, acts also as sufficient evidence of the requisite detrimental reliance. If the common intention is evidenced by an agreement, arrangement or understanding, such as in *Grant v Edwards* or *Eves v Eves*, the claimant must have done something else; something she would not have been likely to do unless she believed she had an interest, and the act of reliance must have resulted in detriment to her. The court in *Eves v Eves*, for example, said that the woman would not have wielded a sledgehammer had she not believed she would get an interest in the property, and in *Chan Pui Chun v Leung Kam Ho*[66] the court found that by devoting herself to Mr Leung's business affairs, and by giving up her own home and moving in with him, all in reliance on his (fraudulent) promise of marriage and a 'dream house', Miss Chan had acted to her detriment and was entitled to a beneficial interest in the property in question.

In *Midland Bank v Dobson*,[67] on the other hand, the court found a common intention, but held that there was no detriment because the wife had not done anything more than the usual domestic duties which were unrelated to the intention that ownership of the house be shared. Similarly, in *Thomas v Fuller-Brown*[68] a man who carried out various pieces of DIY around his partner's home into which he had moved was found not to have acquired a beneficial interest in the property. His actions were found to be the kinds of things a man would have been expected to have done in his home, and not the kinds of things a man would only do if he believed he had an interest in the property. In *James*

---

[64] See *James v Thomas* [2007] EWCA Civ 1212, [2008] 1 FLR 1598; *Morris v Morris* [2008] EWCA Civ 257 and discussion in Harris-Short and Miles (2011: 141–43).

[65] On appeal from [2010] EWCA Civ 578; [2010] 2 FLR 1631. Now see *Jones v Kernott* [2011] UKSC 53 and postscript below p 272.

[66] [2002] EWCA Civ 1075; [2003] 1 FLR 23.

[67] [1986] 1 FLR 171.

[68] [1988] 1 FLR 237.

v Thomas, where the woman's work in the joint business and on improvements to the property was not conduct sufficient to evidence a common intention of her beneficial ownership in the family home, the court commented, 'for completeness', on whether, if they had, they would have been sufficient to meet the detrimental reliance test:

> The true position, as it seems to me, is that she worked in the business, and contributed her labour to the improvements to the property, because she and Mr Thomas were making their life together as man and wife. The Cottage was their home: the business was their livelihood. It is a mistake to think that the motives which lead parties in such a relationship to act as they do are necessarily attributable to pecuniary self-interest.

Q Gender stereotyping can affect whether a party is able to establish detrimental reliance as well as common intention. Harris-Short and Miles comment that a wider range of conduct may be admissible as detrimental reliance in express intention cases than in inferred intention cases (Harris-Short and Miles 2011: 143). Why do you think this might be? See, on gender and constructive trusts, Lawson (1996). How, if at all, would you reform the requirement for detrimental reliance?

Quantifying the Beneficial Interest

The shares to which the parties are entitled once the court finds a constructive trust exists are also determined by the parties' intentions. While it is likely that the Supreme Court in *Jones v Kernott* will address this question, the law at the time of writing is found in *Stack v Dowden*. Baroness Hale said:

> 65 … The approach to quantification in cases where the home is conveyed into joint names should certainly be no stricter than the approach to quantification in cases where it has been conveyed into the name of one only. To the extent that *Walker v Hall*, *Springette v Defoe* and *Huntingford v Hobbs* hold otherwise, they should not be followed.

> 66 … But the questions in a joint names case are not simply 'what is the extent of the parties' beneficial interests?' but 'did the parties intend their beneficial interests to be different from their legal interests?' and 'if they did, in what way and to what extent?' There are differences between sole and joint names cases when trying to divine the common intentions or understanding between the parties. I know of no case in which a sole legal owner (there being no declaration of trust) has been held to hold the property on a beneficial joint tenancy. But a court may well hold that joint legal owners (there being no declaration of trust) are also beneficial joint tenants. Another difference is that it will almost always have been a conscious decision to put the house into joint names. Even if the parties have not executed the transfer, they will usually, if not invariably, have executed the contract which precedes it. Committing oneself to spend large sums of money on a place to live is not normally done by accident or without giving it a moment's thought.

> …

> 69. In law, 'context is everything' and the domestic context is very different from the commercial world. Each case will turn on its own facts. Many more factors than financial contributions may be relevant to divining the parties' true intentions. These include: any advice or discussions at the time of the transfer which cast light upon their intentions then; the reasons why the home was acquired in their joint names; the reasons why (if it be the case) the survivor was authorised

to give a receipt for the capital moneys; the purpose for which the home was acquired; the nature of the parties' relationship; whether they had children for whom they both had responsibility to provide a home; how the purchase was financed, both initially and subsequently; how the parties arranged their finances, whether separately or together or a bit of both; how they discharged the outgoings on the property and their other household expenses. When a couple are joint owners of the home and jointly liable for the mortgage, the inferences to be drawn from who pays for what may be very different from the inferences to be drawn when only one is owner of the home. The arithmetical calculation of how much was paid by each is also likely to be less important. It will be easier to draw the inference that they intended that each should contribute as much to the household as they reasonably could and that they would share the eventual benefit or burden equally. The parties' individual characters and personalities may also be a factor in deciding where their true intentions lay. In the cohabitation context, mercenary considerations may be more to the fore than they would be in marriage, but it should not be assumed that they always take pride of place over natural love and affection. At the end of the day, having taken all this into account, cases in which the joint legal owners are to be taken to have intended that their beneficial interests should be different from their legal interests will be very unusual.

70. This is not, of course, an exhaustive list. There may also be reason to conclude that, whatever the parties' intentions at the outset, these have now changed. An example might be where one party has financed (or constructed himself) an extension or substantial improvement to the property, so that what they have now is significantly different from what they had then.

Baroness Hale here provides a non-exhaustive list of factors for the court to consider when it is searching for the parties' common intention. On the basis of the results of their research, however, Douglas et al question whether it is fair to hold a couple to arrangements which arose and may change from time to time in their relationship in response to economic, childcare or employment circumstances, 'as if they were by common intention' (Douglas et al 2009b: 159).

> **Q** Gardner (2008) suggests that the law now adopts a liberal 'holistic' approach to constructive trusts. Do you agree? Should it? And now see *Jones v Kernott* [2011] UKSC 53.

Constructive Trust or Proprietary Estoppel?

Proprietary estoppel is a claim made in equity that it would be unconscionable for B to act upon his or her rights in the face of his words or actions and A's reasonable detrimental reliance on those words or actions. The leading case is *Thorner v Majors*[69] in which Thorner believed, and, in the view of the court, this belief was reasonable, that his cousin would leave him his farm in his will. Thorner worked on the farm unpaid for almost 30 years. These facts met the law's formal requirement that A reasonably believe that he or she has or is going to get an interest in B's property and acts to his or her detriment on the basis of that belief. What B actually meant by his or her words or conduct is not as important as A's reasonable interpretation of what B said. The principle is that it is unconscionable for B to assert his or her proprietary rights in the face of A's belief and reliance. It is a purely equitable claim and the remedies available to the courts are both proprietary and financial. We can see that proprietary estoppel does not require

---

[69] [2009] UKHL 18; [2009] 2 FLR 405.

any common intention, express or implied, but in other respects it is similar to the common intention constructive trust.[70]

Summary

In property and trust law, then, the court uses gender-neutral principles which reflect the formal equality of the partners. What do these principles mean for men and for women and their ownership of matrimonial or household property? The courts are clear that common ownership is not to be inferred simply because the home was meant to be used as the family home. There is some question about whether or not the courts will *impute* an intention to the parties where one cannot be inferred from their conduct.[71] This issue is surely to be canvassed if not resolved in the forthcoming decision in *Jones v Kernott*. It is an important one, for it may go some way to relieving the restrictions currently on homemakers created by the test for inferring a common intention. As we have seen, that test requires a 'valuable' contribution to the home in order to raise equitable principles. However, for non-earning partners, usually women, as long as only money contributions are considered to be 'valuable' for this purpose, the public/private dichotomy is again invoked. Work done in the private sphere is not considered of value, whereas work done in the public, that which can earn wages, is.

Wong (2003) suggests that there may be a place for human rights law in these cases. She suggests that the Human Rights Act may have indirect horizontal effect such that courts will be required to interpret existing common law or equitable principles in the light of human rights values. This may mean, she argues, that the combination of Articles 8 and 14 ECHR results in the *Rosset*-type test being seen to be discriminatory. Indeed, human rights values such as non-discrimination have already been applied in family law cases to interpret the distribution of property on divorce (Diduck 2001b).[72]

Sawyer suggests another route out of the constructive trust's potential unfairness for women. In the light, she says, of the importance of the best interests of children, and the increasingly acceptable idea that it is right to take into account the care of children when considering property rights, an equitable interest could be founded on the shared parental obligation to bring up children. She goes on to say that 'quantification should start with the realistic notion of the costs of childcare, where the parental obligation to care is discharged by one parent on behalf of the other' (Sawyer 2004: 46–47).

Q How would a court found a constructive trust on the interests of children and parents' obligations to care for them? How would you construct an argument that the constructive trust complies with human rights principles? That it doesn't?

---

[70] On the rights and duties of mortgagees in regard to the family home, particularly in relation to undue influence, see *Barclays Bank v O'Brien* [1994] 1 FLR 1; and *Royal Bank of Scotland v Etridge (No 2)* [2001] UKHL 44; [2002] AC 773; see also Herring (2011: 175–85), Auchmuty (2003, 2010) and Diduck (2010).

[71] See Baroness Hale in *Stack v Dowden*, para 60. And see postscript, below p 272.

[72] See *White v White* [2001] AC 596; [2000] 2 FLR 976 and Chapter 7 below.

Alternatives—1. Unjust Enrichment and the Remedial Constructive Trust

As we have seen, in the same way that the law does not see housework as valuable in terms of wage earning or pension accumulation, it does not see it as valuable in terms of contributions to property ownership. This understanding of value is not only reflected in the law; it is evident in the attitudes of many men and women. In one US study, it was found that divorcing men discuss with their lawyers 'ways to "keep" their property or assets, and women discuss ways to "get" [those] assets' (Gray and Merrick 1996: 243). This view, defining which contributions are of value in property accumulation, is linked to particular ideas of how families are organised and what marriage means. It is a view that has been challenged in other jurisdictions regarding the value placed upon non-monetary contributions to the acquisition or maintenance of property.

The Canadian case of *Pettkus v Becker*[73] is a good example of how a court was able to adapt trust principles to recognise a different and arguably more realistic view of family relationships in which couples only rarely turn their minds to allocating property ownership. Mr Pettkus and Ms Becker were not married, but lived as husband and wife and worked a bee farm together for 19 years. All of the business and residential property was acquired through Mr Pettkus' funds, which he was able to save during the time that Ms Becker paid their rent from her salary. Legal title was in his name. After the acquisition, Ms Becker used her money to purchase new flooring and helped to lay the floor. They worked the business together. The Supreme Court of Canada said the following:

> Turning then to the present case and common intention, the evidence is clear that Mr Pettkus and Miss Becker had no express agreement for sharing economic gain. She conceded there was no specific arrangement with respect to the use of her money. She said: 'No, we just saved together. It was meant to be together, it was ours'. The arrangement 'was without saying anything … there was nothing talked over …' (271)

Q Does their arrangement sound to you like a typical or an atypical family arrangement?

The court went on:

> The finances of each were completely separate … . Uncommitted to marriage or to a permanent relationship it would be difficult to ascribe to Mr Pettkus an intention, express or implied, to share his savings. Miss Becker said they were to 'save together' but the truth is that Mr Pettkus saved at the expense of Miss Becker. (271)

The court did not feel that it needed to find or to impute a common intention where it was impossible or unreasonable to do so. But neither did it feel that this barred Ms Becker from any entitlement to the property. It found that it could use equity to assist her. It preferred to abandon the fiction of a common intention and to utilise a concept that focused more accurately on the real issues between the parties. It adopted the constructive trust as a remedy for the unjust enrichment of Pettkus at the expense of Becker. Unjust enrichment has three requirements: an enrichment of one party; a corresponding detriment to the other part; and the absence of any juristic reason for the enrichment.

---

[73] [1980] 2 SCR 834; (1981) 117 DLR (3d) 257. Page references are to the DLR.

Q How do you feel about abandoning the common intention requirement in these cases? How would Mrs Rosset have fared using this approach?

The court went on:

> Mr Pettkus has had the benefit of 19 years of unpaid labour, while Miss Becker has received little or nothing in return. As for the third requirement, I hold that where one person in a relationship tantamount to spousal prejudices herself in the reasonable expectation of receiving an interest in property and the other person in the relationship freely accepts benefits conferred by the first person in circumstances where he knows or ought to have known of that reasonable expectation, it would be unjust to allow the recipient of the benefit to retain it. (274)

Q Would all wives have a reasonable expectation of receiving an interest in the marital home after doing things that are the 'most natural things in the world' for a wife to do? In 1993 the Supreme Court of Canada again clarified its position regarding household labour as a sufficient contribution to give rise to a constructive trust. The following quote from the case of *Peter v Beblow*[74] captures the court's sentiments:

> The notion that household and child care services are not worthy of recognition by the court fails to recognize the fact that these services are of great value, not only to the family, but to the other spouse … . The notion, moreover, is a pernicious one that systematically devalues the contributions which women tend to make to the family economy. It has contributed to the phenomenon of the feminization of poverty. (346)

Douglas et al suggest something similar. While not endorsing the Canadian approach they invoke the concept of unjust enrichment.

> The essence of unjust enrichment for our purpose is the idea that one party 'gets something for nothing' or enjoys a windfall at the expense of another. This can certainly take the form of a contribution or sacrifice that goes unrecognised, as in *Burns v Burns*. … The continuing criticism of this case lies in the failure of the law to call her partner to account for the benefits he had enjoyed during their relationship, simply because these were not valued in financial terms. But a windfall can also be enjoyed because the law may fail to recognise a *non-contribution*, or it may confer a disproportionate benefit in return for the contribution that has been made. Trusts law itself of course originally sought to recognise the problem of an apparent windfall and to rectify the unfairness that it produces by imposing a trust on the ostensible owner of property, who was not really justified in taking the full benefit of such ownership. But the way that the law of constructive trusts (which is the doctrine to be applied to disputes between couples in intimate relationships), has now been developed by the House of Lords in *Stack v Dowden* means that equity may no longer provide proper redress in such circumstances. … The result of the case is that the law as it currently stands may just as unfairly reward a party who has done little to deserve their share, as penalise a party who has done much but cannot quantify it in the terms required by the technicalities of the case-law. (Douglas et al 2009a: 31–32)

Q Boyd (1994) has suggested, however, that, as progressive as the Canadian decisions appear to be, they tend to reinforce stereotypes of 'traditional family forms' incorporating a breadwinner-dependent philosophy, so that if a woman

---

[74] [1993] 3 WWR 337.

conforms to the dependent role, she is more likely to receive compensation. Does Douglas et al's (2009a) concept of unjust enrichment help to break down such stereotypes while at the same time providing justice for individual non-property-owning women?

Alternatives—2. Community of Property

In many jurisdictions, marriage is viewed as a partnership, and so as a reflection of that philosophy they adopt a system of community of property rather than one of separation of property.[75] It is significant that usually a formal marriage is required to trigger a community of property regime, and that, while the partners remain unmarried, their property remains separate; the introduction of a community of property system would not assist cohabitants. The community of property regime has been described as follows:

> The community of property approach is premised on the assumption that marriage, among other things, is an economic partnership. As such, the partnership or community owns the respective talents and efforts of the spouses. Whatever is acquired as a result of their talents and efforts is shared by and belongs to both of them equally.
>   The essence of a community regime is that the earnings and property acquired by the efforts of either spouse become community property in which each spouse has a present legal interest.
>
> (Payne 1976: 296)

A community of property regime usually results in a complicated system in practice, as elaborate rules tend to be in place governing such matters as the degree to which community property is available to discharge a spouse's contractual obligations or how management of the community property is allocated between the two spouses. It usually includes also the option for the parties to contract out of the regime.

Q What, in your view, are the pros and cons of a community system? Does a community of property system reflect a view of marriage that differs from that reflected by a separate property regime?

IV. STATUTORY REFORM

Statutory variations of the separate property regime in England and Wales have been restricted to two fairly minor amendments: the Married Women's Property Act 1964, which states that money or property bought by a wife out of a housekeeping allowance provided by her husband is to be shared equally between the spouses,[76] and section 37 of the Matrimonial Proceedings and Property Act 1970,[77] which states:

> It is hereby declared that where a husband or wife contributes in money or money's worth to

---

[75] A community of property regime was advocated for England and Wales in the 1950s, led by Kahn-Freund (1955), among others. See also Cretney (2003c) and Eekelaar (2003a).

[76] The Law Commission (1988c) criticised this provision and recommended its repeal.

[77] A similar provision has been incorporated into the Civil Partnership Act 2004 at s 65.

the improvement of real or personal property in which or in the proceeds of sale of which either or both of them has or have a beneficial interest, the husband or wife so contributing shall, if the contribution is of substantial nature and subject to any agreement to the contrary express or implied, be treated as having then acquired by virtue of his or her contribution a share or an enlarged share, as the case may be, in that beneficial interest of such an extent as may have been then agreed, or in default of such agreement, as may seem in all the circumstances just to any court before which the question of the existence or extent of the beneficial interest of the husband or wife arises (whether in proceedings between them or in other proceedings).[78]

Statutory changes with respect to the family home have concentrated upon occupancy rather than ownership. At common law, the owner of a property has rights of occupancy in it, and anyone else living there does so at the owner's discretion. The Family Law Act 1996 provides that all non-owner spouses and civil partners have 'home rights' in the family home, which are the right to occupy it including protection from eviction from it. Non-owner domestic partners do not have home rights, but can gain, in some cases of domestic violence, the right to occupy.[79]

> **Q** Do these statutory interventions go far enough, in your view? Scotland has
> reformed its matrimonial property regime in line with a deferred community
> scheme. A deferred system is one in which property is held separately by the
> partners during marriage, but then, on separation of the partners, a 'snapshot'
> of the family's assets is taken, and the value of all the assets, minus all the debts,
> is split between them. In Scotland the value is normally split equally, while in
> other jurisdictions a more complicated formula may be used. Behind both types
> of system, however, is the notion that both spouses are entitled to an equal
> share of the value of the assets acquired during the marriage. See *Lightbody (or
> Jacques) v Jacques* [1997] 1 FLR 748.

In 1978 the Law Commission recommended a statutory framework for joint ownership of the family home (Law Commission 1978) and in 1988 it recommended, among other things, that 'the purchase of [moveable] property (with some exclusions) by one or both spouses for their joint use or benefit should give rise to joint ownership of property subject to a contrary intention on the part of the purchasing spouse, known to the other spouse'. It also recommended that 'transfer of property by one spouse to the other for their joint use or benefit should give rise to joint ownership of that property subject to a contrary intention on the part of the transferring spouse, known to the other spouse' (Law Commission 1988c: 101). None of these recommendations has been implemented, and in 2002 the Law Commission reported again on the ownership of the family home (Law Commission 2002). This project was originally intended to include the law relating to cohabitation, but it soon became clear that the Commission was really concerned with rights of 'homesharers'. It covered, therefore, the property rights of a broad range of people, not only 'couples'. This, perhaps, was one of the reasons for its rather woolly (non) conclusions. The Commission considered, for example, whether a property approach or a relationship approach would better solve the problem of determining property interests where there are no express arrangements between homesharers as to how property should be owned. With regard to the property approach, it concluded that: 'It is quite simply not

---

[78] See *Pettit v Pettit* [1970] AC 777.
[79] Family Law Act 1996 ss 30–34. See Chapter 12 below.

possible to devise a statutory scheme for the ascertainment and quantification of beneficial interests in the shared home which can operate fairly and evenly across the diversity of domestic circumstances which are now to be encountered' (para 1.31(1)).

This conclusion may not be surprising given that the Commission considered a wide variety of living arrangements. Rather than focus solely upon marriage or marriage-like relationships, it recognised also the possible homesharing rights of 'persons who are not in any sense a "couple", but who live together for mutual support or caring' (para 1.31(4)). In this sense the Commission seemed to be taking our increasingly diverse family practices into account,[80] but just as the law legitimating those relationships as 'family' cannot decide what to do about them,[81] neither could the Law Commission devise a statutory property-sharing scheme that would cope. The Commission first reviewed the current common law position, identified problems with it, then recommended that the current trust for land be retained, but highlighted ways in which it thought the common law could be 'usefully developed' (para 1.28). Before we look at these recommendations, let us examine the difficulties in the present law as identified by the Law Commission:

2.106 'Common Intention' constructive trust

Common intention has been described as a 'myth'. It is certainly difficult to explain every decided case on the basis of the parties' intention being 'express' or 'implied', and there is ample evidence of courts taking an inventive approach to the facts and discovering a common intention where none in truth exists. ...

2.107 The relevance of contributions

... Whilst it seems that a qualifying contribution must be financial in nature, it remains unclear whether it must be directly referable to the acquisition of the property, or, indeed, when a contribution is direct or indirect. It does not seem satisfactory to us that the way in which the parties sharing the home have agreed to administer the household budget should have decisive effect on whether the house is treated as beneficially owned by one or both of them. In some cases, the allocation of financial responsibility could even be deliberately contrived to the advantage of the party with legal title.

2.108 Discrimination against home-makers

The decision in *Burns v Burns* highlights the difficulty faced by those who have shared a home for a long time but who cannot establish the requisite 'common intention' nor prove 'financial' contribution as they have been occupied full-time at home, possibly bringing up children. A strong argument can be made to the effect that the current law discriminates against those who do not earn income from employment.

2.109 The quantification of beneficial entitlement

... [T]he principles of quantification are uncertain, with decisions being made which are (not entirely surprisingly) inconsistent and difficult to reconcile. ...

2.110 The unpredictability of estoppel

The unwillingness of the courts to define precisely the scope of proprietary estoppel means that the doctrine is flexible and can be developed as appropriate. However, the corollary is that certain elements of the doctrine remain unclear and that it is difficult to predict when it will

---

[80] See Chapter 1 above.
[81] See discussion in Chapter 1.

operate. ... Furthermore, the extent to which proprietary estoppel and the common intention constructive trust overlap remains a difficult issue.

2.111 The litigation consequences

The lack of coherent principle does not assist parties or their lawyers in attempts to arrive at a compromise. ...

2.112 The current requirements for establishing the existence of an interest under a trust are not ideally suited to the typical informality of s those sharing a home. (40–42, references omitted)

Q Do you agree with these criticisms? Can you think of any more?

The Commission then made some modest recommendations for useful ways in which the common law could be developed, given these criticisms. First, it suggested that the 'common intention' requirement be kept, despite its highly artificial nature (para 4.24). It thus disagreed with the unjust enrichment approach discussed above. It then recommended that an indirect contribution to the mortgage, such as that made when one party pays household bills, be sufficient to enable courts to infer common intention to share (para 4.26). Finally, it recommended that beneficial entitlement be quantified in a 'holistic' way, looking at the whole course of dealing between the parties (para 4.28).

Q Have any of these recommendations for development of the case law occurred in the courts? Would you recommend any other 'useful development' of the case law?

The Commission also suggested that the 'relationship' or 'status' approach' to home-sharing should not be ignored, however. While accepting 'that there is a very strong case for singling out marriage as a status deserving of special treatment' (para 5.42), it also recommended that the law ought to respond to the 'increasing diversity of living arrangements' in Great Britain. It limited its recommendations in this respect, however, to allowing for the 'formal registration of civil partnerships, or, less formally, a power for the court to adjust the legal rights and obligations of individuals who are or have been living together for a defined period or in defined circumstances' (para 5.43).

Q To what extent have these recommendations been accepted by the government? Do you feel that any more can be done to ensure fairness in determining ownership when people share their home? Do you think the answers lie in a property law approach or in a family/relationship law approach? To what extent are the principles of property law and family law different? To what extent are the divisions between the two artificial in the context of the 'home'. See, on this, Sawyer (2004), Miles (2003), Fox (2003) and Diduck (2005b).

V. CONCLUSION

We have not focused this chapter upon the cases and legislation governing how members of a household earn and distribute income and acquire and hold property. In part, this is because the law does not have much to say about these issues, and assumes that they are a private matter for family members to decide among themselves unless and until the partners go their separate ways. Legal ordering in this event is discussed in later chapters. Rather, we have raised issues here about the implications of the assumptions of family privacy and of formal equality and what they mean for non-earning, and therefore, non-powerful members of families. These members rely upon earning and property-owning members of families for their financial support, and for the most part, the law remains content with this form of familial organisation.

POSTSCRIPT

While this book was in press the Supreme Court rendered its decision in *Jones v Kernott*.[82] It said that where both parties are responsible for the mortgage, 'there is no presumption of a resulting trust arising from their having contributed to the deposit (or indeed the rest of the purchase) in unequal shares. The presumption is that the parties intended a joint tenancy both in law and in equity' (para 25). That presumption 'can be displaced by showing (a) that the parties had a different common intention at the time when they acquired the home, or (b) that they later formed the common intention that their respective shares would change' (para 51(2)). Common intention is to be deduced objectively from the parties' conduct (para 51(3)), but '[i]n those cases where [...] it is not possible to ascertain by direct evidence or by inference what their actual intention was [...] "the answer is that each is entitled to that share which the court considers fair having regard to the whole course of dealing between them in relation to the property".' (para 51(4)) Finally, '[f]inancial contributions are relevant but there are many other factors which may enable the court to decide what shares were either intended [...] or fair [...].' (para 51(5)). In other words, there may be some situations in which a court may impute, rather than infer intention and if it does, it must have regard to fairness.

Where the family home is held in the name of one party only the court must first determine 'whether it was intended that the other party have any beneficial interest in the property at all.' If so, 'the second issue is what that interest is. There is no presumption of joint beneficial ownership' (para 52). The parties' common intention regarding that interest must then be deduced objectively from their conduct, but if the evidence does not show what shares were intended, the court will have to proceed in fairness as at para 51(4) and (5) above.

FURTHER READING

G Douglas, J Pearce and H Woodward, 'Cohabitants, Property and the Law: A Study of Injustice' (2009) 72 *MLR* 24.
L Fox, 'Reforming Family Property—Comparisons, Compromises and Common Dimensions' (2003) *CFLQ* 1.
——, *Conceptualising Home: Theories, Law and Policies* (Oxford, Hart Publishing, 2006).
S Gardner, 'Family Property Today' (2008) 122 *LQR* 422.
S Wong, 'Trusting in Trust(s): The Family Home and Human Rights' (2003) 11 *Feminist Legal Studies* 119.

---

[82] [2011] UKSC 53. All references are to the judgment of Lady Hale and Lord Walker.

7

Dividing the Family Assets

While the law on dividing assets and income on divorce and on dissolution of civil partnership is the same, we will discuss its development in the context of the Matrimonial
Causes Act 1973. We take this approach because the principles, while they apply to both
same-sex and different-sex unions, were developed in the gendered context of marriage
and divorce, and, we argue, reflect that context. Indeed, it will be interesting to see how
they apply in civil partership dissolution proceedings. There are no reported cases to date.

I. HISTORICAL OVERVIEW

We have seen that marital relationships historically were not considered to be relationships
based upon the type of equality we assume today. If there was any idea of equality at all,
it was of the (spurious) 'separate but equal' type according to which each partner assumed
a particular status as the result of the marriage; the husband's status gave him more
economic, public and legal power, and the wife's status gave her moral superiority in
society and responsibility for the family.[1] The parties' economic statuses were dictated by
the doctrine of coverture. Cretney reminds us of Blackstone's authoritative view:

> The effect of the marriage contract (declared by statute to be indissoluble) was, for Blackstone,
> dramatic: the husband and wife became legally a single person, 'the very being or legal exist-
> ence of the woman is suspended during the marriage' … . And, of course, on marriage, the
> wife's assets vested in the husband as his 'sole and absolute property', to 'be disposed of at his
> pleasure'. For Blackstone, marriage was accurately classified among the methods of acquiring
> property. True, it was not quite roses all the way for the husband: he was, for example, liable
> for the wife's pre-marital debts and for her torts; but for this reason the law gave him the power
> to restrain his wife by 'moderate correction' … . Blackstone, nonetheless, assures us that the
> wife's legal disabilities were 'for the most part intended for her protection and benefit', so 'great
> a favourite is the female sex of the laws of England'. (Cretney 2003b: 403)

Unmarried heterosexual couples perhaps had more flexibility to order their private affairs,
including their economic affairs, differently if they wished, and indeed it was this ability
to opt out of the doctrine of coverture which may have encouraged many women to enter

---

[1] See, eg, Stone (1990) and the essays in Smart (1992). The 'traditional family' often eulogised today has
its roots in this marital relationship in which each party's role was separate and clearly understood (Diduck
2003: ch 2).

273

only into informal marriages (Parker 1990).[2] Couples living in lesbian or gay relationships may have kept the nature of their relationships secret, and could, in theory, create a relationship of equality for themselves if they wished.

The husband's economic and legal superiority over the wife, coupled with the moral, if not legal, indissolubility of marriage before the Divorce and Matrimonial Causes Act 1857, meant that, based simply upon his status as husband, he was responsible for maintaining her until her death. She could, however, disentitle herself from maintenance if she committed a matrimonial offence.[3] Finer and McGregor summarise the state of the law at this time:

> The law had two dominant characteristics. First, it subordinated one sex to the other. This was both a cause and an effect of the wider social phenomenon which Mill called the 'subjection of women'—a subjection that was sexual, psychological, economic and domestic, as well as legal, in the midst of which women spent most of their lives (of which they had a far shorter expectation than exists today) occupied with the pains and responsibilities of childbearing and child rearing. The second characteristic of the law, which operated in this respect impartially as between the sexes, was the discrimination its institution created between the rich and the poor. In the sphere of married women's property, the wealthy classes with the aid of their advisors and the Chancery court protected their kin with the marriage settlement, while the common law stripped other women of their possessions. If a marriage broke down, a handful of the richest in the land could win their release from Parliament, and some others, if they could raise the fees and costs, could obtain a legal separation from the Church. The rest had no remedy. The same dichotomy permeated the law related to maintenance. The few women whose marriage was terminated in Parliament obtained—whether themselves guilty or not—a measure of secured financial support. A few others who brought successful petitions to the ecclesiastical courts were awarded decrees of alimony, although these were difficult of enforcement. All the rest of married women who had no separate property—and they were the vast majority—whether living together with or apart from their husbands were, apart from the exiguous protection provided by the doctrine of agency, literally at their husbands' mercy in the financial sense. If the husband was not kind, the wife's only resource was charity, the poor law, or prostitution ... . There developed from this situation, from the mid century onwards, a deliberate legislative drive towards equality: equality within the law for women; equality within the law for people of small means. All major developments in family law from this time onwards have been directed to these ends. (Finer and McGregor 1974: 101)

II. THE MOVE TO EQUALITY

Let us develop Finer and McGregor's statement that all major developments in family law from the mid-nineteenth century have been directed towards equality,[4] for equality can have different meanings to different people. Nineteenth-century legislative reforms created the possibility of divorce in the common law courts,[5] for the award and enforcement of maintenance (alimony) after divorce,[6] and, as we saw in the previous chapter, the law related to married women's property was reformed in this century as well, replacing the

---

[2] And see Chapter 2 above; Probert (2009).
[3] On the history of the Matrimonial offence, see Chapter 3 above.
[4] See also The Honourable Mrs Justice (now Baroness) Hale (1998).
[5] Divorce and Matrimonial Causes Act 1857; and see Chapter 3 above.
[6] Divorce and Matrimonial Causes Act 1857.

doctrine of coverture with that of formal equality and separate property. At this time, formal discrimination in many spheres of public life[7] and as between husband and wife became less and less socially acceptable. On a day-to-day basis, however, and despite an ethos of social equality, it was still women who required and were entitled to maintenance on divorce, and still men who had the obligation and income to provide it.[8] Even into the twentieth-century formal equality between the spouses did not translate into economic equality as the practices of mortgage lenders required that property be purchased in the name of the breadwinner or head of the family (Cretney 2003b), and the ideology of the traditional family meant that few middle-class wives or mothers earned their own income.

Separation of property thus meant that on divorce, husbands usually were entitled to the(ir) property. They still had an obligation to support their former wives, however, and even before the 1970 reforms, judges had discretion as to how to enforce this obligation. If the wife were deemed to be entitled to support, often decided on moral grounds, the judge would then attempt to assess her needs, based on what he determined were her necessaries, given her station in life (Cretney 2003b). Carol Smart indicates that even until the 1960s maintenance obligations were based upon moral grounds.

> A wife was however legally entitled to claim a portion of a man's wage as a dependant under *certain conditions*. She did not have a right to share his wage, nor even to know what he earned, but as a dependant when the marriage broke down and as long as she met certain moral conditions, she was entitled to apply for maintenance. The maintenance could cease on her remarriage, when she became dependent on another man, or could be reduced to below subsistence level if her husband's circumstances changed. Maintenance awards were therefore not based on the wife's need so much as on what she was morally entitled to and what her husband could afford. The common law held that an adulterous wife lost all her rights to maintenance whether the adultery occurred before or after the breakdown of the marriage. However, in practice, statute law had modified this principle somewhat although it depended on the discretion of the judiciary just how much it was modified ... .
>
> In *M v M*[9] the wife lost her right to maintenance because it was discovered that she had had a child by another man eleven years after she and her husband separated. This was in spite of the fact that she had divorced her husband on the grounds of *his* adultery. ...
>
> This differential response to behaviour of husbands and wives undoubtedly contains a moral element ... . Most husbands were (and are) in a much more powerful financial position than their wives. Maintenance, like housekeeping, was in their *gift*. That is to say, it depended to a very great extent on their benevolence and cooperation. (Smart 1984: 89–91)

In 1970 the Matrimonial Proceedings and Property Act was passed. The Act followed the Law Commission's 1969 Report (Law Commission 1969) which recommended that the primary objective for any reform ought to be that the parties' financial positions 'should so far as possible be unaffected by their divorce' (see Law Commission 1980: para 22), the so-called 'minimal loss principle'.[10] So, in addition to a list of factors for courts to consider in making ancillary relief determinations, it included a direction to that effect to courts. Among the list of factors for courts to consider when making awards were the recipient's needs, the payer's ability to pay, and any future obligations or resources each might have. The Act also attempted to address the difficulty with allocating property

---

[7] See, eg, Reform Act 1867; Reform Act 1884; Representation of the People Act 1918.
[8] See generally, Cretney (2003a: ch 10).
[9] [1962] 2 All ER 895.
[10] The 1969 Report's recommendation was enacted in s 25(1) of the MCA 1973.

between the parties and gave the court jurisdiction to make property adjustment orders and orders for the sale of property.

It is important to note at this stage that the law permitted, and still permits, the courts to consider for possible reallocation all of the parties' property, no matter when or how it was acquired. This means that premarital property, property left to a party by way of legacy or gift or property acquired post separation are all theoretically available for division by the courts. The doctrine of separation of property means that any adjustment the courts may make to legal or beneficial ownership of that property is a clear infringement of property rights, but is justified by Parliament in this statute. This property regime is one way in which English and Welsh law is different from that in other jurisdictions, both civil and common law. In these we see systems of community of property, where the parties' property becomes jointly owned on marriage; deferred community property which requires an equal division on death or divorce; or community of acquests, which presumes the divisibility only of assets acquired after the marriage and before the separation.[11] But in many of these systems, we also see provision for the parties to opt out of the property regimes by pre- or postnuptial agreements. This is one further way in which the English/Welsh regime stands out as different: agreements of this type cannot be assumed to be determinative. We will return to these issues below, but they are important to bear in mind as we continue our discussion of the shifts in ancillary relief law over the years.

The 1970 Act was consolidated in 1973 with the Divorce Reform Act 1969 and the resulting Matrimonial Causes Act 1973 (MCA) seemed to shift the ground generally to an approach which focused on the needs and means of the parties, but which still assumed that entitlement to maintenance was based upon a wife's dependence upon her husband. Smart described the developments in these terms:

> It was suggested that during the 1970s the redistribution of family assets was gradually organised more around the concept of need than moral entitlement. Although such a shift is clearly visible, this formulation of the development of case law is somewhat oversimplistic. The major and overriding consideration to affect levels of maintenance is not so much the recipient's need as the donor's ability to pay. (Smart 1984: 113)

She observed that in order to determine both need and ability to pay the Act directed courts to look to, among other things, the future needs and obligations of the spouses or former spouses as well as their earning power and future earning power. The concept of means and needs, therefore, was very flexibly applied in practice. Smart then went on to state:

> The concept of need must therefore be seen as a highly flexible tool and over time the courts can prioritise different needs. For example there may now be occurring a shift away from an emphasis on the needs of the first wife towards the needs of a second family, and there has been a clear shift away from the needs of the spouses to the needs of the children. The 'flexibility' of the concept should not obscure the fact that it appears to have developed in response to the increasingly visible economic vulnerability of the dependent wife or mother. The courts as a whole (with the assistance of legislation) have now come to recognise that the division of labour in the family adversely affects the economic viability of women, particularly when they have children. In so doing they have employed private law to protect her but have rapidly begun to realise that the financial burden this may place on individual men is increasingly unacceptable

---

[11] See further discussion in Chapter 6 above.

to them. This is particularly the case where the man has remarried and has another family to support. The major issue affecting maintenance in the 1970s (and early 1980s) therefore is the extent to which wives, simply because of their marital status, can rely on their right to maintenance on divorce or separation. The extent to which judges have been willing to extinguish this right is not only a reflection of judicial perception of the changing role of women, it may also have an effect on the institution of marriage itself by challenging the taken-for-granted nature of women's dependency in marriage. (ibid: 114)[12]

This extract raises a number of issues. The first is that the legislation left (and still leaves) the determination of all ancillary relief, including maintenance awards, to the discretion of the presiding judge. And, as Smart noted, in the 1970s and 1980s judges were concerned both to ameliorate women's economic vulnerability and to protect men's finances.

Q Apart from the direction in section 25(1) MCA to exercise their powers so as to put the parties in the financial position in which they would have been had the marriage not broken down, there was no direction in the statute to judges to prioritise any of the considerations over others. Would different considerations carry different weight depending upon the facts of the case? On the views of the judge? On the conduct of the parties as assessed by the judge?

The second point we wish to highlight from Smart's extract is that even where considerations other than morality were taken into account, the basis of any maintenance claim was, and still is, the fact of there having been a marriage. Smart suggested, however, that the needs/means approach may have had an effect on the ideological nature of marriage, as the status of wife, although a necessary starting point, was no longer sufficient for a successful maintenance claim.

Q Do you agree with Smart's suggestion that, by beginning to question the assumption of female dependency in maintenance awards, judges can have some influence on the nature of marriage as it is currently practised?

In the 1970s, principles of formal equality in the public sphere[13] eventually led to calls for formal equality to be applied in the private sphere. Interest groups such as Campaign for Justice on Divorce (a divorced men's group) lobbied for a change in the law whereby a woman would not be entitled to maintenance from a man simply because she was at one time married to him. Many feminists also thought that entitlement to maintenance based upon status simply perpetuated women's dependency. It was thought that formal equality in the public sphere meant that women and men, during marriage and after divorce, ought to be able to remain financially independent of one another. The image of the 'alimony drone'[14]—the idle woman living off the hard-earned income of her former husband—was invoked to castigate dependent women in the name of equality principles.

In 1980 the Law Commission recommended 'evolutionary' change to the law, advocating the removal of the minimal loss principle and the inclusion of the requirement that courts give consideration to each party's capacity, actual or potential, to become self-

---

[12] See, further, Eekelaar (1991b).

[13] The Sex Discrimination Act was passed in 1975, the Equal Pay Act in 1970. The election of a woman prime minister and gradual public acceptance of a woman's movement generally led to greater public acceptance of some notions of equality.

[14] 'Divorcees to Lose Meal Ticket', *The Guardian*, 3 November 1983, quoted by Smart (1984).

sufficient after divorce.[15] In addition, the 1979 House of Lords judgment in *Minton v Minton*[16] had made credible, in the social context of the time, the idea which was already becoming established in lower courts: that spouses, on divorce, ought to have a 'clean break' from one another. According to the frequently cited words of Lord Scarman: 'An object of the modern law is to encourage each to put the past behind them and to begin a new life which is not overshadowed by the relationship which has broken down' (608). His words, and the Law Commission's recommendations, captured in law the acceptability of social movements toward equality between the sexes, and the MCA 1973 was amended in 1984 in accordance with this movement. While the guidelines for the exercise of the court's discretion remained substantially unchanged, the legislation repealed the over-riding objective in section 25(1)—the minimal loss principle. It substituted no new objective, but did incorporate new factors for the court to consider: first, the welfare of any children of the marriage; and second, whether imposing a 'clean break' between former spouses would be desirable. As Thorpe LJ wrote extra-judicially in 2009, this reform 'had the obvious consequence of enlarging yet further the ambit of the judge's discretion' (22), yet the policy it expressed—the move from paternalism to autonomy—was wise (24).

The unarticulated model of equality adopted by this new divorce policy was one based upon autonomy of the parties and sameness of treatment, or formal equality. Its liberal origins have been explored in earlier chapters. This approach to equality is based upon the proposition that there are no material differences between men and women in the context of modern, egalitarian marriage, and hence their decision-making autonomy regarding marriage should be respected. On this view, to assume that each partner is entitled to 50% of the family's assets and that women require support from their husbands perpetuates women's inequality. Many who take this view of equality argue that all main-tenance after divorce should therefore be abolished.[17] Indeed, Baroness Deech has maintained this view for over 30 years, and in 2009 wrote:

> Yet we are now in a society where the majority of women, even with children, work or are expected to work, where they claim equal pay and opportunities in employment, where there is contraception to enable a family to be planned and more women are entering higher education and the professions than men. It is inconsistent if at one and the same time family law assumes that a woman can and should stay at home and care for their children and be compensated for that on divorce, and for society to call for women to take 50% of top jobs. (Deech 2009b: 1141)

> One could equally well postulate that the award of large sums of their ex-husband's money to women who have done little other than live is actually a way of punishing the men for leaving them. It is actually considered degrading to women in some quarters and perpetuates the common law proprietary relationship of the husband and wife even after divorce, because of ongoing financial claims and deferred house sale. (ibid: 1142)

This argument, and counter-positions to it, are summarised as follows:

> While the ultimate goal for many feminists may be to abolish maintenance altogether, such a move must occur only when there is no need for support and not be made merely as a conces-sion to the rhetoric of formal sex equality. In order to abolish need, however, we must

---

[15] See Law Commission (1980) and compare with this the Scottish Law Commission Report (1981).
[16] [1979] AC 593.
[17] See, eg, Deech (1977).

restructure fundamentally the relationship between state, family and work. Implicitly, we must not concentrate exclusively upon private support law in order to avoid asking the more basic questions around the division of responsibilities among men, women and society, and around the greater issues of sex equality in the economy generally. O'Donovan has suggested that we must meet five particular conditions in order to abolish the need for maintenance. She advises that the state must: first, ensure the equality of partners during marriage, including financial equality; second, ensure equal participation by both partners in wage earning activities; third, ensure that wages are geared to persons as individuals and not as heads of families; fourth: ensure treatment of persons as individuals and not as dependents by state agencies; and fifth, ensure provision of children by both parents, including financial support, child care, love, attention and stimulation.

Even if one takes a different view and one's goal is not to abolish maintenance entirely, but rather to abolish the systemic economic and social disadvantage for women associated with a systemic gender based division of labour within marriage, similar fundamental changes in the social structure would be necessary. Along with true equity in employment and pay and affordable good quality child care, an adequate valuation of domestic work would mean it would not be necessary that each partner play exactly the same role in wage earning that O'Donovan envisions. Roles in marriage could be adopted based on the partners' actual interests and skills. Maintenance on divorce would still sometimes be necessary, then, but it would no longer overwhelmingly be women who required it and it would no longer result in economic disadvantage for the recipient. Maintenance would be seen as a right, expected and earned, rather than as a gift, act of benevolence or based on a notion of *women's* dependency on *men*.

(Diduck and Orton 1994: 686, references omitted)

Equality, then, can be understood or conceived of in law in different ways. The first view in the above passage envisages that men and women are 'similarly situated' in marriage and for the purposes of market activity, and so equality between them is to be achieved by treating them the same. The second view holds that in some cases, in marriage and the traditional workplace, for example, sameness of treatment results not in equality, but in inequality. This view recognises that some differences of treatment might be required in order to achieve equality, but that those differences are not required because of any assumed inherent differences between men and women;[18] instead they are needed to compensate for differences and disadvantage created by *institutions* such as marriage or structural conditions such as lack of public support for childcare.[19] In this light, different treatment might be necessary to ensure that disadvantage is not suffered by one group disproportionately to another. This has been called substantive equality.[20]

When we factor into these emergent ideas of family equality the further idea of autonomy, the resulting policy picture becomes even more blurred. Herring reminds us of Raz on autonomy:

The ruling idea behind the ideal of personal autonomy is that people should make their own lives. The autonomous person is a (part) author of his own life. The ideal of personal autonomy is the vision of people controlling, to some degree, their own destiny, fashioning it through successive decisions throughout their lives. (Herring 2010b: 257, quoting Raz 1986: 369)

---

[18] As was the case supporting protective labour legislation, for example. See Chapter 6 above.

[19] That women may be rendered vulnerable financially as a result of childcare responsibilities appears to be recognised by the public. See Maclean and Eekelaar (2005).

[20] For an example of how substantive equality arguments have been used successfully in Canadian courts, see Women's Legal Education and Action Fund (1996).

Autonomy is linked with equality because individuals bear equal moral worth. Their autonomous choices must, therefore, be able to be made freely and equally and be respected by law. While this formulation sits comfortably within formal equality, it is also possible, as Diduck explains, to link autonomy with a form of substantive equality by introducing the concept of dignity:

> In *Nova Scotia Attorney General v Susan Walsh and Wayne Bona*[21] a former cohabitant claimed that a matrimonial property law that applied only to married couples violated her right to equality under section 15 of the *Charter of Rights and Freedoms*. The Court disagreed. Dignity, it said, was the underlying value to be protected by the *Charter's* equality guarantee and autonomy was a fundamental expression of dignity. Protecting dignity by protecting autonomous life choices, therefore, was a way to interpret and give meaning to the value of substantive equality. (Diduck 2011: 281–82)

Eekelaar, seeking in 1988 to theorise a basis for equality in maintenance questions, raised two further notions of equality: equality of outcome and equality of opportunity. He suggested, however, that neither of them could be seen as an appropriate objective for maintenance determinations. He defined equality of outcome as the goal that 'each spouse should exit from the marriage at the same economic level as the other' (Eekelaar 1988: 191) and suggested that the major objections to this principle were that it suffered from 'internal contradiction because, by rewarding people with disparate merits and needs equally, the outcome was an even greater inequality' (ibid: 192). He saw equality of opportunity as the ideal that 'each former spouse should be in an equal position to take advantage of the opportunities to enhance her or his economic position in the labour market' (ibid), but this objective too he found artificial. '[T]he prevailing social structure (including, but not only, the labour market) is such that perfect equality of economic opportunity does not in fact pertain as between the sexes' (ibid). He concluded instead that the principle of 'resource sharing' ought to guide courts, in which the 'total combined income of the adults is shared equally among all the family members' (ibid: 197), including children. This vision of equality, then, can be described as one in which equality between the sexes is subordinated to the claims of any children in the family to equality (ibid: 198), and it still assumes ultimately that sameness of treatment is the answer.

Diduck and Orton comment upon Eekelaar's approach as follows:

> In accepting that equality must always mean sameness [either] of treatment or of result, and thus failing to broaden his vision of equality outside of equality in the male patterned market, or to reconceptualise the traditional role of work within the family, it is not surprising that he could not find a basis for equality between the spouses and had to pursue such claims in the name of children. (Diduck and Orton 1994: 688)

In other words, Eekelaar's approach can be criticised because it failed to challenge the type of equality which accepts traditionally male characteristics, realities and work patterns as the ones to which all must aspire in order to receive the social advantages that men, as the currently more dominant social group, enjoy. It failed to ask 'equal to whom?' and why the traditionally male work pattern ought to be the one that is rewarded. His

---

[21] *Nova Scotia Attorney General v Susan Walsh and Wayne Bona* [2002] 4 SCR 325. See now, however, *R v Kapp* [2008] SCC 41, in which the Supreme Court of Canada clarified that while dignity was an essential value underlying the s 15 equality guarantee, it was, on its own, an 'abstract and subjective notion' that makes it difficult to employ as a legal test (paras 21–22).

approach also failed to challenge the institutions, for example that of marriage, which created the disadvantage for one group as compared with the other (Diduck and Orton 1994). Indeed, he has suggested elsewhere that a woman may mitigate her loss from marriage by remarrying (Eekelaar 1991b: 83).

> **Q** Eekelaar's 'resource-sharing' model of equality is based on an acceptance of the currently still dominant model of the husband-provider/wife and children-dependent family. It also entails equal provision for all on divorce. In this respect, the model can be seen as founded on a conception of the family unit as a type of collectivity with shared interests rather than as a group of individuals, each with his or her own individual interests. Indeed, one might suggest that individual equality principles are inappropriate when it comes to family relations, precisely because the family's interests are about the collective welfare of the group and therefore cannot be separated into the rights or interest of the individuals. On the other hand, the idea of autonomy promotes the freedom of choice of individuals in the family. Both can encompass 'equality'. Which approach do you prefer?

A policy of formal equality has informed family law from 1984. As noted above, the Matrimonial and Family Proceedings Act 1984 repealed the old section 25 of the MCA 1973[22] and replaced it with a new section 25 that made the welfare of the child the first consideration in ancillary relief cases,[23] and with a new section 25A which directed courts to consider imposing a clean break between the parties. The MCA 1973 now reads as follows:

25 (1) It shall be the duty of the court in deciding whether to exercise its powers under section 23,[24] 24,[25] 24A[26] or 24B[27] above and, if so, in what manner, to have regard to all the circumstances of the case, first consideration being given to the welfare while a minor of any child of the family who has not attained the age of eighteen.

(2) As regards the exercise of the powers of the court under section 23(a) (b) or (c), 24, 24A or 24B above in relation to a party to the marriage, the court shall in particular have regard to the following matters—

(a) the income, earning capacity, property and their financial resources which each of the parties to the marriage has or is likely to have in the foreseeable future, including in the case of earning capacity any increase in that capacity which it would in the opinion of the court be reasonable to expect a party to the marriage to take steps to acquire;

---

[22] This directed the courts to try to keep the parties in the position they would have been had the divorce not occurred—the so-called principle of 'minimal loss'.

[23] This approach seems to adopt Eekelaar's preferred model.

[24] S 23 enables the court, on granting a decree of divorce, of nullity of marriage, or of judicial separation, to make financial provision orders for a spouse or child of the family, including periodical payments for a specified term, secured periodical payments for a specified term and lump sum payments.

[25] On granting a decree of divorce, a decree of nullity or a judicial separation, the court may make property adjustment orders, including a transfer of property to a spouse or child or other party for the benefit of a child, a settlement of property for the benefit of a spouse or child, and a variation of any prenuptial or postnuptial settlement.

[26] This section gives the court power, where it makes a secured periodical payments order, a lump sum order or a property adjustment order, to order the sale of any property in which or in the proceeds of sale in which either or both spouses has a beneficial interest.

[27] This section gives the court power, on or after granting a decree of divorce or a decree of nullity, to make a pension sharing order.

(b) the financial needs, obligations and responsibilities which each of the parties to the marriage has or is likely to have in the foreseeable future;

(c) the standard of living enjoyed by the family before the breakdown of the marriage;

(d) the age of each party to the marriage and the duration of the marriage;

(e) any physical or mental disability of either of the parties to the marriage;

(f) the contributions which each of the parties has made or is likely in the foreseeable future to make to the welfare of the family, including any contribution by looking after the home or caring for the family;

(g) the conduct of each of the parties, if that conduct is such that it would in the opinion of the court be inequitable to disregard it;

(h) in the case of proceedings for divorce or nullity of marriage, the value to each of the parties to the marriage of any benefit, which, by reason of the dissolution or annulment of the marriage, that party will lose the chance of acquiring.

...

25A (1) Where on or after the grant of a decree of divorce or nullity of marriage the court decides to exercise its powers under section 23(1)(a), (b) or (c), 24, 24A or 24B above in favour of a party to the marriage, it shall be the duty of the court to consider whether it would be appropriate so to exercise those powers that the financial obligations of each party towards the other will be terminated as soon after the grant of the decree as the court considers just and reasonable.

(2) Where the court decides in such a case to make a periodical payments or secured payments order in favour of a party to a marriage, the court shall in particular consider whether it would be appropriate to require those payments to be made or secured only for such term as would in the opinion of the court be sufficient to enable the party in whose favour the order is made to adjust without undue hardship to the termination of his or her financial dependence on the other party.

(3) Where on or after the grant of a decree of divorce or nullity of marriage an application is made by a party to the marriage for a periodical payments or secured payments order in his or her favour, then, if the court considers that no continuing obligation should be imposed on either party to make or secure periodical payments for the other, the court may dismiss the application with a direction that the applicant shall not be entitled to make any future application in relation to that marriage for an order under section 23(1)(a) or (b)[28] above.

So, with the exception of the welfare of children, no factor is prioritised in section 25 over others and, although there is explicit reference to the aim of a clean break where appropriate, no clear or even coherent model of support or property allocation is apparent. Indeed, the factors can be interpreted as supporting different models. Subsections 25(2) (a)–(e) seem to point to a needs-based or income security model in which the obligation to support arises from the marriage itself and the quantum and duration of support from a simple calculation of the parties' needs and means, regardless of the source of those needs and means. Subsections (f)–(h) contain elements of a compensation model in which maintenance should compensate for financial advantages and disadvantages to each party of the roles they undertook in the marriage. Entitlement is not based on the *fact* of the marriage, but rather is a reimbursement or compensation for needs that were created by the way in which the parties structured their marital roles. Finally, section 25A points to a clean-break model in which maintenance, if awarded at all, is meant to be rehabilitative or temporary in order to recognise the parties' presumptively equal ability to move on

---

[28] Orders for periodical payments and secured periodical payments, respectively.

financially from the marital relationship. 'Equality', applied in each of these models takes on very different meanings.

Let us continue with the legislation, focusing on the clean-break principle.

28 (1) Subject in the case of an order made on or after the grant of a decree of divorce or nullity of marriage to the provisions of sections 25A(2) above and 31(7)[29] below, the term to be specified in a periodical payments or secured periodical payments order in favour of a party to a marriage shall be such term as the court thinks fit, except that the term shall not begin before or extend beyond the following limits, that is to say—

(a) in the case of a periodical payments order, the term shall begin not earlier than the date of the making of an application for the order, and shall be so defined as not to extend beyond the death of either of the parties to the marriage or, where the order is made on or after the grant of a decree of divorce or nullity of marriage, the remarriage of the party in whose favour the order is made;

(b) in the case of a secured periodical payments order, the term shall begin not earlier than the date of the making of an application for the order, and shall be so defined as not to extend beyond the death, or where the order is made on or after the grant of such a decree, the remarriage of the party in whose favour the order is made.[30]

(1A) Where a periodical payments or secured periodical payments order in favour of a party to a marriage is made on or after the grant of a decree of divorce or nullity of marriage, the court may direct that the party shall not be entitled to apply under section 31 below for the extension of the term specified in the order. ...

Q Why should remarriage of the payee terminate support? What model or 'ground' for support is envisaged by termination on remarriage?

Symes' analysis, published in 1985, remains pertinent. She acknowledged that the clean-break principle could be seen as 'arguably a logical step forward in the long march towards liberal divorce and sexual equality' (Symes 1985: 46). She went on to argue, however, that it contains within it an internal contradiction which is in danger of creating severe inequity because, in failing to reconsider the nature of marriage at the time it considered the reform of divorce law, those who framed the 1984 reform which introduced it imposed a consequence of solubility (clean break) upon indissoluble (provider/dependant) marriage. She phrased it this way:

Quite clearly, marriage as it has traditionally been practised, is not intended to be ended by divorce. Indeed, traditional housewife marriage has a most potent feature of indissolubility built right into it—dependency ... . The accumulation of responsibilities and obligations, the consequences of an unequal partnership based on dependency—all mean that an absolute severance of the bond without massive adjustment would be manifestly unjust, more likely impossible.

(Symes 1985: 57)

And further:

Divorce in fact takes the lid off marriage, exposes the issue of female dependency and reveals

---

[29] S 31 gives the court power to vary, discharge or suspend orders for financial relief. S 31(7) states that when the court is considering making such an order, it is to have regard to all the circumstances of the case, including the any changes to the factors listed in s 25(1) and (2).

[30] The effect of this is that an unsecured periodical payments order can continue after the death of the payer.

just how much has been taken for granted as appropriate family activity. The process of child-drearing was carried out relatively cheaply in the traditional nuclear family, with the mother usually combining her roles of spouse/parent and homemaker with no direct financial reward. Modern divorce with its emphasis on ultimate self-sufficiency has very rightly called in question the underlying assumptions about this role fusion. For example, is there a legitimate role of homemaker when there are no children? Equally, we must ask, is it just to place the general burden of caring (for children and those of society's dependants who are not in institutions) on women without it being rewarded? ...

Before divorce became pandemic it was possible to avoid these questions of discriminatory role assumptions, although this did not necessarily mean that all was well within the family and that the system worked without injustice. But given our general goal of economic self-sufficiency at the end of marriage, it is imperative that there now be potential if not actual self-sufficiency *throughout* marriage as well. (ibid: 56)

Even if we accept that some notion of equality is appropriate for courts to consider in post-divorce financial and property adjustment, we are faced with the question of why the husband should have to compensate his wife for all the structural inequalities created by society historically, economically and socially. Like Deech (2009b), Ferguson (2008) argues that ancillary relief (and child support) are fundamentally interpersonal rather than social obligations and that it is unjustifiable to use interpersonal obligation as a tool for redressing social inequality. Symes also questioned the appropriateness of trying to rectify systemic inequality through 'private' family law reform. She went on to argue that divorce law cannot provide a substitute for 'humane social policy' incorporating provision for state support. She highlighted female dependency during marriage as a primary reason for the difficulties in adjustment on divorce but maintained that divorce law alone could not provide a solution. For one thing, as she noted, women generally suffer from discrimination in the labour market and with regard to pensions. For another, she said:

In very few cases will financial provision [on divorce] adequately recompense an ex-wife for the many disadvantages she suffers when her marriage ends and distinguishing between specifically marriage-related disabilities and more general ones is not always a simple exercise ... . [Further], [o]nce a party's earning ability has been permanently impaired, clean break divorce is impossible without grave injustice unless adequate state provision (including pensions) compensates for the impairment. The long term effects of such impairment are so profound the task is almost impossible for divorce law in isolation. (Symes 1985: 51)

Others agree that women's equality generally will not be achieved by divorce or family law reform alone, but argue that support law can redress at least some of women's disadvantage on divorce and ought to reflect some fairness as between the parties. '[A]rguing for systemic change does not mean we should continue to tolerate unfairness in the allocation of family resources on separation and divorce. Law must deal with the society it has helped to create and play its part in shaping ideologies it helps to support' (Diduck and Orton 1994: 685). Thus, while ancillary relief cannot, by itself, alter social conditions, it must recognise that family living and family law have some part to play in creating them (Diduck 2011).

This view acknowledges the intimate relationship between public and private responsibility for individual and social well-being. It is feminist in orientation and offers a view of the economic consequences of forming and ending relationships that overtly implicates gender, the social and the political. It reinforces the idea that obligation arises not only from law and private individual choices but also from the moral and social conditions in which that law and those choices are expressed (Diduck 2009a: 204–05; see also Diduck 2009b).

One way to take account of moral and social conditions is to revise assumptions about the *value* of each party's role in the family enterprise:

> To recognize that each spouse is an equal economic and social partner in marriage, regardless of function, is a monumental revision of assumptions. It means, among other things, that caring for children is just as valuable as paying for their food and clothing. It means that organizing a household is just as important as the career rather than quantitatively.
> (Diduck and Orton 1994: 699–700, quoting Abella JA, references omitted)

It would recognise the provision of care in the family as an 'activity of intrinsic value' (Glennon 2009: 193) and as one that confers a benefit on the children, the other partner, the family and society.

Q How does this approach to equality on divorce differ from Eekelaar's? From Symes'? From formal equality? Consider how this approach may influence the trusts cases discussed in Chapter 6.

Equality, then, has been a part of ancillary relief since the 1984 reforms. By the end of the 1990s, however, a trend had developed in the way that courts exercised their wide statutory discretion to distribute the contents of the 'mixed bag' of family wealth in which equality seemed not to be at the forefront. In 2000 District Judge Bird put it this way:

> Housing is normally the most important issue; the housing of the parent with care of the children normally takes priority over that of the other parent, although his/her needs must be met wherever possible. Once housing has been disposed of the reasonable needs of the parties should be considered. The clean break should only be imposed where there is no doubt that the parties will be self-sufficient. Attention must be given to pensions. Where the reasonable needs of the parties have been met there is no justification for further adjustment by the court.
> (Bird 2000: 831)[31]

Q Does equality in any of its forms feature in this approach?

III. FAIRNESS: RETHINKING EQUALITY

Throughout the 1980s and 1990s solicitors were only able to advise their clients that, while there were previous interpretations of the legislation to rely upon, because the matter was entirely within the discretion of the courts, no outcome could be predicted with any accuracy. In the so-called 'big money' cases, this meant that the claimant (usually the wife) would be awarded what the court felt was sufficient to meet her 'reasonable requirements'—no matter what or how she had contributed to the family. Diduck comments:

[31] See also Family Law Committee (1998: para 8.5(a)); Solicitors' Family Law Association (SFLA) (1998: para 23); Association of District Judges (1998: 2).

In *Dart v Dart*, for example, perhaps the leading 'big money' case before *White*, the Court of Appeal stated 'the scheme of [the MCA 1973] must also be set in the wider perspective of history and of the general civil law. In this jurisdiction rights of property are not invaded or reduced by statutory powers save for specific and confined purposes.' This meant that non-propertied wives were required to demonstrate extraordinary or exceptional contribution to the marriage or direct financial contribution to the acquisition of the property in question before they were thought, in fairness, to deserve a share in it. Instead, the breadwinner/dependent ideology prevailed in which so long as her reasonable requirements were met, fairness dictated that she had no further claim to assets, no matter how extensive they were. It was as if the courts felt similar to the way in which many husbands and wives feel when they are negotiating ancillary relief—that it is the husband's money and assets that are being dealt with.

(Diduck 2001b: 174–75, references omitted)

Bennett too regarded the outcome in big money cases as unsatisfactory:

> In case legal advisors are still advising wives that if they make contributions this will make a difference, the salutary experience of reading *Gojkovic* is recommended. The court found that the wife had contributed 50% but she was awarded 27% of the assets ... .
> The award in such cases ... is out of line with most other non-Islamic jurisdictions. At a recent meeting of the International Bar Association, Family Law Committee, on multi-million dollar divorces ... [t]he conclusion was that the award to the wife in nearly 30 jurisdictions around the world would be from 10% to 50%, with the exception of England where it would be 0.6%. (Bennett 1997: 79)

The principles were the same for low- and middle-income families, except that after their housing situation was considered, there was usually little left for redistribution. As in the big-money cases, clean break, welfare, needs and means were the primary factors to be taken into account, but, in practice, this meant that the court would often order the transfer of the husband's interest in the home to the wife for her benefit and that of any children in her care, in exchange for dismissing her claim for ongoing support and dismissing or reducing any claim for child support.[32] Priest noted, however, that:

> Such clean break orders, although made in their hundreds by county court registrars/district judges throughout the UK, were overwhelmingly orders made by consent, and were thus not productive of a reported appellate jurisprudence giving them the clear imprimatur of the Court of Appeal (although indirect support might be derived from authorities such as *Ashley v Blackman* ... and *Delaney v Delaney* ...). They thus formed part of a 'submerged' jurisprudence, evolved and endorsed by practice, and one which gave the lie to the Law Commission's expectation, in 1981, that cases in which a clean break for spousal support would be considered appropriate would be 'comparatively few (and where there were infant children almost non-existent)'. (Law Com No 112, *The Financial Consequences of Divorce, The Response to the Discussion Paper*, para 24). (Priest 1997: 115)

In 2000, however, the ground shifted enormously. In *White v White*[33] the House of Lords can be said to have revolutionised the law of matrimonial property and financial provision. Thorpe LJ (2009) describes it as the House of Lords entering the 'legislative vacuum' left

---

[32] See, eg, *Livesey (formerly Jenkins) v Jenkins* [1985] AC 424 (HL); and the incompatibility of clean-break settlements with the philosophy and application of the CSA 1991 as it was originally applied. See *Crozier v Crozier* [1994] Fam 114; [1994] 2 All ER 362; [1994] 2 WLR 444; [1994] 1 FLR 126; and Chapter 5 above.

[33] [2000] 2 FLR 981 (HL).

by Parliament refusing to act upon its own proposals[34] to review the law of ancillary relief. Diduck (2001b) summarises the facts and history of the case:

> *White v White* was about the breakdown of a 34 year marriage. Mr and Mrs White were both farmers; as the House of Lords stated, 'farming was in their blood'.[35] They acquired their farm one year after marriage with 'a more or less equal'[36] contribution of capital of £2000, a mortgage of £21,000 and an interest-free loan from Mr White's father of £14,000. By the time their applications for ancillary relief came before the court in 1996, their farm was worth approximately £3.5 million. They had executed a formal partnership agreement and traded throughout as equal partners in the farming business. They also farmed together a separate holding called Rexton Farm which Mr White acquired in his sole name from his family, but which was financed substantially by payments out of the partnership income.[37] It was worth £1.25 million. The House of Lords summarised their holdings as follows:
>
> > [T]he overall net worth of Mr and Mrs White's assets was, in round figures, £4.6 million. This comprised, on the figures found and used by the judge: Mrs White's sole property: £196,300 (mostly pension provision); her share of property owned jointly, either directly or through the partnership: £1,334,000; Mr White's share of jointly-owned property: £1,334,000, and Mr White's sole property: £1,783,5000 (mostly Rexton Farm).[38]
>
> On the bases that he did not want to break up an existing farming enterprise, that the wife's desire to have sufficient funds to enable her to continue to farm was unreasonable, and that her reasonable requirements should determine the award, Holman, J awarded her £984,000, or approximately 20% of the total value of the family's assets.
>
> Mrs White successfully appealed to the Court of Appeal. The Court awarded her a total of £1.69 million worth of assets, or approximately 40% of the whole, primarily because she would have received at least £1.52 million had her application proceeded as a formal dissolution of the partnership, rather than under section 25 of the MCA. Indeed, the Court of Appeal was critical of counsel's presentation of the case on this basis, or as a case of 'contribution' rather than 'entitlement', as they put it.[39] Both Mr and Mrs White appealed to the House of Lords, he asking the Court to restore Holman J's order, and she seeking an equal share in all the assets.
>
> (Diduck (2001b: 176–77)

The House of Lords took the opportunity to review the exercise of the discretion given to courts by the MCA. It confirmed that the unstated but nonetheless overriding objective of the legislation was to do 'fairness' between the parties, but it also recognised that 'fairness' was a socially contingent concept; 'fairness' it said, 'like beauty, lies in the eye of the beholder' (989).

> Generally accepted standards of fairness in a field such as this change and develop, sometimes quite radically, over comparatively short periods of time. ... These wide powers [conferred by Parliament in s 25 of the Matrimonial Causes Act 1973] enable the courts to make financial provision orders in tune with current perceptions of fairness. Today there is greater awareness of the value of non-financial contributions to the welfare of the family. There is greater awareness of the extent to which one spouse's business success, achieved by much sustained hard work over many years, may have been made possible or enhanced by the family contribution of the other spouse, a contribution which also required much sustained hard work over many years.

---

[34] Set out in 'Supporting Families' (Home Office 1998).
[35] Ibid, 984.
[36] Ibid.
[37] *White v White* [1998] 2 FLR 310 (CA) 316.
[38] *White v White* [2000] 2 FLR 981 (HL) 985.
[39] *White v White* [1998] 2 FLR 310 (CA) 323, per Butler Sloss, LJ.

> ... In the exercise of these discretions 'the law is a living thing moving with the times and not a creature of dead or moribund ways of thought'. (989–90, references omitted)

Its review of fairness provoked a number of changes in the way courts were meant to exercise their discretion. First, the court challenged specifically the disproportionate weight attached to 'needs' or 'reasonable requirements' that had developed in the case law. It made it clear that this factor was only one among many for the court to consider and should no longer be determinative of a claimant's award.

> I can see nothing, either in the statutory provisions or in the underlying objective of securing fair financial arrangements, to lead me to suppose that the available assets of the respondent become immaterial once the claimant wife's financial needs are satisfied. Why ever should they? If a husband and wife by their joint efforts over many years, his directly in his business and hers indirectly at home, have built up a valuable business from scratch, why should the claimant wife be confined to the court's assessment of her reasonable requirements, and the husband left with a much larger share? Or, to put the question differently, in such a case, where the assets exceed the financial needs of both parties, why should the surplus belong solely to the husband? ... [t]he mere absence of financial need cannot, by itself, be sufficient reason. If it were, discrimination would be creeping in by the back door. In these cases, it should be remembered, the claimant is usually the wife. Hence the importance of the check against the yardstick of equal division.[40] (992)

The gender implications of this finding are important for wives who too often found their 'reasonable requirements' determined according to gendered assumptions about what it was reasonable for a wife to do or to want.[41]

The Lords' second important clarification or revision of the case law was the explicit injection of principles of non-discrimination in the interpretation of 'fairness'.

> In seeking to achieve a fair outcome, there is no place for discrimination between husband and wife and their respective roles. ... [W]hatever the division of labour chosen by the husband and wife, or forced upon them by the circumstances, fairness requires that this should not prejudice or advantage either party when considering para (f), relating to the parties' contributions. ... If, in their different spheres, each contributed equally to the family, then in principle it matters not which of them earned the money and built up the assets. There should be no bias in favour of the money-earner and against the homemaker and the child-carer. (989)

Taken together, these two changes are significant. They mean that it is discriminatory and therefore unfair for an earning spouse merely to meet his non-earning wife's needs out of his capital or salary and then keep any balance that is left over. They promote a very specific meaning of equality. In effect, Lord Nicholls' words are a challenge to the traditional idea that only work done or money earned in the public sphere (ie by means of traditionally male or husband conduct) is valuable and is the norm which wives must reach in order to receive financial benefits from a marriage; it challenges the idea that

---

[40] For discussion of the 'reasonable requirements' principle see the second edition of this book.

[41] An example can be found in *White* itself. At trial Mrs White's reasonable requirements formed the ceiling for her award, and in determining those requirements the court said that it was not reasonable for her to want to continue to farm and to leave a legacy for her children, but it was reasonable for Mr White to do so. As Butler Sloss LJ said in the Court of Appeal, 'In 1998 why should it be reasonable for him to farm and not for her?' (324).

only the person who earns or buys is the rightful owner of family property, and that the other spouse is seeking something to which she is not morally entitled.

Finally, the House of Lords introduced explicitly into ancillary relief law the language of equality. The court was clear that it did not want to establish a presumption of equal sharing in ancillary relief cases. But it was equally clear that judges ought to think about equality:

> [A] judge would always be well-advised to check his tentative views against the yardstick of equality of division. As a general guide, equality should only be departed from if, and to the extent that, there is good reason for doing so. The need to consider and articulate reasons for departing from equality would help the parties and the court to focus on the need to ensure the absence of discrimination. This is not to introduce a presumption of equal division under another guise. (989)

In the result, the House of Lords confirmed the Court of Appeal decision giving Mrs White only approximately 40% of the total assets. The decision that the husband should get the larger share was made at least partly on the basis that the money used to start the business had come from the husband's parents.

Q The court was clearly concerned with the position of homemakers/carers and its decision can be read not only as important for wealthy divorcing couples, but also as important for social policy and other areas of law. To what degree might this case be of value, for example, in cases about acquiring a beneficial interest in the family home? To what degree might it be of symbolic value in thinking about the marital partnership? Refer back to the different 'models' of financial provision. What model of financial provision is adopted in this case? The court did not refer to the Human Rights Act, but to what extent can you see human rights principles or values in its reasoning?

The (equality?) revolution in ancillary relief law did not stop with *White v White*. At the same time as it broke new ground, it upset established norms, especially in big-money cases. Many commented that it increased uncertainty in the law and encouraged litigation (see eg Thorpe, LJ in *Cowan v Cowan*;[42] Eekelaar 2005; Bailey-Harris 2005). Reasonable requirements, they said, was at least certain; how was the value of homemaking contributions to be measured (see eg Eekelaar 2001b, 2003a; Bailey Harris 2003)? *White* thus opened up new areas for argument and raised as many questions as it answered, not only about how the section 25 factors were to be applied in any given case, but also about the constitutional role of the court and the principled basis of ancillary relief itself.

The litigation that resulted in the immediate aftermath of *White* focused primarily upon when a departure from equality would be appropriate and many of these questions are still unresolved. They include whether a departure from equality would be fair if the contribution made by one of the parties could be classified as exceptional, special or 'stellar', whether the duration of the marriage matters, and whether the yardstick applies to all property and contributions.[43] But then in 2006 the House of Lords rendered a second decision on ancillary relief law that attempted to fill in the gaps said to be left by *White*,

---

[42] [2001] 2 FLR 192.
[43] For a discussion of this case law, see the second edition of this book.

and in 2007 the Court of Appeal attempted further clarification. We shall discuss each case in turn.

Miller v Miller; McFarlane v McFarlane[44] considered two cases heard and decided jointly. The Miller's was a short, childless marriage of three years during which the husband built upon his already substantial assets and by the time of the divorce was worth approximately £40 million. The wife had given up her £85,000 per year job in public relations in order to start a family, but suffered a miscarriage. The House of Lords awarded the wife the matrimonial home and sufficient capital to generate for her an annual income of £100,000. The value of this award was approximately £5 million, less than one-sixth of Mr Miller's total wealth. The McFarlane's, on the other hand, was a longer marriage of 16 years. They had three children, the youngest of whom at the time of the divorce was nine years old. At the time of the marriage, each of the partners was in work, he as an accountant, she as a solicitor. She gave up her job, however, afer the birth of their second child and at the time of the divorce had no income. Mr McFarlane's gross partnership income was approximately £1 million per year. They agreed on child support and that their property would be divided in equal shares but their case came before the court on the issue of clean break and her periodical payments. As Cooke describes it:

> She appealed an order that gave her roughly one half of her former husband's net income in periodical payments, but for a term of five years and with the expectation that during that period she would save the excess above her 'needs' towards a deferred clean break. In the Court of Appeal it was held, or perhaps suggested, that the yardstick of equality principle from *White* should apply to periodical payments—although the order made could not be said to have that effect—and thus the case was seen as one in which the application of the yardstick to post-divorce income was in issue. It also raised issues about the importance of the clean break, particularly where there are children; and the legitimacy of using periodical payments for any purpose other than meeting the recipient's income needs. (Cooke 2007: 104)

The House of Lords overturned the five-year term of her award.

Let us now examine the ways in which this case develops the principles emerging from *White*. First, Lord Nicholls reinforces the view that while the court's goal is fairness and fairness is an 'elusive concept', there is no place for gender discrimination within it:

> Fairness is an elusive concept. It is an instinctive response to a given set of facts. Ultimately it is grounded in social and moral values. These values, or attitudes, can be stated. But they cannot be justified, or refuted, by any objective process of logical reasoning. Moreover, they change from one generation to the next. It is not surprising therefore that in the present context there can be different views on the requirements of fairness in any particular case. (para 4)

> The starting point is surely not controversial. In the search for a fair outcome it is pertinent to have in mind that fairness generates obligations as well as rights. The financial provision made on divorce by one party for the other, still typically the wife, is not in the nature of largesse. It is not a case of 'taking away' from one party and 'giving' to the other property which 'belongs' to the former. The claimant is not a supplicant. Each party to a marriage is *entitled* to a *fair* share of the available property. The search is always for what are the *requirements* of fairness in the particular case. (para 9)

---

[44] [2006] UKHL 24; [2006] 1 FLR 1186.

He then goes on to elaborate the requirements of fairness and states that it contains three 'strands': need, compensation and (equal) sharing. Baroness Hale identifies the same three elements of fairness, but she refers to them as the rationales for the redistribution in the first place: 'given that we have a separate property system, there has to be some sort of rationale for the redistribution of resources from one party to another. In my view there are at least three' (para 137). First, Lord Nicholls:

10 ... The first is financial needs. This is one of the matters listed in section 25(2), in paragraph (b): 'the financial needs, obligations and responsibilities which each of the parties to the marriage has or is likely to have in the foreseeable future'.

11. This element of fairness reflects the fact that to greater or lesser extent every relationship of marriage gives rise to a relationship of interdependence. The parties share the roles of money-earner, home-maker and child-carer. Mutual dependence begets mutual obligations of support. When the marriage ends fairness requires that the assets of the parties should be divided primarily so as to make provision for the parties' housing and financial needs, taking into account a wide range of matters such as the parties' ages, their future earning capacity, the family's standard of living, and any disability of either party. Most of these needs will have been generated by the marriage, but not all of them. Needs arising from age or disability are instances of the latter.

12. In most cases the search for fairness largely begins and ends at this stage. In most cases the available assets are insufficient to provide adequately for the needs of two homes. The court seeks to stretch modest finite resources so far as possible to meet the parties' needs. Especially where children are involved it may be necessary to augment the available assets by having recourse to the future earnings of the money-earner, by way of an order for periodical payments.

13. Another strand, recognised more explicitly now than formerly, is compensation. This is aimed at redressing any significant prospective economic disparity between the parties arising from the way they conducted their marriage. For instance, the parties may have arranged their affairs in a way which has greatly advantaged the husband in terms of his earning capacity but left the wife severely handicapped so far as her own earning capacity is concerned. Then the wife suffers a double loss: a diminution in her earning capacity and the loss of a share in her husband's enhanced income. This is often the case. Although less marked than in the past, women may still suffer a disproportionate financial loss on the breakdown of a marriage because of their traditional role as home-maker and child-carer.

Here Lord Nicholls seems to be aware of the literature which shows the drop in women's income and the increase in men's post divorce (Fisher and Low 2009).[45] He goes on:

15. Compensation and financial needs often overlap in practice, so double-counting has to be avoided. But they are distinct concepts, and they are far from co-terminous. A claimant wife may be able to earn her own living but she may still be entitled to a measure of compensation.

This statement offers an interesting perspective on the clean-break principle: at what point ought a claimant's ability to support herself determine the award to which she is entitled?

16. A third strand is sharing. This 'equal sharing' principle derives from the basic concept of equality permeating a marriage as understood today. Marriage, it is often said, is a partnership of equals. In 1992 Lord Keith of Kinkel approved Lord Emslie's observation that 'husband and

---

[45] See also discussion in Chapter 3 above.

wife are now for all practical purposes equal partners in marriage': *R v R* [1992] 1 AC 599, 617. This is now recognised widely, if not universally. The parties commit themselves to sharing their lives. They live and work together. When their partnership ends each is entitled to an equal share of the assets of the partnership, unless there is a good reason to the contrary. Fairness requires no less. But I emphasise the qualifying phrase: 'unless there is good reason to the contrary'. The yardstick of equality is to be applied as an aid, not a rule.

17. This principle is applicable as much to short marriages as to long marriages: see *Foster v Foster* [2003] EWCA Civ 565; [2003] 2 FLR 299, 305, para 19 per Hale LJ. A short marriage is no less a partnership of equals than a long marriage. The difference is that a short marriage has been less enduring. In the nature of things this will affect the quantum of the financial fruits of the partnership.

Here Lord Nicholls states clearly that the yardstick of equality does not apply only to long marriages such as that in *White*. Let us now examine Baroness Hale's interpretation of the three 'rationales for division'.

138. The most common rationale is that *the relationship has generated needs* which it is right that the other party should meet. In the great majority of cases, the court is trying to ensure that each party and their children have enough to supply their needs, set at a level as close as possible to the standard of living which they enjoyed during the marriage (note that the House did not adopt a restrictive view of needs in *White*: see pp 608g to 609a). This is a perfectly sound rationale where the needs are the consequence of the parties' relationship, as they usually are. The most common source of need is the presence of children, whose welfare is always the first consideration, or of other dependent relatives, such as elderly parents. But another source of need is having had to look after children or other family members in the past. Many parents have seriously compromised their ability to attain self-sufficiency as a result of past family responsibilities. Even if they do their best to re-enter the employment market, it will often be at a lesser level than before, and they will hardly ever be able to make up what they have lost in pension entitlements. A further source of need may be the way in which the parties chose to run their life together. Even dual career families are difficult to manage with completely equal opportunity for both. Compromises often have to be made by one so that the other can get ahead. All couples throughout their lives together have to make choices about who will do what, sometimes forced upon them by circumstances such as redundancy or low pay, sometimes freely made in the interests of them both. The needs generated by such choices are a perfectly sound rationale for adjusting the parties' respective resources in compensation.

Note here Baroness Hale's acknowledgement of party autonomy and choice, but also her contextualisation of that choice as being situated in and sometimes affected by its public and private conditions. She goes on:

139. But while need is often a sound rationale, it should not be seen as a limiting principle if other rationales apply. This was the error into which the law had fallen before *White*. Need had become 'reasonable requirements' and thus more generous to the recipient, but it was still a limiting factor even where there was a substantial surplus of resources over needs ... . Counsel would talk of the 'discipline of the budget' and suggestions that a wife's budget might properly contain a margin for savings and contingencies, or to pass on to her grandchildren, were greeted with disbelief.

140. A second rationale, which is closely related to need, is *compensation for relationship-generated disadvantage*. Indeed, some consider that provision for need is compensation for relationship-generated disadvantage. But the economic disadvantage generated by the relation-

ship may go beyond need, however generously interpreted. The best example is a wife, like Mrs McFarlane, who has given up what would very probably have been a lucrative and successful career. If the other party, who has been the beneficiary of the choices made during the marriage, is a high earner with a substantial surplus over what is required to meet both parties' needs, then a premium above needs can reflect that relationship-generated disadvantage.

141. A third rationale is *the sharing of the fruits of the matrimonial partnership*. One reason given by the Law Commission for not adopting any one single model was that the flexibility of section 25 allowed practice to develop in response to changing perceptions of what might be fair. There is now a widespread perception that marriage is a partnership of equals. The Scottish Law Commission found that this translated into widespread support for a norm of equal sharing of the partnership assets when the marriage ended, whatever the source or legal ownership of those assets (Scot Law Com No 67, paras 3.66 to 3.68). A decade earlier, the English Law Commission had found widespread support for the automatic joint ownership of the matrimonial home, even during marriage (*First Report on Family Property—A New Approach*, 1973, Law Com No 52). Earlier still, the checklist of factors accompanying the new powers of property allocation in the Matrimonial Proceedings and Property Act 1970 had introduced the contributions which each party had made to the welfare of the family, including the contribution made by looking after the home and caring for the children. Thirty years later, the authors of *Settling Up* ... found that 'there appeared to be a relatively widespread assumption that an "equal" or 50/50 division was the normal or appropriate thing to do', alongside a recognition of needs and entitlements (but their respondents' views on entitlements might not be quite the same as the lawyers', a point to which I shall return).

142. Of course, an equal partnership does not necessarily dictate an equal sharing of the assets. In particular, it may have to give way to the needs of one party or the children. Too strict an adherence to equal sharing and the clean break can lead to a rapid decrease in the primary carer's standard of living and a rapid increase in the breadwinner's. The breadwinner's unimpaired and unimpeded earning capacity is a powerful resource which can frequently repair any loss of capital after an unequal distribution. (Some references omitted)

Q What views of equality can you identify from Lord Nicholls' speech? From Baroness Hale's?

For the vast majority of divorcing spouses, it is all they can do to meet each party's needs, and the principles by which they do so are clear (Hitchings 2009). These elements of fairness are helpful, however, for determining ancillary relief for parties with significant resources. They do answer one of the questions that arose from *White* regarding the yardstick of equality, conceived here as the equal sharing principle, but they raise others. It is clear, for example, that the equal sharing principle applies to all marriages, regardless of their length, although duration of the marriage may have some effect on the treatment of certain assets. In this connection, the decision was less clear on the question of when departures from equal sharing would be fair. In some cases it would depend on the nature of the asset. Lord Nicholls sought to draw a distinction between matrimonial and non-matrimonial property:

20. ... the courts should be exceedingly slow to introduce, or re-introduce, a distinction between 'family' assets and 'business or investment' assets. In all cases the nature and source of the parties' property are matters to be taken into account when determining the requirements of fairness. The decision of Munby J in *P v P (Inherited Property)* [2005] 1 FLR 576 regarding a family farm is an instance. But 'business and investment' assets can be the financial fruits of a marriage partnership as much as 'family' assets. The equal sharing principle applies to the

former as well as the latter. The rationale underlying the sharing principle is as much applicable to 'business and investment' assets as to 'family' assets.

Matrimonial property and non-matrimonial property

21. A complication rears its head at this point. I have referred to the financial fruits of the marriage partnership. In some countries the law draws a sharp distinction between assets acquired during a marriage and other assets. In Scotland, for instance, one of the statutorily prescribed principles is that the parties should share the value of the 'matrimonial property' equally or in such proportions as special circumstances may justify. Matrimonial property means the matrimonial home plus property acquired during the marriage otherwise than by gift or inheritance: Family Law (Scotland) Act 1985, sections 9 and 10. In England and Wales the Matrimonial Causes Act 1973 draws no such distinction. By section 25(2)(a) the court is bidden to have regard, quite generally, to the property and financial resources each of the parties to the marriage has or is likely to have in the foreseeable future.

22. This does not mean that, when exercising his discretion, a judge in this country must treat all property in the same way. The statute requires the court to have regard to all the circumstances of the case. One of the circumstances is that there is a real difference, a difference of source, between (1) property acquired during the marriage otherwise than by inheritance or gift, sometimes called the marital acquest but more usually the matrimonial property, and (2) other property. The former is the financial product of the parties' common endeavour, the latter is not. The parties' matrimonial home, even if this was brought into the marriage at the outset by one of the parties, usually has a central place in any marriage. So it should normally be treated as matrimonial property for this purpose. As already noted, in principle the entitlement of each party to a share of the matrimonial property is the same however long or short the marriage may have been.

23. The matter stands differently regarding property ('non-matrimonial property') the parties bring with them into the marriage or acquire by inheritance or gift during the marriage. Then the duration of the marriage will be highly relevant. The position regarding non-matrimonial property was summarised in the White case [2001] 1 AC 596, 610:

'Plainly, when present, this factor is one of the circumstances of the case. It represents a contribution made to the welfare of the family by one of the parties to the marriage. The judge should take it into account. He should decide how important it is in the particular case. The nature and value of the property, and the time when and circumstances in which the property was acquired, are among the relevant matters to be considered. However, in the ordinary course, this factor can be expected to carry little weight, if any, in a case where the claimant's financial needs cannot be met without recourse to this property.'

24. In the case of a short marriage fairness may well require that the claimant should not be entitled to a share of the other's non-matrimonial property. The source of the asset may be a good reason for departing from equality. This reflects the instinctive feeling that parties will generally have less call upon each other on the breakdown of a short marriage.

25. With longer marriages the position is not so straightforward. Non-matrimonial property represents a contribution made to the marriage by one of the parties. Sometimes, as the years pass, the weight fairly to be attributed to this contribution will diminish, sometimes it will not. After many years of marriage the continuing weight to be attributed to modest savings introduced by one party at the outset of the marriage may well be different from the weight attributable to a valuable heirloom intended to be retained in specie. Some of the matters to be taken into account in this regard were mentioned in the above citation from the White case. To this non-exhaustive list should be added, as a relevant matter, the way the parties organised their financial affairs.

Flexibility

26. This difference in treatment of matrimonial property and non-matrimonial property might suggest that in every case a clear and precise boundary should be drawn between these two categories of property. This is not so. Fairness has a broad horizon. Sometimes, in the case of a business, it can be artificial to attempt to draw a sharp dividing line as at the parties' wedding day. Similarly the 'equal sharing' principle might suggest that each of the party's assets should be separately and exactly valued. But valuations are often a matter of opinion on which experts differ. A thorough investigation into these differences can be extremely expensive and of doubtful utility. The costs involved can quickly become disproportionate. The case of Mr and Mrs Miller illustrates this only too well.

27. Accordingly, where it becomes necessary to distinguish matrimonial property from non-matrimonial property the court may do so with the degree of particularity or generality appropriate in the case. The judge will then give to the contribution made by one party's non-matrimonial property the weight he considers just. He will do so with such generality or particularity as he considers appropriate in the circumstances of the case.

Lord Nicholls' view of fairness, therefore, is that while the equal sharing principle is presumed to apply to all property acquired during the marriage—that which he calls 'matrimonial property'—courts must be flexible about applying it to 'non-matrimonial property'—that which the parties bring in to the marriage or acquire by inheritance or gift during the marriage. His reference to the *White* comments also means that this distinction seems to be relevant only under the sharing strand of fairness; 'non-matrimonial property' usually will not be treated differently if it is required to meet needs, for example.

Baroness Hale also found that the source or type of property might be relevant to fair decisions about it. Her distinction was slightly different from that of Lord Nicholls, however.

The source of the assets and the length of the marriage

147. Nevertheless, such debates [about valuing contributions] are evidence of unease at the fairness of dividing equally great wealth which has either been brought into the marriage or generated by the business efforts and acumen of one party. It is principally in this context that there is also a perception that the size of the non-business partner's share should be linked to the length of the marriage: see, eg, Eekelaar, 'Asset Distribution on Divorce—the Durational Element' (2001) 117 LQR 552; and 'Asset Distribution on Divorce—Time and Property' [2003] Fam Law 828; and GW v RW (Financial Provision: Departure from Equality) [2003] 2 FLR 108.

148. The strength of these perceptions is such that it could be unwise for the law to ignore them completely. In White v White [2001] 1 AC 596, it was recognised that the source of the assets might be a reason for departing from the yardstick of equality (see p 610c–g). There, the reason was that property had been acquired from or with the help of the husband's father during the marriage, but the same would apply to property acquired before the marriage. In White, it was also recognised that the importance of the source of the assets will diminish over time (see p 611b). As the family's personal and financial inter-dependence grows, it becomes harder and harder to disentangle what came from where. But the fact that the family's wealth consists largely of a family business, such as a farm, may still be taken into account as a reason for departing from full equality: see P v P (Inherited Property) [2004] EWHC 1364 (Fam); [2005] 1 FLR 576. So too may be the nature of the assets, where these are businesses which will be crippled or lose much of their value, if disposed of prematurely in order to fund an equal division: see N v N (Financial Provision: Sale of Company) [2001] 2 FLR 69.

149. The question, therefore, is whether in the very big money cases, it is fair to take some account of the source and nature of the assets, in the same way that some account is taken of the source of those assets in inherited or family wealth. Is the 'matrimonial property' to consist of everything acquired during the marriage (which should probably include periods of pre-marital cohabitation and engagement) or might a distinction be drawn between 'family' and other assets? Family assets were described by Lord Denning in the landmark case of Wachtel v Wachtel [1973] Fam 72, at 90:

> 'It refers to those things which are acquired by one or other or both of the parties, with the intention that there should be continuing provision for them and their children during their joint lives, and used for the benefit of the family as a whole.'

Prime examples of family assets of a capital nature were the family home and its contents, while the parties' earning capacities were assets of a revenue nature. But also included are other assets which were obviously acquired for the use and benefit of the whole family, such as holiday homes, caravans, furniture, insurance policies and other family savings. To this list should clearly be added family businesses or joint ventures in which they both work. It is easy to see such assets as the fruits of the marital partnership. It is also easy to see each party's efforts as making a real contribution to the acquisition of such assets. Hence it is not at all surprising that Mr and Mrs McFarlane agreed upon the division of their capital assets, which were mostly of this nature, without prejudice to how Mrs McFarlane's future income provision would be quantified.

150. More difficult are business or investment assets which have been generated solely or mainly by the efforts of one party. The other party has often made some contribution to the business, at least in its early days, and has continued with her agreed contribution to the welfare of the family (as did Mrs Cowan). But in these non-business-partnership, non-family asset cases, the bulk of the property has been generated by one party. Does this provide a reason for departing from the yardstick of equality? On the one hand is the view, already expressed, that commercial and domestic contributions are intrinsically incommensurable. It is easy to count the money or property which one has acquired. It is impossible to count the value which the other has added to their lives together. One is counted in money or money's worth. The other is counted in domestic comfort and happiness. If the law is to avoid discrimination between the gender roles, it should regard all the assets generated in either way during the marriage as family assets to be divided equally between them unless some other good reason is shown to do otherwise.

151. On the other hand is the view that this is unrealistic. We do not yet have a system of community of property, whether full or deferred. Even modest legislative steps towards this have been strenuously resisted. Ownership and contributions still feature in divorcing couples' own perceptions of a fair result, some drawing a distinction between the home and joint savings accounts, on the one hand, and pensions, individual savings and debts, on the other (Settling Up ...). Some of these are not family assets in the way that the home, its contents and the family savings are family assets. Their value may well be speculative or their possession risky. It is not suggested that the domestic partner should share in the risks or potential liabilities, a problem which bedevils many community of property regimes and can give domestic contributions a negative value. It simply cannot be demonstrated that the domestic contribution, important though it has been to the welfare and happiness of the family as a whole, has contributed to their acquisition. If the money maker had not had a wife to look after him, no doubt he would have found others to do it for him. Further, great wealth can be generated in a very short time, as the Miller case shows; but domestic contributions by their very nature take time to mature into contributions to the welfare of the family.

152. My lords, while I do not think that these arguments can be ignored, I think that they are irrelevant in the great majority of cases. In the very small number of cases where they might

make a difference, of which Miller may be one, the answer is the same as that given in White v White [2001] 1 AC 596 in connection with pre-marital property, inheritance and gifts. The source of the assets may be taken into account but its importance will diminish over time. Put the other way round, the court is expressly required to take into account the duration of the marriage: section 25(2)(d). If the assets are not 'family assets', or not generated by the joint efforts of the parties, then the duration of the marriage may justify a departure from the yardstick of equality of division. As we are talking here of a departure from that yardstick, I would prefer to put this in terms of a reduction to reflect the period of time over which the domestic contribution has or will continue (see Bailey-Harris, 'Comment on GW v RW (Financial Provision: Departure from Equality)' [2003] Fam Law 386, at p 388) rather than in terms of accrual over time (see Eekelaar, 'Asset Distribution on Divorce—Time and Property' [2003] Fam Law 828). This avoids the complexities of devising a formula for such accruals.

Baroness Hale thus preferred to distinguish between 'family assets'—those that are generated by the joint efforts of the parties—and non-family assets. Unlike Lord Nicholls, however, she included in the category of non-family assets investment or business assets generated solely or mainly by the efforts of one partner. This is the approach that has been followed.[46] Like premarital property, inheritances or gifts, non-family assets may be treated differently; a departure from their equality of division may be justified. But, like Lord Nicholls' treatment of 'non-matrimonial' assets, the importance of their designation as non-family assets will diminish over time.

Miller/McFarlane also opened up questions about how the three strands of fairness ought to be balanced. Lord Nicholls:

> There can be no invariable rule on this. Much will depend upon the amounts involved. Generally a convenient course might be for the court to consider first the requirements of compensation and then to give effect to the sharing entitlement. If this course is followed provision for the parties' financial needs will be subsumed into the sharing entitlement. But there will be cases where this approach would not achieve a fair outcome overall. In some cases provision for the financial needs may be more fairly assessed first along with compensation and the sharing entitlement applied only to the residue of the assets. Needless to say, it all depends upon the circumstances. (para 29)

Baroness Hale agreed:

> [T]there cannot be a hard and fast rule about whether one starts with equal sharing and departs if need or compensation supply a reason to do so, or whether one starts with need and compensation and shares the balance. Much will depend upon how far future income is to be shared as well as current assets. In general, it can be assumed that the marital partnership does not stay alive for the purpose of sharing future resources unless this is justified by need or compensation. The ultimate objective is to give each party an equal start on the road to independent living. (para 144).

We can see that the law was developing rapidly in the early 2000s. Concepts of non-discrimination and equality were becoming essential ingredients of 'fairness', which also took into account compensation and assumptions about the 'inherent' nature of the marital partnership. Baroness Hale's statement that 'the ultimate objective is to give each party an equal start on the road to independent living' reinforced also autonomy and the clean-break principle.

---

[46] *H v H* [2007] EWHC 459 (Fam); [2007] 2 FLR 548.

Q Recall that we said earlier that the legislation itself does not disclose any one principled basis or rationale for division of finances and property at all on divorce. Parts of it reveal a needs-based or income security model in which the obligation to support arises from the marriage itself and the quantum and duration of support from a simple calculation of the parties' needs and means, regardless of the source of those needs and means; parts contain elements of a compensation model; and parts point to a clean-break model. In your view, do the judicial interpretations of the MCA 1973 provided by *White* and *Miller/ McFarlane* clarify this question?

We must now look to the third of the recent leading cases on ancillary relief which contributes to that discussion. *Charman v Charman*[47] concerned a 28-year marriage. There were two children of the marriage, both adults at the time of the divorce. When the parties married neither had substantial assets and both were working. The wife quit her employment with local government when their first child was born in 1982. The husband's career prospered enormously. By the time of the divorce, the parties' wealth amounted to £131 million, of which the wife held £8 million and the husband £123 million. The wife at the time of the divorce had no income and sat as a magistrate. The husband's income was approximately £2 million per year. The case arrived at the Court of Appeal on the husband's application to set aside the trial court's award of £40 million to the wife on the grounds, inter alia, that the court failed to take sufficient account of his exceptional or stellar contributions to the making of the family fortune. The court said that in doing so, it was required 'to consider and interpret some of the guidance to the quantification of awards of ancillary relief, especially where the assets are large, given by the House of Lords in *White v White* and, in particular, in *Miller v Miller, McFarlane v McFarlane*' (para 6, per Potter P for the Court). Potter, P goes on:

[63] The best way for us to address Mr Singleton's attack on the judge's treatment of the husband's special contribution is to do so by reference to our interpretation of what is now the proper approach to a case of alleged special contribution, first considering the general nature of the statutory exercise. Two objectives will govern what we say. The first is to be loyal to what we understand to be the spirit as well as the letter of such guidance on the topic as has been given by the House of Lords in *White* and *Miller*, whether or not it is part of the reasoning behind those actual decisions. We say so because there is no doubt that, under that guidance, the House has left much for the courts to develop. The second is to express ourselves as clearly and simply as the subject allows.

[64] 'The yardstick of equality of division', first identified by Lord Nicholls in *White* at p 605G, filled the vacuum which resulted from the abandonment in that decision of the criterion of 'reasonable requirements'. The origins of the yardstick lay in s 25(2) of the Act, specifically in s 25(2)(f), which refers to the parties' contributions: see the preceding argument of Lord Nicholls at p 605D–E. The yardstick reflected a modern, non-discriminatory conclusion that the proper evaluation under s 25(2)(f) of the parties' different contributions to the welfare of the family should generally lead to an equal division of their property unless there was good reason for the division to be unequal. It also tallied with the overarching objective: a fair result.

[65] Although in *White* the majority of the House agreed with the speech of Lord Nicholls and thus with his description of equality as a 'yardstick' against which tentative views should be 'checked', Lord Cooke, at p 615D, doubted whether use of the words 'yardstick' or 'check'

---

[47] [2007] EWCA Civ 503; [2007] 1 FLR 1246.

would produce a result different from that of the words 'guideline' or 'starting point'. In *Miller* the House clearly moved towards the position of Lord Cooke. Thus Lord Nicholls, at 20 and 29, referred to the 'equal sharing principle' and to the 'sharing entitlement'; those phrases describe more than a yardstick for use as a check. Baroness Hale put the matter beyond doubt when, referring to remarks by Lord Nicholls at 29, she said, at 144:

> 'I agree that there cannot be a hard and fast rule about whether one starts with equal sharing and departs if need or compensation supply a reason to do so, or whether one starts with need and compensation and shares the balance.'

It is clear that the court's consideration of the sharing principle is no longer required to be postponed until the end of the statutory exercise. We should add that, since we take the "the sharing principle" to mean that property should be shared in equal proportions unless there is good reason to depart from such proportions, departure is not *from* the principle but takes place *within* the principle.

It seems from these words that 'equal sharing' or the 'yardstick of equality' would now be the starting point in the Court's assessment. But in *B v B*,[48] decided after *Charman*, the Court of Appeal cast doubt upon this interpretation, emphasising its wide discretion and equal sharing as a retrospective yardstick. What is clear is that equal sharing applies to all property, but the designation or source of the property may provide justification to depart from it. Potter P continues:

> [66] To what property does the sharing principle apply? The answer might well have been that it applies only to matrimonial property, namely the property of the parties generated during the marriage otherwise than by external donation; and the consequence would have been that non-matrimonial property would have fallen for redistribution by reference only to one of the two other principles of need and compensation to which we refer in para 68 below. Such an answer might better have reflected the origins of the principle in the parties' contributions to the welfare of the family; and it would have been more consonant with the references of Baroness Hale in *Miller* at 141 and 143 to 'sharing ... the fruits of the matrimonial partnership' and to 'the approach of roughly equal sharing of partnership assets'. We consider, however, the answer to be that, subject to the exceptions identified in *Miller* to which we turn in paras 83 to 86 below, the principle applies to all the parties' property but, to the extent that their property is non-matrimonial, there is likely to be better reason for departure from equality. It is clear that both in *White* at p 605F–G and in *Miller* at 24 and 26 Lord Nicholls approached the matter in that way; and there was no express suggestion in *Miller*, even on the part of Baroness Hale, that in *White* the House had set too widely the general application of what was then a yardstick.

> ...

> [68] In *Miller* the House unanimously identified three main principles which together inform the second stage of the enquiry, namely that of distribution: 'need (generously interpreted), compensation, and sharing', per Baroness Hale at 144; and see, similarly, Lord Nicholls at 10 to 16. The three principles must be applied in the light of the size and nature of all the computed resources, which are usually heavily circumscribing factors.

> [69] It is worthy of note that, although two of them are not expressly mentioned, each of the three distributive principles can be collected from s 25(2), or at any rate from s 25(1) and (2), of the Act and that each of the matters set out in (b) to (h) of s 25(2) can conveniently be assigned to one or another of the three of them.

---

[48] [2008] EWCA Civ 543.

...

[73] Then arises a difficult question: how does the court resolve any irreconcilable conflict between the result suggested by one principle and that suggested by another? Often conflict can be reconciled by recourse to an order for periodical payments: as for example in *McFarlane*, per Baroness Hale at 154. Ultimately, however, in cases in which it is irreconcilable, the criterion of fairness must supply the answer. It is clear that, when the result suggested by the needs principle is an award of property greater than the result suggested by the sharing principle, the former result should in principle prevail: per Baroness Hale in *Miller* at 142 and 144. At least in applying the needs principle the court will have focussed upon the needs of both parties; analogous focus on the Respondent is not present in the compensation principle and we leave for another occasion the proper treatment of irreconcilable conflict between that principle and one of the others. It is also clear that, when the result suggested by the needs principle is an award of property less than the result suggested by the sharing principle, the latter result should in principle prevail: per Lord Nicholls in *Miller* at 28 and 29 and Baroness Hale at 139.

Thus, a court must always be prepared to depart from equal sharing where needs require. The place of compensation relative to needs and equal sharing is more difficult to discern from this decision. Compensation for relationship-generated disadvantage might occur, for example, when a party's needs are met, and so no separate compensatory award is necessary. But as Baroness Hale stated, sometimes compensation will be 'fair' over and above a calculation of needs. What is not clear, however, is whether compensation is always subsumed within equal sharing. Once needs are met, can the compensation strand ever justify a departure from equal sharing?[49]

Charman v Charman also considered how a special contribution to the welfare of the family ought to justify a departure from equality.

[79] It was inevitable, so it seems to us, that the notion of a special contribution should have 'survived' the decision in *Miller*. The statutory requirement in every case to consider the contributions which each party has made to the welfare of the family, as well as those which each is likely to make to it, would be inconsistent with a blanket rule that their past contributions to its welfare must be afforded equal weight. Nevertheless the difficulty attendant upon a comparison of their different contributions and the danger of its infection by discrimination against the home-maker led the House in *Miller* heavily to circumscribe the situations in which it would be appropriate to find that one party had made a special contribution, in the sense of a contribution by one unmatched by the other, which, for the purpose of the sharing principle, should lead to departure from equality. In this regard the House was unanimous

[80] The notion of a special contribution to the welfare of the family will not successfully have been purged of inherent gender discrimination unless it is accepted that such a contribution can, in principle, take a number of forms; that it can be non-financial as well as financial; and that it can thus be made by a party whose role has been exclusively that of a home-maker. Nevertheless in practice, and for a self-evident reason, the claim to have made a special contribution seems so far to have arisen only in cases of substantial wealth generated by a party's success in business during the marriage. The self-evident reason is that in such cases there is substantial property over the distribution of which it is worthwhile to argue. In such cases can the amount

---

[49] In *VB v JP* [2008] EWHC 112 (Fam); [2008] 1 FLR 742 Potter, P considered that compensation arises only as an element of fairness and not as a head of claim in its own right, but that there are circumstances in which it might demand a specific part in the award. In many cases, however, compensation is subsumed within a 'generous assessment of needs' and part of the award is not specifically designated to it (*Lauder v Lauder* [2007] EWHC 1227; [2007] 2 FLR 802).

of the wealth alone make the contribution special? Or must the focus always be upon the manner of its generation? In *Lambert* Thorpe LJ said, at 52:

'There may be cases where the product alone justifies a conclusion of a special contribution but absent some exceptional and individual quality in the generator of the fortune a case for special contribution must be hard to establish.'

From these words we see that a special contribution sufficient to justify a departure from equality would seem to be rare. It may, however, be found simply by the sheer size of the fortune that was generated during the marriage.

Charman v Charman, together with *White* and *Miller/McFarlane*, has generated much discussion and debate. Some has been critical (Deech 2009b; Thorpe LJ 2009), some has been broadly positive (Diduck 2009b), and much has been more cautious and equivocal (Cooke 2007; Miles 2005, 2008; Diduck 2011). Much of the criticism has focused upon the uncertainty the decisions are said to have brought to the law and some have focused upon the unfairness they have created for the wealthy partner (usually husband). These high-profile cases concerning very wealthy individuals have also been reported in the press, again usually reflecting adversely upon their effect on wealthy husbands (eg *The Daily Telegraph* Online 2007, 2011). In many cases, critics have called upon Parliament to re-enter the fray and review the MCA 1973 with a view to reform. The Court of Appeal in *Charman* itself registered its dissatisfaction with the current state of affairs for all the above reasons in the little-used form of a postscript to its judgment. It first noted the law as it stood before *White*:

[106] … The Applicant's reasonable requirements became the focus of the case, throughout its preparation and in its final determination. This method brought predictability and clarity, characteristics that were refined by a mechanism for capitalising the Applicant's future spending requirement, a mechanism inferentially sanctioned by this court in its decision in *Duxbury v Duxbury* [1992] Fam 62n, [1990] 2 All ER 77, [1987] 1 FLR 7. The emphasis on the Applicant's reasonable requirements as the yardstick of the award satisfied the anxiety of judges and others that we should not be drawn into the extravagance of some American states, particularly California, where very large awards were commonplace. This judicial preference for moderation ruled essentially for a generation from the mid 1970s to the year 2000. It suited the society of its day.

But it also reminded us that calls for reform went unheeded during the 1990s, even after the government's *Supporting Families* (Home Office 1998) recommended reforming the MCA 1973, not so as to create any presumptions in law which would unduly fetter judicial discretion, but to include a number of prioritised aims and an overarching objective. The Court in *Charman* went on:

[114] Was the need for reform met by the decision of the House in *White*? The decision deprived practitioners and judges of the old measure of reasonable requirements, offering instead the cross check of equality to ensure fairness and to banish discrimination.

[115] Of course these innovations were well founded on profound social change, particularly in the recognition that marriage is a partnership of equals and that the role of man and woman within the marriage are commonly interchangeable. In the majority of cases the innovations resulting from *White* were timely and beneficial.

[116] However, a social change that was not perhaps recognised in that decision was the extent to which the origins and the volume of big money cases were shifting. Most of the big money

cases pre *White* involved fortunes created by previous generations. The removal of exchange control restrictions in 1979, a policy that offered a favourable tax regime to very rich foreigners domiciled elsewhere, and a new financial era dominated by hedge-funds, private equity funds, derivative traders and sophisticated off-shore structures meant that very large fortunes were being made very quickly. These socio-economic developments coincided with a retreat from the preference of English judges for moderation. The present case well illustrates that shift. At trial Mr Pointer achieved for his client an award of £48 million. Before us he freely conceded that he could not have justified an award of more than £20 million on the application of the reason-able requirements principle. Thus, in very big money cases, the effect of the decision in *White* was to raise the aspirations of the Claimant hugely. In big money cases the *White* factor has more than doubled the levels of award and it has been said by many that London has become the divorce capital of the world for aspiring wives. Whether this is a desirable result needs to be considered not only in the context of our society but also in the context of the European Union of which we are a singular Member State, in the sense that we are a common law jurisdiction amongst largely Civilian fellows and that in the determination of issues ancillary to divorce we apply the *lex fori* and decline to apply the law more applicable to the parties.

This postscript is interesting. First, before *White*, it is arguable that London was the 'divorce capital of the world' for wealthy divorcing husbands; in the *Dart* case Mr Dart fought to ensure his divorce was heard in England because he knew his wife's claim would be limited to the court's determination of her 'reasonable requirements'. Yet this state of affairs was accepted so that we would not be drawn into the 'extravagance' of those jurisdictions where large awards were commonplace. Recall also Bennett's observa-tion in 1997 that awards in 'big money cases' in England were

> out of line with most other non-Islamic jurisdictions. At a recent meeting of the International Bar Association, Family Law Committee, on multi-million dollar divorces ... [t]he conclusion was that the award to the wife in nearly 30 jurisdictions around the world would be from 10% to 50%, with the exception of England where it would be 0.6%. (Bennett 1997: 79)

Secondly, as Herring wonders, it is not clear why the perception of London as the 'divorce capital of the world' for its increased recognition of the value of childcare and need to combat gender discrimination is necessarily a bad thing: if our law is more progressive on these matters than other jurisdictions 'we should celebrate, not complain' (Herring 2011: 243).

Of course since *Charman* was decided in 2007 courts have attempted to work out its principles. Given that the vast majority of ancillary relief disputes do not reach the courts, however, those principles are only the shadow under which settlements are negotiated. Given also that the vast majority of disputes revolve around how to make enough money and property stretch across two households and not around what to do with vast wealth, it is unfortunate that the principles have been developed in these big-money cases. Before we examine how the principles have been interpreted in recent case law, let us review the basic approach to be taken by the courts.

First, the MCA 1973 gives courts broad discretion in matters of ancillary relief. It contains no objectives for the court to meet or guidelines for it to follow, but does contain a list of factors for the courts to consider in exercising their discretion. Apart from the welfare of any child of the marriage, which is to be a court's first consideration, and a duty to consider whether a clean break between the parties would be appropriate, no priority is assigned to any of the other factors. Second, as a result of judicial intervention, an overarching objective has been identified and that is to achieve fairness. Third, fairness contains three strands: needs, compensation and (equal) sharing. The court may then start from a position of equal sharing, but will depart from equality for a number of possible reasons, particularly and importantly, to meet needs.

Let us now look at the types of orders that can be made and how the courts have considered them in the light of these principles.

IV. MAKING THE ORDERS

The first step in any dispute is to identify all the parties' assets. Both parties are expected to make complete disclosure of their financial information before they appear in court.[50] It is only on the basis of full knowledge that they can make any arrangements to settle financial matters between themselves or expect the court to make any order. Rather than litigating, though, the rules and current policy encourage parties to settle.[51] If they are successful, the court will usually abide by their agreement and incorporate it into a consent order if asked to do so.[52] If one of the parties seeks to resile from an agreement previously made, but not yet incorporated in an order of court, the existence of such an agreement becomes a factor in the court's exercise of its discretion in determining overall ancillary relief. The court in this case will not lightly set aside an agreement made between two competent adults after receiving legal advice, but will retain its duty to ensure the overall fairness of the agreement.[53]

Q Negotiations between spouses or former spouses are often characterised by feelings of pain, blame and guilt—feelings that are not taken into account in law's understanding of a 'freely negotiated contract' between two formally equal individuals. Sometimes the parties' bargaining positions are unequal, affected as they may be by differences in economic power, connection with children, or by a stronger desire to end the marriage or a greater desire to make concessions. Feminist critiques of utilising strict formal equality principles in domestic bargaining situations argue that there is a need to take these considerations into account.[54] How could this be done? Further, as we noted above, many men negotiating ancillary matters on divorce felt that it was 'their' money that was being dealt with (Davis et al 1994: 49) and research from the United States found that in divorce 'men discuss with their attorneys ways to "keep" their property or assets, and women discuss ways to "get" assets' (Gray and Merrick 1996: 243). Finally, mothers' pragmatic but short-term concern for their children often outweighs concerns for their longer-term, personal financial welfare (Douglas and Perry 2001). What, if anything, can law or lawyers do about these issues?

[50] Fam Procedure Rules 2010 9.14.
[51] Fam Proc Rules 2010 1. See further Chapter 15 above; and Diduck (2003: ch 6).
[52] S 33A MCA 1973. The court retains its jurisdiction to examine the agreement, however, and will not simply act as a 'rubber stamp'. *Harris v Manahan* [1997] 1 FLR 205.
[53] See *Radmacher v Granatino* [2010] UKSC 42; [2010] 2 FLR 1900, and further discussion below. See also *Xydhias v Xydhias* [1999] 1 FLR 683; *X v X* [2002] 1 FLR 508; *Edgar v Edgar* [1980] 1 WLR 1410; *Smith v McInerney* [1994] 2 FLR 1077; and *Pounds v Pounds* [1994] 1 FLR 775.
[54] See Chapter 6 above and Diduck (1999b).

The MCA 1973[55] states that the court, once it has made a decree of divorce or judicial separation, may make financial provision orders, property transfer orders or orders for the sale of property either by consent of the parties or on application by one of them. On granting a decree of divorce or nullity, it may also make a pension-sharing order. The Civil Partnership Act 2004 gives the Court the same powers.[56]

A financial provision order under MCA 1973 is:

23(1)

(a) an order that either party to the marriage shall make to the other such periodical payments, for such term as may be specified in the order;

(b) an order that either party to the marriage shall secure to the other to the satisfaction of the court such periodical payments, for such term, as may be so specified;

(c) an order that either party to the marriage shall pay to the other such lump sum or sums as may be so specified;

[(d), (e) and (f) repeat these provisions in circumstances for payments to a person, or to a child of the family, for the benefit of that child.]

A property adjustment order is:

24(1)

(a) an order that a party to the marriage shall transfer to the other party, to any child of the family or to such person as may be specified in the order for the benefit of such a child such property as may be so specified, being property to which the first-mentioned party is entitled, either in possession or revision;

(b) an order that a settlement of such property as may be so specified, being property to which a party to the marriage is so entitled, be made to the satisfaction of the court for the benefit of the other party to the marriage and of the children of the family or either of them;

(c) an order varying for the benefit of the parties to the marriage and of the children of the family any ante-nuptial or post-nuptial settlement ... other than one in the form of a pension arrangement ...

(d) an order extinguishing or reducing the interest of either of the parties to the marriage under any such settlement other than one in the form of a pension arrangement ... .

An order for the sale of property is:

24A(1) Where the court makes under section 23 or 24 of this Act a secured periodical payments order, an order for the payment of a lump sum or a property adjustment order, then, on making that order or at any time thereafter, the court may make a further order for the sale of such property as may be specified in the order, being property in which or in the proceeds of sale in which either or both of the parties to the marriage has or have a beneficial interest either in possession or reversion.

An order for sale may contain:

---

[55] They may also use the Domestic Proceedings and Magistrates' Courts Act 1978 for more limited financial relief if they do not wish to divorce. See ss 1–7.

[56] Civil Partnership Act 2004 Sch 5. All of these orders are now called 'financial orders'. Fam Proc Rules 2010 2.3.

24A(2)

(a) provisions requiring the making of a payment out of the proceeds of sale of the property to which the order relates, and

(b) provision requiring any such property to be offered for sale to a person, or class of persons, specified in the order.

Finally, the court may make one or more pension-sharing orders.[57] We shall discuss pensions in more detail below, but for now it suffices that a pension-sharing order is defined as an order which 'provides that one party's (i) shareable rights under a specified pension arrangement, or (ii) shareable state scheme rights, be subject to pension sharing for the benefit of the other party, and (b) specifies the percentage value to be transferred' (MCA 1973 s 21A(1)(a)).

As we saw above, the matters to which the court will have regard are set out in section 25. Let us consider how courts have interpreted these factors to date.

25(1) It shall be the duty of the court ... to have regard to all the circumstances of the case, first consideration being given to the welfare of while a minor of any child of the family who has not attained the age of eighteen.

In this section 'child of the family' includes a child of both parties and any child who has been treated by both parties as a child of their family.[58] In *Suter v Suter and another*[59] the court clarified that 'first' did not mean 'paramount' but rather that the child's welfare was the first in the list of factors to consider.

25(2)(a) the income, earning capacity, property and their financial resources which each of the parties to the marriage has or is likely to have in the foreseeable future, including in the case of earning capacity any increase in that capacity which it would in the opinion of the court be reasonable to expect a party to the marriage to take steps to acquire.

The court may take into account not only current resources, but also those anticipated in the future. It may, for example, in the interests of the parties' ultimate financial independence from each other, require non-earning partners to find work, but it will usually acknowledge the difficulties that primary caretaking parents or homemakers who have been out of the job market for years face in obtaining employment. It may also anticipate increases in the payer's earning level. In *H v H*[60] the court held that a partner's earning capacity could be seen as an asset the other had helped to generate and a share of which, therefore, she was entitled to, if she could show that 'but for' her contribution, he would not be earning what he was. Charles J in taking this approach was concerned that 'the pendulum does not swing too far in favour of wives' (para 96). Other cases have taken a less restrictive approach. In *P v P*[61] the judge awarded the wife, in crude terms, £8.4 million and the husband £8.3 million of the current assets and justified this unequal split by allowing the husband the benefit of any increase in value of most of his remaining assets. He made an exception, though, by stating that the wife was to receive one-third of any

---

[57] MCA 1973 s 24B (1).
[58] MCA 1973 s 52(1).
[59] [1987] 2 FLR 232.
[60] [2008] 2 FCR 714.
[61] [2007] EWHC 2877; [2008] 2 FLR 1135.

amount over the husband's current valuation of shares in the new venture he was proposing to start.

This is also the section under which disputes arise about the relevance of the source of assets. As we saw above, while all assets are to be included, non-matrimonial or non-family assets may be treated differently in any potential division. In *Jones v Jones*[62] the question that faced the Court of Appeal was about post-separation assets in the form of a post-separation increase in the value of the husband's business. The court found that while a spouse's earning capacity may not be capitalised for the purposes of the sharing principle (para 26), the increase in value of the business did fall under the principle because it was a part of the latent value of the business at the time of separation, and therefore a matrimonial asset and not a new venture.

> (b) the financial needs, obligations and responsibilities which each of the parties to the marriage has or is likely to have in the foreseeable future.

As we noted above, need is the only assessment the court has to make in most cases. While it is assessed according to the standard of living the parties enjoyed together,[63] the courts are usually concerned first about housing, particularly to ensure adequate housing for any children of the marriage. If the parties own their home, and there is sufficient equity in it to provide funds[64] on its sale for each of them reasonably to rehouse themselves, the court might order a sale with a direction as to the allocation of the proceeds.[65] In *Piglowska v Piglowski*[66] the House of Lords approved this arrangement, but clarified that there was no right to housing for both parties, particularly where finances did not allow it.

> In *M v B (Ancillary Proceedings: Lump Sum)* [1998] 1 FLR 53, 60, Thorpe LJ said:
>
> > In all these cases it is one of the paramount considerations, in applying the section 25 criteria, to endeavour to stretch what is available to cover the need of each for a home, particularly where there are young children involved. Obviously the primary carer needs whatever is available to make the main home for the children, but it is of importance, albeit it is of lesser importance, that the other parent should have a home of his own where the children can enjoy their contact time with him. Of course there are cases where there is not enough to provide a home for either. Of course there are cases where there is only enough to provide one. But in any case where there is, by stretch and a degree of risk-taking, the possibility of a division to enable both to rehouse themselves, that is an exceptionally important consideration and one which will almost invariably have a decisive impact on outcome.
>
> My Lords, I do not doubt for a moment the sound sense of these remarks. That was a case in which the couple had two children aged 10 and six and the question was whether the wife should have a house which cost £210,000, leaving the husband without enough to buy a property of his own, or a house costing £135,000, leaving the husband £75,000 to buy a property of his own. The Court of Appeal held that the second approach was correct. This is a useful guideline to judges dealing with cases of a similar kind. But to cite the case as if it laid down some rule

---

[62] [2011] EWCA Civ 41; [2011] 1 FLR 1723.
[63] Eg *McCartney v Mills-McCartney* [2008] EWHC 401; [2008] 1 FLR 1508.
[64] Perhaps with the aid of a mortgage.
[65] Eg in *Scallon v Scallon* [1990] FLR 194.
[66] [1999] 1 WLR 13670; [1999] 2 FLR 763.

that both spouses invariably have a right to purchased accommodation is a misuse of authority.

(per Lord Hoffman, 1371–72)

Such an arrangement does have the advantage, say the courts, of furthering 'clean-break' principles. If, however, there would not be sufficient proceeds to allow the primary carer to find suitable accommodation for herself and the children, the court might protect the other party's interest in the home but at the same time allow the carer and child to continue living in it for a specified period of time or until the happening of a specified event.[67] In *Clutton v Clutton*[68] the court referred to this arrangement as a deferred clean break. Finally, the court can order an outright transfer of one party's interest in the home to the other, usually in exchange for some concessions with respect to other assets or future support. If they do not own their home but are renting it from the council, the court also has jurisdiction, under the Family Law Act 1996, to order the transfer of protected, statutory, secure and assured tenancies.[69]

The court will not deal with the home in isolation, therefore. In addition to it being a 'home', it is also considered to be one of the assets to be divided fairly, and so arrangements for dealing with it will be taken in the context of the ancillary relief as a whole.[70]

The court will also be concerned about the sources both of the need and of the available resources to meet that need. In *Miller/McFarlane* Baroness Hale was prepared to give a broad meaning to relationship-generated needs (para 138) and seemed to dismiss from the calculation needs arising from 'extrinsic, unrelated factors such as a disability arising after the marriage has ended' (para 137). It is difficult to find a clear interpretation of this statement, however. The better view is that the court will always consider these questions in its broad discretion. In *North v North*,[71] for example, Thorpe LJ stated that: '[The Respondent] is not an insurer against all hazards nor, when fairness is the measure, is he necessarily liable for needs created by the applicant's financial mismanagement, extravagance or irresponsibility' (para 32). However, he then went on to order payments to a wife after 20 years of divorce when she fell into financial need after moving to Australia and making unwise financial decisions.

When parties re-partner, the court is not permitted to include the resources of their new partners as the parties' resources, but it may take those resources or household contributions into account to reduce the needs of the claimant or free up resources for the respondent. We saw earlier that remarriage of the recipient terminates her periodical payments and while some have suggested that cohabitation ought to have the same effect,[72] until cohabitants acquire a statutory claim against each other, the most a court ought to do is determine not what a new partner is contributing but what he should be contributing

---

[67] As in *Mesher v Mesher and Hall* [1980] 1 All ER 126 where the wife was to remain in the home until the youngest child attained the age of 17, or in *Martin v Martin* [1978] Fam 12 where the wife remained in the home until she no longer needed it or remarried. See also *Elliott v Elliott* [2001] 1 FCR 477 where the court made a Mesher order on the basis of the equality principles in *White* and contrast this with *B v B (Mesher Order)* [2002] EWHC 3106; [2002] 2 FLR 285 where the court declined to make a Mesher order, saying that it would violate the equality principles in *White*. This was because the wife would be making a substantial contribution in the form of childcare for a number of years in the future and this contribution should be recognised. In addition, her childcare responsibilities would inhibit her capacity to build up capital, whereas the husband would be free to accumulate capital.

[68] [1991] 1 All ER 340.

[69] S 53, and Sch 7.

[70] For a fascinating treatment of the 'home' in law, see Fox (2006).

[71] [2007] EWCA Civ 760; [2008] 1 FLR 158.

[72] Per Coleridge J in *K v K* [2006] 4 FLR 288.

so as to reduce the needs of the recipient.[73] Conversely, when considering the parties' respective obligations, a payer's new family may not take priority over the old.[74]

(c) the standard of living enjoyed by the family before the breakdown of the marriage;

(d) the age of each party to the marriage and the duration of the marriage;

(e) any physical or mental disability of either of the parties to the marriage.

These three factors are normally subsumed under needs, although as we have seen, duration of the marriage may also be relevant to the treatment under the sharing principle of non-matrimonial/non-family assets.

(f) the contributions which each of the parties has made or is likely in the foreseeable future to make to the welfare of the family, including any contribution by looking after the home or caring for the family.

It was this factor that the House of Lords in *White* felt was given too little weight relative to the needs factor. Here is where the principle of non-discrimination, as well as the departures from equality have been argued.

(g) the conduct of each of the parties, if that conduct is such that it would in the opinion of the court be inequitable to disregard it.

The type of conduct considered by the courts to be 'inequitable to disregard' can be matrimonial conduct[75] or conduct relating to the family finances or property.[76] It can be conduct which was extremely advantageous for the family,[77] as well as conduct which disadvantages the family or the other party. The House of Lords confirmed in *Miller/McFarlane* that conduct short of this extreme kind is not relevant to fairness. Mrs Miller had argued that it was Mr Miller's affair that that caused the breakdown of the marriage.

The final factor is:

(h) in the case of proceedings for divorce or nullity of marriage, the value to each of the parties to the marriage of any benefit, which, by reason of the dissolution or annulment of the marriage, that party will lose the chance of acquiring.

Here the court would take into account the loss, for example, of pension rights such as widow's or widower's pension as a result of the divorce.

This list of factors is not exhaustive; the court is directed under section 25(1) MCA to take into account all the circumstances of the case. As we have seen, the court will attend to those circumstances in the light of its overarching goal of fairness and fashion an award that utilises one or a combination of the orders available to meet that goal. There are two special issues that arise, however, regarding fairness on relationship breakdown: pensions and marital property agreements.

---

[73] *Grey v Grey* [2009] EWCA Civ 1424; [2010] 1 FLR 1764.

[74] *Vaughan v Vaughan (no 2)* [2010] EWCA Civ 349; [2010] 2 FLR 242.

[75] See *B v B (Financial Provision Welfare of Child and Conduct)* [2002] 1 FLR 555.

[76] See *Beach v Beach* [1995] 2 FLR 160.

[77] *Kokosinski v Kokosinski* [1980] 1 All ER 1106.

The Special Case of Pensions

We saw in Chapter 6 the importance of pensions to a family's well-being in later life. Any rights accumulated under occupational pension plans are included in the 'pot' of assets available for distribution on granting a decree of divorce, dissolution or nullity. There are three ways in which the court (or a settlement agreement) can take pensions into account in that distribution. The first is to offset the value of the pension against another asset or a lump sum which the non-pensioned spouse, usually the wife, can invest for her future.[78] The difficulty with this option is that it is only available for wealthy spouses who have other assets of value, or available income against which to set off their pension. The other difficulty is that it gives the non-pensioned spouse the immediate benefit of an asset from which the pensioned spouse may never benefit. Finally, given the need of carers (usually wives) and children in their care for housing and some security in income in the years immediately following their separation or divorce, there is a trend towards offsetting a claim to future pension entitlement against the home. Lack of pension provision is one of the main casues of poverty for women in later life (Ginn 2002; Price 2011),[79] and divorced women are hit particularly hard: 43% of older divorced women live in poverty and this is directly related to the breadwinner/part-time worker norm, which means poor pension accumulation during marriage because of women's reliance on the breadwinner's pension. On divorce, they have too little time to catch up (Price 2011).

The second option is for the court to order the pension trustees or administrators to earmark a percentage of the pensioner's prospective pension income for the benefit of the non-pensioned party and to make payments to her in that proportion when the sums become payable to him on his retirement.[80] The disadvantage of this type of order is that the parties will not achieve a clean break. Also, if the spouse with the pension dies before it becomes payable, the other spouse will get nothing.

The final main option is pension sharing.[81] The court may make an order splitting the pension into portions representing the proportion it deems fair to allocate to each party. In effect, it creates two pensions out of one and each party becomes responsible to contribute to his or her pension as appropriate from then on. The advantages of this order are that it allows for a clean break, and seems to allow the court to make a fair division of the asset. A disadvantage is that because it requires the parties to continue to build up their separate pensions, it does not resolve the unfair disparities in retirement income between the parties: '[T]he constraints upon a divorced mother's employment and pension building continue' (Ginn 2002: 170; Price 2011). Finally, the courts have said that the MCA 1973 does not require them to make a pension-sharing order[82] and indeed pension-sharing or pension-attachment orders are made in only 7.9% of cases, usually involving only wealthy parties (Price 2011). Furthermore, it is possible that the proposed withdrawal of Legal Aid from marital disputes will exacerbate the problem.

---

[78] *Richardson v Richardson* [1978] 9 Fam Law 86.
[79] See also Chapter 6 above and Douglas and Perry (2001).
[80] MCA 1973 s 25B(4) and (5).
[81] MCA 1973 s 21A. Private occupational pensions can be the subject of this order, as state second pensions.
[82] *T v T (Financial Relief: Pensions)* [1998] 1 FLR 1072.

Prenuptial and Postnuptial Agreements

Part of the call for a review of the law on ancillary relief was also a call for Parliament to review the law on pre- and postnuptial agreements, or 'marital property agreements' (Supporting Familes Home Office 1998; *Charman v Charman* postscript). Parliament duly responded to this call, but while the Law Commission prepared its consultation document, the courts acted. In *Radmacher v Granatino*[83] the Supreme Court decided by a majority of 8–1, Lady Hale delivering a strong dissent, that the prenuptial agreement made in Germany between a German heiress and her French, significantly less wealthy, husband ought to be enforced. The agreement provided that neither party was to acquire any benefit from the property of the other during the marriage or on its termination. The legal principle established, or rather, confirmed by this case was not groundbreaking:

> 7. There can be no question of this Court altering the principle that it is the Court, and not any prior agreement between the parties, that will determine the appropriate ancillary relief when a marriage comes to an end, for that principle is embodied in the legislation. What the Court can do is to attempt to give some assistance in relation to the approach that a court considering ancillary relief should adopt towards an ante-nuptial agreement between the parties
>
> …
>
> 75. *White v White* and *Miller v Miller* establish that the overriding criterion to be applied in ancillary relief proceedings is that of fairness and identify the three strands of need, compensation and sharing that are relevant to the question of what is fair. If an ante-nuptial agreement deals with those matters in a way that the court might adopt absent such an agreement, there is no problem about giving effect to the agreement. The problem arises where the agreement makes provisions that conflict with what the court would otherwise consider to be the requirements of fairness. The fact of the agreement is capable of altering what is fair. It is an important factor to be weighed in the balance. We would advance the following proposition, to be applied in the case of both ante- and post-nuptial agreements, in preference to that suggested by the Board in *MacLeod*:
>
> > '*The court should give effect to a nuptial agreement that is freely entered into by each party with a full appreciation of its implications unless in the circumstances prevailing it would not be fair to hold the parties to their agreement.*' (emphasis in original)

Their reasoning was based upon an appeal to autonomy:

> 78. The reason why the court should give weight to a nuptial agreement is that there should be respect for individual autonomy. The court should accord respect to the decision of a married couple as to the manner in which their financial affairs should be regulated. It would be paternalistic and patronising to override their agreement simply on the basis that the court knows best. This is particularly true where the parties' agreement addresses existing circumstances and not merely the contingencies of an uncertain future.

In the result, the court described as 'obsolete' the traditional view that prenuptial agreements violated public policy because they anticipated a future separation, but did not give up their discretion to determine the weight to be ascribed to them. Prenuptial agreements are now to be treated the same as postnuptial agreements, which always carried weight in the exercise of the court's discretion.

---

[83] [2010] UKSC 42; [2010] 2 FLR 1900. Recall that these agreements were not binding upon the court, but did carry some weight.

As it promised, the court did attempt to give guidance on what may detract from the weight accorded to the agreement. First, 'if an ante-nuptial agreement, or indeed a post-nuptial agreement, is to carry full weight, both the husband and wife must enter into it of their own free will, without undue influence or pressure, and informed of its implications' (para 68). This much seems obvious. But then the court went on:

> Sound legal advice is obviously desirable, for this will ensure that a party understands the implications of the agreement, and full disclosure of any assets owned by the other party may be necessary to ensure this. But if it is clear that a party is fully aware of the implications of an ante-nuptial agreement and indifferent to detailed particulars of the other party's assets, there is no need to accord the agreement reduced weight because he or she is unaware of those particulars. (para 69)

Q Do you agree that full disclosure and independent legal advice may not always be necessary? The provisional proposal of the Law Commission was that a marital property agreement would not be enforceable against a party as a qualifying nuptial agreement unless that party had received material full and frank disclosure of the others party's financial situation (Law Commission 2011a: para 6.74) They left for further consultation the question of whether disclosure could be waived by the parties (ibid: para 6.75). The Commission also proposed that the parties be required to take legal advice before a nuptial contract is valid (ibid: para 6.88).

The Court also held that the standard vitiating factors of duress, fraud or misrepresentation also apply to nuptial agreements,

> but unconscionable conduct such as undue pressure (falling short of duress) will also be likely to eliminate the weight to be attached to the agreement, and other unworthy conduct, such as exploitation of a dominant position to secure an unfair advantage, would reduce or eliminate it. (para 71)

Lady Hale remarked in an earlier case on postnuptial agreements, *MacLeod v Macleod*,[84] that 'family relationships are not like straightforward commercial relationships. They are often characterised by inequality of bargaining power.' She developed this idea in her dissenting judgment in *Radmacher*:

> 135. Some may regard freedom of contract as the prevailing principle in all circumstances; others may regard that as a 19th century concept which has since been severely modified, particularly in the case of continuing relationships typically (though not invariably) characterised by imbalance of bargaining power (such as landlord and tenant, employer and employee). Some may regard people who are about to marry as in all respects fully autonomous beings; others may wonder whether people who are typically (although not invariably) in love can be expected to make rational choices in the same way that businessmen can. Some may regard the recognition of these factual differences as patronising or paternalistic; others may regard them as sensible and realistic. ... *Perhaps above all, some may think it permissible to contract out of the guiding principles of equality and non-discrimination within marriage; others may think this a retrograde step likely only to benefit the strong at the expense of the weak.* (emphasis added)

---

[84] [2008] UKPC 64, [2010] 1 AC 298 at para [42].

Q Is the relationship between the parties in a nuptial agreement relevant? Should they be treated as autonomous economic parties?

Lady Hale reminds us that the object of nuptial agreements is usually to protect the economically stronger party over the weaker.

137. Above all, perhaps, the court hearing a particular case can all too easily lose sight of the fact that, unlike a separation agreement, the object of an ante-nuptial agreement is to deny the economically weaker spouse the provision to which she—it is usually although by no means invariably she—would otherwise be entitled ... . Would any self-respecting young woman sign up to an agreement which assumed that she would be the only one who might otherwise have a claim, thus placing no limit on the claims that might be made against her, and then limited her claim to a pre-determined sum for each year of marriage regardless of the circumstances, as if her wifely services were being bought by the year? ... . *In short, there is a gender dimension to the issue which some may think ill-suited to decision by a court consisting of eight men and one woman.* (emphasis added, references omitted)

Let us continue with the list of factors highlighted by the majority in *Radmacher*, Apart from unequal bargaining power, the court may take into account 'a party's emotional state, and what pressures he or she was under to agree. ... The circumstances of the parties at the time of the agreement will be relevant. Those will include such matters as their age and maturity, whether either or both had been married or been in long-term relationships before' (para 72). Finally 'if the terms of the agreement are unfair from the start, this will reduce its weight, although this question will be subsumed in practice in the question of whether the agreement operates unfairly having regard to the circumstances prevailing at the time of the breakdown of the marriage' (para 73).

Herring describes the *Radmacher* decision as 'controversial' (Herring 2011: 252). He states first, that the benefits of prenuptial agreements appear exaggerated: 'It is far from obvious that having prenups will make the law more certain' (ibid); parties and courts will still be called upon to decide if they are 'fair'. Second, it is not clear that having a prenuptial agreements will reduce the potential for litigation; as we see not least from the list of factors above, there remains broad scope to challenge them in an application for ancillary relief (ibid: 253; see also George et al 2009). Herring also draws attention to the gender implications of prenuptial agreements, particularly in the unpredictable and 'messy' ways we do family: 'Any attempt to set down in advance the responsibilities of the parties could work against the interests of the party who had to undertake unexpected care work. That is likely to be women' (Herring 2011: 253). Lady Hale's dissent highlights these points.

175. ...Marriage is not only different from a commercial relationship in law, it is also different in fact. It is capable of influencing and changing every aspect of a couple's lives: where they live, how they live, who goes to work outside the home and what work they do, who works inside the home and how, their social lives and leisure pursuits, and how they manage their property and finances. A couple may think that their futures are all mapped out ahead of them when they get married but many things may happen to push them off course—misfortunes such as redundancy, bankruptcy, illness, disability, obligations to other family members and especially to children, but also unexpected opportunities and unexplored avenues. The couple are bound together in more than a business relationship, so of course they modify their plans and often compromise their individual best interests to accommodate these new events. They may

have no choice if their marriage is to survive. And these are events which take place while it is still hoped that the marriage will survive. There may be people who enter marriage in the belief that it will not endure, but for most people the hope and the belief is that it will. There is also a public interest in the stability of marriage. Marriage and relationship breakdown can have many damaging effects for the parties, their children and other members of their families, and also for society as a whole. So there is also a public interest in encouraging the parties to make adjustments to their roles and life-styles for the sake of their relationship and the welfare of their families.

The current legal position on pre- and post-nuptial contracts is thus reflected in *Radmacher*. The Law Commission will issue its final report in 2012, and this may recommend a change in position—of course, even if it does, Parliament may or may not act upon it. We shall return briefly to the question of reform of the law on pre- and postnuptial agreements below, but whatever the Law Commission recommends, it seems that our question about the place of equality in the division of marital assets can now be answered in one of two ways. As Lady Hale said in *Radmacher*:

> On the one hand, the sharing principle reflects the egalitarian and nondiscriminatory view of marriage, expressly adopted in Scottish law (in section 9(1)(a) of the Family Law (Scotland) Act 1985 and adopted in English law at least since *White v White*. On the other hand, respecting their individual autonomy reflects a different kind of equality.
>
> (para 178; see also on this Diduck 2011)[85]

V. CHILD SUPPORT

The history of the private responsibility to support children reveals that it was a father's obligation to support his legitimate children, but, as there was no procedure in private law to enforce that obligation until the nineteenth century, it remained in practice more of a moral one.[86] Although the Poor Law Amendment Act 1834 allowed magistrates to make financial orders against non-married fathers, those affiliation proceedings were difficult procedures for the woman concerned (Finer and McGregor 1974; Barton and Douglas 1995: 197).

Even now, after the radical reform of child support law, Millar (1996) places Britain in the category of states which adopt policies indicating a preference for 'private responsibility' when it comes to child support. Indeed, it was the fact that a relatively high

---

[85] Reflecting again on the tension between equality and the autonomy to be able to contract out of it, Lady Hale wrote extrajudicially on the implications of the *Radmacher* decision:

> Finally, therefore, it comes back to what we think marriage is and is for. Is it simply a private arrangement from which each can walk away when they want and without regard to the consequences for the other? Or is it a status in which we all have an interest? Do we want to encourage responsible families, in which people are able to compromise their place in the world outside the home for the sake of their partners, their children and their elderly or disabled relatives, and can be properly compensated for this if things go wrong? I continue to hope that we do. But I wonder whether we really believe in equality in marriage. (Hale 2011: 12)

[86] The Divorce and Matrimonial Causes Act 1857 was the first authority for a court to award maintenance for children of divorced or separated parents. See Finer and McGregor (1974), Barton and Douglas (1995), Cretney (2003a), and MacLean and Eekelaar (1997) on the history of child support. See also the dissenting opinion of Baroness Hale in *R v Secretary of State for Work and Pensions ex parte Kehoe* [2005] UKHL 48.

proportion of a lone parent's income came from benefit and a relatively low proportion from private support (and what this ratio meant both ideologically and materially in terms of the state's budget) that formed the primary driving force behind the implementation of the original Child Support Act in 1991 (CSA).[87] That Act forms the backdrop and framework for the primary legislative provision regarding child support, the Child Maintenance and Other Payments Act 2008. The history behind the CSA 1991 sheds some light on the difficulties the Act was designed to remedy, as well as those that it created.

Most evidence regarding child support awards before the CSA 1991 came into force suggested that the awards varied greatly both in terms of their size and in the proportion they represented of the payer's income, although their variation in the proportion they represented of the recipient's income was not so great (Glendinning et al 1996). Douglas observes that, by the end of the 1980s:

> Many couples reached settlements (often, it seems, approved by the courts in consent orders) whereby the husband/father provided no ongoing maintenance, not only for the wife, but also for the children, in return for giving up his share in the family home. Moreover, even where child maintenance was ordered or agreed, the amounts payable were all too often based on little more than 'gut feeling' as to what it was appropriate to expect a particular parent to pay, rather than on a rational assessment of what the child needed. To add to the inadequacy of the court regime, the Government found widely differing levels of maintenance being set in similar circumstances. As the final straw, they also found that barely a quarter of those required to pay were making regular payments. (Douglas 2004: 203)

Eekelaar also found that 54% of registrars[88] deciding child support claims declined to use any kind of guideline to set the amount, relying instead upon what they termed 'common knowledge' about raising children, and that those who did use guidelines favoured income support levels (Eekelaar 1991b: 95). For the government, these findings amounted to a crisis over a parent's abdication of personal responsibility for his children and a crisis in the rationality and consistency of the court system (Diduck 2003: 172). Lone-parent recipients of maintenance also were dissatisfied with the low levels of support awarded and its inconsistent enforcement, but they also expressed some satisfaction with the control the system allowed them to keep over decisions to claim and to distribute any money they received informally from the non-resident parent (Clarke et al 1994, 1995). Non-resident parents, for their part, also preferred a system that allowed them, even informally, to control the timing and the amount of support paid, and often the way it was spent. These fathers did not view child support as an unconditional obligation, but viewed it as an expression of care for their children, contingent upon the history of the relationship with the mother and thus as mediated through the mother (Bradshaw et al 1999). They often drew a conceptual distinction between paying informally for specific items or days out and paying day-to-day maintenance for children, and were often less inclined to pay maintenance.

Eventually, most observers agreed that 'something ought to be done'; justice was clearly not being done for lone parents or for children (or for the taxpayer!). In 1990 the government issued a White Paper (DSS 1990) linking child support with the welfare of the child and with the responsible behaviour of biological parents. Indeed, it could be

---

[87] See also Children Come First (1990), Keating (1995), Diduck (1995), MacLean and Eekelaar (1993), and MacLean (1994).
[88] Now district judges.

argued that the Act was part of an agenda to 'domesticate' sexually active young men. Rather than adopting other solutions such as the issue of guidelines to courts, the Act it proposed was far more radical. Glendinning et al summarise concisely the main provisions of the original version of the CSA 1991:

— The establishment of the Child Support Agency, responsible for the assessment of all child maintenance payments and their collection where requested.
— The creation of a universally applicable but complex formula to calculate liability for child maintenance. The formula was originally based upon income support levels and did not take into account an 'absent parent's actual expenditure', other than some housing costs. Subsequent amendments to the formula have aimed to reduce the levels of hardship reported by some 'absent parents' and their new families.
— All 'parents with care' claiming means-tested income support, family credit or disability working allowance are *required* to authorize the Secretary of State to recover maintenance from the 'absent parent', and to co-operate with the Child Support Agency in tracing an 'absent parent', assessing and collecting any maintenance owed. Only where a 'parent with care' can demonstrate 'reasonable grounds' for believing that this would cause her or a child to suffer 'harm or undue distress' is this requirement waived.
— Where a 'parent with care' refuses to co-operate without being able to demonstrate a 'risk of harm or undue distress', the personal allowance element of her benefit is reduced by 20% for six months and 10% for a further twelve months. Both the level and the duration of this deduction are to be increased.
— 'Parents with care' on income support have *all* maintenance deducted, pound for pound, from their benefit; 'parents with care' on family credit have £15 maintenance 'disregarded' in calculating their entitlement. (Glendinning et al 1996: 276–77)

This first version of the Act almost immediately encountered difficulties, and was subject to widespread derision. As a result of high-profile media coverage of opposition to the Act, government made a number of changes to it. Glendinning et al summarise the most significant changes made to the Act in the 1995 legislation:

— The introduction of a discretion to 'depart' from the standard maintenance assessment formula in certain closely specified circumstances, to take account of special hardship or other factors.
— Further adjustments to the formula to take greater account of the needs of 'second' partners and children, of an 'absent parent's' travel-to-work costs and of earlier capital property settlements between separating partners.
— From April 1997, lone parents in receipt of income support or the new jobseeker's allowance will be able to build up maintenance 'credits' of £5 a week, which will be repaid as a lump sum when they start working more than sixteen hours a week.

(Glendinning et al 1996: 285)[89]

In 1998 the government published a Green Paper (DSS 1998) proposing further reform of the law of child support. It confirmed the government's commitment to ensuring that parents fulfil their responsibilities for their children and to a non-discretionary system of assessing child maintenance, but it acknowledged that too many difficulties continued to beset the administration of the complicated formula then in use. Its primary solution was to simplify the formula. Even this solution did not work, however, and the Act that fol-

---

[89] See also Clarke et al (1996).

lowed[90] was also subjected to criticism (HC Work and Pensions Committee 2005; Henshaw 2006).

Government's commitment to keeping child support out of the courts remains unshaken, though, and the collection of child support has come to form part of the policy of (private?) responsible parenting to be encouraged by government and an integral part of government's (public?) plan to eradicate child poverty (DWP 2011a). The current statistics are salutory: 1.1 million children in lone-parent families live in relative poverty, and this is 34% of all children in lone-parent families (DWP and DfE 2011: para 1.23). Further, 23% of children in lone-parent families experience persistent poverty compared with about 12% in all families (ibid: para 1.24). More than 50% of children living in separated families have no 'effective financial arrangements' in place at all (DWP 2011b: 1).

It is clear that lone parents (over 90% of whom are women) and their children suffer disproportionate financial hardship relative to the general population. But the question remains: who is responsible for alleviating that hardship? Ferguson (2008) argues that child support is a fundamentally private obligation of the parents.[91] But one could equally argue that the state bears some responsibility, not least under its duties under the UN Convention of the Rights of the Child (Herring 2011: 188–89). The Child Poverty Act 2010 and the coalition government's policy document *A New Approach to Child Poverty* (DWP and DfE 2011) both envision some state responsibility for children's financial well-being, but it is primarily focused upon encouraging parents into work and encouraging parents to meet their personal responsibility.

Q Comment upon the primary role that private maintenance appears to have in the government's plans to eradicate child poverty. In contrast, Fineman has argued:

> Child support is not a viable solution to the problems of child care and dependency. In fact, the theoretical development of child support stands as a diversion to the development of effective policy. On an ideological level, primarily because it is based on the traditional notion of a nuclear family, child support furthers the assumption that dependency is a private matter. Indeed, insistence on child-support policy is an attempt to reconstruct the gendered complementarity of the traditional family through the imposition of the economically viable male. (Fineman 2004: 203)

She then refers to research that demonstrates that on a practical level child support has only a small relationship to child poverty and concludes by saying:

> It may be that we want to establish and collect child support orders for reasons other than that they can in fact substitute for governmental of collective assistance to children in poverty, but in doing so, we should not delude ourselves that we are solving the larger problem. (ibid: 204)

Comment on Fineman's position.

The original CSA 1991 was intended to 'effect a cultural change in attitudes towards maintenance' so that it would no longer be regarded as optional (Keating 1995: 30). The

---

[90] The Child Support Act 1991 as amended by the Child Support, Pensions and Social Security Act 2000.

[91] The Child Support obligation falls on biological parents only. All non-resident unmarried fathers, whether they have parental responsibility or not, are liable for child support. Non-resident former step-parents may be liable to support their former stepchild if they treated the child as a 'child of the family'. MCA 1973 s 52; CPA 2004 Sch 5, para 80(2).

Act created a formula by which maintenance was to be assessed,[92] an agency and officers to administer the assessments,[93] and required all 'persons with care'[94] on state support to co-operate with the Agency or risk a reduction in benefits,[95] while allowing the reduction to be avoided if the Child Support Officer considered that 'there are reasonable grounds for believing that, if she were required to comply, there would be a risk to her or any of her children living with her suffering harm or undue distress as a result of complying'.[96] The Act also removed jurisdiction from the courts to make child support orders where the Child Support Agency has jurisdiction.[97]

However, as we noted above, the difficulties became apparent almost immediately and indicated that the sought-after 'culture change' was not to be forthcoming. There was general lack of public confidence in the scheme (HC Social Security Committee 1994). The Act became the subject of angry, sometimes violent public reaction, when (mostly) non-resident fathers and their 'new families' objected to the increased levels of maintenance they were ordered to pay and to the formula's disregard for 'clean-break' property settlements effected in the past.[98] In addition, as we noted, lone mothers and their children did not appear to be benefiting from the Act (Clarke et al 1996). Indeed, many were worse off.

> For mothers on income support, the lack of a maintenance disregard meant that any maintenance paid had no effect on their income. Indeed, where mothers were just lifted off income support by maintenance, it might drop them into a 'poverty trap'. For some of the mothers who were themselves on family credit, this entitlement had been reduced because they received higher maintenance, but the latter was rarely paid both regularly and at the correct level. Some mothers preferred to suffer the additional hardships of a benefit penalty rather than face the disruption of the assessment process. (Clarke et al 1996: 23–24)

In many cases these financial losses were compounded by indirect losses, particularly of gifts of cash from fathers for the benefit of their children. Further:

> [t]here was no evidence that the Act had had the effect of encouraging any lone mothers to enter employment or to increase their hours of work so that they moved off income support onto family credit. This appeared to be partly because other obstacles to work, such as child care,

---

[92] S 11(2), Sch 1. See also Parker (1991: 36–48) and Eekelaar (1991b: 105–11) for a discussion of different models of child support which could have been employed.

[93] S 11(1), and see also s 13. As a result of 1994 amendments, the Child Support Officer became entitled to make interim assessments: s 12(1) and (1A).

[94] S 3(3): 'A person is a "person with care" in relation to any child, if he is a person—(a) with whom the child has his home; (b) who usually provides day to day care for the child (whether exclusively or in conjunction with any other person); and (c) who does not fall within a prescribed category of persons.' See *C v Secretary of State for Work and Pensions and B* [2002] EWCA Civ 1854; [2003] 1 FLR 829, where being defined as an absent parent or a person with care was not to be considered merely by reference to a family proceedings order, but was considered to be a matter of fact. In this case, the mother had a residence order, the child was in boarding school and the father had roughly shared contact with the child on weekends and during school holidays. The determination should have been based on the level and frequency of care that would have been provided had the child not been in boarding school.

[95] Ss 6 and 46.

[96] S 46(3). On considering the 'risk of harm or undue distress' exemption to the s 6 requirement to co-operate with a Child Support Commissioner stated that 'although the risk must be real as opposed to fanciful, the question is not whether the harm or undue distress would actually happen' (Knights 1997: 121). See also Provan et al (1996).

[97] S 8(3). See also Chapter 5 above.

[98] See, on the public reaction to the CSA 1991, Collier (1994); Wallbank (1997); Diduck (1995).

were a more immediate issue, but also partly because the Agency was unable to guarantee the payment of maintenance to those not on income support. (ibid: 24)

Non-resident parents, who were and are overwhelmingly fathers, objected to the Act as well. Many claimed that the detailed calculations required by the Act insufficiently took account of their new family responsibilities and they objected also to the element in the calculation designated to meet the costs of childcare, believing that it amounted to support for the caretaking parent herself. They felt generally that the formula was inflexible, failing to take account adequately of debts, liabilities and agreements assumed after the breakdown of the relationship.[99]

The policy underlying the original child support scheme was based upon individualisation and privatisation and an attempt at equalisation of parental responsibility for children. The Act was aimed at biological rather than social parents.[100] Although children's welfare was considered briefly in *Children Come First* (1990), it is arguable that alleviating child poverty was not the main impetus behind the scheme,[101] and it is significant that the welfare of the child was not a factor in determining child support.

Q Earlier proposals for reform suggested by the Finer Committee (1974) envisaged a degree of state responsibility for assisting one-parent families living in poverty. The main features of the 'guaranteed maintenance allowance' proposed by the committee were to provide a non-contributory fixed benefit to all one-parent families which would substitute for maintenance payments. Maintenance would be collected by the authority administering the allowance (Finer 1974: vol I, para 5.104, 295–96). Compare and contrast the CSA 1991 provisions with Finer's proposal. Which do you prefer?

Q Do you agree with the Act's focus upon biological rather than social parents?

In 1998 the then new government again reviewed child support and the result was the Child Support, Pensions and Social Security Act 2000. It introduced a simplified formula for calculating maintenance liability; a child maintenance premium which allows families in receipt of benefit to keep up to £10 per week of any maintenance paid before their benefits are reduced; and tougher sanctions for parents who avoid their 'responsibilities'.[102] The 2000 Act did not repeal the 1991 one, but used it as a framework for the new provisions.[103] It is still in use for those applications made before the Child Maintenance and Other Payments Act 2008 (CMOPA) came into force in April 2011 and also remains the framework for that Act.

Based upon the assumptions that '[w]hen parents live together, they normally share

---

[99] For a discussion of the reforms to the Act between 1991 and 2000, see the second edition of this book. See also Diduck (2003: ch 7); Wallbank (1997); Bradshaw *et al* (1999).

[100] Maclean and Eekelaar (1997) reported that the fathers in their study related their obligations to children more closely to the exercise of social parenthood than to biological parenthood.

[101] See Eekelaar (1991b) for different ideological foundations of child support schemes.

[102] In order to collect payments or arrears, the Child Support Agency may obtain a deduction from earnings order (CSA 1991 s 31). To collect arrears, after obtaining a liability order (CSA 1991 s 33), the Agency may levy a distress warrant and the defaulter's goods can be sold (CSA 1991 s 35); register a county court judgment (CSA 1991 s 36); or commit the defaulter to prison or disqualify him from driving for a specified period of time (CSA 1991 ss 39A, 40 and 40A).

[103] For detail of the mechanics of the Act and commentary upon it, see Diduck (2003); Pirrie (2002a, 2002b, 2002c); Wikeley (2000a, 2000b); Wikeley et al (2001).

family expenses' (DSS 1999: ch 2, para 2), they expect to meet their children's needs first (para 3) and they spend roughly 30% of their income on a child (para 5), the level of child maintenance owed by a non-resident parent was set by the 2000 Act at 15% of his net income for one child, 20% for two children, and 25% for three or more children.[104] A non-resident parent's net income is his income remaining after deduction of national insurance, tax and pension contributions, as well as a deduction of 15%, 20% and 25% as above for any children with whom he is currently living in a new relationship. This assessment may be reduced further if the qualifying child stays with the non-resident parent for more than 52 nights per year. That is, if the child stays with the payer 52–103 nights per year, or 1 or 2 nights per week, his payments are reduced by 1/7, if 104–155 nights by 2/7, if 156–174 nights by 3/7 and if 175 nights or more by 1/2. It was hoped that the ease and transparency of the much-simplified calculation would increase compliance and collection rates and that the linking of assessments to overnight contact or 'shared care' would increase both those rates and incidences of shared care (DSS 1999: ch 7, paras 11–12). This formula remains in place under the CMOPA 2008, but the percentages have been reduced to 12% for one child, 16% for two children and 19% for three or more children, and the calculation is based upon gross rather than income.

Let us consider the implications of these changes. First, in the light of the research that illustrates a gender difference in how family income is allocated and parental roles are played out, it could be argued that the assumptions both about how 'intact' families allocate income and that this allocation will continue on separation are unrealistic (Chapter 6 above). Because the primary responsibility for child-rearing tends to fall upon women, they are usually more in tune with the day-to-day financial requirements of childcare (Neale and Smart 2002: 191–95) and exhibit stronger preferences for spending to benefit children (Pahl 1989; Ringen and Halpin 1997; Lister et al 1999; Pahl 2005). Further, because the consequences for many families of the gendered division of childcare is that for fathers, childcare consists mainly of days out or 'fun' times with their children, they may remain happy to buy large items of clothing for school, pay for treats or for one-off presents, but may balk at knowing about or paying for the day-to-day 'maintenance costs' of childcare (Diduck 2003: 168; see also Bradshaw et al 1999). To many, child support, even under the new regime, is still something to 'beat'.

Research in 2002 into how parents perceived the then forthcoming provisions in the 2000 Act indicated that the formula's disregard of the income of the person with care was seen as a source of injustice by non-resident parents (Gillespie 2002). In contrast, they thought that the deduction for shared care might encourage them to think about seeking more staying contact with their children (ibid). As Herring puts it, 'a one-seventh reduction in child support for the cost of a burger and a DVD is a bargain' (Herring 2011: 195, fn 72), while the person with care's financial responsibility is not significantly reduced if the child spends one or two nights away from home. Whether the link drawn between staying contact and support will benefit children is open to debate.

Under the CMOPA 2008 the emphasis remains upon coercing responsible behaviour. And further amendments proposed by the coalition government maintain this focus, but imply an additional element to 'responsibility'—reaching agreement. First, the CMOPA

---

[104] Sch 1 CSA 1991. This is the basic rate and is assessed if the non-resident parent's income is between £200.00 and £2000.00 per week. £2000.00 is the maximum assessable income. If his income is between £100.00 and £200.00 per week, a reduced rate applies. If he earns less than £100.00 per week or receives benefit or allowance, a standard £5.00 per week payment is required. Exceptional claims for costs or for amounts in excess of the maximum can be made to a special tribunal.

2008 replaces the Child Support Agency with a Child Maintenance and Enforcement Commission (CMEC) which is to promote child maintenance and provide information and guidance to parents.[105] The aim is to encourage people to reach private arrangements on child support. The proposed reforms take this 'encouragement' further: where parents are not able reach agreement and wish to use the CMEC, they will be charged a fee the services of the Commission. The proposals are that government will:

11a. Introduce a *gateway* to the statutory maintenance scheme to ensure parents are first supported to take responsibility and make family-based arrangements before resorting to the statutory maintenance system. We will require all applicants to go through this process before accessing the statutory system. Where appropriate, referrals will be made to wider family support services to enable families to find resolution across a range of issues. There would also be a fast-track for the most vulnerable, namely victims of domestic violence.

b. Offer a *package of support* to enable parents to put in place their own financial arrangements. This would include a calculation, based on information from HM Revenue and Customs, on the amount of maintenance to be provided. This service will not operate in isolation—it is intended to complement the gateway and wider family support.

c. Implement *charges for statutory child maintenance* services under the new child maintenance scheme. This proposal builds on the findings of Sir David Henshaw's report for the previous government. The charges proposed are intended to encourage families to make choices in the best interests of their children and the choices can be made at various points which will avoid the application of fees. They will be based on principles of fairness—with a reduced charge for people on benefits. We are also looking at the balance of charges between the parent with care and the non-resident parent, as well as the need to protect particularly vulnerable groups— victims of domestic violence will be exempt from the application charge. This measure along with increased efficiencies will reduce the financial burden on the taxpayer, who currently pays the full cost in transferring maintenance payments, while preserving a statutory scheme for those who need it. (DWP 2011a, emphasis in original, reference omitted)

As Herring comments, whether reaching private agreements is a realistic goal or not remains to be seen (Herring 2011: 198). It is also, we suggest, questionable whether charging for use of child support services will act as an 'incentive' to reach agreement. Herring quotes Wikely who says, 'There is a clear risk, in the absence of adequate advice and support services, that any existing power imbalances between parents will simply be reinforced, to the detriment of children's interests' (ibid: 199). Again, the charging incentive, combined with the proposed withdrawal of Legal Aid from these issues, may only serve to exacerbate this detriment.

The House of Commons Select Committee on Work and Pensions (2011) responded to the reform proposals. Let us examine their responses in detail.

8. In its 2010 Report on child maintenance, our predecessor committee expressed concerns that a reliance on private arrangements might recreate the problems associated with the child maintenance system before the Child Support Act 1991 came into force. As mentioned, the previous Government established the Child Support Agency (CSA) because the courts were considered to have failed to establish fair and consistent maintenance awards, keep such orders up to date and enforce them effectively. We were therefore keen to explore the available evidence on whether family-based arrangements are always more effective than the statutory system.

[105] S 6.

The evidence they found follows:

19. The Centre for Separated Families (CSP) supported the views expressed in Sir David Henshaw's 2006 report (as summarised in chapter 1). They told us that Sir David's report shows that family-based arrangements produced better outcomes and greater compliance than the statutory system and that, as a result, more children would benefit from effective maintenance arrangements. June Venters QC also agreed that family-based arrangements are preferable for parents: 'if parents come to something that they can both live with, that has empowered both of them, then that has to be more likely to succeed in my experience'.

20. However, Caroline Bryson, who has conducted research for the DWP on the impact of child maintenance reform, had found that the evidence pointed to a different conclusion:

> ... there are certain characteristics that suggest that somebody makes a successful private arrangement. Those characteristics are issues like having a better relationship with your ex partner or the nonresident parent, there being contact between the two parents and between the nonresident parent and the child, and higher income families. ... there is a large proportion of the CSA population who do not exhibit those characteristics.

She highlighted evidence from a 2007 survey which showed that:

> 46% of those with a friendly relationship had a private arrangement;
> 19% of those with an unfriendly relationship had a private arrangement.
> 17% of those with an income under £10,000 had a private arrangement;
> 33% of those with an income of between £10,000 and £20,000 had a private arrangement.

21. Janet Allbeson from Gingerbread argued that the reforms would adversely affect families where the parents have never lived together or never had a relationship. Her interpretation of Caroline Bryson's research was that these families were 'far less likely to be able to come to a lasting satisfactory, voluntary private arrangement, particularly when they are on a low income'. Barnardo's argued that family-based arrangements could be particularly problematic when there were changes in parents' circumstances (eg when they find a new partner, move into or out of work, or have another child) and that such situations could lead to the need for renegotiation of payments further down the line, resulting in conflict between parents.

Parents' views on family-based arrangements and statutory support

23. In 2007, our predecessors considered proposed reforms aimed at encouraging separating parents to reach family-based arrangements. Their report highlighted research by the National Centre for Social Research, which found that only 4% of parents with care would be likely to move from the statutory CSA service to private arrangements. The reasons the majority of parents with care were reluctant to move away from the statutory system included:

> They wouldn't feel sure they would get paid (68%)They had a bad relationship with / didn't trust their ex-partner (61%)
> They were not sure they would get the right money (52%)
> They were not sure they would get paid on time (52%)

24. Research conducted by Nick Wikeley and others for DWP found that large numbers of separating parents wanted to involve a third party such as a Government agency in the organisation of their maintenance: 54% of parents with care using the Child Support Agency, and 25% of parents with care who did not use the CSA, wanted to agree maintenance with the help of a Government agency.

25. The Minister offered alternative research, conducted for DWP, which showed that 50% of parents with care and a majority of non-resident parents using the CSA said they would be likely to make a family-based arrangement if they had the help of a trained impartial adviser.

Q Based on this research, are you optimistic that parents will come to agreements on child support?

The Committee's next proposal raised implicit questions about the purpose of child support; that is, is it about ensuring children receive financial support, or is it about instilling responsibility in parents?

14. We suggested to the Minister that the Government introduce a system through which all child maintenance payments were routinely deducted from non-resident parents' wages. She believed that this would not support the Government's objective of encouraging parents to take personal responsibility. She considered that child maintenance arrangements helped keep children in touch with both their parents, and highlighted that deducting payments directly from salaries would place a burden on employers.

15. Nevertheless, we believe that requiring all non-resident parents to pay child maintenance through direct deductions from their salaries or bank accounts could increase the extent to which payments are delivered successfully. This requirement could operate in a similar way to existing types of salary deduction (for example, PAYE tax deductions and pensions or union membership deductions), or, in the case of deductions from bank accounts, in a similar way to a direct debit for a utility bill. We do not believe that this method of collection would necessarily detract from the emphasis on building family relationships; separating parents would still be able to access a range of support and advice services in reaching agreements, and it is arguable that failures to maintain regular child maintenance payments are a source of conflict between separated parents.

16. *A key objective for the Government's child maintenance policy is to ensure that all parents take responsibility for the wellbeing of their children. We believe that ensuring that parents with care receive agreed payments at the correct level on a consistent basis from the non-resident parent is an important element in this. We recommend that the Government considers the introduction of a requirement that child maintenance payments are deducted directly from a non-resident parent's salary or bank account, as we consider that this step would increase the number of payments that are delivered accurately and on time. We recognise that this does not appear within the Government's Green Paper proposals, but we believe it is important for the Government to consider the merits of this option.* (emphasis in original)

The government's response to the Consultation (DWP 2011b) does not address this issue.

Finally, on the proposals to introduce both application and collection charges for use of the system, the Committee concluded:

41. *The Government has decided to introduce application charges as an incentive to parents to use the gateway and to come to a voluntary agreement, and as a disincentive to using the statutory service. We are not convinced that the evidence yet exists to support this approach. The Government will therefore need to monitor carefully the impact of application charges to ensure they have the desired effect.*

42. *Under the Government's proposals, the application charge would fall on the parent with care, even when they had tried all reasonable alternative options to make a family-based arrangement. We believe that the application charge should fall on the non-resident parent, and not the parent with care, in cases where the parent with care has taken all reasonable steps to reach a voluntary agreement.* (emphasis in original)

Collection charges

43. The proposed collection charges would see 7–12% of child maintenance being deducted from

parents with care who use the statutory collection system. Gingerbread argued that 'In circumstances where every penny of maintenance counts, the loss of up to 12% of every payment as a collection charge will further impoverish already disadvantaged children.' This view was shared by Barnardo's, who stated that deducting a percentage of maintenance payments would impact negatively on children's outcomes.

44. The Government has acknowledged that parents with care will effectively be forced to use the statutory collection system if the non-resident parent refuses to pay: the DWP's Equality Impact Assessment stated: 'It is an inherent feature of the child maintenance system that where the non-resident parent is unwilling to pay maintenance voluntarily the full statutory collection service must be used.' The Minister confirmed to us that the Government did not want to deter parents with care from accessing the statutory system if non-resident parents did not co-operate. She told us 'Our intention is not to deter people from using the system if that is the only way that they can get maintenance flowing.'

45. *The Government's proposed collection charges for using the statutory service include both a surcharge on the non-resident parent and a deduction from the payment to the parent with care. We believe that this is excessive and unnecessarily complex and should be replaced by a single, modest administration charge for collection.*

46. *As with application charges, we believe that parents with care who have taken all reasonable steps to come to a voluntary agreement should not have to pay collection charges. In these cases, the collection charge should be borne by the non-resident parent.* (emphasis in original)

Again, the government was undeterred (DWP 2011b).

Until these reforms come into effect, the CSA 1991 and the CMOPA 2008 provide that CMEC will make child support assessments using the formula we noted above if either parent applies for one. If the resident parent is on benefits, no benefit will be deducted from the payments. Finally, CMEC has been given extensive options for enforcement of maintenance, including making deduction orders from bank accounts, liability orders which would then permit seizure of the debtor's goods and charging orders on property. It may disqualify a wilful refuser to pay from driving, confiscate his passport, issue curfew orders and ultimately commit him to prison.

These enforcement mechanisms are important, because once child support is 'taken over' by CMEC, the resident parent to whom arrears may be owed may not take enforcement proceedings herself. This was confirmed by the House of Lords in *R (Kehoe) v Secretary of State for Work and Pensions*.[106] Mr Kehoe had fallen into significant arrears in his child support payments and Mrs Kehoe argued that the (then) Child Support Agency was not enforcing them adequately. She disputed the Act's placement of enforcement exclusively with the Agency and said the scheme violated her Article 6 right to enforce them herself. The House of Lords found against her, saying that resident parents have no such civil right.[107] Subsequent to this decision, the Court of Appeal held also that the Secretary of State owed no duty of care in tort law either to the person with care or the child.[108] Parents are, therefore, in the hands completely of the CMEC; they have no recourse to private law to enforce CMEC assessments.

The CSA 1991 and CMOPA 2008 apply to all 'qualifying' children (CSA 1991 section

---

[106] [2005] UKHL 48. Confirmed by the ECHR in *Kehoe v UK* (App No 2010/06, ECHR) 2008. For further discussion, see Wikeley (2006).

[107] Baroness Hale dissented, holding that support was the right of the child and that that Art 6 was thus engaged and violated.

[108] *Rowley v Secretary of State for the Department of Work and Pensions* [2007] 3 FCR 431.

55). There are residency criteria and also to be a qualifying child he or she must have at least one 'non-resident parent' (section 3(2)). If parentage (obviously, usually fatherhood) is disputed, the CMEC may still make a maintenance calculation against a party if it can presume that he is the father. The situations in which such a presumption can arise are listed in section 26 of the CSA 1991. They include registration as a father; if a scientific test shows that he is the father; an inference drawn from a refusal to take such a scientific test; if he is a 'legal' father pursuant to the HFEA 2008 or if he has been declared to be the father in other proceedings.[109]

Whether or not a child is a qualifying child is important, because if there is a qualifying child for whom a maintenance calculation has been or could be made—ie where CMEC has jurisdiction—the general rule is that courts have no power to make periodical payments for the child. The only exceptions are where the parties make an agreement and wish the court to incorporate it into a consent order, where a top-up order is sought over and above CMEC's maximum calculation based on a gross income of over £3,000 per week, or where the order relates to expenses connected with the child's education or disability. In these cases and where CMEC does not have jurisdiction, the courts may rely upon the DPMCA 1978 (schedule 6), the CPA 2004 (schedule 5) or the MCA 1973 (section 27) if the parents were married or civilly registered, and the Children Act 1989 (schedule 1) regardless of the parents' relationship.[110] The courts always retain jurisdiction, however, to make lump-sum orders and orders in relation to property for the benefit of a child. In all cases, the court has discretion and the child's welfare is not paramount.

VI. REFORM?

Ancillary Relief and Child Support

We have seen that the law on finances and property at the end of relationships has been subject to both judicial and statutory reform. We have seen also, however, that further calls for reform have been voiced, some referring to the 1998 Supporting Families Document. In order to provide greater clarity to the law, that document contained a proposal to add to the section 25 list of factors 'an over-arching objective and set of guiding principles which could make clear the process a judge now follows in determining the allocation of property on divorce' (Home Office 1998: para 4.48).

The proposed objective was for the court to 'exercise its powers so as to endeavour to do that which is fair and reasonable between the parties and any child of the family' (ibid: para 4.49). The proposed set of guiding principles would set out the objectives for the court in making property decisions. They are listed in proposed order of precedence:

> First, to promote the welfare of any child of the family under the age of eighteen, by meeting housing needs of any children and the primary carer, and of the secondary carer; both to facilitate contact and to recognise the continuing importance of the secondary carer's role.

---

[109] See, eg, *Secretary for Work and Pensions v Jones* [2003] EWHC 2163; [2004] 1 FLR 282.

[110] In *T v B* [2010] EWHC 1444 (Fam); [2010] 2 FLR 1966, Moylan J held that a non-resident former lesbian partner who was not a 'female parent' but who had a joint reidence order, was not a 'parent' within the meaning of the Children Act for the purpose of child support liability.

Second, the court would take into account the existence and content of any written agreement about financial arrangements … .

Third … the court would then divide any surplus so as to achieve a fair result, recognising that fairness will generally require the value of the assets to be divided equally between the spouses.

Fourth, the court would try to terminate financial relationships between the parties at the earliest date practicable. (ibid: para 4.49)

Q Have these proposals been all but accepted in the case law that followed them? Do the child support provisions meet these objectives?

As we have seen, reform of ancillary relief law, apart from the law on marital property agreements, appears to be off the government agenda, and reform of child support law is moving forward, but the Law Commission will review in its 11th Programme for reform, commencing in 2012,

> the various means by which court orders for financial provision on divorce or the dissolution of a civil partnership and orders concerning financial arrangements for children are enforced. It will not touch upon the basis for claims, but will consider the legal tools available to force a party to comply with the financial orders made under the Matrimonial Causes Act 1973, the Civil Partnership Act 2004 and the Children Act 1989. (Law Commission 2011b: 15)

We have also seen that reform of the law regarding financial provision for separating cohabitants remains outstanding.

Separating Cohabitants

Cohabitants have no legal obligation to support each other. This means that when they separate, they have no claim to maintenance against their former partner. Adjustment of their property on separation is subject to the laws of property and equity as we saw in Chapter 6. Some say this is as it should be. If cohabitants want the financial benefits of marriage or civil partnership, it is said, they should simply formalise their relationship in this way. These critics say that to offer cohabitants the same remedies as married or civilly registered partners would only undermine marriage. Others say that the law ought to take into account the reality of increased cohabitation and its effects on creating dependencies which, on separation, can result in injustice for the dependant (see Douglas et al 2008; Diduck 2009b).

This injustice or hardship is partially a result of what Barlow et al have called the 'common law marriage myth' (Barlow and James 2004). So far government response is to promote an education campaign to disabuse people of the 'myth'.[111] This is despite attempts in recent years to remedy the disadvantage suffered by dependent or otherwise vulnerable cohabitants on the death of their partner or breakdown of their relationship. The concern was finally taken forward in a 2007 report by the Law Commission. The Law Commission acknowledged that providing remedies for cohabitants either during cohabitation or on its breakdown was controversial. But it also acknowledged that the current legal situation was complex, uncertain and often caused hardship for many.

---

[111] See Barlow et al (2008).

The case for reform

1.7 Recent results of the British Social Attitudes survey indicate that a substantial majority of people in England and Wales think cohabitants should have access to financial relief on relationship breakdown.

1.8 However, some people would say that law reform is unnecessary. They would argue that it would be enough to improve public information and education about the true legal position to enable individuals to make informed choices.

1.9 While improved public awareness of the law is essential, evidence suggests that this strategy is not sufficient, by itself, to deal with the hardship that can arise when cohabitants separate. There will always be reasons why cohabitants do not or cannot take steps to protect themselves. In particular, it is often not feasible for a person simply to 'get married' as his or her partner may not agree to do so. In such circumstances the only alternatives are to put up with the existing position or to leave the relationship. It is not obviously in the interests of the couple, any children involved or society generally for a family to break up in such circumstances.

1.10 Many people think that cohabitants should have access to exactly the same remedies as married couples and civil partners. We do not agree. Although some cohabitants have relationships that many would regard as being similar to those of spouses, there is a broad range of cohabiting relationships, exhibiting different degrees of commitment and interdependence. And cohabitants have not made the distinctive legal and public commitment that marriage entails.

1.11 We have therefore devised a scheme entirely distinct from that which applies between spouses on divorce, that would apply specifically to eligible cohabiting couples who separate.

(Law Commission 2007)

It acknowledged this variable public opinion in its recommendations. It proposed that its scheme should not apply to all cohabitants, but rather only to those who were eligible, eligibility to be determined by either having a child together, or cohabiting for a minimum period of time. It proposed further that cohabitants be able to opt out of the scheme. For all others:

1.17 It would not be sufficient for applicants simply to demonstrate that they were eligible for financial relief and that the couple had not made a valid opt-out agreement disapplying the scheme. In order to obtain a remedy, applicants would have to prove that they had made qualifying contributions to the parties' relationship which had given rise to certain enduring consequences at the point of separation.

1.18 The scheme would therefore be very different from that which applies between spouses on divorce. Simply cohabiting, for however long, would not give rise to any presumed entitlement to share in any pool of property. Nor would the scheme grant remedies simply on the basis of a party's needs following separation, whether by making orders for maintenance or otherwise.

1.19 In broad terms, the scheme would seek to ensure that the pluses and minuses of the relationship were fairly shared between the couple. The applicant would have to show that the respondent retained a benefit, or that the applicant had a continuing economic disadvantage, as a result of contributions made to the relationship. The value of any award would depend on the extent of the retained benefit or continuing economic disadvantage. The court would have discretion to grant such financial relief as might be appropriate to deal with these matters, and in doing so would be required to give first consideration to the welfare of any dependent children.

1.20 We consider that a scheme based on these principles would provide a sound basis on which to address the hardship and other economic unfairness that can arise when a cohabiting relationship ends. It would respond, more comprehensively than the current law can, to the economic impact of the contributions made by parties to their relationship, and so to needs which arise in consequence. Where there are dependent children, the scheme would enable a remedy to be provided for the benefit of the primary carer, and so better protect those children who share their primary carer's standard of living. By making adequate provision for the adult parties, the scheme would give more leeway to the court than it currently has to apply Schedule 1 to the Children Act 1989 for the benefit of the parties' children. (ibid)

While public opinion continues to favour some measure of legal protection for separating cohabitants (Barlow et al 2008), the Law Commission's proposals have not been acted upon by government. Instead, the Labour government announced that it would defer contemplating further reform in this area until it examined the results of a similar measure enacted in Scotland.[112] The coalition government announced in September 2011 that it would not take forward the Law Commission's recommendations.

Marital Agreements: Marriage as Contract?

The law on the enforceability of prenuptial and postnuptial agreements is discussed above. *Radmacher v Granatino* is the leading authority. The Law Commission has still to issue its final report, however, and its consultations have taken that decision into account. It has also taken into account the results of a survey of practioners about the demand for marital agreements, both pre- and post-*Radmacher*, and their practice in respect of them. At the end of 2008, practitioners participating in focus groups reported that the numbers of marital agreements they drafted were not large (Law Commission undated a). In a follow-up survey after the *Radmacher* decision, while the overall numbers were still low, a significant minority (46%, ie 17 of 37) noted an increase in expressions of interest in marital agreements (Law Commission undated b: 5).

The idea of marriage (and civil partnership) as a contractual relation is not new, but it has always been expressed as a type of hybrid relationship. In 1866 in *Hyde v Hyde and Woodmansee* Lord Penzance said 'Marriage has been well said to be something more than a contract, either religious or civil—to be an Institution. It creates mutual rights and obligations, as all contracts do, but beyond that it confers a status' (133). And 150 years later, Lady Hale in *Radmacher v Granatino*[113] said:

[131] … [A]lthough our judgments talk only of marriage and married couples, our conclusions must also apply to couples who have entered into a civil partnership.

[132] The issue may be simple, but underlying it are some profound questions about the nature of marriage in the modern law and the role of the courts in determining it. Marriage is, of course, a contract, in the sense that each party must agree to enter into it and once entered both are bound by its legal consequences. But it is also a status. This means two things. First, the parties are not entirely free to determine all its legal consequences for themselves. They contract into the package which the law of the land lays down. Secondly, their marriage also has legal consequences for other people and for the state.

---

[112] On the first three years of operation of the Scottish legislation, see Wasoff et al (2011).
[113] [2010] UKSC 42.

Marriage and civil partnership seem therefore to be contracts which confer a status. Indeed it is the status aspect which confers many of the legal benefits and burdens. But, as we have seen, party autonomy in setting out the terms of the relationship both at its inception and its end is increasingly encouraged by the law also. What, however, might the complete contractualisation of these relationships mean? It would certainly downplay any residual public interest in marriage/civil partnership, which, as we have seen, probably goes against current social and legal policy. For marriage, it has also been criticised by some feminist commentators, but let us examine the case for the contractarians. It is indeed true that the law insists that marriage, like commercial contracts, must be freely entered into, but that is where the similarities stop and many advocate alleviating the gender-oppressive remnants of traditional marriage by reforming it along the line of contractarian principles. It is thought that marriage could be divested of its gendered over-garments, and redefined according to modern conceptions of respect for the autonomy and equal rights of two individuals who choose to make their lives together. This idea may lie beneath the majority decision in *Radmacher*. David McLellan examines this argument. The proposal he tests is that 'the state could leave most substantive marital rights and obligations to be defined privately, but make the legal system available to resolve disputes arising under the privately created "legislation"' (McLellan 1996: 236, quoting Shuttz, 1982).

> [I]t would allow couples to escape from an outmoded legal tradition through an agreement especially tailored to fit their needs, thus respecting the values of privacy and respect for freedom in the ordering of personal relationships; it would give added authority to an anti-patriarchal and egalitarian stance; and it could be used to confer legitimation and structure on other forms of relationships—homosexual, polygamous, and so on. (McLellan 1996: 237)

However, McLellan then goes on to present the argument against contract marriage. Most importantly, he reminds us that it is premised upon a particular view of the individual and that individual's relationship with others and with the state: '[I]t is closely connected with the political doctrine of minimal government and the Adam Smithian optimism that some hidden hand will promote universal well-being through the pursuit by each of economic self-interest' (ibid: 242–43). It depoliticises the family by removing it into the private sphere of individual bargains where the stronger still rule, but in a non-regulated way (ibid: 242). And finally, it presupposes that the individual bargainers are operating from the proverbial 'level playing field', a presupposition that is belied by the fact that the only women who would be able to negotiate a mutually advantageous relationship with men are those (relatively) few who are economically independent (ibid: 241). McLellan, therefore, concludes by cautioning against the contractualisation of marriage.

The Law Commission is due to report in 2012. While its consultation document (2011c) does propose making agreements enforceable in some circumstances, it reflects a cautious stance on party autonomy:

> 47. We can see force in this argument but there are reasons to be cautious. In particular, the circumstances in which marital property agreements are entered into mean that an act that appears to be autonomous may in fact be tainted by pressure – from a fiancé(e) or spouse, from the wider family and community, or simply from the circumstances surrounding preparations for a wedding. Moreover, autonomous adults may fail to foresee the events of many years of years of marriage; an agreement that was entered into freely, but in ignorance of the future, may not be one that they would have entered had they known how life would unfold.

Q Is this position closer to Lady Hale's or the majority's in *Radmacher*? What is your view of the contractualisation of marriage/civilpartnership? You may wish to refer to Mary Ann Glendon's work, *The Transformation of Family Law* (1989), in which she suggests that state regulation of marriage has so decreased over the years that it may now be seen as a contractual relationship. See also Cretney (2003b).

Q Would it surprise you to learn that cohabitation contracts have always been enforceable in the courts? Why or why not?

VII. CONCLUSION: IS THERE ANY ROLE FOR EQUALITY IN FAMILY ECONOMIES?

Our discussion has proceeded thus far on the basis that equality has had a role to play in the development of rules about the allocation of the economic benefits and burdens of family membership after the partners go their separate ways. We are, in this way, saying something about the nature of the relationship itself. As we said at the beginning of this chapter, rules about the distribution of financial benefits and burdens at the end of a relationship say a great deal about norms in the intact relationship. We saw, for example, how at least three models of property division and financial provision can be distilled from the legislation and we can now link views of marriage and the place of equality within them. Does this mean that the MCA 1973 and CPA 2004 hold all three views of marriage and the proper role of equality in marriage and civil partnership? The first model of property division was a needs-based, income security model, arguably rooted in a breadwinner/dependant 'traditional' view of marriage. It seems that in this model, any notion of equality has little place in determinations of fairness in division of assets. The second was a compensation model, which may be rooted in a partnership philosophy of marriage and in which we can see some idea of substantive equality in determinations of fairness; and the third was a clean-break model which may be rooted in a highly indi-vidualised model of marriage and in which formal equality until recently dominated in determinations of fairness. That no statutory provision at all is made for non-married or non-registered cohabitants seems to suggest that their relationships are outside the scope of legal concern entirely, or at least that it is fair that their relationships remain governed by the common law of formal equality and separate property. Deciding which model is to be applied in any given case depends, says Miles, on 'what we think is the more ideologically acceptable justification for distributing wealth' (Miles 2008: 392) after rela-tionship breakdown. Is it to compensate for the consequences of the roles undertaken during the marriage? In this case, then the Law Commission's proposals on cohabitation make sense for both married/civilly registered partners and cohabitants. Or is it simply that marriage and civil partnership are ultimately insurance-based relationships and there-fore all need is to be provided for? Or is it that domestic relationships are presumed to be 'equal partnerships' and therefore their resources should be divided equally? The case law supports each of these possibilities (Miles 2008; Diduck 2011).

Smith also finds a link between models of marriage and models of financial provision. She says we should expect 'a state's philosophical model of marriage to influence the method it seeks for property division on divorce' (Smith 2000: 215). She identifies five models of marriage:

1. Marriage as Commitment: Marriage is a relationship involving two individuals who have made a lifelong commitment—to each other and to the relationship—that overrides their individual interests in the relationship.
2. Marriage as Partnership: Marriage is a venture designed to promote the interests and development of the individuals who create it.
3. Marriage as Contract: Marriage is a contract of indefinite duration, the continuation of which is subject to the likely changing desires of the individual contracting parties.
4. Marriage as Monarchy: In marriage one must lead and the other must follow, and the leader is accorded the relationship's rights and responsibilities in trust to assure the success of the marriage.
5. Marriage as Democracy: In marriage the spouses are equal to each other in rights, in presumed contributions to the relationship, and in economic and social position; the success of the marriage depends on decisions made by individuals with equal decision-making power. (ibid: 215)

Q Which of these models of marriage are reflected in the MCA 1973? Smith also identifies different models of property division, including an equitable distribution model and an equal division model. She suggests that the first, the equitable distribution model, lies between the partnership and commitment models of marriage: it vests the judge with a wide discretion to distribute property according to needs, and needs are defined in a forward looking way (Smith 2000: 218). She contrasts this with a democracy/partnership model or a democracy/contract model of marriage which would best be served by the equal division model. Comment on Smith's categorisation of marriages and methods of property division. Do her observations and conclusions mean that equality can ever be an appropriate model for property division as long as the commitment model of marriage persists?

If the way the law organises post-separation finances reflects the way it views family living, then there is a reason for advocating substantive equality on separation. The symbolic importance of the law, not necessarily as a direct influence on behaviour, but because it has normative force, means that there are social reasons for being concerned with these private family law decisions. Herring goes so far as to suggest that seeking fairness only between the parties to the divorce may be misguided (Herring 2005a) and Diduck (2009b) locates ancillary relief within in a broader vision of social justice. 'Family' law defines not only individuals' obligations towards one another and their obligations to the family unit as a whole, but also their obligations to society at large. It also defines or regulates the public obligation to families and individual family members and thus raises again the hegemony of liberalism with its emphasis on individuals and its divide between public and private. When we adopt a model of commitment to lifelong relationships we identify a particular role for society to play, or in the case of the private family, not to play, in its support of those individuals and the familial choices they make. In this context, the part that family law and policy are thought to play to alleviate the disadvantage suffered by less powerful members of families—usually the unpaid carers and the cared for—shifts from time to time according to ideas about the nature of the family and its location in society. *White*'s statement, in other words, regarding the (equal) value that ought to be placed on domestic contributions is as important normatively and symbolically as it is financially (Diduck 2009b, 2011), as is *Radmacher's* statement 10 years later about individual autonomy, personal responsibility and the ability to contract out of equality (Hale 2011).

We raised above the arguments that focusing only on private (family) law reform to redress any inequality created by the traditional nuclear family model may not be fair to individual men or even effective for women as a class. Here we wish also to raise the argument that it may actually be counterproductive to gender equality. Even a compensatory approach to maintenance and property division which attributes value to previously unvalued or undervalued home-work and which furthers a type of substantive equality between the spouses may indirectly reinforce the traditional nuclear family model and the inequalities associated with it.

Susan Boyd observes that in cases where compensatory support has been awarded and the feminisation of poverty has been acknowledged, it appears that the state has dealt with the problem (Boyd 1994: 67). She goes on, however:

> Sociologist Margrit Eichler has pointed out that even if the equality principle were fully implemented in family law and women received the full benefit of recognition for their domestic labour, only a tiny minority of women (and children) living in poverty would be assisted ... .
>
> The valuing of women's domestic labour in the family law context is achieved only for a woman who did that work for another person with whom she no longer lives, specifically a male partner. The argument is that her male partner would otherwise be unjustly enriched. Had Ms Peter [see *Peter v Beblow*, referred to in Chapter 6] been a single mother doing much the same work for herself and her children, she would not have had recourse to anyone's property to compensate her. The benefit that society as a whole receives from women's (usually unpaid) domestic labour, particularly in the context of raising children, is thus not recognized. This approach fits with the [Canadian and arguably UK] government's generally neo-conservative anti-statist, pro-market, and pro-'family' approach to child care and economic responsibilities. While courts cannot and perhaps should not impose social programmes, the effect of courts appearing to resolve some social problems through decisions such as *Moge* and *Peter* is to lend ideological support to the state's privatization of financial responsibility.
>
> ...
>
> Increasingly, then, courts and administrative arms of the ... (welfare) state are reinforcing certain private familial responsibilities for women's poverty in the name of feminist values and in part in response to feminist struggle in the courts, while diminishing public societal commitment to alleviating that poverty. Individual men are (again) being held financially responsible to the women they used to live with ... . Women who live more independently from men, or who do not wish to make a private claim upon a man, will almost certainly not be compensated, and woe betide the single mother who cannot find a well-paying job and childcare, and who must therefore rely on welfare. Ideologically, heterosexual relationships—and women's roles as wives and mothers within them—are thus reproduced. (ibid: 67–69)

Q Do you agree with Boyd's analysis? Do you see any role for equality principles in financial and property adjustment after divorce or after separation of unmarried partners? Where same-sex partners separate and dispute the ownership of property, courts thus far have tended to apply the same basic principles as for opposite-sex couples, and often utilise the same sex-role stereotypes,[114] notwithstanding that same-sex partners often organise their domestic and

---

[114] See Chapter 6 above.

employment roles in a non-gendered and more egalitarian way (Dunne 2000). Do you see any scope for change in interpretations of the MCA principles as same-sex partnerships come before the courts? Further, Edwards suggests that the law must also take into account aspects of culture and ethnicity as they form an important part of 'all the circumstances' the court must consider in making financial and property awards. She mentions specifically cultural practices with regard to family property and 'the structural position of Asian women within the private and public world and the specific cultural limitations placed on their opportunities for self-sufficiency and for remarriage' (Edwards 2004: 814). How might the court consider these factors?

FURTHER READING

J CARBONE, 'Feminism, Gender and the Consequences of Divorce' in M Freeman (ed), *Divorce: Where Next?* (Aldershot, Dartmouth, 1996).

A DIDUCK, 'Ancillary Relief: Complicating the Search for Principle' (2011) 38(2) *Journal of Law and Society* 272.

S EDWARDS, 'Division of Assets and Fairness—"Brick Lane"—Gender, Culture and Ancillary Relief on Divorce' (2004) 34 *Fam LJ* 809.

M FINEMAN, *The Illusion of Equality: The Rhetoric and Reality of Divorce Reform* (Chicago, IL, University of Chicago Press, 1991).

C LITTLETON, Reconstructing Sexual Equality' (1987) 75 *California Law Review* 1279.

J MILES, '*Charman v Charman (No 4)*—Making Sense of Need, Compensation and Sharing afer *Miller/ McFarlane*' (2008) *CFLQ* 378.

C SMART, *The Ties That Bind* (London, Routledge and Kegan Paul, 1984).

IM YOUNG, *Justice and the Politics of Difference* (Princeton, NJ, Princeton University Press, 1990).

N WIKELEY, 'Financial Support for Children after Parental Separation: Parental Responsibility and Responsible Parenting' in Probert, Gilmore and Herring, *Responsible Parents and Parental Responsibility* (Oxford, Hart Publishing, 2009).

8

Equal Status under the Children Act 1989: Parental Responsibility

I. INTRODUCTION

In Chapter 4 we examined the concept of parental responsibility and how it is acquired. For the purposes of this chapter, it is important to remember that parental responsibility is a status and is not related to the work of childcare. It empowers a person, usually a parent, to make decisions about the child's upbringing. These decisions relate to many matters in the child's life, from education to healthcare to discipline.

We noted that parental authority is now generally conceived of as existing primarily for the benefit of the child, in that it enables parents to carry out their obligations to their children.[1] Nevertheless, 'the notion that parental authority is of real significance remains powerful' (Cretney 1996a: 136), for who is vested with parental authority shows us whom the law regards as entitled to play a part in a child's upbringing and to make decisions about that child. The allocation of parental authority throws light on the model of the family that is dominant in society and that attracts the imprimatur of the law. It is not surprising, therefore, that the history of the law governing parental status has been marked by the struggle of women against a strict patriarchal hierarchy within the family and towards legal parity with men. Nor is it surprising that more recent years have seen campaigns by men's groups which contend that mothers are now favoured and fathers are being marginalised by the law. This has resulted in a change in the law to vest parental responsibility automatically in most fathers; parental responsibility is conferred on those fathers who jointly register the child's birth. The law has also responded to the changes in family structures to offer the possibility of parental responsibility to step-parents and to same-sex civil partners.[2]

In this chapter, we examine the historical context within which the concept of parental responsibility developed and consider its practical as well as its symbolic significance. Our discussion focuses to a large extent on the theme of equality but it also touches on that of welfare. We will see that it is assumed that it is best for children to have both parents involved in their lives.

---

[1] But see Reece (2009a).
[2] S 4A Children Act 1989.

II. FROM PATERNAL RIGHTS TO SHARED PARENTAL RESPONSIBILITY

Historically, in the eyes of the law, legitimate children belonged to their father, and he had sole rights of custody and control over them. So extensive were these rights that the father was empowered to appoint a guardian, over the mother, to exercise authority over his children on his death.[3] The mother, by contrast, had no parental rights and her legal identity was subsumed under that of her husband.[4] Although by the nineteenth century, the courts did sometimes intervene to restrict the father's rights, this was only where his behaviour was 'exceptionally culpable' (Maidment 1984: 112)[5] so that he forfeited his right to custody.

Mothers' statutory rights emerged piecemeal over the years,[6] beginning, in 1839, with the right, on separation, to apply for access to their children up to full age and to seek custody of children up to the age of 7.[7] The Matrimonial Causes Act 1857, which introduced judicial divorce, gave the court wide discretion to deal with the custody, education and maintenance of children. This discretion was partially extended to cases other than those involving divorce or judicial separation by the Custody of Infants Act 1873. That statute also raised the maximum age at which the courts could award custody of children to their mothers from 7 to 16. In addition, it removed the bar, which existed under the 1839 Act, on custody petitions from adulterous mothers.

In 1886, the Guardianship of Infants Act established mothers as sole guardians of their children where the father died without appointing a guardian. Where a guardian had been appointed by the father or by the court, the mother was entitled to act jointly with him. Moreover, the Act went even further: it 'destroyed the concept of the family as a domestic kingdom ruled by the father' (Bainham 2005: 11). It empowered the court to make such order as it thought fit in relation to the custody or access of an infant 'having regard to the welfare of the infant, and to the conduct of the parents, and to the wishes as well of the mother as of the father'.[8]

The statutory erosion of paternal rights continued into the twentieth century, and the Guardianship of Infants Act 1925 was passed after vigorous campaigning by a leading women's group.[9] This Act explicitly stated in its Preamble that its goal was to establish the principle of equality between men and women in relation to their legitimate children. The Act therefore stipulated that in proceedings before the court concerning the custody or upbringing of an infant, or concerning the property of an infant, the court should have regard to the welfare of the child as the first and paramount consideration and should not consider that the claim of the father was superior to that of the mother or vice versa.

---

[3] The Tenures Abolition Act 1660, as amended by the Wills Act 1837.

[4] See, generally, Maidment (1984: 108ff).

[5] See, eg, *R v Greenhill* (1836) 4 Ad & E 624 where Lord Denman CJ noted that 'the right of the father would not be acted upon where the enforcement of it would be attended with danger to the child; as where there was an apprehension of cruelty, or of contamination by some exhibition of gross profligacy' (640). The fact that the father was involved in an adulterous relationship was not of itself decisive.

[6] For a detailed account of this process, see Maidment (1984: ch 5).

[7] Custody of Infants Act 1839. For an historical account of the passage of this legislation, see Maidment (1984: 113–16).

[8] S 9.

[9] See, for an account of the events leading up to the passing of the legislation, Cretney (1996a).

Q The Guardianship of Infants Acts 1886 and 1925 both introduced the welfare of the child as a consideration in decisions concerning children. What do you think explains the shift from parental status, and paternal authority in particular, to welfare?

It was during the course of the struggle towards gender equality that the welfare principle became prominent and, indeed, Maidment suggests that it developed as a device to sidestep women's claims:

> The welfare of the child principle was ... used in the nineteenth century to deny a mother any right to custody, or even access, because the judges deemed the welfare of the child to be best served by upholding the 'sacred rights of the father' to his children. Conversely the welfare principle was used at this time to dilute women's demands for equal parental rights to their children. Indeed the 1925 Act was a political device to actually deny women equality of parental rights. (Maidment 1984: 107–08)

Accordingly, she argues, the welfare principle developed largely in response to women's claims:

> The rise of the welfare principle could only come in proportion to the fall in the sacred rights of fathers, but this fall did not come essentially out of concern for the interest of the child but out of the fight of women's groups for equality of legal rights. This is not to dismiss the Victorian concern for the welfare of children as hollow or empty, but to say that in this particular context it was in fact a by-product of the women's movement. It may have happened anyway, because other developments in society emphasised the child as a centre of concern (in the nineteenth century largely philanthropic, and in the twentieth largely social and scientific). But as historical fact the emergence of the Guardianship of Infants Act 1925 owes far more to the women's movement than to the child protection movement. (ibid: 146–47)

The welfare principle did benefit mothers. Smart explains that shifts in 'the perception of childhood and the construction of modern "scientific" conceptions of child development' (Smart 1989a: 5) fortified women's claims. The development of new types of knowledge, particularly in the spheres of psychiatry, psychoanalysis, psychology and pedagogics, together with feminist lobbying, combined to enable mothers to make new claims relating to their children:

> These power claims were not rights based like men's claims to children; rather they were formulated around the uniqueness of motherhood and the supposedly natural (biological) bond between the mother and the child she has borne. They also invoked the idea of the interests of the child, interests which were gradually defined as inhering in the quality of physical and emotional care provided for a child. Under this regime the care a mother could provide became valued and hence created a shift in the power nexus of parenthood ... . [A]t the point of marital breakdown, if not during a marriage, the valorisation of motherhood gradually modified men's power in relation to children. (ibid: 6)

Mothering came to be seen in the twentieth century as crucial to the welfare of children and mothers therefore tended to be awarded custody by the courts.[10] Nevertheless, the mother had no automatic parental rights or authority; her rights had to be conferred by

---

[10] See Smart (1989a: 8–9) and Chapter 9 below.

means of a court order. With the passing of the Guardianship Act 1973, mothers were eventually given equal rights and authority with the father 'exercisable by either without the other'.[11] Yet even that statute left unchanged the father's status as natural guardian of his legitimate children. It was not until the enactment of the Children Act 1989 that this rule, which admittedly was more of symbolic than practical importance, was finally abolished.[12] Under the Children Act 1989, married parents, both mothers and fathers, acquire parental responsibility automatically; each is entitled to exercise it independently of the other; and neither loses it on divorce.[13]

> **Q** Why do you think both parents retain parental responsibility equally irrespective of events such as divorce? Does this tell us anything about the dominant ideology of the family? Does it tell us anything about the way we conceive of the welfare of children?

III. EXPLANATIONS FOR THE CHANGE TO SHARED AND ENDURING PARENTAL RESPONSIBILITY

The legal framework that existed prior to the Children Act 1989 had become complex and confusing. The reforms were intended to address a number of problems that had been identified and that were considered by the Law Commission (1988b). For example, the kinds of orders available on separation or divorce varied depending on the nature of the proceedings brought (Law Commission 1988b: para 4.2). Also, it was not clear what powers and responsibilities were conveyed by the various statutes and court orders (ibid: paras 2.10 and 4.3). There were also other concerns. It was observed by professionals that the welfare of children was endangered by parental conflict[14] and it was also felt that court intervention in determining the arrangements for children was of limited use (Hoggett 1994: 9). In addition, children were increasingly coming to be seen as the victims of the breakdown of adult relationships (Roche 1991: 346; Piper 1996b). In consequence, there developed a preference for mediation, thought to reduce conflict, and for arrangements which were thought to go some way towards satisfying children's perceived need for continuity in their relationships with both parents.

The Law Commission, therefore, endorsed three principles: the law should intervene as little as possible; in cases of dispute, it should seek to lower the stakes; and court orders should reduce the opportunities for conflict and litigation in the future (Law Commission 1988b: para 4.5).[15] It also endorsed the 'fundamental principle ... that the primary responsibility for the upbringing of children rests with their parents' (ibid: para 2.1).[16] The role of the state in regulating the relationship between parents and children should be a residual one.

The Law Commission envisaged its reforms as having the effect of providing a realistic framework for decision-making while encouraging the involvement of both parents, even

---

[11] S 1(1) of the Guardianship Act 1973.
[12] S 2(4) of the Children Act 1989.
[13] See further Chapter 4 above.
[14] See further Chapters 9 and 15 below.
[15] See, for discussion, King (1987: 186).
[16] See, further, Eekelaar (1991a) and Chapter 13 below.

after separation or divorce, in the upbringing of their children. It took the view that the incidents of parenthood could not be realistically divided up into different-sized packages and, since '[m]ost parental responsibilities can only be exercised while the parent has the child' (Law Commission 1988b: para 4.8), 'power and responsibility should go hand in hand and largely "run with the child"' (Law Commission 1986: para 4.53(d)). This, it stated (ibid: para 4.53(d)), would be preferable to joint custody, which was gaining in popularity at the time, where one parent had physical care and the other had ill-defined powers to intervene. Accordingly, the legislation gives both parents equal status and each has the capacity to act independently of the other in the absence of a court order to the contrary. In the event of a dispute, a parent may invoke the provisions of section 8 in order to seek its resolution by the court. The statute enables a parent[17] to seek a residence order, determining with whom the child shall live; a contact order, determining whether there may be contact with the child and, if so, what form that contact will take; a specific issue order, settling a specific question which arises concerning parental responsibility for a child; or a prohibited steps order, precluding a person, without the consent of the court, from taking a designated step which could be taken by a parent in exercising parental responsibility.

> [W]e believe it important to preserve the equal status of parents and their power to act independently of one another unless and until a court orders otherwise. This should be seen as part of the general aim of encouraging both parents to feel concerned and responsible for the welfare of their children. A few respondents suggested that they should have a legal duty to consult one another on major matters in their children's lives, arguing that this would increase parental co-operation and involvement after separation or divorce. This is an objective which we all share. However, whether or not the parents are living together, a legal duty of consultation seems both unworkable and undesirable.[18] The person looking after the child has to be able to take decisions in the child's best interests as and when they arise. … In practice, where the parents disagree about a matter of upbringing the burden should be on the one seeking to prevent a step which the other is proposing, or to impose a course of action which only the other can put into effect, to take the matter to court.
>
> (Law Commission 1988b: para 2.10, footnote omitted)

Roche commented that it was assumed that the durability of parental responsibility would contribute to a reduction in disputes over children because there would be less to fight over. The court's powers are restricted to the making of section 8 orders and these do not 'fundamentally disturb' parental responsibility. 'The assumption is that because conflict will be reduced, children will benefit' (Roche 1991: 349). He observed that:

> The legislative change was accompanied by a rhetoric of parenthood which stressed the consensual resolution of disputes between parents over their children. … By definition, parents who fight over such matters are in the wrong. Thus dual-parenting became the new aim of legislation and social policy initiatives and indicated not only how best to resolve disputes over children, but also how the preferred post-divorce arrangements should be organised. (ibid: 346–47)

---

[17] Among others. See s 10 Children Act 1989. This section has been amended to enable step-parents and civil partners who have acquired parental responsibility under s 4A to seek s 8 orders without the leave of the court. Civil partners and step-parents who have treated a child as a child of the family are entitled to apply for residence and contact orders as of right.

[18] But see below on the duty to consult.

IV. PARENTAL RESPONSIBILITY, WELFARE AND EQUALITY

Parental responsibility is assumed to encourage parents to behave more responsibly and to be actively involved in their children's lives. To a large degree, it has been the influence of social science research into the needs of children that has prompted policymakers to adopt what Maclean and Eekelaar (1997: 50) have referred to as the 'new orthodoxy': a conviction that it is important for children's welfare that parents are not in conflict and that both parents participate in their children's upbringing. A number of studies have highlighted the adverse effects of divorce for children and have pointed to conflict between parents as one of the primary sources of these difficulties.[19] They have also pointed to the detrimental effects on children of the loss of a parent, usually the father, on the break-up of the family, and have suggested that for the child to sustain a relationship with both parents after breakdown is important in ameliorating the effects of divorce.[20]

Probably one of the most influential of these studies round the time the Children Act 1989 was being drafted was that of Wallerstein and Kelly, documented in their book, *Surviving the Breakup* (1980).

> Although the initial breakup of the family is profoundly stressful, the eventual outcome depends, in large measure, not only on what has been lost, but on what has been created to take the place of the failed marriage. In full and proper perspective, the effect of the divorce is an index of the success or failure of the participants, parents and children, to master the disruption, to negotiate the transition successfully, and to create a more gratifying family to replace the family that failed. (Wallerstein and Kelly 1980: 304–05)

> Taken as a whole our findings point to the desirability of the child's continuing relationship with both parents during the postdivorce years in an arrangement which enables each parent to be responsible for and genuinely concerned with the well-being of the children. ... Although the influence of the legal structure on the fabric of family life may be considerably less than many persons believe it to be, nevertheless, there is some evidence that legal accountability may influence and shore up psychological and financial responsibility. Furthermore, there is evidence in our findings, that lacking legal rights to share in decisions about major aspects of their children's lives, that many noncustodial parents withdrew from their children in grief and frustration. ...
>
> [W]e offer a view diametrically opposed to that of our esteemed colleagues Goldstein, Freud and Solnit in their book *Beyond the Best Interests of the Child*. ... Our findings regarding the centrality of both parents to the psychological health of children and adolescents alike leads us to hold that, where possible, divorcing parents should be encouraged and helped to shape post-divorce arrangements which permit and foster continuity in the children's relations with both parents. (ibid: 310–11)

Indeed, the conclusions reached by Goldstein, Freud and Solnit (1980a) were very different. They drew attention to the limitations of the law in regulating matters such as the parent–child relationship and warned against the unreliable predictive value of the knowledge on which its judgments can be based (ibid: 50–51). All that can be done, they suggested, is to identify who, amongst the available adults, is or has the capacity to become the child's psychological parent, and so will make the child feel wanted. This would probably be the

---

[19] See further Chapters 10 and 15 below.
[20] See, eg, Hetherington (1979: 855–56).

adult with whom the child has had and continues to have an affectionate bond. Once this decision is made, they argued, it should be final and it should be that parent alone who decides how he or she wishes to raise the child (ibid: 38).

As Maclean and Eekelaar (1997: 51–52) observe, this approach was criticised as leading to an imbalance of power between parents. Also the political climate in the 1970s, with the growth of men's groups, was against it and it had little impact. The 'new orthodoxy', in contrast, continues to find support.[21]

Children's well-being is identified with the preservation of ties with both caretaking and non-resident parents and parental responsibility is regarded as one of the mechanisms for preserving and enhancing the relationship between the non-resident parent and the child.[22] Hence, one of the central justifications for giving divorced non-resident parents (usually fathers) and unmarried fathers parental responsibility was that this would encourage fathers to feel responsible for their children and to be involved in their children's lives. Another was the perception that fairness and justice demanded the equalising of the legal status of both parents. Yet while parental equality is assumed to promote children's welfare, this is not self-evident. Parental responsibility is concerned with decision-making and status[23] rather than childcare or contact after parental separation.[24] And, as Wallbank says, 'equal status does not necessarily translate into equal participation in family life' (Wallbank 2009a: 297).

Nevertheless the observation made by Smart, writing in 1989, that heightened significance was being accorded in the dominant discourse to the involvement or influence of fathers[25] still holds true. She observed that the confluence of a changed deployment of the welfare principle with equality claims have combined to make fathers' claims virtually unanswerable. Fathers' rights groups have argued that the law is biased in favour of mothers and that fathers are being denied equal rights. And their claims have been

---

[21] See Chapter 10 below.

[22] Interestingly, this argument appears to have been extended to non-biological, social parents who were neither married to nor civil partners of the biological parent. See *Re H (Shared Residence: Parental Responsibility)* [1995] 2 FLR 1023; *Re A (A Child) (Joint Residence: Parental Responsibility)* [2008] EWCA Civ 867; [2008] 2 FLR 1593, for instances where the court awarded shared residence to enable the putative father to have parental responsibility. In *Re G (Children) (Shared Residence Order: Parental Responsibility)* [2005] EWCA Civ 462; [2005] 2 FLR 957, the Court of Appeal awarded a shared residence order to the lesbian former partner of the mother of children born into the relationship as a result of artificial insemination. The court pointed out that this order was the only way the former partner could gain parental responsibility. Parental responsibility was crucial, said the court, because without it, the former partner would be marginalised from the children's lives. What is notable about the judgment is the idea that the children's welfare is best served by the involvement of both parents, whatever their sex, and the notion that parental responsibility enables parents to play a role in their children's lives. In all three of these cases, the applicants were clearly already involved parents. However, the importance of biological parenthood over social parenthood was stressed by the House of Lords in the context of a lesbian relationship when reversing the decision in *Re G* and making the child's primary residence the mother's home (*Re G (Children)* [2006] UKHL 43; [2006] 1 WLR 2305).When it comes to biological fathers in particular, it is the case that they, as opposed to social parents, are generally regarded in a special light; this is apparent from the fact that social parents cannot get parental responsibility automatically or through something akin to registration. There must be an agreement or an order of court. Parental responsibility is often granted to biological fathers irrespective of the extent of their past and likely future involvement in their child's life. But see, for a case where a biological father was refused parental responsibility even though he was involved in his child's life, albeit not on a day-to-day basis, *R v E and F (Female Parents: Known Father)* [2010] EWHC 417 (Fam); [2101] 2 FLR 383. For a critical analysis of the case law, see Reece (2009b).

[23] The courts have often approached parental responsibility orders primarily as status-conferring devices.

[24] The previous Labour government's reasoning appears to have been that if parents are made to be responsible, contact will take place. See Wallbank (2009a: 310, 307).

[25] See Smart (1989a: 9).

strengthened by the fact that, increasingly, children's welfare has come to be linked more closely with paternal influence. Noting this shift, Smart stated that:

> [F]or many, to be a father carries very different meanings, emotions and behaviours than in the pre-war period. Such changes have coincided with legal changes in which the father has lost his legal authority whilst being regarded as more and more central to the family in emotional and psychological terms. The father as constituted in legal discourse is no longer the paterfamilias, he is the producer of normal, heterosexual children, the stabilizing anti-delinquency agent, and the bringer of realistic values and the desire for achievement. (Smart 1991: 485–86)

Drawing on the work of Tronto, she distinguished between 'caring for' and 'caring about' children. Mothers typically do more of the physical work of caring for children and, she said, this 'caring for' can be seen as a 'moral practice'. Yet it is assumed to be 'natural' and it is therefore rendered invisible. There is no legitimate language in which mothers can frame moral claims based on this work; mothers are not heard unless they speak in the language of welfare or equality:

> [T]he central and determining metaphors in family law have become the welfare of the child and the importances [sic] of the father as an instrument of welfare and as an individual who earns legal standing. The mother seems to lose her standing. My point is not, of course, that courts or legal policy ignore mothers, nor that mothers have no part to play in the legal proceedings. However, it is not clear to me that there is any longer a language available for mothers to voice their subject position in law. (Smart 1991: 486, footnotes omitted)

> [W]here there is a conflict, there is a tendency for the welfare principle to make the moral claims made by these mothers, based on the work of 'caring for', appear to be statements of self-interest. Equally, the fathers' rights principle makes such claims appear to resemble the unacceptable and 'old-fashioned' appeal to biological motherhood which is now renounced in favour of a policy of equality. The consequence is that such claims are disregarded or silenced. Moreover, the mother is constituted as selfish and self-serving. ...
>   [W]e view women's caring work as a natural attribute which requires little or no substantive acknowledgement, while men's expression of 'caring about' seems increasingly to occupy a sentimental and sacred place in the dominant moral and legal order. (ibid: 494)

Collier has also remarked on the way in which talk of equality and welfare obscures the way in which parenting is actually done. Referring to *Supporting Families* (Home Office 1998), a policy document published by the Home Office when the Labour government was in office, he commented that what was portrayed there was:

> a family marked by the qualities of emotional and sexual equality, mutual rights and responsibilities, a negotiated authority over children, co-parenting and—of particular relevance to discussion of fatherhood—a clear belief in promoting the commitment on the part of both women *and* men to lifelong obligations to children. (Collier 2001: 527)

Men, it is assumed, can parent as well as women, and the law, he noted, has been regarded as having a key role in getting men involved in the family (ibid: 533). Yet, 'there exists a marked disjuncture between the rhetoric of gender convergence and the realities of family practices' (ibid: 537); women remain the primary carers of children (ibid: 542). Indeed men resist change to childcare practices and they resist because it suits them to do so (ibid). The debates about law and the family, which emphasise gender neutrality and equality, are unconnected with the realities of care.[26]

For Sheldon (2001: 114–16), the realities of childcare invalidate the arguments advanced in favour of extending parental responsibility to unmarried fathers who register the birth.[27] While conceding that it cannot be assumed that all unmarried fathers are irresponsible and so undeserving of rights, she says that there is no evidence that all are playing a useful role. It is easier to generalise about mothers because most unmarried mothers do in fact assume an active parenting role. As they are in general the primary carers, it thus makes sense for them to have parental responsibility. The argument that men are unfairly discriminated against is therefore unfounded. Moreover the argument that having parental responsibility makes men play a greater role in childcare has no empirical basis (ibid).

Wallbank too is critical of the amended law for its disregard of the practice of childcare. She states that the change is 'based upon the ethics of justice and fairness as opposed to the ethic of care' (Wallbank 2002: 278). To invoke fairness and justice is to focus on abstract principles and to give prominence to issues of equality and the possession of rights'. This, she says, occurs at the 'expense of a consideration of the practical work that women perform as mothers' (ibid: 280) and, we might add, of the well-being of children.

V. HAVING AND ACQUIRING PARENTAL RESPONSIBILITY

While parents who are married to each other are both automatically vested with parental responsibility,[28] the legal status of parents is different if they do not marry. Section 2(2) of the Children Act 1989 states:

Where a child's father and mother were not married to each other at the time of his birth—

(a) the mother shall have parental responsibility for the child;
(b) the father shall have parental responsibility for the child if he has acquired it (and has not ceased to have it) in accordance with the provisions of this Act.

The ways in which the Act permits an unmarried father[29] to acquire parental responsibility are set out in section 4.

Section 4 provides:

Acquisition of parental responsibility by father.

4(1) Where a child's father and mother were not married to each other at the time of his birth, the father shall acquire parental responsibility for the child if—

---

[26] See also Smart (2006a) and Collier and Sheldon (2008). See also Chapter 10 below.

[27] See below.

[28] S 2(1) Children Act 1989. For further discussion of parental responsibility, including the position of married parents, see Chapters 4, 10 and 11. Special guardians have parental responsibility automatically (s 14C(1) (a) Children Act 1989). This parental responsibility can be exercised to a large extent to the exclusion of any other person with parental responsibility, such as the parents (s 14C(1)(b) Children Act 1989). Prospective adopters with whom a child is placed for adoption also have parental responsibility (s 25 Adoption and Children Act 2002.).

[29] See, for a summary of the debates concerning the desirability or otherwise of granting unmarried fathers automatic parental responsibility, Herring (2011: 362–67).

(a) [except where subsection (1C) applies,][30] he becomes registered as the child's father under any of the enactments specified in subsection 1A;

(b) he and the child's mother make an agreement (a 'parental responsibility agreement') providing for him to have parental responsibility for the child; or

(c) the court, on his application, orders that he shall have parental responsibility for the child.

(1A) The enactments referred to in subsection (1)(a) are—

(a) paragraphs (a), (b) and (c) of section 10(1) and section 10A(1) of the Births and Deaths Registration Act 1953 ... .

[(1C) The father of a child does not acquire parental responsibility by virtue of subsection (1) (a) if, before he became registered as the child's father under the enactment in question—

(a) the court considered an application by him for an order under subsection (1)(c) in relation to the child but did not make such an order, or

(b) in a case where he had previously acquired parental responsibility for the child, the court ordered that he was to cease to have that responsibility.][31]

(2) No parental responsibility agreement shall have effect for the purposes of this Act unless—

(a) it is made in the form prescribed by regulations made by the Lord Chancellor; and

(b) where regulations are made by the Lord Chancellor prescribing the manner in which such agreements must be recorded, it is recorded in the prescribed manner.

(2A) A person who has acquired parental responsibility under subsection (1) shall cease to have that responsibility only if the court so orders.

(3) The court may make an order under subsection (2A) on the application—

(a) of any person who has parental responsibility for the child; or

(b) with the leave of the court, of the child himself,

subject, in the case of parental responsibility acquired under subsection (1)(c), to section 12(4).

(4) The court may only grant leave under subsection (3)(b) if it is satisfied that the child has sufficient understanding to make the proposed application.

There are now also analogous provisions governing the acquisition of parental responsibility by a second female parent where the child is conceived through assisted reproduction and the agreed female parenthood conditions[32] have been met:

4ZA Acquisition of parental responsibility by second female parent

(1) Where a child has a parent by virtue of section 43 of the Human Fertilisation and Embryology Act 2008 and is not a person to whom section 1(3) of the Family Law Reform Act 1987 applies, that parent shall acquire parental responsibility for the child if—

(a) [except where subsection (3A) applies,][33] she becomes registered as a parent of the child under any of the enactments specified in subsection (2);

(b) she and the child's mother make an agreement providing for her to have parental responsibility for the child; or

(c) the court, on her application, orders that she shall have parental responsibility for the child.

---

[30] Provisions in brackets are not yet in force at the time of writing.
[31] Not in force at time of writing.
[32] Human Fertilisation and Embryology Act 2008, s 44.
[33] Words in brackets not in force at time of writing.

Section 12 stipulates:

12 Residence orders and parental responsibility

(1) Where the court makes a residence order in favour of the father of a child it shall, if the father would not otherwise have parental responsibility for the child, also make an order under section 4 giving him that responsibility

(1A) Where the court makes a residence order in favour of a woman who is a parent of a child by virtue of section 43 of the Human Fertilisation and Embryology Act 2008 it shall, if that woman would not otherwise have parental responsibility for the child, also make an order under section 4ZA giving her that responsibility.

(2) Where the court makes a residence order in favour of any person who is not the parent or guardian of the child concerned that person shall have parental responsibility for the child, while the residence order remains in force.

(3) Where a person has parental responsibility for a child as a result of subsection (2), he shall not have the right—

...

(b) to agree or refuse to agree, to the making of an adoption order, or an order under section 84 of the Adoption and Children Act 2002 with respect to the child; or
(c) to appoint a guardian for the child.

(4) Where subsection (1) or (1A) requires the court to make an order under section 4 or 4ZA in respect of the parent of a child, the court shall not bring that order to an end at any time while the residence order concerned remains in force.

For many years, the only ways in which a step-parent could get parental responsibility were by means of adoption or by means of a residence order. However the Act was amended to extend the possibility of gaining parental responsibility to step-parents and to registered civil partners.[34] The change does not apply to a cohabitant who is not the child's parent, however.

4A Acquisition of parental responsibility by step-parent

(1) Where a child's parent ('parent A') who has parental responsibility for the child is married to or a civil partner of a person who is not the child's parent ('the step-parent')—

(a) parent A or, if the other parent of the child also has parental responsibility for the child, both parents may by agreement with the step-parent provide for the step-parent to have parental responsibility for the child; or
(b) the court may, on the application of the step-parent, order that the step-parent shall have parental responsibility for the child.

(2) An agreement under subsection (1)(a) is also a 'parental responsibility agreement' and section 4(2) applies in relation to such agreements as it applies in relation to parental responsibility agreements under section 4.

(3) A parental responsibility agreement under subsection (1)(a), or an order under subsection (1)(b), may only be brought to an end by an order of the court made on the application—

(a) of any person who has parental responsibility for the child; or

---

[34] S 4ZA provides for the acquisition of parental responsibility by a second female parent in cases of assisted reproduction under the Human Fertilisation and Embryology Act 2008.

(b) with the leave of the court, by the child himself.

(4) The court may only grant leave under subsection (3)(b) if it is satisfied that the child has sufficient understanding to make the proposed application.

VI. PARENTAL RESPONSIBILITY, JOINT PARENTING AND THE DUTY TO CONSULT

According to Bainham, the Act was intended to promote joint parenting where both parents have parental responsibility but is deficient in achieving that aim:

> A regime which allows independent decision-making, without prior consultation, may work perfectly well where parents are living together amicably. ... The situation of parental estrangement or divorce is quite different ... . Here there may well not be harmonious relations or any inclination to co-operate. ... It cannot be assumed that an ex-wife will be well disposed to inform her ex-husband (or vice versa) about plans for the child or that, if she does, she will take his views into account when they clash with her own. The chances are that in many (if not most) cases the ... non-residential parent will be kept at a distance and in the dark.
>
> If ... a major aim of the reformed legislation is to strengthen and encourage dual parenting we might have expected to see written into the Act provisions relating to co-operation or consultation ...
>
> Is the reality, perhaps, that parental responsibility can only be exercised meaningfully by a parent who has the physical care of a child? ... If this is right, the focus of attention should really be on what the Act is doing to promote 'time-sharing', a concept alien to English law, whereby the child spends a significant amount of time in the physical care of each parent. If this yardstick is used, the conclusion must again be that there is little real commitment in the legislation to the principle of dual parenting following divorce.
>
> (Bainham 1990: 211–12, footnotes omitted)

Q What do you understand by 'dual parenting'? Would, in your view, provisions relating to consultation and co-operation better promote dual parenting? Is there a difference between decision-making and childcare? Do you agree that dual parenting was the aim of the legislation? Could it be argued that the retreat of the courts and the 'lowering of the stakes' by ensuring that both parents retain parental responsibility on divorce were intended primarily to reduce conflict and to facilitate the resolution of disputes through agreement?

Eekelaar took the view that dual parenting was not the main aim of the legislation The 'stronger imperative', he said, was to promote parental autonomy and the issue of parental co-operation was always meant to be for the parents to work out (Eekelaar 1991b: 129). Yet there are statutory constraints on independent action. For example, placement for adoption and adoption itself cannot take place unless each parent with parental responsibility (and any guardian) consents.[35] The consent of each parent with parental responsibility (and any guardian) is needed for the marriage of a young person aged 16 or 17.[36] A local authority is not permitted to accommodate a child if anyone with parental responsibility

---

[35] Adoption and Children Act 2002 ss 19, 47, 52. But see, eg, *A Local Authority v M and F; The Children (by their Guardian)* [2009] EWHC 3172; [2010] 1 FLR 1355.

[36] Marriage Act 1949 s 3(1A).

is able and willing to provide or arrange for accommodation.[37] Conversely, anyone with parental responsibility can remove the child from local authority accommodation.[38] If a residence order is made it is not possible to change the child's name or remove the child from the UK without the consent of all those with parental responsibility.[39]

Indeed when it comes to change of surname, irrespective of whether the father opposing the change has parental responsibility,[40] consultation and agreement are required, failing which the matter must be resolved by a court.[41] Change of surname is quite often a source of conflict[42] and, according to Hale LJ, the name of a child has come to have too great a symbolic significance. She regretted that it is often suggested that 'fathers need that outward and visible link in order to retain their relationship with, and commitment to, their child. It is a poor sort of parent whose interest in and commitment to his child depends upon that child bearing his name'.[43]

In addition to extending the requirement for agreement on change of name to those without parental responsibility, and so beyond the bounds of the statute, the courts appear to have extended the circumstances in which some element of co-operation is required. Parental responsibility apparently does entail a duty to consult in some situations and does not merely 'run with the child'. Certain forms of medical treatment, namely circumcision[44] and decisions about the MMR (measles, mumps, rubella) vaccine,[45] require consultation. Changing a child's school too is something that a parent cannot do unilaterally. Glidewell LJ held in *Re G (Parental Responsibility: Education)*[46] that because a mother had parental responsibility, she was 'entitled and indeed ought to have been consulted' by the father, with whom the child was living, about taking this 'important step'. In *Re H (Parental Responsibility)*[47] Butler Sloss LJ appeared to consider the duty to consult a wide-ranging one. She said that a father with parental responsibility would have a right to be heard in adoption and in Hague Convention abduction proceedings. In addition, he would have the 'right to be consulted on schooling, serious medical problems, and other important occurrences in a child's life'.[48] However, as Eekelaar has observed, the obligation is ill-defined. He points out that it is not clear what amounts to consultation. Nor is it clear whether information suffices or whether agreement is necessary.[49] There is no indication of what

---

[37] Children Act 1989 s 20(7).

[38] Children Act 1989 s 20(8).

[39] Children Act 1989 s 13.

[40] It seems that if the father does not have parental responsibility, the mother alone can choose the name initially (Bainham 2005: 134). However, changing the name is different. A disputed change should not be made unilaterally without the authorisation of the court, irrespective of parental responsibility: *Dawson v Wearmouth* [1997] 2 FLR 629 (*obiter*); *Re T (Change of Surname)* [1998] 2 FLR 620; *Re C (Change of Surname)* [1998] 2 FLR 656; *Re R (Surname: Using Both Parents)* [2001] EWCA Civ 1344; [2001] 2 FLR 1358.

[41] *Dawson v Wearmouth* [1997] 2 FLR 629.

[42] See, for a more detailed discussion of the case law, Herring (2011: 522–27).

[43] *Re R (Surname: Using Both Parents)* [2001] EWCA Civ 1344; [2001] 2 FLR 1358 para 18. See further on change of name, *Re S (Change of Names: Cultural Factors)* [2001] 2 FLR 1005; *Re W, Re A, Re B (Change of Name)* [1999] 2 FLR 930; *Re A (A Child) (Change of Name)* [2003] EWCA Civ 56; [2003] 2 FLR 1; *Re H (Child's Name: First Name)* [2002] EWCA Civ 190; [2002] 1 FLR 973.

[44] *Re J (Specific Issue Orders)* [2000] 1 FLR 571.

[45] *Re B (A Child) (Immunisation)* [2003] EWCA Civ 1148; [2003] 2 FCR 156.

[46] [1994] 2 FLR 964, 967.

[47] [1998] 1 FLR 855, 859.

[48] Ibid. See also *Re P (A Minor) (Parental Responsibility Order)* [1994] 1 FLR 578, 585, where parental responsibility was considered analogous to joint custody, which entailed consultation.

[49] Herring suggests that it appears from the case law that there is a duty on the resident parent to consult, rather than to obtain the non-resident parent's consent (Herring 2011: 413).

qualifies as important or serious. Finally, he questions how the obligation to consult can be enforced (Eekelaar 2001c: 429).

In reality, in the event of a disagreement over any decision, the parent with whom the child is physically present is usually, in practice, in a better position to put her wishes into effect.[50] Moreover, it seems that in law, if there is a residence order in force, the non-resident parent cannot interfere with the day-to-day upbringing of the child.[51] But the non-caretaking parent is not powerless; provided he is not acting in a manner that is incompatible with a court order,[52] he can, while the child is with him, reverse the care-taking parent's decisions or, in any event, he can challenge them in court.

Q The Law Commission, commenting on the old joint-custody orders, said that these were being described to absent[53] parents as providing 'an important ratification of their continued parental role' and, at the same time, to caregiving parents concerned at the prospect of interference by absent parents as merely 'a matter of words' (Law Commission 1988b: para 4.3). Do you think similar criticisms can be made of shared parental responsibility?

VII. UNMARRIED FATHERS AND PARENTAL RESPONSIBILITY

As we have seen above, all mothers are automatically vested with parental responsibility as are married fathers.[54] Although the possibility was debated in the past,[55] parental responsibility was not conferred automatically on unmarried fathers because of concern to protect vulnerable mothers (LCD 1998: 2). Until relatively recently, unmarried fathers could acquire parental responsibility under section 4 of the Children Act 1989 only through a parental responsibility agreement with the mother or though an order of court. However section 4 has been amended and an unmarried father can now gain parental responsibility automatically if he registers as the child's father.

In the case of married parents, there is a duty on both to register the birth within 42 days.[56] Where the parents are not married to each other at the time of the birth, however, the father has no obligation to register and has no independent right to do so. Normally, he can be registered as the father only if he and the mother attend to register together or, if not, then with the consent of the mother. In the latter case, the mother and the father are each required to provide a declaration that he is the father. Independent registration by either mother or father of the father's name is permitted only where there is a parental responsibility agreement or where a relevant court order can be produced, together with a declaration that it is still in force. The relevant court orders include a parental responsibility order and an order made under Schedule 1 of the Children Act 1989 instructing

---

[50] This is most often the mother. In over 90% of lone-parent families, it is the mother with whom the child lives. See Blackwell and Dawe (2003: para 1.3), Simpson et al (1995: 3).

[51] *Re P (A Minor) (Parental Responsibility Order)* [1994] 1 FLR 578, 585. This appears to be the case even if there is no residence order. See below.

[52] Children Act 1989, s 2(8).

[53] This term has now been replaced by 'non-resident' parents.

[54] Children Act 1989 s 2(1).

[55] See Law Com Report No 118 (1982).

[56] Births and Deaths Registration Act 1953 s 2.

the father to make financial provision for the child.[57] Unless one of these requirements is met, the father's name cannot be entered on the register.[58] However it can be entered at a later stage if the parents jointly request this; if the necessary declarations are made; if there is a parental responsibility agreement; if there is a relevant order of court; or if the parents have married.[59]

Intimations of the move to give parental responsibility to all fathers registered on the birth certificate came with a Consultation Paper (LCD 1998), which noted that the lack of parental responsibility might put fathers at disadvantage in situations like adoption. In addition, it said, parental responsibility 'may be important to people as a symbol of the legal status of parenthood, and it may be a particular source of grievance for some unmarried fathers that they may be forced to support their children financially, whether or not they have acquired parental responsibility under the Children Act 1989' (ibid: 2). It was also noted that few fathers actually got parental responsibility under the Act; the number of agreements and orders was small (ibid: para 53).

As Sheldon says, the anomaly the law was intended to redress was not that there were large numbers of fathers involved in the long-term day-to-day care of children who did not have parental responsibility. Rather it was the fact that there were many men who did not have the rights and status of parental responsibility despite being genetic fathers (Sheldon 2001: 99).[60]

The arguments that prompted the change centred on the issue of fairness and on claims that fathers were being discriminated against.[61] There was also the view that if unmarried fathers were given automatic parental responsibility, this would help to 'promote more involvement by absent fathers in the lives of their children' (Sharp 2001: 610). Without a change in the law, men would continue to be 'condemned as somehow undeserving' and this would only confirm in them the apathy and detachment that leads them to lose contact with their children (ibid). Extra litigation about specific issues would be a price worth paying for justice for fathers and children (ibid).

Another impetus for change[62] was a research study exploring the perceptions held by fathers of their legal status (Pickford 1999). Pickford found that, in her sample, three-quarters of fathers, whether married or unmarried, were not aware that there was a difference in the legal status of married and unmarried fathers. Nor did they know that unmarried fathers did not have parental responsibility (ibid: 145). The reactions of the unmarried fathers on being told of their legal position ranged from surprise to anger to anxiety, and '[o]ften fathers expressed their dissatisfaction in terms of unfairness or injustice', frequently referring to child support (ibid: 152). 'They tended to feel strongly that fathers should have rights if they were expected to bear responsibilities' (ibid). A small number reported difficulties in relation to consent to medical treatment of their children. Few knew of the possibility of entering into a parental responsibility agreement and, in any event, interviewees felt awkward about taking this route as it felt like a betrayal of trust in their partners (ibid).

Pickford maintained that the law was out of step with society's ideas about fatherhood,

---

[57] Ibid, s 10.

[58] Ibid, s 10(1).

[59] Ibid, ss 10A and 14.

[60] But a large number of unmarried fathers appear to live with the mother and child. Also, around 45% of fathers who do not register are in 'some kind of contact' with their children (DWP 2007: para 2).

[61] See Wallbank (2002: 291–92). But note that claims of unjustifiable discrimination under the ECHR failed in *McMichael v UK* (1995) 20 EHRR 205 and *B v UK* [2000] 1 FLR 1.

[62] See Eekelaar (2001c: 426).

that it was unfair and that it was potentially 'destabilising of the parental relationship' (ibid: 158). It could also 'undermine the objective of promoting a sense of involvement and responsibility amongst these fathers' (ibid). She recommended conferring parental responsibility on those fathers who registered the birth jointly with mothers: 'If both parents are prepared to recognise the fact of the man's paternity, it appears in itself a strong argument for such a change, and it would also accord with the views of most people' (ibid: 157). In addition, it would have the effect of giving parental responsibility to most unmarried fathers automatically.

As Pickford predicted, the amendment of section 4 to give registered fathers parental responsibility was very significant in numerical terms. Relatively few parents tended to go down the route of parental responsibility agreements or orders. However, the majority of unmarried parents register their children's births jointly. In a Green Paper published in 2007, *Joint Birth Registration: Promoting Parental Responsibility*, it was reported that '[s]ole registrations in England and Wales constitute about 7 per cent (45,000 children) of total birth registrations each year' (DWP 2007: para 2). Hence the majority of fathers now have parental responsibility. Nonetheless further change was thought necessary. The Births and Deaths Registration Act 1953 was amended by the Welfare Reform Act 2009[63] and regulations were drafted[64] to compel an unmarried woman who has not provided details of the father to provide specified information. This is meant to 'enable the father[65] to be contacted by the registrar, with the aim of entering his details on the register'.[66] The mother is exempt from supplying the designated information only if she makes a declaration that one of the conditions in subsection (4) is met:

(4) Those conditions are—

(a) that by virtue of section 41 of the Human Fertilisation and Embryology Act 2008 the child has no father,
(b) that the father has died,
(c) that the mother does not know the father's identity,
(d) that the mother does not know the father's whereabouts,
(e) that the father lacks capacity (within the meaning of the Mental Capacity Act 2005) in relation to decisions under this Part,
(f) that the mother has reason to fear for her safety or that of the child if the father is contacted in relation to the registration of the birth, and
(g) any other conditions prescribed by regulations made by the Minister.

The new provisions give the father ten days to respond to the Registrar's enquiries and, if he does not, the child can be registered in the mother's name alone. In addition, a man who believes he is the father can ask to be registered and this will be done if the mother confirms his paternity (DfCSF 2009a).

Neither the amendment to the 1953 Act nor the draft 2010 regulations has been brought into force. A consultation was conducted in 2009/2010 about the proposed regulations but, following the change in government, the 'policy for birth registration by unmarried parents is still under consideration' (DfE 2010a: Consultation Results).

The aim of the new changes was to promote the acquisition of parental responsibility

---

[63] Births and Deaths Registration Act 1953, s 2B.
[64] The Registration of Births (Parents not Married and Not Acting Together) Regulations 2010.
[65] Similar provisions were drafted to deal with cases where there is a second female parent.
[66] Welfare Reform Act 2009, Explanatory Notes para 354.

by the relatively small number of fathers who do not gain it under the existing law. The reason for this was, according to the Green Paper, to 'embed a cultural norm that fathers should reach the birth of their child with an expectation that they have a clear responsibility for their child' (DWP 2007: para 19). And '[t]his is a key measure to enhance parental responsibility, promote early engagement in the lives of children and encourage parents to have an ongoing relationship with their children' (ibid: para 23). The White Paper that followed did acknowledge the limits of the law but nevertheless reiterated the aim of involving fathers:

> 10. We recognise that joint birth registration will not change the attitude of those fathers who are determined not to play a part in their child's life. However, we hope that encouraging joint birth registration will support a wider cultural shift so that more fathers see their child as their responsibility. (DfCSF and DWP 2008)

The Green and White Papers, then, focused on promoting responsible parenting. This is an approach based on the assumption that law can change attitudes and behaviour. Elsewhere it has been suggested that parental responsibility orders should be restricted to those fathers who are actually actively engaged in parenting.[67] However, the amendment of section 4 of the Children Act 1989, in extending automatic parental responsibility to most unmarried fathers, has shown that registration of the child's birth is regarded as sufficiently indicative of their commitment (LCD Press Release, 2 July 1998; Wallbank 2002: 277).[68]

Of course, it could be said that most mothers who allow joint registration are willingly allowing their partners to gain parental responsibility; joint registration normally requires the mother's consent. But there is the question of how to ensure that that consent is given freely and not under pressure. There is also the question of how to ensure that mothers know what the legal effect of joint registration is. Furthermore, it is open to doubt whether many mothers will know of their right to seek revocation. And if the new changes are implemented, the pressure on mothers will increase and their consent will be largely irrelevant. For those fathers who do not register, however, it may be that the court's willingness to grant orders may be affected. Masson has already suggested that applicants for parental responsibility orders may, at the very least, be expected to explain why they have not done so (Masson 2003: 581).

VIII. THE UNMARRIED FATHER AND HUMAN RIGHTS

Even if the amendment to the 1953 Act and the draft 2010 regulations are brought into force, unmarried fathers will still be in a legal position that differs from that of mothers and married fathers. In the past, there have been complaints about discrimination and attempts have been made to challenge the legal distinction between unmarried fathers and their married counterparts by using rights discourse.[69] In *B v UK*,[70] however, the ECtHR

---

[67] See Kaganas (1996).

[68] The LCD Press Release (2 July 1998) also states that automatic parental responsibility will encourage such fathers to meet their responsibilities.

[69] See further Choudhry and Herring (2010: 207–08, 323ff).

[70] [2000] 1 FLR 1. See also *McMichael v UK* (1995) 20 EHRR 205.

held a complaint of discrimination under Article 14 ECHR inadmissible. The court declared that there was an 'objective and reasonable justification' (5) for the difference in treatment in relation to automatic parental responsibility. The 'relationship between unmarried fathers and their children', said the court, 'varies from ignorance and indifference to a close stable relationship indistinguishable from the conventional family-based unit' (5). In addition, discrimination against fathers without parental responsibility was justified; fathers with care of their children had different responsibilities from those who merely had contact (6).[71]

Bainham argues that the position taken by the ECtHR and also the English legislation, even after the reform of section 4 of the Children Act 1989, are 'at odds' with the UN Convention on the Rights of the Child (Bainham 2005: 216). He cites Article 7(1), which gives the child, as far as possible, the right, from birth, 'to know and be cared for by his or her parents'. He also refers to Article 18(1) which provides that states should try to 'ensure recognition of the principle that both parents have common responsibilities for the upbringing and development of the child' (ibid). He says that the Convention requires that proof of paternity should give rise to the child's right to know and have a relationship, if possible, with his or her father. Likewise, he suggests, proof of paternity alone should suffice to confer automatic parental responsibility (ibid: 216–17).

This argument hinges on a particular interpretation of 'care' and 'responsibility'. It can only be sustained if parental responsibility is, as Bainham says, seen as primarily a 'status-conferring device' (ibid: 207). It is only if one dissociates the notion of care from material, physical caring activity that the Convention can be read in the way Bainham suggests. And if it is emotional care he is concerned with, it is not clear how parental responsibility will enhance emotional bonds. In addition, it is questionable whether giving an uninterested father parental responsibility will ensure that there is recognition of the principle that he is responsible for his child, except in the most abstract and symbolic way. Nevertheless, as Bainham observes, the law has been moving towards greater rights for unmarried fathers, particularly in the context of adoption (ibid: 217). The consent of a father without parental responsibility to the adoption of his child is not necessary.[72] However regulations stipulate that the adoption agency must, if it considers it appropriate, notify a father without parental responsibility of its decision about whether to place a child for adoption.[73] In addition, certain requirements must be met in respect of a 'parent or guardian' and these apply also to the father without parental responsibility. The adoption agency must, if it considers it appropriate, ascertain his wishes and feelings, offer him counselling and information, and ascertain whether he intends to apply for residence, contact or parental responsibility orders.[74]

The position of unmarried fathers without parental responsibility has also been strengthened as a result of the enactment of the Human Rights Act 1998. In *Re M (Adoption: Rights of Natural Father)*[75] the court observed that in the majority of cases, the father has to be informed of the adoption of his child, however 'unpalatable' this might be for the mother and however 'problematic' for the adoption agency. The duty arises even when the father is unaware of the child's existence. In that case, however, the child's and

---

[71] However, some fathers who do not have parental responsibility do live with their children. See Pickford (1999). This may be less common now that s 4 of the Children Act has been amended.
[72] Adoption and Children Act 2002, s 52(6).
[73] Adoption Agencies Regulations 2005, Reg 19.
[74] Reg 14.
[75] [2001] 1 FLR 745, 755.

the mother's rights under Article 8(2) outweighed the violent father's rights under Article 8 ECHR (right to respect for private and family life) and Article 6 (right to a fair trial).

In *Eski v Austria*[76] the ECtHR held that adoption contrary to an unmarried father's wishes is potentially an infringement of his Article 8 right to family life. However, in this case the father's relationship with the child was not close, whereas she had been living with the stepfather seeking to adopt since the age of six. The father had been given the opportunity to be involved in the proceedings. The decision to grant the adoption was within the margin of appreciation and there had been no violation of Article 8.

Of course, whether the father's rights are engaged at all under the Convention depends on whether there is family life between him and his child that the court deems worthy of protection under Article 8.[77] The existence of family life is subject to a reality test; it is a matter of fact and depends on the presence of close personal ties.[78] The potential for family life also falls within Article 8. There will be family life if the parents have cohabited and the fact that the relationship subsequently breaks down is irrelevant. It seems that the commitment to the mother demonstrated by cohabitation is considered to extend automatically to the new family member. From the moment of the child's birth there exists between the father and child 'a bond amounting to family life'.[79] And this bond may also come into being even if the parents have not cohabited if there are other factors showing a sufficient degree of constancy.[80] In *Lebbink v The Netherlands*[81] the ECtHR said:

35 The Court recalls that the notion of 'family life' under Article 8 of the Convention is not confined to marriage-based relationships and may encompass other *de facto* 'family' ties where the parties are living together out of wedlock. A child born out of such a relationship is *ipso iure* part of that 'family' unit from the moment and by the very fact of its birth. Thus there exists between the child and the parents a relationship amounting to family life.

36 Although, as a rule, cohabitation may be a requirement for such a relationship, exceptionally other factors may also serve to demonstrate that a relationship has sufficient constancy to create de facto 'family ties'. The existence or non-existence of 'family life' for the purposes of Article 8 is essentially a question of fact depending upon the real existence in practice of close personal ties. Where it concerns a potential relationship which could develop between a child born out of wedlock and its natural father, relevant factors include the nature of the relationship between the natural parents and the demonstrable interest in and commitment by the father to the child both before and after its birth. (footnotes omitted)

In *Soderback v Sweden*[82] it appears to have sufficed that, although the father did not live with the child, he showed some commitment to contact. In *Re H; Re G (Adoption: Consultation of Unmarried Father)*[83] the need for cohabitation, or, in its absence, some sign of commitment to the child rather than simply the mother, is clear. The father and mother

---

[76] [2007] ECHR 80.

[77] See *Re J (Adoption: Contacting Father)* [2003] EWHC 199 (Fam); [2003] 1 FLR 933. For an extensive discussion of the concept of family life, see *Singh v Entry Clearance Officer New Delhi* [2004] EWCA Civ 1075; [2004] 3 FCR 72.

[78] *K v United Kingdom* (1987) 50 D&R 199; *K and T v Finland* [2000] 2 FLR 79.

[79] *Keegan v Ireland* (1994) 18 EHRR 342, para 45. See also *Berrehab v The Netherlands* (1989) 11 EHRR 322, para 21.

[80] *Price v United Kingdom*, 55 D&R 224, 234 (Application 12402/86, 9 March 1988). See also *Kroon v The Netherlands* [1995] 19 EHRR 263.

[81] [2004] 3 FCR 59.

[82] (1998) 3 EHRLR 342.

[83] [2001] 1 FLR 646.

of H had cohabited and, although the relationship had ended, the father qualified under Article 8 as having a right to respect for his family life with his child. To have the child adopted without notifying him would be a prima facie breach of his rights. The father also had rights under Article 6. It was held that he should be made aware of the proceedings and given an opportunity to take part. This right could only be overridden in grave cases such as rape or serious domestic violence (para 48). On the other hand, as regards the father of G, his relationship with the mother did not come within the meaning of family life; they had not cohabited and, although it lasted seven years, the relationship lacked commitment. Because he had no right to respect for family life, no obvious issue arose under Article 8 which engaged Article 6.

IX. PARENTAL RESPONSIBILITY ORDERS

The change in the law to allow for automatic parental responsibility for unmarried fathers who register the birth jointly with the mother has enhanced the de facto equality of fathers and mothers and it has reduced the need for parental responsibility orders. The new amendment and regulations, if they come into force, will reduce the need for orders even further. At present orders are still necessary for fathers who were not aware of the pregnancy or birth and who cannot meet the other requirements for registration; for fathers who cannot gain the co-operation of mothers in effecting a joint registration; and for fathers whose registration pre-dated the coming into effect of the amendment to section 4 of the Children Act 1989. Orders will continue to be needed in cases where step-parents and civil partners cannot persuade the parent, or both parents if both have parental responsibility, to enter into an agreement.[84]

A parental responsibility order, like the pre-Children Act parental rights order, is perceived as conferring a status on unmarried fathers[85] in recognition of their concerned and responsible attitude to their children. As the court pointed out in *Re S (Parental Responsibility)*,[86] the 1989 Act places a greater emphasis on responsibility than on rights. However, it is apparent from the decided cases that what is required of fathers is that they conform to a particular image of the 'responsible' father espoused by the courts. And it emerges that the notion of responsibility deployed by the courts is coloured by traditional images of 'good mothers' and 'good fathers'. Butler-Sloss LJ in *Re S* stated that, in seeking a parental responsibility order, the father was asking to assume the 'burden as well as [the] pleasure of looking after his child'; he was showing his willingness to shoulder the weight of his duties by sharing responsibility with the mother (659). Yet the case law reveals an apparently collective judicial vision of the family in which 'good' fathers still

---

[84] Masson argues that there is no logical reason for parental consent rather than notification because the step-parent's acquisition of parental responsibility does not affect the parental responsibility of the biological parent. A system based on notification would have placed the burden of initiating proceedings on the objecting parent instead of the step-parent. Objections by the parent will 'serve to discourage applications, add to the expense and increase bitterness between the parents' (Masson 2003: 582). In any event, she says, courts will be loath to refuse applications, particularly where the step-parent and stepchild have 'family life' for the purposes of Art 8 ECHR (ibid). Bainham (2005) has a different view. He says that because parental responsibility will have to be shared between three instead of two people, this would have the effect of weakening the parental responsibility of the objecting non-resident parent (Bainham 2005: 236). He observes that an agreement is only likely where there is a high degree of co-operation between all the parties (ibid 235).

[85] Also step-parents and civil partners, both men and women (s 4A Children Act 1989).

[86] [1995] 2 FLR 648.

play a limited role in caring for their children. It has been said that 'the demands that parenting put upon a mother are infinite in variety and scale'.[87] In contrast, judicial expectations of fathers are somewhat more modest.

The Responsible Father

As Deech points out, parental responsibilities

> include feeding, washing and clothing the child, putting her to bed, housing her, educating and stimulating her, taking responsibility for arranging babysitting and daycare, keeping the child in touch with the wider family circle, checking her medical condition, arranging schooling and transport to school, holidays and recreation, encouraging social and possibly religious or moral development. (Deech 1992: 8)

She maintains that fathers who do not take on a fair share of these tasks do not know their children sufficiently well to be able to make decisions sensibly about their upbringing. However, it is unlikely that the court in *Re S* envisaged these duties being performed by the non-resident father. Instead, it appears that what is required of 'responsible' fathers is some form of 'commitment'.

This criterion derives from the judgment of Balcombe LJ in *Re H (Illegitimate Children: Father: Parental Rights) (No 2)*.[88] The judge formulated the test to be applied in proceedings concerning parental rights orders under the Family Law Reform Act 1987. This test (often referred to as the CAR test), as well as the case law generally on parental rights orders, has been held to be applicable in interpreting section 4 of the 1989 Act.[89] Balcombe LJ suggested that:

> In considering whether to make an order under s 4 of the 1987 Act, the court will have to take into account a number of factors of which the following will undoubtedly be material (although there may well be others, as the list is not intended to be exhaustive):
> (1) the degree of commitment which the father has shown towards the child;
> (2) the degree of attachment which exists between the father and the child; and
> (3) the reasons of the father for applying for the order. (218)

The courts do not require a great deal to convince them of a father's commitment. Certainly, where fathers take on the physical care of their children, even temporarily, the courts regard this as exceptionally strong evidence. So, in *Re P (A Minor) (Parental Responsibility Order)*,[90] the court found unanswerable the case for the father of a girl aged 5½:

> The father has shown, to use the words of the magistrates, 'great love and concern' for the child. He has striven successfully for contact with her from 1990 onwards. In 1992 he was looking after her on an extensive basis for more than half the week for some months, even though she was then only 4 years old. Now, under the order of the magistrates, he is to have her to stay with him on alternate weekends and for further periods in school holidays. ...

---

[87] *Re L (Contact: Transsexual Applicant)* [1995] 2 FLR 438, 442.
[88] [1991] 1 FLR 214.
[89] See *Re CB (A Minor) (Parental Responsibility Order)* [1993] 1 FLR 920, 923.
[90] [1994] 1 FLR 578. See also *Re CB (A Minor) (Parental Responsibility Order)* [1993] 1 FLR 920.

In the light of the authorities to which I have referred and the far lesser involvement of the fathers in those ... cases in the past and likely future lives of their children, it would seem to me that, subject to the point made by the magistrates to which I will now turn, there is an overwhelming case for an order to be made under s 4 of the Act.

The magistrates based their decision on ... 'the reasons of the father for applying for the order' ... .

Prima facie, if a father is committed to his daughter, as is this father to this daughter, his reasons for applying for an order for parental responsibility will be in order to have his commitment reflected in a formal way ... .

Miss Dooley has to concede that, even if her client was without an order for parental responsibility, he could always apply under s 8 of the Act for a specific issue order or a prohibited steps order relating to matters such as schooling, medical treatment, surname etc; but, says Miss Dooley, that is very much a second best and not properly reflective of the father's position in other respects as an active and committed father. (583–84)

As the judge intimated, the case for an order in these circumstances was exceptionally strong. Generally, where fathers are concerned, the courts do not see commitment and attachment as inextricably bound up with the practical care of children. Fathers who show that they care about their children, support them and, where possible, maintain contact with them stand a good chance of being accommodated within the category of 'committed' fathers. In *Re S (Parental Responsibility)*[91] the father's application, which succeeded on appeal, was formulated on the basis that 'he is very fond of this little girl, that he has always paid money for her, that he takes her out regularly, he has regular contact and that he is thoroughly committed to her' (652). What is more, the very act of applying for parental responsibility was taken as evidence of that dedication and served to fortify his case (659).

That fathers are expected to play only a peripheral part in their children's lives emerges clearly from the case law. The court in *Re E (Parental Responsibility: Blood Tests)*[92] asserted that, where a father has demonstrated constant commitment to his child, has had regular contact and has made financial provision, it is prima facie in the child's best interests that a parental responsibility order be made. One of the reasons for this was that, should the mother die, it would be detrimental to the child if the father had no locus standi. The father, therefore, although he had never lived in the same household as his daughter, was seen as a 'reserve' carer who had to be granted legal status.

Indeed, it was held in *Re C (Minors) (Parental Rights)*,[93] a case involving an application for a parental rights order, that although, on the facts, there was little prospect of the father's being able to exercise any of his rights, this was not a sufficient reason for denying him the formal status he sought. It would have 'real and tangible value', not only as something he could 'cherish for the sake of his own peace of mind, but also as a status carrying with it rights in waiting' which were of value to him and, potentially, to the children (4).[94]

Because parental status is seen as divorced from childcare,[95] the court was able in *Re*

---

[91] [1995] 2 FLR 648.

[92] [1995] 1 FLR 392.

[93] [1992] 1 FLR 1.

[94] See also *Re H (A Minor) (Parental Responsibility)* [1993] 1 FLR 484. There, the father's case for an immediate order was strengthened by the fact that he would not be able to have contact with the child in the foreseeable future. This was because, should he apply at a later stage, the lack of contact would make his case a weak one.

[95] See also *Re H (Paternity: Blood Test)* [1996] 2 FLR 65, 82.

C to make an order in favour of a father who had to be excluded from his children's lives; any involvement would, it was found, have been damaging to the mother and therefore harmful to the children. So even if a father is not in a position to make any practical contribution to his children's lives, the courts see it as imperative to confer on him parental status.[96] The status itself is regarded as important. It is a way of acknowledging paternal concern about, if not actual care of, children. And it is perceived as good for children.

Q Why do you think it might be beneficial for children to confer parental status on non-resident fathers?

X. THE WELFARE OF THE CHILD

Decisions as to whether to make an order giving parental responsibility to someone are governed by the welfare principle in section 1 of the Children Act, although the statute does not explicitly require the courts to apply the checklist in section 1(3). It is clear that the factors enumerated in *Re H* (the CAR test) are subordinate to the welfare principle.[97] However, parental responsibility for fathers is thought to enhance children's well-being, and most applications by fathers are successful. This tendency to grant applications is illustrated by the judgments in *Re G (A Minor) (Parental Responsibility Order)*.[98] The child in question was in care as the mother, and to some extent the father, were having problems with alcohol and drugs. It was anticipated that the mother would undergo a detoxification programme and that the child would be returned to her. The father had contact with his daughter but was adjudged by the court of first instance to have little insight into her needs. The Court of Appeal found that, whatever the failings of the father, they were not sufficiently serious to warrant denying him a parental responsibility order:

> I am quite prepared to accept that the making of a parental responsibility order requires the judge to adopt the welfare principle as the paramount consideration. But having said that, I should add that, of course, it is well established by authority that, other things being equal, it is always to a child's welfare to know and, wherever possible, to have contact with both its parents, including the parent with whom it is not normally resident, if the parents have separated.
>
> Therefore, prima facie, it must necessarily also be for the child's benefit or welfare that it has an absent parent sufficiently concerned and interested to want to have a parental responsibility order. In other words, I approach this question on the basis that where you have a concerned although absent father, who fulfils the other test about which I spoke in *Re H* ... then prima facie it would be for the welfare of the child that such an order should be made ... .
>
> At the end of the day, I come back to what is the purpose of a parental responsibility order. It is to give the unmarried father the rights which would have been automatically his by right if he had been married at the time of the child's birth. ...
>
> [L]et me assume against Mr G that he is awkward, difficult, and thoroughly unresponsive to

[96] In *Re G Parental Responsibility Order)* [2006] EWCA Civ 745; [2006] 2 FLR 1092, the court granted 'suspended parental responsibility' which would come into effect if the mother failed to comply with an instruction to provide the father with information about the child. On appeal it was held that there is no provision in the legislation to make such an order.
[97] *M v M (Parental Responsibility)* [1999] 2 FLR 737, 743.
[98] [1994] 1 FLR 504.

the approaches of the social workers who have the interests of his child at heart: even so I cannot see why that should unfit him to have the order which gives him a locus standi in the life of his child. (508–09)

Q Why do you think the court regarded it significant that, had he been married, the father would automatically have had parental responsibility? Given the degree of commitment and attachment required by the courts, do you agree that it is prima facie in a child's interests that the 'natural father' have a say in his child's upbringing?

There seems to be a feeling among judges that it is natural for biological fathers to be involved in making decisions about their children and that it is almost always best for children that this be so. An order is a means of allowing fathers to discharge their paternal obligations. Certainly, this is the tenor of the judgments in *Re S (Parental Responsibility).*[99]

The case concerned a child, aged 7, whose parents separated some 18 months after the birth. In the following year, the father was convicted of being in possession of obscene pædophilic literature. As a result, the mother terminated contact. However, when it became apparent that this distressed the child, contact was resumed and eventually staying contact was allowed. The father's application for a parental responsibility order was refused on the grounds that it would give him the scope to interfere with the arrangements for the child and would deprive the mother of control over contact. The decision was reversed on appeal. Ward LJ stated:

> It is wrong to place undue and therefore false emphasis on the rights and duties and the powers comprised in 'parental responsibility' and not to concentrate on the fact that what is at issue is conferring upon a committed father the status of parenthood for which nature has already ordained that he must bear responsibility. ...
>
> There is another important emphasis I would wish to make. I have heard, up and down the land, psychiatrists tell me how important it is that children grow up with good self-esteem and how much they need to have a favourable positive image of the absent parent. It seems to me important, therefore, wherever possible, to ensure that the law confers upon a committed father that stamp of approval, lest the child grow up with some belief that he is in some way disqualified from fulfilling his role and that the reason for his disqualification is something inherent which will be inherited by the child, making her struggle to find her own identity all the more fraught. (657) [100]

Butler-Sloss LJ agreed, adding that 'this father should be allowed to share the burden of caring for his daughter' by giving him 'the status in which he can share in the responsibility for the child's upbringing and demonstrate that he will be as good a parent as he can make himself to this little girl' (659).

Q How does the legal status of parental responsibility better enable non-resident or unavailable fathers to fulfil their paternal duties? Do you agree that legal

---

[99] [1995] 2 FLR 648.

[100] See also *Re C and V (Contact and Parental Responsibility)* [1998] Fam Law 10. Compare *Re H (Shared Residence: Parental Responsibility)* [1995] 2 FLR 883, 887. There, the court commented that a boy of 14½ would not be able to comprehend the implications of a shared residence order and the grant of parental responsibility that would accompany it.

labels have the powerful impact on children that Ward LJ suggests they do? Can you think of other factors that might have a greater influence on the child's image of the father? If judges were not so willing to grant orders to all but those fathers considered seriously deviant, would the refusal of an order carry the stigma referred to by the court?

Ward LJ noted that there are few cases where the refusal of an order has been upheld. In those instances where it was, the fathers were 'cruel and callous'[101] or 'outrageous'; they were violent, 'feckless' or intent on sabotaging adoption plans.[102] In *Re T (A Minor) (Parental Responsibility: Contact)*,[103] for example, the father's behaviour was so deplorable that it convinced the court that an order would not be in the child's best interests. He had assaulted the mother while she was pregnant and, on a later occasion, while she had the baby in her arms. He failed to return the child after contact visits, keeping her on one occasion for nine days. He showed no remorse for this action. He failed to discharge his financial obligations to the child and insisted on maintaining control over the expenditure of any money he did provide.

However, there have to be pressing reasons for a court to refuse an order. In *Re H (Parental Responsibility: Maintenance)* the court commented, '[t]he cases show that when a father shows some devotion to his children he should ordinarily be granted a parental responsibility order in the absence of strong countervailing circumstances'.[104] Even the father's failure to support his children, coupled with a refusal to divulge his telephone number so he could be contacted in an emergency, was insufficient to deny him an order. It was enough that he had shown some commitment by attempting to maintain contact and showing an interest in the children's schooling.

The court's reluctance to deny parental responsibility does not, however, denote the existence of a presumption that a 'devoted father will ordinarily be granted an order'.[105] In addition, the three criteria set out in *Re H* were not intended to be the only relevant ones; to adopt that approach would be contrary to the paramountcy principle.[106] In *Re P (Parental Responsibility)*,[107] Hirst LJ said:

> Parental responsibility is not automatically conferred on fathers who are not married to the mothers of their children. There must, accordingly, be criteria against which an application for parental responsibility falls to be judged. The only statutory criteria are (1) that it must be in the interests of the child for such an order to be made, and (2) that the making of a parental responsibility order must be better for the child than making no order. In every case it is a matter of weighing in the balance the various factors ... and deciding, on the facts of the individual case, whether an order for parental responsibility is in the interests of the child ... .

---

[101] *Re T (A Minor) (Parental Responsibility: Contact)* [1993] 2 FLR 450, 456.

[102] See Ward LJ's account in *Re S* at 654–55 of *Re T (A Minor) (Parental Responsibility: Contact)* [1993] 2 FLR 450 and *W v Ealing London Borough Council* [1993] 2 FLR 788. See also *Re P (Terminating Parental Responsibility)* [1995] 1 FLR 1048; *Re P (Parental Responsibility)* [1997] 2 FLR 722. See also *Re H (Parental Responsibility)* [1998] 1 FLR 855, where a father who had injured his child in a manner adjudged to be cruel, and perhaps sadistic, was denied parental responsibility. See also *M v M (Parental Responsibility)* (1999) 2 FLR 237 where the father suffered from serious impediments to his intellectual functioning and was violent. The court said that the element of motivation in the CAR test, as well as the relevant provisions in the Children Act 1989, presupposed a capacity to reason. The father lacked this and was refused parental responsibility.

[103] [1993] 2 FLR 450.

[104] [1996] 1 FLR 867, 872.

[105] *Re H (Parental Responsibility)* [1998] 1 FLR 855, 859.

[106] Ibid, 859–860.

[107] [1998] 2 FLR 96.

Clearly, where a father has shown commitment to a child, has a good relationship with the child and has sound and genuine reasons for wanting parental responsibility, an order granting him that status will not usually be refused. ...

[I]t is the element of irresponsibility in the father's behaviour, or his abuse or likely abuse of parental responsibility which may disqualify him. (109–10)

R v E and F (Female Parents: Known Father)[108] was unusual in that the court refused to grant a parental responsibility order to a biological father who was not guilty of irresponsible or abusive behaviour. The child was conceived as a result of assisted reproduction with the father as sperm donor. The child's home had always been with the mother and her civil partner, although the father and his partner, with whom he had entered into a same-sex marriage in America, had always been involved in the child's life. Indeed until disputes arose between the adults, they all went on holidays together. The father applied for parental responsibility and shared residence while the mother and her partner sought joint residence. The court granted the mother and her partner joint residence and dismissed the father's application. Although the father, who lived in America, had regular contact with the child, had a close relationship with the child and, in the past, had been consulted on important matters, he was not, said the judge, involved in co-parenting. The mother and her partner were the ones who cared for the child and made decisions about his upbringing. Bennett J said:

[43] ... Parenting, in my judgment, involves not just caring emotionally and physically for a child—important though that is—but also taking decisions and exercising rights and responsibilities in relation to that child. In other words, parenting involves exercising responsibilities.

[44] The Law Commission, in recommending the use of the term 'parental responsibility', suggested that it would reflect the everyday reality of being a parent, and would emphasise the responsibilities of all those who were placed in that position ... .

[45] Thus, in the instant case, it is pertinent to ask who were the adults who actually carried out not only the care of Daniel day to day, but also who bore the responsibility of bringing Daniel up and who took the necessary decisions for his welfare? In my judgment, the answer must be Emily and Frances.

[48] I, therefore, conclude that the arrangement arrived in 1999/2000, or in any event before Daniel's conception, was that Emily and Frances were to be his parents. His family was to be Emily and Frances and himself. Richard would have a role to play, and an important one, beyond merely identifying him as Daniel's father in the life of Daniel. I reject the evidence of Richard, supported by John, that he was to be not just Daniel's father, but also one of his parents.

[92] ... I agree that he [the father] is trying to equate the instant case with a post divorce or separation situation. In my judgment, [he] is mistaken.

[93] Furthermore, I accept both Emily and Frances's evidence that they have good reason to perceive the application for parental responsibility as being a direct threat to the autonomy of their family.

[94] ... [I]f parental responsibility were granted to Richard, it is likely that conflicts would arise. ...

[96] During his evidence Richard referred many times to obtaining legal rights, but was unable

---

[108] [2010] EWHC 417 (Fam); [2010] 2 FLR 383.

to show how, in the light of Emily and Frances consulting him on every important decision (save, of course, that of Frances being granted parental responsibility) he would be, practically speaking, in a better position than he was or had been in respect of Daniel's welfare and upbringing or would lead to better decision-making. That is particularly pertinent in the light of the evidence given by Emily and Frances, which I accept, that they will go on consulting him about important matters in Daniel's life.

[103] Accordingly, in my judgment, I am of the opinion that the grant of parental responsibility to Richard is not in Daniel's best interests

What is interesting is that the court here drew a distinction between biological fatherhood and parenthood, attributing far more importance than usual to 'doing' parenthood in the sense of taking responsibility in the form of actual care and decision-making. It seems that post-divorce or post-separation cases could be distinguished on the basis that, in this case, the father had never been part of the child's primary 'nuclear' family What is also interesting is that the court found that parental responsibility would make little difference in reality to the father's position.

XI. EFFECT OF HAVING PARENTAL RESPONSIBILITY

Parental Responsibility and the Non-resident Parent

The Law Commission stated that 'parents should not be regarded as losing their position, and their ability to take decisions about their children, simply because they are separated or in dispute with one another' (Law Commission 1988b: para 2.11). But, as it pointed out, in reality, it is only the parent who has 'practical control' over the child who is in a position to implement any decisions (ibid: para 2.10). So, while both parents have in law the power of independent action (subject to the requirement of consultation in some instances), there are considerable constraints on non-resident parents, many of whom have limited contact with their children, in exercising this power. It is perhaps unlikely that a non-resident parent will be able give effect to a decision made independently and against the wishes of the other parent. And although decisions made by the caretaking parent can be challenged under section 8, the non-resident parent may not even become aware of a decision until it is too late to reverse it. What is more, probably few parents understand what their rights are under the law (Hoggett 1994: 10).

Research conducted in California by Maccoby and Mnookin confirmed that parents might indeed be unaware of what their former spouses or partners are doing. They found that while many parents reported discussing matters such as their children's emotional state, their schooling and their extracurricular activities, there was relatively little discussion about other matters (Maccoby and Mnookin 1992: Table 9.5). They also found that the resident parent was usually the primary decision-maker. Joint decisions were made only in a small number of cases, and then only on major issues (ibid: 221–22). However, there was a discrepancy in perceptions about the division of tasks, the extent of discussion and the way in which decisions were made. Typically, caretaking parents reported less discussion and joint decision-making than the other parents. The authors concluded from this that parents in their sample were probably ignorant of what went on in each other's homes. They went on to say: 'We suspect that residential parents make many routine decisions that the non-residential parent knows nothing about' (ibid: 221). This contention was fortified by their finding that a few years after separation, the most common pattern was what they called 'spousal disengagement' which involved 'parallel parenting' (ibid: 277). Parents avoided conflict by making little or no effort to communicate or to co-operate over childcare (ibid: 233–34). Most importantly, a joint custody order made little difference to the extent of joint decision-making (ibid: 225).

Similar findings were reported in a study carried out in England (Simpson et al 1995). Three approaches to post-divorce parenting were identified: no contact, with fathers reporting that they had lost all contact or had contact only rarely; parallel parenting, where fathers reported contact with children but no communication with their ex-spouses; and communicative parenting, where fathers reported contact accompanied by communication with their ex-spouses (ibid: 23). Of those fathers in the research sample, 27% reported no contact, 27% reported parallel parenting and 46% reported communicative parenting (ibid: 24). Relationships in the first two categories were characterised by hostility and conflict and there was little exchange of information between parents.[109] Although the study focused on fathers who were divorced prior to the coming into force of the Children Act 1989, the researchers maintained that this did not affect its relevance: '[I]t is our contention that the experience of being a father post-divorce is much the same for fathers today as it was for the fathers who took part in this study' (ibid: xv).

Another study, conducted by Maclean and Eekelaar, revealed that there was little joint decision-making among those parents in their sample who were 'formerly married': '[J]oint decision-making of any serious nature probably occurs only in about one in ten cases where contact is regularly exercised, and then usually only on a limited number of issues' (Maclean and Eekelaar 1997: 122).[110]

And it seems that, still, little has changed. More recent research dealing with this issue reveals low levels of joint decision-making, with 78% of parents never discussing their children's problems together (Trinder et al 2005: para 5.5).[111]

It is likely, then, that the concept of parental responsibility does not necessarily facilitate co-operative parenting between separated parents in practice or even, in many cases, give rise to parity in relation to decision-making.[112] The parental responsibility vested in the non-resident parent 'legitimates the actual exercise of parenthood by a natural parent' (Maclean and Eekelaar 1997: 146).[113] However, when the availability of opportunities to engage in such parenting is taken into account, parental responsibility may have no more than symbolic significance for many fathers. This is not to say that it is irrelevant. To vest parental responsibility in non-resident parents may have the intended effect of reducing conflict and encouraging settlement. It may have the effect of mollifying some fathers who would otherwise fight for a court order. It may also persuade resident parents to take cognisance of the non-resident parent's wishes. But the only way those wishes can be

---

[109] However, this was not necessarily a permanent state of affairs. Parents did move between categories and some parents who began in the no-contact category moved up to the communicative category, often via the parallel parenting category (43).

[110] Indeed, Maclean and Eekelaar (1997) found little evidence of widespread joint parenting or joint decision-making generally. This was generally true of parents when they were living together and after they separated, whether they were former spouses or former cohabitants. It was also true of those who had never lived together (Maclean and Eekelaar 1997: 137).

[111] See also Smith (2003).

[112] See Eekelaar (1991b: 135–36).

[113] It also gives the non-resident parent rights in the context of consent to adoption and the right to remove the child from voluntary accommodation against the wishes of the local authority. See above. In addition, it enables the parent to deal with third parties such as doctors. See, generally, Maclean and Eekelaar (1997: 36).

enforced in the absence of actual control of the child and in the face of opposition from the carer, is by means of a section 8 order. And these orders are available to all parents, irrespective of whether they have parental responsibility.[114]

Parental Responsibility and the Resident Parent

The position of the resident parent is far from impregnable. Conflict and poor communication with the other parent can make it difficult to reach satisfactory arrangements or joint plans relating to children (Cockett and Tripp 1994, 1996: 42–43). In such circumstances, the resident parent may be vulnerable to attempts by the non-resident parent to challenge her decisions. However, if parental responsibility of an unmarried father is abused it can be revoked.[115] Alternatively, the mother can apply to court to deal with a specific incident. As Wallbank notes, the burden rests on the mother to institute proceedings in either situation (Wallbank 2001: 281).[116] Given that the Legal Aid, Sentencing and Punishment of Offenders Bill 2010–11 will, if enacted, remove legal aid for most family proceedings, this could render some mothers helpless in the face of paternal intervention in their children's lives. Most disputes, in any event, will have to be assessed to see whether they are suitable for mediation.[117]

As mentioned above, where non-resident fathers wish to challenge mothers' decisions through the legal system, section 8 is their most important resource.[118] Research examining the use of specific issue orders suggests that these are used by non-resident parents to challenge resident parents. The main categories of disputes identified in which the orders are made are children's education, medical treatment, relocation, children's sur-

---

[114] See Chapter 10 below. It is not so much parental responsibility that gives non-resident fathers legal remedies; it is simply parenthood that does so. For parents, the power to challenge decisions in court is not in any way linked in the Act to the concept of responsibility. In terms of s 10(4)(a) of the Act, in addition to persons that have parental responsibility, 'any parent' is entitled to seek a s 8 order. So unmarried fathers without parental responsibility, even the rapist who so exercised the Law Commission (1979: para 3.9), are entitled, without needing to seek the leave of the court, to challenge the caretaking mother's decisions about a child's upbringing. It is arguably, therefore, parenthood coupled with s 8, rather than the possession of parental responsibility, that gives non-resident parents, whether married or unmarried, any real say in relation to their children. See Eekelaar (2001c).

[115] Parental responsibility acquired through birth registration, an agreement or through the court can be removed by a court (Children Act 1989 s 4(2A)). The parental responsibility of a step-parent who is married to or the civil partner of a parent can also be revoked by a court order (s 4A(3)) as can that of a second female parent (s 4ZA(5)). The parental responsibility of mothers and married fathers can only be lost through adoption.

[116] See also Wallbank (2002: 286). Her complaint that fathers who register escape court scrutiny could be applied to fathers who enter into parental responsibility agreements.

[117] See Chapters 10 and 15 below.

[118] The fact that the burden of initiating legal proceedings is placed on the non-resident parent challenging a decision of a resident parent might be some deterrent against interference. However, for a non-resident parent with resources or for one able to negotiate successfully the hurdles of the public funding system, s 8 provides considerable scope for litigation. Indeed, Dewar has pointed out that the Act has increased the opportunity for the 'legalisation' of disputes (Dewar 1992: 356). Any aspect of parental responsibility not already regulated by a court order is open to challenge. The case law seems, on balance, to discourage trivial applications. See *Re C (A Minor) (Leave to Seek S 8 Orders)* [1994] 1 FLR 26; *Re P (A Minor) (Parental Responsibility Order)* [1994] 1 FLR 578. But see *Re HG (Specific Issue Order: Sterilisation)* [1993] 1 FLR 587, 593 where the court stressed the importance of avoiding a restrictive interpretation and of refraining from selecting 'idiosyncratic' situations or events for exclusion from the ambit of a s 8 order. The number of orders made is not inconsiderable. In 2009, there were 7,650 parental responsibility orders, 15,260 prohibited steps orders and 5,390 specific issue orders (MOJ 2010b: Table 2.4). It is not stated how many of these concerned disputes between parents. The number of applications as opposed to orders is not specified. Once the Legal Aid, Sentencing and Punishment of Offenders Bill 2010–11 is enacted, there will probably be fewer cases coming to court.

names and disclosure of information such as the child's medical details (Gilmore 2004). Whether many fathers will be deterred if the availability of legal aid comes to an end remains to be seen. Some fathers even now proceed as litigants in person.

While the availability of section 8 orders is not dependent on the father's having parental responsibility, fathers who do have parental responsibility may be in a better position to acquire information about the child's upbringing and, therefore, to oppose the mothers' decisions.[119] Even the threat of legal proceedings is a potent weapon; a mother who does not have the means to litigate, who is dominated by the father or who is in any way in a weaker bargaining position than he is may feel unable to withstand his demands, however unreasonable.

Grand, a practitioner, suggested that shared parental responsibility can give rise to adverse consequences. He was worried that the way in which the Act is worded seems to invite excessive interference by the non-resident parent in the decision-making of the resident parent. He pointed out that the Act imposes no constraints on the exercise of parental responsibility by the non-resident parent: 'There is no reference to joint responsibility or to sharing responsibility and, on the face of it, what is granted is absolute power, exercisable without reference to the other parent' (Grand 1994: 586).[120] In his view, the legislation could present a real risk that 'irresponsible' non-resident fathers might choose to rely on parental responsibility to reverse the decisions made by resident mothers to the detriment of children's interests (ibid: 587).

Roche's concerns were somewhat different. His disquiet related more to the symbolic force of the status conferred by parental responsibility which could, he said, exacerbate the difficulties resident parents face. He described his concerns in this regard:

> The reality for most mothers is, at best, one of occasional support from their partners in the domestic sphere including those tasks which directly relate to the child. This is not the same thing as shared responsibility for child care, merely assistance. Nevertheless it is still involvement and important. However the father's role is rendered problematic when the adult relationship does break up. ...
>
> If, by symbolically valuing the role of the absent parent, the Act is successful in promoting a continuing and constructive involvement on the part of fathers, it will be of benefit to ex-partners as well as children. ...
>
> While this [parental] responsibility can be exercised independently of the will of the other parent, it is also always potentially open to challenge in the courts via ... Section 8 orders. Whether or not a parent is involved with or has contact with his child, this question of potential involvement, and hence power in relation to the child and the parent the child is living with, is critical.
>
> The argument here is not Bainham's concern over the 'exclusion' of the 'other parent' but whether the Act has made the situation facing the primary carer worse by symbolically re-emphasising the other parent's responsibility and power ... . The parent without day-to-day care of the child will be encouraged to consider himself still involved in the life of the child—indeed this is the very purpose of the new arrangements. However this may operate so as to undermine the position of the primary carer, and the child, whose well-being is inextricably bound up with the well-being of the primary carer economically, emotionally and socially. Mutuality of concerns and action sounds cosy but is this always going to be the case? The

---

[119] See *Re P (Parental Responsibility)* [1998] 2 FLR 96, 110. See also *Re M (Contact: Parental Responsibility)* [2001] 2 FLR 342.

[120] But see above for decisions requiring consultation.

family is not an absence of power but, on the contrary, a nexus of a complex and shifting series of power relations involving adults and children. (Roche 1991: 355–57) [121]

Sheldon, criticising the amendment of section 4, was of the view that, although the risks to mothers are difficult to assess, these should have given the legislature pause before the law was changed (Sheldon 2001: 116)

> **Q** Can a non-resident parent be compelled to assist the primary carer in fulfilling the obligations of parenthood? The Law Commission described the old joint custody as carrying the risk of '"power without responsibility" or, what might be worse, responsibility without power' (Law Commission 1986: para 4.41). Might this be an apt description also of shared parental responsibility?

In contrast, Eekelaar appeared rather sanguine about shared parental responsibility and the potential for applications under section 8 to challenge resident parents (Eekelaar 1991b: 135–36). Indeed, his preference was for all fathers to have automatic parental responsibility (Eekelaar 2001c: 430). He was of the view that biological fathers gain little from obtaining parental responsibility. Their situation is strengthened in some cases such as where children are in local authority accommodation and in adoption proceedings. [122] However, he contended, since fathers, as parents, have legal duties to secure their children's education and to safeguard their health, they must also have concomitant rights to make decisions about these things (ibid: 428). He went on:

> Whatever may have been the experience of some unmarried fathers in Pickford's research, the law must bear some reasonable relationship to social life. The fact that around one million fathers are daily making decisions concerning their children's upbringing cannot surely go unrecognised by the law. The conclusion is irresistible that they do, indeed, have the legal rights necessary to bring up their children.

However, he criticised the way in which the concept of parental responsibility has been interpreted by the courts to impose a duty to consult: [123]

> It may all boil down to symbolism, but it is unsatisfactory to use scarce legal resources to engage in gestures. It must be remembered that cases where fathers make applications for parental responsibility are invariably those where they are living apart from their children. Sometimes they have been in prison. The truth, therefore, is that they believe they are acquiring rights to be directly involved in their children's upbringing, despite living apart from them: that is, a right to be consulted. That would, indeed, be something more than the right to take decisions necessary for bringing up a child, which I have just argued they would have anyway if they were actually bringing the child up. So does parental responsibility give them that right? (Eekelaar 2001c: 428)

However desirable the result which the courts are seeking to achieve might seem to be, it flies in the face of the clear words of s 2(7) of the Children Act 1989. But while I wish to maintain

---

[121] See also Smart (1989a: 21).

[122] And where the mother appoints a guardian (Children Act 1989 s 5(8)). See above on adoption. Local authorities are already obliged to consult unmarried fathers under s 22 of the Children Act 1989 because they are parents. As parents, unmarried fathers have the capacity to apply for s 8 orders as of right (Children Act 1989 10(4)).

[123] See also, for discussion, Maidment (2001).

that the outcome is indeed wrong in law, I also wish to argue that it is undesirable. The mistake is to attempt to cast into legal form an aspiration of good conduct. No one could possibly argue that it would not be a 'good thing' for separated parents to co-operate together as far as possible, and as amicably as possible, over their children's upbringing. So also we could not but applaud a parent who lives apart from his child and who visits the child regularly and lovingly. But we do not impose a legal duty to visit. Even if we believed that imposing such a duty would 'send the right message', the risk would be that by clothing the features of co-operative behaviour in the form of legal duty, people would be encouraged to resort to lawyers over perceived infractions. In any case, how could it be enforced? So we wisely leave this to moral persuasion and the dynamics of the relationship. Precisely the same considerations apply to consultation between separated parents. Provided the relationship is good, and especially where contact takes place, either consultation will occur or the non-residential parent will know what is going on. Cases where problems arise tend to be those where the contact has ceased or is rare … . Suppose there was a generalised legal duty to consult, such as that articulated by Butler-Sloss LJ [in *Re H*][124] … . Will it apply if the non-resident parent has virtually lost touch, or shown no interest in previous communications? What must the parent with the duty do to comply with the duty? What if consultation exacerbates conflict? … . And what would [resident] parents think when they realise that the non-residential parents are under no corresponding duty to take an interest in the children? These are all hard enough questions. They would be made harder by giving the parties an added opportunity for dispute, and incentives to consult solicitors if they believe there has been a failure to comply. In any event, it is difficult to see what enforcement mechanism could be used that is not already available to a non-residential parent who is dissatisfied with how children are being brought up. …

This is not to say that a court could not impose a requirement for consultation appropriate to the circumstances when disposing of a specific dispute within the context of a specific issue order. But a generalised duty is another matter. It threatens to subject parents caring for children to an unnecessary risk of legal harassment and the added anxieties and pressures that would cause in already conflicted situations. …

If the registration gives the father a generalised legal right to be consulted, the mother could be opening herself up to potential trouble in the future. She would be well advised not to agree to have his name recorded, although this would need to be balanced against any difficulty non-registration of his name might cause in establishing paternity, should she subsequently seek child support. (ibid: 429–30)

> **Q** Does Eekelaar's distinction between a right to make decisions and a right to be consulted reflect important differences in principle or is it a distinction based on practical considerations, reliant on the fact that many non-resident fathers are not aware in advance (or at all) of mothers' decisions?

The concerns voiced by commentators about the potential for abuse of power are not often shared by judges; the courts tend to discount the potential for problems when deciding applications for parental responsibility orders.

Parental Responsibility: A Matter of Words?

The courts have been reluctant to accept arguments based on the effects of a parental responsibility order as a reason for refusing applications and they have striven to minimise the practical significance of an order.

---

[124] See above p 345.

In *Re P (A Minor) (Parental Responsibility Order)*[125] the court awarded a parental responsibility order to the father of a child aged 5, rejecting the argument that that this would enable him to interfere in her day-to-day life:

> It is important to be quite clear that an order for parental responsibility to the father does not give him a right to interfere in matters within the day-to-day management of the child's life. Section 2(8) of the Children Act 1989 provides that:
>
>> The fact that a person has parental responsibility for a child shall not entitle him to act in any way which would be incompatible with any order made with respect to a child under this Act.
>
> There is, of course, an order for residence in favour of the mother under the Act and that invests the mother with the right to determine all matters which arise in the course of the day-to-day management of this child's life. (584–85)

Wilson J then went on to observe more generally, without appearing to limit his comments to cases where a residence order has been made:

> It is to be noted that on any view an order for parental responsibility gives the father no power to override the decision of the mother, who already has such responsibility: in the event of a disagreement between them on a specific issue relating to the child, the court will have to resolve it. If the father were to seek to misuse the rights given him under s 4 such misuse could, as a second to last resort, be controlled by the court under a prohibited steps order against him and/or a specific issue order. The very last resort of all would presumably be the discharge of the parental responsibility order. (585)

In *Re S (Parental Responsibility)*[126] Ward LJ stated that the possibility of interference with the day-to-day management of the child's life was irrelevant. In reaching this conclusion he relied on three arguments. First, a parental responsibility order is a mechanism for conferring a status rather than rights; secondly, a non-resident parent has little opportunity in practice to exercise parental responsibility; and, thirdly, any abuse can be restrained by means of a court order.

> It would, therefore, be helpful if the mother could think calmly about the limited circumstances when the exercise of true parental responsibility is likely to be of practical significance. ... There seems to me to be all too frequently a failure to appreciate that the wide exercise of s 8 orders can control the abuse, if any, of the exercise of parental responsibility which is adverse to the welfare of the child. Those interferences with the day-to-day management of the child's life have nothing to do with whether or not this order should be allowed. (657)

Q To what extent will the courts be able to adopt the same reasoning if the Legal Aid, Sentencing and Punishment of Offenders Bill 2010–11 becomes law and legal aid is no longer available for family proceedings?

While section 8 orders[127] are regarded as a useful solution to the problem of interfering

---

[125] [1994] 1 FLR 578.

[126] [1995] 2 FLR 648. Compare *Yousef v The Netherlands* [2003] 1 FLR 210, where the recognition sought by the father was considered a prelude to changing the child's living arrangements, contrary to her best interests. The refusal of recognition did not, therefore contravene Art 8 ECHR.

[127] See, on the use of specific issue orders, Gilmore (2004). It seems that each dispute has to be adjudicated separately. There is authority stating that one parent cannot be given, in advance, the power to make decisions

fathers, they were considered inadequate to constrain a father who intended 'to use a parental responsibility order for improper or inappropriate ends to try to interfere with and possibly undermine the mother's care of the child'.[128] The court accordingly refused to make an order in favour of a father who planned to use it to monitor the child's health, schooling and arrangements for her care.[129] Similarly, in *Re M (Contact: Parental Responsibility)*[130] the court denied the father parental responsibility in relation to his severely mentally disabled daughter on the grounds that he would be very likely to 'misuse it to lend weight to future interference in her care, thus continuing the stress on the mother and potentially undermining her ability to care properly for KM' (365). He and his family saw parental responsibility as conferring rights and would interfere even more than they already had. In what the court referred to as an 'extreme' case like this, it would not suffice to put in place court orders specifying what the father could and could not do (365). The court stated that commitment, attachment and motivation are not the only relevant factors and made it clear that 'parental responsibility is not a reward for the father, but an order which should only be made in the best interests of KM' (365–66).[131]

In contrast, the potential for interference was not treated as relevant and the court focused almost exclusively on the CAR test in *Re J-S (A Child) (Contact: Parental Responsibility)*.[132] The court also thought it significant that it was prepared to grant the father contact. Because of that fact and in the light of the good relationship he had with the child, the 'father should be entitled to play the natural role which fatherhood ordains for him by the very fact of his being a father' (para 50). It was an 'overwhelming' case for granting parental responsibility (ibid).

In *Re D (Contact and Parental Responsibility: Lesbian Mothers and Known Father)*[133] the court granted parental responsibility to a biological father who had answered an advertisement from a lesbian couple seeking a man willing to father a child. The father had contact with the child but, since there was the potential for interference from him in relation to decisions about the child's medical care and schooling, the court made the parental responsibility order subject to the conditions that he would not visit or contact the school or health professionals involved in the care of the child unless he had obtained written consent from the mother and her partner. The main reason for giving the father parental responsibility appears to have been that the court was concerned that he should have some official status in the event that the child might be adopted. The court said that the effect of its order would be to recognise that the mother and her partner were the child's 'day to day parents and he [the father] has no role in her day to day care, whether in relation to decision making or otherwise' (para 93).[134]

For Reece, this decision is strong evidence of what she calls the 'degradation' of

---

in a particular category, such as education: *Re P (Parental Dispute: Judicial Determination)* [2002] EWCA Civ 1627; [2003] 1 FLR 286. See Gilmore (2004), who argues for a different interpretation of the case.

[128] *Re P (Parental Responsibility)* [1998] 2 FLR 96, 110.

[129] Ibid.

[130] [2001] 2 FLR 342.

[131] See also *Re B (Role of Biological Father)* [2007] EWHC 1952 (Fam); [2008] 1 FLR 1015.

[132] [2002] EWCA Civ 1028; [2003] 1 FLR 399.

[133] [2006] EWHC 2; [2006] 1 FCR 556.

[134] Other than schooling and medical care, there appears to be nothing to restrict the exercise of the father's parental responsibility. His independent decision-making capacity in terms of s 2(7) is unaffected and the duty to consult him on important matters remains. It is not even clear whether the duty to consult on education and health is removed. Reece, however, says the decision is inconsistent with the granting of parental responsibility: 'Rather than Mr B having any authority or decision-making power over D, he has actually been ordered to keep away' (Reece 2009b: 90). But see *Re P (A Minor) (Parental Responsibility Order)* above.

parental responsibility. The proliferation of categories of people able to obtain parental responsibility leads her to argue that 'parental responsibility is no longer predominantly about parental authority or decision-making' (Reece 2009b: 94). The process of the 'degradation' of parental responsibility has changed the reasons for conferring it; it is now a form of legitimation. Orders are made in favour of fathers because they need the affirmation implicit in an order, irrespective of whether it has any practical effect. However, she continues, even this function will disappear in relation to fathers, if not other categories of people eligible for parental responsibility, if the amendment of the law regarding registration is implemented; fathers who are unwilling or unsuited to take decisions about their children will be endowed with parental responsibility. The status will no longer imply approval of those fathers, at least as individuals.

So, to summarise, the courts play down the practical significance of parental responsibility yet, in 'extreme' cases, recognise that there is some practical impact; much seems to depend on the court's assessment of the likelihood that the father concerned will in fact use his legal status. Where he is not likely to do so, they reassure resident mothers by stressing the formal, symbolic function of the status. The legislature too has proved keen to endorse paternal status. As a result of the change in the law, and if the amendment is implemented, almost all fathers will have parental responsibility. If parental responsibility creates a wide ranging duty to consult (and the courts seem to be saying it does), it seems that resident mothers will be worse off. In order to consult, the parents will have to communicate more often with each other and this could increase opportunities for conflict. In the event that resident mothers do consult, this will mean that fathers, particularly those who do not have good relationships with their former partners and those who are not close to their children,[135] will have more information than they would otherwise have. For this reason they will be in a better position to challenge decisions. Moreover, a failure to consult could lead to litigation by the aggrieved parent.

XII. CONCLUSION

One of the aims of the Children Act 1989, through the creation of the concept of parental responsibility, is to reduce conflict between parents when their relationship breaks down. With its emphasis on non-intervention by the courts and its endorsement of autonomy for parents, the legislation promotes an expectation that parents will resolve questions relating to child-rearing by agreement. By enshrining in the law an equal and enduring status for both parents, it seeks to ensure that there is less to fight over and that agreement is more likely to be reached. Moreover, by conferring this equal and enduring status on the non-resident parent (usually the father), the law is said to motivate him to remain involved in his children's lives and to encourage the mother to accept that involvement. This goal is, arguably, also at the heart of the courts' growing preoccupation with consultation. It certainly was a justification put forward for extending parental responsibility to unmarried fathers who register the birth. All these aims, namely absence of conflict, agreement and continued involvement, are said to promote the best interests of the children concerned.

Yet in most cases, the extent of involvement of mothers and fathers in their children's

---

[135] Dunn (2003: 24) reports that 'contact *per se* was not significantly linked to fathers' knowledge and influence'. Fathers who had 'affectionate and supportive' relationships with their children knew more about their children's lives.

lives remains very different. And the expectations of mothers and fathers are very different. Indeed, Collier has suggested that in the past the law has been implicated in the construction of the 'good father' as economic provider rather than as carer. The presence expected of fathers, he said, is not physical presence but the presence of 'paternal heterosexual authority' (Collier 1995a: 20). In his later work (Collier 2001), he has shown that the rhetoric has shifted to embrace co-parenting and active paternal participation.[136] And unmarried fathers in particular are increasingly being seen as 'a group who are subject to discrimination, potentially vulnerable and a deserving focus of policy initiatives to protect and strengthen their relationships with their children' (Collier and Sheldon 2008: 178). However, in truth, the involvement facilitated by parental responsibility is primarily concerned with participation in decision-making; the status conferred by parental responsibility lends legitimacy to a non-resident parent's claim to have a say in the upbringing of his children while leaving, often, the responsibility of day-to-day child-care to the mother.

Wallbank, writing of the amendment of section 4 of the Children Act 1989, alleges that the change is part of a wider movement aimed at tying men to children as well as a move from discretion to rules and rights. Parenthood and parental responsibility can be seen, she says,[137] as a way of creating an illusion of permanence in the face of instability[138] amid fears of the breakdown of the traditional family. According to Wallbank, the change to the law 'will do little to promote the relationships between children and fathers in any practical way. However ... significant inroads will be made into the control that women have in relation to their children' (Wallbank 2002: 278).[139]

The law cannot compel fathers to shoulder the responsibility of the practical care of their children. The extent to which it can deliver a joint parenting arrangement is therefore limited. What it does do is establish a framework, of which parental responsibility is a part, in terms of which caretaking mothers are by and large expected to accept whatever degree of involvement with their children that fathers choose for themselves. They are expected to sustain the kind of conflict-free relationship that does not undermine the paternal role.

It is true that the impact in practice of parental responsibility may be limited for many fathers. Nevertheless, parental responsibility does have considerable symbolic force. It serves to affirm paternal status and paternal links with children. It may therefore provide some solace to fathers who might otherwise feel aggrieved and, in doing so, may reduce conflict. Conversely, the extension of the duty to consult may increase conflict. In any event, by equalising the status of both parents, the law might be said to be masking the inequality of the contributions of most mothers and fathers to childcare. It could be said to be rendering invisible mothers' work and to sanction traditional gender roles and child-care patterns. And by promoting an ideal of the post-separation family as one that is conflict-free and in which the non-resident father has an equally important role to that of the mother, it tends to render illegitimate maternal objections to paternal intervention. As a result, it seems, mothers may be expected to bear most of the responsibility for avoiding conflict and to follow the path of acquiescence.

---

[136] See also Collier and Sheldon (2008: 116ff).
[137] Citing Dewar (2000).
[138] See Dewar (2000: 63).
[139] See also Wallbank (2009b).

FURTHER READING

R Collier, 'A Hard Time to Be a Father? Reassessing the Relationship between Law, Policy and Family (Practices)' (2001) 28 *J Law and Society* 520.

S Cretney, '"What Will the Women Want Next?" The Struggle for Power Within the Family 1925–75' (1996) 12 *LQR* 110.

J Eekelaar, 'Rethinking Parental Responsibility' (2001) *Fam Law* 426.

S Gilmore, 'The Nature, Scope, and Use of the Specific Issue Order' (2004) 16 *CFLQ* 367.

F Kaganas, 'Responsible or Feckless Fathers? *Re S (Parental Responsibility)*' (1996) 8 *CFLQ* 165.

S Maidment, 'Parental Responsibility—Is there a Duty to Consult?' (2001) *Fam Law* 518.

J Masson, 'The Impact of the Adoption and Children Act 2002: Part 1—Parental Responsibility' (2003) *Fam Law* 580.

R Pickford, 'Unmarried Fathers and the Law' in A Bainham, S Day Sclater and M Richards (eds), *What is a Parent? A Socio-Legal Analysis* (Oxford, Hart Publishing, 1999).

J Roche, 'The Children Act 1989: Once a Parent Always a Parent?' (1991) *JSW & FL* 345.

S Sheldon, 'Unmarried Fathers and Parental Responsibility: A Case for Reform?' (2001) 9 *FLS* 93.

C Smart, 'The Legal and Moral Ordering of Child Custody' (1991) 18 *J Law and Society* 485.

J Wallbank, 'Clause 106 of the Adoption and Children Bill: Legislation for the 'Good' Father?' (2002) 22 *Legal Studies* 276.

Section 2: Welfare

INTRODUCTION

In the next three chapters we will focus on our second principle or theme: welfare. In Chapter 9 we discuss the welfare principle, a principle that lies at the heart of decision-making regarding children. The welfare of the child is paramount in the context of private law disputes in terms of section 1 of the Children Act 1989; the section applies where decisions are made about children's upbringing. The welfare of the child also applies in public law cases where children are removed into care.

Chapter 9 deals primarily with the welfare principle and its interpretation in private law cases. It traces the development of the welfare principle and seeks to show how its interpretation has been shaped by, first, the demands of women's groups in the nineteenth century for status equal to that of fathers. We then go on to show how its contemporary form has been shaped by notions of equality purveyed by men's and father's rights groups as well as by particular choices within and simplified interpretations of child welfare knowledge. So within the chapter there are also references to the notion of equality but the main concern is with the welfare principle.

Following on from this, and remaining within the same areas of law, is Chapter 10 which discusses the way the welfare principle is applied in private law disputes about children. It argues that the welfare principle is deployed in support of a particular construction of the post-separation family. The 'good' post-separation family is one in which relationships between children and their non-resident parents (usually fathers) are maintained. While in many cases these relationships do in fact promote a child's welfare, their unreflective pursuit can, on occasion, have detrimental consequences for resident parents (usually mothers) and also children.

Chapter 11 deals with a different aspect of welfare and covers both private and public law. It deals with the way notions of children's rights, together with constructions of children as vulnerable and incompetent, along with conflicting constructions of children as autonomous agents, play out in the context of decision-making by children and their participation in legal proceedings. It explores the way in which the welfare of the child dictates that older children be restrained from making decisions that will harm them or damage their prospects. But it also argues that allowing children to challenge the decisions made by their parents opens the family up to outside scrutiny. Similarly, when professionals and courts intervene in decisions about infants with severe disabilities, this intervention in what would normally be the private sphere exposes the family's decisions to outside scrutiny. And the parents' wishes and authority will be overridden if this is considered necessary to safeguard the child's welfare. Again, there are overlaps, this time with the theme of the public/private divide and with the idea that children can be seen as 'being' or as 'becoming'. It was therefore difficult to decide which part of the book this chapter should be in. However, one of the main concerns in it is to examine the way in which welfare is understood or constructed. So this section seemed appropriate.

9

The Welfare Principle

I. INTRODUCTION

The welfare of children has increasingly claimed the attention of policy-makers and law reformers alike in recent decades. Children are portrayed as victims of divorce[1] and of child abuse and their victimisation is presented as the cause of delinquency, maladjustment and under-achievement.[2] These concerns have led to the elevation of the welfare principle to a central and seemingly unassailable position in the law relating to children. Indeed Article 3 of the United Nations Convention on the Rights of the Child[3] sets out the principle that, in all actions concerning children, whether taken by courts, legislatures, administrative bodies or welfare agencies, 'the best interests of the child shall be a primary consideration'.

In this chapter, we examine the welfare principle in the context of private law.[4] We suggest that the way it is applied and interpreted owes less to scientific 'truths' than to understandings of the welfare of children that accord with prevailing beliefs about how families should be structured and what the roles of family members should be. While this chapter is self-evidently focusing on the theme of welfare, it also touches on the public/private theme. Families, and resident mothers in particular, have become increasingly subject to efforts by courts and other agencies to get them to conform to a specific image of the 'good' mother; the welfare of children is seen as society's business and mothers must be made 'responsible'. Yet in contrast to this public concern, there is now a move to keep parents out of court, and get them into mediation instead. This could have the effect of privatising disputes about children.

---

[1] Pryor and Rodgers (2001: 31) refer to 'trauma theories' which focus on divorce or separation as an event and view that event as potentially traumatic for children. They also describe 'life-course theories' which treat parental separation as part of a process over time and not as a single determining event. The dominant view apparent in government documents appears to be that, although most children emerge unharmed, parental separation is potentially damaging if it is not managed 'correctly'. See below.

[2] See, eg, Baroness Butler Sloss (2010).

[3] Ratified by the UK in 1991. It is not part of UK law but the UK government is bound to follow policies that conform broadly to the Convention. See further Bainham (2005: 66–78). Whether the welfare principle as it is currently applied in domestic law is compatible with the Human Rights Act 1998 is contentious. See below.

[4] For discussion of public law, see Chapters 13 and 14 below.

II. LEGISLATION AND THE WELFARE PRINCIPLE

Section 1 of the Children Act 1989 provides:

1. Welfare of the Child

(1) When a court determines any question with respect to—

(a) the upbringing of a child; or
(b) the administration of a child's property or the application of any income arising from it,

the child's welfare shall be the court's paramount consideration.

(2) In any proceedings in which any question with respect to the upbringing of a child arises, the court shall have regard to the general principle that any delay in determining the question is likely to prejudice the welfare of the child.

Section 1(3) goes on to enumerate a checklist of factors to which the court is obliged to have regard in contested section 8 proceedings and Part IV proceedings. This checklist, which is reproduced and discussed in Chapter 10, includes factors such as the ascertainable wishes and feelings of the child, the needs of the child and the ability of the parents to meet those needs, and the likely effect on the child of any change in his or her circumstances.

> **Q** The UN Convention states that the child's best interests shall be a primary
> consideration, whereas the Children Act 1989 states that the child's welfare
> shall be the paramount consideration. How do you interpret each?

In the context of divorce and separation, the Family Law Act 1996 was intended to transform the law in order to uphold what were regarded as fundamental norms, some of which were considered to be important for children's well-being. These norms were enshrined in the general principles set out in section 1:

1. The general principles underlying Parts II and III

The court and any person, in exercising functions under or in consequence of Parts II and III,[5] shall have regard to the following general principles—

...

(c) that a marriage which has irretrievably broken down and is being brought to an end should be brought to an end—
  (i) with minimum distress to the parties and to the children affected;
  (ii) with questions dealt with in a manner designed to promote as good a continuing relationship between the parties and any children affected as is possible in the circumstances. ...[6]
(d) that any risk to one of the parties to a marriage, and to any children, of violence from the other party should, so far as reasonably practicable, be removed or diminished.

Although this provision is still in force at the time of writing, it has no effect since Part

---

[5] Dealing with divorce and separation and with mediation, respectively.
[6] See also s 11(4)(c), which has never been brought into force.

II has never been brought into force and is not expected to be, while Part III has been repealed. Nevertheless it reflects widely held assumptions about children's welfare. Most importantly, the principles have continued to drive government policy: 'Since January 2001,[7] the Government has sought to emphasise its continued commitment to the principles underlying the Family Law Act, looking for alternative ways to provide the support that families want and need' (Walker 2004: 10). This commitment is apparent from the 'key principles' identified by the then Labour government as underpinning its 'agenda for change':

The child's welfare must be the *paramount consideration* in any help, support or intervention given.

A child's welfare is usually best promoted by a continuing and constructive *relationship with both parents,* as long as it is in the child's best interests and safe for all concerned.

Both parents have a responsibility to ensure their child has *constructive contact with the other parent* where contact is in the child's best interests.

Collaborative agreements made between parents should be favoured, as they are likely to work better than those arrangements that flow from court-based resolutions.

Parental separation needs a long-term and *flexible approach*. It is not an event that can be solved by a single unchanging settlement, whether court-imposed or not.

Help, advice and support for parents should be *readily accessible.*

The *wishes and feelings of children* in light of their age and understanding should be considered and taken fully into account. (DCA, DfES and DTI 2005: para 2, emphasis in original)

More recently, in a Practice Direction issued by the President of the Family Division, the aim of the legal process is stated as follows:

1.7 The Revised Programme is designed to assist parties to reach safe agreements where possible, to provide a forum in which to find the best way to resolve issues in each individual case and to promote outcomes that are sustainable, that are in the best interests of children and that take account of their perspectives.[8]

One well-established assumption discernible in these documents is that it is better for parents to reach agreement than to litigate. Indeed, the Children Act 1989 was partly shaped by the assumption that the intrusion of the law into the family can have damaging effects. The statute therefore includes provisions designed to limit judicial intervention in decision-making in relation to arrangements for children. Whereas the law prior to the Act accorded, at least in principle, a leading role to courts in such decisions, even where the parents were not in dispute,[9] now judicial intervention is itself seen as potentially detrimental to children's welfare.

The Law Commission in 1988, for example, indicated that court orders might have the effect of polarising parents and perhaps alienating the child from one or other of them

---

[7] When the demise of the Family Law Act 1996 was announced.

[8] Practice Direction: Revised Private Law Programme [2010] 2 FLR 717. See also para 1.5.

[9] Courts were required to perform a supervisory function and, before granting a divorce, had to approve any agreement reached by the divorcing parents in relation to their children. In practice, the role of the court was of limited significance. See below.

(Law Commission 1988b: paras 3.2–3.3). Consequently, it said, it should not always be assumed that an order should be made. While it would remain open to courts to invoke their powers in uncontested cases, they should do so only where this would be in the child's best interests (ibid: para 3.3).[10] This approach gains expression in section 1(5) of the Children Act 1989, which states that: 'Where a court is considering whether or not to make one or more orders under this Act with respect to a child, it shall not make the order or any of the orders unless it considers that doing so would be better for the child than making no order at all.'

In addition, the Law Commission was of the view that judicial intervention often served little purpose in securing the welfare of children on divorce. While in the 1950s[11] it was considered essential that the courts oversee arrangements for children lest parents fail to put the interests of their offspring first, it is now acknowledged that the courts cannot effectively carry out this function.[12]

It was therefore decided that the court's duty should be pitched at a more modest level; it should simply be required to consider whether to exercise any of its powers under the legislation (Law Commission 1988b: para 3.9). The law was accordingly amended. Where a court decides that it should exercise its powers, it can, in exceptional cases, delay the divorce decree. In the majority of cases, however, said the Commissioners, parents are considered to be the best judges of their children's best interests and there would have to be cogent reasons for setting aside an agreed plan (Law Commission 1988b: para 3.10). The relevant law in relation to divorce and separation proceedings is contained in section 41 of the Matrimonial Causes Act 1973.[13]

41 Restrictions on decrees for dissolution, annulment or separation affecting children

(1) In any proceedings for a decree of divorce or nullity of marriage, or a decree of judicial separation, the court shall consider—

(a) whether there are any children of the family to whom this section applies; and
(b) where there are any such children, whether (in the light of the arrangements which have been, or are proposed to be, made for their upbringing and welfare) it should exercise any of its powers under the Children Act 1989 with respect to any of them.

(2) Where, in any case to which this section applies, it appears to the court that—

(a) the circumstances of the case require it, or are likely to require it, to exercise any of its powers under the Act of 1989 with respect to any such child;

---

[10] An order might be needed 'in the child's own interests, so as to confirm and give stability to the existing arrangements, to clarify the respective roles of the parents, to reassure the parent with whom the children will be living, and even to reassure the public authorities responsible for housing and income support that such arrangements have in fact been made' (Law Commission 1988b: para 3.2).

[11] See Royal Commission on Marriage and Divorce 1951–55 (1956), paras 366–67. The report noted the potentially detrimental effects of divorce on children (para 361) and the possibility that agreements between parents might not safeguard the best interests of their children (para 366). It was considered necessary to focus the minds of parents on the question of their children's welfare and to provide the courts with control over arrangements. In response to this recommendation, s 41 of the Matrimonial Causes Act 1973 was enacted to provide that arrangements made for children on divorce were reviewed by the courts. Before it could make absolute a decree of nullity or divorce, a court had to declare the proposed arrangements 'satisfactory' or the 'best that can be devised in the circumstances'. For a more detailed account of the background to s 41 of the Matrimonial Causes Act 1973, see Law Commission (1986: paras 4.5–4.6). See further Cretney (1989).

[12] The information available to the court was too sparse; the interview with the parent(s) was too perfunctory; the power of the court in practice to produce the desired outcome was limited; and there was no way of guaranteeing that the agreed plan would be observed (Law Commission 1988b: para 3.6).

[13] S 11 of the Family Law Act, which has never been brought into force, is similarly worded.

(b) it is not in a position to exercise the power or (as the case may be) those powers, without giving further consideration to the case, and

(c) there are exceptional circumstances which make it desirable in the interests of the child that the court should give a direction under this section,

it may direct that the decree of divorce or nullity is not to be made absolute, or that the decree of judicial separation is not to be granted until the court orders otherwise.

(3) This section applies to—

(a) any child of the family who has not reached the age of sixteen at the date when the court considers the case in accordance with the requirements of this section; and

(b) any child of the family who has reached that age at that date and in relation to whom the court directs that this section shall apply.

> **Q** Whereas previously it was thought that divorcing parents posed a potential threat to the well-being of their children, it is now assumed that they are usually the people best qualified to judge what is good for their children. How do you explain this change? To what extent do you think this 'hands-off' approach reflects a privatisation of decision-making on divorce?

Section 41 of the Matrimonial Causes Act 1973 is rarely used to withhold a divorce decree.[14] In addition, the provision applies only in cases of separation and divorce and, despite some talk of amending it or devising a new procedure that would apply to contact applications more generally,[15] there has been no change. However, in recent years concern has grown about the safety and appropriateness of consent orders, particularly when the case involves domestic violence or child abuse or both. As a result, where an application is made for an order under section 8 of the Children Act 1989, such as an application determining with whom the child should live or with whom the child should have contact,[16] the Practice Direction: Revised Private Law Programme, issued by the President of the Family Division,[17] sets out some safeguards:

> [1.3] There has been growing recognition of the impact of domestic violence and abuse, drug and alcohol misuse and mental illness, on the proper consideration of the issues in private family law; this includes the acceptance that court orders, even those made by consent, must be scrutinised to ensure that they are safe and take account of any risk factors. Coupled with this is the need to take account of the duty on Cafcass, pursuant to s16A of the Children Act 1989, to undertake risk assessments where an officer of the service (Cafcass officer) suspects that a child is at risk of harm.

So, it seems that the courts' role has become more interventionist of late, even where there is agreement.[18]

In all cases, whether there is agreement or not, when deciding disputes under section 8 of the Children Act, the court is obliged, irrespective of the marital status of or relationship between the parties, to consider the welfare of the child in terms of section 1 of the Children Act 1989:

---

[14] See Fortin (2009a: 242–43) and sources referred to there.
[15] See DCA (2002) Recommendation 13.
[16] See Chapter 10 below.
[17] After consultation with judges, Cafcass (Children and Family Court Advisory and Support Service) and others. See Guidance for Implementation of the Revised Private Law Programme [2010] 2 FCR 504.
[18] However, there is some doubt as to the likely effectiveness of the courts in protecting mothers against domestic violence. See Hunt and Macleod (2008: 12, 175, 185), Kaganas (2011: 74–78).

[2.1] Where an application is made to a court under Part II of the Children Act 1989, the child's welfare is the court's paramount concern. The court will apply the principle of the 'overriding objective' to enable it to deal with a case justly, having regard to the welfare principles involved.[19]

Section 1 of the Children Act 1989 is broad in its scope. It covers cases where questions relating to the upbringing of children arise between parents and also where parents are in dispute with third parties.[20] In addition, it applies in care proceedings and, in that context, is dealt with in more detail in Chapters 13 and 14.[21]

Where applicable, the welfare principle requires the courts to accord overriding importance to the child's best interests.[22] This was not always the criterion by which decisions were made. As Mnookin observes, the history of the legal standards governing disputes over children reveals a dramatic shift from the application of rules to a discretionary system (Mnookin 1975: 233) demanding the 'neutral' (ibid: 235) application of the best interests standard. Arguably, now, despite the pre-eminence of the welfare principle, we are seeing something of a return to rule-like regulation.[23]

III. FROM STATUS TO WELFARE

Until the early nineteenth century, the common law[24] invested fathers with the sole rights of custody and control over their legitimate children. The Court of Chancery had by then acquired powers to make children Wards of Court or Wards in Chancery, as a result of which paternal rights could be restricted and fathers could be deprived of custody.[25] However, although the court's primary consideration was the benefit of the child, intervention to curtail a father's rights was confined to cases in which his conduct was 'exceptionally culpable' (Maidment 1984: 112).[26] In *Re Agar-Ellis*,[27] for instance, the court found itself bound to uphold the 'natural' and 'sacred' rights of fathers, affirming that these should not be interfered with except in extreme cases.[28] Although in these cases the welfare of the child was relevant, it had to be threatened in some serious way to justify interference with paternal rights. In *Re Fynn*, for example, the Vice-Chancellor stated that a court would not intervene unless satisfied that to do so was 'not merely better for the children, but essential to their safety or to their welfare, in some very serious and important

---

[19] Practice Direction. Revised Private Law Programme [2010] 2 FLR 717. The court is required to deal with cases expeditiously, in ways proportionate to the nature, importance and complexity of the case, in ways that ensure the parties are on a equal footing, by allocating an appropriate proportion of the court's resources and without incurring unnecessary expense (para 2.1)

[20] It covers situations such as that which arose in *J v C* [1970] AC 668, a case pre-dating the Children Act 1989. See also *Re K (Adoption and Wardship)* [1997] 2 FLR 221.

[21] The welfare principle in the context of assisted reproduction and adoption is dealt with in Chapters 4 and 5, respectively.

[22] While statutes in the UK use the term 'welfare', the dominant term in North America is 'best interests'. Both terms are used synonymously in the literature in the UK.

[23] See Dewar (2000).

[24] See *Cartlidge v Cartlidge* (1862) 2 Sw & Tr 567; *R v De Manneville* 102 ER 1054, 1055 (KB 1804).

[25] See Pinchbeck and Hewitt (1973: 363ff).

[26] See also ibid: 364ff.

[27] (1883) 24 Ch D 317.

[28] See also *Re Fynn* (1848) 2 De G & SM 457; *Wellesley v Duke of Beaufort*, 2 Bl NS 124; 1 Dow & Cl 152. In *Cartlidge v Cartlidge*, n 24 above, the court held that the discretionary power conferred on the courts by s 35 of the Divorce and Matrimonial Causes Act 1857 should be exercised with reference to the common law rights of the father. Compare *Barnes v Barnes and Beaumont* (1867) 1 Sw & Tr 567.

respect'.[29] Generally, the interests of children were deemed to be best served by paternal custody.

As Maidment observes, the law at this time was less concerned with the wellbeing of children than with protecting the rights of fathers and thereby the social order:

> [I]t is clear that the law was concerned with the enforcement of patriarchal authority and not with the practice of child-care. The common law which gave father absolute rights over wife and children was concerned with the social control of the family and its stability, and with the orderly devolution of property. ...
>
> That the law's insistence on the sacred rights of fathers had nothing to do with the practice of child-care which remained a maternal role, is apparent from the sorts of disputes in which the issues of guardianship and custody arose. ... [F]rom the mid-century onwards the cases all involved fathers who were insistent on controlling the discipline or religious upbringing of the children, which in Victorian society was socially approved behaviour. The courts were not in the slightest concerned with the proper care of the children. Nor were the fathers; they were fighting for higher principles. They were also fighting for control of their sons.
>
> (Maidment 1984: 144–45)

Things did begin to change[30] during the nineteenth century, largely as a result of the struggle mounted by women for equal status in relation to their children.[31] Legislation was passed that enabled mothers to seek custody and access in certain circumstances[32] and, in 1886, the Guardianship of Infants Act empowered the court to make such order as it thought fit 'having regard to the welfare of the infant' as well as the conduct and the wishes of the parents.[33] The divorce courts claimed to apply these principles too.[34] The Guardianship of Infants Act 1925 provided that the court, in deciding any question relating to a child's custody or upbringing, should regard the child's welfare as the 'first and paramount consideration'.[35] While it appears that, initially, the paramountcy principle was introduced to side-step women's calls for equal status,[36] it has continued to inform child law over the years.

IV. THE PARAMOUNTCY OF WELFARE

The paramountcy principle, which has been described as the 'golden thread' running through the Children Act 1989 (Mackay 1989: 505),[37] is interpreted as enshrining the wel-

---

[29] *Re Fynn* (1848) 2 De G & SM 457, 475. See also *Wellesley v Duke of Beaufort* 2 Bl NS, 124; 1 Dow & Cl 152.

[30] For an account of this process, see Maidment (1984: ch 5).

[31] See Maidment (1984: 144–46); Chapter 8 above. Bailey (1994) points out that Caroline Norton, who campaigned for reform of the law, focused not on equality but on the vulnerability of women. Bailey suggests that this approach, rather than a direct challenge to men's rights, may have been the only way to succeed in getting the law changed at that time.

[32] Custody of Infants Act 1839, Divorce and Matrimonial Causes Act 1857, Custody of Infants Act 1873.

[33] S 5(4).

[34] See Maidment (1984: 131).

[35] S 1. See, for a full discussion of the legislation, Cretney (1996a).

[36] See Cretney (1996a); Reece (1996a); Chapter 8 above.

[37] The paramountcy principle has now been introduced into adoption law as well (s 1(2) Adoption and Children Act 2002). It does not, however, apply in committal proceedings where a parent has breached an order of court relating to the child's upbringing (*A v N (Committal: Refusal of Contact)* [1997] 1 FLR 533). Nor does it apply in proceedings relating to financial relief with respect to children (sched 1 para 4 of the Children Act

fare of the child[38] as the determining factor in cases concerning children's upbringing, overriding all others.[39] The formula designating the child's welfare 'first and paramount', contained in the then applicable legislation,[40] was said by Lord MacDermott in *J v C*[41] to mean:

> more than that the child's welfare is to be treated as the top item in a list of items relevant to the matter in question. I think [it] connote[s] a process whereby, when all the relevant facts, relationships, claims and wishes of parents, risks, choices and other circumstances are taken into account and weighed, the course to be followed will be that which is most in the interests of the child's welfare as that term has now to be understood. That is the first consideration because it is of first importance and the paramount consideration because it rules upon or determines the course to be followed. (710)

Although the word 'first' was omitted from the Children Act 1989 because it was said to cause a certain amount of confusion (Law Commission 1988b: para 3.13), the import of section 1 is much the same. It is intended that the court should be guided 'solely by the children's welfare' (Law Commission 1988b: para 3.15) and all relevant factors should be considered in this light.

V. THE HUMAN RIGHTS ACT AND WELFARE

When the Human Rights Act 1998 was enacted, a number of academics suggested that the paramountcy principle might be displaced; there is a view that it is not strictly compatible with the rights framework introduced by the legislation.[42] For example, Swindells et al suggest that 'Article 8 does not support the notion that paramountcy is to be given to the interests of the child' (Swindells et al 1999: para 3, 154).

Article 8 of the ECHR is probably the most important article[43] for the purposes of family lawyers. It reads:

> 1. Everyone has the right to respect for his private and family life, his home and his correspondence.

1989) or to secure accommodation (s 25 of the Children Act 1989). Nor does it apply to the provision of services by local authorities in terms of Part III of the Children Act 1989 (*Re M (A Minor) (Secure Accommodation Order)* [1995] Fam 108). The Child Support Act 1991 specifies only that the Commission must 'have regard' to welfare (s 2).

[38] Where the court has to make a decision in a case involving two children, the question of whose interests should prevail may arise. In *Birmingham City Council v H (A Minor)* [1994] 2 AC 212, the mother of a baby was herself a minor. She wanted contact but the court was of the view that, although it was in her best interests to have contact, it was not in the baby's best interests. The House of Lords took the view that it was the child who was the subject of the proceedings whose welfare was paramount. In this case, the baby's welfare dictated the outcome. Where the interests of two children conflict, and they are both subjects of the proceedings, the court will seek to balance the interests of both. See *Re A (Children) (Conjoined Twins: Surgical Separation)* [2001] 1 FLR 1.

[39] Whether this was the intention behind the introduction of the 'first and paramount' formula into the law is doubted by Cretney (1996a: 129–30).

[40] S 1 of the Guardianship of Minors Act 1971.

[41] [1970] AC 668.

[42] See, eg, Herring (1999). See also Kaganas and Piper (2001) for a critical analysis of the arguments put forward. See, for discussion of the tensions in Australian law between rights and utility in the sense of securing the best possible outcome for children, Dewar (1998: 470–73).

[43] Arts 6 and 14 are also significant, however.

2. There shall be no interference by a public authority with the exercise of this right except such as in accordance with the law and is necessary in a democratic society in the interests of national security, public safety or the economic well being of the country, for the prevention of disorder or crime, for the protection of health or morals, or for the protection of the rights and freedoms of others.

Any interference must be in accordance with the law, in pursuance of a legitimate aim, necessary and proportionate.[44] It seems that in interpreting Article 8, the ECtHR and the (now defunct) European Commission of Human Rights have refrained from polarising the concepts of rights and welfare. Their decisions reveal that they have long considered that the legitimate aim of protecting the health and rights of others extends to the aim of safeguarding the welfare of children, including their emotional and psychological well-being.[45] One case that is often cited, for instance, is *Johansen v Norway*.[46] There, the court referred to the need to 'strike a fair balance' between the interests of the parents and the child. In doing so, it said:

> [T]he court will attach particular importance to the best interests of the child,[47] which depending on their nature and seriousness may override those of the parent. In particular ... the parent cannot be entitled under Article 8 of the Convention to have such measures taken as would harm the child's health and development.

Similarly, in *Hokkanen v Finland*[48] the court stated that, 'Where contacts with the parent might appear to threaten [the child's] interests or interfere with those rights, it is for the national authorities to strike a fair balance between them.' It went on, in effect, to give greatest weight to the child's interests.[49] In *Yousef v The Netherlands*[50] it was held that where the rights of parents and children conflict, the rights of the children must be the 'paramount consideration'.

There are arguments for interpreting the cases restrictively. *Yousef* has been described as an 'isolated and weak decision' (Harris-Short 2005: 357). Herring and Taylor in turn have pointed out that *Johansen* implies that the interests of the child will not always override those of the parents; the decision will depend on the 'nature and seriousness' of the interests concerned (Herring and Taylor 2006: 528).[51] Herring argues that there are important differences between the approach required under the Children Act 1989 and the approach necessitated by the ECHR. He says that in a contact dispute, the starting point under the Convention is the parent's right to family life which will be infringed if contact with his or her child is refused. To justify a breach there must be 'clear and convincing evidence that the contact would infringe the rights and interests of the child or resident parent to such an extent that the infringement was necessary and proportionate' (Herring 2011: 429). Under the Children Act it is assumed that contact is in the child's best interests. He contends that the evidential burden differs depending on which approach is taken

---

[44] See Kaganas and Piper (2001: 259).

[45] See Kaganas and Piper (2001: 258 and n 61).

[46] (1996) 23 EHRR 33, para 78. See also *L v Finland* [2000] 2 FLR 118, 140; *K and T v Finland* [2000] 2 FLR 79, 107; *Elsholz v Germany* [2000] 2 FLR 486, 497.

[47] See also *Glaser v UK* [2001] 1 FLR 153; *Hoppe v Germany* [2003] 1 FCR 176, para 49; *Hendricks v The Netherlands* (1982) D&R 225.

[48] (1995) 19 EHRR 139, para 58.

[49] See Kaganas and Piper (2001: 260).

[50] [2003] 1 FLR 210, para 73. See also *Kearns v France* [2008] 1 FLR 888, para 79.

[51] See also Choudhry and Herring (2010: ch 3).

and that the nature of the questions asked is different. 'Under the Children Act, the question is a factual one—will contact promote the child's welfare?; whereas under the European Convention approach it is a question of legal judgment—whether the harm to the child is sufficient to make the breach "necessary" as understood by the law' (ibid). Fortin agrees with Herring's analysis and states that 'the Convention dictates a process which signally fails to make the child's interests paramount' (Fortin 2009a: 71). In her view, however, children's rights might be susceptible to being interpreted in a way that is compatible with their best interests. She maintains that, however difficult it might be to articulate children's rights, such a step is needed and would also lead to greater transparency in judicial decision-making. A rights perspective would enable the courts to focus more clearly on 'the child's position in relation to the adults involved', and, '[i]n so doing, it should avoid judgments which amount to little more than a series of vague conclusions justified by reference to best interests and welfare' (ibid: 297).

Yet the UK courts do not discern any conflict between the two approaches and continue to operate the paramountcy principle. In *Dawson v Wearmouth*[52] Lord Hobhouse of Woodborough said that nothing in the ECHR requires the court to act otherwise than in accordance with the best interests of the child. In *Re F (Adult: Court's Jurisdiction)*[53] the court clearly prioritised the interests of the child: 'The family life for which Art 8 requires respect is not a proprietary right vested in either parent or child; it is as much an interest of society as of individual family members, and its principal purpose, at least where there are children, must be the safety and the welfare of the child.'

In *Re KD (A Minor) (Ward: Termination of Access)*[54] Lord Oliver said that any conflict between the welfare principle and the human rights jurisprudence was 'semantic only'.[55] In *Re B* Lord Nicholls said that the balancing exercise that must be undertaken under Article 8 of the ECHR does not differ in substance from that required by the welfare principle.[56] And in *CF v Secretary of State for the Home Department*[57] Munby J made it clear that, in his view, the paramountcy principle is entirely compatible with the ECHR and so, also, the Human Rights Act 1998. He referred to an earlier judgment[58] in which he had stated that Strasbourg jurisprudence, like English law, 'has long recognised that, in the final analysis, parental rights have to give way to the child's. He continued:

> That reflects what the Court of Appeal had earlier said in *Re P & Q*[59] at [84]:
>
> > 'The balance to be struck in these cases is between the rights of the parents and the rights of the child … . In striking that balance, the European court has repeatedly stressed that the interests of the child are of crucial importance.'
>
> To this I would only add … that the court has now made clear that, as between parent and child, the child's interests are paramount. As the court said in *Yousef v The Netherlands* (2003) 36 EHRR 20, [2003] 1 FLR 210 at para 73:
>
> > The court reiterates that in judicial decisions where the rights under Art 8 of parents and

---

[52] [1999] 1 FLR 1167, 1182.
[53] [2000] 2 FLR 512, 531.
[54] [1998] 1 All ER 577, 588.
[55] See also *Re B (Adoption by One Natural Parent to Exclusion of Other)* [2002] 1 FLR 196.
[56] *Re B (A Child) (Adoption by One Natural Parent)* [2001] UKHL 70; [2002] 1 All ER 641, para 31.
[57] [2004] EWHC Fam 111; [2004] 2 FLR 517.
[58] *Re S (Adult Patient) (Inherent Jurisdiction: Family Life)* [2002] EWHC Fam 2278; [2003] 1 FLR 292, para 42.
[59] *R(P) v Secretary of State for the Home Department and Another: R(Q) v Secretary of State for the Home Department* [2001] EWCA Civ 1151; [2001] 2 FLR 1122.

those of a child are at stake, the child's rights must be the paramount consideration. If any balancing of interests is necessary, the interests of the child must prevail. (para 48)

It is clear, then, that the courts will not readily relinquish the welfare principle. As Freeman says, the paramountcy principle has 'enormous symbolic importance' and, in the context of litigation over children, 'it is not difficult to construct a right that their welfare should assume overriding importance' (Freeman 2000: 31). It has been suggested that, 'The probability is that under the HRA only those rights of adults involved in disputes that correspond with current understandings of welfare will be upheld' (Kaganas and Piper 2001: 268). And what falls into that category changes.

That understandings of children's best interests are never fixed is something the court had to consider in *CF v Secretary of State for the Home Department*.[60] The judge was presented with an argument that the notion of the child's best interests is not sufficiently certain to comply with the Convention. He examined the principle in *Olsson v Sweden*[61] that, in order for something to be 'in accordance with the law' in terms of Article 8, the law has to be formulated with enough precision to give the individual adequate protection against arbitrary interference. He concluded, obiter, that although what is regarded as in children's best interests changes over time, the welfare principle satisfies this test:

> It may be helpful to bear in mind here Professor Dworkin's distinction between the 'concept' which does not change and changing 'conceptions of the concept' ... . The rule of law demands adequate statement of the 'concept' but recognises and, within appropriate limits, can accommodate the fact that 'conceptions of the concept' may change over time ... . The concept of the child's welfare or best interests as something central to decision-making in respect of the child has of course been part of our law for well over a century ... . Not surprisingly, 'conceptions' of that 'concept'—what Lord Hoffmann would call the 'content'—have changed, and are continuing to change ... . But no one could sensibly suggest that the 'welfare principle' does not meet the *Olsson v Sweden* test. Indeed, it is, as we have seen, a core principle of the Strasbourg jurisprudence. (paras 101–03)

It is to the idea that welfare is socially constructed and to the problems of indeterminacy that we now turn.

VI. THE SCOPE OF THE WELFARE PRINCIPLE

What is encompassed by 'welfare' under the legislation is a very particular understanding of that concept. King and Piper remind us that:

> The broad range of factors—genetic, financial, educational, environmental and relational—which science would recognise as capable of affecting the welfare of a child are narrowed by law to a small range of issues which fall directly under the influence of the judge, the social workers or the adult parties to the litigation process. Among social problem construction theorists the issue is usually presented in terms of political ideology. By reconstructing the social dimension of any issue concerning the welfare of the child in such matters as housing, education, health care and financial security in ways which emphasise individual responsibility and

---

[60] See n 57 above.
[61] (1989) 11 EHRR 259.

the failure to accept that responsibility or perform those duties expected of a child carer, law in capitalist societies effectively depoliticizes social problems and reinforces liberal, individualistic ideology to the detriment of socialist notions of collective or governmental responsibility.

(King and Piper 1995: 50)

Thus the courts confine themselves to consideration of the individual means, behaviour and relationships of the family members involved. The law does not, and indeed King and Piper would argue cannot, attempt to address structural problems such as poverty or gender inequality.

VII. DECIDING WHAT IS GOOD FOR CHILDREN—THE PROBLEM OF INDETERMINACY

Even this restricted conception of welfare presents decision-makers with considerable difficulties. Bereft of any clear rules, such as the old father-right, they are confronted with making choices on the basis of a principle noted for its indeterminacy. This indeterminacy is attributed by Mnookin (1975) to a number of factors.

First, the court is expected to make 'person-oriented', not 'act-oriented' determinations (Mnookin 1975: 250). Instead of deciding on the basis of what it sees to be the true facts of the case, the court is required to make a decision based on its evaluation of the people concerned. It must judge 'the attitudes, dispositions, capacities, and shortcomings of each parent to apply the best-interest standard. Indeed, the inquiry centers on what kind of person each parent is, and what the child is like' (ibid: 251).

Secondly, while adjudication usually requires the determination of past facts, the welfare test demands that the court predict the future. And this prediction must encompass the future relationships between all the protagonists (ibid: 252–53). The future conduct of, say, the father may affect the behaviour of the mother and child. Mnookin highlights the difficulties in operating the welfare test:

[E]ven where a judge has substantial information about the child's past home life and the present alternatives, present-day knowledge about human behaviour provides no basis for the kind of individualized predictions required by the best-interests standard. There are numerous competing theories of human behaviour, based on radically different conceptions of the nature of man, and no consensus exists that any one is correct. No theory at all is considered widely capable of generating reliable predictions about the psychological and behavioural consequences of alternative dispositions for a particular child.

While psychiatrists and psychoanalysts have at times been enthusiastic in claiming for themselves the largest possible role in custody proceedings, many have conceded that their theories provide no reliable guide for predictions about what is likely to happen to a particular child.

(ibid: 258–59)

He goes on:

Even if the various outcomes could be specified and their probability estimated, a fundamental problem would remain unsolved. What set of values should a judge use to determine what is in a child's best interests? If a decision-maker must assign some measure of utility to each possible outcome, how is utility to be determined? ...

[T]he child could be asked to specify those values or even to choose. In some cases, especially those involving divorce, the child's preference is sought and given weight. But to make the child responsible for the choice may jeopardize his future relationship with the other parent. And we often lack confidence that the child has the capacity and the maturity appropriately to determine his own utility.

Moreover, whether or not the judge looks to the child for some guidance, there remains the question whether best interests should be viewed from a long-term or a short-term perspective. The conditions that make a person happy at age seven to ten may have adverse consequences at age thirty. (ibid: 260)

The courts, faced with these imponderables, cannot seek refuge in the certainties of judicial precedent. It is true that the courts have, over time, devised rough guidelines. So, for example, in disputes between parents and third parties, courts tend to take the view that it is in a child's best interests to be brought up by his or her 'natural', meaning biological, parents.[62] But where the dispute is between parents, the courts have abandoned the old formulas. For example, in the past the mother was regarded as the natural caregiver.[63] Although mothers who were adulterous or were considered sexually deviant in other ways were regarded as unfit to care for their children (Brophy 1985: 102–03; Boyd 1991: 87), generally the courts took the view that it was 'better'[64] and in accordance with natural law[65] that small children should be with their mothers. This approach has now, however, been repudiated by the judiciary. Judges have been careful to stress that all considerations must be viewed in the light of the welfare principle; courts are expected to judge each case on its unique merits and to assess the welfare of each child individually without relying on generalisations.[66]

In addition, mindful of the complexities inherent in the exercise of discretion in these cases, appeal courts are reluctant to overturn decisions. *G v G*,[67] a decision of the House of Lords, outlines the limited scope of the appellate jurisdiction in cases concerning children:

The jurisdiction in such cases is one of great difficulty, as every judge who has had to exercise

---

[62] *Re M (Child's Upbringing)* [1996] 2 FLR 441, 453. See also *Re KD (A Minor) (Access: Principles)* [1988] 2 FLR 139. See also *Re K (Adoption and Wardship)* [1997] 2 FLR 221, 228; *Re D (Care: Natural Parent Presumption)* [1999] 1 FLR 134; *Re O (Adoption: Withholding Agreement)* [1999] 1 FLR 451. However, there has been some dispute even over the extent to which biological parents should be preferred. In a case involving a lesbian couple, the court said that, while the fact that one of the women was the child's natural mother did not raise a presumption in her favour when it came to a residence order, it was a significant factor in determining the child's best interests. In the view of Lord Nicholls, 'the court should always have in mind that in the ordinary way the rearing of a child by his or her biological parent can be expected to be in the child's best interests' (*Re G (Children)* [2006] UKHL 43; [2006] 2 FLR 629 para 2). However, Baroness Hale made it clear that this does not mean courts can depart from the paramountcy test: 'The welfare test itself is well able to encompass any special contribution which natural parents can make to the emotional needs of their child, in particular to his sense of identity and self-esteem, as well as the added commitment which knowledge of their parenthood may bring' (para 30). The Supreme Court interpreted this to mean that 'It is only as a contributor to the child's welfare that parenthood assumes any significance' (*Re B (A Child)* [2009] UKSC 5; [2010] 1 FLR 551, para 37). See, for discussion, Everett and Yeatman (2010); Diduck (2007).

[63] Maidment says there was never a maternal preference rule. However, 'in practice the *prima facie* right of the father gave way to the *prima facie* right of the mother from the early part of this century' (Maidment 1984: 156).

[64] *Re L* [1962] 3 All ER 1.

[65] *Re B* [1962] 1 All ER 875.

[66] See *In Re K (Minors) (Children: Care and Control)* [1977] 2 WLR 33, 35; *Re L (Contact: Domestic Violence); Re V (Contact: Domestic Violence); Re M (Contact: Domestic Violence); Re H (Contact: Domestic Violence)* [2000] 2 FLR 334, 342.

[67] [1985] 2 All ER 225.

it must be aware. The main reason is that in most of these cases there is no right answer. All practicable answers are to some extent unsatisfactory and therefore to some extent wrong, and the best that can be done is to find an answer that is reasonably satisfactory. It is comparatively seldom that the Court of Appeal, even if it would itself have preferred a different answer, can say that the judge's decision was wrong, and unless it can say so it will leave his decision undisturbed. ...

[T]he appellate court should only interfere when it considers that the judge of first instance has not merely preferred an imperfect solution which is different from an alternative imperfect solution which the Court of Appeal might or would have adopted, but has exceeded the generous ambit within which a reasonable disagreement is possible. (228–29)

In the absence of defined rules, a court must seek to assess the likely outcomes of the various courses open to it and decide which will best serve the child's interests. Yet these decisions are informed by more than the facts of each particular case. Bradley suggests that the judicial emphasis on the uniqueness of each case is somewhat disingenuous, serving to obscure the values deployed by the court in reaching its conclusions (Bradley 1987: 186).[68] Writers have criticised the welfare test as being subjective and as leaving room for personal prejudice in decision-making.[69] Reece, however, argues that there is a more fundamental problem: '[T]he indeterminacy of children's welfare has allowed other principles and policies to exert an influence from behind the smokescreen of the paramountcy principle' (Reece 1996a: 295–96). These principles and policies are not so much a reflection of subjective prejudice as of a perceived preference in society for the heterosexual nuclear family.[70] Similarly, Thèry, writing about French child custody law, sees the best interest standard less as an expression of the prejudices of individual judges than as a means of regulating the post-separation family:

[T]he practice of referring to 'the interest of the child' as a criterion in judicial decision making has been much criticized and disputed. There are three levels of argument that can be distinguished.

1. For some, it is not so much the principle nor the general criterion as such, but rather the dominant meanings which have been attributed to it. They therefore offer a 'good' interpretation. ... [E]ach position claims its particular version of the 'interest of the child' as the only one in accord with the current state of knowledge. ...

2. At a second level, there are those who dispute the criterion itself. Its indefinable character is seen as giving free rein to the subjectivity of the decision makers. ...

3. Finally, ... there is another group who criticize the criterion itself, not as a subjective and 'empty' concept, but, on the contrary, as a concept overflowing with political and social objectives which, further, have very little to do with the person of the child. ...

These three levels of criticism have a common thread in seeing the criterion as an alibi; an alibi for dominant ideology, an alibi for individual arbitrariness, an alibi for family and more general social policies for which the law serves as an instrument. In my opinion we need to go

---

[68] See, further, King (1987: 189); Eekelaar (1984); Eekelaar (1985).

[69] See Eekelaar (1984: 596); King (1987: 189).

[70] On the one hand, this is changing. The Civil Partnership Act 2004 can be seen as endowing same-sex relationships with legitimacy and acceptability while the inclusion in the Adoption and Children Act 2002 of same-sex couples within the category of adoptive parents endorses their capacity to parent. Increasingly courts are faced with cases involving same-sex relationships and are having to acknowledge new family forms. See, eg, *Re B (Role of Biological Father)* [2007] EWHC 1952 (Fam); [2008] 1 FLR 1015. There is arguably still a preference for the nuclear family but the notion of the nuclear family now extends to same sex parents and their children: See *R v E and F (Female Parents:Known Father)* [2010] EWHC 417 (Fam); [2010] 2 FLR 383. On the other hand, see the discussion in Chapter 1 above on the underlying heteronormativity of the family.

beyond these critiques, which all assume (implicitly or explicitly) that there is such a thing as 'the interest of the child' *per se*. ... Rather we need to examine the relationship between the use of such a criterion and the changing methods of regulation in family affairs.

(Thèry 1989: 81–82)

The concept of 'the interest of the child' necessarily develops into a general image of what the 'good' post-divorce family organization should be, indicating one or more model(s) of family life after divorce. (ibid: 86)

At a more general level, one can distinguish two opposing poles in relation to the 'interest of the child': a logic of substitution which prioritizes the household; and a logic of durability based on the biological family and its history. (ibid: 95)

In the substitution theory, the mother (and more generally, the woman, if one includes the second spouse) remains the person who is the principal means of ensuring the permanence of the child's relationships. According to the logic of durability, paternal and maternal roles are assumed to be equally important and thus less gender specific. (ibid: 99)

Q Thèry concedes that most cases cannot be neatly categorised as applying one or other model, but argues that one or other of the opposed logics is usually dominant. When reading the case law in Chapter 10, consider whether judicial decisions reflect a preference for either model: the model in terms of which the biological family is substituted by the reconstituted family or the model in terms of which the biological family is preserved but reorganised. Could one argue that ideology or politics might play a part in influencing the selection of the model perceived as the 'good' post-separation family?

Developments in law and in policy appear to confirm that the welfare principle is perhaps not as indeterminate as one might think. Dewar argues that there is a growing interest in shifting family law towards a more rights based model and that there is a move away from discretion towards rules:

The factors leading to this growth in rights claims are complex, and include domestic political pressure from organized groups (such as fathers' rights groups seeking greater 'equality' in legal treatment, especially in matters concerning children) [and] the increased relevance of human rights instruments. (Dewar 2000: 68, footnote omitted)

[T]he liberal State's own commitment to privacy has [in the past] made it impossible to formulate clear rules or principles to govern family dissolution—discretion has allowed the underlying issues to remain unresolved. Yet if that is correct, what has changed? It seems that such is the anxiety surrounding the perceived disintegration or decline in 'family values', as well as the financial costs of divorce itself, that families and family law have become central concerns of political debate. As a result, modern legislators have overcome their traditional respect for 'family privacy' and are now more willing than in the late 1970s to issue prescriptions for a 'good divorce'—in particular, that divorcing or separating couples should be rational, altruistic, settlement minded, co-operative and cost-conscious. Part of this prescription for the new model divorce is enshrined in rules, or norms that are increasingly rule-like.

An example of the growing prescriptiveness of family law legislation concerns relationships between children and the non-resident parent after separation or divorce. A striking feature of family law policy in recent years has been the desire to maintain relations between children and the parent with whom they are not living, a relationship that usually involves preserving in law relations between households. This is evident in the child support scheme ..., in the new emphasis on continuing and shared parental responsibility, and on children's 'right' to contact with both parents after parental separation. (ibid: 68–69, footnotes omitted)

The prominence given to the maintenance of this parent-child link is a relatively recent phenomenon—and it is noticeable that the relevant legal provisions are rule-like in nature ... . In this way, modern family law increasingly seeks to radiate messages about how to divorce well, or how the fragmented family should re-form itself. (ibid: 69)

VIII. THE WELFARE PRINCIPLE AND THE 'GOOD' POST-SEPARATION FAMILY

Dewar was writing of Australian law and of the position in England prior to the demise of the Family Law Act 1996. Nevertheless despite the now obscure legal status of section 1, it can still be seen, along with the White Paper, which also emphasises the continuity of relationships between children and both their parents, as giving some indication of the dominant image in this country of the 'good' post-separation or post-divorce divorce family. Recently, the Centre for Social Justice, which might be thought to represent conservative thinking on family policy, has published a review of family law that states:

We ... *suggest legislation should acknowledge that children are most likely to benefit from the* **'substantial involvement'** *of both parents in their lives.* This will be found through contact being of a sufficient frequency and duration so that each parent is able to have this substantial involvement in the child's day-to-day routine and activities.

(Hodson 2009: 28, emphasis in original)

The Coalition government has endorsed the aim of increasing contact, somewhat surprisingly phrasing this in the language of rights and extending its remit to grandparent contact:

We will conduct a comprehensive review of family law in order to increase the use of mediation when couples do break up, and to look at how best to provide greater access rights to non-resident parents and grandparents. (HM Government 2010a: 20)

The Family Justice Review recommended:

[T]here should be a statement in legislation to reinforce the importance of the child continuing to have a meaningful relationship with both parents, alongside the need to protect the child from harm. (Norgrove 2011a: 108)

And while this recommendation has been rejected by the House of Commons Justice Committee (2011: para 71), this was only on the grounds that the law already 'acknowledges that a meaningful, engaged relationship with both parents is generally in a child's best interests'.

The preference for continuity has a history going back about four decades. Courts, like child welfare professionals, have long considered it a priority, when families split up, to preserve links between children and their non-resident biological fathers. Courts hearing contact disputes begin with an 'assumption' in favour of contact or at least that contact is in the child's best interests.[71]

There is also a well-established assumption that conflict is damaging for children and that the 'good' post-separation or post-divorce family should avoid it. Parents who litigate are seen as harming their children and even as failing as parents because they cannot come to a 'sensible' agreement.[72] For example, Baroness Butler-Sloss, speaking extra-judicially, stated as established fact that children of separated parents are harmed and that the parents are to blame. Children whose parents fight over them 'may do less well at school and may find it difficult to make lasting relationships as adults' (Butler-Sloss 2010: 941). Judges deplore cases that remain unresolved and which return to court; such disputes are even regarded as pathological (Kaganas 2010a, 2011). In addition, these 'intractable' contact disputes are considered an illegitimate drain on public funding and legal aid is to be withdrawn in relation to these cases.[73]

To divorce (or separate) 'responsibly' (Reece 2003), parents must come to an agreement that provides for contact. Parents must also maintain a harmonious or at least conflict-free relationship[74] and ensure that their agreement is an enduring one:

> Women and men, in committing to the co-parenting ideal, are to act in ways that are rational, settlement-minded and altruistic. They are to be aware of the social and economic costs of divorce and the risks associated with parental conflict, not least around refusal of contact with the non-resident father. Given that separation should be as harmonious as possible, the object of legal intervention is to reduce conflict, promote consensus between the parties and, where appropriate, facilitate contact between children and the non-resident parent.
>
> (Collier and Sheldon 2008: 158)[75]

The 'good' post-separation family needs a 'good' post-separation mother to sustain it and it is primarily from resident mothers that an altruistic attitude is demanded. Carol Smart gives us some insight into the way the preoccupation with continuity has shaped what is expected of mothers. Not only are they expected to care for their children, they are expected to extend that work to encompass the facilitation of contact by fathers. When mothers refuse to take on this additional task, they become identified as bad or vindictive mothers (Smart 1991: 496). Smart suggests that 'it is assumed that children need fathers so badly that mothers must be prepared to tolerate almost any behaviour. In this form of reasoning, the welfare principle ... diverts attention away from the problem of the "bad" father by creating in its place the "bad" mother' (ibid: 497).

The comments of Boyd, writing in Canada, are apt to describe the demands made of

---

[71] *Re L (Contact: Domestic Violence); Re V (Contact: Domestic Violence); Re M (Contact: Domestic Violence); Re H (Contact: Domestic Violence)* [2000] 2 FLR 334, 367. See on the existence or otherwise of a presumption or assumption of this nature, Gilmore (2008).

[72] See, eg, *Re L (Shared Residence Order)*, [2009] EWCA Civ 20; [2009] 1 FLR 1157, paras 66–70.

[73] Sir Nicholas Wall, interviewed on Law in Action ('What Next for the Family Courts', BBC Radio 4, 19 October 2010), suggested that the government would be justified in withdrawing public funding for intractable disputes which, he said, were damaging for parents and children and which achieved no outcome. The Legal Aid, Sentencing and Punishment of Offenders Bill 2010–11 goes even further. It excludes private children and family matters where there is no domestic violence from the scope of legal aid. The only public funding which will be retained is that made available for mediation. See also MOJ (2010a: para 4.215).

[74] See Kaganas (2010a, 2011).

[75] See also Day Sclater (1999b: 176–77).

British mothers too. She identifies what she calls a 'new ideology of motherhood' according to which 'good' post-separation mothers are expected to be 'reasonable' and to facilitate contact (Boyd 1996: 510). This unrealistic and even oppressive arrangement, she says, involves an attempt to recreate the nuclear family and it places an enormous responsibility on mothers (ibid: 514–15). Moreover, it seems that it is not only mothers who are charged with building the 'good' post-separation family. We have argued elsewhere that some of the responsibility for ensuring that contact 'works' is also now being placed on children; there is an emerging construct of the 'good' child of separation and divorce. This child 'copes' with the upheaval and accedes to contact with the non-resident parent (Kaganas and Diduck 2004).

> **Q** When reading the cases on residence and contact in Chapter 10, consider whether the work of Smart and Boyd accurately describes the attitudes of judges. What factors do you think might be contributing to the construction of these images of 'good' mothers and fathers?

That fathers must be enabled to play a part in their children's upbringing is a conviction that, according to Day Sclater and Piper, can be seen as part of a project to 're-moralise' the family. Anxieties about what is perceived as a crisis in the family, about uncertainty surrounding the role of the father and about the threat to 'traditional' masculinities are, to some extent, assuaged by the new emphasis on the 'rights and responsibilities' of fathers. 'Old' ideas about the biological, two-parent family appear to survive reassuringly amidst the flux of changing families and family forms (Day Sclater and Piper 2000: 147). In a similar vein, Reece suggests that 're-instating the biological father into potentially fatherless families has helped to contain social anxiety about the collapse of the family' (Reece 2006a: 548).

The political acceptability of the ideology of the separate but continuing family is also buttressed by other ideas which are held by diverse groupings for diverse reasons. A number of writers have observed the impact of the image of the new fatherhood, fathers' rights movements and the New Right. The new fatherhood, as Smart (1989a: 16–19) says, relies on the assumption that fathers are increasingly engaged in the work of childcare.[76] Fathers are therefore as capable of looking after their children as mothers are. Fathers' rights advocates, in turn, demand greater rights in relation to their children and complain of discrimination.[77] The New Right, most vocal in the 1980s and 1990s, has been aiming to restore the traditional hierarchy within the family, giving mothers the role of domesticating men and rendering them responsible.[78] More importantly, the 'fatherless family' is associated with 'rising levels of crime, social disorder and the under-achievement of boys' (Collier and Sheldon 2008: 13), and fatherhood is seen as the antidote to a these and a number of other social problems (ibid: 21). All these factors have had a profound influence on perceptions of the 'good' family and all place fatherhood at the centre of this institution. The law, in turn, has increasingly come to be used to promote the 'involved father' instead of focusing, as it did in the past, on the traditional paternal role as economic provider (Collier and Sheldon 2008: 116, 127).

Whether these representations of fatherhood are borne out in the everyday life of most

---

[76] There is evidence that some fathers do become more involved in childcare after divorce than they were during their marriages. See Smart (1999); Walker (2004).

[77] See Geldof (2003). See further Kaganas (2006).

[78] See also Pryor and Rodgers (2001: 7) on what they term the 'conservative' perspective.

families is open to doubt:[79] 'parenting remains in many respects an activity deeply infused with social relations of gender' (Collier and Sheldon 2008: 128). Many men have not changed significantly when it comes to childcare (ibid: 129) and the notion of the 'good' father is still bound up with the role of breadwinner (ibid: 130). As Smart points out, the men's groups which are campaigning for increased contact and demanding that a presumption of shared parenting be enacted are not seeking more paternal involvement during the course of the parental relationship; they focus primarily on the situation after separation:

> This means that the shape of fathers' demands in the early 21st century is not about reconfiguring parenthood as a whole in order that both parents can share the responsibilities and disadvantages—as well as benefits; rather it is a campaign against mothers and a reassertion of paternal privilege which can be exercised at will. (Smart 2006a: ix)[80]

She suggests that, since it is mothers who bear most of the responsibility for childrearing, fathers can fit in quite 'active' parenting around their work and leisure activities. This 'gendered division of labour only becomes a problem for fathers on divorce or separation when the emotionally powerful position of mothers is revealed' (ibid: ix). The demand for residence or more contact after separation therefore leads to conflict. One of the reasons for this is that mothers see fathers as being in the position of 'partially trained apprentice' and find difficulty trusting them with full-time care, at least when children are young (ibid: x). They find difficulty in accepting the genuineness of men's claims that they will become more involved fathers and see these as opportunistic, offering little benefit to children and much harm to mothers (ibid: xii). Fathers, in turn, frame the conflict in terms of justice, fairness and equality, and turn mothers' objections 'into an apparently self-interested, child-harming defence of the status quo' (ibid: xii). They also conflate the interests of fathers and their children (Collier 2006: 68).[81] As Rhoades notes in the Australian context, fathers' groups argue that equal time with both parents is best for children (Rhoades 2006: 131).

For men's groups, the remedy for both children and fathers appears to lie in the law. Smart maintains that this is misguided because the law cannot deal with interpersonal conflicts of this nature. Nevertheless, although as Collier and Sheldon (2006: 26) note, these groups have not got exactly what they want from the law, it appears that they have had an impact on the debate about post-separation parenting.[82] It may be at least in part because of their campaigns that there has emerged a new, 'formal commitment to egalitarianism, gender neutrality and social diversity' (Collier and Sheldon 2008: 13). In particular, 'fatherhood is now widely viewed in legal and social policy as a highly significant resource for children' (ibid: 21). And, as Fineman (1989: 846–47, 861) points out, this claim to the importance of fathers receives crucial support from an apparently neutral source: child welfare science.

---

[79] See Collier and Sheldon (2008: 34); Collier and Sheldon (2006: 18). See Boyd (2003: 172–74) and the research cited there.

[80] See also Boyd (2006: 31–32); Rhoades (2006: 143).

[81] See also Collier (2005).

[82] It seems reasonable to conclude that fathers' campaigns were at least in part influential in the move to increase the powers of the courts to enforce contact, a move that resulted in the amendment of s 11 of the Children Act 1989.

IX. CHILD WELFARE KNOWLEDGE

Fineman (1989), referring to the USA, suggests that child welfare knowledge has been harnessed in support of campaigns by various interest groups. In particular, child welfare knowledge has been coupled with egalitarian arguments to form the basis of a strategy to enhance the position of fathers.

The success in Britain of arguments based on child welfare knowledge and advocating greater emphasis on fatherhood is evidenced by the law governing parental responsibility as well as the law concerning contact and, to a lesser extent, residence. The 'good' post-separation family is portrayed as one that ensures that children's relationships with both parents are preserved. This, it is said, is not just good for parents; child welfare research shows that it is the best arrangement also for children. Claims based on the welfare of children are extremely potent, especially if they bear the hallmark of objective, scientific research. They have accordingly led to a preoccupation in social policy and in the law with ensuring the continued participation of both parents in the upbringing of their child.

King remarks that the ascendancy of child welfare science in the legal arena is hardly surprising given that, with 'the decline of the Church and the growth of pluralism, the only universally accepted truths ... appear to be those manufactured by scientists' (King 1981: 124).[83] Yet what is accepted as scientific 'truth' changes over time:

This term [welfare], used as a criterion for decision-making, carries with it the implicit assumption that it is both possible and necessary to discover the needs of the child. Yet how does one set about defining and assessing children's needs? In the case of physical needs, the answer is relatively straightforward. ... But what of a child's psychological and social needs? How do we know, in the first place, what they are? In our society, the answer to this question in recent years has been to place our faith in the experts, that is, paediatricians like Dr Spock or child psychiatrists like Anna Freud or Albert Solnit. But this answer raises the further question: how do the child experts determine children's needs? 'A combination of theoretical knowledge and empirical observation' would be an intelligent reply, but hardly a satisfactory one, for it does not begin to explain how different experts may come to completely different conclusions not only about the same individual child, but on the needs of children in general. Moreover, theories of child development seem to move in and out of fashion with alarming regularity. ... Suffice it here to make the point that the kinds of behaviour that the experts choose to observe, the hypotheses they choose to formulate and their interpretations of their findings all depend upon the preconceptions they bring with them to the psychology laboratory or field survey. To these preconceptions are added biases of the funding agencies, university departments and hospitals who sponsor and promote research projects.

This leads us then to something of a truism, which nevertheless ought to be stated: except for the basic physical requirements for healthy development, children's needs are socially defined, socially sustained and socially adjusted to conform with prevailing values and expectations. ... A brief glance at some of the child care theories which have won popularity in this country over the past 50 years and the social conditions from which they emerged and within which they were accepted adds further evidence to support this argument. First there was the Truby King regime of the late thirties and early forties:

'Strict four hour feeds, no unnecessary handling beyond nappy changing and feeding and absolutely no cuddling (molly coddling). ...'

It was probably no coincidence that the end of the war in 1945 saw the passing of the Truby

---

[83] See also Fineman (1991: 110–12).

King era. There followed a period when the writings of John Bowlby, a psychiatrist ... were to prove highly influential. ... Bowlby's message was clear and simple. There was no substitute for full-time motherhood. ... It was a message which was rapidly taken up by a popular press critical of the conduct of neglectful working mothers and their 'latch-key' children. It coincided with a widespread feeling that the traditional values associated with the home and family life were under threat, adding the weight of scientific authority to the call for a return to pre-war values. It also coincided with the need for a contraction in the female labour force, made necessary by the return of servicemen and the fact that the government was not in a position to provide day-nurseries for the vast army of potential working mothers.

After King and Bowlby came Dr Spock ... with his emphasis on self-expression and self-indulgence for babies and infants at a time of unprecedented economic growth, confidence and buoyancy in American society. ... More recently, a body of knowledge has emerged disproving Bowlby's more extreme statements about maternal deprivation and suggesting that conflict between parents or growing up in a hostile environment may be far more damaging than the fact of separation of child from mother. Other work has cast doubt on the irreversibility of the effects of damage or deprivation in the early years of life. Significantly perhaps, these ideas are gaining wide dissemination at a time when the number of children affected by divorce has never been higher and state intervention in the family has never been greater.

Three points arise from this discussion of child care theories which are highly relevant to the concept of welfare. ... The first is that doctors and scientists have become authority figures in our society on almost any aspect of human behaviour including the rights and wrongs of child development. In the absence of any absolute morality or universal value system, science and medicine are the only bodies of knowledge which have almost universal appeal. ... It is hardly surprising, therefore, that all the major figures in the recent history of child care have been medically or scientifically qualified.

Secondly, although ideas about what is good or bad for children's healthy mental and social development may be legitimized by the language and trappings of science and medicine, they are neither scientific or medical in the accepted sense. They are rather moralistic and value-laden, emerging from the cauldron of prevailing beliefs and social conditions. ...

The third point is that in order for any particular theory of child development and child care to win recognition, respectability and popular support, the right social conditions must prevail. ... [O]ur society does not consist of a homogeneous collection of people, all sharing the same values and beliefs about child welfare. Bowlby's views on maternal deprivation, for example, were not accepted by working women. ... Yet in a society dominated by men and imbued with the spirit of post-war reconstruction and a desire to return to traditional values, it is not surprising that Bowlby's ideas gained credence despite the opposition of working women. The general principle that one can extract from recent history appears to be that any notion as to what is good or bad for children, above and beyond purely physical matters, if it is to gain popular support and influence policies and practices to a significant degree, must have the backing of powerful groups within society and must be consistent with the objectives of those groups. (King 1981: 109–13, footnotes omitted)

Policy-makers therefore make choices between different research findings. And the theories concerning child welfare that are currently most influential in the context of separation and divorce are those that focus on the damaging effect of interparental conflict[84] and on children's need to know and to maintain relationships with both parents.[85]

Wallerstein and Kelly, for instance, in their book *Surviving the Breakup*, emphasise the psychological importance of both parents (Wallerstein and Kelly 1980: 307) and conclude that, 'where possible, divorcing parents should be encouraged and helped to share post

---

[84] See Piper (1994).
[85] See also Chapter 8 above.

divorce arrangements which permit and foster continuity in the children's relationship with both parents' (ibid: 311). Richards,[86] who has written extensively in the field of childcare and development, also stresses the importance of both parents for children. He argues that a relationship with both parents helps to reduce the emotional trauma of divorce and to avoid disruption of the child's social connections outside the immediate family. The damage inflicted on children by divorce can best be mitigated if parents avoid conflict and continue to play a part in their children's lives.

> Research ... suggests that within a short time of separation many children cease to have a relationship with their father. ... The breaking of established relationships with fathers and other family members may have significant effects on a child's social development and their capacity to form and sustain relationships. ...
> Conflict between parents before and after divorce is associated with poorer outcomes for children. ...
> [P]olicies should aim to encourage the maintenance of a child's existing relationships with parents and the wider family and kin, ensure an adequate income to post-divorce households with children, reduce as far as possible conflict between divorcing parents or, at least, encourage its expression in areas that do not involve children, encourage the provision of emotional and practical support for divorcing parents ... It will not always be desirable to strive to maintain relationships with both parents. ... In rare cases, existing relationships may be detrimental to children if they continue. ..... It is also important to realize that the loss of a parent usually means the permanent loss of half of a child's kin relationships which may have profound ... consequences. (Richards 1994: 307–09)

Conflicting views, such as those propounded by Goldstein, Freud and Solnit (1973), who warned of loyalty conflicts for children and who advocated that the caretaking parent be given the right to decide whether contact should take place, were never widely accepted. Such an approach would, it was said, encourage blackmail and malice on the part of the caretaking parent and preclude co-operation between the parents.[87] Other research highlighting the negative aspects of contact,[88] observing that it allows parents to continue their battles and that it is often stressful for children, has also not had any impact on policy so as to limit support for contact. Nor has the conclusion of Walker et al that too much emphasis is being placed on outcomes (Walker et al 2004: xxxi)[89] and, in particular, on regular physical contact (ibid: 314).

Pryor and Rodgers have reviewed a number of studies in their survey of research into children's lives after parental separation, and their conclusions are in many ways at odds with the current dominant discourse.[90] They point out that research does not support the assumption that contact is necessarily 'good' or that children are damaged if it is not sustained:

> [W]e have established that, in the main, contact with children is good for men and often desired by them, and that children say they want to see their fathers. It is a different question to ask, however, whether it is important for children's well-being that they maintain a relationship with their fathers, especially as so many grow up apparently unscathed by the absence of a father in

---

[86] See also Burgoyne, Ormrod and Richards (1987: ch 4); Richards (1987); Cockett and Tripp (1994, 1996); Hooper (1994).
[87] See Foster (1976); Freeman (1983: 215–19).
[88] See Maidment (1975).
[89] See also 310. See, on the importance accorded to outcomes, Kaganas (2010a).
[90] See also Boyd (2003: 201).

their day-to-day lives. The view is now widely held that frequency and regularity of father–child contact after separation is associated with children's psychological well-being, unless abuse or psychopathology is present. Although positive contact is in itself a good outcome for children who usually want it, the assumption that contact *per se* is measurably good for children does not stand up to close scrutiny. Several studies have found that there is no direct or simple relationship between levels of nonresidential father–child contact and child well-being, while others have reported both positive and negative relationships. This does not mean that contact with fathers is unimportant for children, and these mixed feelings suggest several explanations. First, contact between fathers and children is not necessarily a positive experience for children if the child does not want it or if the relationship is negative. Separation, too, sometimes increases parental conflict, and father-child contact in situations of high parental conflict can be negatively related to well-being, especially for boys.

(Pryor and Rodgers 2001: 214, references omitted)

[F]requency by itself does not have a consistent link with children's well-being, [and so] attention has more recently been given to the *quality* of the father-child relationship ... [I]t is apparent that, apart from economic provision, fathers' contributions to their children's lives depend on more than their mere presence ... [I]t is those aspects of parenting encompassing monitoring, encouragement, love and warmth, that are consistently linked with child and adolescent well-being. (ibid: 215, references omitted, emphasis in original)[91]

Barnett, in her review of the research, suggests that much of it 'yields contradictory or equivocal results' (Barnett 2009a: 51).[92] She argues that the way the welfare of the child is currently constructed is not supported by research but, rather, reflects neoliberal ideology. This rests on the notions of equality, responsibility and citizenship, and assumes equal participation in domestic work by women and men. That assumption, she notes, is not borne out by any empirical evidence; women carry most of the responsibility for childcare and to ignore this prejudices mothers. In addition the emphasis on contact can harm children, especially in cases of domestic violence (Barnett 2009b).

Other academics have also criticised the way research findings are used in the policy-making arena. For example, Fineman (1991) questions the way in which social science research has been deployed to ascribe increased importance to the role of fathers. She maintains, for instance, that the findings reported by Wallerstein and Kelly have been grossly oversimplified by legal policy-makers; rather than revealing maternal incompetence and children's grief at the loss of a father, the study paints a more qualified and complex picture (Fineman 1991: 119–21).

King and Piper also raise issues relating to the interpretation and oversimplification of research but their work focuses specifically on the difficulties inherent in translating child welfare discourse into legal discourse. They argue that the way the law 'thinks' about children is different from the way that child welfare science does. In order for the law to fulfil its functions, such as that of resolving disputes, it has to reconstruct child welfare knowledge so that it 'makes sense' within law. This inevitably leads to reductionism:[93]

The problem for child welfare as science is that, within the legal arena, the information will almost invariably be constructed according to the demands of the legal discourse. ... The law's demand for decisiveness and finality, for winners and losers, for rights and wrongs to be identi-

---

[91] See also Buchanan et al (2001: 5); Walker (2004: 185); Smith (2003: 198).
[92] See also Gilmore (2006b).
[93] Compare James (1992).

fied and exposed to the public gaze in order to further its normative objectives tend to force legal judgments out of the mouths of child welfare representatives. ...

[T]he ... process [of reconstruction] may be seen, not in political terms,[94] but as the inevitable consequence of the autopoietic nature of law and its inability to incorporate external discourses except by reconstructing them. ... Thus the scientific discourse of child welfare in all its richness and complexity is reconstructed as concepts which 'make sense' within law— that is, concepts which further the immediate demands of the law to determine guilt and responsibility, resolve disputes and do justice between litigants. ... This reconstruction process necessarily involves reductionism, and simplification as well as a concentration on the behaviour of individuals. ...

[P]recepts, focusing on mother-child bonding and stability of relationships were used to justify particular outcomes in particular cases, but such outcomes therefore also became the *ratio* for deciding later cases and guidelines for child protection functions. It is consequently easy to trace the emergence and development of a line of cases dealing with 'mother preference' in custody disputes. Similarly, the work of child psychologists concerning the advantages of stability for the child led to the *'status quo principle'*. (King and Piper 1995: 50–51)

So, not only does child welfare science continually reinterpret children's best interests, it in turn is simplified by policy-makers and reinterpreted by the law. Moreover the law not only simplifies child welfare science in its search for clear normative principles, it also makes choices from a range of available principles. It has been argued, drawing on Niklas Luhmann's conceptualisation of risks as decisions leading to avoidable loss (Luhmann 1993: 21–22), that, in the simplified version of child welfare knowledge adopted by law, to deny children contact with non-resident parents and for parents to go down the road of conflict have been constructed as constituting the primary risks to children's welfare on relationship breakdown. It is those risks, rather than others that might be thought to exist, that are addressed by law:

[The legal system] could, for example, have chosen to adopt the principle that contact should not be ordered against the wishes of the resident parent but chose, instead, the opposite. The reason for this must be that a decision to give the resident parent a veto would run counter to the dominant discourse surrounding contact which has been informed by political as well as child welfare imperatives. Currently, government and professional groupings, as well as popular culture reflected in the media, all espouse a particular understanding of the consequences of separation and divorce for children. This understanding has been accorded the status of taken-for-granted truth and cannot fail to impact on the legal system if it is to retain credibility. And the law, in making pronouncements consistent with the dominant discourse, confirms its 'rightness'. Within the dominant discourse and so, also, in the legally reconstituted version of child welfare science, children are damaged by divorce and, increasingly, it is thought that the damage or loss they suffer is exacerbated by conflict or lack of contact. The task for law, then, is to establish the rules and to make the decisions that will avoid or minimise this damage; the legal system must be able to retain public confidence by giving the impression that it can do what is right for children and avert the risks to which they might be exposed. (Kaganas 1999: 109–10)

The use made of the Sturge–Glaser report (Sturge and Glaser 2000) is perhaps instructive. This report was compiled by experts for the court hearing in *Re L*[95] and it drew on 'developmental and psychological knowledge, theory and research' (ibid: 615). Although

---

[94] See pp 393–94 above.
[95] *Re L (Contact: Domestic Violence); Re V (Contact: Domestic Violence); Re M (Contact: Domestic Violence); Re H (Contact: Domestic Violence)* [2000] 2 FLR 334.

it focused primarily on contact in cases involving domestic violence, it also dealt more generally with contact. It states that 'contact can only be an issue where it has the potential for benefiting the child in some way' (ibid: 616) and enumerates both the advantages and the risks of direct and indirect contact. Among the risks is abuse, including emotional abuse where the non-resident parent uses contact to get at the other parent. The report refers, in particular, to the continuation of unhealthy relationships, the risk of undermining the child's sense of stability and continuity as well as the potential for stress affecting children and carers. It suggests that children who do not want contact should be listened to and seems to indicate that it is risky to insist on contact when the parents are implacably at odds. The report also recommends a presumption against contact in domestic violence cases.

The report was extensively relied on by the court in *Re L* but affirmed only selectively. The court decided that the effect of violence should be to 'offset' the presumption or, as Thorpe LJ preferred to call it, the 'assumption' in favour of contact (367). There was mention of other factors that might have the same effect but little prominence was given by the court to the risks mentioned by Sturge and Glaser.[96] Furthermore, the court rejected their recommendation that there be a presumption against contact in domestic violence cases. Likewise, the Practice Directions that followed[97] do not embody such a presumption.

X. ALTERNATIVES TO THE WELFARE PRINCIPLE

That the welfare of children should be paramount has come to be widely accepted as self-evident and beyond question.[98] However, as we have seen, the welfare principle has been criticised on many grounds. One objection is that it allows considerations which are not articulated to affect decision-making. Reece (1996a) maintains that it conceals policy choices. This objection is one that Eekelaar (2002a) would categorise as the 'lack of transparency objection'. But Reece also challenges the paramountcy principle on grounds consistent with what Eekelaar (ibid) terms the 'lack of fairness' objection. Reece (1996a) contends that it is possible to protect children's interests without making their welfare paramount. While more care and attention might be needed to ascertain a child's best interests, since the child may be less able to articulate them, the parents' interests should not be left out of the equation. She finds no justification for allowing adults' rights to be subordinated to children's needs: 'The paramountcy principle must be abandoned, and replaced with a framework which recognizes that the child is merely one participant in a process in which the interests of all the participants count' (ibid: 303).

Herring (1999) too raises questions about both transparency and fairness. He is particularly concerned about how to reconcile clashes between parents' and children's interests in the light of the Human Rights Act. He is also concerned that adults' interests are smuggled into the equation under the guise of children's welfare. He proposes a

---

[96] See further Kaganas (2000: 321–23).

[97] Currently this is Practice Direction (Residence and Contact Orders: Domestic Violence and Harm) [2009] 2 FLR 1400. Indeed the measures adopted to provide safeguards in cases of domestic violence are being scaled down. Finding-of-fact hearings must be held only 'if the court takes the view that the case cannot properly be decided without such a hearing' (President's Guidance (Split Hearings) [2010] 2 FCR 271 para 6).

[98] However, there appears to be no obligation on parents to apply the paramountcy principle when making decisions about their children. See Herring (2011: 419).

modification of the welfare test which he calls a relationship-based welfare approach. He contends that, since families are based on mutual co-operation and support, it is important to encourage children to learn altruism. He also maintains that children's welfare is promoted if their relationships with other family members are fair and just and, to this end, it may be necessary for children to make sacrifices. Decisions should be guided by what is considered a proper parent–child relationship, with children's interests at the forefront of the family's concern.

How 'proper' relationships are identified is not specified and Eekelaar (2002a) points out that Herring's approach involves a balancing of interests but leaves unanswered the question of how they should be balanced. Herring acknowledges this but provides some suggestions as to how his theory could apply in practice. The court would have to consider the relationships at the time of the order as well as the future. Where the child and a parent have an existing relationship, there is more of a case for a contact order than where they do not. The relationship between the parents is also relevant so, for example, violence inflicted on the resident parent must be seen as harmful to the child. In addition, the willingness of the primary carer to permit contact is an important consideration because to compel contact in the face of that parent's resistance will not lead to a 'meaningful on-going relationship'. Finally he says, it is the quality of the contact rather than the kind or level of contact that matters (Herring 2005b: 167).

Eekelaar advocates a different approach:

> The best solution is surely to adopt the course that avoids inflicting the most damage on the well-being of any interested individual … . Under the proposed test, if the choice was between a solution that advanced a child's well-being a great deal, but also damaged the interests of one parent a great deal, and a different solution under which the child's well-being was diminished, but damaged the parent to a far lesser degree, one should choose the second option, even though it was not the least detrimental alternative for the child. (Eekelaar 2002a: 243–44)

Eekelaar qualifies this, however: a solution should not be adopted if the detriments outweigh the benefits to the child unless this is unavoidable. Solutions that harm children are generally unacceptable (ibid). As part of his proposals, Eekelaar then goes on to argue that the notion of welfare should be replaced by that of well-being. He contends that the latter concept can be articulated in a way that gives clearer guidance about the factors to be weighed than the welfare test does. There are some matters, he says, that can be seen as indicators of well-being. For example, for parents to bring up their children serves the well-being of all concerned. However, he goes on, while we can assume that well-being is promoted by maintaining relationships between children and parents, we cannot assume this with regard to establishing a relationship that does not already exist.[99]

The problem here is that, as Eekelaar himself concedes, the transparency question persists. And the same observation can be made of Herring's approach. Who decides, and on what basis, which relationships are important for parents and children? His assumptions are not uncontentious; for example, the courts have certainly at times insisted that to establish a relationship that does not yet exist with a non-resident parent is good for parents and children.

None of these three commentators challenges the use of judicial discretion[100] in

---

[99] See also Eekelaar (2002b).

[100] This discretion is, as mentioned above, constrained by an almost rule-like 'assumption' in favour of contact.

resolving disputes about children. Others have. Writing in the USA in the 1990s, Fineman advocated the abandonment of the best-interests test as unworkable and recommended its replacement, in relation to decisions about the child's residence, with a presumption. The primary caretaker presumption involves a shift from 'person-oriented' to 'fact-oriented' decision-making as well as a shift from discretion to rules:

> The best-interest-of-the-child test must be replaced. ...   One recent suggestion is that custody courts should apply a 'primary-caretaker' rule. This rule has been characterized in different ways, but the essence of the primary-caretaker standard is that children need day-to-day care, and that the parent who has performed this primary care during the marriage should get custody ...
>
> The primary-caretaker standard would not ignore the less essential, secondary contributions of the other parent. They are rewarded by the establishment of visitation periods with the children. Custody, however, can be viewed as a reward for past caretaking behaviour.
>
> The primary-caretaker rule implicitly recognizes that no expert can confidently make the predictions required under the future-oriented best-interest placement, and that past behaviour may in fact be the best indication we have of commitment to the future care and concern for children. ...
>
> In my opinion, a major advantage of the primary-caretaker rule is that it is particularly susceptible to legal analysis because it involves past fact-finding, an inquiry traditionally performed by courts. ...
>
> The rule may currently operate to the advantage of mothers, but, if we value nurturing behaviour, then rewarding those who nurture seems only fair. If fathers are left out, they can change their behaviour and begin making sacrifices in their careers and devoting their time during the marriage to the primary care and nurturing of children. ... In cases in which both parents acted as true primary caretakers, I predict that few custody battles would ensue.
>
> (Fineman 1991: 180–84)[101]

Q How great a departure is the primary caretaker presumption from the status quo principle? From the welfare principle? Does it avoid the application of the welfare principle in contact disputes or in care proceedings? Would its adoption address the issues raised by King and Piper?

Boyd points out that the primary caretaker presumption cannot address the concerns of feminists around contact law. However, what is notable about the primary caretaker approach is that it seeks to ground policy in the reality of childcare (Boyd 1996: 514).[102]

Bainham adopts a very different view,[103] contending that the law should play a normative role and promote the ideal of co-parenting:

---

[101] See, for a more radical proposal, Fineman (1995).

[102] See also Boyd (2003: 211). See Fineman (2004: 191–92). She notes that those contending for shared parenting maintain that fathers' contribution to the upbringing of their children is of equal importance to mothers' contribution. They say that, although fathers contribute in different, mainly economic, ways, they should not be disadvantaged as economic activity takes time away from caring activity. Instead, Fineman asserts that to equalise the chances of the economic provider in disputes over custody is to ignore the detriment already suffered by the primary caretaker because her caring duties have reduced her economic opportunities. Her sacrifice of earning power would be compounded by the loss of the fruits of her caring labour (ibid: 192), while for the economic provider, his contribution enhances his own skills and economic position. Reece (2008: 122) finds this argument unconvincing. She contends that 'caretaking and breadwinning are incommensurable'. The caretaker's economic loss should be compensated by economic means.

[103] See also Ziff (1990).

It may readily be agreed that the existing socio-economic structure of British society militates against the adoption of equal parenting roles within the context of a functioning family. It is incontestable that women are frequently expected to take low paid part-time employment with a built-in expectation that they are the primary providers of child care. Conversely, men are expected to act out the role of breadwinners in full-time employment and not to assume any responsibility for daily child care during the working week. The reality in many families is that the man who might conceivably wish to assume a co-parenting role will find it difficult (if not impossible) to do so. ... But it does not follow from any of this that we must accept [the] view that legal reform should be contingent upon a sea-change in socio-economic policy or parental patterns of behaviour during marriage. It may just as validly be argued that it is a function of law to seek to influence and shape attitudes to the respective roles of parents both during marriage and following divorce. As the Law Commission has said, it is 'an important function of law to provide a model of behaviour which is generally believed to be desirable'. While there may be legitimate disagreement about the efficacy of law in influencing social attitudes (in this case parental behaviour) it is surely right that legislation affecting the family should hold up some normative standard of what society regards as good practice in child-rearing. ...

The search for gender-neutral solutions to the problem of child custody has caused some feminists to argue for a 'primary carer' principle ... .

A better gender-neutral concept in my view is quite simply the concept of 'parenthood' which the 1989 Act ostensibly supports. ... It must be conceded that legislative change cannot of itself convince anyone of the sexual equality implicit in parenthood but it could at least give expression to societal expectations of parental co-operation. (Bainham 1990: 218–19)

This argument is rejected by Boyd:

As for child custody law, recent challenges to feminist work by authors such as Andrew Bainham demonstrate a somewhat simplistic idea of the role of law as positive and expressive. Law is not adequately conceptualized as an instrument of public policy which reacts to social change or dysfunction, and tries to influence the problem. To take this latter view is to ignore the symbolic and discursive effects of law and to treat it as a non-ideological mechanism of social regulation. It omits a consideration of the ways in which law, as a particular discursive field crucial to liberalism and modernism, tends to empower certain discourses over others. (Boyd 1991: 113)

Certainly, in Smart's opinion, the tendency to regard the activity of caring for children as a natural expression of maternal instinct, together with the valorisation of fatherhood, have meant that mothers have 'no legitimate voice unless they speak the language of equal rights (for fathers) or welfare (for children)' (Smart 1991: 498). Anything else is interpreted as a manifestation of selfishness. Similarly, Roche points out that the predominant discourse renders invisible the burdens placed on mothers who are expected to conform to the policy of including fathers: 'If she fails to do so it is she who becomes the problem rather than, for instance, the substance of her well-founded anxieties around contact between the children and their father' (Roche 1991: 358).[104]

Smart and Neale suggest that an 'ethic of care' could be deployed in disputes about children:

An ethic of care is based on responsibilities and relationships, is bound to concrete situations, and is an activity. To operate according to this ethic, one would have to have regard for the discharge of responsibilities, the quality of relationships, the actual situation that people find themselves in and the practice that people have been engaged in. The ethic of care allows for

---

[104] See further Chapter 10 below.

changes to occur in decisions because concrete situations change.

The ethic of justice, on the other hand, focuses on the application of abstract principles from an impartial stance, giving primacy to issues of equality and generalizability ... . It would not be concerned with actualities but with concepts of equality (between men and women) and/or ideals about the welfare of children in general. It would not be concerned with who had done what in terms of providing care, but with identifying whose claim to these abstract principles is the highest. ....

An ethic of care ... would be concerned with who has held responsibility and established relationships, with the actuality of a specific family life and a specific child and with who had actively done the caring. In this formulation responsibility could be economic as well as nurturing, different children in the same family could be treated differently but *theoretical* claims about ability to care would not take precedence over, nor would they be regarded as being as significant as, *actual* past caring behaviour. The quality of the relationship between the parents and between the parents and children would also be part of the equation and the ability of parents to treat each other with dignity and respect would be considered ... . [T]he ethic of care would have a range of different and individuated outcomes while also being just.

(Smart and Neale 1999: 170–71, footnotes omitted, emphasis in original)

The debate about the primary caretaker principle has all but vanished from the public and even the academic agenda.[105] Nor have discussions about the ethic of care[106] featured large of late. On the contrary, the popular imagination has been captured by a notion firmly rooted in the ethic of justice: shared parenting. This is somewhat puzzling, say Kaganas and Piper (2002: 368–69), as it amounts to a resurrection of the old discussions about joint custody in the 1980s. A presumption of joint custody was rejected by the Law Commission (1986) on the grounds that it could operate to the detriment of mothers and, in the absence of genuine shared care, would be purely symbolic.

Welfare and Shared Parenting

The issue of shared parenting was addressed in a Green Paper in 2004 as well as the White Paper that followed it. The then government declared itself unwilling to introduce a statutory presumption:

Some have proposed that legislative change is needed to introduce 'presumptions of contact', to give parents equal rights to equal time with their child after parental separation. Where such arrangements are best for the child, and are agreed between the parents or determined by a court, such arrangements can and should be put in place. The Government does not, however, believe that an automatic 50:50 division of the child's time between the two parents would be in the best interests of most children. In many separated families, such arrangements would not work in practical terms, owing to living arrangements or work commitments. Enforcing this type of arrangement through legislation would not be what many children want and could have a damaging impact on some of them. Children are not a commodity to be apportioned equally after separation. The best arrangements for them will depend on a variety of issues particular to their circumstances: a one-size-fits-all formula will not work. The assumption that both parents have equal status and value as parents is enshrined in current law. The actual arrangements made by courts start from that position. (DCA, DfES and DTI 2004: para 42)[107]

---

[105] But see Fineman (2004).
[106] But see, eg, Sevenhuijsen (2002); Smart (2006b).
[107] See also DCA, DfES and DTI (2005: paras 13–15).

Nevertheless, at the time of writing a private member's bill, the Shared Parenting Orders Bill, is being considered by Parliament. It is intended to create a presumption that shared parenting orders enhance children's welfare. This is unlikely to pass into law given that both the *Family Justice Review* (Norgrove 2011a) and the House of Commons Justice Committee (2011) rejected the possibility of enacting a presumption in favour of shared parenting.[108] However, courts are increasingly making shared parenting orders[109] and mediators are free to suggest shared parenting as a possibility. Some of the criticisms below of a presumption apply also to court orders where parents are in conflict and to the situation where a resident parent is pressured to agree to a shared parenting arrangement.

The original revival and the continuing interest in shared parenting can be largely attributed to the efforts of pressure groups representing fathers. In the submissions made by three organisations, including Families Need Fathers, to the consultation on *Making Contact Work*, it was agued that there should be a presumption of shared parenting, although not necessarily in the form of a 50:50 split. A presumption would, these groups maintained, counter the idea that 'winner takes all' and promote parental involvement. It would amount to recognition of the importance of both parents and, if it were to become the norm, would 'set the tone' for negotiations and would 'remove obstacles' to contact.[110] Another organisation, Fathers4Justice, attracted considerable media attention in a bid to publicise its claims of court bias and injustice. Much publicity has also been given to the contention that the legal system is failing to enforce contact orders against obstructive mothers. In addition, proponents of shared parenting suggest that it would solve the problems posed by so-called parental alienation syndrome (PAS), a phenomenon manifested by the child's rejection of one parent caused mainly by 'brainwashing' by the other, hostile, parent (usually the mother).[111]

The claims made by fathers' rights groups are somewhat surprising, given that most children are in contact with their fathers[112] and given the very strong preference for contact shown by the judiciary,[113] lawyers[114] and other professionals[115] involved with separating

---

[108] See Chapter 10 below.

[109] See Chapter 10 below.

[110] See CASC (2002: appendix 3, paras 3 and 8).

[111] The existence of PAS as a recognised syndrome was rejected in an expert report to the Court of Appeal (Sturge and Glaser 2000). The experts' view was accepted by the court: *Re L (Contact: Domestic Violence); Re V (Contact: Domestic Violence; Re M (Contact: Domestic Violence); Re H (Contact: Domestic Violence)* [2002] 2 FLR 334. See further, Kaganas and Piper (2002: 367).

[112] Hunt and Macleod (2008) review the relevant research and report that the proportion of children without contact is about 30%. At the other end of the spectrum, some children are experiencing quite high levels of contact (ibid: 2). Blackwell and Dawe (2003) report that 17% of non-resident fathers had some form of contact every day, with 8% seeing their child daily, 49% at least weekly and 69% monthly. Between a half and two-thirds had overnight stays at least once a month. Peacey and Hunt (2008) found that even excluding shared care arrangements, 7% of resident parents reported their child had contact with the other parent nearly every day; 34% at least weekly and 45% at least fortnightly. The figures reported by non-resident parents were even higher (8%, 46% and 58%, respectively) (ibid: 2–3). See also Walker (2004: xxiv); Dunn (2003: 18); Blackwell (2003). About 90% of parents do not resort to court proceedings and, of the applications for contact that are made, fewer than 1% are rejected (see DCA, DfES and DTI 2004: paras 21 and 25). One-sixth of applications are made because of an alleged breach of an order (DCA, DfES and DTI 2004: para 26). In the ONS survey, overall, parents were satisfied with their contact arrangements, with almost half saying they were 'very satisfied'. One in 20 parents were 'fairly dissatisfied' with their contact arrangements (Blackwell, 2003). Almost two-thirds of Walker's sample were satisfied (Walker 2004: xxiii, see also 168). See further Mitchell (2004).

[113] See, eg, Davis and Pearce (1999).

[114] See, eg, Wheeler (2004).

[115] See, eg, James et al (2003).

and divorcing couples.[116] Hunt and Macleod were commissioned in 2006 to examine contact cases to establish whether there is any substance to the criticisms made of the courts:

> [T]his research was commissioned in the context of attempts by pressure groups and the parliamentary opposition to introduce a statutory presumption of 'reasonable contact' into the Children Act 1989 and claims that non-resident parents who went to court for a contact order could end up with little or no contact for insubstantial reasons. (Hunt and Macleod 2008: 189)

> [W]e have argued that there can be no doubt that the courts hearing contact applications start from the position that unless there are very good reasons to the contrary contact between a child and their non-resident parent should be promoted. They also make considerable efforts to make that a reality. While they are not always successful in the majority of cases they are. In most of our cases where the outcome was no face to face contact there were either very good reasons for this or the non-resident parent opted out of the proceedings without giving them a proper chance. There are [*sic*] a small proportion of cases which end in no direct contact where this is not the case, but usually the courts will have made considerable efforts to reach a more satisfactory conclusion and will be very loath to give up the attempt. Yet there appears to be a perception that non-resident parents do not get a fair deal from the courts. (ibid: 213)

> There can, we think, be no doubt that the courts operate on, in effect, a presumption of contact, even though this is not in primary legislation. That does not necessarily mean, however, that they are always able to put that presumption into effect. Indeed clearly there will be cases where it would wrong to do so. (ibid: 191)

> However, such circumstances were seen to be extremely rare: in general, even where there was an element of risk, the court would be looking for ways to ensure that face to face contact could take place safely, or failing that, set up arrangements for indirect contact. (ibid: 192).

> Despite the existence of obstacles which can impede the court's attempts to establish face to face contact, the fact remains that most non-resident parents who go to court to seek contact actually get it. This applied to 78% of all completed applications where the outcome was known (207 of 266) and 80% (165 of 206) of first time applications. ... [W]here a case ended with no direct contact expected to take place this was rarely as the result of a court decision made after a contested hearing. (ibid: 204–05)

Moreover, there is no evidence to support the suggestion that it is malevolent mothers who constitute the primary obstacle to contact.[117] Walker's report (Walker 2004)[118] indicates that there are many other reasons for lack of contact. Some fathers in the study experienced difficulty with contact because they could not take the children to their new homes, sometimes because of the presence of a new partner. Distance was also a factor as was the father's work commitments. Communication between the parents was significant: contact stopped when communication was bad and resumed when communication improved. While some mothers would have preferred their former husbands to disappear from their own and their children's lives, most wanted the fathers to contribute more to their chil-

---

[116] See Kaganas and Piper (2002: 370–71).

[117] In an analysis of 300 court files by the DCA, it was found that in around half the cases there was a repeat application and one-third of those were because of alleged breach of court orders (Draft (Children) Contact and Adoption Bill 2005, Regulatory Impact Assessment, para 17).

[118] See also Rhoades (2002).

dren's upbringing (ibid: xxv).[119] Many mothers were disappointed that the fathers made little effort to stay in contact (ibid: 174, 195) Several mothers explained that contact had ceased because of the father's indifference, because the children did not want to see their father or because they had other priorities such as friends of weekend jobs (ibid: xxv).[120]

Hunt and Macleod also found that unreasonable mothers were rarely the reason for problems with contact:

> A degree of hostility to contact on the part of the resident parent (fathers as well as mothers) was seen as being very common when a case first arrives in court. The reasons for this vary widely. Some parents will have well founded safety fears because of domestic violence, drug and alcohol abuse, or child maltreatment. For others the hostility reflects hurt and anger at the breakdown of the relationship, disputes over property and money or a desire to create a new family unit and cut out the biological parent. (Hunt and Macleod 2008: 192)

> Persistent unreasonable hostility, however, was generally seen as quite unusual. (ibid: 193)

> [T]here were very few examples of cases ending in no direct contact where, in our view, the outcome could be regarded as unfair to the non-resident parent in that there were no welfare concerns of sufficient severity to warrant this. (ibid: 193–94).

The researchers also found little evidence of maternal non-compliance with court orders:[121]

> 30 of the sample applications made by non-resident parents (10% of 289) were brought, at least in part, to give effect to orders or agreements made in previous proceedings, of which 10 were asking for a penal notice. Moreover, of all the cases which had concluded by the end of our data collection period 18 (of 292; 6%) were known to have returned to court because of the resident parent's non-compliance with the order or agreement made in the proceedings. (ibid: 205)

It seems, therefore, that the rationales put forward for shared parenting based on bias and on the intransigence of mothers lack substance. In addition, Kaganas and Piper (2002) argue that a presumption of shared parenting would not have the effect of encouraging those fathers who do not want to maintain relationships with their children to do so. It also has potential disadvantages: it might create an imbalance of power between the parents, put pressure on mothers and increase their resentment by downgrading their childcare contributions. It could put mothers as well as children at risk, and it would not solve the problem of parental conflict:

> Many mothers might have very good reasons for opposing shared parenting and these may never come to light or may be minimised in the push for a consent order. Buchanan and Hunt, for example, found that, in their sample, at least one parent reported domestic violence, including harassment and intimidation, in 78% of cases, and, in 56%, there were reports of physical violence. The incidents referred to were rarely minor and in almost two-thirds of cases the violence and fear were present after separation. By the time of the court proceedings, sometimes years after separation, the fear/violence persisted in half the cases but only one-quarter of those

---

[119] See also Walker (2004: 173 and 193). The courts refuse to address a dispute framed in terms of one parent's complaint that the other is insufficiently involved with the children (Pearce, Davis and Barron 1999: 26).

[120] See also Walker (2004: 196, 214); Simpson et al (2003: 204–06).

[121] The authors concede that their figures might be an underestimate but note that the practitioners interviewed did not think non-compliance was common (205).

interviewed cited violence as an issue in the case. So, even if conduct such as domestic violence might be allowed in law to rebut the proposed presumption, evidence of this may not, in practice, come before the court.

In any event, the likelihood that some mothers who oppose contact will be made to agree to it does not necessarily support the claims of the proponents of a presumption of shared parenting that it will be a solution to the problem of conflict over contact. As *Making Contact Work* points out, it is doubtful that the existence of a presumption will prevent acrimonious disagreement between parents who cannot co-operate.

First, it is doubtful whether it will significantly reduce litigation … . Certainly research in the UK shows that 'there has been a remarkable rise both in the number of orders and the number of "disposals" in respect of private law applications under the Children Act'. This would suggest that the existing presumption or assumption in favour of contact has done nothing to stem the tide of litigation and there is no reason to suppose that a statutory presumption of shared parenting will prove more effective in doing so. Mothers who are strongly opposed to any contact at all or who may wish to resist a statutorily mandated split will seek to rebut the presumption in much the same way as they do now.

Secondly, whatever arrangement is embodied in a court order, child care arrangements are unlikely to work or to take place in a conflict-free context, unless the parents espouse this as a goal and are willing to achieve it. A parent might be pressured into agreeing to shared parenting but may resist implementing the arrangement … .

A statutory presumption of shared parenting has, arguably, the potential for an increase in the use of [enforcement] measures. There will be more court orders for contact and, so, more mothers will be exposed to the risk of imprisonment for defying such orders.

(Kaganas and Piper 2002: 272–73, references omitted)

Furthermore, there is no consensus that shared parenting is in the best interests of children generally[122] and so a presumption would constitute a departure from the paramountcy principle (ibid: 376–77). And, it is argued, the courts are likely to see any presumption as incompatible with the Human Rights Act 1998. In the case of *Payne v Payne*[123] Thorpe LJ observed that to create a presumption in favour of one parent would present a risk to the other's right to private and family life in terms of Article 8 of the ECHR and to the right to a fair trial under Article 6.[124]

Australia's Shared Parental Responsibility Act,[125] which creates a presumption that 'equal shared parental responsibility' is in the child's best interests, has, according to Rhoades (2010),[126] led to a number of problems. Shared parenting arrangements are being made in inappropriate cases. These are a source of distress for a significant number of children, particularly where the parents are in conflict. There has been an increase in shared care arrangements 'that do not represent a real consensus between the parties and with which at least one parent (usually the mother) is struggling and unhappy' (Rhoades 2010: 175). Lawyers are finding it difficult to achieve child-centred arrangements because fathers claim to be 'entitled' to a 50:50 division of time. The exception to the presumption where a parent has been violent is being narrowly interpreted (ibid). Parents find difficulty

---

[122] See Neale et al (2003); Gilmore (2006b).

[123] [2001] EWCA Civ 166; [2001] 1 FLR 1052.

[124] See Kaganas and Piper (2002: 378).

[125] The Family Law Amendment (Shared Parental Responsibility Act) 2006.

[126] See also the Chisholm Report which recommends that the 'friendly parent' provision be amended to recognise that some parents need to protect their children. It also states: that, 'instead of suggesting that any particular outcome is likely to be best for children ("one size fits all"), the proposed changes would simply require the court to consider which of the available options in each case would be best for the child' (Chisholm 2009: 8). Cf Gilmore (2006a).

in managing the frequent interaction made necessary by shared care (ibid: 173). And although the paramountcy principle has been retained, the interests of the individual child are not given the attention they should be, says Rhoades (ibid: 176). She advocates a return to judicial discretion in the context of a relational approach:[127]

> In light of the apparently negative consequences of the present legislative scheme, I would agree with Christine Piper that we need a legal framework that allows judges and lawyers to 'approach each case in a position of uncertainty, respecting the complexity and ambiguity of a client's life'. In other words, the law should encourage family law professionals to focus on the particular child and parents, taking account of the affective dimensions of their lives and their relationships with one another and not view these through a pre-determined policy lens about the appropriate form of care arrangement. (ibid: 179, footnote omitted)

> As Herring acknowledges, a relational autonomy approach ..., may be difficult to achieve in practice ... . Michael King and Christine Piper have argued that the system-like nature of law means that it will inevitably oversimplify and distort the complexity of children's lives. Hence the attempt to get decision-makers to think relationally may simply result in this complexity being channelled into a series of binary questions informed by our adversarial traditions, so that, for example, in exploring a parent's own interests and self care needs, a judge might be drawn back into making comparative judgments about the less selfish or more 'friendly' parent. Nor is there any guarantee that a focus on relationships will automatically increase a decision-maker's sensitivity to the emotional and psychological meanings of these relationships for the child in question, having become acculturated to an approach that relies on certain preconceptions about children's interests.
>
> Perhaps the most significant obstacle to the implementation of a relational approach to the 'best interests' principle is its contradiction of the recent direction of family law policy making. ... [I]ts inherently nuanced and contingent understanding of family life is unlikely to be attractive to policymakers (and lobbyists such as fathers' rights groups) who prefer simple messages about socially responsible behaviour ... . At this point I should make it clear that I am not suggesting that broadening the legislative framework will lead to less litigation or more certain outcomes. Quite the opposite ... . Yet as Rosemary Hunter's research tells us, numbers of applications are not an appropriate measure of 'good law' for children, and supporting family law professionals to settle workable arrangements that are a proper fit for the particular client should be the law's role when it comes to raising children, not the achievement of predictability.
> (ibid: 182–83, footnotes omitted)

> [O]ne way forward may be to adopt a relational approach to children's best interests, with the 'object' of producing 'psychologically healthy' parent–child relationships. A possible starting point for enacting such an approach is the New Zealand Care of Children Act's version of the paramountcy principle, which directs decision-makers to investigate the needs of the particular child within his or her particular family circumstances. ...
>
> Clearly a relational approach to children's best interests will not increase the predictability of contested outcomes, nor provide a 'quick fix' for the problems that have arisen. ... But given the growing evidence of harm associated with the 2006 changes for some families, it is imperative that the legislation begin to disrupt the idea that the 'highest truth of good parenting' is facilitation of a shared care arrangement. (ibid: 184, footnotes omitted)

---

[127] See the criticism of the relational approach above.

XI. POLICIES AND RESEARCH

Official policy is informed by the assumed link between contact and welfare. In the United Kingdom, a number of policy documents have been issued dealing with contact, all of which assume and endorse contact as being in the best interests of children. The first of these, published in response to studies highlighting the problem of domestic violence in the context of contact, was a consultation paper followed by a report on contact in cases where there has been domestic violence (CASC 2000).[128] Another consultation paper followed, entitled *Making Contact Work. The Facilitation of Arrangements for Contact Between Children and their Non-residential Parents; and the Enforcement of Court Orders for Contact* (CASC 2001b). The Report of the Committee was then published in 2002: *Making Contact Work. A Report to the Lord Chancellor on the Facilitation of Arrangements for Contact Between Children and their Non-residential Parents and the Enforcement of Court Orders for Contact* (CASC 2002). As the titles suggest, both documents, although they do allude to research on the difficulties surrounding contact, clearly endorse contact as being in the best interests of children. The then government's response likewise prioritised contact (DCA 2002).

Subsequently a Green Paper, (DCA, DfES and DTI 2004) and a White Paper (DCA, DfES and DTI 2005) were published and both documents stressed the importance of contact:

> The Government firmly believes that both parents should continue to have a meaningful relationship with their children after separation as long as it is safe and in the child's best interests. Most parents are able to make arrangements between themselves for the care of their children ... .
>
> In time, it needs to become socially unacceptable for one parent to impede a child's relationship with its other parent wherever it is safe and in the child's best interests. Equally, it should be unacceptable that non-resident parents absent themselves from their child's development and upbringing following separation. (DCA, DfES and DTI 2005: Ministerial Foreword)[129]

The documents demonstrate a commitment to contact as a general 'good' for children. The White Paper does qualify this stance by referring to 'safe' and 'meaningful' contact. The reference to safety is presumably in response to the work of researchers such as Walker[130] and to the Sturge–Glaser report (Sturge and Glaser 2000),[131] which highlights the risks to children in cases of domestic violence. Faced with criticism emanating from women's groups, domestic violence campaigners and some child welfare organisations, judges have been expected to take domestic violence in particular into account to a greater extent than they did in the past.[132] The mantra that is frequently reiterated in policy documents is that contact should be the aim 'as long as it is safe'.[133] So now, alongside the emphasis on promoting contact and settlement, attention is also being paid to safety

---

[128] This issue is dealt with in detail in Chapter 10 below.

[129] See also DCA, DfES, and DTI (2004: para 45) and ibid: Ministerial Foreword, 2.

[130] Referred to in CASC (2001b).

[131] See further Chapter 10 below.

[132] However, the restriction on fact-finding hearings may result in fewer findings of domestic violence. See President's Guidance in Relation to Split Hearings [2010] 2 FCR 271.

[133] See, eg, DCA, DfES and DTI (2005: 5).

by means of measures such as risk assessments,[134] fact-finding hearings[135] and judicial scrutiny of consent orders,[136] as well as the use of indirect or supervised contact.[137] In practice, however, it appears still to be the case that contact is regarded as being almost invariably in children's best interests; unless it can be established that the non-resident parent (usually the father) poses a significant risk,[138] contact will be ordered and, increasingly, enforced

In response to judicial and public dissatisfaction with what was perceived to be judicial inability to prevent obdurate mothers from flouting contact orders,[139] the Children Act 1989 was amended in 2008 to create new orders and new measures to penalise breaches. A court hearing a contact case can make contact activity directions[140] and, on making a contact order, can impose contact activity conditions.[141] A person subject to a contact activity direction or condition is required to 'take part in an activity that promotes contact'.[142] This could include attendance at:

(a) programmes, classes and counselling or guidance sessions of a kind that—
    (i) may assist a person as regards establishing, maintaining or improving contact with a child;
    (ii) may, by addressing a person's violent behaviour, enable or facilitate contact with a child;
(b) sessions in which information or advice is given as regards making or operating arrangements for contact with a child, including making arrangements by means of mediation.[143]

The court may ask a Cafcass officer to monitor compliance with contact activity directions or conditions and to report any breach.[144] Compliance with contact orders may also be monitored and a Cafcass officer can be required, for up to a year, to report breaches of these.[145] Breach of a contact activity condition or a condition attached to a contact order under section 11(7) of the Act constitutes breach of a contact order.[146] Any breach of a contact order may lead to the making of an enforcement order imposing on the parent an

---

[134] Primarily relating to the safety of the child. See, eg, Practice Direction: Revised Private Law Programme, [2010] 2 FLR 717 para 3.9; s 16A Children Act 1989.

[135] See Practice Direction: Residence and Contact Orders: Domestic Violence and Harm [2009] 2 FLR 1400, paras 21–23.

[136] See Practice Direction: Revised Private Law Programme' [2010] 2 FLR 717, paras 1.3, 5.3.

[137] See Practice Direction: Residence and Contact Orders: Domestic Violence and Harm [2009] 2 FLR 1400, paras 26–29.

[138] See, further, Chapter 10 beow. See also, eg, *Re D (Contact: Reasons for Refusal)* [1997] 2 FLR 48 (CA); *Re M (Contact: Violent Parent)* [1999] 2 FLR 321 (FD); *Re L (Contact: Domestic Violence) Re M (Contact: Domestic Violence); Re V (Contact: Domestic Violence) Re H (Contact: Domestic Violence)* [2000] 2 FLR 334; *Re F (Contact)* [2007] EWHC 2543 (Fam); [2008] 1 FLR 1163. In *Re W (Permission to Appeal)* ([2007] EWCA Civ 786, [2008] 1 FLR 406), Wall LJ, setting out to refute claims that the family justice system dispenses injustice, identified the problem as being unreasonable and indeed 'bad' fathers rather than the courts. See also *Re Bradford; Re O'Connell* [2006] EWCA Civ 1199; [2007] 1 FLR 530.; *Re O (Contact: Withdrawal of Application)* [2003] EWHC 3031 (Fam); [2004] 1 FLR 1258 paras 85, 87.

[*Re* W (Contact: Joining Child as Party) [2001] EWCA Civ 1830; [2003] 1 FLR 681, para 10. Cf, eg, *Re J-S (a child) (contact: parental responsibility)* [2002] EWCA Civ 1028; [2002] 3 FCR 433. See further Kaganas (2011).

[139] See Kaganas (2010a)

[140] S 11A Children Act 1989.

[141] S 11C. The same applies when the court varies a contact order.

[142] Ss 11A(3) and 11C(2).

[143] S 11A(5). See also s 11C(5).

[144] S 11G.

[145] S 11H.

[146] Children and Adoption Act 2006, Explanatory Notes, para 30.

unpaid work requirement.[147] Compliance with that too can be monitored.[148] The power to impose an unpaid work requirement is in addition to the courts' normal powers to punish for contempt of court as well as the power to transfer residence from one parent to another.

In order to give effect to the reforms, the Department for Children, Schools and Families (DCSF)[149] commissioned provision for the parenting programmes Making Contact Safe and Making Contact Work. These are

> designed to support attending parents with information on the divorce process, how it can affect them and their children and how to change things for the better. The intention is to encourage safe contact between a child and an individual by the end of the programme. (DCSF undated)

These typically involve two two-hour group-work sessions.[150] There are also intensive, 60-hour-long, domestic violence perpetrator programmes.[151] In addition, information about mediation is provided through the Legal Services Commission.[152]

The court must consider the suitability of the party to engage in the activity prescribed. In practice the Cafcass officer will be likely to have suggested to the court that an activity might be beneficial.[153] The attitude of the person concerned will be a 'key consideration'. In the case of parenting information both parties are required to attend, albeit separately. In the case of domestic violence programmes, the person concerned is required to attend if he has conceded his violence or has been found through a fact-finding process to have been violent. Support services may also be offered to the victim and current partner of the perpetrator.[154]

At the time of writing, although there is no reliable research available, anecdotal evidence suggests that little use has been made of these provisions (Sayers 2009). In addition, it appears that the kinds of intervention available are limited. There may also be insufficient funding available to enable people to attend programmes,[155] particularly in the light of the budgetary constraints imposed by the Coalition government. Nevertheless, the potential for use is there.

While the powers of enforcement have been broadened, it remains the case that the courts are considered a last resort. Indeed, if legal aid is withdrawn from all section 8 cases, with limited exceptions for domestic violence and the representation of children,[156] the number of cases going before the courts may drop dramatically[157] and more cases will probably go to mediation. For those contesting parents able to bring their cases to court the aim is to get parents to reach safe, sustainable agreements.[158]

Practice Directions enjoin the courts to give consideration to the possibilities of alter-

---

[147] S 11J. There is also a power to order financial compensation for financial loss caused by a breach (s 11O).

[148] S 11M.

[149] The DCSF has also designated 10 pilot areas in a project designed to determine how best local services can be co-ordinated for divorcing and separating parents (Walsh 2009).

[150] Cafcass (undated: para 2.2). Resolution also set up pilots for information workshops (Morris 2009).

[151] Cafcass (undated: para 2.2).

[152] DCSF (undated: 7).

[153] Cafcass (undated: para 2.4).

[154] Ibid: para 2.5.

[155] Rhoades' research in Australia shows that parents who are sent by the courts to parenting programmes are a high-conflict group and the programmes that were viewed positively were very resource intensive (2004).

[156] See Legal Aid, Sentencing and Punishment of Offenders Bill 2010–11; MOJ (2010a: para 4.215).

[157] Although the number of litigants in person will probably increase.

[158] Practice Direction: Revised Private Law Programme [2010] 2 FLR 717, para 1.7.

natives to litigation. The Practice Direction governing cases involving allegations of domestic violence empowers the court, with the consent of the person concerned, to direct a party to seek advice or treatment.[159] The Practice Direction issued in terms of the Revised Private Law Programme requires the court at the first hearing in all cases to consider '[w]hat other options there are for resolution eg may the case be suitable for further intervention by Cafcass; mediation by an external provider; collaborative law or use of a parenting plan?'[160] It also refers to the requirement that consideration be given to attendance at Parenting Information Programmes or other activities, whether court ordered in terms of section 11 of the Children Act as amended or not.[161] Most recently, a Pre-Application Protocol[162] has placed an obligation on potential litigants to attend a Mediation Information and Assessment Meeting arranged by a mediator before instituting proceedings in private law disputes involving children. There are limited exceptions to this requirement.[163]

The arrangements made for children are intended to be left largely in the hands of the parents, perhaps with some input from children, and family privacy is to be seen to be left largely intact. But considerable efforts are made by the state, together with the courts, to ensure that the arrangements are the 'right' ones, those that conform to the image of the 'good' post-separation family and therefore those that are assumed to be in the best interests of the children.

This approach, it seems, accords well with Dewar's analysis. The state is aiming to 'radiate' messages about how to separate or divorce well and these messages are rights-oriented and rule-like. The state is seeking to promote 'responsible' decision-making by families, so allowing for the preservation of the liberal ideal of family privacy. At the same time, the state is seeking to promote a particular construction of welfare, one that 'responsible' families will embrace. However, if the proposed cuts in legal aid are implemented, it may become more difficult to ensure that these messages are heard. Some parents may attend mediation but not all will. In such cases the privacy of the family will be reinforced by default.

Promoting 'Responsible' Parenting: Making Contact Work

Research indicates that, that in spite the spread of the settlement culture, litigation over contact has not decreased.[164] It is true that most cases are settled and that, at about 10% of contact arrangements,[165] the proportion of cases that reaches the courts is relatively small. Nevertheless these cases are numerically significant and it is reasonable to assume that these cases are among the most bitterly fought, involving high levels of conflict.[166]

---

[159] Practice Direction: Residence and Contact Orders: Domestic Violence and Harm [2009] 2 FLR 1400. See also the references to treatment in letters of instruction to child mental health professionals or paediatricians in Children Act 1989 proceedings (Practice Direction: Experts in Family Proceedings Relating to Children ANNEX (Drafted by the Family Justice Council) [2009] 2 FLR 1383).

[160] Practice Direction: Revised Private Law Programme [2010] 2 FLR 717, para 5.2(c). At the First Hearing Dispute Resolution Appointment 'the Court, in collaboration with the Cafcass Officer, and with the assistance of any mediator present, will seek to assist the parties in conciliation and in resolution of all or any of the issues between them' (para 4.4).

[161] Ibid: para 5.2(d).

[162] Practice Direction 3A—Pre-Application Protocol for Mediation Information and Assessment.

[163] See further Chapters 10 and 15 below.

[164] See, eg, Bailey-Harris et al (1998: 16).

[165] See Blackwell and Dawe (2003). See also Hunt and Macleod (2008: 92).

[166] See Hunt and Macleod (2008: 3) and references cited there.

This means that the courts, despite doubts about their suitability or efficacy[167] when it comes to conflict within families, are forced to deal with the most difficult cases. And while, if implemented, cuts in legal aid will reduce the number of disputes reaching the courts, many of those cases that do will involve litigants in person or domestic violence or both, cases which are likely to be among the most fraught.

However, there is a growing perception that the nature of the issues in disputes over children means that they are not susceptible of legal resolution. The problems are not legal problems and the solutions are therefore not legal solutions. Policy-makers and judges are now convinced that the reason cases keep returning to court is because the 'underlying' problems have not been addressed. The role of the court has accordingly become more complex. They and those making policy and law see the court's role as not only making decisions about residence and contact but also as endeavouring to change people's attitudes and to help them manage their negative emotions (Kaganas 2010a, 2011). Where traditional judicial strategies such as persuasion or threats fail, courts have been intervening in some cases by referring parties to therapy.[168] This is seen as the best way to ensure not only that contact happens, but that it 'works':

> [T]he demand now is for a solution to a different problem. In the past, the problem was conceived of as a defective, conflict-promoting divorce process centred on fault-based grounds. The solution was to change the divorce law. More recently the problem was characterized as the lack of varied and broad powers of enforcement. The solution identified was to increase those powers. And the solution for the problem of obdurate resident parents has been thought to be to vest the court not only with the power to punish disobedience but also to send parents for interventions designed to change their minds and attitudes. The issues are no longer simply the objective absence of contact or the resort to litigation. Now it is the underlying cause of contact difficulties that is perceived as the problem: the relationship between the family members and the impact it has on their behaviour. What is needed is not only compliance with orders but also 'good' conflict-free contact. This can be achieved only if the parents' relationship problems are addressed, whether therapeutically by means of counselling, or by educating parents. The aim of the Labour government, therefore, was to discover 'how to shift the attitudes of some parents better to focus on the needs of the child and how to develop advice, information, mediation, conciliation and enforcement processes that are much better at doing so'.
>
> The assumption was and remains that even if contact is not working well (or at all), intervention can make it work (or make it work better). And it appears that the family justice system is considered to have a part to play in this process. (Kaganas 2010a: 254–55)

According to Kaganas (ibid: 263), family courts are adopting the characteristics of problem-solving courts,[169] with their therapeutic orientation and an emphasis on solving the underlying problems of the parties. Judges often resort to exhortation and chastise-

---

[167] That the courts have a limited impact on outcomes is confirmed by research conducted by Trinder and Kellet; they found that the amount of court intervention did not determine the amount of contact taking place in the cases they examined (Trinder and Kellet 2007: 20). Both resident and non-resident parents in their sample complained that court orders were not being obeyed. Non-resident parents said this was because resident parents were blocking contact or influencing their children against it. Resident parents maintained that non-resident parents were not sticking to dates and times (ibid: 43). Cantwell argues that the courts do not have the knowledge-base needed to 'make well-informed, child-centred judgments when dealing with parents who separate conflictually' (Cantwell 2010: 86) He also contends that the Cafcass officers who advise the courts do not have a 'credible, evidence-based approach to parental conflict' (ibid: 87). More importantly, courts are not equipped to deal with emotion (Day Sclater and Richards 1995).

[168] See Kaganas (2010a).

[169] These courts emphasise the need to address underlying problems. They focus on outcomes rather than processes. See further Kaganas (2010a).

ment. Kaganas (2010a) points out that even before they were given the power to refer parents for counselling in terms of the amended Children Act 1989, courts were advising parents to manage their emotions or to seek help to do so. It is seen as necessary to control the feelings which give rise to irresponsible behaviour, irrational hostility and conflict in order to ensure that parents accept and fulfil their responsibilities. 'Good' parents are rational and put their children first and so the courts frequently appeal to parents' reasonable side and encourage them to put their own feelings to one side for the sake of their children. Parents who do not overcome their own feelings in order to put their children first may, for example, be told they are failing as parents. And in the case of an intractable dispute, where all else fails, the task of 'solving' the problem is increasingly being delegated by the courts to therapeutic or educational agencies,

This all prompts the question: does it work? Collier has observed that the law's prioritisation of contact has been linked to an increase in disputes; co-parenting which is the product of 'legal or financial coercion' might exacerbate conflict (Collier 2006: 71). May and Smart have noted that the fact that the parents in their study had to remain in contact with each other and even to parent jointly meant that there were constant opportunities for conflict to recur (May and Smart 2007: 71). So the aim of conflict reduction may not be achieved.

Whether the legal process can instil the values of 'responsible parenting' is also open to doubt. Boyd, writing about the Canadian experience, has said that the 'legal system has limited ability to instigate new patterns of parenting' (Boyd 2003: 199). Eekelaar, reviewing the proposals for reform in the UK now embodied in section 11 of the Children Act 1989,[170] commented that 'the recommendations ... signal a significant increase in legal coercion over family arrangements' (Eekelaar 2002b: 272). Yet, he said, similar measures adopted in Australia did not appear to have led to an increase in joint parenting. He concluded that 'it is important not to jump from the fact that an outcome is optimally desirable to the conclusion that it should, therefore, be legally enforceable' (ibid). 'As a general rule', he argued, 'legal coercion should be confined to cases where the actions of a parent threaten to harm a clearly beneficial existing relationship enjoyed by a child' (ibid: 273).

More specifically, parenting programmes and the use of counselling have not been found to be beneficial. In Australia, the court's powers to send recalcitrant resident parents to parenting education programmes have been criticised for impeding mothers' attempts to protect their children by reframing their concerns as manifestations of hostility or over-anxiousness (Rhoades 2007: 137). Nor have such measures been found to change relationships or behaviour for the better. Hunt, reviewing the available research concluded that 'the effectiveness of parent education programmes as a genre has not been conclusively proven' (Hunt 2007: 199). In Germany, contact facilitation,[171] which is coupled with counselling, appears to have little effect on parental relationships or on the durability of contact arrangements (Mueller-Johnson 2007: 120–21).

There is also Australian research that suggests that the underlying reasons for conflict over contact are complex and often relate to domestic violence or to one parent's (usually the resident parent's) concerns about the other's inability to care adequately for the children, or concerns about issues such as substance abuse or mental health problems (Rhoades

---

[170] As they appeared in Making Contact Work (LCD 2000).
[171] In effect, supervised contact.

2002: 75ff).[172] It is debatable whether fears like this would be allayed by information imparting the importance of contact or even by parenting classes. Research conducted in the UK suggests that the reason for contact disputes is not that parents lack education and information about the supposed benefits of contact. In many instances it is that parents believe that they need to engage in the dispute in order to preserve their self-image as 'good' parents or protect their children's best interests.

May and Smart found that some of the parents in their study felt impelled to pursue their cases because of the personal investment they had placed in the conflict itself: 'For some parents the outcome of the court case was tied in with their identity as a moral person and as a "good" parent.' For them, losing the 'parenting contest' would mean being branded a 'bad' or inadequate parent (May and Smart 2007: 73, 75).

Similarly, a study conducted by Day Sclater and Kaganas[173] exploring the dynamics of protracted contact disputes reveals that both mothers and fathers sought to position themselves as good parents and framed their arguments in terms of children's best interests. Mothers who were interviewed had internalised the view that contact is good for children generally. But they resisted contact with *their* children by ex-partners because were convinced it would not be good for those particular children.[174] For example, some doubted fathers' commitment to their children or their capacity to parent. Many recounted incidents of domestic violence. They considered it their duty as good mothers to protect their children from contact.

Fathers who insisted that they should have contact invoked the welfare of their children as a reason. Those who admitted to violence or aggression tended to minimise the impact of their behaviour and still saw themselves as good parents. Some complained about mothers' shortcomings and considered it their role to counteract these perceived faults. Some fathers maintained that it was imperative to fight for contact in order to safeguard their children's best interests generally.

The fact that both mothers and fathers had been to court and that some had failed to achieve the outcomes they sought did not deter them from continuing the battle; they simply saw the courts and the legal system as unfair and biased.

Kaganas refers to this research to suggest that education and counselling might not have the expected or desired effects: '[T]here is no guarantee that parents will hear the messages being conveyed in the way they are meant to' (Kaganas 2011: 92).

XII. CONCLUSION

The welfare principle is a powerful construct, legitimating policy and decision-making on the basis of apparently neutral, scientifically valid criteria. It operates to privilege the biological nuclear family form over other family structures. This image of the family persists even in instances where the nuclear unit has broken down and it is embodied, often to the detriment of caretaking mothers, in legal norms adopted to regulate the post-separation family which prioritise fathers. Mothers who do not embrace these norms are criticised, blamed and, in future, may be given information, education and therapeutic

---

[172] See also Smart and May (2004a). They found that other issues such as housing and child support fuelled disputes.

[173] See Kaganas and Day Sclater (2004); Day Sclater and Kaganas (2003).

[174] See also Trinder (2003: 404).

services to encourage them to do so. Those who resist may face a court with a new armoury of punishments at its disposal.

What will happen to parents who cannot co-operate and agree, who are denied legal aid and who cannot afford to litigate remains to be seen. It seems likely that the scope for applying the welfare principle, and certainly judicial constructions of the welfare principle, will be drastically curtailed in the context of private law. The concerns about promoting contact as well as the efforts to change peoples' attitudes by educating or counselling them will be confined to those parents willing to represent themselves or wealthy enough to pay for representation. The priority accorded to trying to make contact 'work' will be abandoned, the dispute will remain private and resident mothers may be able more easily to resist contact if their children's fathers are not able to fund representation and are not willing and able to represent themselves. However, given the fact that the new Protocol is designed to encourage prospective litigants to mediate, and given that mediators also seek to promote contact, the pressure on resident mothers will continue.

FURTHER READING

A Buchanan et al, Families in Conflict: Perspectives of Children and Parents on the Family Court Welfare Service (Bristol, Policy, 2001).

Baroness Butler-Sloss 'A Child's Place in the Big Society' (2010) *Fam Law* 938.

R Collier and S Sheldon, *Fragmenting Fatherhood: A Socio-legal Study* (Oxford, Hart Publishing, 2008).

G Davis and J Pearce, 'The Welfare Principle in Action' (1999) *Fam Law* 237.

S Day Sclater and F Kaganas, 'Contact: Mothers, Welfare and Rights' in A Bainham et al (eds), *Children and Their Families: Contact, Rights and Welfare* (Oxford, Hart Publishing, 2003).

J Dewar, 'The Normal Chaos of Family Law' (1998) 61(4) *MLR* 467.

——, 'Family Law and its Discontents' (2000) 14 *Int J Law, Policy and the Family* 59.

S Gilmore, 'Disputing Contact: Challenging Some Assumptions' (2008) 20 *CFLQ* 285.

J Eekelaar, 'Beyond the Welfare Principle' (2002) 14(3) *CFLQ* 237.

——, 'Contact—Over the Limit' (2002) *Fam Law* 271.

J Herring, 'The Human Rights Act and the Welfare Principle in Family Law—Conflicting or Complementary?' (1999) 11(3) *CFLQ* 223.

J Hunt and A Macleod, *Outcomes of Applications to Court for Contact Orders after Parental Separation or Divorce* (London, Ministry of Justice, 2008).

F Kaganas, 'Contact, Conflict and Risk' in S Day Sclater and C Piper (eds), *Undercurrents of Divorce* (Aldershot, Ashgate, 1999).

——, '*Re L (Contact: Domestic Violence); Re V (Contact: Domestic Violence); Re M (Contact: Domestic Violence); Re H (Contact: Domestic Violence)*: Contact and Domestic Violence' (2000) 12(3) *CFLQ* 311.

——, 'When it Comes to Contact Disputes, What Are Family Courts For?' (2010) 63 *Current Legal Problems* 234.

——, 'Managing Emotion: Judging Contact Disputes' (2011) 23 *CFLQ* 63.

F Kaganas and S Day Sclater, 'Contact Disputes: Narrative Constructions of "Good" Parents' (2004) 12 *Feminist Legal Studies* 1.

F Kaganas and A Diduck, 'Incomplete Citizens: Changing Images of Post-separation Children' (2004) 67(6) *MLR* 959.

F Kaganas and C Piper, 'Grandparents and Contact: "Rights v Welfare" Revisited' (2001) 15(2) *Int J of Law, Policy and the Family* 250.

——, 'Shared Parenting—A 70% Solution?' (2002) 14(4) *CFLQ* 365.

V May and C Smart, 'The Parenting Contest: Problems of Ongoing Conflict over Children' in M Maclean (ed), *Parenting after Partnering. Containing Conflict after Separation* (Oxford, Hart Publishing, 2007).

B Neale, J Flowerdew and C Smart, 'Drifting Towards Shared Residence?' (2003) *Fam Law* 904.

C Piper, 'Assumptions About Children's Best Interests' (2000) 22(3) *JSWFL* 261.

J Pryor and B Rodgers, Children in Changing Families: Life after Parental Separation (Oxford, Blackwell, 2001).

H Reece, 'The Paramountcy Principle: Consensus or Construct?' (1996) 49 *Current Legal Problems* 267.

H Rhoades, 'The "No Contact Mother": Reconstruction of Motherhood in the Era of the "New Father"' (2002) 16 *Int J Law, Policy and the Family* 71.

——, 'Revising Australia's Parenting Laws: A Plea for a Relational Approach to Children's Best Interests' (2010) 22 *CFLQ* 172.

C Smart and V May, 'Why Can't They Agree? The Underlying Complexity of Contact and Residence Disputes' (2004) 26 *JSWFL* 347.

C Sturge and D Glaser, 'Contact and Domestic Violence—The Experts' Court Report' (2000) *Fam Law* 615.

10

Disputes about Children and the Application of the Welfare Principle

I. INTRODUCTION

The breakdown of a relationship when there are children involved raises questions concerning the arrangements to be made for their care; these are cases where clearly it is the child's welfare that is foremost. And welfare, it is argued, is interpreted to promote what is perceived as the 'good' post-separation family.

Questions about the arrangements for children can arise irrespective of whether each of the parents has parental responsibility.[1] Indeed disputes about children's residence and who will have contact with them can involve litigants who are not parents, such as grandparents and step-parents. Section 8 of the Children Act 1989 makes provision for residence orders stipulating with whom the child shall live and contact orders specifying who will have contact with the child. There is also provision for the making of specific issue orders and prohibited steps orders to settle single-issue disputes such those concerning where the child should be educated. These are dealt with below.

Most section 8 disputes never reach the courtroom since the majority are resolved by agreement.[2] Resources have been made available to potential litigants to encourage them to settle. One such resource is a leaflet, *Parenting Plans*, published by Cafcass (Children and Family Court Advisory and Support Service) containing advice and case histories showing how difficulties have been resolved in various cases (Cafcass undated).

Those who wish to litigate but who cannot afford to do so may not get the public funding they need. At the time of writing, parents may be eligible for public funding only if their dispute is deemed not suitable for mediation. If it is suitable, they may obtain funding for mediation.[3] However, the coalition government plans to cut public funding for all private law disputes except those with an element of domestic violence or forced marriage (MOJ 2010a).[4] There is not even provision for cases where mediation fails or where one party refuses to mediate.[5] Legal aid for mediation will be retained. This may mean

---

[1] See Chapters 4 and 8 above.
[2] See MOJ (2010a: paras 4.208–4.209).
[3] See Chapter 15 below.
[4] These limitations are now embodied in the Legal Aid, Sentencing and Punishment of Offenders Bill, Bill 205.
[5] See House of Commons Committee Debate, Sixth Sitting (19 July 2011) col 202.

that fewer people will have access to the courts. Or it may be that there will simply be more litigants in person. The House of Commons Justice Committee (2011) comments:

> 224. The removal of legal aid from applicants in most private family law cases will increase the number of litigants in person in the family courts. It is self-evident that parents are unlikely to give up applications for contact, residence or maintenance for their children simply because they have no access to public funding. We are concerned that the Ministry of Justice does not appear to have appreciated that this is the inevitable outcome of the legal aid reforms.

In any event, even if the likelihood of a dispute reaching court is lower, the legal principles developed by courts will form the context in which any mediation or negotiation takes place.

II. THE POWER OF THE COURT TO MAKE SECTION 8 ORDERS

Residence and contact orders, along with prohibited steps and specific issue orders, are designated as section 8 orders under the Children Act 1989.[6] Section 10 deals with section 8 orders collectively and sets out the circumstances in which a court is empowered to make such an order. The court can make a section 8 order in family proceedings in which a 'question arises with respect to the welfare of any child'.[7]

Sections 10(4) and (5) provide:

> (4) The following persons are entitled to apply to the court for any s 8 order with respect to a child—
>
> (a)   any parent or guardian [guardian or special guardian] of the child;
> (aa) any person who by virtue of s 4A has parental responsibility for the child;
> (b)   any person in whose favour a residence order is in force with respect to the child.
>
> (5) The following persons are entitled to apply for a residence or contact order with respect to a child—
>
> (a)   any party to a marriage (whether or not subsisting) in relation to whom the child is a child of the family;
> (aa) any civil partner in a civil partnership (whether or not subsisting) in relation to whom the child is a child of the family.
> (b)   any person with whom the child has lived for a period of at least three years;
> (c)   any person who—
>   (i)   in any case where a residence order is in force with respect to the child, has the consent of each of the persons in whose favour the order was made;
>   (ii) in any case where the child is in the care of a local authority, has the consent of that authority; or
>   (iii) in any other case, has the consent of each of those (if any) who have parental responsibility for the child.
>
> (5A) A local authority foster parent is entitled to apply for a residence order with respect to a child if the child has lived with him for a period of at least one year immediately preceding the application.

---

[6] See s 8(2).
[7] S 10(1) Children Act 1989.

(5B) A relative of a child is entitled to apply for a residence order with respect to the child if the child has lived with the relative for a period of at least one year immediately preceding the application.

A parent is entitled as of right to apply for any section 8 order.[8] This capacity has been extended to step-parents and to civil partners who have attained parental responsibility under section 4A.[9] A step-parent, former step-parent,[10] civil partner or former civil partner[11] without parental responsibility who has treated the child as a child of the family is permitted to apply for a residence or contact order as of right. Anyone who does not fall within the scope of the definition of a person who is entitled to seek an order is obliged to apply for the permission of the court to make an application.[12] In addition, whether or not a particular person is entitled to seek an order, and irrespective of whether an application has been launched, a court may, on its own initiative in family proceedings,[13] make an order in favour of any person. Proceedings under the Matrimonial Causes Act 1973 and Civil Partnership Act 2004 are included in the definition of 'family proceedings'.[14] So, while it is open to a person to institute proceedings for a section 8 order at any time, once divorce or dissolution proceedings commence the court also has the power to make such an order on its own initiative.

Sections 10(8) and (9) deal with capacity and the criteria for permission (leave) to apply for an order:

(8) Where the person applying for leave to make an application for a section 8 order is the child concerned,[15] the court may only grant leave if it is satisfied that he has sufficient understanding to make the proposed application for the section 8 order.

(9) Where the person applying for leave to make an application for a section 8 order is not the child concerned, the court shall, in deciding whether or not to grant leave, have particular regard to—

(a) the nature of the proposed application for the section 8 order;
(b) the applicant's connection with the child; [16]
(c) any risk there might be of that proposed application disrupting the child's life to such an extent that he would be harmed by it;[17] and
(d) where the child is being looked after by a local authority—
    (i) the authority's plans for the child's future; and
    (ii) the wishes and feelings of the child's parents.

---

[8] S 10 (4)(a) Children Act 1989.
[9] S 10(4)(aa).
[10] S 10(5)(a).
[11] S 10(5)(aa).
[12] Ss 10(1)(a)(ii), 10(2)(b). The child concerned may apply for a s 8 order with permission of the court in terms of s 10 of the Children Act 1989.
[13] S 10(1)(b). For the definition of 'family proceedings', see s 8(3)–(4).
[14] S 8(4) of the Children Act 1989.
[15] See, on the European Convention on the Exercise of Children's Rights 1996, which promotes rights of participation in proceedings for children, Fortin (2009a: 236–38). See also *Sahin v Germany; Sommerfeld v Germany* [2003] 2 FLR 671.
[16] The more meaningful and important the connection between the applicant and child, the greater the weight to be given to this factor: *Re M (Care: Contact: Grandmother's Application for Leave)* [1995] 2 FLR 86, 95.
[17] The court has considered not just the effect of the application but also the consequences if the application were to succeed *(Re A (A Minor) (Residence Order: Leave to Apply)* [1993] 1 FLR 425, 428). However, in *Re H (Children)* [2003] EWCA Civ 369; 2003 WL 1202504, the Court of Appeal stated that it was the risk of disruption caused by the litigation, and not the possible outcome, that should be considered (para 26).

The legislation thus distinguishes between different categories of applicants for section 8 orders: those who are entitled to apply as of right and those who can apply with the permission of the court. This distinction is designed to control access to the courts. It makes it possible to screen out unmeritorious applications or potentially disruptive litigation while at the same time enabling anyone with a genuine interest in the child's welfare to apply for an order. In deciding whether to grant permission, the court should not focus on the merits of the applicant's case; instead it should make its decision on the basis of the checklist in section 10(9).[18] The court must consider all the factors set out in section 10(9) and is entitled also to consider the welfare checklist in section 1(3).[19] Because an application for permission does not fall within section 1(1), however, the child's welfare is not the paramount consideration.[20] In the case of an application for leave made by a child, the best interests of the child are a significant consideration[21] but section 10(9) does not apply.

Section 9 limits the circumstances under which and the duration for which an order may be made:

> 9(5) No court shall exercise its powers to make a specific issue order or prohibited steps order—
>
> (a) with a view to achieving a result which could be achieved by making a residence or contact order; or
> (b) in any way which is denied to the High Court (by section 100(2)) in the exercise of its inherent jurisdiction with respect to children.
>
> (6) No court shall make any section 8 order which is to have effect for a period which will end after the child has reached the age of sixteen unless it is satisfied that the circumstances of the case are exceptional.
>
> (7) No court shall make any section 8 order, other than one varying or discharging such an order, with respect to a child who has reached the age of sixteen unless it is satisfied that the circumstances of the case are exceptional.

A Settlement Culture

An emphasis on settlement has permeated the family justice system. Where cases do get to court, the aim of the lawyers, the judge and Cafcass is to get the parties to reach an agreement. Negotiation between solicitors, admonishment from the bench, in-court conciliation and reports by Cafcass are all deployed in an effort to make a final hearing avoidable.[22] The new Practice Direction issued pursuant to the Revised Private Law Programme maintains this approach and requires the court at the First Hearing Dispute Resolution Appointment (FHDRA) to consider whether issues can be resolved with the

---

[18] Case law has established that s 10(9) governs the decision whether to grant leave/permission rather than the old test of an arguable case: *Re J (A Child) (Leave to Issue Application for Residence Order)* [2002] EWCA Civ 1346; [2003] 1 FLR 114; *Re H (Children)* [2003] EWCA Civ 369; 2003 WL 1202504.

[19] *North Yorkshire County Council v G* [1993] 2 FLR 732; *Re A (A Minor) (Residence Order: Leave to Apply)* [1993] 1 FLR 425, 428.

[20] *Re A and W (Minors) (Residence Order: Leave to Apply)* [1992] 2 FLR 154; *Re A (Minors) (Residence Order)* [1992] 3 All ER 872; *Re SC (A Minor) (Leave to Seek Residence Order)* [1994] 1 FLR 96. (It appears that *Johnson J in Re C (A Minor) (Leave to Seek S 8 Orders)* [1994] 1 FLR 26 erred on this point.)

[21] Again, the welfare of the child is not of paramount importance. See *Re C (Residence: Child's Application for Leave)* [1995] 1 FLR 927, 931.

[22] See Hunt and Macleod (2008: 168ff). See Chapter 15 below.

assistance of a Cafcass officer or a mediator.[23] It is stipulated that a Cafcass Family Court Advisor (FCA), and where possible a mediator, should attend the first hearing.[24] The court, 'in collaboration with the Cafcass Officer, and with the assistance of any mediator present, will seek to assist the parties in conciliation and in resolution of all or any of the issues between them'.[25] The court must in all cases consider '[w]hat other options there are for resolution eg may the case be suitable for further intervention by Cafcass; mediation by an external provider; collaborative law or use of a parenting plan?'[26] It also refers to the requirement that consideration be given to attendance at Parenting Information Programmes (PIPs) or other activities.[27] PIPs provide 'advice and support' and 'seek to enable parents to take steps towards their own solutions' (Norgrove 2011a: para 5.14).

Once litigation has begun, even if parents agree on the arrangements for their children, the court has a part to play. In terms of section 41 of the Matrimonial Causes Act 1973, and section 63 of the Civil Partnership Act 2004, it has a duty in divorce and dissolution cases, lest unsatisfactory arrangements be permitted to go by default in the absence of parental opposition, to consider whether the court should exercise any of its powers under the Children Act with respect to any children involved.[28]

> **Q** Do you think it necessary to give the courts the power to reject the arrangements made by parents on divorce or dissolution? If so, do you think the courts should have similar powers when cohabiting couples separate?

Safety

In recent years concerns about the safety of children and their carers have come to the fore. This has resulted in the drafting of Practice Directions intended to safeguard children and their carers. In terms of the Practice Direction: Revised Private Law Programme,[29] once an application is issued under Part II of the Children Act 1989, the court must send the documentation to Cafcass so that any safety issues can be identified. Cafcass may need to do a risk assessment[30] and is required to report any safety issues to the court. While the FHDRA is used to try to resolve any issues between the parties, the court and the Cafcass officer have to take any risks into account.[31] If the parties reach an agreement, a consent order will not be made without scrutiny by the court.[32] Finally, there is a Practice Direction dealing specifically with cases where there are allegations or concerns about domestic violence.[33]

---

[23] Practice Direction: Revised Private Law Programme [2010] 2 FLR 717, paras 2.2.and 4.4.

[24] Ibid: para 4.1.

[25] Ibid: para 4.4. See also para 5.2(a).

[26] Ibid: para 5.2(c).

[27] Ibid: para 5.2(d).

[28] The court may direct that a dissolution, divorce or separation order is not made until the court orders otherwise if it appears that its powers under the Children Act should be exercised; that they cannot be exercised or that further consideration is needed before they are exercised; and that there are exceptional circumstances making it desirable in the interests of the child that such a direction be made (s 41(2) of the Matrimonial Causes Act 1973; s 63(2) of the Civil Partnership Act). Although s 41 has been subject to review (see DCA (2002) Recommendation 13), it remains unchanged.

[29] [2010] 2 FLR 717.

[30] S 16A Children Act 1989.

[31] Practice Direction: Revised Private Law Programme [2010] 2 FLR 717, para 4.4.

[32] Ibid: para 5.3.

[33] See below.

Restricting Access to the Court

Section 91(14) of the Children Act 1989 makes provision for the restriction of access to the court so that families can be shielded from repeated applications for orders.[34] It states that when the court disposes of an application under the Act, whether or not it makes an order as a result of the application, it can make an order that no application at all, or no application of a specified type, can be made by the person named in the order in respect of the child named unless the court gives permission.

The judgment in *Re P (Section 91(14) Guidelines) (Residence and Religious Heritage)*[35] sets out guidance for the way in which this provision should be used. Firstly, it should be read in conjunction with section 1(1) which makes the child's welfare paramount. Second, the power to restrict the right of a party to bring proceedings should be used only in exceptional circumstances. It is generally a last resort to be used in cases of 'repeated and unreasonable' applications.[36] However the court can impose the restriction if the welfare of the child requires it to do so, even in cases where there is no past history of unreasonable applications.[37] There would need to be a serious risk that, without the imposition of the restriction, 'the child or the primary carers will be subject to unacceptable strain'.[38] A restriction may be imposed with or without a time limit, but should be proportionate to the harm it is intended to avoid.

The court in *Re P* also considered whether section 91(14) might contravene the Human Rights Act 1998 and the ECHR and concluded that it does not. The applicant is not denied access to the court; the effect of the legislation is to create a partial restriction that prevents the applicant from getting the right to an immediate inter partes hearing.

An order imposing an absolute prohibition does not fall under the section and would have to be made under the court's inherent jurisdiction.[39]

III. THE WELFARE PRINCIPLE

The Children Act 1989 is cast very firmly in the welfare mould. As we have seen, the welfare of the child is paramount in decisions relating to his or her upbringing.[40] This principle, as we have observed,[41] is not susceptible of easy application in any particular case. The problem of indeterminacy, as well as all the other difficulties surrounding the welfare test that we have considered, is imported into the legislation.

The 1989 Act seeks to reduce indeterminacy and to make explicit certain values by codifying 'what society considers the most important factors in the welfare of children' (Law Commission 1988b: para 3.19). A checklist of these factors was incorporated into

---

[34] The court has the power to do this on its own initiative. See *Re C (Prohibition on Further Applications)* [2002] EWCA Civ 292; [2002] 1 FLR 1136.

[35] [1999] 2 FLR 573, 592–93. See also *Re A (Contact: Section 91(14))* [2009] EWCA Civ 1548; [2010] 2 FLR 151.

[36] See also *Re G (Child Case: Parental Involvement)* [1996] 1 FLR 857; *B v B (Residence Order: Restricting Applications)* [1997] 1 FLR 139; *Re A (Contact:Section 91(14))* [2009] EWCA Civ 1548; [2010] 2 FLR 151.

[37] See *Re M (S 91(14) Order)* [1999] 2 FLR 553; *Re F (Children) (Restriction on Applications)* [2005] All ER (D) 42 (Apr).

[38] *Re P* above at 593.

[39] *Re P (S 91(14) Guidelines) (Residence and Religious Heritage)* [1999] 2 FLR 573, 593.

[40] S 1(1) of the Children Act 1989.

[41] See Chapter 9 above.

the statute in the hope that this would provide greater consistency and clarity and to promote a more systematic approach to decision-making by courts. Cafcass officers, such as the FCA, are also required to give consideration to the checklist when carrying out their duties.[42] Section 1(3) provides:

> In the circumstances mentioned in subsection (4), a court shall have regard in particular to—
>
> (a) the ascertainable wishes and feelings of the child concerned (considered in the light of his age and understanding);
> (b) his physical, emotional and educational needs;
> (c) the likely effect on him of any change in his circumstances;
> (d) his age, sex, background and any characteristics of his which the court considers relevant;
> (e) any harm which he has suffered or is at risk of suffering;
> (f) how capable each of his parents, and any other person in relation to whom the court considers the question to be relevant, is of meeting his needs;
> (g) the range of powers available to the court under this Act in the proceedings in question.

Q Do you agree that there is a consensus that these are the most important factors? What would you include in such a checklist? Refer back to some of the explicit and unarticulated principles/assumptions discussed in Chapter 9 above.

While the checklist provides some guidance for the courts and furnishes the backdrop for private negotiations, it is of limited use. As Masson et al (2008a: para 19.014) observe, it merely lists the factors to be considered and does not indicate *how* they should be viewed. It does not prioritise the criteria and courts are still obliged to carry out a difficult balancing exercise. Dewar says that 'the checklist will not eliminate subjective value judgements about parenting and child care arrangements, but may serve to immunise them from challenge on appeal' (Dewar 1992: 366);[43] it may be difficult to overturn a decision reached after consideration of all the criteria (Eekelaar 1991b: 127).

Precisely how the courts are using the checklist is not entirely clear. It appears that something less that meticulous adherence to the checklist is required.[44] In *Re G (Children)*[45] Baroness Hale said:

> [40] My Lords, it is of course the case that any experienced family judge is well aware of the contents of the statutory checklist and can be assumed to have had regard to it whether or not this is spelled out in a judgment. However, in any difficult or finely balanced case ..., it is a great help to address each of the factors in the list, along with any others which may be relevant, so as to ensure that no particular feature of the case is given more weight than it should properly bear.

As the Law Commission indicated (1988b: para 3.19), the checklist is not intended to be exhaustive. In assessing where the child's best interests lie, the courts often rely heavily

---

[42] FPR 2010/2955 R 16.33.

[43] Eekelaar contends that the heavily subjective nature of the power granted to the judge means that, so long as he does not claim to be applying it as a conclusive rule of law, a judge can consider almost any factor which could possibly have a bearing on the child's welfare and assign to it whatever weight he or she chooses (Eekelaar 1991b: 125).

[44] *B v B (Minors) (Interviews and Listing Arrangements)* [1994] 2 FLR 489, 500.

[45] [2006] UKHL 43; [2006] 2 FLR 629. See also *B v B (Residence Order: Reason for Decision)* [1997] 2 FLR 602.

on the opinions of child welfare professionals.[46] The parents might decide to call their own expert witnesses[47] and the court itself can call for a welfare report.[48] This report is compiled by the FCA. The FCA[49] should normally see all those concerned in the case. The report for the court must include recommendations. A court is not bound to follow the recommendations of the FCA. However, if it does decide to depart from the recommendations, the court should hear evidence from the FCA[50] and it should give reasons.[51] Failure to consider the FCA's evidence or to give reasons constitute ground for appeal.

IV. THE NO ORDER PRINCIPLE

Section 1(5) of the Children Act 1989 stipulates that the court should not make an order unless there is some positive advantage to doing so. The courts in dissolution or divorce proceedings do not have a general supervisory role in relation to all arrangements for children on divorce; intervention should be limited to those cases where it is thought necessary. The section does not, however, create a presumption against making an order; the court must simply ask itself whether it is 'better for the child to make the order than to make no order at all'.[52]

Evidently, the intention behind the legislation is to encourage agreement, to limit judicial intervention[53] and to foster the perception that recourse to the courts should be a last resort. However, the retreat of the courts[54] does not mean that the law becomes insignificant. As Mnookin and Kornhauser say, bargaining takes place 'in the shadow of the law' (Mnookin and Kornhauser 1979: 968).

The 'shadow of the law' loomed particularly large over the ill-fated Family Law Act 1996. The statute promoted private settlement and also contained provisions that would have impacted on the negotiating process. While almost nothing remains of the radical new scheme, section 1, setting out the general principles, remains in force. It has no legal effect because it was intended to govern decision-making under Parts II[55] and III.[56] Section 1 requires that those involved in proceedings such as judges and Cafcass officers should have regard to the principle that marriages that have irretrievably broken down should be brought to an end in a way that promotes 'as good a continuing relationship' as possible between the parties and their children. This endorsement of continuity in relationships between parents and children, as well as the rejection of conflict, are principles that still permeate government policy, professional practice and legal decision-making

---

[46] See Buchanan et al (2001: 1). See, on the use of experts, King and Kaganas (1998). See also Chapter 9 above.

[47] See Practice Direction: Experts in Family Proceedings Relating to Children [2009] 2 FLR 1383.

[48] S 7 Children Act 1989. The court is not obliged to request a welfare report.

[49] For a critique of the practice of Children and Family Reporters (now also FCAs), see James et al (2003).

[50] *Re A (Children: 1959 UN Declaration)* [1998] 1 FLR 354. If minded to reject the recommendations of a CAFCASS officer, the court should test any misgivings it might have in the witness box with the officer before deciding (para 79): *Re R (Residence Order)* [2009] EWCA 445, para 79.

[51] *W v W (A Minor: Custody Appeal)* [1988] 2 FLR 505; *Re W (Residence)* [1999] 2 FLR 390.

[52] *G (Children)* [2005] EWCA Civ 1283; [2006] 1 FLR 771, para 10.

[53] See Law Commission (1988b: paras 3.3–4).

[54] Indeed, whether the attempt to reduce litigation has been successful is open to doubt. The statistics show an upward trend since 2005 in the number of children involved in private law disputes (MOJ 2010b: 44). If legal aid is restricted as planned at the time of writing (MOJ 2010a) this could have a dramatic effect, however.

[55] Never brought into force.

[56] Repealed.

relating to separation and divorce. In addition to the case law and the legislation, as Walker observes, there is general agreement on a number of principles that reflect the content of section 1:

> These are: that the law has a responsibility to protect the best interests of children; that parents should be encouraged to reduce any conflict between themselves in order to minimise distress to their children; and that, other than in exceptional circumstances, the relationships children have with both their parents should be maintained and fostered during the upheavals and transitions, and on into post divorce family life. (Walker 2004: 149)

If parents reach agreement, perhaps through mediation or perhaps with the help of lawyers, then, subject to the court's supervisory role (section 41 Matrimonial Causes Act 1973 and section 63 Civil Partnership Act 2004), and subject to the court's duty to scrutinise any agreement before making a consent order,[57] their agreement will stand. Should they fail to agree, litigation may ensue, but court proceedings do not signal unconstrained adversarialism.[58] It is worth bearing in mind that the law is influenced by child welfare knowledge and that the legal process has come to share certain values with mediation; professionals and courts alike increasingly deplore any show of hostility by one parent to the other. According to Pickett, '[n]ot only does law cast its shadow over mediation, but mediation also casts its shadow over law' (Pickett 1991: 28). And both, she argues, are implicated in reinforcing a familial ideology.

V. RESIDENCE

In most cases, parents reach agreement on the question of where the child is to live. The Law Commission (1988b: para 3.2) noted that the number of contested cases is small[59] so that orders are generally not necessary to settle disputes. In the event of a dispute, however, or when certainty is considered desirable, it may be necessary to seek a residence order from the court.

A residence order is defined in section 8 of the Children Act 1989 as 'an order settling the arrangements to be made as to the person with whom a child is to live'. Usually residence is ordered in favour of one parent with contact in favour of the other. A residence order does not have the effect of reallocating parental responsibility between parents; both retain it and the non-resident parent keeps the right to deal directly with third parties such as schools and hospitals (Bainham 1990: 210). Therefore, each parent is, on divorce or dissolution, legally entitled to exercise parental responsibility as before, except to the extent that to do so would conflict with a residence or any other court

---

[57] Practice Direction: Revised Private Law Programme [2010] 2 FLR 717, para 5.3.

[58] See Bailey-Harris et al (1998: 24). Further, Eekelaar, Maclean and Bienart (2000) note that most family law solicitors prefer to promote settlement rather than adversarialism. See also Piper (1999d). See on the role of barristers, Maclean and Eekelaar (2009).

[59] Simpson et al (1995: 25) report that the majority of non-custodial fathers in their sample accepted the status quo regarding residence; approximately 1 in 5 was involved in a dispute about it. In 2003, the number of residence orders granted was 31,966, while only 202 orders were refused (DCA 2003: para 56). 28,160 orders were made and 140 refused in 2009 (MOJ 2010b).

order.[60] *Re P (A Minor) (Parental Responsibility Order)*[61] establishes that a residence order precludes the non-resident parent from interfering with the arrangements for the day-to-day life of the child.[62]

Bainham (2005) comments that:

> In most cases, therefore, despite theoretical equality and the ethos of continuing parental responsibility, it is the resident parent who, for practical purposes, will exercise parental powers. The legislation … . might even be viewed as an attempt at social engineering. It is statutory recognition that ex-spouses remain parents and are expected to be able to distinguish between termination of their own legal and factual relationship and their continuing moral and legal obligations to their children. (Bainham 2005: 153)

Bainham has in the past expressed regret at what he perceived to be a legislative failure to promote dual parenting (Bainham 1990: 212). He took the view that the Children Act should have focused more closely on the concept of time-sharing in the form, perhaps, of a presumption in favour of shared residence. Leaving decisions to parents or, in the event of disagreement, the courts, without establishing a statutory norm of joint parenting, he said, allows many parents to relinquish their parental role (ibid: 213); there is nothing in the legislation to prevent parents continuing 'to agree in droves that mothers should have sole responsibility for the post-divorce care of children' (ibid: 217).

The Children Act does leave open the possibility of shared residence orders on separation: section 11(4) states that where a residence order is made in favour of two or more persons who do not live together, the order may specify the periods of time during which the child is to live in the different households concerned. It appears that this statutory provision has not, in the past, prompted the judiciary to embrace enthusiastically the possibility of shared residence when parents do not live together.[63] However, recent judicial pronouncements indicate that things have been changing. This may be in part a response to the calls being made by fathers' rights groups for the enactment of a presumption of shared parenting.

Q Read Chapter 9. What arguments are there in favour of a presumption of shared residence? What arguments are there against it?

---

[60] See s 2(8) of the Children Act 1989. A residence order does not entitle the person in whose favour it is made to change the child's surname or remove the child from the UK without the written permission of every person with parental responsibility or the leave of the court (s 13(1)). This does not prevent a person with a residence order from removing the child from the UK for a period of less than one month (s 13(2)). A residence order significantly weakens the position of the non-resident parent in cases where the caretaking parent wishes to place the child in local authority accommodation. Normally, a local authority may not provide accommodation if there is someone with parental responsibility able and willing to provide accommodation or to arrange for it to be provided for the child (s 20(7)). Also, if a child is being accommodated, he or she may be removed by any person with parental responsibility (s 20(8)). However, these provisions do not apply if there is a residence order in force (s 20(9)).

[61] [1994] 1 FLR 578, 585.

[62] What qualifies as 'day-to-day' is itself not beyond dispute.

[63] See Baker and Townsend (1996).

VI. APPLYING THE WELFARE PRINCIPLE

Section 1(3) applies to contested section 8 cases.[64] While much of the case law applying the welfare principle pre-dates the Children Act 1989,[65] it remains relevant.[66] Apart from the fact that it introduces a new emphasis on the child's wishes, the checklist, in effect, codifies previous practice. The courts continue to give weight to the same kinds of factors in deciding residence cases as they did in the past when settling custody disputes. They are reluctant to disturb existing arrangements for the care of the child;[67] they tend to try to ensure that siblings are not separated;[68] they consider which parent is more likely to facilitate contact with the other;[69] they consider material wealth but do not regard this as very important;[70] and they disregard matrimonial misconduct that does not affect parenting capacity.[71]

The Checklist—Section 1(3) Children Act 1989

(a) The Child's Wishes and Feelings

The court is obliged to have regard to the 'ascertainable wishes and feelings of the child concerned (considered in the light of [her] age and understanding)'.[72] This item on the checklist echoes the mature minor test deployed in the *Gillick* case.[73] There, the House of Lords emphasised the significance of children's views and accorded to some young people limited autonomy in decision-making, subject to their age and ability to understand the relevant issues. While the court has a duty to consider children's wishes if a section 8 application is contested, there is no obligation on parents to do so; if the parents agree on residence or contact, the children's wishes need not be taken into account by them.

The Law Commission saw potential pitfalls in eliciting children's wishes at all. For example, it said, although the wishes of older children cannot be ignored, children should not be made to feel responsible for the eventual decision, and in any event, a child's views may be unreliable (Law Commission 1988b: para 3.23).[74]

---

[64] See s 1(4)(a) of the Children Act 1989. Strictly speaking, the checklist applies in s 8 proceedings only in contested cases but it seems to influence decision-making generally. Indeed in *Re B (Change of Surname)* [1996] 1 FLR 791 the court held that, although application of the checklist was not mandated in the circumstances before it, nevertheless it remained a 'useful aide mémoire of the factors that may impinge on the child's welfare' (793).

[65] See, for a review of the application of the welfare principle in pre-1989 cases, Law Commission (1986: para 6.38).

[66] See *C v C (A Minor) (Custody: Appeal)* [1991] 1 FLR 223, 230.

[67] *Stephenson v Stephenson* [1985] FLR 1140, 1146; *Re A (A Minor) (Custody)* [1991] 2 FLR 394, 402–03; *Re B (Residence Order: Status Quo)* [1998] 1 FLR 368.

[68] *C v C (Minors: Custody)* [1988] 2 FLR 291; *Re A (A Minor) (Custody)* [1991] 2 FLR 394.

[69] *D v M (A Minor: Custody Appeal)* [1983] Fam 33, 41. See also, eg, the comments made in *Re A (A Minor) (Custody)* [1991] 2 FLR 394, 403. But see *Re B (Residence Order: Status Quo)* [1998] 1 FLR 368. See further below.

[70] *Stephenson v Stephenson* [1985] FLR 1140, 1148. See also *D v M (A Minor) (Custody Appeal)* [1983] Fam 33.

[71] See *Re K (Minors) (Children: Care and Control)* [1977] Fam 179; *S (BD) v S (DJ) (Children: Care and Control)* [1977] Fam 109.

[72] S 1(3)(a).

[73] See Chapter 11 below.

[74] See also Cantwell and Scott (1995), Trinder (1997). However, there is research indicating that children do want to be consulted, particularly about residence. See Smart et al (2001), Hawthorne et al (2003). Gollop et

In the context of section 8 proceedings, the child's wishes do not determine the outcome of the case; the welfare of the child may be found to dictate that an entirely different course be taken. James et al found that Cafcass officers 'attach greater importance to their own judgements about the welfare of the child, which are based on a range of professional principles and personal considerations, than to the child's wishes and feelings' (James et al 2003: 893). The authors state that even if a practitioner considered a child competent to express a view, this view might not be reported if the practitioner felt it conflicted with the child's best interests (ibid).

Judges have generally been wary of speaking directly to children.[75] Recently, however, the Family Justice Council produced 'Guidelines for Judges Meeting Children Who Are Subject to Family Proceedings' (Family Justice Council 2010). These guidelines emphasise that in most cases the child's wishes, needs and feelings are conveyed to the court by means of a report from a Cafcass officer and that nothing in the guidance is intended to 'replace or undermine that responsibility' (ibid: 654). However, judges have a discretion to speak to children directly. When judges are deciding whether to meet with a child, 'chronological age is relevant but not determinative. Some children of 7 or even younger have clear understanding of their circumstances and very clear views which they may wish to express' (ibid).[76] The purpose of meeting with children is not to gather evidence; 'that is the responsibility of the Cafcass officer'. The purpose is 'to enable the child to gain some understanding of what is going on, and to be reassured that the judge has understood him/her' (ibid: 655).

The Human Rights Act 1998, together with the UN Convention on the Rights of the Child 1989,[77] has led to a heightened consciousness of children's rights, however, and this appears to be prompting the courts to accord greater significance to consultation, if not direct judicial contact, with children.[78] There is a view within the courts that 'children should be seen and heard in child cases'.[79] What is more, it is clear that, in some cases, the child's wishes are crucial. In *M v M (Transfer of Custody: Appeal)*[80] the court observed that to ignore the wishes of a 12-year-old and to impose an order to which she was implacably opposed, would provoke her to resist and, possibly, run away.[81] In *Re S (Con-*

---

al (2000), who carried out research in New Zealand, found that parents rarely discussed arrangements with their children. In the UK, Buchanan et al found that most children wanted to be more involved in the decision-making process but fewer than half of those interviewed felt they had been heard by the court and their parents (Buchanan et al 2001: 92). They also found that few children were asked with whom they wanted to live, although more than half were consulted about contact (ibid: 64). However, more and more significance is being accorded to children's views and *Making Contact Work* (The Advisory Board on Family Law 2002: para 3.2.3) states that parents should be advised to inform and consult their children. See, generally, Kaganas and Diduck (2004). For moves to involve children more in mediation, see Chapter 15 below.

[75] See *B v B (Minors) (Interviews and Listing Arrangements)*, [1994] 2 FLR 489. Wall LJ remains 'agnostic' on the question of whether judges should speak to children (Wall 2009). See also Hunter (2007) who questions the advisability of judges speaking to children.

[76] See also *Re W (Abduction: Acquiescence: Children's Objections)* [2010] EWHC 332 (Fam); [2010] 2 FLR 1150 para 37. This was a Hague Convention case, however.

[77] Art 12.

[78] See *Re A (Contact: Separate Representation)* [2001] 1 FLR 715. Depending on the circumstances and the age and maturity of the child, Art 8 ECHR may require courts to ensure that they hear children involved in disputes between their parents. Otherwise a parent could claim that the procedural requirements implicit in Art 8, that there should be adequate protection of the parent's interests in the decision-making process, have not been met. See *Sahin v Germany*; *Sommerfeld v Germany* [2003] 2 FLR 671, para 73.

[79] *Re A (Contact: Separate Representation)* [2001] 1 FLR 715, para 22. See Kaganas and Diduck (2004: 974ff).

[80] [1987] 2 FLR 146.

[81] Pp 152–53. See also *Re F (Minors) (Denial of Contact)* [1993] 2 FLR 677; *Re P (A Minor) (Education)* [1992] 1 FLR 316; *M v M (Defined Contact Application)* [1998] 2 FLR 244.

tact: Children's Views)[82] the court attached considerable importance to the views of teenagers. In *Re R (Residence Order)*[83] the court adopted the approach taken in *Re L, M, V and H.*[84] There the court said that the views of children over 10 carry considerable weight, with children aged 6–10 occupying an intermediate position, while the views of children under 6 are often indistinguishable from those of their main carer (para 57). In *Re R* the Court of Appeal said that the judge below had erred in that he referred to the child's wishes, accepted them and then ignored them. The child was nearly 10, mature and thoughtful. The judge did not justify his rejection of the child's views or, indeed, those of the Cafcass officer. The court upheld the mother's appeal against an order giving residence to the father.

As long as the court explains why it is overriding the child's wishes, the decision is more likely to be upheld on appeal. There are recent cases where the court has transferred residence despite the adamant opposition of the children concerned. These are cases where resident parents are resisting contact between the child and the non-resident parent. The courts appear to consider the preservation of the relationship between the child and the non-resident parent to be more important than the child's distress at being moved from the resident parent.[85] In *S (A Child)*[86] residence of a boy aged almost 12 was moved from the mother, with whom he had always lived, to the father, with whom contact was not taking place. The basis on which the move was ordered was the mother's behaviour regarding contact and the assessment by a psychiatrist that the boy had become 'alienated' from his father. This diagnosis meant, the court said, that the child's objections should not be taken at face value. The Supreme Court agreed. [87]

The wishes of two boys, aged 12 and almost 10, were overridden in *D (Children)*,[88] and the children were removed from a competent and devoted mother,[89] with whom they had always lived, and placed their paternal grandparents. The father was found to have sexually abused his stepdaughter over a period of time. The mother was therefore convinced he was a paedophile who had also abused her sons. In addition, she believed that his parents were also implicated in the abuse. She was said by the expert witnesses to be obsessional and one of them testified that the children would be emotionally harmed by the mother's false belief system. The court recognised that the move would cause 'severe emotional distress in the short term'[90] but considered the harm caused by the mother to be more serious. The court referred to a letter recounting the older child's views and thought this strengthened the case for the move. The child said he was afraid of his father, that the father had abused his brother, that the paternal family did not believe him or his brother and called him a liar. The court took the view that the children were being harmed because they regarded their paternal grandparents as 'ogres'.[91] The only way to

---

[82] [2002] 1 FLR 1156.

[83] [2009] EWCA Civ 445; [2010] 1 FLR 509.

[84] [2000] 2 FLR 334.

[85] But see *Re H (Care Order: Contact)* [2008] EWCA Civ 1245; [2009] 2 FLR 55. The Court of Appeal reversed a decision to make a care order, the basis of which was the mother's refusal to allow contact with the father and maternal grandmother. The court said that the child's wish to be with the mother and her strong attachment to the mother were weighty factors. The court made a residence order in favour of the mother together with a supervision order. The status quo principle, discussed below, is intended to avoid upheaval and associated distress for children.

[86] [2010] EWCA Civ 219.

[87] Ibid: para 27.

[88] [2010] EWCA Civ 496. See, for more detail, the decision of Coleridge J in the High court discussed below: *Re A (Suspended Residence Order)* [2009] EWHC 1676 (Fam); [2010] 1 FLR 1679.

[89] Ibid: para 11.

[90] Ibid: para 10. See also para 15.

[91] Ibid.

avoid the children becoming 'emotional cripples'[92] would be to move them to the grand-parents so that they could develop a normal relationship with them. The predictions of the expert witness and speculative benefits of the move were thus considered to outweigh the distress the children were clearly experiencing as a result of it; one child was described as 'inconsolable'.[93] In effect the relationship not only with the father but with the paternal family was prioritised.

Re A (A Child) (Residence Order)[94] demonstrates that those speculative benefits do not necessarily materialise. The case concerned an 8-year-old boy whose parents had been involved in very protracted contact litigation. The mother was found to have been obstructing contact and was diagnosed by one of the expert witnesses as having a personality disorder; she could not control her feelings towards the father and, although the child had not been harmed, the conflict and 'alienation'[95] would lead to psychological problems. The mother was adjudged a good mother in all respects other than contact. The boy wanted to remain in her care. However, although the recorder was mindful of the distress that would be caused by the move, he ordered it:

> In my judgment, [S] will initially find the move difficult. He will no longer be living with his mother, nor near his friends and maternal grandparents and he will be changing school. There will be some home sickness. This emotionally stable boy will, in my judgment, within a few weeks find that he is otherwise easily able to overcome the initial home sickness or unhappiness. The long-term benefits to him of a move are a good deal more significant and they outweigh the initial homesickness.[96]

The mother's appeal was dismissed. Brissenden, a barrister, recounts the events that followed:

> The mother refused to accept the court's decision and a few months after the move issued proceedings to vary the residence order ... . The boy ... continued to be unhappy in his new home, and by this time was making threats to self-harm. A Section 7 report was ordered and it too treated the judgment of the Court of Appeal as a virtual bar to a change of residence back to mother, reliant as it had been on the diagnosis of personality disorder. Mention was made of the boy's unhappiness, but more significantly, it was apparent from the report that he felt that no one was listening to him, and he was starting to feel worthless and as if his opinion counted for nothing.
>
> It was on this basis that the district judge reluctantly appointed a Rule 9.5 guardian, so that the boy could feel that his voice would be heard, even if it was not acted upon. Fortunately for the child, the guardian did listen to him, and realised that far from the short-term trauma that had been predicted, this child was suffering immensely from the move, and was desperate to live with his mother again ... . The guardian was less concerned with the mother's alleged personality disorder, than with the wishes and feelings of the child. ...
>
> The judge ordered a psychological report to be prepared ... . The boy, whilst on a staying contact with his mother in Kent, threatened to take his own life if he was forced to return to father ... . He was seen by a GP who determined that he certainly had a suicidal intention, and had given serious thought about the means. An emergency hearing was listed, and upon the recommendations of the guardian, and after hearing the tenor of the almost completed psycho-

---

[92] Ibid.
[93] Ibid: para 15.
[94] [2007] EWCA Civ 899; [2008] 1 FCR 599.
[95] Ibid: para 3.
[96] Ibid: para 18.

logist's report, the child was allowed to remain with mother pending the outcome of the final hearing. ...

The boy thrived back home in Kent with his mother and was described by the guardian as 'a different boy ...'. The psychologist's report recommended a variation of the order and a residence order in favour of mother, as the child was suffering severe emotional harm due to the move ... . The guardian went further, and in her report was critical of the original decision to remove the boy from his mother, stating that the decision to change his residence had had a 'profound and negative effect on his developmental and psychological wellbeing' and that this had 'irreparably harmed him'. Following these reports, on the first day of the final hearing (over 2 years after the Court of Appeal ruling), the father consented to a residence order in favour of mother ... .

[W]here there are clear indications, such as in *S (A Child)* [2010] EWCA Civ 219, that the child is resolutely opposed to a change of residence, and is indicating a desire to self-harm, then the need to listen to the child becomes greater, and decisions should be made much more carefully ... .

The general principles were propounded by Butler Sloss LJ in *Re S (Minors)(Access: Religious upbringing)* [1992] 313 (sic)[97] at page 321, a case involving two children aged 13 and 11:

'Nobody should dictate to children of this age, because one is dealing with their emotions, their lives and they are not packages to be moved around. They are people entitled to be treated with respect.'

Yet, packages are what they seem to be.

(b) The Child's Needs

The court has to consider the physical, emotional and educational needs of the child and assess how capable each parent is of meeting those needs. In doing so, it will take into account factors such as the strength of the bonds between the child, the parents and other members of the household.[98]

In cases where there is a dispute between a biological parent and someone who is not a biological parent, the courts have in the past appeared to favour the former.[99] However, the decision in *Re G (Children)*[100] made it clear that the fact that a parent is a 'natural' parent is significant but that there is no presumption in favour of such a parent. This case concerned former lesbian partners who had arranged for donor insemination and who brought up their children together; the residence dispute was between the birth mother of the children and her former partner. Baroness Hale said that the same principles should apply in this case as would apply in relation to a heterosexual relationship (para 7).

She identified three ways in which someone can become a natural parent: genetic, gestational and social/psychological. She said:

[30] ... The statutory position is plain: the welfare of the child is the paramount consideration ... . There is no question of a parental right. As the Law Commission explained, 'the welfare test itself is well able to encompass any special contribution which natural parents can make to the emotional needs of their child' or, as Lord MacDermott put it, the claims and

---

[97] [1992] 2 FLR 313
[98] *Stephenson v Stephenson* [1985] FLR 1140; *Re A (A Minor) (Custody)* [1991] 2 FLR 394.
[99] See *Re KD (A Minor)(Ward: Termination of Access)* [1988] 1 All ER 577, 578; *Re M (Child's Upbringing)* [1996] 2 FLR 441.
[100] [2006] UKHL 43; [2006] 2 FLR 629.

wishes of parents 'can be capable of ministering to the total welfare of the child in a special way'.

[31] None of this means that the fact of parentage is irrelevant ... .

[36] Of course, in the great majority of cases, the natural mother combines all three. She is the genetic, gestational and psychological parent. Her contribution to the welfare of the child is unique. The natural father combines genetic and psychological parenthood. His contribution is also unique. In these days when more parents share the tasks of child rearing and breadwinning, his contribution is often much closer to that of the mother than it used to be; but there are still families which divide their tasks on more traditional lines, in which case his contribution will be different and its importance will often increase with the age of the child.

[37] But there are also parents who are neither genetic nor gestational, but who have become the psychological parents of the child and thus have an important contribution to make to their welfare.

[44] My Lords, I am driven to the conclusion that the courts below have allowed the unusual context of this case to distract them from principles which are of universal application. First, the fact that CG is the natural mother of these children in every sense of that term, while raising no presumption in her favour, is undoubtedly an important and significant factor in determining what will be best for them now and in the future.

Lord Nicholls' words appear to attach even greater weight to the biological relationship:

[2] ... In reaching its decision the court should always have in mind that in the ordinary way the rearing of a child by his or her biological parent can be expected to be in the child's best interests, both in the short term and also, and importantly, in the longer term. I decry any tendency to diminish the significance of this factor. A child should not be removed from the primary care of his or her biological parents without compelling reason. Where such a reason exists the judge should spell this out explicitly.

These judgments, it seems, have led to some confusion. In *Re B (A Child)*[101] Lord Kerr set out to clarify the law in a dispute between the father and grandmother of the child concerned. The judge criticised the fact that the court below had referred to a child's right to be raised by a biological parent, and stressed that the court's duty is to apply the welfare principle (paras 19–23). Lord Nicholls in *Re G* was 'doing no more than reflecting common experience that, in general, children tend to thrive when brought up by parents to whom they have been born' (para 35). Moreover he had said this to be so only in 'the ordinary way' (ibid). This was a case where events did not follow the ordinary way; the child had lived virtually all his life with the grandmother and the father's arrangements to care for him were untested. Upholding the decision to maintain the status quo and keep the child with the grandmother, Lord Kerr said:

[35] ... But many disputes about residence and contact do not follow the ordinary way. There-fore, although one should keep in mind the common experience to which Lord Nicholls was referring, one must not be slow to recognise those cases where that common experience does not provide a reliable guide.

---

[101] [2009] UKSC 5; [2010] 1 FLR 551.

[37] … It is only as a contributor to the child's welfare that parenthood assumes any significance. In common with all other factors bearing on what is in the best interests of the child, it must be examined for its potential to fulfil that aim.

Where a parent has re-partnered, the suitability, in the court's view, of the new partner as a step-parent as well as the child's relationship with him or her will be significant; fathers who can offer a satisfactory mother substitute, for example, tend to be considered better placed than lone fathers to obtain a residence order.[102]

In *Stephenson v Stephenson*[103] the Court of Appeal reversed an order placing a child in the care of her mother. The child had been cared for primarily by her father's cohabitant before being removed by the mother. She was found by the court to have a happy and secure life with the father and his cohabitant. The mother had had limited contact with her and, despite the fact that the father was 'awkward' about it, was said to have abandoned her child. The mother's cohabitant had a criminal record, and was unemployed and had uncertain prospects. Moreover, the court doubted the stability of the mother's relationship with him.

In other reported cases, judges may have been influenced by traditional gender roles and the values associated with these. *May v May*[104] seems to have accorded precedence to those values traditionally associated with the paternal role. The court preferred the care given by the father. It was thought that he would raise the children in a more disciplined way than their mother and her new partner would and that he would provide more stimulation from an educational point of view. The mother lavished affection on the children but her home was more easy-going.

Other decisions have stressed the roles of fathers as earners and of mothers as carers. The courts tend to prefer a parent who is not working full time to one who is.[105] However the prospect of a man, who is capable of working, relying on social security in order to become a full-time carer was apparently anathema to the court. In *B v B (Custody of Children)*[106] a 4½-year-old child had been in the father's care since the breakdown of the marriage over two years earlier. The father was able to devote his time to his son largely because he had lost his job. The court *a quo* had ordered that the child be given into the care of his mother, relying heavily on the father's joblessness. The decision was overturned on appeal, with Oliver LJ stating:

> I do not wish to suggest for a moment that the prospect of an able-bodied man being permanently unemployed is not a relevant consideration, but it does seem to me that in this particular case the judge's emphasis on it showed that he regarded it ultimately as the conclusive consideration. (179)

Cumming-Bruce LJ concurred, remarking obiter:

> I agree with the judge that as a matter of common sense it must usually be sensible to place a small child in the care of an affectionate and sufficiently capable mother who is available to give full-time care, rather than placing the child with a father who, in order to attend the needs of the infant, will have to give up work either altogether or to a great degree. (183–84)

---

[102] See *Stephenson v Stephenson* [1985] FLR 1140.
[103] Ibid.
[104] [1986] 1 FLR 325.
[105] See *Re M (Residence)* [2004] EWCA Civ 1574; [2005] Fam Law 216.
[106] [1985] FLR 166. See also *B v B (Custody of Child)* [1985] FLR 462.

Q Why was it considered not only acceptable, but desirable, for a mother to be available as a full-time carer but not for a father? How might these gendered assumptions be disrupted in same-sex relationships?

A subsequent case[107] suggests that the courts' dislike of reliance on state benefits may extend also to mothers who wish to be full-time carers. In a situation where the man apparently cannot support the post-separation family alone, the court appears to jettison traditional roles rather than countenance the possibility of a drain on the public purse.

May and *B v B* reflect outmoded prejudices and assumptions; similar cases might be decided very differently on the basis of different criteria today. As we saw in Chapter 9 above, perhaps one of the most striking changes is that the courts now seem to be paying more attention to the question of which parent is most likely to facilitate contact. In *V v V (Contact: Implacable Hostility)*[108] the most important factor in transferring residence from the mother to the father appears to have been that the mother was found to have been unreasonably obstructing contact with the father, whereas he would be likely to encourage contact with the mother if the children moved. Also, the father was found to be committed to his children; he could offer 'reasonable' accommodation; he would provide a private education; he had a network of close family members who would help him with childcare; and his working hours were adaptable (para 42).

More generally, as Masson et al observe, courts nowadays rely far more on assessments informed by child welfare knowledge (Masson et al 2008a: para 19.018). It seems that a court, faced with a decision about so important a matter as the relationship between a parent and child, is now expected to seek expert opinion although a report from an FCA would suffice. The ECtHR indicated, in *Elsholz v Germany*,[109] that the national court's refusal to order an independent psychological report in a contact dispute was a factor in its finding that both Article 8 and Article 6 had been breached. Article 8 had been violated because the father had not been sufficiently involved in the decision-making process and Article 6 had been violated because, in the absence of expert evidence, questions of fact and law raised by the case could not be adequately resolved on the basis of the material at the disposal of the German court. The requirements of a fair and public hearing in terms of Article 6 had not been satisfied.

(c) The Likely Effect of Any Change

The checklist instructs the court to consider the likely effect on the child of any change in his or her circumstances. This reflects the long-standing practice of applying what is known as the 'status quo principle'. Courts are very reluctant to disrupt children's lives by moving them from one home to another. As a result, the parent who takes on the care of the children when a relationship breaks down may have an advantage should a dispute over residence arise.

Not surprisingly, in heterosexual relationships, it is mothers who tend to benefit from the status quo principle. The Office for National Statistics reports that, in its research sample, 93% of resident parents were female, whereas 89% of non-resident parents were

---

[107] *Re R (Residence Order: Finance)* [1995] 2 FLR 612.
[108] [2004] EWHC Fam 1215; [2004] 2 FLR 851.
[109] [2000] 2 FLR 486.

male (Blackwell and Dawe 2003: para 1.3).[110] When relationships break down, it is mothers who most often take, or continue to take, responsibility for the care their children.[111] It seems that not many fathers seek residence orders. In Hunt and Macleod's study of contact disputes, only 31% of the applicants, almost all fathers, were also seeking sole or shared residence (Hunt and Macleod 2008: 9). The majority of residence orders were made in favour of mothers (ibid: table 2.24). Smart and May[112] found that, in their study, most applications for residence orders were made by mothers fearing that their children might be removed from their care or attempting to recover a child who had already been removed:

> It was also nearly always the case that the person applying for residence already had the child living with them. When fathers applied for residence, it tended to be in circumstances where the mother was said to be incapable of caring for the child because of mental health problems or substance abuse. Similarly, when grandparents applied for residence, it was in cases where neither parent was able to care for the child. (Smart and May 2004a: 37)[113]

It seems that nothing has changed since Brophy's (1989: 220) work under the pre-Children Act regime. She explained the predominance of custody orders in favour of mothers in terms of maternal caretaking and rejected allegations of discrimination against fathers by the courts. Parents rarely contested custody in court[114] and courts tended to confirm their agreements. In both contested and uncontested cases, custody orders tended to be made on the basis of the status quo principle, with the court electing to leave children with the parent who was caring for them at the time of the proceedings.[115]

The importance attributed to continuity is evident in *Dicocco v Milne*,[116] where the Court of Appeal reversed a decision to award custody[117] to the father. Ormrod LJ stated:

> [I]t is generally accepted by those who are professionally concerned with children that, particularly in the early years, continuity of care is a most important part of a child's sense of security and that disruption of established bonds is to be avoided whenever it is possible to do so. Where, as in this case, a child of 2 years of age has been brought up without interruption by the mother (or a mother substitute) it should not be removed from her care unless there are strong countervailing reasons for doing so. (259–60)

In *Re B (A Child)*[118] the Supreme Court overturned a decision to move a child from living with his grandmother to his father. The change would have led to considerable disruption:

> Transfer of his residence would involve a great deal more than a change of address. Many of the familiar aspects of his life which anchor his stability and sense of security would be changed. The justices were, therefore, right to give significant weight to the desirability of preserving the status quo. This is a factor which will not always command the importance that must be attached

---

[110] See also Walker (2004: table 7.1).

[111] See ibid: 156ff.

[112] See also Smart et al (2003).

[113] The sample comprised 430 cases of which 59% involved residence disputes.

[114] See also Priest and Whybrow (1986: para 4.10).

[115] See also ibid: para 4.11.

[116] (1983) 4 FLR 247. See also *Re B (Residence Order: Status Quo)* [1998] 1 FLR 368; *Re M (Residence)* [2004] EWCA Civ 1574; [2005] *Fam Law* 216; *Re R (Residence Order)* [2009] EWCA Civ 445.

[117] Note that cases which refer to 'custody' pre-date the Children Act 1989. Custody orders are no longer part of the court's repertoire. Instead, courts now have the power to make contact and residence orders.

[118] [2009] UKSC 5; [2010] 1 FLR 551.

to it in the present case but we are satisfied that it was of considerable significance in the debate as to where this child's best interests lay. (para 42)

Of course, the court might decide to move a child if it considers that the existing childcare arrangements are unsatisfactory. Most notably, as we saw in Chapter 9 above, and as is apparent from *S (A Child)* and *Re A (A Child)(Residence Order)* above, courts are becoming increasingly willing to transfer residence in cases where resident parents are designated as being implacably hostile to contact,[119] although such transfers are supposed to be a last resort.[120]

(d) The Child's Age, Sex, Background and Any Characteristics of His Which the Court Considers Relevant

In the past, courts tended to place young children and older girls in the care of their mothers, while older boys were placed with their fathers.[121] However, more recent reported judgments have been, in general, careful to avoid explicit application of the old rules of thumb although there is still a tendency to award residence orders to mothers in cases where the child is very young. In *Re A (A Minor) (Custody)*[122] Butler-Sloss LJ said:

> In cases where the child has remained throughout with the mother and is young, particularly when a baby or toddler, the unbroken relationship of the mother and child is one which it would be very difficult to displace, unless the mother was unsuitable to care for the child. But where the mother and child have been separated, and the mother seeks the return of the child, other considerations apply, and there is no starting point that the mother should be preferred to the father and only displaced by a preponderance of evidence to the contrary. (400)

Q Is Butler-Sloss LJ saying that if a very young child has been in the continuous care of the mother, the court should adopt as its 'starting point' the position that the mother should be preferred to the father except where there is 'a preponderance of evidence to the contrary'? Would this be the same as saying there is a presumption in favour of the mother in those circumstances? Is this merely an application of the status quo principle?

A preference for maternal care was articulated in very clear terms by the House of Lords in *Brixey v Lynas*,[123] a Scots case in which the court had to apply a Scots statutory provision which, like the Children Act 1989, makes the child's welfare paramount. The court cited *Re A* with approval and asserted that, while there is neither a presumption nor a principle that very young children should be with their mothers, the advantages of maternal care must be taken into account.[124]

---

[119] In contrast to the view expressed in *Re B (Residence Order: Status Quo* [1998] 1 FLR 368. There the court said that the overwhelming factor for securing the child's welfare was maintaining the status quo. Difficulties regarding contact had to be 'endured' and 'tackled' by whatever means were possible (371).

[120] *Re A (Residence Order)* [2009] EWCA Civ 1141; [2010] 1 FLR 1083.

[121] See Priest and Whybrow (1986: para 4.24).

[122] [1991] 2 FLR 394. See also *Re W (A Minor) (Residence Order)* [1992] 2 FLR 332; *Re S (A Minor) (Custody)* [1991] 2 FLR 388, 390, 392

[123] [1996] 2 FLR 499.

[124] See, further, 580ff. See also *Re S (A Minor) (Custody)* [1991] 2 FLR 388; *Re A (A Minor) (Custody)* [1991] 2 FLR 394; *Re A (Children: 1959 UN Declaration)* [1998] 1 FLR 354.

[T]he advantage to a very young child of being with its mother is a consideration which must be taken into account in deciding where lie its best interests in custody proceedings in which the mother is involved. It is neither a presumption nor a principle but rather recognition of a widely held belief based on practical experience and the workings of nature. Its importance will vary according to the age of the child and to the other circumstances of each individual case such as whether the child has been living with or apart from the mother and whether she is or is not capable of providing proper care. Circumstances may be such that it has no importance at all. Furthermore it will always yield to other competing advantages which more effectively promote the welfare of the child. However, where a very young child has been with its mother since birth and there is no criticism of her ability to care for the child only the strongest competing advantages are likely to prevail. (505)

The courts are even less likely now to talk in terms of a presumption in favour of the mother. In *Re L*[125] Thorpe LJ remarked that there is a danger that the identification of a presumption in deciding a section 8 case might 'inhibit or distort the rigorous search for the welfare solution'. Instead, he preferred to speak of an 'assumption' in favour of contact in contact disputes. In *Payne v Payne*[126] Thorpe LJ gave a further explanation of his misgivings. To elevate a consideration to a presumption could constitute a breach of a party's rights under Articles 6 and 8 of the ECHR.

In *Re X and Y (Leave to Remove from Jurisdiction: No Order Principle)*[127] the judge raised a different objection to the use of presumptions, arguing that their application is incompatible with section 1(5) of the Children Act 1989. Munby J was of the opinion that, when it comes to decisions hinging on children's best interests, the burden rests on the person seeking a court order to make out a positive case for it. Unless the order would contribute to the child's best interests, no order should be made: 'The proper application of Section 1(5) [of the Children Act 1989] is inconsistent with identifying any particular factor(s) as giving rise to a presumption in favour of making an order or as being all important or only to be displaced by strong countervailing considerations' (148).

There might be factors that are regarded as carrying great weight, he went on. But whether any particular factor might tip the balance one way or another had to be decided on an evaluation of the circumstances rather than by applying a presumption.

In *Re N; A v G and N*[128] the court refused to accept constraints on judicial discretion. It stated that there is no general principle that an 8-year-old boy should be with his father and declined to comment on the research used to support the assertion that a child does better in the care of the same-sex parent.

(e) Any Harm the Child has Suffered or Is at Risk of Suffering

The courts have increasingly come to regard domestic violence, even if not inflicted directly on the child concerned, as damaging and have described it as a failure of parenting.[129] Child abuse might also preclude a parent from obtaining a residence order. In

---

[125] *Re L (Contact: Domestic Violence), Re V (Contact: Domestic Violence), Re M (Contact: Domestic Violence), Re H (Contact: Domestic Violence)* [2000] 2 FLR 334, 364.

[126] [2001] EWCA Civ 166; [2001] 1 FLR 1052, para 40. See also para 25.

[127] [2001] 2 FLR 118.

[128] [2009] EWHC 1807 (Fam); [2010] 1 FLR 272, paras 235–41.

[129] *Re L (Contact: Domestic Violence), Re V (Contact: Domestic Violence), Re M (Contact: Domestic Violence), Re H (Contact: Domestic Violence)* [2000] 2 FLR 334. In the context of public law proceedings, sig-

addition, a parent who resists contact between the child and the non-resident parent may lose residence even if she is otherwise a good parent. So important is contact in the eyes of the courts that they are increasingly prepared to transfer residence to the non-resident parent, or even grandparents, where the resident parent, usually the mother, is considered to be unreasonably obstructing contact. Indeed the courts have even termed mothers' conduct as abusive in some cases and have ordered the local authority to investigate under section 37 of the Children Act 1989. For a full discussion of these cases, see below.

(f) Capacity of Each Parent and Any Other Person the Court Considers Relevant to Meet the Child's Needs[130]

One issue that the courts found particularly troubling until about the mid-1990s was that of the parents' sexual orientation.[131] While a parent's homosexuality did not constitute a bar to the success of an application, parental sexual orientation was perceived as having a significant impact on children's well-being. In *C v C (A Minor) (Custody: Appeal)*[132] the Court of Appeal upheld an appeal by a father against an order awarding custody to the mother on the ground that the trial judge had taken little account of her lesbian relationship. This, according to the court, was plainly wrong as the nature of the relationship was 'an important factor to be put into the balance' (229).

In *Re D (An Infant) (Adoption: Parent's Consent)*[133] the adverse consequences for a child of his father's homosexuality were seen as so severe that his consent to the boy's adoption by the mother and stepfather was dispensed with. Lord Wilberforce in the House of Lords warned that courts should be vigilant to guard against: 'the risk of children, at critical ages, being exposed or introduced to ways of life which ... may lead to severance from normal society, to psychological stresses and unhappiness and possibly even to physical experiences which may scar them for life'.

Neither the notion that homosexual parents are more likely to expose their children to abuse nor the suggestion of 'corruption', making children more likely to grow up homosexual or lesbian, gained currency in the courts.[134] In the past, however, homosexual and lesbian parents were also faced with the argument that children suffer embarrassment and are stigmatised as a result of their parent's sexuality.[135] This argument was coupled with the assertion, in the case of a contest between a homosexual or lesbian parent and a heterosexual parent, that the latter could offer a more 'normal' lifestyle. While the stigmatisation argument was rejected in *B v B (Minors) (Custody, Care and Control)*,[136] the argument invoking the 'normal family' was successfully deployed in the same year.[137]

However, views on same-sex relationships and children's welfare have changed. So, for

---

nificant harm, which is the threshold condition for a care order, has been redefined to include the effects of seeing or hearing domestic violence (s 31 Children Act 1989).

[130] See, eg, *May v May* and *Stephenson v Stephenson* above.

[131] See eg, *Re P(A Minor) (Custody)* [1983] 4 FLR 401; *Re H (A Minor) (Section 37 Direction)* [1993] 2 FLR 541, 545.

[132] [1991] 1 FLR 223.

[133] [1977] AC 602, 629.

[134] See *Re P* [1983] 4 FLR 401; Bradley (1987: 192).

[135] For a comprehensive review of the case law and a critical assessment of the literature, see Reece (1996b).

[136] [1991] 1 FLR 402.

[137] *C v C (A Minor) (Custody: Appeal)* [1991] 1 FLR 223.

example, in *Re D (Contact and Parental Responsibility)*[138] the judge reflected on the fact that neither the courts nor the legislature discriminates against parents and their partners in same-sex relationships:

[31] Same sex family arrangements already receive a considerable degree of recognition from the courts ... . We have come a long way from the days when a mother who began a lesbian relationship might well have found that it meant she was not permitted to have care of her children.

In *Re B (Role of Biological Father)*[139] the biological father, a sperm donor, was the brother of the mother's female partner. He became estranged from the two women and, since he wanted to be involved in the child's life, he sought parental responsibility and contact. The court refused to grant parental responsibility, saying this would lead to conflict. The judge did order contact but it was to be limited so as to protect the autonomy of what the judge referred to as the nuclear family (para 29). In *Re G (Children)*[140] the House of Lords took the view that the dispute between a lesbian mother and her former partner should be decided on the basis of 'principles which are of universal application' and that the courts below had erred by allowing the 'unusual context' of the case to distract them (para 44).

None of these cases involved disputes where a mother and father who are respectively lesbian and heterosexual are contesting residence.[141] It is not entirely inconceivable that, faced with a choice between a same-sex and a heterosexual family, the court would still prefer the more 'normal' family as being more conducive to the child's welfare. However this argument, on its own, is very unlikely to succeed now.[142] In *Salgueiro Da Siva Mouta v Portugal*[143] the ECtHR upheld a claim by a homosexual father under Article 14 ECHR, read with Article 8. He argued that the mother had been given custody of his daughter solely on the ground of his sexual orientation. The Portuguese court had suggested that the father's sexuality presented 'an abnormality' and that the child should not have to grow up in an 'abnormal' situation (para 34). The ECtHR concluded that this showed that the father's sexuality had 'swayed the final decision in a decisive manner' (para 35). The requirement of proportionality between the means used and the aim of safeguarding the child's interests was therefore not satisfied (para 36). One commentator has remarked that this case 'makes it absolutely clear that the sexual orientation of one of the parties to the [contact or residence] proceeding, without more, can no longer be cited as a negative factor' (Wintemute 2000: 620).[144]

---

[138] [2006] EWHC 2 (Fam); [2006] 1 FCR 556.

[139] [2007] EWHC 1952 (Fam); [2008] 1 FLR 1015.

[140] [2006] UKHL 43; [2006] 2 FLR 629.

[141] In *R v E and F (Female Parents: Known Father)* [2010] EWHC 417 (Fam); [2010] 2 FLR 383 the court was faced with a dispute between parents who were both in same-sex relationships. The donor father and his partner were involved in the child's life before they fell out with the biological mother and her partner. He sought a shared residence order but his application was dismissed. The court awarded a joint residence order to the mother and her partner, the adults with whom the child had his home. See also *G v F (Contact and Shared Residence: Applications for Leave)* [1998] 2 FLR 799, where the dispute was between lesbian former partners.

[142] But the ECtHR has held that a refusal to authorise adoption by a homosexual man did not infringe the principle of proportionality, taking into account the child's welfare and the state's margin of appreciation. The court observed that the scientific community was divided over the consequences for children of being adopted by one or more homosexual parents. See *Frette v France* [2003] 2 FLR 9.

[143] (2001) 31 EHRR 47.

[144] See also Marshall (2003: 831–33).

In any event, the cases discussed above are evidence of acceptance of same-sex relationships and the parenting of children within them. English courts are beginning to accept far greater diversity generally when it comes to family forms. In *Singh v Entry Clearance Officer New Delhi*[145] the court commented at length on the nature of family relationships in the context of the ECHR, noting a growth in diversity and multiculturalism, as well as the increase in cohabitation.

The judge went on:

> [62] … [T]here has been a sea-change in society's attitudes towards same-sex unions. Within my professional lifetime we have moved from treating such relationships as perversions to be stamped out … . to a ready acknowledgement that they are entitled not merely to respect but also, in principle, to equal protection under the law: see *Ghaidan v Godin-Mendoza* … [2004] 2 FCR 481 … .

> [63] The result of all this is that in our multi-cultural and pluralistic society the family takes many forms. Indeed in contemporary Britain the family takes an almost infinite variety of forms. Many marry according to the rites of non-Christian faiths. There may be one, two, three or even more generations living together under the same roof. Some people choose to live on their own. People live together as couples, married or not, and with partners who may not always be of the opposite sex. Children live in households where their parents may be married or unmarried. They may be the children of polygamous marriages. They may be brought up by a single parent. Their parents may or may not be their natural parents. Their siblings may be only half-siblings or step-siblings. Some children are brought up by two parents of the same sex. Some children are conceived by artificial donor insemination. Some are the result of surrogacy arrangements. The fact is that many adults and children, whether through choice or circumstance, live in families more or less removed from what until comparatively recently would have been recognised as the typical nuclear family.

> [64] Many of these changes have given rise to profound misgivings in some quarters … . All of those views are entitled to the greatest respect but it is not for a judge to choose between them. The days are past when the business of the judges was the enforcement of morals or religious belief … .

> [65] The law, it seems to me, must adapt itself to these realities … .

The court in this case declared itself unwilling to be influenced by the moral scruples of some groups in society and this judgment is consistent with the policy adopted by the legislature. The Civil Partnership Act 2004[146] creates an institution akin to same-sex marriage and there are statutory provisions catering for same-sex parents. The Adoption and Children Act 2002 makes provision for adoption of unrelated children by same-sex couples[147] as well as adoption by one partner of the other's child.[148] The Human Fertilisation and Embryology Act 2008 and the Children Act 1989 as amended now make provision for the female partners of biological mothers to have the status of parenthood and to have

---

[145] [2004] EWCA Civ 1075; [2004] 3 FCR 72. See also *JM v United Kingdom* [2011] 1 FLR 491.
[146] The refusal to extend marriage to same-sex couples might, however, seen as manifesting a preference for heterosexuality. See Crompton (2004).
[147] S 50, s 51 (2) and s 144(7).
[148] Ss 51(2) and 144(7).

parental responsibility.[149] Same-sex couples, whether civil partners or not, can apply for a parental order in surrogacy cases.[150]

Baroness Hale, reviewing the evolution of the law in relation to homosexual rights, comments that 'we have already reached the stage of recognising same sex relationships for what many will think the most important purpose of regulating family relationships: providing for the care and upbringing of the next generation' (Hale 2004: 134).

VII. SHARED RESIDENCE

In Chapter 9 above we referred to the efforts of fathers' rights groups to have the law changed to introduce a presumption of shared parenting. The government rejected this proposal (DCA, DfES and DTI 2004). However, the courts are becoming increasingly willing to make shared residence orders when parents separate.[151] These orders are not necessarily confined to cases where children spend equal amounts of time with each parent, but they are meant to be used in cases where the children spend substantial periods of time with each.

In the past, the courts tended to shy away from shared residence orders[152] as being contrary to the well-being of children.[153] They conceded that section 11(4) of the Children Act envisaged shared residence orders but maintained a circumspect attitude towards granting them and indicated that they would be inappropriate in most cases.[154] It appears that this view has changed but it is not clear how common shared residence orders are. Hunt and Macleod report that, in their sample, shared residence orders were a 'rarity', something they found surprising in view of the opinion voiced by judges, Cafcass officers and solicitors that these orders were becoming more common (Hunt and Macleod 2008: 28). Thorpe LJ recently noted that 'the recent national survey, "Understanding Society", puts the proportion of equal shared care at 3.1% of the total'.[155]

In *D v D*[156] the court indicated that shared residence would be appropriate provided it reflected the 'reality of [the] children's lives'; this would be sufficient benefit to justify an order (para 34). This shift in emphasis was highlighted by the Court of Appeal in *Re A (Children) (Shared Residence)*:

---

[149] See ss 43–4 Human Fertilisation and Embryology Act 2008. Women in lesbian relationships whose partners conceive children by means of assisted reproduction as a result of treatment under licence are parents of the child provided the agreed female parenthood conditions are met. Civil partners gain the status of parents under s 42 Human Fertilisation and Embryology Act unless they do not consent to the treatment afforded their partners. Civil partners in assisted reproduction cases can acquire parental responsibility in terms of s 2(1A) Children Act 1989. Women in same-sex relationships who are not civil partners can acquire parental responsibility in assisted reproduction cases under s 4ZA Children Act (read with s 2A Children Act 1989). A civil partner of a child's mother in cases not governed by the assisted reproduction provisions can acquire parental responsibility under s 4A Children Act 1989. See Chapter 4 above.

[150] S 54 Human Fertilisation and Embryology Act 2008.

[151] See further Harris and George (2010).

[152] The term 'joint residence' should be used only when the order is made in respect of two people living together, such as a mother and stepfather (*Re K (Shared Residence Order* [2008] EWCA civ 526; [2008] 2 FLR 380 para 15).

[153] See *Riley v Riley* [1986] 2 FLR 429. Compare *J v J (A Minor) (Joint Care and Control)* [1991] 2 FLR 385.

[154] See *Re H (A Minor) (Shared Residence)* [1994] 1 FLR 717; *A v A (Minors) (Shared Residence Order)* [1994] 1 FLR 669 at 672–73, 677.

[155] *MK v CK* [2011] EWCA Civ 793, para 59.

[156] *D v D (Shared Residence Order)* [2001] 1 FLR 495. See para 41.

[10] As I have indicated from the outset, I am very doubtful as to whether the judge in the county court has sufficiently reflected in his approach the shift of emphasis signalled by the decision of this court in *Re D*. There is no doubt at all that there is a need for courts of trial to recognise that there may well be cases that are better suited by a joint residence order than by residence orders to one parent alone. Where there is a proximity of homes and a relatively fluid passage of the children between those two homes, the judicial convention that the welfare of children demanded a choice between one parent or the other as a guardian of the residence order to promote the welfare of the children no longer runs as it used to run. I am in no doubt at all that orders made in the courts of trial should above all reflect the realities.[157]

In *Re F (Shared Residence Order)*[158] Wilson J made it clear that an equal division of time is not necessary: 'Any lingering idea that a shared residence order is apt only where, for example, the children will be alternating between the two homes evenly, say week by week or fortnight by fortnight, is erroneous' (para 34). In addition, the element of proximity was abandoned. Thorpe LJ said:

[21] ... The fact that the parents' homes are separated by a considerable distance does not preclude the possibility that the children's year will be divided between the homes of the two separated parents in such a way as to validate the making of a shared residence order ... . Of course the residence order reflects just that—the place of the children's residence. It is not intended to deal with issues of parental status.[159]

Yet Wilson J pointed to the symbolic significance of a shared residence order:

[32] Speaking for myself, I make no bones about it; to make a shared residence order to reflect the arrangements here chosen by the judge is to choose one label rather than another. Her chosen arrangements for the division of the girls' time could also have been reflected in orders for sole residence to the mother and generous defined contact with the father. But labels can be very important.[160]

And in *A v A (Shared Residence)*[161] Wall J seemed to regard the symbolic function of a shared residence order as important. Making an order in a case involving considerable conflict[162] between the parents, he said:

[124] If these parents were capable of working in harmony, and there were no difficulties about the exercise of shared parental responsibility, I would have ... made no order as to residence ... . Here the parents are not, alas, capable of working in harmony. There must, accordingly, be an order. That order, in my judgment, requires the court not only to reflect the reality that the children are dividing their lives equally between their parents, but also to reflect the fact that

---

[157] [2002] EWCA Civ 1343; [2003] 3 FCR 656.

[158] [2003] EWCA Civ 592; [2003] 2 FLR 397. See also *Re K(Shared Residence Order)* [2008] EWCA Civ 526; [2008] 2 FLR 380.

[159] In *Re G (Residence: Same-Sex Partner)* [2005] EWCA Civ 462; [2005] 2 FLR 957, the court made an order for shared residence in order to confer parental responsibility on the mother's female partner. But see now ss 42–44 Human Fertilisation and Embryology Act 2008; ss 2A, 2(1A), 4A and 4ZA Children Act 1989.

[160] The symbolic impact of an order is referred to also in guidance to the Children Act 1989 (DoH 1991c: para 2.28).

[161] [2004] EWHC Fam 142; [2004] 1 FLR 1195. However, in *Re B (Leave to Remove)* [2006] EWHC 1783 (Fam); [2007] 1 FLR 333, the court refused to make a shared residence order because of the level of conflict between the parents: 'The prospect of this working when the parties cannot talk to each other is very low indeed' (para 170).

[162] Compare *Re O (Contact: Withdrawal of Application)* [2003] EWHC Fam 3031; [2004] 1 FLR 1258, para 8.

the parents are equal in the eyes of the law, and have equal duties and responsibilities towards their children.[163]

In *Re K (Shared Residence Order)*[164] the court cautioned that a shared residence order is sometimes inappropriate but it also subscribed to the notion that a shared residence order provides affirmation of the value of both parents:

> [21] I accept that, although of course a shared residence order gives to one parent no greater control over the child's life than it gives to the other, it is sometimes viewed by a parent intent upon interfering with, or disrupting, the other parent's role in the management of the child's life, as a useful vehicle by which to do so; and I have experience of cases in which parents, although allowed to have substantial contact with the child, are nevertheless rightly refused shared residence on the basis that their motivation seems to be to strike at the other parent's role in the management of the child's life. In any application for an order for shared residence, the court should, in my view, be alert to discern such malign motivation ... . It is, so I consider, profoundly regrettable that the father has been unable to date to give the mother due credit for her achievements ... . But his relative blindness to the mother's achievements is in my view far too light a counterweight to the considerations which militate [*sic*] in favour of placing upon G a stamp that he has two parents of equal importance in the overall direction of his life, notwithstanding that the division of his time between the two homes will remain slightly unequal.

Mostyn J went even further in *Re AR (A Child: Relocation)*:[165]

> [52] I am clearly of the view that a joint or shared residence order should be made. Indeed, such an order is nowadays the rule rather than the exception even where the quantum of care undertaken by each parent is decidedly unequal. There is very good reason why such orders should be normative for they avoid the psychological baggage of right, power and control that attends a sole residence order.

This radical pronouncement was disapproved of by Black LJ in *T v T*:[166]

> 26. In *Re AR (A Child: Relocation)* ..., Mostyn J said that a joint or shared residence order 'is nowadays the rule rather than the exception even where the quantum of care undertaken by each parent is decidedly unequal'. That, in my view, is to go too far. Whether or not a joint or shared residence order is granted depends upon a determination of what is in the best interests of the child in the light of all the factors in the individual case. However, it has certainly been established that it is not a pre-requisite for a shared residence order that the periods of time spent with each adult should be equal and nor is it necessary that there should be co-operation and goodwill between them and shared residence orders have been made in cases where there is hostility.

She went on to warn that shared residence orders can have disadvantages:

> 27. What is profoundly disappointing is to see how, in practice, instead of bringing greater benefits for children, shared/joint residence can simply serve as a further battlefield for the adults in the children's lives so that even when the practicalities of how the child's time should

---

[163] Compare *Re M (Children) (Residence Order)* [2004] All ER (D) 44.
[164] [2008] EWCA Civ 526; [2008] 2 FLR 380.
[165] [2010] EWHC 1346 (Fam); [2010] 3 FCR 131.
[166] [2010] EWCA Civ 1366.

be split are agreed or determined by the court, they continue to fight on over what label is to be put on the arrangement. This can never have been intended when shared/joint residence orders were commended by the courts as a useful tool.

The mother in this case was in a civil partnership. The relationship between the two women and the father of the child deteriorated and a shared residence order was made in favour of the mother and father, with the children living primarily with the mother and her partner. The mother's partner was given parental responsibility, but her application for a residence order jointly with the mother was refused. On appeal, it was argued that in the event of the death of the mother, the father would have control. The father agreed that the mother's partner should also have a residence order in her favour. This plan was endorsed by the judge who made an residence order in favour of the father, the mother and her partner. However, she warned that 'it cannot be anticipated that considerations relating to what may happen in the aftermath of an untimely death will regularly tip the balance in favour of a joint residence order' (para 47).

While the court in *T v T* was concerned about a practical matter, the question that is raised by some of the other cases is the extent to which shared residence orders might be being used by the courts not so much because they benefit children but because they benefit parents and because they 'radiate'[167] the message of co-operation and shared parenting. Certainly some of the judges in Hunt and Macleod's study used shared residence orders to 'send a message' (Hunt and Macleod 2008: 29). Others, however, did not like them and saw applications as a demand for the rights of the parent rather than as an attempt to do what is best for the children (ibid: 30).

Shared residence orders are, as we have seen, not confined to cases where the parents share childcare more or less equally. But where care is actually shared this way, there are also potential problems. Most of those professionals interviewed by Hunt and Macleod had reservations. For example, one solicitor said:

> Some parents come to me and say 'I want 50/50.' We have a lot of cases where they do that. That's where the problem lies, people have this perception that yes, you were living in the house with them and jointly parenting those children and that's all well and good. But you are no longer living in that house with them and the difficulty is that those children have to have a base, they have to have one place which they can call home … . I have dealt with cases where the parents have managed to work it out and they live sufficiently close to the school that they can have a situation whereby the child can stay a couple of nights a week at that parent's home, because they've got their own bedroom there and its all geared up, and then come home. So they have two bases. But that's very rare, and it's only situations where you have the parents who live in proximity, and usually where they get on. Where they're being amicable. Those cases are few and far between. (ibid: 31)

Bridge (1996: 22) asserts that the benefit of a shared residence order must surely be 'parental appeasement, the idea that the "other" parent who none the less cares for the children on a regular basis should not be left feeling he is the loser'. She argues that shared residence may simply be a 'symbolic resolution of parental conflict' (ibid: 13), affording comfort to parents but not necessarily serving the child's best interests:

> After all in any sharing agreement it is the child who has to move, often on a weekly basis,

---

[167] See Dewar (1998: 483).

pack and unpack, and have the wrong clothes in the wrong home at the wrong time. Possibly the only true shared arrangement which has a chance of enhancing the child's welfare is the 'bird's nest' scheme where the child remains in the home and the parents flit in and out on an alternate basis. (ibid: 17, footnote omitted)

Neale et al report findings from their empirical research that, to some extent, bear out Bridge's concerns:[168]

> Shared residence is ... not the same thing as shared parenting. Shared parenting does not require the children to have to spend an equal amount of time with each parent. Shared parenting is defined by degrees of emotional support and collaborative working, not by hours and days......
> So it is important that one does not, in policy terms, allow a slippage in terminology that makes it appear that only shared residence can achieve shared parenting ... .
> [A] regular routine for some [of the children in the authors' sample] meant they knew exactly what to expect but for others it meant an unbearable and inflexible regime. Some of the children relished the feeling of being loved by both parents and understood shared residence as a manifestation of this, but others felt that this was a terrible burden because they became responsible for the emotional well-being of both their parents. Finally, some children thought the arrangement was excellent because it was fair for their parents, but others thought it was dreadful because it was incredibly unfair on them ... .
> Our research suggests ... that solutions to these problems need to be based on a knowledge of the parties involved, rather than adherence to a single principle or rule (such as equality or equal shares). This is most definitely a situation where one size does not fit all.
>
> (Neale et al 2003: 904–05)

Neale et al found that shared care works best where the children's needs are prioritised, arrangements are flexible and the children feel at home in both households. Children, particularly pre-teens, could be 'very content' with shared residence (ibid: 908). But if parents refused to modify the arrangements, this could become an 'intolerable' situation for teenagers who wanted greater freedom from both parents (ibid: 906). The authors also point out that the assumption that shared residence promotes shared parenting is not always well founded: 'Parents who use their children as pawns or who treat them as matrimonial property when the children are 8 or 9, will not necessarily change when the children are 14 or even 18' (ibid: 908).

More recently Trinder, reviewing the research into shared residence, particularly in Australia, concluded:

> What matters more is the quality of parenting and the ability of parents to focus on their children's needs, regardless of the quantity of the child's time that they secure. However, by sending policy messages that shared care is the best option, what has occurred is a shared care paradox where the greatest expansion of shared care has been in precisely those families where shared care is least likely to work and most likely to cause most problems for children. The evidence is particularly strong that rigid shared care arrangements which are most likely to result from court orders may be strongly appreciated by fathers but are not liked by children and may do harm. Contrary to the hopes of some, it would seem that shared care arrangements in high conflict cases are not transformative and instead may merely increase and perpetuate damaging conflict. (Trinder 2010: 495)

---

[168] See also for discussion of other studies, Hunt et al (2009). See also Hunt and Macleod (2008: 29–32).

Shared residence, then, may be used symbolically and bear little relation to the realities of the allocation of responsibility for childcare. Or the order may in some cases reflect the reality of shared care, in which case some children may find the arrangement burdensome. As one Cafcass officer interviewed in Hunt and Macleod's study said: 'I meet lots and lots of fathers who are very keen on the idea of shared care. I meet very few children who are' (Hunt and Macleod 2008: 31).[169]

VIII. CONTACT

When a court makes a sole residence order it may also need to make a contact order in favour of the non-resident parent. A contact order is defined as 'an order requiring the person with whom a child lives, or is to live, to allow the child to visit or stay with the person named in the order, or for that person and the child otherwise to have contact with each other'.[170] The provision is therefore wide enough to encompass visits, staying contact or, where those direct forms of contact are thought inappropriate, telephone calls, letters, cards and gifts. Direct contact which is supervised is also a possibility. In practice, the courts tend to order direct contact in the majority of cases.

In its strict sense supervised contact entails high-vigilance monitoring at a specialist contact centre. Supported contact can also take place at a contact centre or the term might refer to contact that takes place after a handover at a centre (Perry and Rainey 2007: 26). Either way, there is no close monitoring of the interaction between parent and child. There is also a form of informal supervision where the supervision is undertaken by family member or friends.

While supervised contact is used as an interim measure in cases where there are anxieties about the contact parent's behaviour (ibid: 36), courts rarely make such orders as final orders (ibid: 29). Nor do they tend to make final orders for indirect contact. Interim orders are made in 'extreme' circumstances such as cases where the non-resident parent is mentally ill, in prison for a violent offence or the child is vehemently opposed to contact (ibid: 37). The only final orders for indirect contact in their sample were, again, extreme cases where, for instance, the father was in prison and presented a risk to the child and where there were genuine fears of abduction (ibid: 38).

Child Welfare Knowledge

Child welfare knowledge relating to contact was discussed in more detail in Chapter 9 above. It is still the case that, as Maidment (1984: 253) noted, many professionals agree that 'the closer and more normal [the] relationship can be, for example through staying contact, the better it is for the child'.[171] In *Surviving the Breakup*, Wallerstein and Kelly clearly subscribed to this view, commenting that: 'Successful outcome at all ages, which we have equated with good ego functioning, adequate or high self-esteem and no depres-

---

[169] See, for a critique of Australia's legislation which has been interpreted as creating a presumption in favour of shared parenting, Chisholm (2009).

[170] S 8(1).

[171] See further, Chapter 9 above.

sion, reflected a stable, close relationship with the custodial parent and the non-custodial parent' (Wallerstein and Kelly 1980: 215).

They were of the opinion that irregular or infrequent contact damages children and that children are best served by an arrangement that provides them with the supports they would enjoy in an intact family. Co-operation between the parents was found to be crucial to their children's well-being. Richards (1982: 143) pointed to other benefits thought to result from the preservation of ties with both parents: children gain a wider variety of experience and are not deprived of the role model important to the development of gender identity. Freeman (1983: 216) referred to yet another expected advantage, suggesting that a father who has contact with his child is more likely to be willing to support that child financially. *The Exeter Family Study* (Cockett and Tripp 1994, 1996: 62–63) asserted that one of the ways to reduce the adverse outcomes for children whose parents part is to facilitate contact, but only if the child desires it. In an influential report presented to the court in *Re L, M, V and H*,[172] Sturge and Glaser (2000: 3) described the benefits of contact as meeting a number of the needs of the child. These include the need for:

- warmth, approval, feeling unique and special to a parent;
- extending experiences and developing (or maintaining) meaningful relationships;
- information and knowledge;
- reparation of distorted relationships or perceptions.

Not all the available research points to a need for contact between children and non-resident parents, however. Maclean and Eekelaar note that: 'What has not been established is whether a child whose separated parents behave gently and reasonably to her and to one another, but who sees the outside parent rarely or never, somehow does "less well" than a child of similar parents who sees the outside parent often' (Maclean and Eekelaar 1997: 55).

Moreover, Sturge and Glaser advert to a number of possible disadvantages of contact and to the risks associated with it. They mention, for instance, the potential for an escalation of conflict, divided loyalties and the undermining of children's stability and emotional well-being (Sturge and Glaser 2000: 3).

Hunt, in a comprehensive review of research into contact, observes that the evidence of links between contact and children's well-being is contradictory (Hunt 2003: 7). In particular, she points out that most studies show no relationship between frequency of contact and children's well-being (ibid: 8). Other factors might be more important. These include the nature of the arrangements; whether the contact is regular; whether there is a good relationship between the contact parent and the child; the financial position of the resident family; and the degree to which the child is caught up in conflict between the parents (ibid: 8 and 13).[173] Hunt concludes:

> The question of whether contact itself is of value would seem increasingly to be fairly meaningless.
>
> The key questions to address would seem to be what kind of contact, in what circumstances, is good for children and in what ways? What are the disadvantages of contact for children? How do these balance out? Where there is conflict between parents, what form of contact arrangement is least detrimental? (ibid: 66)

---

[172] [2002] 2 FLR 334.
[173] See also Maclean and Eekelaar (1997: 53–57).

Maclean and Eekelaar suggest that the priority accorded to contact is based less on empirical evidence of its beneficial effects on children than on a belief that 'it is wrong to deny children the opportunity to develop a relationship they might possibly value and also wrong to deny the same opportunity to a parent who wanted it' (Maclean and Eekelaar 1997: 148).[174]

The Courts and Contact

As we saw in Chapter 9 above, the attitude of the courts to contact is consistent with the view that contact with their non-resident parents is beneficial, or at least potentially valuable, for children generally. By the early 1970s, the judiciary was endorsing the 'immense value'[175] of contact to children and in *M v M (Child: Access)*,[176] with a rhetorical flourish, Wrangham J declared it to be a right of the child. Subsequent judgments have tended to avoid the language of rights[177] but have instead articulated a 'very strong presumption in favour of maintaining contact between a child and both parents'.[178] Balcombe LJ stated in *Re H (Minors) (Access)*[179] that the court should ask the question: 'Are there any cogent reasons why this father should be denied access to his children; or putting it another way: are there any cogent reasons why these two children should be denied the opportunity of access to their natural father?' (152).

There is no need to show any positive advantage to contact; this is presumed to exist, although in *Re M (Contact: Welfare Test)*[180] the court proposed a balancing exercise relying on the welfare checklist. Wilson J said:

> I personally find it helpful to cast the principles into the framework of the checklist of considerations set out in s 1(3) of the Children Act 1989 and to ask whether the fundamental emotional need of every child to have an enduring relationship with both his parents (s 1(3)(b)) is outweighed by the depth of harm which, in the light, inter alia, of his wishes and feelings (s 1(3) (a)), this child would be at risk of suffering (s 1(3)(e)) by virtue of a contact order. (278–79)

However this approach was not followed[181] and later decisions reiterated the presumption. It was said in *Re O*, for instance, that it is 'almost always' in the interests of the child to have contact with the non-resident parent.[182]

As we saw in Chapter 9, the terminology appears to have changed again but the view articulated in *Re O* persists. In *Re L*[183] Thorpe LJ declared that the existence of a presumption might 'inhibit or distort the rigorous search for the welfare solution' and that a

[174] See further Chapter 9 above; Bailey-Harris et al (1998: 34–35, 41–44); Kaganas (1999).
[175] *M v M (Child: Access)* [1973] 2 All ER 81, 85.
[176] [1973] 2 All ER 81, 85. See also *Re W (A Minor) (Contact)* [1994] 2 FLR 441, 447.
[177] See *Re L (Contact: Domestic Violence); Re V (Contact: Domestic Violence); Re M (Contact: Domestic Violence); Re H (Contact: Domestic Violence)* [2002] 2 FLR 334, 359ff. But see, for example, *V v V (Contact: Implacable Hostility)* [2004] EWHC Fam 1215; [2004] 2 FLR 851, para 47.
[178] *Re M (Contact: Welfare Test)* [1995] 1 FLR 274, 281.
[179] [1992] 1 FLR 148.
[180] [1995] 1 FLR 274.
[181] Except, some years later, in relation to domestic violence and, possibly, other cases involving severe parental deficits. See *Re L (Contact: Domestic Violence); Re V (Contact: Domestic Violence); Re M (Contact: Domestic Violence); Re H (Contact: Domestic Violence)* [2002] 2 FLR 334. See further below pp 484–85.
[182] *Re O (Contact: Imposition of Conditions)* [1995] 2 FLR 124, 128.
[183] *Re L (Contact: Domestic Violence); Re V (Contact: Domestic Violence); Re M (Contact: Domestic Violence); Re H (Contact: Domestic Violence)* [2002] 2 FLR 334, 364.

presumption might be too easy a solution in cases where the decision-maker is unsure what to do. Instead, he said, the word 'assumption' was preferable. He did, however, refer to the 'universal judicial recognition of the importance of contact to a child's development' (364). And Butler-Sloss P in turn endorsed the 'principles' set out in *Re O* (343). These pronouncements, together with the fact that the court required the application of the welfare checklist, as suggested in *Re M*, only in cases where there is evidence sufficient to 'offset' (367, 371) the assumption,[184] suggests that the change in terminology is of little practical significance. This view is borne out by an examination of the words used by a judge in a subsequent case. In *V v V (Contact: Implacable Hostility)*[185] Bracewell J said: 'It is for the mother to establish by credible evidence any basis for denying or restricting contact.'

Not only is contact deemed to be beneficial for children, it is assumed that to deny contact would be to jeopardise the child's welfare.[186] Hence, in *Re F (Minors) (Contact: Mother's Anxiety)*[187] the court referred to 'the risk, well documented by medical and legal literature and cases, that the children could be damaged by not having the right to know their own father'. That this harm might be counterbalanced by other harms which could arise if contact were ordered is not easy to establish.[188] The Court of Appeal in *Re O*[189] indicated that courts should 'not at all readily' accept that the child's welfare might be injured by direct contact and that the likelihood of short-term problems should not be given excessive weight.

> **Q** Do you think that assumptions in favour of contact with non-resident parents, developed in the context of non-resident fathers' claims, can be generalised to same-sex parents? Is there something about the biological relationship between fathers and children that may underlie some of the strength of the assumption? Are there other factors related to the sex of the parents and the 'politics' of motherhood and fatherhood that may be important? See Chapter 9 above. Can you think of any situations in which it might be better for a child not to have contact with a non-resident parent?

The strength of the presumption/assumption in favour of contact has grown over the last two decades[190] and, with the advent of the Human Rights Act 1998, it has been considered necessary to strengthen the law supporting contact even further.[191] A useful survey of the

---

[184] Butler-Sloss P restricted its application to cases involving domestic violence. See pp 342–43.

[185] [2004] EWHC Fam 1215; [2004] 2 FLR 851, para 47. See also *Re O (Contact: Withdrawal of Application)* [2003] EWHC Fam 3031; [2004] 1 FLR 1258, para 4.

[186] It has been argued that conflict and denial of contact have been constructed as the primary risks to children in the context of divorce; other risks have been largely discounted (Kaganas 1999).

[187] [1993] 2 FLR 830, 834.

[188] For an extreme example of the court's concern to facilitate contact, see *Re A (Contact: Witness Protection Scheme)* [2005] EWHC 2189 (Fam); [2006] 2 FLR 551. The court was willing to allow indirect video contact despite the risks to the mother and child. These risks might be alleviated, the judge said, by means of a time delay in the video link as well as electronically altering the child's voice to prevent the father or his relatives from tracking the child and the mother down.

[189] *Re O (Contact: Imposition of Condition)* [1995] 2 FLR 124, 129.

[190] Compare Weyland (1992) with Weyland (1995). Of course, the existence of a contact order does not guarantee that contact will take place. Often, either fathers cease maintaining contact for various reasons or mothers will not permit it to take place. While courts may threaten mothers with imprisonment or the loss of their status as resident parents, fathers still seem to feel that mothers have the upper hand (Simpson et al 1995: 34, 69). See also Geldof (2003); Kaganas (2006); Chapter 9.

[191] See *Re D (Intractable Contact Dispute: Publicity* [2004] EWHC Fam 727; [2004] 1 FLR 1226, paras 35ff.

relevant law under the ECHR is provided by Munby J in *Re D (Intractable Contact Dispute: Publicity)*:[192]

[26] ... It suffices for present purposes if I merely extract a few of the most important points that emerge from the authorities. The first is the principle, long recognised, that, as it was put in Kosmopoulou v Greece [2004] 1 FLR 800 at para [47]:

> ... the mutual enjoyment by parent and child of each other's company constitutes a fundamental element of family life, even if the relationship between the parents has broken down, and domestic measures hindering such enjoyment amount to an interference with the right protected by Art 8 of the Convention.

[27] The second is the principle, also long recognised and most recently stated in *Hoppe v Germany* [2003] 1 FLR 384 at para [54], that, '... in cases concerning a person's relationship with his or her child, there is a duty to exercise exceptional diligence in view of the risk that the passage of time may result in a de facto determination of the matter' ... .[193]

[28] The third is the principle that in private law cases, just as much as in public law cases, Art 8 includes what was described in *Hokkanen v Finland* [1996] 1 FLR 289 at para [55] as: '... a right for the parent to have measures taken with a view to his or her being reunited with the child and an obligation for the national authorities to take such action.'

The court has repeatedly stressed that, as part of their 'obligation ... to take measures to facilitate contact by a non-custodial parent', national authorities 'must do their utmost to facilitate' co-operation between the parents: see *Hokkanen v Finland* at para 58 ... .[194]

[29] The fourth is the general principle enunciated in *Hornsby v Greece* (1997) 24 EHRR 250 ...: '... [T]he right to a court as guaranteed by Art 6 also protects the implementation of final, binding judicial decisions ... . Accordingly, the execution of a judicial decision cannot be unduly delayed.'

[30] These positive obligations extend in principle to the taking of coercive measures not merely against the recalcitrant parent but even against the children ... .

The court [said] in *Hansen v Turkey* [2004] 1 FLR 142 at para [106]: 'Although measures against the children obliging them to reunite with one or other parent are not desirable in this sensitive area, such action must not be ruled out in the event of non-compliance or unlawful behaviour by the parent with whom the children live.'

[31] ... This was elaborated in *Kosmopoulou v Greece* [2004] 1 FLR 800 at para [45]:

> the national authorities' obligation to take measures to facilitate reunion is not absolute, since the reunion of a parent with children who have lived for some time with the other parent may not be able to take place immediately and may require preparatory measures to be taken ... . Whilst national authorities must do their utmost to facilitate ... co-operation, any obligation to apply coercion in this area must be limited since the interests as well as the rights and freedoms of all concerned must be taken into account, and more particularly the best interests of the child and his or her rights under Art 8 of the Convention. Where contact with the parent might appear to threaten those interests or interfere with those rights, it is for the national authorities to strike a fair balance between them.

[32] The test was set out in *Sylvester v Austria* ... [2003] 2 FLR 210 at paras 59–60:

---

[192] [2004] EWHC Fam 727; [2004] 1 FLR 1226.

[193] Munby J also cited, on this point, *Glaser v United Kingdom* [2001] 1 FLR 153, para 93; *Sylvester v Austria* [2003] 2 FLR 210, para 69. See also *Adam v Germany* [2009] 1 FLR 560.

[194] Other cases cited by Munby J on this point included *Glaser v United Kingdom* [2001] 1 FLR 153, para 66; *Hansen v Turkey* [2004] 1 FLR 142, para 98; *Kosmopoulou v Greece* [2004] 1 FLR 800, para 45.

In cases concerning the enforcement of decisions in the realm of family law, the court has repeatedly found that what is decisive is whether the national authorities have taken all the necessary steps to facilitate execution as can reasonably be demanded in the special circumstances of each case. In examining whether non-enforcement of a court order amounted to a lack of respect for the applicant's family life the court must strike a fair balance between the interests of all persons concerned and the general interests in ensuring respect for the rule of law ... .[195]

[35] Not least in the light of the Strasbourg jurisprudence there is no room for complacency about the way in which we handle these cases.

The Approach of the Courts—A Research Study

Despite the clear preference for supporting contact in both domestic and European law, fathers' rights campaigners routinely allege that the courts are corrupt and biased against fathers. These claims, and more specifically the accusation that the courts are allowing resident mothers to flout contact orders with impunity, are regarded as a potential threat to the maintenance of public confidence in the system.[196] A study was commissioned to investigate these allegations (Hunt and Macleod 2008: 3). Hunt and Macleod, using a sample of cases initiated in 2004, examined decision-making in contact cases in the context of 'claims that non-resident parents do not get a fair deal from the family courts in that they may get little or no contact for no good reason' (ibid: 239). They reported that only a small proportion of non-resident parents (10%) might be seen as getting a 'poor deal', but that this tended only to relate to the amount of contact, rather than whether they had contact at all. In addition, unfairness to a parent did not mean unfairness to the child; often it was the child's objections that led to the decision (ibid: 246). Also, where the non-resident parent did not get the order applied for, this was often because he did not co-operate with the court process (ibid: 247).

Far from uncovering bias against fathers (ibid: 253), Hunt and Macleod found that 'the court starts from the position that contact is generally regarded as being in the interests of children and unless there are very good reasons to the contrary, is likely to be ordered at the end of the day' (ibid: 251). Courts operate a '*de facto* presumption' (ibid: 189) and the practitioners interviewed identified only domestic violence or child abuse as factors that might displace it (ibid: 191). Even in those cases the court might order contact if it considered that the risks might be managed (ibid: 192).

The research reveals that persuasion and coercion appeared to be used even in cases where mothers' refusal to co-operate stemmed from justifiable fears. Serious welfare concerns, such as substance abuse, mental illness, child abuse and domestic violence were raised in nearly two-thirds of the cases analysed. Almost half of all the cases involved allegations of domestic violence and in some instances the resident parent raised several welfare issues (ibid: 9).[197] In most of the cases involving allegations of domestic violence, these allegations were admitted, proved or supported by evidence (ibid: 84). Nevertheless 70% of the cases in the sample ended with a contact order (ibid: 11). Most dispositions

---

[195] See also *Maire v Portugal* [2004] 2 FLR 653, paras 70–71.

[196] See, eg, *V v V (Contact: Implacable Hostility)* [2004] EWHC 1215 (Fam); [2004] 2 FLR 851 para 4; *Re D (Intractable Contact Dispute: Publicity)* [2004] EWHC Fam 727; [2004] 1 FLR 1226, para 4.

[197] See also Perry and Rainey (2007). See also House of Common Justice Committee (2011: para 94) which noted that in only 15% of cases was a protective injunction in place.

were for face-to-face contact and half of those allowed staying contact. While some applications were withdrawn, in only one case out of 286 was there an order for no contact (ibid: 13).[198] Of the cases where at least one serious welfare concern was raised, 60% ended with staying or unsupervised visiting contact (ibid: 16). Neither domestic violence nor the objections of children, especially if young, were necessarily considered an obstacle.[199] The courts were seen to 'bend over backwards to try and assist and accommodate fathers' even if violent.[200] Cafcass officers[201] interviewed were concerned that:

> the pro-contact approach [was] marginalising serious welfare issues; losing the focus on the child;[202] downplaying children's clearly expressed and firmly held views; and damaging children through an unwillingness to call a stop to proceedings which are not getting anywhere but are exposing them to prolonged conflict and possibly jeopardising their relationship with their main carer. (Hunt and Macleod 2008: 191)

Where mothers resisted contact, enforcement proceedings appear to have led to its resumption and this was attributed by the researchers, in some cases, to threats of a penal notice[203] or a transfer of residence.[204] However, the study shows that a high proportion of cases were resolved by means of consent orders.[205] The extent to which some of the consent orders reflected genuine agreement must be open to question[206] given that resident parents were put under considerable pressure throughout the legal process. Cafcass worked to get contact started (ibid: 94). Solicitors would try to get the parties to agree and would tell clients that the courts would order contact unless there was good reason not to do so (ibid: 94, 171, 175). Judges impressed on resident parents, even at the first appointment, that contact would be in the interests of the child (ibid: 95). They sought to persuade the resident mother that allowing contact would be 'the right thing to do'; [Y]ou're cajoling, you're persuading, sometimes you think you're more like a social worker than a judge' (ibid: 194). One of the judges interviewed said:

> I think we have a number of cases where a mother will come back to court and say, there's been a consent order, she's not abided by it and she's come back and say she was forced into agreeing it, whether it's by her lawyers, or she feels she was forced by the court to agree. Yes, that does happen. (ibid: 175)

Hunt and Macleod describe cases demonstrating considerable reluctance on the part of the

---

[198] See also 55.

[199] See 19. On the courts' persistence in seeking to overcome the objections of a child, see 199–210.

[200] Solicitor interviewed by Hunt and Macleod (2008: 190). For the comments of professionals, see 190–91.

[201] Cafcass officers appear unlikely to recommend no contact; it seems that within the service there is a tendency to favour contact, in some cases apparently because officers think the court will order it anyway. According to an inspection report by HMICA, the presumption in favour of contact was evident in the practice of Cafcass officers. Cafcass officers interviewed said the presumption was hard to challenge and that they worked on the assumption that courts would order contact (HMICA 2005: para 3.9). Cafcass officers did not sufficiently understand the nature of domestic abuse and their practices put mothers and children at risk (ibid: ch 3).

[202] See also Perry and Rainey (2007: 39).

[203] Although courts were reluctant to impose a penal notice. See Hunt and Macleod (2008: 138, 195–96).

[204] Hunt and Macleod (2008: 148ff, 195). Threats might be made by solicitors (ibid: 143), the courts or by Cafcass (ibid: 175).

[205] At least 85% of the orders made were by consent (p 12). Courts are now supposed to scrutinise consent orders. See Practice Direction: Revised Private Law Programme [2010] 2 FLR 717, para 5.3.

[206] See also Perry and Rainey (2007: 40).

courts and the professionals to concede that the goal of securing contact might not be achievable in some cases (ibid: 165):[207]

> [T]he process of reaching 'agreement' was often slow and fraught with difficulty as resident parents were encouraged, persuaded, pushed or forced into shifting their position. The impetus throughout from the court and Cafcass officers was to try to move contact on, sometimes in very inauspicious circumstances, and while the preferred approach was typically conciliatory a harsher line was sometimes evident when this failed to bring about the desired response.
>
> (ibid: 120)

Given the pressure to which resident mothers were subjected, and the circumstances in which contact was ordered, it might be questioned whether the orders made were always appropriate. Indeed Hunt and Macleod's findings suggest they sometimes were not; there were cases[208] in which the court declined to enforce orders in the context of serious welfare concerns or resistance from the children.

Yet the pressure to ensure that non-resident parents are given contact continues. At the time of writing, there is a Private Member's Bill before parliament, the Children (Access to Parents) Bill 2010–11. This aims to introduce a presumption in favour of contact. [209]

The Checklist

Although the courts appear only to apply it when the assumption in favour of contact is offset,[210] the statute requires that the checklist be applied in all contested contact cases.[211] The focus here is on the factors that have been most prominent in the reported cases.

Child's Wishes and Feelings

Parents seeking contact, and particularly proponents of 'parental alienation syndrome' (PAS),[212] argue that in some cases, children's opposition to contact stems from the influence of their resident parent. The term PAS refers to the situation where a resident parent has influenced a child to the point where the child refuses contact with the other parent. However, PAS is not recognised as a disorder in the UK. Nevertheless, the court may refuse to give effect to children's wishes if these are considered to be the product of the influence of a hostile resident parent.[213] And in a recent case the court declared that the concept of alienation, which does not necessarily entail blaming the resident parent, is now 'mainstream'[214] among experts. This concept is described as follows, a description accepted by the court:

> There are children who show an extraordinary degree of animosity towards a parent with whom they once had a loving relationship. Most of these children will show some or all of [a cluster

---

[207] See, for the description of the cases, 160ff.

[208] Ibid: 71ff, 85–88. See also Rhoades (2002).

[209] See below.

[210] See *Re L (Contact: Domestic Violence); Re V (Contact: Domestic Violence); Re M (Contact: Domestic Violence); Re H (Contact: Domestic Violence)* [2002] 2 FLR 334.

[211] S 1(3) and (4) Children Act 1989.

[212] See, eg, Willbourne and Cull (1997: 807).

[213] See *Re M (Contact: Long Term Best Interests)* [2005] EWCA Civ 1090, [2006] 1 FLR 627.

[214] *Re S (Transfer of Residence)* [2011] 1 FLR 1789, para 46.

of psychological responses]. Within an individual child (and between children in the same family) the presence of the features can vary rapidly over time and place, but in their full manifestation are so surprising and unique as to be unforgettable. The proposed term 'Alienation' applies only to the cluster of psychological responses in the child with no need to presume a deliberate campaign of denigration by one parent. There is now research data supporting a multifactorial aetiology for 'Alienation' following parental separation, involving contributions from both parents and vulnerabilities within the child.[215]

How to deal with an alienated child is something that Bellamy J thought needed 'urgent research' (para 47). One way courts tend to deal with children's objections to contact is to minimise or dismiss them; since contact is assumed to be overwhelmingly beneficial for children, courts[216] are reluctant to allow a child's resistance to it to be decisive.[217] In *Re H (Minors) (Access)*[218] it was said that courts should not be unduly perturbed by the prospect of some distress being caused to children by contact. Balcombe LJ cited (at 151) with approval the judgment of Latey J in *M v M (Child) (Access)*:[219]

[W]here the parents have separated and one has the care of the child, access by the other often results in some upset to the child. Those upsets are usually minor and superficial. They are heavily outweighed by the long-term advantages to the child of keeping in touch with the parent concerned so that they do not become strangers, so that the child later in life does not resent the deprivation and turn against the parent who the child thinks, rightly or wrongly, has deprived him, and so that the deprived parent loses interest in the child and therefore does not make the material and emotional contribution to the child's development which that parent by its companionship and otherwise would make. (88)

So, courts do not always attach much weight to children's wishes, particularly if they are young. 'Courts are very persistent in trying to overcome a child's resistance where this is not seen to be well-founded', say Hunt and Macleod (2008: 199). Often a Cafcass officer will interview or observe the child to see whether the child, despite articulating objections to contact, would in fact be amenable to it or whether the child's concerns can be addressed. Where the child's resistance is more serious, the court may ask for a specialist assessment, there might be therapeutic intervention and indirect contact may be used. Where the resident parent is considered insufficiently supportive of contact, or is thought to be undermining it, threats and persuasion are employed. If none of these strategies work the child may be made a party. In some cases the courts will bow to the child's wishes (ibid).

In *Re S (Transfer of Residence)*[220] Bellamy J reviewed the measure that had been taken in the case before him in 'dealing with' an alienated child:

[49] One possibility that emerges from the research literature is that of transferring care of an alienated child from the resident parent to the non-resident parent. That is, ultimately, the step I decided to take in this case. In my judgment of 4 January I acknowledged the likely difficulties in implementing that order. Since January, three approaches to effecting transfer have been considered in this case: a 'stepping stone' approach involving a period in foster care en route

---

[215] Expert witness quoted by Bellamy J in *Re S (Transfer of Residence)* [2011] 1 FLR 1789, para 43.
[216] See also James et al (2003).
[217] See *M v M (Defined Contact Application)* [1998] 2 FLR 244.
[218] [1992] 1 FLR 148.
[219] [1973] 2 All ER 81.
[220] [2011] 1 FLR 1789.

to transfer of S into the care of his non-resident parent; a therapeutic approach; use of the Tipstaff.

In this case, all efforts to get the child to consent to contact or to engage with his father during contact sessions he was compelled to attend failed. The judge noted that neither interim care orders under section 37 of the Children Act nor therapy were 'one-size-fits-all' solutions (para 55). The use of a tipstaff to transport a *Gillick*-competent child[221] might engage Article 5 of the ECHR (paras 56–58). The court hearing a case involving an alienated child needs expert advice, said Bellamy J but in this case the advice to transfer residence had not had the desired result; the transfer had failed (paras 59–60). One thing that is noteworthy about this case is the extraordinary lengths, including putting the child in foster care, to which all the professionals, the local authrity and the court were prepared to go to in order to make contact work. Poceedings had been ongoing for 10 years and the child was now 12.[222]

Fortin et al found in their study that older children feel aggrieved at the way they are treated by the courts; fewer than a third of those surveyed said that the court had taken proper account of their views and half of those who were older children when their parents divorced said the court had not understood them. Even where a welfare report was prepared children's wishes often remained unknown as the children felt unable to say all that they wanted to (Fortin et al 2006: 220).

Perry and Rainey (2007: 39) suggest that in their efforts to secure the child's long-term welfare by ensuring that contact with the non-resident parent is maintained, courts are failing to pay sufficient attention to the child's short- and medium-term interests. However, long-term emotional injury caused by forcing children to see a parent will militate against contact. In *Re M (Contact: Welfare Test)*[223] the distress of the children, aged 8 and 9, at contact with their mother and their express wish not to see her was crucial to the decision to refuse an order.[224] In *Re S (Contact: Children's Views)*[225] the court refused to make a contact order in respect of a girl aged 16 and made orders for contact by negotiation and agreement in relation to her brothers, aged 14 and 12. These were not, in the end, children, said the court. They were teenagers and the two older ones were, in reality, young adults and should be treated as such; they could make decisions without being pressurised and the 12-year-old should be given some choice commensurate with his age. Young people, the court said, have to be brought up to 'respect the law' and so 'the law must respect them and their wishes, even to the extent of allowing them, as they occasionally do, to make mistakes'.[226] To make an order for contact contrary to their wishes would be counterproductive and the quality of the contact foisted upon them might be poor.[227]

In these cases, the children succeeded in getting their views heard. And while Hunt and Macleod report that children are put under pressure to agree to contact, they also report that direct contact was ordered in fewer than half of the cases in their sample where the child was refusing face to face contact (Hunt and Macleod 2008: 197). That

---

[221] See Chapter 11 below.

[222] The child did say, at a meeting with the father after his return to the mother's care, that he might agree to contact after his GCSEs (para 61).

[223] [1995] 1 FLR 274.

[224] See also *Re F (Minors) (Denial of Contact)* [1993] 2 FLR 677; *Re C (Contact: No Order for Contact)* [2000] 2 FLR 723.

[225] [2002] 1 FLR 1156.

[226] Ibid, 1171.

[227] Ibid, 1169.

children's wishes may be solicited and may have an impact is cause for concern for some; a senior judge has recently expressed the opinion extra-judicially that:

> **the ever increasing emphasis on the sacred cow of listening uncritically to the unfiltered views and wishes of children, including young children, is in serious danger, I think, of undermining the family court's authority and proper function which is to arrive at a decision which is overall, best for the child** ... .
>
> How often did we **used** to read in reports that children didn't want to choose between their parents? We largely ignore that now, I suggest, in favour of forcing children in every case and at every turn to express *'their wishes and feelings'*. Is this a good and child centred development or an uncritical following of fashion and fad, driven more by the ideas of the chattering classes than sound research and, dare I say it, common sense and the real experience of specialists? ...
>
> **If we ... too readily impose the decision on the child, surely we, all of us, are shirking our responsibility to a degree which is bordering on the abusive.** ...
>
> Children expect and are entitled to expect us to make these important decisions without overly and unnecessarily involving them in the process.
>
> (Coleridge 2010: 14–15, emphasis in original)

The Child's Needs and the Ability of the Parents to Meet Them:

Lack of Contact in the Past

The fact that the child has no recollection of the absent parent or that there has been a long period without contact does not preclude an order.[228] However, in *Re L*[229] Thorpe LJ suggested that existing relationships should be treated differently from potential relationships:[230]

> I doubt that sufficient distinction has been made between cases in which contact is sought in order to maintain an existing relationship, to revive a dormant relationship or to create a non-existent relationship. The judicial assumption that to order contact would promote welfare would surely wane across that spectrum. I would not assume the benefit with unquestioning confidence where a child has developed over its early years without any knowledge of its father, particularly if over those crucially formative years a psychological attachment to an alternative father has been achieved. (364)

Disruption for the Child

It appears that the absence of a bond between the non-resident parent and the child may be a significant factor where the possibility of disruption to the child's life is raised. However, the courts seem to have grown reluctant to regard the potential for disruption

---

[228] See *Re D (Contact: Reasons for Refusal)* [1997] 2 FLR 48. See also *Re W (A Minor) (Contact)* [1994] 2 FLR 441; *Re F (Minors)(Contact: Mother's Anxiety)* [1993] 2 FLR 830, 833. Compare the earlier case of *Re SM (A Minor) (Natural Father: Access)* [1991] 2 FLR 333.

[229] *Re L (Contact: Domestic Violence); Re V (Contact: Domestic Violence); Re M (Contact: Domestic Violence); Re H (Contact: Domestic Violence)* [2002] 2 FLR 334.

[230] Although the father's 'intended' relationship with a child, albeit one that has not materialised for reasons not attributable to him, together with his interest in the child and a long relationship with the mother, might suffice to give him a right to family life under Art 8: *Anayo v Germany* (Application No 20578/07 [2011] 1 FLR 1883.

as decisive. The court in *Re SM (A Minor) (Natural Father: Access)*[231] allowed an appeal against an order in favour of the father. Although the father had had contact with the child regularly in the past, the court placed considerable weight on the fact that the child's bond was not with the biological father but with the mother and stepfather. In addition, there was a risk of destabilising the family if contact took place. Yet a few years later, in a case with comparable facts, the court adopted a somewhat different approach. In *Re R (A Minor) (Contact)*[232] the court seemed to accept that contact would lead to disruption but adjourned the father's application with a view to having the child introduced to her father when the risks posed by contact diminished.

The courts have taken into account the negative effects on the family of contact in cases where the child needed a great deal of care and medical attention.[233] They have also done so where the potential disruption was very severe. *Re H (A Minor) (Parental Responsibility)*[234] provides an extreme example.[235] There the stepfather objected so strongly to any contact between father and child that he wrote to the father indicating that his marriage to the mother would be jeopardised if contact continued. The court refused contact in the interests of preserving the child's home life.[236] In *Re H (Contact Order (No 2))*[237] the father, who suffered from Huntington's disease which affected his personality, had threatened suicide and had made preparations to kill the children. The mother testified that she could not cope with the prospect of a contact order and that she had made contingency arrangements for the children lest she suffer a breakdown. The court refused to order direct contact, finding that the effect of an order on the mother's ability to parent and the need to promote her physical and mental health outweighed the need of the children to have direct contact.

Q Read the cases on transfer of residence referred to below. Consider the relative importance accorded by the courts to the risk of disruption and to the aim of achieving contact.

The 'Implacably Hostile' Parent

It is sometimes the case that the resident parent (who is usually the mother in cases of heterosexual parents) seeks to prevent contact between the child and the non-resident parent. This resistance, it is thought, affects the children's attitudes. Where children refuse contact it is sometimes argued that this is because of PAS. In the Sturge–Glaser report, a report compiled by child psychiatrists for the court in *Re L*,[238] the authors indicated that PAS is not recognised and preferred the term 'implacable hostility', a state of affairs in

---

[231] [1991] 2 FLR 333. See also *Re W (A Minor) (Access)* [1989] 1 FLR 163.

[232] [1993] 2 FLR 762. See also *A v L (Contact)* [1998] 1 FLR 361.

[233] *Re F (Contact: Enforcement: Representation of Child)* [1998] 1 FLR 691; *Re C and V (Contact and Parental Responsibility)* [1998] 1 FLR 392.

[234] [1993] 1 FLR 484.

[235] See also *M v M (Parental Responsibility)* [1999] 2 FLR 737. Note, however, that despite the father's condition, he was granted indirect contact. In *M v A (Contact: Domestic Violence)* [2002] 2 FLR 921, it was held that direct contact would adversely affect the emotional stability of the home. However, the father, whose conduct was criticised, and who had convictions for manslaughter and rape as well as dishonesty, was given indirect contact.

[236] See also *Re B (Contact: Stepfather's Opposition)* [1997] 2 FLR 579. See also *Re M (Contact: Violent Parent)* [1999] 2 FLR 321, 332.

[237] [2002] 1 FLR 22.

[238] *Re L (Contact: Domestic Violence); Re V (Contact: Domestic Violence); Re M (Contact: Domestic Violence); Re H (Contact: Domestic Violence)* [2002] 2 FLR 334.

which resident parents resist contact and which can arise for a variety of reasons, some justifiable (Sturge and Glaser 2000: 7–8). The Court of Appeal relied on the report and commented that, while 'some parents, particularly mothers, are responsible for alienating their children from their fathers without good reason',[239] this is a long way from a 'syndrome' requiring the help of mental health professionals. Nevertheless, these mothers are seen as creating an 'insoluble problem'[240] and are regarded as selfish and short-sighted.[241]

Certainly mothers who oppose contact feel that they are put under considerable pressure from solicitors, court welfare officers and mediators to withdraw their objections.[242] And the courts, in particular, have taken an increasingly censorious view of mothers who resist contact.[243] There are, it is true, instances where the mother's opposition to contact has been treated as a reason for denying contact. For example, the court in *Re P (Contact: Discretion)*[244] indicated that contact might be refused if a mother has good reason for her hostility and, even if she does not, where her attitude would make contact damaging for the child. But although the court might refuse contact, the unsatisfactory nature of this situation is often remarked on. *Re D (A Minor) (Contact: Mother's Hostility)*[245] was one such case. The mother said that the father had been violent towards her, drank excessively and took drugs. The judge thought he was now a reformed character although he had certainly behaved in an intimidatory fashion towards the mother and her parents. He had had no contact with his child, aged almost 3, and the mother opposed the application on the grounds that the hatred and fear she felt for him would make contact unworkable and that it would be upsetting and detrimental for the child. On appeal against an order refusing contact, Waite LJ said:

> It is now well settled that the implacable hostility of a mother towards access or contact is a factor which is capable, according to the circumstances of each particular case, of supplying a cogent reason for departing from the general principle that a child should grow up in the knowledge of both his parents. I see no reason to think that the judge fell into any error of principle in deciding, as he clearly did on the plain interpretation of his judgment, that the mother's present attitude towards contact puts D at serious risk of major emotional harm if she were to be compelled to accept a degree of contact to the natural father against her will … .
>
> I share the hope of the trial judge that matters may change for the future, and that the mother herself will come in time to realise that for the long-term benefits of D an upbringing in the knowledge of both his parents may prove to be to his advantage. (7–8)

On other occasions the courts have simply refused to countenance mothers' objections. And at times, the expectations they appear to have of mothers seem oppressive. In *Re P (Contact: Supervision)*[246] the stress occasioned to the mother by contact was held insufficient reason to deny the father supervised contact. The father was violent, racist, anti-Semitic and had in the past threatened to strangle the mother and kill the children.

---

[239] *Re L (Contact: Domestic Violence); Re V (Contact: Domestic Violence); Re M (Contact: Domestic Violence); Re H (Contact: Domestic Violence)* [2002] 2 FLR 334, 351.

[240] Ibid.

[241] See Ingman (1996: 617).

[242] See Smart and Neale (1997); Piper (1993); Hunt and Macleod (2008).

[243] See, generally, Piper (1995). It has been argued that in constructing resident parents as having the power and responsibility for decisions concerning contact, the law has succeeded in characterising uncooperative mothers as posing the main risk to children; they have to be persuaded or compelled to make the 'right' decision (Kaganas 1999: 115).

[244] [1998] 2 FLR 696.

[245] [1993] 2 FLR 1. See also *Re J (A Minor) (Contact)* [1994] 1 FLR 729.

[246] [1996] 2 FLR 314.

However, far from justifying the mother's opposition to contact, the mother's mental state and the history of abuse was treated as placing a 'special burden' (332) on her to accede to contact so that her children could know their father. If she impeded contact, the court said, the children would blame her in later years.

In addition, the courts regard it as imperative not to allow resident parents to defy them. In *Re W (A Minor) (Contact)*[247] the mother indicated that she would disobey an order, contending that the father was incapable of looking after the child and that an order would have a deleterious effect on the stability of the child. The appeal court described the failure of the court below to make an order as an abdication of responsibility and said that the mother had no right to deny the child contact with his father.[248] Moreover, intervention is regarded as essential in some cases to ensure that the passage of time does not become a reason for deciding that it is too late to rescue the relationship between the child and the non-resident parent.[249]

Re O (Contact: Imposition of Conditions)[250] provides a clear statement of the courts' refusal to be dictated to by the resident parent:

> The courts should not at all readily accept that the child's welfare will be injured by direct contact. … Neither parent should be encouraged or permitted to think that the more intransigent, the more unreasonable, the more obdurate and the more unco-operative they are, the more likely they are to get their own way. (129–30)

The court went on to recommend that if direct contact were not possible, there should be indirect contact[251] to ensure that, until direct contact could take place, the child would grow up knowing of the absent parent's love and interest (130).[252]

Making Contact Happen and Enforcement of Contact Orders

Where resident mothers disobey or undermine contact orders, the courts are adopting an increasingly hard line. On occasion, the court has considered some tactics used by mothers resisting contact to be so damaging for children that they warrant a care order. In *Re M (Intractable Contact Dispute: Interim Care Order)*[253] the mother had persuaded the children, falsely, that the father and the paternal grandparents had abused them.[254] As a result, Wall J made an order under section 37 of the Children Act 1989 instructing the local authority to consider whether care proceedings might be appropriate. He had come to the conclusion that the children were suffering significant harm in the mother's care. They were suffering emotional harm because, in particular, the mother was seeking to instil in

---

[247] [1994] 2 FLR 441.

[248] See also *Re F (Minors) (Contact: Mother's Anxiety)* [1993] 2 FLR 830; *Re H (A Minor) (Contact)* [1994] 2 FLR 776.

[249] See *Re S (Unco-operative Mother)* [2004] EWCA Civ 597; [2004] 2 FLR 710, para 17. See also, for a similar pronouncement by the ECtHR, *Maire v Portugal* [2004] 2 FLR 653, para 74.

[250] [1995] 2 FLR 124. See also *V v V (Contact: Implacable Hostility)* [2004] EWHC Fam 1215; [2004] 2 FLR 851, para 47.

[251] See also *Re M (Contact: Supervision)* [1998] 1 FLR 727.

[252] This case clarifies the nature of the conditions that can be imposed in terms of s 11(7) of the Children Act 1989. The court has jurisdiction to compel a mother to send photographs, medical reports and school reports in order to promote meaningful contact between father and child. In addition, the mother could be ordered to write reports to the father. See also *Re M (Contact: Supervision)* [1998] 1 FLR 727.

[253] [2003] EWHC Fam 1024; [2003] 2 FLR 636.

[254] There were also allegations of physical assault and verbal abuse but these were never adjudicated as injunction proceedings were compromised (para 46). The court declined to give any weight to the allegations of domestic violence (para 48).

them the false belief that their father had sexually abused them (para 29). The local authority agreed and an interim care order was made. Residence was then transferred to the father, with a two-year supervision order made in favour of the local authority. The purpose of the care proceedings, said the judge, was to protect the children from significant harm and to restore their relationship with the father. 'In the longer term', he said, 'the aim was to enable the children to retain a good relationship with both parents' (para 20).[255] His judgment, he added, should not be seen as either pro-father or anti-mother (para 23).

Wall J warned that before invoking section 37, the court must be satisfied that there are reasonable grounds for believing that the children are suffering or likely to suffer significant harm in terms of section 31 of the Children Act 1989. In addition, the action contemplated must be in the children's best interests. If the court decides to move the children from one parent to the other, the case must be kept under review (para 11).

The courts have become increasingly ready to transfer residence as a way of dealing with intractable disputes. In *Re C (Residence Order),*[256] for example, the court found that the harm the child was suffering or would suffer if residence were not transferred to the father outweighed the harm she would suffer by being removed from the mother. The court referred to the protests of fathers in many cases coming before it that 'the court is powerless to enforce its orders, quite unable to control the intractable, implacably hostile mother'. It seemed to regard its decision in part as evidence to such fathers that the courts are not powerless:

> Time after time this court has to mollify the angry father, endeavouring to explain that the judge has a broad discretion and that his decision cannot be challenged unless plainly wrong. This time the boot is on the other foot, and if a different conclusion has been reached in this case then let it be shouted out from the rooftops.

Residence was also transferred in *V v V (Contact: Implacable Hostility).*[257] The mother had stopped contact on several occasions, alleging that there had been sexual, physical and emotional abuse of the children, aged 8 and 6, by the father and his relatives. These allegations had led to the involvement of the police, doctors and social services. The court decided that the allegations were unfounded or exaggerated. It also considered the mother responsible for an anonymous campaign to discredit the father and his family. The court said that she had involved the children in false allegations and that she had abused them emotionally by subjecting them to four interviews with the police and visits to hospital which were unnecessary (para 53). The mother, it said, was 'twisted' (para 23). Her concern about the children was feigned and was being used as an excuse to oppose contact. She presented herself as supporting contact but, in reality, was storing up ammunition against the father (paras 22–23). The children had been coached to make allegations (para 22) and their wish to remain with their mother, with whom they had always lived, could not determine the outcome. This was partly because they were young and partly 'because

---

[255] In fact the children were no longer seeing their mother and the court commented that the father and his parents were communicating their hostility to the children. He urged them not to fall into the same 'trap' as the mother had. See paras 173–76.

[256] [2007] EWCA Civ 866; [2008] 1 FLR 211 [24]. See also *Re M (Intractable Contact Dispute: Interim Care Order* [2003] EWHC Fam 1024; [2003] 2 FLR 636 for a case where residence was transferred. In *Re W (Residence; Leave to Appeal)* [2010] EWCA Civ 1280; [2011] 1 FLR 1143, the child was transferred to her grandparents.

[257] [2004] EWHC Fam 1215; [2004] 2 FLR 851.

they have become so enmeshed in the parents' problems and have learnt to say what they think is expected of them'; they were 'tainted by the influence of the mother' (para 44).[258] The court granted a residence order to the father, saying:

[45] If the children move to the father they would be uprooted from the mother's daily care, where they have lived all their lives. They would have to change schools and settle in a new environment with the father and extended family. The mother has more than adequately provided for their needs, except in the relationship with the father. The change would be traumatic ... . If the children stay with the mother ... [t]here would be ... a real risk that the father would become battle-weary and withdraw from the children's lives defeated and demoralised.

[46] If the children move to the father I am satisfied he would actively support generous contact to the mother ... but there is the emotional upheaval for the children to consider ... .

Q What did the court consider to be the greatest risk for the children? Why?

Bracewell J severely criticised those mothers who resist contact and called for more effective measures to enforce orders:

[4] There is a perception among part of the media, and some members of the parents' groups, as well as members of the public, that the courts rubber-stamp cases awarding care of children to mothers almost automatically and marginalise fathers from the lives of their children. There is also a perception that courts allow parents with care to flout court orders for contact and permit parents with residence to exclude the parent from the lives of the children so that the other parent is worn down by years of futile litigation which achieves nothing and only ends when that parent gives up the struggle, or the children are old enough to make their own decisions, assuming they have not been brainwashed in the meantime ... .

[6] ... Unreasonable parents, by definition, are difficult to deal with, and the most intractable situation is undoubtedly the unreasonable mother, but judges currently do not have the tools with which to make progress with the unreasonable mother or sometimes the unreasonable father who can flout or frustrate orders with impunity unless sent to prison.

[7] It appears to me that there are ways in which the problems can be addressed ....They consist of case management ..., judicial continuity, timetabling ..., proactive orders ..., and attaching conditions to residence orders under Section 11(7) of the Children Act 1989 ... . CAFCASS officers, in addition to writing reports ... will be there to monitor the initial stages of contact, help with hand-over arrangements and, if necessary, bring the case back to court ... .

[10] The second way in which improvements can be effected requires legislation ... . Currently, there are only four options available to the court [to enforce orders] and each is unsatisfactory: one, send the parent who frustrates contact to prison, or make a suspended order of imprisonment. This option may well not achieve the object of reinstating contact; the child may blame the parent who applied to commit the carer to prison; the child's life may be disrupted if there is no one capable of or willing to care for the child when the parent is in prison; it cannot be anything other than emotionally damaging for a child to be suddenly removed into foster care by social services from a parent, usually a mother, who in all respects except contact is a good parent. Two, impose a fine on the parent. This option is rarely possible because it is not consistent with the welfare of the child to deprive a parent on a limited budget. Three, transfer

---

[258] The evidence on which the court based this conclusion appears to have been that it considered the allegations unfounded or 'exaggerated'. There may therefore, it seems, have been some deficiencies in the care afforded by the father.

residence. This option is not necessarily available to the court, because the other parent may not have the facilities or capacity to care for the child full-time, and may not even know the child ... . Four, give up. Make either an order for indirect contact or no order at all. This is the worst option of all and sometimes the only one available. This is the option which gives rise to the public blaming the judges for refusing to deal with recalcitrant parents. This option results in a perception fostered by the press that family courts are failing in private law cases and that family judges are anti-father. The truth, however, is that without the weapons to use against what is in essence a small group of obdurate mothers, the ability of judges to do better for fathers is strictly limited.

> **Q** Is the court primarily concerned with the children's best interests in designating the 'do nothing' option as the 'worst'? To what extent is it concerned with countering fathers' rights campaigns and media criticism?

Similar concerns had previously been voiced by Munby J in *Re D (Intractable Contact Dispute: Publicity).*[259] The judge also referred to media coverage, presumably of fathers' rights campaigns, and said:

> There is much wrong with our system and the time has come for us to recognise that fact ... . If we do not we risk forfeiting public confidence. The newspapers ... make uncomfortable reading for us. They suggest that confidence is already ebbing away. We ignore the media at our peril. (para 4)

Both judges favoured removing as many cases as possible from the court arena[260] but called for legislative reform to strengthen the courts' powers to deal with the cases that were litigated. The government response was to publish a White Paper (DCA, DfES and DTI 2005) and legislation followed. Section 16 of the Children Act 1989 was amended so that family assistance orders are no longer reserved for exceptional cases; they can be made for up to a year and the order may, if a contact order is in force, direct the officer dealing with the family to give advice and assistance regarding contact. The officer may also be required to report to the court about contact.

In addition, the Children Act 1989 was amended to create measures to promote contact and compliance with orders.

11A **Contact activity directions**[261]

(1) This section applies in proceedings in which the court is considering whether to make provision about contact with a child by making—

(a) a contact order with respect to the child, or

(b) an order varying or discharging a contact order with respect to the child.

(2) The court may make a contact activity direction in connection with that provision about contact.

---

[259] [2004] EWHC Fam 727; [2004] 1 FLR 1226.

[260] See also the view of Thorpe LJ that the capacity of the family justice system to produce good outcomes in contact disputes is limited. He suggested that investment in therapeutic services might be beneficial (*Re L (Contact: Domestic Violence); Re V (Contact: Domestic Violence); Re M (Contact: Domestic Violence); Re H (Contact: Domestic Violence)* [2002] 2 FLR 334, 366–67).

[261] As long as the court considers making, varying or discharging a contact order, a contact activity direction can be made even if no contact order is made (House of Lords, Children and Adoption Bill Explanatory Notes, para 9). Contact activity conditions can be made only where a contact order is made or varied (s 11C).

(3) A contact activity direction is a direction requiring an individual who is a party to the proceedings to take part in an activity that promotes contact with the child concerned.

(4) The direction is to specify the activity and the person providing the activity.

(5) The activities that may be so required include, in particular—

(a) programmes, classes and counselling or guidance sessions of a kind that—
  (i) may assist a person as regards establishing, maintaining or improving contact with a child;
  (ii) may, by addressing a person's violent behaviour, enable or facilitate contact with a child;
(b) sessions in which information or advice is given as regards making or operating arrangements for contact with a child, including making arrangements by means of mediation.

(6) No individual may be required by a contact activity direction—

(a) to undergo medical or psychiatric examination, assessment or treatment;
(b) to take part in mediation.

...

(9) In considering whether to make a contact activity direction, the welfare of the child concerned is to be the court's paramount consideration.

11C Contact activity conditions

(1) This section applies if in any family proceedings the court makes—

(a) a contact order with respect to a child, or
(b) an order varying a contact order with respect to a child.

(2) The contact order may impose, or the contact order may be varied so as to impose, a condition (a 'contact activity condition') requiring an individual falling within subsection (3) to take part in an activity that promotes contact with the child concerned.

(3) An individual falls within this subsection if he is—

(a) for the purposes of the contact order so made or varied, the person with whom the child concerned lives or is to live;
(b) the person whose contact with the child concerned is provided for in that order; or
(c) a person upon whom that order imposes a condition under section 11(7)(b).

(4) The condition is to specify the activity and the person providing the activity.

(5) Subsections (5) and (6) of section 11A have effect as regards the activities that may be required by a contact activity condition as they have effect as regards the activities that may be required by a contact activity direction.

In terms of these provisions, then, parents can be required to submit to therapeutic or educational intervention. The court can ask a Cafcass officer to monitor compliance with a contact activity direction or condition and to report to the court any failure to comply.[262] It can also require monitoring of a contact order by a Cafcass officer for a period of up to 12 months, with any non-compliance to be reported to the court.[263]

---

[262] S 11G Children Act 1989.
[263] S 11H Children Act 1989.

The Children Act was also amended[264] to broaden the range of measures available to enforce orders. The court's new powers are in addition to powers to alter residence and contact arrangements or to punish for contempt of court.[265] Where a court makes or varies a contact order it is obliged to attach to the order a warning notice which warns of the consequences of failure to comply.[266] If there is a failure to comply, the court can make an unpaid work requirement under an enforcement order[267] and an order for financial compensation.[268] To make an enforcement order, the court has to be satisfied beyond reasonable doubt that a contact order has been breached. Breach of a contact activity condition constitutes breach of a contact order.[269] The court may not make an order if it is satisfied that there is a reasonable excuse for non-compliance.[270] Before making an enforcement order the court must be satisfied that it is necessary to secure compliance and that its likely effect is proportionate to the seriousness of the breach of the contact order.[271] Compliance with enforcement orders can be monitored[272] and there must be a notice warning of the consequences of non-compliance with that order.[273]

Undoubtedly resident and non-resident[274] parents alike can be required to attend information sessions, guidance and counselling. In addition, the Act provides that the resident parent may seek an enforcement order in the same way that a parent seeking contact may.[275] The White Paper preceding the new provisions stated:

> [C]hanging social expectations, as well as Government action, are both needed. In time, it needs to become socially unacceptable for one parent to impede a child's relationship with its other parent wherever it is safe and in the child's best interests. Equally, it should be unacceptable that non-resident parents absent themselves from their child's development and upbringing following separation. (DCA, DfES and DTI 2005: Ministerial Foreword)

This document was developed in the context of heterosexual parenting disputes and the 'gender wars' they have been reported to have inspired. However, it is assumed that its principles will be applied in cases of same-sex parenting disputes. In both situations,

---

[264] By the Children and Adoption Act 2006.

[265] House of Lords, Children and Adoption Bill, Explanatory Notes, para 11.

[266] S 11I Children Act 1989.

[267] S 11J.

[268] S 11O.

[269] See House of Lords, Children and Adoption Bill, Explanatory Notes, para 28.

[270] Even if the defendant has not done what the order required, 'if it was not within his power to do it, issues of *force majeure* are properly to be considered as going to questions of breach rather than reasonable excuse. So, for example, if a parent taking a child for contact is prevented from going on [*sic*] or is delayed by unforeseen and insuperable transport or weather problems—one thinks of the sudden and unexpected grounding of the nation's airlines by volcanic ash—then there will be no breach. Reasonable excuse, in contrast, arises where, although it was within the power of the defendant to comply, he has some good reason, specifically, a "reasonable excuse", for not doing so. A typical case might be where a child suddenly falls ill and the defendant, reasonably in the circumstances, takes the child to the doctor rather than going to contact' (*Re L-W sub nom CPL v CH-W, ML-W, EL-W (by their Guardian ad litem)* [2010] EWCA Civ 1253, para 40). It is necessary to prove breach of an order in terms of s 11J (2) before the question of reasonable excuse in s 11J(3) becomes relevant (para 39).

[271] S 11L Children Act 1989.

[272] S 11M.

[273] S 11N.

[274] S 11A(3) and S 11C(3). The Joint Committee Report recommended that the government give consideration to allowing resident parents to apply to court to impose a contact activity on non-resident parents who fail to discharge their responsibilities to the children (House of Commons, House of Lords 2005, para 38). The language of the Bill admits of an interpretation consistent with this.

[275] S 11J(5) (b)).

though, there can also be little doubt that it is against resident parents (and in the paradigm heterosexual cases specifically resident mothers)[276] that the contact activity provisions and the enforcement mechanisms will primarily be used. It is difficult at present to conceive of a court ordering a reluctant father to attend counselling about how to improve contact or punishing a father who does not visit his children.

The fathers' rights campaigns[277] therefore appear to have had the effect of galvanising the then government and the courts into action against mothers whom they see as obstructive. More punitive as well as therapeutic measures are to be deployed against them. We may well see more cases like *A v N (Committal; Refusal of Contact)*,[278] where the mother was committed to prison for refusing to allow supervised contact with a violent father. In *B v S*[279] the judge said: 'The days are long gone when mothers can assume that their role as carers of children protects them from being sentenced to immediate terms of imprisonment for clear, repeated and deliberate breaches of contact orders.' The Court of Appeal has even gone so far as to make a suspended committal order where the mother, in its view, was 'communicating her views about the father and her hostility to contact to the children'[280] so that they refused contact. The court stated that there was 'a clear obligation upon the mother to assist the children to come to terms with having contact with their father' (242). So, it seems, not only are caretaking mothers expected to obey contact orders, they have a positive duty to see to it that their children want contact. However, much may depend on the wording of the order. In *Re L-W sub nom CPL v CH-W, ML-W, EL-W (by their Guardian ad litem)*[281] it was the father who was the resident parent. He was required to 'allow' the mother to have contact with the child and to make him 'available' accordingly. On several of the occasions in question contact did not take place because the child refused to go. The father took the view that the child should not be forced to comply. The father was appealing against enforcement orders leading to unpaid work requirements, a committal order and compensation orders.

Munby LJ observed that 'allow' means to 'concede' and to 'make available' means to 'put at one's disposal or within one's reach' (para 75). He held that the wording of the order did not place the father under a legal obligation to 'ensure' that contact took place. To find someone guilty of contempt it is necessary to show that the defendant has not done what she/he was required to do and that it was within her/his power to do it (para 34). In addition, the father had not failed to comply for the purposes of an enforcement order or a compensation order. In relation to those occasions where the child refused to see his mother, the father was not in breach; he was in breach only on those occasions when he removed the child from a contact visit and when the child was away at the time allotted for contact (para 80):

> The father did not, on the judge's findings, do anything active or positive to obstruct contact or to prevent it taking place, even if he did little or nothing active or positive to encourage or facilitate it. So how can it be said that the father did not 'allow' contact or that he did not 'make M available'? (para 81)

---

[276] See, for criticism of a mother's resistance to undergoing therapy, *Re S (Unco-operative Mother)* [2004] EWCA Civ 597; [2004] 2 FLR 710.

[277] And, perhaps, to some extent, the European cases on swift enforcement. However, these, of course all refer to a balancing exercise, reasonableness and to the undesirability of proceeding against children's wishes.

[278] [1997] 1 FLR 533.

[279] [2009] EWCA Civ 548; [2009] 2 FLR 1005, para 16.

[280] *F v F (Contact: Committal)* [1998] 2 FLR 237.

[281] [2010] EWCA Civ 1253; [2011] 1 FLR 1095.

The fact that the father may have created a situation over time which led the child to resist contact did not mean he was not allowing contact; the contact did not take place because the child refused (para 85).

The judge was strongly in favour of using committal proceedings where appropriate.[282]

> Committal is—has to be—an essential weapon in the court's armoury in cases such as this. Nothing in this judgment should be seen as a charter for avoiding enforcement of contact orders in whatever is the most appropriate way, including, where appropriate, by means of committal.
> (para 94)

However, in this case, the committal order would have damaging consequences for the child and, even if the father were to go to prison, this would not change the child's mind; he was unrelenting in his refusal to see his mother. The result would be indefinite non-compliance with repeated punishment of the father. Committal of the father to prison would be counterproductive and the order could not stand (paras 100–07).

Munby LJ went on to make a number of comments, obiter:

> 108 ... [I]n relation to committal there is one final observation I should add. A common trope, as we have seen, is that committal in this kind of case is or ought to be a last resort. I agree, but it is important not to misunderstand what is meant by this handy aphorism. Committal should not be used unless it is a proportionate response to the problem nor if some less drastic remedy will provide an adequate solution. But this does not mean that one has to wait unduly before having resort to committal, let alone waiting so long that the moment has passed and the situation has become irretrievable ... . I cannot help feeling that, on occasions, the understandable reluctance to resort to such a drastic remedy as committal means that when recourse to it is first proposed it is too late for committal, whereas a willingness to grasp the nettle by making a committal order at an earlier stage might have ended up making all the difference. I repeat a point I have already made.[283] The threat, or if need be the actual implementation, of a very short period of imprisonment—just a day or two—may at an earlier stage of the proceedings achieve more than the threat of a longer sentence at a much later stage in the process. I do not suggest this as a panacea—this is an area in which there is no panacea—but it is something which, I suggest, is worth keeping in mind.

He went on to refer to other 'techniques' that had been used in earlier cases, mentioning transfer of residence, shared residence and also cessation of contact. He continued:

> 109 ... Since then, of course, the court has been given power (by the amendments to the 1989 Act introduced by the 2006 Act) to make not merely enforcement orders and compensation orders but also contact activity directions in accordance with sections 11A–11G . The effect of these amendments is to give the court a wide range of options in an intractable contact dispute. For example, we understand that CAFCASS is now funding parenting information programmes and that there are in some places in the country parenting classes which seek to educate parents into an appreciation of the damage which polarisation can cause children. Other orders are possible if all this fails. In an appropriate case an order may be made providing for an immediate transfer of residence. More recently this court has endorsed the propriety in an appropriate case of making a suspended residence order, that is, an order providing for a future transfer of

---

[282] He cited, with approval, *A v N* (above), *B v S* (above) and *Re S (Contact Dispute: Committal)* [2004]. EWCA Civ 1790; [2005] 1 FLR 812.

[283] See also *Re D (Intractable Contact Dispute: Publicity)* [2004] EWHC Fam 727; [2004] 1 FLR 1226, paras 56–57.

residence upon the happening (or non-happening) of a defined event: see Re A (Suspended Residence Order) [2009] EWHC 1576 (Fam), [2010] 1 FLR 1679 (appeal dismissed Re D (Children) [2009] EWCA Civ 1551).

The suspended residence order was 'invented' by Coleridge J in *Re A (Suspended Residence Order)*.[284] The mother and father had two sons aged 8 and 11 and the mother had a daughter from a previous relationship. The father was found to have seriously sexually abused his stepdaughter over a period of time. The mother believed he had also abused the two boys, a belief found to be false by the court. She refused to obey various contact orders. The boys did not want to see their father and there had been no contact with him for 2 years and only limited contact with the paternal grandparents. The father and grandparents sought an immediate transfer of residence to the grandparents with a view to gradual reintroduction to the father. It was agreed that the mother's care of the children could not be criticised in any respect other than the fact that she was 'demonising' the father and obstructing contact. One of the expert witnesses was of the opinion that 'a crucial measure of a resident parents [*sic*] "good enough" parenting is whether they promote frequent and continuous contact with the non resident parent' (para 71); he, and the other expert, supported the transfer. The judge said:

[5] Both the court (and I think the father and grandparents) approach this whole matter with a heavy heart. No one, least of all the court, wants to disrupt the children's lives unnecessarily. In most respects they are being brought up well by their mother. They are doing well at their schools and have friends in their locality. And all the father and grandparents have ever really wanted was to play a proper part in the children's lives by way of a proper and regular contact arrangement. The resolution of the whole problem lies in the mother's hands. In the end she has only herself to blame for the position which has been reached. In the end, although the father is certainly causative of the underlying deeply felt hatred felt by the mother for him and so is very far from blameless, it is her fault that the children are in this position and the court is faced by this stark choice as the guardian describes it. The choice comes down, in its essentials, to leaving the children in their present environment where the mother is directly and indirectly 'demonising' the father and the rest of the father's wider family to an extent where the experts in the case now consider they are already suffering significant emotional harm; and the alternative which is to uproot the children from their homes and move them to new schools and a relatively untested base with the grandparents … .

[108] In every respect save one the children have done and are doing well in their mother's care.

[109] The one respect in which she fails dismally is in her resolute opposition to children having a relationship with the whole of the paternal side of their family; father and grandparents. This is not a superficial shortcoming which can be overlooked in the overall balancing exercise. It is, as all the experts agree, a very serious failing and a very damaging deprivation from the boys' point of view. It is driven by her unshakeable conclusion, despite the clearest of findings by the court, that T, and probably N too, have been sexually abused by the father when this is simply not true. By that logic she regards him as a dangerous untreated paedophile who poses a very serious direct risk to the boys.

[110] There is no discernible basis for her opposition to contact with the grandparents save that she sees them as part of the paternal family and such a step as leading eventually to contact with the father … .

[112] This behaviour, left unchecked and undiluted, has already caused and will continue to

[284] [2009] EWHC 1576 (Fam); [2010] 1 FLR 1679.

cause the boys significant emotional harm to a degree which in other circumstances might well lead to their removal to foster carers by a local authority ... .

[114] That state of affairs simply cannot continue. In some cases the court has, as an option, to accept its inability to make an effective order and so abandon further attempts to do so in the children's interest. But in this case for the court to do nothing, in the light of the expert evidence, is not, in my judgment, a responsible option. So there are only two ways ahead; either the mother must change her stance or the children must be physically removed from her daily environment and influence.

[117] Accordingly, there remains only one option; a move to the grandparents with all that entails for their lives.

[118] The effects of such an uprooting are so blindingly obvious to everyone in the case as not to require spelling out again ... . Without doubt a move would be very painful especially in the short term. It would also be harmful, in the longer term, to disrupt their primary attachment to their mother. But would it be as harmful, in the long term, as their being continually and unrelentingly exposed to their mother's false beliefs combined with her unremitting hostility to the paternal family undiluted by contact to them? In the end I do not think so ... .

[121] There is a possibility that if the boys move to their grandparents the mother will distance herself from her sons and restrict her contact with them. I am not really persuaded that the evidence supports that. If, of course, she was to adopt that approach it would be further evidence of her inability to prioritise their needs above her own.

[122] ... As things currently stand, I shall make a residence order in favour of the grandparents.

[123] However, the question still arises as to the date from when such an order might be brought into effect ... . Should the order be suspended in its effect to admit of the slim possibility that the mother will see the sense in not making the children change their whole lives in support of her campaign to exclude the D's from their lives when, if she was to remain intransigent, it would in fact, achieve the opposite result? ...

[125] It seems to me (and the experts) that this 'suspended' course has one very clear advantage; the future residence of the children depends entirely on the mother's and to a lesser extent, the children's decision and action. If she (and they) abide by the court order the children stay with her (with all the obvious advantages). If she ignores it, the suspension on the order will be lifted immediately and the children move to make their home with the grandparents.

Q The expert said that allowing contact was 'a crucial measure' of adequate parenting. Does the court's decision render it *the* crucial measure? Given the research evidence of the benefits of contact (see Chapter 9 above), is the expert's view uncontestable?

Mr Justice Coleridge adopted an approach that prioritised contact over stability in this case. He has made his views known extra-judicially about getting parents and children to obey contact orders and also explained the suspended residence order (Coleridge 2010). In a speech he suggested that the courts' response to the flouting of contact orders has been 'flabby' (ibid: 16) and that a 'three strikes and you are out' policy should be adopted; 'if an order is disobeyed, say, three times, the residence of the child should normally be transferred to the other parent' (ibid: 17). He went on:

The three breaches might take the following route eg

1. *A simple contact order* followed, if that was breached, by

2. *A detailed and closely defined contact order with a very clear warning* (possibly in writing and signed by the judge) followed if that was further breached by

3. *A suspended residence order with conditions of contact attached* which if breached again would lead to immediate change of residence with almost no further recourse to the court. In other words three broken orders.

You may not yet have come across 'the suspended residence order'. It was invented by me last year ... . The Court of Appeal has now given this new tool its blessing on two occasions ... . It works in the same way as a suspended committal order but without the irritating technicalities attached to enforcement by committal. The court attaches clear conditions which if breached lead to immediate removal of the children to the other parent. (17)

There are three conditions I would attach to this suspended residence order approach. Firstly, and obviously, the judge must be satisfied, *at the time the suspended order is made*, that the alternative home is good enough. Secondly, it must be made abundantly clear to the parent concerned that you really mean what you say, and finally there must be judicial continuity throughout. The authority must come from the judge not the process.

I do not, as a rule, favour imprisonment for parents who breach these orders because of the risk of making them martyrs and because it does not actually deal with the problem practically. You are often no further forward after the parent has left prison. But it is sometimes the answer as Munby LJ has reemphasised ... .

A clearly understood process of enforcement, employed quickly and efficiently might, very occasionally, work against the interests of a particular child but the benefits to the general population of children caught up in these cases would be incalculable. ... If it was generally understood that breach of contact orders led to swift and rigorous enforcement, I have no doubt that the situation would drastically and rapidly improve. Children learn quickly enough when their parents really mean business. Similarly their parents need to learn from the courts as well.

(18, emphasis in original)

The approach proposed by Coleridge J is extraordinary. It is the duty of the court under section 1 of the Children Act 1989 to make the welfare of '*the*' child paramount and this surely refers to the child who is the subject of the application before it.[285] In the interests of maintaining the authority of the court and in a bid to change attitudes generally, the judge is proposing to sacrifice the welfare of individual children. Such an approach does not appear to comply with the courts' statutory obligations. Moreover, the criterion of 'good enough' alternative care arguably does not satisfy the paramountcy principle.

Therapeutic Intervention

Coleridge J's speech and the judgments cited above demonstrate a now prevailing hardline punitive approach. However, at the same time, there has been a discernible trend in recent years for the courts to refer both parents and children for therapeutic intervention.[286] As a result of the amendments to section 11 of the Children Act 1989, this option is now available even without the consent of the person concerned. The Act also permits courts to compel parents to attend parenting classes. In addition, the Practice Direction issued in terms of the revised Private Law Programme refers to the requirement that considera-

---

[285] See *Birmingham City Council v H (A Minor)* [1994] 2 AC 212.
[286] See Kaganas (2010a, 2011).

tion be given to attendance at Parenting Information Programmes or other activities, whether court ordered in terms of section 11 of the Children Act as amended or not.[287]

Such interventions may be useful in some instances.[288] However, it appears that the courts might be using therapeutic interventions at least in the hope that this might deal with the 'underlying problems' and persuade resident parents (and children) to accede to contact. Since it is normally the mother who is the resident parent and thus the person opposing contact, it is likely to be the mother who is cast firmly as the person who is at fault or the person who needs to change.

Indeed in the recent case of *Re P (Children)*[289] the Court of Appeal, determined to deal with 'the true underlying issue' (para 36) in a contact case, was willing to consider recommending counselling for a mother whom the judge in the court below had concluded was truthful and not suffering from any mental disorder (para 24). The therapy, it was said, 'might go some little way to assuaging the father's implacable conviction that she is a woman with severe mental problems such as to spill over to the detriment of his children' (para 37). The father, who had been back to court 66 times (para 4), and who had engaged in what the court considered 'less serious' violence (para 5), was expected to seek help in the form of anger management classes. However the court clearly sympathised with his point of view; he needed an arena in which he could 'explain his feelings of anger and bitterness' resulting from the marriage breakdown and difficulties over the children (who were refusing to see him):[290] 'It is enough to make any ordinary man just a little bit angry, but that anger has to be contained ... . hence the need for him to subject himself to what may be the humiliation of counselling and therapy.'[291] His violence was regarded, it seems, as almost within the range of understandable and 'ordinary' responses; it was something to be controlled but not condemned. Moreover, that the mother might be distressed at attending therapy that she appeared not to need, was not mentioned.

This is not the only instance where the courts appear to recommend therapy[292] in a somewhat surprising manner. For example, in *Re W (Permission to Appeal)*[293] the father had been diagnosed with a paranoid personality disorder (paras 55–56). In contrast the mother had been described in the court below as 'an impressive individual' and the judge noted that the way she dealt with a 'highly taxing and demanding issue' showed how 'big a personality' she was (para 56). Nevertheless, Wall LJ endorsed the judge's recommendation that both parties undergo therapy.

Kaganas (2011: 89) comments that it is somewhat worrying that a mother can be told to attend therapy in the absence of any evidence[294] that she needs it, particularly in the light of evidence that failure to engage in therapy can attract adverse legal consequences; a failure to seek help is now a sign of bad parenting. Even before the amendment of section 11 of the Children Act 1989, parents were being warned. In *Re S (Un-co-operative*

---

[287] Practice Direction: Revised Private Law Programme [2010] 2 FLR 717, para 5.2(d).

[288] In particular, it could be helpful to require abusers to attend perpetrator programmes in cases where there is a history of violence.

[289] [2008] EWCA Civ 1431.

[290] One of the children stated that, if his father shouted at him or smacked him, he would curl up and hide his face. He also feared that his father would not return him home after contact (ibid: para 31).

[291] Ibid: para 36. The court also seemed to sympathise with the fact that a 'proud, intelligent father' had been humiliated by the findings of domestic violence against him.

[292] The courts also consider the involvement of the NYAS, which is a step, along with mediation, that is becoming more often seen as leading the parties out of an impasse.

[293] [2007] EWCA Civ 786; [2008] 1 FLR 406.

[294] None was referred to by the court.

Mother)[295] Thorpe LJ said that if the mother refused to attend therapy, 'she must understand that the court may draw adverse inferences against her' (para 22). Of even greater concern is that now, under the amended section 11 of the Children Act 1989, non-compliance with contact activity conditions can attract punitive sanctions. So while courts will be likely to continue to use persuasion and chastisement, parents who refuse to accept therapeutic[296] or educational intervention may now find themselves subject to more coercive measures.[297]

The unremitting focus on getting resident parents to comply stems from the fact that the courts see them as the 'problem'. However Trinder et al (2005) found that parents who are in dispute experience multiple problems. Resident parents in their study tended to say they wanted more contact rather than less. When they wanted contact curtailed, this was because of the perceived lack of commitment of the non-resident parent or, more commonly, because of distress to children and fear of violence. Parents exhibited high levels of anger and distrust, linking children's distress to the other parent's behaviour. The research shows that these cases are not, as non-resident parents characterised them, single-issue disputes about one parent's obstruction of contact. Resident parents saw the contact issue in the context of other concerns.

Rhoades (2002) sees little merit in the measures introduced into section 11. She warns that measures such as these, as well as those that were already being used before the change to the legislation, divert attention from poor parenting during contact visits by non-resident fathers. Her research in Australia showed fathers failing to care adequately for their children or failing to turn up for contact visits at all. These fathers could and did 'breach the terms of contact orders with impunity' (ibid: 78). Moreover, she found that few mothers flouted contact orders and that the most common source of conflict was the resident parent's concern about domestic violence. There were mothers who disobeyed consent orders but in many of these cases the order was amended to place greater restrictions on the father (ibid: 84–85). It may be, then, that at least some of these mothers had been persuaded or pressured into agreeing to inappropriate contact arrangements to begin with.

The measures being adopted to deal with recalcitrant parents, or more specifically mothers, are based on the assumption that they are unreasonable or vindictive, in need of education as to the benefits of contact or in need of treatment. It is assumed that the law can and must help to change their behaviour. It has long been the case that courts have sought to manage the emotions of litigants by castigating parents for harming their children by persisting in their dispute, by appealing to reason, by minimising or rendering illegitimate objections to contact and by designating parents involved in conflict as 'bad' parents (Kaganas 2011). Now they can refer parents to classes and to therapy. However, the basis of the assumption is shaky and the effectiveness of the 'remedy' is doubtful.

Kaganas and Day Sclater (2004) report that, in their study of parents engaged in contact disputes, the 'problem' was not lack of education or mental health difficulties. Instead, both mothers and fathers were interpreting the welfare discourse in ways that enabled

---

[295] [2004] EWCA Civ 597; [2004] 2 FLR 710.

[296] But the court cannot require a person to undergo medical or psychiatric examination, assessment or treatment (s 11A(6) and s 11C(5) Children Act 1989). In any event, whether therapeutic services will be widely available is open to doubt (Sayers 2009). The financial constraints imposed by the coalition government make provision of such services even more unlikely. Rhoades' research in Australia shows that parents who are sent by the courts to parenting programmes are a high-conflict group and the programmes that were viewed positively were very resource intensive (Rhoades 2004).

[297] The potential for punitive use of the provisions is noted by Cantwell (2010: 89–90).

them to see themselves and to be seen as 'good' mothers and fathers. Mothers saw themselves as safeguarding their children's interests and fathers saw it as important not to give up on their children. Mothers had internalised the dominant discourse that contact is good for children but disputed that it was good for *their* children because of the fathers' perceived shortcomings. May and Smart (2007: 73, 75) likewise found that parents' image of themselves as good parents was bound up in their conflict. Parents, then, might not be readily 'educated' or 'helped' to give up the struggle. Indeed, research suggests that education does not change relationships or behaviour. Hunt (2007: 199), reviewing the available research, concluded that 'the effectiveness of parent education programmes as a genre has not been conclusively proven'.

Kaganas suggests that the new measures are both coercive and unlikely to succeed:

> Education and counselling can be experienced as coercive, particularly for mothers who are expected to overcome their objections to contact. But these measures do not necessarily effect change. For one thing, it seems that some parents will always resist the categorisation of themselves as 'bad' or perhaps 'mad'. For another they may respond in unexpected ways to education. This suggests that, as long as the courts are seen and see themselves as having to 'make contact work' by solving the problem of conflict, and therefore needing to provide a 'fix' for the people, emotions and relationships before them, their task will remain, in many instances, an almost impossible one. (Kaganas 2011: 93, footnote omitted)

Q In the cases discussed above, what do the courts appear to consider the primary impediment to beneficial contact? Is it conflict between the parents? The non-resident parent's conduct? The mother's 'implacable hostility'? Smart and Neale (1997) point out that little attention is paid to the 'damage' to children resulting from their fathers failing to take responsibility for them. They argue that contact has become an ideological issue; the 'implacably hostile mother', in refusing to share her child with the father, is 'obstructing the new ideal of the post-divorce family' (ibid: 335). Do you agree? Are not fathers who fail to maintain contact also undermining the ideal?
　　Read Chapter 9 above. Do you think the new measures will lead to more and better contact?

IX. RELOCATION

The relative importance to children of their relationships with resident and non-resident parents is thrown sharply into relief in cases in which a resident parent applies for permission to relocate with the children. Where the resident parent plans to move to another area within the United Kingdom, the courts are empowered to prevent this by imposing a condition under section 11(7) of the Children Act 1989 or by making a prohibited steps order under section 8.[298] However, the courts are reluctant to act in this way and will not restrict the primary carer's freedom to choose her way of life and place of residence unless there are exceptional circumstances:[299]

---

[298] A condition under s 11(7) was considered inappropriate and a prohibited steps order the correct way to achieve the desired result in *Re F (Internal Relocation)* [2010] EWCA Civ 1428; [2011] 1 FLR 1382, para 23.
[299] But see the criticism of the exceptionality criterion in *Re F* (above), paras 25–27.

The first [reason] is that often the notion of such restrictions are simply contrary to good sense and, secondly, because the imposition of restrictions is likely to have an adverse effect on the welfare of the children indirectly through the emotional and psychological disturbance caused to the primary carer by denial of the freedom to exercise reasonable choice.[300]

Where, however, a resident parent seeks permission to move out of the jurisdiction in terms of section 13(1)(b) of the Children Act 1989, a more stringent set of criteria is applied. In deciding whether to grant an application to relocate, the court first considers whether the resident parent's proposals are reasonable and, if they are, it goes on to apply the welfare principle;[301] the child's welfare is paramount.[302]To be regarded as reasonable, the plan to relocate must be practical in the sense of being realistic, and it must be genuine and not motivated by a selfish wish to exclude the other parent.[303] The reasons for the non-resident parent's opposition must also be appraised.[304] One question to consider is whether he or she is motivated by 'genuine concern' for the child's welfare or by some 'ulterior motive'.[305] Another is the potential damage to the non-resident parent's relationship with the child should the move be allowed. If the refusal of an application is likely to have a detrimental impact on the care that the primary carer will be able to give to the child, this consideration will usually outweigh the detrimental impact on the relationship with the other parent if the application is granted.[306] Where the resident parent cares for a child or proposes to care for the child in a new family, the impact of a refusal on the new family or stepparent must also be examined; normally the welfare of the child cannot be secured unless the new family can pursue its goals without unreasonable restrictions.[307] 'Great weight' is attached to the 'emotional and psychological well-being of the primary carer' in evaluating the welfare of the child.[308] However, where the resident parent's primary motive is to get away from the non-resident parent in order to reduce or terminate contact, the court is likely to refuse the application.[309]

It has hitherto been unusual for a court to refuse permission to relocate where the resident parent is in good faith and where her plans are realistic.[310] In the leading case of *Payne v Payne*[311] Thorpe LJ summarised the case law as follows:

---

[300] *Re S (A Child) Residence Order: Condition)* [2001] EWCA Civ 847; [2001] 2 FCR 154, para 16. See also *Re B (Prohibited Steps Order)* [2007] EWCA Civ 1055; [2008] 1 FLR 613.

[301] *Re C (Permission to Remove from Jurisdiction)* [2003] EWHC Fam 596; [2003] 1 FLR 1066, para 24(5). Where more than one child is involved, each child's interests have to be considered separately and where they differ a balancing exercise is required: *Re S (Children)(Relocation: Permission)* [2011] EWCA Civ 454; [2011] 2 FCR 356.

[302] Relocation proceedings may be instituted under s 8 or s 13 of the Children Act 1989. In either case they fall under s 1(1) of the Children Act 1989 and the paramountcy principle applies.

[303] *Payne v Payne* [2001] EWCA Civ 166; [2001] 1 FLR 1052; *Re C (Permission to Remove from Jurisdiction)* [2003] EWHC Fam 596; [2003] 1 FLR 1066.

[304] *Payne v Payne* [2001] EWCA Civ 166; [2001] 1 FLR 1052, paras 40, 85.

[305] Ibid, para 40(b).

[306] *Re C (Permission to Remove from Jurisdiction)* [2003] EWHC Fam 596; [2003] 1 FLR 1066, para 24(9).

[307] *Re B (Removal from Jurisdiction); Re S (Removal from Jurisdiction)* [2003] EWCA Civ 1149; [2003] 2 FLR 643.

[308] *Payne v Payne* [2001] EWCA Civ 166; [2001] 1 FLR 1052, para 41.

[309] See *B v B (Residence: Condition Limiting Geographic Area)* [2004] 2 FLR 979. If this is a secondary motive, it is not fatal to the application. See *Re B (Leave to Remove)* [2006] EWHC 1783 (Fam); [2007] 1 FLR 333, para 179.

[310] But see *Tyler v Tyler* [1989] 2 FLR 158 where the court refused the mother permission to emigrate because the move would deprive the children of a relationship with their father. See also *Re T (Removal from Jurisdiction)* [1996] 2 FLR 352. On same-sex parents, see *G (Children)* [2005] EWCA Civ 462. The court below refused permission for the move. For discussion of recent cases, see Judd and George (2010).

[311] [2001] EWCA Civ 166; [2001] 1 FLR 1052, para 26.

[R]elocation cases have been consistently decided upon the application of the following two propositions:

(a) the welfare of the child is the paramount consideration; and
(b) refusing the primary carer's reasonable proposals for the relocation of her family life is likely to impact detrimentally on the welfare of her dependent children. Therefore her application to relocate will be granted unless the court concludes that it is incompatible with the welfare of the children.

It is thought that, unless the primary carer is psychologically and emotionally stable, the child will not be able to feel secure and stable.[312] Hayes (2006) criticises this approach and argues that it is an unwarranted gloss on the welfare principle that prevents courts exercising their discretion. Herring and Taylor (2006) object to the *Payne* test because, they say, although it purports to be child-centred, it actually protects the adults' interests, especially those of the resident parent. They argue that, to comply with the Human Rights Act 1998, the court must weigh the interests of all those affected by the relocation decision. The rights at issue are Article 8 rights and at the heart of these, say Herring and Taylor, lies the notion of autonomy which encompasses the right to 'develop one's vision of the good life' (Herring and Taylor 2006: 531). Children who are too young to have such a vision should have a right to an 'open future' (ibid). The authors concede that the outcome of the balancing exercise will generally not differ from the results of applying the welfare test. However, they argue that their approach is preferable because it does not rest on 'unsupportable assumptions that identify the interests of one parent with the welfare of the child' (ibid: 532).[313]

Most of the dissatisfaction with *Payne* focuses on the complaint that it favours the resident parent. Increasingly, there has been growing pressure for reform of the law on international relocation (Roche 2010: 978). In *Re D (Children)*[314] Wall LJ referred briefly to the 'perfectly respectable argument' (para 34) that *Payne* places too much emphasis on the wishes of the parent who is seeking to relocate and 'ignores or relegates the harm done to the children by a permanent breach of the relationship which children have with the left-behind parent' (para 33). A more comprehensive attack is to be found in *Re AR (A Child: Relocation)*.[315] Mostyn J referred to *Payne*[316] as:

[7] … tendentious in the true sense of that word ie supplying a tendency, and that tendency is the almost invariable success of the application, save in those cases where it is demonstrably irrational, absurd or malevolent.

He continued:

[8] This ideology has not been uncritically accepted. Indeed there is a strong view that the heavy emphasis on the emotional reaction of the thwarted primary carer represents an illegitimate gloss on the purity of the paramountcy principle. Moreover, some argue that it promotes selfishness and detracts from the importance of co-parenting. Some argue that on the birth of

---

[312] Ibid, para 31.
[313] The test advocated here, however, is also liable to be applied relying on 'unsupportable assumptions' about what best protects children's rights to an 'open future'.
[314] [2010] EWCA Civ 50.
[315] [2010] EWHC 1346 (Fam); [2010] 3 FCR 131.
[316] And the earlier case of *Poel v Poel* [1970] 1 WLR 1469, 1473 which emphasised the importance of protecting the custodial parent's autonomy.

children parents are indentured to sacrifice throughout their minority, but that the one word that is missing from *Payne* is, in fact, *sacrifice*. (emphasis in original)

In March 2010, at an international conference on cross-border family relocation, attended by judges and experts from several countries, a 13-paragraph Declaration was drafted (Roche 2010: 978).[317] Paragraph 3 states that the best interests of the child are paramount and that there should be no presumptions for or against relocation. The 13 factors[318] to be taken into account include the right of the child to maintain relations and direct contact with both parents in a manner consistent with the child's development, unless contact is contrary to the child's bests interests. Factor (ix) is clearly also designed to direct attention to continuity: '[T]he nature of the inter-parental relationship and the commitment of the applicant to support and facilitate the relationship between the child and the respondent after the relocation'.

As Roche points out, little prominence is given to the psychological effect on the resident parent should permission to relocate be refused. At the end of factor (viii) this is only obliquely mentioned: 'The impact of grant or refusal on the child, in the context of his or her extended family, education and social life, and on the parties.'

Mostyn J referred with approval to this declaration in *Re AR* (see para 11), saying:

[11] … It requires the court in a real rather than synthetic way to take into account the impact on both the child and the left behind parent of the disruption of the periodicity and quantum of the prevailing contact arrangement. The hitherto decisive factor for us—the psychological impact on the thwarted primary carer—is relegated to a seemingly minor position at the back end of para 4(viii).

He went on to consider the view expressed in *Re H (a Child)*[319] that the declaration places too little weight on the impact on the child likely to result from the negative impact on an applicant if an order is refused, and went on:

I agree with this, up to a point. Certainly the factor of the impact on the thwarted primary carer deserves its own berth and as such deserves its due weight, no more, no less. The problem with the attribution of great weight to this particular factor is that, paradoxically, it appears to penalise selflessness and virtue, while rewarding selfishness and uncontrolled emotions. The core question of the putative relocator is always 'how would you react if leave were refused?' The parent who stoically accepts that she would accept the decision, make the most of it, move on and work to promote contact with the other parent is far more likely to be refused leave than the parent who states that she will collapse emotionally and psychologically.

The declaration, which by Mostyn J's own admission focuses more on the child's relationship with the non-resident parent than the resident parent's situation, provides, he said, 'a more balanced and neutral approach to a relocation application'.[320] And he went on:

[53] … If one were to draw up a hierarchy of human rights protected by the Convention I would have thought that very near to the top would be the right of a child, while he or she is growing

---

[317] On the potential pitfalls of attempting an internationally agreed approach, see George (2011).

[318] For a list of the factors, see *Re AR (A Child: Relocation)* [2010] EWHC 1346 (Fam); [2010] 3 FCR 131, para 10.

[319] [2010] EWCA Civ 915, para 25.

[320] Ibid.

up, to have a meaningful participation by both of his parents in his upbringing. Although this is (strangely) not explicitly spelt out in the text it must be implicit in the notion of the right to a family life. Recognition of the existence of this very obvious and critically important right is sometimes, so it seems to me, lost in the relocation cases.

A 'balanced' and 'neutral' approach, it seems, means that contact is prioritised over everything else and that 'good' mothers are required to be rational and selfless. The issues could be framed differently:

> [A] tension between a child's right to a close relationship with both parents, and the child's right to be in the care of a well-functioning primary parent, or the freedom of movement of the relocating parent, versus the freedom of movement of the non-moving parent. Or, more provocatively, the right of a non-moving parent to interfere with the relocating parents' freedom of movement. (Henaghan 2011: 232)

Of course, the case law under the Children Act makes it clear that we have to apply the welfare principle rather than rights. Henaghan's proposals for dealing with these cases are, he says, consistent with the welfare principle. He suggests that if the relocating parent is the one who has taken the main responsibility for caring for the child, then that parent should be 'given priority to continue their care' (ibid: 248). Boyd in turn says that whatever approach is taken to resolving relocation disputes, attention must be paid to the realities of the child's life and the care relationships in it (Boyd 2011: 177).

Marilyn Freeman points out that fathers are never expected to relocate to maintain contact. Some mothers seeking to relocate, she says, are fleeing domestic violence and some feel trapped and devoid of support. And while some fathers suffer serious consequences if their children are removed, others who oppose relocation successfully only avail themselves of sporadic contact (Freeman 2010: 248).

The Court of Appeal in *Re W (Children)*[321] was apparently influenced by the research reported by Freeman. It reaffirmed the status of *Payne* as the binding authority in relocation cases. Interestingly, the criticisms of *Payne* and also the judgment of *Re AR* received only fleeting attention.[322] The decision to grant an appeal against a refusal to allow the mother to relocate in this case rested primarily on the ground that the judge had failed to give sufficient weight to the effect on the mother if she were compelled to remain in the UK. Instead the court below had focused too much on the perceived need to build upon the recently established contact between the children and their father. Sir Nicholas Wall P said:[323]

> 99. The judge himself found that the mother would be 'devastated' were her application to be refused. That, in my judgment, is a critical finding. There is also the statement from her health visitor and from her general practitioner, to which the judge makes no reference, No criticism can be made or was made of her relocation plans. It follows that not only was her motivation unimpeachable, but that the plans themselves were plainly in the best interests of the children. Thus all the factors on her side of the scales weigh heavily—and most heavily weighs the effect on the children, through her, of a refusal of permission to relocate.

He went on the give his reasons for his conclusions:

---

[321] [2011] EWCA Civ 345.
[322] Mostyn J's judgment was merely referred to as 'interesting' by Lloyd LJ (para 148).
[323] See also the judgment of Lloyd LJ, paras 156–59.

103. The first is, of course, that when one is looking at the best interests of children, the best interests of their primary carer is a very important consideration and, I have to say, on the facts of this case, clearly outweighs the newly acquired relationship with the left behind parent.

104. Secondly, there was no evidence that the father's relationship with the children would be terminated. The mother's evidence was that the children would visit England and spend a month a year with the father. He would also have the benefit of Skype, telephone and writing, both by Email and letter. These, moreover, are all within the province of the court to *order*—a fact which the judge nowhere considers.

105. Thirdly the judge was in my judgment wrong to assume the impotence of the court either here or in Australia. If either court refused to make a contact order—or rescinded an order already made, it could only do so on the basis that the new order—or lack of it—was in the best interests of the children. As to that, the common evidence was that the continuation and expansion of the relationship was in the best interests of the children, and speaking for myself, I would expect both courts so to order.

106. Equally, in these days of instant communication and internationally established liaison judges, I have more confidence than the judge (he expressed none) that neither court would sit idly by and allow the relationship to wither ... .

108. There is, moreover, a further reason for criticising the judge under this heading. Professor Marilyn Freeman ..., conducted a one year qualitative research project into the question of relocation commencing in June 2008. ... Professor Freeman[324] published an article ... . She asks the direct question: 'Is Relocation in Children's Best Interests?' And the short answer which she gives is: 'we don't know'. She concludes her article with these words:

> 'So we have much work to do. We need to know, firstly, what impact relocation has on the relocated child and, in particular, about children's resiliency in these circumstances. From here, we will need to have the basis for international law to do what it says on the tin: to work in the best interests of the children the law seeks to serve.'

Nobody, I think, could disagree with that. I certainly do not.

109. In my judgment, it follows that the balancing exercise has to be carried out on the facts of the particular case. For the English Judge at first instance the facts may show a case in which the importance of the continuing relationship with a left behind parent tips the scale against relocation. Such cases do, of course, exist: see, for example, the decision of Mostyn J in *Re AR (a child: relocation)* [2010] EWHC 1346, to which the father refers. It is also, I think, worth noting that where the motivation of the relocating parent is found by the court to be inimical to welfare, the court has the power to prevent even a modest internal relocation:—see *Re L (Shared Residence Order)* [2009] 1 FLR 1157.

110. In my judgment, however, this is not one of those cases. In my judgment, performance of the balancing exercise in this points overwhelmingly to relocation being in the best interests of these children.

111. I test that conclusion by a straightforward application of the *Payne v Payne* exercise. I first apply the broad approach advocated by Thorpe LJ ... . The mother's proposals self-evidently are not contrary to the interests of the children, and thus the overwhelming weight of authority is in favour of relocation on the facts as found here.

112. Secondly, I apply the specified test proposed by Thorpe LJ ... . The mother's application is self-evidently genuine. ... It is not motivated by some selfish desire to exclude the father from the children's lives, although there is an anxiety that this may be its consequence. The applica-

---

[324] Freeman (2010).

tion is again self-evidently realistic—that is, founded on practical proposals both well researched and investigated. So the application passes Thorpe LJ's first two tests.

113. The father's opposition must be carefully appraised … . It is plainly genuine. I have rehearsed the evidence of detriment. As I have already pointed out, however, nowhere, however, does the judge consider how the loss of contact with the father would be 'offset by the extension of the children's relationships with the maternal family and homeland', although, as the evidence shows, this is plainly an element in the children's thinking. …

114. What would be the impact on the mother? The judge has found in terms that she would be 'devastated' … .

115. The 'outcome of the second and third appraisals must then be brought into an overriding review of the children's welfare as the paramount consideration'. In my judgment, this discipline point overwhelmingly in favour of relocation … .

117. It is not, of course, a numerical question. Each case turns on its own facts, and the weight to be given to various factors will change from case to case … .

118. I repeat:—the mother has a good case for going. Her proposals are sensible and well thought out. She would be 'devastated' if she and the children cannot go. She is Australian and going back to her family. The children want to go. She is isolated, 'trapped' and depressed in England. Against this has to be balanced the children's relationship with their father and the undoubted diminution in contact which will occur. Once again, whatever test is applied, the answer, in my judgment, is clear.

Finally, he made it clear that too much significance was being attributed to his criticism of *Payne* in the case of *Re D*:[325]

128 … Whilst I do not resile from most of what I have said, I am of the clear view that undue prominence has been accorded to *Re D*, … .

129. Wilson LJ in *Re H (A Child)* [2010] EWCA Civ 915 rightly criticises my use of the word 'ignores', which I retract. It further occurs to me that unless and until we have the research identified by Professor Freeman, and unless and until Parliament imposes a different test to that set out in section 1(1) of the Children Act 1989 (paramountcy of welfare), relocation cases will remain fact specific, the subject of discretionary decisions, and governed by *Pane v Payne*. (emphasis in original)

Relocation and Shared Care

One of the facts relevant to the decision of the court is the existence of a shared residence arrangement. In one case, a request to remove a child was denied because the child was being cared for in a shared care arrangement and, even if the mother did leave the country, it would be in the child's best interests not to experience the disruption of a move.[326] However it was said in another case that a shared residence order is not a bar to relocation.[327]

This issue has now been revisited by the Court of Appeal in *MK v CK*.[328] In this case

---

[325] See above.
[326] *Re Y (Leave to Remove from Jurisdiction)* [2004] 2 FLR 330.
[327] *Re L (Shared Residence Order)* [2009] EWCA Civ 20; [2009] 1 FLR 1157.
[328] [2011] EWCA Civ 793.

Thorpe LJ stated that the guidelines laid out in Payne are posited on the premise that the applicant is the 'primary carer' (para 40); 'Once the care is shared there is not the same dependency and the role of each parent may be equally important' (para 46). He went on:

> 39 As My Lord, Moore-Bick LJ, pointed out in argument, the only principle to be extracted from Payne v Payne is the paramountcy principle. All the rest, whether in paragraphs 40 and 41 of my judgment or in paragraphs 85 and 86 of the President's judgment is guidance as to factors to be weighed in search of the welfare paramountcy.
>
> 40 In family law principles are scarce and generally the more important function of this court is to state guidance. Guidance that directs the exercise of the welfare discretion is equivalent to a statutory checklist. It is valuable if it renders outcomes more predictable and if it supports judges in reaching and explaining discretionary conclusions in a way that is not open to appellate challenge. ...
>
> 57 I fully concur with the reasoning and conclusion of Hedley J.[329] What is significant is not the label 'shared residence' because we see cases in which for a particular reason the label is attached to what is no more than a conventional contact order. What is significant is the practical arrangements for sharing the burden of care between two equally committed carers. Where each is providing a more or less equal proportion and one seeks to relocate externally then I am clear that the approach which I suggested in paragraph 40 in Payne v Payne should not be utilised. The judge should rather exercise his discretion to grant or refuse by applying the statutory checklist in section 1(3) of the Children Act 1989.[330]

Moore-Bick LJ seems to emphasise the fact specific nature of these cases and the contingency of the application of the *Payne* guidance in all cases:

> 86 I accept, of course, that the decision in Payne v Payne is binding on this court, as it is on all courts apart from the Supreme Court, but it is binding in the true sense only for its ratio decidendi. Nonetheless, I would also accept that where this court gives guidance on the proper approach to take in resolving any particular kind of dispute, judges at all levels must pay heed to that guidance and depart from it only after careful deliberation and when it is clear that the particular circumstances of the case require them to do so in order to give effect to fundamental principles. ... As I read it, the only principle of law enunciated in Payne v Payne is that the welfare of the child is paramount; all the rest is guidance. Such difficulty as has arisen is the result of treating that guidance as if it contained principles of law from which no departure is permitted. Guidance of the kind provided in Payne v Payne is, of course, very valuable both in ensuring that judges identify what are likely to be the most important factors to be taken into account and the weight that should generally be attached to them. It also plays a valuable role in promoting consistency in decision-making. However, the circumstances in which these difficult decisions have to be made vary infinitely and the judge in each case must be free to weigh up the individual factors and make whatever decision he or she considers to be in the best interests of the child. As Hedley J said in Re Y, the welfare of the child overbears all other considerations, however powerful and reasonable they may be. I do not think that the court in Payne v Payne intended to suggest otherwise.

Black LJ is more reluctant to sideline *Payne*:

---

[329] In *Re Y* (above).
[330] He also referred to the argument that the mobility of the non-resident parent should be considered; could he also relocate? See para 47.

96 ... Where my reasoning and that of Thorpe LJ diverge is in relation to point ii), in particular in relation to the treatment of Payne v Payne. Thorpe LJ considers that Payne should not be applied in circumstances such as the present and that the judge should instead have applied the dicta of Hedley J in Re Y. For my part, as will become apparent, I would not put Payne so completely to one side. Whilst this makes no difference to the outcome of this case, it may not be without significance more generally.

97 I have found it helpful first to consider Payne in its historical context, which begins with Poel v Poel [1970] 1 WLR 1469. In these early cases I detect a struggle to reconcile a disinclination to interfere with the reasonable choice of the parent with custody as to how, and in particular where, they should live with the undoubted principle that the welfare of the child is the primary consideration in deciding whether to give that parent permission to move to live outside the jurisdiction. The answer to the conundrum was found in the conviction that the child's welfare was inextricably bound up with the happiness of the custodial parent and the stability of the home that he or she could provide and that that happiness and stability would be likely to be threatened if the parent was compelled to adopt a manner of life that he or she reasonably did not want. ...

141 The first point that is quite clear is that, as I have said already, the principle—the *only* authentic principle—that runs through the entire line of relocation authorities is that the welfare of the child is the court's paramount consideration. Everything that is considered by the court in reaching its determination is put into the balance with a view to measuring its impact on the child.

142 Whilst this is the only truly inescapable principle in the jurisprudence, that does not mean that everything else—the valuable guidance—can be ignored. It must be heeded for all the reasons that Moore-Bick LJ gives but as guidance not as rigid principle or so as to dictate a particular outcome in a sphere of law where the facts of individual cases are so infinitely variable.

143 Furthermore, the effect of the guidance must not be overstated. Even where the case concerns a true primary carer, there is no presumption that the reasonable relocation plans of that carer will be facilitated unless there is some compelling reason to the contrary, nor any similar presumption however it may be expressed. Thorpe LJ said so in terms in Payne and it is not appropriate, therefore, to isolate other sentences from his judgment, such as the final sentence of paragraph 26 ('Therefore her application to relocate will be granted unless the court concludes that it is incompatible with the welfare of the children') for re-elevation to a status akin to that of a determinative presumption. It is doubly inappropriate when one bears in mind that the judgments in Payne must be read as a whole, with proper weight given to what the then President said. She said that she wished to reformulate the principles since they may have been expressed from time to time in too rigid terms with the word 'presumption' over-emphasising one element of the approach (paragraph 82) whereas the criteria in s 1 Children Act govern the application (paragraph 83) and there is no presumption in favour of the applicant (paragraph 84). Dame Elizabeth referred, of course, to the effect on the parent with residence (paragraphs 83 and 84) but she also stressed that the relationship with the other parent is highly relevant and that there are many other factors which may arise in an individual case (paragraph 84). I detect in her discussion of the factors and in her summary at paragraph 85 no weighting in favour of any particular factor. She said that the reasonable proposals of the parent with a residence order wishing to live abroad carry 'great weight' whereas the effect on the child of denying contact with the other parent is 'very important' but I do not infer from that phraseology any loading in favour of the reasonable proposals as opposed to the effect of the loss of contact.

144 Payne therefore identifies a number of factors which will or may be relevant in a relocation case, explains their importance to the welfare of the child, and suggests helpful disciplines to

ensure that the proper matters are considered in reaching a decision but it does not dictate the outcome of a case. I do not see Hedley J's decision in Re Y as representative of a different line of authority from Payne, applicable where the child's care is shared between the parents as opposed to undertaken by one primary carer; I see it as a decision within the framework of which Payne is part. It exemplifies how the weight attached to the relevant factors alters depending upon the facts of the case.

145 Accordingly, I would not expect to find cases bogged down with arguments as to whether the time spent with each of the parents or other aspects of the care arrangements are such as to make the case 'a Payne case' or 'a Re Y case', nor would I expect preliminary skirmishes over the label to be applied to the child's arrangements with a view to a parent having a shared residence order in his or her armoury for deployment in the event of a relocation application. The ways in which parents provide for the care of their children are, and should be, infinitely varied. In the best of cases they are flexible and responsive to the needs of the children over time. When a relocation application falls to be determined, all of the facts need to be considered.

146 Despite my rather different view of Payne from that of Thorpe LJ, I agree with him that the judgment and the exchange with counsel that follows do not demonstrate that all the relevant factors were put properly in the balance. In particular, the contribution that the father was making to the children's welfare and the advice of the CAFCASS officer received insufficient attention. ...

147 I should make clear that in this case, I have been addressing only the issue of relocation outside this jurisdiction. The so-called 'internal relocation' cases have followed a slightly different path, outside the reach of Payne , and such argument as there may be about them is not for today. In so far as we were referred to that line of authorities, the reference was, I thought, rather too oblique to justify giving any prominence to it in the present context.

It seems, then, that within the judicial opinions we can discern competing visions of children's welfare as well as concerns about privileging resident parents' (usually mothers') interests. In the case of shared care, whether one adopts the approach of Thorpe LJ or Black LJ, it is likely that the perceived benefits of preserving the relationship between the respondent and child will weigh more heavily against the reasonableness of the plans of the parent wishing to relocate, the genuineness of her motives and the effect on her of a refusal of permission. However, while Thorpe LJ appears willing to rely on section 1(3) alone in shared care cases, Black LJ would still expect the court, whether in a shared care or a primary caretaker case, to apply the guidelines in the context of the welfare test. The latter approach may accord more prominence to the interests of the applicant. For example, on Thorpe's approach in shared care cases, the court would not be expected to pay attention specifically to the reasonableness of the relocation plans of the applicant or the nature of her motives.Ultimately, however, the decision of the court on either approach will depend to a large extent on the degree to which courts see children's well-being as being bound up with that of the parent who wishes to relocate.

X. VIOLENCE AND CHILD ABUSE

Buchanan et al (2001: 17) reported that one of the main reasons that led mothers in their research sample to oppose fathers' proposals about childcare was domestic violence.

Mothers' fears might relate to their own safety[331] and to that of their children. Similarly, Trinder et al (2005) found that mothers in their sample reported high levels of domestic violence, with some violence beginning after separation. Women referred to risks to both themselves and their children. Nevertheless contact was seldom supervised. Hester and Radford (1992) pointed to studies indicating that children who witness violence inflicted on their mothers suffer profound effects[332] and that men who are violent to their partners may also be violent to their children. In their own research, carried out between 1992 and 1995, they found that the children of half the women in their sample[333] had been physically and/or sexually abused by the women's partners and most had witnessed violence to their mothers (Hester and Radford 1996: 5, 9). Often, abuse or neglect occurred during contact visits (ibid: 10–11, 22).[334] Yet many of the professionals interviewed 'had a strong commitment to the idea of maintaining contact for children with non-resident fathers, even where there had been child abuse and the children were afraid' (ibid: 23).

Their study also confirms that there is a risk that contact may be used by fathers as an opportunity to continue harassment or abuse of their partners. The majority of women in their sample were assaulted by their husbands or partners after separation and '[a]ll of the post-separation violence was linked in some way to child contact' (ibid: 3).[335] In some instances, children were forced to aid their fathers in abusing their mothers (ibid: 10).

In spite of this, they found, most mothers did not hamper, and even facilitated, contact with violent partners provided they believed that it would benefit their children (ibid: 24–25). Nevertheless, when women did oppose contact, the problem was predominantly defined by professionals and courts alike as the mothers' hostility rather than the violence of their partners and its effect on the children.[336] Professionals failed to see any link between the welfare of children and the safety of their caretaking mothers.

Similar findings are reported in relation to a study conducted in 1995 by Rights of Women (Anderson 1997).[337] Mothers who had been abused were not generally opposed to contact but the wishes of those who were, and the wishes of their children, appeared to have little impact on outcomes. The author of the report commented that, '[i]t seems that the ideological assumption of the importance of contact with the father is so strong that cases are rarely dismissed as being without merit, however extreme the circumstances' (ibid: 8).

> **Q** Consider the cases concerning the 'implacably hostile' parent above. Do they bear out Hester and Radford's contention that it is the mother's hostility that is defined as the problem rather than the violence?

---

[331] Buchanan et al (2001: 15) found high levels of violence in their sample. This was frequent in many cases and often severe. For some mothers in the study the fear still persisted a year after court proceedings began (ibid: 61). Fortin et al (2006: 218) record that, in their study, domestic violence was common across social class at some stage in divorce. And, while many cases involving violence did not even reach court, it was more likely that those involving extreme violence or violence linked to mental illness would.

[332] See also Humphreys and Harrison (2003b: 240).

[333] See also McGee (2000) who interviewed women and children who had experience of domestic violence. In over 70% of cases the children had witnessed their mothers being physically assaulted. Over half the children were found to have been physically abused themselves and emotional abuse was found in almost two-thirds of the families. A significant proportion of the children had been subjected to controlling behaviour and some had been sexually abused.

[334] For an example of such a case, see *G v C (Residence Order: Committal)* [1998] 1 FLR 43.

[335] See also pp 8, 26–27.

[336] See pp 23–26. But see also *Re T (A Minor) (Parental Responsibility: Contact)* [1993] 2 FLR 450.

[337] It remains the case that contact with children is a precipitating factor in domestic violence incidents and violence occurs in the context of contact (Stanley et al 2010: 11).

Subsequent to the publication of research studies such as these and partly as a result of their findings,[338] concern about violence to women and children in the context of divorce increased. Campaigners publicised the research and called for protection.[339] Mediators and the court welfare service, now Cafcass, began to address the problem.[340] Legislation was also introduced acknowledging the need for protection. After initial opposition from the government on the ground that it was not relevant to divorce and separation,[341] a provision dealing with domestic violence was inserted into the 'general principles' contained in section 1 of the Family Law Act 1996.[342] However, this provision is of no obvious effect, given the fate of the 1996 Act. More significant is the amendment of the Children Act 1989: the definition of 'harm' in section 31 was expanded to include 'impairment suffered from seeing or hearing the ill-treatment of another'.[343] Although this provision does not apply to section 8 proceedings, the definition contained in it is included in the Practice Direction now governing contact and residence cases where domestic violence issues are raised.[344] Even prior to the publication of the original Practice Direction in 2008, reported judgments on contact began to reveal a growing awareness of the risks to mothers and children.

In *Re D (Contact: Reasons for Refusal)*[345] the Court of Appeal dismissed an appeal against a refusal to order direct contact.[346] The court accepted that the father presented a risk of physical harm to the child, or of physical harm to the mother to an extent that the child would be indirectly harmed. The court declined to treat this case simply as one involving an implacably hostile mother. Hale J remarked that the way in which that term is used is sometimes misleading and continued:

> It is ... an umbrella term that sometimes is applied to cases not only where there is hostility, but no good reason can be discerned either for the hostility or for the opposition to contact, but also to cases where there are such good reasons. In the former sort of case the court will be very slow indeed to reach the conclusion that contact will be harmful to the child. It may eventually have to reach that conclusion but it will want to be satisfied that there is indeed a serious risk of major emotional harm before doing so. It is rather different in the cases where the judge or the court finds that the mother's fears, not only for herself but also for the child, are genuine and rationally held; as indeed the court did in this case. (53)

There developed a greater readiness to accept that experiences of violence can have a lasting and traumatising effect so that mothers' opposition to contact becomes explicable and justifiable (Kaganas and Day Sclater 2000: 633).[347] And, in taking mothers' fears

---

[338] See *Re L (Contact: Domestic Violence); Re V (Contact: Domestic Violence); Re M (Contact: Domestic Violence); Re H (Contact: Domestic Violence)* [2002] 2 FLR 334, 369.

[339] Reece (2006a) argues that the almost exclusive focus on violence by feminist campaigners has redounded to women's detriment. The campaigns did not challenge the image of the unreasonable, implacably hostile mother and allowed women resisting contact to be placed into two categories: domestic violence victims and unreasonable women. Reece contends that, rather than framing arguments against contact in the research about domestic violence, feminist campaigners should advance explicitly autonomy based arguments criticising the ways in which women are expected to sustain the nuclear family even after it has broken up.

[340] See Chapter 15 below.

[341] See Bird and Cretney (1996: para 1.17).

[342] S 1(d) Family Law Act 1996.

[343] After consultation, see CASC (1999) and CASC (2000).

[344] See below.

[345] [1997] 2 FLR 48. For the law in Scotland, see *S v M (Access Order)* [1997] 1 FLR 980.

[346] See also *Re M (Contact: Family Assistance: McKenzie Friend)* [1999] 1 FLR 75.

[347] See *Re K (Contact: Mother's Anxiety)* [1999] 2 FLR 703, 708.

more seriously, the courts also began to examine the behaviour of the fathers concerned (ibid); 'violent fathers are now expected to deal with drink and drug problems and to confront their violence in counselling or therapy' (ibid). In *Re M (Contact: Violent Parent)*,[348] for example, Wall J stated:

> Often in these cases where domestic violence has been found, too little weight ... is given to the need for the father to change ... a father, like this father, must demonstrate that he is a fit person to exercise contact, that he is not going to destabilise the family, that he is not going to upset the children and harm them emotionally. (333)

The new focus on violence was central to the decision of the Court of Appeal in *Re L*.[349] Dame Butler Sloss P said:

> The family judges and magistrates need to have a heightened awareness of the existence of and consequences (some long term), on children of exposure to domestic violence between their parents or other partners. There has, perhaps, been a tendency in the past for courts not to tackle allegations of violence and to leave them in the background on the premise that they were matters affecting the adults and not relevant to issues regarding the children. The general principle that contact with the non-resident parent is in the interests of the child may sometimes have discouraged sufficient attention being paid to the adverse effects on children living in the household where violence has occurred. It may not necessarily be widely appreciated that violence to a partner involves a significant failure in parenting[350]—failure to protect the child's carer and failure to protect the child emotionally.
>
> In a contact or other s 8 application, where allegations of domestic violence are made which might have an effect on the outcome, those allegations must be adjudicated upon and found proved or not proved. It will be necessary to scrutinise such allegations which may not always be true or may be grossly exaggerated.[351] If however there is a firm basis for finding that violence has occurred, the psychiatric advice becomes very important.[352] There is not, however, nor should there be, any presumption that, on proof of domestic violence, the offending parent has to surmount a prima facie barrier of no contact. As a matter of principle, domestic violence of itself cannot constitute a bar to contact. It is one factor in the difficult and delicate balancing exercise of discretion ... . In cases of proved domestic violence, as in cases of other proved harm or risk of harm to the child, the court has the task of weighing in the balance the seriousness of the domestic violence, the risks involved and the impact on the child against the positive factors (if any), of contact between the parent found to have been violent and the child. In this context, the ability of the offending parent to recognise his past conduct, be aware of the need to change and make genuine efforts to do so, will be likely to be an important consideration. (341–42)

Dame Butler-Sloss P found that in the cases before her, the mothers' fears were 'reasonable' and that this distinguished them from 'implacable hostility' cases (343). In reaching

---

[348] [1999] 2 FLR 321. See also *Re H (Contact: Domestic Violence)* [1998] 2 FLR 42, 57.

[349] *Re L (Contact: Domestic Violence); Re V (Contact: Domestic Violence); Re M (Contact: Domestic Violence); Re H (Contact: Domestic Violence)* [2002] 2 FLR 334.

[350] This phrase echoes the word used in the Sturge–Glaser report that was before the court.

[351] In the research conducted by Buchanan et al (2001), half of the mothers interviewed reported violence or fear at the time proceedings commenced (ibid: 15) and for some, the fear persisted a year later (ibid: 61). Only a quarter regarded domestic violence as an issue in the proceedings (ibid: 15). So, rather than mothers making false allegations in proceedings, it seems that many mothers who have suffered abuse do not raise the matter in court.

[352] But see Saunders and Barron (2003: 8) on the appropriateness of this kind of expert evidence.

her conclusions she endorsed Wilson J's approach in *Re M (Contact; Welfare Checklist)*,[353] which involved using the section 1(3) checklist. This, she said, was 'a useful summary of the proper approach to a contact application where domestic violence is a factor'.[354]

Thorpe LJ, like Dame Butler-Sloss P, was careful not to elevate domestic violence cases to a special category, 'Domestic violence', he said. 'is one of a catalogue of factors that may operate to offset the assumption for contact but it has not been separately categorised ..., nor ... should it be' (367). Like Butler-Sloss P, he rejected the recommendation in the Sturge–Glaser report that, where a parent is or has previously been violent, there should be an assumption against contact. Instead he said: 'In my opinion the only direction that can be given to the trial judge is to apply the welfare principle and the welfare checklist, section 1(1) and (3) of the Children Act 1989, to the facts of the particular case' (370). The effect of domestic violence, along with other serious misconduct or deficiencies, would be to 'offset' the 'assumption' in favour of contact and to activate the checklist:

> [T]he factors that may offset the assumption in favour of contact are probably too legion to be either listed or categorised. Abuse must form the largest compartment: as well as physical abuse of the other parent and/or the child there is equally sexual and emotional abuse within the family. Then there is the self abuse of either drugs or alcohol and the failure to maintain sexual boundaries appropriate to the development of the child. Additionally mental illness or personality disorder may be a dominant factor as may be malign motives prompting the applicant to pursue a seemingly justifiable application for the covert purpose of threatening or dominating the primary carer. This uncomprehensive catalogue only demonstrates that the factor of domestic violence must be kept in proportion. (370)

So, on the basis of the President's judgment, the checklist must be used in cases where domestic violence has been proved. Thorpe LJ's obiter dictum appears more wide-ranging; it enumerates a number of factors that would invite the application of section 1(3). Nevertheless, both judges agree that the court should have discretion to award contact in cases of violence and, it seems, it is only in the exceptional cases that the assumption is offset; in cases not covered by the exceptions, the presumption/assumption in favour of contact persists.

The Labour government made it clear that it did not wish to introduce a presumption of no contact in cases where it has not been established that contact will be safe for all involved (DCA, DfES and DTI 2005: preamble to para 20).[355] However, guidelines for the courts substantially reflecting the judgments in *Re L* were published.[356] Despite this, concern mounted after the publication of a report on 13 cases in which 29 children were murdered by their fathers during contact.[357] It was clear in 11 of these cases that domestic violence was involved yet in five of them contact was ordered by the court. In three of those, contact was ordered by consent.[358] Investigation by the Family Justice Council revealed that the guidelines in *Re L* were being 'more honoured in the breach than the

---

[353] [1995] 1 FLR 274, 278–79. See above p 580.

[354] *Re L* 342–43.

[355] Compare s 60(3) of the New Zealand Care of Children Act 2004. The New Zealand legislation contains a presumption against unsupervised contact in cases of violence. See, further, Perry (2006). See also Radford et al (1999: 33); Saunders (2001); Saunders and Barron (2003: 61).

[356] CASC (2002).

[357] Saunders (2004). See also Wall (2009).

[358] Craig (2007: 1).

observance'.[359] Practice Directions followed and Practice Direction (Residence and Contact Orders: Domestic Violence and Harm)[360] now applies to all cases involving contact or residence where there are allegations of or concerns about domestic violence:

> [2] The practice set out in this direction is to be followed in any case in which it is alleged, or there is otherwise reason to suppose, that the subject child or a party has experienced domestic violence perpetrated by another party or that there is a risk of such violence. For the purpose of this direction, the term 'domestic violence' includes physical violence, threatening or intimidating behaviour and any other form of abuse which, directly or indirectly, may have caused harm to the other party or to the child or which may give rise to the risk of harm. ('Harm' in relation to a child means ill-treatment or the impairment of health or development, including, for example, impairment suffered from seeing or hearing the ill-treatment of another: Children Act 1989, ss 31(9), 105(1).)

The court is required to make findings on allegations of domestic violence that could affect its order (para 3). All applications for residence or contact must be sent by the court to Cafcass for screening and the results of this or any risk assessment must be placed before the court (paras 6–7). Consent orders should not be made by the court without scrutiny and consideration of any risks to the child (paras 4–5). Where domestic violence is raised as an issue in contact or residence proceedings, the court should consider calling for a Cafcass report unless this is not necessary to safeguard the child's interests (para 16). The court must consider whether the child should be made a party to the proceedings and be separately represented (para 17). Where any allegation of domestic violence is disputed, the court has to decide whether it is necessary to conduct a fact-finding hearing.[361] In deciding on interim contact, it must use the welfare checklist and also give particular consideration to the risks to the child (para 19).[362] The court should consider whether any contact ordered should be supervised or supported. It should endeavour to ensure that risks to the child are minimised and that the safety of the child and the resident parent is secured before, during and after contact.[363] At the final hearing, the court, where there are findings of fact, should apply the checklist in the light of those findings, giving particular consideration to the risks to the child. An order for contact should only be made if the court is satisfied that the 'physical and emotional safety' of the resident parent and the child can, 'as far as possible, be secured before, during and after contact'.[364] The court has to consider the effect of any violence proved on the child and the resident parent. In deciding whether the violence has been proven on a balance of probability, the court takes into account only those facts that are proven to that standard. Anything not proven on a balance of probability is taken out of the equation on the basis that it did not

---

[359] Ibid: 6.

[360] [2009] 2 FLR 1400

[361] The court has a discretion: *Re C (Domestic Violence: Fact-Finding Hearing)* [2009] EWCA Civ 994; [2010] 1 FLR 1728. Where the allegations are serious, the court should not terminate the hearing without hearing all available evidence: *Re R (Family Proceedings: No Case to Answer)* [2009] EWCA Civ 1619; [2009] 2 FLR 83, para 14.

[362] Interim contact, even supervised, is normally inappropriate if the allegations (if true) would be relevant to whether contact should be ordered and, if so, what kind: *S v S (Interim Contact)* [2009] EWHC 1575 (Fam); [2009] 2 FLR 1586, para 10. For a case where interim contact was ordered despite the fact that there was evidence that the father had taken out a contract on the mother, see *Re T (Wardship: Review of Police Protection Decision) (No 1)* [2010] 1 FLR 1017. See subsequently *Re T (Wardship: Review of Police Protection Decision) (No 2)* [2008] EWHC 196 (Fam); [2010] 1 FLR 1026.

[363] Practice Direction, paras 18–20.

[364] Ibid, para 26.

occur; there is 'no room for finding that the alleged event "might have happened"'.[365] In deciding whether to order contact, the court must also have regard to whether the non-resident parent's motivation is to continue his violence, or his intimidation or harassment of the other parent. It must consider what the contact parent's behaviour is likely to be like during contact and its effect on the child. Whether the contact parent appreciates the effect of the violence on the other parent and the child is also relevant, as is the attitude of the contact parent to past violence and whether he has the capacity to change.[366]

If direct contact is not considered appropriate, the court must consider making an order for indirect contact.[367] When direct contact is ordered in cases involving domestic violence, the court has to consider whether it should be supervised and whether conditions should be attached (such as seeking treatment or advice). In terms of the Practice Direction this is subject to any necessary consent being given.[368] However, under the amended section 11 of the Children Act 1989, the court can make contact activity directions or conditions to compel attendance at counselling or a perpetrator programme irrespective of consent.

The potential for protection offered by the Practice Direction has now been somewhat reduced. The President of the Family Division, expressing concern that split hearings[369] are 'taking place when they need not do so' and 'are taking up a disproportionate amount of the court's time and resources',[370] has issued guidance[371] for the courts. This states 'a fact-finding hearing is a working tool designed to assist them to decide the case. Thus a fact-finding hearing should only be ordered if the court takes the view that the case cannot properly be decided without such a hearing.'[372] If allegations of domestic violence are unlikely to affect the court's decision, there is no need for a separate fact-finding hearing.[373] Even if a fact-finding hearing is thought by the court to be necessary, it need not be held separately from the substantive hearing.[374] So courts are now perhaps less likely to investigate allegations of domestic violence thoroughly. Moreover, given the levels of understanding within the courts and among Cafcass officers about domestic violence, there may be many cases where mothers and children are put at risk. An inspection report published in 2005, for example, reported that the nature of domestic abuse was 'not sufficiently understood by most Cafcass officers' (HMICA 2005: 8).

---

[365] *Re T (Wardship: Impact of Police Intelligence)* [2009] EWHC 2440 (Fam), para 72. See also *Re B (Care Proceedings: Standard of Proof)* [2008] KHL 35; [2008] 2 FLR 141.

[366] Practice Direction, para 27.

[367] Ibid, para 29.

[368] Ibid, para 28.

[369] 'A split hearing is a hearing divided into two parts, during the first of which the court makes findings of fact on issues either identified by the parties or the court, and during the second part of which the court, based on the findings which it has made, decides the case. A "fact-finding hearing" is the first limb of a split hearing' (President's Guidance (Split Hearings) [2010] 2 FCR 271, para 4).

[370] Ibid, para 1.

[371] President's Guidance (Split Hearings) [2010] 2 FCR 271. This is designed to set out good practice; it is not binding (ibid, para 3).

[372] Ibid, para 6. See also *AA v NA and Others* [2010] EWHC 1282 (Fam); [2010] 3 FCR 327, para 18.

[373] President's Guidance, para 8.

[374] Ibid, para 7.

Harm to the Child

Where it is alleged that a child has been sexually[375] or otherwise[376] abused by the non-resident parent, or where the child has been harmed by witnessing domestic violence, the court may deny contact altogether. According to Thorpe LJ in *Re L*,[377] proof of domestic violence or abuse serves to 'offset' the 'assumption' in favour of contact. However, harm to the child is not necessarily a bar to contact and, in order to avoid terminating contact completely, the court has in the past sometimes ordered supervised or indirect contact. In *L v L (Child Abuse: Access)*,[378] for example, the court allowed supervised contact, finding that there was a close bond between father and daughter, that she showed no ill-effects and that contact was in her best interests.[379] In *Re L*[380] the Court of Appeal refused to allow direct contact in any of the four cases before it. In the first case, *Re L*, the father had engaged in serious and sadistic violence to the mother and there were risks of emotional harm to the child (345–46). In the second, *Re V*, the child continued to be distressed and traumatised by the experience of having witnessed a knife attack on his mother (348). In the third, *Re M*, the court found that if the child were forced to have contact, this would have a detrimental effect on him (353). And in the fourth, *Re H*, the father had made serious threats against the mother who was afraid of him and feared he would abduct the children. In addition, contact could expose the children to a clash of cultures (357). Nevertheless, the orders for indirect contact[381] made by the lower courts were considered appropriate in all four situations.

The Effects of Re L and of the Safeguards

Kaganas, commenting on *Re L*, suggested that whether it would help victims of violence and abuse would depend on whether the courts develop better knowledge about the dynamics of domestic violence. In *Re L* itself, it appears from the President's judgment that, in order to avoid being labelled 'implacably hostile', the resident parent needs to show not only that her fears are 'genuine' but also 'reasonable' (Kaganas 2000: 318–19).[382] This, arguably, does not take sufficient account of the experiences of some victims. Cessation of violence does not automatically bring women's fears to an end and some abused women may suffer post-traumatic stress giving rise to disproportionate anxiety. In any event, whether fears are regarded as reasonable depends on the court's understanding of violence and awareness of post-separation violence. It also depends on the court's assessment of the seriousness of the violence. Also relevant is whether the court sees domestic violence in terms of mutual combat: 'Fears are less likely to be perceived as "genuine" if the parties are seen as equals engaged in a fight. Fears are also less likely to be seen as

---

[375] *S v S (Child Abuse: Access)* [1988] 1 FLR 213.

[376] See *In re A (Contact: Domestic Violence)* [1998] 2 FLR 121 where the father's assault on one of the children as well as his violence against the mother were relevant to the court's decision to deny contact.

[377] *Re L (Contact: Domestic Violence); Re V (Contact: Domestic Violence); Re M (Contact: Domestic Violence); Re H (Contact: Domestic Violence)* [2002] 2 FLR 334.

[378] [1989] 2 FLR 16.

[379] See also *Re H (Minors) (Access: Appeals)* [1989] 2 FLR 174. For a critical appraisal of the courts' reluctance to deny contact, see Jones and Parkinson (1995).

[380] *Re L (Contact: Domestic Violence); Re V (Contact: Domestic Violence); Re M (Contact: Domestic Violence); Re H (Contact: Domestic Violence)* [2002] 2 FLR 334.

[381] See also in the context of care proceedings, *Re G (Domestic Violence: Direct Contact)* [2000] 2 FLR 865.

[382] See also *Re H (A Child: Contact: Mother's Opposition)* [2001] 1 FCR 59.

"genuine" if it is assumed that they cease once the violence has stopped' (ibid: 319). In addition, the fact that only proof of violence rather than evidence of risk suffices to 'offset' the assumption may leave women and children vulnerable. This restrictive test is, Kaganas argues, consistent with a 'general reluctance to curtail contact' (ibid: 318). Butler-Sloss P, for instance, warns in *Re L* of the danger of the 'pendulum swinging too far against contact where domestic violence has been proved' (342). There is, therefore, a possibility that 'the balancing exercise which the court is required to undertake under Section 1(3) might be deployed in a way that continues to accord contact greater weight than other considerations, such as the impact on resident mothers of past violence' (ibid).

Subsequent research examining the impact of *Re L* and of the Guidelines (now replaced by the Practice Direction) suggests that, while there were some improvements, courts have continued to prioritise contact over protecting abused women and children. A survey conducted by Women's Aid Federation of England (Saunders 2001) asked 127 refuge projects about the experiences of abused women and children in the period of approximately one year after *Re L* had been decided. Only 11 (8%) thought court practice had generally improved, while 66 (50%) said it had stayed the same. 61 (48%) said that, if contact was ordered despite allegations of abuse, adequate measures were not being taken to ensure the safety of the child and resident parent, while only three projects said they were. Most projects said their local contact centre provided only 'low vigilance' contact, as opposed to supervised contact. Nearly half reported that they knew of cases where a man used contact proceedings to track down his former partner. 30 (23%) said that they knew of abused women who were ordered to hand over their children for contact visits even though they were on the Child Protection Register as a result of abuse by the father. 45 projects reported that children had been harmed during contact visits.

Similar results emerged from a subsequent survey by Women's Aid (Saunders with Barron 2003).[383] This involved sending questionnaires in 2003 to refuges and domestic violence services, asking about their views concerning contact and residence proceedings since the Guidelines were first introduced in 2001.[384] There were 178 responses. The key findings of the study were that very few respondents thought that appropriate measures were being taken to secure the safety of the child and resident parent; children were not being listened to if they resisted contact; children were being required to have contact with fathers who had caused their names to be put on the child protection register or who had committed offences against children; children were being sent to live with violent parents; and violent parents used contact to track down their former partner (ibid: 5).

Smart and May concluded from the study that they conducted that, 'the courts operate under an assumption in favour of contact and it appears that, before the courts take the step of denying or restricting contact, they require substantial proof of harm potentially caused to the child by contact' (Smart and May 2004a: 41). And where courts do restrict contact, research findings raise questions about the safety of the measures currently being used to do so. Fortin et al reported that fathers' violence continued and orders designed to protect mothers and children such as those imposing supervision were simply disobeyed (Fortin et al 2006: 218).

Perry and Rainey's 2007 study showed an 'increased likelihood of an order for supervised or supported or indirect contact being made in cases in which violence featured, although many such cases simply resulted in an order for direct, unsupervised contact'

---

[383] See also Humphreys and Thiara (2002: 87ff).
[384] See CASC (2001a).

(Perry and Rainey 2007: 40). Indirect contact, they say, was seen by the judges 'as the last resort—a means of "opening the door" to contact in a situation where there seemed to be good reason not to order direct contact immediately' and to keep the possibility open even if there was no prospect of re-establishing direct contact (ibid: 37). The sorts of cases where indirect contact was used were 'extreme' such as cases of mental illness and imprisonment for a violent offence (ibid). Their research, conducted between 2003 and 2005, showed a lack of attention to allegations of violence. And although, as they say, the courts do sometimes restrict contact in cases of violence or abuse, research suggests that there is a possibility that if the court does make a contact order, even a supervised contact order, it will not necessarily ensure that either the resident mother or the child will be safe.

XI. CONTACT CENTRES

Contact centres were introduced largely in response to the perception that family break-down was increasing and that fathers were losing contact with their children, particularly when they had no suitable place to meet (Humphreys and Harrison 2003b: 239). Some contact centres offer high-vigilance supervision while others are low-vigilance supported centres.[385] A source of concern for commentators is that supported contact centres have been inappropriately used for families with a history of severe domestic violence (Humphreys and Harrison 2003a: 420–21). What is more, the courts, centre co-ordinators and fathers all put pressure on mothers to shift to more open arrangements (ibid: 422), which might be even less safe.

Humphreys and Harrison (2003b: 244) found that violence was being minimised or made invisible. One problem was that centre coordinators were not always aware of the history of violence. This could be because the woman never revealed it or because professionals, such as Cafcass officers and solicitors, did not pass on information about violence (ibid: 245). Another problem is that perpetrators deny or minimise violence and, often, there was no evidence corroborating the woman's allegations (ibid: 246–47). And even if there was evidence of violence, it was not always assessed by professionals and coordinators as relevant to contact (ibid: 248). Risks were not adequately investigated (ibid: 249–50) and, in any event, a pro-contact stance could override concerns about safety (ibid: 250).

These problems feature also in the research conducted by Perry and Rainey (2007: 39). Judges made extensive use of supported or supervised contact as a short-term measure designed to assuage the anxieties of resident parents before moving on to unsupervised contact (ibid: 36). Cases involving allegations of violence were more likely to be seen to warrant supported or supervised contact, as were cases where contact had been problematic before the proceedings (ibid). The authors observe:

> There were no 'typical' cases in which supervised contact was ordered. Some of the cases in which supervised or supported contact was used were highly problematic, involving high levels of conflict, allegations of inappropriate parenting, lack of parenting ability, fear on the part of the children, severe mental illness on the part of the non-resident parent, and so on. In others,

[385] Humphreys and Harrison (2003b: 241–42). Some supported centres do provide high levels of observation. See Humphreys and Harrison (2003a: 421).

the supervision or support was ordered to overcome practical obstacles less linked to the child's welfare, and more to do with the fact that the parents had thus far proved themselves incapable of putting contact into practice without assistance.

Supervised contact presents its own problems, not least of which is how the supervision is to be provided. There are also questions as to the level of supervision, and its purpose. Use of contact centres can be problematic in that many centres are set up and equipped to offer support for contact, but not to offer supervised contact. ... There can be problems, too, with relying on family or friends to provide supervision. If the purpose of such supervision is protection of the child, it is questionable as to what extent a grandparent or friend will be in a position to offer that protection. There is also the danger of the partisan nature of the designated supervisor. The contact parent's parents are likely to be loyal to the contact parent, unlikely to believe he or she constitutes a genuine threat to the child, and less likely to believe that supervision is really necessary. A friend or relative of the resident parent, on the other hand, may seek to undermine the relationship between the contact parent and the child by interpreting the necessity to provide supervision in such a way that it makes the whole contact experience extremely hard for the contact parent. (ibid: 36–37)

XII. SPECIFIC ISSUE ORDERS

While most disputes in the reported cases appear to revolve around contact, there can be disputes about specific decisions such as a child's schooling. These disputes can be resolved by means of specific issue orders or prohibited steps orders.

Section 8(1) provides that: '"a specific issue order" means an order giving directions for the purpose of determining a specific question which has arisen, or which may arise, in connection with any aspect of parental responsibility for a child'.

The court is empowered to give directions in order to resolve disputes. An order must relate to matters encompassed by parental responsibility such as medical treatment or education.[386] However, an order should be sought only for important matters. In *Re C (A Minor) (Leave to Seek Section 8 Orders)*[387] the court refused an application for leave made by a child wishing to go on holiday against her parents' wishes, indicating that orders should not be sought for trivial matters[388] or for the purpose of 'micro-managing' the child's life.[389] Orders can be sought in circumstances that, before the Children Act 1989, would have necessitated wardship proceedings;[390] they can be used to address serious and

---

[386] *Re R (A Minor) (Blood Transfusion)* [1993] 2 FLR 757; *Re O (A Minor) (Medical Treatment)* [1993] 2 FLR 149; *Re A (Specific Issue Order: Parental Dispute)* [2001] 1 FLR 121. A specific issue order may also be sought in relation to a change of surname: *Re PC (Change of Surname)* [1997] 2 FLR 730. In *Re HG (Specific Issue Order: Sterilisation)* ([1993] 1 FLR 587, 593) the court stressed that the notion of parental responsibility should not be interpreted restrictively.

[387] [1994] 1 FLR 26.

[388] See also *Re C (Residence: Child's Application for Leave)* [1995] 1 FLR 927, 931.

[389] See *Re N; A v G and N* [2009] EWHC 1807 (Fam); [2010] 1 FLR 272. See para 108. The court dismissed the father's application for specific issue orders and prohibited steps orders dealing with matters such as the homework in which subjects each parent should supervise and whether the mother should be forbidden to be on the premises when the child was having lessons.

[390] Cases where parents withhold consent to medical treatment may be brought before the court by a local authority where the child is at risk. See *Re R (A Minor) (Blood Transfusion)* [1993] 2 FLR 757, where the court held that a specific issue order was the appropriate mechanism for deciding whether the child of Jehovah's Witnesses should receive a blood transfusion. See *Re O (A Minor) (Medical Treatment)* [1993] 2 FLR 149 for a case where the court regarded the inherent jurisdiction as more appropriate.

sensitive questions. In *Re HG (Specific Issue Order: Sterilisation)*[391] the court was asked to decide whether a young woman with limited mental capacities should be sterilised. Although there was no dispute between the parents, said the court, this was a matter that could and should be brought before it under section 8. A dispute between parents as to what the child's religious affiliation and upbringing should be can also be resolved by means of a specific issue order.[392]

XIII. PROHIBITED STEPS ORDER

A prohibited steps order is defined in section 8(1) as: 'an order that no step which could be taken by a parent in meeting his parental responsibility for a child, and which is of a kind specified in the order, shall be taken by any person without the consent of the court'.

This order is modelled on the wardship jurisdiction.[393] A prohibited steps order is less wide-ranging in nature than wardship, however. Whereas the effect of wardship is to require any important decisions relating to the child to be brought before the court, a prohibited steps order places only those matters named in the order under the court's supervision. While an order may be directed at any person, not just someone with parental responsibility, it can only be made in respect of those steps that could be taken by a parent in meeting his or her parental responsibility for a child. So, for example, an order can be used to prevent someone, who is not party to the proceedings and who does not live with a child, from having contact with the child.[394] However, it cannot forbid parents to have contact with each other, because contact between parents has nothing to do with the exercise of parental responsibility.[395] It can also be used to prevent a parent moving with the child to a different area[396] or to forbid a change of school (Masson and Morris 1992: 32).[397]

It has been suggested that, because an order can prohibit only those steps that a parent could take in exercising parental responsibility, it cannot extend into those spheres where the minor is mature enough to make the relevant decision. For example, Masson and Morris (1992: 32) contend that 'an order could stop a person allowing a child to have cosmetic surgery or engage in a dangerous sport but would not be effective to prevent a mature young person making such a decision for himself'. Yet the wording of the section refers to the steps that could be taken by *a* parent and not *the* parent. This could be interpreted as referring to the parental responsibility of parents generally, rather than to the powers of the particular parent concerned, whose child might happen to be a mature minor. Moreover, in his comments in *Re R*, Lord Donaldson indicated that the court, 'in the exercise of its wardship or statutory jurisdiction', has the power to override the decisions of a *Gillick* competent minor as well as those of parents.[398] This suggests that the

---

[391] [1993] 1 FLR 587.

[392] In *Re J (Specific Issue Orders: Child's Religious Upbringing and Circumcision)* [2000] 1 FLR 571, the court dismissed an application made by Muslim father for a specific issue order that his son be circumcised.

[393] Law Commission (1988b: para 4.20).

[394] *Re H (Prohibited Steps Order)* [1995] 1 WLR 667.

[395] *Croydon London Borough Council v A (No 1)* [1992] 2 FLR 341.

[396] See s 1 of the Child Abduction Act 1984 and s 13 of the Children Act 1989 for consent requirements for the removal of a child from the jurisdiction. See, eg, *Re B (Prohibited Steps Order)* [2007] EWCA Civ 1055; [2008] 1 FLR 613.

[397] See *Re G (Parental Responsibility: Education)* [1994] 2 FLR 964.

[398] [1992] 1 FLR 190, 200. See also 199.

courts may be unwilling to accept an interpretation constraining their powers under section 8 in the manner suggested. If they do, it will remain open to a party to invoke the inherent jurisdiction.

XIV. SECTION 8 ORDERS AND EDUCATION: WHO DECIDES?

It is clear that disputes about education can be dealt with by means of specific issue or prohibited steps orders[399] and, as Gilmore (2004) notes, a number of reported specific issue cases are concerned with education. He examines the factors that are taken into consideration by the courts in deciding such cases:

> Each case very much depends on its own facts, but factors that have been highlighted in the case-law as relevant in such cases include: the timing of any proposed change of school and its effect on the child; the distance, and ease of travelling, to any relevant school(s); and, where the dispute is as to whether the education should be publicly or privately funded, the parents' current and ongoing ability to meet any school fees.[400] It has been said that where a child has recently changed school, compelling reasons will be required for further disruption to the child's schooling.
>
> Some of the disputes have a bicultural dimension, where parents of different nationalities and/or cultures are seeking to ensure that their own culture is reflected in the child's education. In general, the courts appear, in such cases, to have attempted to ensure some balance regarding the child's access to both cultures.[401] (Gilmore 2004: 379–80)

Gilmore (2004) raises the question of whether the court awarding a specific issue order has to make the decision itself or whether it can delegate decision-making power to someone else such as one of the parents. The case law on this is not clear.

In *H-D (Children)*[402] Hale LJ refused permission to appeal against a specific issue order which stated that the mother could control the choice of the children's schools and religious upbringing (para 13). Similarly, in *Re W (Children) (Education: Choice of School)*[403] the Court of Appeal approved an order that the children should attend the school of the mother's choice, although Hale LJ remarked that the purpose of specific issue orders is normally to 'decide the issue and not give the right of exclusive decision to one parent or the other'.[404]

Yet Thorpe LJ took a very different position in *Re P (Parental Dispute: Judicial Determination)*.[405] He allowed an application for permission to appeal against an order directing that questions about the children's education arising in the future should be finally determined by the mother following consultation with the father. He took the view that this amounted to 'the plainest failure to adjudicate' (para 6). The order was 'unprincipled' (para 11) and the result an abdication of the court's 'primary obligation to decide'

---

[399] See, eg, *M v H (Education Welfare)* [2008] EWHC 324 (Fam); [2008] 1 FLR 1400.

[400] See *Re W (Children) (Education: Choice of School)* [2002] EWCA Civ 1411; [2002] 3 FCR 473.

[401] See *Re A (Specific Issue Order: Parental Dispute)* [2001] 1 FLR 121.

[402] [2001] EWCA Civ 402.

[403] [2002] EWCA Civ 1411; [2002] 3 FCR 473.

[404] At para 5. Thorpe LJ concurred. See also *Re H (A Child: Parental Responsibility)* [2002] EWCA Civ 542, para 16.

[405] [2002] EWCA Civ 1627; [2003] 1 FLR 286.

(para 8).[406] The final decision had to be made by the judge and it was not permissible to 'appoint one of the parents with more or less absolute responsibility' (para 11), so empowering one and disempowering the other (para 12).

Reviewing these cases and noting the potential for contradictory interpretations of the judgments, Gilmore suggests that *Re P* should not be read as precluding entirely an order in the terms granted by the court below. He ventures that the decision was 'unprincipled' because the court below had failed to consider the question before it and simply delegated the decision. He argues that a specific issue order 'can and ought to be able to, empower others to determine a question'. But he concedes that the position is not entirely clear (Gilmore 2004: 370–71).

XV. THE FAMILY JUSTICE REVIEW

At the time of writing, there are signs that the law will change significantly and that specific issue orders may become central to litigation about children. Concerns about the mounting numbers of contact disputes that end up in court (and indeed return to court many times), about the associated cost and about the appropriateness of courts to deal with such cases have grown. A panel was set up to examine the family justice system and to make recommendations to change what is perceived as a 'system under strain' (Norgrove 2011 Executive Summary: p 5, para 59). The *Family Justice Review Interim Report* (Norgrove 2011a)[407] sets out what are seen to be the issues that need to be resolved and, in the context of private law disputes says:

> 11. In private law, many fail to resolve conflict independently and turn to court for judicial determination. Unfortunately, this often starts off a lengthy adversarial process with conflict potentially becoming more entrenched. Evidence shows such combative processes harm the children involved and may deepen the rifts that already exist between parents. The number of applications to court has increased steadily in recent years. In 2006 there were over 111,000 children involved in applications for private law orders. In 2009 this had increased to over 137,000. These figures point to an increasing reliance on court processes in the resolution of disputes between couples.[408]

> 12. The family justice system is also expensive, both for individuals and the state. We have no accurate figures for this, as for so much else about family justice, but we have estimated the cost to government alone (excluding the no doubt significant private costs) as £1.5 billion in 2009–10, of which roughly £0.95 billion is for public law and £0.55 billion for private.

> 103. We need to be realistic about the limitations of the state in dealing with these cases. Judges can provide resolution of issues, by virtue of a court order, and judicial determination in family relations is unavoidable in the most difficult cases, but it is a blunt instrument. The very process of achieving a determination may itself cause further harm to the individuals involved and the arrangements may not be successful in the long term. (Norgrove 2011 Executive Summary)

Among the measures suggested is that there be a single family court (ibid: para 46; Report: para 3.152) and that court social work services become part of the family justice

---

[406] See also para 11.
[407] See further Chapters 9 and 15.
[408] See also the Report, para 5.8.

system, subsuming the role currently performed by Cafcass (Norgrove 2011a Executive Summary: para 37; Report: para 3.104).[409] There is a recommendation for an online information helpline and hub to help parents resolve the issues confronting them. Among other things this would be used to give 'clear guidance' to parents about their responsibilities and to give them information about the cost of litigation as well as about alternative forms of dispute resolution, including mediation and Separated Parents Information Programmes (PIPs) (Norgrove 2011a Executive Summary: para 114).[410] If parents wish to go to court, they will, if the recommendations are implemented, have to be assessed by a mediator to establish the most appropriate way of resolving the case. This might be mediation, collaborative law or, in cases where there are safety concerns or a serious imbalance of power, the court (ibid: para 115). After being assessed, parents will be required to attend a PIP where they will be told about the court process and the cost it entails. Parents, the panel notes, are often deterred from litigation when they know about the effect on children, the cost and that the judge will not necessarily condemn their former partner (ibid). If necessary parents should go to mediation or another accredited method of dispute resolution such as collaborative law sessions (ibid: para 119).

While the proposed process is designed to keep parents out of court, the panel members did consider what changes should be made in respect of the orders available to courts where cases do reach them. In particular they explored the possibility of introducing legislation to 'strengthen the rights of children to a continuing relationship with both parents (and others, for example grandparents)[411] after separation' (ibid: para 107). However there appears to be no enthusiasm for a presumption in favour of shared residence.[412] The panel referred to evidence 'about the significant damage done to children when legislation creates expectations about a substantial sharing of time against the wishes of the parent with whom the child mostly lives' (ibid). It concluded:[413]

5.73 Trinder[414] suggests that research indicates early or pre-existing parent or family characteristics predict subsequent pathways and outcomes ... . It appears that if parents share parental care fully before separation, they are more likely to do so successfully after separation. The panel sees that there are limits as to what legislation can achieve if this approach to parenting is not taken prior to separation.

5.74 In our view, achieving 'shared parenting' in those cases where it is safe to do so is a matter of raising parental awareness at the earliest opportunity. This is intended to manage expectations and move towards recognition of parental responsibilities rather than parental rights, as

---

[409] Further change is said to be necessary, according to the response of the House of Commons Justice Committee (2011).

[410] See also the Report, para 5.59.

[411] The panel decided not to recommend removal of the requirement that grandparents seek permission before applying to court (Report, paras 5.79ff). However, at the time of writing there is a Private Member's Bill before Parliament entitled the Grandparents (Access Rights) Bill 2010–11. Its purpose and content are not yet public.

[412] At the time of writing a Private Member's Bill is before Parliament. It is entitled the Children (Access to Parents) Bill 2010–11 and it is intended to require courts and local authorities to operate a presumption that 'the rights of a child include the right to grow up knowing and having access to and contact with both of the parents involved in the residence or contact case concerned, unless exceptional circumstances are demonstrated that such contact is not in the best interests of the child; to create an offence if a relevant body or person does not operate under or respect such a presumption' (http://services.parliament.uk/bills/2010-11/childrenaccess-toparents.html, accessed 27 April 2011).

[413] See also the Report, para 5.68ff, and the Executive Summary, para 108.

[414] Trinder (2010).

opposed to making any significant changes to the welfare principle of section 1 of the Children Act 1989, or to the approach of the courts.

5.75 Our proposals are designed to enhance the regard given to the status of shared parental responsibility and to shift the focus of potentially warring parents so that consideration is given to how this responsibility is practically shared post-separation.

5.76 Based on the experiences of Sweden and Australia, the panel has concluded that no legislation should be introduced that creates or risks creating the perception that there is a parental right to substantially shared or equal time for both parents.

5.77 But we do see merit in inserting a general statement of intent, similar to the delay principle, into the Children Act 1989. This would reflect the case law on contact, reinforcing the importance of the child continuing to have a meaningful relationship with both parents, alongside the need to protect the child from harm.

5.78 Such a statement would guide parents when coming to their own arrangements, whether or not they seek assistance via mediation or alternative dispute resolution. It would also reinforce the starting point of the courts, which has been recognised in case law, for the minority of cases that do require judicial determination. This amendment would require courts to take into account:

> the benefit to a child of having a meaningful relationship with both of his or her parents; and
> the need to protect the child from physical or psychological harm. (Norgrove 2011a Report)

112. *Residence and contact orders should no longer be available to parents who have PR for their child, but disputes over the division of a child's time between parents should instead be resolved by a specific issue order.* This is intended to reduce both the likelihood of long and unfocused hearings, and to move from a sense of a 'winner' in terms of 'awarding' residence and contact.[415]

113. We plan to give further thought to how disputes should be resolved where fathers do not have PR. Our expectation is that a *father without PR who wishes the court to consider the child living with him (currently a residence order) should first apply for PR, and then negotiate for this to be included in the Parenting Agreement, or apply for a specific issue order. The full range of the four orders under section 8 of the Children Act 1989 should remain open to a father who does not have PR or to other non-parental relatives.*

(Norgrove 2011a Executive Summary, emphasis in original)

The House of Commons Justice Committee (2011), responding to the recommendations made in the *Review* appeared to doubt the utility of intervention and information given by means such as the proposed hub but it has endorsed the recommendation not to enact a presumption in favour of shared parenting:

65. The evidence shows that courts rarely deny contact between child and parent. Most applications that result in no contact are abandoned by the applicant parent. In our view this reflects the reality of the cases that come before the court. In the majority of cases it will be in a child's best interests to have meaningful contact with both parents. In cases where a parent constitutes a danger to his or her child, either directly or through failing to protect them from others, the courts must remain free to refuse, or specify the arrangements for, contact in order to protect the child.

---

[415] See also Report, para 5.95.

66. The Australian experience of introducing a shared parenting presumption shows that it does not contribute to children's well-being, which, in our view, must be the paramount aim and objective of the family courts. We believe therefore that the best interests of the child should remain the sole test applied by the courts to any decision on the welfare of children in the family justice system.

It has rejected the recommendation that there be a statement in the legislation to guide parents:

71. We do not see any value in inserting a legislative statement reinforcing the importance of the child continuing to have a meaningful relationship with both parents, alongside the need to protect the child from harm, into the Children Act 1989. Such a statement is not intended to change the current position as the law already acknowledges that a meaningful, engaged relationship with both parents is generally in a child's best interests. The Panel has concluded that the family court system is allowing contact in the right cases; in our view nothing should be done that could undermine the paramount importance of the welfare of the child.

XVI. CONCLUSION

The Committee is correct that the law already acknowledges the need for continuing relationships and the suggestion in the *Review* could have changed little. It is already the case that parents (mothers) are being pressured to agree contact arrangements. It is already the case that parents (mothers) tend to internalise the normative message that contact is good for children in general. As we saw above, it is not lack of education that fuels contact disputes. In addition, it must be doubtful that abandoning contact and residence orders in favour of specific issue orders, as suggested in the *Review*, will make much difference either. What would essentially be a change in terminology is unlikely to have a significant effect;[416] the change from 'custody' to residence and contact orders certainly did not. What might change the section 8 landscape is the proposed restriction on legal aid.

POSTSCRIPT

While this book was in press the *Family Justice Review. Final Report* was published (Norgrove 2011b). This reiterates many of the recommendations in the Interim Report such as the creation of an information hub, as well as the use of Parenting Agreements, Mediation Information and Assessment Meetings and PIPs. However it does contain some changes. The Report makes it clear that the need for grandparents to apply for permission before making an application for contact should remain (Executive Summary para 110). It also makes it clear that there should be no presumption of shared parenting and withdraws its earlier suggestion that the legislation be amended to emphasise the importance to children of a 'meaningful' relationship with both parents (Executive Summary para 109). Such a change could lead to increased litigation, misunderstanding of the law and added complications (Report paras 4.29ff). Most radically, the Report recommends that residence and contact orders be abolished. However, instead of substituting these with specific issue orders as suggested in the Interim Report, the Final report recommends the

---

[416] But see Report, para 5.94.

introduction of a 'child arrangements order'. Specific issue orders and prohibited steps orders would remain. The new order would 'would encompass all arrangements for children's care in private law' (Report para 4.60). If this is warranted by the scope of the order, fathers without parental responsibility would be vested with it (para 4.64). In our view, the introduction of a 'child arrangements order' could fuel litigation or at least disputes over its contents. The potential breadth of its scope could lead to arguments between parents not only about where the child will live or who the child should spend time with, but over more specific matters as well.

FURTHER READING

J DEWAR, 'The Normal Chaos of Family Law' (1998) 61 *MLR* 467.

J FORTIN, C RITCHIE and A BUCHANAN, 'Young Adults' Perceptions of Court-ordered Contact' (2006) 18 *CFLQ* 211.

M HESTER and L RADFORD, *Domestic Violence and Child Contact Arrangements in England and Denmark* (Bristol, Policy, 1996).

C HUMPHREYS and R THIARA, *Routes to Safety* (Bristol, WAFE, 2002).

C HUMPHREYS and C HARRISON, 'Squaring the Circle—Contact and Domestic Violence' (2003) *Fam Law* 419.

——, 'Focusing on Safety—Domestic Violence and the Role of Child Contact Centres' (2003) 15 *CFLQ* 237.

J HUNT and A MACLEOD, *Outcomes of Applications to Court for Contact Orders after Parental Separation or Divorce* (London, Ministry of Justice, 2008).

F KAGANAS, 'Contact, Conflict and Risk' in S Day Sclater and C Piper (eds), *Undercurrents of Divorce* (Aldershot, Ashgate, 1999).

——, '*Re L (Contact: Domestic Violence; Re V (Contact: Domestic Violence); Re M (Contact: Domestic Violence); Re H (Contact: Domestic Violence)*: Contact and Domestic Violence' (2000) 12 *CFLQ* 311.

——, 'Judgment: *Re L (A Child: Domestic Violence)*' in R Hunter, C McGlynn and E Rackley (eds), *Feminist Judgments: From Theory to Practice* (Oxford, Hart Publishing, 2010).

F KAGANAS and A DIDUCK, 'Incomplete Citizens: Changing Images of Post Separation Children' (2004) 67 (6) *MLR* 959.

M KING and F KAGANAS, 'The Risks and Dangers of Experts in Court' (1998) *Current Legal Issues* 221.

B NEALE, J FLOWERDEW and C SMART, 'Drifting Towards Shared Residence?' (2003) *Fam Law* 904.

C PIPER, 'Ascertaining the Wishes and Feelings of the Child' (1997) *Fam Law* 796.

——, 'Assumptions About Children's Best Interests' (2000) 22 *Journal of Social Welfare and Family Law* 261.

——, 'Commentary on Re L' in R Hunter, C McGlynn and E Rackley (eds), *Feminist Judgments: From Theory to Practice* (Oxford, Hart Publishing, 2010).

L RADFORD, S SAYER and AMICA, *Unreasonable Fears? Child Contact in the Context of Domestic Violence: A Survey of Mothers' Perspectives of Harm* (Bristol, WAFE, 1999).

H RHOADES, 'The "No-Contact Mother": Reconstructions of Motherhood in the Era of the "New Father"' (2002) 12 *Int J Law, Policy and the Family* 71.

B ROCHE, 'International Relocation: Case for a Payne-less Future?' (2010) *Fam Law* 978.

H SAUNDERS and J BARRON, *Failure to Protect? Domestic Violence and the Experiences of Abused Women and Children in the Family Courts* (Bristol, WAFE, 2003).

C SMART and V MAY, 'Residence and Contact Disputes in Court' (2004) *Fam Law* 36.

C SMART and B NEALE, 'Arguments Against Virtue—Must Contact Be Enforced?' (1997) *Fam Law* 332.

C SMART et al, *Residence and Contact Disputes in Court* (London, Department for Constitutional Affairs, DCA Research Series No 6/03, 2003).

L TRINDER et al, A Profile of Applicants and Respondents in Contact Cases in Essex (London, DCA Research Series 1/05, 2005).

11

Decisions about Children's Upbringing

I. INTRODUCTION

We later discuss how the law moved from protecting paternal authority to safeguarding children's[1] welfare,[2] so that child protection came to be seen as a legitimate reason for intervention in the family.[3]

Talk about child protection has at times been couched in terms of children's rights,[4] but since the 1970s a number of commentators have sought to expand the concept of children's rights to embrace the notion of self-determination.[5] The views of the children's liberationists of that era, who advocated the same sorts of rights for children as there are for adults, have not been widely accepted. As Fortin says, 'many contemporary writers are now chary of claiming for children a moral right to autonomy identical to that claimed by adults' (Fortin 2009a: 19).[6] There are, she says, 'good theoretical grounds' for this caution:

> Few deny that mature children are often able to take on far more responsibility than many adults give them credit for … . [But] few philosophers today consider that children have the competence for complete autonomy and some see paternalism as having an important role to play in restricting their powers of self-determination. (ibid)

Herring points out that even the more moderate versions of child liberation theory are difficult to apply. According to this more moderate account, differences should not be based on age alone but can be based on competence or understanding. However, says Herring (2011: 435–36), competence can be difficult to assess on a case-by-case basis.[7]

Of course, children's rights/interests need not be promoted at all and their views can legally be ignored as long as the family's decision-making remains in the private domain.[8]

---

[1] In this chapter the words 'children' and 'minor' are used to denote those under the age of 18.
[2] See Chapter 13 below.
[3] See Chapters 13 and 14 below.
[4] See Freeman (1983: 18–19).
[5] See the discussion in Freeman (1983: 22–24). For a comprehensive discussion of children's rights, see Fortin (2009a: chs 1 and 2). See also Herring (2011: 435–43); Bainham (2005: 97ff).
[6] See also Bainham (2005: 100).
[7] This is nevertheless the basis of the *Gillick/Fraser* test. See below.
[8] Only a minority of children are consulted about arrangements that affect them when parents separate. See May and Smart (2004: 305–06) and references cited there. Smart and Neale found that for many children it was important to be given information and to participate in making arrangements after parental separation or divorce (Smart and Neale 2000: 165). See also Buchanan and Hunt (2003: 372–73).

But there is some recognition that it might be beneficial to consult children about matters affecting them[9] and there has been a proliferation of research seeking to reveal children's experiences in the context of, for example, domestic violence or parental separation. Sociologists of childhood have sought to explore notions of agency in relation to children.[10] Constructions of children and childhood have changed to accommodate images of children as actively influencing the shape of their own lives, the lives of those around them and the societies in which they live. And, for some years now, legal theorists working within a rights framework have been grappling with the competing images of children and young people as rational and competent on the one hand, and, on the other hand, as irrational and vulnerable. They have sought to theorise ways in which competent young people can be empowered to make their own choices about their lives and, at the same time, can be protected from their own folly and from abuse by others.

Freeman, for example, has identified four categories of rights. These are rights to welfare; rights to protection; rights which adults have (eg to vote); and autonomy rights (Freeman 1983: 40). Children, he said, can be assumed to want to be given the chance to mature into 'a rationally autonomous adulthood and [to] be capable of deciding on [their] own system of ends as free and rational beings' (ibid: 57). They would want to be shielded from decisions that would frustrate this goal and so should not be permitted to exercise their rights in a way that would prevent them from achieving it (ibid).

Eekelaar has spoken of three interests which might be said to form the foundation of rights claims. The 'basic interest' refers to '[g]eneral physical, emotional and intellectual care' (Eekelaar 1986: 170) from immediate caregivers. The second interest, whereby children's capacities should be developed to their best advantage, is termed the 'developmental interest' (ibid). Finally, he said, children have an interest in choosing their own lifestyles free of adult control: the 'autonomy interest' (ibid: 171). In the event of the child's autonomy interest conflicting with the developmental or basic interests, the latter interests should prevail. He argued that few adults would retrospectively want to have been allowed to make choices that would have prejudiced their life chances. Eekelaar subsequently developed his theory to take greater account of children's interest in making choices (Eekelaar 1994a). He devised the concept of 'dynamic self-determinism'. This is based on an understanding of children's best interests that allows scope for the child to determine what those interests are. He maintained that the 'very fact that the outcome has been, at least partly, determined by the child is taken to demonstrate that the outcome is in the child's best interests' (ibid: 48). It should be the competent child's decision that should determine the issue under consideration, but this should be subject to two limitations. The child's decision must be compatible with the law and with the interests of others. And the child should not be permitted to make decisions 'contrary to his or her *self-interest*, … narrowly defined in terms of physical or mental well-being and integrity' (ibid: 57).

We can see in both Freeman's and Eekelaar's analyses of children's rights the difficulties encountered in seeking to reconcile the competing images of children and childhood, the competing imperatives of self-determination and protection. The law too has had to confront this dilemma and the issue of children's autonomy has proved particularly problematic (Douglas 1992: 570). In general, the law continues to maintain a paternalistic stance; children are perceived as being in need of protection both from themselves and from others. They lack full legal capacity and decisions about their upbringing are normally entrusted to the adults who are responsible for them.

---

[9] See Fortin (2009a: 7).
[10] See Chapter 4 above.

Yet the law has increasingly come to treat the child, and the older child in particular, as an individual whose views, which might conflict with those of other family members, should be taken seriously. The *Gillick* case[11] gave us the concept of the competent minor, and legislation gives prominence to the wishes of the child. In relation to private law proceedings,[12] relevant statutory provisions include the checklist in section 1 of the Children Act 1989, requiring that, in opposed section 8 applications, the court should take into account the wishes and feelings of the child.[13] In addition, young people, if of sufficient understanding, can invoke the jurisdiction of the court to oppose parental decisions about them.[14] This possibility is not welcomed by some commentators. Guggenheim[15] argues, for instance, that his 'parental rights doctrine' would ensure that 'the important decisions in [children's] lives will be made by those who are most likely to know them best and to care the most for them'. The alternative of state oversight and intervention which would attend the public assertion of rights, he contends, will not serve children well (Guggenheim 2005: 46):

> Children do not need rights within the family. What they need are rules that work. Keeping families free from state oversight will do more for children than encouraging litigation and judicial intervention. (ibid: 249)

The principle of family autonomy continues to find expression in the law,[16] but 'parental power' can now be challenged by children as well as by the child protection machinery (Bell 1993: 398). Yet, allowing young people access to the courts does not in itself cause family tension and breakdown as alleged by some. On the contrary, says Fortin, where court proceedings are brought it is likely that family relationships are already damaged. And in those cases, 'it is better to be a rights-holder than to "depend on the kindness and favors of others"' (Fortin 2009a: 11).[17] 'Rights are important', says Freeman, 'because they recognise the respect their bearers are entitled to. To accord rights is to respect dignity: to deny rights is to cast doubt on humanity and on integrity' (Freeman 2007a: 7).[18] 'Rights are important', he continues, 'because those who have them can exercise agency. Agents are decision-makers' (ibid: 8).

Article 12 of the United Nations Convention on the Rights of the Child[19] is intended to promote participation in decision-making by children; it provides:

> 1. States parties shall assure to the child who is capable of forming his or her own views the right to express those views freely in all matters affecting the child, the views of the child being given due weight in accordance with the age and maturity of the child.
>
> 2. For this purpose the child shall in particular be provided the opportunity to be heard in any judicial and administrative proceedings affecting the child, either directly, or through a repre-

---

[11] See below at pp 506ff.

[12] S 1(3) of the Children Act 1989 also applies to child protection proceedings under Part IV. In relation to private law, see also ss 20(6), 22(5), 26, 46(3)(d), 61(2) and 64(2).

[13] S 1(3)(a) of the Children Act 1989.

[14] See below.

[15] For critical reviews of Guggenheim's book, see Freeman (2006). For a critique of Guggenheim's focus on the law as a solution to intergenerational problems, see King (2007).

[16] Eg in the non-intervention principle contained in s 1(5) of the Children Act 1989. The emphasis on mediation in relation to decisions about children also supports the idea of family autonomy but it is notable that opinion is moving in favour of involving children in the process. See Chapter 15 below.

[17] Citing Bandman (1973). See Fortin (2009a: 11, fn 51).

[18] See also Freeman (2010).

[19] This has not been incorporated into domestic law and is of persuasive force only (Fortin 2009a: 47–48).

sentative or an appropriate body, in a manner consistent with the procedural rules of national law.

Fortin points out, however, that the provision offers scope for restricting autonomy because it refers to children's 'age and maturity' (Fortin 2009a: 43).[20] She also notes that the mechanisms to enforce Convention obligations are weak (ibid: 46ff), and that the government has exploited internal inconsistencies within the Convention (ibid: 48) and has failed to make people aware of its contents (ibid: 54).[21] Moreover, although children's rights are also protected by the Human Rights Act 1998 and by the ECHR, and although the ideas in the ECHR concerning autonomy are influencing domestic courts in the context of decisions about adolescents (ibid: 25), the Convention is not specific to children and not designed to promote their autonomy.[22] And as far as the Children Act 1989 is concerned, Piper asserts that the introduction of provisions requiring consideration of children's wishes and feelings was mainly intended to add 'the child's perspective to the operation of the welfare test'; the law is primarily concerned with children's welfare (Piper 1999b: 79).

The law, and also government policy, emphasise children's participation in, rather than control of, decision-making (Roche 1999: 58). This 'new right to a conversation', Roche says, avoids the difficulty of choosing between self-determination and paternalism: the languages of rights and welfare converge (ibid: 58–59). The child's best interests require a consideration of that child's wishes: 'The child's right to participate, as opposed to making the decision, is integral to their welfare as well as respectful of their liberty rights' (ibid: 59).

This participation is limited. In particular, although this may be changing somewhat, the courts have tended to seem uncomfortable with the notion of the child as an active participant in decision-making and in legal proceedings.[23] It has often been assumed that children should not have the 'burden' of saying what they want[24] and that 'court is a bad place for children' (Piper 1999c: 396). Indeed, it seems that in some ways, children's participation may be becoming even more restricted, particularly as a result of the increasing privatisation of disputes between parents about their children on divorce or separation. Increasingly, parents are being encouraged to make their own arrangements when it comes to childcare after divorce or separation.[25] If they cannot agree they are exhorted to settle their differences without resorting to court; they are told to use mediation or alternative dispute resolution (ADR). This, say Harold and Murch, may lead to the marginalisation of the child.[26] Unless mediators and in-court conciliators involve children

---

[20] See also the Charter of Fundamental Rights of the European Union (2000/C 364/01). Art 24 makes children's welfare a 'primary consideration' and states that children's views will be taken into consideration in accordance with their 'age and maturity'. The UK has opted out and is not bound by this convention (Protocol 30 on the Application of the Charter of Fundamental Rights of the European Union to Poland and the United Kingdom).

[21] See UN Committee on the Rights of the Child (2002: para 29). The Committee states that the obligations under Art 12 have not been consistently incorporated into legislation such as that dealing with divorce and adoption. Also, it says, the right to independent legal representation is not 'systematically exercised'. For more recent criticism of compliance, see UN Committee on the Rights of the Child 2008.

[22] On children's rights and the ECHR, see Fortin (1999); Fortin (2009a: ch 2); Fortin (2011).

[23] See Roche (1995: 285); Newsline (2003: 296).

[24] See Mr Justice Coleridge (2010: 15).

[25] See Piper (1999c). See further Chapter 10 above and Chapter 15 below.

[26] See Chapter 15. See also Dame Butler-Sloss with Fiddy (2001: 16).

directly, they will often have to rely on parents' perceptions of their children and these may not be reliable (Harold and Murch 2005: 199).[27]

Even if children are permitted to participate in mediation or ADR, the problem remains that the process may fail to check or compensate for power imbalances within the family and, as a result, children could be disadvantaged relative to the more powerful adults involved. Concerns arise also from the fact that the separating or divorcing family is being closed off from public scrutiny.

Arguably, it is the ability to invite this scrutiny that is regarded as the most important aspect of giving children a say. It appears that neither the courts nor Parliament have so much endorsed children's autonomy rights as opened up the private family, and parental conduct, in particular, to 'new forms of surveillance' in some areas, making the family more susceptible to regulation (Lyon and Parton 1995: 40, quoting Alan Prout). Children's rights can be invoked to intervene in the private family to protect children.[28] Indeed, Nelken has suggested that, whatever the concerns about increasing children's autonomy, in the medium term the idea of children's rights has led to increased control by welfare professionals over the child (and we would say, over the family). This development, he argued, was consistent with what he saw as a trend to undermine the control of parents in favour of the 'psy' professions (Nelken 1998: 318).

While Nelken's observations remain valid today, another trend has developed alongside the paternalistic one he noted. Government policy has, during the last decade, placed great emphasis on the desirability of families and the individuals within them taking responsibility for themselves and for bettering the society in which they live. Increasingly, we think, children's participation is coming to be seen as a way of 'civilising' children, transforming them into responsible citizens and removing the potential threat to society they could pose through delinquency and social exclusion.[29] There is, in some spheres and particularly in relation to the youth justice system, a 'move away from a paternalistic model of regulation that stresses the essential passivity of youth toward the cultivation of a more active subjectivity within young people who will be required to take more responsibility for their lives' (Vaughan 2000: 348).[30] In addition, children are supposed to be able to develop their citizenship qualities through having a voice in shaping policy[31] as a result of the creation, by the Children Act 2004, of the office of Children's Commissioner. Yet, at the same time, as we shall see in this chapter, children are still perceived as vulnerable. It is notable that while the Equality Act 2010 provides protection from various forms of discrimination, including age discrimination, it does not extend to children in this respect. The government explained:

> Age discrimination provisions do not extend to the under 18s because it is almost always appropriate to treat children of different ages in a way which is appropriate to their particular stage of development, abilities, capabilities and level of responsibility.

---

[27] See Chapter 15 below.

[28] But see Cooper (1998: 85) who argues that rights can drive a wedge between family members and 'unwisely' cast them in the role of adversaries. See also Guggenheim (2005).

[29] See Kaganas and Diduck (2004).

[30] Vaughan argues that in relation to criminal liability, we are treating children more like autonomous adults but that the effect of this is to enable young people to be regulated more intensively than before (Vaughan 2000: 359).

[31] See also the references to increasing participation of children and consultation with them by government, local authorities and civil society generally, UN Committee of the Rights of the Child (2002: para 29).

Children of different ages have different needs, which should be reflected by the support and services they receive. (HM Government 2010b: para 7, 11)

Within law, policy and sociology, then, there has emerged a 'blended' image of the child incorporating two previously competing images (Kaganas and Diduck 2004: 961). The first is the child as incompetent, dependent and vulnerable. This child is one whose welfare is to be prioritised over rights because he or she is not yet fully capable of exercising rights competently. This image is rooted in ideas of the child as 'becoming' a rational and competent subject. The second image, espoused by sociologists of childhood, is that of the child as 'being'. On this view children are capable of agency, of affecting their environments, attachments and identity. Both these constructs contribute to the image of the child in law (ibid: 961–62).[32] In this chapter we explore, primarily within the contexts of decision-making and representation, the tensions between the notion of the child as 'becoming', who is vulnerable and whose welfare must be protected, and the child as 'being', who must have his or her rights respected and who must be accorded a measure of autonomy.[33] The chapter also touches on the tensions between welfare and autonomy as well as the tensions between children's autonomy and family privacy. In the context of medical treatment of neonates, it raises the issue of the privacy and autonomy of the family in circumstances where the life of the infant is at stake.

II. PARENTAL RESPONSIBILITY AND DECISION-MAKING

As we saw in Chapters 4 and 8 above, parental responsibility confers on a person 'all the rights, duties, powers, responsibilities and authority which by law a parent of a child has in relation to the child and his property'.[34] This includes the capacity to make decisions concerning the child's education and to consent to medical treatment.[35] Each parent may act independently of the other in meeting his or her responsibility[36] but it appears that parental responsibility confers a right to be consulted or informed about important matters such as education and some medical procedures, including vaccination and circumcision, and perhaps, all important matters in the child's life.[37]

Parental responsibility does not confer absolute powers on anyone who holds it. The law makes provision for a child as well as other interested parties to challenge parental decisions in court.[38] In addition, young people themselves have limited capacity to make decisions concerning medical treatment. It was in relation to medical decisions that the first significant moves were made to confer on children some autonomy and it is to that subject we now turn.

---

[32] See Freeman (2010: 9–15).

[33] See further, Diduck (2003: ch 4).

[34] S 3(1) of the Children Act 1989. On theories explaining why it is parents who have rights and responsibilities, see Herring (2011: 402–05).

[35] See pp 175–76 above.

[36] S 2(7) of the Children Act 1989.

[37] *Re G (Parental Responsibility: Education)* [1994] 2 FLR 964; *Re H (Parental Responsibility)* [1998] 1 FLR 855, 859. See pp 344–46 above.

[38] In some cases, the local authority has instituted proceedings to obtain a ruling on a question relating to a child's medical treatment. See, eg, *Re C (HIV Test)* [1999] 2 FLR 1004.

III. THE COMPETENT MINOR AND MEDICAL TREATMENT

Where adults are concerned, unless there are exceptional circumstances, the consent of the patient is essential to any medical examination or treatment. In the absence of valid consent, any examination or treatment constitutes an assault and renders the doctor liable in tort.[39] The law's emphasis on the autonomy of the individual and the right to physical integrity is reflected in the rule that competent adults have an absolute right to choose whether or not to undergo medical treatment, for any reason, rational or irrational or for no reason at all, even if their decisions lead to their own deaths.[40] Although in recent years the courts have shown themselves at times ready to find this presumption rebutted,[41] it is presumed that adults are competent to make these decisions.

The position of children is very different, however. The adults responsible for the child are empowered to decide on his or her medical treatment.[42] The Children Act 1989 gives some authority to temporary carers to make such decisions,[43] but, apart from this statutory exception and the exception recognised under the doctrine of necessity,[44] the consent of someone with parental responsibility is normally required before a child can be medically examined or treated.[45] Depending on the seriousness with which the treatment decision is viewed, the decision may be one in relation to which each person with parental responsibility is obliged to consult the other.[46] Where the parents are in dispute, one can institute section 8 proceedings in the form of an application for a specific issue order or a prohibited steps order to challenge the other's decision. The decision of the court is made on the basis of the welfare principle, taking into account any expert evidence before it as well as other considerations.[47]

There are circumstances in which parents have a positive duty to ensure that their children receive medical treatment,[48] but otherwise it is within their discretion to give or

---

[39] See *In Re T (Adult: Refusal of Treatment)* [1992] 3 WLR 782, 787; *Re B (Consent to Treatment: Capacity)* [2002] EWHC Fam 429; [2002] 1 FLR 1090.

[40] See *Sidaway v Board of Governors of the Bethlem Royal Hospital and the Maudsley Hospital* [1985] AC 871, 904–05; *Re T (An Adult) (Consent to Medical Treatment)* [1992] 2 FLR 458, 460; *Re MB (Medical Treatment)* [1997] 2 FLR 426, 432; *St George's Healthcare NHS Trust v S; R v Collins, ex parte S* [1998] 2 FLR 728; *Re JT (Adult: Refusal of Medical Treatment)* [1998] Fam Law 23; *Re AK (Medical Treatment: Consent)* [2001] 1 FLR 129; *Re B (Consent to Treatment: Capacity)* [2002] EWHC Fam 429; [2002] 1 FLR 1090.

[41] See *In re T (Adult: Refusal of Treatment)* [1992] 3 WLR 782; *Re MB (Medical Treatment)* [1997] 2 FLR 426. But see *St George's Healthcare NHS Trust v S; R v Collins, ex parte S* [1998] 2 FLR 728; *Re B (Consent to Treatment: Capacity)* [2002] EWHC Fam 429; [2002] 1 FLR 1090.

[42] Where a child is in care, the local authority shares parental responsibility with the parents. See Chapter 14 below.

[43] S 3(5) enables a temporary carer to arrange for medical assistance in an emergency resulting from, eg, an accident but does not authorise consent to major elective surgery (see Law Commission 1988b: para 2.16).

[44] A doctor may treat a patient in an emergency without first obtaining the necessary consents if this is necessary to save life or safeguard health. See *F v West Berkshire Health Authority* [1989] 2 All ER 545, 564 and 566.

[45] Where treatment is undertaken without consent, the cause of action lies in tort and would have to be based on trespass to the child's person. See further Bainham (2005: 318).

[46] Presumably serious surgery would qualify. The courts appear to be expanding the categories of medical procedures that warrant consultation: eg immunisation (*Re C (Welfare of Child: Immunisation)* [2003] EWCA Civ 1148; [2003] 2 FLR 1095) and circumcision of a boy (*Re J (Specific Issue Orders: Child's Religious Upbringing and Circumcision)* [2000] 1 FLR 571). Female circumcision is illegal: Female Genital Mutilation Act 2003.

[47] *Re C (Welfare of Child: Immunisation)* [2003] EWCA Civ 1148; [2003] 2 FLR 1095. See O'Donnell (2004) for a critical appraisal of this exercise in *Re C*.

[48] Children and Young Persons Act 1933 s 1. See Chapter 4 above.

withhold[49] consent.[50] However, the law has, consonant with changing perceptions of children, come to embrace the idea that children's wishes should be heeded and, in some circumstances, be allowed, in the event of conflict, to prevail over those of their parents.[51]

Older minors are empowered by statute to consent to medical procedures.[52] Section 8 of the Family Law Reform Act 1969 provides that:

> 8(1) The consent of a minor who has attained the age of sixteen years to any surgical, medical or dental treatment.[53] ... shall be as effective as it would be if he were of full age; and where a minor has by virtue of this section given an effective consent to any treatment it shall not be necessary to obtain any consent for it from his parent or guardian. ...
>
> ...
>
> (3) Nothing in this section shall be construed as making ineffective any consent which would have been effective if this section had not been enacted.

It is in the courts, in judgments interpreting the statutory rules and expounding on the common law, that the law on medical decision-making is being shaped. This process began with the landmark decision of the House of Lords in *Gillick v West Norfolk and Wisbech Area Health Authority*.[54]

Gillick/*Fraser Competence*

The *Gillick* case arose out of the decision of the then Department of Health and Social Security to issue to Area Health Authorities a memorandum of guidance on family planning which indicated that, in 'exceptional' circumstances, a doctor could lawfully prescribe contraception to girls under 16 without their parents' knowledge or consent. Victoria Gillick, a mother of daughters under the age of 16, objected to the guidance and sought a declaration that it was unlawful. The arguments put forward on her behalf were, first, that a doctor acting on the guidance would be guilty of a criminal offence;[55] secondly, that children under the age of 16 years could not validly consent to medical treatment; and, thirdly, that the guidance could or did adversely affect her rights as a parent. Mrs Gillick failed in the court of first instance but the Court of Appeal allowed her appeal. The case

---

[49] O'Donnell (2004) points out that in relation to minor issues, both parents can agree to withhold treatment. In relation to major matters, their decision can be challenged in court. Where the parents are in dispute, even minor matters become justiciable and the courts do not tend to show any preference for endorsing the views of the primary carer.

[50] They have the power to consent to therapeutic treatment and, it seems, non-therapeutic treatment where this is for the benefit of the child (Bainham 2005: 316–17). Herring suggests that a parent cannot give effective consent to a procedure that is detrimental to the child (Herring 2011: 457). Some procedures, such as sterilisation that is not incidental to other medical treatment, require the consent of the court. See the discussion in *Re HG (Specific Issue Order: Sterilisation)* [1993] 1 FLR 587, 594–95.

[51] Compare *Nielsen v Denmark* (1988) 11 EHRR 175. The ECtHR held that a 12 year old could be confined to a closed ward on the authority of his mother and against his wishes. His Art 5 rights were not infringed and his mother's Art 8 rights included the right to exercise parental authority. Fortin (2009a: 160) suggests that it is unlikely that medical teams could shelter behind *Nielsen* if they rely on parental consent to detain an uncooperative, but *Gillick/Fraser*-competent, child.

[52] See also in the context of public law, ss 38(6) and 43(8) of the Children Act 1989.

[53] It appears that organ donations are not within the scope of this provision. See Fortin (2009a: 151).

[54] [1986] 1 AC 112.

[55] By encouraging the commission of unlawful sexual intercourse contrary to s 28 of the Sexual Offences Act 1956.

went before the House of Lords, where the majority rejected the argument based on the criminal law and focused on the other two issues. By a majority of three to two, the DHSS's appeal was upheld and a test based on competence rather than chronological age was adopted to determine capacity.

On the question of capacity, Lord Fraser of Tullybelton had this to say:

> The contention on behalf of Mrs Gillick was that section 8(1) [of the Family Law Reform Act 1969] shows that, apart from the subsection, the consent of a minor to such treatment would not be effective. But I do not accept that contention because subsection (3) leaves open the question whether consent by a minor under the age of 16 would have been effective if the section had not been enacted. (167)

> It would ... appear that, if the inference which Mrs Gillick's advisers seek to draw ... is justified, a minor under the age of 16 has no capacity to authorise any kind of medical advice or treatment or examination of his own body. That seems to me so surprising that I cannot accept it in the absence of clear provisions to that effect. It seems to me verging on the absurd to suggest that a girl or a boy aged 15 could not effectively consent, for example, to have a medical examination of some trivial injury to his body or even to have a broken arm set. Of course the consent of the parents should normally be asked, but they may not be immediately available. Provided the patient, whether a boy or a girl, is capable of understanding what is proposed, and of expressing his or her own wishes, I see no good reason for holding that he or she lacks the capacity to express them validly and effectively and to authorise the medical man to make the examination or give the treatment which he advises. After all, a minor under the age of 16 can, within certain limits, enter into a contract. He or she can also sue and be sued, and can give evidence on oath. Moreover, a girl under 16 can give sufficiently effective consent to sexual intercourse to lead to the legal result that the man involved does not commit the crime of rape ... .
>
> Accordingly, I am not disposed to hold now, for the first time, that a girl aged less than 16 lacks the power to give valid consent to contraceptive advice or treatment, merely on account of her age. (169)

He then went on to consider the question of parental rights and duties, pointing out that parental rights existed, not for the benefit of the parent, but for the benefit of the child. They were justified, he said, only in so far as they enabled the parent to perform parental duties (170). He cited (at 172) with approval the dictum of Lord Denning in *Hewer v Bryant*[56] to the effect that the rights of parents were 'dwindling' rights 'which the courts will hesitate to enforce against the wishes of the child, and the more so the older he is. It starts with a right of control and ends with little more than advice'. Lord Fraser then continued:

> Once the rule of the parents' absolute authority over minor children is abandoned, the solution to the problem in this appeal can no longer be found by referring to rigid parental rights at any particular age. The solution depends upon a judgment of what is best for the welfare of the particular child. Nobody doubts, certainly I do not doubt, that in the overwhelming majority of cases the best judges of a child's welfare are his or her parents. Nor do I doubt that any important medical treatment of a child under 16 would normally only be carried out with the parents' approval. ... But there may be circumstances in which a doctor is a better judge of the medical advice and treatment which will conduce to a girl's welfare than her parents. ...
>
> The only practicable course is to entrust the doctor with a discretion to act in accordance

[56] [1970] 1 QB 357, 369.

with his view of what is best in the interests of the girl who is his patient. He should, of course, always seek to persuade her to tell her parents that she is seeking contraceptive advice, and the nature of the advice that she receives. At least he should seek to persuade her to agree to the doctor's informing the parents. But there may well be cases, and I think there will be some cases, where the girl refuses either to tell the parents herself or to permit the doctor to do so and in such cases, the doctor will, in my opinion, be justified in proceeding without the parents' consent or even knowledge provided he is satisfied on the following matters: (1) that the girl (although under 16 years of age) will understand his advice; (2) that he cannot persuade her to inform her parents or to allow him to inform the parents that she is seeking contraceptive advice; (3) that she is very likely to begin or to continue having sexual intercourse with or without contraceptive treatment; (4) that unless she receives contraceptive advice or treatment her physical or mental health or both are likely to suffer; (5) that her best interests require him to give her contraceptive advice, treatment or both without the parental consent. (173–74)

> **Q** Who, according to Lord Fraser, should decide whether advice or treatment should be given? Is it the parents, the girl or the doctor? What criteria should form the basis of this decision?

Lord Scarman, like Lord Fraser, rejected the interpretation of section 8(3) of the Family Law Reform Act 1969 put forward on Mrs Gillick's behalf. And like Lord Fraser, he adopted the view that parental rights existed only for the purpose of fulfilling duties; parental rights, he said, could be challenged or even overridden if not exercised in accordance with the welfare principle (184). However, his judgment can be read as conveying a clearer endorsement of young people's autonomy:[57]

> The underlying principle of the law was exposed by Blackstone and can be seen to have been acknowledged in the case law. *It is that parental right yields to the child's right to make his own decisions when he reaches a sufficient understanding and intelligence to be capable of making up his own mind on the matter requiring decision.* (186, emphasis added)

> *I would hold that as a matter of law the parental right to determine whether or not their minor child below the age of 16 will have medical treatment terminates if and when the child achieves a sufficient understanding and intelligence to enable him or her to understand fully what is proposed.* It will be a question of fact whether a child seeking advice has sufficient understanding of what is involved to give a consent valid in law. Until the child achieves the capacity to consent, the parental right to make the decision continues save only in exceptional circumstances. Emergency, parental neglect, abandonment of the child, or inability to find the parent are examples of exceptional situations justifying the doctor proceeding to treat the child without parental knowledge and consent. ...
>
> When applying these conclusions to contraceptive advice and treatment it has to be borne in mind that there is much that has to be understood by a girl under the age of 16 if she is to have legal capacity to consent to such treatment. It is not enough that she should understand the nature of the advice which is being given: she must also have a sufficient maturity to understand what is involved. There are moral and family questions, especially her relationship with her parents; long-term problems associated with the emotional impact of pregnancy and its termination; and there are the risks to health of sexual intercourse at her age, risks which contraception may diminish but cannot eliminate. It follows that a doctor will have to satisfy himself that she is able to appraise these factors before he can safely proceed upon the basis that she has at law capacity to consent to contraceptive treatment. (188–89, emphasis added)

---

[57] But see Gilmore (2009).

Q How do you interpret the italicised passages in this judgment? In whom does Lord Scarman say the capacity to decide resides? Do you think most adults have the kind of knowledge required of girls under 16? Could a young person who makes a decision that to adult eyes appears detrimental to her interests still qualify as '*Gillick* competent' or, as it is often now termed, 'Fraser competent'? How would you advise a doctor who asked you whether she was required to comply with the clear and confidential request of a mature and intelligent 15-year-old girl for contraceptive treatment, when she was not sure that it would be in the girl's best interests to become sexually active?

While the *Gillick* case concerned medical decisions, it was interpreted by some commentators as recognising young people's capacity to make their own choices and it was thought that this autonomy might extend to other spheres.[58] For example, the reasoning in *Gillick* was used in *Roddy*[59] to reach a decision to allow a girl, not quite 17 years old, to make public her story about her time in care. She was of an age and of sufficient maturity, and had sufficient understanding, to decide for herself. Herring is of the view that the implication of that case is that *Gillick* is 'of general application' (Herring 2011: 459). Eekelaar, writing soon after *Gillick*, also thought the case very significant for children's autonomy:

> The significance of Lord Scarman's opinion with respect to children's autonomy interests cannot be over-rated. It follows from his reasoning that, where a child has reached capacity, there is no room for a parent to impose a contrary view, *even if this is more in accord with the child's best interests*. For its legal superiority to the child's decision can rest only on its status as a parental right. But this is extinguished when the child reaches full capacity. More importantly, the argument catches the court itself ... . The inherent jurisdiction of the High Court to intervene in the lives of children rests on the doctrine of the Crown's role as *parens patriae*. But on what principle can the Crown retain the parental jurisdiction when the parent himself has lost it, not through deprivation, but due to the superior right of the child? The primary question ... can no longer be: what is in the best interests of the child? It must be, has the child capacity to make his own decisions?
>
> This recognition of the autonomy interests of children can be reconciled with their basic and developmental interests only through the empirical application of the concept of the acquisition of full capacity. This, as Lord Scarman made clear, may be no simple matter. The child must not only understand the nature of the transaction, but be able to evaluate its implications. Intellectual understanding must be supplemented by emotional maturity. It is easy to see how adults can conclude that a child's decision which seems, to the adult, to be contrary to his interests, is lacking in sufficient maturity. In this respect, the provision of the simple test of age to provide an upper limit to the scope of a supervisory, paternalistic power has advantages. ... [C]ould we not say that it is on balance better to subject all persons to this potential inhibition up to a defined age, in case the failure to exercise the restraint unduly prejudices a person's basic or developmental interests? It avoids judgments in which question [*sic*] of fact and value will be impenetrably mixed. But the decision, it seems, has been taken. Children will now have, in wider measure than ever before, that most dangerous but most precious of rights: the right to make their own mistakes. (Eekelaar 1986: 181–82, emphasis in original)

---

[58] But see Gilmore (2009).
[59] *Re Roddy (A Child) (Identification: Restriction on Publication)* [2003] EWHC 2927 (Fam); [2004] 2 FLR 949. See paras 56–57.

Q Explain what Eekelaar means when he refers to the mixing of questions of fact and value.

The concept of '*Gillick* competence'[60] is a flexible one, enabling the courts to demand capacity commensurate with the gravity of the consequences of the decision in question.[61] On occasion, the levels of understanding demanded have been very high. For example, in *Re E (A Minor) (Wardship: Medical Treatment)*[62] the court overruled the refusal of a Jehovah's Witness, a few months short of his 16th birthday, to accept blood transfusions. Ward J (as he then was) found that the boy, who suffered from leukaemia, was intelligent and realised he might die without transfusions. Nevertheless, he was not sufficiently competent because he did not have a full understanding of the manner of his death and the extent of his own and his family's suffering.[63] Similarly, a Jehovah's Witness aged 15½ was held not to be '*Gillick* competent' because she too had an insufficient understanding of the manner of her death and the pain and distress that would attend it. Moreover, she was child-like in hoping for a miracle to save her.[64] In *Re L (Medical Treatment: Gillick Competency)*[65] another Jehovah's Witness, aged 14, failed the test of *Gillick* competence because she did not have enough knowledge of the details of the 'horrible' way in which she would be likely to die. She did not have the requisite knowledge because the surgeon did not tell her.[66] Nevertheless this contributed to the court's decision. It was also influenced by the fact that she lived a sheltered life among her family and under the influence of a religious congregation.

In *Re M (Medical Treatment: Consent)*[67] the court was faced with the refusal of a 15½ year old girl to consent to a heart transplant. She explained her refusal saying she did not want to have someone else's heart and that she did not want to take medication for the rest of her life. The court was at pains to point out that she was intelligent and that her views should carry 'considerable weight' (1100). Nevertheless, she was judged to be 'overwhelmed by her circumstances and the decision she was being asked to make' (ibid). It appears from this, although the court did not rule explicitly on M's competence, that it considered her to be lacking the competence necessary to make the decision. In any event, the girl's mother had consented to the treatment and the court simply went on to state that despite the risks of the surgery and of organ rejection, and despite the risk that M might resent what had been done to her, the alternative of certain death meant that the operation would be in her best interests and should go ahead.

Q Although there is evidence that the courts may on occasion be willing to intervene in adults' decisions to refuse treatment, the way they have applied the '*Gillick*/Fraser competence' test appears to be more rigorous than the test used to determine adult competence. Why do you think this might be? The court in

---

[60] On the concept of competence in relation to young children and adolescents, see Fortin (2009a: 81ff).

[61] See *Re S (A Minor) (Consent to Medical Treatment)* [1994] 2 FLR 1065, 1076. This test has been applied also in relation to adult capacity. See *In re T (Adult: Refusal of Treatment)* [1992] 3 WLR 782, 799; *Re MB (Medical Treatment)* [1997] 2 FLR 426, 437.

[62] [1993] 1 FLR 386.

[63] This patient, when he reached the age of 18, is reported to have exercised his right to refuse blood and died. See *Re S (A Minor) (Consent to Medical Treatment)* [1994] 2 FLR 1065, 1075.

[64] *Re S (A Minor) (Consent to Medical Treatment)* [1994] 2 FLR 1065.

[65] [1998] 2 FLR 810.

[66] Herring (2011: 451, n 421) reports that the BMA has suggested that doctors should not withhold information for fear of distressing a young patient.

[67] [1999] 2 FLR 1097.

Re E remarked that courts 'should be very slow to allow an infant to martyr himself' (394). Do you think this explains their approach? Do these decisions bear out Eekelaar's concern that the unacceptability of the young person's decision could lead to a finding of incapacity? Do you agree with Bridge (1999: 591), who suggests that the application of the competence tests is a 'sham' because the court makes its decision on the basis of outcome and its view of the child's welfare?

Q Fortin suggests that society has an interest in protecting young people until they reach the age of majority and that it might be more honest to accept that a patient is *Gillick* competent but to override his or her wishes all the same (Fortin 2009a: 155).[68] Do you agree?

The 'Retreat' from Gillick

Eekelaar and Herring have interpreted the *Gillick* decision as giving the competent child the right to make mistakes. However, judges in subsequent cases have balked at this prospect and have interpreted the decision restrictively. The Court of Appeal has taken the view that *Gillick* establishes only that a competent child can give valid consent to medical treatment; it does not give the child a right to veto the administration of treatment. A distinction had to be drawn between cases where children consent to treatment and where they refuse it. A competent child's refusal to undergo treatment can be overridden by a person with parental responsibility. What is more, whether it is a competent minor's consent or refusal that is in question, his or her decision can be overridden by a court exercising its inherent jurisdiction or, it seems, on an application for an order under section 8 of the Children Act 1989.[69] The court needs first to consider whether the child is competent but, even if the child is competent, the court must apply the welfare principle. Where it is in the child's interests to do so, the court can override the child's wishes and, indeed, those of the parents.

In *Re R (A Minor) (Wardship: Medical Treatment)*[70] the court was asked to consider whether a 15-year-old girl was entitled to refuse treatment in the form of medication. She was admitted to an adolescent psychiatric unit and diagnosed as psychotic. The unit made it clear that, if she was to remain a patient in its care, it should have a free hand in the administration of medication, whether she consented to it or not. During a lucid interval,

---

[68] See also Bridge (1999a: 594).

[69] The use of the inherent jurisdiction is said to be appropriate at least in relation to older children (CAAC 1992/93: 68). The wardship jurisdiction was successfully invoked to override a minor's refusal to undergo medical treatment in *Re R (A Minor) (Wardship: Medical Treatment)* [1992] 1 FLR 190. Alternatively, proceedings can be brought under the inherent jurisdiction or under s 8, perhaps in the form a specific issue order (see *Re K, W and H (Minors) (Medical Treatment)* [1993] 1 FLR 854, 859; *Re HG (Specific Issue Order: Sterilisation)* [1993] 1 FLR 587). In *Re O (A Minor) (Medical Treatment)* [1993] 2 FLR 149, the court took the view that applications such as that in question, concerning an infant child of Jehovah's Witnesses requiring blood transfusions, should ordinarily be made under the inherent jurisdiction. Where a local authority is the applicant and is seeking a result that could be achieved by means of a specific issue order, the use of the court's inherent jurisdiction is unnecessary and inappropriate. In any event, cases where the fundamental beliefs of the parents might be overridden should be heard *inter partes* and in the High Court wherever possible *(Re R (A Minor) (Blood Transfusion)* [1993] 2 FLR 757). See further Children Act Advisory Committee Report (1992/93: 67–68).

[70] [1992] 1 FLR 190.

the girl indicated that she did not wish to take the drugs prescribed for her. A consultant psychiatrist reported that if she failed to continue with the treatment, her more florid psychotic behaviour was likely to recur. The court found that she was not competent, even if she was capable of passing the *Gillick* test on good days; her fluctuating mental disability rendered her incompetent.[71] In any event, whether she was competent or not, the wardship court was empowered to override her decision. Lord Donaldson commented obiter on the implications of the *Gillick* case and on the question of whether a minor could validly refuse treatment:

> [C]onsent by itself creates no obligation to treat. It is merely a key which unlocks a door. Furthermore, whilst in the case of an adult of full capacity there will usually only be one keyholder, namely the patient, in the ordinary family unit where a young child is the patient there will be two keyholders, namely the parents, with a several as well as a joint right to turn the key and unlock the door. If the parents disagree, one consenting and the other refusing, the doctor will be presented with a professional and ethical, but not with a legal, problem because, if he has the consent of one authorised person, treatment will not without more constitute a trespass or a criminal assault. (196)

> ... Lord Scarman [in *Gillick*] was discussing the parents' right '*to determine* whether or not their minor child below the age of 16 will have medical treatment' (my emphasis). ... A right of determination is wider than a right to consent. The parents can only have a right of determination if *either* the child has no right to consent, ie is not a keyholder, *or* the parents hold a master key which could nullify the child's consent. I do not understand Lord Scarman to be saying that, if a child was '*Gillick*-competent', to adopt the convenient phrase used in argument, the parents ceased to have an independent right of consent, as contrasted with ceasing to have a right of determination, ie a veto. In a case in which the '*Gillick*-competent' child refuses treatment, but the parents consent, that consent *enables* treatment to be undertaken lawfully, but in no way determines that the child shall be so treated. In a case in which the positions are reversed, it is the child's consent which is the enabling factor, and again the parents' refusal of consent is not determinative. If Lord Scarman intended to go further than this and to say that in the case of a '*Gillick*-competent' child, a parent has no right either to consent or to refuse consent, his remarks were obiter, because the only question in issue was Mrs Gillick's alleged right of veto. Furthermore, I consider that they would have been wrong.[72] (197–98, emphasis in original)

> **Q** Is the interpretation of Lord Scarman's judgment persuasive? Douglas (1992: 575) suggested that, if a parent has no right to 'determine' whether a child should undergo treatment, it does not make sense to say that that parent can give valid consent to it. She also argued that to override a refusal means having to interfere with a person's intellectual and physical autonomy and that, therefore, a person's refusal should be given greater weight than consent. Do you agree?

---

[71] Fortin points out that an amendment to the Mental Health Act 1983, s 131(2) means that if a doctor wishes to force a 16 or 17 year old to be admitted to a hospital for treatment for a mental disorder, he or she must use the mental health legislation, as in the case of adults. The legislation does not preclude the medical team from administering unwanted treatment once the adolescent has been admitted. However, the Mental Health Code advises doctors not to rely on parental consent but to seek authorisation by using mental health legislation or to seek authorisation from the court (Fortin 2009a: 161).

[72] Staughton LJ doubted this interpretation.

Lord Donaldson went on to consider the power of the court:

> In many cases of wardship, the parents or other guardians will be left to make decisions for the child, subject only to standing instructions to refer reserved matters to the court ... and to the court's right and, in appropriate cases, duty to override the decision of the parents or other guardians. If it can override such consents, as it undoubtedly can, I see no reason whatsoever why it should not be able, and in an appropriate case willing, to override decisions by '*Gillick*-competent' children who are its wards or in respect of whom applications are made for, for example, s 8 orders under the Children Act 1989. (199)

Lord Donaldson developed this line of reasoning further and applied it to a case involving a girl aged 16 and so competent in terms of the 1969 Act. In *In Re W (A Minor) (Medical Treatment: Court's Jurisdiction)*[73] the local authority sought authorisation from the court, exercising its inherent jurisdiction, to treat a girl suffering from anorexia nervosa without her consent.[74] This time, however, Lord Donaldson referred only briefly to the position of parents. He conceded that his interpretation of Lord Scarman's judgment in *Gillick* might be wrong and that, as far as the common law was concerned, Lord Scarman might have said that the consent of those with parental responsibility would not be effective in the face of the minor's refusal. However, he went on, the question before him concerned the power of the court to authorise treatment, something not decided in *Gillick*.

The first question he addressed was whether section 8 of the Family Law Reform Act 1969 had the effect of depriving those with parental responsibility of the power to consent to the treatment of the young person. His analysis of the wording of the provision and a review of its history[75] persuaded him that it did not and that parents retained the ability to give valid consent. Power to give valid consent may vest concurrently in more than one person:

> On reflection I regret my use in *In Re R* ... of the keyholder analogy because keys can lock as well as unlock. I now prefer the analogy of the legal 'flak jacket' which protects the doctor from claims by the litigious whether he acquires it from his patient who may be a minor over the age of 16, or a '*Gillick* competent' child under that age or from another person having parental responsibilities which include a right to consent to treatment of the minor. Anyone who gives him a flak jacket (that is, consent) may take it back, but the doctor only needs one and so long as he continues to have one he has the legal right to proceed ... .
>
> Hair-raising possibilities were canvassed of abortions being carried out by doctors in reliance upon the consent of parents and despite the refusal of consent by 16- and 17-year-olds. Whilst this may be possible as a matter of law, I do not see any likelihood taking account of medical ethics, unless the abortion was truly in the best interests of the child. ... Despite the passing of the Children Act 1989, the inherent jurisdiction of the court could still be invoked in such a case to prevent an abortion which was contrary to the interests of the minor. (767–68)

Q Could a pregnant teenager invoke the Human Rights Act and the European Convention on Human Rights to protect her from undergoing an abortion against her will?

Lord Donaldson went on to affirm the importance of taking into account the wishes of

---

[73] 1992] 3 WLR 758.

[74] There was a care order in force which meant that she could not be made a ward of court. See 762.

[75] For criticism of the court's analysis, see Thornton (1993).

young people. The welfare of young people, he said, requires that they be given 'the maximum degree of decision-making which is prudent' (770). Balcombe LJ in turn remarked that it would normally be in the best interests of a competent minor to respect his or her 'integrity as a human being and not lightly override its decision on such a personal matter as medical treatment' (776).

Q How does this rationale for respecting young people's decisions differ from the reasons we respect adult's decisions?

Nevertheless, irrespective of the child's capacity, the court has the power to impose whatever decision best serves the child's interests.[76] Lord Donaldson suggested that anorexia is a condition that is capable of destroying the ability to make an informed choice. But in any event, he held, the court could override W's choice:

> There is ample authority for the proposition that the inherent powers of the court under its parens patriae jurisdiction are theoretically limitless and that they certainly extend beyond the powers of a natural parent. ... There can therefore be no doubt that it has power to override the refusal of a minor, whether over the age of 16 or under that age but *'Gillick* competent'. (769)

His summary of his decision included the following points:

> 4. Section 8 of the Family Law Reform Act 1969 gives minors who have attained the age of 16 a right to consent to surgical, medical or dental treatment. Such a consent cannot be overridden by those with parental responsibility for the minor. It can, however, be overridden by the court. ...
>
> 5. A minor of any age who is *'Gillick* competent' in the context of particular treatment has a right to consent to that treatment which again cannot be overridden by those with parental responsibility, but can be overridden by the court. ...
>
> 6. No minor of whatever age has power by refusing consent to treatment to override a consent to treatment by someone who has parental responsibility for the minor and a fortiori a consent by the court. Nevertheless such a refusal is a very important consideration in making clinical judgments and for parents and the court in deciding whether themselves to give consent. Its importance increases with the age and maturity of the minor.[77] (772)

The 'theoretically limitless'[78] power of the high court exercising its inherent jurisdiction was again successfully invoked in *South Glamorgan County Council v W and B*.[79] In that case, it was held that section 38(6) of the Children Act 1989, giving children the right to refuse to submit to an examination or assessment, did not in any way affect the inherent jurisdiction of the court. A competent minor subject to an interim care order could be assessed, treated and restrained against her will.

---

[76] *In Re W (A Minor) (Medical Treatment: Court's Jurisdiction)* [1992] 3 WLR 758, 776. See also *Re L (Medical Treatment: Gillick Competency)* [1998] 2 FLR 810, 813. Bridge (1999a: 594) suggests that a court would be unwilling to overrule a young person's objections where the proposed procedure is complex, ongoing and would require the patient's co-operation.

[77] In *Re P (Medical Treatment: Best Interests)* [2003] EWHC Fam 2327; [2004] 2 FLR 1117, the court overrode the objections of a 17-year-old Jehovah's witness to treatment with blood or blood products. The court declared itself reluctant to overrule his wishes but did so on the basis of his best interests.

[78] For discussion about the inherent jurisdiction and the circumstances in which the court will not exercise its jurisdiction, see Masson et al (2008a: para 18-052).

[79] [1993] 1 FLR 574.

What Douglas (1992) has termed the 'retreat' from *Gillick* may have been slowed or perhaps halted by the decision in *R (Axon) v The Secretary of State for Health and the Family Planning Association*.[80] However, the case concerned consent to medical treatment, not refusal and therefore is distinguishable from *Re R* and *In Re W*. The facts of the case were similar to those in *Gillick* but the court now had to take account of the Human Rights Act 1998. The court reaffirmed the principles established in *Gillick* and appeared to advocate respect for the decisions of teenagers (Taylor 2007). Ms Axon, a mother, mounted a challenge, similar to that pursued by Mrs Gillick, to Department of Health Guidance. The Guidance was intended to reflect the decision in *Gillick* and stated that young people under 16 could receive advice and treatment on sexual matters without parental consent or knowledge, provided that the young person concerned understood the advice and its implications and that the advice or treatment was in their best interests. Ms Axon contended that doctors had no duty of confidentiality to children in relation to sexual matters except where disclosure would damage the child's health. She also alleged that the Guidance went further than *Gillick* in excluding parental knowledge. Finally she argued that the Guidance infringed parents' Article 8 ECHR rights.

The court held that *Gillick* had impliedly rejected the contention that medical professionals should inform a young person's parents (para 55). Further, the reasoning in *Gillick* 'was that the parental right to determine whether a young person will have medical treatment terminates if and when the young person achieves a sufficient understanding and intelligence to understand fully what is proposed' (para 56), with the result that doctors could provide advice and treatment without parental knowledge or consent. The approach in *Gillick*, said Silber J, is not confined to sexual matters and applies to all forms of medical advice and treatment, including abortion (paras 86–87, 90–91).

What is particularly interesting about the judgment in *Axon* is the fact that the court, referring to *Mabon*,[81] indicated that there is now greater appreciation of young people's autonomy and right to participate in important decisions (para 76). While the facts in *Mabon* were very different, he said, the comments in that case 'illustrate that the right of young people to make decisions about their own lives by themselves at the expense of the views of their parents has now become an increasingly important and accepted feature of family life' (para 79).

In relation to the alleged contravention of Article 8, Silber J said that 'any right to family life on the part of a parent dwindles as their child gets older and is able to understand the consequence of different choices and then to make decisions relating to them' (para 129). Any right to be notified depends on matters such as the child's age and understanding (para 130):

[132] There is nothing in the Strasbourg jurisprudence which persuades me that any parental right or power of control under Art 8 is wider than in domestic law, which is that the right of parents, in the words of Lord Scarman, 'exists primarily to enable the parent to discharge his duty of maintenance, protection and education until he reaches such an age as to be able to look after himself and make his own decisions' (see *Gillick* at 185E and 250 respectively). The parental right to family life does not continue after that time and so parents do not have Art 8 rights to be notified of any advice of a medical professional after the young person is able to look after himself or herself and make his or her own decisions. This leads to the next question which is whether the 2004 Guidance interferes with those rights.

---

[80] [2006] EWHC 37 (Admin); [2006] 2 FLR 206.
[81] See below.

Even if the parents' rights were interfered with, this interference was justified under Article 8(2), For one thing, to remove confidentiality would deter young people from seeking advice and treatment with resulting harm to health. He concluded with guidance based on that of Lord Fraser in *Gillick*:

[154] Thus, my task has been to determine the circumstances in which a medical professional could advise or treat a young person for sexual matters when all attempts to enable their parents to be notified and consulted have failed. The solution to this task is to be found in the decision of the House of Lords in *Gillick*, by which I am bound and which for the reasons, which I have sought to explain, provides much guidance on the circumstances in which medical advice and treatment can be given without parental knowledge or consent on contraception, on sexually transmissible diseases and on abortion. This leads to the conclusion that the medical professional is entitled to provide medical advice and treatment on sexual matters without the parents' knowledge or consent provided he or she is satisfied of the following matters:

(1) that the young person although under 16 years of age understands *all* aspects of the advice. ...

(2) that the medical professional cannot persuade the young person to inform his or her parents or to allow the medical professional to inform the parents that their child is seeking advice and/or treatment on sexual matters. ...

(3) that ... the young person is very likely to begin or to continue having sexual intercourse with or without contraceptive treatment or treatment for a sexually transmissible illness ;

(4) that unless the young person receives advice and treatment on the relevant sexual matters, his or her physical or mental health or both are likely to suffer. ...

(5) that the best interests of the young person require him or her to receive advice and treatment on sexual matters without parental consent or notification.

[156] Thus there are two important aspects of the requirements which I have set out in para [154], above. First, these guidelines have to be strictly observed and, second, if they are not, the medical professional concerned can expect to be disciplined by his or her professional body. The 2004 Guidance is not unlawful ... . Thus, for the reasons which I have sought to explain, the claimant is not entitled to the relief which she seeks.

Taylor welcomes the decision but contends that the analysis of Article 8 may be misconceived. Silber J appears to be saying that family life ceases when the child reaches maturity. However, whether there is family life is a matter of fact and it can persist after the child grows up, depending on the relationship between parents and child. In any event, young people under 16 are likely to be dependent on and to live with their parents, and so the members of the family would enjoy family life together. However, proof of family life alone would not suffice to impugn the Guidance because Ms Axon would have to show that 'respect' for her family life included the right to control her children and that any interference with this was unjustified. Taylor argues, on the basis of the decision in *Hokkanen v Finland*,[82] that 'once the child is competent to make a particular decision for herself, respect for family life does not require parental knowledge or consent in relation to that decision' (Taylor 2007: 91).

Taylor comments that it is not clear whether *Axon* will affect the courts' decisions where they see the autonomy interests of a young person as conflicting with his or her

---

[82] (1995) 19 EHRR 139.

welfare. Herring notes the remarks of the judge (at para 56) suggesting that if a child is competent the parent has no right to determine what treatment will be given. But, he says, this is an obiter statement of a first instance judge and is it cannot overrule the established line of court of appeal cases (Herring 2009: 455). In any event, it may be that the word 'determine' will continue to be interpreted narrowly to exclude only a veto, as before.

The approach of the court in cases such as *In Re W* meets with the approval of Lowe and Juss (1993): [83]

> After all, it is perhaps all too easily forgotten that, in the final analysis, a child is still only a child. Moreover, the entire thesis based on the premise of Lord Scarman's child of 'sufficient understanding and intelligence' who is able 'to understand fully what is proposed' is, it is submitted, in one sense open to question. Is a child of sufficient understanding and intelligence if he or she acts irrationally? Is autonomy meaningful if it is irrational? ... To those who question how a child can be held able to give a valid consent yet be unable to exercise a power of veto, we would reply that there *is* a rational distinction to be made between giving consent and withholding it. We must start with the assumption that a doctor will act in the best interests of his patient. Hence, if the doctor believes that a particular treatment is necessary for his patient, it is perfectly rational for the law to facilitate this as easily as possible and hence allow a '*Gillick* competent' child to give a valid consent, and also to protect the child against parents opposed to what is professionally considered to be in its best medical interests. In contrast, it is surely right for the law to be reluctant to allow a *child* of whatever age to be able to veto treatment designed for his or her benefit particularly if a refusal would lead to the child's death or permanent damage. In other words, the clear and consistent policy of the law is to protect the child against wrong-headed parents and against itself with the final safeguard, as *Re W* unequivocally establishes, of giving the court the last word in cases of dispute.
>
> (Lowe and Juss 1993: 871–72, emphasis in original)

Bridge, reviewing the case law, also argues that it is right that the courts should be able to override objections by parents and young people to treatment in a life-or-death situation; as a society, we take the view that a young person should be given the opportunity to grow up to make up his or her own mind. 'In a life and death situation the court, as society's representative, is unlikely to allow parents, or the almost competent teenager, to choose death,' she says (Bridge 1997: 318). Yet she is very uneasy about the fact that parents can consent effectively to treatment to which the young person objects. As the law stands, she maintains, 'the treatment of young people remains in the hands of parents, healthcare professionals and ultimately medical ethics' and parents, in particular, occupy too powerful a position (ibid: 313, 329).

> **Q** It is established law that the capacity of an adult cannot be impugned solely on the ground that the decision in question is irrational.[84] Why should it be different where a young person is concerned? Who decides whether the parent or child is being 'wrong-headed' as Lowe and Juss (1993) call it? Could there be a divergence of opinions on this question?[85]

The effect of the cases is to leave intact the presumption created by section 8 of the 1969

---

[83] See also Fortin (2009a: 157–58).
[84] See p 505.
[85] See Douglas (1992: 576).

Act[86] that children over the age of 16 have the capacity to consent to medical treatment, enabling a doctor willing to do so to administer it.[87] However, a refusal to undergo treatment will be ineffective if overridden by someone with parental responsibility.[88] In the case of a minor under the age of 16, the law does not confer competence unless the child passes the *Gillick* test. If the child is deemed *Gillick*/Fraser competent, he or she is in a position analogous to that of the competent minor over the age of 16. In either case, an unwilling adolescent can be subjected to treatment pursuant to the consent of a parent who, in some cases, may not be the best judge of that young person's best interests. And not all would assume that doctors always know best. Doctors are, however, unlikely to treat too readily.[89] There is Department of Health Guidance that advises doctors not to rely on the consent of the parents to the medical treatment of 16–18 year olds.[90] Also, any decision about the medical treatment of a child, whether made by a parent or by the child, can be overturned by the court. In practice, though, most cases where a parent consents to treatment will not be brought before the court[91] and, as Herring says, if the matter is not taken to court it is the doctor's view that will prevail (Herring 2011: 458).

Fortin argues that an adolescent forced to undergo treatment may be able to invoke the ECHR successfully. Article 8 guarantees the right to 'physical and moral integrity' but, Fortin says, the medical team could contend that the treatment is necessary to save the patient's life under Article 8(2) (Fortin 2009a: 159). She suggests, however, that the patient could rely on Article 3 because forcing treatment on a patient could involve 'inhuman or degrading treatment'. This is the case as regards competent and incompetent adults[92] and, according to Fortin, the same principle could apply to minors (ibid).[93] Similarly, it might be possible to rely on Article 5, which protects the right to liberty and security of the person, in cases involving restraint or detention (ibid: 159–60). She concludes that 'the principle established in *Re R* and *Re W* [and the *South Glamorgan* case][94] is vulnerable to challenges based on Articles 3 and 5 and 8 of the ECHR, combined with Article 14'. A *Gillick*/Fraser-competent minor might argue that he or she is as intellectually mature as an adult and so is entitled to the same protection from forcible treatment as are adult patients (ibid: 160). Failure to provide it would infringe those articles and constitute discrimination on the grounds of age contrary to Article 14 (ibid). However, she goes on to

---

[86] See Brazier and Bridge (1996: 90).

[87] But no doctor can be required to treat a child, whether by the court, the parents, the child or anyone else: *Re R (A Minor) (Wardship: Medical Treatment)* [1992] 1 FLR 190, 200; *R v Cambridge District Health Authority, ex parte B* [1995] 1 FLR 1055; *Re C (Medical Treatment)* [1998] 1 FLR 384.

[88] As one commentator observes, however, it is doubtful whether a doctor would be willing to carry out intrusive treatment against the wishes of an articulate and intelligent teenager (Downie 1997: 500). Fortin reports that the BMA instructs doctors to ensure that the decision is the patient's 'own independent choice' (Fortin 2009a: 149).

[89] See also Fortin (2009a: 149) for discussion of the converse situation. She contends that doctors would be reluctant to treat minors on the basis of their consent alone.

[90] Department of Health (2008: para 36.33); see also Department of Health (2009: 34, para 15), discussed by Fortin (2009a: 161–62).

[91] Balcombe LJ said in *Re W (A Minor) (Medical Treatment: Court's Jurisdiction)* [1992] 3 WLR 758, 782 that in the event of a conflict, where the child refuses consent but a parent gives it, the jurisdiction of the court should always be invoked. However, it has since been held that a doctor with consent from someone with parental responsibility need not bring legal proceedings (*Re K, W and H (Minors) (Medical Treatment)* [1993] 1 FLR 854, 859).

[92] See *Herczegfalvy v Austria* (1992) 15 EHRR 437.

[93] See *R (On the Application of Burke) v The General Medical Council* [2004] EWHC Admin 1879; [2004] 2 FLR 1121, paras 58, 80, 145–49, 178, where the court explicitly refers to inhuman or degrading treatment of babies as well as incompetent adults; awareness on the part of the victim is not necessary to found liability.

[94] Based on Art 5 (Fortin 2009a: 179).

suggest that courts faced with adolescents refusing to accept life-saving treatment might be able to invoke Article 2, which creates a duty to take reasonable steps to preserve life. This could outweigh the patient's rights under Articles 3 and 5 (ibid: 162).

Fortin suggests that the success of a challenge under the ECHR may depend on the impact of the ideas emerging from the decision of the ECHR in *Pretty v United Kingdom*.[95] She says that although that case involved an adult seeking legal endorsement of assisted suicide, 'arguably the general principles voiced by the Court apply equally to children' (Fortin 2011: 182). The concept of private life under Article 8, said the court, covers a person's physical and psychological integrity and the provision encompasses the right to self-determination, or 'the notion of autonomy' (para 61). These ideas were considered in the judgment of Munby J in *Roddy*.[96] That case concerned a young woman who wanted to be identified in a newspaper article. Munby J indicated that courts should take young people's Convention rights seriously (para 46). It was held that it was the court's duty not only to recognise but to defend the right of a child who has sufficient understanding to make an informed choice (para 57). However, as Fortin points out, *Roddy* did not concern a decision that posed a risk to life and how Munby J would have dealt with such a case is unknown.

In summary, then, the law recognises, to some extent, the autonomy interests of the minor in the context of medical decisions. However the child's wishes are not decisive. The ultimate arbiter is, in those cases of dispute that are brought before it, the court. A court will take account of a competent minor's wishes and 'approach its decision with a strong predilection to give effect to the child's wishes'. Indeed, courts will also regard an incompetent child's wishes as material.[97] However, although the court takes cognisance of the child's views, it makes its decision on the basis of the welfare principle. The effect of the case law, then, by allowing the mature minor's wishes to be overridden, may be said to entrench paternalism in the law.

Ultimately a child who makes a decision which is thought to endanger his or her life or seriously jeopardise his or her welfare will be seen more as 'becoming' than as 'being'.

IV. MEDICAL TREATMENT OF NEONATES AND BABIES

Introduction

Very sick babies are treated differently from older children. They are indeed 'becoming'; they cannot make decisions and they cannot communicate, and therefore others, usually parents, make choices for them. Some commentators, such as Fortin, have even suggested that very small infants have not yet taken on the mantle of 'personhood' (Fortin 1998: 414).

Section 1 of the Children and Young Persons Act 1933 renders parents liable to criminal prosecution if they fail to provide adequate medical assistance for their children. More often, however, the question of medical treatment arises in the context of civil law

---

[95] [2002] 2 FLR 45.

[96] *Re Roddy (A Child) (Identification: Restriction on Publication)* [2003] EWHC 2927 (Fam); [2004] 2 FLR 949.

[97] In *Re W (A Minor) (Medical Treatment; Court's Jurisdiction)* [1992] 3 WLR 758, 776.

when the court may be asked to override the parents' lack of consent to treatment.[98] Conversely, in some cases, the courts are asked for guidance where the doctors do not consider that treatment would benefit the patient but the parents want their seriously ill baby to be treated. The court may make a decision under its inherent jurisdiction, wardship or under section 8 of the Children Act 1989.

It is largely as a result of technological developments that the courts are being asked to make these difficult decisions. In years gone by, medical science could not help seriously disabled infants. However, babies whose survival in previous years would have been unthinkable, can now be kept alive. But their lives can, in some cases, be painful and dependent on technology (Wells 1988: 325).

Wells observed in 1988 that non-treatment of severely disabled neonates had become far from uncommon. Brazier (2006: para 6.2) cites authority suggesting that the same remains true today. This may indicate that, as a society, we view neonates and very young babies in a different light from older children and adults. The sanctity of human life is a principle that informs all decisions about life and death, whether they relate to infants or others. However, as Wells has noted, the principle is not absolute (Wells 1988: 330) and it may be that we are more ready to allow infants to die than, say, older children.[99]

Infants and 'Personhood'

Dworkin, although he does not deal specifically with medical treatment, argues that we do see the death of an infant differently from the death of an older child or adult. He espouses a sanctity of life approach, maintaining that we see each human life as being inviolable. This, he says, is because each human is the result of complex creative investments (Dworkin 1993: 84). Each human life is the product of the creative force of nature[100] and also of human creativity. A life is the sum of natural evolution, of the human intelligence of parents, of self, of other people and of culture (ibid: 82). Any premature end to a life, once it has begun, is intrinsically bad and a waste of the investments made in that life (ibid: 73–74, 81, 84, 88).

Most people think that everyone has an equal right to life, says Dworkin (ibid: 85). But, he goes on, we also think that 'some cases of premature death are greater tragedies than others' (ibid: 84–85). We believe that there is a greater waste of life when a young person dies than when an old person dies (ibid: 85). And he goes on to point out that, 'it is terrible when an infant dies but worse, most people think, when a three-year-old child dies and worse still when an adolescent dies' (ibid: 87). The waste of life is often greater and more tragic because of what has already happened in the past, he says. The death of an adolescent girl is worse than the death of an infant girl because the adolescent's death frustrates the investments she and others have already made in her life in terms of, say, emotional attachments and future plans (ibid). The 'frustration is greater if it takes place after rather than before the person has made a significant personal investment in his own life, and less if it occurs after any investment has been substantially fulfilled' (ibid: 88).

---

[98] If the threshold conditions are satisfied, a local authority may take the child into care in which case it can consent, or if the child is being accommodated, the local authority can seek a specific issue order under the Children Act for the treatment.

[99] Actively taking steps to kill a seriously ill infant is prohibited by the criminal law. But see *Re A (Children) (Conjoined Twins: Surgical Separation)* [2000] 4 All ER 961.

[100] Or, for those who are religious, God.

If one applies Dworkin's reasoning to the case of seriously ill infants, therefore, it could be suggested that it would make the frustration worse if life were allowed to continue because this would add to the wasted investments made by the child and by others in a life that will inevitably end early.[101] In some cases, then, a choice of premature death could minimise the frustration of life and, rather than compromising the doctrine of the sanctity of life, would uphold it.

Other scholars have focused on the notion of personhood. Wells reviewed various arguments taking this approach. She referred to the view that, although they are human, newborn babies are not 'persons'. According to this thesis, this is because they lack, for instance, an awareness of self as a present and future being (Wells 1988: 331). They are entitled to protection but the moral obligations owed to them are different and there may be 'less compelling reasons for their full protection than there are for protecting fully-fledged persons' (ibid).[102] Alternatively, she observed, newborns can be seen as being entitled to partial or even full protection, not because they qualify as persons, but because they have the potential to become full persons (ibid).

The notion that only 'persons' with the capacity for consciousness and rationality command serious moral concern is rejected by other commentators.[103] In the Nuffield Report, the moment of birth, which is easy to identify, was designated as the significant moral and legal point for making decisions about preserving life (Brazier 2006: paras 2.19, 9.5). In addition, no baby, 'however profound his or her disability or bodily deformity, should be classified as non-human' (ibid: para 8.14).

Whether or not one agrees with the construction of infants as non-persons or potential persons, and whether or not one agrees that they should be treated differently,[104] the question of whether a severely disabled baby should be kept alive at all costs is a very difficult one. It is one that parents, the medical profession and courts are increasingly having to face. For all involved, whether it is an infant or an older person whose life is at stake, the decision is an agonising one.

In all cases involving infants,[105] the test for deciding whether he or she should be treated is the infant's best interests.

The Best Interests Test

There is a strong presumption in favour of preserving life but there are circumstances in which it does not apply. The least contentious of these is where, as in *Re C (a minor)*

---

[101] See Dworkin (1993: 90–91). He also argues that ending a life might be a way of upholding the sanctity of life if a person's life would 'go worse' if left alive without being conscious. However, this argument relies primarily on judging the situation through the eyes of the patient as a conscious, competent person (see Dworkin 1993: ch 7). To extrapolate this approach to newborns is not possible unless one applies a fictitious version of the subjective test, something which our courts do not generally appear willing to do in cases of non-treatment of infants (see below).

[102] See also Kuhse (1987), who argued that human life is sacred only in that it is a prerequisite for rationality, the holding of ideals and the ability to be a moral being.

[103] See, eg, Price (2001: 640).

[104] Views on disability appear to be changing according to Read and Clements (2004). This in turn could be affecting the way we treat disabled infants. Fortin (2009a: 382) says that attitudes to mental impairment have changed and it is unlikely nowadays that treatment will be refused or infants be allowed to die because of mental impairment.

[105] And incompetent older children and adults.

(wardship: medical treatment),[106] the child was dying and any treatment could do no more than postpone death for a short while; death was inevitable and life could be only marginally prolonged. It is well established that the presumption in favour of preserving life does not apply where treatment would be 'futile'.[107] The second category, about which some uncertainty has been expressed,[108] is where a child's faculties have been entirely destroyed.[109] In both these categories of cases the court may well find that it is in the child's best interests to be allowed to die with dignity.[110]

What the courts have found most difficult are cases where the infant, although 'gravely disabled is not dying'.[111] In the case of *Re B*[112] the court was of the view that it should not withhold consent to treatment which could enable a child to survive a life-threatening condition unless the quality of the child's subsequent life would be 'intolerable to the child', 'bound to be full of pain and suffering' and 'demonstrably so awful that in effect the child must be condemned to die' (929–30).

The notion of intolerability was rejected in *Wyatt v Portsmouth NHS Trust*[113] where the court said it should not be deployed as a gloss on or as a supplementary test to the best-interests test. Nevertheless, the court said, it could be a valuable guide in the search for best interests. This in turn was rejected in *An NHS Trust v MB*[114] where Holman J said it was not possible to both exclude the concept as a gloss or supplementary test while still treating it as a 'valuable guide': 'If it means no more than that the conclusion that it is in the best interests of the patient to be allowed to die should only be reached in a clear and strong case' then it added nothing to the reasoning already used by courts in these cases (para 17).

The concept of 'intolerability' was referred to in *Re J (A minor) (Wardship: Medical Treatment)*,[115] and was used in conjunction with another test which has also found little favour. The baby concerned had suffered very severe brain damage. He was likely to develop paralysis of both his arms and legs. He appeared to be blind and was likely to be deaf. He was unlikely ever to be able to speak or to develop even limited intellectual abilities. It was, however, likely that he could feel pain. He was expected to die before his teens. The court made it clear that the sanctity of life doctrine is not absolute and noted that there are cases in which 'it is not in the interests of the child to subject it to treatment which will cause increased suffering and produce no commensurate benefit'.[116] Instead of using an objective test to decide whether this was such a case, the court looked

---

[106] [1989] 2 All ER 782.

[107] *Re L (Medical Treatment: Benefit)* [2004] EWHC Fam 2713; [2005] 1 FLR 491, para 12. Any obligation under Art 2 ECHR to provide life-sustaining treatment is subject to this qualification (*R (On the Application of Burke) v The General Medical Council and Others* [2004] EWHC Admin 1879; [2004] 2 FLR 1121, paras 152–62). 'Futile' in this context appears to include cases where death will inevitably ensue soon and where the patient is in a persistent vegetative state. But it also seems to include the situation where the intolerability test is satisfied (see below).

[108] See *Re J (A minor) (Wardship: Medical Treatment)* [1990] 3 All ER 930, 938.

[109] Ibid, 944–45.

[110] See *R (On the Application of Burke) v The General Medical Council* [2004] EWHC Admin 1879; [2004] 2 FLR 1121, para 116.

[111] Ibid, para 105.

[112] [1990] 3 All ER 927; [1981] 1 WLR 1421.

[113] [2005] EWCA Civ 1181; [2006] 1 FLR 554, paras 76 and 91.

[114] *An NHS Trust v MB (A Child Represented by Cafcass as Guardian ad litem)* [2006] EWHC 507 (Fam); [2006] 2 FLR 319.

[115] [1991] Fam 33; [1990] 3 All ER 930; [1991] 2 WLR 140.

[116] [1990] 3 All ER 930, 938.

at the situation 'from the assumed point of view of the patient'.[117] This is referred to as the 'subjective test' or the 'substituted judgment test'.

> I consider that the correct approach is for the court to judge the quality of the life the child would have to endure if given the treatment and decide whether in all the circumstances such a life would be so afflicted as to be intolerable to that child. I say 'to that child' because the test should not be whether the life would be intolerable to the decider. The test must be whether the child in question, if capable of exercising sound judgment, would consider the life intolerable ... . It takes account of the strong instinct to preserve one's life even in circumstances, which an outsider, not himself at risk of death, might consider unacceptable. (All ER 945)

The use of this test in cases where the patient has never been competent has been criticised.[118] A New York court, for example, discussing the issue of treatment for a patient with profound learning difficulties, thought it unrealistic to ask what the patient would want if, for a 'miraculous moment', he could comprehend his plight.[119]

English courts have also disapproved of the subjective test.[120] Similarly, what seems to be akin to, albeit the converse of, the substituted judgment test was rejected in *NHS Trust v A*.[121] There Holman J stated that the case had to be decided by means of the application of an objective best interests test: 'I am not deciding what decision I might make for myself if I was, hypothetically, in the situation of the patient; nor for a child of my own if in that situation' (para 40(iii)).

In the main, the case law makes it clear that the decision must be made on the basis of the child's best interests, objectively assessed. The concept of best interests has been interpreted broadly to include medical emotional, social, ethical, moral and welfare considerations.[122] Many of the reported decisions place a great deal of importance on the quality of life of the child concerned. If treatment was likely to prolong life, the courts would often weigh this in the balance with the projected quality of life of the child and the suffering treatment might inflict.[123] However, the judgment of Ward LJ in *Re A (Children) (Conjoined Twins: Surgical Separation)*[124] exhibits considerable unease about making this a deciding factor and he attempts to fashion a more rigid version of the sanctity of life principle.

---

[117] Ibid.

[118] See Wells et al (1990).

[119] See ibid: 1545, referring to the case of *Re Storar* 52 NY 2d 353; 420 NE 2d 64 (1981). See also Rhoden (1988).

[120] The test was rejected by the House of Lords in *Airedale NHS Trust v Bland* [1993] 1 FLR 1026, 1043 and Ward LJ doubted whether it was still good law in *Re A (Children) (Conjoined Twins: Surgical Separation)* [2000] 4 All ER 961, 999. But see *Wyatt v Portsmouth NHS Trust* [2005] EWCA Civ 1181; [2006] 1 FLR 554, para 87. See also *A National Health Service Trust v D* [2000] 2 FLR 677, 686–87.

[121] [2007] EWHC 1696 (Fam); [2008] 1 FLR 70.

[122] See *Wyatt v Portsmouth NHS Trust* [2005] EWCA Civ 1181; [2006] 1 FLR 554, para 79; *R (On the Application of Burke) v The General Medical Council and Others* [2004] EWHC Admin 1879; [2004] 2 FLR 1121, paras 116 and 213, *Re L (Medical Treatment: Benefit)* [2004] EWHC Fam 2713; [2005] 1 FLR 491, para 12. The Nuffield Report recommends that professionals take into account factors such as whether the child will be capable of sustaining relationships with other people, whether the baby can experience pleasure and what support is available to provide for the care of the child (Brazier 2006: Executive Summary, paras 29–30).

[123] See, eg, *A National Health Service Trust v D* [2000] 2 FLR 677, 687. See also Brazier (2006: para 8.20). This Report indicates that infants should not be subjected to burdensome treatment where the child's life would be 'bereft of any of those features that give meaning and purpose to human life' (para 2.13) or the life will be one of great suffering and the family believes that further treatment is 'more than can be borne' (para 2.14). Nor is treatment warranted where intervention would do no more that delay death for a short time (para 2.12). On the right to die, see Wilson (1995).

[124] [2000] 4 All ER 961.

The Court of Appeal was faced here with a very unusual and a very sad case. Jodie and Mary were conjoined twins. Jodie was capable of an independent existence but Mary was dependent on her sister to live. If they were not separated, both would die as Jodie could not support both her own and her sister's life; her heart would fail. If the operation were performed, Mary would certainly die. The doctors caring for the twins wanted to operate to separate the babies but the parents, for religious reasons, refused to consent.

The court found that the operation would allow Jodie to enjoy a normal life expectancy and, in prolonging her life, would be in her best interests (996). However, Ward LJ balked at the suggestion in the court below that Mary's life, if she were not separated from her twin, would be 'worth nothing to her' and espoused what he considered the 'true principle of sanctity of life' (999). It meant, he said, that 'each life has inherent value in itself and the right to life, being universal, is equal for all of us' (1000). Nevertheless, he acknowledged that the doctrine leaves room for the withdrawal or withholding of treatment in some situations.

Drawing on the work of Keown,[125] an academic in the field of law and medical ethics, Ward LJ argued that there is a distinction between saying that treatment would be worthwhile and saying that the patient's life would be worthwhile (1000–1). Mary's life, irrespective of how diminished her capacity to enjoy it and how desperate her circumstances, still had its 'own ineliminable value and dignity' (1002). Moreover, it was certainly not in her best interests that she undergo an operation to separate her from her twin, a procedure that would result in her death (1004).[126]

In order to reach a conclusion the court had to strike a balance between the twins. The equal right to life of each of the twins had to be weighed in the balance. But there were other considerations that tipped the scales. Ward LJ said he was precluded by the sanctity of life doctrine from comparing the worth of one life with the other. But he could take into account the worthwhileness of the treatment:

> When considering the worthwhileness of the treatment, it is legitimate to have regard to the actual condition of each twin and hence the actual balance sheet of advantage and disadvantage which flows from the performance or the non-performance of the proposed treatment. Here it is legitimate, as John Keown demonstrates, and as the cases show, to bear in mind the actual quality of life each child enjoys and may be able to enjoy. In summary, the operation will give Jodie the prospects of a normal expectation of a relatively normal life. The operation will shorten Mary's life but she remains doomed for death. ... [The] balance is heavily in Jodie's favour. ... [T]he balancing exercise I have just conducted is *not* a balancing of the quality of life in the sense that I value the potential of one human life above another ... . In this unique case it is, in my judgment, impossible not to put in the scales of each child the manner in which they are individually able to exercise their right to life. Mary may have a right to life, but she has little right to be alive. She is alive because, and only because ... she sucks the lifeblood of Jodie and she sucks the lifeblood out of Jodie. She will survive only as long as Jodie survives.

---

[125] According to Keown, treatment can be withdrawn where it is 'disproportionate'. This would be where the treatment is futile or excessively burdensome. A treatment is futile if it offers 'no reasonable hope of therapeutic benefit' and excessively burdensome 'if, for example, it would cause great pain' (Keown 2000: 71). Also, if a proposed treatment offers 'no reasonable hope of improving the patient's condition or "quality of life", there is no duty to administer it' (ibid). By this, he says he means that we should not ask whether the patient's life is worthwhile but whether, 'Given this patient's quality of life or condition, does this treatment offer a reasonable prospect of improving it?' (ibid). See also Keown (1997).

[126] This chapter deals only with the family law aspects of the case. The court also had to make important findings in relation to the criminal law.

Jodie will not survive long because constitutionally she will not be able to cope. Mary's parasitic living will be the cause of Jodie's ceasing to live. (1010, emphasis in original)

The best interests of the twins[127] therefore demanded that the chance of life be given to Jodie, who was capable of accepting it, even if that meant sacrificing the life of the other twin, who could not (1011).[128]

Price (2004) comments that Ward LJ has misunderstood Keown's position. Keown is attempting, in Price's view, to confine the decision-making criteria purely to medical questions such as the efficacy of the treatment and the extent of prolongation of life. For Price, Keown's approach cannot be sustained.[129] If one accepts that the sanctity of life principle is not absolute, he says, questions about the patient's quality of life must inevitably come into play. He agrees that it is the treatment rather than the patient that must be evaluated. But whether treatment is worthwhile cannot be assessed without taking into account the patient's overall condition, including any disability (Price 2001: 642–43). He maintains that Ward LJ's formulation of the decision-making criteria does not follow Keown's argument (ibid: 642). According to the approach adopted by Ward LJ, quality of life still enters the equation, albeit at a different stage; it has to be considered when deciding whether the treatment is worthwhile.

In cases decided since, Ward's analysis has not been referred to and the courts seem to be making their decisions based on the child's best interests informed by an assessment of the child's likely quality of life. In *An NHS Trust v MB*[130] the child was 18 months old, almost entirely incapable of movement and was being fed through a tube. The prognosis was that he might survive for a few years or might die soon. His condition was deteriorating and the doctors took the view that his quality of life was so poor he should no longer be kept alive and the tube enabling him to breathe should be removed. The parents did not agree and were of the opinion that, although the child showed pain and distress, he also showed pleasure, recognised family members, and responded to stimuli such as music and television.

Holman J observed that cases decided in the past had involved brain-dead or severely brain-damaged patients; to his knowledge no court had previously been asked to approve withdrawal of life support, against the wishes of the parents, of a 'conscious child with sensory awareness and assumed normal cognition and no reliable evidence of any significant brain damage' (para 11). Holman J held that cases of this kind involved the upbringing of a child and that the paramountcy principle applied. However, he also went on to say that the case law determining when a patient should be allowed to die could be set out in ten propositions:

Among these were the following:

[16] ...

(iv) The matter must be decided by the application of an objective approach or test.

(v) That test is the best interests of the patient. Best interests are used in the widest sense

---

[127] There is some slippage here in Ward LJ's judgment as he had previously indicated that surgery was not in Mary's best interests.

[128] For a critique of the rights analysis used, see Munro (2001). On the withdrawal of treatment and Art 2 ECHR, see *An NHS Trust v M; An NHS Trust v H* [2001] 2 FLR 367.

[129] He also questions whether it is possible to determine sensibly whether treatment is futile or the suffering it creates is excessive.

[130] *An NHS Trust v MB (A Child Represented by Cafcass as Guardian ad litem)* [2006] EWHC 507 (Fam); [2006] 2 FLR 319.

and include every kind of consideration capable of impacting on the decision. These include, non-exhaustively, medical, emotional, sensory (pleasure, pain and suffering) and instinctive (the human instinct to survive) considerations.

(vi) It is impossible to weigh such considerations mathematically, but the court must do the best it can to balance all the conflicting considerations in a particular case and see where the final balance of the best interests lies.

(vii) Considerable weight (Lord Donaldson of Lymington MR referred to 'a very strong presumption') ... must be attached to the prolongation of life because the individual human instinct and desire to survive is strong and must be presumed to be strong in the patient. But it is not absolute, nor necessarily decisive; and may be outweighed if the pleasures and the quality of life are sufficiently small and the pain and suffering or other burdens of living are sufficiently great.

There is no distinction between withdrawing and withholding life support, he said, and the best interests test applies to both situations (para 20). He had asked those involved in the cases to draw up a list of benefits and burdens/disadvantages and after considering these, he came to the conclusion, even taking into account future deterioration, that it would not at that time be in the child's best interests to withdraw ventilation with the immediate result that the child would die (para 89). In the event that the child in future would need more painful measures to stay alive, it would be in the child's interests to withhold those procedures even though he would probably die (para 91).

While the child's life was full of discomfort and was 'helpless and sad' (para 100), he must be taken to have age-appropriate cognition; he had a relationship with his parents; and he gained some pleasure from sight, touch and sound (para 101). The burdens did not outweigh the benefits. Indeed 'as his life does still have benefits, and is his life, it should be enabled to continue' (para 102). One of the factors influencing this decision was that the child already had 'an accumulation of experiences and the cognition to gain pleasure from them' (para 106).

In both *MB* and a later case, *NHS Trust v A*,[131] Holman J stressed that each case is fact specific. However, Fortin suggests that *MB* appears to reflect a new approach in that it emphasises cognition and experience. This seems to echo, to some extent, Dworkin's approach. However, as Brazier (2006: para 8.36) points out, the fact that a child or infant has cognitive function might mean that his or her suffering is greater than if there were no cognitive function.[132]

The baby in *NHS Trust v A* had less experience of life but better prospects than the child in *MB*. She was suffering from a condition from which she would die by about the age of one. However if she were to undergo a bone marrow transplant, she would have a 50% chance of a normal life. Her parents opposed the treatment because the infant had already undergone very unpleasant treatment and they did not want her to suffer the pain and distress the transplant would cause. They were also convinced she would die during the treatment or that it would not be successful and she would die anyway. Finally, they were concerned that she would be rendered infertile and this, in their eyes, would negate 'part of ... the benefit and privilege of being a woman' (para 46).

Holman J said that he hoped the girl would, if she survived, agree with him that it was better to be alive and infertile than to be dead (para 50). The potential benefit if the transplant were successful would be 'not merely prolongation of life by a few months or

---

[131] [2007] EWHC 1696 (Fam); [2008] 1 FLR 70.
[132] See also Fortin (2009a: 379–80).

even years, but the prospect of a full, whole life into adulthood with a normal life expectancy' (para 61). Against this he weighed the potential disadvantages of pain and suffering, the possible failure of the treatment, the risk of death that it posed and other consequences such as infertility. He concluded that it was in the baby's overall best interests that the doctors be authorised to carry out the treatment. He reiterated the ten propositions set out in *MB* and, in a passage implicitly informed, perhaps, by notions of both quality of life and futility or otherwise of treatment, he said:

> [70] If a BMT [bone marrow transplant] could only prolong by a relatively short period her life; or if it would leave her alive but probably seriously impaired (eg significantly brain damaged) then I would or might take a different view. But, in my view, a 50% prospect of a full, normal life (even though infertile) when set against the certainty of death before the age of 1 or 1½, does in this case outweigh all other considerations and disadvantages. If the opportunity of a BMT is not taken, a very real prospect of a full life, weighed against certain death, will have been lost for a few more months of babyhood. A is more than merely a baby. She is a living human being, with a future as well as a present, to whom, despite her disease, modern medicine and science may be able to give a full life. ... I am convinced that A should be given that opportunity. I hope that the parents will feel able to accept my judgment.

Certainly, quality of life appears to have been the main consideration in *Re RB*,[133] where the judge approved of the father's decision to withdraw his opposition to the course of action proposed by the mother and the medical professionals. The infant could not breathe without ventilation, could not move and could not express distress. If the child underwent the procedure initially supported by the father the child would suffer discomfort and pain but would be unable to show it. He would also be subjected to additional procedures. The infant, it was decided, should be allowed to die.

The Parents, the Doctors and the Courts

We have seen that the courts will apply the best interests test in deciding on the medical treatment of infants. However, the courts are not necessarily involved in such decisions. Where there is no dispute, the case need not be brought before the court. Ward LJ said in *Re A* that despite the fact that the medical team disagreed with the parents' insistence that nature should be allowed to take its course, it would have been open to them to 'bow to the weight of the parental wish'.[134] It was within the hospital's discretion, rather than its duty, to seek a judicial ruling.[135]

Similarly, it is open to the parents to accept medical opinion. The Court of Appeal put it this way in *R v Portsmouth Hospitals NHS Trust Ex Parte Glass*:

> There can be no doubt that the best course is for a parent of a child to agree on the course which the doctors are proposing to take, having fully consulted the parent and for the parent to fully understand what is involved. ... If that is not possible and there is a conflict, and if the

---

[133] [2009] EWHC 3269 (Fam); [2010] 1 FLR 946, paras 7, 10.

[134] [2000] 4 All ER 961, 987. The view of the Nuffield working party was that parents do have an interest in decisions about their children, that their wishes should be given some weight but that the child's best interests must take priority (Brazier 2006: Executive Summary, para 10).

[135] The proceedings were initiated under the court's inherent jurisdiction.

conflict is of a grave nature, the matter must then be brought before the court so the court can decide what is in the best interests of the child concerned. (910)[136]

In the situation where the doctors wish to treat but the parents do not agree, it is not possible to proceed without parental consent. Doctors cannot, except in an emergency, simply ignore a parent's objections to treatment. The case has to be taken before the court,[137] failing which the treatment will amount to a violation of the patient's rights to respect for private life and physical integrity.[138]

Where the jurisdiction of the court is invoked, ultimately it is the judge who has to decide.[139] But where the medical team do not consider treatment to be appropriate, not even the court can compel them to administer it.[140] If the parents want their child to be treated contrary to their doctors' advice, they will need to instruct another doctor who is prepared to treat. In particular, there is no obligation on the medical profession to treat where treatment would be futile, and so not in the patient's best interests.[141]

As a general rule, the courts places considerable weight on the medical evidence and tend to accede to the clinical judgement of the doctors,[142] although, as we shall see in *Re T* below, the medical position is not determinative. In particular, members of the medical profession have no expertise in assessing the range of non-medical considerations that must inform a decision.[143]

The weight that courts place on parental wishes varies. It is clear that when the court comes to adjudicate, 'there must always be a real possibility of an outcome at variance with parental wishes'.[144] In *Re A*[145] Ward LJ said:

> Since the parents have the right in the exercise of their parental responsibility to make the decision, it should not be a surprise that their wishes should command very great respect. Parental right is, however, subordinate to welfare ... .
>
> [I]t is perhaps useful to repeat the passage in the judgment of Bingham MR in *Re Z (a minor) (freedom of publication)* [1995] 4 All ER 961 at 986 ... . Bingham MR said:

---

[136] [1999] 2 FLR 905. See also *R (On the Application of Burke) v The General Medical Council and Others* [2004] EWHC Admin 1879; [2004] 2 FLR 1121, para 202.

[137] *Re A (Children) (Conjoined Twins: Surgical Separation)* [2000] 4 All ER 961, 987. It seems likely that where a child is in care and the local authority has parental responsibility, that parental responsibility does not suffice for making life and death decisions and the case should go to court, irrespective of the parents' views (*Re B (Medical Treatment)* [2008] EWHC 1996 (Fam); [2009] 1 FLR 1264).

[138] *Glass v United Kingdom* [2004] 1 FCR 553.

[139] *Portsmouth NHS Trust v Wyatt and Wyatt, Southampton NHS Trust Intervening* [2004] EWHC Fam 2247; [2005] 1 FLR 21, paras 16 and 33.

[140] See n 87 above. See also *A National Health Service Trust v D* [2000] 2 FLR 677, 686.

[141] *Airedale NHS Trust v* [1993] 1 FLR 1026. See also *Re L (Medical Treatment: Benefit)* [2004] EWHC Fam 2713; [2005] 1 FLR 491, para 12.

[142] See, eg, *Re J (A Minor) (Wardship: Medical Treatment)* [1991] 1 FLR 366; [1990] 3 All ER 930; *Re C (Medical Treatment)* [1998] 1 FLR 384. In *Airedale NHS Trust v Bland* [1993] 1 FLR 1026, 1042, the House of Lords referred to the greater experience that doctors have in these matters, compared with judges. In *Re L (Medical Treatment: Benefit)* the court urged the mother to 'listen to what is proposed by those who have a great deal of medical and nursing experience' ([2004] EWHC Fam 2713; [2005] 1 FLR 491, para 32). For a case where the parents were persuaded, see *Re MM (Medical Treatment)* [2000] 1 FLR 224. See also Brazier (2006) para 8.31.

[143] *R (On the Application of Burke) v The General Medical Council* [2004] EWHC Admin 1879; [2004] 2 FLR 1121, paras 93, 116 and 213.

[144] *Re Wyatt (No 3)(A Child) (Medical Treatment: Continuation of Order)* [2005] EWHC Fam 693; [2005] All ER (D) 278, para 12. See also *Re A (Children) (Conjoined Twins: Surgical Separation)* [2000] 4 All ER 961, 1010.

[145] *Re A (Children) (Conjoined Twins: Surgical Separation)* [2000] 4 All ER 961, 1006.

I would for my part accept without reservation that the decision of a devoted and responsible parent should be treated with respect. It should certainly not be disregarded or lightly set aside. But the role of the court is to exercise an independent and objective judgment. If that judgment is in accord with that of the devoted and responsible parent, well and good. If it is not, then it is the duty of the court, after giving due weight to the view of the devoted and responsible parent, to give effect to its own judgment ... .

That is the law. That is what governs my decision. (1007–08)[146]

The courts have tended to override parental wishes where they consider that the parent's decision would harm or endanger the child. So, for example, in *Re R (a minor) (blood transfusion)*[147] the court authorised the use of blood products in treating the 10-month-old daughter of Jehovah's Witnesses, whose religious convictions precluded them from countenancing such treatment.[148]

However, in a case that attracted considerable criticism, the court appeared to be guided primarily by the mother's wishes. In *In Re T (A minor) (Wardship: Medical Treatment)*[149] the parents, both healthcare professionals and having jobs in a distant Commonwealth country, refused to consent to liver transplant surgery for their 17-month-old son, even though unanimous medical opinion said the child would not live beyond the age of 2½ without the transplant. The trial judge authorised the treatment, but the Court of Appeal overruled the trial court. Butler-Sloss LJ said that unanimous medical opinion was 'that the prospects of success were good and that this operation was in the best interests of the child' (506). The issue before the court was whether it should overrule the decision of the parents and give consent to the operation.

The judge in a careful, comprehensive and sensitive judgment, reviewed the reasons for the mother's refusal to consent and said ... . 'Whilst I can understand her difficulties, I conclude that her refusal to accept the unanimous advice of the doctors is not the conduct of a reasonable parent.' (506)

However Butler-Sloss LJ differed:

[I]t is clear that when an application under the inherent jurisdiction is made to the court the welfare of the child is the court's paramount consideration. The consent or refusal of consent of the parents is an important consideration to weigh in the balancing exercise to be carried out by the judge.
... In my view ... the judge erred in his approach to the issue before the court. He accepted the unchallenged clinical opinion of the three consultants and assessed the reasonableness of the mother's decision against that medical opinion. (509)

But ... the reasonableness of the mother was not the primary issue. This mother and this child are one for the purpose of this unusual case and the decision of the court to consent to the operation jointly affects the mother and son and it also affects the father. The welfare of this child depends on his mother. The practical considerations of her ability to cope with supporting the child in the face of her belief that this course is not right for him, and the requirement to return probably for a long period to this country, either to leave the father behind and lose his

---

[146] See also *J v C* [1969] 1 All ER 788; *Re D (A Minor) (Wardship: Sterilisation)* [1976] 1 All ER 326, 333.
[147] [1993] 2 FLR 757.
[148] See also *Re B (A Minor) (Wardship: Medical Treatment)* [1990] 3 All ER 927; *Re S (A Minor) (Medical Treatment)* [1993] 1 FLR 376.
[149] [1997] 1 FLR 502, and see Michalowski (1997) and Fox and McHale (1997).

support or to require him to give up his job and seek one in England were not put by the judge into the balance when he made his decision. (510)[150]

> ... The welfare of the child is the paramount consideration and I recognise the very strong presumption in favour of a course of action which will prolong life, and the inevitable consequences for the child of not giving consent. But to prolong life ... is not the sole objective of the court and to require it at the expense of other considerations may not be in a child's best interests ... . I believe that the best interests of this child require that his future treatment should be left in the hands of his devoted parents. (512)

Waite LJ stated:

> It can only be said safely that there is a scale, at one end of which lies the clear case where parental opposition to medical intervention is prompted by scruple or dogma of a kind which is patently irreconcilable with principles of child health and welfare widely accepted by the generality of mankind; and that at the other end lie highly problematic cases where there is genuine scope for a difference of view between parent and judge ... the greater the scope for genuine debate between one view and the other the stronger will be the inclination of the court to be influenced by a reflection that in the last analysis the best interests of every child include an expectation that difficult decisions affecting the length and quality of its life will be taken for it by the parent to whom its care has been entrusted by nature. (513–14)

> **Q** Is there a difference in the reasoning of Butler-Sloss LJ and that of Waite LJ in *Re T*? Do either or both of them adopt a test different from the other cases we have considered?

It seems unlikely that the reasoning in *Re T* will be followed in the future.[151] The ten propositions formulated in *MB*[152] and *NHS Trust v A*[153] include a statement that although the views of the parents may have 'particular value' because they know the patient so well, the court 'needs to be mindful that the views of any parents may ... be coloured by their own emotion or sentiment'. Moreover,

> Their ... wishes, however understandable in human terms, are wholly irrelevant to consideration of the objective best interests of the child save to the extent in any given case that they may illuminate the quality and value to the child of the child–parent relationship.

Fortin suggests that *Re T* had undermined the principle that parents do not have the final say over whether their children should live or die and that *NHS Trust v A* has restored that principle (Fortin 2009a: 385).

O'Donnell maintains that parental qualities, such as reasonableness,[154] are treated as

---

[150] This approach has been criticised for failing to recognise the independent interests of the child. See Downie (2000: 200).

[151] Although in other contexts the welfare of the child is seen by some commentators as bound up with the welfare of those caring for them. See, eg, Freeman (2006: 95) and references therein.

[152] *An NHS Trust v MB (A Child Represented by Cafcass as Guardian ad litem)* [2006] EWHC 507 (Fam); [2006] 2 FLR 319.

[153] [2007] EWHC 1696 (Fam); [2008] 1 FLR 70, para 40(x).

[154] See also Fox and McHale (1999: 702). Ward LJ in *Re A (Children) (Conjoined Twins: Surgical Separation)* [2000] 4 All ER 961, 1009 emphasised that, despite their religious foundation, the parents' objections had some substance; 'this is not a case where opposition [by the parents] is "prompted by scruple or dogma"' when he declared that their wishes did not accord with the children's best interests.

relevant in deciding what weight to ascribe to their wishes (O'Donnell 2004: 224–25). Commentators have noted that parental objections founded in religious belief appear to be more easily discounted by the courts as 'scruple or dogma'. They are more likely to take seriously any objections voiced by articulate professionals such as the parents in *Re T*.[155] These commentators question whether religious and ethical beliefs ought to be downgraded and also whether it should be so readily accepted that educated parents are being reasonable.[156]

V. CHILDREN IN COURT

Listening to Children[157]

The Revised Private Law Programme[158] states that it is designed to assist parents to 'reach safe agreements where possible', and to 'promote outcomes that are sustainable, that are in the best interests of children and that take account of their perspectives'. It goes on to require the court to 'give judicial consideration of the way to involve the child'[159] and to consider how the child's wishes and feelings are to be ascertained.[160] The reality is, however, that in private law cases, the court tends to rely on the evidence of the parties, usually the parents, and if ordered, a welfare report from Cafacass.[161] There is no obligation on the court to order such a report and, indeed report writing has been downgraded in the push to promote conciliation and parental agreement (Fortin 2009a: 254). It may be the case that the court knows little of the child's wishes and feelings if no report is produced. The Interim Report of the *Family Justice Review* states that children should, 'as early as possible in a case, be offered a menu of options to lay out the ways in which they could—if they wished—make their views known' (Norgrove 2011a: para 3.12). It does not, however, specifically recommend any additions to the options currently available. However, there does seem to be increasing readiness on the part of the judiciary to hear children's views themselves.[162] There are now guidelines applicable in both private and public law proceedings for judges who are prepared to talk to children. They are meant to:

> encourage judges to enable children to feel more involved and connected with proceedings in which important decisions are made in their lives and to give them an opportunity to satisfy themselves that the Judge has understood their wishes and feelings and to understand the nature of the Judge's task. (Judge Bellamy, Judge Platt and District Judge Crichton 2010)

---

[155] Fortin (1998: 415) points out that the parents in another case, who were asking for treatment to continue as required by their beliefs as Orthodox Jews, were treated very differently and their wishes were overruled (*Re C (Medical Treatment)* [1998] 1 FLR 384). In *Re C (HIV Test)* [1999] 2 FLR 1004, however, the parents' wishes were overruled because they flew in the face of accepted medical opinion.

[156] See Downie (1999); Fox and McHale (1997); Fortin (1998); Bridge (1999b).

[157] For detailed discussion, see Fortin (2009a: ch 7).

[158] Practice Direction: Revised Private Law Programme [2010] 2 FLR 717, para 1.7. This governs private law cases such as disputes under s 8 Children Act 1989.

[159] Ibid, paras 2.2(f), 5.5(b).

[160] Ibid, para 5.5(a).

[161] Under s 7 Children Act 1989.

[162] See *Re A (Contact: Separate Representation)* [2001] 1 FLR 715, 721. See also Dame Butler-Sloss with Fiddy (2001). See further Chapter 10 above.

This suggests that children should be seen to reassure them that they have been heard and to give them a greater understanding of the courts task; the purpose is not to allow children to exercise autonomy.[163]

Party Status and Separate Representation

Ordinarily, children cannot bring or defend proceedings in their own right; they need to be represented by an adult. In public law proceedings the court must appoint a children's guardian unless satisfied that it is not necessary to do so in order to safeguard the child's interests.[164] The children's guardian is a Cafcass officer.[165] In private law proceedings children can be given party status if the court considers this to be in the child's best interests.[166] If the child is the applicant or has been made a party to proceedings in relation to which he or she is the subject, a children's guardian must be appointed.[167] If the child is a party but is not the subject of proceedings, the child must have a litigation friend to conduct the proceedings on his or her behalf.[168] A litigation friend may be appointed in private law proceedings by the court and may be the Official Solicitor, a Cafcass officer or some other person.[169] Otherwise, if not court-appointed, the litigation friend must be someone who:

(a) can fairly and competently conduct proceedings on behalf of the child;
(b) has no interest adverse to that of the child; ...[170]

More unusually, children may instruct their own solicitors. This can occur, as Fortin explains (Fortin 2009a: 257), where the child is a party and the court considers the child mature enough to instruct a solicitor without the help of a children's guardian. It may also occur where the child initiates section 8 proceedings such as residence proceedings.[171]

In the past courts have tended to use their power to order separate party status sparingly[172] and recent practice directions appear to have been designed to restrict children's participation as separate litigants. Practice Direction 16A[173] makes it clear that making a child a party to proceedings is 'a step that will be taken only in cases which involve an

---

[163] On the question of whether judges should speak to children in private law cases see Chapter 10 above; Hunter (2007); Raitt (2007).

[164] Family Procedure Rules 2010, R 16.3. '"Specified proceedings" has the meaning assigned to it by section 41(6) of the 1989 Act and rule 12.27' (R 2.3).

[165] Ibid, R 16.17.

[166] Ibid, R 16.2.

[167] Ibid, R 16.4. In such cases the guardian might be a Cafcass officer, the Official Solicitor or some other person. The guardian must be able to conduct the case fairly and competently and must not have any interests adverse to the child (ibid, R 16.24.).

[168] Ibid, R 16.5.

[169] Ibid, R 16.11.

[170] Ibid, R 16.9

[171] The government proposes to retain legal aid for the separate representation of children, even if the proposed reforms limiting legal aid in family cases are implemented (MOJ 2010a: paras 4.105–4.106). See Legal Aid, Sentencing and Punishment of Offenders Bill 2010–11, Sched 1, Part 1, para 13.

[172] See Bellamy and Lord (2003). See also Dame Butler-Sloss with Fiddy (2001: 14). In *Re A (Contact: Separate Representation)* [2001] 1 FLR 715, Hale LJ stated that in cases where parents are separating, children need to be heard and may need someone 'to orchestrate an investigation of the case on their behalf' (721). However this does not, she said, mean that they need separate representation. Often, the parents or the Cafcass officer can meet their needs (ibid). see District Judge Adam (2011: 257–58).

[173] Which has superseded a similarly worded practice direction published in 2004.

issue of significant difficulty and consequently will occur in only a minority of cases' (para 7.1). Before taking this step the court should consider alternatives, such as asking the Cafcass officer to do more or to make a referral to social services or to obtain expert evidence (ibid). The court must also be mindful of the fact that separate representation of the child may cause delay and must put this risk in the balance when assessing the child's best interests (para 7.3).

The Practice Direction provides guidance as to what circumstances might justify making an order to make the child a party (para 7.2). Examples given of cases where taking this step might be appropriate include those where the Cafcass officer recommends such a measure; where the child has a standpoint or interests that cannot be represented by the adult parties; where there is an intractable dispute over contact or residence, including where contact has ceased or there is evidence of 'irrational but implacable hostility' to contact or the child 'may be suffering harm associated with the contact dispute'; where the wishes of the child cannot be adequately represented by means of a report; where there are serious allegations of physical, sexual or other abuse of the child or there are allegations of domestic violence not amenable to resolution with the help of a Cafcass officer; where there is an older child opposed to the court's proposed course of action; where there are complex issues such as medical or mental health issues; where the conflicting interests of children are in issue; where there is a contested issue about scientific testing; or where there is an international dimension other than child abduction, and it may be necessary to hold discussions with overseas authorities or courts.

According to Harold and Murch, writing of the similarly worded Practice Direction that has now been replaced by the 2010 one, the reluctance to order separate representation evidenced in the restriction of its use to cases involving 'serious difficulty', together with the then government's attempt to limit the use of welfare reports, 'herald[ed] a new low in the official response to the demands of Article 12(2) of the UN Convention on the Rights of the Child' (Harold and Murch 2005: 203).[174]

Powers and Duties of Children's Guardian and Litigation Friend

The powers and duties of the children's guardian are set out in the Family Procedure Rules 2010:

16.20.—Powers and duties of the children's guardian

(1) The children's guardian is to act on behalf of the child upon the hearing of any application in proceedings to which this Chapter applies with the duty of safeguarding the interests of the child.

(2) The children's guardian must also provide the court with such other assistance as it may require.

(3) The children's guardian, when carrying out duties in relation to specified proceedings, other than placement proceedings, must have regard to the principle set out in section 1(2) and the matters set out in section 1(3)(a) to (f) of the 1989 Act as if for the word 'court' in that section there were substituted the words 'children's guardian' ... .

---

[174] But see Whybrow (2004), who argues that party status for the child, as opposed to use of the guardian/ Cafcass officer, serves no purpose unless the child is competent to instruct a solicitor.

(5) The children's guardian's duties must be exercised in accordance with Practice Direction 16A.

(6) A report to the court by the children's guardian is confidential.

Practice Direction 16A expands upon the guardian's duties and these differ, depending on whether the proceedings in question are public or private law proceedings. Where the guardian is appointed in public law proceedings, such as care applications, the relevant provisions are contained in Part 3 of the Practice Direction. This requires the guardian to contact or seek to interview such persons as the guardian thinks appropriate or who have been identified by the court. The guardian must obtain appropriate professional assistance.[175] Unless a solicitor has been appointed, the guardian must appoint one. He or she must instruct the solicitor and advise the child.[176] The children's guardian also has duties to the court. He or she must advise the court as to the child's wishes; the child's level of understanding where relevant; and the options available in relation to the child as well as their suitability.[177]

There are different provisions setting out the duties of a children's guardian who is appointed under rule 16.4, namely where the child is a party to and the subject of private law proceedings. These are contained in Part 4 of the Practice Direction. The guardian must conduct proceedings 'fairly and competently' and must have no interests adverse to those of the child. All the guardian does in relation to the proceedings must be for the child's benefit.[178] The duties of a litigation friend, set out in Part 2 of the Practice Direction, are the same as those of the children's guardian in private law proceedings.

It seems that the description by the court in *Re CT* of the functions of what were the next friend and the guardian ad litem, now termed the litigation friend and the children's guardian, is still relevant. In *Re CT (A Minor) (Wardship: Representation)* the court said:

> A next friend or guardian does not in those circumstances act merely as the child's representative. He has an independent function to perform, and must act in what he believes to be the minor's best interests, even if that should involve acting in contravention of the wishes of a minor who is old enough to articulate views of his own … . He owes a loyalty which has by its very nature to be divided: to the child whose views he must fully and fairly represent; and to the court, which it is his duty to assist in achieving the overriding or paramount objective of promoting the child's best interests.[179]

Separate Representation and the 'Mature' Minor

Children themselves may initiate proceedings with the leave of the court under section 10(8) of the Children Act 1989. Normally they have to be assisted by a litigation friend or children's guardian. But there is another route to separate representation open to children who are judged sufficiently mature. Under Rule 16.6 of the Family Procedure Rules 2010, the child can apply to begin or defend proceedings or act as a party without the

[175] Practice Direction 16A 2010, para 6.1.
[176] Ibid, para 6.2.
[177] Ibid, para 6.6.
[178] Ibid, para 7.6.
[179] [1993] 2 FLR 278, 280–81.

guidance of such an adult representative or, if one is already in place, to dispense with that person's services.[180]

(a) Permission to Apply for a Section 8 Order

Children may apply for leave, or what is now in the Rules termed 'permission', to seek section 8 orders.[181] In order to be granted permission, the child must satisfy the court that he or she has sufficient understanding. And even if the court is so satisfied, it still has a discretion whether to grant permission.[182]

Children's applications for permission are now subject to the 'overriding objective' of the new Family Procedure Rules 2010 and, according to District Judge Adam (2011: 247), previous authorities, and particularly older cases, on family procedure may not necessarily be good law anymore. The overriding objective set out in Rule 1.1 is to '[enable] the court to deal with cases justly, having regard to any welfare issues involved'. Dealing with cases justly entails, among other things, dealing with cases fairly, expeditiously and in a way that is proportionate to the importance and complexity of the issues involved. The parties must be placed on an even footing but court resources and cost saving are also relevant. It is therefore possible that cases concerning permission might be decided differently now and it is with this in mind that we consider the older law. However, it seems likely that the court's concerns in the cases discussed below are likely to remain concerns and the balancing exercise seems consistent with the new objective.

In *Re C (Residence: Child's Application for Leave)*[183] the court indicated that such cases should be approached cautiously, taking into account the child's best interests but not making them paramount.[184] It is necessary to balance the child's wish to be heard and to have her views taken into account against the possible detrimental effects of, for example, being cross-examined or hearing evidence it would be better not to hear. In addition, judges have declared themselves conscious of the need to protect children from their own lack of insight and maturity.[185]

It appears also that the courts are wary of intervening in the relationship between parent and child. In *Re C (A Minor) (Leave to Seek Section 8 Orders)*[186] a girl of almost 15 sought leave to apply for a residence order to enable her to live with a friend's family rather than with her parents. She also sought leave to apply for a specific issue order allowing her to go on holiday with the friend's family. Johnson J refused leave in relation to the residence order indicating that this was something that would be better resolved through discussion within the family. Moreover, leave to seek a specific issue order might be interpreted by the girl as giving her 'some advantage against her parents' in a situation where she should be dealing directly with her parents rather than seeking the intervention of the court.[187] He also took the view that the jurisdiction was intended to be exercised

---

[180] See below.

[181] S 10(8) Children Act 1989.

[182] *Re SC (A Minor) (Leave to Seek Residence Order)* [1994] 1 FLR 96; *Re N (Contact: Minor Seeking Leave to Defend and Removal of Guardian)* [2003] 1 FLR 652.

[183] [1995] 1 FLR 927.

[184] The court made it clear that s 10(9) of the Children Act 1989 does not apply in the case of an application by the child concerned in the case.

[185] See *Re C (Residence: Child's Application for Leave)* [1995] 1 FLR 927, 929, citing *Re S (A Minor) (Independent Representation)* [1993] 2 FLR 437. See also *Re A (Care: Discharge Application by Child)* [1995] 1 FLR 599, 601.

[186] [1994] 1 FLR 26.

[187] Ibid, 29.

only in relation to matters of some importance and that a dispute over a holiday was too trivial to warrant the granting of leave.

Q Sawyer has written that '[t]here can be no simple answer as to when and how the child should be heard when the State intervenes in the family' (Sawyer 1995: 194). She pointed out that '[t]he empowerment of the child as active participant in proceedings represents a distortion of the usual power-structure of the family which may of itself provoke tension' (ibid: 192).[188] Family stability may be affected as might the child's life within the family (ibid: 193). She concluded that '[a]ny process by which the State or any outside body ... becomes involved in resolving internal family disputes, must recognise the child's subjectivity without ignoring the implications of the child's position of emotional dependency within the family' (ibid: 194). Do you see any similar concerns reflected in *Re C* above?

(b) Representation of Children

Whether or not a minor is competent to run a case unassisted by an adult representative, leave/permission of the court to initiate an application must be sought under section 10(8). Where the minor is competent, however, additional rules apply to allow him or her to participate in litigation proceedings without such a representative: rules of court authorise a minor in certain circumstances to conduct certain family proceedings, including proceedings under the inherent jurisdiction and section 8, without the intervention of a litigation friend or a children's guardian. The effect is to enable the child to instruct a solicitor directly. In order to do so, the child must get the permission of the court or be judged by a solicitor,[189] who has agreed to be instructed by the child, to have sufficient understanding.[190]

The duties of the child's solicitor are enumerated in detail in the Family Procedure Rules 2010 R 16.29. The solicitor must take instructions from the children's guardian, if there is one. However if there is no guardian, or if the solicitor is satisfied that a child wishes to give instructions which conflict with those of the children's guardian and is able to do so, the solicitor must take instruction from the child.

To obtain permission to litigate without a guardian or litigation friend the child must show that he or she 'has sufficient understanding to conduct the proceedings concerned or proposed without a litigation friend or children's guardian'.[191] If this standard is satis-

---

[188] See also Sawyer (1999: 111–12).

[189] It is the court that has the ultimate right to decide whether a child has the capacity to instruct a solicitor (*Re CT (A Minor) (Wardship: Representation)* [1993] 2 FLR 278, 289). The minor must be able not only to instruct the solicitor as to his or her views, but also to give instructions on various matters arising in the course of the case: *Re H (A Minor) (Role of Official Solicitor)* [1993] 2 FLR 552. The court, if it later finds it is not satisfied that the child still has sufficient understanding, can appoint a litigation friend or children's guardian (R 16.6(8)–(10)).

[190] FPR 2010 R 16.6. If a child already has a litigation friend or children's guardian in an ongoing case, the child can seek the premission of the court to continue without the litigation friend or children's guardian (FPR 2010 R 16.6(5)). Again, the test is whether the child has sufficient understanding to conduct the proceedings without a litigation friend or children's guardian (FPR 2010 R 16.6(6)). This is in essence the same test as that under s 10 of the Children Act 1989 (*Re N (Contact: Minor Seeking Leave to Defend and Removal of Guardian)* [2003] 1 FLR 652). For a case where the child, aged 7, was considered too young to instruct a solicitor, see *Re W (Contact: Joining Child as a Party)* [2001] EWCA Civ 1830; [2003] 1 FLR 681.

[191] FPR 2010 R 16.6(6).

fied, the court 'will' grant the application.[192] However, the courts have set a high standard in the past when judging competence.[193] In *Re S (A Minor) (Independent Representation)*[194] the court held that *Gillick* competence was the appropriate measure for the child's understanding (447). But Sir Thomas Bingham said that where 'sound judgement' calls for the kind of insights that only maturity and experience can bring, the court and the solicitor should be 'slow' to conclude that the child's understanding is sufficient (444).[195] The court went on in terms that clearly convey the tensions between the images of the autonomous and the vulnerable child, the child as 'being' and as 'becoming':[196]

> [C]hildren are human beings in their own right with individual minds and wills, views and emotions, which should command serious attention. A child's wishes are not to be discounted or dismissed simply because he is a child. He should be free to express them and decision-makers should listen. Second is the fact that a child is, after all, a child. The reason why the law is particularly solicitous in protecting the interests of children is that they are liable to be vulnerable and impressionable, lacking the maturity to weigh the longer term against the shorter, lacking the insight to know how others will react in certain situations, lacking the experience to match the probable against the possible. (448)

However, there are some cases where the court appears to have come down on the side of autonomy.[197] The most striking declarations in favour of young people's autonomy can be found in *Mabon v Mabon*,[198] a Court of Appeal case. Although this was decided under the old rules of court, the words of Thorpe LJ remain relevant:

> 23. There are a number of factors which pointed strongly towards the grant of separate representation in the present case. The applicants were at the date of judgment aged respectively 17, 15, and 13. What remained was a disposal hearing … . [W]ithout separate representation how were they to know what their parents were contending for: were there cross-applications for residence, what were the contact applications? It was simply unthinkable to exclude young men from knowledge of and participation in legal proceedings that affected them so fundamentally. They had been seen by an experienced family practitioner who had no doubts as to the sufficiency of their understanding: hardly surprising given that they are educated, articulate and reasonably mature for their respective ages … .

> 25. … In our system we have traditionally adopted the tandem model for the representation of children who are parties to family proceedings, whether public or private. First the court appoints a guardian ad litem who will almost invariably have a social work qualification and very wide experience of family proceedings. He then instructs a specialist family solicitor who, in turn, usually instructs a specialist family barrister. This is a Rolls Royce model and is the envy of many other jurisdictions. However its overall approach is essentially paternalistic. The

---

[192] Ibid.
[193] See *Re H (A Minor) (Guardian ad Litem: Requirement)* [1994] 4 All ER 762, 765.
[194] [1993] 2 FLR 437.
[195] See also *Re N (Contact: Minor Seeking Leave to Defend and Removal of Guardian)* [2003] 1 FLR 652.
[196] Children themselves differ on whether they wish to attend court and whether they wish to speak to the judge (Newsline 2003: 295–96).
[197] See *Re H (A Minor)(Guardian ad Litem: Requirement)* [1994] 4 All ER 762, esp 767. See also *Re CT (A Minor)(Wardship: Representation)* [1993] 2 FLR 278 where the court made it clear that a minor's capacity to instruct a solicitor goes beyond the Children Act 1989 to include wardship proceedings; wardship proceedings could not be used to impose a guardian ad litem on a competent 13½-year-old girl. However, allowing a young person separate representation does not necessarily mean that he or she will be permitted to give evidence in court. See *Re O (Care Proceedings: Evidence)* [2003] EWHC Fam 2011; [2004] 1 FLR 161.
[198] [2005] EWCA Civ 634; [2005] All ER (D) 419.

guardian's first priority is to advocate the welfare of the child he represents. His second priority is to put before the court the child's wishes and feelings. Those priorities can in some cases conflict. In extreme cases the conflict is unmanageable. That reality is recognised by the terms of [rules of court]. ... [T]he focus is upon the sufficiency of the child's understanding in the context of the remaining proceedings.

26. In my judgment the Rule is sufficiently widely framed to meet our obligations to comply with both Article 12 of the United Nations Convention and Article 8 of the ECHR, providing that judges correctly focus on the sufficiency of the child's understanding and, in measuring that sufficiency, reflect the extent to which, in the 21st Century, there is a keener appreciation of the autonomy of the child and the child's consequential right to participate in decision making processes that fundamentally affect his family life ... .

28. The guidance given by this court in *Re S* ... on the construction of [the rules of court] is now twelve years old. Much has happened in that time. Although the United Kingdom had ratified the UN Convention some fifteen months earlier, it did not have much impact initially and it is hardly surprising that it was not mentioned by this court on the 26 February 1993. Although the tandem model has many strengths and virtues, at its heart lies the conflict between advancing the welfare of the child and upholding the child's freedom of expression and participation. Unless we in this jurisdiction are to fall out of step with similar societies as they safeguard Article 12 rights, we must, in the case of articulate teenagers, accept that the right to freedom of expression and participation outweighs the paternalistic judgment of welfare.

29. In testing the sufficiency of a child's understanding I would not say that welfare has no place. If direct participation would pose an obvious risk of harm to the child arising out of the nature of the continuing proceedings and, if the child is incapable of comprehending that risk, then the judge is entitled to find that sufficient understanding has not been demonstrated. But judges have to be equally alive to the risk of emotional harm that might arise from denying the child knowledge of and participation in the continuing proceedings ... .

32. In conclusion this case provides a timely opportunity to recognise the growing acknowledgement of the autonomy and consequential rights of children, both nationally and internationally. The Rules are sufficiently robustly drawn to accommodate that shift. In individual cases trial judges must equally acknowledge the shift when they make in individual cases a proportionate judgment of the sufficiency of the child's understanding.

Wall LJ added:

40. ... I am in no doubt at all that in the overwhelming majority of cases in which it is appropriate for children to be separately represented, what has become known as the 'tandem model' of representation serves the interests of those children extremely well. The child has the input of expertise from the different disciplines of lawyer and guardian, who are able, with the court's permission, to call on additional expertise and advice where necessary. In public law proceedings, Section 42 of the Children Act 1989 gives the guardian sweeping powers of investigation on the child's behalf. At the same time, the child concerned is protected from the corroding consequences of adversarial litigation. Children are not required to give evidence and be cross-examined: they do not have access to the sensitive documentation generated by the case. This system is, of course, paternalistic in approach, but it usually works well, in my experience, even in cases where the child has sufficient understanding to participate in the proceedings concerned without a guardian.

41. However, the [rules of court] sensibly make provision for the circumstance in which the guardian and the children concerned fall out, as has happened in this appeal ... .

43. ... [T]he judge seems to me, with all respect to him, to have perceived the case from the perspective of the adults. From the boys' perspective, it was simply impossible for the guardian to advance their views or represent them in the proceedings. He would, no doubt, faithfully report to the judge what the boys were saying, but the case he would be advancing to the judge on their behalf would be (or was likely to be) directly opposed to what the boys were actually saying.

44. In these circumstances, I do not agree with the judge that the only advantage from independent representation was 'perhaps the more articulate and elegant expression of what I already know'. That analysis overlooks, in my judgment, the need for the boys on the facts of this particular case to emerge from the proceedings (whatever the result) with the knowledge that their position had been independently represented and their perspective fully advanced to the judge.[199]

As Fortin says, overall, the ways in which children's wishes in private law cases are conveyed to the court are 'fragmented and arbitrary' (Fortin 2009a: 248). The 'tandem model' discussed in *Mabon* applies in cases which qualify as 'specified proceedings' under section 41 of the Children Act 1989 and has been largely confined to public law cases. Its application was potentially extended to section 8 cases when section 41 of the Children Act 1989 was amended by section 122 of the Adoption and Children Act 2002 to allow for the inclusion of section 8 applications in the category of 'specified proceedings'. This is an enabling provision, however, and so far it has not led to the inclusion of section 8 cases to put them on a par with public law cases. Nevertheless, according to Fortin, recent years have seen Cafcass 'replicating the public law system of tandem representation as closely as possible for children in private law cases'. A child in such cases 'is normally assisted by a Cafcass officer acting as his guardian ad litem,[200] together with a private solicitor (or a solicitor from Cafcass Legal) acting as his legal advocate' (Fortin 2009a: 259). Fortin was writing when the old rules were in operation and it remains to be seen whether the practice she observed will continue.

In any event, whether the 'tandem model' better enables children in private law proceedings to convey their views to the court is open to question. James et al found that Cafcass officers in their study operated within the context of a 'universal model of childhood and "the child"' (James et al 2003: 890). They attached more importance to their own judgements about the welfare of the child, which were based on professional principles and personal considerations, than on the children's wishes and feelings (ibid: 893).[201] They also focused on the family as a group as their priority rather than on the individual child (ibid: 894). The authors concluded that there are obstacles in the way of any attempt to 'make real' children's 'rights' to be heard in judicial proceedings (ibid: 895). Masson,

---

[199] Judges have tended to be reluctant to discuss what children want directly with them. See the discussion in Freeman (2001: 198).

[200] See *Re A (Contact: Separate Representation)* [2001] 1 FLR 715, paras 20–22. This case was unusual in that the child was only 4½. but the court made her a party and appointed the NYAS (National Youth Advocacy Service) as her guardian.

[201] Compare May and Smart (2004), where children's views were sometimes important in the context of residence and contact. However, they note that, while older children did influence outcomes, younger children tended to make an impact only if their views were consistent with other evidence and were in agreement with the welfare professional's assessment. Otherwise their views were disregarded (ibid: 315), although the authors say it is not clear whether this was because of their status as children or because it 'would be genuinely unsafe to place too much weight on their views' (ibid). They also express concerns elsewhere that assumptions concerning children's welfare take the place of consultation with children (Smart and Neale 2000: 168). See also Sawyer (2000). See further on children's wishes and feelings in the context of residence and contact, Chapter 10 above.

in the context of public care proceedings, reported that solicitors regarded the guardian and not the child as their client and that they spent little or no time with the children concerned (Masson 2000: 480). Guardians and solicitors were reluctant to view as competent children whose wishes are considered to conflict with their best interests (ibid: 486).

The 'tandem model' is, then, essentially a paternalistic one and it is not designed to give the child an independent voice. But as the court in *Mabon* made clear, it does not preclude the need to allow the mature minor to act as an autonomous litigant in appropriate cases. An older minor might, for instance, express disagreement with the guardian.[202] *Mabon* may herald a time when greater priority will be given to recognising young people as autonomous. According to Fortin, 'few courts will prevent "elderly" children from dispensing with the services of a [children's] guardian ... in cases where they are already involved in parental litigation' (Fortin 2009a: 269).

Children's Evidence

There are concerns about the direct participation of children in family proceedings generally,[203] and the tension between viewing the child as vulnerable and incompetent on the one hand and as an autonomous actor on the other is very evident in the case law relating to children as witnesses, particularly in the reported child protection cases.

Children are considered unreliable witnesses in cases which involve much documentation and also hearsay.[204] In addition, the risk of harm to the child is thought to be too high in most cases. For example, in *LM (By Her Guardian) v Medway Council, RM and YM* [205] the court said:

> The correct starting point ... is that it is undesirable that a child should have to give evidence in care proceedings and that particular justification will be required before that course is taken. There will be some cases in which it will be right to make an order. In my view they will be rare. (para 44)

Instead, video recordings of 'Achieving Best Evidence' (ABE) interviews are used in care cases:

> The near-contemporaneous account, given in response to open-ended questioning, in relaxed and comfortable surroundings, is considered inherently more likely to be reliable than an account elicited by formal questioning in the stressful surroundings of a courtroom months if not years after the event. Unlike criminal proceedings, however, it is 'rare' for the child to be called for cross-examination in family proceedings.[206]

---

[202] However, Masson reports that research in relation to care proceedings revealed that guardians were reluctant to express their views to the child concerned or to show the child the report. This meant that the child would not even know whether there was a disagreement (Masson 2000: 486). Children were also discouraged from seeking separate representation (ibid: 486–87). Children had little influence on the process or the outcome (ibid: 492). The welfare orientation within the proceedings coupled with a belief that legal proceedings are damaging for children meant that they were excluded from participation (ibid). It may be that things have changed since then, however.

[203] See, eg, Hunter (2007); Norgrove (2011a: para 3.13).

[204] *Re W (Children) (Abuse: Oral Evidence)* [2010] UKSC 12; [2010] 1 FLR 1485, para 10.

[205] [2007] EWCA Civ 9; [2007] 1 FLR 1698.

[206] *Re W (Children) (Abuse: Oral Evidence)* [2010] UKSC 12; [2010] 1 FLR 1485, para 10.

However, it has now been held by the Supreme Court in *Re W (Children) (Abuse: Oral Evidence)*[207] that a presumption or starting point that children should not be called contravenes the human rights of all concerned and cannot be retained as part of the law:

[22] ... That cannot be reconciled with the approach of the European Court of Human Rights, ... Article 6 requires that the proceedings overall be fair and this normally entails an opportunity to challenge the evidence presented by the other side. But even in criminal proceedings account must be taken of the Art 8 rights of the perceived victim: see *SN v Sweden (Application No 34209/96)* (2002) 39 EHRR 304. Striking that balance in care proceedings may well mean that the child should not be called to give evidence in the great majority of cases, but that is a result and not a presumption or even a starting point.

[23] The object of the proceedings is to achieve a fair trial in the determination of the rights of all the people involved. Children are harmed if they are taken away from their families for no good reason. Children are harmed if they are left in abusive families. This means that the court must admit all the evidence which bears upon the relevant questions ... .

[24] When the court is considering whether a particular child should be called as a witness, the court will have to weigh two considerations: the advantages that that will bring to the determination of the truth and the damage it may do to the welfare of this or any other child ... . [T]he welfare of the child is ... a relevant consideration, albeit not the paramount consideration in this respect. ... [T]he object of the proceedings is to promote the welfare of this and other children. The hearing cannot be fair to them unless their interests are given great weight.

[25] In weighing the advantages that calling the child to give evidence may bring to the fair and accurate determination of the case, the court will have to look at several factors. One will be the issues it has to decide in order properly to determine the case ... . Another will be the quality of the evidence it already has. Sometimes there may be enough evidence to make the findings needed whether or not the child is cross-examined. Sometimes there will be nothing useful to be gained from the child's oral evidence ... . The quality of any ABE interview will also be an important factor, as will be the nature of any challenge which the party may wish to make. The court is unlikely to be helped by generalised accusations of lying, or by a fishing expedition in which the child is taken slowly through the story yet again in the hope that something will turn up, or by a cross-examination which is designed to intimidate the child and pave the way for accusations of inconsistency in a future criminal trial. On the other hand, focused questions which put forward a different explanation for certain events may help the court to do justice between the parties. Also relevant will be the age and maturity of the child and the length of time since the events in question, for these will have a bearing on whether an account now can be as reliable as a near-contemporaneous account, especially if given in a well-conducted ABE interview.

[26] The age and maturity of the child, along with the length of time since the events in question, will also be relevant to the second part of the inquiry, which is the risk of harm to the child. Further specific factors may be the support which the child has from family or other sources, or the lack of it, the child's own wishes and feelings about giving evidence, and the views of the child's guardian and, where appropriate, those with parental responsibility. We endorse the view that an unwilling child should rarely, if ever, be obliged to give evidence. ... [T]he court is entitled to have regard to the general evidence of the harm which giving evidence may do to children, as well as to any features which are particular to this child and this case. ...

[27] But on both sides of the equation, the court must factor in what steps can be taken to improve the quality of the child's evidence and at the same time to decrease the risk of harm

---

[207] Ibid.

to the child. These two aims are not in opposition to one another. The whole premise of Achieving Best Evidence and the special measures in criminal cases is that this will improve rather than diminish the quality of the evidence to the court ... .

[28] ... There are things that the court can do but they are not things that it is used to doing at present. It is not limited by the usual courtroom procedures or to applying the special measures by analogy. The important thing is that the questions which challenge the child's account are fairly put to the child so that she can answer them, not that counsel should be able to question her directly. One possibility is an early videoed cross-examination as proposed by Pigot. Another is cross-examination via video-link. But another is putting the required questions to her through an intermediary. This could be the court itself, as would be common in continental Europe and used to be much more common than it is now in the courts of this country.

[29] In principle, the approach in private family proceedings between parents should be the same as the approach in care proceedings. However, there are specific risks to which the court must be alive. Allegations of abuse are not being made by a neutral and expert local authority which has nothing to gain by making them, but by a parent who is seeking to gain an advantage in the battle against the other parent. This does not mean that they are false but it does increase the risk of misinterpretation, exaggeration or downright fabrication. On the other hand, the child will not routinely have the protection and support of a Cafcass guardian ... .

In *Re J (Child Giving Evidence)*[208] the court, applying the judgment in *Re W*, reiterated that the best interests of the child, while not paramount, are 'extremely important' (para 27). The Article 6 rights of all the parties to a fair trial pointed, in that case, to allowing the child to give evidence. While the court had to consider any harm that might result from his giving evidence, it also had to take account of the welfare benefits if he did so. He wanted to give evidence, was sufficiently mature to do so and would feel a profound sense of injustice if he were not permitted to testify.

VI. CONCLUSION

When it comes to children's autonomy and decision-making, much depends on the extent to which they are viewed as competent. Infants are clearly not seen in this way; they are seen as 'becoming'. Their parents have the right and responsibility to decide all matters relating to their upbringing but, when the decision is a life or death one, and it is challenged by the professionals, it can no longer be kept within the private family. The ultimate arbiter is the court and the basis on which the decision is made is the court's assessment of the child's best interests.

In the case of older children, the tensions between their construction as 'becoming' and as 'being' become more apparent. The law and the courts are increasingly open to endorsing the capacity of young people to make decisions and to be viewed as social actors. Nevertheless, it is more often a case of showing willingness to allow children to participate in the 'conversation' than a willingness to allow them to make decisions. And again, when it comes to questions of life and death and the professionals and parents disagree, it is the court rather than the child or the private family that decides.

---

[208] [2010] EWHC 962 (Fam); [2010] 2 FLR 1080.

FURTHER READING

C Bridge, 'Parental Powers and the Medical Treatment of Children' in C Bridge (ed), *Family Law Towards the Millennium: Essays for PM Bromley* (London, Butterworths, 1997).

——, 'Religious Beliefs and Teenage Refusal of Medical Treatment' (1999) 62 *MLR* 585.

——, 'Religion, Culture and Conviction—The Medical Treatment of Young Children' (1999) 11 *CFLQ* 1.

J Bridgeman, 'Old Enough to Know Best?' (1993) 13 *Legal Studies* 69.

G Douglas, 'The Retreat from *Gillick*' (1992) 55 *MLR* 569.

J Eekelaar, 'The Interests of the Child and the Child's Wishes: The Role of Dynamic Self-determinism' (1994) 8 *Int J Law and the Family* 42.

J Fortin, '*Re C (Medical Treatment)*: A Baby's Right to Life' (1998) 10 *CFLQ* 411.

——, 'Rights Brought Home for Children' (1999) 62 *MLR* 350.

——, *Children's Rights and the Developing Law* (Cambridge: Cambridge University Press, 2009) Part Two.

M Freeman, 'The Human Rights of Children' (2010) 63 *Current Legal Problems* 1.

AL James, A James and S McNamee, 'Constructing Children's Welfare in Family Proceedings' (2003) *Fam Law* 889.

F Kaganas and A Diduck, 'Incomplete Citizens: Changing Images of Post-separation Children' (2004) 67 *MLR* 959.

J Keown, 'Beyond *Bland*: A Critique of the BMA Guidance on Withholding and Withdrawing Medical Treatment' (2000) 20 *Legal Studies* 66.

H Kuhse, *The Sanctity of Life Doctrine in Medicine* (Oxford, Clarendon Press, 1987).

V May and C Smart, 'Silence in Court?—Hearing Children in Residence and Contact Disputes' (2004) *Fam Law* 305.

V Munro, 'Square Pegs in Round Holes; The Dilemma of Conjoined Twins and Individual Rights' (2001) 10 *Social and Legal Studies* 459.

D Nelken, 'Afterword: Choosing Rights for Children' in G Douglas and L Sebba (eds), *Children's Rights and Traditional Values* (Aldershot, Ashgate, 1998).

C Piper, 'Barriers to Seeing and Hearing Children in Private Law Proceedings' (1999c) *Fam Law* 394.

——, 'Ascertaining the Wishes and Feelings of the Child' (1997) *Fam Law* 796.

D Price, 'Fairly Bland: An Alternative View of a Supposed "Death Ethic" and the BMA Guidelines' (2001) 21 *Legal Studies* 618.

C Smart and B Neale, '"It's My Life Too"—Children's Perspectives on Post-divorce Parenting' (2000) *Fam Law* 163.

C Wells, 'Whose Baby Is It?' (1988) 15 *JLS* 323.

C Wells, P Alldridge and D Morgan, 'An Unsuitable Case for Treatment' (1990) *NLJ* 1544.

Section 3: The Public/Private Divide

INTRODUCTION

The next four chapters all focus on the public/private divide. Chapters 12 and 13, dealing with domestic violence and child abuse, respectively, examine the way in which each of these phenomena came to be constructed as a problem warranting intervention in the private family. Both chapters, along with Chapter 14, covering child protection, explore the extent to which the notion of family privacy may be affecting the way in which the law is currently implemented. These chapters all examine the way in which government policy, professional practice and the law struggle to balance respect for family privacy and autonomy with the perceived need to intervene to protect the vulnerable. Chapter 15 also raises issues surrounding the public/private divide; it examines the way in which what were previously considered disputes which had to be resolved by the courts, or by means of agreements overseen the courts, are becoming increasingly privatised. The chapter considers the extent to which this privatisation by means of alternative dispute resolution (ADR), and mediation in particular, can expose vulnerable parties to exploitation and oppression, and lead to unfair settlements. The private nature of ADR means that there is no outside scrutiny of the process and in some cases, of the agreements; power imbalances may remain unaddressed. The chapter points to the fact that the professional ethos among mediators and court personnel prioritises the aim of ensuring that relationships between children and non-resident parents are maintained. It argues that in the context of such an ethos, resident mothers are subject to considerable pressure to agree to contact.

While the focus of this part is family law's negotiation of the public/private divide, the chapters also touch on the other themes in this book. For example, Chapter 15 looks at the power imbalances within mediation, and Chapter 12 considers the status of women and men in the context of domestic violence. Chapters 13 and 14 clearly raise the issue of welfare in the way that child abuse is constructed and the way the concept of significant harm is applied in the courts. Welfare is also central, of course, to the way child protection processes operate and on what assumptions.

12

A Public or Private Matter?
Domestic Violence

I. INTRODUCTION

The term 'domestic violence' is widely used, and will be used here,[1] to describe abuse between partners in an intimate relationship.[2] Like child abuse, abuse of women in intimate relationships has not always been seen as a social problem demanding remedial action by the state and its agents. It has come to be constructed as such through the efforts, first, of 'moral entrepreneurs'[3] and, more recently, of feminists. The success of those efforts was a product of social and economic change and, in particular, changes in the way women and their place in the family were seen. Women had to be seen as individuals rather than adjuncts of their husbands before they could be seen as requiring protection from spousal abuse. In addition, the abuse of women in the family had to be constructed as representing so serious a problem that intervention in the private domain of the family to deal with it was justified.

Until the nineteenth century, the ideal of family privacy, an ideal central to the philosophy underlying the liberal state, largely shielded the family from state intervention.[4] Feminist writers have frequently pointed to the notion of the family as a private domain as one of the primary obstacles, initially, to the designation of domestic violence as a social problem, and, latterly, to devising a response to it.[5] The ideal of family privacy, as O'Donovan says, rests on certain assumptions about family life; the home 'is thought to be a private place, a refuge from society, where relationships can flourish untrammelled

---

[1] This term has been criticised for masking the gendered nature of the violence but, as one writer has pointed out, the other terms frequently used in this context, such as battered wife, are also unsatisfactory (Smith 1989: 1). The use of 'victim' rather than 'survivor' is criticised by some commentators as well. See Burton (2008a: 124).

[2] This category will be taken to include cohabiting and married couples, ex-partners and couples who have never lived together. This chapter, with its focus on gendered aspects of domestic violence, will not address violence between same-sex couples. Nor will it deal with other violence that could be seen as domestic violence, such as abuse of children or elderly or disabled family members (see, on elder abuse, eg, Special Edition on Elder Abuse (1995) 2(3) *Social Work in Europe*; Decalmer and Glendenning 1993; Herring 2011: 731ff)). As the Home Office has pointed out, these forms of abuse are different from partner abuse and are dealt with differently (Home Office 2000: para 1.12). Some reference will be made to children in this chapter since child abuse is linked to partner abuse. However, child abuse is covered separately in Chapter 13 below. This chapter will not deal with abuse of parents by teenage children either. To focus on this issue in the context of domestic violence risks marginalising partner abuse (see Home Office 2000: para 1.13).

[3] See Chapter 13 below.

[4] See also Chapter 13 below.

[5] See Dobash and Dobash (1997: 7).

by public interference' (O'Donovan 1985: 107). In order for domestic violence to be seen as a problem justifying, and even demanding, state intervention, these assumptions had to be challenged.

In this chapter, we consider what behaviours are categorised as domestic violence and trace the way in which domestic violence came to be constructed as a social problem. We then go on to examine the law designed to address the problem and the way in which it is implemented. We consider the ways in which the notion of family privacy has kept the issue of domestic violence hidden or has led agencies such as the police to ignore it in the past. And we go on to consider how, more recently, the notion of privacy has been invoked to question the use of the law in some cases. This chapter also touches on the theme of equality, pointing out that women's status and constructions of masculinity have been implicated in the existence of and understandings of domestic violence.

II. WHAT IS DOMESTIC VIOLENCE?

Definition

What is regarded as abusive in the context of intimate relationships has changed over time. Early concern focused on wife-beating but attention is now directed at a broader range of behaviour. For example, Hester and Radford identify 'a range of abusive behaviours' such as 'emotional cruelty, controlling and demeaning behaviour including withholding of money, attempts at strangulation and threats to kill' (Hester and Radford 1996: 7). Sev'er (1997) also refers to controlling behaviour and examines tactics such as intimidation, threats, stalking, destruction of property and using children to induce guilt in or to threaten the woman.

There is no definition of domestic violence for all legal purposes, but the broad working definition in the Crown Prosecution Service *Policy for Prosecuting Cases of Domestic Violence* (CPS 2009) is one that has been agreed by government and used by agencies involved in dealing with domestic violence:[6]

> 2.2 The Government definition of domestic violence against both men and women (agreed in 2004) is:
>
>> 'any incident of threatening behaviour, violence or abuse [psychological, physical, sexual, financial or emotional] between adults who are or have been intimate partners or family members, regardless of gender or sexuality.'
>
> 2.3 An adult is any person aged 18 years and over and family members are defined as mother, father, son, daughter, brother, sister and grandparents, whether directly related, in-laws or step-family. The definition is supported by an explanatory text that makes it clear that domestic violence includes female genital mutilation, forced marriage and so-called 'honour crimes'.

We see in this definition two notable recent additions to the kinds of behaviour classified as domestic violence. The first is the practice of compelling someone to marry against his or her will. The Forced Marriage (Civil Protection) Act 2007 added Part IVA to the

---

[6] See also Home Office (2005: para 10) and ACPO, NPIA (2008: 7) for a similar definition, but excluding the explicit reference to honour-based violence, female genital mutilation and forced marriage. See, for other definitions, Donovan and Hester (2011: 28).

Family Law Act 1996. Part IV embodies the civil law offering protective remedies in cases of domestic violence and the provisions of Part IVA are very similar. Force is defined as including 'threats or other psychological means'.[7]

The second is so-called 'honour'-based violence. However, the Home Affairs Select Committee has indicated that this 'differs from domestic violence in that it is often perpetrated by more than one individual, from the victim's own family or wider community' (Home Affairs Select Committee 2008: para 9).

More recently, the government focused its attention on violence against women and girls,[8] including, but not restricted to, domestic violence. It adopted a definition that reflects the gendered nature of such violence:

> Violence against women and girls is a gender-based crime which requires a focused and robust cross-government approach underpinned by a single agreed definition. It is for this reason that we are using the United Nations (UN) Declaration (1993) on the elimination of violence against women to guide our work across all government departments: *'Any act of gender-based violence that results in, or is likely to result in, physical, sexual or psychological harm or suffering to women, including threats of such acts, coercion or arbitrary deprivation of liberty, whether occurring in public or in private life'.* The declaration enshrines women's rights to live without the fear of violence and abuse and the United Kingdom's ratification of the UN Convention on the Elimination of all Forms of Discrimination against Women (CEDAW) upholds this principle. This is the first time that government has agreed to work to a single definition and we will specifically include girls in our approach. (Home Office 2010: 5, emphasis in original)[9]

In the Foreword to this same document, it is stated that, 'Every day women experience fear, or the aftermath of horrific crimes against them. ... This suffering is a form of gender inequality and it is wrong.' We can discern clearly the influence of feminism in this 'official' thinking about domestic violence. We see this influence also in 'official' acceptance that domestic violence is not merely a sudden outburst of anger but is a manifestation of power and control in many cases.

> Typically the violence involves a pattern of abusive and controlling behaviour which tends to get worse over time. It can take a number of forms. Some are directly and indirectly physical, such as assault, indecent assault, rape, destruction of property and threats. Some are non-physical, such as destructive criticism, pressure tactics, belittling, breaking trust, isolation, oppressive control of finances and harassment. The physical manifestations of domestic violence are criminal offences; the non-physical forms may also amount to offences, under the Protection from Harassment Act 1997.[10] (Home Office 2000a: para 1.15)

Perpetrators and Victims

Domestic violence is conceived of primarily as a problem of men's abuse of women.[11]

---

[7] S 63A(6) Family Law Act 1996.

[8] Previously intimate violence against girls, as opposed to women, was not given much attention.

[9] See also *EU Guidelines on Violence against Women and Girls and Combating All Forms of Discrimination Against Them* (2008: para 2).

[10] See below.

[11] In a survey conducted across the European Union, 25% of those surveyed said that they knew a woman within their circle of friends and family who had been a victim of domestic violence (TNS Opinion and Social 2010: para 1.2).

Men's groups argue that women are as violent as men are, that men are victims of domestic violence and that their plight is being ignored by the state. However, Kaganas (2006) contends that, while these groups are concerned about abuse of men, they neither produce evidence that this is a major social problem nor place protection high on their agenda. Instead, she says, they use the equivalence argument mainly to obscure the issue of gender in the context of domestic violence and as a weapon in their campaign for shared parenting and contact with children.[12]

Although there is evidence that, in a comparatively small number of cases, women abuse men,[13] and although researchers have documented abuse within same-sex relationships,[14] the available research suggests that domestic violence is overwhelmingly directed by men against women.[15]

Mirrlees-Black, in her analysis of a computerised self-completion questionnaire included in the 1996 British Crime Survey, found prevalence figures for violence against men that were similar to those for violence against women: 26% of women and 17% of men in her study had suffered physical (use of force) or non-physical violence (frightening threats) from a partner at some time (Mirrlees-Black 1999: 18). However, women tended to suffer more severe abuse than men did. Women were far more likely to be 'chronic' victims, suffering repeated abuse (ibid: 25). Women were 'much more likely to report choking, strangling and suffocation and being forced to have sex' (ibid: 37). In addition, women were more likely to be injured than men (ibid). Far more women than men were frightened during the incident and they remained upset by it for longer (ibid: 39); women were more likely to be 'living in fear of their partners' (ibid: 20). Only 11% of 'chronic' male victims and 5% of 'intermittent' male victims, compared with 80% of 'chronic' female victims and 52% of 'intermittent' female victims, said they had been 'very frightened'. These figures suggest that many of the 'threats' reported by men did not make them feel threatened. Mirrlees-Black suggests that it may be that men tend to report more trivial incidents (ibid: 61). She also speculates that men may suffer less serious consequences because of their greater physical strength, or that they are less likely to admit to serious outcomes (ibid: 62). In any event, she says, men are far more likely to be in a position to leave an abusive relationship than women are (ibid).

A study conducted by Walby and Allen, examining responses from the computerised self-completion questionnaire which was included in the 2001 British Crime Survey, also found that 'women are the overwhelming majority of the most heavily abused group' (Walby and Allen 2004: vii). According to this report, it is largely women who 'suffer multiple attacks and are subject to more than one form of inter-personal violence' (ibid: 11).[16] Of those respondents who had been subject to four or more incidents of domestic violence, 89% were women (ibid: vii).[17] Women also outnumbered men when it came to

---

[12] See p 402 above.

[13] Helplines have been set up for men. See, eg, Men's Advice Line—Respect (www.mensadviceline.org.uk/mens_advice.php, accessed 17 January 2011). A report published in 2004 revealed that only 1.5% of cases of partner abuse on the CPS files involved assaults on men by women. However, there were numerous counter-allegations by male defendants against women at the time of reporting an incident or at a later interview (HMcpsi and HMIC 2004: para 7.9).

[14] See, eg, Eaton (1994: 195), Donovan et al (2006), Donovan and Hester (2011).

[15] See Mirrlees-Black et al (1996), Law Commission (1992a: para 2.1(a)), Home Office (2000a: para 1.17), Walby and Allen (2004), Barnish (2004: paras 2.1–2.3).

[16] See further pp 18, 29–31.

[17] See further Walby and Allen (2004: 23, 25). Domestic violence also appears to affect women's health but not men's (ibid: 87).

severe injury and mental or emotional harm.[18] Ten times more women than men reported potentially life-threatening violence (ibid: 19). The number of sexual assaults against women greatly exceeded those against men.[19] Women were more likely to be subjected to aggravated stalking,[20] by an 'intimate or former intimate'.[21] They were more likely to suffer post-separation violence. Also, far more women than men reported being frightened of threats (ibid: 19).

The findings from the 2005/06 British Crime Survey self-completion module on domestic violence, sexual assault and stalking are similar.[22] Women were more likely to have experienced all three forms of abuse than men. More women than men reported being abused by their partners and being subject to multiple forms of abuse. Fifty-four per cent of women who were subject to sexual violence reported that the perpetrator was a partner or former partner (Jansson 2007).[23]

A study carried out by Dobash and Dobash led them to conclude that it 'is impossible to construe the violence of men and women as either equivalent or reciprocal' (Dobash and Dobash 2004: 343). All the women in the study had been victims of repeated violence inflicted by their male partners, yet just under half had not used violence against the men concerned, none had used sexual violence and only a few had used serious violence. The women's violence was often in self-defence. The men usually reported that the women's violence was 'inconsequential', generally infrequent and they experienced few negative consequences (ibid: 343–44). [24]

Hester conducted a study of cases reported to the Northumbria police and tracked the couples in the sample from 2001 to 2007. The majority of sole perpetrators on the police files were men. Men were far more likely to be repeat perpetrators while most of the women who were recorded as sole perpetrators instigated only one recorded incident. She observes that 'the intensity and severity of violence and abusive behaviours from the men was much more extreme' (Hester 2009: 8). Men's violence, she says 'tended to create a context of fear and related to that, control'. This was not the case where women were perpetrators. Few women used threats or harassment. However, she notes, 'women were much more likely to use a weapon, although this was at times in order to stop further violence from their partners'. It appeared also that female perpetrators were more likely to have mental health or other health issues (ibid). Male victims were less likely to be afraid (ibid: 11). In cases where both parties were perpetrators, men were more likely to be repeat abusers and were more likely to engage in severe harassment and abuse post-separation (ibid: 13).

All these studies, then, reveal that violence between men and women is asymmetrical.[25] And the reason for gender differences, feminist writers argue, can be found in hierarchical notions about relationships between men and women, notions that have a long historical pedigree.

---

[18] Walby and Allen (2004: viii). See further, ibid: 33–37.

[19] See ibid: vii. Of the women who were raped, 45% were raped by a husband or partner and 9% by a former husband or partner (ibid:ix).

[20] Cases where there was violence in addition to stalking.

[21] Thirty seven per cent in the case of women compared with 8% in the case of men (Walby and Allen 2004: ix, 61).

[22] See also Simmons et al (2002: vii, 12), Walker et al (2009: para 3.4).

[23] Similar results are recorded by Hoare and Jansson (2008).

[24] See also Gadd et al (2002). Many of the men in this study described the abuse from their partners as 'rare and relatively inconsequential' and few perceived themselves as victims (ibid: 3).

[25] For judicial acknowledgement of this, see Wall (2005: 30).

III. HISTORICAL BACKGROUND

The Legal Position of Husbands and Wives

It appears that, until relatively recently, violence by men against their wives, provided it fell within permissible bounds, was considered socially acceptable and was condoned by the church and by the law:

> It is impossible to say who first declared that wives could and should be beaten by their husbands or when this practice began; it is equally difficult to find any historical period in which there were no formulas stating the form such beatings should take and specifying the conditions under which a wife was deserving of a good clout. (Dobash and Dobash 1979: 31)

The most frequently cited formula is the 'rule of thumb', according to which, it is said, it was lawful for a man to beat his wife provided the 'stick were no thicker than his thumb' (Stone 1977: 326). While it is doubted that this rule ever actually existed (Doggett 1992: 8), there is evidence that a certain amount of violence against wives was tolerated.[26] Doggett (1992: 5), for example, quotes from a manual of procedure published by Sir Anthony Fitzherbert in 1516 which indicates that husbands were entitled to subject their wives to reasonable chastisement. What was considered reasonable, according to Doggett's review of seventeenth-century authority, appears to have included 'a high degree of violence' (ibid: 6). With the rise of Protestantism, however, wife-beating came to be frowned on by theologians and authors of marriage manuals alike:

> It was ... the 'Homily on Marriage' that was probably the most influential manual, reaching the largest audience for the longest period of time. The inferior character, rights, and status of wives were clearly stated in this document, which was ordered by the crown to be read in church every Sunday from 1562 onward. In it, the wife's subjection and obedience were made a primary necessity for a happy Christian marriage, but husbands were advised, for the sake of domestic peace, not to exercise the right to beat their wives but rather to remember women's weak and inconstant character when dealing with them. (Dobash and Dobash 1979: 55, footnotes omitted)

Despite moral injunctions to abjure violence, according to Dobash and Dobash (1979: 56) wife-beating remained widespread. Yet there does appear to have been a move to deny it legitimacy. This normative shift was manifested both in the law and in the attitudes of the community. Violence that went beyond generally accepted limits sometimes provoked a community response and, by the nineteenth century, rituals[27] of public shaming or ridicule in the form of the *chiavari*[28] or 'rough music'[29] were being directed at abusive husbands (Thompson 1972: 290). Legal measures to combat violence were also deployed. Doggett (1992: 11) reports that it had become common for women in the eighteenth century to swear the peace against their husbands; the aggressor was required to enter into

---

[26] See, eg, Freeman (1979: 128).

[27] These rituals were also used to shame wives who were thought to be dominating their husbands.

[28] In which the offender might be paraded through the town astride a pole or seated backwards on a donkey, pelted with mud, thrown into a pond or beaten (Doggett 1992: 112).

[29] The offender's home would be surrounded by a crowd beating on pots and chanting verses (Dobash and Dobash 1979: 58; Doggett 1992: 112).

a recognisance, promising to pay a sum of money if he failed to keep the peace.[30] And in the nineteenth century, legislation was introduced to punish wife-beating.

Nevertheless, whatever its limits, and these may never have been precisely defined, reasonable chastisement remained legal and its demise only finally became evident by the 1880s, says Doggett (1992: 15). Even so, husbands remained immune from prosecution if they raped their wives[31] and were still legally entitled to exercise a right of reasonable confinement. Blackstone (1778: 445) suggested that the power of correction had come to be doubted in the 'politer reign' of Charles II but that the right to restrain for 'gross misbehaviour' remained. In *Re Cochrane*[32] the court appeared to go even further, upholding 'the *general* right of the husband to the control and custody of his wife'.[33] Doggett (1992: 22–24) suggests that this right was abridged only if the parties entered into a separation agreement (except if the wife was guilty of certain types of misbehaviour) or if the husband behaved unreasonably by, for instance, confining his wife in a madhouse. A wife imprisoned by her husband and who felt herself to be unreasonably confined could be brought before the court pursuant to a writ of habeas corpus. Criminal prosecution was also possible. For wives seeking a more permanent escape, a separation agreement might provide an appropriate remedy. However, for wives whose husbands would not enter into such an agreement, it was necessary to petition the ecclesiastical courts for a separation *a mensa et thoro* on the grounds of cruelty.[34] In 1857 judicial divorce was introduced but for a wife to divorce her husband, she had to show he had committed aggravated adultery.[35]

IV. EXPLANATIONS FOR THE HUSBAND'S RIGHTS

Doggett (1992: 74) points out that in the Middle Ages, common lawyers unabashedly wrote of the husband's power over his wife. For example, one writer observed that the position of a wife 'whilst in the power of her Husband' was such that she could 'in no measure oppose or controvert his will' (de Glanville 1812: 281).

However, Blackstone, in the eighteenth century, explained the husband's powers in less forthright terms. He said that the husband's rights of chastisement and confinement arose out of the doctrine of coverture:

> The husband, also, (by the old law) might give his wife moderate correction. For, as he is to answer for her misbehaviour, the law thought it reasonable to intrust him with this power of restraining her, by domestic chastisement, in the same moderation that a man is allowed to correct his apprentices or children; for whom the master or parent is also liable in some cases to answer. But this power of correction was confined within reasonable bounds, and the husband

---

[30] This did not mean that wife-beating was a criminal offence, but it did mean that a remedy was provided for abused wives—see Clark (1992: 192); Doggett (1992: 12).

[31] *R v Clarence* (1889) 22 QBD 23, 51.

[32] (1840) 8 Dowl 630, cited by Doggett (1992: 15–16).

[33] Quoted by Doggett (1992: 15–16).

[34] Cruelty, says Doggett (1992: 31), was strictly interpreted until the late eighteenth century. The definition was gradually relaxed and in the mid-nineteenth century the idea of mental cruelty began to develop (Doggett 1992: 32).

[35] Adultery coupled with, eg, cruelty, incest, bigamy or rape (s 27 of the Divorce and Matrimonial Causes Act 1857).

was prohibited from using any violence to his wife [except in so far as he may lawfully and reasonably do so in order to correct and chastise his wife]. (Blackstone 1778: 445)

This power stemmed from the doctrine of the unity of the spouses:

> By marriage, the husband and wife are one person in law: that is, the very being or legal exist-ence of the woman is suspended during the marriage, or at least is incorporated and consolidated into that of her husband: under whose wing, protection, and cover, she performs every thing.
> (ibid: 442).

Thus, a 'husband was not simply *permitted* to control his wife's behaviour—he was *expected* to control it. In return for the power over her which the state allowed him, he was required to answer for her conduct' (Doggett 1992: 57–58).[36] 'In the eyes of the law, a husband and wife constituted *not two individuals, but one*' (ibid: 83) and this doctrine, argues Doggett, served, in the seventeenth century, to mask the contradiction between the emerging principle of individualism and the subordination of wives (ibid: 77 and 83).

The right of the husband sexually to coerce his wife, while also rooted in women's subordination, was explained differently. In 1736 Sir Matthew Hale found its origin in a fiction of consent: '[b]ut the husband cannot be guilty of rape committed by himself upon his lawful wife, for by their mutual matrimonial consent and contract the wife hath given up herself in this kind unto her husband, which she cannot retract' (Hale 1971: 629).

This fiction survived as part of the law, albeit in modified form, until 1991.[37] Law reform to prohibit wife-beating came far earlier, and we now turn to examine the way violence perpetrated by husbands on their wives came to be constructed as a social problem demanding action by the state and its agents.

V. THE EMERGENCE OF WIFE-BEATING AS A SOCIAL PROBLEM

According to Doggett (1992: 111), wife-beating became a matter of public concern from about the mid-nineteenth century. Extensive coverage in legal and popular journals of cases of assaults appeared and legislation was enacted to afford some protection to vic-tims. In 1853, the Act for Better Prevention and Punishment of Aggravated Assaults upon Women and Children introduced new penalties for wife-beating.[38]

Clark (1992: 196) explains the readiness of the state to engage in more extensive regu-

---

[36] The subordinate status of wives was reflected in a number of legal rules. One of these was that, until 1828, a wife who killed her husband was guilty of petit treason but a husband who killed his wife was guilty only of murder 'because of the obedience which in relation of law is due from the wife to the husband' (East 1972: 336). See also Stephen (1883: 34–35).

[37] See pp 563–64.

[38] This gave, one commentator observed, women the same protection that had already been accorded to animals (see Freeman 1979: 129). It seems that, rather than use their powers of imprisonment, courts continued to prefer the peace bond and deferred sentencing as sanctions. Edward Cox, a London magistrate, in his 1877 work *The Principles of Punishment* (Cox 1984), felt that a criminal justice response would exacerbate the tensions between the spouses and make future cohabitation even more difficult (ibid 103–04). In any event, most of the men who came before him for beating their wives had been grievously provoked, he thought (ibid: 101). Similar concern with family unity and assertions of provocation have echoed down the years. See pp 558, 562–63 and 565 below.

lation of violence in the family in terms of pressure coming from a middle class motivated by evangelicalism and humanitarianism. However, they were also, according other commentators, motivated by anxieties evoked by the urban poor. Doggett (1992: 20) emphasises the preoccupation of reformers with the idea that the working class was degenerate and posed a threat to public order.[39] Whereas previously wife-beating had been seen and tolerated as part of working-class family life, now it came to be deplored. In the context of concerns about an increase in public violence generally, wife-beating was, she says, regarded by the upper and middle classes as threatening; it was seen as but one facet of generalised savagery among the working classes. Moreover, it was feared that this savagery might spill over into the streets and that children exposed to it would become delinquent. Doggett's explanation echoes those discussed in Chapter 13 below relating to concerns about child abuse. Like concern about child abuse, concern about abuse of women is, therefore, largely attributed to social anxiety and the perception that intervention in the family would be a lesser evil than the threat to social order that some families would present unless they were regulated.

Nevertheless, it appears that the movement for women's rights also contributed to change and that the work of liberal reformers such as John Stuart Mill, Harriet Taylor Mill and Frances Power Cobbe had an impact.[40] Cobbe, certainly, is credited with influencing the content of the Matrimonial Causes Act 1878.[41] These reformers shared many of the assumptions held by other commentators, believing, for example, that violent abuse was mainly confined to the working class.[42] But, unlike the parliamentarians seeking reform, these 'moral entrepreneurs'[43] were not simply arguing for the cessation of violence against women. They were challenging what they saw as the causes of violence: patriarchy and women's inferior legal, social and economic status. Mill and Taylor argued that women lacked adequate legal protection because they were deprived of their rights under the social contract.[44] Marriage was seen as curtailing those rights further. For example, in *The Subjection of Women*, published in 1869, John Stuart Mill wrote:

[A] female slave has (in Christian countries) an admitted right, and is considered under a moral obligation, to refuse to her master the last familiarity. Not so the wife: however brutal a tyrant she may unfortunately be chained to ... he can claim from her and enforce the lowest degradation of a human being, that of being made the instrument of an animal function contrary to her inclinations. (Mill 1975: 463)

Marriage is not an institution designed for a select few. ... The vilest malefactor has some wretched woman tied to him, against whom he can commit any atrocity except killing her, and, if tolerably cautious, can do that without much danger of the legal penalty. (ibid: 467)

The law of servitude in marriage is a monstrous contradiction to all the principles of the modern world. (ibid: 521)

Cobbe, in 1878, published 'Wife Torture in England' in which she presented a horrifying

---

[39] See also Pahl (1985b: 42).
[40] See, for a more detailed account, Dobash and Dobash (1979: 64ff). See also Stark and Flitcraft (1996: 43ff).
[41] See Doggett (1992: 130–31).
[42] See ibid: 126.
[43] See pp 616–17 below.
[44] See Clark (1992: 202).

catalogue of cases of abuse. Her discussion of the causes of wife-beating reverberates in the writings of modern feminists, highlighting as it does the proprietary attitudes of husbands to wives and prevailing beliefs in the privacy of the family:

> The general depreciation of women as a sex is bad enough, but in the matter we are considering, the special depreciation of wives is more directly responsible for the outrages they endure. The notion that a man's wife is his PROPERTY, in the sense in which a horse is his property ... is the fatal root of incalculable evil and misery. Every brutal-minded man, and many a man who in other relations of life is not brutal, entertains more or less vaguely the notion that this wife is his thing. ... It is even sometimes pleaded on behalf of poor men, that they possess nothing else but their wives, and that, consequently, it seems doubly hard to meddle with the exercise of their power in this narrow sphere! (Cobbe 1878: 62–63, emphasis in original)

The inadequacy of the law and the leniency shown to abusers by magistrates came in for criticism and Cobbe set out to draft a Bill designed to give women an escape route from abuse.[45] The Matrimonial Causes Act of 1878, based on that Bill, empowered magistrates to grant judicial separation with maintenance[46] to a wife whose husband had been convicted of an aggravated assault on her, if satisfied that the future safety of the wife was imperilled.[47]

In addition, the 1884 Matrimonial Causes Act removed the power of the court to imprison a spouse for a refusal to obey an order for restitution of conjugal rights.[48] Relying on this new legislation, the Court of Appeal held, in *R v Jackson*,[49] that a husband now had no right, if indeed he ever had, to seize and detain his wife until she agreed to restore to him his conjugal rights. While a husband might be entitled to 'restrain' his wife from dishonouring him by, for example, going with another man, he had no right to imprison her.[50] Moreover, said Lord Esher, he did not believe it had ever been the law that a husband had a right to beat his wife (682).

VI. THE MODERN EMERGENCE OF DOMESTIC VIOLENCE AS A SOCIAL PROBLEM

Although in the early years of the twentieth century violence against women was taken up as an issue by both British and American suffragists,[51] 'it virtually disappeared from the agenda of "social" problems between 1920 and 1970' (Smith 1989: 5).[52] One of the principal reasons for its reappearance on the agenda was the growth of the women's movement in the late 1960s and 1970s. The modern version of the nineteenth-century

---

[45] See Doggett (1992: 130–31).

[46] The wife could also be awarded custody of children under the age of 10 (s 4).

[47] In 1895, this proviso was removed by the Summary Jurisdiction (Married Women) Act 1895.

[48] Previously, wives seeking to escape abusive husbands could be imprisoned for failing to return to them. After the 1884 Act was passed, the refusal to comply simply rendered that spouse guilty of desertion.

[49] [1891] 1 QB 671.

[50] *R v Reid* (1972) 56 Cr App R 703 finally established that, on the basis of Jackson, a husband could be convicted of kidnapping his wife, whether or not the spouses were living apart: 'The notion that a husband can, without incurring punishment, treat his wife ... with any kind of hostile force is obsolete' (707).

[51] See Dobash and Dobash (1979: 74).

[52] Pahl (1985c: 42–43) suggests that this may be attributable to the low status of women during the period concerned and the 'high degree of regard for the privacy of the home and the sanctity of marriage'.

'moral entrepreneurs', acting to bring domestic violence to public attention and to present it as a problem requiring amelioration by the state and its agents, were primarily feminists.

In 1971, Chiswick Women's Aid was established in a house made available by the local council (Dobash and Dobash 1979: 1). It was in the course of conversations there that some women began to reveal that they had been subjected to serious violence at the hands of their male partners.[53] In response to their stories, Chiswick Women's Aid, headed by Erin Pizzey, opened the Chiswick refuge. Feminist activists set out to establish further refuges and to raise public awareness about domestic violence.[54] Pizzey's book, *Scream Quietly or the Neighbours Will Hear* (1974), contributed to this awareness and, by 1974, public pressure demanded that the government respond to the problem. A Parliamentary Select Committee was accordingly set up in 1975 to hear evidence and to make recommendations.[55]

Since the 1970s, the efforts of feminist campaigners and researchers working in the field of domestic violence have been directed at moving it up the political and legal agenda.[56] They have advocated law reform. They have also sought to change the practices and attitudes of those involved in implementing the law as well as the responses of other professionals.[57]

In order to redefine domestic violence as a serious social problem requiring action by public agencies, it has been necessary to transform prevailing perceptions of domestic violence as a relatively uncommon phenomenon and as a private family matter, often trivial in nature. Feminist writers have therefore consistently stressed that, although it has been a largely hidden problem,[58] domestic violence affects significant numbers of women[59]

---

[53] For a detailed account, see Dobash and Dobash (1992: 25ff).

[54] See ibid: 27.

[55] Ibid: 112–13.

[56] See Itzin (2000); Kaganas (2006). For an account of the efforts of Women's Aid, see Harwin and Barron (2000). For an account of the efforts of Southall Black Sisters, see Patel (2000). Women's Aid, for example, has responded to numerous government documents and consultation papers and has published widely in the field of domestic violence.

[57] See generally on the impact of feminist perspectives, Hanmer and Itzin (2000). Researchers have highlighted the links between woman abuse and child abuse as well as the violence that occurs in the context of contact with children. They have also argued for change to the defences for murder in the context of domestic homicide committed by abused women. See McColgan (1993); O'Donovan (1993); Kaganas (2002); Law Commission (2003). See Hester et al (1994) and Harne and Radford (1994) on contact. See further Chapter 10 above.

[58] See Stanko (1988); Mooney (2000: 24–25). Over half the victims in the British Crime Survey had told no one of the most recent attack (Mirrlees-Black 1999: 51). Most who did tell anyone told friends or relatives. Many did not seek help from a professional agency (ibid: 63). The police are told of only 1 in 8 incidents (ibid). In the 2008/09 British Crime Survey, 42% of victims of all violent offences reported the incident to police, compared with 16% of domestic violence victims (Thompson 2010: fn 3). Underreporting may be explained by a number of factors. Those suggested include a desire to preserve the relationship, a wish to protect privacy, financial dependence on the perpetrator and fear that contact with officialdom could lead to the removal of the victim's children by social services. It is also likely that many victims are physically prevented from reporting and that the fear of reprisals is a strong deterrent. Some may feel that the end result of the process does not justify the ordeal of going through the criminal justice system. There are also suggestions that victims from some ethnic groups as well as lesbian, gay, transgender and bisexual victims may fear a hostile response from the authorities. See, on barriers to seeking help, Paradine and Wilkinson (2004: paras 1.2.4, para 5.1). A significant proportion of victims of sexual assault tell no one and are unlikely to report to the police (Povey et al 2009: 62)

[59] For example, the government, relying on the figures revealed by British Crime Surveys, has accepted that 1 in 4 women experiences domestic violence during her lifetime (Home Office 2003: 8; Home Office, *Violence against Women and Girls*, undated). Relying on the 2008–09 British Crime Survey (Walker et al 2009), the government noted that domestic violence accounts for 14% of all violent incidents and that repeat victimisation is common (Home Office 2009: 4). See also on prevalence Mooney (1994). Reviewing the literature, Stanko et

(and their children)[60] in profound ways. The effects of domestic violence have been found to range from social isolation, fear and depression to permanent disability[61] or death,[62] and, it is argued, domestic violence should therefore be taken seriously. Feminist campaigners and scholars have sought to displace the image of the idealised family as a haven from the outside world and to present it as a potentially dangerous arena. And the danger, they contend, is primarily to women. They argue that the roots of domestic violence can be traced to women's inferior status and to dominant constructions of masculinity. For this argument to gain ground, it has been necessary to challenge the view that domestic violence is usually attributable to dysfunctional families or to the individual pathology of the parties.[63]

VII. THE 'CAUSES' OF DOMESTIC VIOLENCE[64]

Some proponents of theories locating the 'causes' of domestic violence in the individual explain it in terms of an inter-generational cycle of violence.[65] Others have sought explanations in biology, citing chromosomal structure or testosterone levels.[66] Yet others look to the character of the abuser. Perpetrators are said to suffer from mental illness;[67] to abuse drugs or alcohol;[68] or to act as a result of frustration or stress brought about by factors such as unemployment or poverty.[69] Alternative explanations have been sought in the character of the victim, who might be described as masochistic or addicted to violence.[70] Further, women who are bad housekeepers or who 'nag' might be seen to provoke violence.[71] Indeed, family systems theorists, who adopt what has been termed a 'family violence' approach (Dobash and Dobash 1992: 258), locate the genesis of violence in the

---

al concluded that '[i]n general, the research suggests that many women may experience threats or assaults from partners during their relationships, while a small number (two to five percent) report serious, frequent attacks' (Stanko et al 1998: 14). They estimated in their study of Hackney that in 1996 1 in 9 women there suffered domestic violence of some kind (ibid: 22).

[60] Hester (2009: 16) reports that in 55% of the cases recorded in her sample, children were present when violence or abuse took place. In cases of post-separation violence, issues relating to child contact arose in 30%. See also Humphreys (2000); McGee (2000); Mullender (2000); Mullender et al (2002); Paradine and Wilkinson (2004: para 1.4.2).

[61] See Paradine and Wilkinson (2004: para 1.4.1); Hester et al (2000: para 1.8). Humphreys and Thiara's research (2003: 200) shows that women may fear for their emotional well-being or mental health. Many fear for their lives or for the lives of their children. Some fear they might kill the abuser.

[62] According to Thompson (2010: para 2.3), relying on homicide figures, '47 per cent of the 3,249 women murdered since 1995, and 12 per cent of the 6,806 men, were killed by a partner or ex-partner'. The Home Office (2003: 9) states that on average, two women per week are killed by a male partner or former partner and that almost half of all female murder victims are killed by a partner or former partner. Of all murders of men, about 8% occur in a domestic context but some women who kill may have done so in self-defence or after a history of abuse. See also Home Office (2000a: para 1.18); Home Office (2002: paras 8.4–8.5); Flood-Page and Taylor (2003: 3); Paradine and Wilkinson (2004: para 1.2.2); Walby (2004: pp 27ff).

[63] For a fuller discussion of dominant stereotypes, see Edwards (1996: ch 5, esp 178–79). For discussion of the various explanations that have been put forward, see Hearn (1998: 17–33).

[64] See also Barnish (2004: paras 3.1–3.2).

[65] For a discussion of this theory, see Morley and Mullender (1994: 37–38).

[66] Neither explanation is convincing. See Hearn (1998: 18–19).

[67] See, eg, *Lomas v Parle* [2003] EWCA Civ 1804; [2004] 1 FLR 812, para 51: 'Those who molest others are usually trapped in an obsessional emotional state'.

[68] Alcohol featured strongly in the cases analysed by Hester (2009).

[69] See, eg, Borkowski et al (1983: ch 5).

[70] See Pizzey and Shapiro (1982). Compare Pahl (1985a: 5).

[71] See Borkowski et al (1983: ch 5).

interaction between family members.[72] According to this view, it is the family that is violent and women are as likely as men to be the aggressors.[73] These claims lead to an understanding of domestic violence in terms of mutual combat, an understanding that underlies the greater use of arrest of both parties in the USA under mandatory arrest statutes and the use, in the British civil courts, of cross-undertakings[74] in cases where the woman uses violence to protect herself.[75] It also leaves room for the view that mediation between parties to resolve their disputes is appropriate.[76]

Dobash and Dobash (1992: ch 8; 2004),[77] amongst others, attempt to counter such claims and argue that research focusing on the parity of men's and women's violence, which tends to rely on what is called the 'Conflict Tactics Scale' (CTS), is deficient. In studies which use an 'act-based approach' such as the CTS, respondents are required to indicate whether they had done any of the things referred to in a list of items intended to measure conflict, violence and abuse. The items listed might range from calm discussion, through acts such as throwing things, to the use of a knife or gun. The results of the studies have been interpreted as suggesting that there is little difference in the extent to which men and women engage in these acts (Straus and Gelles 1990).[78]

However, Browne (1987: 6–9) indicates that these studies are misleading. Women, she says, underestimate the extent of the violence they have suffered. Moreover, men under-report the extent of the violence they have committed and overestimate their partners' violence in order to justify their own.[79] Dobash and Dobash (1992: 275–81; 2004: 330–31) in turn say the act-based research is not geared to establishing the context in which acts of violence take place and fails to distinguish between acts of aggression and self-defence.[80] Nor does it discriminate adequately between different types of violence; Dobash and Dobash (1992: 280) note that two slaps are treated as equivalent to two knife attacks. In addition, they say, it ignores the motives behind actions and therefore does not take account of the possibility that an act, such as throwing something, may not be intended to harm or intimidate. Allied to this is the problem that no attention is paid to determining whether the act causes injury and, if so, whether the injury is serious. Acts of sexual violence, which are almost invariably perpetrated against women, are excluded from some assessments.[81] Finally, act-based research fails to reveal the 'constellation of abuse' that characterises men's violence against women and that includes 'a variety of additional intimidating, aggressive and controlling' behaviour (Dobash and Dobash 2004: 328).

Stark and Flitcraft (1996: 64–65) are also critical of family violence research and point out that there is no evidence of a hidden population of battered men in police reports, medical records or clinical samples. They argue that there is a difference between domestic violence against women and other forms of violence:

[72] See, for an account of this approach, Dobash and Dobash (1992: 238–39).
[73] See, eg, Straus (1993). For a discussion of relevant research, see Dobash and Dobash (1992: ch 8).
[74] Undertakings by both parties that they will not molest or interfere with each other.
[75] See, on the use of cross-undertakings, Barron (1990: 57).
[76] Compare Kaganas and Piper (1994).
[77] See also Kurz (1993).
[78] See generally, on this research, Dobash and Dobash (1992: 258–61), Dobash and Dobash (2004), Kurz (1993), Hester *et al* (2000: para 1.3), Brush (1993).
[79] See also Dobash and Dobash (2004: 344).
[80] See also Kurz (1993: 258).
[81] Mirrlees-Black (1999) reports that it is overwhelmingly women who suffer serious abuse, injury and sexual abuse.

Only women attacked by their partners exhibit the syndrome of multiple injuries, medical problems, isolation, psychosocial problems, and almost paralyzing terror we identify with battering ... . Battering is not about fighting ... . Fighting occurs in many ... families and relationships without jeopardizing the liberty of those involved ... . In contrast, battering occurs when persons have been forcibly isolated from potentially supportive kin and peer relations and become locked, like hostages, into situations in which objectification, subordination and continued punishment are inevitable. Physical fighting presents a moral concern; battering presents a political reality. Unlike the battered husband, the abused woman cannot escape because her situation is mediated by reproduction and enforcement of her dependent status through all society. (Stark and Flitcraft 1996: 27–28)

Johnson (2008: 2) too suggests that the kind of violence perpetrated primarily against women is different. He also suggests that differences between the findings of feminist researchers and family violence researchers can be attributed to their choice of different research populations. He maintains that there are four different types of intimate violence. In what he terms 'intimate terrorism' the perpetrator uses violence as part of a strategy to gain general control over his partner while the partner does not. In 'violent resistance' the partner is violent and controlling (an intimate terrorist) and the other partner (usually the woman) uses violence to resist. In 'mutual violent control' each party uses violence in an attempt to gain control over the other. This is rare (ibid: 12). In situational couple violence, one or both parties may be violent but neither is trying to gain control over the other (ibid: 5).

Intimate terrorism is characterised by a pattern of control that can include isolating the victim, demeaning and humiliating her, depriving her of control over economic resources and intimidating her. The physical violence coupled with these other forms of abuse ensures that the victim feels trapped; she knows that her partner will go to any lengths to maintain control (ibid: 7–10).[82] In heterosexual relationships this is the kind of violence perpetrated 'almost entirely by men, not women' (ibid: 2).[83] It is intimate terrorism that characterises cases found in refuges, emergency rooms and legal settings. Feminist researchers draw their samples from such settings and it is intimate terrorism that they mean when they refer to domestic violence (ibid: 3, 6).

Situational couple violence is not a manifestation of control but of the escalation of specific conflicts; a disagreement may give rise to frustration leading to violence, for example, or violence may simply be used to win the argument (ibid: 11). This is the kind of violence that is more likely to emerge from general social surveys and this is the kind of evidence on which family violence theorists rely (ibid: 3). So, says Johnson, family violence theorists and feminist researchers have been studying two different phenomena and this explains the difference in their findings (ibid: 3). Those involved in intimate terrorism are unlikely to participate in social surveys. Situationally provoked violence does not generally call for police intervention, visits to emergency rooms, court orders or escape to a refuge (ibid: 19). However, there are cases where men's situational violence is sufficiently severe that it leads to injury and results in the victim resorting to protective measures (ibid: 21).

Researchers adopting a feminist perspective see domestic violence (usually in the form of what Johnson would call intimate terrorism) as an extension of male power and control,

---

[82] See further 26–30.
[83] In those cases where the woman also used violence this was less frequent and less severe (30).

control that is 'historically and socially constructed' (Dobash and Dobash 1979: 15).[84] According to Hearn, male violence is intimately bound up with notions of masculinity: 'Men's doing of violence to women simultaneously involves "being a man" and symbolically showing "being a man"' (Hearn 1998: 37). It is a manifestation of dominance and also perpetuates dominance. And according to Johnson (2008: 32), intimate terrorists are impulsive, accepting of violence, hostile to women and 'traditional in their sex role attitudes'. They may also be possessive or simply determined to get their own way.

Hearn argues that men's use of violence reflects the power relations that exist in 'normal' family life (Hearn 1998: 36). As Dobash and Dobash point out, although the status of women has changed, there are still widely held beliefs about the hierarchical nature of family relationships (Dobash and Dobash 1979: 76). Men who use violence, the Dobashes argue, are simply living up to cultural norms that endorse dominance and the enforcement of that dominance (ibid: 22–24).

That these norms exist is borne out by a research study conducted by Burton et al (1998).[85] They found that almost one in four young men[86] thought it would be acceptable to hit a woman if she had 'slept with' someone else. A substantial proportion thought it would be acceptable to hit a woman or force her to have sex if she was his wife or girlfriend. Women who nagged or were 'disrespectful' were also seen as deserving of abuse.

Dobash and Dobash contend (1979: 96) that their research findings[87] demonstrate that abusive husbands exhibit a sense of 'possessiveness, domination and "rightful" control' over their wives.[88] They report that the men they interviewed tended to minimise the seriousness of their violence and to justify it in as being necessary to achieve the purpose of '"shutting her up", getting a meal or having sex' (Dobash and Dobash 1998: 167). The women they interviewed reported that the arguments that preceded the first violent incident (Dobash and Dobash, 1979: 95) and those that followed (ibid: 98) were primarily associated with husbands' possessiveness, their sexual jealousy, their ideas about wives' domestic duties or their ideas about how money should be allocated.[89] In particular, women's resistance to men's demands or failure to fulfil those demands might lead to violence (Hearn 1998: 36, 127–28).[90] For example:

> It would start off with him being angry over trivial little things, a trivial thing like cheese instead of meat on a sandwich, or it might be the way your face just looked for a second at him, or something, and then he'd just give you one across the face, always across the face.
>
> (Dobash and Dobash 1979: 100)

Women were not expected to challenge their husbands and, if they did, they might be silenced by force:

---

[84] Marital rape too is perceived as an abuse of power. See Russell (1990, originally 1982: 4 and 123ff).

[85] See also Mullender et al (2002: 70–74); Barter et al (2009); McCarry (2009).

[86] Twelve per cent of young women concurred.

[87] Arising out of a study conducted in Scotland.

[88] See also Ptacek (1988).

[89] See further, Dobash and Dobash (1998: 144ff). See also Pahl (1985b: 36–39), who found links between control of money by husbands and more general attempts at control and subordination.

[90] However, Hearn also found evidence of simple misogyny (Hearn 1998: 135).

Q: What made you violent towards her?
A: ... her being clever and cocky with me.   (Hearn 1998: 129)[91]

Campbell's (1992) study of woman killing also focuses on men's proprietariness and dominance[92] and, according to Wilson and Daly (1992), separation increases the risk of woman killing because it challenges male sexual proprietariness; it entails the woman moving out of the man's control. Polk, in a study of violence conducted in Australia, found two 'dominant forms of sexual ownership' (Polk 1994: 56). One category of cases involved violence, fuelled by rage, and aimed at controlling women. The cases he put into this group included cases where women were killed after they ended the relationship and cases where women were killed because they were suspected of infidelity. The other category involved severely depressed men who, before committing suicide, killed their female partners (ibid: 57). In both categories, he notes, the woman is seen as a possession (ibid: 189). In contrast, the few women who killed their sexual partners tended to be reacting to abuse by that partner.[93]

> **Q** Why do feminist researchers emphasise issues of power and control as well as the predominance of men amongst assailants and women amongst victims?

An important element in the construction of social problems is the designation of their 'causes'.[94] Whether violence is seen as pathological or an expression of uncontrollable rage or sexual jealousy brought on by the conduct of the victim, or whether it is seen as a manifestation of proprietary control, has significant implications for the way it is dealt with by agencies such as the police and the legal system.

Radford's account of a case that went to trial in England in 1982 can be used to illustrate the point. The victim, Mary Bristow, was clubbed with a meat tenderiser, smothered with a pillow and strangled. Peter Wood, a former lover, was charged with her murder. On the night of the murder, Peter had gone into the house when she was out and had awaited her homecoming. He told the court that they had made love but that when she rejected his suggestion that they should have a monogamous relationship, he had decided to kill her. In his summing up, the judge endorsed the view that Mary brought her death upon herself.

'Mary Bristow,' he said,

> with an IQ of 182, was a rebel from her middle-class background. She was unorthodox in her relationships, so proving that the cleverest people aren't always very wise. Those who engage in sexual relationships should realise that sex is one of the deepest and most powerful human emotions, and if you're playing with sex you're playing with fire ...

In drawing a distinction for the jury between murder and manslaughter, he explained, '... There is a difference between a villain shooting a policeman, and a husband killing his wife or lover at a stage when they can no longer cope.' (Radford 1992: 231–32)

---

[91] See also Dobash and Dobash (1979: 103).
[92] In her Ohio sample, 64% of cases involved male jealousy, which, she suggests, is related to a wish to control and possess the woman concerned. Male dominance was a factor in 18% of cases. Included in this category were a case where the woman refused to fetch the perpetrator more wine and one where the woman rejected her assailant's sexual advances. In only 7% of cases did the victim precipitate the violence by producing a weapon.
[93] See also Browne (1987: 9–11, 35, 180–83).
[94] See further, Chapter 13 below.

Q Wood was convicted of manslaughter. Might a judge adopting a feminist analysis have instructed the jury differently?

What this account illustrates is that the construction of male aggression or male sexuality as uncontrollable and linked to biological make-up serves to normalise violence and to diminish male culpability.[95] It also leads to victim-blaming. Women who 'inflame' male passions are seen to be courting danger. Similarly women who 'provoke' men through their 'nagging' or infidelity are regarded as contributing to their fate.

Feminist commentators reject explanations relying on pathology or on victim-blaming. Instead, by explaining violence in terms of male dominance and proprietariness, they seek to locate the blame firmly in the perpetrator and in dominant constructions of masculinity which inform the way in which men are socialised. More fundamentally, by linking violence to women's subordinate status in the family and in society generally, they aim to effect a social transformation.

VIII. EQUALITY WITHIN MARRIAGE—THE ABOLITION OF THE MARITAL RAPE EXEMPTION

Feminist reformers have met with notable success in campaigning for formal, if not substantive, equality within marriage. However, the last bastion of husbands' legal sovereignty over their wives fell only relatively recently. It was only in 1991, in the case of *R v R (Rape: Marital Exemption)*[96] that it was finally held without qualification[97] that a husband could be convicted of raping his wife.

Apart from Hale's statement (p 554 above), a number of modern justifications for retaining the marital rape exemption were advanced in the literature prior to its abolition. These have been extensively canvassed by other writers[98] and only a brief outline of the debate will be offered here. First, fears existed that, without this protection, husbands would be vulnerable to charges fabricated by malicious wives. Secondly, it was argued that evidentiary problems would arise if rape in marriage were a crime. Thirdly, it was contended that prosecution for rape would jeopardise the possibility of reconciliation between the spouses. Fourthly, it was said that adequate remedies already existed in the law and, finally, some commentators took the view that all violence between husband and wife should be dealt with by family law.

The House of Lords in *R v R* took the view quite simply that the exemption was anachronistic, pointing out that women's status had changed since Hale's time and that to say that a woman consented irrevocably to sexual intercourse with her husband was 'unacceptable' in modern times; marriage had come to be regarded as 'a partnership of equals' (484). The court finally brought down the last legal rule upholding husbands' dominion over the private family.

---

[95] See Stanko (1985: 9).

[96] [1991] 4 All ER 481. See, now, Sexual Offences Act 2003 ss 1–4. See also Law Commission (1992b).

[97] The exemption was modified in a number of decisions. See, eg, *R v Clarke* [1949] 2 All ER 448; *R v Miller* [1954] 2 QB 282; *R v O'Brien* [1974] 3 All ER 663; *R v Steele* (1976) 65 Crim App R 22; *R v Roberts* [1986] Crim L Rev 188; *R v Sharples* [1990] Crim L Rev 198. See, on sexual acts other than rape, Edwards (1996: 187–89).

[98] See, eg, Scutt (1976); Glasgow (1979–80); Geis (1978); Freeman (1981).

IX. THE CRIMINAL JUSTICE SYSTEM

Wife-rape has been declared illegal. The view that domestic violence is an understandable response to 'provocation' or a lapse in self-control has become less prevalent. Domestic violence has been firmly established as a serious social problem and the state must therefore be seen to be dealing with it. The involvement of the criminal justice system has increasingly come to be seen as an appropriate response to the problem.

Yet, as we shall see, the notion of family privacy persists to some extent and this, as well as prevailing understandings of violence between intimates, has significantly affected the way in which both civil and criminal law operate in practice.

Some of the acts designated as domestic violence by feminist commentators, such as constant and severe criticism, belittling and withholding money for essentials, do not fall within the criminal law.[99] Nevertheless, abuse can constitute a criminal offence ranging from harassment,[100] common assault, through aggravated assault, assault occasioning actual bodily harm, grievous bodily harm and unlawful wounding to manslaughter or murder.[101] However, those involved in implementing the criminal law have traditionally regarded the context of the private relationship within which domestic violence occurs as rendering it less serious or as not warranting a criminal justice response at all.

The Police

The police, in particular, have in the past been loath to respond to abuse of a woman as a crime. They tended to take the view that a criminal justice response was appropriate only in exceptional cases and that domestic violence should be dealt with by social services and family counselling agencies.[102] Police intervention in such cases was seen, first, as a waste of time because women often withdrew their complaints,[103] and, secondly, as an unwarranted and potentially damaging invasion into the private sphere of the family.[104] The typical response, then, was to refuse to arrest and to treat the assault as a private and/or civil matter (Dobash and Dobash 1979: 214).

The view held by many officers that domestic violence cases did not involve 'real crimes'[105] and that they were unlikely to proceed to prosecution gave rise to a reluctance on the part of the police to record them as crimes (Edwards 1996: 194).[106] Often, the police would see their role as a conciliatory one, calming the situation down.[107] If a woman indicated that she wanted more done, she might be pressed on whether she really wanted to take legal action and might be given time to 'think it over' (Faragher 1985: 117). These strategies had the effect of leaving the woman unprotected and in a state of

---

[99] See Stanko et al (1998: 12).

[100] See Protection from Harassment Act 1997.

[101] See Offences Against the Person Act 1861.

[102] See Dobash and Dobash (1992: 150).

[103] A joint inspection of police and the CPS revealed that in 44% of cases dealt with by the CPS, the victim made a withdrawal statement (HMcpsi and HMIC 2004: para 6.15). See also Cretney and Davis (1997a).

[104] See, eg, House of Commons, Select Committee on Violence in the Family (1975: 366, 369).

[105] See further, Bossy and Coleman (2000: 29–31).

[106] For a summary of research, see Edwards (1996: 195–96). See also Edwards (1989).

[107] See Borkowski et al (1983: 192); London Strategic Policy Unit, Police Monitoring and Research Group (1986: 3).

fear.[108] Racist attitudes on the part of the police exacerbated matters for ethnic minority women.[109]

Smith, reviewing the earlier research on police practice, commented:

> Reluctance [by the police] to intervene was, to a large part, shaped by notions and assumptions about the role of women in society and, in particular, within families as wives and mothers; the importance attached to 'family life' and the consequent perceived need for families to stay intact; and the privacy traditionally accorded families in which state intervention is seen as being mainly inappropriate unless it is designed to help families stay together. (Smith 1989: 85)

> [A]lthough domestic violence is not *simply* a crime problem, it nevertheless remains such a problem. If the criminal justice system does not treat it as seriously as other crime problems ... then the criminal justice system may signal to other agencies and to the wider public that domestic violence is a problem with which we should not be too concerned. ... Although it seems unlikely that the response of the criminal justice system *on its own*, will be sufficient to combat domestic violence or to deal with the diverse problems it brings in its wake, it is arguable that that response is nevertheless both necessary and potentially very important. The symbolic nature of law—its declaratory and denunciatory functions—is important in shaping climates of opinion. The criminal law is after all a normative statement. It sets the boundaries of acceptable behaviour. (ibid: 89, emphasis in original)

Police policy[110] has changed in response to criticism and, officially, domestic violence is no longer viewed as a private matter. For some years now, the police have been expected to be more interventionist[111] and pro-arrest policies were developed along the lines of those introduced in North America.[112] An inspection report published in 2004 focusing on the investigation and prosecution of domestic violence cases noted that considerable strides had been made in the development of policies designed to ensure that incidents are taken seriously (HMcpsi and HMIC 2004: 6).

At the time the report was published, over 90% of police forces had domestic violence officers/co-ordinators within established units, playing a mainly supportive role, acting as a point of contact with the police for the victim and liaising with other support services (ibid: para 3.1).[113] In addition, all police officers are obliged to adhere to the revised Home Office Circular on domestic violence (Home Office 2000b). This circular makes it clear

---

[108] See Borkowski et al (1983: 192).

[109] For a discussion of the particular problems created by racism, see Mama (1989: 304). See also Humphreys and Thiara (2002: 49).

[110] However, within the police service, domestic violence work has low status (HMcpsi and HMIC 2004: para 3.4).

[111] See Home Office (1990b); Edwards (1996; 192–93).

[112] In the USA, feminist campaigns centred around increased use of criminal sanctions and included the tactic of suing police departments for failing to implement assault laws. See further Walsh (1995). In response, some states expanded police powers of arrest while others made arrest mandatory. Pro-arrest polices were adopted by police forces, and in some areas 'no-drop' policies prevented the dropping of charges except in exceptional circumstances (see Morley and Mullender (1992: 266–68). These pro-arrest policies gained considerable support as a result of a well-publicised research project, the 'Minneapolis Experiment', carried out by Sherman and Berk (1984). On comparing three possible police responses to domestic violence—arrest, advice/mediation and separating the parties—the researchers found arrest to be most effective in reducing repeat offending. They therefore recommended that police should operate on the basis of a presumption in favour of arrest. In Canada, researchers reported favourably on the effects of a pro-charge policy adopted in London, Ontario (see further Morley and Mullender (1992: 267). However, Morley and Mullender point out that attempts to replicate the Sherman and Berk study have failed (ibid: 270).

[113] The police attending an incident generally provide information to victims or make referrals to helping organisations (HMcpsi and HMIC 2004: para 3.26).

that the police should not treat an incident less seriously because it has occurred in a domestic setting. It stipulates that an incident should only be 'no-crimed' if there is clear evidence that an offence did not take place. It instructs officers at the scene to speak to the parties separately and in a way that ensures that the victim will not be overheard. It stresses that the police should not act as conciliators. It requires the police to ask the victim if she wishes to take the matter to court. However, it also emphasises the importance of gathering photographic and other forensic evidence so as to reduce the need to rely on the victim's willingness and ability to testify. In addition, it creates a presumption in favour of arrest in all but exceptional cases. It states that where the authority to arrest exists,[114] and where evidence is present, the offender should normally be arrested and a decision not to do so should be recorded and justified.

However, the inspectors observed that often these policies were not reflected in practice (ibid: 6). They concluded that, overall, 'the priority given to domestic violence locally was variable' (ibid: 10). The inspectors found that call-handlers in police control rooms sometimes failed to prioritise calls appropriately and, as a result, police responses to reports of domestic violence could be too slow. This meant that victims' first contact with the police could be unsatisfactory (HMcpsi and HMIC 2004: paras 2.1–2.5). Not all police officers understood force policy and responses to incidents varied with individual officers.[115] Few, with the exception of specialist officers, 'had any real understanding of the dynamics of domestic violence' (ibid: para 2.18). Police practice relating to arrest varied between forces, with arrests being made in 13–63% of cases where, potentially, there could have been arrests (ibid: para 2.21). Case histories were seldom provided to officers attending incidents and they were seldom made aware of court orders, bail conditions or injunctions unless the victim told them (ibid: paras 2.23–2.24). The inspectors noted that there was 'potentially, a significant under-recording of domestic violence crime' (ibid: para 2.28). In particular, potential offences under the Protection from Harassment Act 1997 were being missed and officers showed inadequate understanding of the legislation (ibid: para 6.4). Where a crime was recorded, only 21% of offenders were charged (ibid: para 6.6).[116] Decisions as to whether a crime would be recorded or a charge preferred were usually based on the victim's wishes and willingness to co-operate (ibid: para 6.9). Enhanced, or what the report referred to as 'effective' evidence gathering rarely featured in police practice, with few officers recording injuries or taking photographs of the scene (ibid: paras 2.30–2.32).[117] Poor investigation meant that corroborative evidence was lacking, leading to reliance on the victim's testimony. If she proved unwilling to proceed, the Crown Prosecution Service (CPS) would often take the view that the case was unlikely to succeed in court and it was dropped (ibid: para 1.16). The inspectors reported that, partly because of this, the attrition rates in these cases was consistently higher than for most other crimes (ibid: para 1.16).

A few years later, the Home Affairs Committee observed that although there had been progress in the police response, 'the experience of individual victims remains varied, and depends to a great degree on the commitment and knowledge of the individual officer'.[118]

---

[114] All offences, including common assault, are now covered by s 24 Police and Criminal Evidence Act 1984.

[115] Humphreys and Thiara (2000: 55ff) report that the experiences of the women in their study varied considerably. In particular, while many reported positive change in the attitude of police, this often depended on whether they qualified as 'good' victims in the eyes of the police.

[116] When 'missed' crimes were taken into account, the figure dropped to 10% (HMcpsi and HMIC 2004: para 6.9). Hester et al (2003) report that in their study, less than a third of arrests led to criminal charges.

[117] See also Hester et al (2003).

[118] Quoted in Home Department (2008: para 50).

It recommended training of all police officers.[119] In response to these criticisms the government indicated that training was being reviewed (Home Department 2008: para 51) and the Association of Chief Police Officers (ACPO) recently issued updated *Guidance on Investigating Domestic Abuse* (ACPO, NPIA 2008) which is intended to improve police practice.[120] It requires call-takers to be trained and supplies a list of questions that need to be asked when a call is taken (paras 1.1, 2.2). It warns about the link between child abuse and domestic abuse (para 1.2). It states that officers attending the scene must be apprised of any domestic violence history including any court orders (para 2.4). It notes that police are under a duty to take positive action to secure the safety of victims and children in order to satisfy their obligations under the Human Rights Act 1998[121] as well as the law of negligence. Under the Police and Criminal Evidence Act 1984 (PACE), it says, an arrest will normally be necessary where an offence has been committed (para 3.1). The decision whether to arrest lies with the officer, and victims should not be asked whether they want the offender to be arrested. If an arrest is not made, the officer must record the reasons and provide the victim with an explanation. The victim and/or children must be referred to helping agencies. Officers should focus on gathering evidence and should not rely only on the victim's statement (para 3.1). They should consider taking photographs or using video to record evidence (paras 3.4, 4.3.2). The victim must be spoken to separately where the perpetrator cannot overhear (para 3.8). Previous withdrawals of support for prosecution should not influence the decision whether to arrest (para 3.8). Nor should the victim's willingness to testify (para 3.10). When faced with counter-allegations, officers should consider whether the victim acted in self-defence (para 3.10.1). Officers should avoid arresting both parties without conducting an investigation to determine who was the primary aggressor (para 3.10.2). Closed-circuit television can be used to protect vulnerable victims at risk of further harm (para 4.6.2). All domestic abuse cases should be referred to duty prosecutors if the threshold test is met. The threshold test requires custody officers to decide whether there is at least a reasonable suspicion that the suspect has committed an offence, and, if there is, whether it is in the public interest to charge that suspect (para 5.3.1). Cautions should rarely be considered appropriate (para 5.3.3). Risk factors should be analysed when deciding on police bail and the primary consideration should be the protection of the victim, any children and the suspect (para 5.3.4). If bail is granted, bail conditions, such as a prohibition on contacting the victim, should be considered (para 5.3.5). If the case is discontinued, the victim must be notified. (para 5.3.7).[122]

Stanley et al report cases where the police response was slow (Stanley et al 2010: paras 5.3.1, 5.3.3) but they did find that the perpetrator was arrested in the majority of cases (para 5.4.2). Officers reported that even where the victim retracted her statement the CPS was prepared to prosecute; other evidence was used (para 5.4.3).

The police also co-operate with other agencies in an effort to protect those at risk; they are part of multi-agency risk assessment conferences (MARACs). These are meetings held to bring together on one occasion all agencies involved in the case in question. The

---

[119] See ibid: para 51.

[120] This does not supplant the Home Office Circular (Home Office 2000b)

[121] The notion of private life under Art 8 of the ECHR extends to cover attacks on physical and moral integrity. States have a duty to protect individuals from such attacks and have to provide an adequate legal framework. Failure of the authorities to implement and enforce the law constitutes infringement of Art 8: *A v Croatia Application 55164/08* [2011] 1 FLR 407. See also *Hajduova* v *Slovakia (Application No 2660/03)* (2011) I FLR 1247.

[122] See Criminal Justice System (2005).

meeting produces a risk-management plan to reduce the risk of harm and repeat victimisation (ACPO, NPIA 2008: para 6.2.3).[123] Independent domestic violence advisors (IDVAs), located in the voluntary sector, work alongside the police and other agencies to provide independent support for victims identified as high risk who are going through the criminal justice process (ACPO, NPIA 2008 para 6.2.5)

The new Guidance retains an emphasis on proactive policing. In addition, section 24 of PACE has been amended to increase police powers of arrest:

24 Arrest without warrant: constables

(1) A constable may arrest without a warrant—

(a) anyone who is about to commit an offence;
(b) anyone who is in the act of committing an offence;
(c) anyone whom he has reasonable grounds for suspecting to be about to commit an offence;
(d) anyone whom he has reasonable grounds for suspecting to be committing an offence.

(2) If a constable has reasonable grounds for suspecting that an offence has been committed, he may arrest without a warrant anyone whom he has reasonable grounds to suspect of being guilty of it.

(3) If an offence has been committed, a constable may arrest without a warrant—

(a) anyone who is guilty of the offence;
(b) anyone whom he has reasonable grounds for suspecting to be guilty of it.

(4) But the power of summary arrest conferred by subsection (1), (2) or (3) is exercisable only if the constable has reasonable grounds for believing that for any of the reasons mentioned in subsection (5) it is necessary to arrest the person in question.

(5) The reasons are—

(a) to enable the name of the person in question to be ascertained (in the case where the constable does not know, and cannot readily ascertain, the person's name, or has reasonable grounds for doubting whether a name given by the person as his name is his real name);
(b) correspondingly as regards the person's address;
(c) to prevent the person in question—
    (i)   causing physical injury to himself or any other person;
    (ii) suffering physical injury;
    (iii) causing loss of or damage to property;
    (iv) committing an offence against public decency (subject to subsection (6)); or
    (v)   causing an unlawful obstruction of the highway;
(d) to protect a child or other vulnerable person from the person in question;

However, pro-arrest policies have been criticised by some as having the effect of endangering women. Not only might arrest fail to deter violence,[124] but it might also put women at risk of reprisals from an irate partner (Morley and Mullender 1992: 270–71; Hoyle 1998: 189–90).

Hoyle and Sanders (2000) conducted research in 1996–97, interviewing victims of

---

[123] It is planned at the time of writing that every domestic abuse death will be automatically reviewed
[124] Maxwell, Garner and Fagan (2002: 70) found a correlation between arrest and a consistent but modest reduction in repeat offences against the victim. However, they concede that many offenders are not deterred by police involvement or arrest (ibid: 71–72). See also Hanmer et al (1999: 37). Generally, however, research on this is inconclusive (Paradine and Wilkinson 2004: para 5.2).

domestic violence to discover what response they wanted when they called the police to an incident. Over half the women interviewed wanted the offender to be arrested but a significant minority did not. Furthermore, most of the women who wanted an arrest did not want a prosecution (ibid: 22).[125] The authors concede that the choice not to pursue arrest or prosecution was often a result of being in a coercive relationship. However, these were rational choices prompted by fear, by community or familial pressure or by the fact that the women were isolated and had no resources (ibid: 21, 29).[126] The best thing for these women, say Hoyle and Sanders, would be to help them to change their circumstances so that they can make different choices (ibid: 21). To this end, they say, a range of measures is necessary. Arrest only helped to reduce violence if combined with other measures such as perpetrator programmes (ibid: 30).[127] They assert that the pro-arrest stance is mainly of symbolic value (ibid: 30),[128] although it is useful in giving the women time and space to decide what to do. Support from domestic violence officers and the use of bail conditions could help to ensure that the time is used constructively (ibid: 31). Pro-arrest policies, on their own, may fail some women.[129]

Research is now emerging in relation to domestic violence in same-sex relationships. Donovan and Hester found that among their sample of interviewees recalling past experiences, those who gave the most negative accounts of police intervention were gay men who had called the police eight years previously. More mixed responses were reported by two interviewees who had called the police five years previously (Donovan and Hester 2011: 39–40). The authors conclude that it is difficult to assess the effects of changed police policy. They do say, however, that the people they spoke to tended not to report abuse, either because they did not see police intervention as appropriate or because they did not expect a sympathetic response (ibid: 40).

The Crown Prosecution Service

The CPS has revised its policy on prosecuting domestic violence in a way that accords recognition to the interests of victims. The current version, published in 2009, states: '[T]he CPS understands that domestic violence is very serious, and that it can inflict lasting trauma on victims and their extended families. We want people to know that our aim is to prosecute domestic violence cases effectively' (CPS 2009: para 1.5).

The CPS decides upon the charge to be pursued (CPS 2009: para 3.6) and, whereas in the past, reduced charges were common,[130] charging is now, it has been said, generally

---

[125] This was usually because the arrest had had the desired effect on the assailant's behaviour or because of fear that prosecution would not end the violence and could even provoke more (Hoyle and Sanders 2000: 23). The main reason women did not want to make a statement or wanted to withdraw a statement was fear of retaliation. Others did not want to pursue the legal route because they had separated. Some, however, said they wanted to save the relationship (ibid: 24).

[126] See Hester et al (2000: para 1.11). See also Richards (2004: paras 4.3.3 and 5.3.3).

[127] See below.

[128] But see Dobash (2003: 316), who emphasises both the symbolic force and the 'real' consequences of the use of the criminal law.

[129] Indeed, there is evidence from the USA and Canada that mandatory arrest policies have resulted in increased rates of arrest of both men and women. See Chesney-Lind (2002: 83).

[130] See Paradine and Wilkinson (2004: para 6.1). A survey carried out in 2001 amongst workers in the domestic violence sector, such as refuge workers, evoked complaints about the downgrading of charges from an 'overwhelming majority' of respondents (Barron 2002: 17).

appropriate (HMcpsi and HMIC 2004: para 7.53).[131] In deciding whether to proceed with the case, the prosecutor has to apply two tests. Crown prosecutors must be satisfied that there is enough evidence to provide 'a realistic prospect of conviction'. If the case satisfies this requirement they must go on to consider whether the prosecution is necessary in the public interest. When considering the public interest test, the prosecutor should always take into account 'the consequences for the victim of the decision whether or not to prosecute, and any views expressed by the victim or the victim's family' (CPS 2009: paras 4.4–4.6). If the evidential test is passed and the victim is willing to give evidence, a prosecution will 'almost always' be mounted (ibid: para 6.4). The CPS may ask that the defendant be kept in custody or that the court impose bail conditions (ibid: paras 7.7, 7.11–7.12). It may ask the court for special measures to be implemented such as the use of a screen to protect the witness from intimidation in court (ibid: paras 11.14–11.18). Support such as a meeting with the prosecutor is intended to increase the confidence of the witness (ibid: para 11.31).

Where the victim withdraws support for the prosecution,[132] and where it is suspected that she has been pressured to do so, the police will be asked to investigate (ibid: paras 5.11, 5.15); they are required to take a statement to determine whether the victim had been put under pressure.[133] If the victim insists on withdrawing the complaint, the prosecutor is required to consider whether the case can proceed in her absence and whether it is in the public interest to proceed (ibid: para 5.12).[134] The more serious a case, the more likely a prosecution, irrespective of the victim's wishes (ibid: para 5.17). In serious cases the prosecution may consider requiring the victim to give evidence or may seek to use the victim's statement in court (ibid: paras 5.19–5.20).[135] If the victim withdraws support for the prosecution but there is enough evidence to proceed, a decision may be made to continue with the prosecution but 'the safety of the victim and any children and young person will be a key factor' (ibid: para 6.3).

Finally, measures have been put into place to improve witness care. Victims are supposed to be offered the opportunity to articulate the effects on them of the violence in personal statements (CPS 2009: para 11.38ff). Also, victims are supposed to be kept informed about the progress of their cases (ibid: ch 13). Where the CPS makes a decision not to charge on the basis of the evidence it has received from the police, or decides to drop or substantially to amend a charge, the policy document states that the CPS will inform the victim in writing of the decision and the reasons for it (ibid: para 3.8).

The CPS has been found wanting in the past. The joint inspectorate made a number of criticisms: the majority of CPS files did not include personal statements from victims (HMcpsi and HMIC 2004: para 2.44); breaches of bail conditions were not acted on (ibid: para 7.5); and prosecutors still appeared to accept bind-overs in some cases when it would have been more appropriate to pursue criminal proceedings (ibid: para 7.68).

It seems that the CPS does not necessarily drop charges if the victim does not want to

---

[131] But see Barron (2002: 17). Her respondents reported that charges were often downgraded or dropped.

[132] One in three out of all failed prosecutions for domestic violence in 2009/10 failed because the victim refused to testify or retracted (Starmer 2011).

[133] See CPS (2009: para 5.11), ACPO, NPIA (2008: para 4.4.5). Police shortcomings in this regard have been noted in the past (HMcpsi and HMIC 2004: para 2.45).

[134] See Stanley et al (2010: para 5.4.3).

[135] However, the court may be unwilling to take this step in the light of the potential repercussions for the victim should she testify against her abuser. See James (2007).

proceed (ibid: para 6.15).[136] However, it seems from the findings of the joint inspection report (ibid: para 6.11)[137] and the Home Affairs Committee Report (Home Department 2008: para 69) that it is only a small proportion (5%) of domestic violence incidents that lead to prosecution and conviction. This is disputed by the government which gives a rate of 19% for 2008. From charge to conviction, the national average rate of conviction was over 70% in 2008 (ibid: para 69).[138] Yet while conviction rates have improved over the years, the courts are still coming in for criticism.

The Courts

The Court of Appeal has indicated that domestic assaults should be treated as seriously as other assaults.[139] Nevertheless, high acquittal rates, the frequent use of bind-overs, the use of plea-bargaining and the leniency of sentences have been observed by a number of researchers and, it has been suggested, these practices make victims feel let down by the court process.[140]

Hester et al (2006: 4) reported a high attrition rate between arrest and conviction. They also found that bind-overs were common and that repeat domestic violence offenders were likely to be sentenced to community service.

More recently, the Home Affairs Committee observed that 'sentencing of domestic violence perpetrators seems to be variable, and often to result in a fine or other monetary penalty, frequently for risibly small amounts'.[141] It also referred to 'ignorance or inadequate sentencing by judges and magistrates' as obstacles for victims wishing to pursue cases through the courts.[142] The Committee also recorded that its members had 'heard accounts of ignorance and misunderstanding amongst some lawyers, judges and magistrates with regard to domestic violence'.[143] It recommended training in all aspects of domestic violence including violence in contact cases, forced marriage and 'honour'-based violence.

Improvements have been made in some parts of the country; specialist domestic violence courts (SDVCs) operate in a number of magistrates' courts.[144] They specialise in

---

[136] The CPS is often unwilling to proceed with a prosecution if the victim indicates that she does not wish to co-operate. There are a number of reasons for acceding to the woman's wishes. Her failure to co-operate is seen as making a conviction unlikely. In addition, it is recognised that the victim may be put at risk as a result of a prosecution. Cretney and Davis (1997b: 88), while suggesting that failure to proceed on the part of the CPS means that the symbolic force of the law is not being deployed to condemn domestic violence, nevertheless take the view that compelling women to testify is not helpful. Victims should, however, receive the support and encouragement that would enable them to go through with the prosecution process. This would produce a higher conviction rate which, coupled with appropriate penalties, would convey the message that domestic violence cannot be tolerated.

[137] See also Hester et al (2003).

[138] The Director of Public prosecutions reports that the number of prosecutions has increased and that conviction rates have risen from 49% in 2002 to 72% in 2009/10. There was a successful outcome in 73% of cases involving an IDVA and in 66% of cases involving an IDVA there was a cessation or reduction in violence (Starmer 2011).

[139] *R v Cutts* [1987] Fam Law 311.

[140] See Cretney and Davis (1996: 171); Cretney and Davis (1997a: 153); Hoyle (1998: 191–93); Humphreys and Thiara (2002: 51); Hester et al (2003). The joint inspectorate found that some cases were discontinued when a bind-over was ordered (HMcpsi and HMIC 2004: para 6.15). The acquittal rate was significantly higher than the national average (ibid: para 6.17).

[141] Quoted in Home Department (2008: para 74).

[142] Quoted in ibid: para 75.

[143] Quoted in ibid: para 78.

[144] There were 141 such courts in place as of 1 April 2010 (CPS 2010: 20).

dealing with domestic abuse cases, providing IDVAs, prosecutors, magistrates, legal advisers and police officers who specialise in domestic abuse cases. These courts normally either fast-track domestic violence cases or cluster them together (ACPO, NPIA 2008: para 8.3.5)

> In essence, the specialist court programme is a *co-ordinated community response* to DV which combines both criminal justice and non-criminal justice interventions and forms a multi-agency response that creates greater victim safety and brings perpetrators to account.
>
> (Barran et al 2006: 4, emphasis in original)

Cook et al (2004) observed that more custodial sentences and community penalties were being imposed in specialist courts. Victim satisfaction increased[145] but the specialist courts had no effect on the level of charges or the rate of victim withdrawals. However, as Burton says, withdrawal after receiving appropriate advice and support is better than a decision to withdraw without such knowledge and support (Burton 2008a: 114). She found that the main advantage of the specialist court from the perspective of the victims was the presence of an advocate to give them the support they needed (ibid: 122).

A study of Croydon's specialist court suggested that sentencing practices improved and bind-overs were not used. The court was using compliance hearings to review the perpetrator's compliance with community orders requiring attendance at a perpetrator programme. As a result the magistrates received feedback on compliance and the perpetrator received encouragement to complete the programme (Vallely et al 2005).[146]

Perpetrator programmes have increasingly come to be seen as a productive way of dealing with offenders. However, these programmes have the effect of stopping violence only for some men.[147]

Perpetrator Programmes

There are two types of perpetrator programmes in the UK: criminal justice programmes and community-based programmes (Respect 2010a). Criminal justice programmes are usually run by probation or prison staff and these take only referrals from the court as part of a sentence imposed pursuant to a conviction for a violent or abusive act. Community-based programmes are generally run by the voluntary sector and take self-referrals as well as referrals from children's services, family courts and other sources (ibid). Anger management programmes, educational programmes for men and couples counselling are not perpetrator programmes and are not appropriate, according to Respect.[148] Anger management programmes, which are often favoured by the courts,[149] are concerned with managing anger[150] and not with safety or with stopping violence (ibid). [151]

---

[145] See also the research discussed by Burton (2008a: 117ff).

[146] See also Burton (2006).

[147] See the research discussed by Burton (2008a: 130ff).

[148] Respect sets national standards for voluntary organisations providing perpetrator programmes (Respect 2010b). Respect is the 'UK membership association for domestic violence perpetrator programmes and associated support services') (ibid)

[149] See, eg, *Lomas v Parle*, n 67 above, para 51.

[150] These may fail to address the question of why the man is angry and the appropriateness of the anger (Dobash et al 2000: 45). It could be argued that they misconstrue the genesis of the violence. The violence may stem from a wish to control the victim rather than from an inability to exercise self-control.

[151] See Dobash *et al* (2000: 291–93).

Respect has issued a briefing paper stating that not all services are working to minimum safety standards (Respect 2010b). The organisation sets as the minimum the existence of an 'integrated partner support service' (ISS) and a system of risk assessment and management (ibid). An ISS runs alongside the perpetrator programme and is a service whereby the service provider remains in touch with the perpetrator's current or former partner. In this way she can be supported and he (the perpetrator) can be more easily monitored and, if necessary, the risks he poses can be reassessed.

Mullender and Burton (2000) say that research into perpetrator programmes shows no conclusive evidence of success.[152] Dobash et al, on the other hand, take a more positive view. Their research revealed that, while a 'concerted criminal justice response involving arrest and prosecution may affect the subsequent violence of men' (Dobash et al 2000: 300), 'in comparison with other criminal justice sanctions, participation in one of the programmes is more likely to reduce the incidence and frequency of violence and associated controlling behaviours' (ibid: 301). The authors point out (ibid: 304), however, that programmes must be integrated into the criminal justice mechanisms dealing with domestic violence. The process of being arrested, charged, prosecuted and sentenced to attendance at a programme, with the threat of increased sanctions in the event of failure, provides an incentive to change.[153] In contrast, they say, there is a high attrition rate in relation to voluntary attendance at programmes. For example, some abusers enter voluntary counselling in order to persuade their partners to return home or not to leave home. They drop out when they achieve this aim (ibid). Without court sanctions, most perpetrators do not attend for long enough to make any lasting changes (Adams 2000: 315).

In a briefing paper reviewing the available research, Respect (2010a) cite Dobash et al (2000) as well as other studies, and conclude that men who are mandated to attend a programme are more likely to complete it and those who complete a programme are more likely to stop using violence. The paper also refers to other forms of mandate such as threats by social services action to remove children, or the threat of not being allowed contact with children, if the perpetrator does not attend.[154]

X. THE PROTECTION FROM HARASSMENT ACT 1997

This legislation, initially introduced to deal with stalking, covers a broad range of conduct and one of its main uses has been in relation to domestic violence.[155] It is particularly useful in cases of post-separation violence.[156] The legislation embodies a combination of criminal law and civil law measures. The statute prohibits the pursuit of a course of conduct that amounts to harassment[157] and creates two offences: harassment contrary to this prohibition[158] and putting a person in fear of violence.[159]

---

[152] See also Bowen (2011).

[153] See also Dobash (2003: 316–17).

[154] However, this kind of threat is likely to impact on the mother as well.

[155] See Harris (2000: 9). However Humphreys and Thiara (2002: 51) report little use of the Act in relation to women in their sample. Barron (2002: 18) also found the Act to be under-used.

[156] Harris (2000: 9) reports that most cases concern 'the unwanted attentions of ex-partners' as well as harassment by neighbours.

[157] S 1 Protection from Harassment Act 1997.

[158] S 2.

[159] S 4.

Section 1 prohibits any person from engaging in a course of conduct which he or she knows, or ought reasonably to know,[160] constitutes harassment. 'Harassment' is not defined, save that section 7 provides that it includes alarming or causing distress to a person and that harassment may take the form of either words or conduct.[161] This is taken to encompass 'unwanted telephone calls, letters or gifts, vandalism of property or harassment of family and friends' (Harris 2000: 1–2). These types of conduct may be accompanied by threats and are often linked to controlling behaviour and abuse (ibid: 2). Conviction may result in imprisonment or a fine.

Section 2 makes it an offence[162] to pursue a course of conduct in breach of the prohibition against harassment in section 1.[163] Section 4 makes it an offence to pursue a course of conduct that puts a person in fear of violence. This offence is committed where the perpetrator knows or ought reasonably to know that such fear will be induced.[164] The police can arrest where they have the power to do so under PACE.

According to section 7, a 'course of conduct' must involve conduct on at least two occasions. The fewer the incidents and the wider spread they are over time, the less likely it is that a finding of harassment will be made.[165] In *R v Hills*[166] the court was unconvinced that the evidence was enough to link the two incidents relied on so as to show a course of conduct. One of the main considerations in reaching this conclusion appears to have been that the parties' relationship was continuing. Otton LJ remarked that the case before him was remote from the 'stalking' for which he said the Act was intended and he seemed unwilling to include ongoing violent relationships within the scope of the legislation. He said that it could be applied to cases where a person made

> a nuisance of himself to a partner or wife when they have become estranged. However in a situation such as this, when they were frequently coming back together and intercourse was taking place ... it is unrealistic to think that this fell within the stalking category which either postulates a stranger or an estranged spouse. (para 31)

The Act also makes provision for orders designed to prevent a person from behaving in certain ways. Section 5 empowers the court to make restraining orders when dealing with persons convicted of an offence, which need not necessarily be an offence under the Act. For the purpose of protecting the victim of the offence or any other person from conduct amounting to harassment or conduct which will cause a fear of violence, the court can prohibit the defendant from doing anything described in the order. The court could, for example, prohibit the defendant from contacting the victim or visiting her home.[167] Under section 5A(1) the court can even make a restraining order where the defendant is acquitted of an offence if it considers it necessary to do so to protect a person from harassment by the defendant. Sections 5(5) and 5A(2) make it an offence for a defendant, without reasonable excuse, to do anything in contravention of a restraining order.

In addition to its criminal law provisions, the Protection from Harassment Act also

---

[160] This is an objective test judged by the standard of a reasonable person: *R v Colohan* [2001] EWCA Crim 1251; [2001] 2 FLR 757.

[161] It appears to be similar in scope to the concept of molestation. See below, p 579.

[162] The penalty is a term of imprisonment of up to six months or a fine or both (s 2(2)).

[163] The offence is not committed if the act does not qualify as harassment, eg if it is reasonable (see s 1(3)).

[164] Defences are set out in s 4(3).

[165] See *Lau v Director of Public Prosecutions* [2000] 1 FLR 799, 801.

[166] [2001] 1 FLR 580.

[167] See Harris (2000: 5).

created a tort of harassment; in terms of section 3, an actual or apprehended breach of section 1 may form the basis of a civil claim. The court is empowered to award damages and to grant an injunction restraining the defendant from pursuing conduct that amounts to harassment. It is an offence to breach such an injunction without reasonable cause.[168] An alternative method[169] of enforcing an injunction is for the victim to go to court to apply for a warrant of arrest in terms of section 3(3).

The 1997 Act has advantages over other available measures in cases of domestic violence. Since the offence of harassment is potentially very broad, the police need not be concerned with determining whether the assailant's act falls within the definition of assault. In addition, because it is the police who take action when an offence under the statute is committed, and not the victim, there is no need for a person subject to violence to finance civil proceedings for a non-molestation order or to apply for legal aid. So, provided the police understand and are not reluctant to exercise their powers, and provided the CPS and the courts take domestic violence seriously,[170] the Act can provide a cheap and quick remedy.

Harris's research into the use of the legislation revealed that some 41% of cases involved parties who were intimately known to each other, usually ex-partners. In 94% of cases in her sample involving 'intimates', the suspect was male (Harris 2000: 11 and table 2.2). The most common reason for harassment was that the complainant had decided to end the relationship with the suspect (ibid: 17).

Q Do you consider that Harris's findings mirror the findings of researchers attributing domestic violence to male proprietary control?

Harris evaluated the operation of the legislation several years ago and the findings must therefore be treated with some care as practices may have changed. She found similar problems to those identified in relation to the operation of the criminal justice system in domestic violence cases generally. She found that the police did not have background information when they attended an incident (Harris 2000: 21–22), information that could be relevant to establishing a course of conduct. There was some confusion among the police as to what the requirements of the Act are (ibid: 20). There was extensive use of bail conditions but suspects were simply rebailed where these conditions were breached (ibid: 34). The attrition rate was high as a result of lack of evidence and the decisions of complainants not to proceed (ibid: 29–30). Bind-overs were common (ibid: 31) and there was some evidence of down-charging (ibid: 46). The most common sentence was a conditional discharge, although this was often combined with a restraining order (ibid: xviii, 37). And although complainants were generally kept informed of developments by the police (ibid: 26), they were not told of the outcome of a trial or whether a restraining order had been made (ibid: 38).

There was some disagreement among those surveyed by Harris as to whether it was appropriate to use the criminal rather than the civil provisions in the Act. The police tended to be willing to use the criminal law but complained of being thwarted when cases reached the CPS or the courts. The judiciary, in particular, seemed to assume that harassment should be dealt with as a civil matter (ibid: 48). Some magistrates in turn felt that

---

[168] S 3(6) and s 3(9).
[169] Criminal proceedings and contempt of court proceedings are mutually exclusive (s 3(7)–(8)).
[170] See, on sentencing under the Protection from Harassment Act 1997, *Liddle v Hayes* [2000] 1 Cr App R(S).

criminalising harassment could lead to unfounded and vindictive accusations. Police and prosecutors were also wary of what they termed 'paranoid' women who 'read more into another's behaviour than was perhaps warranted' (ibid: 42). This view is somewhat surprising in the light of the fact that Harris found that few women knew of the Act or what to expect when they made a report to the police. And about half of the victims interviewed had 'endured the unwanted behaviour for a significant period before they decided to report it' (ibid: 19). The fear of vindictive women is also surprising given the high attrition rate noted by Harris.

Q Can you think of other areas of the law where women have traditionally assumed to be irrational, untrustworthy or vindictive?

XI. CRIMINAL OR CIVIL PROCEEDINGS?

The criminal justice system has been criticised both for failing to be sufficiently robust in dealing with domestic violence offenders and offering too little support to their victims. The Law Commission, reviewing the role of the law in domestic violence cases, expressed the view that the criminal law, being primarily concerned with punishment, might be inappropriate in many cases; most victims simply 'want the violence to stop and they want protection' (Law Commission 1992a: para 2.9). Civil law, it thought, could be framed to provide a flexible framework enabling account to be taken of the different needs of different victims (ibid). Cretney and Davis, in turn, point out that the criminal law, with its focus on discrete incidents, is not always appropriate for dealing with what may have been a long history of violence (Cretney and Davis 1995: 84).

Feminist commentators[171] have expressed unease at giving priority to civil remedies for domestic violence, suggesting that this approach reinforces the notion that it is not a criminal matter and that it diverts attention away from necessary reform of the criminal process. Nevertheless, there is research indicating that women feel that they have benefited from using the civil law. In addition, there are advantages in the lower standard of proof and in the fact that orders can be tailored to meet a variety of problems (Humphreys and Kaye 1997: 405).

Q What role do you see for the criminal justice system in domestic violence cases? Why?

XII. CIVIL LAW

The High Court has always had jurisdiction to grant injunctions where it is just and expedient to do so[172] and county courts acquired the same powers through statute.[173] However, the exercise of these powers was subject to limitations. Pursuant to the recom-

---

[171] See, eg, Humphreys and Kaye (1997: 405).
[172] S 37(1) Supreme Court Act 1981, declaratory of the existing law.
[173] S 38(1) County Court Act 1984.

mendations made in 1975 by the Select Committee on Violence in the Family, legislation designed specifically to improve the civil law protection of victims of domestic violence was passed.[174] These laws enabled women to seek injunctions without first instituting divorce or separation proceedings. An order could be sought to prevent one partner molesting the other or the children. In addition, it was possible to apply for an ouster[175] order excluding the abuser from the common home and even from the area in which it was situated. A power of arrest could be attached by the court to an order, authorising a police constable to arrest without warrant a person whom he or she had reasonable cause to suspect was in breach of an injunction.

However, a number of problems were identified in relation to the scope of the civil law and its implementation.[176] In 1992, the Law Commission described the then existing civil remedies as complex, confusing and lacking integration (Law Commission 1992a: para 1.2). Post-separation violence was not adequately addressed.[177] The criteria for the award of ouster orders placed too much emphasis on the seriousness of the conduct of the abuser rather than on its effects on the applicant. Also children's interests were given insufficient weight (ibid: para 2.26).

Barron (1990), reporting on an empirical study investigating the effectiveness of legal protection for victims of domestic violence, found deficiencies in the remedies and services provided. She criticised the way in which the legislation relating to ousters was being applied, observing that, whereas non-molestation orders were granted fairly readily, anything more than that could be difficult to obtain. Courts were reluctant to deprive a man of 'his' home, she said, quoting one judge as saying that ousters 'are remedies of the last resort' (Barron 1990: 50). Judges also referred to such orders as 'Draconian'.[178]

Q What does the emphasis on property rights tell us about the seriousness with which the courts have tended to view domestic violence?

Barron reported that once obtained, orders often proved ineffective.[179] Neither the police nor the courts, she observed, provided the back-up necessary to enforce them (Barron 1990: 65). Often, orders, especially ex parte orders, had no power of arrest attached (ibid: 55) and, in the absence of a power of arrest, the response from the police was found to be particularly weak. Courts, in turn, were reluctant to send men to prison for breach of an injunction or undertaking (ibid: 69).[180] Instead, judges appeared to stress the need for amicable agreement (ibid: 69, 123).

---

[174] The Domestic Violence and Matrimonial Proceedings Act 1976 and the Domestic Proceedings and Magistrates Courts Act 1978. The Matrimonial Homes Act 1967 (incorporated in and extended by the Matrimonial Homes Act 1983), although not designed primarily to provide remedies for victims of abuse, came to be designated the principal Act governing ousters.

[175] Or in the magistrates' court, an exclusion order which was somewhat more limited in scope.

[176] See, generally, Edwards (1996: 213ff).

[177] See, eg, Peacock (1998: 629). Post-separation violence is common. For example in a study undertaken by Humphreys and Thiara, more than three quarters of the women surveyed suffered post-separation violence (Humphreys and Thiara 2003: 199).

[178] Law Commission (1992a: para 2.26).

[179] But see Humphreys and Kaye (1997: 405).

[180] *Neil v Ryan* [1998] 2 FLR 1068; *Hale v Tanner* [2000] 2 FLR 879; *Lomas v Parle* [2003] EWCA Civ 1804; [2004] 1 FLR 812, *Wilson v Webster* [1998] 1 FLR 1097.

XIII. THE FAMILY LAW ACT 1996

In the wake of considerable criticism of the law, Part IV the Family Law Act 1996[181] was enacted with the intention of addressing the difficulties identified.[182] It has since been amended to make provision for the advent of civil partnership and also to extend the definition of cohabitants to same-sex couples.

The Act provides for two basic types of remedy, 'non-molestation orders' and 'occupation orders', and eligibility for either order is restricted to 'associated persons'. A non-molestation order prohibits molestation, and an occupation order regulates occupation of the family home.[183] Before going on to discuss these orders, however, it is important to note that, in the past, courts have tended to accept undertakings from alleged abusers rather than make orders.[184] An undertaking is a promise made by a party to the court and is enforceable in the same way as a court order[185] but a power of arrest cannot be attached to an undertaking.[186] Researchers have found in the past that undertakings were being accepted even in inappropriate cases where there is considerable risk to the applicant.[187] This practice should now have ended with the enactment of section 46(3A).[188]

Non-Molestation Order

Section 42 of the Family Law Act 1996 defines a non-molestation order and specifies the proceedings in the course of which an order may be made:

42.—Non-molestation orders.

(1) In this Part a 'non-molestation order' means an order containing either or both of the following provisions—

(a) provision prohibiting a person ('the respondent') from molesting another person who is associated with the respondent;

(b) provision prohibiting the respondent from molesting a relevant child

(2) The court may make a non-molestation order—

(a) if an application for the order has been made (whether in other family proceedings or without any other family proceedings being instituted) by a person who is associated with the respondent; or

(b) if in any family proceedings to which the respondent is a party the court considers that the

---

[181] On the use of anti-social behaviour orders under the Crime and Disorder Act 1998, see Burton (2008c).

[182] Some modifications to the Law Commission's recommendations were necessitated by a campaign by a tabloid newspaper and a minority of Conservative MPs alleging that the original Bill (the Family Homes and Domestic Violence Bill 1995) undermined 'family values' (Murphy 1996: 845).

[183] The High Court, county courts and magistrates' courts all have jurisdiction under the Act (s 57). However, the jurisdiction of magistrates' courts is slightly limited: see s 59.

[184] The Family Law Act 1996 makes provision for this practice to continue. S 46(1) provides that '[i]n any case where the court has power to make an occupation order or non-molestation order, the court may accept an undertaking from any party to the proceedings'.

[185] S 46(4).

[186] See p 596 below.

[187] See Humphries (2001). See also Humphreys and Thiara (2002: 54).

[188] See below.

order should be made for the benefit of any other party to the proceedings or any relevant child even though no such application has been made ... .

(5) In deciding whether to exercise its powers under this section and, if so, in what manner, the court shall have regard to all the circumstances including the need to secure the health, safety and well-being—

(a) of the applicant; and

(b) of any relevant child.

Nowhere in the Act is the term 'molestation' defined. The Law Commission took the view that a definition was unnecessary and might prove to be overly restrictive (Law Commission 1992a: para 3.1). It has been held that the term implies 'deliberate conduct which is aimed at a high degree of harassment ... so as to justify intervention by the court'.[189] The courts have, over the years, treated a wide range of behaviour as 'molestation':

Examples of ... 'non-violent' harassment or molestation cover a very wide range of behaviour. Common instances include persistent pestering and intimidation through shouting, denigration, threats or argument, nuisance telephone calls, damaging property, following the applicant about and repeatedly calling at her home or place of work. Installing a mistress into the matrimonial home with a wife and three children, filling car locks with superglue, writing anonymous letters and pressing one's face against a window whilst brandishing papers have all been held to amount to molestation. The degree of severity of such behaviour depends less upon its intrinsic nature than upon it being part of a pattern and upon its effect on the victim.[190]

(Law Commission 1992a: para 2.3, footnotes omitted)

A non-molestation order may be granted to an 'associated person'[191] in free-standing proceedings, or in the course of family proceedings,[192] whether on application or on the court's own initiative.

'Associated Persons'

The Law Commission took the view that the often intense nature of family or domestic relationships made it necessary to provide special remedies and procedures in cases of violence or molestation.[193] The category of 'associated persons' was accordingly devised to identify those relationships. Section 62(3) provides:

---

[189] *C v C (Non-molestation Order: Jurisdiction)* [1998] 1 FLR 554, 556–57.

[190] See, eg, on the meaning of molestation: *Vaughan v Vaughan* [1973] 1 WLR 1159; *Horner v Horner* [1982] Fam 90; *George v George* [1986] 2 FLR 347; *Smith v Smith* [1988] 1 FLR 179; *Johnson v Walton* [1990] 1 FLR 350.

[191] Children under 16 may themselves apply for non-molestation or occupation orders with leave (s 43). See, for criticism of the leave requirement, Murphy (1996: 850–51).

[192] S 63(1) defines 'family proceedings' as proceedings related to children under the court's inherent jurisdiction and proceedings under the enactments specified in s 63(2). They include proceedings under the Matrimonial Causes Act 1973, Part IV of the Family Law Act 1996 and Parts I, II and IV of the Children Act 1989. Proceedings under Part V of the Children Act are not included but there is one exception. S 42(3) of the Family Law Act 1996 stipulates that 'family proceedings' include proceedings in which the court has made an emergency protection order under s 44 of the Children Act 1989 which includes an exclusion requirement.

[193] See, Hayes (1996), Law Commission (1992a: paras 3.8–3.27). It was thought inappropriate in such cases to require victims to rely on the court's jurisdiction under s 37 of the Supreme Court Act 1981 or s 38 of the County Courts Act 1984. These provisions provide limited assistance to those who fall outside the scope of the Family Law Act 1996. Because injunctions are generally only granted in support of an existing legal right (but see *Burris v Azadani* [1995] 1 WLR 1372), the victim normally has to prove that the respondent's behav-

For the purposes of this Part, a person is associated with another person if—

(a)   they are or have been married to each other;

(aa) they are or have been civil partners of each other

(b)   they are cohabitants or former cohabitants;

(c)   they live or have lived in the same household, otherwise than merely by reason of one of them being the other's employee, tenant, lodger or boarder;

(d)   they are relatives;[194]

(e)   they have agreed to marry one another (whether or not that agreement has been terminated);[195]

(ea) they have or have had an intimate personal relationship with each other which is or was of significant duration[196]

[eza] they have entered into a civil partnership agreement (as defined by section 73 of the Civil Partnership Act 2004) (whether or not that agreement has been terminated);[197]

(f)   in relation to any child, they are both persons falling within subsection (4);[198] or

(g)   they are parties to the same family proceedings (other than proceedings under this Part).

The definition of cohabitants and former cohabitants in section 62(1)(a) includes same-sex couples, that is 'two persons who are neither married to each other nor civil partners of each other but are living together as husband and wife or as if they were civil partners'.

The concept of 'associated persons' has been interpreted by the courts to take account of the Law Commission's concern to deal with the heightened stresses engendered by disputes between those in close relationships.[199] In *Chechi v Bashier*[200] the Court of Appeal held that a dispute between brothers and their families fell within the ambit of the

---

iour amounts to a tort such as battery, assault, trespass or nuisance. See *Wilkinson v Downton* [1897] 2 QB 57; *Siskina (Owners of cargo lately laden on board) v Distos Compania Naviera SA* [1979] AC 210.

[194] This term is very widely defined in s 63(1) as: '(a) the father, mother, stepfather, stepmother, son, daughter, stepson, stepdaughter, grandmother, grandfather, grandson or granddaughter of that person or of that person's spouse, former spouse, civil partner or former civil partner, or (b) the brother, sister, uncle, aunt, niece, nephew or first cousin (whether of the full blood or of the half blood or by marriage or civil partnership) of that person or of that person's spouse, former spouse, civil partner or former civil partner, and includes, in relation to a person who is cohabiting or has cohabited with another person, any person who would fall within paragraph (a) or (b) if the parties were married to each other or were civil partners of each other.'

[195] There is a time limit of three years after termination of the agreement; no application for either a non-molestation or an occupation order can be made after this period has elapsed (s 42(4) and s 33(2)).

[196] Added by the Domestic Violence, Crime and Victims Act 2004 s 4. This may or may not be a sexual relationship. The provision does not cover platonic relationships or one-night stands (House of Lords 2003–04: Domestic Violence, Crime and Victims Bill, Explanatory Notes, para 31).

[197] There is a time limit of three years after termination (s 332A).

[198] A person falls within subs (4) if he or she is a parent of the child or has or has had parental responsibility for the child. Since the enactment of the Family Law Reform Act 1987 s 1, the term 'parent' has included the unmarried father; he is a parent even if he does not have parental responsibility. An order may be sought against an unmarried father by the mother of the child irrespective of the fact that the parents have never lived together. The Act also makes provision for the situation where an adoption agency has the power to place a child for adoption, where a placement order has been made or where a child has been adopted. Two persons are associated with each other if one is the natural parent and the other is the child or an adoptive parent, a person who has applied for an adoption order or a person with whom the child has been placed for adoption (s 62(5)).

[199] Reece (2006) argues that the definition is too wide because it obscures the special nature of the relationships which the protective legislation was originally intended to target: those characterised by the isolation and inequality that are features of spousal and quasi-spousal relationships. However, Burton (2008a:19) points out that inequality is not confined to spousal and cohabitant relationships. She suggests that the definition overlaps with Madden Dempsey's conceptualisation of domestic violence in its 'strong sense'. According to Madden Dempsey, violence 'is best understood in terms of three distinct elements: violence, domesticity, and structural inequality' (Madden Dempsey 2006: 306).

[200] [1999] 2 FLR 489.

Act because, although the quarrel was about land, the family relationship fuelled it and kept it alive. In *G v G (Non-Molestation Order: Jurisdiction)*[201] the court held that the parties qualified as former cohabitants under section 62(3)(b) even though the relationship had not been stable (543). Wall J took the view that:

> where domestic violence is concerned, they [the justices] should give the statute a purposive construction and not decline jurisdiction, unless the facts of the case before them are plainly incapable of being brought within the statute. Part IV of the 1996 Act is designed to provide swift and accessible protective remedies to persons of both sexes who are the victims of domestic violence, provided they fall within the criteria of S 62. It would, I think, be most unfortunate if S 62(3) was narrowly construed so as to exclude borderline cases where swift and effective protection for the victims of domestic violence is required. This case is, after all, about jurisdiction; it is not about the merits. (543)

Section 42(5) sets out in broad terms the matters to which the court should have regard in deciding whether to grant an order:

> In deciding whether to exercise its powers under this section and, if so, in what manner, the court shall have regard to all the circumstances including the need to secure the health,[202] safety and well-being—
>
> (a) of the applicant; and
> (b) of any relevant child.

The intention behind the wording of the section is to ensure that the courts focus on the effects of the respondent's behaviour on those around him rather than on the nature of the conduct itself. This approach, said the Law Commission, is consistent with the 'trend in family law towards providing protection from harm rather than punishment or blame' (Law Commission 1992a: para 3.6).[203]

Q Why should family law not be concerned with punishment or blame?

Should the court decide that the circumstances warrant a non-molestation order, it will go on to consider the scope and duration of an appropriate order. The order 'may be expressed so as to refer to molestation in general, to particular acts of molestation, or to both'.[204] Typically, courts will frame orders to prohibit the respondent from intimidating, harassing or pestering the applicant and from encouraging someone else to do so (Platt 2000: 908).

---

[201] [2000] 2 FLR 533.

[202] Defined in s 63(1) as including physical or mental health.

[203] The court may refuse an injunction where it considers it would have undesirable consequences. In *Chechi v Bashier* [1999] 2 FLR 489, the judge was held to have been justified in refusing a non-molestation order because granting such an order would have meant that he would have had to attach a power of arrest under s 47(2)(b). In the circumstances, this would have given the applicant unacceptable power over the respondents which he would be likely to abuse. In *Banks v Banks* [1999] 1 FLR 726 the court refused to make a non-molestation order because the wife's abusive behaviour was a result of her mental condition. She had no control over her conduct and so the order would serve no purpose. However it is not necessary that the person subject to the injunction has a detailed understanding of the court's powers. It suffices if he understands that he is not permitted to do the act concerned and that he will be punished if he does (*P v P (Contempt of Court: Mental Capacity)* [1999] 2 FLR 897).

[204] S 42(6).

If specific acts are complained of, these are likely to be referred to in the order as well.[205] The order 'may be made for a specified period or until further order'.[206]

Occupation Order

An occupation order excluding an abusive associated person from the home, part of it or the area in which it is situated may be sought in the course of family proceedings or as a free-standing application.[207] As the Law Commission pointed out, these orders are particularly important in domestic violence cases where the parties live together: '[A]n occupation order ousting the respondent from the home will often be the only way of supporting a non-molestation order and giving the applicant effective protection' (Law Commission 1992a: para 4.6). By contrast, the utility of occupation orders was doubted by many of those from within refuge-providing organisations who responded to Barron's questionnaire. These orders were relatively rarely sought by women entering refuges, many of whom wished to be rehoused where they could not be traced by their abusers (Barron 2002: 7).

In relation to occupation orders the Act draws a distinction between an applicant who qualifies as a 'person entitled' and one who does not. The powers of the court differ according to which category the applicant falls into and are more extensive where she has some interest recognised in law or in equity in the property. Moreover, the categories of non-entitled persons eligible to seek an occupation order are restricted to former spouses, former civil partners, cohabitants and former cohabitants.

The Law Commission (1992a: para 4.7) favoured drawing a distinction between entitled and non-entitled applicants for two reasons. First, an occupation order can 'severely restrict the enjoyment of property rights' and this interference is 'more difficult to justify' where the applicant has no right to occupy the premises. Secondly, it was said, the purpose of an occupation order is generally different in the two cases. In the case of an applicant who is entitled, an order has a purpose beyond short-term protection; it regulates occupation of the home until a decision is made as to the medium- or long-term disposition of the property and, in some circumstances, lasts indefinitely. In the case of non-entitled applicants, an order is 'essentially a short term measure of protection intended to give then time to find alternative accommodation or, at most, to await the outcome of an application for a property law remedy' (ibid).

'Person Entitled'

A person falls into this category either by virtue of an interest recognised by the general law or by virtue of home rights under section 30 of the Family Law Act 1996. Section 30 comes into operation where one spouse or civil partner is entitled to occupy the home, whether by reason of a beneficial estate or interest, contract or statute, and where the other is not so entitled. The spouse or civil partner who is not so entitled[208] is given home

---

[205] See Freeman (1996b: 86).

[206] S 42(7).

[207] See s 39(2).

[208] S 30(9) provides that a person with an equitable interest should be treated, for the purposes of determining home rights, as if she is not entitled to occupy the home. In relation to former spouses and civil partners, see s 35(11). In relation to cohabitants and former cohabitants, see s 36(11).

rights.[209] These comprise the right, if in occupation, not to be excluded from the house, or any part of it, without the leave of the court and the right, if not in occupation, to enter and occupy the property with the leave of the court.[210]

If the applicant is a 'person entitled', she can seek an occupation order against anyone with whom she is associated, provided the home is or has been or was intended to be their common home:

33.—Occupation orders where applicant has estate or interest etc or has home rights.

(1) If—

(a) a person ('the person entitled')—
  (i) is entitled to occupy a dwelling-house by virtue of a beneficial estate or interest or contract or by virtue of any enactment giving him the right to remain in occupation, or
  (ii) has home rights in relation to a dwelling-house, and
(b) the dwelling-house—
  (i) is or at any time has been the home of the person entitled and of another person with whom he is associated, or
  (ii) was at any time intended by the person entitled and any such other person to be their home,

the person entitled may apply to the court for an order containing any of the provisions specified in subsections (3), (4) and (5).

(2) If an agreement to marry is terminated, no application under this section may be made by virtue of section 62(3)(e) by reference to that agreement after the end of the period of three years beginning with the day on which it is terminated.

(2A) If a civil partnership agreement (as defined by section 73 of the Civil Partnership Act 2004) is terminated, no application under this section may be made by virtue of section 62(3) (eza) by reference to that agreement after the end of the period of three years beginning with the day on which it is terminated.

(3) An order under this section may—

(a) enforce the applicant's entitlement to remain in occupation as against the other person ('the respondent');
(b) require the respondent to permit the applicant to enter and remain in the dwelling-house or part of the dwelling-house;
(c) regulate the occupation of the dwelling-house by either or both parties;
(d) if the respondent is entitled as mentioned in subsection (1)(a)(i), prohibit, suspend or restrict the exercise by him of his right to occupy the dwelling-house.
(e) if the respondent has home rights in relation to the dwelling-house and the applicant is the other spouse or civil partner, restrict or terminate those rights;
(f) require the respondent to leave the dwelling-house or part of the dwelling-house; or
(g) exclude the respondent from a defined area in which the dwelling-house is included.

---

[209] No such rights arise if the home has at no time been, and which at no time was intended to be, the parties' matrimonial or civil partnership home (s 30(7)). However, if the relationship breaks down before the parties move into a home which they intended to be their home, the non-entitled party does gain home rights. If only one party, say the non-entitled spouse, intended the home to be the matrimonial home and the other did not, it is not clear whether home rights will arise.
[210] S 30(2)(a) and (b). A spouse or civil partner with home rights may pay rent, mortgage payments or other outgoings and these payments are as good as if made by the other spouse or civil partner (s 30(3)).

(4) An order under this section may declare that the applicant is entitled as mentioned in subsection (1)(a)(i) or has home rights.

(5) If the applicant has home rights and the respondent is the other spouse or civil partner, an order under this section made during the marriage or civil partnership may provide that those rights are not brought to an end by—

(a) the death of the other spouse or civil partner; or

(b) the termination (otherwise than by death) of the marriage or civil partnership.

The court can, therefore, make a declaratory order in terms of section 33(4) or a regulatory order in terms of section 33(3).[211] A declaratory order simply states that the applicant is entitled to occupy the home. To enforce the right to occupy, or to exclude the respondent, an applicant must look to the provisions governing the regulatory orders.

The court has wide powers under section 33(3). An order under section 33(3)(a) could be combined with a declaratory order and would be appropriate where the respondent interferes or threatens to interfere with the applicant's right to occupy under the general law or section 30.[212] Section 33(3)(b) applies where the applicant has been excluded from the home[213] or part of it. The power under section 33(3)(c) to make an order regulating occupation of the home enables the court to direct which parts of the home may be used by each party and to prescribe those parts of the home that one or other party may not enter.[214] Section 33(3)(d) empowers the court to override the respondent's property rights and deny, suspend or restrict the exercise of those rights. A respondent's home rights can be restricted or terminated in terms of section 33(3)(e). In addition, the respondent may be excluded from the home or from a specified area surrounding it. The order may be made for a specified period or until the happening of a specified event or until further order.[215]

The court does not always have a discretion as to whether to make an order. The Act stipulates that if what is known as the 'balance of harm' test is satisfied, the court is obliged to make an occupation order. Section 33(7) provides:

If it appears to the court that the applicant or any relevant child is likely to suffer significant harm attributable to conduct of the respondent if an order under this section containing one or more of the provisions mentioned in subsection (3) is not made, the court shall make the order unless it appears to it that—

(a) the respondent or any relevant child is likely to suffer significant harm if the order is made; and

(b) the harm likely to be suffered by the respondent or child in that event is as great as, or

---

[211] See Law Commission (1992a: para 4.1).

[212] See Bird (1996a: para 3.3).

[213] Or has been threatened with exclusion (Bird 1996a: para 3.3).

[214] See Bird (1996a: para 3.3). See, eg, *G v G (Occupation Order: Conduct)* [2000] 2 FLR 36.

[215] S 33(10). Because home rights cease to exist when a marriage or civil partnership is terminated, a spouse or civil partner who is otherwise not entitled to occupy the home would then be restricted, as a non-entitled former spouse or civil partner, to a remedy under s 35. S 33(5) accordingly provides that an order made during the marriage or civil partnership may stipulate that the home rights are not brought to an end by termination of the marriage or civil partnership. The court may exercise its powers under subs (5) 'where it considers that in all the circumstances it is just and reasonable to do so' (s 33(8)). Normally, should the parties divorce or terminate their civil partnership, questions concerning the home will be finalised by means of a property adjustment order rather than under this jurisdiction (Bird 1996a: para 3.4). In relation to orders extending rights of occupation beyond the death of the other party, the Law Commission commented that, generally, a time limit would be appropriate (Law Commission 1992a: para 4.3).

greater than, the harm attributable to the conduct of the respondent which is likely to be suffered by the applicant or child if the order is not made.[216]

The 'balance of harm test' was designed to remedy the defects complained of in the old legislation.[217] That legislation, said the Law Commission, was 'unsatisfactory' in that the criteria for granting orders did not afford adequate protection to victims of violence and gave insufficient weight to the interests of children (Law Commission 1992a: para 4.23).

> In cases where the question of significant harm does not arise, the court would have power to make an order taking into account the ... factors set out above;[218] but, in cases where there is a likelihood of significant harm, this power becomes a duty ... . It is likely that a respondent threatened with ouster on account of his violence would be able to establish a degree of hardship (perhaps in terms of difficulty in finding or unsuitability of alternative accommodation or problems in getting to work). But he is unlikely to suffer significant harm, whereas his wife and children who are being subjected to his violence or abuse may very easily suffer harm if he remains in the house. In this way the court will be treating violence or other forms of abuse as deserving immediate relief, and will be directed to make an order where a risk of significant harm exists. (ibid: para 4.34)

Broadly speaking, the court has to balance the extent of the harm likely to result if the order is not granted against the extent of the harm likely to result if it is granted. If the applicant succeeds in showing significant harm and that it is attributable to the respondent's conduct, then the court must grant an order unless the respondent can show that the harm he (or a relevant child) will suffer as a result of an order being granted is equal to or greater than the harm to the applicant (or relevant child) if the order is not granted. If he can show this, the court has a discretion as to whether to grant the order and the case falls to be decided under section 33(6). [219]

Similarly, where the applicant cannot show significant harm or where she cannot show that the harm is attributable to the respondent's conduct, the court has a discretion whether to grant an order. In deciding whether to make an order, the court is required to have regard to of the factors enumerated in subsection (6):

> In deciding whether to exercise its powers under subsection (3) and (if so) in what manner, the court shall have regard to all the circumstances including—
>
> (a) the housing needs and housing resources of each of the parties and of any relevant child;[220]
> (b) the financial resources of each of the parties;[221]
> (c) the likely effect of any order, or of any decision by the court not to exercise its powers under

---

[216] The Act does not, however, restrict the court's discretion as to the type of order it makes.

[217] The Matrimonial Homes Act 1983. See *Richards v Richards* [1984] 1 AC 174.

[218] These factors are now contained in s 33(6)(a)–(c). Conduct was not included in the criteria recommended by the Law Commission.

[219] *Chalmers v Johns* [1999] 1 FLR 392, 396; *G v G (Occupation Order: Conduct)* [2000] 2 FLR 36, 41.

[220] In *G v J (Ouster Order)* [1993] 1 FLR 1008, 1018–19, Purchas J expressed the view that the court should not regard its task as solving a housing problem. However, the courts have in the past tended to be more ready to exclude a party who has alternative accommodation (see *Scott v Scott* [1992] 1 FLR 529). Moreover, an application by a wife might be more likely to be refused if the local authority has an obligation to rehouse her but not her husband. See also *Wooton v Wooton* [1984] FLR 871. However, the respondent's conduct may tip the balance in favour of an order despite his lack of alternative housing *(Thurley v Smith* [1984] FLR 875). But see *B v B (Occupation Order)* [1999] 1 FLR 715, where the interests of the abuser's child tipped the balance against an order.

[221] See *Baggot v Baggot* [1986] 1 FLR 377.

subsection (3), on the health, safety or well-being of the parties and of any relevant child;[222] and

(d) the conduct of the parties in relation to each other and otherwise.[223]

Applying the 'Balance of Harm Test'

'Significant harm' is a concept derived from the Children Act 1989.[224] While 'harm' is defined in both the Children Act 1989 and the Family Law Act 1996, neither statute contains a definition of 'significant'. The term has been interpreted in the context of the Children Act 1989 as 'considerable, noteworthy or important'[225] and it is appears that this definition is being applied in interpreting the Family Law Act 1996 too.[226] 'Harm' is defined in section 63(1) of the Family Law Act 1996 and a distinction is drawn between persons who are under and over the age of 18:

'harm'—

(a) in relation to a person who has reached the age of eighteen years, means ill-treatment or the impairment of health; and
(b) in relation to a child, means ill-treatment or the impairment of health or development;
  'health' includes physical or mental health;
  'ill-treatment' includes forms of ill-treatment which are not physical and, in relation to a child, includes sexual abuse.

Q Would sexual abuse of an adult constitute 'ill-treatment'?

In the case of the applicant, the harm must be attributable to the conduct[227] of the respondent, whereas the harm to the respondent that may be taken into account is 'harm in the widest sense, for example, the harm which might be suffered as a result of being evicted' (Bird 1996a: para 3.8). It appears that the harm suffered by an applicant or relevant child engendered by having to live in unsuitable accommodation after fleeing the violence of the respondent can be attributed to the respondent's conduct and will also be weighed in the balance.[228] However, in the light of the definition of harm, any upset or inconvenience to an applicant by, for instance, having to leave the home is unlikely to qualify as significant harm.

Once the court has assessed the harm to the applicant or relevant child it goes on to assess the harm to the respondent or relevant child. The court then has to consider whether the harm likely to be suffered by the respondent or relevant child if the order is granted

---

[222] See *O'Connell v O'Connell* (unreported 28 August 1998).

[223] See *Thurley v Smith* [1984] 1 FLR 875. But see *E v E (Ouster Order)* [1995] 1 FLR 224, where the court refused to exclude a husband from the home despite the fact that he had attempted to rape his wife. On the facts, it was decided that it would suffice to order that the wife should have exclusive use of a bedroom and that the husband should be prohibited from entering it. In *Scott v Scott* [1992] 1 FLR 529 it was held that, since an ouster would be the only way of preventing the husband from breaching a non-molestation order, it was correct to grant one.

[224] See ss 31 and 105 Children Act 1989.

[225] DoH (1991c: para 3.19); *Humberside County Council v B* [1993] 1 FLR 257, 263.

[226] *Chalmers v Johns* [1999] 1 FLR 392, 398.

[227] Conduct that is unintentional can cause harm within the meaning of the section. What matters is the effect of the conduct on the applicant or children rather than the intention of the respondent: *G v G (Occupation Order: Conduct)* [2000] 2 FLR 36, 40.

[228] *B v B (Occupation Order)* [1999] 1 FLR 715.

is equal to or greater than the harm likely to be sustained by the applicant or relevant child if it is not.

If it is found that it is the applicant who is likely to suffer the greater harm, the court is obliged to make an order. If not, the court has a discretion and will exercise this in the light of all the circumstances, including the specific matters referred to in section 33(6).

A 'Draconian' Order

Under the old legislation, courts were reluctant to exclude parties (usually men) from their homes, stressing the 'Draconian'[229] nature of such an order. In *Wiseman v Simpson*,[230] for example, the Court of Appeal declared that, although violence or molestation was not a prerequisite for making an ouster order, it was not just or reasonable to make such a Draconian order simply because the applicant had a greater need for accommodation.[231]

While the criteria in section 33(6) are somewhat broader than those applied previously, it appears that courts regard occupation orders in the same light as they did ousters—as drastic measures to be used sparingly. In *Chalmers v Johns*[232] Thorpe LJ described the new occupation order as 'Draconian' like its predecessors and continued, '[i]t remains an order that overrides proprietary rights and … it is an order that is only justified in exceptional circumstances'. What would qualify as exceptional is not clear (Humphries 2001: 544). However, the judgment in *G v G (Occupation Order: Conduct)*[233] seems to imply that little other than violence will suffice.[234] Upholding a decision to refuse an occupation order and confirming an order regulating shared occupation of the home, Thorpe LJ said:

> This was not a case in which the wife had suffered any violence at the hands of the husband. It has been said time and time again that orders of exclusion are draconian and only to be made in exceptional cases. Add to that the judge's assessment that the friction between the parties was only the product of their incompatible personalities and the heightened tensions that any family has to live with whilst the process of divorce and separation is current, and the judge's conclusion is plainly justified. (41)

And even if there has been violence, the court will not necessarily grant an order. In *B v B*[235] the wife was denied an occupation order. Kaganas (1999a) says that the wife was refused the order because she had fled the husband's violence, and was now safe, albeit in poor accommodation. This meant the court felt able to say that, because the child living with the husband would suffer harm if they had to leave the home, the order should not be granted. This outcome is criticised by Kaganas (1999a) because the court, in judging significant harm, did not take into account the violence the wife suffered before she left or the risk of violence should she return. *Chalmers v Johns* was also a case involving violence but was, in the view of Thorpe LJ, 'in the range of domestic violence a slight case' (397). Decisions, it seems, are being made in the same way that they were before

---

[229] See *Davis v Johnson* [1979] AC 264, 302–03. Indefinite exclusion of a sole owner from his property has been seen as particularly drastic. See *Wiseman v Simpson* [1988] 1 WLR 35, 44.

[230] [1988] 1 WLR 35.

[231] See also *Blackstock v Blackstock* [1991] Fam Law 415.

[232] [1999] 1 FLR 392, 397. See, for critical comment, Kaganas (1999a).

[233] [2000] 2 FLR 36.

[234] See also *Re Y (Children) (Occupation Order: Conduct)* [2000] 2 FLR 36.

[235] *B v B (Occupation Order)* [1999] 1 FLR 715.

the 1996 Act (Humphries 2001: 544). Burton (2008a: 25) comments that where there are divorce proceedings pending between the parties, the courts prefer not to make an occupation order. This, she says, is 'unfortunate' because 'violence can escalate at the point of separation'.

However, a recent judgment evidences a somewhat different approach from the earlier cases. In *G v G (Occupation Order)*[236] the husband was verbally abusive, domineering and controlling but not physically violent. The wife instituted divorce proceedings and a decree nisi was granted. The wife sought a non-molestation order and an occupation order under section 33(6). She claimed that the situation in the husband's ancestral family home where the parties were living separate lives was intolerable and stressful, but she did not argue that she or the children would suffer significant harm if an order were not granted. Instead she was asking the court to exercise its discretion to make an order. The husband was wealthy, he had alternative accommodation available, and he had failed to offer to make any arrangements for alternative accommodation for the wife and children, although she had agreed to move out of the home if he did offer her an alternative. The court below granted the order and the husband argued, on appeal, that it had not taken sufficient account of the seriousness of an occupation order. The court said that separation of the parties was necessary, that the seriousness of an order is greatest where the spouse against whom it is made has no alternative accommodation, that because the husband had alternative accommodation and was refusing to make any available to the wife and children, an order was appropriate; it was the only way of effecting a separation. The duration of his exclusion from the home was something under the control of the husband. The difference in this case, it seems, was the availability to the husband of alternative accommodation and the considerable resources he had to provide a home for himself as well as the wife and children. The duration of his exclusion would be as short as he chose to make it.

Non-entitled Former Spouse or Former Civil Partner

The category of 'associated persons' includes former spouses[237] and former civil partners.[238] The non-entitled applicant would have no recognised interest in the home and any home rights would have terminated when the marriage or civil partnership ended.[239] An application for an occupation order in these circumstances would be dealt with under section 35. That section makes provision for cases involving former spouses or former civil partners where one is entitled to occupy the home[240] and the other is not.

The court, in relation to non-entitled persons, has to engage in a two-stage decision-making process.[241] First, it has to decide whether the applicant should be granted 'occupation rights'.[242] If it decides in favour of the applicant, it then goes on to consider whether to make a regulatory order.

The first stage is dealt with under subsections (3) and (4). Before considering the possibility of a regulatory order, the court must make what is in effect a declaration that the

---

[236] [2009] EWCA Civ 976, [2011] 1 FLR 687.
[237] S 62(3)(a).
[238] S 62(3)(aa).
[239] S 33(5) can be used to avoid this happening. See above.
[240] It must have been, at any time, or have been intended to be their matrimonial or civil partnership home (s 35(1)(c)).
[241] In practice, the process may often be telescoped (Law Commission 1992a: para 4.18).
[242] See Law Commission (1992a: para 4.18).

applicant is entitled to occupy the home. If she is in occupation, the order must include provision giving her the right not to be evicted or excluded from the home or any part of it for the period specified in the order. It must also prohibit the respondent from excluding her.[243] If she is not in occupation, the order must give her the right to enter and occupy the home for the period specified and it must require the respondent to allow her to exercise that right.[244]

In deciding whether to make an order making provision of the kind mentioned in subsection (3) or (4), the court must, in terms of section 35(6), have regard to all the circumstances including:

(a) the housing needs and housing resources of each of the parties and of any relevant child;
(b) the financial resources of each of the parties;
(c) the likely effect of any order, or of any decision by the court not to exercise its powers under subsection (3) or (4), on the health, safety or well-being of the parties and of any relevant child;
(d) the conduct of the parties in relation to each other and otherwise;
(e) the length of time that has elapsed since the parties ceased to live together;
(f) the length of time that has elapsed since the marriage or civil partnership was dissolved or annulled; and
(g) the existence of any pending proceedings[245] between the parties—
  (i) for an order under section 23A or 24 of the Matrimonial Causes Act 1973 (property adjustment orders in connection with divorce proceedings etc);
  (ia) for a property adjustment order under Part 2 of Schedule 5 to the Civil Partnership Act 2004;
  (ii) for an order under paragraph 1(2)(d) or (e) of Schedule 1 to the Children Act 1989 (orders for financial relief against parents); or
  (iii) relating to the legal or beneficial ownership of the dwelling-house.

The court, if it decides to make an occupation rights order, must then go on to consider whether a regulatory order is appropriate. Under section 35(5), it has the power to make an order regulating the occupation of the house; prohibiting, suspending or restricting the exercise by the respondent of his right to occupy; requiring the respondent to vacate the home or part of it; or excluding the respondent from a defined area in which the home is situated.

Section 35(8) places an obligation on the court to make an order under subsection (5) in certain circumstances. Such an order is mandatory if it appears to the court that, unless provision is made under subsection (5), the applicant or a relevant child is likely to suffer significant harm attributable to the respondent's conduct. This obligation comes into being unless unless the harm suffered by the respondent or child as a result would be as great or greater.

If the court is not obliged to make an order under section 35(8), then, as under section 33, it still has the discretion to make one. In deciding whether to include a subsection (5) provision in its order, the court must have regard to all the circumstances including the matters referred to in subsection 6(a)–(e).[246]

---

[243] S 35(3).
[244] S 35(4).
[245] If an order settling the financial and property arrangements between the parties is to be made in the near future, the court is less likely to make an occupation order. See *Chalmers v Johns* [1999] 1 FLR 392; *G v G (Occupation Order: Conduct)* [2000] 2 FLR 36.
[246] S 35(7).

An order in favour of a former spouse of former civil partner, unlike one in favour of a spouse or civil partner, cannot exceed six months in duration. The reason for this appears to be that occupation remedies for non-entitled parties are seen as 'a relatively short term measure of protection, just to give sufficient time to find alternative accommodation or to await the outcome of property proceedings' (Law Commission 1992a: para 4.19). However, an order may be extended for further periods of up to six months each.[247]

Non-entitled Cohabitant or Former Cohabitant

Cohabitants and former cohabitants qualify as 'associated persons' in terms of section 62(3)(b). This section applies in cases where the parties are cohabitants or former cohabitants, and where one party is entitled to occupy the home[248] and the other is not. The provisions of section 36 are identical to those of section 35 in many ways. The two-stage process is common to both sections. The court must decide whether to give the applicant occupation rights[249] and then consider whether to make a regulatory order in terms of subsection (5). And in deciding whether to make provision for occupation rights under subsection (3) or (4) many of the matters that the court is directed to consider under section 36(6) are the same as those specified in section 35(6). The court must have regard to housing needs and resources[250] as well as financial[251] resources. It must consider the likely effects of its decision on the health, safety and well being of the parties and any relevant child;[252] the conduct of the parties;[253] the length of time that has elapsed since the parties lived together;[254] and the existence of pending proceedings between the parties.[255]

However, there are significant differences. First, section 36(6) also provides that the court must have regard to:

(e) the nature of the parties' relationship and in particular the level of commitment involved in it;
(f) the length of time during which they have cohabited;
(g) whether there are or have been any children who are children of both parties or for whom both parties have or have had parental responsibility.[256]

> **Q** Why should a person be more or less deserving of the right to occupy the home depending on the duration of the relationship, on whether the relationship was more or less committed or on whether the parties have had children together?

The second difference is that an order containing a subsection (5) provision is entirely within the court's discretion; there are no circumstances in which it is obliged to make one. The court is simply directed,[257] in exercising this discretion, to have regard to all the

---

[247] S 35(10).
[248] It must be the home in which they cohabit or have cohabited or intended to cohabit: s 36(1)(c).
[249] S 36(3) and (4).
[250] S 36(6)(a).
[251] S 36(6)(b).
[252] S 36(6)(c).
[253] S 36(6)(d).
[254] S 36(6)(h).
[255] S 36(6)(i).
[256] The wording suggests that children who have grown up are intended to be covered.
[257] In terms of s 36(7).

circumstances, including the factors listed in subsection 6(a)–(d), and to apply the balance of harm test.[258] There is no duty on the court to make an order even if the applicant or relevant child would suffer considerably more harm by its failure to do so than the respondent or child would suffer if it did make an order.

> **Q** Why is the need for an occupation order apparently less pressing in a case involving cohabitants or former cohabitants than in a case involving spouses/civil partners or former spouses/civil partners?

Finally, the duration of an order is limited to six months and it can be extended only once for up to six months.[259]

> **Q** Why is the duration of occupation orders in favour of cohabitants limited to a maximum of 12 months?

The legislation appears to be designed to offer protection more readily to those cohabitants who can produce evidence of commitment to the relationship. An applicant who has lived with the respondent for a long time or who has had children or shared parental responsibility with him would, it seems, find it easier to obtain an order than one who has not.

The effect of section 36(6)(e) is not clear. It might be seen in the same light as its predecessor, section 41, which was drafted in similar terms and has been repealed. That was, said Freeman (1996b: 83), 'an ideological statement' stemming from the *Daily Mail*-inspired opposition to the 1995 Family Homes and Domestic Violence Bill.[260] He doubted its significance in practice but expressed concern that cohabitants might be labelled uncommitted if, for example, they kept separate bank accounts.

Neither Party Entitled to Occupy

This situation could arise where, for example, the parties are squatters, where their right of occupation has been terminated,[261] where neither party wishes to assert a right to occupy or where such a right cannot be proved.[262] Section 37 deals with spouses/civil partners and former spouses/civil partners while section 38 deals with cohabitants and former cohabitants.

Both sections empower a court to make an order requiring the respondent to allow the applicant to enter and remain in the home[263] or part of it; regulating the occupation of the

---

[258] Contained in s 36(8).

[259] S 36(10). While a year may be sufficient time to find alternative accommodation in most cases, this limitation may prejudice a cohabitant with special needs for whom the home has been purpose-built or specially adapted (Murphy 1996: 849).

[260] A group of Conservative MPs opposed that Bill on the ground that it undermined marriage because, they said, it improved the position of cohabitants. As Freeman wryly comments, '[t]hat some of the provisions they identified had been the law since 1976 either escaped their attention or was deemed irrelevant' (Freeman 1996b: 4).

[261] See Bird (1996a: para 3.27).

[262] See Freeman (1996b: 78).

[263] In relation to spouses/civil partners or former spouses/civil partners it must be or have been the matrimonial/civil partnership home (ss 37(1)(a), 38(1)(a)). In relation to cohabitants or former cohabitants it must be the home in which they cohabit or have cohabited (s 38(1)(a)).

home; requiring the respondent to leave the home or part of it; or excluding the respondent from a defined area in which the home is situated.[264]

In deciding whether to make an order in cases involving spouses/civil partners or former spouses/civil partners, the court is required to apply sections 33(6) and (7).[265]

In deciding whether to exercise its powers in a case involving cohabitants, the court must have regard to all the circumstances including housing needs and resources, financial resources, the effect of its decision on the health, safety and well-being of those concerned and the conduct of the parties.[266] It is also required to apply the balance of harm test[267] but is not mandated to make any order.

An order under section 37 cannot be made for a period exceeding six months but may be extended for one or more periods of up to six months.[268] An order under section 38 may not exceed six months in duration but may be extended once for up to six months.[269]

Children

A 'relevant child' would have to be considered in applying any provisions, such as the balance of harm test, which make reference to such a child.[270]

A child might be able to apply for an order against a parent as they are 'associated persons'.[271] However, a child under the age of 16 would need the permission of the court. This would be granted only if she were adjudged to have sufficient understanding under section 43 to make the application and even if the court were satisfied that she does, it is still at liberty to refuse permission.[272]

Should a child[273] make an application for an occupation order, it is not at all clear from the legislation what criteria the court should apply in deciding whether to grant it. An occupation order is defined in section 39 as an order made under a number of specified sections, all but one of which refer to spouses/civil partners or cohabitants. The one exception refers to parties who are 'entitled' to occupy and, presumably, a child with, say, a beneficial interest in property would qualify. Other than that, the Act is silent on this matter. A court applying the Northern Ireland legislation,[274] the terms of which are similar to those of the Family Law Act 1996, held that since the child was not 'entitled' and did

---

[264] Ss 37(3) and 38(3).

[265] S 37(4).

[266] S 38(4).

[267] Contained in s 38(5).

[268] S 37(5).

[269] S 38(6).

[270] If an applicant is not eligible under the Family Law Act 1996 to apply for an occupation order, it is nevertheless possible to exclude a respondent to protect children's interests. It was held in *C v K (Inherent Powers: Exclusion Order)* [1996] 2 FLR 506 that the court's jurisdiction under s 37 of the Supreme Court Act 1981 or under s 38 of the County Courts Act 1984 can be invoked in support of the rights and duties conferred by a residence order. A person may be restrained from interfering with the exercise of parental responsibility of a person who has a residence order.

[271] S 62(4). A stepchild does not appear to qualify under this provision unless the stepparent has acquired parental responsibility.

[272] It is likely that the court will consider whether it would be more appropriate for the other parent to institute proceedings for a non-molestation order. This was considered necessary by a court interpreting the legislation applicable in Northern Ireland, the terms of which are similar to those of the Family Law Act 1966. See *Re Alwyn (Non-molestation Proceedings by a Child)* [2009] NI Fam 22; [2010] 1 FLR 1363.

[273] Whether under 16, with leave of the court, or between the ages of 16 and 18, as of right.

[274] Family Homes and Domestic Violence (Northern Ireland) Order 1998.

not fall within the categories of non-entitled applicants, his application had to be dismissed.[275]

In addition, the Children Act 1989[276] was amended by the 1996 Act to create a new power to include an exclusion requirement in an emergency protection order or an interim care order. This permits the removal from the home of a suspected abuser instead of the child. Exclusion requirements are considered in more detail in Chapter 14 below.

Applications by Third Parties

Should a victim of violence be unable to bring proceedings herself because, for example, she feels too vulnerable, there is provision for rules of court to prescribe persons or categories of persons who may act on her behalf. This provision had not yet been implemented at the time of writing and there is debate about whether this measure would help victims or further disempower them.[277] Most service providers, such as lawyers and refuge workers, interviewed by Burton thought action should not be permitted without the victim's consent (Burton 2008a: 50). But if this were a requirement, much of the benefit of third-party applications could be lost; the victim would have a measure of control of the case and so be open to intimidation and reprisals (ibid).

Ancillary Provisions

A court, when making an occupation order[278] or at any time after doing so, is empowered to make an ancillary order imposing obligations on either party regarding maintenance and repair of the property;[279] payment of rent, mortgage and other outgoings;[280] and the payment of what amounts to occupation rent to a party excluded from a property which he or she would otherwise have been entitled to occupy.[281] In addition, the court may grant either party possession of the furniture or other contents of the home.[282] However, it seems that there is no way to enforce an order made under section 40 for payment of money to a third person, such as a mortgagee. In *Nwogbe v Nwogbe*[283] the husband was ordered to pay the rent, water rates, council tax and certain arrears relating to the property. He failed to do this and the wife applied for his committal for contempt of court. The court held that it did not have the power to commit him to prison. Nor could it make an attachment of earnings order. The court remarked that this is a serious omission from the statute that required urgent attention but no change has yet been made in this respect.

---

[275] *Re Alwyn (Non-molestation Proceedings by a Child)* [2009] NI Fam 22; [2010] 1 FLR 1363.
[276] Ss 38A and 44A Children Act 1989.
[277] S 60 FLA 1996. See Burton (2008a: 48ff).
[278] Whether under ss 33, 35 or 36 (see s 40(1)).
[279] S 40(1)(a)(i).
[280] S 40(1)(a)(ii).
[281] S 40(1)(b).
[282] S 40(1)(c).
[283] [2000] 2 FLR 744.

Orders Without Notice[284]

Normally, an applicant must comply with rules of court specifying the notice to be given to the respondent of proceedings. The general rule is that a court should not make an order without giving those likely to be affected by it the opportunity to be heard. However, in some circumstances the court may grant an order without notice.[285] The situations in which this step might be necessary are, according to the Law Commission, where the remedy is needed urgently or where the applicant, although she may not need the order itself as a matter of urgency, is so frightened of the respondent that she needs protection in order to pursue her remedy.[286]

Prior to the Family Law Act 1996, it was clear that ex parte orders would be granted only in limited circumstances.[287] However, although under the new legislation the remedy of an order without notice remains discretionary, its wording leaves open the possibility that the courts could grant such orders more readily. Section 45(1) provides that both occupation and non-molestation orders may be made without notice (ex parte) where the court considers it 'just and convenient to do so'. In deciding whether to make such an order, the court must, in terms of section 45(2), have regard to all the circumstances including any risk of significant harm to the applicant or a relevant child, attributable to the respondent's conduct, if the order is not made immediately; whether, unless the order is made immediately, it is likely that the applicant will be deterred or prevented from proceeding; and whether there is reason to believe the respondent is evading service and the applicant or child will be prejudiced by delay. Barron maintained some years ago that occupation orders were not very often made without notice (Barron 2002: 7–8) but the figures for the county courts in 2009 show that about twice as many applications were received without notice as were received on notice (MOJ 2010b: table 2.8).

Enforcement

Breach of a court order constitutes contempt of court, punishable by imprisonment.[288] The court in *Hale v Tanner*[289] set out guidelines for dealing with such cases:

> (26) [T]hese cases have to come before the court on an application to commit … . Not surprisingly, therefore, the court is directing its mind to whether or not committal to prison is the appropriate order. But it does not follow from that that imprisonment is to be regarded as the automatic consequence of the breach of an order. Clearly it is not. There is, however, no principle that imprisonment is not to be imposed at the first occasion … . Nevertheless, it is a common practice, and usually appropriate in view of the sensitivity of the circumstances of these cases, to take some other course on the first occasion … .
>
> (29) [T]he length of the committal has to depend upon the court's objectives. There are two objectives always in contempt of court proceedings. One is to mark the court's disapproval of

---

[284] This term is used now although the Act still refers to ex parte orders.

[285] The potential difficulties of effecting service are described by Barron (1990: 22–23).

[286] Law Commission (1992a: paras 5.6 and 5.8).

[287] See *Ansah v Ansah* [1977] 2 WLR 760; Practice Note (Matrimonial Cause: Injunction) [1978] 1 WLR 925. The Law Commission noted that in practice, ex parte ouster orders were particularly rare (Law Commission 1992a: para 5.5).

[288] But see Burton (2008a) discussed below.

[289] [2000] 2 FLR 812.

the disobedience to its order. The other is to secure compliance with that order in the future. Thus, the seriousness of what has taken place is to be viewed in that light as well as for its own intrinsic gravity ... .

(36) An important part of the exercise is that the contemnor should understand[290] the importance of keeping court orders, of not breaking them and the likely consequences if they are so broken ... .

(38) It is rare, when one looks at the reported cases, to find sentences of 6 months' imprisonment in the context of much more serious breaches than took place in this case. One tends to find, even in cases of violence causing quite significant injury, a shorter sentence.

There are difficulties and delays involved in enforcing orders through civil contempt proceedings,[291] and the Family Law Act was framed to include significant reforms. First, it makes provision for greater use to be made of powers of arrest.[292] Secondly, it provides for the involvement of the police in enforcing orders even where there is no power of arrest.[293] Thirdly, it gives the courts the power to remand[294] and, if bail is granted, to require compliance with requirements considered necessary to prevent interference with witnesses or to prevent the obstruction of justice by other means.[295]

Power of Arrest

A power of arrest can be attached by the court to one or more provisions of an occupation order. If a power of arrest is attached, a constable may arrest a perpetrator without warrant if he or she has reasonable cause to suspect that that person is in breach of any provision to which the power is attached.[296] The respondent must be brought before the court within 24 hours of his arrest[297] and the court may punish him for contempt. The power of arrest serves the purpose of providing a short route to the power to commit for contempt of court and also has the effect of removing the abuser from the scene.[298]

The court is obliged to attach a power of arrest in certain circumstances:

47. **Arrest for breach of order**

(2) If—

(a) the court makes an occupation order; and
(b) it appears to the court that the respondent has used or threatened violence against the applicant or a relevant child.

it shall attach a power of arrest to one or more provisions of the order unless satisfied that in

---

[290] See, on capacity to understand, *P v P (Contempt of Court: Mental Capacity)* [1999] 2 FLR 897.

[291] See Women's National Commission (1985: para 108ff); Barron (2002: 8).

[292] Prior to the Family Law Act 1996, the courts were reluctant to attach powers of arrest. See *Lewis v Lewis* [1978] 1 All ER 729. They were normally limited to three months in duration: Practice Note (Domestic Violence: Power of Arrest) [1981] 1 WLR 27.

[293] In the past, those engaged in putting committal orders made by the High Court and the county court into effect were the officers of those civil courts, and they were not available outside working hours. It was only the magistrates' courts that could involve the police.

[294] S 47(7)(b) and (10). This power was previously restricted to magistrates' courts.

[295] S 47(12).

[296] S 47(6).

[297] S 47(7)(a).

[298] *Re H (Respondent Under 18: Power of Arrest)* [2001] 1 FLR 641.

all the circumstances of the case the applicant or child will be adequately protected without such a power of arrest.

It seems that courts may not be willing to interpret 'violence' as including emotional abuse[299] but it appears that any physical violence suffices to satisfy subsection 2(b).[300] If there is violence or a threat of violence, the court is required to attach a power of arrest unless satisfied that the applicant or relevant child would be adequately protected without one. If a power of arrest were attached, a copy of the occupation order to which the power of arrest is attached must be delivered to a local police station.[301]

There is a view that orders without a power of arrest are so difficult to enforce that they are 'virtually useless' (Barron 2002: 8). Nevertheless there are a number of situations in which no power of arrest is attached. First, the court retains complete discretion in cases that do not fall within section 47(2), such as those where there has been no actual or threatened violence. Secondly, a power of arrest will not be attached where, in terms of section 47(2), the court is satisfied that the applicant or child is adequately protected without one. Thirdly, in the case of orders made without notice, the presumption in favour of a power of arrest does not operate and the court's discretion is limited; it may make an order if violence has been used or threatened and there is a risk of significant harm, attributable to the conduct of the respondent, if the power of arrest is not attached immediately.[302] Fourthly, the power of arrest might be attached only to certain provisions of the order. Finally, it is not possible to attach a power of arrest to an undertaking[303] and the courts still appear to be accepting undertakings readily. However, the Act does provide that if a power of arrest is appropriate, the court cannot accept an undertaking instead of making an occupation order.[304] A new section 46(3A) was enacted by which breach of a non-molestation order was made an arrestable offence.[305] In terms of that provision, the court is not permitted to accept an undertaking instead of making a non-molestation order in any case where it appears to the court that the protection of an order carrying penalties for breach is appropriate.[306]

Barron (2002: 8) found that powers of arrest were 'by no means universally obtainable'. However they do seem to be granted in more than half of the cases where occupation orders are made.[307] If no power of arrest is attached, then, in the event of breach, the court is empowered to issue a warrant for arrest.[308]

---

[299] See Barron (2002: 8); Humphries (2001: 542).

[300] See Bird (1996a: para 5.3).

[301] R 10.10 of the Family Procedure Rules 2010/2955. Copies of non-molestation orders must also be delivered to the police station.

[302] S 47(3). The violence as well as the risk of significant harm must relate to the applicant or a relevant child.

[303] S 46(2). Barron (2002: 8) suggests that powers of arrest are not normally attached to ex parte (now without notice) orders. Arrest of a person before the order has been served on him may be unlawful and a breach of his human rights (Platt 2000: 907–08).

[304] S 46(3).

[305] See below.

[306] See below.

[307] In 2005 and 2006 the county courts attached powers of arrest to around 10 times more orders than the number of orders made without. From 2007 the proportion dropped and in 2009 there were 2,616 orders made with power s of arrest and 1587 without (MOJ 2010b: table 2.9). It may that courts are making non-molestation orders together with occupation orders in terms of s 42(4A). See below.

[308] Committal proceedings for contempt of court are also possible.

Warrant for Arrest

The court is empowered under section 47(8), on application, to issue a warrant of arrest if satisfied that the respondent has breached an order or an undertaking.[309] If a court does decide to issue a warrant of arrest, this would enable the court to involve the police in the enforcement process.

Offence of Breaching a Non-molestation Order

The difficulties of enforcing orders were noted by the government:

> [G]iven that the power of arrest is often only attached to specific parts of an order, police officers may be unclear whether they can arrest the respondent or not. Moreover, information on orders and powers of arrest is not recorded centrally, and the arrangements for passing such information between police forces can be inconsistent. If no power of arrest was attached, the victim has to apply to the civil court for an arrest warrant, which can put the victim at risk of further violence until the warrant is issued. (Home Office 2003: para 46)

In order to ameliorate the problems, common assault was made an offence[310] and the Family Law Act 1996 was amended by the insertion of a new section 42A to make breach of a non-molestation order an offence:

42A Offence of breaching non-molestation order

(1) A person who without reasonable excuse does anything that he is prohibited from doing by a non-molestation order is guilty of an offence.

(2) In the case of a non-molestation order made by virtue of section 45(1),[311] a person can be guilty of an offence under this section only in respect of conduct engaged in at a time when he was aware of the existence of the order.

(3) Where a person is convicted of an offence under this section in respect of any conduct, that conduct is not punishable as a contempt of court.

(4) A person cannot be convicted of an offence under this section in respect of any conduct which has been punished as a contempt of court.

The effect of this is that the police can arrest without a warrant or a power of arrest. Alternatively the victim can apply for a warrant of arrest for contempt of court.[312] The Act does not make breach of an occupation order an offence because a history of violence or molestation is not required for such an order (House of Lords Session 2003–04: para 26). However section 42(4A) is intended to ensure that those victims who need the protection that an immediate arrest offers will be given it. The court is required, when considering whether to make an occupation order, to consider whether it should exercise its power to make a non-molestation order on its own initiative. In addition, the Act

---

[309] S 46(4) provides that an undertaking is enforceable as if it were an order of court.
[310] Now covered by s 24 of the Police and Criminal Evidence Act.
[311] This deals with orders without notice.
[312] See House of Lords (Session 2003–04: paras 23–25). But see s 42A(3).

introduces a measure designed to prevent the court accepting an undertaking in a case where an arrest power is warranted. Section 46(3A) provides:

> The court shall not accept an undertaking under subsection (1) instead of making a non-molestation order in any case where it appears to the court that—
>
> (a) the respondent has used or threatened violence against the applicant or a relevant child; and
> (b) for the protection of the applicant or child it is necessary to make a non-molestation order so that any breach may be punishable under section 42A.

According to Burton, the criminalisation of breaches of non-molestation orders shows that domestic violence is seen as a serious matter and it also opened up a new range of sentencing options to the courts, including sending an offender to a perpetrator programme (Burton 2008a: 53).

Attention has also been directed at changing the sentencing practices of the courts. The Sentencing Guidelines Council published *Overarching Principles. Domestic Violence* to provide sentencing guidance. The document states:

> This guideline makes clear that offences committed in a domestic context should be regarded as being no less serious than offences committed in a non-domestic context. Indeed, because an offence has been committed in a domestic context, there are likely to be aggravating factors present that make it more serious. (Sentencing Guidelines Council 2006a: i)

Courts may take into account the history of the relationship. Aggravating factors include the abuse of trust and power, although these factors will be of less relevance when the parties have been separated for a long time. Other aggravating factors are the impact on children; a proven history of violence or threats in a domestic setting; the use of contact with a child to instigate an offence; the fact that the victim is forced to leave home; and a history of breaching orders. The court may mitigate the sentence in some cases where the victim genuinely wants the relationship to continue but, generally, it is the seriousness of the offence and not the victim's wishes that dictates the sentence. Mitigating factors include good character and also provocation. The inclusion of provocation leaves open the possibility that courts may reduce a sentence if they consider that a man has endured excessive 'nagging' from his partner (Burton 2008a: 64).

Sentencing guidelines have also been published which are specifically directed at breach of non-molestation orders under section 42A of the Family Law Act 1996 and breach of restraining orders under the Protection from Harassment Act 1997 (Sentencing Guidelines Council 2006b). Aggravating factors include the vulnerability of the victim; the impact on children; a proven history of violence or threats; the use of contact with children to perpetrate the abuse; and the fact that a victim is forced to leave the home. The mitigating circumstances listed are that there has been a long period of compliance or the victim initiated the contact. Custody is the starting point in cases where violence has been used.[313]

Q The changes to policies within the criminal justice system and the reform of the legislation governing the civil law appear to be intended to increase protection for victims of abuse. How do you reconcile these changes with the changes

---

[313] For an example of the application of the guidelines, see *Attorney General's Reference (No 80 of 2009); Also known as R v Singh Moore (Harpal)* [2010] EWCA Crim 470.

designed to encourage mediation on divorce (see Chapter 15 below) and the emphasis on contact with fathers and on disciplining the 'implacably hostile' mother in contact cases (see Chapter 10 above)?

Evaluating the Law

Researchers have sought to evaluate the Family Law Act and the results of studies carried out in the early years of its operation suggest qualified approval. Burton (2008a: 39ff) reports on her earlier research written up in 2002 and for the purposes of which service-providers were questioned. They said that it was relatively easy to get orders in cases of physical abuse, but not in other cases. In particular, solicitors advising victims were telling them they needed to prove physical abuse to get a remedy. And the general perception among solicitors was that it was difficult to get an occupation order unless there was evidence of severe violence, and almost impossible to get an occupation order at all without notice.[314] Enforcement was also a problem; service-providers were of the view that the police were not using their powers of arrest properly and that, on occasion, they adjudicated on incidents, dismissing them as 'too trivial to warrant action' (ibid: 41). The courts did not treat breaches seriously and punishments often took the form of fines. If imprisonment was used, usually only for repeated breaches, the sentences were for short terms. In another study, conducted among domestic violence workers (Barron 2002), the majority of those surveyed thought that the 1996 Act had improved protection (ibid: 5). However, the general view was that orders are only effective if the perpetrator has some respect for the law and if the police are prepared to enforce the order (ibid: 9). Powers of arrest are seen to be crucial to effectiveness.[315]

These conclusions are mirrored in Humphreys and Thiara's research. They reported that the orders available under the civil law were found to be helpful in many cases in their sample:

The [quantitative] data suggest that there was a group of women who found protection orders effective. In fact, over one-third (36%) of those who used protection orders said that they were very helpful and the abuse stopped. A further 39% said that they were of some help; that although they were breached, the abuse may have been less or they felt more protected … .

There is evidence in both the quantitative and the qualitative data that a significant group of women are finding effective (or some) protection using civil remedies. A total of 73% of this sample of women said that they would apply for an order if they needed one in the future, though many (60% who answered the question) said that they would have preferred a third party to take the order on their behalf to relieve them of the dangers and responsibilities of invoking legal proceedings against their partner or ex-partner … .

[H]owever … for those women who were suffering chronic post-separation violence, civil protection orders had little impact. Over a third of the women (36%) completing the question-naire found that abuse was continuing. Twenty five per cent of those who used orders found them of no help; the abuse continued and police or the courts were unhelpful in acting upon breaches. These women experienced themselves to be outside protection, a finding mirrored in other research which indicates significant disillusionment with the effectiveness of orders … .

Women who were unable to access orders also failed to gain protection. This included

---

[314] However, the success rate of without notice applications does not seem very low. See DCA (2006: table 5.9).

[315] See Bossy and Coleman (2000: para 3.3).

women who found them too expensive, who lacked knowledge of the orders, who were afraid to take court proceedings for fear of making the abuse worse, and whose immigration status precluded them from access. Interestingly, the data on the use of non-molestation orders shows that in spite of significant improvements to protection orders under the Family Law Act, 1996 ... there has not been an increase in the actual number of civil protection orders granted under the legislation ... . The increasing financial cost of legal services is posited as a significant factor inhibiting use.[316] (Humphreys and Thiara 2003: 203–05, references omitted)

Humphreys and Thiara concluded that:

The effectiveness of protection orders for some women suggests that there is a group of men who respond to cultural norms and the legislative framework and who do not want to be seen to step outside the law. The shame brought to the family or the impact on employment provide significant restraining factors. More assertive action on breaches could impact relatively quickly on making more of these orders effective It is also important to recognise that all the women in this study had the support of outreach services and that they therefore had access to information, advocacy and on-going support. ... [I]t is difficult in the extreme for women to take legal action and give evidence about violence and abuse without support. (ibid: 209)

The authors went on to consider the law in general and its effect on determined abusers:

[A] smaller group of chronic and serious offenders were unresponsive to normative frameworks. 'Brushes' with the law which result in being charged with minor offences, cautions, binding over or short custodial sentences had no effect and in fact served to reinforce the abuser's belief that there are no effective constraints or sanction on his behaviour. They can increase the dangers to women, who will be seen to have 'transgressed' by having called the police or given evidence against the abuser. Moreover poor and ineffective action from law enforcement and prosecution services may serve to confirm a woman's belief that she is outside help and, therefore, has no option other than to seek to appease the abuser. (ibid: 210)

Whether the most recent changes in the law have had the effect of increasing protection for victims is open to question. Hester et al (2008: 18) found that in the short period after implementation covered by their study, there did not appear to be an overall increase in the number of arrests for common assault. In addition, there appeared to be a decrease in the number of applications for non-molestation orders. However, the majority of victims' advocates said the criminalisation of breaches 'encouraged more women to report breaches' (ibid: 20). Victims were generally in favour of the new law and some saw it as having the potential to force the police to 'do something' (ibid: 23, 28).

His Honour Judge Platt (2008: 643) and Burton (2008b) report a steep decline in the number of applications for non-molestation orders from 2007 when section 42A was implemented.[317] Both suggest that the criminalisation of breach of a non-molestation order may have affected victims' willingness to apply for an order. However, they do not entirely dismiss other possible explanations.[318] His Honour Judge Platt (2008: 643) speculates that improvements in the criminal justice response to domestic violence may be leading to a move away from the civil courts. Burton suggests that the explanation may

---

[316] Ibid: para 3.4.
[317] See also Platt (2008: 643). However, the total number of applications for domestic violence remedies increased from 2008 to 2009 and the number of non-molestation applications increased by 10% in that period (MOJ 2010b: 52)
[318] See also Burton (2009).

lie in the quality of the advice victims are receiving. She says there is evidence that some solicitors who do not specialise in domestic violence cases 'give inappropriate advice or unsympathetic treatment' to victims (Burton 2008b: 4). In addition some women may be deterred for seeking orders because they do not see them as effective or because of concerns about cost (ibid).

Reviewing the research, Burton observes:

> [N]ow that there are criminal penalties for breach, respondents may be more inclined to contest applications, which might either put victims off making applications and/or result in fewer orders being made. Victims of domestic abuse want the abuse to stop, they do not necessarily want their partner criminalised. It has been argued that criminalisation reduces victims' choices and is disempowering because, for example, victims might be concerned that the CPS will prosecute breaches against their wishes.

She goes on to suggest that, even if those interviewed by Hester et al (2008) are correct that section 42A is encouraging the reporting of breaches, this may not help victims:

> This will only work if victims believe that the police and CPS take breaches of non-molestation orders seriously. Victims interviewed by Hester et al had variable experiences of the police response to breaches; some saying the police were unsure about the scope of the powers and unwilling to make arrests, others reporting the police were responding well to the breach (but that new assault charges arising out of the breach were not being rigorously pursued by the CPS). It is possible that victims may be less willing to pursue non-molestation orders, not so much because they fear that prosecutions will take place against their wishes, but because they are unable to get the criminal justice agencies to pursue a prosecution for breach and are left with an order that they cannot enforce themselves. ... As yet there is no reliable empirical evidence on the police and CPS response to breaches, but the Home Affairs Select Committee on domestic violence received anecdotal evidence that the police are using cautions rather than prosecuting breach; a practice it condemned. The lack of empirical evidence suggests that the implementation needs to be kept under review. (Burton 2008b: 16–17, references omitted)

Platt also points to deficiencies in the way in which the criminal justice system deals with cases of breach. There is no mechanism for informing the police and the CPS of the evidence upon which the original injunction was granted. What may appear to be a minor and isolated incident could be part of a much more serious pattern of which they are unaware. Wrong charging decisions and decisions to caution result (Platt 2008: 644). Charging decisions are made with inadequate information and a failure to appreciate the risk posed by the defendant can lead to the defendant being bailed by magistrates to return to the family home occupied by the victim (ibid: 646). And the fact that the accused has a right to trial by jury leads to significant delays, giving him time to subject the victim to emotional blackmail. In addition, the lapse of time makes it more likely that a victim, who wants to get on with her life, will make a withdrawal statement (ibid*)*.

XIV. A CO-ORDINATED RESPONSE—FURTHER REFORM

Humphreys and Thiara suggested that, while the law has an important part to play, a co-ordinated response with community support, civil protection and criminal justice is needed (Humphreys and Thiara 2003: 210). Some indication of what might be included in

such a response can be seen in the priorities enumerated by the domestic violence survivors who participated in an internet consultation (Bossy and Coleman 2000). They made
it clear that they wanted domestic violence to be treated seriously by the criminal justice
system. They also wanted changes made to the law relating to contact with children to
ensure that women and children were not endangered post-separation.[319] In addition to
legal measures, they wanted more publicity and information to be made available about
sources of support. Finally, they wanted better access to accommodation as well as more
support services in the form of refuges, outreach services and advocacy.

Steps were taken by the Labour government to promote a more co-ordinated response:

Early identification and intervention

Raising awareness of domestic violence with a wide range of practitioners and providing appropriate training and tools is key to early identification and intervention. During this year routine
enquiry about domestic violence when taking a social history in antenatal clinics, mental health
services and 22 accident and emergency departments was rolled out … .

New materials were launched for schools and for young people to raise awareness of forced
marriage … .

Work also began on developing guidance on sex and relationships education as part of the
Personal, Social, Health Education and the Government invested in the expansion of parent
support advisors to support families across a range of issues including domestic violence. …

Building capacity within the domestic violence sector

… In 2007–08 the Supporting People Programme provided over £64.5m of housing related
support services for women at risk of domestic violence … .

The Forced Marriage Unit continued to provide advice and support … . There continued to be
a significant level of cross-Government activity including a series of honour-based violence
roadshows … .

Improving the criminal justice response to domestic violence

Improving the criminal justice response to domestic violence can have a significant impact on
achieving protection for victims and on bringing perpetrators to justice. The Specialist Domestic
Violence Court (SDVC) programme continued to expand and by the end of March there were
122 SDVCs … .

The Crown Prosecution Service met its target of 72% for successful prosecutions and the
number of unsuccessful outcomes in domestic violence cases fell significantly, alongside a
reduction in cases that have been discontinued. A new training programme was developed and
the domestic violence Policy and Guidance on Prosecuting Cases of Domestic Violence refreshed,
accompanied by a new victim and witness leaflet. … A significant achievement for the Police
was the development and adoption by ACPO of the Domestic Abuse, Stalking and Harassment
and Honour-Based Violence (DASH) risk assessment model. A Domestic Violence Enforcement
Campaign was launched on 16 December in 10 force areas and a national TV campaign ran at
the same time. …

Supporting victims through the criminal justice system and managing perpetrators

Providing specialist support to victims and enabling them access to a range of services can have

---

[319] See further Chapter 10 above.

a profound effect on their feelings of safety and engagement with the criminal justice system. Independent Domestic Violence Advisers (IDVAs) are trained specialists whose goal is the safety of victims. Their focus is to provide a service to victims who are at high risk of harm; addressing their safety needs and helping them to manage the risks that they face. Delivery of accredited training for IDVAs continues to be delivered by the Coordinated Action Against Domestic Abuse (CAADA).

A Multi-Agency Risk Assessment Conference (MARAC) is a multi-agency meeting which has the safety of high risk victims of domestic violence as its focus. The number of MARACs increased ... to over 200 by the end of March 2009. (Home Office 2009: Executive Summary)

Q Can you identify the 'causes' of domestic violence that are apparently accepted by the government in adopting some of these measures?

Domestic Violence Protection Notices and Orders

A new initiative is being piloted at the time of writing. The Home Affairs Committee recommended the introduction of orders which allow the police to remove the perpetrator from the home for a specified period (Home Department 2008: para 85). This, it said, should be used in conjunction with sanctuary schemes (ibid: para 86). The Home Office reports that, currently, domestic violence protection orders are being piloted,[320] allowing the police, and subsequently the court, to ban, for a limited period, alleged abusers from returning to the home. It is notable that, while both the police and the courts must consider the opinion of the person they are acting to protect, the notice and the subsequent order can be made without that person's consent. These new measures might be effective in giving victims time to consider their options without their having to consider the consequences of arrest.

Section 24 of the Crime and Security Act 2010 empowers an authorising officer to issue a Domestic Violence Protection Notice (DVPN):

(2) A DVPN may be issued to a person ('P') aged 18 years or over if the authorising officer has reasonable grounds for believing that—

(a) P has been violent towards, or has threatened violence towards, an associated person, and
(b) the issue of the DVPN is necessary to protect that person from violence or a threat of violence by P.

(3) Before issuing a DVPN, the authorising officer must, in particular, consider—

(a) the welfare of any person under the age of 18 whose interests the officer considers relevant to the issuing of the DVPN (whether or not that person is an associated person),
(b) the opinion of the person for whose protection the DVPN would be issued as to the issuing of the DVPN,
(c) any representations made by P as to the issuing of the DVPN, and
(d) in the case of provision included by virtue of subsection (8), the opinion of any other associated person who lives in the premises to which the provision would relate.

(4) The authorising officer must take reasonable steps to discover the opinions mentioned in subsection (3).

---

[320] See Home Office (undated) *Domestic Violence Protection Notices and Orders*. The pilots began on 30 June 2011.

(5) But the authorising officer may issue a DVPN in circumstances where the person for whose protection it is issued does not consent to the issuing of the DVPN.

(6) A DVPN must contain provision to prohibit P from molesting the person for whose protection it is issued.

(7) Provision required to be included by virtue of subsection (6) may be expressed so as to refer to molestation in general, to particular acts of molestation, or to both.

(8) If P lives in premises which are also lived in by a person for whose protection the DVPN is issued, the DVPN may also contain provision—

(a) to prohibit P from evicting or excluding from the premises the person for whose protection the DVPN is issued,
(b) to prohibit P from entering the premises,
(c) to require P to leave the premises, or
(d) to prohibit P from coming within such distance of the premises as may be specified in the DVPN.

(9) An 'associated person' means a person who is associated with P within the meaning of section 62 of the Family Law Act 1996.

A constable must apply to the magistrates' court for a Domestic Violence Protection Order within 48 hours and the DVPN remains in force until the application is determined. A constable may arrest without warrant a person whom she/he has reasonable grounds to believe is in breach of a DVPN.[321]

28 Conditions for and contents of a domestic violence protection order

(1) The court may make a DVPO if two conditions are met.

(2) The first condition is that the court is satisfied on the balance of probabilities that P has been violent towards, or has threatened violence towards, an associated person.

(3) The second condition is that the court thinks that making the DVPO is necessary to protect that person from violence or a threat of violence by P.

(4) Before making a DVPO, the court must, in particular, consider—

(a) the welfare of any person under the age of 18 whose interests the court considers relevant to the making of the DVPO (whether or not that person is an associated person), and
(b) any opinion of which the court is made aware—
    (i) of the person for whose protection the DVPO would be made, and
    (ii) in the case of provision included by virtue of subsection (8), of any other associated person who lives in the premises to which the provision would relate.

(5) But the court may make a DVPO in circumstances where the person for whose protection it is made does not consent to the making of the DVPO.

(6) A DVPO must contain provision to prohibit P from molesting the person for whose protection it is made.

(7) Provision required to be included by virtue of subsection (6) may be expressed so as to refer to molestation in general, to particular acts of molestation, or to both.

[321] S 25.

(8) If P lives in premises which are also lived in by a person for whose protection the DVPO is made, the DVPO may also contain provision—

(a) to prohibit P from evicting or excluding from the premises the person for whose protection the DVPO is made,

(b) to prohibit P from entering the premises,

(c) to require P to leave the premises, or

(d) to prohibit P from coming within such distance of the premises as may be specified in the DVPO.

(9) A DVPO must state that a constable may arrest P without warrant if the constable has reasonable grounds for believing that P is in breach of the DVPO.

(10) A DVPO may be in force for—

(a) no fewer than 14 days beginning with the day on which it is made, and

(b) no more than 28 days beginning with that day.

(11) A DVPO must state the period for which it is to be in force.

XV. FORCED MARRIAGE

In recent years concern has begun to grow about what is now perceived to be a problem warranting the attention of the law: forced marriage. Forced marriage is not the same as arranged marriage, which is considered acceptable. Forced marriage, by contrast, is abusive. It can involve physical, sexual, psychological or financial abuse (Kazimirski et al 2009: para 1.1). The majority of forced marriages involve a female victim and about one-third of cases handled by the Forced Marriage Unit involve victims under the age of 18 (ibid: para 1.1). Lord Lester, who introduced the private members' bill that became the Forced Marriage (Civil Protection) Act 2007, said:

> The serious social evil which the Bill seeks to combat and remedy is the forcing of children and young adults to marry against their will. It gives rise to gross abuses of human rights especially affecting children and young people of either sex within our British Asian communities and elsewhere. It involves inhuman and degrading treatment and punishment of those who resist coercion, even their murder. It is a form of domestic violence and there is a direct link between forced marriages and honour killings.[322]

The 2007 Act amended the Family Law Act and Part IVA was introduced, modelled on Part IV.

Forced marriages are voidable because of lack of consent.[323] However, the new statutory provisions are designed to protect, by means of a civil order,[324] a person from being

---

[322] House of Lords, Hansard 26 Jan 2007, Col 1319.

[323] Where the applicant cannot rely on s 12C MCA 1973, the court can declare that the marriage is not valid under its inherent jurisdiction (*Re P (Forced Marriage)* [2011] EWHC 3467 (Fam); [2011] 1 FLR 2016; see also *P v H*, Annex 1 to the judgment in *Re P*).

[324] Criminalisation was considered undesirable because it would force the issue underground, leaving victims isolated. Also it would prevent family reconciliation and some victims would be deterred from seeking help if their families might be subject to criminal charges (House of Lords, Hansard 10 May 2007, col GC 231).

forced into marriage or a person who has already been forced into marriage. The marriage need not be legally binding but could, for example, be a religious ceremony.[325]

63A Forced marriage protection orders

(1) The court may make an order for the purposes of protecting—

(a) a person from being forced into a marriage or from any attempt to be forced into a marriage; or

(b) a person who has been forced into a marriage.

(2) In deciding whether to exercise its powers under this section and, if so, in what manner, the court must have regard to all the circumstances including the need to secure the health, safety and well-being of the person to be protected.

(3) In ascertaining that person's well-being, the court must, in particular, have such regard to the person's wishes and feelings (so far as they are reasonably ascertainable) as the court considers appropriate in the light of the person's age and understanding.

(4) For the purposes of this Part a person ('A') is forced into a marriage if another person ('B') forces A to enter into a marriage (whether with B or another person) without A's free and full consent.

(5) For the purposes of subsection (4) it does not matter whether the conduct of B which forces A to enter into a marriage is directed against A, B or another person.

(6) In this Part—

'force' includes coerce by threats or other psychological means (and related expressions are to be read accordingly); and
'forced marriage protection order' means an order under this section.

An order can be formulated to deal with whatever circumstances are before the court; it may contain whatever terms are considered appropriate.[326] These terms can relate to conduct within and/or outside England and Wales. They can relate to more than one person and can bind any persons who 'force or attempt to force, or may force or attempt to force, a person to enter into a marriage' as well as anyone 'involved'.[327] The statute gives a non-exhaustive list of activities that could be classified as involvement:

(3) For the purposes of subsection (2) examples of involvement in other respects are—

(a) aiding, abetting, counselling, procuring, encouraging or assisting another person to force, or to attempt to force, a person to enter into a marriage; or

(b) conspiring to force, or to attempt to force, a person to enter into a marriage.

An application for an order may be made in family proceedings or as a free-standing application and an order can be made by the court on its own initiative when hearing another matter.[328] An application may be made as of right by the person protected by the order or by 'a relevant third party'.[329] And, unlike section 60, on which it is modelled, the

---

[325] S 63S Family Law Act 1996.
[326] S 63B(1).
[327] S 63B(2).
[328] S 63C(6).
[329] S 63C(2).

third-party provision has been given effect: local authorities have been designated relevant third parties.[330] Local authorities do not, unlike other third parties,[331] need the leave of the court to apply. Orders may be made without notice on grounds similar to those governing the orders in Part IV.[332] The court can accept an undertaking instead of making an order but not if a power of arrest is appropriate.[333] A power of arrest must be attached if the court 'considers that the respondent has used or threatened violence against the person being protected or otherwise in connection with the matters being dealt with by the order'[334] unless it considers that the person will be adequately protected without one.[335]. The court is not obliged to attach a power of arrest on an application made without notice but may do so if it considers that the respondent has used or threatened violence and that there is a risk of significant harm to a person, attributable to conduct of the respondent, if the power of arrest is not attached.[336] If a power of arrest is not attached a warrant of arrest may be issued for contempt of court in the event of a breach.[337] It is not only the person protected who may apply for a warrant but also an 'interested party', which may be a local authority or, with permission, any other person.[338]

What is perhaps notable about the forced marriage legislation is the possibility of third-party applications as well as the possibility of enforcement by third parties. Although the court has to take into account the victim's wishes in deciding whether to make an order, the victim's consent is not required for proceedings to be instituted, for an order to be made or for an order to be enforced. This may reflect the concern of the legislature for the victims who appear to be predominantly young and who are often coerced by family members and may not be in a position to assert their will. In some cases, the victim may have been taken out of the country and so will not be in a position to institute proceedings.

XVI. FAMILY PRIVACY REVISITED

The law, and increasingly government policy, clearly countenance intervention in the family and domestic violence is now a matter of public concern. Yet commentators have observed that implementation of both law and policy has remained marked by a persisting reluctance to interfere or to interfere decisively. This is something that the Law Commission has referred to in the past with concern; it remarked that legal remedies can be undermined by the way in which the law is implemented in practice; women may be deterred from proceeding and the law can be made ineffective if the reactions of those working in the area are 'affected by particular perceptions of male and female roles or an ambivalence about the propriety of legal or police intervention in the family' (Law Commission 1992a: para 2.8).

Some of this reluctance to take domestic violence seriously may be attributable to a

---

[330] Family Law Act 1996 (Forced Marriage) (Relevant Third Party) Order 2009.
[331] S 63C(3) Family Law Act 1996.
[332] S 63D.
[333] S 63D.
[334] S 63H(1)(b).
[335] S 63H(2).
[336] S 63H(3)–(4).
[337] S 63J.
[338] S 63J.

continuing perception of the family as private. Schneider asserts that the 'rhetoric of privacy has masked inequality and subordination' (Schneider 1994: 39) and continues:[339]

> The rationale of privacy legitimates and supports violence against women; woman abuse reveals the violence of privacy. Privacy justifies the refusal of the state to intervene, of judges to issue restraining orders,[340] of neighbours and friends to intervene or to call the police, of communities to confront the problem. (ibid: 53)

But, she says, there are aspects of the concept of privacy that abused women may not wish to relinquish. While they want to be free of abuse, they also want the freedom to choose whether to continue with or end their intimate relationships (ibid: 53). Similarly, it has been argued that women should not be compelled to testify against their wishes[341] and that third-party applications should not be made possible without the victim's consent.[342] At present, however, women who do not go through with legal proceedings attract criticism. The question often asked is why the woman does not simply leave. Yet not all women seeking help want to leave (Stanko et al 1998: 43).

> Mahoney (1994: 59) contends that the preoccupation with exit from the relationship ignores the dangers and difficulties associated with leaving; it assumes that leaving is both possible and will bring safety. On the contrary, she says, the violence may continue as part of an attempt to reassert control over the woman. Moreover for women to redefine their loved ones as abusers is a difficult decision, particularly if there are children; the welfare of children is widely believed to be bound up in their relationships with their fathers. To many women, the best course appears to be to seek to improve the relationship with their partners. Mandatory participation in legal proceedings or discounting victims' wishes can, it is argued, be coercive and have the effect of disempowering or even revictimising the women concerned.[343]

So, while it is widely thought that women who seek help from outside agencies should not be denied it, feminist writing brings into question the desirability of intervening against the victim's wishes. This approach, it might be suggested, may not be appropriate in cases of serious violence where the public interest demands the intervention of the criminal law. Stanko refers to the variations of violence in arguing that the law should provide a flexible range of resources for abused women. It appears to be in this context that she contends that the law should leave to those women the decision as to whether and to what extent the abuse should become a matter for public concern:

> It is essential that we begin to explore the variations and nuances of men's violence to women. ... [M]en's dangerousness varies. ... [T]his demands flexible services to women at various stages of exiting from violence. It means that we take seriously the hold of emotional attachments (Ellis and DeKeseredy (1997) call this loyalty/love) and be willing to work with and through these attachments without losing patience with women for not leaving. Moreover, we must promote a variety of mechanisms that support women's own voices, which guide them and us through that crucial and dangerous stage of separation. (Stanko 1997: 634).

---

[339] See also Pahl (1985c: 191).
[340] The US equivalent of injunctions.
[341] See Ellison (2003: 767–68).
[342] See Burton (2003: 146–47); Barron (2002: 10).
[343] See Ellison (2003: 767–68); Burton (2003: 146–47).

XVII. HOUSING

Often, victims of abuse who lack resources flee the home to stay with friends or family or in a refuge. Although the government denied the allegation made by the Home Affairs Committee that there is a 'desperate shortage' of refuge provisions, it did agree to commission research into the matter (Home Department 2008: para 55).

Attention has also been paid to the provision of more long-term accommodation. Some women may not wish to return home even if the abuser is removed because they fear that the abuse will continue as long as their abusers know where they are. There are sanctuary schemes designed help victims stay in their homes if they wish to do so, provided it is safe and the perpetrator has left. These schemes also help to prevent homelessness but concerns have been expressed that they may be used to save costs in cases where the victim would be safer if rehoused.[344]

> The main feature of a scheme is the creation of a 'sanctuary room', providing a safe room or sanctuary from where victims can call and wait for the arrival of the police. Additional security can also be provided, eg, locks on windows and doors, gated security to the outside of a property, fire hammers, fire blankets and emergency lighting. Sanctuary schemes are implemented by LAs [local authorities], in partnership with the police, the Fire and Rescue Service and a specialist domestic abuse service, with support provided throughout the process.
>
> (ACPO, NPIA 2008: para 5.4.6)

For those women with limited financial resources who do not want to return home, or for whom it is not safe to do so, the only way of securing accommodation may be through the homelessness legislation. A person can apply under the Housing Act 1996 to the local housing authority for accommodation if she is eligible.[345] Provided she can show that she is unintentionally homeless and that she is in priority need, the authority has a duty to house her.[346] She will qualify as homeless if she has nowhere to stay.[347] Section 175(3) provides that a 'person shall not be treated as having accommodation unless it is accommodation which it would be reasonable for him to continue to occupy'. Section 177 states:

177.— Whether it is reasonable to continue to occupy accommodation.

(1) It is not reasonable for a person to continue to occupy accommodation if it is probable that this will lead to domestic violence or other violence against him, or against—

(a) person who normally resides with him as a member of his family, or

(b) any other person

Hence a person who has fled from a violent relationship is likely to be found unintentionally homeless because she could not reasonably have been expected to remain in the home.[348]

---

[344] Harris-Short and Miles (2007; online update 2009: para 4.5.3).
[345] See Chapter 5 above for a fuller discussion of housing.
[346] S 193 Housing Act 1996.
[347] See s 175 Housing Act 1996.
[348] See s 191 Housing Act 1996. But see *R (on the application of Hassan) v Croydon LBC* (2009) 12 *JHL* D56–57. There the court found that the applicant had been subjected to domestic violence but that this was not the reason she left home. She was therefore intentionally homeless.

An issue that has arisen, however, is what is meant by domestic violence. *The Homelessness Code of Guidance for Local Authorities* says:

> Section 177(1A) provides that violence means violence from another person or threats of violence from another person which are likely to be carried out. Domestic violence is violence from a person who is associated with the victim and also includes threats of violence which are likely to be carried out. Domestic violence is not confined to instances within the home but extends to violence outside the home. (DfCLG 2006: para 8.19)

The concept of domestic violence has been interpreted widely in a recent case, where the Supreme Court rejected the narrow definition previously used in housing cases. In *Yemshaw v Hounslow London Borough Council (Secretary of State for Communities and Local Government and another intervening)*[349] the Supreme Court referred to the broad definition of domestic violence adopted by the Home Office (2005) and continued:

> 27 'Violence' is a word very similar to the word 'family'. It is not a term of art. It is capable of bearing several meanings and applying to many different types of behaviour. These can change and develop over time. There is no comprehensive definition of the kind of conduct which it involves in the Housing Act 1996: the definition is directed towards the people involved. The essential question ... is whether an updated meaning is consistent with the statutory purpose ... . In this case the purpose is to ensure that a person is not obliged to remain living in a home where she, her children or other members of her household are at risk of harm. A further purpose is that the victim of domestic violence has a real choice between remaining in her home and seeking protection from the criminal or civil law and leaving to begin a new life elsewhere.

> 28 That being the case, it seems clear to me that, whatever may have been the position in 1977, the general understanding of the harm which intimate partners or other family members may do to one another has moved on. The purpose of the legislation would be achieved if the term 'domestic violence' were interpreted in the same sense in which it is used by Sir Mark Potter P, the President of the Family Division, in his [Practice Direction] suitably adapted to the forward-looking context of sections 177(1) and 198(2) of the Housing Act 1996: '"Domestic violence" includes physical violence, threatening or intimidating behaviour and any other form of abuse which, directly or indirectly, may give rise to the risk of harm.'

> 34 ... It has been recognised for a long time now that it is dangerous to ignore what may appear to some to be relatively trivial forms of physical violence. In the domestic context it is common for assaults to escalate from what seems trivial at first. ... But of course, that is not every case. Isolated or minor acts of physical violence in the past will not necessarily give rise to a probability of their happening again in the future. This is the limiting factor. Sections 177 and 198 are concerned with future risk, not with the past.

> 36 ... Was this, in reality, simply a case of marriage breakdown in which the claimant was not genuinely in fear of her husband; or was it a classic case of domestic abuse, in which one spouse puts the other in fear through the constant denial of freedom and of money for essentials, through the denigration of her personality, such that she genuinely fears that he may take her children away from her however unrealistic this may appear to an objective outsider? This is not to apply a subjective test ... . The test is always the view of the objective outsider but applied to the particular facts, circumstances and personalities of the people involved.

---

[349] [2011] UKSC 3; [2011] 1 WLR 433.

In addition to being homeless, the applicant has to show priority need to activate the local authority's duty to house her. A pregnant woman and a person who has a dependent child living with her, or who has a child who could reasonably be expected to live with her, are classified as having priority need.[350] Persons who qualify as vulnerable are also in priority need.[351] A person may be vulnerable as a result of having to stop occupying accommodation 'because of violence from another person or threats of violence from another person which are likely to be carried out' (DfCLG 2006: para 10.2(ix)). What matters is the probability of violence 'and not actions which the applicant could take (such as injunctions against the perpetrators)' (DfCLG 2006: para 10.28).

> 10.13. *It is a matter of judgement whether the applicant's circumstances make him or her vulnerable. When determining whether an applicant in any of the categories set out in paragraph 10.12 is vulnerable, the local authority should consider whether, when homeless, the applicant would be less able to fend for him/herself than an ordinary homeless person so that he or she would suffer injury or detriment, in circumstances where a less vulnerable person would be able to cope without harmful effects.* (DfCLG 2006, emphasis in original)

> 10.29. In considering whether applicants are vulnerable as a result of leaving accommodation because of violence or threats of violence likely to be carried out, a housing authority may wish to take into account the following factors:
>
> (i) the nature of the violence or threats of violence (there may have been a single but significant incident or a number of incidents over an extended period of time which have had a cumulative effect);
> (ii) the impact and likely effects of the violence or threats of violence on the applicant's current and future well being;
> (iii) whether the applicant has any existing support networks, particularly by way of family or friends. (ibid)

If a person cannot show priority need, she may still seek accommodation under the local authority's normal allocation scheme.[352]

Reform of the system of allocating social housing is now being considered. The Localism Bill 2010–11 currently before Parliament gives local authorities more discretion to decide who should be eligible for social housing.[353] However, they will continue to be required to afford 'reasonable preference' to vulnerable groups (DfCLG 2010: para 4.11; DfCLG 2011: para 1.16).[354] There are no plans to change the homelessness priority need groups (DfCLG 2010: para 6.10; DfCLG 2011: paras 4.34-5). What is proposed is that local authorities be permitted to bring their homelessness duty to an end by offering rented accommodation in the private rented sector without the applicant's prior consent (DfCLG 2010: para 6.11; but see DfCLG 2011: para 6.11).[355]

---

[350] DfCLG (2006: para 10.2). See also s 189(1) Housing Act 1996 and the Homelessness (Priority Need for Accommodation) (England) Order 2002.

[351] S 189(1)(c).

[352] See s 167 Housing Act 1996. See also s 166A to be inserted—see cl 128 Localism Bill 2010–11.

[353] See s 160ZA Housing Act 1996 to be inserted—see cl 127 Localism Bill 2010–11.

[354] It is also proposed that there be a power to pass regulations if the need arises (DfCLG 2010: para 4.11).

[355] Cl 193 Housing Act 1996 as amended by s 129 Localism Bill 2010–11.

XVIII. CONCLUSION

Abuse of women, through the efforts of the early 'moral entrepreneurs', and more recently, feminists, has come to be constructed as a social problem[356] demanding a response from government and from various public agencies. The nineteenth-century campaigns began the process by making the phenomenon of wife abuse visible and by challenging long-held convictions about the appropriate status of women; for change to be possible, women had to be seen not simply as adjuncts to the patriarch but as meriting protection in their own right. In the twentieth and twenty-first centuries, the process has also been characterised by an emphasis on gender inequality, and researchers and commentators have sought to reconceptualise domestic violence as an abuse of power and an expression of possessiveness. The efforts of the reformers have been successful, in that abuse in intimate relationships is now less likely to be seen by the police and by the courts as an excusable lapse. Moreover, the explanation of domestic violence in terms of power and control has now gained widespread acceptance. However, feminist efforts to establish gender inequality as the 'cause' of the problem have been less successful; it is still primarily conceived of as a problem of individuals. Despite the new emphasis on education, the 'solution', for government, the police and professionals in the field, therefore lies primarily in the treatment and/or punishment of those individuals rather than in (significantly less manageable) far-reaching social change.

Perhaps one of the most crucial factors in the construction of domestic violence as a social problem has been the challenge to the conception of the family as a private haven. Although this is still the most potent image of the family, the home is now also perceived as a potentially dangerous place, especially for women and children, and, as such, it is not immune to outside intervention.

Yet there is a tendency to trivialise domestic violence and there is a failure to understand its dynamics. In addition, it is possible that the ideal of family privacy has continued to inhibit those charged with implementing measures to protect women. The civil and criminal justice systems in particular have come in for criticism for failing to help those seeking protection from domestic violence. In response to these criticisms, policies have changed and the law has been reformed to increase levels of intervention and to toughen the measures available to combat domestic violence. Yet some changes, such as the introduction of pro-arrest and no-drop policies, as well as the criminalisation of non-molestation orders, have provoked yet more criticism. These policies, it is said, do little to support women or to protect them, and at the same time they disempower victims. Women who bring violence into the public arena, sometimes because seeking outside intervention is the only way they can attempt to renegotiate their relationships, are unable to retreat easily back into privacy.

To refuse to intervene and to withhold help from abused women clearly leaves them exposed to risk. In addition, non-intervention is symbolically damaging for all women. Yet to force victims into the public arena of the criminal law or to insist that they leave their abuser before taking them seriously can also have damaging consequences. It is argued that when and the extent to which violence is made public should be a decision for the woman and not for outside agencies. Whether to invoke the criminal law or civil law or both should be the woman's choice. And women who choose to remain with their

---

[356] See, eg, Dobash and Dobash (1992: 285 and 288).

violent partners should be able to receive safe, confidential advice and support.[357] What is needed are mechanisms that make it easier and safer for abused women who wish to do so to obtain advice, to seek legal remedies and to access support networks and housing.[358] These needs have to some extent been addressed by government initiatives. However it remains a matter for concern that the new policies, as well as the law, will not always be implemented in practice.

FURTHER READING

M BARNISH, *Domestic Violence: A Literature Review* (London, HM Inspectorate of Probation, 2004).

J BARRON, *Five Years On: A Review of Legal Protection from Domestic Violence* (Bristol, WAFE, 2002).

J BOSSY and S COLEMAN, *Womenspeak. Parliamentary Domestic Violence Internet Consultation: Report of the Main Findings* (Bristol, WAFE, 2000).

M BURTON, 'Third Party Applications for Protection Orders in England and Wales: Service Provider's Views on Implementing Section 60 of the Family Law Act 1996' (2003) 25 *JSW&FL* 137.

——, *Legal Responses to Domestic Violence* (London, Routledge-Cavendish, 2008).

——, *Domestic Abuse. Literature Review* (Leicester: University of Leicester, 2008) www.legalservices. gov.uk/docs/fains_and_mediation/DomesticAbuseLiteratureReview.pdf (accesed 24 January 2011).

RE DOBASH, 'Domestic Violence: Arrest, Prosecution and Reducing Violence' (2003) 2 *Criminology & Public Policy* 313.

RE DOBASH and RP DOBASH, The Politics and Policies of Responding to Violence Against Women' in J Hanmer et al (eds), *Home Truths About Domestic Violence: Feminist Influences on Policy and Practice: A Reader* (London, Routledge, 2000).

——, 'Women's Violence to Men in Intimate Relationships. Working on a Puzzle' (2004) 44 *Brit J Criminol* 324.

J HARRIS, *An Evaluation of the Use and Effectiveness of the Protection from Harassment Act 1997*: Home Office Research Study 203 (London, Home Office, 2000).

M HESTER, *Who Does What to Whom? Gender and Domestic Violence Perpetrators* (Bristol, University of Bristol in association with the Northern Rock Foundation, 2009).

M HESTER et al, *Domestic Violence: Making it Through the Criminal Justice System* (University of Sunderland, Northern Rock Foundation and International Centre for the Study of Violence and Abuse, 2003).

C HOYLE and A SANDERS, 'Police Response to Domestic Violence: From Victim Choice to Victim Empowerment?' (2000) 40 *Brit J Criminol* 14.

C HUMPHREYS and R THIARA, *Routes to Safety: Protection Issues Facing Abused Women and Children and the Role of Outreach Services* (Bristol, WAFE, 2002).

——, 'Neither Justice nor Protection: Women's Experiences of Post-separation Violence' (2003) 25 *JSWFL* 195.

M JOHNSON, *A Typology of Domestic Violence: Intimate Terrorism, Violent Resistance and Situational Couple Violence* (Hanover, NH, University Press of New England, 2008).

F KAGANAS, 'Domestic Violence, Men's Groups and the Equivalence Argument' in A Diduck and K O'Donovan (eds), *Feminist Perspectives on Family Law* (Abingdon, Routledge-Cavendish, 2006)

R LEWIS, RE DOBASH and K CAVANAGH, 'Law's Progressive Potential: The Value of Engagement with the Law for Domestic Violence' (2001) 10 *Social and Legal Studies* 105.

M MADDEN DEMPSEY, 'What Counts as Domestic Violence—A Conceptual Analysis' (2006) 12 *William and Mary Journal of Women and the Law* 301.

---

[357] See Women's Aid (2003: 25).
[358] See Morley and Mullender (1992: 271).

——, *Prosecuting Domestic Violence. A Philosophical Analysis* (Oxford, Oxford University Press, 2009).

K PARADINE and J WILKINSON, *Research and Literature Review: Protection and Accountability: The Reporting, Investigation and Prosecution of Domestic Violence Cases* (London, Her Majesty's Crown Prosecution Service Inspectorate (HMCPSI), Her Majesty's Inspectorate of Constabulary (HMIC), Centrex, 2004).

N STANLEY, P MILLER, H RICHARDSON FOSTER and G THOMSON, *Children and Families Experiencing Domestic Violence: Police and Children's Social Services' Responses* (London, NSPCC, 2010).

13

A Public or Private Matter? Child Abuse

I. INTRODUCTION

Child abuse has come to be seen as a social problem[1] demanding the attention of governments and legislators and justifying state intervention in what is regarded as the private realm of the family. Yet this was not always so. It was not until the nineteenth century that the ill-treatment of children within the family became a matter of public concern. It appears that there were two preconditions for this development. First, perceptions of children had to change, and, secondly, there had to be a change in attitudes to family privacy. It was in the eighteenth century that the image of the child as vulnerable and in need of protection began to emerge. And even then, family privacy and parental, specifically paternal, authority largely shielded the family from outside intervention. It was not until the late nineteenth century that the protection of children came to be regarded as a legitimate reason for intervening in the family. Since then, the ill-treatment of children within the family has been regarded as a matter of public concern. However, the focus of concern has changed over the years; definitions of the harm from which children have been thought to need protection have been shaped by the nature of specific campaigns and by the state of knowledge about children at particular times.

In this chapter, we trace the way in which child abuse has come to be constructed as a social problem so serious that state intervention is seen not only as permissible but, indeed, as a moral and legal imperative. We then explore definitions of child abuse which have come to be accepted as justifying intervention in the family. We go on to examine the response of the state to the problem of child abuse and the roles of professionals and the law in regulating the family. Finally, we consider contemporary moves to shift the

---

[1] Official statistics tend to underestimate the prevalence of abuse. A study published by the NSPCC (Cawson et al 2000) was devised with the aid of the CTS (see Chapter 12 above). A quarter of the sample had experienced at least one form of violent behaviour such as being hit with an implement, punched, kicked, knocked down, shaken or deliberately burned or scalded. 78% of the violent treatment occurred at home, most often at the hands of mothers and fathers. One-fifth reported that they had suffered injury on at least one occasion (Cawson et al 2000: 8). 7% were assessed as having been seriously abused and 14% as experiencing intermediate abuse (ibid: 9). 6% were assessed as suffering serious absence of care with 9% experiencing intermediate absence of care (ibid: 11). 6% were considered to have experienced emotional abuse (ibid: 15). Sexual abuse by relatives affected about 4% (ibid: 17). See also Creighton (2004). The NSPCC estimates that an average of 79 children are killed every year in England and Wales and that in 78% of child homicides in 2000/01, the parents were the main suspects (Creighton and Tissier 2003 p 2). More recently the NSPCC (2011) has reported that more than 1 in 8 young people between the ages of 11 and 17 have been severely maltreated by a parent or guardian; 1 in 20 have experienced contact sexual abuse; 1 in 10 have been severely neglected. The way in which prevalence is gauged depends on the definitions of abuse used. Not all children who experience what could be classed as abuse are within the child protection system and so do not appear in official statistics.

focus of attention from child protection to the prevention of abuse. While this chapter focuses mainly on the theme of the public/private divide, it also raises issues of welfare, addressing questions of what is considered harmful to children.

II. THE CONSTRUCTION OF SOCIAL PROBLEMS

According to social construction theorists, social conditions do not in themselves constitute social problems. Rather, these conditions may or may not be constructed as problems. Behaviour is categorised as deviant and as presenting a social problem when policymakers perceive it as transgressing public morality or as a threat to social order, and as necessitating social action to control it.[2] The process which leads to this outcome is described by Manning:

> [T]he promotion of social conditions as social problems typically occurs through perceived grievances being organised into claims which various groups bring to the state. The legitimacy of those claims is heavily influenced by mass media interpretations of public opinion, and the priorities and interests of government departments in terms of existing policies, perceived voter preference and major power blocks. (Manning 1985a: 22)

Manning's description is a contemporary one but, as we shall see, the process of identifying certain conditions as problems, endeavouring to have them generally accepted as such and campaigning for change pre-dates the mass media age. Crucial to this process have been the efforts of individuals or groups of people, those whom Becker refers to as 'moral entrepreneurs':

> Deviance—in the sense … of publicly labeled wrongdoing—is always the result of enterprise. Before any act can be viewed as deviant, and before any class of people can be labeled and treated as outsiders for committing the act, someone must have made the rule which defines the act as deviant. Rules are not made automatically. Even though a practice may be harmful in an objective sense to the group in which it occurs, the harm needs to be discovered and pointed out. People must be made to feel that something ought to be done about it. Someone must call the public's attention to these matters, supply the push necessary to get things done, and direct such energies as are aroused in the proper direction to get the rule created. (Becker 1963: 162)[3]

The emergence of child abuse as a social problem has traditionally been traced to the efforts of campaigners who, at different times, have included philanthropists,[4] professional groupings[5] and feminist activists. Their success, however, cannot be fully explained out-

---

[2] See Gordon (1989: 27). See also Gusfield (1975).

[3] The activities of an enterprising individual or group 'can properly be called "moral enterprise" for what they are enterprising about is the creation of a new fragment of the moral constitution of society, its code of right and wrong' (Becker 1963: 145). Becker's analysis stresses the crusading spirit of 'moral entrepreneurs', suggesting that they typically believe that 'their mission is a holy one' (ibid: 148) and that they tend to be members of a dominant class seeking to improve the status of those 'beneath' them (ibid: 149). However, Manning's analysis, based on the work of Spector and Kitsuse, does not imply missionary zeal and refers to the role of pressure groups other than elites (Manning 1985a: 19). While Becker's analysis is apt in relation to nineteenth-century philanthropists, Manning's better describes twentieth-century developments.

[4] See Simey (1951); Mowat (1961).

[5] An account of the involvement of professional groupings in the construction of social problems is offered by Dickson (1968). He argues that agencies have a tendency to extend their power so that their enterprise arises

side the context of changes in political and economic conditions. In particular, their messages would, it seems, have gone unheeded without significant changes in perceptions of children and of the family.

III. CONSTRUCTIONS OF CHILDHOOD[6]

Parton states that '[v]alues are crucial ... in whether and how a situation is defined as a problem' (Parton 1985: 6). According to Pinchbeck and Hewitt, one of the significant changes in our values over the last two centuries has been in our attitude to children (Pinchbeck and Hewitt 1973: 347).

The fact that, for centuries, children lacked statutory protection from abuse, is, they say, explicable in the light of the nature of parent–child relationships in pre-industrial England. Children were regarded as the property of their parents. They were seen as tainted with original sin and harsh discipline and punishment were considered necessary to correct waywardness.[7] Moreover, from about the age of 7, children were gradually initiated into the world of adult work (Cunningham 1995: 79) and, to that extent, it appears that, as Pinchbeck and Hewitt suggest, they were seen as 'little adults' (Pinchbeck and Hewitt 1973: 348).

The French historian Ariès argues that our concept of childhood is a modern invention emanating from seventeenth-century Europe; there was no notion of childhood in medieval times:

> [I]n medieval society, the idea of childhood did not exist; this is not to suggest that children were neglected, forsaken or despised. The idea of childhood is not to be confused with affection for children: it corresponds to an awareness of the particular nature of childhood, that particular nature which distinguishes the child from the adult ... . In medieval society this awareness was lacking. That is why, as soon as the child could live without the constant solicitude of his mother, his nanny or his cradle-rocker, he belonged to adult society. (Ariès 1962: 128)

Ariès is criticised for drawing on material that documents the, probably unrepresentative, life of Louis XIII, and because his research was confined to records compiled exclusively by male authors who may have had little contact with children.[8] A more fundamental criticism is that, as Ariès himself acknowledges, childhood has been recognised through the ages as a separate stage of human existence.[9] Instead of interpreting his evidence to show that there was no concept of childhood in the Middle Ages, he should, says Archard (1993: 19), have concluded only that what was lacking was our concept of childhood. It is our concept of childhood that demands as a morally appropriate way of treating children that there be a separation of adult and children's worlds (ibid: 20).[10]

---

from bureaucratic pressures. Both Becker's and Dickson's theories are referred to in the context of child abuse by Parton (1985: 6–9). He discusses both the crusading efforts of philanthropists in the nineteenth century and the efforts of groupings within the medical profession to secure their professional status during the twentieth century. See further below.

[6] See further, Piper (2008: ch 2).
[7] See also Cunningham (1995: 55).
[8] See Freeman (1983: 12).
[9] See Cunningham (1995: 32).
[10] See generally Archard (1993: chs 2 and 3).

It was during the eighteenth century that this separation began to occur. There was a shift 'from a prime focus on the spiritual health of the child to a concern for the development of the individual child' (Cunningham 1995: 62). The key to this shift, says Cunningham, was the secularisation of attitudes to childhood and children and the decline in belief in original sin (ibid: 61).[11] The writings of Locke, Rousseau and the Romantics in turn contributed to an emphasis on the individuality of the child and to a belief that childhood should be a happy, carefree time.[12] According to Cunningham, the introduction of compulsory schooling in the late nineteenth century was crucial in transforming the meanings attached to childhood by removing children, in principle at least, from the workforce (ibid: 17).[13] Most importantly, mass attendance at school made children 'visible' to medical professionals, sociologists and philanthropic workers, who saw that the school could be used as a 'laboratory' to produce 'scientific' knowledge (Hendrick 2003: 22). The Child Study movement, formed in the 1890s, subjected childhood to 'scientific' scrutiny, using the techniques of natural history and spearheading the use of 'observation, classification and experiment' (ibid: 23). It popularised the notion that the child's conception of the world differed from that of adults and that there were marked stages in normal development (ibid). During the nineteenth century, says Hendrick, the child was widely perceived as characterised by 'ignorance, incapacity and innocence' (ibid: 21).[14] Helping children became a priority among charitable organisations: 'Because children were thought to be innocent ... they could easily be victimised. Because children were thought to be malleable ... they could be molded into good citizens' (Gordon 1989: 29).

And as 'scientific' knowledge grew, doctors and psychologists were beginning to define children 'in an apparently "scientific" manner, thereby making it difficult for lay persons to dispute their findings' (Hendrick 2003: 23). This, perhaps, marked the ascendancy of expertise in the arena of child protection which is so evident today.

IV. CHILD CONCERN AND THE ROLE OF THE STATE

Protection through 'Tutelage'

The protection of family members regarded as vulnerable to cruelty and neglect presents the liberal state with a problem. The question it faces is 'how child-rearing can be made into a matter for public concern and its quality can be monitored without destroying the ideal of the family as a counterweight to state power, a domain of voluntary, self-regulating actions' (Dingwall et al 1983: 214–15).[15] As Dingwall et al point out, one possible solution to the abuse of power within the family is to give to vulnerable members greater access to outside agencies. This solution preserves family autonomy because privacy is

---

[11] But see Cox (1996: 203).

[12] See Cunningham (1995: 62ff).

[13] Schools, family and youth organisations such as the Scouts and the Boys Brigade were seen as the 'proper' places for children to take them off the street. This 'privatising' of children became a part of the idea of childhood in the nineteenth century (Prout 2005: 36).

[14] Rex and Wendy Stainton Rogers (1992) in their discussion of the contemporary construction of children as vulnerable and dependent challenge the assumption that this is necessarily evidence of progress; it was the understanding of children as different from adults that made corporal punishment of children acceptable at a time when it had become unthinkable for adults.

[15] See further Archard (1993: 9) and Chapter 1 above.

breached only at the behest of a family member. However, while some abused women may actively seek help from outside agencies, access to outside agencies is a particularly ineffective means of protecting children. In many cases, protection from parental abuse can be gained only by means of surveillance of the family by outside agencies (ibid: 216).

According to the French writer Donzelot (1980), drawing on Foucault's theoretical ideas, one way in which this has been achieved has been through the operation of what he refers to as 'the tutelary complex'. He observes that during the nineteenth century, there was a transition from government *of* the family to government *through* the family (Donzelot 1980: 92). Philanthropy, he says, was a deliberately depoliticised strategy for establishing public services without undermining the liberal definition of the state. Families were used as agents for conveying social norms into the private sphere of the home. Philanthropic organisations penetrated the family in the name of hygienic and educative protection. By means of the technique of moralisation, charity was made available, but only to those families whose shortcomings were not judged to be the result of moral failure. Through the process of normalisation, families were inculcated with approved norms by means of education and, sometimes, legislation. Complaints, usually by women against men, facilitated entry into the home. Tutelage, involving the monitoring and surveillance of families to assess levels of compliance, made possible coercive intervention. The family's automomy was preserved only if it observed approved norms; resistance or non-compliance were seen as evidence of deviance.[16]

Philanthropic bodies gradually lost their principal role in 'civilising' the family and, according to Cunningham, the state began to take on itself the primary responsibility for child-saving at the end of the nineteenth century (Cunningham 1995: 137). Philanthropy was largely replaced by a new series of professions[17] that emerged in the late nineteenth century and early twentieth centuries, including the 'psy' professions[18] and social work. Increasingly, the regulation of the family has fallen to those with professional expertise 'underpinned by the power of a claim to truth' (Rose 1987: 71) and backed up by legal sanctions. This sphere of activity, termed 'the social' by Donzelot, was seen as enabling the liberal state to maintain its legitimacy while protecting family members.

Q In the light of Donzelot's analysis, to what extent can the family be said to constitute a private domain?

The 'Cruelty Act': Protecting Children or Protecting Society?

The first major statute regulating the care of children in their families was the Prevention of Cruelty to and Protection of Children Act 1889. Prior to this, the state had intervened little in the family which was seen as being under the rule of the patriarch.[19]

Why intervention became a moral and a political possibility is not entirely clear. According to Cunningham, the reasons included 'concern about population levels; worry about the level of "civilization" of the masses; desire to breed a race capable of competing in the 20th century', as well as concern for the children themselves (Cunningham 1995: 137). He observes that the industrial revolution first brought the 'new ideology of child-

---

[16] See further Dingwall et al (1983: 215–17).
[17] However, many professionals work for charitable bodies.
[18] Such as psychiatry.
[19] But see, on Poor Law children, Frost and Stein (1989: 21–24).

hood' into play in policy-making (ibid: 138), an ideology at the heart of which lay a commitment to the view that childhood was significant in determining the kind of adult the child would become and that childhood attracted its own rights and privileges (ibid: 41).

Initially, however, the focus was not on abuse within the family, but on those visible 'children without a childhood':[20] children who were working in factories and in mines.[21] These new workplaces were seen as presenting not only physical but moral dangers; they were seen as sources of 'deprivation and depravity' (Piper 1999a: 37). Pursuant to scandals around baby farming, legislation was also passed against infanticide.[22] This, as Piper (1999a: 42–43) observes, was directed against single, unmarried mothers and commercial nurses. The reluctance to breach the privacy of the 'normal' family continued. In 1871, for instance, Lord Shaftesbury, a leading philanthropist, condemned the evils of child abuse. Yet he stated that they were 'of so private, internal and domestic a character as to be beyond the reach of legislation'.[23] To change this view, 'it was necessary to show how little of the sacredness of family life existed among the more depraved, and the manner in which a man exercised his right to do what he would with his own'.[24]

Explanations of the concern about child cruelty that emerged during the late nineteenth century have centred on the social anxiety engendered by social instability.[25] This was linked to disquiet about the urban masses (Piper 1999a: 46). In particular, it was linked to ideas about the socialisation of children. Children who grew up in urban slums were seen as a potential threat to the moral order; they could not but grow up unhealthy and depraved.[26] Intervention in the family came to be seen 'as a lesser evil' than the risk that 'the entire moral framework of society [might be undermined] ... unless selected families were regulated' (ibid).[27]

Societies for the prevention of cruelty to children were set up locally in the 1880s and the National Society for the Prevention of Cruelty to Children (NSPCC) was formed in 1889. The NSPCC, says Hendrick:

> was of vital importance in reshaping public opinion away from the view that the family was inviolate, towards a view which recognised that if the ideal of the family were to be realised, then a certain amount of interference by outside bodies was essential for the purposes of education and, occasionally, prosecution. (Hendrick 2003: 32)

Child protection legislation, modelled on the earlier legislation against cruelty to animals, was promoted by the NSPCC and enacted.[28] The Prevention of Cruelty to and Protection of Children Act 1889 reflects, say Eekelaar et al, primarily moral rather than welfarist concerns: 'Child and animal cruelty were morally corrupting and for such moral delinquency parents were to lose their rights to their children' (Eekelaar et al 1982: 74). The

---

[20] This phrase was used by Douglas Jerrold in 1840 to describe factory children. Quoted by Cunningham (1995: 144).

[21] See, eg, the Health and Morals of Apprentices Act 1802.

[22] Infant Life Protection Act 1872.

[23] Quoted in Pinchbeck and Hewitt (1973: 622).

[24] Gertrude Tuckwell (1894), *The State and Its Children*, p 127, quoted by Pinchbeck and Hewitt (1973: 623).

[25] But see also Hendrick (2003: 24–25).

[26] See Hendrick (2003: 8–9, 25).

[27] See also Hendrick (2003: 24–25).

[28] See ibid: 26.

1889 Poor Law (Children) Act in turn gave guardians authority to assume parental rights over Poor Law children.[29]

> Q Do the analyses discussed above suggest that the primary justification for intervention in the family was seen as the protection of children from abuse or the protection of society from moral disintegration?

Shifting Patterns of Concern

Child cruelty and neglect were now firmly on the political agenda but, in the ensuing years, policies oscillated between prevention and protection, between working with families and rescuing children from their families.

The turn of the century saw concern focusing not only on urban degeneration and child-saving but also on a different aspect of the national interest. This change stemmed largely from anxieties about the fitness of the working class for manual labour and military service; in particular, the Boer War revealed general unfitness among the recruits. The new priorities included all-round efficiency, public health, nutrition, hygiene and responsible parenthood (Hendrick 2003: 15, 68–69). Children were seen as potential assets of the nation and so state welfare provision for children increased. The state became more interventionist, providing support in the form of school meals[30] for example, while also taking on an active role in rescuing children subject to cruelty. The Prevention of Cruelty to Children Act 1904 and the 1908 Children Act gave local authorities powers to remove children from their families.[31]

There emerged a child guidance movement and, as psychological and psychiatric interest in children grew, treatment of children and their families came to be seen as crucial in problem cases; when parents failed to provide the 'correct environment', 'mental disturbance' was thought to ensue (Hendrick 2003: 107). By 1933, the legislators' gaze had shifted once again to delinquency and this continued to occupy their attention for many years. The Children and Young Persons Act 1933 was concerned more with young offenders than with the victims of cruelty or neglect (Parton 1985: 39; Hendrick 2003: 119). Both offenders and non-offenders were thought to need treatment (Hendrick 2003: 116) and those children who were considered to be at risk were usually removed from the family.

That policy changed with the Second World War. The evacuation of children from the cities revealed to many the scale of deprivation of urban children, and it was argued that this was too widespread to be dealt with by removing children from their families. 'Problem' families could be helped to provide better childcare (Hendrick 2003: 140). Further, the dislocation of wartime led to concern that families should be together. The 1948 Children Act gave expression to this new approach.[32] Prevention, rather than rescue, became the focal point. Yet concern continued to centre on delinquency rather than protection.[33]

During the 1950s through to the 1970s, coercive intervention was seen as a last resort;

---

[29] See Parton (1985: 35).
[30] Education (Provision of Meals) Act 1906. See also Hendrick (2003: 66ff).
[31] See Parton (1985: 37–38).
[32] See ibid: 42–43; Hendrick (2003: 139).
[33] See the report of the Ingleby Committee (1960).

the emphasis was on working with the family (Parton 1991: 20). But there had to be intervention. Indeed, Hendrick argues that, running throughout the history of concern to protect children, has also been a thread of concern about what children might become without it: 'The child victim was nearly always seen as harbouring the possibility of another condition, one that was sensed to be threatening to moral fibre, sexual propriety, the sanctity of the family, the preservation of the race, law and order, and the wider reaches of citizenship' (Hendrick 2003: 7).[34]

Q Does a focus on delinquency imply concern to protect children or to protect society from children?

V. CHILD ABUSE—THE BEGINNINGS OF CONTEMPORARY CONCERN

The image of the child as victim has emerged strongly since the 1970s and, as child welfare knowledge has expanded, the ways in which children are seen to be victimised have multiplied. Whereas early concerns about children focused on child cruelty and neglect, more recent concerns have centred on a wider range of harms to children, encompassed in the term 'child abuse'. The catalyst for the contemporary wave of concern was the publication in 1974 of the report of the inquiry into the death of Maria Colwell (Secretary of State for Social Services 1974). As Parton notes, however, the groundwork had already been laid in the preceding decades.[35]

This groundwork was primarily the achievement of members of the medical profession. In 1961, the term 'battered child syndrome' was coined by Dr C Henry Kempe in the United States. The following year he and his colleagues argued that the syndrome was found in children who had been subjected to severe physical abuse, usually by a parent. As Parton (1985: 51) points out, the label defined abuse as an illness. Attention was deflected from social and cultural factors that might be considered significant in explaining abuse (ibid: 52).

In Britain, this 'syndrome' was also medicalised and it was not until the death of Maria Colwell, aged 7, at the hands of her stepfather, that child abuse emerged as a major social problem (ibid: 68).

Reaction to this event, Parton says, 'took on the proportions of a moral panic' (ibid: 70). The case, he suggests, 'provided a focus for the expression of a range of social anxieties'. These anxieties, echoing those expressed during the nineteenth century, were 'concerned with the collapse of the "English way of life", the growth in violence, the decline in individual and social discipline and morality, and the need to re-establish the traditional family' (ibid: 81).

Whereas previously abuse was conceptualised as a 'medical and social welfare problem' (ibid: 97) to which the solution was the treatment and rehabilitation of the family, the Maria Colwell case led to a downgrading in the importance of the blood-tie (ibid: 98) and an increased willingness to remove children from their families. In addition, rehabilitation of children with their parents became less of a priority. Research suggesting that children

---

[34] See further Piper (2008).
[35] See Parton (1985: ch 3), for a detailed discussion.

in care tended to be left to 'drift' (Rowe and Lambert 1973) contributed to a move towards permanency, necessitating timely and decisive action to place the child in a new family. The 1975 Children Act reflected this shift and attempted to give local authorities greater powers to intervene between parents and children.[36]

The Children Act 1989 heralded another change, with the emphasis on working with families wherever possible. And, according to Hendrick (2003), the Bulger case has led to a preoccupation with socialisation. That case involved the murder of a toddler by two young boys and it gave rise to concerns within the then Labour government about the children of the 'socially excluded'. It has led, says Hendrick, to increasing efforts to ensure that children are '"protected" from becoming antisocial' and 'early intervention' to achieve this aim is presented as being in children's best interests (Hendrick 2003: 244).

The early intervention agenda is inextricably linked with the notion of 'safeguarding' and these are implicated in what Parton has described as 'the emergence of the "preventative state"' (Parton 2006: 6). 'Investment' in children (Piper 2008), primarily by putting in place mechanisms for early intervention to guard against poor outcomes, became a priority. However, it is not only the state which must strive to ensure good outcomes; it is incumbent on parents to accept the help offered to improve their parenting (ibid: 100ff). Parents are regarded as being responsible for raising well-functioning and responsible citizens[37] and, as Reece (2005) says, they are seen as accountable for failures. Whether the Coalition government will continue to see investment as a priority is open to doubt but the accountability of parents is unlikely to diminish.

Sexual Abuse

The history of concern about child sexual abuse differs somewhat from that of concern about physical cruelty and neglect. In the nineteenth century one of the corrupting influences that preoccupied reformers was that of sex. However, concern seems to have centred on moral harm rather than on the child's psychological or even physical state. Controversy surrounding the Contagious Diseases Acts (1864, 1866, 1869), designed to control prostitution, generated debate about juvenile prostitution (Hendrick 2003: 34). Purity campaigners turned their attention to this subject and the Criminal Law Amendment Act 1885 was passed to raise the age of consent to 16 for girls and to make it an offence to procure a girl younger than 21 (ibid: 35). The privacy of the family and Victorian beliefs in the 'almost sacred nature of domesticity' (ibid: 38) meant that legislation outlawing incest was passed only in 1908.[38] This legislation, too, stemmed from concerns about purity and public morality rather than child welfare.[39]

However, allegations of incest were thought to be the product of children's fantasies, a response widely attributed to the writings of Freud which focused on Oedipal fantasies.[40] According to Smart, the medical profession explained venereal disease in babies and children by reference, for example, to mothers kissing their children's genitals and passing on

---

[36] See ibid: 116.

[37] See Piper (2008: 47–48, 51) on the image of children as responsible actors in society.

[38] The Punishment of Incest Act 1908. Smart (1989b: 54) argues that the legislation focused on the unnaturalness of the offence rather than simply the protection of children.

[39] See Hendrick (2003: 39–40).

[40] See Freeman (1989b: 86). For an account of Freud's abandonment of his initial explanation of hysteria in terms of childhood sexual abuse in favour of a theory of seduction fantasies, see Howitt (1993: 10ff).

infections received from their husbands (Smart 1999b: 395). Symptoms suffered by children in institutions were attributed to poor hygiene (ibid). Smart argues that there was an awareness of adult–child sexual contact but that early feminist campaigners found themselves unable to change medical opinion or legal and common-sense perceptions of harm (ibid: 405) and of childhood. Legal discourse, for instance, characterised children as unreliable witnesses who, in any event, were likely to be 'partly responsible for the minor lapse in adult behaviour' of which they complained (ibid: 399). Smart suggests that throughout the 1920s and 1930s it was 'assumed that children simply forgot what had happened to them or they were perceived as becoming "vicious"' (ibid: 404); although there was some understanding that they were 'damaged', they were in fact seen as wicked (ibid).

Opinions about harm, it seems, remained divided even into the 1950s. The Kinsey Report, published in 1953, revealed that sex between adults and children did take place but said that it was difficult to understand, except in terms of cultural conditioning, how children might be disturbed by sexual contact. The Report went on to suggest that children were harmed more by the reactions of the police and other adults than by the sexual contact itself (Kinsey Report 1953: 121). It was only towards the 1980s that child sexual abuse within the family began to be seen as a social problem in the United Kingdom.[41]

The new factors accounting for this included a growing feminist movement in the 1970s and a more general focus on victims and their experiences. It was through the efforts of rape crisis groups and incest survivor groups that sexual abuse began to be brought to public attention (MacLeod and Saraga 1988: 18; Smart 1989b: 56) and with the help of prominent figures within medicine and psychiatry, it came to be seen as a child protection issue. The media too contributed to the construction of sexual abuse as a social problem: a BBC progamme, *Childwatch*, was followed by the launch of Childline, a national freephone number set up to help abused children.[42] These events in turn contributed to knowledge about sexual abuse and its prevalence.

VI. DEFINING ABUSE

We see, then, that that the abuse of children has come to be seen as a social problem, initially largely through the efforts of moral campaigners, and later through the efforts of professionals, the media and feminist groups. However, what constitutes abuse is not self-evident;[43] only certain types of harm to children have come to be categorised as abuse and as requiring remedial action by the state.

King (1997: 31) points out that 'there is a moral judgment implicit in the word "abuse"'. It is, he says, by definition a wrong to be prevented and, if possible, eliminated. It follows, then, that agencies of the liberal state are expected to protect children from and to prevent or to punish those activities or events defined as abusive. Before going on to consider the strategies adopted to combat abuse, it is crucial to identify what is regarded as constituting abuse.

As King observes, 'in itself, the term "abuse" tells us nothing whatsoever about the way that certain kinds of behaviour come to be defined as abusive (and, therefore,

---

[41] See Parton (1991: 85).
[42] See ibid: 91ff.
[43] Gelles (1975: 364–65) points out that abuse is socially constructed.

immoral) within society at any one time' (ibid). With the possible exceptions of killing or deliberate maiming, there are few kinds of behaviour that would be universally classified as child abuse (ibid: 34).

In a liberal state, the definition of abuse, says Archard (1993: 148), should not impose unreasonable demands on those who care for children, otherwise the majority of parents will not be able to avoid being designated abusers. In particular, the legal definition of abuse has to be confined to serious matters:

> '[A]buse', as legally defined, will normally trigger State intervention. Since it is presumed that children in a liberal society will, normally and in the first instance, be brought up within families by their parents, such intervention will be into families and against the wishes of the parents. As we have seen, intervention can consequently be represented as violating parental and familial rights. 'Abuse' must thus be something serious enough to warrant such intervention. We might call this the 'threshold requirement'. (Archard 1993: 149)

What qualifies as 'serious' is largely determined by child welfare knowledge:

> [L]iberal arguments assume and invoke an understanding of childhood as a distinct phase of life in which the individual is dependent, less than fully formed as an individual, but nonetheless endowed with rights as an individual ... . In turn, parents have rights in respect of their children, but also responsibilities for organising their welfare in an appropriate manner. Public intervention is justified where harm is or is likely to be suffered by the child concerned, where criteria of 'harm' and those of 'best interests of the child' are determined by particular forms of knowledge of what constitutes childhood and appropriate child development.
>
> (Ashenden 2004: 55)

Q Which of the following would you define as child abuse and why? Smacking a child? Hitting a child with a belt? Bullying by other children at school? A stranger exposing himself to a child? In which of these circumstances would you counsel coercive state intervention? Does your answer correspond with your definition of abuse?

The line designating the threshold is continually being redrawn. As we have seen, what is considered abusive varies over time: 'Today's abuse includes much that was yesterday's punishment' (Gordon 1989: 177). A Department of Health publication comments that '[s]ociety continually reconstructs definitions of maltreatment which sanction intervention' (DoH 1995b: 15) and observes that new types of abuse have been 'discovered' over the years (ibid: 20). The 'discovery' of neglect was followed by 'discoveries' of physical abuse, sexual abuse and then emotional maltreatment.[44] And the boundaries of 'abuse' have continued to expand. That society's perceptions of what harms children have changed is perhaps illustrated in the reform of the law relating to corporal punishment, which is no longer permitted in schools,[45] and in the reduction in scope of the defence of 'reasonable punishment'.[46] Also, the definition of 'harm' in section 31(9) of the Children Act has

---

[44] Consideration was given to adding ritual or satanic abuse to the list but this was rejected as a separate category. See DoH (1995b: 21).

[45] See s 548 Education Act 1996.

[46] S 58 of the Children Act 2004 has removed the defence of reasonable punishment in relation to criminal offences other than common assault and has restricted the use of the defence in the sphere of tort law.

been amended to cover impairment suffered by children as a result of witnessing or hearing domestic violence.[47]

In addition, the circumstances in which and the settings within which state intervention is regarded as appropriate are expanding too. This is apparent from the expansion of categories enumerated in *Working Together to Safeguard Children*, a document devised and revised by government departments, the most recent version of which was published in 2010.[48] In the current version, professionals are given advice on child protection and the investigation of abuse in a number of different contexts. These include bullying and abuse of children by other children or young people (DfCSF 2010: ch 11). Advice is also given about dealing with situations where children are affected by gang activity, where there is fabricated or induced illness, institutional abuse, abuse in foster care, organised or multiple abuse,[49] abuse of disabled children, domestic violence, forced marriage and 'honour-based violence', trafficking and female genital mutilation (DfCSF 2010: ch 6)

Of course, female genital mutilation is tolerated in—and indeed is a crucial part of a woman's integration into—some societies; notions of abuse vary between cultures. Deliberate facial scarring of a child would be considered abusive in modern Western industrial societies. Yet in traditional sub-Saharan African cultures, ritual scarification is regarded as a form of beautification and it is an important part of tradition and cultural identity in these societies.[50]

Moreover, not all behaviour recognised as harmful to children is seen as falling within the definition of abuse. And those factors that cannot be attributed to the behaviour of specific individuals are not addressed in the context of child protection at all. As King (1997: 33–34) says, pollution, poverty and lack of access to good education have not attracted the label of child abuse and are not therefore part of the child protection agenda even though, in the long run, these factors may be just as harmful as a severe beating or emotional deprivation.[51]

'Significant Harm'

The concept of 'significant harm' rather than the notion of abuse marks the threshold for the purposes of coercive legal intervention in the family to protect children.[52] This concept is defined in relatively unspecific terms in section 31 of the Children Act 1989. However, some indication of what might be covered can be found in the more detailed description of those acts considered abusive provided in *Working Together*. It provides detailed guidance for professionals and agencies charged with safeguarding and protecting

---

[47] Attention has increasingly focused on the effects on children of living with domestic violence. Hester and Radford (1996: 9) report that, from the accounts of the women in their study, 'it is apparent that living in circumstances of domestic violence can be directly abusive to children. ... Men who are violent to their wives and partners may be directly physically or sexually abusive to the children. Or they may use the children to further the violence and abuse against wives/partners. Children may be assaulted in their attempt to protect their mothers from abuse. Witnessing violence to their mothers can also be emotionally abusive to children.' See also Mullender and Morley (1994); Parkinson and Humphreys (1998); McGee (2000).

[48] Like its predecessors, it was issued under s 7 of the Local Authority Social Services Act 1970. It does not have statutory force but should be complied with in the absence of exceptional circumstances.

[49] Defined as 'abuse involving one or more abusers and a number of children' (DfCSF 2010: para 6.10).

[50] See King (1997: 34); Archard (1999: 84); Freeman (1995).

[51] See also Birchall (1989: 10); Archard (1993: 151).

[52] See ss 31, 43 and 44 of the Children Act 1989. See further Chapter 14 below. In relation to the criminal law, see Chapter 4 above.

children. It sets out to provide working definitions of the main categories of abuse and neglect:

1.32 Abuse and neglect are forms of maltreatment of a child. Somebody may abuse or neglect a child by inflicting harm, or by failing to act to prevent harm. Children may be abused in a family or in an institutional or community setting, by those known to them or, more rarely, by a stranger for example, via the internet. They may be abused by an adult or adults, or another child or children.

Physical abuse

1.33 Physical abuse may involve hitting, shaking, throwing, poisoning, burning or scalding, drowning, suffocating, or otherwise causing physical harm to a child. Physical harm may also be caused when a parent or carer fabricates the symptoms of, or deliberately induces, illness in a child.

Emotional abuse

1.34 Emotional abuse is the persistent emotional maltreatment of a child such as to cause severe and persistent adverse effects on the child's emotional development. It may involve conveying to children that they are worthless or unloved, inadequate, or valued only insofar as they meet the needs of another person. It may include not giving the child opportunities to express their views, deliberately silencing them or 'making fun' of what they say or how they communicate. It may feature age or developmentally inappropriate expectations being imposed on children. These may include interactions that are beyond the child's developmental capability, as well as overprotection and limitation of exploration and learning, or preventing the child participating in normal social interaction. It may involve seeing or hearing the ill-treatment of another. It may involve serious bullying (including cyberbullying), causing children frequently to feel frightened or in danger, or the exploitation or corruption of children. Some level of emotional abuse is involved in all types of maltreatment of a child, though it may occur alone.

Sexual abuse

1.35 Sexual abuse involves forcing or enticing a child or young person to take part in sexual activities, not necessarily involving a high level of violence, whether or not the child is aware of what is happening. The activities may involve physical contact, including assault by penetration (for example, rape or oral sex) or non-penetrative acts such as masturbation, kissing, rubbing and touching outside of clothing. They may also include non-contact activities, such as involving children in looking at, or in the production of, sexual images, watching sexual activities, encouraging children to behave in sexually inappropriate ways, or grooming a child in preparation for abuse (including via the internet). Sexual abuse is not solely perpetrated by adult males. Women can also commit acts of sexual abuse, as can other children.

Neglect

1.36 Neglect is the persistent failure to meet a child's basic physical and/or psychological needs, likely to result in the serious impairment of the child's health or development. Neglect may occur during pregnancy as a result of maternal substance abuse. Once a child is born, neglect may involve a parent or carer failing to:

• provide adequate food, clothing and shelter (including exclusion from home or abandonment);
• protect a child from physical and emotional harm or danger;
• ensure adequate supervision (including the use of inadequate care-givers); or
• ensure access to appropriate medical care or treatment.

It may also include neglect of, or unresponsiveness to, a child's basic emotional needs.

(DfCSF 2010)

In their study, Masson et al found that the most common ground invoked by children's social care services was neglect, followed by emotional abuse, then physical abuse and then sexual abuse. At least two types of harm were alleged in two-thirds of cases (Masson et al 2008b: 37). Whether any particular instance or instances of ill-treatment will be regarded as falling within the scope of significant harm and as warranting coercive intervention depends on how the professionals (and the courts) evaluate the behaviour:

> 1.28 There are no absolute criteria on which to rely when judging what constitutes significant harm. Consideration of the severity of ill-treatment may include the degree and the extent of physical harm, the duration and frequency of abuse and neglect, the extent of premeditation, and the presence or degree of threat, coercion, sadism and bizarre or unusual elements. ... Sometimes, a single traumatic event may constitute significant harm, for example, a violent assault, suffocation or poisoning. More often, significant harm is a compilation of significant events, both acute and long-standing, which interrupt, change or damage the child's physical and psychological development. Some children live in family and social circumstances where their health and development are neglected. For them, it is the corrosiveness of long-term emotional, physical or sexual abuse that causes impairment to the extent of constituting significant harm. In each case, it is necessary to consider any maltreatment alongside the child's own assessment of his or her safety and welfare, the family's strengths and supports, as well as an assessment of the likelihood and capacity for change and improvements in parenting and the care of children and young people. (DfSCF 2010, footnote omitted)

> 1.29 To understand and identify significant harm, it is necessary to consider:
> - the nature of harm, in terms of maltreatment or failure to provide adequate care;
> - the impact on the child's health and development;
> - the child's development within the context of their family and wider environment;
> - any special needs, such as a medical condition, communication impairment or disability, that may affect the child's development and care within the family;
> - the capacity of parents to meet adequately the child's needs; and
> - the wider and environmental family context. (DfCSF 2010)

In any event, the 'state remains selective in its concerns' (DoH 1995b: 15). Although a duty is imposed in terms of section 17 of the Children Act 1989 to alleviate disadvantages stemming from conditions such as homelessness and poverty,[53] these disadvantages are not of themselves regarded as constituting abuse.

VII. THE 'CAUSES' OF CHILD ABUSE

Manning explains that an important element in the construction of social problems is the choice of explanations for those problems and of appropriate solutions. Indeed, he suggests, 'a major influence on the emergence of a successful social problem is the availability of a promising solution for it—in many cases the solution determines the problem rather than vice versa' (Manning 1985b: 162). The tendency is to designate as a cause that which

---

[53] See also the government's 'Sure Start' programme (Home Office 1998: paras 1.36–1.44).

can be tackled to achieve the desired change in the 'most convenient, economic or efficient way possible' (ibid: 164), a way that typically leaves the broader status quo unchanged (ibid: 165). Hence, the process of constructing child abuse as a social problem has involved not only categorising certain behaviours as abusive, but also selecting those behaviours which are amenable to causal explanations that suggest manageable solutions.

The earlier literature on the 'causation' of child abuse may be seen as postulating two major models: the 'psychological model' and the 'sociological model' (O'Donnell and Craney 1982: 185). The model of causation espoused naturally determines what strategies for combating abuse appear appropriate. As we shall see, the models that have influenced policy and professional practice have focused on the particular family and the individuals within it.[54] It follows that the 'solution' to the problem is seen as lying within the family; either it can be rehabilitated or the child must be separated from it. This 'solution' appears, on the face of it, more manageable for the state and less disruptive of the status quo than the wide-ranging economic, social or cultural reforms suggested by other models of causation. However, as we shall see, it assumes that the problem family or individual can be identified and this is by no means an easy task.

Neglect, Physical and Emotional Abuse

The 'psychological model', which locates the principal cause of abuse in the psychological make-up of the abuser and which suggests that there are particular psychiatric categories specifically associated with child abuse, has been largely discounted. For example, Parton, reviewing the literature, observes that writers who maintain that abusers suffer from personality disorders cannot agree on what these are (Parton 1985: 135).[55]

The 'sociological model' embraces a variety of theoretical positions, but each of the analyses suggest that radical change, whether social, economic or cultural, is necessary to deal with abuse. Straus, Gelles and Steinmetz (1981), writing on violence in families, maintain that it is far from abnormal and arises from the interaction of culture, family structure, stress and social learning. It is argued that it is in the family that people learn to be violent. The prevalence of violence within families is a result of the fact that people tend to see intra-familial violence generally and corporal punishment of children[56] in particular, as normal and acceptable.[57] Freeman (1983: 124) argues that children are still seen as objects and that it is therefore not surprising that they are abused. Writers such as Parton (1985: 175) contend that child abuse is strongly related to class, inequality and poverty, and, more specifically, the stress and frustration engendered by difficult economic and social conditions.

Q Are the two major models mutually exclusive?

A number of the various models put forward since the Second World War to explain why

---

[54] See also Hendrick (2003: 169).

[55] See also Gelles (1973: 614).

[56] But see s 58 Children Act 2004. In *A v United Kingdom (Human Rights: Punishment of Child)* [1998] 2 FLR 952, the European Court of Human Rights held that a boy who had been subjected to severe beatings had suffered ill-treatment within the purview of Art 3 of the Convention for the Protection of Human Rights and Fundamental Freedoms.

[57] See also Gelles (1979: 39); Gelles (1992).

children are maltreated are summarised[58] in a Department of Health document: *Child Protection. Messages from Research* (DoH 1995b: 21–22). The document goes on to indicate that single-cause explanations, whether relying on pathology, stress, poverty, environment or the characteristics of the victim, have largely been supplanted by an 'integrated model':[59]

> Integrated model: Today, it is broadly accepted that a combination of social, psychological, economic and environmental factors play a part in the abuse or neglect of children. ... Families overwhelmed and depressed by social problems form the greatest proportion of those assessed and supported by child protection agencies. Not included in this group is a small proportion with very different characteristics, such as those in which a parent has serious psychiatric problems or a predisposition to family violence. (DoH 1995b: 21–22)

Working Together (DfCSF 2010: ch 9) lists various 'sources of stress for children and families' which could contribute to poor parenting. These include social exclusion, domestic violence, mental illness or learning disability of a parent or carer and substance misuse by the caretaking adults. Davies and Ward note that problems can be compounded by 'other stressors' such as 'financial or housing problems and unsupportive or inadequate social and familial networks' (Davies and Ward 2011: 4).[60]

> **Q** What 'solutions' do these formulations of the problem suggest? Davies and Ward argue, like many others, that multi-agency and multi-disciplinary responses are needed (Davies and Ward 2011: 12ff). How would this help?

Sexual Abuse

Since sexual abuse has been found to be spread more evenly across social classes than other forms of abuse,[61] explanations have centred less on factors such as poverty than on the characteristics of the families themselves. However, competing explanations, emerging from feminist theory, stress male power and suggest strategies entailing social and cutural change.[62]

Sexual abuse, like other types of abuse, is thought by some to be learned behaviour.[63] Other explanations have been put forward by proponents of family systems theory.[64] The family is seen as a system and sexual abuse occurs when that system breaks down: 'sexual abuse is a *symptom* of what is wrong in the family, or even a "solution" to the dysfunction' (Macleod and Saraga 1988: 33). Furniss, a proponent of systems theory, draws a distinction between 'conflict-avoiding' and 'conflict-regulating' families. Sexual abuse, he maintains, functions either to avoid conflict between the parents or to help to regulate it. In conflict-avoiding families, sexual abuse 'takes the pressure off the precarious sexual relationship between the parents' (Furniss 1991: 56); the role of sexual partner

---

[58] For detailed discussion of the various models, see Freeman (1983: ch 4); Parton (1985: chs 6 and 7).
[59] See also DoH (2000: para 2.24).
[60] See also Masson et al (2008b: 20).
[61] See Freeman (1989b: 97).
[62] Eg, Freeman suggests that the 'socialisation processes which construct images of masculinity need to be re-examined' (Freeman 1989b: 116) and that the status of children should be improved (ibid: 117).
[63] See Briggs (1995).
[64] See, for discussion, MacLeod and Saraga (1988).

is delegated to a child. In conflict-regulating families, the sexually abusive relationship helps to decrease conflict and prevents the break-up of the adults' relationship.

Feminist writers point out that this account blames mothers for the abuse of their children by fathers; they are seen as being responsible for the behaviour of their menfolk. They are described as withdrawing, being punitive and as denying men their conjugal rights, while men are described as acting on uncontrollable sexual urges.[65]

The feminist analysis, in contrast, finds the explanation of sexual abuse in the way in which male sexuality is constructed.[66] Feminist writers emphasise the fact that sexual abusers are predominantly male[67] while their victims are predominantly female[68] and assert that masculinity and male sexuality are associated with dominance:

> Generally boys and men learn to experience their sexuality as an overwhelming and uncontrollable force; they learn to focus their sexual feelings on submissive objects, and they learn the assertion of their sexual desires, the expectation of having them serviced. Obviously this is a crude account of a complex phenomenon ... . Thus all men do not abuse.
>
> (MacLeod and Saraga 1988: 41)

A more sophisticated account is provided by Liddle (1993). Drawing on the concept of 'cathexis', meaning the social organisation of desire, he suggests that 'dominant processes of masculinization ... create a momentum toward the cultivation of sets of desires compatible with adult–child sex' (Liddle 1993: 116). This is because male sexual desire is constructed in a way that links it with 'themes of performance, superiority and achievement' (ibid: 112). The feelings and needs of partners and the possible harm caused by a sexual encounter are accorded little significance (ibid: 114). However, there is nothing inevitable about child sexual abuse, he says; men who abuse choose to do so.

It appears that it is the feminist analysis that has, at least to some extent, prevailed. Official documentation indicates that sexual abuse is now seen in terms of power and exploitation. This is apparent from *Protecting the Public*, the White Paper which preceded the enactment of the Sexual Offences Act 2003. Although this relates to the criminal law, it can be seen as reflecting contemporary thinking generally. Children are regarded as vulnerable and abusers are seen as predatory. The assumption that there has been an abuse of power persists in cases involving children irrespective of consent: [69]

> [48] There may be circumstances where sexual activity takes place with the ostensible consent of both parties but where one of the parties is in such a great position of power over the other that the sexual activity is wrong and should come within the realms of the criminal law. The most obvious cases involve children and vulnerable people with learning disabilities or mental disorders. (Home Office 2002)

Section 13 of the Sexual Offences Act 2003 introduces a new offence: 'Child sex offences committed by children or young persons'. Sections 25 and 26 create the new offences of 'Sexual activity with a child family member'[70] and 'Inciting a child family member to

---

[65] See MacLeod and Saraga (1988: 36–37).

[66] See Smart (1989b: 50). Compare Howitt (1993: 108).

[67] See Finkelhor (1986: 126ff). See also Briggs (1995: ch 8).

[68] See Finkelhor and Baron (1986: 61–64).

[69] Piper (2000) argues that children are seen as 'unsexualised' in our society and there is little room, in our conception of childhood, for self-willed sexual activity.

[70] Replacing incest under the Sexual Offences Act 1956.

engage in sexual activity',[71] respectively. These are also explained in terms of power and exploitation:

> [52] ... While it is recognised that much sexual activity involving children under the age of consent might be consensual and experimental and that, in such cases, the intervention of the criminal law may not be appropriate, the criminal law must make provision for an unlawful sexual activity charge to be brought where the sexual activity was consensual but was also clearly manipulative. (Home Office 2002)

> [58] ... Familial sexual abuse of a child will capture the sexual abuse and exploitation of children within the family unit. It is recognised that the balance of power within the family and the close and trusting relationships that exist make children particularly vulnerable to abuse within its environment. (ibid)

Q What response does this explanation suggest is needed?

VIII. THE 'HIGH-RISK' FAMILY

As we have seen, theories of causation entailing radical social, economic or cultural change have had little impact on the law, the politics or the practice of child protection. The perspective that has predominated in shaping policy and social work practice, and which can be discerned in the 'integrated model', locates the primary 'causes' of child abuse firmly within the family.[72]

The child protection system assumes that the family or individual family members can be 'diagnosed'. It assumes that, in consequence, abuse can be predicted, or at least identified, and abusers can be offered treatment. It places reliance on health and welfare professionals who are seen as having the requisite expertise to fulfil these tasks and so protect children.[73] In particular, it relies on professionals to identify high-risk cases.[74] Indeed, the assumed ability to do so is fundamental to the belief that children can be protected and that this can be achieved without undermining the philosophy underlying the liberal state: 'In theory, the identification of the actual or potentially dangerous individual or family provides the mechanism for both ensuring that children are protected while also avoiding unwarrantable interventions' (Parton 1992: 103).

Part of the expertise of professionals charged with identifying high-risk cases is their knowledge of 'risk factors' that are said to serve as indicators of such cases. Factors that have been identified in the past have included signs in children; unplanned and unwanted pregnancy; abuse of the parent during childhood; a history of violence; and social and economic stress.[75] And as social science knowledge changes, those factors categorised as risk factors change. So, for example, social exclusion,[76] substance abuse by parents and mental illness are now seen as major risk factors.[77] In addition, it is now accepted that

---

[71] Replacing the offence of incitement to commit incest, s 54 Criminal Law Act 1977.
[72] See Parton (1985: 132–33).
[73] Ibid: 149.
[74] See, eg, London Borough of Brent (1985: 289).
[75] See Parton (1985: 135–36); DoH (1995a: 14).
[76] 'Social exclusion', the terminology used in *Working Together*, refers to the disadvantage associated with poverty, social isolation and racism (DfCSF 2010: para 9.16).
[77] See DoH (2000: para 2.21); Sinclair and Bullock (2002: 18); DfCSF (2010: para 10.16).

children living in violent families are exposed to increased risk; men who abuse their partners are likely to abuse children as well.[78] Children who witness domestic violence are also considered damaged as a result. *Working Together*, reflecting the Labour government's focus on social exclusion, adds yet more risk factors. These include involvement in crime, 'poverty, debt, inactivity or worklessness and low aspirations', 'poor housing and homelesssness' and poor school attendance (DfCSF 2010: para 10.16).[79]

The *Framework for the Assessment of Children in Need and their Families* (DoH 2000) is intended to assist professionals to judge whether a child is in need, whether the child is suffering or likely to suffer significant harm, what action should be taken and what services would best meet the needs of the child and the family (ibid: viii). It embodies what is described as an ecological approach and requires assessments to take account of three domains:

- The child's developmental needs;
- The parents' or caregivers' capacities to respond appropriately;
- The wider family and environmental factors. (ibid: para 1.40)

The assessment is therefore one that examines not only the personal characteristics of the parents and children but also highlights factors such as income, employment and community resources. Cooper et al suggest that it is a positive innovation which 'has the potential to raise the standard of assessment' (Cooper et al 2003: 18).[80] Nevertheless, it does not make identifying child abuse or the risk of abuse an easy task.

Identifying and Predicting Child Abuse

Davies and Ward urge that early recognition of abuse is essential to avoid long-term damage to children (Davies and Ward 2011: 4). They suggest that teachers and health professionals are particularly well placed to identify problems (ibid: 5). *Working Together*, which is targeted at a variety of professionals and child welfare professionals in particular, states that knowledge about how to respond to concerns about child maltreatment:

> develops over time, informed by research, experience and the critical scrutiny of practice. Sound professional practice involves making judgements supported by evidence: evidence derived from research and experience about the nature and impact of maltreatment, and when and how to intervene to improve outcomes for children; and evidence derived from a thorough assessment of a specific child's health, development and welfare, and his or her family circumstances.
>
> (DfCSF 2010: para 9.1)

However, the difficulty that besets the child protection system is that, while professional knowledge and expertise are assumed to facilitate the accurate identification or prediction of child abuse, this assumption is, it seems, unfounded. Nor is it always apparent what 'works' in terms of intervention.

A number of child abuse inquiries have concluded that child welfare professionals have

---

[78] See DoH (2000: para 2.22); DfCSF (2010: para 10.16).
[79] See also Cafcass (2010: para 3.3).
[80] See also Sinclair and Bullock (2002: 26).

failed to carry out their tasks satisfactorily. For example, Lord Laming, in his report after the death of Peter Connelly (then known only as Baby P) said:

> It would be unreasonable to expect that the sudden and unpredictable outburst by an adult towards a child can be prevented. But that is entirely different from the failure to protect a child or young person already identified as being in danger of deliberate harm. The death of a child in these circumstances is a reproach to us all. (Laming 2009: 3)

Failures, says Ashenden (2004: 11, 19), are often attributed to lack of resources and inadequate training. They provoke criticisms of workers[81] as well as recommendations for better training[82] and closer supervision.[83] However, at times, a more fundamental problem is identified: an insufficient knowledge base. This deficit, says Ashenden, calls into question the very legitimacy of intervention in the family by child protection agencies. Such crises in child protection lead to calls for more research and the development of better predictive techniques.[84] 'Better' experts are summoned before inquiries to evaluate the expertise and professionalism of the experts and professionals involved in the case and who are deemed to have failed. These 'better' experts are seen as offering the promise of more 'reliable' expertise. In this way, says Ashenden, the legitimacy of the system is restored.[85]

King (1995b) suggests that child welfare professionals are faced with an impossible task. They must, however, give the impression that they are able to accomplish their professional goals successfully, he says. He too maintains that the need to give the impression that the child protection system can 'work' leads to the accumulation of ever more extensive 'knowledge' about child abuse which is used to legitimate decisions. And when things go wrong, he says, organisations adopt coping strategies such as the introduction of increasingly detailed regulation.[86] These strategies serve to convince the members of these organisations, as well as the outside world, that mistakes arise from remediable faults, such as inefficiency or failure to observe the proper procedures, rather than the uncertainties inherent in child protection work (King 1997: 439–40).[87]

Yet Cooper et al (2003: 13) complain that procedures come to dominate decision-making[88] partly because they also operate to give some protection to professionals if things go wrong.[89] However, the risk-averseness that these rules represent and that permeates the child protection system, say Cooper et al, has detrimental effects on practice:

> Systems of risk assessment and management are oriented almost entirely to minimising risk of extreme failure, and never to promoting creative and acceptable risk taking in pursuit of good outcomes for children. Equally, the systems of professional accountability are … almost never

---

[81] See London Borough of Brent (1985: 289); London Borough of Greenwich (1987: 106–07); Laming (2003). See also Sinclair and Bullock (2002: 40); Laming (2009: para 1.7); Davies and Ward (2011: 9ff).

[82] See, eg, Laming (2003: Recommendations 14, 31 and 37); Laming (2009: 5 and paras 5.9ff).

[83] See, eg, Laming (2003: Recommendation 30); Laming (2009: paras 2.12, 3.15).

[84] See, eg, London Borough of Brent (1985: 288–89). See also Audit Commission (1994).

[85] See Ashenden (2004: 164).

[86] See further on the proceduralisation of social work, King (1997: ch 4). On the use of regulations, see Smith (2000).

[87] As Becker (1963: 157) observes, those charged with enforcing rules devised to deal with social problems must be able to show that their attempts at enforcement are 'effective and worthwhile', while at the same time demonstrating that the problem still exists and that their services are still needed to control it.

[88] See also Cooper et al (2003: 18–19). Cooper et al also refer to the mechanisms relied on by professionals in order to cope with the uncertainties inherent in child protection; they tend to 'fall back into denial, optimism, a checklist mentality or the use of other unhelpful defensive risk avoidance techniques' (ibid: 59).

[89] See ibid: 11.

[oriented] to encouraging responsibility (in the sense of [professional] autonomy) or [acknowledge] the inevitability of failure. In short, these methodologies are ill adapted to the complexity, uncertainty and indeterminacy of the functions to which they are applied.

(Cooper et al 2003: 57)

So failures are inevitable because predicting abuse is very difficult,[90] as a Department of Health publication, *Child Abuse: A Study of Inquiry Reports 1980–1989*, acknowledges:

It is not possible confidently to predict who will be an abuser, for the potential for abuse is widespread and often triggered by the particular conjunction of circumstances which is unpredictable. Almost anyone with whom the professionals work could be an abuser, and when an incident 'breaks' it is also easy to look back with the confidence of hindsight and to see cues that were missed, small mistakes and tell tale signs. (DoH 1991: 63)

An examination of 40 serious case reviews involving cases where children died or were seriously injured came to similar conclusions. Of the cases studied, only one was classified as 'highly predictable' and three were 'highly preventable' (Sinclair and Bullock 2002: 46, 96).[91] The authors observe that the predictive value of known indicators of abuse is limited (ibid: 17–18). The likelihood of abuse depends on an 'interplay of a range of factors' and it is not possible to determine the significance of particular features or characteristics (ibid: 18). They go on to say that: 'Even if the forecasts of future abuse were accurate, attempts to predict which of those children would be murdered or suffer serious injury are virtually impossible' (ibid). As the Foreword to the study says, '[i]n some cases, the abuse occurred out of the blue, in others it occurred in a context of low level need and occasionally it arose in situations where it seemed to have been "waiting to happen"' (ibid: i).

The study conducted by Masson et al, based on data derived from court files from 2004, bears testimony to the difficulty of predicting sudden deteriorations in children's conditions. Forty two per cent of cases were 'unplanned crisis interventions' (Masson et al 2008b: 25). Only a small number of cases came 'out of the blue'. In the majority of cases the families were known to social services and there had been some social services involvement in the past.

The families in these cases were typically those described by Olive Stevenson as 'bumping along the bottom' which may make up a large proportion of the caseloads of Children's Services Departments, but only a few of which deteriorate, often suddenly, to a point where a court application becomes necessary as a matter of urgency. (ibid: 26, references omitted)[92]

Sinclair and Bullock fall into the category of those calling for more knowledge and better practice. What they say is that, although child deaths are 'unpredictable and unpreventable', more could be known and done (Sinclair and Bullock 2002: 62, 64). Cooper et al take a different approach, stressing the need to concentrate on outcomes rather than diagnosis and risk (Cooper et al 2003: 59–60).

---

[90] See also Sutton (1981); Howitt (1993: 31). For Howitt (ibid: 123–24), though, the problem goes deeper than the possibility of mistaking warning signals. He maintains that it is the child protection process that is at fault and that produces 'errors'.

[91] Twelve of the 40 children were 'completely unknown to their local social services department at the time of the incident' (Sinclair and Bullock 2002: 27).

[92] See also Brophy (2006: 17).

We shall see later in this chapter that the more recent child protection policy documents, and the Munro Review (DfE 2011f) in particular, do indeed stress outcomes rather than procedures. But the likelihood is, perhaps, that outcomes will become one of the criteria against which professionals' performance will be evaluated, so increasing accountability. Furthermore, the identification of children at risk is still seen as a central function of child welfare professionals. Therefore, it may well be that future child abuse inquiries will focus on professionals' failure to achieve satisfactory outcomes as well as their failure to identify risk. It is likely that there will be continued calls for yet further research, greater knowledge and more training in an ongoing effort to secure both objectives.[93]

IX. THE ROLE OF PROFESSIONALS AND THE LAW: THE CHILDREN ACT 1989

The Children Act 1989—The Background

The Children Act 1989 is part of the continuing drive to show that the child protection system can function effectively to protect children and that it can accomplish this goal with the minimum of coercive state intervention. It was enacted at least in part in response to what were seen as flaws in the practices and procedures adopted by child protection personnel as well as deficiencies in the law.

The Review which preceded the Act (DHSS 1985) emphasised that, in most cases, the interests of children are best served by allowing them to be brought up by their families and that parents should be allowed 'to undertake their natural and legal responsibility to care for their own children' (ibid: para 2.8).[94] Even where a child could not remain at home, the emphasis should be on working 'in partnership with rather than in opposition to his parents, and to work towards his return to them' (ibid). '[T]he state', it went on, 'should only be able compulsorily to intervene where the child is being or is at risk of being harmed if it does not' (ibid: para 2.15).

> **Q** Is the use of the word 'natural' significant? To what extent does the approach adopted in the Review reflect adherence to the notion of family privacy?

At the same time that these policies promoting the autonomy of the family and voluntary co-operation were being formulated, a number of inquiries into child deaths during the 1980s stressed the need to intervene decisively to protect children at risk. The inquiry into the death of Jasmine Beckford (London Borough of Brent 1985) criticised social workers for operating under the 'rule of optimism'. The operation of this rule, identified by Dingwall et al (1983), leads professionals to assume that parents love their children and that they are 'honest, competent and caring' (Dingwall et al 1983: 89). Instead, the Beckford Report stated, social workers should be able to identify 'high-risk' cases and, in such

---

[93] See below.

[94] These principles are echoed in Art 9 of the UN Convention on the Rights of the Child. This states that children should not be separated against their will from their parents, except by process of law, and only where necessary in their best interests. Abuse and neglect are cited as justifiable reasons for separating children from parents. Where so separated, children have a right to contact with their parents except where contrary to their best interests.

cases, '[s]ociety should sanction … the removal of such children for an appreciable time' (London Borough of Brent 1985: 289). Similarly, the inquiry into the death of Kimberly Carlile (London Borough of Greenwich 1987),[95] who was abused by her stepfather, criticised social workers for failing to be alert to danger signals.

While these inquiries criticised social services for doing too little too late, the Cleveland crisis[96] raised very different isssues. During 1987, a paediatrician based in Cleveland, with the help of a colleague, began to use a new and controversial method of diagnosing sexual abuse. Their use of the reflex anal dilatation test, along with other indicators, led to the diagnosis of an unprecedented number of children as having been sexually abused. There were not enough resources to deal with the number of children taken into emergency care as a result. This led to a public 'crisis'. Carol Smart observes that: 'Although it appears on the surface to be a panic about child sexual abuse within the family, it was in fact a panic over parents' rights. … What appeared to be a concern for children became deflected into a concern to protect the nuclear family from any outside interference' (Smart 1989b: 62).

The report of the inquiry set up as a result of the events in Cleveland (Butler-Sloss 1988) had a significant effect on the content of the Children Act 1989. The report is perhaps most notable for its emphasis on the importance of the law in cases of child abuse and, in particular, the importance of parents' rights. It emphasised the need for parents to be kept informed and, where appropriate, to be consulted by the professionals involved in the investigation; it stated that parents should always be advised of their rights of appeal or complaint in respect of any decisions made; and it instructs social services to confirm important decisions in writing and to give parents the opportunity to take legal advice (p 246). Nevertheless the report, like those that preceded it, went on to affirm that, 'Social workers have a duty in law to ensure the protection of children where they have cause to believe that there is a high risk of further immediate abuse' (Butler-Sloss 1988: para 13.4).

Q Are the messages coming out of the Jasmine Beckford inquiry and the Cleveland Report contradictory? How can the law ensure that children are protected while still protecting parents' 'inherent rights'?

The Children Act 1989

The Children Act 1989 was passed in the context of political pressure favouring a reorientation of policy away from interventionism towards a greater emphasis on family autonomy. Intervention between parent and child was again increasingly becoming conceived of as interference with the natural order of things. Nevertheless, it was considered a necessary evil to prevent or terminate a worse evil: child abuse. The only justification for coercive intervention, therefore, would be 'reliable' evidence of abuse or the risk of abuse.

It has been said that the Act 'strikes a new balance between family autonomy and the protection of children' (DoH 1989: iii). This assessment is reiterated in the more recent Family Justice Review:

---

[95] See also London Borough of Lambeth (1987).
[96] Like the events in Rochdale and the Orkneys. See SSI (1990); Clyde (1992).

The Children Act 1989 establishes mechanisms to strike a balance between the family's autonomy and the state's role in protecting children. Wherever possible and appropriate, children should be brought up by their own families. Care proceedings are to be brought only when necessary. (Norgrove 2011a, Executive Summary and Recommendations: para 57)

The balance referred to is most apparent in the stress on 'partnership' with families. At the centre of the notion of partnership is the promotion of co-operation and consultation between all those concerned with child protection, including local authorities, parents and the children themselves.[97] The discussion that follows focuses on partnership between local authorities and parents.

Q What do you understand by the term 'partnership'?

Partnership

We will argue that partnership serves a dual function. First, it promotes the ideology that it is the family, rather than the state, that should be responsible for children. Secondly, it enables the liberal state to maintain its legitimacy by restricting coercive intervention in families while still regulating them.

Partnership is discussed extensively in government publications such as the Guidance and Regulations that supplement the Children Act 1989 and, although the legislation itself contains no reference to the term, it includes a number of measures designed to give effect to the partnership philosophy. Local authorities have a duty to promote the upbringing of children within their families and, in order to facilitate this, to provide support for families of children in need.[98] This duty extends to providing accommodation for children in need[99] in a way that does not stigmatise the parents or restrict their parental responsibility.[100] If parents ask for help this should not be seen as a sign of failure but rather as a sign of responsible parenting (DfCSF 2010: para 1.5).

Section 20(7) provides that a local authority may not provide accommodation against the wishes of a person who has parental responsibility for the child and who is willing and able to provide or to arrange for accommodation. Section 20(8) stipulates that any person who has parental responsibility for a child may at any time remove that child from local authority accommodation. As the White Paper that preceded the Act states, local authority accommodation should:

> be seen as a positive response to the needs of families and not as a mark of failure either on the part of the family or those professionals and others working to support them. An essential characteristic of this service should be its voluntary character, that it should be based clearly in continuing parental agreement and operate as far as possible on a basis of partnership and co-operation between the local authority and parents. (DHSS 1987: para 21)

---

[97] See Kaganas (1995); Masson (1995).

[98] S 17.

[99] S 20.

[100] The only powers that can be exercised by a local authority are those delegated to it by the parents (s 2(9)) or the power to do what is reasonable in the circumstances for the purpose of safeguarding or promoting the child's welfare (s 3(5)). The Act repealed s 3 of the Child Care Act 1980 which enabled local authorities to assume parental rights over children in what was known as 'voluntary care' by means of an administrative process. It also abolished the old statutory requirement that a parent wishing to remove a child from 'voluntary care' give notice to the local authority of this intention.

Even where there is some risk to a child, the policy behind the Act is that coercive intervention should be avoided if possible. Schedule 2 to the Act (para 7) directs local authorities to take reasonable steps to reduce the need to bring proceedings for care or supervision orders. Section 1(5) of the Act, which embodies the 'no order' principle, enjoins the court to refrain from making orders unless there is some positive advantage to the child in doing so: 'Where a court is considering whether or not to make one or more orders under this Act with respect to a child, it shall not make the order or any of the orders unless it considers that doing so would be better for the child than making no order at all.'

As far as child welfare professionals are concerned, *Working Together* makes it clear that they should not normally intervene unless invited to do so by the family. They are expected to respond to requests for help from children and parents, and to do so as early as possible, but they should avoid coercion:

> 1.6 A wide range of services and professionals provide support to families in bringing up children. Sometimes children will seek out and ask for help and advice themselves. However, in the great majority of cases, it will be the decision of parents when to ask for help and advice on their children's care and upbringing. As well as being responsive to children's direct requests for help and advice, professionals also need to engage with parents at the earliest opportunity when doing so may prevent problems or difficulties becoming worse. Only in exceptional cases should there be compulsory intervention in family life—for example, where this is necessary to safeguard a child from significant harm. Such intervention should—provided this is consistent with the safety and welfare of the child—support families in making their own plans for the welfare and protection of their children. (DfCSF 2010)

Therefore, parents should be involved in choosing the appropriate form of intervention. Local authorities should try to avoid instituting court proceedings and:

> 3.3 Before making an application for a care or supervision order a local authority is expected to seek legal advice and to communicate with the parents (and child, if of sufficient age and understanding) the nature and extent of their concerns. Prior to submitting an application to the court, and where the short term safety and welfare of the child permits, the local authority should send a 'Letter Before Proceedings' to the parents, the contents of which should also be explained carefully and directly to the parents … . The purpose of such a letter is to enable the parents to obtain legal assistance and advice, prior to a meeting with the local authority, the intention of which is either to deflect proceedings or, at least, to narrow and focus the issues of concern. (DfCSF 2008).

Even in cases where there is a finding of 'significant harm' to the child and compulsory intervention in the form of an emergency protection order, care order or supervision order is necessary, local authority social services are still expected to work in partnership with parents. For example, parents are normally entitled to have contact with their children while they are in local authority care[101] and also to have a say in their upbringing.[102] While the local authority acquires parental responsibility pursuant to an emergency pro-

---

[101] S 34.
[102] See, eg, s 22(4).

tection order[103] or a care order,[104] the parents still retain their parental responsibility, albeit in a curtailed form, in terms of section 2(6).

> **Q** Why do parents who have been found wanting in respect of their ability to care for their child retain parental responsibility when that child is taken into local authority care? Why are local authorities expected to work in partnership with such parents? What is the practical significance of these measures?

Partnership—The Emphasis on Parental Responsibility

Eekelaar (1991a) argues that the Act encompasses two concepts of responsibility. First, what he calls *'responsibility (1)'*, refers to the duties parents have to take care of and provide for their children. *'Responsibility (2)'*, on the other hand, refers to the idea that parents are entitled to bring up their children without interference from others or the state.

Reviewing the provisions of the Children Act 1989, as well as the official documentation that followed it, he concludes that the legislation evidences an emphasis on *'responsibility (2)'*. In support of this contention, he draws attention to the fact that the law conceives of parental responsibility as individual responsibility; it vests in parents, or, in their absence, other individuals in preference to the state. He also notes that parental responsibility may not be voluntarily surrendered to the state and that parental responsibility remains in parents when care of their children is shared with the state.

> The truth of the situation where parental responsibility has been assumed by an authority under a Care Order is that the parent is unable to exercise *responsibility (1)*: indeed, he has been deprived of the opportunity to do so because he has failed to exercise it competently. The 'responsibility' which the parent retains under the Act is *responsibility (2)*. But, split from *responsibility (1)*, this second sense of responsibility appears nakedly ideological. ... [I]t is a statement that, despite realities, it remains the parent's rather than the authority's role to look after the child, either because that is what nature ordained ('their very parenthood') or because it is a desirable social ordering. (Eekelaar 1991a: 45, emphasis in original)

He goes on to question the suggestion that the reduction of control over parents will encourage them to behave more 'responsibly' towards their children:

> In other words, [it is said] that the promotion of *responsibility (2)* encourages *responsibility (1)*, or, as the Secretary of State put it: 'The Bill's emphasis on the primary function of parenthood will, we hope, sharpen our perceptions and highlight the obligation on parents to care for their children and bring them up properly' (House of Commons Debates, vol 151, col 1107). ... [This] ... may reflect a deeper belief that, given freedom from state regulation, parents will *naturally* care for their offspring; that the fact of parenthood itself provides sufficient assurance. It may be asked whether the historical record justifies such a view. (ibid: 49–50, emphasis in original)

> **Q** Where does the Children Act 1989 place primary responsibility for children—in the private or the public sphere?

---

[103] S 44(4)(c).
[104] S 33(3)(a).

Partnership—Regulating the Family

While Eekelaar sees partnership in terms of a withdrawal of the state and the placing of primary responsibility for children on families, official documentation gives prominence to the ideas of family autonomy and empowerment.

Working Together states:

Involving children and families

In the process of finding out what is happening to a child it is important to listen to the child, develop a therapeutic relationship with the child and through this gain an understanding of his or her wishes and feelings. The importance of developing a co-operative working relationship is emphasised so that parents or caregivers feel respected and informed; they believe staff are being open and honest with them and in turn they are confident about providing vital information about their child, themselves and their circumstances. The consent of children or their parents/caregivers, where appropriate, should be obtained for sharing information unless to do so would place a child at risk of suffering significant harm. Similarly, decisions should also be made with their agreement, whenever possible, unless to do so would place the child at risk of suffering significant harm. (DfCSF 2010: para 5.5, 135)

Recent guidance lists among the principles of good social care practice the following:

- Parents should be expected and enabled to retain their responsibilities and to remain as closely involved as is consistent with their child's welfare, even if that child cannot live at home either temporarily or permanently.
- If children have to live apart from their family, both they and their parents should be given adequate information and helped to consider alternatives and contribute to the making of an informed choice about the most appropriate form of care.
- Continuity of relationships is important and attachments should be respected, sustained and developed. (DFE 2010b: para 1.5)

The *Guidance* goes on:

1.6 These principles reflect the intention in the 1989 Act, that parents should be encouraged to exercise their responsibility for their child's welfare in a constructive way and that where compulsory intervention in the family is necessary it should, where possible, support rather than undermine the parental role. The 1989 Act places a strong emphasis on the local authority working in partnership with parents when undertaking their statutory functions. (DFE 2010b)

The Labour government repeatedly endorsed the role of the family as primarily responsible for raising children and the subsidiary role of the state in helping the family to do so. The Children's Plan, initially drawn up in 2007, set out:

a series of guiding principles—that parents bring up children, not government; that all children have the potential to succeed; that children and young people need to be safe, healthy and enjoy life; that all children and families deserve services that work together for them; and that it is always better to prevent failure than tackle a crisis later. (DfCSF 2009b: 3) [105]

---

[105] See also DfES (2004c: 2); DfES (2004d: para 1.2); DfCSF (2010: 2).

Partnership, according to this account, is a way of respecting the rights of families and the children in them as well as a way of furthering children's beat interests.

Partnership can take several forms. *Working Together* stipulates that families must be told of agencies that give advice and provide advocacy (DfCSF 2010: para 10.5); they should be given all the information they need to understand the child protection process (ibid: para 10.7); and their racial, ethnic and cultural identities should be taken into account, although professionals '*must be clear that child abuse cannot be condoned for religious or cultural reasons*' (ibid: para 10.9, emphasis in original).

Children's involvement,[106] in particular, is addressed along with that of other family members:

> 5.5 Work to safeguard and promote the welfare of children should be:
>
> • *Child centred*
>
> ... The child should be spoken and listened to, and their wishes and feelings ascertained, taken into account (having regard to their age understanding) and recorded when making decisions about the provision of services. Some of the worst failures of the system have occurred when professionals have lost sight of the child and concentrated instead on their relationship with the adults. (DfCSF 2010)

In the *Challenge of Partnership*, the Department of Health identified four approaches: providing information to families; involvement of family members; participation of family members; and partnership (DoH 1995a: para 2.7).[107] It acknowledges that involvement may sometimes be 'predominantly passive and amount to little more than receiving information, having a non-contributory presence at meetings, endorsing other people's decisions or making minor decisions' (ibid: para 2.12). According to Munro, 'the main part of child protection work is helping parents provide better care'; professionals must be authoritative and ask challenging questions while at the same time engaging with parents to help them 'improve their parenting capacity' (DfE 2011f: para 2.24).

However, the more concerns about the children rise, the more limited the role of the family members in deciding what should be done.

Partnership

> 2.13 The objective of any partnership between families and professionals must be the protection and welfare of the child; partnership should not be an end in itself. From the outset workers should consider the possibility of a partnership with each family based on openness, mutual trust, joint decision making and a willingness to listen to families and to capitalise on their strengths. However, words such as equality, choice and power have a limited meaning at certain points in the child protection process. There are times when professional agencies have statutory responsibilities that they have to fulfil and powers that they have to use for the benefit of the child. (DoH 1995a: para 2.13)

Q You were asked about your understanding of partnership above. Has this understanding changed? Are the partners in the child protection process equals? To what extent are parents empowered? To what extent are children empowered?

---

[106] S 53 Children Act 2004, amended the Children Act 1989, ss 17, 20 and 47 to place more emphasis on children's wishes and feelings.

[107] The term 'partnership' appears to have two meanings in this document, one more general and one more specific.

Kaganas[108] argues that choice and power lie largely in the hands of the child protection professionals. For example, the Letter Before Proceedings is meant to focus on ways to avoid litigation but by getting the parents to see things from the point of view of the professionals and to adjust their behaviour accordingly (Kaganas 2010b: 60). Partnership with parents who do not co-operate is minimal:

> [N]ot all the parties have the freedom to choose whether to enter into a partnership relationship. It is the professional partners who decide whether it is fitting to extend an offer of partnership to the family members. On the basis of their assessment of the family, they decide whether partnership is possible and, if so, to what extent. They also largely determine the tasks that family members must perform in order to sustain the partnership. In all this, they are free to discount the views and wishes of their supposed partners. But a rebellious family that refuses to work with the professionals or attempts to ignore their views will find that it cannot safely do so; it will simply be subjected to coercive measures. For those judged irresponsible and unreasonable, the partnership, if it exists at all, will be of the most rudimentary nature. Clearly, then, the partnership is largely controlled by the professional partners. (Kaganas 1995: 11)

Lindley and Richards, although they concede that *Working Together* ensures that parents have information, also question whether it is possible for a 'true partnership' to develop:[109]

> The term 'partnership' implies equality between partners. Yet it is inevitable that when the state intervenes in family life on a compulsory basis such equality is not achievable, because ultimately, such intervention may involve the local authority overriding the parents' wishes.
>
> (Lindley and Richards 2000: 222)

> [Social workers] are expected to make inquiries about the child's safety and welfare, whilst simultaneously empowering parents to be actively involved in the planning and decision-making process. When the inquiries result in a plan being made which is prescriptive about how the parents should care for their child, the local authority is effectively placing restrictions on how they may exercise their parental responsibility. Social workers are therefore being required to empower people whose power they are themselves circumscribing. (ibid: 223)

> Parents are expected to co-operate with any assessment, planning and monitoring which the local authority may require … otherwise they risk an application being made for a compulsory order … .
>
> Although it may be conducted under the guise of partnership and agreement, the degree of informal coercion exercised in these circumstances can be quite considerable. Indeed, the familiar practice of persuading parents to agree to their child being accommodated, with the threat of a compulsory order being applied for if they do not comply, has been documented.
>
> (ibid: 224, reference omitted)[110]

---

[108] See also Aldgate (2001: 67).

[109] The authors suggest that advice and advocacy for parents can enhance partnership. They report that parents and social workers find this helpful and that such work can 'ease communication with the parents, and help them to understand the issues and engage in partnership' (Lindley and Richards 2000: 225). However, it is not apparent from their findings that parents are necessarily empowered as a result; it seems, rather, that they are often persuaded to 'come round' to the professionals' point of view. Indeed, in Lindley et al (2001: 182), it is reported that most advocates in the study encouraged parents to co-operate in most cases. While parents were, for instance, helped to express themselves and to participate in meetings, they were also helped to understand the risk, to accept the professionals' decisions and to understand the local authority social services' view (ibid: 185).

[110] See also Aldgate (2001: 51). According to the research conducted by Brophy, accommodation is used, in at least some local authorities, as an alternative to applying for court orders (Brophy 2006: 53). Parents reported being subjected to pressure to agree to accommodation under threat of court proceedings (ibid: 53–54).

Masson (2005: 78) suggests that pressure to agree, uncertainty about what has been agreed and lack of independent advice and external scrutiny may lead to oppressive social work practice. In addition, parents may agree to arrangements they are not able to maintain.

For King, partnership is a useful device for the professionals because it facilitates surveillance of the family without disturbing the balance between the family and the state.

> To appreciate the importance of this device for politics and thus for government, we need to refer to ... the paradox of child protection and respect for parental rights. Seen in the light of these seemingly incompatible objectives, what the notion of partnership does is to allow officials to intrude upon the privacy of family life, while maintaining intact the structure of parental and family rights. ... This is not to suggest in any way that partnership arrangements are necessarily one-sided. The agreements may well place parents or other care-givers in a better position to secure support and services for themselves and for the child than might have been the case if the responsibilities to the social services department had not been specified in a semi-formal manner.
>
> It hardly needs to be stated, however, that local authority social service departments charged by government with the protection of children have much to gain from entering into partnership arrangements with parents. Partnership operates for them as an observation post sited in the midst of family life from where, under ideal conditions, all the activities of the family may be noted, and reported back to case conferences and planning meetings. Partnership then allows the social worker to play the part of an ethologist, while leaving the political environment, the delicate balance between family and state, between private and public, largely undisturbed.
>
> (King 1995a: 149–50, footnotes omitted)

'Partnership failure' provides proof of the parents' deficiencies and hence the justification for the intrusion into the private sphere and 'all the information that the social services and other agencies acquired during the partnership is now reproduced in court in the form of evidence that the child is being abused or neglected' (ibid: 150).

Q To what extent do these analyses reflect Donzelot's concept of tutelage?

X. FAMILY SUPPORT AND THE CHILDREN ACT 2004

The Children Act 1989 was shaped in part by child abuse scandals. The Children Act 2004, on the other hand, largely owes its very existence to yet another such scandal.[111] Victoria Climbie died after being subjected to horrific abuse by a great-aunt and her cohabitant. The Report of the inquiry that followed concluded that 'in general, the legislative framework for protecting children is basically sound' (Laming 2003: para 1.30). However, it severely criticised the professionals involved in the case for failing to adhere to good practice, for poor investigative standards and for poor communication. The fault, said Lord Laming, who headed the inquiry, lay not in the law but its implementation (ibid: para 1.30). He made a number of recommendations aimed at improving co-operation, partnership and the sharing of information between agencies. He also recommended setting up new agencies. And he made it clear that family support was a crucial: 'It is not possible to separate the protection of children from wider support to families. Indeed,

---

[111] See DfES (2004c: 4). It was also a response to an inspection report.

often the best protection for a child is achieved by the timely intervention of family support services' (ibid: para 1.30).

A move from a focus on child protection to one on prevention through family support had been the subject of debate for some time.[112] But it was after the publication of the Laming Report that the then government moved family support much further up the policy agenda. In 2003, it published a Green Paper, *Every Child Matters* (DfES 2003), that contained proposals not only to overhaul the child protection machinery but to increase the services available to families and to promote early intervention:

> 4. As Lord Laming's recommendations made clear, child protection cannot be separated from policies to improve children's lives as a whole. We need to focus both on the universal services which every child uses, and on more targeted services for those with additional needs. The policies set out in the Green Paper are designed both to protect children and to maximise their potential. ... It aims to reduce the numbers of children who experience educational failure, engage in offending or anti-social behaviour, suffer from ill-health, or become teenage parents.
>
> 5. We need to ensure we protect children at risk within the framework of universal services.
>
> (DfES 2003: Executive Summary)

The Green Paper set out five desirable outcomes for children that have influenced policy since:

> 1.3 ...
> * *being healthy:* enjoying good physical and mental health and living a healthy lifestyle
> * *staying safe:* being protected from harm and neglect and growing up able to look after themselves
> * *enjoying and achieving:* getting the most out of life and developing broad skills for adulthood
> * *making a positive contribution:* to the community and to society and not engaging in anti-social or offending behaviour
> * *economic well-being:* overcoming socio-economic disadvantages to achieve their full potential in life. (DfES 2003, emphasis in original)

By the time the ensuing White Paper appeared, a new post of Minister for Children, Young People and Families had been created, signifying the importance the government was attaching to family and child issues.[113] The White Paper, *Every Child Matters: Next Steps* (DfES 2004a), outlined new legislation, which was to become the Children Act 2004. Reporting on the consultations that were carried out, it stated:

> 1.12 There is a strong consensus in support of ... a sharper focus on prevention and early intervention. ...
>
> 3.6 ... we need to shift away from associating parenting support with crisis interventions to a more consistent offer of parenting support throughout a child and young person's life. We will work towards a mix of universal and targeted parenting approaches including advice and information, home visiting and parenting classes ... .
>
> 3.33 ... Our aim is to achieve a culture change where practitioners and managers focus creatively on whether outcomes have improved rather than whether centrally determined processes have been adhered to. (DfES 2004a)

---

[112] See, eg, DoH (1998: para 1.2).
[113] See DfES, DoH and Home Office (2003: para 19).

The Children Act 2004 established the legal framework within which these changes were to take place. It created the office of Children's Commissioner.[114] Section 2 stipulates that the function of the Commissioner is to promote awareness of the views and interests of children on issues such as health and protection from harm and neglect. Part 2 of the Act focuses on the child protection system and on services for children. Section 10 places a duty on all children's services authorities in England[115] to promote co-operation between agencies. Information sharing is promoted as a means of helping to track children and follow up concerns more effectively; section 12 provides for the setting up of databases containing information about children and young people.[116]

New mechanisms for assessment were created for individual professionals working with children. The Common Assessment Framework[117] was intended to 'provide a national, common process for early assessment' (DfES 2004d: para 3.30). The idea is that the professional who first deals with a child who is thought to be in need or at risk, such as a head-teacher, can make an initial assessment before deciding whether it is necessary to refer the case to children's services. If the case is referred, then there is another guide to assessment that must be adhered to by local authority social workers:[118] the *Framework for the Assessment of Children in Need and their Families*.[119] This sets out an 'ecological' approach which must be adopted by child protection professionals in assessing children to determine whether they are in need or at risk.

Sinclair and Bullock point to the challenges of applying this framework. They argue that professionals need to know whether some of the specified factors are more important than others, whether they are more dangerous in combination and what interventions meet particular needs (Sinclair and Bullock 2003: 62). It is clear, therefore, that however helpful guidance and frameworks might be, child welfare professionals are still required to exercise considerable judgement and powers of interpretation in the context of a complex knowledge base that offers little certainty.

To summarise, the policy is to ensure that children and families are provided with universal services to meet their needs and to prevent the risk of children suffering harm. Within this universal service, targeted services are supposed to meet the more pressing needs of children at risk. To this end, guidance is provided to show professionals how to assess children.

XI. EARLY INTERVENTION

Increasingly, therefore, partnership has taken the form of encouraging parental co-operation with early intervention, where families are helped through education and advice to achieve the preferred outcomes. The education and advice are made available through services such as through Sure Start Centres and Family Intervention Projects.[120] These

---

[114] S 1 Children Act 2004.

[115] For the law relating to Wales, see Part 3 Children Act 2004.

[116] See further DfES (2004d: paras 3.33–3.36).

[117] See Chapter 14 below.

[118] Other agencies which might be involved in helping with assessments under s 27 of the Children Act 1989, such as health authorities, are also required to be aware of the *Framework* (DoH 2000: ix).

[119] See above and Chapter 14 below.

[120] See DfCSF (2009b: 4–5, 46); DfE (2011f: paras 2.27–2.28); Chapter 5 above. See below.

services are intended to be universal,[121] with targeted services aimed at families in difficulty. [122]

> 10.17 Early action to prevent and address problems for children and young people is critical to
> stop children living in these circumstances having poor outcomes in life. This means a co-ordi-
> nated approach across services to identify and intervene early with families with children who
> are at the greatest risk of having poor outcomes. An agreed list of warning signs which could
> prompt concerns being raised about a child's welfare (such as a permanent exclusion from
> school, repeated truancy or involvement in anti-social behaviour, knife crime, violence, and/or
> gangs) should identify that whole family intervention may be necessary to safeguard and
> promote a child's welfare. Targeted parenting and family support is provided through services
> such as Family Intervention Projects (FIPs) and parenting programmes and services as set out
> in the local authority's Parenting Strategy. (DfCSF 2010)

While programmes such as parenting programmes and Sure Start are voluntary, they do
entail an attempt to get parents to engage and to change. For example:

> 10.23 ... The ability of workers to engage parents effectively and consistently and to achieve
> 'buy in' to what is often a demanding and rigorous change management programme, is crucial
> to the success of any intervention. There is considerable skill, tenacity, determination and toler-
> ance required by parenting practitioners and key workers who will need to identify the
> appropriate drivers for change in their clients. (DfCSF 2010)

Kaganas argues that, while many families are undoubtedly helped by these services and
by these interventions, they facilitate surveillance:

> This aspect of family policy could lead to greater intrusion in the family. It is aimed at breaching
> the ramparts of the private family to inculcate in parents 'better' attitudes to their children and
> to promote 'better' childcare practices ... . [I]t seems that it is now ... considered acceptable to
> seek to intervene in families other than those posing an immediate risk to children. It seems
> that whereas previously family policy was concerned primarily with ensuring that parents did
> no harm to their children, the state is now demanding more: parents are expected to do good ... .
> And where parents are considered deficient in some way, there is now a preoccupation with
> effecting change. Problem, potential problem or marginalised families must be moulded into
> better families in order to transform them into suitable environments for raising children ... .
>   What is new about the current policy is the scope of its reach; the new re-moralisation
> project is embedded in an ambitious project to improve parenting throughout the nation by
> means of universal and targeted services. ...
>   These initiatives expose parents to monitoring and to intervention by welfare professionals
> in circumstances where there are few safeguards in place and no real counterweight to the
> power of those professionals. More specifically new measures have the potential to make more
> families, or, to be more accurate, more mothers, visible and susceptible to varying levels of
> surveillance and coercion to transform them into 'good' mothers.
>   (Kaganas 2010b: 43–44, footnote omitted)

There are outreach and home visiting services which are used to 'persuade parents to

---

[121] At the time of writing, financial constraints are leading to a scaling down of services with, for example,
the closure of some Sure Start centres and this has led to public consternation. See, eg, Richardson (2011a,
2011b).
[122] See further, Davies and Ward (2011: 7ff).

access services' and to 'get them to participate regularly in the relevant Sure Start Services' (Ball and Niven 2011: Key Findings). Where families are considered to be in difficulty, the response is to provide early and intensive intervention.[123] Here, there is an element of coercion. The family is expected to accept help and, if they do not, they are deemed irresponsible: '[T]he parent of an at-risk child should be given support, but it is also incumbent on them to take this support'. What is required is 'a clear sense of personal responsibility ...with clear consequences if those responsibilities are not met' (HM Government 2006: para 3.66).

Moreover, as Hendrick[124] says, the image of the child as victim and the image of the child as threat tend to go in tandem and the services provided are often described as means of preventing social exclusion.[125] Even section 10 of the Children Act 2004 refers to children's contribution to society.

So, yet again, the construction of the child embraces two images. And children, moulded in both of those images, it seems, must be made increasingly visible. The family remains private but the aim is to draw more and more families and their children into public arenas to take advantage of the services offered.[126] It appears that the tutelary system has been expanding in a bid by the state to ensure that children become neither victims nor threats.

XII. FAMILY GROUP CONFERENCES

The Public Law Outline[127] states that, where it is in the child's interests, and where the court considers it appropriate, the parties should be encouraged to use alternative dispute resolution. The utility of such an approach in many cases is open to doubt; as Masson points out, 'lack of parental co-operation with child protection services is a key factor in the initiation of care proceedings, and ... planning for children without court orders requires good co-operation with their parents' (Masson 2007: 420).

One extra-judicial mechanism that has been used for some years, and which is said to empower families, is the family group conference.[128] This is deployed as a means of making decisions about children 'at risk' as well as 'in need'.[129] The functions of the family group conference are described in *Working Together*:

> 10.2 A family group conference (FGC) is a decision making and planning process whereby the wider family group makes plans and decisions for children and young people who have been identified either by the family or by service providers as being in need of a plan that will safeguard and promote their welfare. FGCs do not replace or remove the need for child protection conferences, which should always be held when the relevant criteria are met. FGCs may be valuable, for example:
>
> • for children in need, in a range of circumstances where a plan is required for the child's future welfare;

---

[123] See DfES (2007: para 2.16).
[124] See p 622 above.
[125] See above. See also, eg, DoH (2000: x).
[126] Family policy has come increasingly to focus on children. See Chapter 5 above.
[127] Practice Direction. Public Law Proceedings Guide to Case Management: April 2010, para 3.20(14).
[128] See DfE (2010b: 49).
[129] See Lupton et al (1995: para 2.5.3).

- where section 47[130] enquiries do not substantiate concerns about significant harm but where support and services are required; and
- where section 47 enquiries progress to a child protection conference, the conference may agree that an FGC is an appropriate vehicle for the core group to use to develop the outline child protection plan into a fully worked-up plan. (DfCSF 2010)

First introduced in New Zealand and based on traditional Maori practice, the family group conference process gives the task of decision-making to the family rather than the child-care professionals. The family decide who should attend and the group may include friends and neighbours as well as family members.

Q Refer to Chapter 15 below. To what extent is this process similar to mediation? To what extent might it give rise to similar problems?

The procedure has evoked some anxiety among professionals about imbalances of power within the family and the risk that some members will be silenced or dominated by others (Lupton et al 1995: para 5.2.6). One study reveals that this did occur in a minority of cases (ibid: para 5.6.4). Some family members interviewed also indicated that family tension and hostility created problems (ibid). Nevertheless, there is research that indicates that there is general satisfaction among families and professionals with family group conferences.[131] In particular, proponents of the model argue that among its virtues is the fact that it extends the partnership principle and empowers families (ibid: para 6.1). While parental involvement in the form of partnership can appear 'tokenistic' (ibid: para 2.2.8), the family group conference procedure is promoted as transferring power 'from the hands of faceless state officials to the family and the community' (King 1997: 140).

Yet, on closer analysis, this transfer is limited. There are certain decisions that the family is not permitted to make. *Working Together* makes it clear that it is the professionals who set the parameters of the discussion:

10.3 It is essential that all parties are provided with clear and accurate information, which will make effective planning possible. The family is the primary planning group in the process. Family members need to be able to understand what the issues are from the perspective of the professionals. The family and involved professionals should be clear about:

- what the professional findings are from any core assessment of the child and family;
- what the family understands about their current situation;
- what decisions are required;
- what decisions have already been taken;
- the family's scope for decision-making, and whether there are any issues/decisions which are not negotiable; and
- what resources are or might be available to implement any plan. Within this framework, agencies and professionals should agree to support the plan if it does not place the child at risk of suffering significant harm, and if the resources requested can be provided.

(DfCSF 2010)

That it is the professionals who have the final say means that the family unit is allowed to make decisions only within the confines of predefined notions of what is harmful to children (King 1997: 158). The privacy of the family can be preserved only within con-

---

[130] See Chapter 14 below.
[131] See Lupton et al (1995); Crow and Marsh (1997).

straints set by the professionals and the law. Where the child's safety is at stake, the family is not permitted to operate autonomously within its 'black box' (ibid: 159). In addition, Welbourne has noted that the research on the outcomes for children of FGC decision-making is lacking and there are no safeguards; there is no external scrutiny such as judicial scrutiny of these decisions, provided they are accepted by the local authority (Welbourne 2008: 342–43)

XIII. LOCAL AUTHORITY ACCOUNTABILITY

Negligence

Local authorities owe a duty of care to the children for whom they are responsible. They are expected to exercise their discretion in placing children and making decisions about them in a reasonable manner. Failure to do so could result an action in tort for negligence.[132] In *Barrett v Enfield London Borough Council*[133] the House of Lords ruled that an action in negligence is available in relation to decisions taken by a local authority about the upbringing of a child while already in care. The negligence alleged in that case consisted of the way the plaintiff was placed with various unsuitable foster parents and in children's homes as a child, without being adopted or placed with his relatives. There were also allegations about the local authority's failure to enable him to see his mother and a failure to provide psychiatric treatment. He argued that as a result he had suffered psychiatric injury. The court held that, in principle, the exercise of a statutory discretion could give rise to a duty of care. The possibility of a viable cause of action in negligence was confirmed by the court in *S v Gloucestershire County Council*,[134] a case in which two adults claimed that the foster fathers with whom they had been placed as children had sexually abused them. They sued in negligence claiming that they had suffered long-term damage as a result of their abuse.

The Human Rights Act 1998

Much of the jurisprudence that has developed around the European Convention for the Protection of Human Rights and Fundamental Freedoms 1950 can be seen as consistent with the notion of partnership and with the aim of family participation in decision-making. It also reinforces the idea that compulsory intervention should be a last resort.

The Human Rights Act 1998 incorporates most of the provisions of the ECHR and provides remedies for individuals whose rights have been infringed. Section 6(1) stipulates

---

[132] Local authorities have a duty of care to the children they deal with. They also have a duty of care to the foster parents with whom they place children. In *W v Essex County Council* [2000] 1 FLR 657, the House of Lords held that the foster parents had an arguable case because the local authority had placed a known sexual abuser with them, without informing them of the boy's history, and in the knowledge that the foster parents had stipulated that they did not want to foster children who were known to be or suspected of being sexual abusers. The boy allegedly abused the foster parents' children. See also *A and B v Essex County Council* [2003] 1 FLR 615; *NXS v Camden London Borough Council* [2009] EWHC 1786 QB; [2010] 1 FLR 100.

[133] [1999] 2 FLR 426.

[134] *S v Gloucestershire County Council: Tower Hamlets London Borough Council and Havering London Borough Council* [2000] 1 FLR 825.

that it is unlawful for a public authority to act in a way that is incompatible with a Convention right, unless, as a result of the contents of primary legislation, it could not have acted differently.[135] Courts and local authorities are classified as public authorities and so are bound by the Act. A person who claims that a public authority has acted or proposes to act unlawfully in contravention of his or her rights may rely on the Convention rights within the context of existing legal proceedings or may bring a free-standing application.[136]

The Human Rights Act has created a cause of action for those harmed by the failure of a local authority to intervene to protect them. In *Z and Others v United Kingdom*[137] it was held by the ECtHR that the failure of a local authority to protect children from serious, long-term neglect and abuse constituted a violation of Article 3, which prohibits torture, or inhuman or degrading treatment or punishment, and which requires the state to intervene to prevent ill-treatment of which the authorities knew or ought to have known.[138]

However, most of the case law focuses on protection of the family from intervention. The rights that are invoked most frequently in child protection cases are those enshrined in Articles 6 and 8. Article 6 states that everyone is entitled to a fair and public hearing in the determination his or her civil rights and obligations, or any criminal charge. This extends to a right to be involved in decisions to make, continue or discharge care orders.[139] Decisions about the child while a care order is in force may or may not affect the child's or the parents' rights.[140] The proceedings have to be examined as a whole to determine whether they were fair.[141]

Article 8 gives everyone a right to respect for private and family life. Case law has established that the 'mutual enjoyment by parent and child of each others' company constitutes a fundamental element of family life'.[142] The article also prohibits interference by a public authority with the rights to respect for private and family life, except to the extent that it is in accordance with the law, necessary in a democratic society and for the protection of health or morals, or for the protection of the rights and freedoms of others. The notion of necessity implies that the interference must correspond to a pressing social need and must be proportionate to a legitimate aim.[143] The reasons for interfering must be

---

[135] S 6(2)(a).

[136] S 7. Remedies are set out in s 8. Proceedings against local authorities under s 7 should be considered a longstop; other mechanisms such as judicial review may be appropriate: *Re S (Minors) (Care Order: Implementation of Care Plan); Re W (Minors) (Care Order: Adequacy of Care Plan)* [2002] UKHL 10; [2002] 1 FLR 815, para 62. Judicial review itself should only be considered when local authority actions cannot be challenged by other means such as through the provisions of the Children Act 1989: *Re M (Care Proceedings: Judicial Review)* [2003] EWHC Admin 850; [2003] 2 FLR 171. See also *Re L (Care Proceedings: Human Rights Claims)* [2003] EWHC Fam 665; [2003] 2 FLR 160.

[137] [2001] 2 FLR 612.

[138] Paras 74–75. This applies only if the local authority should have been aware of the abuse: *DP and JC v United Kingdom* [2003] 1 FLR 50, para 114. Nor is there a failure to protect the child's physical or moral integrity in breach of Art 8 unless the local authority ought to have been aware of the abuse: *DP and JC v United Kingdom* [2003] 1 FLR 50, para 119. See, also, on breach of Art 3 as a result of physical punishment, *A v United Kingdom (Human Rights: Punishment of Child)* [1998] 2 FLR 952.

[139] *Re S (Minors) (Care Order: Implementation of Care Plan); Re W (Minors) (Care Order: Adequacy of Care Plan)* [2002] UKHL 10; [2002] 1 FLR 815, paras 75–76.

[140] Ibid, paras 77–79. Decisions about contact and rehabilitation do affect rights.

[141] *Re V (Care: Pre-Birth Actions)* [2004] EWCA Civ 1575; [2005] 1 FLR 627.

[142] *W v United Kingdom* (1987) 10 EHRR 29, para 59; *Johansen v Norway* (1996) 23 EHRR 33, para 52; *K and T v Finland* [2001] 2 FLR 707, para 151; *P, C and S v United Kingdom* [2002] 2 FLR 631, para 113.

[143] *W v United Kingdom* (1987) 10 EHRR 29, para 60; *Re W and B; Re W (Care Plan)* [2001] EWCA Civ 757; [2001] 2 FLR 582, para 54; *Haase v Germany* [2004] 2 FLR 39, para 88.

'relevant' and 'sufficient'.[144] Protection of the interests of children can, potentially, justify interference as it is a legitimate aim; it falls within the ambit of the expressions 'protection of health' and the 'protection of the rights and freedoms of others'.[145] Consideration of what is in the best interests of the child is of 'crucial importance'.[146] Mistaken judgements or assessments by professionals do not of themselves constitute infringements of Article 8:

> The authorities, both medical and social, have duties to protect children and cannot be held liable every time genuine and reasonably held concerns about the safety of children vis-à-vis members of their family are proved, retrospectively, to have been misguided. [147]

Kaganas, reviewing the case law, maintains that the Human Rights Act does little to strengthen parental rights (Kaganas 2010b: 44). While the ECtHR and domestic courts have been willing to criticise procedural defects, and precipitate action such as removal of children without sufficient notice, failure to involve parents in the process and restrictions on contact with children in care, they have been less ready to question the merits of decisions to put children in care; the welfare principle tends to prevail (ibid: 46–47). Applications for Emergency Protection Orders (EPOs) and care orders[148] are almost invariably granted.[149] Police, social workers and the courts alike are reluctant to leave children in what has been assessed by the professionals and experts to be a risky situation.

XIV. REFORMING THE SYSTEM

Alongside a review of the court system,[150] the government commissioned a review of the social work child protection system. A central question was 'what helps professionals make the best judgments they can to protect a vulnerable child?' (DfE 2011f: Executive Summary, para 1). Munro, who conducted this review, has called for a move from a 'compliance to a learning culture' (DfE 2011f: Preface). This involves, she says, 'moving from a system that has become over-bureaucratised and focused on compliance to one that values and develops professional expertise and is focused on the safety and welfare of children and young people' (DfE 2011f: Executive Summary, para 1). The child protection

---

[144] *K and T v Finland* [2001] 2 FLR 707, para 154; *P, C and S v United Kingdom* [2002] 2 FLR 631, para 114.

[145] *Olsson v Sweden (No 2)* (1992) 17 EHRR 134, para 119 (Commission), and para 84 (Court); *Haase v Germany* [2004] 2 FLR 39, para 87. See also See *Re D (Unborn Baby)* [2009] EWHC 446 (Fam); [2009] 2 FLR 313.

[146] *K and T v Finland* [2001] 2 FLR 707, para 154. However, it appears that the courts should take into account the effects on the parents' relationship of a care order when engaging in the balancing exercise, particularly if it would entail their permanent separation: *Mr JD, Mrs JD v City and County of Swansea, KD (A Child by her Children's Guardian)* [2011] EWCA Civ 34. The headnote summarises the view of the appeal court: 'the effect of the judge's order ... was to require the permanent breakdown of the parents' marriage, as well as to provide that K's future relationship with the father should be of an attenuated nature. Whether addressed through the prism of art 8 of the Convention or under s 1(1) and (3) of the Children Act 1989, the judge's decision had to be one of last resort.'

[147] *AD and OD v UK* [2010] 2 FLR 1, para 84. See also *MAK and RK v United Kingdom* [2010] 2 FLR 451.

[148] See further Chapter 14 below.

[149] See Masson et al (2007: 177, 207). See also Masson et al (2008b: para 55).

[150] See Norgrove (2011a). This is discussed in Chapter 14 below.

system has in recent times, she says, been shaped by four main driving forces which have created a 'defensive system' (ibid: para 3):

- the importance of the safety and welfare of children and young people and the understandable strong reaction when a child is killed or seriously harmed;
- a commonly held belief that the complexity and associated uncertainty of child protection work can be eradicated;
- a readiness, in high profile public inquiries into the death of a child, to focus on professional error without looking deeply enough into its causes; and
- the undue importance given to performance indicators and targets which provide only part of the picture of practice, and which have skewed attention to process over the quality and effectiveness of help given. (ibid: para 2)[151]

Attention should shift, she argues, from following procedures to checking whether children and young people are being helped (ibid: para 4). Among other things, she recommends that the government should revise both *Working Together* and the *Framework for the Assessment of Children in Need* so as to remove the constraints to local innovation and professional judgement presented by nationally designed assessment forms and national performance indicators (ibid: para 21, Recommendation 1). She also recommends that a new inspection framework should examine the child's experiences and also 'look at the effectiveness of the help provided to children, young people and their families' (ibid: Recommendation 3).

What is notable about this review is the acknowledgement and acceptance of uncertainty. As Munro observes, 'Future predictions about abusive behaviour are necessarily fallible' (DfE 2011f: para 1.1).[152] Uncertainty arises at two stages. First, abuse and neglect often occur in the privacy of the home and so cannot easily be identified. Family autonomy and privacy are valued and so monitoring children's safety, especially in the early years, is difficult because professionals have to rely on parental co-operation (ibid: para 1.12). Second, uncertainty arises when making predictions about children's future safety: 'The big problem for society (and consequently for professionals) is establishing a realistic expectation of professionals' ability to predict the future and manage risk of harm to children and young people' (ibid: para 1.13). Even where it is established that harm is occurring, it is difficult to decide whether the child can be protected at home or whether it is necessary to remove him or her (ibid). It is not possible to eradicate risk but only to 'try to reduce the possibility of harm' (ibid). Hindsight distorts our judgement (ibid: para 1.14) and we tend to explain bad outcomes in terms of human error (ibid: para 1.15). The solution then becomes finding ways to control people so they do not make these mistakes (ibid: para 1.16). The managerialist concern with targets and performance indicators has meant that the focus is not on children's needs (ibid: para 1.21).[153] What is needed instead is to allow professionals scope to exercise their judgement (ibid: para 1.27):[154]

8.4 The priority given to process over practice has led to insufficient attention being given to whether children and young people are benefiting from the services they receive. Any future reform programme must make outcomes for children and young people the prime measure of

---

[151] See also DfE (2011f: para 1.7).
[152] See also paras 2.32–2.33.
[153] See also para 1.16.
[154] However, she goes on to recommend 'clearly understood procedures' when agencies work together. See para 8.8.

whether the system is working well. ... In place of the current system, which has been a part of the compliance culture, there should be more attention given to learning and adapting. This will require practitioners, and leaders in particular, to learn to expect the possibility of error.

Whether these recommendations will be implemented remains to be seen. However, as Munro observes, it is a 'major challenge ... to make the system less "risk averse" and more "risk sensible"' (ibid: para 8.26). If professionals are given more opportunity to exercise their skill and judgement, if they are assessed according to outcome, and if procedures become more local and flexible, as she recommends, this will probably not change the perceptions of failure and blame. The response to Peter Connelly's death and that of other children in high-profile cases suggests that the media, politicians and the public are more likely to focus on the duty to protect than the inevitability of bad outcomes in some cases. Outcomes such as a child death will probably continue to be blamed on human error and calls will be made for better training and knowledge. Indeed the Munro Review itself recommends these.

XV. CONCLUSION

Changes in images of childhood have led to the perception that children must be protected; child abuse has been successfully constructed as a major social problem. Along with this, more recent years have seen government initiatives to tackle poverty and social exclusion and so efforts are being made to provide universal services for children. However, it remains the case that the obligation of the state to intervene in order to protect children from harm is conceived of more narrowly; the notion of abuse is confined to acts perpetrated by individuals.[155] This might be explained, applying Manning's analysis, by the fact that it is in relation to these types of harm that 'entrepreneurial' efforts have been concentrated and that publicity has been greatest. In addition, what are seen as appropriate measures to combat these types of harm have been capable of accommodation within the political agenda of the state.

This accommodation has not been without its difficulties. Measures to protect children potentially threaten the autonomy of the family which, in the liberal state, must also be protected. The history of child protection reveals an ever-present tension between the ideal of family privacy and a perceived need to respond to the problem of abuse. Moreover, the scope of the problem is expanding; child welfare knowledge is constantly changing and leading to the 'discovery' of new categories of abuse.

However, while child welfare knowledge is contributing to the construction of new problems, it also constitutes the modern justification for breaching the privacy of the family to deal with these problems. The state has to be seen to be responding to concerns by 'doing something' about abuse, and this it does through the agency of its social workers. They work within a legal framework which precludes coercive intervention in the absence of 'reliable' evidence of abuse or a risk of abuse.[156] The law sets thresholds and child welfare workers are charged with the almost impossible task of determining whether these have been crossed. Unlike the philanthropists of old, however, they do not

---

[155] Including the behaviour of individuals within institutions. See Report of the National Commission of Inquiry into the Prevention of Child Abuse (1996: para. 2.42); Utting (1997).

[156] See further Chapter 14 below.

rely on moral judgements to justify their actions. Instead, they rely on what is regarded as more 'scientific' knowledge. Child welfare knowledge enables social workers, and other child welfare professionals working in the child protection arena, to be presented and to present themselves as having the expertise necessary to determine which children are at risk. This apparent ability to judge when intervention is needed allows them to be seen as protecting children without unwarranted intrusions into family life.

We have noted a trend to curtail coercive intervention and to emphasise working with the family. The concept of partnership is evidence of this trend. And now the aim is to provide help for families and children in an attempt to pre-empt any need at all for coercive intervention. However, it is doubtful whether the trend to minimise coercion implies a lessening in regulation of the family. Partnership can be seen as facilitating surveillance and the expanded services to help families, too, can be seen in this light, at least to the extent that they survive the current financial cuts. As Gillies (2008) says, the Labour government saw (and we would say also the coalition government continues to see) deviancy and poor outcomes as being rooted in inadequate parenting. Government sees itself as responsible for ensuring that families (and in Gillies' view specifically working-class families and mainly mothers) raise their children to approved standards. Unregulated parents, she says are thought to 'spawn damaged anti-social children destined to live a life of poverty and crime', whereas responsible parenting enables children to flourish. On this reasoning, she says, 'only the most selfish, uncaring or stupid would reject advice and guidance designed to improve their children's life chances' (Gillies 2008: 100)

The measures designated as parenting support could therefore be seen as functioning to strengthen what Donzelot referred to as the 'tutelary complex' and may serve as a means of inculcating families with approved norms. While the ideology of privacy of the family remains strong and family autonomy is underwritten by the law, the private family will continue to be regulated to encourage it to conform to public norms informing the image of the responsible family.

FURTHER READING

D ARCHARD, 'Can Child Abuse Be Defined?' in M King (ed), *Moral Agendas for Children's Welfare* (London, Routledge, 1999).

S ASHENDEN, *Governing Child Sexual Abuse: Negotiating the Boundaries of Public and Private, Law and Science* (London, Routledge, 2004).

J EEKELAAR, 'Parental Responsibility: State of Nature or Nature of the State?' (1991) *JSW&FL* 37.

N PARTON, *Safeguarding Childhood: Early Intervention and Surveillance in Modern Society* (Basingstoke, Palgrave Macmillan, 2006).

C PIPER, *Investing in Children. Policy, Law and Practice in Context* (Devon, Willan Publishing, 2008).

F ROBERTSON ELLIOT, 'The Family: Private Arena or Adjunct of the State' (1989) 16 *J of Law and Society* 443.

N ROSE, 'Beyond the Public/Private Division: Law, Power and the Family' (1987) 14 *J of Law and Society* 61.

14

Child Protection

I. INTRODUCTION

This chapter incorporates the theme of welfare as well as that of the public/private divide. As we saw in Chapter 13 above, child protection raises questions about what is harmful to children as well as the issues of when and to what extent it is appropriate for agencies representing the state to intervene in the family. This chapter focuses on the process of child protection, the moves to try to secure good outcomes for children and also the relevant law.

The primary agency[1] responsible for child protection, the prevention of abuse and neglect, the investigation of cases and the initiation of court proceedings is the local authority.[2] So, for example, while the Children Act 1989 empowers the police to take children at risk into police protection for up to 72 hours, the local authority has to be notified of such cases and if, after inquiry, the police consider it necessary to apply for an emergency order, this is done on behalf of the local authority.[3] It is, therefore, the local authority that is charged with endeavouring to ensure that children are not being abused or at risk of being abused.

However, it is important to keep in mind that a number of agencies, including NHS trusts,[4] health authorities, police and probation, are all required to have regard to the need to 'safeguard and promote the welfare of children' when carrying out their normal functions. This duty, embodied in section 11 of the Children Act 2004, rests on both the agencies and those individuals working within them.

---

[1] Art 19 of the UN Convention on the Rights of the Child places a duty on states to take measures, including administrative and legislative measures to protect children from violence, injury, abuse and maltreatment. There is also a requirement that states provide for social programmes to provide support for the child and the child's carers, as well as forms of prevention and identification, treatment and, if necessary, judicial involvement.

[2] Local Authority Social Services Act 1970, Sch 1. The NSPCC is designated an 'authorised person' and is therefore permitted to initiate care proceedings. However, it rarely does so.

[3] S 46. Of course, the police would be the principal agency involved in a criminal investigation concerning abuse.

[4] At the time of writing abolition of NHS Trusts was under consideration by the Coalition government.

II. FROM 'RISK' TO 'NEED'?

We have discussed the concept of child abuse as a social construction and the contingency of the definition of abuse.[5] However, even if there are shared understandings about the concept of abuse, the problem remains as to how to determine whether it has occurred or whether there is a risk of a future occurrence. The difficulties lie in identifying or predicting harm as discussed in Chapter 13 above. Here we will focus on the processes currently in place to structure decision-making. Munro, in a recent review of the child protection system, says that the rules and guidance published by government departments were put in place in an attempt to control people in order to attempt to eliminate human error. This goal, she says, is unattainable: risk cannot be eliminated—it can only be reduced. The system currently in place, she argues, is overbureaucratised and does not leave sufficient scope for professional judgement (DfE 2011f).[6]

One of the documents criticised by Munro is *Working Together to Safeguard Children*, which provides guidance for agencies and professionals working in the field of child welfare and protection. It contains detailed instructions for handling cases of children in need, and cases of abuse or suspected abuse. Part 1, with which this chapter deals, is statutory guidance and must be complied with by local authorities carrying out their social services functions unless there are exceptional circumstances justifying departure from it (DfCSF 2010: 25).

Working Together has gone through various incarnations since the first version was published in 1991. One of the notable changes is a shift from a focus on child protection to safeguarding. This, in turn, reflects a partial policy shift away from requiring a focus on risk to a perception that universal services for all children, alongside targeted services for children in need or at risk, provide a more effective framework for promoting the welfare of children and avoiding abuse.[7]

Cooper et al have observed that social work has come to be characterised by risk assessment and risk avoidance (Cooper et al 2003: 59). Social workers are afraid to make mistakes; they fear leaving children in dangerous situations and they fear removing children from their families unnecessarily. Cooper et al maintain that 'fear of failure has shaped child protection practice in England and Wales for several decades' (ibid: 10) and that 'the system encourages social workers to protect their own position' (ibid: 11), at the cost, presumably, of doing what they think is best for families.

This preoccupation with avoiding risk has for some years met with criticism in government documents: '[R]isks must be taken in order to get a more successful outcome for the child by keeping various avenues of family support firmly in mind when child protection enquiries are underway' (DoH 1995b: 52). In addition, rather than confining themselves primarily to child protection, with its attendant focus on risk assessment, workers were urged to 'tackle the wider welfare requirements of children and families' (ibid: 48). A shift from protection to prevention in the form of increased provision of services was advocated in a Department of Health publication, *Child Protection. Messages From Research*:

---

[5] See Chapter 13 above.

[6] For a more detailed discussion of the Munro Report, see Chapter 13 above.

[7] See DfCSF (2010: paras 3.8–3.10). See Chapter 13 above.

The research studies suggest that too much of the work undertaken comes under the banner of child protection. ... A more useful perspective [is one according to which] much early work is viewed as an enquiry to establish whether the child in need might benefit from services. ...

The focus would be on the overall needs of children rather than a narrow concentration on the alleged incident. (DoH 1995b: 54–55)

This shift has led to a widening of the remit of local authorities to encompass the promotion of children's best interests alongside child protection. Local authorities and professionals are expected to help children achieve outcomes that might be seen as promoting the 'good' life and responsible citizenship while avoiding social exclusion. These outcomes, which are now embodied in the Children Act 2004, are enumerated in Chapter 13 (p 645) of this book. *Working Together* sets out what is needed to achieve them:

1.3 To achieve the five *Every Child Matters* outcomes, children need to feel loved and valued, and be supported by a network of reliable and affectionate relationships. They need to feel they are respected and understood as individual people and to have their wishes and feelings consistently taken into account. If they are denied the opportunity and support they need to achieve these outcomes, children are at increased risk not only of an impoverished childhood, but also of disadvantage and social exclusion in adulthood. Abuse and neglect pose particular problems.

(DfCSF 2010)

To fulfil their potential children must be safeguarded and their welfare promoted. *Working Together* explains what is meant by this:

1.20 *Safeguarding and promoting the welfare of children* is defined for the purposes of this guidance as:

- protecting children from maltreatment;
- preventing impairment of children's health or development;
- ensuring that children are growing up in circumstances consistent with the provision of safe and effective care;

and undertaking that role so as to enable those children to have optimum life chances and to enter adulthood successfully.

1.21 Protecting children from maltreatment is important in preventing the impairment of health or development though that in itself may be insufficient to ensure that children are growing up in circumstances consistent with the provision of safe and effective care. These aspects of safeguarding and promoting welfare are cumulative, and all contribute to the outcomes set out in paragraph 1.1 ... .

1.23 *Child protection* is a part of safeguarding and promoting welfare. This refers to the activity that is undertaken to protect specific children who are suffering, or are likely to suffer, significant harm.

1.24 Effective child protection is essential as part of wider work to safeguard and promote the welfare of children. However, all agencies and individuals should aim to proactively safeguard and promote the welfare of children so that the need for action to protect children from harm is reduced. (DfCSF 2010)

The aim is to improve the lives of children generally and to provide additional, targeted support for children in need and children at risk. Yet despite the breadth of the new remit, Munro says that, 'social work services remain heavily biased towards dealing with child protection, and family support services have failed to materialise at the rate intended' (DfE 2011f: para 8.14). She tells us that preventative services are more effective than reactive ones in reducing abuse and neglect (ibid: paras 5.1–5.2). Early help also improves children's life chances; it minimises adverse experiences for children and prevents irreparable damage to them. In addition it is cost effective. Sure Start Children's Centres, in particular, she says, are 'well placed to provide early help for children and families' (ibid: para 5.18).[8] These provide a therapeutic and holistic service 'accessible to all families but focused on those in greatest need' (ibid: para 5.19). Other services providing useful help include Home Start and Community Service Volunteers (ibid: para 5.21).

There have been a number of other initiatives[9] such as the establishment of Family Nurse Partnerships, Family Intervention Programmes,[10] and *Connexions* to provide services for children and families. In addition, the Children Act 1989 imposes obligations on local authorities to provide services. The nature of these is outlined in Part III of the Act and they include daycare and accommodation. In particular, local authorities are required,[11] in terms of section 17, to provide services for 'children in need' and their families:[12]

17.—Provision of services for children in need, their families and others.

(1) It shall be the general duty of every local authority (in addition to the other duties imposed on them by this Part)—

(a) to safeguard and promote the welfare of children within their area who are in need; and

(b) so far as is consistent with that duty, to promote the upbringing of such children by their families, by providing a range and level of services appropriate to those children's needs.

(2) For the purpose principally of facilitating the discharge of their general duty under this section, every local authority shall have the specific duties and powers set out in Part 1 of Schedule 2.

(3) Any service provided by an authority in the exercise of functions conferred on them by this section may be provided for the family of a particular child in need or for any member of his family, if it is provided with a view to safeguarding or promoting the child's welfare … .

(4A) Before determining what (if any) services to provide for a particular child in need in the exercise of functions conferred on them by this section, a local authority shall, so far as is reasonably practicable and consistent with the child's welfare—

(a) ascertain the child's wishes and feelings regarding the provision of those services; and

(b) give due consideration (having regard to his age and understanding) to such wishes and feelings of the child as they have been able to ascertain … .

(6) The services provided by a local authority in the exercise of functions conferred on them

---

[8] However, doubts have been expressed about the extent to which Sure Start benefits children: BBC Radio 4 (11 July 2011).

[9] See HM Treasury (2005: paras 5.1–5.21).

[10] See Laming (2009: para 3.14); DfCSF (2010: paras 10.25–10.29).

[11] With the help of other authorities, if necessary. See s 27 Children Act 1989; Children Act 2004.

[12] However, an assessment does not give rise to a right, enforceable by an individual, to services to meet those assessed needs; s 17 merely sets out duties of a general character intended to benefit children in the area generally. In particular, the local authority has no obligation to provide residential accommodation for individual children and their families in cases where the parents are homeless; an authority providing accommodation for a child is not under a duty to accommodate the family as well: *R (on the application of G) v Barnet London Borough Council; R (on the application of W) v Lambeth London Borough Council; R (on the application of A) v Lambeth London Borough Council* [2003] UKHL 57; [2004] 1 FLR 454. On the relationship between local authorities' powers to accommodate and immigration law, see *M v London Borough of Islington and Secretary of State for the Home Department* [2004] EWCA Civ 235; [2004] FLR 867.

by this section may include [providing accommodation and] giving assistance in kind or, in exceptional circumstances, in cash. ...

(10) For the purposes of this Part a child shall be taken to be in need if—

(a) he is unlikely to achieve or maintain, or to have the opportunity of achieving or maintaining, a reasonable standard of health or development without the provision for him of services by a local authority under this Part;

(b) his health or development is likely to be significantly impaired, or further impaired, without the provision for him of such services; or

(c) he is disabled,

and 'family', in relation to such a child, includes any person who has parental responsibility for the child and any other person with whom he has been living.

(11) For the purposes of this Part, a child is disabled if he is blind, deaf or dumb or suffers from mental disorder of any kind or is substantially and permanently handicapped by illness, injury or congenital deformity or such other disability as may be prescribed; and in this Part—

'development' means physical, intellectual, emotional, social or behavioural development; and

'health' means physical or mental health.

Despite this statutory duty to help children in need even if they are not at risk of serious harm, in practice, and in the context of limited resources, local authorities seem to have concentrated services on those children deemed to be at risk of abuse or neglect.[13] Cooper et al for example, remarked in 2003 that 'most resources are still focused on high risk situations and crises' (Cooper et al 2003: 21). It is unlikely that this has changed. Moreover, it seems that universal and targeted services are being scaled down as a result of the economic constraints on local authorities; these have already led to the closure of some Sure Start Children's Centres.[14]

Moreover, it remains the case that professionals have to identify children who are at risk. For one thing, *Working Together* states that compulsory intervention should be confined to 'exceptional cases' such as those where a child has to be protected from significant harm (DfCSF 2010: para 1.6). For another, all agencies are expected to be alert to 'potential indicators of abuse or neglect' (ibid: para 1.14). So, while the local authorities are expected to turn their attention to the provision of services to families and children generally, they are still charged with the duty to protect children at risk and to intervene early to avert that risk.[15]

Children in Need or at Risk—Assessment

Everybody who has contact with children, such as GPs,[16] needs to recognise and know how to act on evidence of impairment of a child's health or development (DfCSF 2010: para 5.8). In assessing the child, use should be made of the Common Assessment Framework (CAF):[17]

---

[13] See Audit Commission (1994: paras 44, 48, 59).
[14] Discussed on BBC Radio 4 (11 July 2011).
[15] See Chapter 13 above.
[16] See DfCSF (2010: para 2.65).
[17] See also Chapter 13 above.

Where it is considered a child may have additional needs, with the consent of the child, young person or parents/carers, practitioners may undertake a common assessment in accordance with the national practice guidance to assess these needs and to decide how best to support them. The findings from the common assessment may however give rise to concerns about a child's safety and welfare. Practitioners should be particularly concerned regarding children whose parents or caregivers are experiencing difficulties in meeting their needs as a result of domestic violence, substance misuse, mental illness and/or learning disability. (DfCSF 2010: para 5.12)

If the child is not found to be 'in need', the possibility of offering services should be considered (ibid: para 4.14). If it is thought that the child may be 'in need', a referral to children's social care should be made, provided the parents consent. If the child is believed or suspected to be suffering significant harm, a referral to children's social care should always be made (ibid: para 5.14). Undertaking a CAF is not a prerequisite for a referral (ibid: para 5.17). And:

> [w]hile professionals should seek, in general, to discuss any concerns with the child and family and, where possible, seek their agreement to making referrals to local authority children's social care, *this should only be done where such discussion and agreement-seeking will not place a child at increased risk of suffering significant harm.* (ibid: para 5.18, emphasis in original)[18]

Where a case is referred[19] to children's social care services,[20] whether by members of the public, schools or otherwise, the referral has to be taken seriously (DoH 1995a: paras 4.10–4.11). The professionals are obliged to undertake an initial assessment,[21] which may be followed by a more detailed, core assessment. In undertaking this task, staff should apply the *Framework for the Assessment of Children in Need and their Families* (DoH 2000: para 3.9). This identifies three domains that have to be considered: the child's developmental needs; the parents' or caregivers' capacity to respond appropriately; and the wider family and environmental factors (ibid: para 1.40). In attempting to determine whether a child has been abused, professionals have to rely on evidence such as physical symptoms and injuries as well as the child's development and the adequacy of parental care. They also have regard to factors such as the relationships between the family members, the home environment and the circumstances of the alleged injury. But evidence is often inconclusive and can be interpreted in different ways. As Munro points out, '[w]hile the forms set out what information is needed, organisations have given less attention to helping frontline staff know how to collect and analyse it' (DfE 2011f: para 6.8). Currently, whether cases proceed through the child protection system appears to be dependent on whether certain risk factors are present.[22] Factors such as 'difficulties being experienced in the family/household due to domestic violence, mental illness, substance misuse and/or learning disability' (DfCSF 2010: para 5.32) are frequently referred to.

It appears that intervention does not necessarily follow even in cases where risk indicators are present. Stanley et al (2010: Executive Summary, 14), whose study focusing on children and families experiencing domestic violence took place between 2007 and 2009,

---

[18] See also para 5.35. See the limits to partnership discussed in Chapter 13 above.
[19] Unlike many US states, the UK does not have laws making the reporting of suspected child abuse mandatory.
[20] See DfCSF (2010: para 5.12).
[21] Which could be limited to phone calls to, eg, the school and GP.
[22] See, eg, DoH (1995b: 33–34). Compare earlier research that revealed a 'rule of optimism' (p 636 above).

say that the practitioners[23] they surveyed reported that very few families were receiving services from social work services and emphasised the need for early intervention. Masson et al, whose research data was derived from court files relating to applications made in 2004 (ie children considered at risk), found that most families in their sample were offered services but that in 41% of these cases help was refused, particularly where this related to treatment for substance misuse or therapeutic help with mental health difficulties (Masson et al 2008b: 29). Davies and Ward found that intervention where children are at risk can be 'indecisive or delayed' (Davies and Ward 2011: Executive Summary, 1). And where intervention is given and accepted, this 'may be offered for too short a period or withdrawn too abruptly' (ibid: 10).

Where the local authority can, it should provide services to the family on a voluntary basis (DCSF 2010: para 1.6) However, if the local authority is not satisfied that the child will be safe under a voluntary arrangement, it may apply to court for an order empowering it to intervene coercively.

III. LEGAL CRITERIA FOR THE GRANTING OF COURT ORDERS

Court orders permitting compulsory intervention are available only if the statutory criteria centred on significant harm or a likelihood of significant harm are met. In addition, the court must apply the welfare test in section 1[24] of the Children Act 1989 and must, in accordance with section 1(5), be satisfied that making the order would be better for the child than making no order.[25] The term 'significant' is not defined in the legislation but it has been interpreted to mean 'considerable, noteworthy or important'.[26] 'Harm' is defined in Section 31:

31(9) In this section—

...

'harm' means ill-treatment or the impairment of health or development including, for example, impairment suffered from seeing or hearing the ill-treatment of another;[27]
'development' means physical, intellectual, emotional, social or behavioural development;
'health' means physical or mental health; and
'ill-treatment' includes sexual abuse and forms of ill-treatment which are not physical.

(10) Where the question of whether harm suffered by a child is significant turns on the child's health or development, his health or development shall be compared with that which could reasonably be expected of a similar child.[28]

---

[23] Independent Domestic Violence Advocates, police and children's services staff (10).

[24] The checklist in s 1(3) applies in relation to care proceedings but not to emergency cases dealt with under Part V of the Act.

[25] See p 639 above.

[26] See *Humberside County Council v B* [1993] 1 FLR 257, 263. See further *Re MA (Care Threshold)* [2009] EWCA Civ 853; [2010] 1 FLR 431.

[27] This is intended to cover cases where children witness domestic violence.

[28] So, eg, a greater degree of care may be expected for a child with brittle bone disease or a disability. On the impact of the statutory criteria on different ethnic groups, see Brophy et al (2003). See also Brophy (2003).

IV. IMMEDIATE PROTECTION AND INVESTIGATION

The first concern of the child protection professionals should be to ensure that the child is safe.[29] It will sometimes emerge in the early stages that emergency action is needed (DfCSF 2010: para 5.36). In other situations, referrals may lead to no further action, to monitoring, to the provision of services from an appropriate agency,[30] and/or to a fuller initial assessment of the needs and circumstances of the child, which may in turn be followed by section 47 enquiries (ibid: para 5.39).

The initial assessment is intended to determine whether the child is at risk of significant harm, is in need, or requires services. It is also used to determine whether a 'further, more detailed' core assessment is warranted (ibid: para 5.38). The core assessment builds on the initial assessment and examines the most important needs of the child and the parents' capacity to respond appropriately to them (ibid: para 5.48).[31] Both the initial and the core assessment should be undertaken in accordance with the *Framework for the Assessment of Children in Need and their Families* (DoH 2000).

Where it is suspected that the child is suffering is or is likely to suffer significant harm, the local authority is obliged to carry out an investigation in terms of section 47 of the Children Act 1989 'to enable it to decide whether it should take any action to safeguard and promote the welfare of the child' (DfCSF 2010: para 5.50).[32] The child should always be seen and interviewed (ibid: para 5.64), normally with the knowledge of the parents. Exceptionally, where the child might be threatened or coerced, where evidence might be destroyed or where the child does not want the parent involved, the child will be seen without the knowledge of the parent (ibid: para 5.67).

47 Local authority's duty to investigate

(1) Where a local authority—

(a) are informed that a child who lives, or is found, in their area—
    (i) is the subject of an emergency protection order; or
    (ii) is in police protection; or … .
(b) have reasonable cause to suspect that a child who lives, or is found, in their area is suffering, or is likely to suffer, significant harm,

the authority shall make, or cause to be made, such enquiries as they consider necessary to enable them to decide whether they should take any action to safeguard or promote the child's welfare.[33]

---

[29] The decision should normally be made after consulting available records and discussion with professionals or services, such as the police (DfCSF 2010: para 5.34). Permission should be sought from the parents before discussing the referral with other agencies unless this would expose the child to significant harm (ibid: para 5.35). A decision about how to proceed must be made within one working day (ibid: para 5.34).

[30] Agencies such as housing and education authorities are required to give help when requested to do so by the local authority, provided this is compatible with their other duties and does not unduly prejudice the discharge of their other functions (s 27 Children Act 1989). see Chapter 5 above.

[31] See further DfCSF (2010: paras 5.62, 5.121).

[32] See further DfCSF (2008: paras 4.73ff).

[33] The child's wishes and feelings must be taken into account in determining what action should be taken (s 47(5A)). S 47 governs the local authority's duties in cases where it is alerted to the possibility of abuse. Concern about a child might also arise in the course of family proceedings such as s 8 proceedings. S 37 of the Children Act 1989 provides that, where it appears to the court in any family proceedings that it might be appropriate to make a care or supervision order in relation to a child, the court may direct the appropriate local authority to undertake an investigation into the child's circumstances. If the local authority decides, after investigating, not to apply for a care or supervision order, it must inform the court of the reasons for that

If, at this or any earlier or later stage, there is a 'risk to the life of a child or a likelihood of serious immediate harm, an agency with statutory child protection powers[34] *should act quickly to secure the immediate safety of the child*' (DfCSF 2010: para 5.51, emphasis in original). A strategy discussion must be held with the police and other relevant agencies either before the action is taken or as soon as possible afterwards.[35] This meeting is the forum for deciding whether criminal proceedings should be pursued, whether a section 47 enquiry should be undertaken, whether a core assessment should be made as part of the section 47 enquiry[36] or continued if already started under section 17, and what action is required to safeguard or promote the child's welfare and/or what interim services to provide (DfCSF 2010: para 5.57). It may be possible to keep the child safe in the home if, for example, the alleged perpetrator leaves,[37] or, in appropriate cases, the local authority must seek to remove the child pursuant to a voluntary arrangement or an emergency protection order.[38] 'Police powers should only be used in exceptional circumstances where there is insufficient time to seek an EPO or for reasons relating to the immediate safety of the child' (DfCSF 2010 para 5.53).

Impeding Access to the Child

Section 47(4) of the Children Act 1989 places an obligation on a local authority conducting enquiries under section 47(1) to take such steps as are reasonably practicable to gain access or ensure that access is gained to the child, unless satisfied that they already have sufficient information. Section 47(6) provides that where, in the course of section 47 enquiries, the person conducting the enquiry is refused access to or denied information about the whereabouts of the child, the authority has a duty to apply for an emergency protection order (EPO), a child assessment order, a care order or a supervision order unless they are satisfied that the child's welfare can be satisfactorily safeguarded without doing so.

Section 44(1)(b) provides that where section 47(1) enquiries are being made and those enquiries are being frustrated by access to the child unreasonably being refused, and the applicant has reasonable cause to believe that access to the child is required as a matter of urgency, the court may make an emergency protection order.

The local authority should apply for an EPO only where access is required as a matter of urgency. If the aim is to assess the child but the child is not considered to be in immediate danger, the appropriate order would be a child assessment order (DfCSF 2008: para 4.35).

The local authority or NSPCC may apply for permission from the court to enter premises to search for a child who is the subject of an EPO[39] or another child who they

---

decision and of the services or assistance they have provided or intend to provide and of any other action taken or proposed to be taken. The court no longer has the power it had prior to the Children Act to commit children to care in matrimonial and domestic proceedings.

[34] The local authority, the police or the NSPCC.

[35] See further DfCSF (2010: paras 5.56–5.59). The strategy discussion can take place 'following a referral or at any other time' (ibid: para 5.57).

[36] 'The core assessment is the means by which a s 47 enquiry is carried out' (ibid: para 5.62).

[37] In which case the local authority may provide assistance, including financial assistance to find alternative accommodation (Sch 2, para 5, to the Children Act 1989).

[38] See DfCSF (2010: para 5.52–5.53).

[39] S 48(3) Children Act 1989.

think ought to be.[40] Any attempt to obstruct such a search intentionally is a criminal offence and the police can be given a warrant to assist the authorised person.[41] In addition, in other situations where time is of the essence, the local authority might ask the police to take the child into police protection rather than seek an emergency order from the court.[42]

A constable, if he or she has reasonable cause to believe that a child would otherwise be likely to suffer significant harm, can take that child into police protection for up to 72 hours.[43] A constable taking a child into police protection in terms of the Children Act 1989 must inform, as soon as possible, the local authority, the parents and the child about what steps have been taken. The child must be taken to a refuge or local authority accommodation.[44] A designated officer must investigate the case and the child must then be released unless that officer is satisfied that there is reasonable cause to believe the child would be likely to suffer significant harm if released. If so satisfied, the designated officer can apply for an EPO on behalf of the local authority, whether they are aware of this or not. Alternatively, the local authority, apprised of the situation and obliged to investigate in terms of section 47, might apply for an order itself or ask the police to do so on its behalf.[45] The designated officer must, while the child is in police protection, allow what that officer considers reasonable contact between the child and the persons specified in section 46(10), if that is considered in the child's best interests.

Masson et al report that police protection powers are used primarily when the police 'stumble' on a situation or when they are requested to take action by the local authority. This might be because it is thought that an application for an EPO would be too slow or because the events in question occur outside court hours (Masson et al 2004: 6–7).

The Outcome of the Investigation

The professionals must judge the needs of the child as well as the risks. Once they have completed an investigation, the professionals may decide that there is no cause for concern, or that the parents can be helped to care adequately for their child(ren), in which case they should consider whether the family needs support and services:

> 1.10 Children have varying needs that change over time. Judgements on how best to intervene when there are concerns about harm to a child will often, and unavoidably, entail an element of risk—at the extreme, of leaving a child for too long in a dangerous situation or of removing a child unnecessarily from his or her family. The way to proceed in the face of uncertainty is through competent professional judgements, based on a sound assessment of the child's needs and the parents' capacity to respond to these—including their capacity to keep the child safe from significant harm—and the wider family circumstances.

> 1.11 Effective measures to safeguard children are those that also promote their welfare. They should not be seen in isolation from the wider range of support and services already provided and available to meet the needs of children and families:[46]

---

[40] S 48(4) Children Act 1989.
[41] See DfCSF (2008: para 4.48).
[42] See ibid: para 4.64ff; DfCSF (2010: para 5.53).
[43] S 46 Children Act 1989. See also ss 17(1)(e) and 24 Police and Criminal Evidence Act 1984.
[44] Although Masson et al (2004: 7) report that most are taken initially to a police station.
[45] S 47(3)(c).
[46] See also DfCSF (2010: para 5.75).

- enquiries under section 47 of the Children Act 1989 may reveal significant unmet needs for support and services among children and families. These should always be explicitly considered, even where concerns are not substantiated about significant harm to a child, if the child and/or their family so wishes; and
- if processes for managing concerns about individual children are to result in improved outcomes for children, then effective plans for safeguarding and promoting children's welfare should be based on a wide-ranging assessment of the needs of the child, including the child's wishes and feelings, whether they are suffering or likely to suffer significant harm, parental capacity and their family circumstances. (DfCSF 2010)

Alternatively, there may be concerns, but the evidence is lacking. Then the decision may be to monitor the family (DfCSF 2010: para 5.76). Or it may be that the child has suffered significant harm but can be protected without the need for compulsory intervention: 'In the great majority of cases, children remain with their families following section 47 enquiries even where concerns about abuse or neglect are substantiated' (ibid: para 5.72).[47] Where, however, it is judged that the child remains at risk of significant harm, the local authority must call a child protection conference (ibid: para 7.81).[48]

The Child Protection Conference

The responsibility for convening a child protection conference[49] rests with the local authority children's social care. The function of the conference is described in *Working Together*:

5.82 The initial child protection conference brings together family members, the child who is the subject of the conference (where appropriate) and those professionals most involved with the child and family, following section 47 enquiries. Its purpose is:

- to bring together and analyse, in an inter-agency setting, the information which has been obtained about the child's developmental needs and the parents' or carers' capacity to respond to these needs to ensure the child's safety and promote the child's health and development, within the context of their wider family and environment;
- to consider the evidence presented to the conference and … make judgements about the likelihood of the child suffering significant harm in future and decide whether the child is continuing to, or is likely to, suffer significant harm; and
- to decide what future action is required in order to safeguard and promote the welfare of the child, including the child becoming the subject of a child protection plan, what the planned developmental outcomes are for the child and how best to intervene to achieve these.

(DfCSF 2010)

Family members and carers may be invited to attend. Parents should normally be invited and helped to participate with the assistance, if they so wish, of a friend, supporter or advocate (ibid: para 5.86).[50] Children, depending on their age and understanding, may also

---

[47] See also ibid: paras 5.77–5.79.

[48] There is no legal requirement to call child protection conferences. However, they are an important part of the child protection process.

[49] There is no reference to child protection conferences in the Children Act 1989 but they are referred to in many of the guidance documents such as *Working Together*.

[50] Family members might be excluded if, for example, a parent is the alleged abuser, where there are high levels of conflict between family members, or where there is a risk of violence or intimidation (DfCSF 2010: paras 5.87–5.88).

attend and bring a friend, advocate or supporter (ibid). In any event, the child's wishes and feelings should be conveyed to the conference (ibid).

The task of the conference is to decide whether the child has suffered or is likely to suffer significant harm (ibid: para 5.97).[51] If the answer is in the affirmative, a formal child protection plan will be needed (ibid: para 5.99) and the conference must formulate an outline plan (ibid: para 5.102). In addition, the conference must decide whether the child should be accommodated or whether any legal action is needed (ibid: para 5.103). Alternatively, the conference might reach the conclusion that a child protection plan is not necessary but that services should be provided for the child and for the purposes of helping the family meet the child's needs. In such a case a child in need plan may be drawn up (ibid: para 5.104).

If a child protection plan is deemed necessary, a lead statutory body (either local authority children's social care or the NSPCC) and a lead social worker must be appointed. A core group of professionals and family members must be identified by the conference to develop and implement the child protection plan. The conference must also decide how the child and family members should be involved in the assessment, planning and implementation process, and what advocacy or help should be available to them. In its outline child protection plan, the conference must indicate what needs to change in order to ensure that the child's welfare is safeguarded (ibid: para 5.105).

The aim of the child protection plan[52] devised by the core group pursuant to the assessment is to:

- ensure the child is safe from harm and prevent him or her from suffering further harm by supporting the strengths, addressing the vulnerabilities and risk factors and helping meet the child's unmet needs;
- promote the child's health and development, i.e. his or her welfare; and
- provided it is in the best interests of the child, to support the family and wider family members to safeguard and promote the welfare of their child. (ibid: para 5.122)

The plan should set out who needs to do what. As long as a child protection plan remains in place, it has to be reviewed at regular intervals (ibid: para 5.136) The plan should take into account the wishes of the child and the family 'insofar as they are consistent with the child's welfare' (ibid: para 5.124). The lead social worker must make every effort to ensure that the child and parents understand the planned outcomes and that the parents are prepared to co-operate. If they are not, the local authority must consider what action, 'including the initiation of family proceedings', is needed to safeguard the child's welfare (ibid). While the expectation is that efforts will be made to work with parents, it is clear that the partnership is shaped by the professionals:

5.127 Parents should be clear about the evidence of significant harm which resulted in the child becoming the subject of a child protection plan, what needs to change and about what is expected of them as part of implementing the plan for safeguarding and promoting their child's welfare. All parties should be clear about the respective roles and responsibilities of family members and different agencies in implementing the plan. The parents should receive a written copy of the plan so that they are clear about who is doing what when and the planned outcomes for the child. (ibid)

---

[51] See para 5.98 for the test to be applied in determining the risk of future harm.
[52] Where a child is the subject of a child protection plan, the child's case record must be recorded on the local authority's IT system (DfCSF 2010: para 5.150).

Partnership is impossible in some cases. For example, partnership cannot work if there is continued hostility to professional intervention or lack of motivation to be involved in planning for the child's future. Allegations of sexual abuse; denial of abuse where there is evidence that it occurred; or persistent violence on the part of a man towards the children or his partner may preclude partnership (DoH 1995a: paras 8.17–8.20).

V. ACCOMMODATING CHILDREN

Guidance for professionals states that interventions should be based on assessments of what would work best to achieve good outcomes for the child (DfCSF 2010: para 5.128). Measures taken might include therapy for the child and, in abuse cases, the abuser (ibid: para 5.131). A key issue is whether the child's needs can be met within the family and within timescales that are appropriate for the child (ibid: para 5.133). If the child cannot be cared for safely by his or her caregivers, the child will be removed while work is undertaken with the child and family (ibid: para 5.130). If change cannot be achieved fast enough, the child may be placed away from home on a long-term basis (ibid: para 5.133). This could be done with a voluntary arrangement or by means of a court order.

Court proceedings, according to *The Challenge of Partnership*, do not necessarily put an end to partnership. A new kind of partnership may be negotiated in which the worker 'makes explicit her or his control' (DoH 1995a: para 8.16). The family can co-operate in building a safer environment for the child or accept the child's long-term or permanent removal (ibid).

Provided the parents are co-operative, it is likely that the professionals will consider it unnecessary to seek a court order. They may choose to seek to avert any need for compulsory measures by monitoring the family and by providing assistance.[53] If it is considered too risky to leave the child in the same home as the suspected abuser, the local authority may offer to accommodate the child away from the home under section 20 of the Children Act 1989:

Provision of accommodation for children: general

20.—(1) Every local authority shall provide accommodation for any child in need within their area who appears to them to require accommodation as a result of—

(a) there being no person who has parental responsibility for him;

(b) his being lost or having been abandoned; or

(c) the person who has been caring for him being prevented (whether or not permanently, and for whatever reason) from providing him with suitable accommodation or care. ...[54]

(3) Every local authority shall provide accommodation for any child in need within their area who has reached the age of 16 and whose welfare the authority consider is likely to be seriously prejudiced if they do not provide him with accommodation.

(4) A local authority may provide accommodation for any child within their area (even though

---

[53] See Sch 2, para 4(1), to the Children Act 1989; Sch 2, para 7(a)(i).

[54] This would include parents who cannot care for their children as a result of illness and parents who need respite from caring for their child. Respite care is used by parents of children who need constant attention, such as children with disabilities, and by parents of children with behavioural problems.

a person who has parental responsibility for him is able to provide him with accommodation) if they consider that to do so would safeguard or promote the child's welfare. ...

(6) Before providing accommodation under this section, a local authority shall, so far as is reasonably practicable and consistent with the child's welfare—

(a) ascertain the child's wishes and feelings regarding the provision of accommodation; and

(b) give due consideration (having regard to his age and understanding) to such wishes and feelings of the child as they have been able to ascertain.

Accommodation may be a short-term measure to enable the parents to deal with their problems. In those cases where the child cannot return home, accommodation in a residential establishment or foster home[55] is provided as a long-term measure. In either event, a child can only be accommodated in terms of section 20 if those with parental responsibility consent. However, whether consent is always freely given is open to doubt; some parents may be faced with the prospect of a care or supervision order as an alternative.[56] The child's views must always be given consideration before a decision is made about his or her future (DFE 2010c: paras 1.11–1.12).

Parents retain their parental responsibility while their child is being accommodated, and the voluntary nature of accommodation is evident in a number of the provisions in section 20. A local authority may not provide accommodation for a child if a person with parental responsibility objects and is willing and able to provide accommodation or to arrange for it to be provided.[57] And once accommodation is being provided, any person with parental responsibility for the child may remove him or her.[58] The only circumstances in which these provisions do not apply are where a child who has reached the age of 16 agrees to the accommodation[59] or where a person who has a residence order, who is a special guardian or who has the care of the child pursuant to an order under the High Court's inherent jurisdiction, agrees to it.[60]

While the child is being accommodated, neither the local authority nor a foster parent acquires parental responsibility. However, the Act allows for the delegation of parental responsibility in full or in part[61] and provides authority for carers to make routine decisions: section 3(5) states that a person who does not have parental responsibility but has care of the child may do what is reasonable in the circumstances in order to safeguard or promote the child's welfare.[62]

When a child is accommodated, a written care plan is drawn up setting out the arrangements for the child's care.[63] In so far as it is reasonably practicable, it should be agreed

---

[55] See s 22 s 22A for the duty owed by local authorities regarding accommodation of children who are being looked after or in their care.

[56] See Masson et al (2004: 58–60); Lindley and Richards (2000: 224); Bainham (2011: 374–75).

[57] S 20(7).

[58] S 20(8). Masson et al found that, where children at risk were being accommodated, parents who sought to remove their children contrary to an agreement faced the possibility of proceedings for an emergency protection order (Masson et al 2004: 69). The authors recommend that parents have access to legal advice or independent advocacy before entering agreements (ibid: 77).

[59] S 20(11).

[60] S 20(9).

[61] S 2(9).

[62] It may be that this provision could be used to prevent a parent from removing a child from accommodation, eg if the parent is aggressive, violent or drunk. See HC Deb, 18 May 1989, Standing Committee B, col 148. But see Masson et al (2008: para 17.051).

[63] S 4 The Care Planning, Placement and Case Review (England) Regulations 2010, SI 959/2010 .

with the parent(s) or person with parental responsibility.[64] While children who are looked after by the local authority[65] should normally be placed with their parents or someone with parental responsibility,[66] this does not apply if such an arrangement would not be consistent with the child's welfare or would not be reasonably practicable.[67] In that event, the local authority should give preference to placing the child with a 'relative, friend or other person connected with C and who is also a local authority foster parent'.[68] If this is not an option, the placement may be with a local authority foster parent who is not connected with the child or in a children's home. The placement should not disrupt the child's education; it should be near the child's home; and if the child has a sibling who is being accommodated, then with that sibling.[69] In addition, the Act requires the local authority, before making any decisions about a child, in so far as is reasonably practicable, to ascertain and give due regard to the wishes of the child, in the light of his or her age and understanding, and the parents.[70]

The new *Guidance* places considerable emphasis on avoiding care proceedings, on alternative dispute resolution and on kinship care. Where recourse to the courts is contemplated, the child and family must be consulted:

> 3.3 Before making an application for a care or supervision order a local authority is expected to seek legal advice and to communicate with the parents (and child, if of sufficient age and understanding) the nature and extent of their concerns. Prior to submitting an application to the court, and where the short term safety and welfare of the child permits, the local authority should send a 'Letter Before Proceedings' to the parents, the contents of which should also be explained carefully and directly to the parents ... . The purpose of such a letter is to enable the parents to obtain legal assistance and advice, prior to a meeting with the local authority, the intention of which is either to deflect proceedings or, at least, to narrow and focus the issues of concern. It is recognised, of course, that there will be some emergency and other situations where the welfare of the affected child will not permit even a brief period for such correspondence and direct discussions to take place. ...

> 3.6 The scheme for care and supervision proceedings is founded on a number of principles. The first is that the local authority can only intervene in the care and upbringing of a child without the parents' agreement if the authority obtains a court order following proceedings in which the child, his parents and others who are connected with the child are able fully to participate. The proceedings should establish what action, if any, is in the child's interests, and the procedure must be fair to all concerned. The term 'care' is used in the Act in relation to a child who is the subject of a care order. This term does not extend to cover a child accommodated by a local authority under voluntary arrangements (section 105(1) of the Act).

---

[64] S 4(4) The Care Planning, Placement and Case Review (England) Regulations 2010, SI 959/2010 .

[65] 'A child is looked after by a local authority if s/he is in their care by reason of a care order or is being provided with accommodation under section 20 of the 1989 Act for more than 24 hours with the agreement of the parents, or of the child if s/he is aged 16 or over (section 22(1) and (2) of the 1989 Act)' (DfE 2010c: para 1.20).

[66] S 22C(3) Children Act 1989.

[67] S 22C(4) .

[68] S 22C(6)(a) read with s 22C(7)(a). Placement with a connected person is thought to promote continuity, to preserve the child's sense of belonging to a wider network, to make it more likely that bonds exist or will develop, and to make it less likely that the child will be rejected if problems arise (DfE 2010c: para 3.12). But see para 3.13.

[69] S 22C(8). See further DfE (2010c: paras 3.21–3.23).

[70] S 22(4) and (5). A local authority refusal to consult with a parent or keep him informed was held to be an irregularity that did not render the decisions made void in *Re P (Children Act 1989, ss 22 and 26: Local Authority Compliance)* [2000] 2 FLR 910.

3.7 Secondly, the local authority has a general duty, under section 17 of the Act, to promote the upbringing of children in need by their families so far as this is consistent with its duty to safeguard and promote the welfare of children, in particular through the provision of family support services to children in need and their families. This means that voluntary arrangements for the provision of services to the child and his family including the consideration of potential alternative carers should always be fully explored prior to making an application under section 31, provided that this does not jeopardise the child's safety and welfare. ... It is possible that care proceedings may be avoided altogether or that a different application, such as for a special guardianship order or a residence order, made by a relative or carer, may be more appropriate, rather than a care order application by the local authority.

...

3.24 ... Parents, the child (if they are of sufficient age and understanding) and others with a legitimate interest in the child's future should, as far as possible, be involved in the preapplication assessment processes and should, to the extent that it is possible to do so, be consulted on the local authority's plans for the child. Thus, even before the local authority reaches a decision that it should apply for a care or supervision order, parents will already have been made aware of the local authority's concerns about the child. Before reaching such a decision, the local authority should have taken such steps as are possible, perhaps through a family group conference or other family meeting, to explore whether care for the child can be safely provided by a relative or friend ... .

3.25 Where the local authority decides, having sought and considered legal advice, that it intends to apply for a care or supervision order, the local authority must immediately notify that decision to the parents and others with parental responsibility for the child ... .

3.26 The parents (and any others with parental responsibility for the child), on receipt of the local authority's written notification of its intention to apply for a care or supervision order, (known as the 'Letter Before Proceedings') ... are entitled to non-means tested publicly funded legal advice at 'Level 2', which covers liaison and negotiations with the local authority.

(DfCSF 2008)

The House of Commons Justice Committee, commenting of the *Family Justice Review* (Norgrove 2011a), remarked on the lack of knowledge as to the effectiveness of interventions with parents (such as the letter before proceedings) designed to avoid the need to take care proceedings.

91. We agree with the Interim Report that further research is required on a range of measures which could potentially help parents to make changes which could resolve pubic law cases without taking children into care, or without proceedings. We are particularly interested in the wider use of "letters before proceedings". However, the Department has no data on how often they are used, what the barriers are to their wider use, or how effective they are. Given that receiving a letter before proceedings confers entitlement to non-means-tested legal aid we find this lack of any evidence base particularly surprising. We recommend that the Government should commission such research. (House of Commons Justice Committee 2011)

Welbourne's concerns are different. She is concerned that the new procedures might deter local authorities from considering section 31 applications.

A move toward informal agreements could benefit some children, but [it] also has implications for their rights. There is no simple equation between the promotion of informal kinship care and children's right to family life, and there is protection for the child's welfare interests in a court setting which is absent in alternative methods of dispute resolution. It is argued that the changes ... will collectively make it much less likely that children, their parents and carers will be offered the legal safeguards available through the courts, even when it would be in their best interests to have them. (Welbourne 2008: 336, footnote omitted)

Under new rules, parents, but not children, will have access to legal advice once they have received a letter of intention to commence section 31 proceedings from the local authority. Children will not have a court-appointed guardian unless and until court proceedings have commenced, so any arrangements for their care, made in response to the local authority's threat of legal action, will be made without the benefit of an independent advocate for the child. Parents, as sole holders of parental responsibility, will be the only people empowered to make choices for their children. (ibid: 338–39, footnotes omitted)

Three key aspects of a court hearing are absent [in alternative dispute resolution processes]: (a) independence of the person making or ratifying the decision about the child's best interests; (b) independent representation of the child and parents; and (c) enforceability of decisions made. Decisions may be reached in 'informal' processes that seriously affect parents' and children's family life, but they are decisions that may be lawfully disregarded by parents, leaving children at continuing risk of serious harm. Agreements need to be carefully monitored for compliance, but there is no right of access to the child following negotiated agreements, and no statutory requirement that local authorities carry out regular reviews or systematically follow up the placement. (ibid: 350–51)

VI. COURT ORDERS: EMERGENCY PROCEEEDINGS

Child Assessment Order

This order[71] is designed to facilitate assessment of children about whom there are concerns and whose parents do not co-operate voluntarily. The child assessment order authorises assessment of the child[72] and requires that any person in a position to produce the child do so and comply with any directions specified in the order.[73] Only a local authority or, in theory, the NSPCC may apply for an order.[74] The child's welfare is the paramount consideration and although the checklist in section 1(3) of the Children Act does not apply to Part V of the legislation, professionals are expected to bear in mind that Part V orders may be followed by other proceedings where the checklist does apply (DfCSF 2008: para 4.9).

---

[71] This order had no equivalent under the pre-Children Act scheme; it was introduced pursuant to a recommendation in the report of the Kimberley Carlile inquiry, see London Borough of Greenwich (1987: ch 25).

[72] S 43(7) Children Act 1989. A child, if of sufficient understanding to make an informed decision, can refuse to submit to the assessment (s 43(8)). But see *South Glamorgan County Council v W and B* [1993] 1 FLR 574.

[73] S 43(6) Children Act 1989. Deliberate failure to comply with an order may suffice to satisfy the grounds for an emergency protection order. In cases of extreme emergency, it may be necessary to call on the police to exercise their powers under s 46 Children Act 1989 (see p 666 above) or their powers under the Police and Criminal Evidence Act (s 17(1)(e)) to enter and search premises if there is a threat to life and limb. See DfCSF (2008: para 4.22).

[74] See DfCSF (2008: para 4.11).

43 **Child assessment orders**

(1) On the application of a local authority or authorised person for an order to be made under this section with respect to a child, the court may make the order if, but only if, it is satisfied that—

(a) the applicant has reasonable cause to suspect that the child is suffering, or is likely to suffer, significant harm;

(b) an assessment of the state of the child's health or development, or of the way in which he has been treated, is required to enable the applicant to determine whether or not the child is suffering, or is likely to suffer, significant harm; and

(c) it is unlikely that such an assessment will be made, or be satisfactory, in the absence of an order under this section.

An order cannot have effect for more than seven days[75] and the child may be kept away from home only if it is necessary for the purposes of assessment, and then only for the period specified in the order.[76] If the child is to be kept away from home, the order should contain directions concerning contact.[77]

Child assessment orders are intended to be used where there is reasonable cause to suspect significant harm, [78] but there is insufficient information available for a care or supervision order and the child is not thought to be at immediate risk (DfCSF 2008: para 4.13). The purpose of an order is to enable the local authority (or NSPCC) to ascertain how the child is:

4.10 … Its use is most relevant in circumstances where:

- the child is not thought to be at immediate risk, to the extent that removal from his parents' care is required;
- the local authority considers that an assessment is required but his parents have refused to co-operate; and
- it is intended to allow the local authority to find out enough about the state of the child's health or development or the way in which he has been treated to decide what further action, if any, it should take. It should not be used where the circumstances of the case suggest that an application for an EPO or a care or supervision order would be more appropriate. ….

4.12 A child assessment order will usually be more appropriate where the suspected harm to the child appears to be longer-term and cumulative rather than sudden and severe. The examples of such circumstances include:

- a persistent concern about a child who appears to be failing to thrive;
- parents who are ignorant of or unwilling to face up to possible harm to their child arising from his state of health or development; or
- the existence of some evidence that the child may be subject to continuing or periodic wilful neglect or abuse, but not to such an extent as to place him at serious immediate risk.

(DfCSF 2008)

The advantage of the child assessment order was thought to be that it is less interventionist than emergency protection orders and interim care or supervision orders (ibid: para

---

[75] S 43(5).

[76] S 43(9).

[77] S 43(10).

[78] As opposed to 'believe', which is the requirement for an emergency protection order (EPO). See DfCSF (2008: para 4.11).

4.24). For example, it does not confer parental responsibility on the local authority the way an emergency protection order does. However, it does not appear to be used often, apparently because social workers are reluctant to alienate parents who might otherwise co-operate and because a time limit of seven days is too short to allow for a reliable assessment (Dickens 1993: 91).[79]

Section 43(4) provides that a child assessment order should not be made if the court is satisfied that there are grounds for an emergency protection order and considers that it ought to make such an order instead.[80] For example:

> A parent's refusal to allow a social worker to see a child about whom there is serious concern (as opposed to an objection to the child being examined or assessed) may indicate that the child is at immediate risk of significant harm, and justify an application for an EPO.
>
> (DfCSF 2008: para 4.13)

Emergency Protection Order

The provisions of the Children Act reflect a consensus that the emergency powers of local authorities should be circumscribed. According to the *Guidance*, '[a]n application for an EPO is a very serious step. It should not be regarded as being an automatic response in a case of suspected child abuse or as a routine first step to initiating care proceedings' (DfCSF 2008: para 4.27).

The emergency protection order is designed to 'enable the child, in an emergency, to be removed from where he is or to be kept where he is if, and only if, this is necessary to provide immediate short-term protection' (ibid para 4.25).[81] The criteria for granting an EPO are summarised in the *Guidance:*

> [T]he court must be satisfied that there is reasonable cause to believe that the child is likely to suffer significant harm (defined by reference to section 31) or that access to the child by a person authorised to seek access has been frustrated in circumstances where the child might be suffering significant harm. (DfCSF 2008: para 4.26(a))

The Children Act 1989 provides:

Orders for emergency protection of children

44.—(1) Where any person ('the applicant') applies to the court for an order to be made under this section with respect to a child, the court may make an order if, but only if, it is satisfied that—

(a) there is reasonable cause to believe that the child is likely to suffer significant harm if—
    (i) he is not removed to accommodation provided by or on behalf of the applicant; or
    (ii) he does not remain in the place in which he is then being accommodated;[82]
(b) in the case of an application made by the local authority—
    (i) enquiries are being made with respect to the child under section 47(1)(b); and

---

[79] See also Lavery (1996). See also *Re B (A Minor) (Care Order: Criteria)* [1993] 1 FLR 815.
[80] See also DfCSF (2008: para 4.20).
[81] See particularly the judgments of Munby J in *X Council v B (Emergency Protection Orders)* [2004] EWHC 2015 (Fam) and McFarlane J in *Re X: Emergency Protection Orders* [2006] EWHC 510 (Fam); [2006] 2 FLR. 701. See below.
[82] Eg, a hospital.

(ii) those enquiries are being frustrated by access to the child being unreasonably refused to a person authorised to seek access and that the applicant has reasonable cause to believe that access to the child is required as a matter of urgency.

According to the *Guidance*:

> There is a clear distinction to be drawn between the significant harm test in section 44(1)(a) and the test set out in subsections (b) and (c).[83] The former test is objective, that is, there must be reasonable cause to believe the child is at risk of significant harm. In the latter, the test is subjective and it will depend on whether the applicant has reasonable cause to believe that access to the child is required as a matter of urgency. The test in relation to significant harm looks to the future. In other words, the EPO is necessary to protect the child from the likelihood of suffering significant harm. Past or present significant harm is relevant to the extent that it indicates that the child is likely to suffer significant harm in the near future.
>
> (DfCSF 2008: para 4.39)

An application for an EPO may in some circumstances be made without notice and the court will, in making its decision, apply the welfare principle in section 1(1)[84] as well as the no-order principle in section 1(5). If granted, an order would be made for a period of up to eight days, with the possibility of an extension not exceeding a further seven days.[85] An application to discharge the order may be made,[86] but there is no provision for appeal either against the granting of or refusal of an order.[87]

The order operates as a direction to any person in a position to do so to comply with any request to produce the child.[88] It may authorise the applicant to enter premises to search for the child and any other child thought to be there who the court is satisfied is at risk.[89] All emergency protection orders authorise, for the purposes of safeguarding the welfare of the child,[90] removal of the child to accommodation provided by the applicant or the prevention of the removal of the child from the place where he or she is.[91] The *Guidance* notes that in cases where an EPO is sought to prevent the removal by parents of a child from accommodation provided by the local authority under section 20, 'the court may apply a less severe test than in cases where the child is to be removed from the parents' direct care' (DfCSF 2008: para 4.27).

The order gives the successful applicant, usually the local authority, parental responsibility for the child.[92] This can be exercised only in so far as is necessary to safeguard or

---

[83] S 44(1)(c) contains provisions similar to those in s 44(1)(b) and applies where the application pursuant to an enquiry is made by an authorised person (the NSPCC). Unlike the local authority, however, the applicant must satisfy the court about the existence of reasonable cause for suspicion.

[84] The checklist in s 1(3) is, strictly speaking, not applicable.

[85] S 45. An extension is permitted only where the court has reasonable cause to believe the child will suffer significant harm if the order is not extended. A children's guardian will be appointed under s 41 to safeguard the interests of the child in the proceedings.

[86] S 45(8).

[87] S 45(10). See *Essex County Council v F* [1993] 1 FLR 847. See also *Re P (Emergency Protection Order)* [1996] 1 FLR 482.

[88] S 44(4)(a).

[89] Sub-s 48(3) and (4). In terms of s 48(9), a warrant may be obtained if it appears to the court that a person trying to exercise powers under an EPO has been frustrated by being refused entry to premises or access to the child or that he or she is likely to be frustrated in this way. The warrant will authorise any constable to assist, using reasonable force if necessary.

[90] S 44(5)(a).

[91] S 44(4)(b). It is an offence intentionally to obstruct the exercise of these powers (s 44(15)).

[92] S 44(4)(c). Anyone can apply for an order but in practice the 'vast majority' of applications are likely to be made by local authorities (DfCSF 2008: para 4.30).

promote the welfare of the child[93] and the parents retain their parental responsibility.[94] The court may give directions with respect to assessment of the child as well as contact.[95] Subject to any such direction, the applicant must allow reasonable contact.[96]

In *X Council v B (Emergency Protection Orders)*[97] the court urged that decisions to make EPOs should not be made lightly. Munby J acknowledged that the removal of children in terms of such orders is in principle compatible with the ECHR and there may be cases where an application without notice is justified (para 35).[98] However, he said, '[a]n EPO, summarily removing a child from his parents, is a terrible and drastic remedy' (para 34). He considered that defects in the statutory scheme, such as the absence of a right of appeal, make it all the more important that courts approach applications with 'anxious awareness of the extreme gravity of the relief being sought and a scrupulous regard for the European Convention Rights of both the child and the parents' (para 41). The judge went on to comment generally on the way that the law should be applied:

[57] ...

(i) An EPO, summarily removing a child from his parents, is a 'draconian' and 'extremely harsh' measure, requiring 'exceptional justification' and 'extraordinarily compelling reasons'. Such an order should not be made unless the FPC is satisfied that it is both necessary and proportionate and that no other less radical form of order will achieve the essential end of promoting the welfare of the child. Separation is only to be contemplated if immediate separation is essential to secure the child's safety: 'imminent danger' must be 'actually established' ... .

(iii) Any order must provide for the least interventionist solution consistent with the preservation of the child's immediate safety.

(iv) If the real purpose of the local authority's application is to enable it to have the child assessed then consideration should be given to whether that objective cannot equally effectively, and more proportionately, be achieved by an application for, or by the making of, a CAO under s 43 of the Children Act 1989.

(v) No EPO should be made for any longer than is absolutely necessary to protect the child. Where the EPO is made on an ex parte (without notice) application very careful consideration should be given to the need to ensure that the initial order is made for the shortest possible period commensurate with the preservation of the child's immediate safety ... .

(vii) Save in wholly exceptional cases, parents must be given adequate prior notice of the date, time and place of any application by a local authority for an EPO. They must also be given proper notice of the evidence the local authority is relying upon.

(viii) Where the application for an EPO is made ex parte the local authority must make out a compelling case for applying without first giving the parents notice. An ex parte application will normally be appropriate only if the case is genuinely one of emergency or other great urgency— and even then it should normally be possible to give some kind of albeit informal notice to the

---

[93] S 44(5)(b).

[94] See DfCSF (2008: para 4.41).

[95] S 44(6). A child, if of sufficient understanding to make an informed decision, may refuse to submit to an examination or other assessment (s 44(7)). But see *South Glamorgan County Council v W and B* [1993] 1 FLR 574. The court also has the power to impose conditions in relation to contact and may direct that there shall be no assessment (s 44(8)).

[96] S 44(13).

[97] [2004] EWHC Fam 2015; [2005] 1 FLR 341.

[98] See also, eg, *Haase v Germany* [2004] 2 FLR 39. See also Masson et al (2004: 21–22).

parents—or if there are compelling reasons to believe the child's welfare will be compromised if the parents are alerted in advance to what is going on.[99]

(ix) The evidential burden on the local authority is even heavier if the application is made ex parte ... .

(xii) ... The local authority must apply its mind very carefully to whether removal [of the child] is essential in order to secure the child's immediate safety. ... .

(xiii) ... [Sections 44(10)(a) and (11)(a) impose] on the local authority a continuing duty to keep the case under review day by day so as to ensure that parent and child are separated no longer than is necessary to secure the child's safety ... .

(xiv) Section 44(13) of the Children Act 1989 requires the local authority, subject only to any direction given by the FPC under s 44(6), to allow a child who is subject to an EPO 'reasonable contact' with his parents. Arrangements for contact must be driven by the needs of the family, not stunted by lack of resources.

These points were approved in *Re X (Emergency Protection Orders):*[100]

Emergency Protection Orders: good practice guidance

100 For ease of reference I will now draw together the observations I have made with some additional guidance:

(a) The 14 key points made by Munby J in *X Council v B* should be copied and made available to the justices hearing an EPO on each and every occasion such an application is made; ... .

(c) Mere lack of information or a need for assessment can never of themselves establish the existence of a genuine emergency sufficient to justify an EPO. The proper course in such a case is to consider application for a Child Assessment Order or issuing s 31 proceedings and seeking the court's directions under s 38(6) for assessment; ... .

(f) Where the application is made without notice, if possible the applicant should be represented by a lawyer, ...

(j) Cases of emotional abuse will rarely, if ever, warrant an EPO, let alone an application without notice;

(k) Cases of sexual abuse where the allegations are inchoate and non-specific, and where there is no evidence of immediate risk of harm to the child, will rarely warrant an EPO;

(l) Cases of fabricated or induced illness, where there is no medical evidence of immediate risk of direct physical harm to the child, will rarely warrant an EPO;

(m) Justices faced with an EPO application in a case of emotional abuse, non specific allegations of sexual abuse and/or fabricated or induced illness, should actively consider refusing the EPO application on the basis that the local authority should then issue an application for an interim care order.

---

[99] In *Haase v Germany* [2004] 2 FLR 39, para 95, the ECtHR said that 'it may not always be possible, because of the urgency of the situation, to associate in the decision-making process those having custody of the child. Nor may it even be desirable, even if possible, to do so if those having custody of the chid are seen as the source of an immediate threat to the child.' However, it must be shown that there was reason to think that the circumstances justified removal of the child without prior consultation (ibid).

[100] [2006] EWHC 510 (Fam); [2006] 2 FLR 701.

Clearly, these judgments were intended to protect the family from state intervention which is unwarranted or which takes place in the absence of legal representation. However, according to Masson, there have been unintended consequences. The restrictions imposed by the judges, along with the demands placed on local authorities in terms of procedure by the Public Law Outline,[101] have led to an increased use of police protection. As a result, emergency measures are being taken with no representation or court scrutiny (Masson 2010b).

In keeping with the preference for voluntary as opposed to compulsory measures, where there are concerns that emergency intervention might be needed because of suspected abuse, the local authority should consider providing services and/or accommodation to the suspected abuser rather than removing the child (DfCSF 2008: para 4.28). In addition, the Children Act 1989 provides that, rather than social services having to remove the child from the home, the court can order that the suspected abuser be excluded instead. Section 44A of the Children Act 1989 provides that an exclusion requirement can be included in an EPO. It may exclude a person from the home or a defined area in which the home is situated. It may also prohibit that person from entering the home. In addition, the court may, in terms of section 42(2)(b) and section 42(3) of the Family Law Act 1996, make a non-molestation order where this would benefit the child.

An exclusion requirement can be included, in the case of an EPO made under section 44(1)(a), if there is reasonable cause to believe that, if the relevant person[102] is excluded from the child's home, the child will not be likely to suffer significant harm if not removed from or kept out of the home. In the case of an order made under section 44(1)(b),[103] there must be reasonable cause to believe that enquiries will cease to be frustrated if the relevant person is excluded. A further condition for the inclusion of an exclusion requirement is that there is someone in the home, whether a parent or not, who consents to it and who is willing and able to care for the child.[104] The exclusion requirement ceases to have effect when the emergency protection order does and may be made for a shorter period.[105] A power of arrest can be attached to it permitting a constable to arrest without warrant any person reasonably believed to be in breach.[106] Alternatively, the court may accept an undertaking which is enforced through contempt proceedings.[107]

VII. CARE PLANS

Before making an order, the court must be satisfied that the order would be in the child's best interests[108] and that to make that order is better for the child than making no order at all.[109] It is therefore imperative that the court is aware of the local authority's proposed

---

[101] Practice Direction. Public Law Proceedings Guide to Case Management: April 2010. This is a revised version of the one discussed by Masson.

[102] In a case where suspicion is not directed at a particular individual such as one of the parents, there is no 'relevant' person who might sensibly be excluded. An exclusion requirement would not, therefore, be appropriate.

[103] Or s 44(1)(c).

[104] S 44A(2)(b) of the Children Act 1989.

[105] S 44A(4).

[106] Sub-s 44A(5) and (8).

[107] S 44B.

[108] Sub-s 1(1) and (3).

[109] S 1(5).

course of action should an order be granted. Where an application is made pursuant to which a care order can be made,[110] the local authority must present a care plan to the court outlining the child's needs and indicating how these are to be met. The plan should give details of matters such as where the child is to live and what arrangements for contact will be made.[111] Parents who wish to challenge a care plan on human rights grounds should normally do so under section 7(1)(b) of the Human Rights Act 1998 within the context of the care proceedings.[112] Where the court disagrees with the care plan it can refuse to make the order.[113] However, if the court thinks a care order is necessary, then, at least where the disagreement relates to contact, over which the court retains control, the order should be made.[114]

VIII. THE CHILDREN'S GUARDIAN

Section 41(1) stipulates that the court must appoint an Cafcass officer for the child unless satisfied that it is not necessary to do so in order to safeguard his or her interests.[115] In public law cases, this officer is the children's guardian.[116] The guardian would normally be a qualified and experienced social worker. He or she is under a duty to safeguard the interests of the child[117] and to represent the child. Normally, the child's solicitor is appointed and instructed by the guardian.[118] While the role of the guardian is fairly limited in emergency proceedings,[119] it is very significant in care and supervision proceedings, involving, among other things, an investigation into all the circumstances and the writing of a report for the court.[120]

---

[110] A supervision order can be made on application for a care order and vice versa (s 31(5)).

[111] The obligation to prepare a care plan is now embodied in statute: s 31A Children Act 1989. The obligation arises where an application is made on which a care order may be made, but not when the application is for an interim care order. No care order may be made until the court has considered a s 31A plan (s 31(3A)). See also DfCSF (2008: para 3.42); *Manchester City Council v F* [1993] 1 FLR 419; *Re J (Minors) (Care: Care Plan)* [1994] 1 FLR 253.

[112] *Re L (Care Proceedings: Human Rights Claims)* [2003] EWHC Fam 665; [2003] 2 FLR 160. See also *Re V (Care Proceedings: Human Rights Claims)* [2004] EWCA Civ 54; [2004] 1 FLR 944 para 8; *R (CD) v Isle of Anglesey County Council)* [2004] EWHC Admin 1635; [2005] 1 FLR 59.

[113] *Re J (Minors) (Care: Care Plan)* [1994] 1 FLR 253, 258; *Re B (Supervision Order: Parental Undertaking)* [1996] 1 FLR 676. But see *Re M (Care Order: Freeing Application)* [2003] EWCA Civ 1874; [2004] 1 FLR 826 para 20(iv).

[114] *Re K (Care Proceedings: Care Plan)* [2007] EWHC 393 (Fam).

[115] This duty arises in relation to 'specified proceedings' enumerated in s 41(6). These include applications for care or supervision orders, applications to discharge these orders and proceedings under Part V.

[116] Prior to the creation of Cafcass, this role was carried out by a guardian ad litem, who was a member of a panel set up by the local authority.

[117] S 41(2)(b).

[118] However, if the child is of sufficient understanding to instruct a solicitor and those instructions conflict with the guardian's, the solicitor must follow the child's instructions See Chapter 11 above. See also *Re P (Representation)* [1996] 1 FLR 486.

[119] There may not be a guardian appointed in emergency proceedings. See *X Council v B (Emergency Protection Orders)* [2004] EWHC 2015 (Fam); [2005] 1 FLR 341, para 37.

[120] For a more detailed account of the guardian's role and that of Cafcass generally, see Cafcass (2010). See, in particular, the importance attached to children's views and representation (ibid: para 2.3).

IX. INTERIM ORDERS

Interim orders should not be regarded as routine. An interim order amounts to compulsory intervention in the family and is similar in effect to full care or supervision orders (DfCSF 2008: para 3.44). Interim orders can be made for up to eight weeks and can be extended for four-week periods.[121]

These orders are used, for example, where ongoing intervention is needed after an EPO expires or after the expiry of a period of police protection (ibid). Section 38(1) provides that the court may make an interim order where proceedings relating to an application for a care or supervision order are adjourned[122] or where a direction is given under section 37(1). To make an interim order, the court has to be satisfied only that there are reasonable grounds for believing that the child's circumstances meet the criteria in section 31(2) for granting a care or supervision order.[123] This test is less strict than that governing the making of a full order; for that, the court requires proof of the matters referred to in section 31(2). If the court makes a residence order in favour of relatives, it must make an interim supervision order unless satisfied that the child's welfare will be safeguarded without it.[124] The judge dealing with an interim care application should limit the enquiry to matters that cannot await trial. In addition, in order to justify removal of a child by means of an interim order, the court must be satisfied that the child's safety demands immediate separation.[125]

Where the court makes an interim care order, it may include an exclusion requirement[126] if satisfied that there is reasonable cause to believe that, if a particular person is excluded from the home, the child will cease to suffer, or cease to be likely to suffer, significant harm. There must be some other person in the home, whether a parent or not, who consents to the exclusion requirement and who is able and willing to care for the child adequately. A power of arrest may be attached. Alternatively the court may accept an undertaking, in which case a power of arrest cannot be attached.[127]

---

[121] S 38(4) and (5).

[122] The court has the power to order or prohibit assessments of the child (s 38(6) and (7)), although the older child has the capacity to refuse. But see *South Glamorgan County Council v W and B* [1993] 1 FLR 574. The court's jurisdiction extends to all assessments that involve the child and are directed at providing the court with the information it needs in order to reach a proper decision at the final hearing of the application for a full care order. This can entail assessment of the child within the family in a residential institution. The local authority cannot refuse to make such an assessment on the grounds of lack of resources (*Re C (A Minor) (Interim Care Order: Residential Assessment)* [1996] 3 WLR 1098). An application under s 38(6) can engage Arts 6 and 8 of the European Convention. In many cases the parents' only hope of averting a care order and adoption may lie in the successful completion of an assessment. The fate of the child may rest on this (*Re G (Interim Care Order: Residential Assessment)* [2004] EWCA Civ 24; [2004] 1 FLR 876).

[123] S 38(2). See *Oxfordshire County Council v S* [2003] EWHC Fam 2174; [2004] 1 FLR 426. The test in s 1(5) also applies.

[124] S 38(3).

[125] *Re LA (Care: Chronic Neglect)* [2009] EWCA Civ 822; [2010] 1 FLR 80; *Re F (Care Proceedings: Interim Care Order)* [2010] EWCA Civ 826; [2010] 2 FLR 1455. These cases re-establish a clear rule and clarify the confusion caused by the test of 'imminent risk of really serious harm' used in *Re L (A Child) (Care Proceedings: Removal of Child)* [2007] EWHC 3404 (Fam); [2008] 1 FLR 575.

[126] S 38A.

[127] See s 38B.

Bainham (2011) argues that the interim care application is a crucial 'battle'. Care cases take many months because of the time taken to file evidence as well as the need for parental and kinship assessments and drug and alcohol testing. While these take place, the interim order tends to be renewed. The practice of the lower courts, he says, does not conform to the test enunciated by the Court of Appeal. In *Re B (Interim Care Order)* it was stressed that an interim order is just that. It lasts for eight weeks and subsequent orders can last for four. A parent is entitled to argue that an order should not be extended and the court should extend an order only after considering 'whether the continued removal of [the child] from the care of her parents is proportionate to the risk of harm to which she will be exposed if she is allowed to return to her parents' care'.[128] If the order is extended on successive occasions, circumstances change and, Bainham says, it becomes unlikely that the child will be returned home. He expresses concern that this state of affairs often comes about because parents agree to an interim care order, often under pressure. They may feel compelled to co-operate with the local authority or be convinced that any opposition is unlikely to succeed in court. This is in spite of the fact that, many cases of, say, emotional abuse or a family living in unhygienic conditions, probably do not, according to Bainham, warrant immediate separation. Local authorities are, he suggests, often seeking interim orders in order merely to gain parental responsibility and almost anything negative in the parents' history can be sufficient to cross the statutory threshold.

Q If Bainham is correct, would parents be better off contesting interim care orders rather than co-operating?

X. CARE AND SUPERVISION ORDERS—THRESHOLD CRITERIA

Where a court is faced with an application for a care or supervision order, the court has to determine whether the requirements of section 31 have been met. If they have, the court has a discretion whether or not to grant the order and must exercise that discretion in accordance with section 1. These two stages have been referred to as the 'threshold' stage and the 'welfare' stage, respectively.[129] The process may take the form of a split hearing, involving a finding of fact hearing to determine whether the threshold criteria under section 31 have been met and then a final hearing to decide the outcome of the care application.[130]

The court may not make a care order empowering the local authority to remove the child from the family without considering the Article 8 ECHR rights of the adults and children of the family. The judge 'must not sanction such an interference with family life unless he is satisfied that it is both necessary and proportionate and that no other less

---

[128] *Re B (Interim Care Order)* [2010] EWCA Civ 324; [2010] 2 FLR 283, para 21.
[129] *Re M and R (Child Abuse: Evidence)* [1996] 2 FLR 195, 202.
[130] See *Re L (Care Proceedings: Risk Assessment)* [2009] EWCA Civ 1008; [2010] 1 FLR 790, para 40.

radical form of order' would promote the child's welfare.[131] Indeed, it has been said that any application under Part IV of the Children Act 1989 engages Articles 6 and 8 ECHR.[132] However, it appears that cases brought almost always succeed. Masson et al report that in their sample, consisting of court files relating to applications made in 2004, the threshold for intervention was not found to have been met in only one (Masson et al 2008b: 34). The threshold criteria were contested in only a minority of cases at final hearing (ibid: 55).

Section 31(2) sets out the threshold conditions and provides that:

A court may only make a care order or supervision order if it is satisfied—

(a) that the child concerned is suffering, or is likely to suffer, significant harm; and

(b) that the harm, or likelihood of harm, is attributable to—

    (i) the care given to the child, or likely to be given to him if the order were not made, not being what it would be reasonable to expect a parent to give him; or

    (ii) the child's being beyond parental control.

The section, then, allows for an order to be made not only in circumstances where the child is already suffering harm but also where there is no evidence of existing or past harm but there is a risk of future harm. In determining whether the threshold criteria are satisfied,[133] there will normally be expert evidence to assist the judge.[134] It is not sufficient if the 'significant harm'[135] test is met. In addition, the court must be satisfied that the harm is attributable to some parental deficit.[136]

'Is Suffering'

The relevant time for determining whether a child 'is suffering' significant harm was considered by the House of Lords in *Re M (A Minor) (Care Orders: Threshold Conditions)*.[137] When the child concerned in that case, G, was 4 months old, his father murdered his mother[138] and was then sentenced to life imprisonment. The mother's cousin, Mrs W, took over the care of the older children in the family but felt unable to look after

---

[131] *Re B (Care: Interference with Family Life)* [2003] EWCA Civ 786; [2004] 1 FCR 463, para 34. See also *Re V (Care Proceedings: Human Rights Claims)* [2004] EWCA Civ 54; [2004] 1 FLR 944, para 8. See further on the Human Rights Act, Chapter 13 above. See also, on proportionality, the Public Law Outline: Practice Direction. Public Law Proceedings Guide to Case Management: April 2010.

[132] *Re V (Care Proceedings: Human Rights Claims)* [2004] EWCA Civ 54; [2004] 1 FLR 944, para 8.

[133] Hearsay evidence is admissible in cases of this kind. See s 96(3) of the Children Act 1989; The Children (Admissibility of Hearsay Evidence) Order 1993, SI 1993/621. Failure to observe guidelines for interviewing children is likely to reduce or undermine entirely the probative value of any conclusions drawn from the interview (*Re E (A Minor) (Child Abuse: Evidence)* [1991] 1 FLR 420; *Re A and Others (Minors) (Child Abuse: Guide-Lines)* [1992] 1 FLR 439).

[134] While the court is not obliged to accept the expert's view, it must not reject it without a sound basis and an explanation for doing so (*Re M-W (Care Proceedings: Expert Evidence)* 2010 EWCA Civ 12; [2010] 2 FLR 46). See also on expert evidence *A Local Authority v S* [2009] EWHC 2115 (Fam); [2010] 1 FLR 1560; *East Sussex County Council v K and Others* [2005] EWHC Fam 144; [2005] All ER D (201) (Mar). See also *Re Y and K (Split Hearing: Evidence)* [2003] EWCA Civ 669; [2003] 2 FLR 273.

[135] The meaning of this term is considered on p 663 above.

[136] The burden is on the local authority to prove that an injury is non-accidental; it is not up to the parents to disprove an allegation of non-accidental injury: *Re C and D (Photographs of Injuries)* [2011] 1 FLR 990.

[137] [1994] 2 FLR 577.

[138] The court has produced guidelines for cases where one parent kills the other. A care order should be sought in all such cases. See *Re A and B (One Parent Killed by the Other)* [2011] 1 FLR 783.

G as well. G was accordingly sent to foster parents and the local authority applied for a care order. He later went to live with Mrs W who had changed her mind. With the support of the local authority, she applied for a residence order. However, the child's father argued that G should be adopted. The question that had to be decided was whether the section 31 threshold test was satisfied, since G was being adequately cared for at the time the court had to make a decision and was not *at that time* suffering significant harm.

Reviewing the provisions of the Act, and section 31(2) in particular, Lord Mackay LC said:

> I would conclude that the natural construction of the conditions in s 31(2) is that where, at the time the application is to be disposed of, there are in place arrangements for the protection of the child by the local authority on an interim basis which protection has been continuously in place for some time, the relevant date with respect to which the court must be satisfied is the date at which the local authority initiated the procedure for protection under the Act from which these arrangements followed. If after a local authority had initiated protective arrangements the need for these had terminated, because the child's welfare had been satisfactorily provided for otherwise, in any subsequent proceedings it would not be possible to found jurisdiction on the situation at the time of initiation of these arrangements. It is permissible only to look back from the date of disposal to the date of initiation of protection as a result of which local authority arrangements had been continuously in place thereafter to the date of disposal. It has to be borne in mind that this in no way precludes the court from taking account at the date of the hearing of all relevant circumstances. The conditions in sub-s (2) are in the nature of conditions conferring jurisdiction upon the court to consider whether or not a care order or supervision order should be made. Conditions of that kind would in my view normally have to be satisfied at the date on which the order was first applied for. (583)

> It is true ... that it is now permissible under the second branch of s 31(2)(a) to look to the future even if no harm has already occurred in the past. This is an important difference from the previous legislation but in my opinion to read the present legislation as the Court of Appeal has done [ie that the harm had to be present at the time of the disposal of the case] is substantially to deprive the first branch of s 31(2)(a) of effect. ... It is also clear that while Parliament added the new provisions looking to the future without any necessary connection with harm already suffered, it wished to retain the first branch in respect of harm which the child is suffering. (586)

The court decided that the child was suffering significant harm at the relevant time and held that a care order should be made despite the fact that he was now being well cared for.

In *Re G (Care Proceedings: Threshold Conditions)*[139] the Court of Appeal held that although the threshold had to have been crossed at the time of the initial intervention, the local authority was entitled to rely on information obtained after that date, and even on later events, if those later events were capable of proving the state of affairs at the date of the first intervention.

'Is Likely to Suffer'

In Chapter 13 above we discussed the difficulties of predicting those events that we designate as child abuse. Nevertheless, when the courts decide cases based on the ground

---

[139] [2001] EWCA Civ 968; [2001] 2 FLR 1111.

that the child is 'likely to suffer significant harm', they are in effect making predictions. And it appears that they may be prepared, in the course of this exercise, to look far into the future.[140] The way in which they establish the boundary between what is sufficiently 'likely' and what is not is through rules of evidence. The date at which this likelihood is assessed is the date on which the local authority initiated protective arrangements, provided these remain continuously in place until disposal of the case by the court.[141]

What suffices to prove likelihood was considered by the House of Lords in *In Re H and Others (Minors) (Sexual Abuse: Standard of Proof)* [142] (sometimes called *Re H* or *Re H and R*). This case concerned four sisters and stepsisters. The oldest, D1, alleged that she had been sexually abused and raped by her stepfather, Mr R, the father of two of her siblings. He was charged and acquitted but the local authority proceeded with applications for care orders for the younger girls. The local authority rested its case solely on the alleged abuse of D1, arguing that there was at least a substantial risk that Mr R had sexually abused her and that the others were likely to be harmed too. The House of Lords held that the threshold criteria were not satisfied.

Delivering the majority judgment, Lord Nicholls first considered the meaning of the word 'likely' in the statute. He concluded that it refers to 'a real possibility, a possibility that cannot sensibly be ignored having regard to the nature and gravity of the feared harm in the particular case' (585).[143] He then went on to deal with the standard of proof and held that cases must be proved on a balance of probabilities. He addressed the question of what information counts as a 'fact' for the purposes of determining likelihood of harm.[144] He noted that, although the judge in the court below suspected that the abuse did occur, the local authority, on whom the burden of proof rested, had failed to establish that it had. Upholding the decision of the Court of Appeal, he said:

I have indicated that unproved allegations of maltreatment cannot form the basis for a finding by the court that either limb of s 31(2)(a) is established. It is, of course, open to a court to conclude there is a real possibility that the child will suffer harm in the future although harm in the past has not been established. There will be cases where, although the alleged maltreatment itself is not proved, the evidence does establish a combination of profoundly worrying features affecting the care of the child within the family. In such cases it would be open to a court in appropriate circumstances to find that, although not satisfied the child is yet suffering significant harm, on the basis of such facts as are proved there is a likelihood that he will do so in the future.

This is not the present case. The three younger girls are not at risk unless D1 was abused by Mr R in the past. If she was not abused there is no reason for thinking the others may be. ... To decide that the others are at risk because there is a possibility that D1 was abused would be to base the decision, not on fact, but on suspicion: the suspicion that D1 *may* have been abused. (591–92)

Lord Browne-Wilkinson, dissenting, said:

[T]he facts relevant to an assessment of risk ('is likely to suffer ... harm') are not the same as the facts relevant to a decision that harm is in fact being suffered ... . The combined effect of

---

[140] See *Re H (A Minor) (S 37 Direction)* [1993] 2 FLR 541, 548.
[141] *Southwark London Borough Council v B* [1998] 2 FLR 1095.
[142] [1996] AC 563, sub nom *Re H and R (Child Sexual Abuse: Standard of Proof)* [1996] 1 FLR 80.
[143] See also *Re R (Care Order Threshold Criteria)*[2009] EWCA Civ 942; [2010] 1 FLR 673.
[144] See also *East Sussex County Council v K and Others* [2005] EWHC Fam 144; [2005] All ER D (201) (Mar).

a number of factors which suggest that a state of affairs, though not proved to exist, may well exist is the normal basis for assessment of future risk. To be satisfied of the existence of a risk does not require proof of the occurrence of past historical events but proof of facts which are relevant to the making of a prognosis.

Let me give an example, albeit a dated one. Say that in 1940 those responsible for giving air-raid warnings had received five unconfirmed sightings of approaching aircraft which might be enemy bombers ... . The facts relevant to the assessment of such risk [of an air-raid] were the reports ..., not the truth of such reports. They could well, on the basis of these unconfirmed reports, have been satisfied that there was a real possibility of an air-raid. (572–73).[145]

The approach adopted by Lord Nicholls was criticised by commentators. For example, Hayes argued:

In the usual kind of case there will be a number of concerns that cumulatively lead a local authority to believe that a child is suffering, or is likely to suffer, significant harm. However, if each allegation of fact on its own does not satisfy the balance of probabilities test then, applying Lord Nicholls of Birkenhead's analysis, there are no facts to support a finding of risk of future harm and the court is powerless to proceed. It is suggested that this is not a safe approach to risk taking with children. (Hayes 2004: 66)[146]

Nevertheless, in *Re M and R (Child Abuse: Evidence)*[147] the Court of Appeal approved the approach adopted in the House of Lords in *In Re H* and held that it applied at the welfare stage of the court's deliberations in the same way that it did at the threshold stage. An attempt was made at the welfare stage of this case to reintroduce allegations of sexual abuse. An item in the welfare checklist, section 1(3)(e), refers to any harm the child has suffered or is at risk of suffering. The court, in considering that provision, 'can only have regard to any harm that the child has suffered or is at risk of suffering if satisfied on the balance of probabilities that such harm or risk of harm in fact exists' (205). Although the judge in the court below had concluded that there was a 'real possibility' that sexual abuse had occurred, the Court of Appeal held that this did not suffice:

If ... the court concludes that the evidence is insufficient to prove sexual abuse in the past, and if the fact of sexual abuse in the past is the only basis for asserting a risk of sexual abuse in the future, then it follows that there is nothing except suspicion or mere doubts to show a risk of future sexual abuse. (203)

Apart from his insistence that all facts needed to show a likelihood of harm be proved on a balance of probabilities, Lord Nicholls in *In Re H* went on to make what proved to be an even more contentious observation:[148]

When assessing the probabilities the court will have in mind as a factor, to whatever extent is appropriate in the particular case, that the more serious the allegation the less likely it is that the event occurred and, hence, the stronger should be the evidence before the court concludes that the allegation is established on the balance of probability. ... A stepfather is usually less likely to have repeatedly raped and had non-consensual oral sex with his under-age stepdaughter

---

[145] Baroness Hale in *Re B* (below) took the view that this conclusion was dependent on the context ([2008] UKHL 35; [2008] 2 FLR 141, para 55).

[146] See also Keating (1996).

[147] [1996] 2 FLR 195. Affirmed in *Re S-B (Children)* [2009] UKSC 17; [2010] 1 FLR 1161.

[148] See, eg, the dissent of Lord Lloyd (577) and Keating (1996).

than on some occasion to have lost his temper and slapped her. Built into the preponderance of probability standard is a serious degree of flexibility in respect of the seriousness of the allegation.

Although the result is much the same, this does not mean that where a serious allegation is in issue the standard of proof required is higher. It means only that the inherent probability or improbability of an event is itself a matter to be taken into account when weighing the probabilities and deciding whether, on balance, the event occurred. (586)

As a consequence of this statement, there was some confusion in the courts regarding the standard of proof[149] but this has now been definitively cleared up by two important decisions. It is now settled that the burden of proof is a simple balance of probabilities, irrespective of whether an applicant is seeking to prove that a child *is* suffering significant harm or *is likely* to suffer significant harm. In assessing the likelihood of future significant harm, nothing but facts proven on a balance of probabilities will be taken into account.[150] However, it suffices if those facts, proven on a balance of probabilities, go to show a real possibility of future harm. In contrast, if what is sought to be relied on is past or present harm (the child is suffering or has suffered significant harm), the harm itself must be proven on a balance of probabilities.

In deciding whether a fact has been proven on a balance of probabilities, the court will take into account the inherent improbability of events. However, it will assess that inherent improbability within the context of the available evidence. Once context is taken into account, it may be clear in a particular case that the event alleged, however serious or however unusual, did indeed occur. So, while the seriousness of the misconduct and gravity of the harm remain relevant to the inherent probability that the alleged events occurred, the evidence may point to the occurrence of the events and they therefore cease, as was said in *Re B* (below), to be improbable. Moreover, just because an allegation is serious, it does not follow that the events or acts alleged are improbable or that an allegation is untrue.

In *Re B (Care Proceedings: Standard of Proof)*,[151] Baroness Hale said:

32 In our legal system, if a judge finds it more likely than not that something did take place, then it is treated as having taken place. If he finds it more likely than not that it did not take place, then it is treated as not having taken place … .

54 … The threshold is there to protect both the children and their parents from unjustified intervention in their lives. It would provide no protection at all if it could be established on the basis of unsubstantiated suspicions … . If Parliament had intended that a mere suspicion that a child had suffered harm could form the basis for making a final order, it would have used the same terminology of "reasonable grounds to suspect" or "reasonable grounds to believe" as it uses elsewhere in the Act … .

59 To allow the courts to make decisions about the allocation of parental responsibility for

---

[149] In *Re ET (Serious Injuries: Standard of Proof)* [2003] 2 FLR 1205, the court suggested that the difference between the civil and the criminal standard is 'largely illusory'. That contention was firmly rejected in *Re U (Serious Injury: Standard of Proof); Re B* [2004] EWCA Civ 567; [2004] 2 FLR 263, where the court reasserted that the standard is the balance of probabilities in accordance with the test set out in *Re H*. See also *Re T (Abuse: Standard of Proof)* [2004] EWCA Civ 558; [2004] 2 FLR 838, para 28.

[150] Keating argues that the court's insistence that the threshold criteria cannot be satisfied by anything less than proven facts rather than a real possibility that the events alleged occurred means that the law is unable to protect some children from 'possible but unproven harm' (Keating 2009: 231).

[151] [2008] UKHL 35; [2008] 2 FLR 141.

children on the basis of unproven allegations and unsubstantiated suspicions would be to deny them their essential role in protecting both children and their families from the intervention of the state, however well intentioned that intervention may be. It is to confuse the role of the local authority, in assessing and managing risk, in planning for the child, and deciding what action to initiate, with the role of the court in deciding where the truth lies and what the legal consequences should be. I do not underestimate the difficulty of deciding where the truth lies but that is what the courts are for ... .

70 ... [T]he standard of proof in finding the facts necessary to establish the threshold under section 31(2) or the welfare considerations in section 1 of the 1989 Act is the simple balance of probabilities, neither more nor less. Neither the seriousness of the allegation nor the seriousness of the consequences should make any difference to the standard of proof to be applied in determining the facts. The inherent probabilities are simply something to be taken into account, where relevant, in deciding where the truth lies.

71 As to the seriousness of the consequences, they are serious either way. A child may find her relationship with her family seriously disrupted; or she may find herself still at risk of suffering serious harm. A parent may find his relationship with his child seriously disrupted; or he may find himself still at liberty to maltreat this or other children in the future.

72 As to the seriousness of the allegation, there is no logical or necessary connection between seriousness and probability. Some seriously harmful behaviour, such as murder, is sufficiently rare to be inherently improbable in most circumstances. Even then there are circumstances, such as a body with its throat cut and no weapon to hand, where it is not at all improbable. Other seriously harmful behaviour, such as alcohol or drug abuse, is regrettably all too common and not at all improbable. Nor are serious allegations made in a vacuum. Consider the famous example of the animal seen in Regent's Park. If it is seen outside the zoo on a stretch of greensward regularly used for walking dogs, then of course it is more likely to be a dog than a lion. If it is seen in the zoo next to the lions' enclosure when the door is open, then it may well be more likely to be a lion than a dog.

73 In the context of care proceedings, this point applies with particular force to the identification of the perpetrator. It may be unlikely that any person looking after a baby would take him by the wrist and swing him against the wall, causing multiple fractures and other injuries. But once the evidence is clear that that is indeed what has happened to the child, it ceases to be improbable. Someone looking after the child at the relevant time must have done it. The inherent improbability of the event has no relevance to deciding who that was. The simple balance of probabilities test should be applied.

In *Re S-B (Children)*[152] the same issue was considered again by the Supreme Court. Baroness Hale again noted the need, on the one hand, to protect children from harm and, on the other, the need to protect children and their families from the injustice and harm that could result from unwarranted removal.

This case concerned two children. The older child had suffered bruising and was removed from his parents, whereas the baby had not suffered any harm. However, he had also been removed and the issue in question was whether he would be likely to suffer harm if returned to his mother, now separated from the father. Baroness Hale set out the relevant law:

[8] The leading case on the interpretation of these conditions is the decision of the House of Lords in *Re H (Minors) (Sexual Abuse: Standard of Proof)* ... [1996] 1 FLR 80. Three proposi-

---

[152] [2009] UKSC 17; [2010] 1 FLR 1161.

tions were established which have not been questioned since. First, it is not enough that the court suspects that a child may have suffered significant harm or that there was a real possibility that he did. If the case is based on actual harm, the court must be satisfied on the balance of probabilities that the child was actually harmed. Second, if the case is based on the likelihood of future harm, the court must be satisfied on the balance of probabilities that the facts upon which that prediction was based did actually happen. It is not enough that they may have done so or that there was a real possibility that they did. Third, however, if the case is based on the likelihood of future harm, the court does not have to be satisfied that such harm is more likely than not to happen. It is enough that there is:

> 'a real possibility, a possibility that cannot sensibly be ignored having regard to the nature and gravity of the feared harm in the particular case' (per Lord Nicholls of Birkenhead, at ... 95 ...)

[9] Thus the law has drawn a clear distinction between probability as it applies to past facts and probability as it applies to future predictions. Past facts must be proved to have happened on the balance of probabilities, that is, that it is more likely than not that they did happen. Predictions about future facts need only be based upon a degree of likelihood that they will happen which is sufficient to justify preventive action. This will depend upon the nature and gravity of the harm: a lesser degree of likelihood that the child will be killed will justify immediate preventive action than the degree of likelihood that the child will not be sent to school.

[10] The House of Lords was invited to revisit the standard of proof of past facts in *Re B (Care Proceedings: Standard of Proof)* ..., [2008] 2 FLR 141, where the judge had been unable to decide whether the alleged abuse had taken place. The suggestion that it would be sufficient if there were a 'real possibility' that the child had been abused was unanimously rejected. The House also reaffirmed that the standard of proof of past facts was the simple balance of probabilities, no more and no less.

Another question that the court must answer, where harm to a child has been established, is whether that harm is significant. In addition, there is the question of how likely it is that there will also be future significant harm. These questions arose in *Re MA (Care Threshold)*.[153] The parents in this case were found to have been holding a girl, A, aged 4 or 5, apparently brought from Pakistan as a hostage in a family dispute. They were found to have physically and sexually abused her. The parents had three children of their own. The eldest, M, aged nearly 4, was found to have been hit and kicked by the mother and the father on several occasions.

Hallett LJ found that M had not suffered significant harm:

[39] I confess that my first reaction on reading the papers was to question how any reliance could be placed on the untested allegations of a three-year-old child. Reasonable physical chastisement of children by parents is not yet unlawful in this country. Slaps and even kicks vary enormously in their seriousness. A kick sounds particularly unpleasant, yet many a parent may have nudged their child's nappied bottom with their foot in gentle play, without committing an assault. Many a parent will have slapped their child on the hand to make the point that running out into a busy road is a dangerous thing to do. What M alleged, therefore, was not necessarily indicative of abuse. It will all depend on the circumstances.

[153] [2009] EWCA Civ 853; [2010] 1 FLR 431.

Ward LJ accepted that there had been harm[154] but he also accepted the view of the judge that it had not been significant:

> [60] ... It sounds terrible. It could speak of a persistent campaign of abuse causing real suffering. But it could equally amount in fact to no more than a handful of isolated minor acts of chastisement forgotten as soon as administered ... . Yes, it amounts to ill-treatment and therefore to harm as defined in s 31(9) of the Act yet despite intensive outside intervention in this family's life, no one ever saw a mark on that little girl and the stark fact is that she appeared to be, and it is worth repeating it, 'well-nourished, well cared for and with close attachments to her parents'.
>
> [61] So was the harm significant? That was for the judge to decide. In my judgment, he was fully entitled to come to the conclusion he did. I am inclined to think I may well have come to the same conclusion myself.

Ward LJ then went on to determine whether it was likely that M would suffer significant harm in the future:

> [62] What of the likelihood of significant harm? Here the 'shocking' ill-treatment of A is also relevant. But A's position in that household was so shrouded in mystery that only the judge who had so signally failed through no fault of his to get to the bottom of the complexity, only he was in the position to judge the extent to which it was likely these parents would treat their own children as they had treated this strange interloper. He concluded that they were not likely to mete out barbarous treatment to their own flesh and blood. I am far from satisfied he erred in so doing.

This assessment appears to have been based on the fact that the children appeared well-nourished, well-cared for and to be attached to their parents (para 42). However Wilson LJ, in a dissenting judgment, declared himself 'staggered' (para 34) at the conclusions of the court below:

> [35] ... The conduct of the parents towards A was so grossly abnormal as to show a capacity for cruelty towards children which, surely, gives rise to a real possibility that it would also be directed towards their own children. As the judge observed, the evidence did not enable him to explain why the parents had thus ill-treated A and accordingly it gave him no platform for a conclusion that it would not be likely to be replicated towards their own three children. Indeed to some extent it had already begun to be replicated: for, again for reasons which remained disturbingly unexplained, the parents had embarked upon a course of physical ill-treatment of their oldest child when she had been aged only two. There is no need to take issue with the judge's conclusion, arguably surprising though it also was, that the emotional harm suffered by her as a result of the physical abuse of her was otherwise than of a significant character. For me, the conclusion inexorably driven by the combination of the gross ill-treatment of A and of the ill-treatment of M is that all three children were *likely* to suffer significant emotional and physical harm.

Masson strongly criticises the majority decision. The fact that the children were well fed and had no signs of injury did not mean that they were not likely to suffer significant harm. The majority of the court did not 'address the reasons for considering that M was

---

[154] He rejected the interpretation by the court below of the judgment of Lord Nicholls in *In Re H* to the effect that the threshold for establishing the significance of harm was low (para 52).

likely to suffer significant ill-treatment: the number of incidents, their deliberate nature and the lack of any explanation by the parents for their behaviour' (Masson 2010b: 294).[155] The fact that reasonable chastisement is not illegal was not relevant as in this case the parents could give no explanation for their actions and so these actions were not reasonable. Moreover, she says, the case gives cause for concern as it might deter local authorities from applying to court (ibid: 297). Also it might indicate that courts are becoming unwilling to find the threshold met unless there are already signs of abuse. This, Masson argues, contradicts the future orientation of the Act; the Act provides for intervention before the harm occurs (ibid: 295).

Standard of Parental Care

For a care or supervision order, it is not enough to establish that a child has suffered significant harm, or is at risk of suffering significant harm. To make an order under section 31(2)(b)(i), the court must be satisfied that the significant harm or risk of significant harm is attributable to the standard of care given to the child and that this care is not what would be reasonable to expect a parent to give that child. The test is not what would be reasonable for the parents in question but for a hypothetical parent. And the hypothetical parent is a reasonable parent: the greater the child's needs, the higher the standard of care that would be expected. Parents whose care falls below the requisite standard and who do not seek or use appropriate services are covered by the provision, as are parents who unreasonably fail to protect their child from abuse by a third party. It is not relevant that the parent might be doing his or her 'incompetent best' or might be suffering from a disability or mental impairment; the standard must be met and the Disability Discrimination Act 1995 is not applicable.[156] However, the parents' care should not be regarded as having been unreasonable in cases of minor shortcomings; a '*substantial* deficit' in the standard of care must be evident (DHSS 1985: para 5.15).

> 3.40 ... If the issue is the adequacy of parenting, there must be a direct connection between the harm suffered (or likely to be suffered) by the child and the care given by the parent. Harm caused solely by a third party is not therefore relevant, unless the parent could have been expected to intervene to prevent it and, unreasonably, did not do so. The quality of care given to the child will be compared with what it would be reasonable to expect a parent, having regard to the child's needs, to give the child. 'Care' is not defined but in the context is interpreted as including responsibility for making proper provision for the child's health and welfare (including promoting his physical, intellectual, emotional, social and behavioural development) and not just meeting basic survival needs. (DfCSF 2008)

Q Would the provision cover a blind lone mother? Parents who are poor? A family in which the father frequently beats the mother?[157]

---

[155] See also Keating (2011), particularly in relation to the cultural relativism apparent in the judgment of Ward LJ.

[156] *Re D (Care Order: Evidence)* [2010] EWCA Civ 1000, [2011] 1 FLR 447.

[157] Domestic violence is relevant to risk but is not probative that the violent parent perpetrated an act of child abuse; it does not demonstrate a propensity towards violence against small children (*Lancashire County Council v R* [2008] EWHC 2959 (Fam); [2010] 1 FLR 387).

There have been a number of cases in recent years in which the court has been faced with the situation where there is evidence of significant harm but it is not clear who the perpetrator is. *In Re B (Minors) (Care Proceedings: Practice)*[158] was a case where the court could not be certain which of the parents had harmed the child. It nevertheless made a care order: 'A finding that it must have been either father or mother means ... that the child is at risk from both.' In *Lancashire County Council v B*[159] the child's care was shared between the parents and a childminder and it was not apparent which of these carers had inflicted the child's injuries. The House of Lords dealt with this problem by adopting a relatively broad interpretation of section 31(2)(b). Lord Nicholls rejected an interpretation put to him that he said could lead to successful care proceedings in a case where parents temporarily entrust a child to someone they reasonably think is suitable. He also rejected a formulation that would preclude a care order despite repeated abuse of a child, simply because the perpetrator could be one of two or more people and so could not be identified (588).

> I consider that a permissible and preferable interpretation of s 31(2)(b)(i), between the two extremes, is as follows. The phrase 'care given to a child' refers primarily to the care given to the child by a parent or parents or other primary carers. That is the norm. The matter stands differently in a case such as the present one, where care is shared and the court is unable to distinguish in a crucial respect between the care given by the parents or primary carers and the care given by other carers. Different considerations from the norm apply in a case of shared caring where the care given by one or other of the carers is proved to have been deficient, with the child suffering harm in consequence, but the court is unable to identify which of the carers provided the deficient care. In such a case, the phrase 'care given to the child' is apt to embrace not merely the care given by the parents or other primary carers; it is apt to embrace the care given by any of the carers ... .
>
> I recognise that the effect of this construction is that the attributable condition may be satisfied where there is no more than a possibility that the parents were responsible for inflicting the injuries which the child has undoubtedly suffered ... . I recognise that this interpretation of the attributable condition means that parents who may be wholly innocent, and whose care may not have fallen below that of a reasonable parent, will face the possibility of losing their child ... . [But] it by no means follows that because the threshold conditions are satisfied the court will go on to make a care order ... .
>
> But, so far as the threshold conditions are concerned, the factor which seems to me to outweigh all others is the prospect that an unidentified, and unidentifiable, carer may inflict further injury on a child he or she has already severely damaged. (589–90)

Lord Clyde in turn said:

> What the subsection requires is the identification of the incidence of harm, or the risk of harm, attributable to the care of the child, not the identification of the hand which caused, or may be likely to cause, it ... .
>
> [T]he function of the section is to define the jurisdiction of the court ... . The making of the order requires a much more careful consideration of the case with regard in particular to the matters specified in s 1(3) of the Act, subject always to the paramount consideration of the child's welfare, as specified in s 1(1). So it is reasonable to allow a degree of latitude in the scope of the jurisdictional provision. (592–93)

---

[158] [1999] 1 WLR 238, 249.
[159] [2000] 1 FLR 583.

The test to be applied, both at the threshold stage and the welfare stage, before treating someone as posing a potential risk is 'whether there is a real possibility or likelihood that one or more of a number of people with access to the child might have caused the injury to the child'.[160] In other words, 'is there a likelihood or real possibility that A or B or C was the perpetrator or a perpetrator of the inflicted injuries?'[161]

So, although it is not proved as a fact which of the carers caused the harm or is likely to do so, anyone in relation to whom there is a real possibility is designated as posing a risk.[162] This was confirmed by the House of Lords in *Re O and N; Re B*.[163] As in *In Re H*, the court was concerned with the nature of what counts as evidence. But it was doing so at the welfare stage and in the context of an unidentified perpetrator case. Lord Nicholls reiterated the test in *In Re H*; where significant harm or likelihood of significant harm are in question, the court can only have regard to facts proved to the requisite standard (paras 16–18).[164] He also went on to comment obiter, that in cases where the threshold criteria are satisfied on one ground, but not on another, the unproven allegation cannot be taken into account at the welfare stage under section 1(3)(e) (paras 37–38). However, he said, different policy considerations might apply in determining the matters the court can take into account when assessing risk under different statutory provisions. Thus it appears that the courts take a more flexible approach when it comes to the question of attributing harm. The *Lancashire* case shows that this is so at the threshold stage. And *Re O and N; Re B* shows this is so at the welfare stage:

[26] The first area concerns cases of the type involved in the present appeals, where the judge finds a child has suffered significant physical harm at the hands of his parents but is unable to say which. I stress one feature of this type of case. These are cases where it has been proved, to the requisite standard of proof, that the child is suffering significant harm or is likely to do so.

[27] Here, as a matter of legal policy, the position seems to me to be straightforward. Quite simply, it would be grotesque if such a case had to proceed at the welfare stage on the footing that, because neither parent, considered individually, has been proved to be the perpetrator, therefore the child is not at risk from either of them. This would be grotesque because it would mean the court would proceed on the footing that neither parent represents a risk even though one or other of them was the perpetrator of the harm in question.

[28] That ... would mean that, in 'uncertain perpetrator' cases, the court decides that the threshold criteria are satisfied but then lacks the ability to proceed in a sensible way in the best interests of the child. The preferable interpretation of the legislation is that in such cases the court is able to proceed at the welfare stage on the footing that each of the possible perpetrators is, indeed, just that: a possible perpetrator ... .

[33] ... The approach adopted in *Re H* ... is not apt at the welfare stage in 'uncertain perpetrator' cases.

---

[160] *North Yorkshire County Council v SA* [2003] EWCA Civ 839; [2003] 2 FLR 849, para 26. 'Likelihood' and 'real possibility' were treated as synonymous by the court.

[161] Ibid.

[162] Evidence that emerges at a late stage helping to identify the perpetrator may lead to a rehearing; it is in the public interest that the perpetrator be identified (*Re K (Non-accidental Injuries: Perpetrator: New Evidence)* [2004] EWCA Civ 1181; [2005] 1 FLR 285).

[163] [2003] UKHL 18; [2003] 1 FLR 1169.

[164] The court also rejected the suggestion that in cases of this type, the court should find one or both parents guilty of failure to protect the child and assess the future risk on that basis: 'Inability to identify the perpetrator is not always accompanied by a finding of failure to protect' (para 30).

The question of the unknown perpetrator was revisited in *Re S-B*[165] and Baroness Hale approved the approach taken in the *Lancashire* case, *Re O and N* and *Re B*: it is the care of the primary carers or, in cases of shared care, all those carers, that is in issue. She then went on to consider the standard of proof applicable in the identification of the perpetrator(s).

[34] ... [T]he same approach is to be applied to the identification of perpetrators as to any other factual issue in the case. This issue shows quite clearly that there is no necessary connection between the seriousness of an allegation and the improbability that it has taken place. The test is the balance of probabilities, nothing more and nothing less.

[35] Of course, it may be difficult for the judge to decide, even on the balance of probabilities, who has caused the harm to the child. There is no obligation to do so. As we have already seen, unlike a finding of harm, it is not a necessary ingredient of the threshold criteria. As Wall LJ put it in *Re D (Care Proceedings: Preliminary Hearing)* [2009] EWCA Civ 472, [2009] 2 FLR 668, at para [12], judges should not strain to identify the perpetrator as a result of the decision in *Re B*:

'If an individual perpetrator can be properly identified on the balance of probabilities, then ... it is the judge's duty to identify him or her. But the judge should not start from the premise that it will only be in an exceptional case that it will not be possible to make such an identification.'

[40] ... [I]f the judge cannot identify a perpetrator or perpetrators, it is still important to identify the pool of possible perpetrators. Sometimes this will be necessary in order to fulfil the 'attributability' criterion. If the harm has been caused by someone outside the home or family, for example at school or in hospital or by a stranger, then it is not attributable to the parental care unless it would have been reasonable to expect a parent to have prevented it. ......

[43] ... If the evidence is not such as to establish responsibility on the balance of probabilities it should nevertheless be such as to establish whether there is a real possibility that a particular person was involved. When looking at how best to protect the child and provide for his future, the judge will have to consider the strength of that possibility as part of the overall circumstances of the case.

It was held in *Lancashire County Council v D and E*[166] that it does not suffice if there is medical evidence that the most likely cause of the injuries was an abusive act and that there is a 'pool of possible perpetrators'. In this case, the evidence such as the timing of events did not 'fit' the allegations of the local authority which were accordingly held not to have been proved.

So, to summarise, the court must consider the care given by those who have taken on the 'task of looking after the child',[167] whether those are parents or shared carers, in assessing attributability. Then the court must attempt to identify who the perpetrator was on a balance of probability. If this is not possible, the court must seek to identify a pool of possible perpetrators and establish a real possibility that a particular person caused the harm.

Q Is the approach taken in these cases consistent with the approach in cases such as *In Re H*, which set as a precondition for compulsory intervention in the family,

---

[165] [2009] UKSC 17; [2010] 1 FLR 1161.
[166] [2008] EWHC 832 (Fam); [2010] 2 FLR 196.
[167] *Lancashire County Council v B* [2000] 1 FLR 583, 592.

the requirement that there is proof that the child is likely to suffer significant harm? Does it appear that the courts are more willing to countenance a risk that the child might suffer harm in the future than to risk leaving a child in what might be a dangerous situation where harm has already been proved?

XI. EFFECTS OF A CARE ORDER

Although many children subject to care orders remain at home,[168] a child may be removed to be cared for elsewhere if this is thought necessary. The aim, however, should be to reunite the family if and when this becomes possible.[169] Care orders invest local authorities with parental responsibility and, although parents retain their parental responsibility,[170] their ability to exercise it is significantly curtailed.[171]

Effect of care order

33—(1) Where a care order is made with respect to a child it shall be the duty of the local authority designated by the order to receive the child into their care and to keep him in their care while the order remains in force.

...

(3) While a care order is in force with respect to a child, the local authority designated by the order shall—

(a) have parental responsibility for the child; and
(b) have the power (subject to the following provisions of this section)[172] to determine the extent to which
  (i) a parent, guardian or special guardian of the child; or
  (ii) a person who by virtue of section 4A has parental responsibility for the child,
  may meet his parental responsibility for him.

(4) The authority may not exercise the power in subsection (3)(b) unless they are satisfied that it is necessary to do so in order to safeguard or promote the child's welfare.

(5) Nothing in subsection 3(b) shall prevent [a person mentioned in that provision who has care of the child] from doing what is reasonable in all the circumstances of the case for the purpose of safeguarding or promoting his welfare.

There is little scope for challenging local authority decisions concerning children in care. However, the statute imposes obligations on local authorities designed to promote partner-

---

[168] Such placements are governed by the Care Planning, Placement and Case Review (England) Regulations 2010/959, Regs 15–20. The parents must be assessed. See DfE (2010: paras 3.70–3.76). Following assessement, appropriate services must be included in the childcare plan (ibid: para 3.78).
[169] *Re C and B (Children) (Care Order: Future Harm)* [2001] 1 FLR 611, para 34. See Basic Guidance to Good Practice in Care Proceedings Across London [2011] 1 FLR 201, paras 45–49.
[170] See ss 2(5) and (6).
[171] S 2(8) precludes those with parental responsibility from exercising it in a way that is incompatible with a court order. See also s 33(3)(b) below.
[172] These relate to determining the child's religion, consenting to the child's adoption and appointing a guardian (s 33(6)). In addition, consent from every person with parental responsibility or the leave of the court is necessary before the child's surname can be changed and before the child can be removed from the UK (ss 33(7) and (8)).

ship with parents and children. Section 22C applies to all children 'looked after' by local authorities, and this term refers to children in care as well as to children being accommodated (DfE 2010c: para 1.20). Consultation with parents and children in making decisions is required where reasonably practicable. Before a child is placed in terms of section 22C, a placement plan must be drawn up specifying how the placement is intended to contribute to meeting the child's needs and how parenting tasks are to be shared between the carer and the local authority.[173] Even where a child is subject to a care order, the parents retain parental responsibility and so should be included in discussions about responsibility for decisions about the child (DfE 2010c: para 3.144). In addition, the complaints procedures mandated by section 26(3) are open to children and the parents of children who are being looked after both voluntarily and under care orders.[174]

The local authority looking after a child must arrange for that child to live with a parent, a person with parental responsibility, a relative or a friend, unless this is not reasonably practicable or consistent with the child's welfare.[175] If this is not possible, foster care or residential care are used. Residential care is thought to be appropriate for older children (DfE 2010c: para 3.96). Any accommodation that is provided must be near the child's home and siblings must be accommodated together whenever this is reasonably practicable and consistent with children's welfare.[176]

Contact with their families is widely regarded as important to children's well-being while in care and it has been found to be a significant factor in facilitating the successful rehabilitation of children with their families (DfCSF 2008: para 3.72).[177] The statute therefore places considerable emphasis on preserving links between children and their families.[178] Schedule 2, paragraph 15 imposes a duty on local authorities, in so far as is reasonably practicable and consistent with the child's welfare, to 'endeavour to promote contact' between a child who is being looked after and his or her family and friends.[179] Section 34 empowers courts to make contact orders[180] and also creates a presumption[181] of contact between children in care and their parents:

34. **Parental contact etc with children in care**

(1) Where a child is in the care of a local authority, the authority shall (subject to the provisions of this section) allow the child reasonable contact with—

(a)   his parents;

---

[173] Care Planning, Placement and Case Review (England) Regulations 2010/959 Reg 9; DfE (2010c: para 3.128).

[174] Research suggests that complaints procedures are rarely understood or used (DoH 1995b: 46). See, further, Williams and Jordan (1996).

[175] S 22C. See Basic Guidance to Good Practice in Care Proceedings Across London [2011] 1 FLR 201, paras 50–52.

[176] S 22C.

[177] See also Bullock et al (1993: 100).

[178] This is in conformity with Art 9(3) of the UN Convention on the Rights of the Child which requires states to respect the rights of a child to maintain personal relations and direct contact with parents unless this is contrary to the child's best interests.

[179] It is for the local authority to justify refusing contact to family members such as grandparents (*Re M (Care: Contact: Grandmother's Application for Leave)* [1995] 2 FLR 86).

[180] If appropriate, the court can impose conditions on contact (s 34(7)). If reasonable contact is appropriate, there is no need to make an order (*Re S (A Minor) (Care: Contact Order)* [1994] 2 FLR 222).

[181] See *Re Y (Child Orders: Restricting Applications)* [1994] 2 FLR 699 for an extreme example of circumstances rebutting this presumption. The Guidance refers to the difficulties that can arise when contact takes place within the carer's home and suggest that arrangements must 'be sensitive' to the needs of carers and their families as well as those of parents (DfE 2010c: para 3.142).

(b)   any guardian or special guardian of his;

(ba)   any person who by virtue of section 4A has parental responsibility for him;

(c)   where there was a residence order in force with respect to the child immediately before the care order was made, the person in whose favour the order was made; and

(d)   where, immediately before the care order was made, a person had care of the child by virtue of an order made in the exercise of the High Court's inherent jurisdiction with respect to children, that person.

If the local authority[182] wishes to refuse contact to such a person, it has to apply to court.[183] It is only in an emergency that contact can be justifiably denied without the authority of the court and then only for seven days.[184] Any restrictions on contact may damage the parent/child relationship; such measures constitute an interference with family life under Article 8 ECHR and so warrant strict scrutiny. In particular, '[c]utting off all contact and the relationship between the child or children and their family is only justified by the overriding necessity of the interests of the child'.[185]

XII. CHALLENGING LOCAL AUTHORITY DECISIONS IN COURT

While decisions about whether to grant, refuse or discharge a care order, as well as decisions about contact, lie in the hands of the courts, all other decision-making while the child is in care is within the discretion of the local authority.[186] In particular, section 9(1) prevents parents from seeking to resolve disputes with local authorities by means of prohibited steps or specific issue orders: 'No court shall make any Section 8 order, other than a residence order, with respect to a child who is in the care of a local authority.' Judicial review is possible[187] but the court's inherent jurisdiction cannot be invoked to challenge decisions.[188] Moreover, the court cannot make a care order subject to conditions that the local authority implement it in a particular way.[189]

A question that has arisen is whether the court can oversee the activities of local authorities, particularly in the event of a change to the care plan or a failure to implement

---

[182] A child is also entitled to seek termination of contact (s 34(4)).

[183] S 34(4). See *Re E (A Minor) (Care Order: Contact)* [1994] 1 FLR 146, where a local authority's application to refuse contact to parents was denied although there was no prospect of rehabilitation. Compare *Re L (Sexual Abuse: Standard of Proof)* [1996] 1 FLR 116, 127. See also *Re S (Care: Parental Contact)* [2004] EWCA 1397; [2005] 1 FLR 469.

[184] S 34(6).

[185] *Re C and B (Children) (Care Order: Future Harm)* [2001] 1 FLR 611, para 34.

[186] Decisions about children who are looked after, whether as a result of care proceedings or because they are accommodated, are made by the local authority in consultation with the child and parents. However, in the event of a dispute, children who are accommodated can be removed by the parents and the local authority is generally in a weaker position as it does not have parental responsibility. Disputes about children in care are therefore potentially more likely to arise. Some parents of accommodated children might be persuaded to agree to decisions by the threat of care proceedings.

[187] But it should not normally be used to seek to prevent proceedings for an emergency or care order from being instituted (*Re M (Care Proceedings: Judicial Review)* [2003] EWHC Admin 850; [2003] 2 FLR 171). See, on the right to complain against a decision not to apply for a care order, *R v East Sussex County Council, Ex Parte W* [1998] 2 FLR 1082.

[188] *A v Liverpool City Council* [1982] AC 363. A dispute over the scope of parental responsibility may be resolved under the court's inherent jurisdiction (*Re M (Care: Leave to Interview Child)* [1995] 1 FLR 825).

[189] *Re T (A Minor) (Care Order: Conditions)* [1994] 2 FLR 423.

it. The court cannot make a care order without first considering the care plan.[190] However, once a care order is made, control by the courts is largely lost.

This was the issue before the House of Lords in *Re S (Minors); Re W (Minors)*.[191] There were two appeals. In *Re S* the care plan was devised to facilitate rehabilitation of the children with the mother but none of the assistance envisaged, such as therapy, was forthcoming. In *Re W* the judge had described the care plan as 'inchoate' because it involved considerable uncertainty.

When the cases went on appeal, the Court of Appeal introduced two innovations. First, it provided guidelines intended to give courts a wider discretion to make interim, rather than final, care orders. Secondly, it introduced the notion of 'starred' care plans. Once the care order was made, the court said, the essential milestones of the care plan would be identified and starred. If a starred milestone was not reached within a reasonable time, the case could be brought back to court by the children's guardian or the local authority. This, thought the court, would be interpreting the Children Act 1989 so that it would be compatible with the European Convention.

The House of Lords disagreed and said this about the 'starring' of care plans:

> [27] ... [A] court cannot have day to day responsibility for a child. The court cannot deliver the services which may best serve a child's needs. Unlike a local authority, a court does not have close, personal and continuing knowledge of the child. The court cannot respond with immediacy and informality to practical problems and changed circumstances as they arise. Supervision by the court would encourage 'drift' in decision making ... . Nor does a court have the task of managing the financial and human resources available to a local authority ... .

> [42] I have ... noted, as a cardinal principle of the [Children] Act [1989], that the courts are not empowered to intervene in the way local authorities discharge their parental responsibilities under final care orders. Parliament entrusted to local authorities, not the courts, the responsibility of looking after children who are the subject of care orders. To my mind the new starring system would depart substantially from this principle ... . In short, under the starring system the court will exercise a newly-created supervisory function.

The court went to consider the degree of scrutiny that should be applied to care plans:

> [99] Despite the inevitable uncertainties, when deciding whether to make a care order the court should normally have before it a care plan which is sufficiently firm and particularised for all concerned to have a reasonably clear picture of the likely way ahead for the child for the foreseeable future ... . If the parents and the child's guardian are to have a fair and adequate opportunity to make representations to the court on whether a care order should be made, the care plan must be appropriately specific.

> [102] ... [T]he court must always maintain a proper balance between the need to satisfy itself about the appropriateness of the care plan and the avoidance of 'over-zealous investigation into matters which are properly within the administrative discretion of the local authority'.[192] (references omitted)

The House of Lords went on to point out that the mere failure to adhere to a care plan

---

[190] S 31(3A) and s 31A Children Act 1989. See further pp 679–80 below.
[191] *Re S (Minors) (Care Order: Implementation of Care Plan); Re W (Minors) (Care Order: Adequacy of Care Plan)* [2002] UKHL 10; [2002] 1 FLR 815.
[192] Norgrove (2011a: para 66) calls for a reduction in the level of scrutiny by the courts of care plans. See futher p 705 below.

does not necessarily violate human rights; there might be good reason such a change of circumstances.[193] However, if things go really wrong in the local authority's exercise of parental responsibility, this might entail a violation of Article 8 rights. This could be addressed by judicial review or, as a last resort, by proceedings under section 7 of the Human Rights Act (para 62).

However, there is a lacuna in the legislation, according to the court. Where decisions vitally affect the parent–child relationship, the scrutiny afforded by judicial review might not be sufficiently strict to satisfy the standards set by the Strasbourg court (para 79), although a remedy for breach of Article 8 rights might be available under sections 7 and 8 of the Human Rights Act 1998 (paras 80–81). There is also another lacuna in that young children who have no parent or guardian willing or able to challenge local authority decisions do not have their rights protected (para 86).

Changes have now been made to the law dealing with reviews of cases which may help to monitor the way plans are being implemented. There are now regulations requiring every local authority to appoint an independent reviewing officer to review cases.[194] They have the power to refer those cases which cannot be resolved to their satisfaction to Cafcass. Most disputes are resolved through the dispute-resolution procedure, use of the complaints procedure or by instituting an application under the Children Act 1989 (DfE 2010c: para 4.41).

XIII. SUPERVISION ORDERS

A supervision order[195] does not give the supervisor, the local authority,[196] parental responsibility. The effect of an order is to make it the duty of the supervisor to 'advise, assist and befriend the supervised child' and to take such steps as are reasonably necessary to give effect to the order.[197] An order lasts for up to a year but can be extended to cover a total of three years.[198] Orders may affect the child and the 'responsible person', defined as any person with parental responsibility and any other person with whom the child is living.[199]

What might be contained in an order is set out in Schedule 3. It may require the child

---

[193] However, when there is any significant change to the care plan or to the child's living arrangements, the parents must be properly involved in the decision-making and must have an opportunity to put forward their views (*Re G (Care: Challenge to Local Authority's Decision)* [2001] EWHC Fam 551; [2003] 2 FLR 42, para 43). See further on the case law under the Human Rights Act 1998, Chapter 13 above.

[194] Care Planning, Placement and Case Review (England) Regulations 2010/959. In relation to children who are looked after, the first review must take place within 20 working days of the child becoming looked after. The second review must take place not more than three months after the first. Subsequent reviews must be at six-monthly intervals (Reg 33). See, for arrangements involving voluntary placements, Arrangements for Placement of Children by Voluntary Organisations and Others (England) Regulations 2011/582, Reg 18.

[195] Supervision orders can be granted only when the significant harm test is satisfied. Where concerns about a family emerge in the course of family proceedings, usually in the context of private law proceedings, the court is empowered to make a family assistance order in terms of s 16. This jurisdiction exists in any proceedings in which the court has the power to make a s 8 order, which would include care proceedings as well as various private law proceedings. The court cannot make such an order unless every person named in the order, other than the child, consents. The order requires an officer of the local authority to be made available to advise, assist and befriend those named in it.

[196] See Children Act 1989 Sch 3, para 9.

[197] Ss 35(1)(a) and (b).

[198] Children Act 1989 Sch 3, para 6.

[199] Ibid, para 1.

to comply with directions given by the supervisor about where to live, what places to attend and in which activities to participate.[200] So the supervisor could, for example, require the child to take part in educational activities. The child could also be required to allow the supervisor to visit.[201] However, although the child can be required to undergo psychiatric and medical examination and treatment, this must be specifically provided for in the order.[202] Obligations can be imposed on the responsible person too if he or she consents. In that event, the order may include a requirement that he or she take reasonable steps to ensure that the child comply with the supervisor's and the court's directions. It may also require the responsible person to attend to take part in specified activities.[203]

There is no prescribed means of enforcing directions given under a supervision order. The statute states only that when the order is not complied with or becomes unnecessary, the supervisor is required to apply to court to vary or discharge it.[204] If the child is considered to be at risk, the local authority would apply for an emergency protection order or a care order in the usual way.

> 3.83 There is no prescribed remedy for breach of a requirement set out in the order itself or of a local authority's direction. In case of breach, the local authority would have to consider whether to apply to the court to vary or discharge the order (section 35(3)). If the supervisor is prevented from visiting the child or having reasonable contact with him under paragraphs 8(1) (b) and (2)(b) of Schedule 3, he may apply to the court for a warrant under section 102. The warrant is intended to enable the person concerned to exercise his powers. If the supervisor considered that urgent action should be taken to protect the child, he should consider whether to apply for an emergency protection order (section 44) or ask a constable to take the child into police protection under section 46. (DfCSF 2008)

XIV. CARE ORDER OR SUPERVISION ORDER?

In cases where it is thought safe to leave the child in the home, it is open to the court to make either a care order or a supervision order. However, the court should begin with a preference 'for the less interventionist rather than the more interventionist approach'.[205] In *Re W (A Minor) (Interim Care Order)*[206] the court indicated that wherever possible, a supervision order should be made rather than a care order: 'It is only if the supervision order appears unlikely to be sufficient to obviate the risk that the court should go on to make a care order.' This approach has since been endorsed as being in conformity with the Human Rights Act 1998. As Hale LJ observed in *Re C and B (Children) (Care Order: Future Harm)*, state intervention in family life is permissible under Article 8 ECHR only if it is in accordance with the law; is in pursuit of a legitimate aim; and is necessary in a democratic society. This last requirement is interpreted as emphasising that the interven-

---

[200] Ibid, para 2.
[201] Ibid, para 8.
[202] Ibid, paras 2(3), 4 and 5.
[203] Ibid, para 3.
[204] S 35(1)(c).
[205] *Re O (Care or Supervision Order)* [1996] 2 FLR 755, 760; *Oxfordshire County Council v L (Care or Supervision Order)* [1998] 1 FLR 70.
[206] [1994] 2 FLR 892, 898. See also *Re B (Care or Supervision Order)* [1996] 2 FLR 693, 698.

tion has to be proportionate to the legitimate aim.[207] What the court has to decide is whether a supervision order is a proportionate response to the risk presented.[208]

The more 'serious'[209] care order is needed in cases where the risk to the child is grave,[210] where intensive monitoring of the child is needed, where responsibility for safeguarding the child should be entrusted to the local authority under section 22 and where the local authority needs to have parental responsibility.[211] Other considerations are the extent to which the parents are willing to co-operate and give consent to any 'requirements' under a supervision order as well as whether the court considers that an effective sanction in the event of non-compliance is needed.[212] Supervision orders rely on the co-operation of the family, whereas care orders give the local authority coercive powers. In cases where it is not considered safe to leave the child at home, the only option is a care order.[213]

Q Refer to Chapter 13 above as well as the Human Rights Act 1998. Why should there be a preference for a less interventionist order?

XV. EXCLUDING THE ABUSER—THE FAMILY LAW ACT 1996, SECTION 8 ORDERS UNDER THE CHILDREN ACT 1989 AND INHERENT JURISDICTION

There may be cases where one parent abuses the child but the other could, given the opportunity, care for or be helped to care for the child in a manner considered satisfactory. These cases might be best dealt with by leaving the child at home with the non-abusing parent and ousting the abuser. The abuser might be persuaded to leave voluntarily and the local authority may be able assist financially or provide alternative accommodation.[214] It is open to the non-abusing parent, provided he or she qualifies under Part IV of the Family Law Act 1996,[215] to seek an occupation order excluding the abuser from the family home so as to protect the child. Indeed, section 43 provides that children themselves may apply for occupation orders with leave of the court. However, the grounds on which

---

[207] *Re C and B (Children) (Care Order: Future Harm)* [2001] 1 FLR 611, paras 33–34.

[208] *Re O (Supervision Order)* [2001] EWCA Civ 16; [2001] 1 FLR 923, para 28. See also *Re C (Care Order or Supervision Order)* [2001] 2 FLR 466. See also *Re T (Care Order) [2009]* EWCA Civ 121; [2009] 2 FLR 574.

[209] *Re B (Care or Supervision Order)* [1996] 2 FLR 693, 698.

[210] Where the risk is low, a supervision order will be granted in preference to a care order. See *Re C (Care Order or Supervision Order)* [2001] 2 FLR 466; *Re O (Supervision Order)* [2001] EWCA Civ 16; [2001] 1 FLR 923.

[211] *Re S(J) (A Minor) (Care or Supervision Order)* [1993] 2 FLR 919. See also *Re S (Care or Supervision Order)* [1996] 1 FLR 753 where it was held that a supervision order would not confer on the child the degree of protection considered necessary.

[212] *Re V (Care or Supervision Order)* [1996] 1 FLR 776, 786. In *Re O (Care: Discharge of Care Order)* [1999] 2 FLR 119, the mother was co-operative and also the children needed to be relieved of the threat posed by a care order of being removed from their parent.

[213] Once a care order is made, it remains in force until the child reaches the age of 18 unless it is brought to an end earlier by an order of court (s 91(12)). A care order may be discharged on application to the court under s 39. The making of a residence order discharges a care order (s 91(1)). A care order has no effect while a placement order is in force (Adoption and Children Act 2002 s 29(1)).

[214] Children Act 1989 Sch 2 para 5.

[215] See Chapter 12 above.

occupation orders may be granted in favour of children are not clear from the statute.[216] There is no power to exclude a parent from the family home under the child protection provisions of the Children Act 1989 except under sections 38A and 44A.

Wardship and the Court's Inherent Jurisdiction

The provisions of Parts IV and V of the Children Act 1989 were intended to set out a comprehensive code for the protection of children at risk. The aim of the legislation was to allow compulsory intervention in the family only where the strict threshold criteria could be satisfied.[217] The use of section 8 orders was to be confined largely to disputes between private individuals and the extensive use of wardship by local authorities in public law cases to supplement or even circumvent the statutory provisions governing child protection was to be curtailed.

Wardship derives from the *parens patriae* duty of the state to protect minors; the state has an interest in seeing that children are properly brought up and educated.[218] Originally used as a means of protecting the property of wealthy orphans, the wardship jurisdiction of the High Court was increasingly invoked in the years prior to the Children Act 1989 in complex cases concerning children.[219] Section 100 was framed to put a stop to this practice although it left the High Court with its inherent jurisdiction, of which wardship is a part. The inherent jurisdiction can be invoked to decide single-issue disputes, whereas wardship places the child's life under the supervision of the court; all important decisions must be brought before the court. Local authorities, while they normally cannot seek wardship,[220] are permitted to invoke the court's residual inherent jurisdiction where there are no statutory provisions applicable to the situation in question.

Section 100 states:

100(2) No court shall exercise the High Court's inherent jurisdiction with respect to children—

(a) so as to require a child to be placed in the care, or put under the supervision of a local authority; or

(b) so as to require a child to be accommodated by or on behalf of a local authority; or

(c) so as to make a child who is the subject of a care order a ward of court; or

(d) for the purpose of conferring on any local authority power to determine any question which has arisen, or which may arise, in connection with any aspect of parental responsibility for a child.

(3) No application for any exercise of the court's inherent jurisdiction with respect to children may be made by a local authority unless the authority have obtained the leave of the court.

(4) The court may only grant leave if it is satisfied that—

(a) the result which the authority wish to achieve could not be achieved through the making of any order of a kind to which subsection (5) applies; and

---

[216] See pp 592–93 above.

[217] See Law Commission (1988b: paras 4.51–4.52); DHSS (1987: para 5).

[218] See *Hope v Hope* (1854) 4 De GM & G 328, 344–45.

[219] See, on wardship generally, Lowe and Douglas (2007: ch 16).

[220] But see *Re W and X (Wardship: Relatives Rejected as Foster Parents)* [2003] EWHC Fam 2206; [2004] 1 FLR 415. There was a need in this case for 'external control' and a care order was not possible in the circumstances.

(b) there is reasonable cause to believe that if the court's inherent jurisdiction is not exercised with respect to the child he is likely to suffer significant harm.

(5) This subsection applies to any order—

(a) made otherwise than in the exercise of the court's inherent jurisdiction; and

(b) which the local authority is entitled to apply for (assuming, in the case of any application which may only be made with leave, that leave is granted).

Local authorities' use of section 8 orders is limited by section 9:

9(2) No application may be made by a local authority for a residence order or contact order and no court shall make such an order in favour of a local authority. ...

...

(5) No court shall exercise its powers to make a specific issue order or prohibited steps order—

(a) with a view to achieving a result which could be achieved by making a residence or contact order; or

(b) in any way which is denied to the High Court (by section 100(2)) in the exercise of its inherent jurisdiction with respect to children.

There have been occasions when local authorities have attempted to protect children by means of section 8 orders or through the inherent jurisdiction instead of using care or supervision orders. In particular, these cases have raised the issue of whether an abuser can be excluded from the home.

In *Nottinghamshire County Council v P*[221] the Court of Appeal was faced with a situation where, although the children in question were considered to be at risk of sexual abuse from their father, the local authority declined to seek a supervision or a care order. Instead it applied for a prohibited steps order, requiring the father not to live in the same home as the children and not to have contact with them except under specified conditions. The court held that such an order was precluded by section 9 as the same results could be achieved by means of a residence and a contact order.[222] Moreover, as a matter of policy, where children are found to be at risk, the court said, local authorities should seek care or supervision orders as only these orders confer those powers necessary to protect children. A prohibited steps order was therefore inappropriate. A residence order in favour of the mother, who opposed the exclusion of the father, gave the local authority no powers and was also inappropriate. The court expressed concern that where the local authority resists taking steps to obtain a care or supervision order, there is nothing the court can do to protect children.

This case establishes that a section 8 order cannot be used to remove a parent from the family home. However, it has been held in a much-criticised decision that the inherent jurisdiction can be invoked to this end. In *Re S (Minors) (Inherent Jurisdiction: Ouster)*[223] the court, for the purposes of section 100(4)(a), found that the result that the local authority wished to achieve was to oust an abuser from the family home. Since there was no statutory power under the Children Act to do so, section 100(4)(a) was satisfied. However Dewar (1995: 66) contends that the 'result' that the local authority wanted could have been characterised more broadly as the protection of the children. Section 31 proceedings

---

[221] [1993] 2 FLR 134.

[222] An order that there shall be no contact falls within the definition of a contact order (at 143).

[223] [1994] 1 FLR 623.

are designed to accomplish this objective and therefore the inherent jurisdiction should not have been invoked. Moreover, Roberts (1995) says, in the light of the *Nottinghamshire* case, the inherent jurisdiction, like section 8 orders, should not be used as an alternative to the statutory powers to protect children at risk.

The High Court's inherent jurisdiction and section 8 have been successfully deployed to prohibit a person outside the family from communicating with or having contact with children.[224] However, while these cases might be interpreted as authority for excluding non-family members by those means,[225] it is questionable whether local authorities will be able in future to obtain orders to exclude parents except as a temporary measure under sections 44A and 38A of the Children Act 1989.

XVI. REFORMING THE SYSTEM

While the framework established by the Children Act 1989 continues to be well regarded, the family justice system is thought to be in need of reform. A Family Justice Review was set up and its interim report had been recently published at the time of writing. This Report states that the family justice system is under strain and is not working (Norgrove 2011a: Executive Summary, para 7).[226] There are problems of delay, cost, confusion for adults and children, and lack of trust, among others (Report, para 2.28). Ways to ameliorate these problems by using alternatives to the courts, or at least traditional courts, are suggested. For instance the Report endorses the use of Family Group Conferences and also recommends investigating the use of mediation. In addition, it remarks that the Family Drug and Alcohol Court model, which involves a problem-solving approach, shows promise and that it could potentially be rolled out (Norgrove 2011a: Executive Summary and Recommendations, para 98). However, the main focus of attention is the overhaul of the whole family justice system. There are recommendations, for example, for the creation of a family court (ibid: para 46). It is also suggested that Cafacass be subsumed in a new Family Justice Service as part of court social work services (ibid: para 37).[227]

In relation to public law, the Report notes the use of additional assessments and multiple experts[228] in a bid to reduce uncertainty:

> Judges have a natural tendency to look for certainty and support in making these difficult and emotionally demanding judgments, perhaps through a human desire to have the decision made unavoidable. This has been exacerbated by lack of trust in the judgement of local authority social workers, driven by concerns over the poor presentation of some assessments coming from often under-pressure staff. This increases the tendency to commission more reports and delay decisions. There is a hope that the combination of time and more expert advice will reconcile

[224] See *Devon County Council v S* [1994] 1 FLR 355. See also *Re H (Prohibited Steps Order)* [1995] 1 FLR 638 where it was held that a prohibited steps order could be made against the abuser, the mother's former partner, to the effect that he should have no contact with the children.

[225] See Roberts (1995: 247–48).

[226] See, in the context of private law, Chapter 12 above and Chapter 15 below.

[227] See Norgrove (2011a: Executive Summary and Recommendations, paras 19ff).

[228] Masson et al report that experts were appointed in 90.0% of the cases in their sample (Masson et al 2008b: 49). The court is expected to control the use and cost of experts (Practice Direction. Public Law Proceedings Guide to Case Management: April 2010, para 3.20).

parents to accept a decision or at least to go along with it.
                    (Norgrove 2011a: Executive Summary and Recommendations, para 64)

It also criticises the tendency of the court to duplicate effort by scrutinising the detail of care plans drawn up by local authorities with the result that local authorities do not do some of the work because they know the court will order that they repeat it (ibid: para 66). Instead of trying to predict the future, courts should focus on the fundamental question of whether a care order is in the child's best interests; other means exist for dealing with future events and changes (ibid: paras 72.77–72.79). Courts should also be limited in their use of additional reports and expert witnesses (ibid: paras 89–92).

The House of Commons Justice Committee endorsed this view:

257. We are convinced that there are unnecessary expert reports in some family cases. We note the Minister's comments that greater use could be made of non-expert witnesses, including foster carers. However, foster carers have a distinct role from that of experts, and while they can be a valuable source of information they cannot replace experts in those cases where there is a genuine need for expertise. (House of Commons Justice Committee 2011)

The Committee reflected that, while common sense might suffice in some cases, it has its limits and expert testimony may be required in others (ibid: para 2.55). However, if judges trusted social workers more, they would not need so many expert reports (ibid: para 2.50).

Q Will limiting the court's use of expert evidence increase the uncertainty about risks surrounding child protection cases?

XVII. CONCLUSION

We have seen throughout this examination of the child protection process a tension between the aim of protecting children and the aim of respecting the privacy and integrity of the family. There is always a preference for co-operation, partnership and voluntary measures. And this preference is increasingly being driven by concerns about cost and delay. What changes will follow from the Family Justice Review remain to be seen. However, the emphasis on alternative dispute resolution in the form of mediation and Family Group Conferences will remove some cases from the courts and so will reduce oversight of the decisions of the professionals. It may also reduce the accountability of local authorities. Parents are unlikely in many cases to take the initiative and the risk of challenging local authorities in court.

In addition to concerns about the position of parents, there are concerns about children. Increased resort to kinship care may mean that children are placed at risk; the families of dysfunctional parents may themselves be dysfunctional.

In the end, the fates of both parents and children are determined by the judgments of the professionals and, sometimes, the courts. Their decisions have to be made in the context of the competing aims of protecting children and the aim of preserving family privacy and autonomy. They also have to be made in the context of unpredictability and uncertainty. Protecting children is a risky business.

POSTSCRIPT

While this book was in press, the *Family Justice Review. Final Report* was published (Norgrove 2011b). It confirms the recommendation in the Interim Report for a single family court (Executive Summary para 36) and stresses the need for judicial continuity, with the same judge hearing all aspects of a case (para 33). It acknowledges the central role of the court in child protection cases (Executive Summary para 59, Report para 3.18) but makes it clear that judges should only focus on 'core issues' such as whether the child should live with the parents or other family members, whether the child should be removed into care and whether there should be contact between the child and any person (Executive Summary paras 62–3). The Report goes on to suggest that consideration be given to the amendment of s 34 of the Children Act 1989 to enable siblings to apply for contact without the leave of the court (Report para 3.43).

Perhaps the most radical proposal reflects the concern in the Report about the effects of delay in child protection cases. The report recommends a six month time limit for the completion of care and supervision proceedings, with some exceptions such as where cases are complex (Report para 3.64ff). Interim orders will last for up to six months (ibid para 3.57). In addition, the Report endorses the use of the Letter before Proceedings (para 81) and Family Group Conferences (Executive Summary para 98). Finally, it recommends that mediation be piloted (para 99) and that there be a limited roll-out of the Family Drug and Alcohol Court (para 100).

FURTHER READING

J Brophy, J Jhutti Johal and C Owen, 'Assessing and Documenting Child Ill-treatment in Ethnic Minority Households' (2003) *Fam Law* 756.

M King and F Kaganas, 'The Risks and Dangers of Experts in Court' [1998] *Current Legal Issues* 221.

J Masson, M Winn Oakley and K Pick, *Emergency Protection Orders: Court Orders for Child Protection Crises* (Coventry, Warwick University, 2004).

J Masson with D McGovern, K Pick and M Winn Oakley, *Protecting Powers. Emergency Intervention for Children's Protection* Chichester (NSPCC, Wiley, 2007).

J Masson, J Pearce and K Bader with O Joyner, J Marsden and D Westlake, *Care Profiling Study*, Ministry of Justice Research Series 4/08 (London, Ministry of Justice, 2008).

D Norgrove (Chair) (2011) *Family Justice Review. Final Report* (London, Ministry of Justice).

N Stanley, P Miller, H Richardson Foster and G Thomson, *Children and Families Experiencing Domestic Violence: Police and Children's Social Services' Responses* (London, NSPCC, 2010).

15

A Public or Private Matter—Alternative Dispute Resolution and Negotiation

I. INTRODUCTION

We have discussed elsewhere[1] the dilemma that the liberal state faces in seeking to regulate the family while at the same time preserving, or at least appearing to preserve, family privacy. Divorce, like marriage, has long been regarded as a public matter and as necessitating legal intervention. However, there has been a gradual move over the years to the partial privatisation and de-legalisation of the process. The introduction of no-fault divorce and the special procedure for undefended divorces,[2] for example, evidence this trend. More recently, there has been a move to privatise disputes arising from the termination of adult relationships; money and children have become private matters too. There is a remarkable degree of consensus about the limitations of law and the courts in dealing with family disputes, particularly disputes about children. There is a widely held view that, wherever possible, cases should be kept out of the courts and that the parties should be encouraged to reach their own agreements. The most well-established mechanisms for achieving settlements are lawyer negotiation,[3] mediation and in-court conciliation.[4] In the past few years, there has also been a growth in the use of collaborative law.

A decade ago, Davis wrote that it was becoming increasingly difficult to distinguish between 'legal services and mediation, between the mainstream and the "alternative"' (Davis 2000: 3). He went on:

> Any applicant to the court in respect of children or money will now be deflected to one of a variety of negotiating opportunities. These may or may not be on court premises, and the mediation label may or may not be attached. ... [C]ustomers of mediation services may find that their mediator is in fact a lawyer ... . Even if the mediator's academic antecedents are impeccably 'social' it is likely that he or she will be a good deal preoccupied with achieving agreements which can be presented to the court as constituting formal legal settlement. So we have mediation in the law, and we have law in mediation; or to put this another way, we have deflection

---

[1] See, eg, Chapter 9 above.

[2] Almost all divorces are undefended (see p 82 above) and public funding is not available to defend a divorce petition.

[3] This crucial means of resolving disputes is often omitted in the discourse surrounding ADR, which generally focuses on processes such as mediation.

[4] The term 'conciliation' was originally used to refer to both in-court and out-of-court schemes. It was then replaced by the term 'mediation'. Now it appears that the term 'conciliation' has been resurrected in relation to in-court schemes, while 'mediation' is used to refer to independent schemes.

from the formal and formalisation of the informal. That is either an impressive convergence of practice and of principle, or it is a very fine mess, depending on how one looks at it. (ibid: 3)

Whether it is a 'mess' or not, alternative dispute resolution (ADR) is still seen as the best way to deal with family disputes and diversion from court has become an even greater priority.[5] In a speech delivered in 2010, Jonathan Djanogly, the Parliamentary Under-Secretary of State at the Ministry of Justice, set out the government's plans to support mediation and said:

> We need to work together to build the case for mediation and other forms of dispute resolution so that it is adopted by the many and not just the few. It is true that court is still often viewed as the place to resolve conflict but I think we are beginning to see a shift. … Awareness of mediation is growing, albeit slowly, and with the financial situation forcing us all to tighten our belts, the benefits of avoiding costly, distressing court actions cannot be overplayed.
>
> (Walsh 2011)

With anticipated restrictions on access to legal aid,[6] and the proposals in the *Family Justice Review Interim Report* (Norgrove 2011a),[7] it is likely that fewer disputes will find their way into court. The recommendations of the *Family Justice Review* are dominated by concerns about the proliferation of private law disputes, particularly about children, as well as delay and cost.

If the recommendations of the *Review* are implemented, a Family Justice Service will be created. This must provide the 'information and tools' needed to enable people to resolve their disputes without going to court (Norgrove 2011a: Executive Summary, para 32) and it must 'procure publicly funded mediation' (ibid: para 33). Rather than going to court for orders such as contact and residence orders, parents will be expected to access an online information helpline and hub to help them resolve their dispute. The hub will, among other things, tell them about the cost of litigation and about alternative forms of dispute resolution, such as mediation and Separated Parents Information Programmes (PIPs) (ibid: para 114).[8] If parents wish to go to court, they will have to be assessed by a mediator to establish the most appropriate way of resolving the case. This might be mediation, collaborative law or, in cases where there are safety concerns or a serious imbalance of power, the court (ibid: para 115). After being assessed, parents will be required to attend a PIP where they will be told about the court process and the cost it entails. Parents will then, if necessary, attend mediation or another accredited method of dispute resolution such as collaborative law sessions (ibid: para 119). Unlike the assessment and the PIP, mediation will not be compulsory but 'the aim must be that this becomes normality' (ibid).

> 121. Only in cases where parents are unable to agree about a specific aspect of a Parenting Agreement, or in those cases where an exemption is raised by a trained professional, will one or both of the parties be able to apply to court for a determination on a *specific issue* … .

---

[5] See Family Procedure Rules 2010/2955 R 3.1–3.3.

[6] See Chapter 10 above. Legal aid for the purposes of legal proceedings will not be available for disputes about finance or children, unless there is an element of violence. There is no exception for situations where mediation fails or if one party refuses to attend mediation (Legal Aid, Sentencing and Punishment of Offenders Bill 2010–11). Legal aid will be available for mediation.

[7] See further Chapter 10 above.

[8] See also the Report, paras 5.14, 5.59.

125. Judges will retain the power to order parties to attend a mediation information session and *may make cost orders where it is felt that one party has behaved unreasonably.*

(ibid, emphasis in original)

Those in dispute about property and money matters '*should access the information hub and be assessed for mediation* in the same way' as those in dispute about children (ibid: para 128, emphasis in original).

Clearly, the recommendations are aimed at diverting cases from court and promoting ADR[9] and, in the case of disputes about children, parenting agreements:[10]

104. There has been a move within the current private law system to recognise that cases can and often should be diverted away from the courts where it is safe to do so. The range of support available to allow separating families to resolve disputes outside court has developed over the years to include mediation, collaborative law and Separating Parents Information Programmes. These services can support parties to resolve issues themselves through discussion and negotiation that may be more sustainable and at lower cost than going to court. At present, though, many people are made aware of these alternatives only after they have entered the court system, by which time attitudes and behaviours may be entrenched and significant cost has already been incurred.

105. The state cannot fix fractured relationships or create a balanced, inclusive family life after separation where this was not the case before separation. Court is generally not the best place to resolve these disputes. Where possible, disputes should be resolved independently or using dispute resolution services such as mediation, when it is safe to do so. Parents who choose to use the court system must understand it will not be a panacea. Courts will only make an order where this is in the best interests of a child. Further, where the court does make an order, this may well not be in line with one or both parents' expectations or wishes. People need to expect that court should be a last resort, not a first port of call.[11]

The House of Commons Justice Committee, responding to the recommendations made in the *Review*, appeared to doubt the utility of intervention and information given by means such as the proposed hub:

106. More support for separating parents could reduce the number of cases reaching court and reduce the negative impact of separation on children. However, there is currently a lack of evidence as to which early interventions are most effective. There is also the risk that some of the numerous cases where one parent has no contact could be diverted into court ... .

107. Currently only one in ten separating parents resolves their disputes in court. The evidence we received is that a large number of these parents have multiple problems. This means that they are unlikely to be diverted from court by anything other than intensive intervention. In addition, there are many cases involving safeguarding concerns which should not be diverted from court. Some parents could be diverted from court by low-level intervention, but the Government should be realistic about the impact of any proposals on the number of private law cases reaching court. (House of Commons Justice Committee 2011)

Even more problematic was the requirement to meet with a mediator:

160. The Interim Report is walking a fine line between strongly encouraging the use of media-

---

[9] See, eg, Executive Summary, para 39.
[10] See Executive Summary, para 111; Report, paras 590ff.
[11] See also the Report, paras 5.2, 5.58, 5.60.

tion, and making it compulsory for those who do not qualify for an exemption. Given the mixed evidence around the effectiveness of mediation, especially in difficult cases, we cannot support it being made compulsory. We call on the Family Justice Panel to clarify that while attendance at Information Meeting or Assessment for Mediation sessions and a Separated Parenting Programme should be compulsory (with some limited exemptions), all parents should be free to apply to the court after those have taken place. (ibid)

Here, we trace the development of ADR as the 'officially' approved means of settling practical arrangements when partners separate. We focus primarily on mediation, in-court conciliation and settlement through negotiations by lawyers. We also consider, more briefly, collaborative law, Financial Dispute Resolution and parenting agreements. In the course of examining these forms of private ordering,[12] we highlight the problems that can arise out of the privatisation of decision-making.

II. ALTERNATIVE DISPUTE RESOLUTION

The Background to the Rise of Mediation and ADR

The seemingly inexorable rise in divorce rates since the Second World War led to a re-evaluation of both the grounds for divorce and the procedures by which divorces were granted.[13] Initially, efforts at reform were directed at promoting reconciliation between spouses as well as at reducing costs to public funds and relieving pressure on the legal system.

This preoccupation with marriage saving was reflected in the Divorce Reform Act 1969. Section 3 required solicitors to certify whether or not they had discussed the possibility of reconciliation with their clients and had offered to refer them to counselling. In addition, courts were empowered to adjourn proceedings while parties attempted reconciliation. However, as Eekelaar and Dingwall have observed, in the context of a legal system intent on expediting cases and containing costs, these provisions were 'an almost immediate dead letter' (Eekelaar and Dingwall 1988: 11). Attention shifted instead, during the 1970s, to what was then called 'conciliation'. This term is now used in relation to in-court services but other schemes are generally referred to as 'mediation'.

Rather than concentrating on trying to save marriages, reformers became concerned with facilitating the settlement of disputes arising on marriage breakdown with as little conflict as possible. The increase in divorce was acknowledged to be the product of apparently irreversible social change such as the economic emancipation of women through participation in employment; the availability of social security support to those women who would otherwise be unable to leave their marriages; and a growing perception that the purpose of marriage should be emotional fulfilment.[14] Preserving unhappy marriages was no longer the main priority for the state. Equally important, it was thought, was the provision of a means by which relationships could be dissolved and differences settled with as little acrimony as possible.

---

[12] For a discussion of family group conferences in the context of child protection, see pp 648–50 above.
[13] See, generally, Eekelaar and Dingwall (1988).
[14] See, eg, ibid: 15.

Since the mid-1970s, when the first conciliation services were established,[15] mediation has increasingly come to be seen as an appropriate forum for the settlement of family disputes.

Forms of ADR

Mediation is currently the most favoured mechanism for settling, or managing, family disputes. Collaborative law is also being used but its use appears limited. In the past, various other mechanisms were trialled but largely without success. Parenting plans were introduced to show parents what kinds of arrangements work and to help them reach agreement.[16] These are available through Cafcass and are also used by mediators, However, their use has been 'ad hoc' (Norgrove 2011a: para 5.90) and the *Family Justice Review* recommends parenting agreements instead. A Family Advice and Information Service (FAInS), intended to facilitate early resolution of disputes, was piloted in the 2000s. Solicitors were meant to act as a one-stop shop, directing people to other services where appropriate. However little change in practice resulted, partly because the service networks did not exist (Walker et al 2007).

We will consider mediation at some length. As Davis has observed: 'The main "story" of private family law over the past two decades has been the emergence of mediation. This has attracted massive interest in its own right, and it has also greatly influenced the work of family lawyers and the family courts' (Davis 2000: 1). However, we will first distinguish mediation from other forms of ADR, some of which are discussed in more detail later in this chapter.

Mediation

Mediation is intended to facilitate joint decision-making by the parties. It was used in the UK, initially, primarily in seeking to resolve disputes about children. However, its scope has been broadened to address issues of property and finance[17] as well as 'other practical issues' and it aims to 'achieve longer-term agreements through improved communication and co-parenting' (LSC undated, *What Is Family Mediation?*). Out-of-court mediation is conducted away from court premises. Services[18] are staffed mainly by professionals with counselling, social work or legal backgrounds. Lawyers who mediate, however, operate primarily in the private profit-making sector, rather than in the not-for-profit sector.

---

[15] For an account of the history of mediation in England and Wales, see the Newcastle Conciliation Project Unit Report (1989: paras 2.21ff).

[16] See DCA, DfES and DTI (2005: para 31).

[17] Mediation involving only property and finance tends to be more formal and oriented towards fact finding than child-related mediation (Dingwall and Greatbach 2000: 233). In the study conducted by Davis and colleagues, which began in 1997 and which was published in 2000, 85% of cases referred for mediation concerned disputes about children and 33% of cases had a financial or property dispute as a component (Davis et al 2001b: 111). Of those cases that were actually mediated, 67% involved an attempt to resolve issues about children (ibid: 112). Walker et al (2004) found that 38% of mediation users were hoping to resolve child-related and financial issues. 28% were concerned only about finances and 20% only about children. 14% were not clear about why they had been referred to mediation at all (ibid: 131–32). 38% of those who attended mediation did so on the advice of their solicitors (ibid: 132).

[18] The UK College of Family Mediators (now the College of Mediators) was formed to validate professional standards in the private and not-for-profit sectors.

Comprehensive mediation[19] was developed in response to the growing perception that issues around children cannot be sensibly dealt with without also addressing questions of finance and property. Each impacted on the other. In addition, it was thought, the benefits of mediation about children might be lost if parties were left to deal with disputes over assets through traditional adversarial channels

Mediation is described in a report by Walker et al:

> Family Mediation is a process in which an impartial third person, the mediator, assists couples considering separation or divorce to make arrangements, to communicate better, to reduce conflict between them, and to reach their own agreed joint decisions. The issues to be decided may concern separation, the divorce, the children, finance and property.
>
> The mediator has no stake in any disputes, is not identified with any of the competing interests, and has no power to impose a settlement on the participants, who retain authority to make their own decisions.
>
> Couples enter mediation voluntarily, to work together on the practical consequences of family breakdown, and to reach proposals for settlements which may then be endorsed by their legal representatives and the court, wherever appropriate. Mediation offers an alternative to negotiation by solicitors and to adjudication through the court, but is not a substitute for legal advice and representation. (Walker et al 1994: facing page)

Parkinson stresses that agreements are not binding and that parties are encouraged to seek legal advice:

> Mediation is intended to encourage co-operation and reduce long-running disputes. The Memorandum of Understanding drawn up by a mediator at the conclusion of a mediation sets out proposed terms of settlement that can be confirmed by legal advisors in open correspondence, legally binding agreement or consent order. Legal advisors provide a system of checks and balances, with clients encouraged to take advice between mediation meetings as well as at the end. Legal advice is not invariably needed on minor details of contact arrangements. ... The confidentiality and legal status of written summaries of mediation outcomes need to be clearly stated so that legally binding agreements can be drafted by lawyers with minimal delay and cost and without risks of premature or ill-informed concessions. (Parkinson 2011a: 92)

The process of mediation is shaped by a number of underlying ideas, the most prominent among which have been described by Simon Roberts as follows:

> that family disputes should be approached in a spirit of restraint rather than antagonism; that those in dispute should retain responsibility for decision-making rather than surrender this to third parties; that there are advantages in informality of process; that the focus of third-party intervention should be upon relationships rather than specific issues and vice versa; that outcomes should be founded in agreement and compromise rather than coercion; that the handling of disputes should be taken out of the hands of specialists; that there should be a move from state ordering to private ordering, from a legal to a non-legal world. (Roberts 1983: 538)[20]

---

[19] Services have adopted differing models of comprehensive mediation. A lawyer might act as a co-mediator together with, eg, a welfare professional, or might act as a consultant who is not directly involved in mediation sessions. See, further, Walker et al (1994: 15–16); Roberts (1997: 34–37). Dingwall and Greatbach comment that mediators in their study showed limited abilities to advise on financial matters and frequently referred issues to solicitors (Dingwall and Greatbach 2000: 233; Dingwall and Greatbach 2001: 379). While solicitor mediators do deal with both children and finance, they have tended to deal mainly with finance and property (Davis et al 2000d: 36).

[20] See also Davis and Roberts (1988: 6).

Mediation therefore differs from forms of ADR such as arbitration where the final decision is made by a third party, the arbitrator. It is also distinguished from other forms of intervention to deal with family breakdown.

Financial Dispute Resolution

Mediation differs from the process of financial dispute resolution (FDR).[21] This is restricted to financial matters and the parties' representatives attend together with their clients. FDR is in effect an attempt, normally before a district judge, to reach a negotiated settlement. FDR does not require the consent of the parties,[22] whereas mediation in Britain is voluntary.

Lawyer Negotiation

Mediation is different from the process of negotiation and dispute settlement often conducted by lawyers because, in mediation, the negotiation is undertaken by the parties themselves. Although they are assisted by the mediator, it is the parties, it is said, who control the outcome. By contrast, when cases are settled by lawyers, it is the lawyers who conduct negotiations, often in the absence of their clients (Davis and Roberts 1988: 8).

Collaborative Law

This is a process of negotiation in which lawyers and their clients participate. It is described in the *Family Justice Review*:

[5.25] Collaborative law is a process in which a divorcing couple and their lawyers agree not to go to court, but instead work as a team to find solutions aimed at enabling them to move forward. In the event that they are unable to reach a solution by this method, the parties must instruct alternative lawyers to take their case to trial (with of course an increase in costs). Collaborative law is more directive than mediation and allows lawyers to be present in the discussion process

[5.26] ... A benefit of the process is that it is not driven by a timetable imposed by the court. There is no incentive for the lawyer to escalate the case since the parties must instruct new lawyers if the matter does go to court. (Norgrove 2011a)

Therapy and Counselling

Mediation must also be distinguished from family therapy or counselling.[23] Whereas therapeutic intervention is predicated on the assumption that the parties or the family have a problem requiring treatment, mediation proceeds from the assumption that the parties

---

[21] See below.

[22] See, further, Coleridge et al (1996); Singer (1996).

[23] Roberts (1983: 552) points out, however, that it is not always possible to draw a clear line between intervention in the form of giving advice and counselling and intervention to facilitate joint decision-making.

are competent to define the issues and to arrive at a negotiated solution (Davis and Roberts 1988: 8).

Moreover, since mediation does not concern itself with delving into the psyche[24] but is rather concerned with managing practical arrangements, it is essentially forward looking. Since, in general, it is less concerned with *why* the relationship has broken down than with the consequences of that breakdown, it is usually not conducted in a way that encourages parties to rehearse the past and to express their hurt and resentment.[25] As Marian Roberts says, 'excessive or prolonged' excursions into such matters may 'seriously impede rational exchange and lead to a deterioration of relations, rather than any improvement' (Roberts 1997: 25). Indeed, Dingwall and Greatbach (2000: 251) remark that mediation is often seen as a 'quasi-legal, dispute resolving intervention'.

In-court Conciliation

In-court conciliation is carried out on court premises by court personnel. Cafcass officers (with a mediator if available) attend the First Hearing Dispute Resolution Appointment (FHDRA). At this hearing, the court must consider 'whether and the extent to which the parties can safely resolve some or all of the issues with the assistance of the Cafcass officer and any available mediator'.[26] There must be at every FHDRA a period in which 'the Cafcass officer, with the assistance of any mediator and in collaboration with the court, will seek to conciliate and explore with the parties the resolution of all or some of the issues between them'.[27] The court, together with the Cafcass officer, and any mediator present, 'will seek to assist the parties in conciliation and in resolution of all or any of the issues between them'. Any remaining issues will be identified and the Cafcass officer will recommend means to resolve these. Directions will then be given for their future resolution.[28] FHDRAs were said to be helpful in the *Family Justice Review* interim report, and so worth retaining (Norgrove 2011a: para 5.146).

III. MEDIATION

Mediation—A Voluntary Process?

We have seen that once parties get to court and attend the FDHRA, they will be expected to consider conciliation. However, it is now also the case that before court proceedings are even instituted, an applicant is obliged to consider mediation. Parties are expected to reach agreement without a hearing having to take place at all

The government has refrained from making mediation compulsory.[29] However, the new

---

[24] See Booth (1985: para 3.11).

[25] That mediators are not concerned about reconciliation was observed by Dingwall and Greatbach (2000: 241).

[26] Practice Direction, The Revised Private Law Programme [2010] 2 FLR 717, para 2.2(a).

[27] Ibid, para 5.2(a).

[28] Ibid, para 4.4.

[29] This has long been the preferred approach. See DCA, DfES and DTI (2005: para 50). See also University of Newcastle's Conciliation Project Unit's report (1989; para 20.19); the Law Commission (1990); and the Lord Chancellor's Department (1995a). Among the cases where mediation was considered potentially unsuitable by

requirement to consider mediation, discussed below, is likely to add to the pressure disputing parties may find themselves under to avoid litigation. Mediators may strongly influence clients to undergo mediation. There are, say Davis et al, 'hidden pressures' because clients are in 'advice-seeking mode' and they fear that they might be 'ill-advised' not to accept the mediator's suggestions (Davis et al 2000f: 214).[30] In addition, the judiciary are clearly in favour of mediation and may be willing to exert some pressure on the parties to consider participating and adjourn proceedings which have already commenced to enable them to do so.[31]

There are also financial incentives designed to persuade people to engage in mediation to resolve their disputes before they ever get to court. For those seeking public funding, it is necessary to consider mediation before legal funding can become available. The incentives to consider mediation were introduced in the Family Law Act 1996 and survive the demise of Parts II and III in a slightly different form.

Community Legal Services funding is regulated by the Legal Services Commission Funding Code Criteria (LSC 2007a) and Funding Code Decision Making Guidance (Family) (Section 20) (LSC 2007b). Section 8 of the Access to Justice Act 1999 specifies the principles that must shape the criteria for funding and subsection (3) states that '[t]he criteria set out in the code shall reflect the principle that in many family disputes mediation will be more appropriate than court proceedings'.[32]

The Funding Code Guidance (LSC 2007b: section 20.1(2)) states that '[t]he primary aim of funded Family Services is to help people resolve disputes concerning children and family relationships at the earliest opportunity and in the most appropriate way, where possible without litigation'. Funding is available for mediation in cases which have been assessed as suitable by a mediator (ibid: section 20.9(3)ff). However, all applications for legal funding for court proceedings must be assessed for suitability for mediation before the application for funding is made (ibid: section 20.16). And funding may be refused if mediation is considered more suitable than legal representation (LSC 2007a: para 11.12.3). It is only if a case falls within the specified exceptions that an assessment meeting with a mediator need not take place (LSC 2007b: 20.16(3)). The exemptions cover cases such as those where a mediator has assessed the case as unsuitable for mediation or in certain cases involving domestic violence (ibid: section 20.16(4)).

So, in effect, those seeking public funding must be assessed to determine whether mediation is suitable and they may not be able to access funding for other services unless mediation has been ruled out. This used to mean that those seeking public funding were in a different position from wealthier parties who could decide to pursue their case in court.

It now the case, however, that the position of those who are publicly funded and those who are self-funded has been harmonised (Norgrove 2011a: para 5.24) Prospective applicants to court, whether self-funding or publicly funded, are required to attend a meeting to learn about mediation before taking the case to court, on the assumption that this will

---

the Law Commission were cases involving exploitation of the weaker party by the stronger, cases where this would lead to delay and also where courts might postpone difficult and painful cases which ought to be decided quickly. See Law Comm (1990: paras 5.34–5.7).

[30] Davis et al report that, from their research, it is apparent that giving people a choice of processes at a time of crisis is to expect them to focus on matters they do not understand (Davis et al 2001a: 266–67).

[31] For an unusual case, see *Al-Khatib v Masry* [2004] EWCA Civ 1353; [2005] 1 FLR 381.

[32] See also s 4 which states that it is the most appropriate service that must be funded if more than one is available.

'potentially [reduce] the number of cases which go on to court' (Norgrove 2011a: para 5.24).[33]

This change is embodied in a new Practice Direction setting out a Pre-Application Protocol[34] designed to compel prospective litigants to 'ensure, as far as possible, that all parties have considered mediation as an alternative means of resolving their disputes'.[35] All potential applicants for an order are required to consider, with a mediator, whether the dispute might be capable of being resolved by means of mediation.[36] Applicants must therefore attend a Mediation Information and Assessment Meeting, if invited to do so, before commencing proceedings. They will be required to attend a meeting unless they fall within the exceptions set out in Annex C. Such a meeting may be attended by both parties together or separately, where necessary.[37] If the applicant initiates court proceedings, the mediator must complete a form confirming the applicant's attendance at the meeting or setting out the reasons for any failure to attend.[38] The court will want to know at the first hearing whether mediation has been considered by the parties. It can take into account any failure to comply with the protocol and may refer the parties to a meeting with a mediator before the proceedings go any further.[39] Attendance at a mediation assessment meeting can be ordered as a contact activity under sections 11A and 11C of the Children Act 1989.[40]

There are exceptions. Attendance at a meeting is not required where the mediator considers the case unsuitable because the other party refuses to attend a meeting and consider mediation; where the mediator decides the case is not suitable for a meeting; or a mediator has decided, within the previous four months that it is not suitable for a meeting or for mediation.[41] Also excluded are cases where the applicant does not know the whereabouts of the other party[42] or where the application is made without notice.[43] A meeting is not required where social services are involved because of child protection concerns in respect of a child who would be the subject of the application.[44] There are also exemptions that are designed to afford some protection to applicants from having to mediate in cases of domestic violence or imminent harm. An applicant is exempt from attending where there has been an allegation of domestic violence which has resulted in a police investigation or civil proceedings for protection within the previous 12 months.[45] There is also an exemption where the prospective application is urgent.[46] This is defined as where:

---

[33] The *Family Justice Review* recommends compulsory assessment by a mediator for party attendance at a PIP or other dispute resolution with cost penalties for those who behave 'unreasonably' by not attending (Norgrove 2011a: paras 5.125–5.126).

[34] Practice Direction 3A—Pre-application Protocol for Mediation Information and Assessment (2011).

[35] 'Introduction', para 2(1)(c).

[36] Ibid, para 4.1.

[37] Protocol, para 6.

[38] Ibid, para 8.

[39] 'Introduction', para 4.1.

[40] Independent Mediation: Information for Judges, Magistrates and Legal Advisor (2011) *Fam Law* 301.

[41] Practice Direction 3A—Pre-application Protocol for Mediation Information and Assessment (2011) Annex C, paras 1–3. On contact activity conditions and directions, see Chapter 10 above.

[42] Annex C, para 7.

[43] Ibid, para 9.

[44] Ibid, para 11.

[45] Ibid, para 4.

[46] Ibid, para 10.

(a) there is a risk to the life, liberty or physical safety of the applicant or his or her family or his or her home; or

(b) any delay caused by attending a Mediation Information and Assessment Meeting would cause a risk of significant harm to a child, a significant risk of a miscarriage of justice, unreasonable hardship to the applicant or irretrievable problems in dealing with the dispute (such as an irretrievable loss of significant evidence).

The House of Commons Justice Committee noted research by Hunt and Macleod (2005):

94. ... In a 2005 study, 53% of women reported physical or emotional abuse as a cause of the separation, with actual or fear of violence continuing post-separation for 40% of women. Actual violence or fear of violence prior to the application was reported by 24% of women who had not reported violence during the relationship. The study noted that despite the high levels of domestic violence only about 15% of cases had an injunction or protective order. ...

97. We received evidence that a large number of private law cases that currently reach court involve families with multiple problems. A high percentage of cases involve domestic violence or other child protection concerns. Care must be taken that any measures to divert cases from court only seek to do so where that is in the best interests of the child. This will be more complex than simply screening for domestic violence.

(House of Commons Justice Committee 2011)

> **[Q]** Consider the Protocol as well as the conditions upon which the availability of public funding for legal services depends. Do you think their effect is simply that of encouraging mediation or do you think they could have the effect of putting pressure on the parties to mediate? Consider the limitation in the Protocol to cases of domestic violence that have led to police involvement or civil protection proceedings. Do you think this is adequate to protect an applicant from the disadvantages outlined below of mediation in cases of domestic violence?

Research conducted in the late 1990s, when equivalent rules to the current rules on legal funding existed,[47] showed that, while there was an increase in these intake assessments, the significant number of cases deemed unsuitable meant that the number of mediations proper did not grow noticeably (Davis et al 2000c).[48] Also revealing are the findings of the researchers whose evaluation of the impact of information meetings held under the Family Law Act 1996 contributed to the abandonment of the provisions dealing with divorce and mediation.[49] Walker and her team found that information 'may' have encouraged some people to attempt mediation or counselling (Walker et al 2004: 123). However most recipients of information about mediation still consulted a solicitor and 85% engaged one (ibid). The Family Law Act 1996 was intended to make mediation an 'integrated part of the divorce process' (LCD 1995a: 42) and one of the factors that led the Lord Chancellor to announce he would ask for the repeal of Part II was the fact that greater numbers of people were not encouraged to attend mediation as a result of the information meetings (ibid: 131). What is more, to his disappointment, the research studies indicated that 39%

---

[47] Requiring attendance at a meeting to consider mediation.

[48] See also Davis et al (2000d: 33).

[49] The legislation required a party embarking on the divorce process to attend an information meeting at least three months before making a statement of marital breakdown. The other party, if applying to court regarding a child, property or finance, or if contesting an application, was also supposed to attend a meeting. One of the purposes of this meeting was to inform the parties about mediation.

of people were more likely to consult a solicitor after attending an information meeting (Diduck 2003: 111).

Walker et al suggest that recommendations by solicitors are more effective in getting people to attend mediation than the provision of information about it (Walker et al 2004: 132). In any event, they remark, 'most people will choose not to use mediation' (ibid: 131). Only 10% of those responding to the survey carried out by Walker and her co-researchers had attended mediation and a further 2% had gone to a preliminary meeting with a mediator but did not engage in the mediation process (ibid). Walker et al speculate that 'there is little prospect of increasing the use of mediation so long as attendance remains voluntary' (ibid: 134). And they do not think the solution lies in compulsion; mediation has little prospect of success in cases where parties with little faith in the process are forced to participate.[50]

It might be thought surprising, in the light of this research, that a requirement to attend a Mediation Information and Assessment Meeting has now been introduced for all prospective litigants. Dingwall (2010), reviewing the available research, concludes that a requirement that a potential applicant meet initially with a mediator is unlikely to lead to increased mediation. Parkinson (2011a) disputes this. She maintains that the new process is not likely to be as unsuccessful as the old information meetings and, in any event, low conversion figures from initial meetings to actual mediation should not be viewed negatively. First, she argues that information meetings were not successful because they were not individualised, because people confused mediation with counselling and because in many cases disputes had not yet arisen. The Mediation Information and Assessment Meetings take place when there is already a dispute in existence. Secondly, while she acknowledges that after legal funding restrictions were introduced, referrals to mediation increased but the number of mediated cases did not (Parkinson 2011b: 196),[51] she says this does not denote failure. She suggests that some parties do not go on to mediation because they have reached an agreement or are getting along more amicably. And even where this is not the case, the initial meeting will not have been a waste of time because people appreciate being listened to (Parkinson 2011a: 90).

More fundamentally, Dingwall also challenges the assumption underlying the new procedure—that mediation is effective. He argues that the change ignores the lack of evidence of effectiveness and also the move away from compulsion to mediate in other jurisdictions. It is to the claims in favour of mediation that Dingwall says are unconvincing that we now turn.

Why Mediation?

A number of diverse needs and pressures led to the development of mediation as a 'better' way of dealing with the consequences of family breakdown.

The notion of family privacy was significant in explaining early support for mediation. According to Parkinson (1985: 245), for example, mediation reinforced the private family against threatened intrusion by the 'powerful system of state control'. Party control was

---

[50] See Walker et al (2004: 140).
[51] See also Walker et al (2007: 11).

seen as central, with disputants being able to shape their own outcomes.[52] And Mnookin saw liberal philosophy as fundamental to support for private ordering:

> Let me begin with the arguments supporting the presumption in favour of private ordering. The core reason is rooted in notions of human liberty. Private ordering is supported by the liberal idea that individuals have rights, and should largely be left free to make of their lives what they wish. (Mnookin 1984: 366)

However, there were also a number of other pressures at work. One factor,[53] particularly prominent in the debates leading up to the enactment of the Family Law Act 1996,[54] was financial. The soaring legal aid bill for divorce provided the impetus to look for cheaper alternatives to lawyers and courts (Davis and Roberts 1988: 10; Piper 1996a: 64).[55] In addition, courts were struggling under the burden of the growing number of cases. It was thought that court time could be saved if there were a higher number of settlements (Davis and Roberts 1988: 10). In fact, research conducted by Bevan et al calls both these supposed advantages into question. They found that mediation had almost no effect on the likelihood of a full legal aid certificate being awarded (Bevan et al 2001: 187) and there was almost no effect on legal costs (ibid: 188).[56]

There were other arguments in favour of mediation, however. The adversarial system has been said to inflame conflict.[57] In addition, the effectiveness of court intervention was thought to be limited. Pressure of time meant that courts were unable to enquire into arrangements for children. More significantly, there were doubts whether it was appropriate for courts even to attempt to make such enquiries; parents were more likely to know what was best for their children.[58] In any event, court-ordered arrangements were frequently found to break down (Gingerbread and Families Need Fathers 1982: 19–21) and it was thought that agreements voluntarily reached by the parties themselves would be more likely to endure than arrangements foisted on them from an external source.[59] Mediation therefore came to be regarded not only as the solution to political, financial and administrative problems, but also as better for the parties and their children.

Q Can the preference for mediation be reconciled with the welfare principle?

As Piper (1996a: 65) notes, proponents of mediation have tended to rely chiefly on arguments focusing on the welfare of children. Children are seen as the victims of divorce and the divorce system, with its adversarial, conflictual character, is thought to exacerbate the damage caused to them.[60] In contrast, mediation is thought to encourage parents to put the needs of their children first. Davis and Roberts explain:

---

[52] See CPU (1989: 276).

[53] Another factor, which will not be dealt with here, was pressure coming from various professional groupings such as probation officers. For details see Piper (1996a: 66); Davis and Roberts (1988: 11).

[54] But see also the Report of the Interdepartmental Committee on Conciliation (1983); Newcastle Conciliation Project Unit Report (1989).

[55] See LCD (1995a: para 5.20).

[56] But see Fisher and Hodson (2001).

[57] See Norgrove (2011a: paras 5.30–5.32).

[58] See Piper (1993: 12); Piper (1996a: 65–66).

[59] See Parkinson (1983: 23). See also Piper (1993: 12).

[60] See, eg, LCD (1995a: para 5.2). There is evidence that conflict does harm children (Hunt and Trinder 2011, cited in Norgrove 2011a: para 5.28).

[C]onciliation[61] has been identified with a greater concentration on the needs of children, bringing home to parents the hurt and perhaps even the long-term damage that may result from their continuing quarrelling, or the abandonment of all links between the children and the non-custodial parent. ... Many mediators are motivated, at least in part, by a perception that conflict between separated parents is bad for children; indeed, this is a quite explicit part of the case advanced on behalf of conciliation services. (Davis and Roberts 1988: 10–11)

This focus on reducing conflict[62] is given expression in the Code of Practice of the College of Mediators (2008), which states:

2.2 Mediation also aims to assist participants to communicate with one another now and in the future and to reduce the scope or intensity of dispute and conflict.

2.3 Mediators should have regard to the ethics of mediation in that it should be carried out in a way that:

• minimises distress to the participants and any others involved;
• promotes as good a relationship between the participants and any others involved as possible;
• removes or diminishes any risk of abuse to any of the participants or others involved, and
• avoids unnecessary cost to the participants.

This case for mediation has proved very persuasive. The White Paper that preceded the Family Law Act 1996 stated:[63]

Conflict is harmful to children and the Government is of the view that the reduction of conflict should be high on the list of objectives for a good divorce process. ...

It is also important that, where there are children, parents learn early to communicate during the process of making arrangements for a life apart. ... Research shows that the children who do best are those whose parents are able to talk together. ...

Research has established that communication between a couple is improved by their being able to say things face to face in mediation. (LCD 1995a: paras 5.16–5.18)

Mediation, then, is regarded as a 'civilising'[64] process, reducing conflict, facilitating communication, promoting agreement and safeguarding the best interests of children. However, the talk about mediation, according to Davis et al, conflates two different kinds of activity. The first is that of 'mediation as an aid to private communication' (Davis et al 2001a: 265). The outcomes are meant to be 'better understanding, agreement on a variety of specific issues, and improved capacity to negotiate in future, and less conflict' (ibid). The second 'involves the attempted settlement of contested legal proceedings'. This latter activity, the authors suggest, is best regarded as part of the court procedure, intended, to 'divert cases from trial' (Davis et al 2000e: 136), and, like most procedural devices, to minimise legal costs and 'advance the settlement process' (Davis et al 2001a: 265).

Not all the professed aims and outcomes rank equally in importance. Mediation appears nowadays to be focusing less on the relationships between the parties or empowerment of clients and more on the aims of settlement and diversion from court. 'Client empower-

---

[61] They are referring to what is now called mediation.
[62] Mediation and other forms of ADR are perceived as means of managing conflict (see, eg, Smart and May 2004b: 358–59). References to party control and autonomy are now rare.
[63] See also LCD (1993: para 4.5); Home Office (1998: para 4.41).
[64] See Walker et al (1994: 9); CPU (1989: 276).

ment' say Dingwall and Greatbach, has given way to 'managed settlement seeking' (Dingwall and Greatbach 2001: 379).

So, on the one hand commentators have observed of mediation that the autonomy it purports to confer on the parties is illusory; the assumptions underlying mediation, its focus on settlement and the norms espoused by mediators permeate the mediation process and influence its outcome. On the other hand, fears have been expressed that, in the absence of partisan representation by lawyers and of formal legal safeguards, imbalances of power between the parties remain unchecked because of mediator non-intervention and the welfare of children is jeopardised.

Autonomy and Control

The potential for mediator influence in the process and outcome of mediation was high-lighted some years ago by Simon Roberts.[65] He suggested that the mere presence of the mediator must have an impact on negotiations and that this impact is likely to be ampli-fied by the activities of the mediator; minimal intervention by mediators is rare:

> Once the mediator goes on to provide a normative framework for discussion, however sparse, the universe within which bilateral negotiation would have taken place is profoundly changed. This transformation is taken further if he helps to clarify issues … . Many mediators will see it as necessary to a settlement that the disputants' view of their predicament be transformed; and so deliberately set out to do this, offering evaluations of past conduct or future options, and identifying what they consider to be the appropriate outcome.
>
> In so far as the mediator succeeds in transforming the disputants' view of the quarrel, he comes to share with them control over the outcome. (Roberts 1983: 549)

The College of Mediators Code of Practice states that mediators should be neutral as to the outcome of mediation (2008: para 4.2). Yet research suggests that neutrality may be difficult to achieve. Certainly, Piper's empirical study of child-focused mediation revealed considerable mediator control:

> What became apparent was that the 'facts' supplied by parents were used by mediators with prior beliefs, stemming from a normative framework, about the problem and its solution. Full parental responsibility for the process and outcome could then be possible only in the hypo-thetical case where what was supplied by parents was acceptable to mediators. (Piper 1993: 190)

And Marian Roberts has warned mediators against adopting a directive role:

> Mediators are not neutral. … They have their own values and attitudes. Influenced by prevailing research findings, they are likely to adopt a strong pro-contact stance in the belief that it is better, on the whole, for children to have a continuing relationship with both parents after separation and divorce. In most cases, these values are shared by parents themselves. However, mediators should not brow-beat parents with research evidence or with warnings of emotional damage or of the harmful effects of litigation. The exertion of overt influence is incompatible with the facilitating role of the mediator. (Roberts 1997: 124)[66]

---

[65] See also Grillo (1991).
[66] See also Roberts (1997: 84); Dingwall and Greatbach (2000).

Dingwall and Greatbach (2001: 380) report that the mediation clients in their sample considered mediators impartial.[67] But what they go on to say bears out the view that mediators are not neutral as to outcome:

> Mediators, however, clearly had views about outcomes. We have called these 'the parameters of the permissible'. Within these, clients were left to work out their own deals, but the client who stepped outside could face heavy mediator pressure. For example, mediators may not be greatly concerned whether a contact agreement specifies one weekend in three or one weekend in four. A residential parent who refuses any contact, however, has breached the parameters and will be pressed to return to them. The parameters seemed to be broader for financial issues, probably because houses and cash are more easily divisible than children. (ibid)[68]

Neale and Smart too point out that:

> Mediation is not value-free. It operates (at present) only marginally in the shadow of the law but centrally in the shadow of social welfare ideology. Indeed it may operate as 'a cover for value laden tampering with family life', with mediators exerting subtle pressure on clients to conform to current welfare notions. (Neale and Smart 1997: 383, footnote omitted)

Walker et al found that even in relation to money matters, mediators deployed various strategies to get parties to rethink arrangements of which they disapproved (Walker et al 1994: 106). It appears that the process the researchers refer to as 'coming round' (ibid: 97) involved, at least to some extent, a transformation in the perceptions of the parties to accommodate ideas more acceptable to mediators (Piper 1996a: 77).

Clearly, then, research suggests that the parties are not necessarily empowered by mediation and that the norms of the mediators tend to shape the agreement forged between the parties. Some commentators who have observed the process have also identified an element of control.[69] Bottomley, for instance, contended that the privatisation of family disputes masks continuing supervision of families which is rendered benevolent by notions of welfare (Bottomley 1985: 163): '[T]he process of de-legalization is not one of de-regularization but is a shift from one form of social discipline to another' (Bottomley 1984: 300). Her critique points to the potency of mediation in purveying particular norms and underwriting particular images of the family.

Dominant Norms

Because mediation can be used to promote particular ideologies of the family, it can be viewed as a means of social control. Moreover, the ideology that has been observed to be dominant in mediation has, it is argued, potentially damaging implications for women. The focus on children is seen as a denial of women's identities distinct from motherhood. It also leads to a preference for a particular model of joint parenting and a presumption in favour of contact, an approach that helps to perpetuate the power of fathers.[70] Several women told Walker and her colleagues, for example, that they felt pressured to come to

---

[67] This means that they did not favour one party over the other.
[68] See further, Dingwall and Greatbach (2000: 242–45).
[69] See Sanders (1997: 8).
[70] See Roberts (1996). See also Pickett (1991: 29–33). Davis et al (2000e: 100) speculate that that the slight preference for mediation over solicitor negotiation by the men in their research sample might suggest that

an agreement (Walker et al 2004: 138) and, we can surmise, although the researchers do not tell us so, that these women agreed to contact; usually, mothers are expected by professionals, including mediators, to agree to contact.[71] The emphasis on jointness ignores the unequal contributions of fathers and mothers to parenting prior to separation. It also places the burden of absorbing any strain and inconvenience caused by contact on mothers (Piper 1988: 491–92). For, although Smart (1999) in her study found that some fathers became more involved in childcare after divorce, the reconstruction of the family in the mould of the 'continuing-but-separated' family leaves intact in many cases the traditional divisions of labour, enabling fathers to continue as decision-makers while leaving mothers as primary caretakers.[72]

Q Read Chapter 10 above on residence and contact. Do you think that courts might be said to espouse the same familial ideology as mediators?

Power and Mediation

While interventionism by mediators is seen by some as opening the way to social control and as disempowering the parties, particularly mothers, non-interventionism can present dangers for the weaker party: 'The stronger party may be enabled to force a coercive settlement on the weaker' (Roberts 1983: 557). Trinder et al (2006) report that in their study of in-court conciliation:

> Resident parents[73] reported less choice about entering the process, more anxiety beforehand, more tension in the meeting, less able to say all they wanted to and more likely to report being pressured into an agreement by their ex-partner. (Trinder et al 2006: Executive Summary, iii)

This is a problem that has frequently been adverted to in the context of mediation by feminist writers warning that women are often in the weaker bargaining position and that to ignore this perpetuates inequalities in power.[74]

Bryan (1992), writing in the United States, has asserted that women are disadvantaged in numerous ways. They tend to earn less than men; they are less likely to be employed in jobs that develop negotiating skills; they have lower self-esteem; and they are more care oriented, focusing on relationships and sacrificing other goals in order to keep the peace. Men's greater status promotes dominant behaviour and their experience in the public sphere enhances their authority and their ability to negotiate. These disadvantages are compounded by the familial ideology informing mediation:

> Mediation proponents seductively appeal to women's socialized values by speaking softly of relatedness. Yet mediation exploits wives by denigrating their legal entitlements, stripping them of authority, encouraging unwarranted compromise, isolating them from needed support, and

mediators might be more supportive of the arguments advanced by non-resident parents, who are usually fathers.

[71] See, eg, Dingwall and Greatbach (2001: 380), quoted above.

[72] See Pickett (1991: 32).

[73] Who are usually mothers.

[74] See Bottomley (1985: 179); Hilton (1991: 29). Davis et al (2000e: 85) report that a higher proportion of women found mediation about children matters upsetting than found solicitor negotiations upsetting. However, a significant proportion of women found mediation satisfactory overall. See below.

placing them across the table from their more powerful husbands and demanding that they fend for themselves. The process thus perpetuates patriarchy by freeing men to use their power to gain greater control over children, to implant more awareness of male dominance into women's consciousness, and to retain more of the marital financial assets than men would obtain if lawyers negotiated divorce settlements. (Bryan 1992: 523)

Although concerns about adequate representation arise also in the legal arena,[75] the problems are more acute in mediation because the process occurs in private, without the presence of partisan lawyers and without access to appeal (Bruch 1988: 120).

The lawyers interviewed by Walker et al (2007) expressed concern about the position of the weaker party in mediation:

[S]olicitors ... noted that the mediators' lack of legal knowledge, especially when one party took the lead in mediation, sometimes produces an agreement which is unfair to the weaker party and leaves that person feeling unable to backtrack. There is a general sense that the quality of mediators varies to the extent that some of the less competent can end up producing damaging outcomes for clients:

> Clients complain about the quality of the CAFCASS [mediation] service, being bullied, forced into meeting abusers and a lack of understanding of the relevant history. (FAInS practitioner)

When solicitors noted other disadvantages to mediation, the word 'intimidation' cropped up frequently. This was especially so in the context of potential power struggles at mediation and initial imbalances of power. Solicitors are of the view that a power imbalance can result in an unfair settlement and can be destructive of relationships when one party ends up agreeing to a settlement in order to reach a compromise and please the mediator—to 'do the right thing'.

(Walker et al 2007: 111)

Disadvantages cited also included the pressure to reach agreement. Solicitors are concerned that this is particularly so for the vulnerable client, who may feel forced or pressured into agreeing to a detrimental or unfair settlement. ...

Delay was also perceived to be a problem with mediation. One solicitor in the second survey noted that 'time could be lost through mediation in an unsuitable case, assets thus dissipated and a status quo develop[ed] with respect to the children'. Solicitors noted that mediation often prolongs matters where it is already obvious that things are not going to be resolved. When delay is caused by mediation it then has the knock-on effect of delaying negotiations between solicitors and so wastes even more time. Waiting for an appointment for mediation after referral creates a further delay so far as some solicitors are concerned.

Solicitors also noted that a mediated agreement is not always comprehensive. This may be due in part to the inability of a client to negotiate finances, particularly given that mediation provides no compulsion to make full and frank disclosure. Agreements are often reached at mediation without proper disclosure. (ibid: 112)

Q Do you think these findings cast doubt of the cost benefits claimed for mediation, at least for those not reliant on legal aid. Those who are may not have access to court.[76]

---

[75] Indeed, Roberts (1997: 158) has pointed out that different inequalities may be created. The parties' resources might be unequal as might be the skill of their lawyers.

[76] See n 6 and p 715 above.

Q Do you agree that women are more likely to be in a weaker bargaining position than men?

Roberts does not recommend mediation in cases where there is a serious imbalance in bargaining power such as those involving domestic violence, those where a sense of guilt makes a party liable to agree to prejudicial arrangements and those where cultural norms deny women decision-making authority (Roberts 1997: 129). However, Davis and Roberts had previously found the feminist critique relating to power to be largely unsubstantiated. The mediators they observed 'controlled the ebb and flow of negotiation' and 'in some cases, the "weaker" party did, indeed, feel empowered' (Davis and Roberts 1989: 306).[77] Moreover, Marian Roberts has argued that bargaining power involves a complex interplay of forces and is constantly shifting. 'Rarely are the disadvantages or advantages stacked all one way, nor should it be assumed, either, that where one party has superior "endowments" of one sort or another that power will necessarily be used, let alone exploited' (Roberts 1996: 239).

The power of mediators to control the process of mediation is not perceived as a source of reassurance by some critics. Grillo (1991: 1592), for example, has suggested that the mediator may not have sufficient understanding of the power dynamic in the relationship to know whether or how to intervene. Davis et al (2000f: 217) have suggested that oppression or undue pressure could be problems and remarked that some mediators in their study found this difficult to handle. Some of the women clients questioned indicated that they felt intimidated irrespective of the strategy they used to resolve the outstanding issues; whatever they did could lead to punitive consequences (ibid). This finding, along with Walker et al's research (above), brings into question claims that mediators can and do redress serious imbalances of power.

The issue is particularly troubling in cases where there has been a history of domestic violence. Such instances present the starkest examples of inequality of bargaining power and the greatest likelihood that power will be exploited.

Domestic Violence and Mediation

1. Outlining the Problems

The prevalence of domestic violence should not be underestimated.[78] Davis et al state that in their sample mediation suppliers reported being aware of allegations of domestic violence in 31% of cases (Davis et al 2000c: 28). There were also reports of fear of violence in 19% of cases (ibid: 29). These percentages are slightly higher, perhaps because screening is better, than the 23% noted by Walker et al some years earlier (Walker et al 1994: 62). That such cases can be dealt with easily is belied by the evidence of at least one of their interviewees, who said:

> Signals were being given to [the mediator] which he didn't take up. I was too afraid of my husband to state the nature of my anxieties—mentioning it would have prompted more. [The mediator] was asking us to go away and discuss the very things which provoked him to

---

[77] See further Roberts (1997: 120–21, 160–62).
[78] See Chapters 10 and 12 above. See Kaganas and Piper (1994: 268).

violence—the children and the house ... on our own when in fact that's what we'd gone there for. (ibid)

Q Do you think the problem in this case was that the mediator apparently was not aware of the history of violence? Do you think mediation could have been made fair and safe for the wife if he had been aware?

There are strong arguments for saying that mediation is not appropriate where relationships have been characterised by sustained violence. These were summarised by Kaganas and Piper:

> The basic elements of mediation have been described as voluntary participation, equality or rough parity of bargaining power, neutrality on the part of the mediator, and confidentiality. ... It has been pointed out that these fundamental principles are in the main incompatible with protecting the interests of victims of abuse. ...
>
> First, it is argued that the existence of a violent relationship undermines the voluntary nature of mediation. Victims have no real choice. They are not free to act contrary to their partner's wishes in either electing or rejecting mediation. Nor are they really free to terminate it once it has commenced ... . Secondly, it is said that, in the context of abuse, mediation cannot achieve its principal aim: co-operation for mutual benefit. Because an abuser devalues his victim ... he is able to dismiss her point of view ... . Thirdly, it is feared that in place of co-operation, mediation might lead to capitulation by the weaker party. Disputes over matters such as child [residence or contact] can form part of an ongoing effort to assert control and exact concessions from the other party.... Victims may be unable even to articulate their wishes and needs and may, through fear or to avoid conflict, yield to their husbands' demands. Seen in this light, it becomes clear that 'mediation empowers only the already more powerful husband' ... and is detrimental to the interests of abused women ... .
>
> The ability of mediators to redress the balance is doubtful. In the first place the mediator may not even be aware of the dynamics of the parties' relationship: 'Even the most sensitised mediator cannot be expected to identify and interpret the ... innuendo of threat or coercion' which might be present in a look or gesture ... . Where mediators do intervene, their efforts are generally confined to promoting procedural equality and this does not redress the power imbalance ... . The substantive inequality remains and, in circumstances of this kind, mediation does not result in genuine agreement.
>
> The concerns of mediators to remain neutral and to avoid allocating blame not only leads to a failure to confront problems of power and domination, it can have the effect of exacerbating them. The absence of any challenge to the abuser's conduct can be interpreted as condoning it. ...
>
> That this might have the effect of compounding the danger to the victim becomes evident when it is remembered that violence often escalates during and after separation.
>
> (Kaganas and Piper 1994: 266–67, references omitted)

The authors concluded that, while those victims of violence who feel sufficiently confident to participate in mediation should be given the opportunity to do so, mediation should not be extended to cases in which the impact of violence on the victim negates any benefits of the process. It is crucial, they said, that services devise methods to determine not only whether abuse has occurred but also the levels of fear experienced by the victim and whether that fear leads her to modify her behaviour to placate the abuser (ibid: 272–73). In order to determine whether the effect of violence is such that the victim is rendered unable to assert herself and to negotiate effectively, the authors adopted the concept of a culture of battering developed by Fischer et al (1993). Three elements need to be present for a culture of battering to be established: actual abuse of whatever type; a systematic pattern of domination; and the victim's denial and minimisation of abuse:

[W]here a relationship is characterised by these features, mediation holds no promise of a satisfactory outcome for the victim. Mediators cannot compensate, however well trained and aware, for the damage done to anyone who has not only suffered the direct effects of abuse but who has also been systematically controlled over time and who has not been able to acknowledge the abuse. (Kaganas and Piper 1994: 271)

Screening for violence is important as information about a background of violence may not emerge in other ways. Victims of domestic violence are often reluctant to seek court orders or even to reveal their plight.[79]

As Kaganas and Piper point out:

Victims as well as abusers tend to minimise or deny violence: voluntary disclosure is relatively unusual. Researchers have advanced a number of possible explanations for this. First, to acknowledge violence by disclosing it, is to acknowledge that the relationship in which so much has been invested cannot continue. Disclosure may therefore signify too much personal loss for it to be psychologically possible. Moreover, while some victims may refrain from seeking help for fear of retaliation, others may still be emotionally bound to their partners; Ellis and DeKeseredy refer to the loyalty/love that victims often feel. The possibility that victims do not disclose during the course of their relationships is significant on divorce: it means that there is no 'official' evidence in the form of court orders or criminal proceedings that abuse occurred. This, in turn, makes it less likely that the abuse will be discovered on divorce.

Secondly, even on divorce the victim/survivor may not expect to be believed or taken seriously. Thirdly, she may fear being labelled a failure—a misplaced sense of shame therefore inhibits disclosure. Fourthly, she may have fears that she will lose her children. Fifthly, it may be difficult for her to redefine an intimate partner as an abuser, particularly if he is the father of her children. Finally, she may not disclose because she does not conform to her own stereotypes of battered women. (Kaganas and Piper 1999: 188, references omitted)

Ellis and Stuckless (1996: 77–80) have suggested that mediation services that employ screening, coupled with, in the cases they do take on, support for the party with weaker bargaining power and monitoring for abusive behaviour, may mitigate the effects of power imbalances. They also have said that voluntary mediation can play a part in reducing 'postprocessing abuse' (ibid: 58). However, mediation can be inappropriate and even dangerous in cases where mediators do not ask about violence, do not understand its impact and do not have the skill to deal with the issues (Young 1996, cited in Hester et al 1997: 59–60).

2. Professional Practice

Screening policies are now in place: mediators are expected to 'assess whether there are risks of domestic violence, imbalance between the parties or child protection issues that require immediate diversion to the court process' (Norgrove 2011a: para 5.127).

The screening policy document issued by the College of Mediators states that there must be screening both before and during mediation (College of Mediators 1999: A3, B3).

[79] See further Women's Project (1998: 9–12).

Mediators are not only required to screen for violence but also to counter its effects in mediation. The College of Mediators Code of Practice (2008), for example, states:

> 4.8.1 In all cases, mediators must seek to discover through a screening procedure whether or not there is fear of abuse or any other harm and whether or not it is alleged that any participant has been or is likely to be abusive towards another. Where abuse is alleged or suspected mediators must discuss whether any participant wishes to take part in mediation and information about available support services should be provided.

> 4.8.2 Where mediation does take place, mediators must uphold throughout the principles of voluntariness of participation, fairness and safety and must conduct the process in accordance with this section. In addition, steps must be taken to ensure the safety of all participants on arrival and departure.

The screening document defines abuse widely and focuses on the perspective of the victim:

> [B]ehaviour that seeks to secure power and control for the abuser and the impact of which is to undermine the safety, security, self esteem and autonomy of the abused person. Domestic violence contains elements of the use of any or all of physical, sexual, psychological, emotional, verbal or economic intimidation, oppression or coercion. (College of Mediators 1999: C)

> D Principles of Screening for Domestic Abuse

> 1.1 Mediators must routinely screen for abuse before a decision is taken to proceed with mediation.

> 1.2 Screening must take place separately with each participant.

> 1.3 In reaching a decision about whether to proceed, priority should be given to the individual's perception of abuse over any judgement about levels of severity or types of abuse.

> 1.4 If in any doubt about the appropriateness of mediation the mediator could consult with his/her supervisor and if doubt still remains, must not proceed … . (College of Mediators 1999)

Early research after the introduction of screening policies showed that these had limited impact on the attitudes and practices of a large proportion of mediators (Hester et al 1997). Dingwall and Greatbach (2000, 2001) found that violence was not treated as being of much significance when the issue was raised in mediation sessions:

> [F]ew mediators routinely asked whether violence was an issue. When the issue arose it tended to be marginalised, as found in previous research. No case was terminated on this ground. Mediators clearly had some difficulty in knowing where to draw a line between 'acceptable' and 'unacceptable' levels of conflict in the relationship. (Dingwall and Greatbach 2001: 381)[80]

Davis et al (2000f: 216) report that if violence was revealed, mediators still encouraged people to consider mediation, although they did suggest some safety measures. However '[i]n order for mediation to be ruled out on the grounds of past violence, clients had to make quite strong claims that they were in fear of the other party' (ibid: 217).

If Parkinson is correct, things have changed within mediation:

---

[80] See further, Dingwall and Greatbach (2000: 245–48).

All recognised mediators who are members of Approved Bodies should by now have had training. Specialist training equips mediators to recognise different forms of domestic violence, including psychological and emotional abuse, and to identify risks for an adult and/or child requiring immediate referral to other services and agencies. Screening for domestic violence and child protection issues needs awareness of different forms of abuse and carefully graduated questions to enable concerns to surface. Individuals may fear disclosing domestic violence and might face reprisals if confidentiality is not handled extremely carefully. The mediator's use of language is particularly important. The word 'violent' should be avoided unless the client uses it, because behaviour seen by some as violent may be seen by others as normal. For some people, violence means physical violence, whereas some abused women have said they found unremitting verbal and psychological abuse even more harmful. There are at least five different categories of domestic abuse. Mediation may be suitable in some situations with appropriate conditions and safeguards, but strongly contra-indicated in other categories.

(Parkinson 2011a: 90)

And while it is possible that things may have changed more recently in the practices of Cafcass officers, a report published in 2005 found these to be deficient. An inspection into the services provided by Cafcass found that there was no systematic risk assessment process and that the focus on agreement-seeking meant that, according to the women in the study, insufficient attention was paid to safety. The inspectors found, from their observations, that there was insufficient understanding of the nature of domestic violence and lack of attention to safety planning. The report concluded that:

This report finds an inherent danger arising from the current policy emphasis on seeking mediated agreements between parents in ever larger numbers of disputed family proceedings. We conclude that ensuring the safety of both children and adults receives insufficient consideration—this was a strong and consistent message from the women survivors of domestic violence who we consulted. We consider that arrangements for assessing the risks associated with allegations of domestic violence need markedly strengthening ... .

As this inspection shows, there is a risk that individuals within agencies sometimes find it easier to down-play or even ignore the presenting signs of domestic violence.

(HMICA 2005: Chief Inspector's Foreword)

Solicitors appear to have been be no more adept at identifying cases involving violence.[81] Davis et al (2000f: 217) observed that solicitor mediators barely touched on the question of violence.

In spite of their criticisms of the professionals, Davis et al (2000e: 58) were not entirely convinced of the dangers posed by domestic violence in the context of mediation. They found that, in their study, 71% of clients who said they feared violence reported that they had felt able to say what they wanted to say in mediation: 'Reported fear of violence was not on this evidence associated with reduced ability to communicate freely' (ibid: 70). They also observed that although fear of violence featured in a great many of the cases they surveyed, it appeared, 'for the most part to be overcome in mediation' (ibid: 137). Women's responses to mediation were, 'on the whole', slightly more positive than those of men (ibid).

Nonetheless, even Davis et al found that those clients who feared violence were about twice as likely to find mediation upsetting than those who did not (ibid: 75). And Walker et al's informants provided even less reassuring information. They did not necessarily find

---

[81] See Kaganas and Piper (1999). But see Walker et al (2007).

that fear of violence was overcome and some reported feeling intimidated (Walker et al 2004: 138)[82].

> **Q** The Legal Aid, Sentencing and Punishment of Offenders Bill 2010–11, if enacted, will remove legal aid for cases involving disputes about finance and children. There are exemptions, among others, for cases where one party has been abused by the other or is at risk of being so abused.[83] How do you think victims will be able to show they fall within this category? Do you think many victims will fail to disclose altogether?

Mediation and Children's Welfare

Trinder et al (2006), in their study of in-court conciliation, found that, while the overall agreement rate was high and while only a fifth of these agreements had not worked at all six months later, parental satisfaction rates were not high and that this was relevant to children's welfare; simply having contact was not predictive of child well-being They commented:

> [T]he conciliation session and the adoption of new contact arrangements had little impact on parental relationship quality, shared decision making and contact problems. It is these issues, rather than the mere quantity of contact, that are most likely to impact on children's adjustment. The quantity of contact alone was not related to child wellbeing in this study ... .
>
> In-court conciliation is effective in reaching agreement and ensuring contact but, *regardless of model*, has limited impact on the key co-parenting factors that will make contact work for children. This in itself should not come as a surprise. The service that parents receive is very brief and is not designed to address relationship issues.
>
> (Trinder et al 2006: Executive Summary, 4, emphasis in original)

In a follow-up study, two years after those in the study attended in-court conciliation, Trinder and Kellett (2007) found that contact was taking place in the majority of cases. However, in about 10% of cases it had not been possible to establish contact. Contact was more likely to be taking place in what had been the easier cases to start with. Even in cases where there was contact, the majority of cases had required further intervention and, in 40% of them, there had been further litigation. About 60% of agreements had been dropped or had broken down, mostly because either one or more parents or children had not supported it. The majority of parents reported poor relationships, lack of confidence in the other's parenting and little shared decision-making. Many parents remained in conflict even if they did not relitigate.

They conclude:

> In short, conciliation is an effective way of reaching agreements and restoring contact over the short-term but is often followed by further litigation and has very limited impact on making contact actually work well for children. (Trinder and Kellett 2007: Executive Summary, iv)

When it comes to mediation, similar problems are likely to exist. In addition, the agreed

---

[82] See also Walker et al (2007).
[83] Sched 1 Part 1, para 10(1).

arrangements may not be in children's best interests. And because mediation is private, there is the potential effect of removing from public scrutiny the issue of the best interests of the children concerned.

Mediation, like other forms of private ordering, is premised on the assumption that parents know what is best for their children and fails to acknowledge that the needs of parents and children are not always synonymous.[84] And the agreement, although not binding unless it is formalised or brought before the court, may not necessarily come before a judge.

Harold and Murch (2005: 199) have expressed concern that the increased emphasis on mediation and ADR may marginalise the child. The child's views and wishes are usually not canvassed. Unless mediators and in-court conciliators involve children directly, they will often have to rely on parents' perceptions of their children and these perceptions may not be reliable.

Article 12 of the UN Convention on the Rights of the Child gives the child a right to express an opinion and have it taken into account. In relation to the FHDRA, the judge is obliged to consider ways to involve the child[85] but we do not know how this requirement works in practice. In relation to mediation, some mediators do consider direct participation by children but most tend to rely on the adults concerned to relay children's views.[86] The College of Mediators Code of Practice (2008) stipulates:

4.7.4 Mediators must encourage the participants to consider children's own wishes and feelings. Where appropriate, they may discuss with the participants whether and to what extent it is proper to involve the children themselves in the mediation process in order to consult them about their wishes and feelings.

4.7.5 If, in a particular case, the mediator and participants agree that it is appropriate to consult any child directly in mediation, the mediator should be trained for that purpose, must obtain the child's consent and must provide appropriate facilities.

Dingwall and Greatbach found in their study that there were no cases where children were seen by the mediator, although the 'idea' was discussed in two cases.[87] They did observe a focus on children's interests, however:

[T]he children's perspectives were distinguished and discussed in 52 of the 56 cases where they were relevant. Since the 1980s mediators seem to have become much better at separating what might in general be good for children[88] and what parents claim would be good for children and in dealing with these separately. (Dingwall and Greatbach 2001: 381)[89]

Again, there may have been some changes. According to Parkinson:

There are different ways in which children and young people may meet with a family mediator or, in some services, with a child counsellor who is part of the family mediation team

---

[84] See Piper (1994: 101); Richards (1995b); Douglas et al (1996: 130).

[85] Practice Direction: Revised Private Law Programme [2010] 2 FLR 717, para 2.2(f).

[86] On training schemes for mediators to get them to help parents to consult their children or for mediators to consult children directly, see Fisher (1996: 14); Piper (1994); Piper (1996: 375); Roberts (1997: 141–42); Piper (1999b: 91–92).

[87] See also Douglas et al (2000: 191).

[88] This would appear to embrace an assumption that contact is good for children. See above pp 721ff.

[89] See further, Dingwall and Greatbach (2000: 248–49).

(L Parkinson [2006] Fam Law 483–488). Opportunities for individual children or siblings need to be considered carefully with their parents first of all, before an invitation is offered to a child. Children see confidentiality as a major issue and if they are to be seen on their own, a written agreement needs to be signed by both parents covering confidentiality and arrangements for any feedback. These conditions also need to be explained to and accepted by the child. Many children in these situations are used to managing their divided lives and can be helped to consider messages that they wish to give to their parents without causing hurt or explosions of anger. Australian researchers (McIntosh J et al, 'Child-Focused and Child-Inclusive Divorce Mediation—Comparative Outcomes' (2008) 46 *Family and Conciliation Courts Review* 105–124) compared child-focused mediation, in which children did not take part directly, with child-inclusive mediation in which children met with a child counsellor. In both groups in the year following mediation, the researchers found lasting reductions in levels of conflict and improved management of disputes as reported by the parents and the children. The child-inclusive group showed more significant improvements in parental and child-parent relationships, particularly between fathers and children, and more noticeable benefits in children's developmental recovery from high-conflict separation. (Parkinson 2011b: 24)

The Harmonious Divorce/Separation?

As we have seen, mediation is conceived of primarily as a means of reducing conflict, facilitating settlement and, to some extent, as a way of improving communication between warring parties. Since the early days of its deployment in family disputes, efforts have been made to differentiate it from other forms of intervention. In 1989, for instance, the Newcastle study into conciliation stated that the objectives of conciliation, as it was then generally termed, 'are not reconciliation, adjudication, arbitration or counselling as such although each of these may play a part in the settlement of a dispute' (CPU 1989: 276).

Mediation and conciliation are premised on the ability of the participants to negotiate in a rational way, unclouded by hostility, and, particularly in the case of child-related issues, to put the interests of the children first. The assumption is that not only is it more cost-efficient than the traditional legal route to dispute resolution, but it is better at reducing conflict and promoting co-operation.

Day Sclater, however, raises the question whether the harmonious divorce can be promoted by removing it from the realm of the adversarial system or whether, to some extent, polarisation, opposition and conflict may be part of the psychology of divorce (Day Sclater 1999a: 162)—and, presumably, separation. She goes on to suggest that, not only are negative emotions an undeniable reality in many family break-ups, but that the drive to reduce conflict and the refusal to countenance expressions of anger and hostility in dispute-resolution processes may be detrimental to participants. Exhortations to co-operate can be experienced as persecutory (Day Sclater 1999b: 183). Conflict may be implicated in the process of rebuilding of the self (Day Sclater 1999a: 176). And the ideal of parental harmony for the sake of the children operates to delegitimise feelings of anger that could be important for survival and recovery (see 1999a: 170; 1999b: 180). A refusal to allow parties to dwell on past wrongs could also deprive parties of a helpful strategy: the reinterpretation of the past (1999a: 173; 1999b: 150). Often the marriage is viewed negatively from the vantage point of the present, so making it possible to see the break-up more positively and as a route out of an oppressive relationship (1999a: 175). A focus on the future 'sits uneasily with the need to revisit and reinterpret the past' that is essential to recovery (1999b: 177).

Day Sclater found that those who underwent mediation fared less well psychologically than those who relied on a solicitor from the start. She speculates that one explanation for this could be that 'the barrier to the expression of hostile emotions, posed by the discourses of welfare and harmony, runs counter to ordinary coping strategies, thus militating against the achievement of psychological separation and emotional resolution' (Day Sclater 1999b: 149).[90] The participants are not given the opportunity to tell their stories. Instead these stories are 'reframed' during the course of mediation to fit in with the discourse of welfare and harmony (ibid: 150).

She comments that our

> inability to accept the emotional complexities of divorce … lead us either to trivialise it (as in booklets distributed to divorcing parents which tell them that they must 'put their feelings to one side for the children's sake'), or to pathologise it, as when 'conflict' is regarded as a dangerous, abnormal and avoidable. (Day Sclater 1999a: 180).

In both cases, she says, we try to render emotions manageable and we 'deny the realities of family breakdown' (ibid).

Other commentators have suggested that mediation be adapted to take account of emotion. Dingwall and Greatbach (2000: 251), for example, thought that mediators probably require training in counselling or related skills to deal with clients' distress. And it seems that some mediators too are suggesting that clients' emotions should be acknowledged. Also, they say, that this 'emotional work' has the added advantage of helping to achieve settlements (Wilson 2004).[91]

IV. NEGOTIATING THROUGH LAWYERS

Solicitors frequently refer clients to mediation. However, often, rather than do that and rather than litigate, they negotiate agreements on behalf of their clients.[92] Lawyers play a pivotal role in dealing with disputes arising on divorce and separation. Walker (2004: 122), reporting on the results of a large study into the information meeting pilots, says that over 80% of those in the research sample who applied for divorce consulted a solicitor.[93] Whether or not people had received information about services such as mediation beforehand made little difference to the statistics.

Traditionally lawyers are seen as implicated in fomenting conflict through partisanship and adversarialism. This view is apparent in a government document published in 1998, which announced a commitment to ensuring that the divorce process 'does not make the situation worse for the family … by for example encouraging litigation or making children pawns in a fight between parents'. To that end, it said, it is important to reduce conflict and to strengthen mediation as an alternative to lawyer negotiation (Home Office

---

[90] See also Day Sclater (1999a: 177).

[91] This appears to be a return to a position rejected in earlier years. See, eg, Roberts (1997: 25), referred to above, p 714. Wilson (2010) argues for a need to address the past in mediation concerning finances.

[92] See Bailey-Harris *et al* (1998: ch VII). The majority of ancillary relief applications lead to a negotiated outcome. See Davis et al (2000b). It is claimed that solicitors settle at least 90% of their cases (Davis et al 2001a: 265–66).

[93] Most respondents did likewise (Walker 2004: 122).

1998: para 4.41). However, it is questionable whether the dichotomy set up between lawyer negotiation and mediation is defensible.[94]

Within the context of family break-up most lawyer negotiations no longer take the form of 'a bipartisan process involving constructive but hard bargaining to secure the client's interests' (Neale and Smart 1997: 383). Neale and Smart observed, as long ago as 1997, that conceptions of 'good' legal practice had changed to emphasise the welfare principle in the law and the growth of mediation (ibid). Indeed 'good' lawyering has come to resemble mediation.[95] The Resolution Code of Practice (2005), requires solicitors to:

> deal with each other in a civilised way and to encourage their clients to put their differences aside and reach fair agreements. Experience shows that agreed solutions are more likely to work in the long term than any arrangements imposed by a Court. If the family has to resort to the Court to resolve their dispute, it is best for all concerned that any proceedings are conducted in a constructive and realistic way to minimise conflict and distress as far as possible.
>
> (Law Society 2006: Appendix 2)

Davis et al suggest that solicitors dealing with disputes about contact or residence do not follow 'unreasonable' or confrontational instructions. In their sample,

> 66% of informants said that their solicitor had acted 'completely' in their interests. This is a lower percentage than one might expect given that the solicitor is, after all, a partisan who acts on his client's instructions. It reflects the fact that family lawyers temper their partisanship quite considerably. They also see themselves as representing the children's interests, as sponsoring 'reasonable' solutions, and as having a responsibility to rein in their client's worst excesses.
>
> (Davis et al 2000e: 85)

Neale and Smart's research led them to conclude that the image of the 'good' lawyer has become that of the welfarist, impartial and conciliatory practitioner (Neale and Smart 1997: 378). This, they said, has led many lawyers to focus on the welfare of the child, as they understand it, and on joint parenting and agreement as opposed to litigation. Practice among the solicitors participating in their study varied, with some adopting a traditional adversarial approach and others being flexible, steering a middle course between traditional lawyering and 'good' lawyering. Yet others adhered rigidly to the approaches characterising 'good' lawyering. This inflexible 'good' lawyering can, the authors contended, be 'bad' for clients in some cases: 'The "good" solicitor who is more concerned about enforcing [*sic*] co-parenting and avoiding litigation may not be disposed to accept that some parents have good grounds for denying contact. In fact the sympathies of such solicitors may well lie with the parent who has been denied contact' (ibid: 393). Clients, they suggested, could be left unsupported and vulnerable.[96] In support of their argument, they quoted a family law specialist describing his approach to contact disputes:

> I think the only time that I lay down the law and I'm heavy handed is if I've got a mother whose

---

[94] Maclean and Eekelaar (2009).

[95] See Wright (2007). King (1999) observed, eg, that clients were encouraged to be 'sensible'. Lawyers try to reduce tensions and try to achieve the best deal for clients only within the confines of the normative standards of the law (Eekelaar et al 2000: 184–85).

[96] See also Davis et al (1994: 261). The authors point out that inequality between parties is not always redressed in negotiations between lawyers. Much depends on the ability and commitment of the legal advisor. In addition, the ability of each party to withstand delay is important. Typically, women need an order resolving the dispute while men are content to allow a stalemate to continue.

[*sic*] not allowing contact ... *I try to beat everybody into submission* ... . The prospect of the court ever backing [a contact order] up with [committal proceedings] is very unlikely, but *I would never tell the mum that* ... What you hope is that the judge will be strong enough *to frighten the socks off mum* ... I've got a particularly difficult case at the moment where the mother has ... been subject to *what seems to be some nasty incidents of violence and fled the area specially to get away* ... . There's been no contact for eight months in respect of a child who's just two ... . Now persuading her to get contact up and running again is very, very difficult. And, in fact, we [the two lawyers] were able to arrange that ... .

Q: Who were you acting for?

A: I was acting for mum. ... (ibid: 394, emphasis in original)

This account appears to demonstrate that some solicitors, like mediators, put considerable, and perhaps more explicit, pressure on mothers to accede to contact. However, it seems that their understanding of what they consider reasonable may be communicated to fathers as well. Davis et al (2000e: 99) report that only half the men who reached agreement through a solicitor said that it was in the best interests of the children, compared with two-thirds of those who went to mediation. Men (34%) were also far less likely than women (69%) to be satisfied that the agreement reached was 'completely reasonable' (ibid: 100).[97] From this, the authors infer that 'solicitors bring some pressure to bear on their male clients, requiring them to modify their initial stance in order to bring this more into line with norms of settlement in child contact disputes' (ibid: 99).

V. THE OUTCOMES AND THE CLIENT'S VIEW

Both mediation/conciliation and solicitor negotiation are aimed at avoiding litigation. Yet it appears that support among professionals for ADR and negotiation is stronger than support among members of the public. Resolution reported that in its survey, only 55% of people thought it was 'very important to avoid a court battle' (Cross 2005: 168). In particular, public understanding of and support for mediation is limited. Davis et al (2000f: 202–03) observed that, whereas those who attended mediation of their own accord or who were referred by solicitors or, in some cases, the court, appeared knowledgeable about the process and came at a time that was right for them, clients who were referred to assessment meetings as a condition of receiving public funding were less knowledge-able, less conciliatory and less motivated. Diduck comments that:

> This finding is significant to the extent that government enthusiasm for mediation was based in large part upon mediators' enthusiasm, which seems now to have been the result of their experience of a self-selecting and unrepresentative clientele. The actual families that they now encounter may represent the less than ideal altruistic, rational and free-willed individuals of government expectations. (Diduck 2003: 112)

Davis and his colleagues sought to compare client responses to mediation with responses to representation by a solicitor. Their findings indicate that the public do not necessarily find mediation more attractive. They remark that '[f]or mediation to work it is probably necessary that both parties feel able to negotiate directly with each other in good faith'

---

[97] Fear of violence did not alter these proportions except very marginally.

(Davis et al 2001a: 112). They found that in fact there were high levels of mistrust of former partners among their panel of clients. Those participating in the study also doubted their former partners' commitment to resolving the disputed issues (ibid). Similar factors were cited by Walker et al's informants as reasons for not attending mediation. Some, however, said they did not need mediation as they could make their own arrangements. Others referred to the fear of intimidation by the other spouse. The main reason given was the unwillingness of other party to attend (Walker et al 2004: 133).

The experiences of those who did attend mediation were not noticeably better than the experiences of those who went to solicitors. Solicitors were rated as 'very helpful' in explaining options by 60% of clients questioned, compared with 35% of mediators' clients (Davis et al 2000e: 83). 69% of solicitors were said to have understood their clients' problems 'very well' as opposed to 51% of mediators (ibid). The researchers found that 81% of their sample would recommend seeing a solicitor to others in the same position, compared with 71% of mediation clients (ibid: 86).[98] Of those engaged in financial disputes, 84% said they would recommend seeing a solicitor, compared to 68% of mediation customers who said the same of going to mediation (ibid: 89). Overall, solicitors scored higher than mediators.[99] The authors suggest that although, particularly in disputes concerning children, solicitors restrain clients whom they consider unreasonable,

> [a]t the same time they remain partisan and this, probably, is the reason they tend to score higher than mediators on most of these measures. People feel they need partisanship, and even if it is muted, they like it. People who opt for mediation are also positive on the whole, but approval ratings across the board are not quite as high. This is no reflection on mediators, or indeed on mediation. It is just an indication of the kinds of help that people value most highly at this particular time. Some people value both, but there is a tendency to value lawyers more. It might be more accurate to say that they value partisanship more.[100] Mediation, in comparison, is like castor oil—everyone says it is good for you, but that does not mean you have to like it. (Davis et al 2000e: 85)

However, according to Wright, solicitors in her sample who were dealing with financial and property disputes were non-partisan and conciliatory; they appeared to have 'absorbed some of the ethos behind mediation' and something akin to a hybrid profession may be emerging (Wright 2007: 490). Solicitors see their role as negotiating, or helping their clients to negotiate, a fair solution. And, Wright says, it may be that they set out to persuade clients to adopt what they, the solicitors, see as an appropriate solution, which might be very different from what either of the disputing parties wanted originally (ibid: 485). Wright observes that agreements were not always fair and solicitors failed to address imbalances of power. She suggests that this is because, in line with mediation principles, solicitors seek to avoid conflict and to preserve the relationship between the parties. These were often the clients' goals too. However, Wright says that the aim of fairness may be being subordinated to the aim of preserving an unconflicted relationship; solicitors should do more to protect the long-term interests of their clients rather than sacrificing those to the short-term goal of conflict avoidance. Indeed it appears that clients are less satisfied

---

[98] They caution that, if people were compelled to attend mediation, satisfaction rates with the process would be likely to be lower (Davis, 2000).

[99] Walker reports that 'satisfaction with solicitors was higher than satisfaction with mediators, but not as high as satisfaction with counsellors' (Walker et al 2004: 130).

[100] See further Walker et al (2004: 127–28). Some people felt that their solicitor was not partisan enough, whereas others said that their solicitor had been too partisan and had caused unnecessary conflict.

with solicitors who adopt a strongly conciliatory approach than with those who are more partisan. Nevertheless, clients tended to value the presence of their solicitors:

> This hybrid professional group, with their specific skills, may be uniquely placed to build on the willingness of clients to negotiate the terms of their settlement directly with their spouse. This study found that clients are willing to do this when supported by a solicitor. This support consisted of three main elements: first, the imparting of information in relation to legal entitlements; secondly, as a 'shield' to protect them from spousal conflict/hostility; and, thirdly, as a 'fallback' system should the negotiations fail. Clients did not appear willing to assume responsibility for negotiating the final outcome without such support, and when interviewed were strikingly emphatic that they could not have proceeded via mediation. Clients instead preferred to conduct their negotiations in the 'shadow of their solicitor'. (ibid: 491)

It seems that solicitors are becoming more like mediators and that this may not be beneficial in all ways for their clients and that some clients may not even like it.

Mediation can only claim limited success when it comes to outcomes as well. Agreement rates in mediation in the study by Davis et al were not very high. In cases involving children, Davis et al report a rate of 45%, dropping to 40% where the informant reported fear of violence (Davis et al 2000e: 77). The agreement rate in respect of financial issues was 34% (ibid: 80). Walker et al report that only 30% of clients stopped mediation because they felt it had achieved its objectives and 30% said it was not achieving anything (Walker et al 2004: 135). 46% of users were helped to find solutions to their problems but only about 25% resolved all the issues raised (ibid: 136).[101]

The proportion of agreements seems to be higher in in-court conciliation cases.[102] Trinder et al (2006) found agreement in their in-court conciliation study on all or some issues in 76% of cases. In the follow-up study by Trinder and Kellett (2007), there were agreements in 79% of cases. However, two-thirds of parents reported that additional intervention had been necessary in the two years since conciliation (ibid: 10). The reason that agreements broke down or changed was mainly that the parent(s) or child(ren) did not support the arrangement, rather than being an adaptive change to a change in circumstances. Re-litigation occurred in 40.2% of cases (ibid: 11). These results suggest an inability on the part of the parents to renegotiate agreements themselves; ADR was therefore not equipping them do so (ibid: 13).

Davis et al (2000e) considered the durability of the agreements reached in mediation and the likelihood of their renegotiation. Overall, 59% of those who had been in mediation about children said they thought they would be able to modify the agreement when necessary but, for those in the group who feared violence, the percentage was lower: only 43% of those who feared violence thought they could renegotiate (Davis et al 2000e: 80). In fact, when people from the same sample of mediation clients were interviewed a second time, it was only in about 20% of all those cases where the agreement had broken down[103] that the parties had managed to negotiate a new one (ibid). 65% of those who used solicitor negotiations to reach agreement said they thought they would be able to renego-

---

[101] The figure of 28% is cited elsewhere (Walker et al 2004: 142).

[102] Trinder et al (2006: 1) point out that, compared to mediation, in-court conciliation tends to produce higher rates of agreement and say this is indicative of greater pressure. In-court conciliation also tends to produce lower levels of satisfaction with the agreement and with the process. However, the authors do say that two studies comparing mediation with in-court conciliation did not find a substantial difference in satisfaction rates.

[103] The agreement had broken down in 9 out of 29 cases (Davis et al 2000e: 80).

tiate when necessary. When interviewed later, 72% said their agreements had lasted and 20% of those that did not were renegotiated (ibid: 106).

Davis et al suggest that their findings:

> cast doubt on one of the central claims made on behalf of mediation, namely that it delivers *durable* agreements and, furthermore, that it improves couples' capacity to negotiate together in future. On this evidence, which admittedly is subject to various possible qualifications, mediation does not deliver this any more effectively than do lawyers. Given that mediation is in so many instances a relatively fleeting intervention, this is hardly surprising.
>
> (Davis et al 2000e: 101, emphasis in original)

The research findings of Walker and her colleagues also raise doubts about the durability of agreements. Contact arrangements were particularly prone to break down, 'often because residential parents feel that they [were] pushed into reaching agreements about which they [were] not happy' (Walker et al 2004: 142). This calls into question the fairness of the original agreements. It may be, as Genn has said, that mediation is not about 'just settlement'; it is 'just about settlement' (Rozenberg 2008).

Walker et al also found little evidence to support the wider claims often made for mediation. People, particularly if they had failed to reach an agreement, 'did not feel that attending mediation had helped to make divorce less distressing,[104] or that it had helped them to improve communication, share decision-making about parenting, reduce conflict or avoid going to court' (Walker et al 2004: 140–41).

Finally, Davis et al go on to call into question another claim made in favour of mediation, namely that it saves costs:

> Does mediation, overall, save money on lawyer services? Answer: we do not think so. Engaging in mediation is not of itself associated with reduced legal costs, although there appears on the face of it to be an association between mediation *agreement* and reduced cost.
>
> Is mediation a service which people value? Yes it is, by those who choose to avail themselves of it. However, efforts to shepherd a much larger section of the relevant population into the arms of mediators have not proved cost-effective. This is partly because of client resistance, and partly because the chosen mechanism is so inefficient as a means of securing the engagement of both parties.[105] (Davis et al 2000e: 138, emphasis in original)

Davis and his colleagues suggest that mediation should be seen as an 'aid to private communication' rather than as a means of saving costs and diverting cases from trial (Davis et al 2000b: paras 29–30). We should not, they say, expect mediation to reduce significantly the demand for legal services. Many people simply do not feel that the conditions for fair resolution of their dispute through reasonable discussion exist. They turn to lawyers and the courts as a means of countering strategies such as 'lying, evasion or threat' used by their former partners. Mediation is not seen as being able to respond adequately to such levels of conflict and, therefore, 'there is little prospect of mediation replacing lawyers—or certainly not of its replacing them effectively' (ibid: para 30.5)

Walker draws similar conclusions, suggesting that mediation will continue to be used

---

[104] Some of Walker's informants complained that their solicitor had ignored the 'stressful, emotive issues' surrounding divorce (Walker et al 2004: 128).

[105] The main reasons for cases to be designated unsuitable were that the former partner was uncooperative, unwilling to compromise or did not attend (Davis et al 2000a: para 15.3). Failure to reach agreement also increases cost (ibid: para 31.3).

by only a minority, while the majority, including those who go to mediation, will continue to depend on legal services (Walker et al 2004: 145). However, it must now be noted that if the Legal Aid, Sentencing and Punishment of Offenders Bill becomes law, many will not have access to legal services.

The *Family Justice Review* acknowledges that there is insufficient evidence of the cost, benefits and effectiveness of mediation (Norgrove 2011a: paras 5.102–5.103). It also concedes that the evidence for the durability of agreements compared to court outcomes is limited (ibid: para 5.105). The panel also reports hearing evidence that 'some people are reluctant to use ADR such as mediation because they think the court will be more effective'. However, the panel speculates that the name 'alternative dispute resolution' puts people off because the word 'alternative' implies secondary (ibid: para 5.122). The solution it recommends is rebranding ADR as 'Dispute Resolution Services'; this, says the report, could 'minimise one deterrent to their use' (ibid: para 5.123).

This raises the question why, when the word 'mediation' is used so often, this does not operate to remove the deterrent thought to be inherent in the term 'alternative dispute resolution.' This, specifically, is one the main forms of ADR offered to the public and yet the public remains resistant. It also raises the question as to how likely it is that a change of name will change people's minds. It is less likely to be the terminology that deters people than the fact that they want the reassurance of having someone, a solicitor, who is at least partly on their side when they are in distress and seeking someone to help them deal with a situation fraught with mistrust.

VI. ALTERNATIVE DISPUTE RESOLUTION: THE OTHER ALTERNATIVES AVAILABLE

Collaborative Law

This is a relatively recent addition to the ADR mechanisms available to settle family-related disputes. It was first introduced into the UK in 2003 and the process is being promoted by Resolution (Resolution, undated). In this process, both parties are represented by lawyers whose aim is to settle the case. All four participants enter into a participation agreement in which they agree not to go to court while the process is ongoing (LNTV 2005a: 3; Resolution, undated; Resolution 2009: Summary). The agreement also stipulates that if a settlement is not reached, neither lawyer can take the case to court. The parties have to instruct different legal representatives for that purpose (LNTV 2005a).[106]

The parties set out to negotiate a settlement in a series of round-table meetings known as 'four-way' meetings (Resolution, undated). The parties and their lawyers all negotiate face-to-face. There is no set timetable and the parties negotiate at their own pace (LNTV 2005a: 5; Resolution, undated). If necessary, other professionals will be asked to assist. These could be pensions advisors, accountants and others who can advise in financial matters (Resolution, undated). There are also other professionals who can be asked to assist with difficulties engendered by the family dynamics. The role of family consultants is seen as 'crucial' (LNTV 2005a: 3). They are likely to come from 'therapeutic, social

---

[106] The process was praised by the judge in *S v P*, Royal Courts of Justice, 30 July 2008 (transcript).

work and counselling backgrounds' and many have mediation experience (ibid). Their contribution to the process involves helping parties and their lawyers deal with some of the emotional fall-out of the separation or divorce (ibid). It is this involvement of a variety of professionals and the therapeutic element that differentiates collaborative family law from lawyer negotiation and mediation. It also differs from mediation in that each party has a lawyer to provide advice and support.

According to Tesler, writing in the United States, collaborative law meets the needs of both clients and legal practitioners (who find it easier to adapt to collaborative law than to mediation):

> [C]lients appear to want the advantages of a contained, settlement-orientated, creative, private, respectful process without sacrificing the benefits of having a committed legal advocate at their sides. For that reason Collaborative Law appeals to clients who may hesitate to commit to a dispute resolution process facilitated solely by a neutral mediator. (Tesler 2004: 318)

> The role of the lawyer shifts ... to guide for negotiations and manager of conflict ... . Good collaborative lawyers detach from outcome and judge their success by the degree to which both collaborative lawyers succeed in working effectively with all participants ... . at an appropriate pace, toward a mutually beneficial and acceptable outcome. (ibid: 328)

Nevertheless, collaborative law is not suitable for everyone and it is up to the practitioners to screen out inappropriate cases (LNTV 2005a: 4). Such cases might involve highly conflicted former partners (LNTV 2005b). Also, cases involving child abuse or domestic violence may not be suitable (LNTV 2005a: 4). How active this screening is, is not clear; one practitioner interviewed on a College of Law training DVD remarked that most unsuitable clients screen themselves out (LNTV 2005b). This may be cause for concern[107] but at least, unlike in the case of mediation, the party who is not the abuser does have a lawyer who should be alert to any prejudice to their interests or to those of the children. Imbalances of power may not be as stark as those that can potentially exist in the context of mediation.

Concerns have also been expressed about other limitations of the process. There is a risk that the lack of a timetable can lead to abuse of the process by means of delay. There is no way of ensuring that honest disclosure of assets or other information is made (LNTV 2005a: 5). Nor is there any way in which the child's wishes and views are being conveyed other than through the parents (ibid).

Research commissioned by Resolution (2009), covering the period 2006–07, shows that while the number of cases is increasing, it is still not high.[108] Most clients were well educated and economically active. 80% of cases completed in 2006–07 were settled and so were 90% of more recent cases. Practitioners thought the cases had been completed more cheaply and more quickly than they would have been through lawyer-negotiated settlements or court proceedings. However, there were reservations, and lawyers stressed the need for screening.

---

[107] Women's Aid has expressed concerns that the emphasis on promoting agreement through collaborative law 'is likely to mean that fears about domestic violence will continue to be minimised or ignored' (DCA, DfES and DTI 2005: para 41).

[108] The survey produced estimates of between approximately 1,440 and 2,870 cases opened, and between approximately 970 and 1,950 completed.

At one level, this involved being on the alert for issues of domestic violence or abuse, mental health problems, or alcohol or drug abuse. But more generally, prerequisites were felt to be: sufficient trust and respect between the parties; some mutual recognition of needs rather than positional stances; a lack of unrealistic expectations; ability to communicate with and to be civil towards each other, and a shared concern for the welfare of any children and for their relationships with both parents.

Lawyers also stressed that the collaborative approach involved important qualitative shifts in the client–lawyer relationship. Whilst the collaborative lawyer's primary responsibility remained to their client, they also had to let go of partisanship, and do their best to ensure that the interests of both parties, and particularly any children involved, were addressed. This required a high degree of trust between the lawyers; each needed to be confident that the other would look out for the interests of their client. It also meant that clients needed to know that they may experience their lawyer speaking against them, or speaking up for the other party's interests.

A key advantage of collaborative law was felt to be that it allowed the parties to devise their own solutions, without having outcomes imposed by a court—or arrived at via negotiations in which one or other party felt backed into a corner. Examples of a number of outcomes were given which lawyers said either could not, or almost certainly would not, have been achieved via litigation or conventional negotiations.

Nevertheless, legal norms were still considered important in providing a framework for clients in negotiations, and a 'reality check' if expectations were unrealistically high or low. Collaborative lawyers therefore saw the provision of legal advice as an essential element of their role. But the nature, timing and presentation of legal advice all needed careful consideration to prevent it leading to negotiations becoming polarised through the adoption of strong positions by one or both parties.

Another important issue was the role of emotions in collaborative law—not only because the parties were brought together in four-way meetings, but also because the client-led nature of the process made it important to understand how emotions might affect parties' approaches to negotiations. With regard to the latter in particular, lawyers were increasingly keen to involve other professionals, such as family consultants and mediators, in helping clients to address issues which they (the lawyers) were not qualified to help with. (Similar considerations applied to bringing in independent financial advisers, on matters such as pension sharing).

(Resolution 2009)

Of the small number of (mainly female) clients interviewed for this study, most felt their level of participation was commensurate with their wishes and they were satisfied with both lawyers. Some stressed that whether the process worked for them depended on the quality of the lawyers.

This research suggests that collaborative law is probably best suited to the less difficult cases; clients who were interviewed chose it because they did not want an acrimonious divorce. It is probably not suited to families with multiple problems. It is therefore doubtful that it is suited to the majority of cases.

In addition, it must raise some of the same issues as lawyer negotiation; much must depend on the lawyers' constructions of what is 'best' for the parties and children. Also, it is clear that discussions take place 'in the shadow of the law', and it can be speculated that a strong emphasis on child contact is probably a feature.

A focus on the welfare of the family as a whole is apparent in the Canadian context. Wiegers and Keet say that the emphasis on 'familial welfare' and harmony can pressure more vulnerable parties into abandoning legitimate claims and can be particularly disadvantageous for victims of abuse; it can exacerbate their unwillingness or impaired ability to communicate (Wiegers and Keet 2008: 746). The sensitivity of the lawyers and the quality of their screening is crucial when it comes to cases involving oppressive imbalances of power or domestic violence. The lawyers in their study showed varied levels of awareness of domestic violence and abuse and some did not screen (ibid: 753). Nor was there consensus in their sample of lawyers on what would constitute a power imbalance sufficient to make a case unsuitable for collaborative law (ibid: 751–52).

Financial Dispute Resolution

This process is designed to facilitate agreement in settling financial matters arising out of divorce. It is triggered when a case is brought to court and it is managed by the district judge. After originally being piloted in the 1990s, FDR now forms part of the standard procedure. It entails, ideally, strict control by the judge to ensure that matters are resolved as quickly and 'justly'[109] as possible. Justice demands that the parties are on an even footing. The aim is also to save expense and to deal with cases in a manner proportionate to the amounts involved and to the complexity and importance of the issues.[110]

The parties are obliged to attend a first appointment, with their solicitors, before the district judge. This appointment is meant to be used 'to define the issues and save costs'.[111] The court, if it considers it appropriate to do so, may then direct that the case be referred for a FDR appointment. This is held 'for the purposes of discussion and negotiation'[112] and the parties must use their 'best endeavours to reach agreement'.[113] It is only if a consent order is not possible that the case will go on to a final hearing. A different judge must preside over the final hearing.

Parenting Agreements

While a parenting agreement is not a means of resolving disputes, parenting agreements are included here because they are meant to reduce areas of dispute. They are not yet part of the settlement process; the use of parenting agreements is one of the proposals put forward by the *Family Justice Review* (Norgrove 2011a: paras 5.90ff).

It is proposed that parenting agreements be drawn up by parents to set out how they 'will jointly exercise their parental responsibility following separation' (ibid: paras 5.90–5.91). The panel thought this would encourage parents to discuss the incidents of parental responsibility 'with a view to identifying matters of agreement or disagreement'. It would also focus parental attention on the care of the child rather than on their own status. The agreement is meant to set out in advance what the parents will do and who will make what decisions so that 'the number of disputed issues is reduced' (ibid: para 5.91). Children are expected to participate in the process of drawing up the agreement, taking into account their age and understanding.

---

[109] FPR 2010/2955 R1.1.
[110] Ibid.
[111] R 9.15(1)
[112] R 9.17(1).
[113] R 9.17(6).

VII. CONCLUSION

Private ordering, in political and professional discourse, is generally considered to be a beneficial development. There is much good practice that bears out this judgement. However, there is an element of coercion in some of the schemes to engage in the process of ADR and to agree to the types of post-separation family arrangements preferred by the professionals. While private ordering enables parties to avoid the stress and expense of litigation and while it may often enable parties to retain some measure of autonomy, it may be a far from perfect solution in some cases of family break-up. To speak of family privacy and family autonomy is to assume that the family is capable of making decisions as a unit. However, the interests and desires of different family members may be very different and may even be irreconcilable. To contain decision-making and dispute resolution in the private sphere means that the formal safeguards designed to ensure that each party's case is heard are absent. Imbalances of power may be left unredressed and a party unable to articulate his or her point of view is disadvantaged. In addition, a party may 'agree' out of fear or exhaustion to arrangements that could be damaging. Moreover, the familial norms purveyed by some professionals engaged in mediation, negotiation and other forms of ADR may place pressure on one party, usually the mother, to agree to arrangements that are not in her (or possibly her child's) interests.

POSTSCRIPT

While this book was in press the *Family Justice Review: Final Report* was published (Norgrove 2011b). This reiterates many of the recommendations in the Interim Report such as the creation of an information hub (paras 4.11, 4.74–4.79), as well as the use of Parenting Agreements (paras 4.12, 4.49–4.54), Mediation Information and Assessment Meetings (paras 4.83–4.85) and PIPs (paras 4.87–4.90). However, in spite of an expressed preference for mediation to resolve disputes (paras 4.94–4.99), it also expresses considerable concern about the proposed changes to the availability of legal aid (paras 4.175–4.183).

FURTHER READING

G Davis et al, *Monitoring Publicly Funded Family Mediation: Report to the Legal Services Commission* (London, Legal Services Commission, 2000).

G Davis, R Fitzgerald and S Finch, 'Mediation Case Profiles' in G Davis, *Monitoring Publicly Funded Family Mediation: Report to the Legal Services Commission* (London, Legal Services Commission, 2000).

G Davis, G Bevan and J Pearce, 'Family Mediation—Where do We Go from Here?' (2001) *Fam Law* 265.

G Davis, S Finch and R Fitzgerald, 'Mediation and Legal Services—The Client Speaks' (2001) *Fam Law* 110.

S Day Sclater, 'Experiences of Divorce' in S Day Sclater and C Piper (eds), *Undercurrents of Divorce* (Aldershot, Ashgate, 1999).

——, *Divorce: A Psychosocial Study* (Aldershot, Ashgate, 1999).

G Douglas et al, 'Safeguarding Children's Welfare in Non-contentious Divorce: Towards a New Conception of the Legal Process?' (2000) 63 *MLR* 177.

J Eekelaar, M Maclean and S Beinhart, *Family Lawyers: The Divorce Work of Solicitors* (Oxford, Hart Publishing, 2000).

F Kaganas and C Piper, 'Divorce and Domestic Violence' in S Day Sclater and C Piper (eds) *Undercurrents of Divorce* (Aldershot, Ashgate, 1999).

M Maclean and J Eekelaar, *Family Advocacy: How Barristers Help the Victims of Family Failure* (Oxford, Hart Publishing, 2009).

C Piper, 'How Do You Define a Family Lawyer?' (1999) 19 *Legal Studies* 93.

S Roberts, 'Alternative Dispute Resolution and Civil Justice: An Unresolved Relationship' (1993) 56 *MLR* 452.

C Smart and V May, 'Why Can't They Agree? The Underlying Complexity of Contact and Residence Disputes' (2004) 26 *JSW&FL* 347.

L Trinder and J Kellett, *The Longer-term Outcomes of In-court Conciliation*, Ministry of Justice Research Series 15/07 (London, Ministry of Justice, 2007).

L Trinder, J Connolly, J Kellett, C Notley and L Swift, *Making Contact Happen or Making Contact Work? The Process and Outcomes of In-Court Conciliation*, DCA Research Series 3/06 (London, DCA, 2006).

Bibliography

ABORTION RIGHTS (undated) 'Pregnant and Considering Abortion?', www.abortionrights.org.uk/content/view/16/109/ (accessed 1 August 2011).

ACKERS, L (2000) 'From "Best Interests" to Participatory Rights—Children's Involvement in Family Migration Decisions' 12 *CFLQ* 167.

ADOPTION RESEARCH INITIATIVE (2010) *Summary 10: Supporting Direct Contact After Adoption* (London, ARI).

ASSOCIATION OF CHIEF POLICE OFFICERS AND NATIONAL POLICING IMPROVEMENT AGENCY (ACPO, NPIA) (2008) *Guidance on Investigating Domestic Abuse*, www.acpo.police.uk/documents/crime/2008/2008004CRIIDA01.pdf (accessed 14 February 2011).

ADAM, BD (2004) 'Care, Intimacy and Same-sex Partnership in the 21st Century' 52 *Current Sociology* 265.

ADAM, D District Judge (2011) 'The Family Procedure Rules 2010: A District Judge's Perspective' *Fam Law* 244.

ADAMS, BN (1975) *The Family: A Sociological Interpretation*, 2nd edn (Chicago, IL, Rand McNally).

ADAMS, D (2000) 'The Emerge Program' in J Hanmer, and C Itzin with S Quaid and D Wigglesworth (eds), *Home Truths About Domestic Violence: Feminist Influences on Policy and Practice: A Reader* (London, Routledge).

ADAMS, L, MCANDREW, F and WINTERBOTHAM, M (2005) *Pregnancy Discrimination at Work: A Survey of Women* (London, Equal Opportunities Commission).

ADVISORY GROUP ON MARRIAGE AND RELATIONSHIP SUPPORT (2002) *Moving Forward Together: A Proposed Strategy for Marriage and Relationship Support for 2002 and Beyond* (Lord Chancellor's Department, London, The Stationery Office).

ALDGATE, J (2001) *The Children Act Now: Messages from Research* (London, The Stationery Office).

ALSTON, P, PARKER, S and SEYMOUR, J (1992) *Children, Rights and the Law* (Oxford, Clarendon Press).

ANCILLARY RELIEF ADVISORY GROUP (1998) *Report to the Lord Chancellor by the Ancilliary Relief Advisory Group* (London).

ANDERSON, L (1997) *Contact between Children and Violent Fathers: In Whose Best Interests? Rights of Women Research Report on the Operation of the Children Act 1989 in Circumstances of Domestic Violence* (London, Rights of Women).

ANDERSON, M (1980) 'The Relevance of Family History' in M Anderson (ed), *The Sociology of the Family: Selected Readings*, 2nd edn (Harmondsworth, Penguin).

ANDERSON, S, (1984) 'Legislative Divorce—Law for the Aristocracy' in GR Rubin and D Sugarman (eds), *Law, Economy and Society, Essays in the History of English Law 1750–1914* (Abingdon, Professional Books).

ANITHA, S and GILL, A (2009) 'Coercion, Consent and the Forced Marriage Debate in the UK' 17 *Fem Legal Studies* 165.

ANTHIAS F and YUVAL-DAVIS, N (in association with H Cain) (1993) *Racialized Boundaries* (London, Routledge).

ARCHARD, D (1993) *Children: Rights and Childhood* (London, Routledge).

—— (1999) 'Can Child Abuse Be Defined?' in M King (ed), *Moral Agendas for Children's Welfare* (London, Routledge).

ARCHBISHOP OF CANTERBURY'S GROUP (1966) *Putting Asunder—A Divorce Law for Contemporary Society* (London, Society for Promoting Christian Knowledge, CUP).

ARIÈS, P (R Baldick trans) (1962) *Centuries of Childhood* (London, Jonathan Cape).

ASHENDEN, S (2004) *Governing Child Sexual Abuse: Negotiating the Boundaries of Public and Private, Law and Science* (London, Routledge).

ASHWORTH, A (1995) *Principles of Criminal Law*, 2nd edn (Oxford, Clarendon Press).

ASSOCIATION OF DISTRICT JUDGES (1998) 'Submission of Association of District Judges' Appendix 8 to the *Report to the Lord Chancellor by the Ancillary Relief Advisory Group* (London).

ATWOOD, M (1985) *The Handmaid's Tale* (Toronto, McClelland and Stewart).

AUCHMUTY, R (2003) 'When Equality is not Equity: Homosexual Inclusion in Undue Influence Law' 11 *Feminist Legal Studies* 163.

—— (2004) 'Same-sex Marriage Revived: Feminist Critique and Legal Strategy' 14 *Feminism and Psychology* 101.

—— (2008a) 'What's So Special abut Marriage? The Impact of *Wilkinson v Kitzinger*' 4 *CFLQ* 475.

—— (2008b) 'The Married Women's Property Acts: Equality Was Not the issue' in R Hunter (ed), *Rethinking Equality Projects in Law: Feminist Challenges* (Oxford, Hart Publishing).

—— (2009) 'Beyond Couples' 17 *Feminist Legal Studies* 205.

—— (2010) '*Royal Bank of Scotland plc v Etridge* (No 2)' in R Hunter, C McGlynn and E RACKLEY (eds), *Feminist Judgments From Theory to Practice* (Oxford, Hart Publishing).

AUDIT COMMISSION (1994) *Seen But Not Heard: Co-ordinating Community Child Health and Social Services for Children in Need: Detailed Evidence and Guidelines for Managers and Practitioners* (London, HMSO).

—— (1996) *Counting to Five: Education of Children Under Five* (London, HMSO).

BAAF (2005) British Association for Adoption and Fostering, www.baaf.org.uk/info/stats/England

BACCI, CA (1990) *Same Difference* (Sydney, Allen & Unwin).

BACKHOUSE, C (1991) *Petticoats and Prejudice: Women and Law in Nineteenth Century Canada* (Toronto, Women's Press).

BAILEY, MJ (1994) 'England's First Custody of Infants Act' 20 *Queen's L J* 391.

BAILEY-HARRIS, R (1999) 'Third Stonewall Lecture—Lesbian and Gay Family Values and the Law' *Fam Law* 560.

—— (2003) 'Case Comment' *Fam Law* 386.

—— (2005) 'The Paradoxes of Principle and Pragmatism: Ancillary Relief in England and Wales' 19 *Int J of Law, Policy and the Family* 229.

BAINHAM, A (1985) 'The Balance of Power in Family Decisions' 45 *CLJ* 262.

—— (1990) 'The Privatisation of the Public Interest in Children' 53 *MLR* 206.

—— (1995) 'Contact as a Fundamental Right' 54 *CLJ* 255.

—— (1999) 'Parentage, Parenthood and Parental Responsibility: Subtle, Elusive, Yet Important Distinctions' in A Bainham, S Day Sclater and M Richards (eds), *What is a Parent?* (Oxford, Hart Publishing).

—— (2005) *Children: The Modern Law*, 3rd edn (Bristol, Jordan).

—— (2008a) 'What Is the Point of Birth Registration?' 20 *CFLQ* 449.

—— (2008b) 'Arguments about Parentage' 67 *CLJ* 322.

—— (2011) 'Interim Care Orders: Is the Bar Set too Low?' *Fam Law* 374.

BAKER, A and TOWNSEND, P (1996) 'Post-Divorce Parenting—Rethinking Shared Residence' 8 *CFLQ* 217.

BALA, N (1998) 'Canada: Child Support Guidelines, Parental Mobility, and Redefining Familial Relationships' in A Bainham (ed), *The International Survey of Family Law* (London, Martinus Nijhoff).

BANDA, F (2003) 'Global Standards: Local Values' 17 *Int J of Law, Policy and the Family* 27.

BARLOW, A and DUNCAN, S (2000a) 'New Labour's Communitarianism, Supporting Families and the "Rationality Mistake": Part I' 22(2) *JSWFL* 23.

—— and —— (2000b) 'New Labour's Communitarianism, Supporting Families and the "Rationality Mistake": Part II' 22(2) *JSWFL* 129.

—— and JAMES G (2004) 'Regulating Marriage and Cohabitation in 21st Century Britain' 67 *MLR* 143.

——, Duncan, S, and James, G (2002) 'New Labour, the Rationality Mistake and Family Policy in Britain' in A Carling, S Duncan and R Edwards (eds), *Analysing Families: Morality and Rationality in Policy and Practice* (London, Routledge).

——, Duncan, S, James, G and Park A (2005) *Cohabitation, Marriage and the Law* (Oxford, Hart Publishing).

——, Bourgoyne, C, Clery, E and Smithson, J (2008) 'Cohabitation and the Law: Myths, Money and the Media' in A Park et al (eds) *British Social Attitudes: the 24th Report* (London, Sage).

Barn, R (2000) 'Race, Ethnicity and Transracial Adoption' in A Treacher and I Katz (eds), *The Dynamics of Adoption* (London, Jessica Kingsley).

Barnett, A (2009a) 'The Welfare of the Child Revisited: In Whose Best Interests? Part 1' *Fam Law* 50.

—— (2009b) 'The Welfare of the Child Revisited: In Whose Best Interests? Part II' *Fam Law* 135.

Barnish, M (2004) *Domestic Violence: A Literature Review* (London, HM Inspectorate of Probation).

Bar-On, A (1997) 'Criminalising Survival: Images and Reality of Street Children' 26 *J of Social Policy* 63.

Barran, D et al (2006) *Specialist Domestic Violence Court Programme Manual* (London, The Stationery Office).

Barrett, B and Melrose, M (2003) 'Courting Controversy—Children Sexually Abused through Prostitution—Are they Everybody's Distant Relatives but Nobody's Children?' 15 *CFLQ* 371.

Barrett, M and Macintosh, M (1991) *The Anti-Social Family*, 2nd edn (London, Verso).

Barron, J (1990) *Not Worth the Paper? The Effectiveness of Legal Protection for Women and Children Experiencing Domestic Violence* (Bristol, Women's Aid Federation of England).

—— (2002) *Five Years On: A Review of Legal Protection from Domestic Violence* (Bristol, Women's Aid Federation of England).

Barry, N (1995) 'Justice and Liberty in Marriage and Divorce' in R Whelan (ed), *Just a Piece of Paper? Divorce Reform and the Undermining of Marriage* (London, IEA Health and Welfare Unit).

Bart, P and Moran, E (eds) (1993) *Violence Against Women: The Bloody Footprints* (London, Sage).

Barter, C, McCarry, M, Berridge, D and Evans, K (2009) *Partner Exploitation and Violence in Teenage Intimate Relationships* (Bristol, NSPCC and University of Bristol).

Bartholomew, BW (1958) 'Legal Implications of Artificial Insemination' 21 *MLR* 236.

Barton, C (1997) 'When Did You Next See Your Father? Emigration and the One-parent Family—*Re T (Removal from Jurisdiction); Goertz v Gordon (formerly Goertz)*' 9 *CFLQ* 73.

—— (1998) 'Third Time Lucky for Child Support?—The 1998 Green Paper' *Fam Law* 668.

—— (2000) 'Adoption—The Prime Minister's Review' 30 *Fam Law* 731.

Barton, C and Douglas, G (1995) *Law and Parenthood* (London, Butterworths).

Bastin, G (1996) 'Europe and the CSA' *Fam Law* 678.

BBC News Online (2005) 'Call for Women-friendly Pensions' 21 April 2005, http://news.bbc.co.uk/1/hi/business/4469405.stm.

BBC News (13 April 2011) *All Domestic Abuse Deaths to have Multi-agency Review*, www.bbc.co.uk/news/uk-13058300 (accessed 13 April 2011).

BBC News Europe (2011) 'Malta Votes "Yes" in Divorce Referendum', www.bbc.co.uk/news/world-europe-13588834 (accessed 4 August 2011).

BBC Radio 4 (11 July 2011) *Analysis. Unsure About Sure Start.*

Beck, U and Beck-Gernsheim, E (1995) *The Normal Chaos of Love* (Cambridge, Polity).

—— and —— (2002) *Individualization* (London, Sage).

Becker, HS (1963) *Outsiders: Studies in the Sociology of Deviance* (New York, NY, Free Press).

Beihal, N, Ellison, S, Baker, C and Sinclair, I (2009) 'Characteristics, Outcomes and Meanings of Three Types of Permanent Placement—Adoption by Strangers, Adoption by Carers and Long-Term Foster Care', *Research Brief* (London, DCSF).

Bell, V (1993) 'Governing Childhood: Neo-liberalism and the Law' 22 *Economy and Society* 390.

Bellamy, C, District Judge and Geoff, District Judge (2003) 'Reflections on Family Proceedings Rule 9.5' *Fam Law* 265.

BELLAMY, C, Judge, PLATT, J, Judge and CRICHTON, N, District Judge (2010) 'Talking to Children: The Judicial Perspective' *Fam Law* 647.

BENNETT, F (2002) 'Gender Implications of Current Social Security Reforms' 23 *Fiscal Studies* 559.

—— (2005) *Gender and Benefits, Equal Opportunities Commission Working Paper Series No 30* (London, Equal Opportunities Commission).

BENNETT, M (1997) 'Life After Dart' *Fam Law* 79.

BERGER, PL and KELLNER, H (1980) 'Marriage and the Construction of Reality' in M Anderson (ed), *The Sociology of the Family*, 2nd edn (Harmondsworth, Penguin).

BEST, R (1995) 'Direct Consultation with Children: A Progress Report on Training Modules' 5 *Fam Mediation* 8.

BEVAN, G, DAVIS, G, and FENN, P (2001) 'Can Mediation Reduce Expenditure on Lawyers?' *Fam Law* 186.

BEVERIDGE, Sir WILLIAM (1942) *Social Insurance and Allied Services*, Cmd 6404 (London, HMSO).

BIGGART, L and O'BRIEN, M (2009) *Fathers' Working Hours: Parental Analysis from the Third Work–Life Balance Employee survey and Maternity and Paternity Rights and Benefits Survey of Parents* (London, BIS).

BIRCHALL, E, (1989) 'The Frequency of Child Abuse—What do We Really Know?' in O Stevenson (ed), *Child Abuse: Public Policy and Professional Practice* (Hemel Hempstead, Harvester Wheatsheaf).

BIRD, R (1996) *Domestic Violence: The New Law: Part IV of the Family Law Act 1996* (Bristol, Jordans).

—— (2000) 'Ancillary Relief Outcomes' 30 *Fam Law* 831.

BISSET-JOHNSON, A and BARTON, C (1995) 'The Divorce White Paper' *Fam Law* 349.

BLACKSTONE, W (1778) *Commentaries on the Laws of England*, 8th edn (Oxford, Clarendon Press).

BLACKWELL, A and DAWE, F (2003), *Non-Resident Parental Contact* (London, ONS).

BOCK, G (1991) 'Antinatalism, Maternity and Paternity in National Socialist Racism' in G Bock and P Thane (eds), *Maternity and Gender Policies: Women and the Rise of the European Welfare States* (London, Routledge).

BODER, R and CHILDS, M (1996) 'Paying for Procreation: Child Support Arrangements in the UK' 4 *Feminist Legal Studies* 131.

BOND, A (1996) 'Working for the Family? Child Employment Legislation and the Public/Private Divide' 4 *JSWFL* 291.

BOOTH, Mrs Justice (1985) *Report of the Matrimonial Causes Procedure Committee* (London, HMSO).

BORKOWSKI, M, MURCH, M, and WALKER, V (1983) *Marital Violence: The Community Response* (London, Tavistock).

BOSELY, S (1996) 'Labour Floats Plans to Improve Parenting', *The Guardian,* 14 November.

BOSSY, J and COLEMAN, S (2000) *Womenspeak. Parliamentary Domestic Violence Internet Consultation: Report of the Main Findings* (Bristol, Women's Aid Federation of England).

BOTTOMLEY, A (1984) 'Resolving Family Disputes: A Critical View' in M Freeman (ed), *State, Law and Family: Critical Perspectives* (London, Tavistock and Sweet & Maxwell).

—— (1985) 'What Is Happening to Family Law? A Feminist Critique of Conciliation' in J Brophy and C Smart (eds), *Women in Law: Explorations in Law, Family and Sexuality* (London, Routledge and Kegan Paul).

BOWEN, E (2011) *The Rehabilitation of Partner Violent Men* (Chichester, Wiley-Blackwell).

BOWLBY, J (1953) *Child Care and the Growth of Love* (Harmondsworth, Penguin).

BOYD, D (1990) 'Blaming the Parents' 2 *J Child Law* 65.

BOYD, S (1991) 'Some Postmodernist Challenges to Feminist Analyses of Law, Family and State: Ideology and Discourse in Child Custody Law' 10 *Canadian J Family Law* 79.

—— (1994) '(Re)Placing the State: Family, Law and Oppression' 9 *Canadian J Law and Society* 39.

—— (1996) 'Is there an Ideology of Motherhood in (Post) Modern Child Custody Law?' 5 *Social and Legal Studies* 495.

—— (2003) Child Custody, Law and Women's Work (Oxford, Oxford University Press).

—— (2006) '"Robbed of their Families"? Fathers' Rights Discourses in Canadian Parenting Law Reform Processes' in R Collier and S Sheldon (eds), *Fathers' Rights Activism and Law Reform in Comparative Perspective* (Oxford, Hart Publishing).

—— (2007) 'Gendering Legal Parenthood: Bio-genetic Ties, Intentionality and Responsibility' 25 *Windsor Yearbook of Access to Justice* 63.

—— (2011) 'Relocation, Indeterminacy and Burden of Proof: Lesson from Canada' 23 *CFLQ* 155.

BPAS (2011) 'Statistics Briefing (6): Provision, Funding and Geographical Location' *Abortion Review* (25 May 2011) www.abortionreview.org/index.php/site/article/966/ (accessed 1 August 2011).

—— (undated) 'About Bpas' *Abortion Review*, www.abortionreview.org/index.php/site/about/18/ (accessed 1 August 2011).

BRADLEY, D (1987) 'Homosexuality and Child Custody in English Law' 1 *Int J of Law and the Family* 155.

—— (1996) *Family Law and Political Culture* (London, Sweet & Maxwell).

BRADLEY, H (1997) 'Gender and Change in Employment: Feminization and its Effects' in RK Brown (ed), *The Changing Shape of Work* (Basingstoke, MacMillan).

BRADNEY, A (1994) 'Duress, Family Law and the Coherent Legal System' 57 *MLR* 473.

BRADSHAW, J and MILLAR, J (1991) *Lone Parent Families in the UK DSS Research Report No 6* (London, HMSO).

——, STIMSON, C, SKINNER, C and WILLIAMS, J (1999) *Absent Fathers?* (London, Routledge).

BRANNEN, J et al (1994) *Employment and Family Life: A Review of Research in the UK (1980–1994) Department of Employment Research Series No 41* (London, University of London).

BRAZIER, M (Chair) (2006) *Critical Care Decisions in Fetal and Neonatal Medicine: Ethical Issues* (London, Nuffield Council on Bioethics).

—— and BRIDGE, C (1996) 'Coercion or Caring: Analysing Adolescent Autonomy' 16 *Legal Studies* 84.

——, CAMPBELL, A and GOLOMBOK, S (1998) *Surrogacy: Review for Health Ministers of Current Arrangements for Payments and Regulation, Report of the Review Team*, Cmd 4068 (London, HMSO).

BREUGEL, I (1994) 'Sex and Race in the Labour Market' in M Evans (ed), *The Woman Question*, 2nd edn (London, Sage).

BRIDGE, C (1996) 'Shared Residence in England and New Zealand—A Comparative Analysis' 8 *CFLQ* 12.

—— (1997) 'Parental Powers and the Medical Treatment of Children' in C Bridge (ed), *Family Law Towards the Millennium: Essays for PM Bromley* (London, Butterworths).

—— (1999a) 'Religious Beliefs and Teenage Refusal of Medical Treatment' 62 *MLR* 585.

—— (1999b) 'Religion, Culture and Conviction—The Medical Treatment of Young Children' 11 *CFLQ* 1.

—— and SWINDELLS, H (2003) *Adoption: The Modern Law* (Bristol, Jordans).

BRIDGEMAN, J (1993) 'Old Enough to Know Best?' 13 *Legal Studies* 69.

BRIGGS, F (1995) *From Victim to Offender: How Child Sexual Abuse Victims Become Offenders* (Australia, Allen & Unwin).

BRINDLEY, B (2001) 'Black and White in Pensions' *Fam Law* 462.

BRISSENDEN, C (2010) 'Changing Residence—A Judgment of Solomon' *Family Law Week*, www.familylawweek.co.uk/site.aspx?i=ed57393 (accessed 18 November 2010)

BROPHY, J (1985) 'Child Care and the Growth of Power: The Status of Mother in Child Custody Disputes' in J Brophy and C Smart (eds), *Women in Law: Explorations in Law, Family and Sexuality* (London, Routledge and Kegan Paul).

—— (1989) 'Custody Law, Child Care, and Inequality in Britain' in C Smart and S Sevenhuijsen (eds), *Child Custody and the Politics of Gender* (London, Routledge).

—— (2003) 'Diversity and Child Protection' *Fam Law* 674.

—— (2006) *Research Review: Child Care Proceedings under the Children Act 1989 DCA Research Series 5/06* (London, Department of Constitutional Affairs).

BROWN, S (2010) 'Marriage and Child Well-being: Research and Policy Perspectives' 72 *J Marriage and the Family* 1059.

BROWNE, A (1987) *When Battered Women Kill* (New York, The Free Press).

BRUCH, C (1988) 'And How Are the Children? The Effects of Ideology and Mediation on Child Custody Law and Children's Well-Being in the United States' 2 *Int J of Law and the Family* 106.

BRUSH, LD (1993) 'Violent Acts and Injurious Outcomes in Married Couples: Methodological Issues in the National Survey of Families and Households' in P Bart and E Moran (eds), *Violence Against Women: The Bloody Footprints* (London, Sage).

BRYAN, P (1992) 'Killing Us Softly: Divorce Mediation and the Politics of Power' 40 *Buffalo Law Review* 441.

BUCHANAN, A, HUNT, J, BRETHERTON, H and BREAM, V (2001) *Families in Conflict: Perspectives of Children and Parents on the Family Court Welfare Service* (Bristol, Policy).

BUDGEON, S and ROSENEIL, S (2004) 'Editors' Introduction: Beyond the Conventional Family' 52 *Current Sociology* 127.

BULLOCK, R, LITTLE, M and MILHAM, S (1993) *Going Home: The Return of Children Separated from their Families* (Aldershot, Dartmouth).

BURGHES, L (1993) *One-parent Families: Policy Options for the 1990s* (York, Joseph Rowntree Foundation).

BURGOYNE, C (2004) 'Heart-strings and Purse-strings: Money in Heterosexual Marriage' 14 *Feminism and Psychology* 165.

—— and MILLAR, J (1994) 'Enforcing Child Support Obligations: The Attitudes of Separated Fathers' 22 *Policy and Politics* 95.

BURGOYNE, J, ORMROD, R and RICHARDS, M (1987) *Divorce Matters* (Harmondsworth, Penguin).

BURNS, M, BOURGOYNE, C and CLARKE, V (2008) 'Financial Affairs? Money Management in Same-sex Relationships' 37 *Journal of Socio-Economics* 481.

BURTON, M (2003) 'Third Party Applications for Protection Orders in England and Wales: Service Providers' Views on Implementing Section 60 of the Family Law Act 1996' 25 *JSWFL* 137.

—— (2006) 'Judicial Monitoring of Compliance: Introducing "Problem Solving" Approaches to Domestic Violence Courts in England and Wales' 20 *Int J of Law, Policy and the Family* 366.

—— (2008a) *Legal Responses to Domestic Violence* (London, Routledge-Cavendish).

—— (2008b) *Domestic Abuse. Literature Review* (Leicester, University of Leicester) www.legalservices.gov.uk/docs/fains_and_mediation/DomesticAbuseLiteratureReview.pdf (accessed 24 January 2011).

—— (2008c) '*R (Rabess) v Commissioner of the Police for the Metropolis*—"Scream Quietly or the Neighbours Will Hear": Domestic Violence, "Nuisance Neighbours' and the Public/Private Dichotomy Revisited" *CFLQ* 95.

—— (2009) 'Civil Law Remedies for Domestic Violence: Why Are Applications for Non-Molestation Orders Declining?' 31 *JSWFL* 109.

BURTON, S and KITZINGER, J with KELLY, L and REGAN, L (1998) *Young People's Attitudes Towards Violence, Sex and Relationships: A Survey and Focus Group Study* (Edinburgh, Zero Tolerance Charitable Trust).

BUTLER, B (1989) 'Adopting an Indigenous Approach' 13 *Adoption and Fostering* 27.

BUTLER-SLOSS, E (1988) *Report of the Inquiry into Child Abuse in Cleveland 1987*, Cmd 412 (London, HMSO).

BUTLER-SLOSS, BARONESS E (2010) 'A Child's Place in the Big Society' *Fam Law* 938.

—— and FIDDY, A (2001) 'The ChildRIGHT Interview' December *Childright* 14.

CABINET OFFICE AND HOME OFFICE (1999) *Living Without Fear: An Integrated Approach to Tackling Violence against Women* (London, Cabinet Office).

CAFCASS (undated) *Guidance to Cafcass Practitioners on their Roles in Supporting the Courts in their Use of the Section 11A Provisions, Children Act 1989 (as inserted by the Children and Adoption Act 2006)* www.flba.co.uk/__data/assets/pdf_file/0003/60627/Presidents_Guidance_-_New_Provisions_ introduced_by_Part_1_Children_and_Adoption_Act_2006.pdf (accessed 28 July 2011).

CAIRNS, J (ed) (1965) *The Nineteenth Century 1815–1914* (New York, Free Press).

CAMPBELL, JC (1992) '"If I Can't Have You, No One Can": Power and Control in Homicide of Female Partners' in J Radford and DEH Russell (eds), *Femicide: The Politics of Woman Killing* (Buckingham, Open University Press).

CAMPBELL-BARR, V and GARNHAM, A (2010) *Childcare: A Review of What Parents Want* (Manchester, EHRC)

CAMPION, MJ (1995) *Who's Fit to Be a Parent?* (London, Routledge).

CANAAN, C (1992) *Changing Families, Changing Welfare* (Hemel Hempstead, Harvester Wheatsheaf).

CANTILLON, S and NOLAN, B (1998) 'Are Married Women More Deprived than their Husbands?' 27 *J of Social Policy* 151.

CANTWELL, B (2010) 'The Emotional Safeguarding of Children in Private Practice' *Fam Law* 84.

—— and NUNNERLY, M (1996) 'A New Spotlight on Family Mediation' *Fam Law* 177.

—— and SCOTT, S (1995) 'Children's Wishes, Children's Burdens' 17 *JSWFL* 337.

CARBONE, J (1996) 'Feminism, Gender and the Consequences of Divorce' in M Freeman (ed), *Divorce: Where Next?* (Aldershot, Dartmouth).

CARLING, A (2002) 'Family Policy, Social Theory and the State' in A Carling, S Duncan and R Edwards (eds), *Analysing Families: Morality and Rationality in Policy and Practice* (London, Routledge).

CASC (Children Act Sub-Committee of the Advisory Board on Family Law) (1999) *Consultation Paper on Contact Between Children and Violent Parents* (London, The Stationery Office).

—— (2000) *A Report to the Lord Chancellor on the Question of Parental Contact in Cases where there is Domestic Violence* (London, The Stationery Office).

—— (2001a) *Guidelines for Good Practice on Parental Contact in Cases where there is Domestic Violence. Section 5 of Report of Children Act Sub-committee to Lord Chancellor on the Question of Parental Contact in Cases where there is Domestic Violence* (London, Lord Chancellor's Department).

—— (2001b) *Making Contact Work. A Report to the Lord Chancellor on the Facilitation of Arrangements for Contact Between Children and their Non-residential Parents and the Enforcement of Court Orders for Contact* (London, Lord Chancellor's Department).

—— (2002) *Guidelines for Good Practice on Parental Contact in Cases where there is Domestic Violence* (London, Department of Constitutional Affairs).

CAWSON, P, BROOKER, S and KELLY, G (2000) *Child Maltreatment in the United Kingdom: A Study of the Prevalence of Abuse and Neglect: Executive Summary* (London, NSPCC).

CENTRE FOR SOCIAL JUSTICE (2010) 'Green Paper on the Family' (London, Centre for Social Justice)

—— (2011) 'History and the Family: Setting the Record Straight. A Rebuttal to the British Academy Pamphlet *Happy Families?*' (London, Centre for Social Justice).

CHARLES, N (1994) 'The Housing Needs of Women and Children Escaping Domestic Violence' 23 *J of Social Policy* 465.

CHESNEY-LIND, M (2002) 'Criminalizing Victimization: The Unintended Consequences of Pro-arrest Policies for Girls and Women' 1 *Criminology & Public Policy* 81.

Chisholm, R (2009) *Family Courts Violence Review* (Australian Government).

CHODOROW, N (1978) *The Reproduction of Mothering: Psychoanalysis and the Sociology of Gender* (Berkeley, CA, University of California).

CHOUDHRY, S (2003) 'The Adoption and Children Act 2002, The Welfare Principle and the Human Rights Act 1998—A Missed Opportunity?' 15 *CFLQ* 119.

—— and HERRING, J (2010) *European Human Rights and Family Law* (Oxford, Hart Publishing).

CLARK, A (1992) 'Humanity or Justice? Wife Beating and the Law in the Eighteenth and Nineteenth Centuries' in C Smart (ed), *Regulating Womanhood: Historical Essays on Marriage, Motherhood and Sexuality* (London, Routledge).

CLARKE, K, GLENDINNING, C and CRAIG, G (1994), 'Child Support, Parental Responsibility and the Law: An Examination of the Implications of Recent British Legislation' in J Brannen and M O'Brien (eds), *Childhood and Parenthood* (London, University of London Institute of Education).

——, CRAIG, G and GLENDINNING, C (1995), 'Money Isn't Everything. Fiscal Policy and Family Policy in the Child Support Act' 29 *Social Policy and Administration* 26.

——, —— and —— (1996) *Small Change: The Impact of the Child Support Act on Lone Mothers and Children* (London, Family Policy Studies Centre).

CLARKE, L (1989) 'Abortion: A Rights Issue?' in D Morgan and WR Lee (eds), *Birthrights: Law and Ethics at the Beginning of Life* (London, Routledge).

CLARKSON, C and KEATING, H (1994) *Criminal Law: Text and Materials*, 3rd edn (London, Sweet & Maxwell).

CLIVE, E (1980) 'Marriage: An Unnecessary Legal Concept?' in J Eekelaar and S Katz (eds), *Marriage and Cohabitation in Contemporary Societies* (Toronto, Butterworths).

CLYDE, J (1992) *The Report of the Inquiry into the Removal of Children from Orkney in February 1991* (Edinburgh, HMSO).

COBBE, FP (1878) 'Wife Torture in England' 32 *Contemporary Review* 55.

COCKETT, M and TRIPP, J (1994, 1996) *The Exeter Family Study: Family Breakdown and its Impact on Children* (Exeter, University of Exeter Press).

COLERIDGE, MR JUSTICE (2010) 'Let's Hear It for the Child; Restoring the Authority of the Family Court, Blue skies and Sacred Cows', speech given at Association of Lawyers for Children, 21st Annual Conference, www.alc.org.uk/uploads/KEYNOTE_20102.pdf (accessed 27 July 2011).

COLERIDGE et al (1996) 'FDR—The Pilot Scheme' *Fam Law* 746.

COLLEGE OF MEDIATORS (1999) *Domestic Abuse Screening Policy*, www.collegeofmediators.co.uk/index. php?option=com_rokdownloads&view=file&Itemid=18&id=11:college-of-mediators-domestic-abuse-screening-policy (accessed 28 July 2011).

Small Change: The Impact of the Child Support Act on Lone Mothers and Children (2008) *Code of Practice* www.collegeofmediators.co.uk/index.php?option=com_rokdownloads&view=file&Itemid=18&id=5:code-of-practice (accessed 28 July 2011).

COLLIER, J, ROSALDO, M and YANAGISAKO, S (1982) 'Is There a Family? New Anthropological Views' in M Thorne and M Yalom (eds), *Rethinking the Family: Some Feminist Questions* (London, Longman).

COLLIER, R (1994) 'The Campaign Against the Child Support Act, "Errant Fathers" and "Family Men"' *Fam Law* 384.

—— (1995a) '"Waiting Till Father Gets Home": The Reconstruction of Fatherhood in Family Law' 4 *Social and Legal Studies* 5.

—— (1995b) *Masculinity, Law and the Family* (London, Routledge).

—— (1999) 'The Dashing of a "Liberal Dream"?—The Information Meeting, the "New Family" and the Limits of Law' 11 *CFLQ* 257.

—— (2001) 'A Hard Time to Be a Father? Reassessing the Relationship between Law, Policy and Family (Practices)' 28 *J Law and Society* 520.

—— (2005) 'Fathers 4 Justice, Law and the New Politics of Fatherhood' 17 *CFLQ* 511.

—— (2006) ' "The Outlaw Fathers Fight Back": Fathers' Rights Groups, Fathers 4 Justice and the Politics of Family Law Reform—Reflections on the UK Experience' in R Collier and S Sheldon (eds), *Fathers' Rights Activism and Law Reform in Comparative Perspective* (Oxford, Hart Publishing).

—— (2010) *Men, Law and Gender, Essays on the 'Man' of Law* (London, Routledge).

—— and SHELDON, S (2006) 'Father's Rights, Fatherhood and Law Reform - International Perspectives' in R Collier and S Sheldon (eds), *Fathers' Rights Activism and Law Reform in Comparative Perspective* (Oxford, Hart Publishing)

—— and —— (2008) *Fragmenting Fatherhood. A Socio-Legal Study* (Oxford, Hart Publishing).

COMMISSION FOR RACIAL EQUALITY (1994), *Annual Report*.

—— (2005) Statistics Labour Market, www.cre.gov.uk/duty/reia/statistics_labour.html.

CONWAY, HL (1996) 'Presumption of Legitimacy and Blood Tests' *Fam Law* 228.

—— (1997) 'The Future for Judicial Separation' *Fam Law* 48.

COOK, D et al (2004) *Evaluation of Specialist Domestic Violence Courts/Fast Track Systems* (London, Crown Prosecution Service and Department of Constitutional Affairs).

COOK, R, DAY SCLATER, S and KAGANAS, F (2003a) 'Introduction' in R Cook, S Day Sclater and F Kaganas (eds), *Surrogate Motherhood: International Perspectives* (Oxford, Hart Publications).

——, —— and —— (eds) (2003b) *Surrogate Motherhood: International Perspectives* (Oxford, Hart Publications).

COOKE, E (2007) '*Miller/McFarlane*: Law in Search of Discrimination' 19 *CFLQ* 98.

COOPER, A, HETHERINGTON, R and KATZ, I (2003) *The Risk Factor: Making the Child Protection System Work for Children* (London, Demos).

COOPER, D (1998) 'More Law and More Rights: Will Children Benefit?' 3 *Child and Family Social Work* 77.

—— and HERMAN, D (1991) 'Getting "The Family Right": Legislating Heterosexuality in Britain, 1986–1991' 10 *Canadian J of Family Law* 41.

CORNISH, W and CLARK, G (1989) *Law and Society in England 1750–1950* (London, Sweet & Maxwell).

COSSMAN, B (1990) 'A Matter of Difference: Domestic Contracts and Gender Equality' 28 *Osgoode Hall Law Journal* 303.

—— and RYDER, B (2001) 'What is Marriage-like Like? The Irrelevance of Conjugality' 18 *Canadian J of Family Law* 269.

COX, C (1990) 'Anything Else Is not Feminism: Racial Difference and the WMWM' 1 *Law and Critique* 237.

COX, EW (1984) *The Principles of Punishment, as Applied in the Administration of Criminal Law, by Judges and Magistrates* (New York, Garland).

COX, R (1996) *Shaping Childhood: Themes of Uncertainty in the History of Adult–Child Relationships* (London, Routledge).

CRAIG, J (2007) '*Everybody's Business'—How Applications for Contact Orders by Consent Should be Approached by the Court in Cases Involving Domestic Violence. The Family Justice Council's Report and Recommendations to the President of the Family Division* (Family Justice Council), www.family-justice-council.org.uk/docs/contactsummary.pdf (accessed 18 November 2010).

CRIMINAL JUSTICE SYSTEM (2005) *The Code of Practice for Victims of Crime.*

CREIGHTON, S (2003) *Child Protection Statistics 3: Child Protection Outside the Home* (London, NSPCC).

—— (2004) 'Prevalence and Incidence of Child Abuse: International Comparisons', NSPCC Information Briefings.

—— and TISSIER, G (2003) 'Child Killings in England and Wales', NSPCC Information Briefings.

CRETNEY, A and DAVIS, G (1995) *Punishing Violence* (London, Routledge).

—— and —— (1996) 'Prosecuting Domestic Assault' *Crim L Rev* 162.

—— and —— (1997a) 'Prosecuting Domestic Assault: Victims Failing Courts, or Courts Failing Victims?' 36 *Howard Journal* 146.

—— and —— (1997b) 'The Significance of Compellability in the Prosecution of Domestic Assault' 37 *Brit J Criminology* 75.

CRETNEY, S (1989) 'Privatizing the Family: The Reform of Child Law' *Denning Law Journal* 15.

—— (1990) 'Divorce and the Low Income Family' *Fam Law* 377.

—— (1995a) '"Tell Me the Old, Old Story"—The Denning Report, 50 Years On' 7 *CFLQ* 163.

—— (1995b) 'The Divorce White Paper—Some Reflections' *Fam Law* 302.

—— (1996a) '"What Will the Women Want Next?" The Struggle for Power Within the Family 1925–1975' 12 *LQR* 110.

—— (1996b) 'Divorce Reform in England: Humbug and Hypocrisy or a Smooth Transition' in M Freeman (ed), *Divorce: Where Next?* (Aldershot, Dartmouth).

—— (2003a) *Family Law in the Twentieth Century: A History* (Oxford, Oxford University Press).

—— (2003b) 'The Family and the Law—Status or Contract?' 15 *CFLQ* 403.

—— (2003c) 'Community of Property Imposed by Judicial Decision' 119 *LQR* 349.

CROMPTON, L (2004) 'The Civil Partnerships Bill 2004: The Illusion of Equality' *Fam Law* 888.

CROSS, L (2005) 'New Year's Resolution for the SFLA' *Fam Law* 167.

CROW, G and MARSH, P (1997) *Family Group Conferences, Partnership and Child Welfare: A Research Report on Four Pilot Projects in England and Wales* (Sheffield, University of Sheffield Partnership Research Programme).

CROWN PROSECUTION SERVICE (CPS) (2009) *CPS Policy for Prosecuting Cases of Domestic Violence.*

—— (2010) *Violence Against Women Crime Report 2009–2010*.

CUNNINGHAM, H (1995) *Children and Childhood in Western Society Since 1500* (London, Longman).

CYPU (2001) *Learning to Listen: Core Principles for the Involvement of Children and Young People* (London).

DAILY TELEGRAPH (2007) 'Call for Divorce Review After Record Payout' 25 May 2007.

DALY, C (1997) 'Too Little Too Late' 135 *Childright* 14.

DALY, M (1994) 'A Matter of Dependency: Gender in British Income Maintenance Provision' 28 *Sociology* 779.

—— and SCHEIWE, K (2010) 'Individualisation and Personal Obligations—Social Policy, Family Policy, and Law Reform in Germany and the UK' 24 *Int J of Law, Policy and the Family* 177.

DAVIDOFF, L, DOOLITTLE, M, FINK, J and HOLDEN, K (1998) *The Family Story: Blood, Contract and Intimacy, 1830–1960* (London, Longman).

DAVIES, C (1993) 'Divorce Reform in England and Wales: A Visitor's View' *Fam Law* 331.

DAVIES, J (ed) (1993) *The Family: Is it Just Another Lifestyle Choice?* (London, IEA Health and Welfare Unit).

DAVIS, G (2000) 'Introduction' in G Davis, G Bevan, S Clisby, Z Cumming, R Dingwall, P Fenn, S Finch, R Fitzgerald, S Goldie, D Greatbatch, A James and J Pearce, *Monitoring Publicly Funded Family Mediation: Report to the Legal Services Commission* (London, Legal Services Commission).

DAVIS, G and ROBERTS, M (1988) *Access to Agreement* (Milton Keynes, Open University Press).

—— and —— (1989) 'Mediation and the Battle of the Sexes' *Fam Law* 305.

—— and PEARCE, J (1999) 'The Welfare Principle in Action' *Fam Law* 237.

——, CRETNEY, S and COLLINS, J (1994) *Simple Quarrels: Negotiating Money and Property Disputes on Divorce* (Oxford, Clarendon Press).

——, PEARCE, J, BIRD, R, WOODWARD, H and WALLACE, C (2000a) Ancillary Relief Outcomes' 12 *CFLQ* 43.

——, BEVAN, G, CLISBY, S, CUMMING, Z, DINGWALL, R, FENN, P, FINCH, S, FITZGERALD, R, GOLDIE, S, GREATBATCH, D, JAMES, A and PEARCE, J (2000b) *Monitoring Publicly Funded Family Mediation: Report to the Legal Services Commission* (London, Legal Services Commission).

——, FITZGERALD, R and FINCH, S (2000c) 'Monthly Monitoring' in G Davis et al, *Monitoring Publicly Funded Family Mediation: Report to the Legal Services Commission* (London, Legal Services Commission).

——, —— and —— (2000d) 'Mediation Case Profiles' in G Davis et al, *Monitoring Publicly Funded Family Mediation: Report to the Legal Services Commission* (London, Legal Services Commission).

——, FITZGERALD, R, FINCH, S and BEVAN, G (2000e) 'The Panel' in G Davis et al, *Monitoring Publicly Funded family Mediation. Report to the Legal Services Commission* (London, Legal Services Commission).

——, PEARCE, J and GOLDIE, S (2000f) 'An Analysis of Intake' in G Davis et al, *Monitoring Publicly Funded family Mediation. Report to the Legal Services Commission* (London, Legal Services Commission).

——, BEVAN, G and PEARCE, J (2001a) 'Family Mediation—Where do We Go from Here?' *Fam Law* 265.

——, FINCH, S and FITZGERALD, R (2001b) 'Mediation and Legal Services—The Client Speaks' *Fam Law* 110.

DAY SCLATER, S (1999a) 'Experiences of Divorce' in S Day Sclater and C Piper (eds), *Undercurrents of Divorce* (Aldershot, Ashgate).

—— (1999b) *Divorce: A Psychosocial Study* (Aldershot, Ashgate).

—— and PIPER, C (eds) (1999) *Undercurrents of Divorce* (Aldershot, Ashgate).

—— and —— (2000) 'Remoralising the Family?—Family Policy, Family Law and Youth Justice' 12 *CFLQ* 135.

—— and KAGANAS, F (2003) 'Contact Mothers: Welfare and Rights' in A Bainham et al (eds), *Children and Their Families: Contact, Rights and Welfare* (Oxford, Hart Publishing).

—— and RICHARDS, M (1995) 'How Adults Cope with Divorce: Strategies for Survival' *Fam Law* 143.

DE GLANVILLE, R and BEAMES J (trans) (1812) *A Treatise on the Law and Customs of the Kingdom of England* (London, Valpy).

DEAKIN, S and MORRIS, G (1998) *Labour Law*, 2nd edn (London, Butterworths).

DECALMER, P and GLENDENNING, F (eds) (1993) *The Mistreatment of Elderly People* (London, Sage).

DEECH, R (1977) 'The Principles of Maintenance' 7 *Fam Law* 229.

—— (1992) 'The Unmarried Father and Human Rights' 4 *J of Child Law* 3.

—— (1994) 'Comment: Not Just Marriage Breakdown' *Fam Law* 121.

—— (1996) 'Property and Money Matters' in M Freeman (ed), *Divorce: Where Next?* (Aldershot, Dartmouth).

DEECH, BARONESS R (2009a) 'Divorce—A Disaster?' *Fam Law* 1048.

—— (2009b) 'What's a Woman Worth? *Fam Law* 1140.

—— (2010) 'Cohabitation' *Fam Law* 39.

DENNIS, N and ERDOS, G (1993) *Families Without Fatherhood* (London, IEA Health and Welfare Unit).

DEPARTMENT FOR CHILDREN, SCHOOLS AND FAMILIES AND DEPARTMENT OF WORK AND PENSIONS (2008) *Joint Birth Registration: Recording Responsibility*, Cm 7293 (London, HMSO).

DEPARTMENT FOR CHILDREN, SCHOOLS AND FAMILIES (2005) *Replacement Children Act 1989 Guidance on Private Fostering* (London, The Stationery Office).

—— (2007) *A Study into the Views of Parents into the Physical Punishment of Children* (London, The Stationery Office).

—— (2008) *The Children Act 1989. Guidance and Regulations Volume 1. Court Orders* (London, The Stationery Office)

—— (2009a) *Consultation. The Registration of Births (Parents not Married and not Acting Together) Regulations 2010* (London, HMSO).

—— (2009b) *The Children's Plan Two Years on: A Progress Report* (London, The Stationery Office).

—— (2010) *Working Together to Safeguard Children. A Guide to Inter-Agency Working to Safeguard and Promote the Welfare of Children* (London, The Stationery Office).

—— (undated) 'Government Response to the Consultation on the Proposals for the New Subsidy Arrangements to Support Individuals Taking Part in Contact activities Directed or so Ordered by the Courts', www.dcsf.gov.uk/.../Contact%20Activity%20Summary%20of%20Responses%20Final.doc *(accessed 10 May 2010).*

DEPARTMENT FOR COMMUNITIES AND LOCAL GOVERNMENT (DfCLG) (2006) *Homelessness Code of Guidance for Local Authorities*, www.communities.gov.uk/documents/housing/pdf/152056.pdf (accessed 1 March 2011)

—— (2010) *Local Decisions: A Fairer Future for Social Housing. Consultation* (London, DfCLG Publications).

—— (2011) *Local Decisions: Next Steps Towards a Fairer Future for Social Housing. Summary of Responses to Consultation* (London, DfCLG Publications)

DEPARTMENT OF CONSTITUTIONAL AFFAIRS (2003) *Judicial Statistics* (London, The Stationery Office).

—— (2006) *Judicial Statistics (Revised) England and Wales for the Year 2005*, Cm 6903 (London, The Stationery Office).

——, DfES and DTI (2004) *Parental Separation: Children's Needs and Parents' Responsibilities*, Cm 6273 (London, The Stationery Office).

——, DfES and DTI (2005) *Parental Separation: Children's Needs and Parents' Responsibilities: Next Steps, Report of the Responses to Consultation and Agenda for Action*, Cm 6452 (London, The Stationery Office).

DEPARTMENT FOR EDUCATION (2010a) Consultation Results, www.education.gov.uk/consultations/index.cfm?action=conResults&consultationId=1666&external=no&menu=3 (accessed 21 March 2011).

—— (2010b) *Family and Friends Care: Statutory Guidance for Local Authorities* (London, The Stationery Office).

—— (2010c) *The Children Act 1989. Guidance and Regulations Volume II. Care Planning, Placement and Case Review* (London, The Stationery Office).

—— (2011a) *Adoption Statutory Guidance* (London, The Stationery Office).

—— (2011b) *Adoption National Minimum Standards* (London, The Stationery Office).

—— (2011c) *Adoption and Special Guardianship England DataPack* (London, The Stationery Office).

—— (2011d) *Fostering Services National Minimum Standards* (London, The Stationery Office).

—— (2011e) *The Children Act 1989 Guidance and Regulations Volume 4: Fostering Services* (London, The Stationery Office).

—— (2011f) *The Munro Review of Child Protection: Final Report. A Child-Centred System.* Cm 8062 (London, The Stationery Office).

DEPARTMENT FOR EDUCATION AND SKILLS (2003) *Every Child Matters*, Cm 5860 (London, The Stationery Office).

—— (2004) Local Authority Circular LAC (2004) 27.

—— (2004a) *Every Child Matters: Next Steps* (London, The Stationery Office).

—— (2004b) *Statistics of Education: Referrals, Assessments and Children and Young People on Child Protection Registers: Year Ending 31 March 2004* (London, The Stationery Office).

—— (2004c) *Every Child Matters: Change for Children* (London, The Stationery Office).

—— (2004d) *The Children Act Report 2003* (Nottingham, DfES).

—— (2007) *Care Matters: Time for Change*, Cm 7137 (London, HMSO).

——, DOH and HOME OFFICE (2003) *Keeping Children Safe: The Government's Response to the Victoria Climbie Inquiry Report and Joint Chief Inspectors' Report Safeguarding Children*, Cmd 5861 (London, The Stationery Office).

DEPARTMENT OF THE ENVIRONMENT (1993) *Housing Consequences of Relationship Breakdown* (London, HMSO).

DEPARTMENT OF THE ENVIRONMENT, TRANSPORT AND THE REGIONS AND DEPARTMENT OF SOCIAL SECURITY (2000) *Quality and Choice: A Decent Home for All: The Housing Green Paper* (London, DETR and DSS).

DEPARTMENT OF HEALTH (1989) *An Introduction to the Children Act 1989* (London, HMSO).

—— (1991) *Child Abuse: A Study of Inquiry Reports 1980–1989* (London, HMSO).

—— (1995a) *The Challenge of Partnership in Child Protection: Practice Guide* (London, HMSO).

—— (1995b) *Child Protection—Messages from Research* (London, HMSO).

—— (1996) *Allocation of Housing Accommodation: Homelessness: Code of Guidance on Parts VI and VII of the Housing Act 1996* (London, HMSO).

—— (1998) *Working Together to Safeguard Children: New Government Proposals for Inter-Agency Co-operation: Consultation Paper* (London, The Stationery Office).

—— (2000) *Framework for the Assessment of Children in Need and their Families* (London, The Stationery Office).

—— (2002) *Protecting the Public*, Cmd 5668 (London, The Stationery Office).

—— (2008) *Code of Practice: Mental Health Act 1983* (London, The Stationery Office).

—— (2009) *Reference Guide to Consent for Examination or Treatment* (London, The Stationery Office).

——, HOME OFFICE and WELSH ASSEMBLY GOVERNMENT (2003) *Adoption: National Minimum Standards* (London, The Stationery Office).

—— and WELSH OFFICE (1992) *Review of Adoption Law: Report to Ministers of an Interdepartmental Working Group* (London, HMSO).

—— and WELSH OFFICE (1996) *Adoption—A Service for Children: Adoption Bill, A Consultative Document* (London, Department of Health).

—— and WELSH OFFICE, HOME OFFICE, LORD CHANCELLOR'S DEPARTMENT (White Paper) (1993) *Adoption: The Future*, Cmd 2288 (London, HMSO).

DEPARTMENT OF HEALTH AND SOCIAL SECURITY (1985) *Review of Child Care Law: Report of Ministers of an Inter-departmental Working Party* (London, HMSO).

—— (1987) *The Law on Child Care and Family Services*, Cmd 62 (London HMSO).

DEPARTMENT OF SOCIAL SECURITY (1997) *Statistics 1997* (London, The Stationery Office).

—— (1998) *Children First: A New Approach to Child Support*, Cmd 3992 (London, The Stationery Office).

—— (1999) *A New Contract for Welfare: Children's Rights and Parents' Responsibilities* (London, The Stationery Office).

DEPARTMENT OF TRADE AND INDUSTRY (1998) *Fairness at Work*, Cmd 3968 (London, The Stationery Office).

—— (WOMEN AND EQUALITY UNIT) (2003a), *Civil Partnership: A Framework for the legal recognition of same-sex couples* (London, DTI Home Office).

—— (2003b) *Responses to Civil Partnership* (London, The Stationery Office).

—— (2005) *Work and Families, Choice and Flexibility: A Consultation Document* (London, The Stationery Office).

DEPARTMENT OF WORK AND PENSIONS (2007) *Joint Birth Registration: Promoting Parental Responsibility*, Cm 7160 (London, HMSO).

—— (2006) *The Gender Impact of Pension Reform*, www.dwp.gov.uk/docs/genderimpactassessment. pdf (accessed 29 July 2011).

—— (2009) *State Pension Reform. Equality Impact Assessment*, www.dwp.gov.uk/docs/ia-state-pension-reform-09.pdf (accessed 29 July 2011).

—— (2010a) *21st Century Welfare*, Cm 7913 (London, The Stationery Office).

—— (2010b) *Universal Credit: Welfare that Works*, Cm 7957 (London, The Stationery Office).

—— (2011a) *Strengthening Families, Promoting Parental Responsibility: The Future of Child Maintenance*, Cm 7990 (London, The Stationery Office).

—— (2011b) *Government's Response to the Consultation on Strengthening Families, Promoting Parental Responsibility: The Future of Child Maintenance*, Cm 8130 (London, The Stationery Office).

—— INFORMATION DIRECTORATE (2010) *Households Below Average Income 1004/95–2008/09.*

—— and DFE (2011) *A New Approach to Child Poverty: Tackling the Causes of Disadvantage and Transforming Families' Lives*, Cm 8061 (London, The Stationery Office).

DERMOTT, E (2006) 'What's Parenthood Got To Do With It? Men's Hours of Paid Work' 57 *British Journal of Sociology* 619.

DEWAR, J (1989) 'Fathers in Law? The Case of AID and Fatherhood' in D Morgan and WR Lee (eds), *Birthrights: Law and Ethics at the Beginning of Life* (London, Routledge).

—— (1995) 'Local Authorities, Ouster Orders and the Inherent Jurisdiction—*Re S (Minors) (Inherent Jurisdiction Ouster)*' 7 *J of Child Law* 64.

—— (1998) 'The Normal Chaos of Family Law' 61 *MLR* 467.

—— (2000) 'Family Law and its Discontents' 14 *Int J of Law, Policy and the Family* 59.

DICKENS, B (1987) 'Legal Aspects of Surrogate Motherhood: Practices and Proposals', Paper presented at the UK National Committee of Comparative Law 1987 Colloquium 'Legal Regulation of Reproductive Medicine', Cambridge, 15–17 September.

DICKENS, J (1993) 'Assessment and Control of Social Work: An Analysis of Reasons for Non-use of the Child Assessment Order' *JSWFL* 88.

DICKSON, DT (1968) 'Bureaucracy and Morality: An Organizational Perspective on a Moral Crusade' 16 *Social Problems* 143.

DIDUCK, A (1990) '*Carnigan v Carnigan*: When Is a Father Not a Father?' *Man Law Journal* 580.

—— (1993) 'Legislating Ideologies of Motherhood' 2 *Social and Legal Studies* 461.

—— (1995) 'The Unmodified Family: The Child Support Act and the construction of Legal Subjects' 22 *J Law and Society* 527.

—— (1997) 'In Search of the Feminist Good Mother' 7 *Social and Legal Studies* 129.

—— (1998) 'Conceiving the Bad Mother: "The Focus Should Be on the Child to be Born"' 32 *University of British Columbia Law Review* 1999.

—— (1999a) 'Justice and Childhood: Reflections on Refashioned Boundaries' in M King (ed), *Moral Agendas for Children's Welfare* (London, Routledge).

—— (1999b) 'Dividing the Family Assets' in S Day Sclater and C Piper (eds), *Undercurrents of Divorce* (Aldershot, Ashgate).

—— (2001a) 'A Family by Any other Name … or Starbucks Comes to England' 28 *J Law and Society* 290.

—— (2001b) 'Fairness and Justice for All? The House of Lords in *White v White*' 9 *Feminist Legal Studies* 173.

—— (2003) *Law's Families* (Cambridge, Cambridge University Press).

—— (2005a) 'Shifting Familiarity' 58 *Current Legal Problems 235.*

—— (2005b) 'There's No Place Like Home', unpublished paper presented to LSA Annual Meeting, Chicago, USA.

—— (2007) '"If Only We Can Find the Appropriate Terms to Use the Issue Will be Solved": Law, Identity and Parenthood' 19 *CFLQ* 458.

—— (2008a) 'Family Law and Family Responsibility' in J Bridgeman, H Keating and C Lind (eds), *Responsibility, Law and the Family* (Dartmouth, Ashgate).

—— (ed) (2008b) *Marriage and Cohabitation: Regulating Intimacy, Affection and Care* (Dartmouth, Ashgate).

—— (2009a) 'Public Norms and Private Lives: Rights, Fairness and Family Law' in J Wallbank, S Choudhry and J Herring (eds), *Rights, Gender and Family Law* (London, Routledge-Cavendish).

—— (2009b) 'Relationship Fairness' in A Bottomley and S Wong (eds), *Changing Contours of Domestic Life, Family and Law. Caring and Sharing* (Oxford, Hart Publishing).

—— (2010) 'Commentary on *Royal Bank of Scotland plc v Etridge* (No 2)' in R Hunter, C McGlynn and E Rackley (eds), *Feminist Judgments From Theory to Practice* (Oxford, Hart Publishing).

—— (2011) 'Ancillary Relief: Complicating the Search for Principle' 38 *J Law and Society* 272.

—— and O'DONOVAN K (2006) 'Introduction' in A Diduck and K O'Donovan (eds), *Feminist Perspectives on Family Law* (Abingdon, Routledge-Cavendish).

—— and ORTON, H (1994) 'Equality and Support for Spouses' 57 *MLR* 681.

DINGWALL, R (2010) 'Divorce Mediation: Should We Change Our Mind?' 32 *JSWFL* 107.

—— and EEKELAAR, J (1988) 'Families and the State: An Historical Perspective on the Public Regulation of Private Conduct' 10 *Law and Policy* 341.

—— and GREATBACH, D, (2000) 'The Mediation Process' in G Davis, *et al*, *Monitoring Publicly Funded Family Mediation: Report to the Legal Services Commission* (London, Legal Services Commission).

—— and —— (2001) 'Family Mediators—What Are They Doing?' *Fam Law* 378.

——, EEKELAAR, J and MURRAY, T (1983) *The Protection of Children: State Intervention and Family Life* (Oxford, Blackwell).

DNES, AW (1997) *The Division of Marital Assets Following Divorce with Particular Reference to Pensions*, LCD Research Series No 7/97 (London, Lord Chancellor's Department).

DOBASH, RE (2003) 'Domestic Violence: Arrest, Prosecution and Reducing Violence' 2 *Criminology & Public Policy* 313.

—— and DOBASH, RP (1979) *Violence Against Wives* (New York, Free Press).

—— and —— (1992) *Women, Violence and Social Change* (London, Routledge).

—— and —— (1998) 'Violent Men and Violent Contexts' in RE Dobash and RP Dobash (eds), *Rethinking Violence Against Women* (London, Sage).

—— and —— (2000) 'The Politics and Policies of Responding to Violence Against Women' in J Hanmer, et al (eds), *Home Truths About Domestic Violence: Feminist Influences on Policy and Practice: A Reader* (London, Routledge).

—— and —— (2004) 'Women's Violence to Men in Intimate Relationships. Working on a Puzzle' 44 *Brit J Criminology* 324.

DOBASH, RP, DOBASH, RE, CAVANAGH, K and LEWIS, R (2000) 'Confronting Violent Men' in J Hanmer et al (eds), *Home Truths About Domestic Violence: Feminist Influences on Policy and Practice: A Reader* (London, Routledge).

DOGGETT, ME (1992) *Marriage, Wife-Beating and the Law in Victorian England* (London, Weidenfeld & Nicolson).

DONOVAN, C and HESTER, M (2011) 'Seeking Help from the Enemy: Help-seeking Strategies of those in Same-Sex Relationships who have Experienced Domestic Abuse' *CFLQ* 26.

——, HESTER, M, HOLMES, J AND McCARRY M (2006) *Comparing Domestic Abuse in Same Sex and Heterosexual Relationships* (Bristol, University of Bristol).

DONZELOT, J and HURLEY, R (trans) (1980) *The Policing of Families* (London, Hutchinson).

DOUGLAS, G (1991) *Law, Fertility and Reproduction* (London, Sweet & Maxwell).

—— (1992) 'The Retreat from *Gillick*' 55 *MLR* 569.

—— (1993) 'Assisted Reproduction and the Welfare of the Child' 46 *Current Legal Problems* 53.

—— (1994) 'The Intention to be a Parent and the Making of Mothers' 57 *MLR* 636.

—— (1996) 'Comment on *Re Q*' *Fam Law* 207.

—— (2004) *An Introduction to Family Law,* 2nd edn (Oxford, Oxford University Press).

—— and LOWE, NV (1992) 'Becoming a Parent in English Law' 108 *LQR* 414.

—— and PERRY, A (2001) 'How Parents Cope Financially on Separation and Divorce—Implications for the Future of Ancillary Relief' 13 *CFLQ* 67.

—— and SEBBA, L (1998) *Children's Rights and Traditional Values* (Aldershot, Ashgate).

——, MURCH, M, SCANLAN, L and PERRY, A (2000) 'Safeguarding Children's Welfare in Non-contentious Divorce: Towards a New Conception of the Legal Process?' 63 *MLR* 177.

——, PEARCE, J and WOODWARD, H (2009a) 'Cohabitants, Property and the Law: A Study of Injustice' 72 *MLR* 24.

——, —— and —— (2009b) 'Money, Property, Cohabitation and Separation. Patterns and Intentions' in J Miles and R Probert (eds), *Sharing Lives, Dividing Assets* (Oxford, Hart Publishing).

DOWNIE, A (1997) 'The Doctor and the Teenager—Questions of Consent' *Fam Law* 499.

—— (1999) 'Consent to Medical Treatment —Whose View of Welfare?' *Fam Law* 818.

DUNCAN, S, EDWARDS, R, REYNOLDS, T and ALLDRED, P (2003) 'Motherhood, Paid Work and Partnering: Values and Theories' 17 *Work, Employment and Society* 309.

DUNN, J (2003) 'Contact and Children's Perspectives on Parental Relationships' in A Bainham et al (eds), *Children and Their Families: Contact, Rights and Welfare* (Oxford, Hart Publishing).

DUNNE, G (1999) 'A Passion for "Sameness"? Sexuality and Gender Accountability' in EB Silva and C Smart (eds), *The 'New' Family?* (London, Sage).

—— (2000) 'Opting into Motherhood: Lesbians Blurring the Boundaries and Transforming the Meaning of Parenthood and Kinship' 14 *Gender and Society* 11.

DWORKIN, R (1995) *Life's Dominion: An Argument about Abortion and Euthanasia* (London, Harper Collins).

EAGLETON, T (1991) *Ideology: An Introduction* (London, Verso).

EAST, EH (1972) *Pleas of the Crown*, vol 1, ed PR Glazebrook (London, Professional Books).

EASTON, S (1976) 'Explaining Ideology' 2 *Sociological Analysis and Theory* 187.

EATON, M (1994) 'Abuse by Any Other Name: Feminism, Difference, and Intralesbian Violence' in MA Fine and R Myktiuk (eds), *The Public Nature of Private Violence: The Discovery of Domestic Abuse* (London, Routledge).

EDWARDS, R and DUNCAN, S (1996) 'Rational Economic Man or Lone Mothers in Context? The Uptake of Paid Work' in EB Silva (ed), *Good Enough Mothering? Feminist Perspectives on Lone Motherhood* (London, Routledge).

——, GILLIES, V and RIBBENS MCCARTHY, J (1999) 'Biological Parents and Social Families: Legal Discourses and Everyday Understandings of the Position of Step-parents' 13 *Int J of Law, Policy and the Family* 78.

EDWARDS, S (2004) 'Division of Assets and Fairness—"Brick Lane"—Gender, Culture and Ancillary Relief on Divorce' 34 *Fam Law* 809.

EDWARDS, SSM (1989) *Policing Domestic Violence* (London, Sage).

—— (1996) *Sex and Gender in the Legal Process* (London, Blackstone Press).

EEKELAAR, J (1984) '"Trust the Judges": How Far Should Family Law Go?' 47 *MLR* 593.

—— (1985) 'Custody Appeals' 48 *MLR* 704.

—— (1986) 'The Emergence of Children's Rights' 6 *OJLS* 161.

—— (1988) 'Equality and the Purpose of Maintenance' 15 *J Law and Society* 188.

—— (1991a) 'Parental Responsibility: State of Nature or Nature of the State?' *JSWFL* 37.

—— (1991b) *Regulating Divorce* (Oxford, Clarendon Press).

—— (1994a) 'The Interests of the Child and the Child's Wishes: The Role of Dynamic Self-determinism' 8 *Int J of Law and the Family* 42.

—— (1994b) 'Third Thoughts on Child Support' *Fam Law* 99.

—— (1996) 'The Family Law Bill—The Politics of Family Law' *Fam Law* 45.

—— (1998) 'Should Section 25 be Reformed?' *Fam Law* 469.

—— (1999) 'Family Law: Keeping Us "On Message"' 11 *CFLQ* 387.

—— (2000) 'Uncovering Social Obligations: Family Law and the Responsible Citizen' in M Maclean (ed), *Making Law For Families* (Oxford, Hart Publishing).

—— (2001a) 'Back to Basics and Forward into the Unknown' *Fam Law* 30.

—— (2001b) 'Asset Distribution on Divorce—The Durational Element' 117 *LQR* 552.

—— (2001c) 'Rethinking Parental Responsibility' *Fam Law* 426.

—— (2002a) 'Beyond the Welfare Principle' 14 *CFLQ* 237.

—— (2002b) 'Contact—Over the Limit' *Fam Law* 271.

—— (2003a) 'Asset Distribution on Divorce—Time and Property' 33 *Fam Law* 838.

—— (2003b) 'Contact and Adoption Reform' in A Bainham et al (eds), *Children and Their Families: Contact, Rights and Welfare* (Oxford, Hart Publishing).

—— (2005a) 'Shared Income After Divorce: A Step Too Far' 121 *LQR* 1.

—— (2005b) '*Miller v Miller*: The Descent into Chaos' *Fam Law* 870.

—— (2006) *Family Law and Personal Life* (Oxford, Oxford University Press).

—— (2007) 'Why People Marry: The Many Faces of an Institution' 41 *FLQ* 413

—— and MACLEAN, M (2004) 'Marriage and the Moral Bases of Personal Relationships' 31 *J Law and Society* 510.

——, DINGWALL, R and MURRAY, T (1982) 'Victims or Threats? Children in Care Proceedings' *JSWL* 68.

——, MACLEAN, M and BEINART, S (2000) *Family Lawyers: The Divorce Work of Solicitors* (Oxford, Hart Publishing).

EICHLER, M (1990) 'The Limits of Family Law Reform or, The Privatization of Female and Child Poverty' 7 *Canadian Family Law Quarterly* 59.

ELLIS, D and STUCKLESS, N (1996) *Mediating and Negotiating Marital Conflicts* (London and California, Sage).

ELLISON, G, BARKER, A and KULASURIYA, T (2009) *Work and Care: A Study of Modern Parents, EHRC Research Report 15* (Manchester, EHRC).

ELLISON, L (2003) 'Responding to Victim Withdrawal in Domestic Violence Prosecutions' *Crim LR* 760.

ELLISON, R (1996) 'Pensions and Divorce—The New Regulations' *Fam Law* 502.

ELLMAN, IM (1997) 'The Misguided Movement to Revive Fault Divorce and Why Reformers Should Look Instead to the American Law Institute' 11 *Int J of Law, Policy and the Family* 216.

ENGELS, F (1978) *The Origin of the Family, Private Property and the State* (Peking, Foreign Language Press).

EQUAL OPPORTUNITIES COMMISSION (1995) *The Life Cycle of Inequality: Women and Men in Britain* (Manchester, EOC).

ERIKSON, EH (1980) *Identity and the Life Cycle* (London, Norton).

EQUALITY AND HUMAN RIGHTS COMMISSION (EHRC) (2009a) *Working Better*, www.equalityhumanrights.com/advice-and-guidance/here-for-business/working-better/ (accessed 29 July 2011)

—— (2009b) *Monitoring Update on the Impact of the Recession on Various Demographic Groups*, www.equalityhumanrights.com/uploaded_files/research/impact_of_the_recession.pdf (accessed 29 July 2011) (London, Equalities Office).

—— (2010) *How Fair Is Britain?* Executive Summary, www.equalityhumanrights.com/key-projects/how-fair-is-britain/full-report-and-evidence-downloads/#How_fair_is_Britain_Equality_Human_Rights_and_Good_Relations_in_2010_The_First_Triennial_Review (accessed 29 July 2011).

EVERETT, K and YEATMAN, L (2010) 'Are Some Parents More Natural than Others?' 22 *CFLQ* 290.

FAMILY JUSTICE COUNCIL (2010) 'Guidelines for Judges Meeting Children Who Are Subject to Family Proceedings' *Fam Law* 654.

FARAGHER, T (1985) 'The Police Response to Violence against Women in the Home' in J Pahl (ed), *Private Violence and Public Policy: The Needs of Battered Women and the Response of the Public Services* (London, Routledge and Kegan Paul).

FAWCETT SOCIETY, THE (2011) Single Mothers: Singled Out. The Impact of 2010–15 Tax and Benefit Changes on Women and Men (London, The Fawcett Society).

FEIJTEN, P, BOYLE, P, GRAHAM, E and GAYLE, V (2011) *Differences in Mental Health between Adults in Stepfamilies and 'First Families'* (ESRC Centre for Population Change, London, ESRC).

FERGUSON, L (2008) 'Family, Social Inequalities and the Persuasive Force of Interpersonal Obligation' 22 *Int J of Law, Policy and the Family* 61.

FERRI, E and SMITH, K (1996) *Parenting in the 1990s* (London, Family Policy Studies Centre).

FINEMAN, MA (1989) 'The Politics of Custody and the Transformation of American Custody Decision Making' 22 *University of California, Davis* 829.

—— (1991) *The Illusion of Equality: The Rhetoric and Reality of Divorce Reform* (Chicago, IL, University of Chicago Press).

—— (1995) *The Neutered Mother, the Sexual Family and Other Twentieth Century Tragedies* (London, Routledge).

—— (2004) *The Autonomy Myth* (New York, The New Press).

—— and KARPIN, I (eds) (1995), *Mothers in Law: Feminist Theory and the Legal Regulation of Motherhood* (New York, NY, Columbia University Press).

FINER, M (1974) *Report on the Committee on One Parent Families*, Cmd 5629 (London, HMSO).

—— and McGREGOR, OR (1974) *History of the Obligation to Maintain*, Appendix 5 in M Finer, *Report of the Committee on One Parent Families*, Cmd 5629 (London, HMSO).

FINKELHOR, D (1986) 'Abusers: Special Topics' in D Finkelhor et al (eds), *A Sourcebook on Child Sexual Abuse* (CA, Sage).

—— and BARON, L (1986) 'High Risk Children' in D Finkelhor et al (eds), *A Sourcebook on Child Sexual Abuse* (CA, Sage).

FIONDA, J (ed) (2001a) *Legal Concepts of Childhood* (Oxford, Hart Publishing).

—— (2001b) 'Youth and Justice' in J Fionda (ed), *Legal Concepts of Childhood* (Oxford, Hart Publishing).

FISCHER, K, VIDMAR, N and ELLIS, R (1993) 'The Culture of Battering and the Role of Mediation in Domestic Violence Cases' 46 *SMV Law Review* 2117.

FISH, DG (1997) 'Child Abuse—A Legal Practitioners' Guide' *Fam Law* 665.

FISHER, T (1996) 'The Rights of the Child in Mediation and Divorce' *Child Care Forum* No 9.

—— and HODSON, D (2001) 'Family Mediation—Did it Make Things Better?' *Fam Law* 270.

FISHER, D and GRUESCU, S (2011) *Children and the Big Society* (London, ResPublica).

FISHER, H and LOW, H (2009) 'Who Wins, Who Loses and Who Recovers from Divorce? in J Miles and R Probert (eds), *Sharing Lives, Dividing Assets* (Oxford, Hart Publishing).

FLATLEY, J, KERSHAW, C, SMITH, K, CHAPLIN, R and MOON, D (2010) *Home Office Statistical Bulletin. Crime in England and Wales 2009/10*, www.homeoffice.gov.uk/publications/science-research-statistics/research-statistics/crime-research/hosb1210/ (accessed 13 April 2011) (London, Home Office).

FLETCHER, R (1973) *The Family and Marriage in Britain: An Analysis and Moral Assessment*, 3rd edn (Harmondsworth, Penguin).

FLOOD-PAGE, C and TAYLOR, J (eds) (2003) *Crime in England and Wales 2001/2002: Supplementary Volume* (London, Home Office).

FORTIN, J (1994) '*Re F*: "The Gooseberry Bush Approach"' 57 *MLR* 296.

—— (1998) '*Re C (Medical Treatment)*: A Baby's Right to Life' 10 *CFLQ* 411.

—— (1999) 'Rights Brought Home for Children' 62 *MLR* 350.

—— (2004) 'Children's Rights: Are the Courts Now Taking Them More Seriously?' 15 *KCLJ* 253.

—— (2009a) *Children's Rights and the Developing Law*, 3rd edn (Cambridge, Cambridge University Press).

—— (2009b) 'Children's Right to Know their Origins—Too Far Too Fast?' 21 *CFLQ* 336.

—— (2011) 'A Decade of the HRA and its Impact on Children's Rights' *Fam Law* 176.

——, Ritchie, C and Buchanan, A (2006) 'Young Adults' Perceptions of Court-ordered Contact' 18 *CFLQ* 211.

Foster, H (1976) 'A Review of "Beyond the Best Interests of the Child"' 12 *Williamette Law Journal* 545.

Fowler, E and Stewart, S (2005) 'Rule 9.5 Separate Representation and NYAS' *Fam Law* 49.

Fox, L (2003) 'Reforming Family Property—Comparisons, Compromises and Common Dimensions' 15 *CFLQ* 1.

—— (2006) *Conceptualising Home: Theories, Law and Policies* (Oxford, Hart Publishing).

Fox, M and McHale, J (1997) 'In Whose Best Interests?' 60 *MLR* 700.

Fox, R (1992) *Reproduction and Succession: Studies in Law, Anthropology and Society* (London, Transaction).

Fox-Harding, L (1996) *Family State and Social Policy* (Basingstoke, MacMillan).

Fredman, S (1994) 'A Difference with Distinction: Pregnancy and Parenthood Reassessed' 110 *LQR* 106.

—— (1997) *Women and the Law* (Oxford, Clarendon Press).

Freeman Marilyn (2010) 'Relocation and the Child's Best Interests' *International Family Law Journal* 247.

Freeman, MDA (1979) *Violence in the Home* (Aldershot, Gower).

—— (1981) '"But If You Can't Rape Your Wife, Who[m] Can You Rape?": The Marital Rape Exemption Re-examined' 15 *FLQ* 1.

—— (1983) *The Rights and Wrongs of Children* (London, Frances Pinter).

—— (1985) 'Towards a Critical Theory of Family Law' 38 *Current Legal Problems* 153.

—— (1989a) 'Is Surrogacy Exploitative?' in S McLean (ed), *Legal Issues in Human Reproduction* (Aldershot, Gower).

—— (1989b) 'Cleveland, Butler-Sloss and Beyond—How Are we to React to the Sexual Abuse of Children?' 42 *Current Legal Problems* 85.

—— (1995) 'The Morality of Cultural Pluralism' 3 *Int J Children's Rights* 1.

—— (ed) (1996) *Divorce: Where Next?* (Aldershot, Dartmouth).

—— (1997a) *The Moral Status of Children* (Leiden, Brill).

—— (1997b), 'Family Values and Family Justice' 50 *Current Legal Problems* 315.

—— (2000) 'The End of the Century of the Child?' 53 *CLP* 505.

—— (2000) 'Feminism and Child Law' in J Bridgeman and D Monk (eds), *Feminist Perspectives on Child Law* (London, Cavendish Publishing).

—— (2001) 'The Child in Family Law' in J Fionda (ed), *Legal Concepts of Childhood* (Oxford, Hart Publishing).

—— (2006) 'Review Essay: What's Right with Rights for Children' *Int J Law in Context* 89.

—— (2007) 'Why it Remains Important to Take Children's Rights Seriously' 15 *Int J Children's Rights* 5.

—— (2010) 'The Human Rights of Children' 63 *Current Legal Problems* 1.

—— and Lyon, C (1983) *Cohabitation without Marriage* (Aldershot, Gower).

Freud, A, Solnit, AJ and Goldstein, J (1973) *Beyond the Best Interests of the Child* (New York, NY, Free Press).

Freud, S (1905) *Three Essays on the Theory of Sexuality*, vol VII in J Strachey (ed and tr), *The Standard Edition of the Complete Psychological Works of Sigmund Freud* (London, Hogarth).

Frost, N and Stein, M (1989) *The Politics of Child Welfare: Inequality, Power and Change* (London, Harvester Wheatsheaf).

Frug, MJ (1992) *Postmodern Legal Feminism* (London, Routledge).

Fudge, J and Glasbeek, HJ (1992) 'The Politics of Rights: A Politics with a Little Class' 1 *Social and Legal Studies* 45.

Furedi, F (2004) *Therapy Culture* (London, Routledge).

Furniss, T (1991) *The Multi-Professional Handbook of Child Sexual Abuse: Integrated Management, Therapy and Legal Intervention* (London, Routledge).

GABB, J (2005) 'Locating Lesbian Parent Families: Everyday Negotiations of Lesbian Motherhood in Britain' 12 *Gender, Place and Culture* 419.

GADD, D, FARRALL, S, DALLMORE, D and LOMBARD, N (2002) *Domestic Abuse against Men in Scotland* (Edinburgh, Scottish Executive).

GALLAGHER, B, CHRISTMANN, C, FRASER, C and HODGSON, B (2003) 'International and Internet Child Sexual Abuse and Exploitation—Issues Emerging from Research' 15 *CFLQ* 353.

GARDNER, S (2008) 'Family Property Today' 122 *LQR* 422.

GEIS, G (1978) 'Rape-in-Marriage: Law and Law Reform in England, the United States, and Sweden' 6 *Adelaide LR* 284.

—— and BINDER, A, (1991) 'Sins of their Children: Parental Responsibility for Juvenile Delinquency' 5 *Notre Dame Journal of Law Ethics and Public Policy* 303.

GELDOF, B, (2003) 'The Real Love that Dare Not Speak its Name' in A Bainham et al (eds), *Children and Their Families: Contact, Rights and Welfare* (Oxford, Hart Publishing).

GELLES, RJ (1973) 'Child Abuse as Psychopathology: A Sociological Critique and Reformulation' 43 *American Journal of Orthopsychiatry* 611.

—— (1975) 'The Social Construction of Child Abuse' 45 *American J Orthopsychiatry* 363.

—— (1979) *Family Violence* (Thousand Oaks, CA, Sage).

—— (1992) *The Violent Home: A Study of Physical Aggression between Husbands and Wives* (Thousand Oaks, CA, Sage).

GEORGE, P (1997) 'In All the Circumstances—Section 25' *Fam Law* 729.

GEORGE R (2011) 'Practitioners' Views on Children's Welfare in Relocation Disputes: Comparing Approaches in England and New Zealand' 23 *CFLQ* 178.

——, HARRIS, P and HERRING, J (2009) 'Pre-nuptial Agreements: For Better or for Worse?' *Fam Law* 934.

GHANDHI, PR and MACNAMEE (1991) 'The Family in UK Law and the International Covenant on Civil and Political Rights' 5 *Int J of Law and the Family* 104.

GIBB, F (2005) 'Lesbian's Former Lover Wins Right to Share Child', *The Times*, 8 April.

GIBBONS, J, CONROY, S and BELL, C (1995) *Operating the Child Protection System: A Study of Child Protection Practices in English Local Authorities* (London, HMSO).

GIDDENS, A (1992) *The Transformation of Intimacy* (Cambridge, Polity).

GILBERT, G (1993) 'Housing for Children' 5 *J of Child Law* 166.

GILLESPIE, G (2002) 'Child Support—When the Bough Breaks' *Fam Law* 528.

GILLIGAN, C (1982) *In a Different Voice* (Cambridge, MA, Harvard University Press).

GILLIES, V (2008) 'Perspectives on Parenting Responsibility: Contextualizing Values and Practices' 35 *J Law and Society* 95.

GILLIS, J (1985) *For Better or for Worse: British Marriages 1600 to the Present* (Oxford, Oxford University Press).

—— (1997) *A World of Their Own Making, A History of Myth and Ritual in Family Life* (Oxford, Oxford University Press).

GILMORE, S (2004) 'The Nature, Scope, and Use of the Specific Issue Order' 16 *CFLQ* 367.

—— (2006a) 'Court Decision-making in Shared Residence Order Cases: A Critical Examination' 18 *CFLQ* 478.

—— (2006b) 'Contact/Shared Residence and Child Well-being: Research Evidence and its Implications for Legal Decision-making' 20 *Int J of Law, Policy and the Family* 344.

—— (2008) 'Disputing Contact: Challenging Some Assumptions' 20 *CFLQ* 285.

—— (2009) 'The Limits of Parental Responsibility' in R Probert, S Gilmore and J Herring (eds), *Responsible Parents and Parental Responsibility* (Oxford, Hart Publishing).

GINGERBREAD and FAMILIES NEED FATHERS (1982) *Divided Children: A Survey of Access to Children After Divorce.*

GINN, J (2002) 'Do Divorced Women Catch Up in Pension Building?' 14 *CFLQ* 157.

—— (2003) 'Parenthood, Partnership Status and Pensions: Cohort Differences among Women' 37 *Sociology* 493.

—— and ARBER, S (1996) 'Patterns of Employment, Pensions and Gender: The Effect of Work History on Older Women's Non-State Pensions' 10 *Work, Employment and Society* 469.

GIOVANNONI, JM and BECERRA, R (1979) *Defining Child Abuse* (New York, Free Press; London, Collier Macmillan).

GITTINS, D (1993) *The Family in Question: Changing Households and Familiar Ideologies*, 2nd edn (Basingstoke, Macmillan).

GLASGOW, JM (1979–80) 'The Marital Rape Exemption: Legal Sanction of Spousal Abuse' 18 *J Family Law* 565.

GLENDINNING, C, CLARKE, K and CRAIG, G (1996) 'Implementing the Child Support Act' 18 (3) *JSWFL* 273.

GLENDON, MA (1989) *The Transformation of Family Law* (Chicago, IL, University of Chicago Press).

GLENNON, L (2000) *'Fitzpatrick v Sterling Housing Association Ltd*—An Endorsement of the Functional Family?' 14 *Int J of Law, Policy and the Family* 226.

—— (2008) 'Obligations Between Adult Partners: Moving from Form to Function?' 22 *Int J of Law, Policy and the Family* 22.

—— (2009) 'The Limitations of Equality Discourses on the Contours of Intimate Relations' in J Wallbank, S Choudhry and J Herring (eds) *Rights Gender and Family Law* (London, Routledge-Cavendish).

GOLDSTEIN, J (1980) *Before the Best Interests of the Child* (London, Burnett Books).

——, FREUD, A and SOLNIT, AJ (1980a) *Beyond the Best Interests of the Child* (London, Burnett Books).

——, —— and —— (1996) *The Best Interests of the Child: The Least Detrimental Alternative* (New York, Free Press).

GOODE, J (1993) *World Changes in Divorce Patterns* (New Haven, CT, Yale Univeristy Press).

GOODMAN, A and GREAVES, E (2010) *Cohabitation, Marriage and Child Outcomes* (London, Institute for Fiscal Studies).

GORDON, L (1989) *Heroes of their Own Lives: The Politics and History of Family Violence: Boston 1880–1960* (New York, Penguin Books).

GOVERNMENT STATISTICAL OFFICE (1998) *Population Trends*, 91 (London, The Stationery Office).

GRABHAM, E and SMITH, J (2010) 'From Social Security to Individual Responsibility (Part Two): Writing Off Poor Women's Work in the Welfare Reform Act 2009' 32 *JSWFL* 81.

GRACE, S (1995) *Policing Domestic Violence in the 1990s, Home Office Research Study No 139* (London, HMSO).

GRAND, A (1994) 'What Is this Thing Called Parental Responsibility?' *Fam Law* 586.

GRASSBY, M (1991) 'Women in their Forties: The Extent of the Right to Alimentary Support' 30 *Reports of Family Law 3d* 369.

GRAY, C and MERRICK, S (1996) 'Voice Alterations, Why Women Have More Difficulty than Men with the Legal Process of Divorce' 34 *Family and Conciliation Courts Review* 240.

GREGSON, N and LOWE, M (1994) *Servicing the Middle Classes: Class, Gender and Waged Domestic Labour in Contemporary Britain* (London, Routledge).

GRIFFITHS, DL and MOYNIHAN, FJ (1963) 'Multiple Epiphysial Injuries in Babies ("Battered Baby Syndrome")' *British Medical Journal* 1558.

GRILLO, T (1991) 'The Mediation Alternative: Process Dangers for Women' *Yale Law Journal* 1545.

GUGGENHEIM, M (2005) *What's Wrong with Children's Rights?* (Harvard, Harvard University Press).

GUSFIELD, JR (1975) 'Categories of Ownership and Responsibility in Social Issues: Alcohol Abuse and Automobile Use' 5 *Journal of Drug Issues* 290.

HALE, Dame B (1996) *From the Test Tube to the Coffin: Choice and Regulation in Family Life* (London, Sweet & Maxwell).

—— (1998) 'Private Lives and Public Duties: What Is Family Law For?' 20 *JSWFL* 125.

—— (2004) 'Homosexual Rights' 16 *CFLQ* 125.

—— (2011) 'Equality and Autonomy in Family Law' 33 *JSWFL* 3.

HALE, Sir MATTHEW (1971) *Historia Placitorum Coronae*, vol 1, ed PR Glazebrook (London, Professional Books).

HALL, A (2008) 'Special Guardianship and Permanency Planning: Unforeseen Consequences and Missed Opportunities' 20 *CFLQ* 359.

HALL, JG and MARTIN, DF (1990) 'Child Delinquency and Parental Responsibility' 154 *Justice of the Peace* 604.

HAMILTON, AC and SINCLAIR, M (1991) *Report of the Aboriginal Justice Inquiry of Manitoba* (Winnipeg, Province of Manitoba).

HAMILTON, C (1996) 'Marriage, Wardship and "Best Interests"' 123 *Childright*.

—— and WATT, B (2004) 'The Employment of Children' *CFLQ* 135.

HANCOCK, E (1982) 'Sources of Discord Between Attorneys and Therapists in Divorce Cases' 6 *Journal of Divorce* 115.

HANMER, J, GRIFFITHS, S and JERWOOD, D (1999) *Arresting Evidence: Domestic Violence and Repeat Victimisation: Police Research Series, Paper 104* (London, Policing and Reducing Crime Unit).

—— and ITZIN, C with QUAID, S and WIGGLESWORTH, D (eds) (2000) *Home Truths About Domestic Violence: Feminist Influences on Policy and Practice: A Reader* (London, Routledge).

HARDING, R (2010) '*Wilkinson v Kitzinger*' in R Hunter, C McGlynn and E Rackley (eds), *Feminist Judgments From Theory to Practice* (Oxford, Hart Publishing).

HARNE, L and RADFORD, J (1994) 'Reinstating Patriarchy: The Politics of the Family and the New Legislation' in A Mullender and R Morley (eds), *Children Living with Domestic Violence* (London, Whiting & Birch).

—— and —— (1997) *Valued Families: The Lesbian Mothers' Legal Handbook* (London, Women's Press).

HAROLD, G and MURCH, M (2005) 'Inter-parental Conflict and Children's Adaptation to Separation and Divorce: Theory, Research and Implications for Family Law, Practice and Policy' 17 *CFLQ* 185.

HARRIS, J (2000) *An Evaluation of the Use and Effectiveness of the Protection from Harassment Act 1997: Home Office Research Study 203* (London, Home Office).

HARRIS, N (2007) *Education, Law and Diversity* (Oxford, Hart Publishing).

HARRIS, P and GEORGE, R (2010) 'Parental Responsibility and Shared Residence Orders: Parliamentary Intentions and Judicial Interpretations' *CFLQ* 151.

HARRIS-SHORT, S 'Family Law and the Human Rights Act 1998: Judicial Restraint or Revolution?' (2005) 17 *CFLQ* 329.

—— (2010) '*Evans v Amicus Healthcare*' in R Hunter, C McGlynn, and E Rackley (eds), *Feminist Judgments From Theory to Practice* (Oxford, Hart Publishing).

—— and MILES, J (2007) *Family Law* (Oxford, Oxford University Press); (2009) Online Updates, ch 4 'Domestic Violence', www.oup.com/uk/orc/bin/9780199277162/resources/updates/ch04_1009.pdf (accessed 28 February 2011).

—— and —— (2011) *Family Law Text, Cases and Materials* (Oxford, Oxford University Press).

HARRISON, K (1995) 'Fresh or Frozen: Lesbian Mothers, Sperm Donors and Limited Fathers' in M Fineman and I Karpin (eds), *Mothers in Law: Feminist Theory and the Legal Regulation of Motherhood* (New York, Columbia University Press).

HARTRAIS, L (1994) 'Comparing Family Policy in Britain, France and Germany' 23 *J of Social Policy* 135.

HARWIN, N and BARRON, J (2000) 'Domestic Violence and Social Policy: Perspectives from Women's Aid' in J Hanmer et al (eds), *Home Truths About Domestic Violence: Feminist Influences on Policy and Practice: A Reader* (London, Routledge).

HASKEY, J (2005) 'Living Arrangements in Contemporary Britain: Having a Partner Who Usually Lives Elsewhere and Living Apart Together (LAT)' 122 *Population Trends* 35.

—— and LEWIS, J (2006) 'Living Apart-Together in Britain: Context and Meaning' 2 *Int J of Law in Context* 37.

HATTEN, W, VINTER, L and WILLIAMS, R (2002) *Dads on Dads: Needs and Expectations at Home and at Work* (London, Equal Opportunities Commission).

HAVAS, E (1995) 'The Family as Ideology' 29 *Social Policy and Administration* 1.

HAYES, M (1994) '"Cohabitation Clauses" in Financial Provision and Property Adjustment Orders—Law, Policy and Justice' 110 *LQR* 124.

—— (1996) 'Non-molestation Protection—Only Associated Persons Need Apply' *Fam Law* 134.

—— (2004) '*Re O and N; Re B*—Uncertain Evidence and Risk-taking in Child Protection Cases' 16 *CFLQ* 63.

—— (2006) 'Relocation Cases: Is the Court of Appeal Applying the Correct Principles?' 18 *CFLQ* 351.

—— and WILLIAMS, C (1999) *Family Law: Principles, Policy and Practice* (London, Butterworths).

HAYES, P (2003) 'Giving Due Consideration to Ethnicity in Adoption Placements—A Principled Approach' 15 *CFLQ* 255.

—— (1995) 'The Ideological Attack on Transracial Adoption in the USA and Britain' 9 *Int J of Law and the Family* 1.

HEARN, J (1998) *The Violences of Men: How Men Talk About and How Agencies Respond to Men's Violence to Women* (London, Sage).

HENAGHAN M (2011) 'Relocation Cases—The Rhetoric and the Reality of a Child's Best Interests—A View from the Bottom of the World' 23 *CFLQ* 226.

HENDRICK, H (2003) *Child Welfare: Historical Dimensions, Contemporary Debate* (Bristol, Policy).

HENRICSON, C and BAINHAM, A (2005) *The Child and Family Policy Divide, Tensions, Convergence and Rights* (York, Joseph Rowntree Foundation).

HENSHAW, D (2006) *Recovering Child Support: Routes to Responsibility* (London, DWP).

HM COURT SERVICE INSPECTORATE (HMCSI) (2003) *Seeking Agreement. Children and Family Court Advisory and Support Service (CAFCASS). A Thematic Review by MCSI of the Operation of Schemes Involving CAFCASS at an Early Stage in Private Law Proceedings*, www.cafacass.gov.uk (accessed 6 June 2005).

HM CROWN PROSECUTION SERVICE INSPECTORATE (HMCPSI), HM INSPECTORATE OF CONSTABULARY (HMIC) (2004) *A Joint Inspection of the Investigation and Prosecution of Cases Involving Domestic Violence*.

HM GOVERNMENT (2006) *Reaching Out: An Action Plan on Social Exclusion* (London, Cabinet Office).

HM GOVERNMENT (2010a) *The Coalition: Our Programme for Government*, www.cabinetoffice.gov.uk/sites/default/files/resources/coalition_programme_for_government.pdf (accessed 14 March 2011) (London, The Stationery Office)

—— (2010b) *Children's Rights: Government Response to the Committee's Twenty-fifth Report of Session 2008–9* (London, The Stationery Office)

HM INSPECTORATE OF COURT ADMINISTRATION (HMICA) (2005) *Domestic Violence, Safety and Family Proceedings. A Thematic Review of the Handling of Domestic Violence Issues by the Children and Family Court Advisory and Support Service (CAFCASS) and the Administration of Family Court in Her Majesty's Court Service (HMCS)*, www.hmica.gov.uk/files/HMICA_Domestic_violence_linked1.pdf (accessed 5 October 2010 (London, HMICA).

HM INSPECTORATE OF PROBATION (1997) *Family Court Welfare Work: Report of a Thematic Inspection* (London, Home Office).

—— (2003) *Every Child Matters.*

—— (2004) *Child Poverty Review* (London, The Stationery Office).

—— DfES, DWP and DTI (2004) *Choice for Parents, the Best Start for Children: A Ten Year Strategy for Childcare* (London, HM Treasury).

HERRING, J (1998) '"Name this Child"' *CLJ* 266.

—— (1999) 'The Human Rights Act and the Welfare Principle in Family Law—Conflicting or Complementary?' 11(3) *CFLQ* 223.

—— (2003) 'Connecting Contact: Contact in a Private Law Context' in A Bainham et al (eds), *Children and their Families: Contact, Rights and Welfare* (Oxford, Hart Publishing).

—— (2005a) 'Why Financial Orders on Divorce Should be Unfair' 19 *Int J of Law, Policy and the Family* 218.

—— (2005b) 'Farewell Welfare?' 27 *JSWFL* 159.

—— (2010a) 'Sexless Family Law' 11 *Lex Familiae* 3.

—— (2010b) 'Relational Autonomy and Family Law' in J Wallbank, S Choudhry and J Herring (eds), *Rights, Gender and Family Law* (London, Routledge-Cavendish).

—— (2011) *Family Law*, 5th edn (Essex: Longman Law Series).

—— and TAYLOR, R 'Relocating Relocation' (2006) 18 *CFLQ* 517.

HESTER, M (2009) *Who Does What to Whom? Gender and Domestic Violence Perpetrators* (Bristol, University of Bristol in association with the Northern Rock Foundation).

—— and RADFORD, L (1996) *Domestic Violence and Child Contact Arrangements in England and Denmark* (Bristol, Policy).

—— et al (1992) 'Domestic Violence and Access Arrangements for Children in Denmark and Britain' *JSWFL* 57.

—— et al (1998) 'Domestic Violence and Child Contact' in A Mullender and R Morley (eds), *Children Living with Domestic Violence* (London, Whiting & Birch).

——, PEARSON, C and HARWIN, N (2000) *Making an Impact: Children and Domestic Violence: A Reader* (London, Jessica Kingsley).

——, HANMER, J, COULSON, S, MORAHAN, M and RAZAK, A (2003) *Domestic Violence: Making it Through the Criminal Justice System* (University of Sunderland, Northern Rock Foundation and International Centre for the Study of Violence and Abuse).

——, WESTMARLAND, N, GANGOLI, G, WILKINSON, M, O'KELLY, C, KENT, A and DIAMOND, A (2006) *Domestic Violence Perpetrators: Identifying Needs to Inform Early Intervention* (Bristol, University of Bristol).

——, WESTMARLAND, N, PEARCE, J and WILLIAMSON, E (2008) *Early Evaluation of the Domestic Violence, Crime and Victims Act 2004*, Ministry of Justice Research Series 14/08.

HETHERINGTON, EM (1979) 'Divorce: A Child's Perspective' 34 *American Psychologist* 851.

HIBBS, M, BARTON, C and BESWICK, J (2001) 'Why Marry?—Perceptions of the Affianced' *Fam Law* 197.

HILL, M (1980) *Understanding Social Policy* (Oxford, Robertson).

HILTON, N (1991) 'Mediating Wife Assault: Battered Women and the New "Family"' 9 *Canadian J Family Law* 29.

HITCHINGS, E (2009) 'Chaos or Consistency? Ancillary Relief in the "Everyday" Case' in J Miles and R Probert (eds), *Sharing Lives, Dividing Assets* (Oxford, Hart Publishing).

HODSON, D (2009) *Every Family Matters. An In-Depth Review of Family Law in Britain* (London, Centre for Social Justice).

HOGGETT, B (1994) 'Joint Parenting Systems: The English Experiment' 6 *J Child Law* 8.

HOLCOMBE, L (1983) *Wives and Property: Reform of the Married Women's Property Acts* (Toronto, University of Toronto Press).

HOME DEPARTMENT (2008) *The Government Reply to the Sixth Report from the Home Affairs Committee Session 2007–08 HC 263, Domestic Violence, Forced Marriage and "Honour"-based Violence*, Cm 7450.

HOME OFFICE (1990a) *Crime Justice and Protecting the Public*, Cmd 965 (London, HMSO).

—— (1990b) *Domestic Violence*, Home Office Circular 60/1990 (London, Home Office).

—— (1993) *Information on the Criminal Justice System in England and Wales, Digest 2*.

—— (1994) *National Standards for Probation Service Family Court Welfare Work* (London, HMSO).

—— (1997) Press Release, 5 June.

—— (1998) *Supporting Families: A Consultation Document* (London, The Stationery Office).

—— (1999) *Supporting Families: Responses to the Consultation Document* (London, The Stationery Office).

—— (2000a) *Domestic Violence: Break the Chain Multi-Agency Guidance for Addressing Domestic Violence* (London, HMSO).

—— (2000b) 'Domestic Violence: Revised Circular to the Police', Home Office Circular No 19/2000 (London, Home Office).

—— (2002) *Justice for All* (London, HMSO) Cm 5563.

—— (2003) *Safety and Justice: The Government's Proposals on Domestic Violence*, Cm 5847 (London, HMSO).

—— (2005) *Domestic Violence: A National Report*.

—— (2009) *National Violence Delivery Plan. Progress Report 2008–09*, http://webarchive.nation-alarchives.gov.uk/20100418065544/http://homeoffice.gov.uk/documents/dom-violence-delivery-plan-08-09.html (accessed 21 January 2011).

—— (2010) *Call to End Violence Against Women and Girls* (London, The Stationery Office).

—— (undated) 'What We're Doing', www.homeoffice.gov.uk/crime/violence-against-women-girls/what-we're-doing/ (accessed 26 January 2011).

—— (undated) *Violence against Women and Girls*, www.homeoffice.gov.uk/crime/violence-against-women-girls/ (accessed 2 March 2011).

—— (undated) *Domestic Violence Protection Notices and Orders*, www.homeoffice.gov.uk/crime/violence-against-women-girls/dv-protection-orders/ (accessed 28 July 2011).

HOME OFFICE RESEARCH DEVELOPMENT STATISTICS (2010) http://rds.homeoffice.gov.uk/rds/violence-women.html (accessed 13 January 2011).

Hooper, C (1994) 'Do Families Need Fathers? The Impact of Divorce on Children' in A Mullender and R Morley (eds), *Children Living with Domestic Violence* (London, Whiting & Birch).

HOUSE OF COMMONS COMMITTEE DEBATE, SIXTH SITTING (19 July 2011) *Legal Aid, Sentencing and Punishment of Offenders Bill*, www.publications.parliament.uk/pa/cm201011/cmpublic/leg-alaid/110719/pm/110719s01.htm (accessed 26 July 2011) (London, House of Commons).

HOUSE OF COMMONS SELECT COMMITTEE ON VIOLENCE IN THE FAMILY (1975) *Report from the Select Committee on Violence in Marriage, Vol II, Report, Minutes of Evidence and Appendices* (London, HMSO).

HOUSE OF COMMONS SELECT COMMITTEE ON SCIENCE AND TECHNOLOGY (2004) Written Evidence, May 2004; *Memorandum from the Department of Health* www.publications.parliament.uk/pa/cm200405/cmse-lect/cmsctech/7/7we02.html.

HOUSE OF COMMONS SELECT COMMITTEE ON WORK AND PENSIONS (2011) *The Government's Proposed Child Maintenance Reforms* (London, The Stationery Office).

HOUSE OF COMMONS, SOCIAL SECURITY COMMITTEE (1993) *The Operation of the Child Support Act* (HC 69) (London, HMSO).

—— (1994) *The Operation of the Child Support Act: Proposals for Change* (HC 470 1994–95) (London, HMSO).

—— (1998) *Pensions on Divorce* (HC 869) (London, The Stationery Office)

HOUSE OF COMMONS AND HOUSE OF LORDS (2005) *Joint Committee on the Draft Children (Contact) and Adoption Bill, Session 2004–05, Volume 1: Report* HC 400-I, HL Paper 100-I (London, The Stationery Office).

HOUSE OF COMMONS JUSTICE COMMITTEE (2011) *Sixth Report. Operation of the Family Courts*, http://jor-danpublishing.communigatormail2.co.uk/jordanspublishinglz//lz.aspx?p1=0584302S3921&CC=&w=8165&cID=0&cValue=1 (accessed 21 July 2011).

HOWITT, D (1993) *Child Abuse Errors—When Good Intentions Go Wrong* (Piscataway, NJ, Rutgers University Press; Harvester, Wheatsheaf).

HOYLE, C (1998) *Negotiating Domestic Violence: Police, Criminal Justice and Victims* (Oxford, Oxford University Press).

—— and SANDERS, A (2000) 'Police Response to Domestic Violence: From Victim Choice to Victim Empowerment?' 40 *Brit J Criminology* 14.

HUDSON, P and LEE, WR (1990) 'Women's Work and the Family Economy in Historical Perspective' in P Hudson and WR Lee (eds), *Women's Work and the Family Economy in Historical Perspective* (Manchester, Manchester University Press).

HUMAN FERTILISATION AND EMBRYOLOGY AUTHORITY (2009) *Code of Practice—Guidance Notes* (London, HFEA).

—— (2010) *Fertility Facts and Figures 2008* (London, HFEA) (accessed July 2011).

—— (2011) *Donor Statistics* (London, HFEA) (accessed July 2011).

HUMPHREYS, C (2000) *Child Protection and Woman Protection: Links and Schisms: An Overview of the Research* (Bristol, Women's Aid Federation of England).

HUMPHREYS, C and HARRISON, C (2003a) 'Squaring the Circle—Contact and Domestic Violence' *Fam Law* 419.

—— and —— (2003b) 'Focusing on Safety—Domestic Violence and the Role of Child Contact Centres' 15 *CFLQ* 237.

—— and THAIRA, R (2002) *Routes to Safety: Protection Issues Facing Abused Women and Children and the Role of Outreach Services* (Bristol, Women's Aid Federation of England).

—— and —— (2003) 'Neither Justice nor Protection: Women's Experiences of Post-separation Violence' 25 *JSWFL* 195.

HUMPHRIES, M (2001) 'Occupation Orders Revisited' *Fam Law* 542.

HUNT, A (1985) 'The Ideology of Law: Advances and Problems in Recent Applications of the Concept of Ideology to the Analysis of Law' 10 *Law and Society Review* 11.

HUNT, J (2003) *Researching Contact* (London, One Parent Families).

—— (2007) 'Intervening in Litigated Contact: Ideas from Other Jurisdictions' in M Maclean (ed), *Parenting after Partnering. Containing Conflict after Separation* (Oxford, Hart Publishing).

—— and MACLEOD, A (2005) *Outcomes of Applications to Court for Contact Orders After Parental Separation or Divorce,* Briefing Note.

—— and —— (2008) *Outcomes of Applications to Court for Contact Orders After Parental Separation or Divorce* (London, Ministry of Justice),

—— and TRINDER, L (2011) *Chronic Litigation Cases: Characteristics, Numbers, Interventions. A Report for the Family Justice Council.*

——, MASSON, J and TRINDER, L (2009) 'Shared Parenting: The Law, the Evidence and Guidance from Families need Fathers' *Fam Law* 831.

HUNTER, R (2007) ' 'Close Encounters of a Judicial Kind: "Hearing" Children's "Voices" in Family Law Proceedings' 19 *CFLQ* 283.

INDUSTRIAL RELATIONS SERVICES (1995) 596 *Employment Trends* (London, Industrial Relations Services).

INGLEBY REPORT (1960) *Report of the Committee on Children and Young Persons*, Cmd 1191 (London, HMSO).

INGLEBY, R (1992) *Solicitors and Divorce* (Oxford, Oxford University Press).

INGMAN, T (1996) 'Contact and the Obdurate Parent' *Fam Law* 615.

INTERDEPARTMENTAL COMMITTEE ON CONCILIATION (1983) *Report* (London, HMSO, 1983).

ITZIN, C (2000) 'Gendering Domestic Violence: The Influence of Feminism on Policy and Practice' in J Hanmer et al (eds), *Home Truths About Domestic Violence: Feminist Influences on Policy and Practice: A Reader* (London, Routledge).

JACKSON, E et al (1993) 'Financial Support on Divorce: The Right Mixture of Rules and Discretion?' 7 *Int J of Law and the Family* 230.

—— (2001) *Regulating Reproduction: Law, Technology and Autonomy* (Oxford, Hart Publishing).

—— (2002) 'Conception and the Irrelevance of the Welfare Principle' 65 *Modern Law Review* 176.

—— (2006) 'What Is a Parent?' in A Diduck and K O'Donovan (eds), *Feminist Perspectives on Family Law* (Abingdon, Routledge-Cavendish).

JAMES, A (1992) 'An Open or Shut Case? Law as an Autopoetic System' 19 *J Law and Society* 271.

—— (1999) 'Parents: A Children's Perspective' in A Bainham, S Day Sclater and M Richards (eds), *What Is a Parent?* (Oxford, Hart Publishing).

JAMES, AL, JAMES A and MCNAMEE, S (2003) 'Constructing Children's Welfare in Family Proceedings' *Fam Law* 889.

JAMES, B (2007) 'Prosecuting Domestic Violence' *Fam Law* 456.

JAMES, C (2009) *Ten Years of Family Policy—1999–2009* (London, Family and Parenting Institute).

JAMES, S (1994) 'Women's Unwaged Work—The Heart of the Informal Sector' in M Evans (ed), *The Woman Question*, 2nd edn (London, Sage).

JENKS, C (1996) *Childhood* (London, Routledge).

JOHNSON, L (1997) 'Expanding Eugenics or Improving Health Care in China: Commentary on the Provisions of the Standing Committee of the Gansu People's Congress Concerning the Prohibition of Reproduction by Intellectually Impaired Persons' 24 *J Law and Society* 199.

JOHNSON, M (2008) *A Typology of Domestic Violence: Intimate Terrorism, Violent Resistance and Situational Couple Violence* (Hanover, NH, University Press of New England).

JOLLY, SC (1994) 'Cutting the Ties—The Termination of Contact in Care' 16 *JSWFL* 299.

—— and SANDLAND, R (1994) 'Political Correctness and the Adoption White Paper' 24 *Fam Law* 30.

JONES, C (2010) 'The Identification of 'Parents' and 'Siblings': New Possibilities under the Reformed Human Fertilisation and Embryology Act' in J Wallbank, S Choudhry, and J Herring (eds), *Rights, Gender and Family Law* (Abingdon, Routledge).

—— (2011) 'The (im)Possible Parents in Law' in C Lind, H Keating, and J Bridgeman (eds), *Taking Responsibility: Law and the Changing Family* (Farnham, Ashgate).

JONES, E and PARKINSON, P (1995) 'Child Sexual Abuse, Access and the Wishes of Children' 9 *Int J of Law and the Family* 54.

JOSEPH ROWNTREE FOUNDATION (1996) 'The Relationship between Family Life and Young People's Lifestyles' *Social Policy Research* 95.

JOSHI, H and DAVIES, H (1992) 'Pensions, Divorce and Wives' Double Burden' 6 *Int J of Law and the Family* 289.

JUDD, F and GEORGE, R (2010) 'International Relocation: Do We Stand Alone?' *Fam Law* 63.

KAGANAS, F (1995) 'Partnership under the Children Act 1989—An Overview' in F Kaganas, M King and C Piper (eds), *Legislating for Harmony: Partnership under the Children Act 1989* (London, Jessica Kingsley).

—— (1996) 'Responsible or Feckless Fathers? *Re S (Parental Responsibility)*' 8 *CFLQ* 165.

—— (1999a) 'Contact, Conflict and Risk' in S Day Sclater and C Piper (eds), *Undercurrents of Divorce* (Aldershot, Ashgate).

—— (1999b) '*B v B (Occupation Order)* and *Chalmers* v *Johns* Occupation Orders Under the Family Law Act 1996' 11 *CFLQ* 193.

—— (2000) '*Re L (Contact: Domestic Violence; Re V (Contact: Domestic Violence); Re M (Contact: Domestic Violence); Re H (Contact: Domestic Violence)*: Contact and Domestic Violence'12 *CFLQ* 311.

—— (2002) 'Domestic Homicide, Gender and the Expert' in A Bainham, S Day Sclater and M Richards (eds), *Body Lore and Laws* (Oxford, Hart Publishing).

—— (2006) 'Domestic Violence, Men's Groups and the Equivalence Argument' in A Diduck and K O'Donovan (eds), *Feminist Perspectives on Family Law* (Abingdon, Routledge-Cavendish).

—— (2010a) 'When it Comes to Contact Disputes, What Are Family Courts For?' 63 *Current Legal Problems* 234.

—— (2010b) 'Child Protection, Gender and Rights' in J Wallbank, S Choudhry and J Herring (eds), *Rights, Gender and Family Law* (Abingdon, Routledge).

—— (2011) 'Managing Emotion: Judging Contact Disputes' 23 *CFLQ* 63.

—— and DAY SCLATER, S (2000) 'Contact and Domestic Violence—The Winds of Change?' *Fam Law* 630.

—— and —— (2004) 'Contact Disputes: Narrative Constructions of "Good" Parents' 12 *Feminist Legal Studies* 1.

—— and DIDUCK, A (2004) 'Incomplete Citizens: Changing Images of Post-separation Children' 67(6) *MLR* 959.

—— and MURRAY, CM (1991) 'Law, Women and the Family: The Question of Polygyny in a New South Africa' *Acta Juridica* 116.

—— and PIPER, C (1994) 'Domestic Violence and Divorce Mediation' *JSWFL* 265.

—— and —— (1999) 'Divorce and Domestic Violence' in S Day Sclater and C Piper (eds), *Undercurrents of Divorce* (Aldershot, Ashgate).

—— and —— (2001) 'Grandparents and Contact: "Rights v Welfare" Revisited' 15 *Int J of Law, Policy and the Family* 250.

—— and —— (2002) 'Shared Parenting—A 70% Solution?' 14 *CFLQ* 365.

KAHN FREUND, O (1955) 'Matrimonial Property in England' in W Friedmann (ed), *Matrimonial Property Law* (Toronto, Carswell).

KANDEL, RF (1994) 'Which Came First: The Mother or the Egg? A Kinship Solution to Gestational Surrogacy' 47 *Rutgers Law Review* 165.

KATZ, I (2000) 'Triangles of Adoption The Geometry of Complexity' in A Treacher and I Katz (eds), *The Dynamics of Adoption* (London, Jessica Kingsley).

KAZIMIRSKI, A, KEOGH, P, KUMARI, V, SMITH, R, GOWLAND, S, PURDON, S with KHNUM N (2009) *Forced Marriage—Prevalence and Service Response*, Research Report DCSF-RR128, www.education. gov.uk/publications/eOrderingDownload/DCSF-RR128.pdf (accessed 17 February 2011) (London, DCSF).

KEATING, H (1995) 'Children Come First?' 1 *Contemporary Issues in Law* 29.

—— (1996) 'Shifting Standards in the House of Lords: *Re H and Others (Minors) (Sexual Abuse: Standard of Proof)*' 2 *CFLQ* 157.

—— (2009) 'Suspicions, Sitting on the Fence and Standards of Proof' *CFLQ* 230.

—— (2011) '*Re MA*: The Significance of Harm' *CFLQ* 115.

KEMPE, CH et al (1962) 'The Battered Child Syndrome' 181 *Journal of the American Medical Association* 17.

KENWAY, P, MACINNES, T, FOTHERGILL, S and HORGAN, H (2010) *Working-age 'Welfare': Who Gets It, Why and What It Costs* (London, Joseph Rowntree Foundation).

KEOWN, J (1997) 'Restoring Moral and Intellectual Shape to the Law after *Bland*' 113 *LQR* 481.

—— (2000) 'Beyond *Bland*: A Critique of the BMA Guidance on Withholding and Withdrawing Medical Treatment' 20 *Legal Studies* 66.

KEWLEY, A (1996) 'Pragmatism Before Principle: The Limitations of Civil Law Remedies for the Victims of Domestic Violence' 18 *JSWFL* 1.

KING, M (1981) 'Welfare and Justice' in M King (ed), *Childhood, Welfare and Justice* (London, Batsford Academic and Educational).

—— (1987) 'Playing the Symbols–Custody and the Law Commission' *Fam Law* 186.

—— (1995a) 'Essay Review: *Child Abuse Errors; When Good Intentions Go Wrong*: by Dennis Howitt (New York: Harvester Wheatsheaf 1992)' 86 *British J Psychology* 437.

—— (1995b) 'Partnership in Politics and Law: A New Deal for Parents?' in F Kaganas, M King and C Piper (eds), *Legislating for Harmony: Partnership under the Children Act 1989* (London, Jessica Kingsley).

—— (1997) *A Better World for Children* (London, Routledge).

—— (1999) '"Being Sensible": Images and Practices of the New Family Lawyer' 28 *J of Social Policy* 249.

—— (2007) 'Review Article. The Right Decision for the Child' (70) *MLR* 857.

—— and KAGANAS, F (1998) 'The Risks and Dangers of Experts in Court' *Current Legal Issues* 221.

—— and PIPER, C (1995) *How the Law Thinks about Children*, 2nd edn (Aldershot, Arena).

KINGDOM, E (1991) *What's Wrong with Rights* (Edinburgh, Edinburgh University Press).

KINSEY, A et al (1953) *Sexual Behavior in the Human Female* (Philadelphia, PA, WB Saunders).

KLEANTHOUS, V (2003) 'SFLA Mediation Annual Conference' *Fam Law* 849.

KLINE, M (1995) 'Complicating the Ideology of Motherhood: Child Welfare Law and First Nation Women' in M Fineman and I Karpin (eds), *Mothers in Law: Feminist Theory and the Legal Regulation of Motherhood* (New York, Columbia University Press).

KNIGHTS, E (1997) 'Child Support Update' *Fam Law* 120.

KOHLBERG, L (1984) 'The Psychology of Moral Development: The Nature and Validity of Moral Stages', in *Essays on Moral Development*, vol 2 (London, Harper & Row).

KURZ, D (1993) 'Social Science Perspectives on Wife Abuse: Current Debates and Future Directions' in PB Bart and EG Moran (eds), *Violence Against Women: The Bloody Footprints* (London, Sage).

KUHSE, H (1987) *The Sanctity of Life Doctrine in Medicine* (Oxford, Clarendon Press).

LA VALLE, I, CLERY, E and HUERTA M (2008) *Maternity Rights and Mothers' Employment Decisions*, Department of Work and Pensions Research Report 496 (London, The Stationery Office).

LACLAU, E and MOUFFE, C (1985) *Hegemony and Socialist Strategy: Towards a Radical Democratic Politics* (London, Verso).

LAFAUCHEUR, N (2004) 'The French "Tradition" of Anonymous Birth: The Lines of Argument' 18 *Int J of Law, Policy and the Family* 319.

LAMING, Lord (2003) *The Victoria Climbie Report* (London, The Stationery Office).

—— (2009) *The Protection of Children in England: A Progress Report*, HC330 (London, The Stationery Office).

LANGDRIDGE, D and BLYTHE, E (2001) 'Regulation of Assisted Conception Services in Europe: Implications of the New Reproductive Technologies for "the Family"' 23 *JSWFL* 45.

LAVERY, R (1996) 'The Child Assessment Order—A Reassessment' 8 *CFLQ* 41.

LAW COMMISSION (1966) No 6, *Reform of the Grounds of Divorce—The Field of Choice*, Cmd 3123 (London, HMSO).

—— (1969) No 25, *Financial Provisions in Matrimonial Proceedings* (London, HMSO).

—— (1978) No 86, *Third Report on Family Property: The Matrimonial Home (Co-ownership and Occupancy Rights) and Household Goods* (London, HMSO).

—— (1979) No 74, *Illegitimacy* (London, HMSO).

—— (1980) No 103, *The Financial Consequences of Divorce: The Basic Policy* (London, HMSO).

—— (1981) No 112, *The Financial Consequences of Divorce: The Response to the Discussion Paper* (London, HMSO).

—— (1982) No 118, *Illegitimacy* (London, HMSO).

—— (1985a) No 91, *Guardianship: Working Paper* (London, HMSO).

—— (1985b) *Review of Child Law: Guardianship* (London, HMSO).

—— (1986) No 96, *Family Law: Review of Child Law: Custody* (London, HMSO).

—— (1988a) No 170, *Facing the Future: A Discussion Paper on the Grounds for Divorce* (London, HMSO).

—— (1988b) No 172, *Family Law: Review of Child Law: Guardianship and Custody* (London, HMSO).

—— (1988c) No 175, *Family Law: Matrimonial Property* (London, HMSO).

—— (1990) No 192, *Family Law: The Ground for Divorce* (London, HMSO).

—— (1992a) No 207, *Family Law: Domestic Violence and Occupation of the Family Home* (London, HMSO).

—— (1992b) No 205, *Criminal Law: Rape Within Marriage* (London, HMSO).

—— (1995) No 139, *Criminal Law: Consent in the Criminal Law*, Consultation Paper (London, HMSO).

—— (1996) *The Treatment of Pension Rights on Divorce*, Consultation Paper (London, HMSO).

—— (2002) No 278, *Sharing Homes: A Discussion Paper*, Cmd 3345 (London, The Stationery Office).

—— (2003) No 173, *Partial Defences to Murder. Consultation Paper* (London, The Law Commission).

—— (2007) *Cohabitation: The Financial Consequences of Relationship Breakdown LC 307* (London, The Stationery Office).

—— (2011a) Marital_Property_Agreements_Consultation www.justice.gov.uk/lawcommission/docs/cp198_(accessed 19 July 2011).

—— (2011b) *Eleventh Programme of Law Reform Law*, Com 330 (London, The Stationery Office).

—— (2011c) *Marital Property Agreements. A Consultation Paper Executive Summary.* Consultation Paper No 198.

—— (undated a) *Law Commission Report. A Study of the Views and Approaches of Family Practitioners Concerning Marital Property Agreements*, www.justice.gov.uk/lawcommission/docs/hitchings-report.pdf (accessed 29 July 2011).

—— (undated b) *Law Commission Report (2). Marital Property Agreements. A Supplemental Enquiry*, www.justice.gov.uk/lawcommission/docs/hitchings-report-supplementary.pdf (accessed 29 July 2011).

LAW COMMISSION OF CANADA (2002) *Beyond Conjugality: Recognizing and Supporting Close Personal Adult Relationships* (Ottawa, Law Commission of Canada).

LAW SOCIETY, Family Law Sub-Committee (1979) *A Better Way Out: Suggestions for the Reform of the Law of Divorce and Other Forms of Matrimonial Relief; for the Setting Up of a Family Court; and for its Procedure* (London, The Law Society).

——, Family Law Committee (1998) *Maintenance and Capital Provision on Divorce, The Family Law Committee's Submission to the Ancillary Relief Advisory Group*, Appendix 10 to *Report to the Lord Chancellor by the Ancillary Relief Advisory Group* (London, The Law Society).

—— (2002) *Cohabitation: The Case for Clear Law* (London, The Law Society).

—— (2003) *Financial Provision on Divorce: Clarity and Fairness, Proposals of Reform* (London, The Law Society).

—— (2011) *Family Law Protocol*, www.lawsociety.org.uk/documents/downloads/dynamic/familylaw-protocol.pdf (accessed 28 July 2011) (London, The Law Society).

LAWSON, A (1996) 'The Things We Do for Love: Detrimental Reliance in the Family Home' 16 *Legal Studies* 218.

LEGAL AID BOARD (1995) *Family Transaction Criteria*, Issue no 2.

LEGAL SERVICES COMMISSION (2007a) *Funding Code Criteria.*

—— (2007b) *Funding Code Decision Making Guidance (Family) (Section 20).*

—— (undated) *What Is Family Mediation?*, www.legalservices.gov.uk/docs/fains_and_mediation/UnderstandingPubliclyfundedFamilyMediation.pdf (accessed 28 July 2011).

LEMMINGS, D (1996) 'Marriage and the Law in the Eighteenth Century: Hardwicke's Marriage Act 1753' 39 *The Historical Journal* 339.

LEVY, A and KAHAN, B (1991) *The Pindown Experience and the Protection of Children: The Report of the Staffordshire Child Care Inquiry 1990* (London, HMSO).

LEWIS, J (1980) *The Politics of Motherhood: Child and Maternal Welfare in England 1900–1939* (London, Croom Helm).

—— (1991) 'Models of Equality for Women: The Case of State Support for Children in Twentieth Century Britain' in G Bock and P Thane (eds), *Maternity and Gender and Policies: Women and the Rise of the European Welfare States* (London, Routledge).

—— (1992) 'Women and Late-Nineteenth Century Social Work' in C Smart (ed), *Regulating Womanhood: Historical Essays on Marriage, Motherhood and Sexuality* (London, Routledge).

—— (1996) 'Marriage Saving Revisited' *Fam Law* 423.

—— (1999) *Marriage, Cohabitation and the Law: Individualism and Obligation*, Lord Chancellor's Department Research Series No 1/99 (London, The Stationery Office).

—— (2002) 'Individualisation, assumptions about the existence of an adult worker model and the shift towards contractualism' in A Carling, S Duncan and R Edwards (eds), *Analysing Families: Morality and Rationality in Policy and Practice* (London, Routledge).

—— (2004) 'Adoption: The Nature of Policy Shifts in England and Wales 1972–2002' 18 *Int J of Law, Policy and the Family* 235.

—— (2009) *Work–Family Balance, Gender and Policy* (Cheltenham, Edward Elgar).

LEWIS, J, DATTA, J and SARRE, S (1999) *Individualism and Commitment in Marriage and Cohabitation*, Lord Chancellor's Department Research Series No 8/99 (London, Stationery Office).

LIDDLE, AM (1993) 'Gender, Desire and Child Sexual Abuse: Accounting for the Male Majority' 10 *Theory, Culture and Society* 103.

LIM, H (1996) 'Messages from a Rarely Visited Island: Duress and Lack of Consent in Marriage' 4 *Feminist Legal Studies* 195.

LIND, C and HEWITT, T (2009) 'Law and the Complexities of Parenting: Parental Status and Parental Function' 31 *JSWFL*, 391.

LINDLEY, B (1997) 'Open Adoption—Is the Door Ajar?' 9 *CFLQ* 115.

—— and RICHARDS, M (2000) 'Working Together 2000—How will Parents Fare under the New Child Protection Process?' 12 *CFLQ* 213.

——, RICHARDS, M and FREEMAN, P (2001) 'Advice and Advocacy for Parents in Child Protection Cases—What is Happening in Current Practice?' 13 *CFLQ* 167.

LINTON, R. (1949) 'The Natural History of the Family' in R Anshen (ed), *The Family: Its Function and Destiny* (New York, Harper & Bros).

LISTER, R, GOODE, J and CALLENDER, C (1999) 'Income Distribution within Families and the Reform of Social Security' 21 *JSWFL* 203.

LITTLETON, C (1987) 'Reconstructing Sexual Equality' 75 *California Law Review* 1279.

LNTV (2005a) 'Family Law: Collaborative Family Law' Programme 1125, LNTV Times.

—— (2005b) 'Family Law: Collaborative Family Law' Programme 1125, LNTV DVD.

LONDON BOROUGH OF BRENT (1985) *A Child in Trust: Report of the Panel of Inquiry Investigating the Circumstances Surrounding the Death of Jasmine Beckford* (London, London Borough of Brent).

LONDON BOROUGH OF GREENWICH (1987) *A Child in Mind: Protection of Children in a Responsible Society: The Report of the Commission of inquiry into the circumstances surrounding the death of Kimberley Carlile* (London, London Borough of Greenwich and Greenwich Health Authority).

LONDON BOROUGH OF LAMBETH (1987) *Whose Child? The Report of the Panel Appointed to Inquire into the Death of Tyra Henry* (London, London Borough of Lambeth).

LONDON STRATEGIC POLICY UNIT, POLICE MONITORING AND RESEARCH GROUP (1986) *Briefing Paper No 1: Police Response to Domestic Violence* (London, London Strategic Policy Unit).

LORD CHANCELLOR'S DEPARTMENT (1993) *Looking to the Future: Mediation and the Ground for Divorce: a Consultation Paper*, Cmd 2424 (London, HMSO).

—— (1995a) *Looking to the Future: Mediation and the Ground for Divorce: The Government's Proposals*, Cmd 2799 (London, HMSO).

—— (1995b) *Legal Aid: Targeting Need: The Future of Publicly Funded Help in Solving Legal Problems in Disputes in England and Wales; a Consultation Paper*, Cmd 2854 (London, HMSO).

—— (1996) 'Introduction', in *Marriage and the Family Law Act 1996: The New Legislation Explained* (London, Lord Chancellor's Department).

—— (1997) Press Release, 13 June.

—— (1998) *Consultation Paper 1: Court Procedures for the Determination of Paternity, 2: The Law on Parental Responsibility for Unmarried Fathers* (London, HMSO).

—— (1999) *Settling Finances on Divorce: Modernising The Role of the Court* (London, The Stationery Office).

—— (2002) *LCD Guidelines for Good Practice on Parental Contact in Cases where there is Domestic Violence* (London, Lord Chancellor's Department).

LOVELAND, I (1996) 'The Status of Children as Applicants under the Homelessness Legislation—Judicial Subversion of Legislative Intent?' 8 *CFLQ* 89.

LOWE, NV (1997) 'The Meaning and Allocation of Parental Responsibility—A Common Lawyer's Perspective' 11 *Int J of Law, Policy and the Family* 192.

—— (2001) 'Children's Participation in the Family Justice System—Translating Principles into Practice' 12 *CFLQ* 137.

—— and DOUGLAS, G (2007) *Bromley's Family Law* (Oxford, Oxford University Press).

—— and Juss, S (1993) 'Medical Treatment—Pragmatism and the Search for Principle' 56 *MLR* 865.

LUHMANN, N (1993) *Risk: A Sociological Theory*, trans Barrett R (New York, Walter de Gruyter).

LUPTON, C, BARNARD, S and SWALL-YARRINGTON, M (1995) *Family Planning? An Evaluation of the Family Group Conference Model, Report No 31* (Portsmouth, Social Services Research and Information Unit, University of Portsmouth).

LYON, C and PARTON, N (1995) 'Children's Rights and the Children Act 1989' in B Franklin (ed), *The Handbook of Children's Rights: Comparative Policy and Practice* (London, Routledge).

MAAS, R (1997) 'What God has Joined ...' *Taxation* 387.

MACCOBY, E and MNOOKIN, R (1992) *Dividing the Child: Social and Legal Dilemmas of Custody* (Cambridge, MA, Harvard University Press).

MACEY, M (1995) '"Same Race" Adoption Policy: Anti-racism or Racism?' 24 *J of Social Policy* 473.

MACKAY, Lord (1989) 'Perceptions of the Children Bill and Beyond' 139 *NLJ* 505.

MACLEAN, M (1994) 'The Making of the Child Support Act of 1991: Policy Making at the Intersection of Law and Policy' 21 *J Law and Society* 505.

—— and KURCZEWSKI, J (eds) (1994) *Families, Politics and the Law* (Oxford, Oxford University Press).

—— and EEKELAAR, J (1993) 'Child Support: The British Solution' 7 *Int J of Law and the Family* 205.

—— and —— (1997) *The Parental Obligation: A Study of Parenthood Across Households* (Oxford, Hart Publishing).

—— and —— (2004) 'The Obligations and Expectations of Couples Within Families: Three Modes of Interaction' 26 *JSWFL* 117.

—— and —— (2005) 'Taking the Plunge: Perceptions of Risk Taking Associated with Formal and Informal Partner Relationships', Social Contexts and Response to Risk Network Working Paper 2005/7 (Canterbury, University of Kent School of Social Policy, Sociology and Social Research).

—— and —— (2009) *Family Law Advocacy: How Barristers Help the Victims of Family Failure* (Oxford, Hart Publishing)

MACLEOD, M and SARAGA, E (1988) 'Challenging the Orthodoxy: Towards a Feminist Theory and Practice' 28 *Feminist Review* 16.

MADDEN DEMPSEY, M (2006) 'What Counts as Domestic Violence—A Conceptual Analysis' 12 *William and Mary Journal of Women and the Law* 301.

—— (2009) *Prosecuting Domestic Violence. A Philosophical Analysis* (Oxford, Oxford University Press).

MAHONEY, M (1991) 'Legal Images of Battered Women: Redefining the Issue of Separation' 90 *Michigan Law Review* 1.

—— (1994) 'Victimization or Oppression? Women's Lives, Violence and Agency' in MA Fineman and R Myktiuk (eds), *The Public Nature of Private Violence: The Discovery of Domestic Abuse* (New York, Routledge).

MAIDMENT, S (1975) 'Access Conditions in Custody Orders' 2 *Brit J Law and Society* 182.

—— (1984) *Child Custody and Divorce: The Law in Social Context* (London, Croom Helm).

—— (1998) 'Parental Alienation Syndrome—A Judicial Response?' *Fam Law* 264.

—— (2001) 'Parental Responsibility—Is there a Duty to Consult?' *Fam Law* 518.

MAINE, HS (1917) *Ancient Law* (London, Dent).

MALOS, E and HAGUE, G (1993) *Domestic Violence and Housing: Local Authority Responses to Women and Children Escaping Violence in the Home* (Bristol, Women's Aid Federation England, and School of Applied Social Studies, University of Bristol Press).

MAMA, A (1989) *The Hidden Struggle: Statutory and Voluntary Sector Responses to Violence Against Black Women in the Home* (London, London Race and Housing Research Unit).

MAMASHELA, M (2003) *The Practical Implications and Effects of The Recognition of Customary Marriages Act No 120 of 1998,* School of Development Studies University of Natal – Durban Research Report No 59 (Pietermaritzburg, Law School University of Natal).

MANNING, N (1985a) 'Constructing Social Problems' in N Manning (ed), *Social Problems and Welfare Ideology* (Aldershot, Gower).

—— (1985b) 'Reconstructing Social Problems: Policy Failure, Ideology and Social Knowledge' in N Manning (ed), *Social Problems and Welfare Ideology* (Aldershot, Gower).

MARCHANT, R and KIRBY, P (2004) 'The Participation of Young Children: Communication, Consultation and Involvement' in B Neale (ed), *Young Children's Citizenship* (York, Joseph Rowntree Foundation).

MARSHALL, A (2003) 'Comedy of Adoption—When Is a Parent not a Parent?' *Fam Law* 840.

MARSHALL, S (1994) 'Whose Child Is it Anyway?' in D Morgan and G Douglas (eds), *Constituting Families* (Stuttgart, Franz Steiner Verlag).

MARTIN, A. (1996) 'Pensions and Divorce' *Fam Law* 432.

MASSON, J (1989) 'Old Families into New: A Status for Step-parents' in MDA Freeman (ed), *State, Law and Family* (London, Tavistock).

—— (1995) 'Partnership with Parents: Doing Something Together Under the Children Act 1989' in F Kaganas, M King and C Piper (eds), *Legislating for Harmony: Partnership under the Children Act 1989* (London, Jessica Kingsley).

—— (1996a) 'Right to Divorce and Pension Rights' in M Freeman (ed), *Divorce: Where Next?* (Aldershot, Dartmouth).

—— (1996b) 'Representations of Children' *CLP* 245.

—— (2000) 'Representation of Children in England: Protecting Children in Child Protection Proceedings' 34 *Fam LQ* 467.

—— (2002) 'Police Protection—Protecting Whom?' 24 *JSWFL* 157.

—— (2003) 'The Impact of the Adoption and Children Act 2002: Part 1—Parental Responsibility' *Fam Law* 580.

—— (2005) 'Research—Emergency Intervention to Protect Children: Using and Avoiding Legal Controls' *CFLQ* 75.

—— (2007) 'Reforming Care proceedings—Time for a Review' *CFLQ* 411.

—— (2010a) '(Mis)understandings of Significant Harm' 19 *Child Abuse Review* 291.

—— (2010b) 'Emergency Protection: The Impact of Court Control on Safeguarding Children' *Fam Law* 1088.

——, WINN OAKLEY, M and PICK, K (2004) *Emergency Protection Orders: Court Orders for Child Protection Crises* (Coventry, Warwick University).

—— with McGOVERN, D, PICK, K and WINN OAKLEY, M (2007) *Protecting Powers. Emergency Intervention for Children's Protection* Chichester (NSPCC, Wiley).

——, BAILEY-HARRIS, R and PROBERT R (2008a) *Cretney. Principles of Family Law* (London, Sweet & Maxwell).

——, PEARCE, J and BADER, K with JOYNER, O, MARSDEN, J and WESTLAKE, D (2008b) *Care Profiling Study*, Ministry of Justice Research Series 4/08 (London, Ministry of Justice).

MAXWELL, CD, GARNER, JH and FAGAN, JA (2002) 'The Preventive Effects of Arrest on Intimate Partner Violence: Research, Policy and Theory' 1 *Criminology & Public Policy* 51.

MAY, V and SMART, C (2004) 'Silence in Court?—Hearing Children in Residence and Contact Disputes' *Fam Law* 305.

—— and —— (2007) 'The Parenting Contest: Problems of Ongoing Conflict over Children' in M Maclean (ed), *Parenting after Partnering. Containing Conflict after Separation* (Oxford, Hart Publishing).

MAYHEW, P, MAUNG, MA and MIRRLEES-BLACK, C (1993) *The 1992 British Crime Survey* (London, HMSO).

MAYHEW, P and PERCY, A (1996) *The 1996 British Crime Survey: England and Wales* (London, HMSO).

McCANDLESS, J and SHELDON, S (2010a) '"No Father Required"? The Welfare Assessment in the Human Fertilsation and Embryology Act 2008' 18 *Fem Legal Studies* 201.

—— (2010b) 'The Human Fertilisation and Embryology Act 2008 and the Tenacity of the Sexual Family Form' 73 *Modern Law Review* 175.

McCARRY, M (2009) 'Justifications and Contradictions: Understanding Young People's Views of Domestic Violence' 11 *Men and Masculinities* 325.

McCULLOCH, J (2004) 'Protection Before Punishment' *Fam Law* 64.

McGEE, C (2000) *Childhood Experiences of Domestic Violence* (London, Jessica Kingsley).

McGLYNN, C (1996) 'Pregnancy Dismissal and the *Webb* Litigation' 2 *Feminist Legal Studies* 220.

McGREGOR, OR (1957) *Divorce in England* (London, Heinemann).

McLEAN, S (ed) (1989) *Legal Issues in Human Reproduction* (Aldershot, Dartmouth).

McLELLAN, D (1996) 'Contract Marriage—The Way Forward or Dead End?' 23 *J Law and Society* 234.

McCOLGAN, A (1993) 'In Defence of Battered Women who Kill' 13 *OJLS* 508.

MEREDITH, P (2001) 'Children's Rights and Education' in J Fionda (ed), *Legal Concepts of Childhood* (Oxford, Hart Publishing).

MICHALOWSKI, S (1997) 'Is it in the Best Interests of a Child to Have a Life-saving Liver Transplantation? *Re T (Wardship: Medical Treatment)*' 9 *CFLQ* 179.

MILES, J (2003) 'Property Law v Family Law: Resolving the Problems of Family Property' 23 *Legal Studies* 624.

—— (2008) '*Charman v Charman (no 4)*—Making Sense of Need, Compensation and Sharing after *Miller/McFarlane*' *CFLQ* 378.

MILL, JS (1975) 'The Subjection of Women' in JS Mill, *Three Essays* (London, Oxford University Press).

MILLAR, J and WARMAN, A (1996) *Family Obligations in Europe* (London, Family Policy Studies Centre).

—— (1996) 'Mothers, Workers, Wives: Comparing Policy Approaches to Supporting Lone Mothers' in EB Silva (ed), *Good Enough Mothering?* (London, Routledge).

MILLBANK, J (2008) 'The Role of the "Functional Family" in Same-sex Family Recognition Trends' *CFLQ* 155.

MINISTRY OF JUSTICE (2010a) *Proposals for the Reform of Legal Aid in England and Wales*, Cm7967 (London, The Stationery Office).

—— (2010b) *Judicial and Court Statistics 2009*, www.justice.gov.uk/publications/judicialandcourtstatistics.htm?format=hi-vis (accessed 19 April 2011).

MIRRLEES-BLACK, C (1999) *Domestic Violence: Findings from a New British Crime Survey Self-completion Questionnaire, Home Office Research Study 191* (London, Home Office).

MITCHELL, J, District Judge (2004) 'Contact in Practice' *Fam Law* 662.

MITCHELL, M, DICKENS, S and O'CONNOR, W (2009) *Investigating the New Legislative Environment for Same Sex Couples* (London, National Centre for Social Research).

MNOOKIN, RH (1975) 'Child Custody Adjudication: Judicial Functions in the Face of Indeterminacy' 39 *Law and Contemporary Problems* 226.

—— (1979) 'Bargaining in the Shadow of the Law: The Case of Divorce' *CLP* 65.

—— (1984) 'Divorce Bargaining: The Limits on Private Ordering' in J Eekelaar and S Katz (eds), *The Resolution of Family Conflict: Comparative Legal Perspectives* (Toronto, Butterworths).

—— and KORNHAUSER, L (1979) 'Bargaining in the Shadow of the Law: The Case of Divorce' 88 *Yale LJ* 950.

MONAGHAN, K 'Commentary: *Wilkinson v Kitzinger*' in R Hunter, C McGlynn and E Rackley (eds), *Feminist Judgments From Theory to Practice* (Oxford, Hart Publishing).

MONK, D (2009) 'Regulating Home Education: Negotiating Standards, Anomalies and Rights' 21 *CFLQ* 155.

MOONEY, J (1994) *The Hidden Figure: Domestic Violence in North London* (London, Islington Council).

—— (2000) 'Revealing the Hidden Figure of Domestic Violence' in J Hanmer et al (eds), *Home Truths About Domestic Violence: Feminist Influences on Policy and Practice: A Reader* (London, Routledge).

MORE, G (1993) '"Equal treatment" of the Sexes in European Community Law: What Does Equal Mean?' 1 *Feminist Legal Studies* 45.

MORGAN, DHJ (1996) *Family Connections* (Cambridge, Polity).

—— (1999) 'Risk and Family Practices: Accounting for Change and Fluidity in Family Life' in EB Silva and C Smart (eds), *The 'New' Family?* (London, Sage).

MORGAN, D (1989) 'Surrogacy: An Introductory Essay' in D Morgan and R Lee (eds), *Birthrights: Law and Ethics at the Beginnings of Life* (London, Routledge).

—— (1990) *Discovering Men* (London, Routledge).

MORGAN, P (1995) *Farewell to the Family? Public Policy and Family Breakdown in Britain and the USA* (London, IEA Health and Welfare Unit).

—— (1996) *Who Needs Parents? The Effects of Childcare and Early Education on Children in Britain and the USA* (London, IEA Health and Welfare Unit).

MORLEY, R (1993) 'Recent Responses to "Domestic Violence" Against Women: A Feminist Critique' 5 *Social Policy Review* 177.

—— and MULLENDER, A (1992) 'Hype or Hope? The Importation of Pro-arrest Policies and Batterer's Programmes from North America to Britain as Key Measures for Preventing Violence against Women in the Home' 6 *Int J of Law and the Family* 265.

MORRIS, A and NOTT, S (1995) *All My Worldly Goods: A Feminist Perspective on the Legal Regulation of Wealth* (Aldershot, Dartmouth).

MORRIS G (2009) 'Resolution: Parenting After Parting: Information Workshops for Parents' *Fam Law* 984.

MOUNT, F (1982) *The Subversive Family: An Alternative History of Love and Marriage* (London, Cape).

MOWAT, C (1961) *The Charity Organization Society 1869–1913: Its Ideas and Work* (London, Methuen).

MUELLER-JOHNSON, K (2007) 'Enabling Contact: The Involvement of Psycho-social Professionals in Supporting Contact in Germany' in M Maclean (ed), *Parenting after Partnering. Containing Conflict after Separation* (Oxford, Hart Publishing).

MULLENDER, A (1994) 'Domestic Violence and Children: What Do We Know from Research?' in A Mullender and R Morley (eds), *Children Living with Domestic Violence: Putting Men's Abuse of Women on the Child Care Agenda* (London, Whiting & Birch).

—— (2000) *Reducing Domestic Violence ... What Works? Meeting the Needs of Children*, Policing and Reducing Crime Briefing Note (London, Home Office).

—— and BURTON, S (2000) *Reducing Domestic Violence ... What Works? Perpetrator Programmes*, Policing and Reducing Crime Briefing Note (London, Home Office).

—— and MORLEY, R (eds), (1994) *Children Living with Domestic Violence: Putting Men's Abuse of Women on the Child Care Agenda* (London, Whiting & Birch).

—— and PASCALL, G (1996) 'Women and Homelessness: Proposals from the Department of the Environment' 18 *JSWFL* 327.

——, HAGUE, G, IMAM, U, KELLY, L, MALOS, E and REGAN, L (2002) *Children's Perspectives on Domestic Violence* (London, Sage).

MÜLLER-FREIENFELS, W (2003), 'The Emergence of *Droit de Famille* and *Familienrecht* in Continental Europe and the Introduction of Family Law in England' *Journal of Family History* 31.

MULINARI, D and SANDELL, K (2009) 'A Feminist Re-reading of Theories of Late Modernity: Beck, Giddens and the Location of Gender' *Critical Sociology* 493.

MUNRO, V (2001) 'Square Pegs in Round Holes; the Dilemma of Conjoined Twins and Individual Rights' 10 *Social and Legal Studies* 459.

MURPHY, J (1996) 'Domestic Violence: The New Law' 59 *MLR* 845.

—— (2000) 'Child Welfare in Transracial Adoptions: Colour-blind Children and Colour-blind Law' in J Murphy (ed), *Ethnic Minorities their Families and the Law* (Oxford, Hart Publishing).

—— (2004) 'Same-sex Marriage in England: A Role for Human Rights?' 16 *CFLQ* 245.

MURRAY, C (2004) 'Same-sex Families: Outcomes for Children and Parents' *Fam Law* 136.

MYKITIUK, R (2001) 'Beyond Conception: Legal Determinations of Filiation in the Context of Reproductive Technologies' 39 *Osgoode Hall Law Journal* 771.

NASH, M (1991) 'Pronatalism and Motherhood in Franco's Spain' in G Bock and P Thane (eds), *Maternity and Gender and Policies: Women and the Rise of the European Welfare States* (London, Routledge).

NATIONAL CHILDREN'S BUREAU (1994) *Statistics: Under Fives and Pre-school Services in England and Wales 1994* (London).

NATIONAL COMMISSION OF INQUIRY INTO THE PREVENTION OF CHILD ABUSE (1996) *Childhood Matters: Volume 1: The Report* (London, The Stationery Office)

NEALE, B (2004) 'Executive Summary' in B Neale (ed), *Young Children's Citizenship* (York, Joseph Rowntree Foundation, 2004).

—— and SMART, C (1997) '"Good" and "Bad" Lawyers? Struggling in the Shadow of the New Law' 19 *JSWFL* 377.

—— and —— (2002) 'Caring, Earning and Changing: Parenthood and Employment after Divorce' in A Carling, S Duncan and R Edwards (eds), *Analysing Families: Morality and Rationality in Policy and Practice* (London, Routledge).

——, FLOWERDEW, J and SMART, C (2003) 'Drifting Towards Shared Residence?' *Fam Law* 904.

NEIL, E (2003) 'Adoption and Contact: A Research Review' in A Bainham, B Lindley, M Richards and L Trinder (eds), *Children and their Families: Contact, Rights and Welfare* (Oxford, Hart Publishing).

—— (2009) 'Post-adoption Contact and Openness in Adoptive Parents' Minds: Consequences for Children's Development' 39 *Br J Social Work* 5.

——, COSSAR, J, JONES, C, LORGELY, P and YOUNG, J (2011) *Supporting Direct Contact After Adoption* (London, British Association for Adoption and Fostering).

NELKEN, D (1998) 'Afterword: Choosing Rights for Children' in G Douglas and L Sebba (eds), *Children's Rights and Traditional Values* (Aldershot, Ashgate).

NEWCASTLE CONCILIATION PROJECT UNIT REPORT (1989) *Report to the Lord Chancellor on the Costs and Effectiveness of Conciliation in England and Wales* (London, Lord Chancellor's Department).

NEWSLINE (2003) 'President's Address' *Fam Law* 294.

NORGROVE, D (Chair) (2011a) *Interim Report of the Family Justice Review* (London, Ministry of Justice).

NORGROVE D (Chair) (2011b) *Family Justice Review. Final Report* (London, Ministry of Justice).

NORRIE, A (1993) *Crime, Reason and History* (London, Butterworths).

O'BRIEN, M and SHEMILT, I (2003) *Working Fathers: Earning and Caring* (London, Equal Opportunities Commission).

O'DONNELL, C and CRANEY, J (1982) 'The Social Construction of Child Abuse' in C O'Donnell and J Craney (eds), *Family Violence in Australia* (Cheshire, Longman).

O'DONNELL, K (2004) 'Case Commentary—*Re C (Welfare of Child: Immunisation)*—Room To Refuse? Immunisation, Welfare and the Role of Parental Decision Making' 16 *CFLQ* 213.

O'DONOVAN, K (1984) 'Wife Sale and Desertion as Alternatives to Judicial Marriage Dissolution' in J Eekelaar and S Katz (eds), *The Resolution of Family Conflict* (Toronto, Butterworths).

—— (1985) *Sexual Divisions in Law* (London, Weidenfeld & Nicolson).

—— (1993a) 'Law's Knowledge: The Judge, The Expert, The Battered Woman, and the Syndrome' 20 *Journal of Legal Studies* 427.

—— (1993b) *Family Law Matters* (London, Pluto).

—— (2000) 'Constructions of Maternity and Motherhood in Stories of Lost Children' in J Bridgeman and D Monk (eds), *Feminist Perspectives on Child Law* (London, Cavendish).

—— and MARSHALL, J (2006) 'After Birth: Decisions About Becoming a Mother' in A Diduck and K O'Donovan (eds), *Feminist Perspectives on Family Law* (London, Routledge-Cavendish).

O'NEILL, O (1979) 'Begetting, Bearing and Rearing' in O O'Neill and W Ruddick (eds), *Having Children* (New York, Oxford University Press).

OAKLEY, A (1985) *The Sociology of Housework* (Oxford, Blackwell).

OFFICE FOR NATIONAL STATISTICS (2005a) *Population Trends, Spring 2005* (London, Office for National Statistics).

—— (2005b) Annual Online edition, *General Household Survey.*

—— (2007) *Social Trends No 38.*

—— (2010a) *Civil Partnerships in the UK 2009. Statistical Bulletin.*

—— (2010b) *Statistical Bulletin. Fertility.*

—— (2010c) *Statistical Bulletin. Adoption.*

—— (2011a) *Statistical Bulletin. Families and Households in the UK 2001–2010.*

—— (2011b) *Marriages.*

—— (2011c) *Divorces in England and Wales, 2009.*

OFFICE OF THE DEPUTY PRIME MINISTER (2002) *Revision of the Code of Guidance on the Allocation of Accommodation* (London, ODPM).

OKIN, SM (1989) *Justice, Gender and the Family* (New York, Basic Books).

OLSEN, F (1983) 'The Family and the Market: A Study of Ideology and Legal Reform' 96 *Harvard Law Review* 1497.

—— (1992) 'Children's Rights: Some Feminist Approaches to the United Nations Convention on the Rights of the Child' in P Alston, S Parker and J Seymour (eds), *Children, Rights and the Law* (Oxford, Clarendon Press).

PAGELOW, M (1990) 'Effects of Domestic Violence on Children and their Consequences for Custody and Visitation Agreements' 7(4) *Mediation Quarterly* 347.

PAHL, J (1985a) 'Introduction' in J Pahl (ed), *Private Violence and Public Policy: The Needs of Battered Women and the Response of the Public Services* (London, Routledge and Kegan Paul).

—— (1985b) 'Marital Violence and Marital Problems' in J Pahl (ed), *Private Violence and Public Policy: The Needs of Battered Women and the Response of the Public Services* (London, Routledge and Kegan Paul).

—— (1985c) 'Violence Against Women' in N Manning (ed), *Social Problems and Welfare Ideology* (Aldershot, Gower).

—— (1989) *Money and Marriage* (Basingstoke, Macmillan).

—— (2005) 'Individualisation in Couple Finances: Who Pays for the Children?' 4 *Social Policy and Society* 381.

PAONE, G (2006) HESA-ETUI Newsletter.

PARADINE, K and WILKINSON, J (2004) *Research and Literature Review: Protection and Accountability: The Reporting, Investigation and Prosecution of Domestic Violence Cases* (London, Her Majesty's Crown Prosecution Service Inspectorate (HMCPSI), Her Majesty's Inspectorate of Constabulary (HMIC), Centrex).

PARENTLINE PLUS (2005) *Stepfamilies: New relationships new challenges* (London, Parentline Plus).

PARKER, S (1987) 'The Marriage Act 1753: A Case Study in Family Law-making' 1 *Int J of Law and the Family* 133.

—— (1990) *Informal Marriage, Cohabitation and the Law 1750–1989* (Basingstoke, MacMillan).

—— (1991) 'Child Support in Australia: Children's Rights or Public Interest' 5 *Int J of Law and the Family* 24.

PARKINSON, L 'Conciliation: Pros and Cons (I)' (1983) 13 *Fam Law* 22.

—— (1985) 'Conciliation in Separation and Divorce' in W Dryden (ed), *Marital Therapy in Britain, vol II* (London, Harper & Row).

—— (2011a) 'ADR Professional: Family Mediation: Ideology or New Discipline? Part I' *Fam Law* 88.

—— (2011b) 'ADR Professional: Family Mediation: Ideology or New Discipline? Part II' *Fam Law* 196.

PARKINSON, P and HUMPHREYS, C (1998) 'Children Who Witness Domestic Violence—The Implications for Child Protection' 10 *CFLQ* 147.

PARRY, ML (1993) *The Law Relating to Cohabitation*, 3rd edn (London, Sweet & Maxwell).

PARSONS, T (1949) 'The Social Structure of the Family' in R Anshen (ed), *The Family: Its Function and Destiny* (New York, Harper).

—— (1992) 'The Contemporary Politics of Child Protection' *JSWFL* 100.

PARTON, N (1985) *The Politics of Child Abuse* (Basingstoke, Macmillan Education).

—— (1991) *Governing the Family: Child Care, Child Protection and the State* (Basingstoke, Macmillan Education).

PASCALL, G (1997) *Social Policy: A New Feminist Analysis* (London, Routledge).

—— and MORLEY, R (1996) 'Women and Homelessness: Proposals from the Department of the Environment' 18 *JSWFL*, 189.

——, LEE, S, MORLEY, R and PARKER, S (2001) 'Changing Housing Policy: Women Escaping Domestic Violence' 23 *JSWFL* 293.

PATEL, P (2000) 'Southall Black Sisters: Domestic Violence Campaigns and Alliances Across the Divisions of Race, Gender and Class' in J Hanmer et al (eds), *Home Truths About Domestic Violence: Feminist Influences on Policy and Practice: A Reader* (London, Routledge).

PATEMAN, C (1988) *The Sexual Contract* (Cambridge, Polity).

PAYNE, J (1976) 'Family Property Reform as Perceived by the Law Reform Commission of Canada' 9 *Chitty's Law Journal* 289.

PEACOCK, G (1998) 'Domestic Abuse Research' *Fam Law* 628.

PEOPLE AND SCIENCE POLICY LTD (2006) Report on the Consultation on the Review of the Human Fertilsation and Embryology Act 1990 (London, People and Science Policy Ltd).

PERFORMANCE AND INNOVATION UNIT (2000) *Prime Minister's Review of Adoption* (London, Cabinet Office).

PERRY, A (2006) 'Safety First? Contact and Family Violence in New Zealand: An Evaluation of the Presumption against Unsupervised Contact' 18 *CFLQ* 1.

—— and RAINEY, B (2007) 'Supervised, Supported and Indirect Contact Orders: Research Findings' *Int J of Law, Policy and the Family* 21.

PETCHESKY, R (1987) 'Foetal Images: The Power of Visual Culture in the Politics of Reproduction' in M Stanworth (ed), *Reproductive Technologies: Gender, Motherhood and Medicine* (Cambridge, Polity).

PHILIPPS, L (2002) 'Tax Law and Social Reproduction: The Gender of Fiscal Policy in an Age of Privatization' in J Fudge and B Cossman (eds), *Privatization, Law and the Challenge to Feminism* (Toronto, University of Toronto Press).

PHOENIX, A (1996) 'Social Constructions of Lone Motherhood: A Case of Competing Discourses' in EB Silva (ed), *Good Enough Mothering? Feminist Perspectives on Lone Motherhood* (London, Routledge).

PIAGET, J and COOK, M (trans) (1952) *The Origins of Intelligence in Children* (New York, International Universities Press).

PICKETT, E (1991) 'Familial Ideology, Family Law and Mediation: Law Casts More than a "Shadow"' 3 *Journal of Human Justice* 27.

PICKFORD, R (1999) 'Unmarried Fathers and the Law' in A Bainham, S Day Sclater and M Richards (eds), *What Is a Parent? A Socio-legal Analysis* (Oxford, Hart Publishing).

PINCHBECK, I and HEWITT, M (1973) *Children in English Society, vol II* (London, Routledge and Kegan Paul).

PIPER, C (1988) 'Divorce Conciliation in the UK: How Responsible Are Parents?' 16 *Int J of Sociology of Law* 477.

—— (1993) *The Responsible Parent: A Study in Divorce Mediation* (Hemel Hempstead, Harvester Wheatsheaf).

—— (1994) '"Looking to the Future" for Children' 6 *J of Child Law* 98.

—— (1995) 'Court of Appeal: *In Re O (A Minor) (Contact: Imposition of Conditions)'*, *The Times*, 17 March 1995, 17 *JSWFL* 355.

—— (1996a) 'Norms and Negotiation in Mediation and Divorce' in MDA Freeman (ed), *Divorce: Where Next?* (Aldershot, Dartmouth).

—— (1996b) 'Divorce Reform and the Image of the Child' 33 *J Law and Society* 364.

—— (1997) 'Ascertaining the Wishes and Feelings of the Child' *Fam Law* 796.

—— (1999a) 'Moral Campaigns for Children's Welfare in the 19th Century' in M King (ed), *Moral Agendas for Children's Welfare* (London, Routledge).

—— (1999b) 'The Wishes and Feelings of the Child' in S Day Sclater and C Piper (eds), *Undercurrents of Divorce* (Aldershot, Ashgate).

—— (1999c) 'Barriers to Seeing and Hearing Children in Private Law Proceedings' *Fam Law* 394.

—— (1999d) 'How Do You Define a Family Lawyer?' 19 *Legal Studies* 93.

—— (2000) 'Historical Constructions of Childhood Innocence: Removing Sexuality' in E Heinze (ed), *Of Innocence and Autonomy: Children, Sex and Human Rights* (Aldershot, Ashgate).

—— (2006) 'Feminist Perspectives on Youth Justice' in A Diduck and K O'Donovan (eds), *Feminist Perspectives on Family Law* (London, Cavendish).

—— (2008) *Investing in Children* (Devon, Willan Publishing).

—— and KAGANAS, F (1997) 'Family Law Act 1996, Section 1(d)—How Will "They" Know if there is a Risk of Violence?' 3 *CFLQ* 179.

PITT, G (1997) *Employment Law*, 2nd edn (London, Sweet & Maxwell).

PIZZEY, E (1974) *Scream Quietly or the Neighbors Will Hear* (Harmondsworth, Penguin).

—— and SHAPIRO, J (1982) *Prone to Violence* (Hamlyn Paperbacks).

PLANT, R (2003) 'Citizenship and Social Security' 24(2) *Fiscal Studies* 153.

PLATT, HH Judge J (2002) 'Human Rights and Part IV of the Family Law Act 1996' *Fam Law* 905.

—— (2008) 'The Domestic Violence Crime and Victims Act 2004 Part 1: Is it Working?' *Fam Law* 642.

POLK, K (1994) *When Men Kill: Scenarios of Masculine Violence* (Cambridge, Cambridge University Press).

POND, C and SEARLE, A (1991) *The Hidden Army: Children at Work in the 1990s* (London, Low Pay Unit).

PORTANTI, M and WHITWORTH, S (2009) *A Comparison of the Characteristics of Childless Women and Mothers in the ONS Longitudinal Study in Population Trends 136* (London, ONS).

POVEY, D (ed), COLEMAN, K, KAIZA, P and ROE, S (2009) *Homicides, Firearm Offences and Intimate Violence 2007/08 (Supplementary Vol 2 to Crime in England and Wales 2007/08)* (London, Home Office).

PRICE, D (2001) 'Fairly Bland: An Alternative View of a Supposed "Death Ethic" and the BMA Guidelines' 21 *Legal Studies* 618.

—— (2007) 'Closing the Gender Gap in Retirement Income: What Difference will Recent UK Pension Reforms Make? 36 *J of Social Policy* 561.

—— (2009) 'Pension Accumulation and Gendered Household Structures' in J Miles and R Probert (eds), *Sharing Assets, Sharing Lives* (Oxford, Hart Publishing).

—— (2011) 'UK Pension Reform: Implications for Family Law', Paper presented at the Child and Family Law Quarterly Seminar, King's College London.

PRIEST, J (1993) *Families Outside Marriage*, 2nd edn (Bristol, Family Law, Jordan).

—— (1997) 'Capital Settlements and the CSA – Part I' *Fam Law* 115.

—— and WHYBROW, JC (1986) *Custody Law in Practice in the Divorce and Domestic Courts, Supplement to Law Commission WP No 96 Family Law Review of Child Law: Custody* (London, HMSO).

PRIOR, G and FIELD, J (1996) *Department of Social Security Research Report No 50 Pensions and Divorce* (London, HMSO).

PROBERT, R (2002) 'When Are we Married? Void, Non-existent and Presumed Marriages' 22 *Legal Studies* 398.

—— (2004a) 'Families, Assisted Reproduction and the Law' 16 *CFLQ* 273.

—— (2004b), 'Family Law—A Modern Concept?' *Fam Law* 901.

—— (2009) *Marriage Law and Practice in the Long Eighteenth Century. A Reassessment* (Cambridge, Cambridge University Press).

PROUT, A (2005) *The Future of Childhood* (London, Routledge Falmer).

—— and JAMES, A (2003) 'A New Paradigm for the Sociology of Childhood? Provenance, Promise and Problems' in A James and A Prout (eds), *Constructing and Reconstructing Childhood* (London, Routledge).

PROVAN, B et al (1996) *The Requirement to Co-operate: A Report on the Operation of the 'Good Cause' Provisions, In-house Report 14* (London, Department of Social Security Research Branch).

PRYOR, J and RODGERS, B (2001) *Children in Changing Families: Life after Parental Separation* (Oxford, Blackwell).

PTACEK, J (1988) 'Why Do Men Batter their Wives?' in K Yllo and M Bograd (eds), *Feminist Perspectives on Wife Abuse* (London, Sage).

PURVIS, T and HUNT, A (1993) 'Discourse, Ideology, Discourse, Ideology, Discourse, Ideology …' 44 *British Journal of Sociology* 473.

RADFORD, J (1992) 'Retrospect on a Trial' in J Radford and DEH Russell (eds), *Femicide: The Politics of Woman Killing* (Buckingham, Open University Press).

RADFORD, L, SAYER, S and AMICA (1999) *Unreasonable Fears? Child Contact in the Context of Domestic Violence: A Survey of Mothers' Perspectives of Harm* (Bristol, Women's Aid Federation of England).

RAFFERTY, A and WIGGAN, J (2011) 'Choice and Welfare Reform: Lone Parents' Decision-making around Paid Work and Family Life' 40 *J of Social Policy* 275.

RAGONE, H (2003) 'The Gift of Life: Surrogate Motherhood, Gamete Donation and Constructions of Altruism' in R Cook, S Day Sclater and F Kaganas (eds), *Surrogate Motherhood: International Perspectives* (Oxford, Hart Publishing).

RAITT, F (2007) 'Hearing Children in Family Law Proceedings: Can Judges Make a Difference?' *CFLQ* 204.

RANDALL, V (1996) 'Feminism and Child Daycare' 25 *J of Social Policy* 485.

RAZ, J (1986) *The Morality of Freedom* (Oxford, Oxford University Press).

READ, J and CLEMENTS, (2004) 'Demonstrably Awful: The Right to Life and the Selective Non-treatment of Disabled Babies and Young Children' 31 *J Law and Society* 482.

REECE, H (1996a) 'The Paramountcy Principle: Consensus or Construct?' 49 *Current Legal Problems* 267.

—— (1996b) 'Subverting the Stigmatization Argument' 23 *J Law and Society* 484.

—— (2003) *Divorcing Responsibly* (Oxford, Hart Publishing).

—— (2006a) 'UK Women's Groups' Child Contact Campaign: "So Long as it is Safe"' 18 *CFLQ* 538.

—— (2006b) 'The End of Domestic Violence' 69 *MLR* 770.

—— (2008) 'The Autonomy Myth: A Theory of Dependency' 20 *CFLQ* 109.

—— (2009a) 'Parental responsibility as Therapy' Fam Law 1167.

—— (2009b) 'The Degradation of Parental Responsibility' in R Probert, S Gilmore and J Herring (eds), *Responsible Parents and Parental Responsibility* (Oxford, Hart Publishing).

REHMAN J (2007) 'The Sharia, Islamic Family Laws and International Human Rights Law: Examining the Theory and Practice of Polygamy and Talaq' 21 *Int J of Law, Policy and the Family* 108.

RESPECT (2010a) *Respect Briefing Paper: Evidence of Effects of Domestic Violence Perpetrator Programmes on Women's Safety*, www.respect.uk.net/data/files/resources/respect_briefing_paper_ on_the_evidence_of_effects_of_perpetrator_programmes_on_women_revised_18th_march_10.pdf (accessed 14 February 2011).

—— (2010b) *Respect Briefing Paper on Unsafe Domestic Violence Perpetrator Interventions*, www. respect.uk.net/data/files/respect_paper_on_unsafe_domestic_violence_perpetrator_interventions.pdf (accessed 14 February 2011).

REEVES, J (1993) 'The Deviant Mother and Child: The Development of Adoption as an Instrument of Social Control' 20 *J Law and Society* 412.

REGAN, MC (1999) *Alone Together: Law and the Meanings of Marriage* (Oxford, Oxford University Press).

RESOLUTION (2005) *Code of Practice*, www.resolution.org.uk/site_content_files/files/code_of_practice_22.2.07_final.pdf (accessed 28 July 2011).

—— (2009) *Collaborative Law in England and Wales: Early Findings.*

—— (undated) 'Collaborative Law', www.resolution.org.uk/editorial.asp?page_id=53 (accessed 19 July 2011).

REYNOLDS, J and MANSFIELD, P (1999) *The Effect of Changing Attitudes to Marriage on Its Stability, Lord Chancellor's Department Research Series 2/99, vol 1* (London, The Stationery Office).

RHOADES, H (2002) 'The "No-Contact Mother": Reconstructions of Motherhood in the Era of the "New Father"' 12 *Int J of Law, Policy and the Family* 71.

—— (2004) 'Contact Enforcement and Parenting Programmes—Policy Aims in Confusion?' 16 *CFLQ* 1.

—— (2006) 'Yearning for Law: Fathers' Groups and Family Law Reform in Australia' in R Collier and S Sheldon (eds), *Fathers' Rights Activism and Law Reform in Comparative Perspective* (Oxford, Hart Publishing).

—— (2007) 'The Changing Face of Contact in Australia' in M Maclean (ed), *Parenting after Partnering. Containing Conflict after Separation* (Oxford, Hart Publishing).

—— (2010) 'Revising Australia's Parenting Laws: A Plea for a Relational Approach to Children's Best Interests' 22 *CFLQ* 172.

RHODEN, NK (1988) 'Litigating Life and Death' 102 *Harv LR* 375.

RICHARDS, L (2004) *Getting Away with It: A Strategic Overview of Domestic Violence Sexual Assault and 'Serious' Incident Analysis* (London, Metropolitan Police Service).

RICHARDS, M (1982) 'Post-divorce Arrangements for Children: A Psychological Perspective' *JSWL* 133.

—— (1987) 'Children, Parents and Families: Developmental Psychology and the Re-ordering of Relationships at Divorce' 1 *Int J of Law and the Family* 295.

—— (1996) 'Divorce Numbers and Divorce Legislation' *Fam Law* 151.

—— (1994) 'Divorcing Children: Roles for Parents and the State' in M Maclean and J Kurczewski (eds), *Families, Politics and the Law: Perspectives for East and West Europe* (Oxford, Clarendon Press).

—— (1995) 'Private Worlds and Public Interests—The Role of the State in Divorce' in A Bainham, D Pearl and R Pickford (eds), *Frontiers of Family Law* (Chichester, John Wiley and Sons).

—— (2011) *Rights of Women Response to the Consultation 'Proposals for Reform of Legal Aid in England and Wales'* (London, Rights of Women).

RINGIN, S and HALPIN, B (1997) 'Children, Standard of Living and Distributions in the Family' 26 *J of Social Policy* 21.

ROBERTS, D (1993) 'Racism and Patriarchy in the Meaning of Motherhood' 1 *J Gender and the Law* 1.

ROBERTS, M (1995) 'Ousting Abusers—Children Act 1989 or Inherent Jurisdiction? *Re H (Prohibited Steps Order)*' 7 *CFLQ* 243.

—— (1996) 'Family Mediation and the Interests of Women—Facts and Fears' *Fam Law 239.*

—— (1997) *Mediation in Family Disputes: Principles of Practice*, 2nd edn (Aldershot, Arena).

ROBERTS, S (1983) 'Mediation in Family Disputes' 46 *MLR* 537.

—— (1993) 'Alternative Dispute Resolution and Civil Justice: An Unresolved Relationship' 56 *MLR* 452.

ROCHE, B 'International Relocation: Case for a Payne-less Future?' (2010) *Fam Law* 978.

ROCHE, J (1991) 'The Children Act 1989: Once a Parent Always a Parent?' *JSWFL* 345.

—— (1995) 'Children's Rights: In the Name of the Child' 17 *JSWFL* 281.

—— (1999) 'Children and Divorce: A Private Affair?' in S Day Sclater and C Piper (eds), *Undercurrents of Divorce* (Aldershot, Ashgate).

RODGER, J (1995) 'Family Policy or Moral Regulation' 15 (1) *Critical Social Policy* 5.

ROSE, N (1987) 'Beyond the Public/Private Division: Law, Power and the Family' 14 *J Law and Society* 61.

ROSENEIL, S (2004) 'Why We Should Care about Friends: An Argument for Queering the Care Imaginary in Social Policy' 3(4) *Social Policy and Society* 409.

—— and BUDGEON, S (2004) 'Cultures of Intimacy and Care beyond "The Family": Personal Life and Social Change in the Early 21st Century' 52 *Current Sociology* 135.

ROTHMAN, BK (1989) *Recreating Motherhood: Ideology and Technology in a Patriarchal Society* (New York, WW Norton).

ROWE, J (1966) *Parents, Children and Adoption* (London, Routledge and Kegan Paul).

ROYAL COMMISSION ON DIVORCE AND MATRIMONIAL CAUSES (1853) *Report*, Parliamentary Papers 1852–53, vols 40–42.

—— (1912) *Report*, Parliamentary Papers 1912–13, vols 18–20.

—— (1992) *Report on Family Law* No 135 (Edinburgh, HMSO).

ROYAL COMMISSION ON MARRIAGE AND DIVORCE (1956) *Report*, Parliamentary Paper 1951–56, Cmd 9678 (London, HMSO).

ROZENBERG, J (2008) 'Dame Hazel Genn Warns of "Downgrading" of Civil Justice' *Law Society Gazette* (18 December), www.lawgazette.co.uk/opinion/joshua-rozenberg/dame-hazel-genn-warns-039down-grading039-civil-justice (accessed 20 July 2011)

RUDDICK, S (1997) 'The Idea of Fatherhood' in HL Nelson (ed), *Feminism and Families* (London, Routledge).

RUMNEY, P (2003) 'Progress at a Price: The Construction of Non-stranger Rape in the Millberry Sentencing Guidelines' 66 *MLR* 870.

RUSSELL, DEH (1990) *Rape in Marriage* (Bloomington and Indianapolis, Indiana University Press).

SALFORD, H (2002) 'Concepts of Family under EU Law—Lessons from the ECHR' 16 *Int J of Law, Policy and the Family* 410.

SANDERS, A (1997) 'First Principles Revisited' 7 *Family Mediation* 8.

SANDLAND, R (2003) 'Crossing and not Crossing: Gender, Sexuality and Melancholy in the European Court of Human Rights' 11 *Feminist Legal Studies* 191.

SARAT, A and FELSTINER, WLF (1995) *Divorce Lawyers and their Clients* (Oxford, Oxford University Press).

SAYERS, B (2009) 'In Practice: Contact Activities' *Fam Law* 617.

SAUNDERS, H (2001) *Making Contact Worse?* (Bristol, Women's Aid Federation of England).

—— (2004) *Twenty-nine Child Homicides: Lessons Still to be Learnt on Domestic Violence and Child Protection* (Bristol, Women's Aid Federation of England).

—— with BARRON, J (2003) *Failure to Protect? Domestic Violence and the Experiences of Abused Women and Children in the Family Courts* (Bristol, Women's Aid Federation of England).

SAWYER, C (1995) 'The Competence of Children to Participate in Family Proceedings' 7 *CFLQ* 180.

—— (1999) 'Conflicting Rights for Children? Implementing Welfare, Autonomy and Justice Within Family Proceedings' 21 *JSWFL* 99.

—— (2000) 'An Inside Story: Ascertaining the Child's Wishes and Feelings' *Fam Law* 170.

—— (2004) 'Equity's Children—Constructive Trusts for the New Generation' 16 *CFLQ* 31.

SCHECHTER, M and ROBERGE, L (1976) 'Sexual Exploitation' in R Helfer and C Kempe (eds), *Child Abuse and Neglect: The Family and the Community* (Cambridge, MA, Ballinger).

SCHNEIDER, EM (1994) 'The Violence of Privacy' in MA Fineman and R Myktiuk (eds), *The Public Nature of Private Violence: The Discovery of Domestic Abuse* (London, Routledge).

SCHUURMAN, M (2003) 'Children's Rights in the Constitution for Europe' *Childright* 10.

SCOTT, J and DEX, S (2009) 'Paid and Unpaid Work. Can Policy Improve Gender Inequalities?' Relationships' in J Miles and R Probert (eds), *Sharing Lives, Dividing Assets* (Oxford, Hart Publishing).

SCOTT, KM, WELLS, JE, ANGERMEYER, M, BRUGHA, TS, BROMET, E, DEMYTTENAERE, K, DE GIROLAMO, G, GUREJE, O, HARO, JM, JIN, R, KARAM AN, KOVESS, V, LARA, C, LEVINSON, D, ORMEL, J, POSADA-VILLA, J, SAMPSON, N, TAKESHIMA, T, ZHANG, M and KESSLER, RC (2010) 'Gender and the Relationship between Marital Status and First Onset of Mood, Anxiety and Substance Use Disorders' 40 *Psychological Medicine* 1495.

SCOTTISH LAW COMMISSION (1981) Report No 67, *Aliment and Financial Provision* (Edinburgh, HMSO).

SCUTT, JA (1976) 'Reforming the Law of Rape: The Michigan Example' 50 *Australian LJ* 615.

SECRETARY OF STATE FOR HEALTH (2000) *Adoption: A New Approach—A White Paper*, Cmd 5017 (London, The Stationery Office).

SECRETARY OF STATE FOR SOCIAL SERVICES (1974) *Report of the Committee of Inquiry into the Care and Supervision Provided in Relation to Maria Colwell* (London, HMSO).

SENTENCING GUIDELINES COUNCIL (2006a) *Overarching Principles: Domestic Violence. Definitive Guideline.*

—— (2006b) *Breach of a Protective Order, Definitive Guideline.*

SEV'ER, A (1997) 'Recent or Imminent Separation and Intimate Violence against Women: A Conceptual Overview and Some Canadian Examples' 3 *Violence Against Women* 566.

SEVENHUIJSEN, S (1998) *Citizenship and the Ethics of Care* (London, Routledge).

—— (2002) 'A Third Way? Moralities, Ethics and Families' in A Carling, S Duncan and R Edwards (eds), *Analysing Families: Morality and Rationality in Policy and Practice* (London, Routledge).

SHAH, P (2003) 'Attitudes to Polygamy in English Law' 52 *International and Comparative Law Quarterly* 369.

SHARP, D (2001) 'Parental Responsibility—Where Next?' *Fam Law* 606.

SHAW, C (2004) 'Interim 2003-based National Population Projections for the United Kingdom and Constituent Countries' *Population Trends* (London, Office for National Statistics) 118.

SHELDON, S (1993) 'Who Is the Mother to Make the Judgment? The Construction of Woman in English Abortion Law' (1993) 1 *Feminist Legal Studies* 3.

—— (1996) 'Subject Only to the Attitude of the Surgeon Concerned: The Judicial Protection of Medical Discretion' 5 *Social and Legal Studies* 95.

—— (1997) *Beyond Control: Medical Power and Abortion Law* (London, Pluto).

—— (1999) '*Re*Conceiving Masculinity: Imagining Men's Reproductive Bodies in Law' 26 *J Law and Society* 129.

—— (2001) 'Unmarried Fathers and Parental Responsibility: A Case for Reform?' 9 *Feminist Legal Studies* 93.

—— (2004) 'Gender Equality and Reproductive Decision-Making' 12 *Feminist Legal Studies* 303.

—— (2005) 'Fragmenting Fatherhood: The Regulation of Reproductive Technologies' 68 *MLR* 523.

—— (2006) 'Reproductive Choice: Men's Freedom, Women's Responsibility?' in JR Spencer and A du Bois-Pedain (eds), *Freedom and Responsibility in Reproductive Choice* (Oxford, Hart Publishing).

—— (2009) 'From "Absent Objects of Blame" to "Fathers Who Want to Take Responsibility": Reforming Birth Registration Law' 31 *JSWFL* 373.

—— (2010) 'Commentary on *Evans v Amicus Healthcare*' in R Hunter, C McGlynn and E Rackley (eds), *Feminist Judgments From Theory to Practice* (Oxford, Hart Publishing).

SHERMAN, LW and BERK, RA (1984) 'The Specific Deterrent Effects of Arrest for Domestic Assault' 49 *American Sociological Review* 261.

SHIPMAN, B and SMART, C (2007) '"It's Made a Huge Difference": Recognition, Rights and the Personal Significance of Civil Partnership' 12 *Sociological Research Online*.

SHULTZ, M (1982) 'Contractual Ordering of Marriage: A New Model for State Policy' 70 *California Law Review* 227.

SILVA, EB (ed), (1996) *Good Enough Mothering? Feminist Perspectives on Lone Motherhood* (London, Routledge).

SIMEY, M (1951) *Charitable Effort in Liverpool in the Nineteenth Century* (Liverpool, University Press).

SIMON, Sir J (1996) *With All my Worldly Goods*, Holdsworth Club, Presidential Address, University of Birmingham in B Hoggett et al, *The Family, Law and Society: Cases and Materials*, 4th edn (London, Butterworths).

SIMMONS, J et al (2002) *Crime in England and Wales 2001/2. Home Office Statistical Bulletin.*

SIMPSON, B, JESSOP, J and MCCARTHY, P (2003) 'Fathers after Divorce' in A Bainham et al (eds), *Children and Their Families: Contact, Rights and Welfare* (Oxford, Hart Publishing).

SIMPSON, B, MCCARTHY, P and WALKER, J (1995) *Being There: Fathers after Divorce* (Newcastle upon Tyne, University of Newcastle upon Tyne, Relate Centre for Family Studies).

SINCLAIR, R and BULLOCK, R (2002) *Learning from Past Experience—A Review of Serious Case Reviews* (London, Department of Health).

SINGER, L (1996) 'FDR and the Holy Grail' *Fam Law* 751.

SMART, C (1984) *The Ties That Bind* (London, Routledge and Kegan Paul).

—— (1987) '"There Is, Of Course, the Distinction Dictated by Nature": Law and the Problem of Paternity' in M Stanworth (ed), *Reproductive Technologies: Gender, Motherhood and Medicine* (Cambridge, Polity).

—— (1989a) 'Power and the Politics of Child Custody' in C Smart and S Sevenhuijsen (eds), *Child Custody and the Politics of Gender* (London, Routledge).

—— (1989b) *Feminism and the Power of Law* (London, Routledge).

—— (1991) 'The Legal and Moral Ordering of Child Custody' 18 *J Law and Society* 485.

—— (1992) 'Disruptive Bodies and Unruly Sex: The Regulation of Reproduction and Sexuality in the Nineteenth Century' in C Smart (ed), *Regulating Motherhood: Historical Essays on Marriage, Motherhood and Sex* (London, Routledge).

—— (1999a) 'The "New" Parenthood: Fathers and Mothers after Divorce' in EB Silva and C Smart (eds), *The 'New' Family?* (London, Sage).

—— (1999b) 'A History of Ambivalence and Conflict in the Discursive Construction of the "Child Victim" of Sexual Abuse' 8 *Social and Legal Studies* 391.

—— (2006a) 'Preface' in R Collier and S Sheldon (eds), *Fathers' Rights Activism and Law Reform in Comparative Perspective* (Oxford, Hart Publishing).

—— (2006b) 'The Ethic of Justice Strikes Back: Changing Narratives of Fatherhood' in A Diduck and K O'Donovan (eds), *Feminist Perspectives on Family Law* (London, Glass House Publications).

—— (2007) *Personal Life* (Cambridge, Polity).

—— (2009) 'Family Secrets: Law and Understandings of Openness in Everyday Relationships' 38 *J of Social Policy* 551.

—— and MAY, V (2004a) 'Residence and Contact Disputes in Court' *Fam Law* 36.

—— and —— (2004b) 'Why Can't They Agree? The Underlying Complexity of Contact and Residence Disputes' 26 *JSWFL* 347.

—— and NEALE, B (1997) 'Arguments Against Virtue—Must Contact be Enforced?' *Fam Law* 332.

—— and —— (1999) *Family Fragments?* (Cambridge, Polity).

—— and —— (2000) '"It's My Life Too"—Children's Perspectives on Post-divorce Parenting' *Fam Law* 163.

—— and SEVENHUIJSEN, S (eds), (1989) *Child Custody and the Politics of Gender* (London, Routledge).

——, NEALE, B and WADE, A (2001) *The Changing Experience of Childhood: Families and Divorce* (Cambridge, Polity).

——, MAY, V, WADE, A and FURNISS, C (2003) *Residence and Contact Disputes in Court, DCA Research Series No 6/03* (London, Department for Constitutional Affairs).

SMITH, C (2000) 'The Children (Protection from Offenders) (Miscellaneous Amendments) Regulations 1997: New Alliances in the Management of Risk and Uncertainty' 22 *JSWFL* 367.

—— and LOGAN, J (2002) 'Adoptive Parenthood as a "Legal Fiction"—Its Consequences for Direct Post-adoption Contact' 12 *CFLQ* 281.

SMITH, DK (2001) 'Superannuating the Second Sex: Law, Privatisation and Retirement Income' 64 *MLR* 519.

SMITH, L (2010) 'Clashing Symbols? Reconciling Support for Fathers and Fatherless Families after the Human Fertilisation and Embryology Act 2008' 22 *CFLQ* 46.

SMITH, LJF (1989) *Domestic Violence: An Overview of the Literature. Home Office Research Study No 107* (London, HMSO).

SMITH, M (2003) 'New Stepfamilies—A Descriptive Study of a Largely Unseen Group' 15 *CFLQ* 185.

SMITH, R (2004) 'Hands-off Parenting?—Towards a Reform of the Defence of Reasonable Chastisement in the UK' 16 *CFLQ* 261.

SOCIAL SERVICES INSPECTORATE, DEPARTMENT OF HEALTH (1990), *Inspection of Child Protection Services in Rochdale* (Manchester, Department of Health).

SOCIAL WORK IN EUROPE (1995) 2(3) *Special Edition on Elder Abuse.*

SOCIETY FOR PROMOTING CHRISTIAN KNOWLEDGE (1966) *Putting Asunder—A Divorce Law for Contemporary Society* (Cambridge, Cambridge University Press).

—— (1998) 'Proposals for Reform of Ancillary Relief Law', Appendix 11 to *Report to the Lord Chancellor by the Ancillary Relief Advisory Group* (Orpington, SFLA).

SPEIGHT, S, SMITH, R, LA VALLE, I, SCHNEIDER, V and PERRY, J with COSHALL, C and TIPPING, S (2009) *Childcare and Early Years Survey of Parents 2008, Research Report DCSF-RR136* (London, Department for Children, Schools and Families/National Centre for Social Research).

SPENSKY, M (1992) 'Producers of Legitimacy: Homes for Unmarried Mothers in the 1950s' in C Smart (ed), *Regulating Womanhood: Historical Essays on Marriage, Motherhood and Sex* (London, Routledge).

STAINTON ROGERS, R and STAINTON ROGERS, W (1992) *Stories of Childhood: Shifting Agendas of Child Concern* (London, Harvester Wheatsheaf).

STANKO, E (1985) *Intimate Intrusions: Women's Experience of Male Violence* (London, Routledge and Kegan Paul).

—— (1988) 'Hidden Violence Against Women' in M Maguire and J Pointing (eds), *Victims of Crime: A New Deal?* (Milton Keynes, Open University Press).

—— (1997) 'Should I Stay or Should I Go? Some Thoughts on the Variants of Intimate Violence' 3 *Violence Against Women* 629.

—— et al (1998) *Counting the Costs: Estimating the Impact of Domestic Violence in the London Borough of Hackney* (Wiltshire, Crime Concern).

STANLEY N, MILLER P, RICHARDSON FOSTER H and THOMSON G (2010) Children and Families Experiencing Domestic Violence: Police and Children's Services Responses (London, NSPCC).

STANWORTH, M (1987) 'Reproductive Technologies and the Deconstruction of Motherhood' in M Stanworth (ed), *Reproductive Technologies: Gender, Motherhood and Medicine* (Cambridge, Polity in association with Blackwell).

STARK, E and FLITCRAFT, A (1996) *Women at Risk: Domestic Violence and Women's Health* (London, Sage).

STARMER, K (2011) *Domestic Violence: The Facts, the Issues, the Future*, Speech by the Director of Public Prosecutions, Keir Starmer QC, www.cps.gov.uk/news/articles/domestic_violence_-_the_facts_the_issues_the_future/ (accessed 13 April 2011).

STARR, S (2011) 'HFEA Makes First Set of Decisions Following Donation Review' *Bionews* 616, www. bionews.org.uk/page_102199.asp (accessed 29 July 2011).

STEPHEN, Sir JAMES FITZJAMES (1883) *A History of the Criminal Law of England, vol III* (London, Clay Sons & Taylor).

STONE, L, (1977) *The Family, Sex and Marriage in England, 1500–1800* (London, Weidenfeld & Nicolson).

—— (1979) *The Family, Sex and Marriage in England 1500–1800* (London, Harper & Rowe).

—— (1990) *Road to Divorce* (Oxford, Oxford University Press).

STRATHERN, M (1992) *Reproducing the Future: Anthropology, Kinship and the New Productive Technologies* (Manchester, Manchester University Press).

STRAUS, M (1993) 'Physical Assaults by Wives: A Major Social Problem' in R Gelles and D Loseke (eds), *Current Controversies on Family Violence* (London, Sage).

—— and GELLES, R (1990) 'Societal Change and Change in Family Violence from 1975 to 1985 as Revealed in Two National Surveys' in M Straus and R Gelles (eds), *Physical Violence in American Families* (New Brunswick, NJ, Transaction).

——, GELLES, R and STEINMETZ, SK (1981) *Behind Closed Doors: Violence in the American Family* (New York, Anchor/Doubleday).

STRICKLAND, S (2011) 'Conscientious Objection in Medical Students: A Questionnaire Survey' *J Medical Ethics* 1 (accessed online 28 July 2011 http://press.psprings.co.uk/jme/july/jme42770.pdf).

STURGE, C and GLASER, D (2000) 'Contact and Domestic Violence—The Experts' Court Report' *Fam Law* 615.

STYCHIN, C (2006) 'Family Friendly? Rights, Responsibilities and Relationship Recognition' in A Diduck and K O'Donovan (eds), *Feminist Perspectives on Family Law* (London, Cavendish).

SUPPERSTONE, M and O'DEMPSEY, D (1994) *Immigration: The Law and Practice*, 3rd edn (London, Longman).

SUTTON, A (1981) 'Science in Court' in M King (ed), *Childhood, Welfare and Justice* (London, Batsford Academic and Educational).

SYMES, P (1985) 'Indissolubility and the Clean Break' 48 *MLR* 44.

TNS OPINION AND SOCIAL (2010) *Special Eurobarometer 344.Domestic Violence against Women Report* (Brussels, TNS Opinion and Social).

TALLIN, GPR (1956) 'Artificial Insemination' 31 *Canadian Bar Review* 1.

TASKER, FL and GOLOMBOK, S (1991) 'Children Raised by Lesbian Mothers: The Empirical Evidence' *Fam Law* 184.

TAYLOR, R (2007) 'Reversing the Retreat from Gillick? R (Axon) v Secretary of State for Health' *CFLQ* 81.

TEN BROEK, J (1963–64) 'California's Dual System of Family Law: Its Origin, Development and Present Status' 16 *Stanford Law Review* 257.

TESLER, P (2004) 'Collaborative Family Law' 4 *Pepperdine Dispute Resolution Law Journal* 317.

THANE, P (2010) *Happy Families? History and Family Policy* (London, British Academy).

THÉRY, I (1989) '"The Interest of the Child" and the Regulation of the Post-Divorce Family' in C Smart and S Sevenhuijsen (eds), *Child Custody and the Politics of Gender* (London, Routledge).

THOBURN, J (2003) 'The Risks and Rewards of Adoption for Children in the Public Care' 15 *CFLQ* 391.

THOMAS, A (2010) 'International Relocation: Gain a new Country but Lose a Child' *Fam Law* 982.

THOMAS, P and COSTIGAN, R (1990) *Promoting Homosexuality: Section 28 of the Local Government Act 1988* (Cardiff, Cardiff Law School).

THOMPSON, EP (1972) 'Rough Music' 27(1) *Annales: ESC* 286.

THOMPSON, G (2010) *Domestic Violence Statistics, SN/SG/950* (House of Commons Library).

THOMPSON, M (1996) 'Employing the Body: The Reproductive Body and Employment Exclusion' 5 *Social and Legal Studies* 243.

——, VINTER, L and YOUNG, V (2005) *Dads and their Babies: Leave Arrangements in the First Year: Working Paper Series No 37* (London, Equal Opportunities Commission).

THORNTON, R (1993) 'Minors and Medical Treatment—Who decides?' 52 *CLJ* 34.

THORPE, The Rt Hon Lord Justice (2009) 'London—The Divorce Capital of the World' *Fam Law* 21.

TONNIES, F and JACOBY, EG (ed and tr) (1974) *On Social Ideas and Ideologies* (New York, Harper & Row).

TRAVIS, A (2011) 'Sham Marriages Targeted in Church of England Crackdown' *The Guardian* 12 April 2011.

TRINDER, L (1997) 'Competing Constructions of Childhood: Children's Rights and Children's Wishes in Divorce' 19 *JSWFL* 291.

—— (2003) 'Working and Not Working Contact after Divorce' in A Bainham et al (eds) *Children and Their Families: Contact, Rights and Welfare* (Oxford, Hart Publishing).

—— (2010) 'Shared Residence: A Review of Recent Research Evidence' *CFLQ* 475.

—— and KELLETT, J (2007) *The Longer Term Outcomes of In-court Conciliation. Ministry of Justice Research Series 15/07* (London, Ministry of Justice).

——, CONNOLLY, J, KELLETT, J and NOTLEY, C (2005) *A Profile of Applicants and Respondents in Contact Cases in Essex, DCA Research Series 1/05* (London, Department of Constitutional Affairs).

——, CONNOLLY, J, KELLETT, J, NOTLEY, C and SWIFT, L (2006) *Making Contact Happen or Making Contact Work? The Process and Outcomes of In-Court Conciliation, DCA Research Series 3/06* (London, Department of Constitutional Affairs).

TRISELIOTIS, J (2000) 'Identity Formation and the Adopted Person Revisited' in A Treacher and I Katz (eds), *The Dynamics of Adoption* (London, Jessica Kingsley).

—— (2002) 'Long-term Foster Care or Adoption? The Evidence Examined' 7 *Child and Family Social Work* 23.

——, FEAST, J and KYLE, F (2005) *The Adoption Triangle Revisited. A Study of Adoption, Search and Reunion Experiences (Summary)* (London, BAAF).

UN COMMITTEE ON THE RIGHTS OF THE CHILD (1995) *Consideration of Reports of States Parties: United Kingdom of Great Britain and Northern Ireland, CRC/C/15* (Geneva, Centre for Human Rights).

—— (2002) *Concluding Observations of the UN Committee on the Rights of the Child on the United Kingdom's Second Periodic Report (CRC/C/15/Add.188)* www.unhchr.ch.

—— (2008) *Concluding Observations of the Committee on the Rights of the Child: United Kingdom of Great Britain and Northern Ireland, CRC/C/GBR/CO/4* (Geneva, Centre for Human Rights).

UN DEPARTMENT OF PUBLIC INFORMATION (1996) *Platform for Action and the Beijing Declaration.*

UNIVERSITY OF EAST ANGLIA IN ASSOCIATION WITH THE NATIONAL CHILDREN'S BUREAU (2005) *Children's Trusts: Developing Integrated Services for Children in England, Research Report No 617* (Norwich, University of East Anglia).

URSEL, J (1992) *Private Lives, Public Policy: 100 Years of State Intervention in the Family* (Toronto, Women's Press).

UTTING, Sir W (1997) *People Like Us: The Report of the Review of the Safeguards for Children Living Away From Home* (London, The Stationery Office).

VALLELY, C, ROBINSON, A, BURTON, M and TREDIDGA, J (2005) *Evaluation of Domestic Violence Pilot Sites at Caerphilly (Gwent) and Croydon* (London, Crown Prosecution Service).

VAUGHAN, B (2000) 'The Government of Youth: Disorder and Dependence?' 9 *Social and Legal Studies* 347.

VEITCH, E (1976) 'The Essence of Marriage – A Comment on the Homosexuality Challenge' 5 *Anglo-American Law Review* 41.

VOGLER, C (2009) 'Managing Money in Intimate Relationships' in J Miles and R Probert (eds), *Sharing Lives, Dividing Assets* (Oxford, Hart Publishing).

VOGLER, C, BROCKMANN, M and WIGGINS, R (2008) 'Managing Money in New Heterosexual Forms of Intimate Relationships' 37 *Journal of Socio-Economics* 552.

WADE, J, DIXON, J and RICHARDS, A (2009) *Implementing Special Guardianship Research Brief* (London, Department for Children, Schools and Families).

WALBY, C and SYMONS, B (1990) *Who Am I? Identity, Adoption and Human Fertilisation: Discussion Series no 12* (London, British Agencies for Adoption and Fostering) in Hoggett et al, *The Family, Law and Society* (London, Butterworths, 1996).

WALBY, S (2004) *The Cost of Domestic Violence* (London, Department for Trade and Industry).

—— and ALLEN, J (2004) *Domestic Violence, Sexual Assault and Stalking: Findings from the British Crime Survey: Home Office Research Study 276* (London, Home Office).

WALKER, A, FLATLEY, J, KERSHAW, C and MOON, D (2009) *Crime in England and Wales 2008/9. Home Office Statistical Bulletin 11/09* (London, Home Office).

WALKER, J (1996) 'Is There a Future for Lawyers in Divorce?' 10 *Int J of Law, Policy and the Family* 52.

—— (2001) *Information Meetings and Associated Provisions within the Family Law Act 1996: Summary of the Final Evaluation Report* (London, The Stationery Office, Lord Chancellor's Department).

—— et al (2004) *Picking up the Pieces: Marriage and Divorce: Two Years After Information Provision* (London, Department of Constitutional Affairs).

——, McCARTHY, P and TIMMS, N (1994) *Mediation: the Making and Remaking of Co-operative Relationships – An Evaluation of the Effectiveness of Comprehensive Mediation* (Newcastle Upon-Tyne, Relate Centre for Family Studies, University of Newcastle).

WALKER, J, McCARTHY, P, FINCH, S, COOMBES, M, RICHARDS, M and BRIDGE, C (2007) *The Family Advice and Information Service: A Changing Role for Family Lawyers in England and Wales? Final Evaluation Report* (Newcastle, Newcastle Centre for Family Studies).

WALL, The Rt Hon Lord Justice (2005) 'Enforcement of Contact Orders' *Fam Law* 26.

—— (2009) 'Making Contact Work in 2009' *Fam Law* 590.

WALLBANK, J (1997) 'The Campaign for Change of the Child Support Act 1991: Reconstituting the "Absent" Father' 6 *Social and Legal Studies* 191.

—— (2002) 'Clause 106 of the Adoption and Children Bill: Legislation for the "Good" Father?' 22 *Legal Studies* 276.

—— (2004) 'Reconstructing the HFEA 1990: Is Blood Really Thicker than Water?' 16 *CFLQ* 387.

—— (2009a) 'Parental Responsibility and the Responsible Parent: Managing the "Problem" of Contact' in R Probert, S Gilmore and J Herring J (eds), *Responsible Parents and Parental Responsibility* (Oxford, Hart Publishing).

—— (2009b) '"Bodies in the Shadows": Joint Birth Registration, Parental Responsibility and Social Class' *CFLQ* 267.

—— (2010) 'Channelling the Messiness of Diverse Family Lives: Resisting the Calls to Order and De-centreing the Hetero-normative Family' 32 *JSWFL* 353.

WALLERSTEIN, JS (1991) 'The Long-term Effects of Divorce on Children: A Review' 30 *Journal of the American Academy of Child and Adolescent Psychiatry* 349.

—— and LEWIS, J (1998) 'The Long-term Impact of Divorce on Children: A First Report From a 25-Year Study' *Family and Conciliation Courts Review* 368.

—— and KELLY, JB (1980) *Surviving the Breakup: How Children and Parents Cope with Divorce* (London, Grant McIntyre; New York, Basic Books).

—— and BLAKESLEE, S (1989) *Second Chances* (London, Bantam).

WALSH, E (2009) 'Newsline Extra: Support for Separated Parents' *Fam Law* 1220.

—— (2011) 'Newsline Extra: The Government and Mediation' *Fam Law* 101.

WALSH, K (1995) 'The Mandatory Arrest Law: Police Reaction' 16 *PACE L Rev* 97.

WARIN, J, SOLOMON, Y, LEWIS, C and LANGFORD, W (1999) *Fathers, Work and Family Life* (London, Family Policy Studies Centre, Joseph Rowntree Foundation).

WARNOCK, Dame Mary (Chair) (1984) *A Question of Life: The Warnock Report on Human Fertilisation and Embryology, Report of the Committee of Inquiry into Human Fertilisation and Embryology* (Oxford, Blackwell).

WARREN, T (2003) 'Working Part-time: Achieving a Successful "Work–Life" Balance?' 55 *Sociology* 99.

WASOFF, F, MILES, J and MORDAUNT, E (2011) *No Longer Living Together: How Does Scots Cohabitation Law Work in Practice?*, University of Cambridge, Faculty of Law Research Paper Series, Paper 11/02.

WEEKS, J (2002) 'Elective Families: Lesbian and Gay Life Experiments' in A Carling, S Duncan and R Edwards (eds), *Analysing Families: Morality and Rationality in Policy and Practice* (London, Routledge).

——, DONOVAN, C and HEAPHY, B (1999) 'Everyday Experiments: Narratives of Non-heterosexual Relationships' in EB Silva and C Smart (eds), *The 'New' Family?* (London, Sage).

WEITZMAN, L (1985) *The Divorce Revolution: The Unexpected Social and Economic Consequences for Women and Children in America* (New York, Free Press).

WELBOURNE, P (2008) 'Safeguarding Children on the Edge of Care: Policy for Keeping Children Safe after the *Review of the Child Care Proceedings System, Care Matters* and the *Carter Review of Legal Aid*' *CFLQ* 335.

WELDON-JOHNS, M (2011) 'The Additional Maternity Leave Regulations 2010: A New Dawn or More "Sound-bite" Legislation' 33 *JSWFL* 25.

WELLS, C (1988) 'Whose Baby Is It?' 15 *J Law and Society* 323.

——, ALLDRIDGE, P and MORGAN, D (1990) 'An Unsuitable Case for Treatment' *NLJ* 1544.

WEYLAND, I (1992) 'Contact within Different Legal Contexts' *Fam Law* 138.

—— (1995) 'Judicial Attitudes to Contact and Shared Residence since the Children Act 1989' *JSWFL* 445.

WHEELER, D (2004) 'Can We Make Contact Work?' *Fam Law* 601.

WHELAN, R (ed) (1995) *Just a Piece of Paper? Divorce Reform and the Undermining of Marriage* (London, IEA Health and Welfare Unit).

WHINCUP, M. (1991) *Modern Employment Law*, 7th edn (Oxford, Butterworth-Heinemann).

WHYBROW, J (2004) 'Children, Guardians and Rule 9.5' *Fam Law* 504.

WICKS, The Rt Hon Malcolm, MP, Minister of State for Pensions (2004) Speech to TUC Conference Women and Pensions.

WIEGERS, W and KEET, M (2008) 'Collaborative Family Law and Gender Inequalities: Balancing Risks and Opportunities' 46 *Osgoode Hall LJ* 733.

WIKELEY, N (2000a) 'Child Support—The New Formula, Part I' *Fam Law* 820.

—— (2000b) 'Compliance, Enforcement and Child Support' *Fam Law* 888.

—— (2001) 'Children and Social Security Law' in J Fionda (ed), *Legal Concepts of Childhood* (Oxford, Hart Publishing).

—— (2002) *Wikeley, Ogus and Barendt's: The Law of Social Security* (London, Butterworths).

—— (2006) 'A Duty But Not a Right: Child Support after *R (Kehoe) v Secretary of State for Work and Pensions*' 18 *CFLQ* 287.

—— (2007) 'Family Law and Social Security' in R Probert (ed), *Family Life and the Law* (Dartmouth, Ashgate).

——, BARNETT, S, BROWN, J, DAVIS, G, DIAMOND, I, DRAPER, T and SMITH, P (2001) *National Survey of Child Support Clients, Research Report No 152* (London, Department for Work and Pensions) (Summary of Report: www.dwp.gov.uk/asd/asd5/152summ.html).

WILLBOURNE, C and CULL, L (1997) 'The Emerging Problem of Parental Alienation' *Fam Law* 807.

WILLIAMS, C and JORDAN, H (1996) 'Factors Relating to Publicity Surrounding the Complaints Procedure under the Children Act 1989' 8 *CFLQ* 337.

WILLIAMS, F (2004) *Rethinking Families* (London, Calouste Gulbenkian Foundation).

WILLIAMS, G (1983) *Textbook of Criminal Law*, 2nd edn (London, Stevens & Sons).

WILLIAMS, PJ (1991) *The Alchemy of Race and Rights* (Cambridge, MA, Harvard University Press).

—— (1994) 'Spare Parts, Family Values, Old Children, Cheap' 28 *New England Law Review* 913.

WILLOW, C (2004) 'Consulting with Under 12s: A Mapping Exercise' in B Neale (ed), *Young Children's Citizenship* (York, Joseph Rowntree Foundation).

WILSON, B (2004) 'Emotion, Rationality and Decision-making in Mediation' *Fam Law* 682.

—— (2005) 'Dispute "Ripeness", Timing and Mediation' *Fam Law* 162.

—— (2010) 'Unfinished Business: Mediating the Past' *Fam Law* 201.

WILSON, M and DALY, M (1992) 'Till Death Do Us Part' in J Radford and DEH Russell (eds), *Femicide: The Politics of Woman Killing* (Buckingham, Open University Press).

WILSON, W (1995) 'Is Life Sacred?' 12 *JSWFL* 131.

WINDEBANK, J (1996) 'To What Extent Can Social Policy Challenge the Dominant Ideology of Mothering? A Cross-national Comparison of Sweden, France and Britain' 6(2) *Journal of European Social Policy* 147.

WINTEMUTE, R (2000) 'Lesbian and Gay Inequality 2000: The Potential of the Human Rights Act 1998 and the Need for an Equality Act' 6 *EHRLR* 603.

WOMAN'S OWN (1987) 31 October.

WOMEN'S AID FEDERATION OF ENGLAND (2003) *Response to 'Safety and Justice', the Government's Consultation Paper on Domestic Violence* (Bristol, Women's Aid Federation of England).

WOMEN'S LEGAL EDUCATION AND ACTION FUND (1996) *Equality and the Charter: Ten Years of Feminist Advocacy before the Supreme Court of Canada* (Toronto, Emond Montgomery).

WOMEN'S NATIONAL COMMISSION (1985) *Violence Against Women, Report of an ad hoc Working Group* (London, Cabinet Office, 1985).

WOMEN'S PROJECT (1998) *Bridges or Barriers* (Weston-Super-Mare, Women's Project).

WONG, S (2003) 'Trusting in Trust(s): The Family Home and Human Rights' 11 *Feminist Legal Studies* 119.

—— (2009) 'Caring and Sharing: Interdependency as a Basis for Property Redistribution? in A Bottomley and S Wong (eds), *Changing Contours of Domestic Life* (Oxford, Hart Publishing).

WRIGHT, K (2007) 'The Role of Solicitors in Divorce: A Note of Caution' *CFLQ* 481.

YNGVESSON, B (1997) 'Negotiating Motherhood: Identity and Difference in "Open" Adoptions' 31 *Law and Society Review* 33.

YOUNG, IM (1990) *Justice and the Politics of Difference* (Princeton, NJ, Princeton University Press).

YOUNG, K (1996) *Research Evaluation of Family Mediation Practice and the Issue of Violence* (Attorney-General's Department, Australia).

ZIFF, B (1990) 'The Primary Caretaker Presumption: Canadian Perspectives on an American Development' 4 *Int J of Law and the Family* 186.

ZIPPER, J and SEVENHUIJSEN, S (1987) 'Surrogacy: Feminist Notions of Motherhood Revisited' in M Stanworth (ed), *Reproductive Technologies: Gender, Motherhood and Medicine* (Cambridge, Polity).

Index

Introductory Note

References such as '178–9' indicate (not necessarily continuous) discussion of a topic across a range of pages. Wherever possible in the case of topics with many references, these have either been divided into sub-topics or only the most significant discussions of the topic are listed. Because the entire work is about 'family law' the use of this term (and certain others which occur constantly throughout the book) as an entry point has been minimised. Information will be found under the corresponding detailed topics.